Malaysia

The British Documents on
the End of Empire Project
gratefully acknowledges
the generous assistance of
the Leverhulme Trust.

The Project has
been undertaken
under the auspices
of the British Academy.

BRITISH DOCUMENTS ON THE END OF EMPIRE

General Editor S R Ashton
Project Chairman A N Porter

Series B Volume 8

Malaysia

Editor
A J STOCKWELL

Published for the Institute of Commonwealth Studies
in the University of London

London: TSO

First published 2004

© The Stationery Office 2004

Introduction © A J Stockwell, 2004

Documents from The National Archives © Crown copyright

Crown copyright material used by permission of The National Archives under licence from the Controller of Her Majesty's Stationery Office

All Rights Reserved. No part of this publication may be reproduced, stored in a retrieval system, or transmitted in any form or by any means, electronic, mechanical, photocopying, recording or otherwise without the permission of the Publishers

Applications for reproduction of government documents in this work should be addressed to the Copyright Officer, The National Archives, Kew, Richmond, Surrey TW9 4DU

Applications for reproduction of any other part of this work should be addressed to the publisher: The Stationery Office, St Crispins, Duke Street, Norwich, NR3 1PD

ISBN 0 11 290581 1

British Library Cataloguing in Publication Data
A CIP catalogue record for this book is available from the British Library

If you wish to receive future volumes from the British Documents on the End of Empire project, please write to TSO, Standing Order Department, PO Box 29, St Crispins, Duke Street, NORWICH NR3 1GN, or telephone on 0870 600 5522, quoting classification reference numbers 04 03 017 and 04 03 018

Published by TSO (The Stationery Office) and available from:

Online
www.tso.co.uk/bookshop

Mail, Telephone, Fax & E-mail
TSO
PO Box 29, Norwich NR3 1GN
Telephone orders/General enquiries: 0870 600 5522
Fax orders: 0870 600 5533
Email: book.orders@tso.co.uk
Textphone: 0870 240 3701

TSO Shops
123 Kingsway, London WC2B 6PQ
020 7242 6393 Fax 020 7242 6394
68–69 Bull Street, Birmingham B4 6AD
0121 236 9696 Fax 0121 236 9699
9–21 Princess Street, Manchester M60 8AS
0161 834 7201 Fax 0161 833 0634
16 Arthur Street, Belfast BT1 4GD
028 9023 8451 Fax 028 9023 5401
18–19 High Street, Cardiff CF10 1PT
029 2039 5548 Fax 029 2038 4347
71 Lothian Road, Edinburgh EH3 9AZ
0870 606 5566 Fax 0870 606 5588

TSO Accredited Agents
(see Yellow Pages)

and through good booksellers

Printed in the UK by the Stationery Office, London

ID 158701   11/04   C4   990622

Contents

MALAYSIA AND ITS NEIGHBOURS

Foreword

The main purpose of the British Documents on the End of Empire Project (BDEEP) is to publish documents from British official archives on the ending of colonial and associated rule and on the context in which this took place. In 1945, aside from the countries of present-day India, Pakistan, Bangladesh and Burma, Britain had over fifty formal dependencies; by the end of 1965 the total had been almost halved and by 1985 only a handful remained. The ending of Britain's position in these formal dependencies was paralleled by changes in relations with states in an informal empire. The end of empire in the period at least since 1945 involved a change also in the empire as something that was more than the sum of its parts and as such formed an integral part of Britain's domestic affairs and international relations. In publishing official British documents on the end of empire this project is, to a degree, the successor to the two earlier series of published documents concerning the end of British rule in India and Burma which were edited by Professors Mansergh and Tinker respectively. The successful completion of *The transfer of power* and *The struggle for independence*,[1] both of which were based on British records, emphasised the need for similar published collections of documents important to the history of the final stages of Britain's association with other dependencies in Africa, the Middle East, the Caribbean, South-East Asia and the Pacific. These documents are crucial research tools for scholars both from sovereign independent states which emerged from colonial rule as well as those from Britain itself. BDEEP is also set in the much wider context of the efforts made by successive British governments to locate Britain's position in an international order. Here the empire, both in its formal and informal senses, is viewed as an instrument of the domestic, foreign and defence policy of successive British governments. The project is therefore concerned with the ending of colonial rule in individual territories as seen from the British side at one level, and the broader political, economic and strategic considerations involved in that at another.

Despite the similarities, however, BDEEP differs in significant ways from its predecessors in terms both of presentation and content. The project is of greater magnitude than that undertaken by Professor Mansergh for India. Four major differences can be identified. First, the ending of colonial rule within a dependent empire took place over a much longer period of time, extending into the final years of the twentieth century while having its roots in the Second World War and before. Secondly, the empire consisted of a large number of territories, varying in area, population, wealth and in many other ways, each with its own individual problems but often with their futures linked to those of neighbouring territories and the

---

[1] Nicholas Mansergh et al, eds, *Constitutional relations between Britain and India: the transfer of power 1942–47* 12 vols (London, 1970–1983); Hugh Tinker, ed, *Constitutional relations between Britain and Burma: the struggle for independence 1944–1948* 2 vols (London, 1983–1984).

growing complexity surrounding the colonial empire. Thirdly, while for India the documentary record for certain matters of high policy could be encapsulated within a relatively straightforward 'country' study, in the case of the colonial empire the documentary record is more diffuse because of the plethora of territories and their scattered location. Finally, the documents relating to the ending of colonial rule are not conveniently located within one leading department of state but rather are to be found in several of them. As the purpose of the project is to publish documents relating to the end of empire from the extensive range and quantity of official British records, private collections and other categories of non-official material are not regarded as principal documentary sources. In BDEEP, selections from non-official material will be used only in exceptional cases to fill gaps where they exist in the available official record.

In recognition of these differences and also of the fact that the end of empire involves consideration of a range of issues which operated at a much wider level than that normally associated with the ending of colonial rule in a single country, BDEEP is structured in two main series along with a third support series. Series A represents the general volumes in which, for successive British governments, documents relating to the empire as a whole are be published. Series B represents the country or territory volumes and provides territorial studies of how, from a British government perspective, former colonies and dependencies achieved their independence and countries which were part of an informal empire regained their autonomy. In addition to the two main documentary series, a third series—series C—has been published in the form of handbooks to the records of the former colonial empire which are deposited at The National Archives (formerly the Public Record Office). Series C consists of two volumes which form an integral part of BDEEP and also serve as former PRO guides to the records. Together they enable scholars and others wishing to follow the record of the ending of colonial rule and empire to pursue their inquiries beyond the published record provided by the general studies in series A and the country studies in series B. Volume one of the handbooks, a revised and updated version of *The records of the Colonial and Dominions Offices* by R B Pugh which was first published in 1964, is entitled *Records of the Colonial Office, Dominions Office, Commonwealth Relations Office and Commonwealth Office* (1995). It covers over two hundred years of activity down to 1968 when the Commonwealth Office merged with the Foreign Office to form the Foreign and Commonwealth Office. Volume two, entitled *Records of the Cabinet, Foreign Office, Treasury and other records* (1998), focuses more specifically on twentieth-century departmental records and also includes references to the records of inter-departmental committees, commissions of inquiry and international organisations. The two volumes were prepared under the direction and supervision of Dr Anne Thurston, at the time honorary research fellow at the Institute of Commonwealth Studies in the University of London, and more recently executive director of the International Records Management Trust.

In the two main series the research is organised in stages. Stage one, covering the years 1925–1957, is now complete and consists of three general volumes and five country volumes, collectively published in twenty-one individual parts. In series A there are volumes on *Imperial policy and colonial practice 1925–1945* in two parts (1996), *The Labour government and the end of empire 1945–1951* in four parts (1992), and *The Conservative government and the end of empire 1951–1957* in three parts (1994). In series B there are volumes on *Ghana* in two parts (1992), *Sri Lanka* in two parts (1997), *Malaya* in three parts (1995), *Egypt and the defence of the Middle East* in three parts (1998) and the *Sudan* in two parts (1998). Starting in 1999, the project began publishing volumes in a second stage which covers the period 1957–1964. Here there are five volumes, a general volume on the *Conservative government and the end of empire 1957–1964* in two parts (2000), and country volumes on the *West Indies* in one part (1999), *Nigeria* in two parts (2001), *Malaysia* in one part (2004) and Kenya. Research for a third and final stage, covering the years 1964–1971, began in 2000. It consists of a general volume and country volumes on Central Africa, Southern Africa, the Pacific (Fiji), and the Mediterranean (Cyprus and Malta).

The criteria which have been used in selecting documents for inclusion in individual volumes are explained in the introductions written by the specialist editors. These introductions are more substantial and contextual than those in previous series. Each volume also lists the sources searched at The National Archives. However, it may be helpful to outline the more general guiding principles which have been employed. BDEEP editors pursue several lines of inquiry. There is first the end of empire in a broad high policy sense in which the empire is viewed in terms of Britain's position as a world power and of the inter-relationship between what derives from this position and developments within the colonial dependencies. Here Britain's relations with the dependencies of the empire are set in the wider defence, economic and foreign policy contexts of Britain's relations with the United States, with Europe, and with the Commonwealth and United Nations. Secondly, there is investigation into colonial policy in its strict sense. Here the emphasis is on those areas which were specifically—but not exclusively—the concern of the leading department. In the period before the administrative amalgamations of the 1960s,[2] the leading department of the British government for most of the dependencies was the Colonial Office; for a minority it was either the Dominions Office and its successor, the Commonwealth Relations Office, or the Foreign Office. Colonial policy included questions of economic and social development, questions of governmental institutions and constitutional structures, and administrative questions concerning the future of the civil and public services and of the defence forces in a period of transition from European to indigenous control. Finally there is inquiry into the development of political and social forces within colonies, the response to these and the transfer of governmental authority and of legal sovereignty from Britain to its colonial dependencies as these processes were understood and interpreted by the British government. Here it should be emphasised that the purpose of BDEEP is not to document the history of colony politics or nationalist movements in any particular territory. Given the purpose of the project and the nature of much of the source material, the place of colony politics in BDEEP is conditioned by the extent to which an awareness of local political situations played an overt part in influencing major policy decisions made in Britain.

Although in varying degrees and from different perspectives, elements of these various lines of inquiry appear in both the general and the country series. The aim in both is to concentrate on the British record by selecting documents which illustrate

---

[2] The Colonial Office merged with the Commonwealth Relations Office in 1966 to form the Commonwealth Office. The Commonwealth Office merged with the Foreign Office in 1968 to form the Foreign and Commonwealth Office.

those policy issues which were deemed important by ministers and officials at the time. General volumes do not normally treat in any detail of matters which will be fully documented in the country volumes but some especially significant documents do appear in both series. The process of selection involves an inevitable degree of sifting and subtraction. Issues which in retrospect appear to be of lesser significance or to be ephemeral have been omitted. The main example concerns the extensive quantity of material devoted to appointments and terms of service—salaries, gradings, allowances, pension rights and compensation—within the colonial and related services. It is equally important to stress certain negative aspects of the official documentary record. Officials in London were sometimes not in a position to address potentially significant issues because the information was not available. Much in this respect depended on the extent of the documentation sent to London by the different colonial administrations. Once the stage of internal self-government had been reached, or where there was a dyarchy, the flow of detailed local information to London began to diminish.

Selection policy has been influenced by one further factor, namely access to the records at The National Archives. Unlike the India and Burma series and the current Foreign and Commonwealth Office series of Documents on British Policy Overseas (DBPO), BDEEP is not an official project. In practice this means that while editors have privileged access (in the form of research facilities and requisitioning procedures) to the records at The National Archives, they do not have unrestricted access. For files which at the time a volume is in preparation are either subject to extended closures beyond the statutory thirty years or retained in the originating department under section 3(4) of the Public Records Act of 1958, editors are subject to the same restrictions as all other researchers. Apart from cases where files or series of files are withheld, official weeding processes now tend to remove sentences or paragraphs from public view, rather than the whole document; such omissions are indicated in footnotes. To date access has not impeded the research undertaken by the project to any significant degree, and the project has been successful in securing the release of a number of hitherto withheld documents from the Historical Section of the Cabinet Office and the Records and Historical Department of the Foreign and Commonwealth Office.

A thematic arrangement of the documents has been adopted for the general volumes in series A. The country volumes in series B follow a chronological arrangement; in this respect they adopt the same approach as was used in the India and Burma series. For each volume in both series A and B a summary list of the documents included is provided. The headings to BDEEP documents, which have been editorially standardised, present the essential information. Together with the sequence number, the file reference (in the form of the call-up number at the Archives and any internal pagination or numeration) and the date of the document appear on the first line.[3] The second and subsequent lines record the subject of the document, the type of document (letter, memorandum, telegram etc), the originator (person or persons, committee, department) and the recipient (if any). A subject entry in a heading in single quotation marks denotes the title of a document as it

---

[3] The call-up number at the Archives precedes the comma in the references cited. In the case of documents from FO 371, the major foreign office political class, the internal numeration refers to the jacket number of the file.

appears in the original. An entry in square brackets denotes a subject indicator composed by the editor. This latter device has been employed in cases where no title is given in the original or where the original title is too unwieldy to reproduce in its entirety. Security classifications and, in the case of telegrams, times of despatch and receipt, have generally been omitted. In the headings to documents and the contents lists, ministers are identified by the name of the office-holder, not the title of the office (ie, Mr Macleod, not secretary of state for the colonies).[4] In the same contexts, officials are identified by their initials and surname. In general volumes, ambassadors, governors, high commissioners and other embassy or high commission staff are cited in the form Sir H Foot (Cyprus). Footnotes to documents appearing below the rule are editorial; those above the rule, or where no rule is printed, are part of the original document. Each volume provides an initial summary list of which principal offices were held by whom, and a separate series of biographical notes (at the end) for major figures who appear in the documents. Other figures are identified in editorial footnotes on the occasion of first appearance. Link-notes, written by the volume editor and indented in square brackets between the heading and the beginning of a document, are often used to explain the context of a document. Technical detail or extraneous material has been extracted from a number of documents. In such cases omission dots have been inserted in the text and the document is identified in the heading as an extract. Occasional omission dots have also been used to excise purely mechanical chain-of-command executive instructions and some redundant internal referencing has been removed, though much of it remains in place, for the benefit of researchers. No substantive material relating to policy-making has been excised from the documents. In general the aim has been to reproduce documents in their entirety but where available space is a major constraint on editors, a consideration which applies particularly in the case of general volumes, where the documentation is voluminous, this is not always possible, and some purely factual information may be omitted. It must also be emphasised in this context that the BDEEP volumes do not remove the necessity for researchers to study the original records themselves. The footnote reference 'not printed' is used only in cases where a specified enclosure or an annex to a document has not been included. Unless a specific cross-reference or note of explanation is provided, however, it can be assumed that other documents referred to in the text of the documents included have not been reproduced. Obvious typing errors in the original are in the main silently corrected, but abbreviations and contractions stand. Each volume has a list of abbreviations together with a consolidated index, and country volumes include a chronology of principal events.

One radical innovation, compared with previous Foreign Office or India and Burma series, is that BDEEP reproduces many more minutes by ministers and officials.

Crown copyright material is used by permission of The National Archives under licence from the Controller of Her Majesty's Stationery Office. All references and dates are given in the form recommended in guidelines from The National Archives.

*   *   *   *

---

[4] This is an editorial convention, following DBPO practice. Very few memoranda issued in their name were actually written by ministers themselves, but normally drafted by officials.

Formally launched in 1987, BDEEP has been based since its inception at the Institute of Commonwealth Studies. The work of the project is supervised by a Project Committee chaired by Professor Andrew Porter, Rhodes professor of imperial history in the University of London. Professor Porter succeeded Professor Anthony Low, formerly Smuts professor of the history of the Commonwealth in the University of Cambridge, who retired in November 1994. Professor Michael Crowder became the first general editor while holding a visiting professorship in the University of London and a part-time position at Amherst College, Massachusetts. Following his untimely death in 1988, Professor Crowder was replaced as general editor by Professor David Murray, pro vice-chancellor and professor of government at the Open University, who played a critical role in establishing a secure financial base for the project and in negotiating contracts with the volume editors and the publisher. His invaluable advice and expertise in dealing with the early manuscripts are acknowledged with particular gratitude. Mrs Anita Burdett was appointed as project secretary and research assistant. She was succeeded in September 1989 by Dr Stephen Ashton who previously worked with Professors Mansergh and Tinker during the final stages of the India and Burma series. Dr Ashton replaced Professor Murray as project director and general editor in 1993.

The project benefited from an initial pump-priming grant from the British Academy. Thanks are due to the secretary and Board of the Academy for this grant and for the decision of the British Academy to adopt BDEEP as one of its major projects. The Academy made a further award in 1996 which enabled the project to employ a research assistant on a fixed term contract. The Managers of the Smuts Memorial Fund in the University of Cambridge are also to be acknowledged. They made possible the workshop from which the project developed and they have since provided a further grant for work on two of the stage two volumes. The principal funding for the project in stages one and two has been provided by the Leverhulme Trust and the volumes are a tribute to the support provided by the Trustees. A major debt of gratitude is owed to the Trustees. In addition to their generous grants to cover the major costs of both stages, the Trustees agreed to a subsequent request to extend the duration of the first grant, and also provided a supplementary grant which enabled the project to secure Dr Ashton's appointment. It is thanks largely to the Leverhulme Trust that BDEEP has developed into one of the country's most successful historical research projects.

Members of the Project Committee, who meet annually at the Institute of Commonwealth Studies, have provided valuable advice and much needed encouragement. Professor Low, the first chairman of the Committee, made a singular contribution, initiating the first exploratory meeting at Cambridge in 1985 and presiding over subsequent developments in his customary constructive but unobtrusive manner. Professor Porter continues in a similar vein and his leadership and experience are much appreciated by the general editor. The director and the staff of the Institute of Commonwealth Studies have provided administrative support and the congenial surroundings within which the general editor works. The editors of volumes in both stages one have benefited considerably from the researches undertaken by Dr Anne Thurston and her assistants which resulted in the publication of the two handbooks. Although BDEEP is not an official project, the general editor wishes to acknowledge the support and co-operation received from the Historical Section of the Cabinet Office and the Historical and Records

Department of the Foreign and Commonwealth Office. He wishes also to record his appreciation of the spirit of friendly co-operation received from the editors of DBPO. Dr Ronald Hyam, editor in stage one of the general volume on the post-war Labour government and co-editor of the stage two volume on the Conservative government, played an important role in the compilation of the house-style adopted by BDEEP and his contribution is acknowledged with gratitude. Thanks also are due to The Stationery Office for assuming publishing responsibility and for their expert advice on matters of design and production. Last, but by no means least, the contribution of the chief executive and keeper of the records and the staff, both curatorial and administrative, at The National Archives must be emphasised. Without the facilities and privileges afforded to BDEEP editors at the National Archives, the project would not be viable.

S R Ashton
Institute of Commonwealth Studies
October 2003

Malaysia

Schedule of Contents

Abbreviations

ADO	Assistant District Officer
ANZAM	Australia, New Zealand and Malaya
ANZUS	Australia, New Zealand, United States (Pact)
ASA	Association of Southeast Asia
BARJASA	Barisan Rakyat (Ra'ayat) Jati Sarawak
BBC	British Broadcasting Corporation
BDCC(FE)	British Defence Co-ordinating Committee (Far East)
BDEEP	British Documents on End of Empire Project
BNB	British North Borneo
BS/BSS/BS(S)	Barisan Sosialis (Singapore) (Socialist Front)
BUNAP	Borneo Utara National Party (North Borneo National Party)
C	Cabinet memorandum/memos, Conservative (Macmillan) government, 1957–1963
CAB	Cabinet
CC	Cabinet conclusions (minutes), Conservative (Macmillan) government, 1957–1963
CCO	Clandestine Communist Organisation (Sarawak)
CCP	Chinese Communist Party
CDC	Colonial Development Corporation
CD(&)W	Colonial Development and Welfare
CEC	Central Executive Committee
CENTO	Central Treaty Organisation
CH	Companion of Honour
C in C	commander in chief
CMG	Companion of the Order of St Michael and St George
Cmnd	Command (parliamentary) paper
CO	Colonial Office
col	colonial

com-gen	commissioner-general
COS	Chiefs of Staff
CPC	Colonial Policy Committee (Cabinet, UK)
CPM	Communist Party of Malaya (see MCP)
CRO	Commonwealth Relations Office
DCC	Defence Co-ordinating Committee (see also BDCC(FE))
Dept	department
DO	Defence Committee (Cabinet, UK); CRO file series; District Officer
DOPC	Defence and Oversea Policy Committee (Cabinet, UK)
DSB	Director, Special Branch
DSE	Official Committee, Future Development in SE Asia
DTC	Department of Technical Co-operation
ECAFE	Economic Commission for Asia and the Far East
EEC	European Economic Community
EFTA	European Free Trade Area
FCO	Foreign and Commonwealth Office
FMS	Federated Malay States
FO	Foreign Office
FRUS	*Foreign Relations of the United States*
FSU	Factory and Shopworkers' Union (see SFSWU)
GATT	General Agreement on Tariffs and Trade
GCMG	Knight Grand Cross of the Order of St Michael and St George
GM	Greater Malaysia Committee
GMD	Greater Malaysia Discussions
GMT	Greenwich mean time
GNP	gross national product
gov	governor
gov-gen	governor-general
govt	government
HC	high commissioner
HCUKKL	high commissioner for the UK in Kuala Lumpur
HH	His Highness

HM	Her/His Majesty
HMG	Her Majesty's Government
HMOCS	Her Majesty's Oversea Civil Service
H of C Debs	*House of Commons Debates* (Hansard)
IBRD	International Bank for Reconstruction and Development (World Bank)
ICFTU	International Confederation of Free Trades Union
ILO	International Labour Organisation
IMF	International Monetary Fund
IMP	Independence of Malaya Party
ITC	Inter-Territorial Conference
ISC	Internal Security Council
JCS	Joint Chiefs of Staff
JIC	Joint Intelligence Committee
JPC	Joint Planning Staff
KBE	Knight Commander of the Order of the British Empire
KCMG	Knight Commander of the Order of St Michael and St George
KL	Kuala Lumpur
Kt	Knight
Lab	Labour Party
MAS	Malay Administrative Service
memo	memorandum
MCA	Malayan (Malaysian) Chinese Association
MCP	Malayan Communist Party (see CPM)
MCS	Malayan (Malaysian) Civil Service
MIC	Malayan (Malaysian) Indian Congress
MoD	Ministry of Defence
MP	Member of Parliament
MSCC	Malaysia Solidarity Consultative Committee
NATO	North Atlantic Treaty Organisation
NB	North Borneo
nd	no date
nn	no name; no number

NUSU	Nanyang University Students' Union
OAG	Officer administering government
OBA	Old Boys' Associations (Singapore)
OEEC	Organisation for European Economic Co-operation
OM	Order of Merit
OP/OPC	Oversea Policy Committee (Cabinet Committee)
OPD	Oversea Policy and Defence (Cabinet Committee)
O/S	Overseas
OSAS	Overseas Service Aid Scheme
PANAS	Party Negara Sarawak
PAP	People's Action Party (Singapore)
PAPAS	Party Pesaka Anak Sarawak (also PESAKA)
PESAKA	Party Pesaka Anak Sarawak (also PAPAS)
PKI	Partai Kommunis Indonesia (Indonesian Communist Party)
PM	prime minister
PMIP	Pan-Malayan Islamic Party
PNI	Partai Nasional Indonesia (Indonesian Nationalist Party)
PP	*Parliamentary Papers*
PPP	People's Progressive Party
PPS	parliamentary private secretary
PPSO	Preservation of Public Security Ordinance
PRB	Party Rakyat (Ra'ayat) Brunei (Brunei People's Party)
PREM	Prime Minister's Office files at PRO
PRM	Party Rakyat (Ra'ayat) Malaya (Malayan People's Party)
PRO	Public Record Office
PUS	permanent under-secretary
QC	Queen's Counsel
r	reigned
RAF	Royal Air Force
RN	Royal Navy
SABAPA	Sabah Alliance
SATU	Singapore Association of Trade Unions
SBWU	Singapore Bus Workers' Union

SCA	Sarawak Chinese Association
SCMSSU	Singapore Chinese Middle School Students' Union
SCPA	Singapore Country People's Association
SEATO	South East Asia Treaty Organisation
SGEU	Singapore General Employees' Union
SFSWU	Singapore Factory and Shop Workers' Union
SIC	Sabah Indian Congress
SLO	security liaison office/officer
SNAP	Sarawak National Party
S of S/ Ss of S	secretary of state/secretaries of state
SPA	Singapore People's Alliance
SRRA	Singapore Rural Residents' Association
STUC	Singapore Trade Union Congress
STUWC	Singapore Trade Union Working Committee
SUPP	Sarawak United People's Party
T	Treasury
tel	telegram
TNKU	Tentera Nasional Kalimantan Utara (National Army of North Kalimantan)
TUC	Trade Union Congress
UDP	United Democratic Party (Malaya)
UK	United Kingdom
UMNO	United Malays National Organisation (Malaya)
UNKO	United National Kadazan Organisation (Sabah)
UN(O)	United Nations (Organisation)
UNPMO	United National Pasok Momogun (United National Party of Sons of the Soil, Sabah)
UNRWA	United Nations Relief and Works Agency
UNTAB	United Nations Technical Assistance Board
UPP	United People's Party (Singapore)
US(A)	United States (of America)
USNO	United Sabah National Organisation
USSR	Union of Soviet Socialist Republics
WEU	Western European Union

Principal Holders of Offices 1957–1963

UNITED KINGDOM

Ministers in Conservative governments Jan 1957– Sept 1963

(a)   *Cabinet ministers*

Prime minister	Mr H Macmillan (10 Jan 1957–13 Oct 1963)
Chancellor of Exchequer	Mr P Thorneycroft (13 Jan 1957) Mr D Heathcoat Amory (6 Jan 1958) Mr J Selwyn Lloyd (27 July 1960) Mr R Maudling (13 July 1962)
S of S foreign affairs	Mr J Selwyn Lloyd (20 Dec 1955) Earl of Home (27 July 1960)
S of S colonies	Mr A Lennox-Boyd (30 July 1954) Mr I Macleod (14 Oct 1959) Mr R Maudling (9 Oct 1961) Mr D Sandys (13 July 1962) (office held jointly with S of S Commonwealth relations)
S of S Commonwealth relations	Earl of Home (12 Apr 1955) Mr D Sandys (28 July 1960) (office held jointly with S of S colonies from 13 July 1962)
Minister of defence	Mr D Sandys (13 Jan 1957) Mr H Watkinson (14 Oct 1959) Mr P Thorneycroft (13 July 1962)

(b)   *Junior ministers*

Colonial Office

Minister of state	Earl of Perth (17 Jan 1957) Marquess of Lansdowne (20 Apr 1962)

Parliamentary under-secretary of state   Mr J Profumo (18 Jan 1957)
                                           Mr J Amery (1 Dec 1958)
                                           Mr H Fraser (28 Oct 1960)
                                           Mr N Fisher (16 July 1962)

Commonwealth Relations Office

Minister of State   Mr C J M Alport (22 Oct 1959–1 Mar
                                              1961)
                                           Duke of Devonshire (6 Sept 1962)

Parliamentary under-secretary of state   Mr C J M Alport (18 Jan 1957)
                                           Mr R H M Thompson (22 Oct 1959)
                                           Duke of Devonshire (28 Oct 1960–6 Sept
                                              1962)
                                           Mr B Braine (9 Feb 1961–16 July 1962)
                                           Mr J D Tilney (16 July 1962)

(c) *Cabinet Committee on Greater Malaysia*

The Cabinet (Ministerial) Committee on Greater Malaysia, chaired by the prime
minister, met twice in Nov 1961 to prepare for talks with the Malayan government in
London later that month and a third time in Mar 1962 to consider a letter from Lord
Cobbold. Otherwise ministers considered Malaysian policy in the Defence
Committee, Colonial Policy Committee, Future Policy Committee, Oversea Policy
Committee and ad hoc meetings.

2. *Civil servants*

(a) *Secretary to the Cabinet*   Sir Norman Brook (1947–1962)
                                              Sir Burke Trend (1963–1972)

(b) *Colonial Office*

Permanent under-secretary of state   Sir John Macpherson (1956–1959)
                                           Sir Hilton Poynton (1959–1966)

Deputy permanent under-secretary   Sir Hilton Poynton (1948–1959)
   of state (joint)   Sir John Martin (1956–1965)
                                           Sir William Gorell Barnes (1959–1963)

Assistant under-secretary of state   E Melville (1917–1961)
   with superintending responsibility   C G Eastwood (1962)
   for Far East   W I J Wallace (1963)

Assistant secretary, head of Far
    Eastern Dept

J B Johnston (1956–1957)
W I J Wallace (1956–1962)
J D Higham (1963)

(c)   *Commonwealth Relations Office*

Permanent under-secretary of state

Sir Gilbert Laithwaite (1955–Aug 1959)
Sir Alexander Clutterbuck (Sept 1959–
    1961)
Sir Saville Garner (Jan 1962–1968)

Deputy permanent under-secretary
    of state (joint)

Sir Henry Lintott (1956–1963)
Sir Algernon Rumbold (1958–1966)
Sir Neil Pritchard (July–Nov 1961; 1963–
    1967)
Sir Arthur Snelling (1962–1966)

Assistant under-secretary of state
    with superintending responsibility
    for Malaya

A W Snelling (1957)
D W S Hunt (1960)
N Pritchard (1961)
G P Hampshire (1962)
C S Pickard (1963)

Assistant secretary, head of dept covering
    SE Asia

G W St J Chadwick (1957)
C S Pickard (1958)
W J Smith (1960)
R C Omerod (1961–1962)
A A Golds (1963)

(d)   *Foreign office*

Permanent under-secretary of state

Sir Frederick Hoyer Millar (1957–1962)
Sir Harold Caccia (1962–1965)

(e)   *Ministry of defence*

Permanent secretary

Sir Richard Powell (1956–1959)
Sir Edward Playfair (1960–1961)
Sir Robert Scott (1961–1963)

Chief of defence staff

Sir William Dickson (1958–1959)
Earl Mountbatten of Burma (1959–1965)

(f) *Cabinet (Official) Committee on Greater Malaysia*

This interdepartmental committee of officials was set up by direction of the prime minister to examine Tunku Abdul Rahman's proposal for the creation of a 'Greater Malaysia' incorporating Malaya, Singapore and the Borneo territories. Chaired by the permanent under-secretary, CRO (first Clutterbuck and then Garner) and composed of representatives from the CO, FO, MoD and Treasury, it met for the first time on 27 Sept 1961 and was dissolved on 22 Oct 1963.

SOUTH EAST ASIA

1. *British officials in SE Asia and some other postings*

(a) *SE Asia, 1957–1963*

Commissioner-general	Sir Robert Scott (1955–1959)
	Earl of Selkirk (1959–1963)
Deputy commissioner-general	A M MacKintosh (1956–1960)
	Sir Denis Allen (1959–62)
	A C S Adams (Nov 1962)

(b) *Federation of Malaya, 1957–1963*

High commissioner	Sir Geofroy Tory (1957–1963)
Deputy high commissioner, KL	R C W Hunt (1957–1959)
	E Crombie (1960–1961)
	M J Moynihan (1961–1963)
Deputy high commissioner, Penang, terminated Oct 1962	D J King (1957–1959)
	J R Williams (1959–1962)

(c) *Singapore, 1957–1959*

Governor	Sir William Goode (1957–1959)
Chief secretary	E B David (1957–1959)

Singapore, 1959–63

Yang di-pertuan negara	Sir William Goode (3 June–2 Dec 1959)
UK commissioner	Earl of Selkirk (1959–1963)

| UK deputy commissioner | H T Bourdillon (1959–1961) |
| | P B C Moore (1961–1963) |

(d)　*Brunei*

High commissioner	Sir Anthony Abell (1950–1959)
	Sir Dennis White (1959–1963)
	A M MacKintosh (1963–1964)
Resident	J O Gilbert (1954–1958)
	D C White (1958–1959)

(e)　*North Borneo*

Governor	Sir Roland Turnbull (1954–1960)
	Sir William Goode (1960–1963)
Chief secretary	R N Turner (1956–1963)

(f)　*Sarawak*

Governor	Sir Anthony Abell (1950–1959)
	Sir Alexander Waddell (1959–1963)
Chief secretary	J H Ellis (1955–1958)
	J C H Barcroft (1958)
	F D Jakeway (1959–1963)

(g)　*Federation of Malaysia, 1963*

| High commissioner | Viscount Head |

Deputy high commissioner, KL	J R A Bottomley
Deputy high commissioner, Singapore	P B C Moore
Deputy high commissioner, Eastern Malaysia (Kuching)	H P Hall

(h)　*Select list of other British officials overseas*

| Ambassador, Washington | Sir Harold Caccia (1956–1961) |
| | Sir David Ormsby-Gore (1961–1965) |

Permanent representative, UN	Sir Pierson Dixon (1954–1960) Sir Patrick Dean (1960–1964)
Permanent representative, UN Trusteeship Council	Sir Andrew Cohen (1957–1960) Sir Hugh Foot (1961–1962)
Ambassador, Jakarta	Sir Leslie Fry (1959–1963) Sir Andrew Gilchrist (1963–1966)
Ambassador, Manila	J (Sir John) Pilcher (1959–1963)

2. SE Asian governments, 1957–1963

(a) Brunei

Head of state	HH Sultan Omar Saifuddin III (r 1950–1967)
Mentri besar/chief minister under 1959 constitution	Datu Perdana Mentri Ibrahim Jafar (1959–1961) Datu Seri Paduka Awang Haji Marsal bin Maun (Aug 1961–1967)

(b) Federation of Malaya

(i) Head of state and Cabinet ministers, Aug 1957– Sept 1963

Yang di-pertuan agong	HM Tuanku Abdul Rahman of Negri Sembilan (1957–1960) HM Hisamuddin Alam Shah of Selangor (1960) HM Syed Putra of Perlis (1960)
Prime minister	Tunku Abdul Rahman (1957–Apr 1959, Aug 1959–1963) Tun Razak (Apr–Aug 1959)
Deputy prime minister	Tun Razak (1957–Apr 1959, Aug 1959–1963)
Minister of external affairs	Tunku Abdul Rahman (1957–Apr 1959, Aug 1959–1963) Dr Dato Ismail (Apr–Aug 1959)
Minister of defence	Tun Razak (1957–1963)

Minister of internal security/ home affairs	Dr Dato Ismail (1961–1963)
Minister of finance	H S Lee (1957–1959) Tan Siew Sin (1959–1963)

(ii)   Officials, 1957–1963

Permanent secretary, PM's Department	Dato Abdul Aziz bib Haji Abdul Majid (1957–1963)
Permanent secretary, Ministry of External Affairs	Othman bin Mohamed (1957–1959) Ghazali Shafie (1959–1963)
Permanent secretary, Ministry of Defence	F Brewer (1957–1959) R G K Thompson (1959–1961) Abdul Kadir bin Shamsudin (1961–1963)
High commissioner, London	Dato Nik Kamil (1957–1958) Tunku Yaacob (1958–1963)
Ambassador in Washington and permanent representative at UN	Dr Dato Ismail (1957–1959) Dato Nik Kamil (1959–1962) Dato Ong Yoke Lin (1962)

(c)   Singapore, 1957–1963

Head of state/Yang di-pertuan negara	Sir William Goode (3 June–2 Dec 1959) Yusof bin Ishak (2 Dec 1959; president of Republic of Singapore, 1965)
Chief minister to May1959	Lim Yew Hock (1956)
Prime minister from June 1959	Lee Kuan Yew
Deputy prime minister from June 1959	Toh Chin Chye

(c)   Federation of Malaysia, 16 September 1963

(i)   Heads of state and ministers

Yang di-pertuan agong	HM Syed Putra of Perlis
Prime minister & minister of external affairs	Tunku Abdul Rahman

Deputy prime minister & minister of defence	Tun Razak
Minister of internal security & interior	Dr Dato Ismail
Minister of finance	Tan Siew Sin
Federal minister for Sabah affairs	Peter Lo
Federal minister for Sarawak affairs	Temenggong Jugah anak Barieng
Sabah, head of state	Datu Mustapha bin Harun
Sabah, chief minister	Donald Stephens
Sarawak, head of state	Datu Abang Haji Openg
Sarawak, chief minister	Stephen Kalong Ningkan
Singapore, head of state	Yusof bin Ishak
Singapore, prime minister	Lee Kuan Yew

(ii) *Officials*

Permanent secretary, PM's Department	Dato Abdul Aziz bib Haji Abdul Majid
Permanent secretary, Ministry of External Affairs	Ghazali Shafie
Permanent secretary, Ministry of Defence	Abdul Kadir bin Shamsudin
High commissioner, London	Tunku Yaacob
Ambassador in Washington and permanent representative at UN	Dato Ong Yoke Lin

Chronological Table of Principal Events

1957

Jan	Harold Macmillan forms government
Mar–Apr	Constitutional talks in London result in agreement on self-government for Singapore
Mar	Bermuda conference between Macmillan and Eisenhower restores Anglo–American special relationship after Suez crisis
	Treaty of Rome for formation of European Common Market
Apr	New constitution for Sarawak comes into force including legislature with an elected majority
	Party Rakyat Brunei holds first congress
Aug	Independence of the Federation of Malaya
Oct	Anglo–Malayan Defence Agreement signed
Dec	Cabinet Colonial Policy Committee authorises public discussion of closer association in North Borneo and Sarawak
	PAP wins 13 seats in Singapore City Council election

1958

Jan	Federation of West Indies inaugurated
May	London talks settle the constitution for the self-governing State of Singapore

1959

Apr	Malaya and Indonesia sign treaty of friendship (ratified 30 Apr 1960)
May	People's Action Party wins 43 out of 51 seats in elections to Singapore legislative assembly
June	Singapore becomes self-governing with Lee Kuan Yew as premier
	SUPP formed in Sarawak
Aug	Alliance (under Tunku Abdul Rahman) wins Malayan federal elections with reduced majority
Sept	Promulgation of Brunei constitution and Anglo–Brunei agreement
Oct	Conservatives (under Macmillan) win British general election with increased majority
Nov–Dec	Elections in Sarawak on multi-tier basis

1960

Feb	Harold Macmillan's 'wind of change' speech in Cape Town
Apr	PANAS formed in Sarawak
June	Tunku Abdul Rahman raises possibility of Greater Malaysia with Lord Perth

July   Belgium sends troops to Congo
              Cabinet Colonial Policy Committee discuss Greater Malaysia proposal
              Official end of twelve-year Malayan emergency
Oct   Lord Monckton's report on Central African Federation
Nov   Sir R Scott reports to ministers on future developments in SE Asia

1961

Jan   J F Kennedy inaugurated as president of USA
              Duncan Sandys visits Kuala Lumpur for talk about merger
Apr   Further discussions on Greater Malaysia in Cabinet Colonial Policy
              Committee
              Ong Eng Guan defeats PAP in Hong Lim by-election, Singapore
              SNAP formed in Sarawak
May   Tunku Abdul Rahman publicly proposes Greater Malaysia, 27 May
              South Africa leaves Commonwealth
June   Lee supports Tunku's proposal, 3 June
              Macmillan welcomes Tunku's proposal in parliamentary statement, 20 June
July   Tunku's goodwill visit to Borneo territories
              David Marshall defeats PAP in Anson by-election, Singapore
              PAP dissidents meet Lord Selkirk, 'Eden Hall tea party'
              Lee Kuan Yew wins vote of confidence in Singapore's legislative assembly
              Formation of the Malaysia Solidarity Consultative Committee, 23 July
              (meets Aug–Feb 1962)
              Formation of the Barisan Sosialis, Singapore
Aug   UNKO formed in North Borneo
Aug–Sept   Discussions between Malaya and Singapore resulting in broad agreement
              on merger
Sept   Jamaicans vote in referendum to secede from Federation of West Indies
              First meeting of Greater Malaysia (Official) Committee
              Macmillan's memo, 'Our foreign and defence policy for the future', 29 Sept
Sept–Oct   Lee Kuan Yew's radio broadcasts, 'Battle for merger'
Oct   Reginald Maudling succeeds Iain Macleod as secretary of state for colonies
              Malayan house of assembly approve concept of Greater Malaysia, 18 Oct
              Greater Malaysia (Official) Committee reports to ministers, 20 Oct
Nov   Singapore white paper on proposed terms for merger
              London talks between British and Malayan governments on Malaysia,
              20–22 Nov
Dec   Singapore legislative assembly votes in favour of Malaysia
              USNO formed in North Borneo
              BARJASA formed in Sarawak

1962

Jan   Appointment of Commission of Enquiry, North Borneo and Sarawak
              (Cobbold Commission)
              Sir John Martin and Ian Wallace visit Borneo territories and Singapore
Feb   Report of MSCC broadly favours Malaysia
Feb–Apr   Cobbold Commission tours Sarawak and North Borneo, 18 Feb–18 Apr

Mar	Harold Watkinson visits Kuala Lumpur and Singapore for defence talks
	Tunku accuses British officers in Borneo of hampering progress towards Malaysia
Apr	Federation of West Indies dissolved
	Philippines house of representatives makes formal claim upon North Borneo
May	Cobbold Commission reconvenes in the UK
June	Lord Cobbold submits report to Harold Macmillan and Tunku Abdul Rahman (21 June)
July	Harold Macmillan reshuffles Cabinet ('night of the long knives') and Sandys becomes secretary of state for the colonies (in addition to Commonwealth secretary)
	Lee Kuan Yew wins vote in legislative assembly on referendum bill
	Lee Kuan Yew successfully defends referendum for merger at UN
	Brunei legislative council supports participation in merger talks
	Neutrality of Laos guaranteed at conclusion of Geneva Conference
	President Macapagal (Philippines) suggests Maphilindo (grouping of Malaya, Philippines and Indonesia)
	London talks result in Anglo–Malayan agreement on Malaysia, 31 July
Aug	Publication of joint statement on Malaysia and Cobbold Report, 1 Aug
	Inter-Governmental Committee set up under Lord Lansdowne; first meeting, 30 Aug
	Party Rakyat wins Brunei elections
	Netherlands and Indonesia reach agreement on West Irian dispute
Sept	Singaporeans vote for Malaysia in a referendum, 1 Sept
	Legislatures of North Borneo and Sarawak approve Malaysia in principle
	Commonwealth premiers endorse British negotiations to join EEC
Oct	Transfer of West Irian to UN (later to Indonesia, 1 May 1963)
	Formation of Sabah Alliance Party
	Formation of Sarawak United Front (Sarawak Alliance, Nov 1962)
Nov	Tunku's second goodwill visit to North Borneo and Sarawak
Dec	Dean Acheson says Britain has lost an empire but failed to find a role, 5 Dec
	Brunei rising, 8 Dec
	President Kennedy and Macmillan meet at Nassau and agree that US shall provide Britain with Polaris missiles instead of Skybolt
	Britain acknowledges Nyasaland's right to secede from Central African Federation

1963

Jan	De Gaulle vetoes UK application to join EEC
	Dr Subandrio announces Indonesia's 'confrontation' towards Malaysia, 20 Jan
Feb	Operation 'Cold Store' leads to mass arrests of communists and their supporters in Singapore
	Quadripartite talks on Malaysia in Washington (Australia, New Zealand, United Kingdom and United States)
	Publication of the Report of the Inter-Governmental Committee (Lord Lansdowne), 27 Feb

Feb–Mar   Talks between Brunei and Malaya result in heads of agreement
Mar   Executive Working Group on Malaysian matters set up in Whitehall
          Sarawak's Council Negri and North Borneo's legislative council approve
          Malaysian entry terms as set out in Lansdowne report
Apr   Angus MacKintosh succeeds Dennis White as high commissioner of
          Brunei
          Sir Henry Lintott's financial mission to Kuala Lumpur, 6–14 Apr
May   Anglo–Malayan talks in London on financial provision for Malaysia
          Tunku Abdul Rahman and Sukarno meet in Tokyo
May–June Lansdowne visits KL for talks
June   Foreign ministers of Malaya, Philippines and Indonesia meet in Manila
          IBRD mission (Jacques Rueff) reports on economic aspects of Malaysia
          Talks in Kuala Lumpur between Malaya and Singapore and between
          Malaya and Brunei reach deadlock and Tunku suggests 'Little Malaysia'
          Off-shore oil discovered in Brunei
July   London talks result in the Malaysia Agreement without Brunei, 9 July
          Conclusion of elections in North Borneo and Sarawak
          British Parliament enacts legislation for Malaysia
July–Aug Manila Summit between Tunku Abdul Rahman, Sukarno (Indonesia) and
          Macapagal (Philippines), 30 July–5 Aug
Aug   Macmillan and Kennedy correspond on Indonesian opposition to
          Malaysia
          Britain, US and USSR sign nuclear test ban treaty
          Federal Parliament enacts legislation for Malaysia
          Completion of British orders in council for constitutions of Sabah,
          Sarawak and Singapore, and for compensation to overseas officers in
          North Borneo and Sarawak
          Postponement of Malaysia
          UN mission on Borneo opinion, arrives in Kuching on 16 Aug
          Duncan Sandys makes prolonged visit to KL, departs London 23 Aug
          Lee Kuan Yew unilaterally declares Singapore's independence on 31 Aug
          Sabah and Sarawak achieve de facto self-government pending formation
          of Malaysia
Sept   Yang di-pertuan agong appoints heads of state for Sabah and Sarawak
          Publication of the report of the UN mission to North Borneo and
          Sarawak, 14 Sept
          Inauguration of Malaysia, 16 Sept
          Indonesian mob storms British embassy in Jakarta, 16–18 Sept
          People's Action Party wins general election in Singapore, 21 Sept

Introduction*

The documents in this collection tell the story of the making of Malaysia from the records and perspectives of British policy-makers. They narrate developments from the achievement of Malayan independence in 1957 to the inauguration six years later of a greater state incorporating Malaya, Singapore, Sabah (North Borneo) and Sarawak. In so doing they reveal how statements of intent became detailed plans and the extent to which these plans were brought to fruition. That some called it a 'Grand Design' suggests a coherent scheme of decolonisation and, in so far as it was, it appeared to be effective; after all, Britain managed to withdraw from remaining dependencies in Southeast Asia while retaining interests and influence there.

At first sight, therefore, the formation of Malaysia may appear to have been the completion of unfinished business and the last, rather predictable, chapter in the history of colonial empire in Southeast Asian. It came at the end of a spate of decolonisation by the Macmillan government and at a time when European powers were generally eager to detach themselves from overseas dependencies if, indeed, they had not already done so. In fact, the principal components of the Malaysia project had previously passed beyond colonialism: Malaya had been independent since 31 August 1957 and, although sovereignty over Singapore lay with Britain until its transfer to Malaysia, the island enjoyed internal self-government from June 1959. Brunei (which had been expected to join the federation until the Sultan pulled out on the eve of the signing ceremony) was a protected state with its own sovereign ruler and, therefore, beyond British jurisdiction. Of the participating countries, only North Borneo and Sarawak were crown colonies, and, in a manner of speaking, only North Borneo and Sarawak were being decolonised. Indeed, as the final touches were put to Malaysia, the British presented it to the United Nations, not as a new state, but as an extension of an existing member-state, that is to say an extension of the

* During the course of research for this volume I have incurred debts to many people and institutions. I wish to thank Shigeru Akita, Mandy Banton, Matthew Jones, Yoichi Kibata, Albert Lau, Edwin Lee, Roger Louis, Mohd Samsudin, Andrew Porter, Kumar Ramakrishna, Tim Ross, the late Ralph Smith, and Nicholas White. I am especially grateful to the BDEEP general editor, Stephen Ashton, for his support and expert guidance throughout the preparation of this volume. I received a generous grant of sabbatical leave from Royal Holloway, University of London to enable me to complete the volume and invaluable assistance from the Bodelian Library (Rhodes House), British Library, Churchill Archives Centre at Cambridge, The National Archives (Public Record Office), and the library of the School of Oriental and African Studies. My research has benefited from discussion at the Imperial History Seminar (University of Cambridge), the Imperial History Seminar (Institute of Historical Research, London), the seminar on 'South Asia and the Modern World-System' (University of Tokyo, Bunkyo-ku, Nov 2000), the workshop on 'Nation-building Histories' (Institute of Southeast Asian Studies, Singapore, Sept 2002), and a meeting of the Royal Society for Asian Affairs (Feb 2003). Parts of articles published in the *Journal of Imperial and Commonwealth History*, 26, 2 (1998), *Asian Affairs*, 24, 3 (2003), and *Modern Asian Studies*, 38, 4 (2004) were drawn from material used for this volume. Finally, I thank Jane, whose encouragement has sustained me through the years of research and writing.

independent Federation of Malaya to which Sabah (North Borneo), Sarawak and Singapore merely acceded. In short, the creation of Malaysia appears to have been an undramatic piece of house-keeping, an operation to tidy up the remnants of empire.

But the documents expose another, rougher side to the story: one in which policy-making snagged on the contradictions of multiple objectives; one in which Britain was buffeted by the conflicting demands of local politicians and interventions from outside; one in which events frequently brought planning to a standstill and deadlock fostered despondency; one in which resistance was met by guile or coercion, and the prospect of failure provoked desperate measures; one in which not all of Britain's objectives were fulfilled while some of its fears were realised. Indeed, the Malaysia that was inaugurated on 16 September 1963 failed wholly to satisfy any of the parties to it. It was neither forged through nationalist struggle, nor did it reflect a homogeneous national identity. Rather it was the product of grudging compromise and underpinned by only fragile guarantees; its formation was peppered with resistance and that it came into being at all was regarded by many at the time as a close-run thing.

Taken altogether the 227 documents in this collection are perhaps the equivalent in size to a few of the bulkier files amongst the thousands consulted during the research for this volume. Selection has, therefore, been brutal but it has been guided by the overarching quest for those papers which shed light on the reasons, manner and timing of the key decisions to end empire and create the successor state of Malaysia. In providing a continuous record of such decisions, the editor has, firstly, struck a balance between the principal themes of colonial obligations and imperial interests, secondly, placed Malaysian policy in the context of domestic, regional and global problems, thirdly, included material from various departments and levels of government, and, finally, covered crises and the unexpected as well as the measured products of calm deliberation.

The documents are presented in chronological order and arranged in five chapters. Each chapter deals with a distinct period which ends at the apparent closure of one issue and at the start of another phase in policy-making. Chapter 1 covers the tentative steps towards territorial integration following Malayan independence and culminates in Tunku Abdul Rahman's public initiative on 27 May 1961. The second chapter, which is dominated by Anglo–Malayan discussions, concludes with the joint statement following the London talks of November 1961. This publicised an undertaking to proceed with Malaysia provided conditions about the future of Singapore and the interests of Borneo peoples were met. Chapter three focuses, though not to the exclusion of other problems, on the Cobbold enquiry into Borneo opinion. During this period the crisis in Anglo–Malayan relations, which was provoked by the Commission's report, combined with the deterioration in Lee Kuan Yew's position in Singapore to threaten a break-down which was averted by the two agreements (one public and the other secret) reached at the London conference at the end of July 1962. Over the next year (chapter 4), the detailed membership terms and constitutional provisions were worked out in inter-governmental discussions between Malaya and Singapore, between Malaya and Brunei, and between Britain, Malaya and the Borneo colonies. Steady progress towards the formal agreement on 9 July 1963 was disrupted, however, by the Brunei revolt, mass arrests in Singapore, opposition from Indonesia and the Philippines, and the decision of the Sultan of Brunei not to join the federation. The roller-coaster then entered its shortest but bumpiest passage (chapter 5) as the result of the Tunku's decision to postpone inauguration pending a UN inquiry.

The chronological account given by the documents is supported by a narrative which is reproduced as the appendix to this collection. Entitled 'The origins and formation of Malaysia', this paper was produced in 1970 by the Research Department of the FCO and, like the other documents here, its availability was subject to the provisions of the 'thirty year rule'. It represents considerable research and the investment of much staff time but no explanation is provided for its origins and purpose, about which one can only speculate. It may have been used to provide background to the continuing dispute between Malaysia and the Philippines over sovereign jurisdiction in Sabah (formerly North Borneo); a few lines on this subject (Appendix, paragraph 141) have been retained under section 3(4) of the Public Records Act of 1958. On the other hand, it should be noted that the dispute amounts to a relatively brief section of the paper. Since narrative is well served by the appendix as well as by the chronological arrangement of the documents, this introduction approaches the making of Malaysia from two different angles: the first part, Aspects of Policy, discusses the notion of the 'Grand Design', economic factors, defence issues and the making and implementation of the Malaysia policy. The second part, Dimensions of Merger, examines the Malaya-Singapore axis, Anglo–Malayan differences over the decolonisation of Borneo, the United Nations mission and, finally, Brunei's decision not to join.

1 Aspects of Policy
The 'Grand Design': awaiting an initiative

> Our ultimate objective is a Confederation between the five present territories of the Federation of Malaya, Singapore, Sarawak, North Borneo and Brunei. We have already agreed that this should be achieved in two stages: first by the combination of (a) Singapore and the Federation and (b) the three Borneo Territories as separate entities; and second, by bring [sic] together these two groups under one appropriate constitutional government.
> [Malcolm MacDonald, 2 April 1955 [1]]

The inauguration of the Federation of Malaysia on 16 September 1963 was the culmination of a long-held objective of British government. Consolidation of disparate Southeast Asian dependencies became a principle of policy during wartime planning for the post-war region and was pursued erratically and unsuccessfully over the next fifteen years. Six months after the fall of Singapore to Japan, the Foreign Office and Colonial Office agreed on the desirability of a union of the Malay States, Straits Settlements and Borneo territories. Although the final plans for the post-war reoccupation of Southeast Asia fell far short of such a union, the government created a structure for regional co-ordination in the office of the governor-general (later commissioner-general) and looked forward to the eventual creation of what Malcolm MacDonald called a self-governing 'British dominion of Southeast Asia'. The post-war separation of Singapore and Malaya was deeply regretted in many quarters—not least on economic grounds—but the prospect of their merger was kept alive by the commissioner-general and by community leaders. Cautious attempts were made to link the three Borneo territories, on the one hand, and, on the other, to encourage politicians in Malaya and Singapore to discuss the feasibility of merging island with peninsula. It was envisaged that Malaya and Singapore would unite in advance of the Borneo territories, and that integration of the two blocs lay some distance in the future on account of their unequal political and economic development. An alternative approach was to encourage the amalgamation of all five territories, without the preliminary formation of the Malayan and Borneo blocs, but until 1961 this was generally regarded as unrealistic. In any case, closer association was expected to be a long-drawn-out process. Periodically, the British tried to stimulate local interest in the concept, but they knew it would be counter-productive to impose a scheme or to issue a directive and they steadfastly refrained from forcing the pace.[2]

Notwithstanding declarations of intent, however, progress was slow. Malays of the peninsula mistrusted domination by Singapore's Chinese; Singaporeans feared their subordination as the twelfth state in a Malay-controlled federation; business interests of peninsula and island pulled in different directions; the Sultan of Brunei was on his guard against loss of both sovereignty and oil revenue; non-Malay indigenous peoples of Borneo had little love for Malays, while British governors of North Borneo and Sarawak were adamant that their charges should be given sufficient, if unspecified, time to prepare for merger. Momentum was lost during the worst years of the Malayan emergency (1948–1960) when territories drifted further apart and their separateness was reinforced by vested interests. In 1953 a Joint Co-ordinating Committee was established to prepare for the merger of island and peninsula largely because General Templer (high commissioner, Malaya, 1952–1954) and the Chiefs of Staff sought to integrate the defence and internal security of Malaya and Singapore.[3] At the same time fresh impetus was given to the integration of the Borneo dependencies; in April 1953 MacDonald succeeded to the extent of establishing the twice-yearly Inter-Territorial Conference for the co-ordination of policies and common services. Neither initiative bore fruit. MacDonald was tireless and infinitely optimistic in the pursuit of what he called 'our grand design', but on his departure from Southeast Asia in 1955 it still seemed a long way off.[4] If the union of Malaya and Singapore presented difficulties, those related to its assimilation of the Borneo territories were even greater: politically and economically they diverged from each other and lagged far behind Singapore and Malaya. In March 1956 the Sultan of Brunei publicly rejected the idea of a Borneo federation with the result that the Colonial Office temporarily shelved a proposal for a Standing Joint Council to take over from the Inter-Territorial Conferences. Meanwhile, Malaya and Singapore went their separate ways. In August 1957 the Federation achieved independence on its own and in 1957–1958 two constitutional conferences placed Singapore on course to be a self-governing state in 1959. Thus empire ended in Malaya before three frequently-stated pre-conditions for decolonisation were in place: firstly, the state of emergency had not ended; secondly, a genuine multi-racial movement and sense of nationhood had yet to emerge; thirdly, fusion with Singapore and the Borneo territories seemed more distant than ever.

Nevertheless, the British did not abandon the goal of regional consolidation. Three months after Malayan *merdeka* (independence), the secretary of state for the colonies returned to the question of the closer association of the Borneo territories. Still wary of forcing the pace, Alan Lennox-Boyd recommended to the Cabinet Colonial Policy Committee the encouragement of public debate in the two colonies about their future (documents 1, 2). Following radio broadcasts by the governors (3), the

Legislative Councils of North Borneo and Sarawak set up committees to ascertain popular reaction to the idea of territorial integration. Largely owing to inter-ethnic mistrust, the response was unenthusiastic. The chief obstacle once again proved to be the Sultan of Brunei who resented current supervision by personnel from the Sarawak government and suspected that further integration would result in the distribution of oil revenue to poorer neighbours. When he returned to Brunei in December 1958, MacDonald (who was then high commissioner in New Delhi), noted impressive developments since his last visit just over three years before as well as 'a pleasing change in the Sultan himself'. He observed 'that his face reveals a much more mature, self-confident character than before. Nor did I see in his eyes any hint of the madness which one should perhaps look for in a member of the Royal House of Brunei' (5, see also 6). On these grounds MacDonald based a hope that his highness might yet be persuaded to espouse closer association.

In fact, however, Omar Ali Saifuddun explored the possibility of a different link-up—a special relationship with the Federation of Malaya. In 1958–1959 he granted a loan of M\$100 million to the federal government which in turn seconded civil servants to take the place of British expatriates in the fledgling modern state of Brunei. Omar Ali also entertained Malay Sultans at the opening of the new mosque in Brunei Town, visited Kuala Lumpur and received as his guest in Brunei the Yang-di Pertuan Agong (the king of Malaya).[5] The British had mixed feelings about this Brunei-Malaya rapprochement: on the one hand it might constitute a breach of the 1905–1906 arrangement whereby Britain had assumed control of Brunei's external relations; on the other hand, it might usefully prepare Borneo for the ultimate stage in regional consolidation. In any case, British officials had very little say in the matter after Omar Saifuddin reinforced his autonomy by promulgating a written constitution on 29 September 1959. 'Brunei is now in practice no longer a Colonial Office responsibility', remarked a former high commissioner. 'She will go her own way' (16, see also 4 and 9).

As one cadre of senior officials was replaced by another at the end of 1959 and the beginning of 1960—Scott by Selkirk as commissioner-general, Turnbull by Goode as governor of North Borneo, Abell by Waddell as governor of Sarawak and by White as high commissioner of Brunei—there was a general assessment of the prospects for territorial consolidation. Scott suggested that the resurrection of the idea would be something for the in-coming governors of North Borneo and Sarawak to address (11, 12, 14, 16, 17).[6] While he emphasised 'that the future holds great promise for the Borneo Territories in conjunction and danger if they fail to unite', he reiterated 'that no pressure should be put upon the Sultan to drive him in the direction of closer association' (11). Abell summed up the position as follows: 'The case for a form of closer association is as strong today as it ever was; the arguments used in its favour are as unassailable as they ever were but the practical difficulties have grown immeasurably and will continue to grow unless we do something about them.' Abell went further, however, in arguing that the time had come for London to take the lead: 'I think it is essential that Her Majesty's Government should have a policy in this matter which her representatives in Borneo should be instructed to follow. If we are allowed to drift further apart we may find, as in the case of Malaya and Singapore that the gulf is too wide to bridge' (16). Two months later, Sir Denis Allen (out-going deputy commissioner-general) similarly urged Whitehall to take the lead: 'I confess to some uneasiness whether, if ... our attitude remained simply one of "wait and see", we might not find ourselves missing important opportunities when the critical moment came.' He continued: 'if we wish to use our remaining influence in those territories to steer events in one direction rather than another we ought to begin soon' (18).

The long-awaited initiative came from an unexpected quarter when Tunku Abdul Rahman, prime minister of Malaya, explored the idea of a super-federation of Malaya, the Borneo territories and possibly Singapore too. The Tunku was known to be hostile to a bilateral merger with Singapore, but in 1958–1959 his interest in the 'Grand Design' may have been stirred by the possibility—deemed by British officials to be unlikely—of Sukarno mounting a claim to northern Borneo on the lines of his bid for Western New Guinea (7, 8, 10 and 19). While it may have been tempting to move immediately to their ultimate objective—ie the integration of all five territories—British representatives in Southeast Asia felt that the Tunku's proposal was unrealistic and even dangerous. Premature union with Malaya would set back the steady development of North Borneo and Sarawak which, it was held, would be better served by colonial rule for many years to come. 'On the whole', commented Sir John Martin of the Colonial Office in a letter to Sir Denis Allen in Singapore, 'benevolent neutrality, but with "later rather than now" the motto, seems our right policy in this matter' (20).[7] For the time being the Tunku was persuaded that the federation's assimilation of the Borneo territories should remain a long-term goal with an unspecified target date. Nevertheless, while in London for the Commonwealth Prime Ministers' Conference in May–June 1960, the Tunku raised the subject in a talk with Lord Perth, minister of state for colonial affairs (21, 22). Ministers might have allowed the matter to drop once again had it not been for Selkirk's intervention.

Selkirk, who had only recently taken up his appointment in Southeast Asia, recognised the difficulties in merger: tension arising from communal and economic differences, doubts over the future of the Singapore base and obligations to protect the 'more primitive peoples' of Borneo. With respect to the last issue, he foresaw 'the possible danger of running into a situation somewhat similar to that in the Central African Federation', a comparison which would frequently be drawn by British policy-makers during the course of the next three years. On the other hand, he felt their membership of a 'Greater Malaysia' would provide the Borneo territories with much-needed protection, for, even if they were to achieve independence on their own, they would not be able to defend themselves without British assistance (23). Defence and security were the key issues for Selkirk. It was most important to 'give a measure of stability to the area' which was threatened by territorial fragmentation and particularly by the political instability of Singapore. Now at last the Tunku, who hitherto had raised all manner of objections to merger, offered an opportunity for some movement in this direction to which, Selkirk was confident, Lee Kuan Yew's government in Singapore would 'readily agree'. Inchoate though the Tunku's proposal was, the commissioner-general urged ministers to examine it 'very closely and urgently'.

Selkirk's entreaty had its effect in that on 27 July the matter was considered by the Colonial Policy Committee, chaired by the prime minister and with the commissioner-general present (24, 25, 27). There was, however, no dramatic shift in approach. On the advice of officials, Iain Macleod presented a cautious paper. The secretary of state went only so far as to incline to the view that 'the idea of an association of the five territories was likely to provide the least unsatisfactory future' both for the Borneo peoples and for Britain, and that it might pave the way for the merger of Malaya and Singapore which now seemed unlikely except within a wider federation. He argued that 'we ought to go slowly' because 'there are so many unknowns here' and 'far too many imponderables for us to be certain'. Rather than issue a policy statement, he instructed Selkirk to consult the governors of North Borneo and Sarawak and the high commissioner of Brunei. Having conferred at a meeting in Kuching, which was attended by Lord Perth, on 25 October Selkirk formally requested ministerial endorsement of broad lines of a policy gradually leading to the political association of the five territories (30). At the end of January 1961, after the matter had been aired in the annual conference at Eden Hall (the commissioner-general's residence), Selkirk followed up his October despatch with another. Now he was more insistent that, against a backdrop of Singapore's deteriorating internal security, 'Her Majesty's Government should decide urgently what its attitude should be towards the Grand Design'. He feared that, unless ministers responded positively to Lee Kuan Yew's commitment to merger, Singapore's prime minister would be challenged, possibly toppled, by the extreme left. He also reported encouraging signs that the Malayan government was coming round to the view that its own well-being depended on stabilising Singapore through merger (32, 33, also 47).

Ever since Malayan independence, British interest in closer association had focused but snagged on the Borneo territories. From early 1961, however, the potential insecurity of Singapore concentrated attention on the other dimension of the 'Grand Design'—the union of Malaya and Singapore. Since the Tunku would not contemplate the latter without being sure of the former, the British faced a dilemma: an accelerated advance towards 'Greater Malaysia' would have grave repercussions on Borneo, but delay could be fatal for Singapore (26, 31, 36). In mid-April 1961, on the recommendation of Macleod, the Colonial Policy Committee deferred a decision pending further consultations, this time with the Australian and New Zealand governments and also with the Tunku, Lee Kuan Yew and other local notables (34, 35). Ministers had not turned their backs on the 'Grand Design', but they were reluctant to run the risk of pressing ahead with it until they had were assured that it had significant support and a reasonable chance of success.

The determination driving the 'Grand Design' at this stage lay in Southeast Asia, not in London, and more in Singapore than in Kuala Lumpur. A few days after the Colonial Policy Committee had confirmed its cautious approach and had authorised Selkirk to take soundings locally, Lee Kuan Yew himself broached the matter with the Tunku. Lee was faced with dissent in his party and opposition to his government, and it was imperative to persuade the Tunku of the need for an early agreement on merger in principle. After their meeting and having consulted Selkirk and Philip Moore (Selkirk's deputy), Lee composed a secret paper on how merger might be achieved which he completed on 9 May and despatched to Kuala Lumpur (37). Although the commissioner-general had doubts about its practicality, especially regarding the integration of the Borneo territories for whose closer association he recommended a number of immediate measures (36), a break-through was in the offing. Tun Razak, Malaya's deputy prime minister, accepted Lee's arguments and in turn convinced the Tunku that Malaya could no longer stand alone. In a speech to foreign correspondents at the Singapore Press Club on 27 May 1961, Tunku Abdul

Rahman announced his conversion to 'Greater Malaysia' in general but unmistakable terms. He later described its 'electrifying' effect: 'Suddenly everyone was sitting bolt upright, hardly believing their ears. ... My reference so discreetly but publicly to "Malaysia" took all the territories by storm.'[8] Tory was delighted: 'Given his violent prejudice hitherto this represents almost miraculous change of heart. As suspected, now penny has dropped.' He urged ministers to seize the opportunity and press ahead towards long-held objectives, for, while the Tunku was 'perhaps moving ahead faster than we were prepared to go... we have more hope of steering him if we go along with him than if we try to restrain him at this juncture' (39).

Although the integration of the five territories had long been pivotal to British strategy in the region, the mood in London was neither triumphant nor even optimistic. For years ministers had awaited a local initiative; but, now that it had been offered, the way forward was unclear and success uncertain. The Tunku, by contrast, tried to force the pace. Unnerved by the deteriorating situation in Singapore, he wanted an early decision on the Borneo territories and, with the zeal of a convert, he pressed the British government for an explicit policy statement (41, 46). While Selkirk was anxious not to waste this chance, he and other British officials in the region were appalled by the Tunku's haste with respect to North Borneo and Sarawak (40, 42–44, 47, 48, 55, 58). At home ministers were careful not to give the impression of wanting Malaysia either forthwith or at all costs. In any case, they preferred to enter negotiations without having first revealed their fundamental *desiderata*. Macmillan, therefore, parried the Tunku's demands while he awaited the views of the Australian and New Zealand governments (51–53, 57). When, however, the Tunku made it clear that he would not engage in talks without a firm British commitment to Malaysia, Macmillan, who had so far merely welcomed the proposal in a parliamentary statement at the end of June, had no option but to adopt it as a principle of policy (61, 63, 66, 67). It was not until the end of September, four months after the Tunku's public announcement, that the British prime minister set in train formal preparations for Anglo–Malayan discussions (60, 62, 71, 75–78).

The 'Grand Design' might have appeared to offer a future for Singapore and the Borneo territories, long-term security for Malaya and guarantees for Britain's interests and influence in the region, yet at this stage it was more a rhetorical flourish than a template for territorial integration, let alone for nation-building. Duncan Sandys for one criticised the term as 'pretentious and vague'.[9] In itself, 'Grand Design' did not provide practical answers to the pressing questions now facing ministers and their officials. How was continued British use of the Singapore base to be guaranteed? How was the union of independent Malaya and the British dependency of Singapore to be effected? How were the Borneo territories to be integrated within Malaysia without contravening British trusteeship obligations to their peoples? What were the likely costs and benefits of Malaysia?

Economic aspects

My own personal feeling is that the economic aspects of these proposals are not likely to be of paramount importance.
[C C Lucas (Treasury), 21 Aug 1960 [10]]

The making of Malaysia was not simply a colonial issue. It has to be considered, as it was by politicians and policy-makers at the time, against a backdrop of balance of payments problems and galloping defence costs, of the Cold War and the special relationship with the US, of Commonwealth allegiances and the anti-colonialism of the UN. Strategies of decolonisation could help Britain address these other problems if, by moving from formal to informal empire, it found a new role in the world.[11] With respect to Southeast Asia, the 'Grand Design' for a 'Greater Malaysia' might perpetuate Britain's influence in the post-colonial period. Those in British governing circles who welcomed Malaysia did so on account of its expected benefits for Britain. It was these very expectations, on the other hand, that moved Malaya's Socialist Front, Singapore's Barisan Sosialis and Brunei's Party Rakyat to condemn Malaysia as neo-colonialism, as the pursuit of imperialism by other means. The charge that it was 'in fact, nothing but a smokescreen behind which the old colonialist activities continue' was also energetically articulated by the Indonesian government and the Soviet bloc in the United Nations. A month after its inauguration, Khrushchev condemned Malaysia as 'a new form of the old colonialist policy'. He continued: 'The British imperialists want to hold onto their colonial domination in South East Asia, and in creating this State they are merely changing the label'.[12] Associated with the transparent polemic of President Sukarno's rickety regime, these claims may now appear an easy target.[13] Nevertheless, the economic aspects of neo-colonialism have found support in so much of the scholarly literature, that their significance in driving and shaping British policy should be reassessed.

Certainly there is plenty of data indicating that British business continued to dominate the trade, investment, planting and mining sectors of the 'Greater Malaysia' region and enjoyed a favourable position in the post-colonial state of Malaya. Indeed, British business had huge assets in the Federation, Singapore and the Borneo territories. British private capital investment in Malaya was estimated at about £400 millions (compared with £335 millions in India and £108 in Pakistan) while British exports were approximately £60 millions or, according to another evaluation, about 22 per cent of Malaya's total imports. At the time of Malayan independence British officials emphasised the country's value as a source of essential raw materials and a substantial dollar-earner.[14] After independence economic links between Malaya and the United Kingdom intensified and, when the British government was calculating its financial settlement for Malaysia in 1963, Sir Geofroy Tory (high commissioner in Kuala Lumpur) advocated generous provision on the ground that Britain had 'a very big financial stake in Malaya and a considerable vested interest in the maintenance of a stable and prosperous Malayan economy' (170).

In the long-term, however, Malaya's economic importance for Britain was on the wane.[15] Whereas Britain had valued Malaya for the dollar-earning capacity of rubber and tin (it had been the principal dollar-earner at the onset of the communist insurrection), by 1960 'the importance of Malayan dollars to the strength of sterling had now declined with the spread of convertibility'.[16] Competition with synthetic rubber tended to drive down the price of natural rubber and make it a decreasingly attractive investment. A similar trend towards substitution affected Malayan tin exports. As the significance for Britain of Malaya's dollar earnings diminished and interest faded in commercial development within the sterling area, so Malayan investment groups diversified into western economies in the 1950s. British exports to the region also fell off conspicuously and, although this trend was reversed, the improvement was short-lived. When Sardon Jubir (Malaya's minister of transport) visited London in May 1961 with an estimated purse of £17 million, the British government laid on a 'show', including a meeting with Macmillan, in an attempt to win contracts for manufacturing industry in the UK. Although Sardon was impressed, he admitted that, in order to escape accusations of neo-colonialism, British business had to be exceptional to win contracts in post-colonial Malaya.[17] So far as capital contracts were concerned, it was reported that 'British firms have not secured any major civil engineering contracts in Malaya' and only one, Taylor Woodrow, had shown an interest in tendering for the construction of the international airport at Subang (outside Kuala Lumpur).[18] At the same time British capital was losing its bargaining power. Until the early 1960s British business was said to be enjoying a honeymoon with independent Malaya, a relationship that was reinforced by its contributions to the Alliance's election expenses. Yet a mood of pessimism affected British businessmen who foresaw difficulties ahead such as economic nationalism, or economic mismanagement, or the rise of Islamic fundamentalism, or the revival of communist insurgency.[19]

Britain's economic importance for Southeast Asia and the region's economic significance for Britain were declining together. All the more reason, one might think, for the government to promote British enterprise, as, indeed, they did by sending out trade missions to the area in 1961. It is not surprising, therefore, that Malaysia has been described as the extension of the neo-colony of Malaya. For example, Greg Poulgrain has stated that one of the guiding principles in the decolonisation of Southeast Asia was 'that the new political leaders who assumed the reins of power when the Colonial Office departed should be known to be amenable to continued British investment'.[20] Yet the records are almost silent on the economic benefits which the 'Grand Design' might bring to Britain. Of course, historians should look outside government files for information on the views of businessmen, but, had their activities significantly affected policy-making, it is reasonable to assume that the impact would have been noted in the official papers. In contrast, however, to the documents at The National Archives on Malaya for 1948 which reveal business pressures on government for firm action over communist insurgency, those for 1960–1963 contain relatively little on business relations with government. There is, indeed, hardly any evidence of representations from manufacturers seeking contracts, or from traders concerned about possible tariff changes, or from investors apprehensive about the likely nationalisation of foreign assets. Even the concerns of Brunei Shell appear to have been peripheral to the pre-occupations of policy-makers: company spokesmen informed the high commissioner and CO officials of their hopes and fears, but these did not alter the course of British policy. Although one of the principal reasons for the collapse of the negotiations over Brunei's entry into Malaysia was the dispute over the allocation of mineral revenues between federal and state governments, it was the political rather than the economic aspects of this issue that principally exercised British policy-makers. In any case, until the discovery of rich, off-shore deposits was confirmed in June 1963, the prognosis of Brunei Shell throughout the planning of Malaysia was that mineral sources were in decline and that oil was a diminishing asset. 'The oil will not last for ever' (25; also 165). In short, there is nothing in the record of policy-making to suggest that the government set out to advance business interests, or was swayed by the concerns of British companies, or thoroughly explored the likely impact of territorial integration on British trade and investments, or made use of British business connections to further its case.

When Whitehall first addressed the economic aspects of the 'Grand Design', it concentrated on its implications for the component territories (in terms of development, tariffs and inter-territorial trade) rather than its possible benefits for the United Kingdom. Officials at the Treasury, CO and CRO formed the view early on that the economic aspects of the Malaysia proposal were 'not likely to be of paramount importance', since the 'concept is essentially a political one and it is on political considerations that it will stand or fall'. With this in mind, they expected political integration to produce economic difficulties for the territories involved. Primary producers of Malaya and Borneo might suffer from internal competition. Furthermore, without safeguards or assistance, the economic inferiority of the Malay community might be aggravated. In addition, burgeoning industries in the peninsula might be nipped in the bud by those in Singapore. Officials presciently foresaw that the benefits that Malaya might derive from 'Brunei's money bags' would be counter-balanced by the costs of North Borneo and Sarawak. With respect to the United Kingdom's economic interests, however, they reckoned that these 'would be little affected either way'.[21]

Although economics were subordinated to political issues, they were nonetheless an important aspect of strategies for territorial integration. Thus, as part of the drive to consolidate Borneo interests, activities and services, in March 1961 a small committee chaired by J L Rampton (who had been seconded from the Treasury as financial adviser to the British high commission in Kuala Lumpur) recommended new machinery to facilitate economic co-operation. It also proposed a free trade arrangement for North Borneo and Sarawak and this led to the creation of a common market in January 1962 and the appointment of H P Hall to serve as co-ordinator based in Jesselton (36). British officials took a close interest in the IBRD mission, led by Jacques Rueff, which was originally appointed to examine the feasibility of closer economic co-operation between Malaya and Singapore and which later extended its scope to include the Borneo territories. Its proposal for a common market would be a bone of contention between Malaya and Singapore in the final run-up to Malaysia, as would worries about the migration of Singapore's surplus population to other parts of the new federation (143, 185, 191, 220).

Once agreement had been achieved in July 1962 on the principles of federation, a key matter to be decided was the size of the colonial dowry. Lord Lansdowne (minister of state for colonial affairs) urged generosity towards North Borneo and Sarawak because Britain was withdrawing from them before they were ready for independence on their own (146). The Treasury saw financial assistance, not as a way of reinforcing Britain's hold on the Malaysian economy, but as an unavoidable burden: 'We have reluctantly had to accept that, up to the creation of Malaysia and at any rate for a short while thereafter, we have an inescapable responsibility to help the new state in the military field as a legacy of our Colonial responsibilities.'[22] The federal government, which was already committed to an expensive five-year plan at a time when the price of rubber was dropping sharply and its balance of payments was deteriorating, would require outside assistance in order to meet the defence and internal security budget of Malaysia. 'The Malayans', it was reported, 'are seriously afraid that they are being asked to take on more than they can manage, and they are afraid that the United Kingdom may not appreciate the scale of their difficulties when it comes to negotiation.' (165, also 170, 173) Macmillan assured the Tunku that 'we are anxious to do what we can, within the limits of our capabilities, to help you with the kind of difficulties which you foresee'. Just as emergent Malaysia faced financial problems, so, too, did Britain.[23] When ministers succumbed to pressure to increase their offer, they did so for political purposes, in order, as Lansdowne put it, to buy good will (170, 173–177, 179, 181, 196).

Throughout the planning of Malaysia, one set of economic considerations was invariably subordinated to another: the possibility of future economic benefits took second place to the reality of public expenditure. British exports, overseas investments and control of extractive industry were secondary objectives; priority was given to the reduction of defence costs. The mantra is repeated in every assessment of British obligations in the region and of the region's costs and benefits for Britain: 'expenditure in South and South East Asia, largely for military purposes, was high in comparison with our earnings from investment in, and trade with, the area as a whole'.[24] By 1960 'there was no material asset in the area essential to our national economy to compare with, for example, oil in the Middle East. ... Rubber and tin were no longer essential to our balance of payments and we were spending money in the area for political reasons rather than for any prospect of financial gain' (28). In the list of five general aims, which were itemised in October 1960 by Sir Robert Scott's Committee on Future Developments in Southeast Asia, trade and economic development appeared after the containment of communism, maintenance of western influence and the preservation of peace and the security of non-communist societies. (29) A year later the prime minister himself identified economic interests as the third of three general objectives of overseas policy, and in so doing had in mind particularly 'our oil interests in the Persian Gulf'. (65). The costs of Southeast Asian defence commitments far outweighed any economic benefits, as Sir Arthur Snelling (deputy under-secretary, CRO) pointed out:—

> The resources of the area, especially rubber, oil and tin, are considerable but not indispensable. British trade with South East Asia is only about 3 per cent of our total trade. The foreign exchange we earn from our investments in all countries in Asia between West Pakistan and Japan is smaller than the foreign exchange we disperse for defence purposes in the same area. The conclusion is inescapable that our defence expenditure in the Far East is now out of all proportion to our economic stake there (166).

Summarising overseas commitments in a paper for the Cabinet Defence Committee in mid-June 1963, Sir Burke Trend (Cabinet secretary) pointed out that, while Britain had a wide measure of commercial interests in the Far East, no single interest carried the same importance as Middle East oil. Furthermore, defence costs in the Far East were far higher than in the Middle East: 'Our expenditure in the Far East, at a level more than twice that of our expenditure in the Middle East, is therefore devoted primarily to maintaining a politico-military position, based on Singapore' (180).

The record establishes that what was uppermost in the official mind at this time was not British investments, nor the dollar-earnings of rubber and tin, nor the reactions of plantation and mining companies, but rather the security of the region and the expense of maintaining it. The documents reveal an indifference to the economic potential of Malaysia, on the one hand, and, on the other, an overwhelming anxiety about the cost of defence commitments. The government's priority was to reduce public expenditure, not to promote private enterprise. Senior officials, ministers and the prime minister himself were attracted to the 'Greater Malaysia' scheme on account of the solution it seemed to offer to a particularly knotty problem of maintaining regional stability at minimum cost to the British taxpayer. By the early 1960s it was recognised that British trade and investments were reducing in a region which was becoming less and less valuable to Britain as a supplier of primary products, as a market for manufactured goods and as a dollar-earner, and more and more expensive so far as defence commitments were concerned. The prospects for the 'Grand Design' were, therefore, assessed from the strategic perspective not the economic. Bases not markets, security not commerce, international influence not investment opportunities dominated the thinking of British ministers and officials.

Defence strategy [25]

> One final point: why are we continuing to retain armed forces in this area at all? I put this question to one of the shrewdest Chinese in Singapore. After a little thought he said: first, in the interest of Malaysia; secondly, in the interest of America; thirdly, in the interest of Australia; fourthly, in the interest of New Zealand; and lastly in the general interest of the United Kingdom. I agree with this assessment. Our interest is not so much in the extent of our economic investments and trade as in our vested interest in world peace. If we accept this as the basis of our policy in the Far East, I believe our whole position would become more natural and understandable to the people of the area.
> [Lord Selkirk to Harold Macmillan, 3 Sept 1963 [26]]

If ending empire was a device to enable Britain to maintain global influence on the cheap, by the early 1960s it had not adequately reduced either overseas expenditure or overseas expectations. As a result Britain was suffering the strain of punching above its weight in world affairs. Two years after the 1957 defence review, which had shifted resources from conventional to nuclear weaponry with the intention of cutting military expenditure yet retaining commitments east of Suez,[27] Macmillan initiated a major study of future overseas policy. He first primed senior civil servants and Chiefs of Staff in June 1959 [28] and the review gathered momentum after the Conservatives' landslide victory in the general election of October. When the ministerial Cabinet Future Policy Committee met for the first time on 23 March 1960, it considered a wide-ranging paper produced by a group of senior officials chaired the Cabinet secretary, Sir Norman Brook.[29] This spawned a number of inter-departmental committees to study specific regions. One of these was the Committee on Future Developments in Southeast Asia which was set up in June under the chairmanship of the former commissioner-general of Southeast Asia, Sir Robert Scott.

Instructed to review the likely course of developments in the region during the next ten years as well as British aims and the means to secure them, the Scott Committee produced a summary report in mid-October and its final report in November (28, 29).[30] In addition to general aims held in common with western allies (the containment of communism, maintenance of western influence, preservation of peace and reinforcement of non-communist societies, fostering trade, political stability and economic development), the Scott Report identified a number of commitments peculiar to the region: membership of the Southeast Asia Treaty

Organisation, the Anglo–Malayan Defence Agreement of 1957, the ANZAM arrangements with Australia and New Zealand for the defence of the Malayan area, and the Geneva Agreement for Indo–China (which Britain had co-chaired in 1954 and would do so again when the Geneva Conference resumed to consider the crisis in Laos in 1961–1962). With the US taking the lead in Southeast Asian defence, Britain would be obliged to play its part, particularly in the internal security and external defence of dependencies, in supporting the strategic deterrent against China and in contributing to any SEATO land operations.

Macmillan was keen to maintain the momentum of this review of future policy as well as to impress the new American president, J F Kennedy, with his grasp of world affairs. During the Christmas recess of 1960–1961 he drafted a major 'think piece' which he 'half-jokingly' entitled 'The Grand Design'. In this paper he set out 'all the economic, political and defence problems confronting the free world' and, in the realisation that Britain could no longer fulfil its policing role, emphasised the 'interdependence' of the western alliance.[31] His concern was not simply to cut his coat according to his cloth or merely to live within his means—such shibboleths had pervaded policy reviews since the Second World War—but rather to discover a way, a middle way perhaps, of reducing expenditure without losing influence. This conundrum lay at the heart of another paper, 'Our Foreign and Defence Policy', which he presented to the Cabinet Future Policy Committee in September 1961 (65, also 68, 70). This was an attempt to establish criteria for assessing the importance of traditional activities and for the most effective deployment of limited resources. It was becoming clear, though not yet to all ministers of overseas departments, that the reduction of expenditure would necessitate the reduction of commitments, rather than run the risk of spreading resources too thinly.

How far did the 'Grand Design' for 'Greater Malaysia' match the greater design for British future policy? The compelling attraction of 'Greater Malaysia' was the prospect of both retaining influence and reducing expenditure (45). It would secure Singapore from subversion, reinforce the Commonwealth and enhance British relations with, as well as influence upon, the United States. Escaping from costly responsibilities for needy dependencies, Britain might yet sustain its position in the front line of the Asian Cold War. As the US ambassador to Malaya put it cryptically, but approvingly, in a telegram to Washington, 'UK objective will be to continue to play dominant role in local defense picture at reduced cost.'[32] Reducing military costs was imperative, as Lord Selkirk observed from his vantage point in Singapore: 'we are stretched to a point where our strength might snap under the strain' and 'our present position would be highly perilous were it not for our basic dependence on the USA'. The commissioner-general was desperate to disabuse those who 'still seem to assume that we are in a position to mount an expedition from Singapore and Malaya as it were from a secure base'(54). Singapore's constitution was due for review in the spring of 1963: were the island to remain separated from the peninsula, it would be exposed to riot and revolution, and might offer a bridgehead for Chinese communism. If, on the other hand, Singapore were to merge with Malaya, both the island and Britain's military base on it would be safe. In Selkirk's view, long-term defence interests would be better served through the implementation of the 'Grand Design' than by upholding the status quo.

The strategic case for Malaysia did not go uncontested. The Chiefs of Staff, at least to begin with, disputed the supposed advantages of the 'Grand Design' and expressed concern lest the run-down of Britain's presence in Singapore would discourage friends and allies (45). Julian Amery shared these misgivings. As a backbencher in 1953 Amery had argued against evacuation from the Suez Canal Zone on the grounds that it would both jeopardise access to the base and diminish Britain's prestige in the Middle East and beyond, bringing an end to the Commonwealth as 'an independent force in the world'.[33] As minister of state at the Colonial Office, Amery had been centrally involved in the long and complex negotiations whereby Britain retained 'in perpetuity' the bases of Akrotiri and Episcopi in the independent republic of Cyprus. Now secretary of state for Air, Amery argued that the project for 'Greater Malaysia' would weaken Britain's title to the Singapore base and consequently reduce Britain's capacity to influence developments in Southeast Asia. 'The fact remains that if we want to contribute to keeping the communists out of South East Asia and if we want to maintain our influence with Australia and New Zealand on the one hand and the United States on the other, we must have the effective use of Singapore. Without it our influence in the area could sink to the level of that of France.'[34] In his view, Singapore's integration within Malaysia would place intolerable limitations on Britain's use of the base.

The pros and cons of Singapore's merger with Malaya seemed finely balanced. Some, like Selkirk, held that the Singapore base would be reinforced by membership. Others, like Amery, maintained that it would be undermined. Yet others (such as the Joint Planning Staff of the Chiefs of Staff) reckoned that, whatever happened, 'Singapore, in or out of the "Grand Design", will eventually become unreliable as a main base'.[35] Advantages and disadvantages seemed evenly balanced; the Joint Planning Staff of the COS reached the conclusion that the 'Grand Design' was 'the least harmful of the possible developments', [36] while the prime minister himself concluded that 'the matter was one of great difficulty since it seemed likely that we should be faced with grave problems whether or not Greater Malaysia were achieved' (74). When Macleod had pointed out to the Colonial Policy Committee in late July 1960 that merger would end Britain's constitutional right to the base (25), ministers had noted that it might be easier to maintain defence facilities in Singapore by a treaty concluded with a new Federation of Malaysia of which Singapore was a part (27). This option was explored further as officials and ministers prepared for the first round of formal talks with Tunku Abdul Rahman regarding his proposal for territorial integration.

After several postponements the Anglo–Malayan talks took place in London on 20–22 November 1961 (79–84). At their conclusion the two prime ministers issued a joint statement accepting Malaysia as a desirable aim. They also set out two fundamental conditions for the proposed state: firstly, the views of the peoples of North Borneo and Sarawak should be ascertained; secondly, the Anglo–Malayan Defence Agreement of 1957 should be extended to all territories of the new federation. As regards the second of these conditions, particular care was taken over the wording of the arrangements governing the Singapore base. The British government, which was determined to play its full part in SEATO, did not wish to be restricted in its use of the base. The delegation from Malaya, which had steadfastly remained outside SEATO, was anxious lest the sovereignty of Malaysia were impaired at the outset by British military activities that did not accord with Malaya's national interest. Each side sought to preserve its freedom and also to avoid future embarrassment—the British with their SEATO allies, the Malayans with their electorate—but it proved difficult to reconcile Anglo–Malayan differences in a public statement without leaving some things unsaid. The final version stated:—

> the Government of the Federation of Malaysia will afford to the Government of the United Kingdom the right to continue to maintain the bases and other facilities at present occupied by their Service authorities within the State of Singapore and will permit the United Kingdom to make such use of these bases and facilities as the United Kingdom may consider necessary for the purpose of assisting in the defence of Malaysia, and for Commonwealth defence and for the preservation of peace in South East Asia. [37]

Although it did not spell out rights, powers and purposes, the British were satisfied by the Joint Statement. Its general phraseology amply covered their strategic needs, while the omission of explicit terms reduced, so they hoped, the scope for political controversy. The British government set immense store by this Joint Statement on defence; it guided subsequent discussions over the next eighteen months and was reproduced word for word in article 6 of the final and binding Malaysia Agreement of 9 July 1963.[38]

Nevertheless, the Joint Statement of November 1961 by no means resolved all the questions related to the future of the Singapore base. First of all, Anglo–Malayan differences were immediately exposed when, to the consternation of Sandys (Commonwealth secretary) and Watkinson (minister of defence), the Tunku and Tun Razak (deputy prime minister and minister of defence) were tempted to reassure their public that Britain's use of the base would be subject to a Malaysian veto (85, 86). Secondly, continuing doubts about the future reliability of Singapore caused the Chiefs of Staff to examine the feasibility of alternative sites for a military base, such as the island of Labuan or northern Australia. Thirdly, not only did Singapore's political instability draw the British further into the management of the internal security of a territory that was already internally self-governing, but ministers were also persuaded to authorise the deployment of British troops for internal security operations after the inauguration of Malaysia. They took this unusual decision because emergent Malaysia lacked resources. Nevertheless, although ministers attempted to minimise the risks by stipulating that they would intervene only at the express invitation of the independent government of Malaysia, it was clear that any such move would expose Britain to international opprobrium, accusations of neo-colonialism, complex political and legal difficulties as well as unknown financial burdens (167).[39]

Just over a year after the Anglo–Malayan Joint Statement, the Anglo–American agreement at Nassau established new strategic parameters for British defence policy and gave a further twist to the review of overseas commitments. Crucial to Britain's global position was the possession of an independent nuclear deterrent and, at Nassau in December 1962, Macmillan succeeded in persuading Kennedy to provide Britain with Polaris in place of the discredited Skybolt. Meeting at Chequers on 9 February 1963, the Cabinet Defence Committee considered future policy, firstly, on the assumption that expenditure on the strategic deterrent had been largely settled at Nassau and, secondly, in the light of current balance of payments difficulties. While the costs of maintaining forces East of Suez made withdrawal tempting, ministers accepted that savings would have to be set against likely political and economic consequences. As regards the Far East, since Singapore had a four-fold role to play (with respect to Malaysia, SEATO, Indonesia, and Hong Kong), any substantial retrenchment would be regarded 'as a major political defeat'. It would have a 'serious effect' on Australia, New Zealand and the United States, encourage 'the spread of Communism' and amount to the abandonment of Malaysia. The Defence Committee accepted, nevertheless, that the defence budget should be contained, if possible, within a limit of 7 per cent of the GNP and it commissioned studies of, firstly, the costs and value of the Aden base and, secondly, the political and economic consequences of withdrawal from, or substantial reduction of forces in, the Far East.

The question of retrenchment in the Far East was referred to the Official Oversea Co-ordinating Committee for which Sir Arthur Snelling (deputy under-secretary at the CRO) wrote a comprehensive review of the many issues with which ministers and officials had been grappling throughout the planning and implementation of the Malaysia project. Having identified policy objectives and summarised the political and military arguments for and against withdrawal, Snelling proceeded to assess the extent to which non-military methods (for example diplomacy and aid) and a more effective redistribution of the load between allies might lighten Britain's budget from the mid-1960s onwards. Of his many conclusions, three stand out: firstly, defence costs far outweighed economic benefits from the region; secondly, total British military withdrawal would have 'disastrous political and military effects, particularly in the face of Indonesian pressure'; and, thirdly, few objectives could be achieved by entirely non-military methods. Damned if they left, the British risked being damned if they stayed (166).

By this time Britain's sponsorship of Malaysia was being contested by Indonesia, the Philippines and at the United Nations, with the result that Australia, New Zealand and the United States were reluctant to give Britain their wholehearted support (160–163).[40] It was now becoming clear that unless Indonesia were appeased through tripartite talks with Malaya and the Philippines or through UN mediation, the creation of Malaysia was likely to increase Britain's defence costs instead of reducing them (168, 169). Defence estimates were continuing to rise inexorably. When the Cabinet Defence Committee resumed its consideration of future policy on 19 June 1963, forecasts indicated that defence expenditure would breach the limit of 7 per cent of the GNP (180). Maudling (chancellor of the Exchequer) argued strenuously for cuts but Home (foreign secretary) reminded his colleagues: 'We have rejected the idea that we should choose between Europe and a world role.'[41] In spite of the need to make cuts, the committee saw no prospect of savings with respect to either the independent deterrent or Europe and it dismissed the possibility of early withdrawal from Singapore. Although Macmillan hoped that the burden of protecting Malaysia might be mitigated by drawing further on the support of Australia and New Zealand and by negotiating a political understanding with Indonesia, the Malaysian die was cast and the final agreement was due for signature within a few weeks.

The making and implementation of policy

It is Rhodesia all over again.
[Harold Macmillan 5 Apr 1962 [42]]

Malaysia was forged in a furnace of conflicting objectives and mounting pressures. It was the product of prolonged and frequently interrupted negotiations that oscillated between Britain and Southeast Asia. London remained the seat of sovereignty (as regards North Borneo, Sarawak and Singapore) and also the scene of the principal conferences. Talks were held here in November 1961, July 1962, May and July 1963 when the principal differences between the prospective members of Malaysia, as well as between them and Britain, were addressed and up to a point resolved. But much of the power in the new federation was brokered and many of the crucial details of membership were worked out in the region itself, where inter-governmental discussions took place between Malaya and Singapore, between Malaya and Brunei, and between Britain, Malaya and the Borneo territories.

The capacity of the British government to control the final outcome, or even to adjudicate between contesting leaders, was reduced by its declining power in Southeast Asia and also by its conflicting commitments there. While there was consensus that the fundamental purposes in promoting Malaysia were to stabilise Singapore, secure the base and safeguard the interests of the Borneo peoples, there was a profusion—sometimes confusion—of British views regarding the balance to be struck between these objectives and also with respect to the manner and speed of their implementation. Policy-making for Malaysia, therefore, became a process of arbitrating between competing views within British government as well as between the competing interests of participating territories. British perspectives were affected by departmental responsibilities, for example, whether they were for imperial defence or colonial welfare. Political considerations and military costs were two of the factors that caused disagreement. For example, when Whitehall began to take Malaysia seriously in early 1961, officials at the Ministry of Defence, which was hoping for political change in order to reduce military expenditure, fretted at what they took to be a willingness in the CO, CRO and FO to accept the status quo. [43] Yet attitudes did not coalesce for long round this stark polarity: opinion within defence circles was itself divided over the merits of retrenchment east of Suez, while any unanimity in the other oversea departments regarding the primacy of political issues collapsed over their interpretations. Two and a half years later, when plans for Malaysia had been completed but when its future appeared to hang by a thread, a Foreign Office official writing to the British ambassador in Jakarta noted worrying differences between Whitehall departments:—

> I have a strong feeling, from looking back through recent telegrams before dictating this letter, that we are not altogether *en rapport* with you and Singapore about our basic Malaysia policy ... lack of understanding could quite easily have arisen because of the fact that the Colonial Office often reflect a rather different focus from that of the Foreign Office and Commonwealth Relations Office so that there is quite a lot of room for doubt as to what Her Majesty's Government want. [44]
> ...

The most serious clashes occurred between the Colonial Office and Commonwealth Relations Office, especially with respect to the Borneo territories. Each had responsibility for different, yet interlocking, elements of the 'Grand Design'. The Colonial Office was accountable for the crown colonies of North Borneo and Sarawak, and to a lesser extent (in that they were internally self-governing from 1959) for Singapore and Brunei. The CRO supervised British relations with sovereign Malaya and liaised with Australia and New Zealand regarding the defence of their Near North. The welfare of the Borneo peoples and the well-being of the

Commonwealth pulled planners in opposite directions; whereas the CRO pressed for the early creation of Malaysia, the CO advocated delay until the conditions were right. These differences were pronounced at every level: in the region, Whitehall and Cabinet.

British approaches were also affected by location—be it London, or Kuala Lumpur, or Singapore, or Jesselton, or Kuching, or Brunei Town—and were influenced by territorial pre-occupations as well as by institutional loyalties. Lord Selkirk and Philip Moore (commissioner-general and deputy) had regular confabulations with Lee Kuan Yew in Singapore, as did Sir Geofroy Tory (high commissioner to Malaya) with Tunku Abdul Rahman in Kuala Lumpur. Sir William Goode (North Borneo), Sir Alexander Waddell (Sarawak) and Sir Dennis White (Brunei) conveyed the diverse interests of the Borneo peoples both to the CO and at regional gatherings convened by Selkirk. Selkirk, who reported directly to the prime minister with respect to the co-ordination of foreign, colonial, Commonwealth and defence policies, urged speed in the implementation of the 'Grand Design' for the sake of regional stability.[45] He was also anxious to ensure an effective presence for Britain in Southeast Asia once Malaysia had been formed and the commissioner-general's office had been wound up (88, 90, 171). By contrast, Goode and Waddell emphasised a much more measured approach in the interests of indigenous peoples. Of the two governors, Goode was more influential—or more 'difficult'—but both expressed the fear that the CRO would have no compunction in standing aside while Tunku Abdul Rahman colonised Borneo. On at least one occasion Goode argued against a role for the CRO in North Borneo since it would undermine local confidence (104) and both Borneo governors let it be known that they had 'no high opinion' of Sir Geofroy Tory.[46] As British high commissioner in Kuala Lumpur, Tory's job was, of course, to convey to the CRO the views of the Tunku and his Cabinet. Sometimes, however, he appeared to champion the Malayan cause. Alastair Morrison, Sarawak's information officer, described him as 'a mediocre man... who, as viewed from Sarawak, seemed at times to regard himself as a supernumerary member of the Tunku's staff'.[47] Indeed, Ghazali Shafie (permanent secretary at Malaya's Ministry of External Affairs) valued Tory as providing a more direct line to the heart of Whitehall than did the Malayan high commissioner in London. Ghazali has also recalled how, during the London conference that followed the Cobbold inquiry, Tory did 'his best, short of being accused of being a Malayan ambassador'. [48]

In Whitehall, Sir John Martin, who had served briefly in the MCS during the 1930s and had risen to the rank of deputy permanent under-secretary by 1956, was the most senior CO official closely involved in Malaysia policy. He was assisted by E Melville, C G Eastwood and particularly W I J Wallace, who was an old Burma hand and head of the Far Eastern Department from 1956 to the end of 1962 when he was promoted to assistant under-secretary with superintending responsibilities for the Far East. Accompanied by Wallace, Martin conducted an assessment of Borneo opinion preparatory to the Cobbold Mission and he was subsequently the administrative anchor of Lansdowne's Inter-Governmental Committee. Martin stalwartly defended the Borneo interest in inter-departmental discussions but was hampered in this by indifferent ministerial leadership. Sir Saville (Joe) Garner, permanent under-secretary at the CRO from January 1962, was better placed; he chaired the Greater Malaysia (Official) Committee and enjoyed a close working relationship with a strong secretary of state.

During this period the CRO was led by two secretaries of state. Lord Home, confidant of the prime minister, was particularly exercised by the international aspects of the 'Grand Design' which he continued to follow when he became foreign secretary in July 1960. Home was succeeded at the CRO by Duncan Sandys who, as a former minister of defence, also took a keen interest in the broader context of Malaysia policy. By contrast, notwithstanding the activity of Lord Perth (minister of state for colonial affairs) at an early stage in the project, before July 1962 none of the colonial secretaries took the lead in promoting the 'Grand Design'. Alan Lennox-Boyd went no further than cautiously to foster the closer association of the Borneo territories. Iain Macleod was the most pro-active of the three but was pre-occupied with Africa. Reginald Maudling led the department for less than a year and during that time showed little interest in Southeast Asia unless prompted. In the minds of ministers from other departments, the CO became identified with a fastidious interpretation of trusteeship obligations which they found to be irksome. Even Macmillan felt that the zeal with which governors and colonial administrators championed the Borneo peoples betrayed an inability to appreciate the wider, international picture and Britain's reduced place in it.

Policy-making for Malaysia, therefore, was by no means the preserve of any one department. As has been seen in the discussion of its economic and strategic aspects, the CO, CRO, FO, Ministry of Defence and Treasury were all involved. Distinctive departmental approaches converged upon, and up to a point were resolved within, the Cabinet and its committees, notably the Colonial Policy Committee, Defence Committee and the ad hoc Greater Malaysia Committee, all of which were chaired by the prime minister. The Colonial Policy Committee was replaced at the end of June 1962 by the Oversea Policy Committee whose more wide-ranging terms of reference were to consider questions of oversea policy (other than defence policy and external economic policy) which concerned more than one of the oversea departments. Each ministerial committee was shadowed by an official committee (ie an inter-departmental committee composed of officials). For example, the Greater Malaysia (Official) Committee (September 1961 to October 1963), which was chaired by the permanent under-secretary at the CRO, briefed ministers for the London talks of November 1961 and of July 1962 and also assessed the Cobbold and Lansdowne Reports on Borneo. The OPC was supported by the Oversea (Official) Co-ordinating Committee which was chaired by A L M Cary (deputy secretary, Cabinet Office) and consisted of representatives of the Treasury, FO, CRO, CO, Ministry of Defence, Board of Trade and Department of Technical Co-operation. The Co-ordinating Committee met ten times in the second half of 1962 and examined in particular: the economic aid requirements of North Borneo, Sarawak and Singapore; the strength of the Malaysian armed forces; the extent to which Malaya would be in a position to contribute financially to the defence and development of Malaysia. The defence implications of the Malaysia project were also scrutinised by the Chiefs of Staff Committee (chaired by the chief of the defence staff) and its planning staff, and were informed by reviews produced by the prime minister's Future Policy Committee and by Sir Robert Scott's Committee on Future Developments in Southeast Asia.

The extent of Macmillan's involvement in the making of Malaysia is remarkable. It indicates the departmental complexities of the project as well as its significance for Britain's international standing. During 1961–1963 Malaysia policy disturbed the prime minister and was addressed by the Cabinet on many more occasions than had

Malayan matters previously, even during the twelve-year communist emergency. The prime minister chaired Cabinet committees dealing with Malaysia, presided over constitutional conferences and corresponded directly with the prime minister of Malaya. At key moments—in the run-up to the London talks of November 1961, before and during the London conference in July 1962 and following the Manila summit in August 1963—Macmillan personally intervened to save the project from foundering. But the host of problems claiming his attention— balance of payments difficulties, Cold War crises, Britain's independent nuclear deterrent, European membership, the decolonisation of Africa, by-election defeats, the Profumo scandal—meant that, though he was fully briefed by the Cabinet secretary and his private office, it was inconceivable that the prime minister should attempt to direct policy. Nevertheless, the ominous parallels which he and his colleagues could not avoid drawing between Malaysia and the Central African Federation convinced Macmillan that a senior figure should assume overall charge. Having recognised that it was impossible for Central Africa to be handled by two secretaries of state and still reeling under the intolerable burden which that had placed on himself, Macmillan accepted that as regards Malaysia 'we must do all we can to avoid a repetition of the Federation of Rhodesia and Nyasaland'.[49]

The Central African Federation differed from the Malaysian 'Grand Design' in that its problems centred upon the entrenched position of white settlers, dominated colonial affairs for over a decade and spilled into Britain's domestic politics, even inducing two colonial secretaries to threaten resignation. In many other respects, however, the schemes were similar. Both federations appeared to offer stability to a strategically significant area, yet provoked inter-territorial and inter-racial resentments. Moreover, each was dominated by a single, independent or semi-autonomous territory, Malaya in the one and Southern Rhodesia in the other. In addition, each experienced unrest (the Brunei revolt and the Nyasaland emergency), mass arrests of suspected subversives (operation 'Coldstore' and operation 'Sunrise'), a proconsular resignation (White from Brunei and Armitage from Nyasaland), and a commission of inquiry (Cobbold in Borneo and Monckton in Central Africa). Furthermore, both were targets of international criticism and, finally, both suffered from continual tension between two lead departments—the CO and CRO. In March 1962 Macmillan attempted a fresh start by transferring the affairs of Central Africa from the CRO and CO to the new Central Africa Office under R A Butler. Nevertheless Central Africa 'haunted, not to say poisoned' the last years of his premiership [50] and similarities between it and Malaysia depressed him further. In spite of regular inter-departmental communication, policy-making for Malaysia suffered from the same lack of cohesion as did that for Central Africa. As the possibility of Malaysia's unravelling grew more likely and Macmillan awaited an opportunity to appoint a ministerial supremo, Duncan Sandys was itching to take charge. The moment came in mid-July 1962 when, facing economic problems and increasing unpopularity,[51] Macmillan uncharacteristically lost his nerve and so bungled the dismissal of his chancellor of the Exchequer, Selwyn Lloyd, that he proceeded to sack one third of his Cabinet in 'the night of the long knives' which seriously damaged his reputation for 'unflappability' and left him exhausted and demoralised.[52] This domestic crisis had important repercussions for Malaysian planning; Thorneycroft replaced Watkinson as minister of defence and, more significantly, Maudling was succeeded at the Colonial Office by Sandys who now combined this position with that of

Commonwealth relations. Although the CO and CRO were not amalgamated until 1966, responsibility for Malaysia was hereafter vested in a single Cabinet minister.

By the time Sandys assumed overall control of Malaysia, the project had been designed but had yet to be delivered. During the next fourteen months the principal role of the secretary of state would be that of enforcer and trouble-shooter. Tough, energetic and a perfectionist who did nothing by halves, Sandys shouldered a massive workload as territory after territory claimed his attention. Used by successive Conservative prime ministers as 'a kind of political commando',[53] Sandys spared neither himself nor his staff in efforts to resolve crises and achieve agreement. Even with Sandys at the helm, however, ambiguity and drift were not eradicated from the Malaysian project. In February 1963 de Zulueta, the prime minister's private secretary for overseas matters, considered that 'the whole Malaysian situation looks to me to be getting out of hand' (164). Indeed, the completion of technical matters were in danger of becoming an irrelevance in the face of the Brunei revolt, Indonesian confrontation, Singapore's security problems and America's lukewarm support. The conduct and implementation of Britain's policy still lacked coherence and direction; too many Whitehall departments had their fingers in the pie and momentum had slackened. The Greater Malaysia Committee, which was a deliberative rather than executive group, now seldom met since the time for deliberation had been succeeded by a time for execution. Yet the execution of policy faltered. Moreover, the lack of co-ordination and drive in Whitehall had been compounded by the decision to wind up the British Defence Coordinating Committee Far East.[54] To get the project back on course, de Zulueta suggested the appointment of an executive committee 'under a powerful chairman' such as Edward Heath, who, as chief whip and then lord privy seal with FO responsibilities, had acquired a reputation for getting things done. Sir Burke Trend, who had recently taken over from Sir Norman Brook as Cabinet secretary, ruled out a ministerial appointment on the grounds that it would conflict with Sandys' role and instead proposed an inter-departmental executive working group of officials. While existing Cabinet Committees would continue to deal with broad policy issues, the function of the executive group would be to ensure prompt, day-to-day action on the international, Commonwealth, colonial and defence aspects of Malaysia. It met for the first time on 5 March and thereafter on a frequent, even daily, basis with the result that by early May 1963 inter-departmental co-ordination had markedly improved.[55]

If lack of co-ordination was an impediment to the making of policy, lack of clout was an obstacle to its implementation. As in the transfer of power to Malaya in 1955–1957, so with the creation of Malaysia in 1961–1963, the British found they could not dictate terms. Such an argument may be difficult to sustain in the light of instances of forceful intervention such as military action in Brunei, the arrest of Barisan supporters in Singapore and the detention of members of the Clandestine Communist Organisation and their sympathisers within the Sarawak United People's Party.[56] Yet the weight of evidence indicates the limitations of Britain's power as well as British forebodings about the untoward effects of the use of force. When crises blew up Britain was often wrong-footed and vulnerable; for example, the Brunei revolt turned out to be a close-run thing, while ministers were most reluctant to sanction arrests in Singapore on account of the world-wide criticism operation 'Coldstore' would provoke. Moreover, far from being in the driving-seat during the run-up to Malaysia, British ministers and officials frequently felt that they were being taken for a ride by Lee Kuan Yew, the Tunku, or the Sultan of Brunei. When Sultan Omar Saifuddin decided at the last minute against joining, there was simply nothing the British government could do to induce him to change his mind. Similarly, although British administrators were appalled by Kuala Lumpur's colonial designs upon the Borneo territories, they were scarcely in a position to halt them and were hard-pressed even to moderate them. When Lee Kuan Yew unilaterally declared independence two weeks before Malaysia Day, the British circumspectly turned a blind eye to his 'brinkmanship'. It was, after all, because Britain's interest in Malaysia derived from its loss of power in the region that the Malaysia it got was not exactly the Malaysia it wanted.

Lacking compliant proxies and mistrustful of *force majeure*, the British relied on painstaking negotiations in order to reconcile the contradictory objectives of the participating territories. Months of discussions and consultations identified interests, assessed opinion, established principles, brokered compromises and eventually resulted in an uneasy agreement on the nature of the new federation. Its constitution was not the fulfilment of nationhood but a structure for nation-building. Ultimately nationhood would legitimate the state; at the moment of its inauguration, however, Malaysia was a state without a nation. In his advocacy of Malaysia in May 1961, Lee Kuan Yew foresaw the new federation instilling 'pride in a more powerful and viable state' which 'would give a boost to nation-building' (37). This point was echoed some weeks later by the Tunku: 'It is a matter for emphasis that such a federation, comprising a grand total of nearly ten million, in an area of 130,000 square miles, as against a Federation of 50,000 square miles, will have the effect of creating a greater importance in the hearts and minds of the people of these territories and a national pride which would go a long way in building up a feeling of loyalty to the country.' (46) As Lord Cobbold commented in his conclusions to the Commission's report, 'It is a necessary condition that, from the outset, Malaysia should be regarded by all concerned as an association of partners, combining in the common interest to create a new nation but retaining their own individualities.'[57] But, given the strength of those individualities, perhaps the most that could be expected of Malaysia was a federation of nations rather than a nation-state. By setting out at length and in detail the provisions for federal and state institutions, citizenship, legislative powers, administrative arrangements, financial and public services, the protection of the special interests of the Borneo states and Singapore, and temporary arrangements covering a transitional period for the Borneo states and Singapore, the Malaysia agreement of July 1963 allocated powers and apportioned responsibilities, acknowledged majority interests and safeguarded minority rights, enshrined public service and reduced opportunities for corruption and arbitrary rule. In short, the constitution of Malaysia was an elaborate set of contracts concluded after prolonged and elaborate multi-lateral negotiations. It may subsequently have disappointed many, provoked active opposition in some quarters and been breached later by its very guardians, but the complex, inter-active process of its making refutes the stark simplicity of the charge that the British government devised Malaysia both single-mindedly and single-handedly. When Goode urged a tougher approach to the Tunku, Macmillan rejected the suggestion as misplaced: 'the whole mood is based on a false assessment of our power' (117).

What resources could it draw upon when differences seemed irreconcilable and the scheme appeared to be on the verge of collapse? Little more, it seemed, than force of personality. At three moments of crisis Malaysia was salvaged by Sandys administering bruises while Macmillan applied the balm. The first occasion was in July 1962 when the Tunku was pulled back from the brink of withdrawal at a hastily arranged lunch at Chequers. The second came a year later when Sandys broke the deadlock in talks between Malaya and Singapore by calling the participants to London for arbitration. On this occasion, only a few days remained before the Malaysia Agreement was due to be signed and he applied his technique of meticulously reading through proposals sentence by sentence with all concerned sitting round a table in all-night meetings 'in order to wear down the opposition and grind out the solution he wanted'.[58] 'It was', Lee Kuan Yew recalled, 'his method of dealing with stubborn parties, wringing concessions from both sides until they finally reached agreement' and, Lee added, 'not unlike what the communists did to us at committee meetings'.[59] While he could be 'forceful and, where necessary, brutal',[60] Sandys was 'by no means deficient in charm'[61] for he knew that ultimate success lay in patience.

The final crisis came in August 1963 when the Tunku agreed at the Manila Summit to postpone Malaysia until a United Nations inquiry had ascertained the wishes of the Borneo peoples. Macmillan despatched his secretary of state to Kuala Lumpur to 'hold the Tunku's hand', as Sandys put it to the Australian premier, Robert Menzies.[62] In fact several crises kept Sandys in the region for about four weeks. These were: firstly, the danger the Tunku might put off the inauguration of Malaysia indefinitely in order to appease Sukarno; secondly, the risk Lee Kuan Yew ran in irretrievably damaging relations with Malaya by taking advantage of the postponement of Malaysia Day to strengthen the terms of Singapore's membership; and, thirdly, the dispute between Malayan and Sarawakian politicians over the selection of Sarawak's first head of state. By now the Tunku was said to be 'suffering seriously from cold feet' (221) and 'in a highly emotional and touchy state' (214) but Sandys knocked heads together with 'many rough words on all sides' (224) in a series of last-minute deals. Greatly relieved that Malaysia did not come unstuck at the eleventh hour, Macmillan congratulated Sandys on having 'done wonders' and despatched an emollient message to the Tunku.[63] Notwithstanding the celebrations on 16 September (226, 227), Sandys' earlier, unceremonious conduct rankled with the Tunku for some time to come (224).

2 Dimensions of Merger
Malaya and Singapore

> The PAP are of course co-operating closely with the Alliance in pushing through the Malaysia scheme, but in their political outlook the Alliance and the PAP are like oil and water.
> [Sir Geofroy Tory, 18 June 1962 [64]]

Throughout history the island of Singapore has fluctuated in its relationship with the Malayan peninsula, sometimes in union with it and sometimes in isolation from it. When Stamford Raffles established a British settlement there in 1819, it was severed from what remained of the Johor empire but a few years later the East India Company linked it with Penang and Malacca to form the Straits Settlements. In the 'high colonial' period administrative and economic rivalry between the Straits

Settlements and the Federated Malay States led to a tension between their capitals—Singapore and Kuala Lumpur—that has waxed and waned ever since.

While there were strong reasons for including Singapore in the post-war Malayan Union, it was omitted principally on account of its Chinese population which would have challenged Malay paramountcy in the peninsula. Instead, Singapore was established as a crown colony on its own. Its first elections were held in 1948, when 6 representatives were elected to a legislature of 23 member. The constitution of 1955 provided for a Council of Ministers who were collectively accountable to a Legislative Assembly with an elected majority. Under this arrangement David Marshall of the Labour Front became the first chief minister but he held office for only fourteen months. It was a period of labour and student unrest and Marshall was a mercurial figure. He resigned in June 1956 after talks with the British had broken down over his demand for self-government.[65] Lim Yew Hock, also of the Labour Front, then took over. In spite of his apparent success in countering subversion and negotiating the advance of Singapore to internal self-government at the London conferences of 1957 and 1958, Lim was defeated in the 1959 elections by the People's Action Party (PAP) led by Lee Kuan Yew.

An English-educated Chinese meritocrat, Lee Kuan Yew had practised law and acted as legal adviser to many trade unions before becoming Singapore's first prime minister. His career has become synonymous with the growth of independent Singapore; for example, Lee's memoirs for the period to 1965 are called *The Singapore story*. Sometimes he appears to have taken on single-handedly the enemies of his country, but he was ably assisted by Toh Chin Chye (deputy prime minister), Goh Keng Swee (minister of Finance) and S Rajaratnam (minister of culture). Singapore was now self-governing in all domestic matters including internal security, although the Internal Security Council (on which Britain, Malaya and Singapore were all represented) had power to take decisions which were binding on the Singapore government. Lee's government started with the advantages of popular support and strong leadership. The PAP had appealed to the electorate because it was 'founded on principle, not opportunism'[66] and it now commanded an apparently unassailable majority on the Legislative Assembly (43 of 51 seats). Exuding confidence and also a 'sober dignified dedication to the task of governing for the benefit of the masses', it made an immediate impact (13, 15, 33, 38). It also faced immense problems, notably a rising population, increasing unemployment, economic problems and plenty of activists looking to subvert the government. Like Marshall and Lim Yew Hock before, Lee rode the tiger of communism which threatened to devour him as it had them. Unlike his predecessors, however, Lee adopted the strategy of absorption and containment, at least at first. Thus he refused to take office as prime minister until the British governor released eight detainees (including Lim Chin Siong) with whom he had been closely associated and some of whom he tried to neutralise by appointing to government posts. A meticulous planner who was by no means averse to taking staggering risks, Lee sought to win the support of workers without alienating businessmen, to attract the Chinese-educated without offending the westernised middle class, to pursue socialist policies without becoming the handmaiden of communism, to achieve independence without losing British support, to cultivate Malayan nationalism without sacrificing Singapore's interests. He may have resorted to dramatic gestures, cynical stratagems and the rhetoric of anti-colonialism to distract attention from his dilemmas, but he rarely lost his instinct for what was politically possible.

ıtion of Singapore was due for review in the spring of 1963. The next
rely be independence; anything less would have been unacceptable to
people of Singapore. Yet, because the island was regarded as too small and
therefore too vulnerable to survive on its own, many believed that union with the
peninsula was essential to the island's future stability and prosperity. Lee himself
consistently and strenuously advocated independence through merger with Malaya.
He was also convinced that it should come sooner rather than later, since the
communists, who opposed closer association with the staunchly anti-communist
regime in Kuala Lumpur, were working to undermine his government, cause dissent
in the PAP and stir up unrest amongst the workforce. Lee assiduously wooed the
Malayan government but the more he pressed his case the more it resisted, and as his
domestic position worsened so the Tunku steadfastly kept his distance.

While there is more to the story of merger than the relationship between the two
prime ministers, it contributed as much as their policies to the initiation, set-backs
and outcome of the Malaysia proposal. In addition to a common antipathy towards
communism, they shared a mistrust of each other. Although they occasionally
relaxed together on the golf course, Tunku Abdul Rahman and Lee Kuan Yew were
never close—the Tunku's bonhomie was not Lee's style, while the former was
frequently overawed by the intellectual brilliance of the latter. The Tunku's
background, temperament and working methods were very different from those of
Lee. Son of the former Sultan of Kedah, the Tunku had acquired the reputation of a
playboy in his youth. As a statesman, he was frequently 'breezy and charming ... and
determined to avoid close discussion on any particular problem'.[67] He was also
content to leave the detail of policy-making and government to others. The anchor of
his administration was his deputy, Tun Abdul Razak, who was also minister of
defence during this period and who led the Malayan delegation through the more
arduous negotiating sessions. Dr Ismail bin Dato Abdul Rahman, the Malayan
representative on the ISC, participated in many of the key meetings while Tan Siew
Sin, minister of finance, was central to financial and commercial discussions. As
minister for external affairs as well as prime minister, the Tunku delegated
generously to Ghazali Shafie, permanent secretary since 1959. At the Ministry of
Defence, Abdul Kadir bin Shamsudin succeeded Robert Thompson as the top civil
servant in April 1961. In addition to Thompson, other British expatriates were
employed by the federal government including Claude Fenner (Police) and C M
Sheridan (attorney-general).

If not a painstaking administrator, the Tunku was an astute politician and an
emollient national leader. He had negotiated the independence settlement and before
that the formation of the Alliance of three communal parties (United Malays National
Organisation, Malayan Chinese Association, Malayan Indian Congress) which
dominated politics until its reformulation as the Barisan National (national front) in
1973–1974.[68] As prime minister of independent Malaya his priorities were to prevent
racial conflict and a recrudescence of communist insurgency. Domestic politics in
large measure determined the Tunku's approach to closer association with
neighbouring territories. As leader of the United Malays National Organisation, the
dominant party in the governing Alliance, the Tunku was somewhat unnerved by
electoral setbacks in 1959. This is largely to be explained by changes in the electorate
which had doubled since the first federal elections in 1955 and included seven times
the number of Chinese voters. In the state elections of 1959 the Pan–Malayan Islamic

Party won Kelantan and Trengganu, and, while the Alliance just clung to a two-thirds' majority in the federal house of representatives (which was essential in order to carry any constitutional amendment), the 30 opposition members in the 104-seat parliament included 13 from the Pan–Malayan Islamic Party and 8 from the Socialist Front. Tunku Abdul Rahman was naturally attentive to Malay hostility to any kind of union with Chinese-dominated Singapore. He feared it would end Malay paramountcy in the federation, undermine his leadership of the Malay community and rekindle the insurgency that had only recently ended after a twelve-year state of emergency. He was also sensitive to the expansionist aspirations of the leaders of the PMIP who, while eschewing merger with Singapore, looked forward to the achievement of *Melayu raya*, a greater Malay world embracing kith, kin and co-religionists overseas. UMNO's Chinese partner in the Alliance (the MCA) also looked askance at their southern neighbour and were alarmed by the possibility of political annihilation at the hands of the PAP and economic subordination to the business interests of Singapore. Amongst Malayans in general there was a desire to bring to an end the federation's commercial dependence on Singapore and a 'craving for economic self-sufficiency'—a desire for a major port, an international air-port, a national industrial policy, a federal stock exchange (32).

An ardent cold-warrior, Abdul Rahman also regarded Singapore as a potential Cuba endangering the non-communist Malay world. He abhorred the unruliness of its labour relations and mistrusted the socialism and international neutralism of its leader. For all these reasons, the Malayan prime minister would probably have preferred the indefinite continuation of arrangements whereby the island's defence remained Britain's responsibility while its internal security was administered by the Internal Security Council on which the Malayan government had a representative. Yet, although in his heart of hearts he may have believed that Britain would never allow Singapore to fall to communism, he was sufficiently alarmed by that possibility to consider merger as a way of strengthening Lee Kuan Yew's non-communist regime and thereby reinforcing regional stability. It was Lee Kuan Yew's deteriorating position that convinced the Tunku of the need to absorb the restless island in order to control it. At the end of April 1961, Lee's former minister of national development, Ong Eng Guan, contested the Hong Lim by-election and, capitalising on labour disputes, anti-colonialism and support for separate independence, he defeated the PAP candidate. Although Hong Lim was a serious reverse for the strategy of 'independence through merger', Lee was determined to push on with it because information from 'The Plen' (a high-level contact within the Singapore communist organisation) indicated that the communists would exploit delay to foment unrest.[69] In the end the Tunku was persuaded to have Lee inside, rather than outside, the Malaysian tent on condition that his presence be offset by the inclusion of the Borneo territories (37, 39).[70]

If the PAP had been shaken by the Hong Lim by-election, it was rocked by subsequent reverses. The Tunku's speech of 27 May 1961 exacerbated Lee domestic troubles. Rebels within the PAP rejected the Malaysia initiative and at the Anson by-election on 15 July Lim Chin Siong and other PAP assemblymen transferred their support from the PAP candidate to David Marshall who was campaigning for 'independence *before* merger'. Marshall's victory left Lee and his colleagues 'pretty broken men, extremely jumpy and uncertain of their political future' (50). They cast about for scapegoats—the Malayan government and the British—for their difficulties. After the Anson by-election, a delegation of four PAP dissidents met Selkirk at the so-called 'Eden Hall tea-party'. They sought a reassurance that the British would not suspend the constitution and impose direct rule in a situation where Lee fell from power and they succeeded in forming a government (49, 50). Fearing that the British would ditch him, Lee accused them of machiavellian conspiracy and called for a vote of confidence in the Legislative Assembly which he won after an all-night session, although he was 'within an ace of falling' (72). By the end of the month the dissidents had defected to form the Barisan Sosialis, leaving Lee with a majority of one in the assembly (26 out of 51). It was 'a staggering reverse' (72). Clearly, Lee Kuan Yew had 'not been successful in riding the communist tiger and was in danger of being gobbled up' (55). As the Barisan exploited a network of contacts by retaining control over many PAP constituency organisations and as it shifted its stance on Malaysia to one unrealistically promoting a 'full merger', Lee abandoned the strategy of containing communism and embarked on confrontation which would culminate in February 1963 with the arrest of some 120 suspects, including Lim Chin Siong. In the meantime, however, and with his back to the wall, he battled for merger on several fronts: through marathon radio broadcasts; in a victorious, if controversial, referendum; by an appearance before the UN's Committee of Seventeen in July 1962; and at talks with the Malayan government on the terms and conditions of Malaysian membership.

Apart from matters relating to the military base and the operation of AMDA, by and large the British left the Malayan and Singapore governments to work out on their own the terms and conditions of Singapore's membership of Malaysia. Sovereignty in Singapore still lay with Britain and would in due course be transferred by an act of parliament, but the British refrained from intervening in merger talks unless they reached deadlock, as they did in June and again in September 1963. To begin with, however, inter-governmental discussions made good progress. On 23 August 1961 the Tunku and Lee reached preliminary agreement on the principle of merger as well as on the degree of autonomy to be retained by Singapore. In September a working party was established to examine the detailed arrangements and by November—just before the first Anglo–Malayan conference in London—Heads of Agreement were drawn up and set out in a Singapore white paper (59).[71] Using the 'Ulster model', Singapore was allowed to keep its free-port status, control its labour and education policies, and retain a large proportion of its revenue to cover these functions. Enjoying greater autonomy than other states within the federation, it would have fewer seats in the federal parliament than its population warranted. Moreover, its citizens would be known as 'Malaysian nationals' (not 'Malaysian citizens') and would therefore be ineligible to vote outside Singapore. When these terms were presented to the Singapore Legislative Assembly on 6 December 1961, they were carried by 33 to 0, with 18 Barisan supporters absenting themselves (79, 87). Because the Barisan attacked the 'unequal citizenship' terms and pressed for 'genuine merger', Lee sought popular endorsement through a referendum. The referendum was a risky course for a weak and unpopular government, but, having improved the chances of success by restricting the questions to alternative forms of merger and by counting all blank or spoiled ballot papers as votes in support of the government's line, his policy won a ringing endorsement of policy (131).

Whereas Lee Kuan Yew was a consistent and single-minded advocate of merger, the Tunku blew hot and cold (64). After his dramatic announcement on 27 May 1961, the commitment of the Malayan prime minister wobbled. Each of the three major London conferences on Malaysia—November 1961, July 1962 and July 1963—was almost sabotaged by a threat from Abdul Rahman to pull out of the project altogether. He constantly needed reassurance on what were for him three fundamental conditions: firstly, the participation of the Borneo territories, secondly, the exclusion of Singapore from federal politics, and, thirdly, federal control of Singapore's internal security. Internal security was the burning issue which forged the rapprochement between Singapore and Kuala Lumpur in May 1961 but prised them apart thereafter. Both the Tunku and Lee opposed communism but they did so in different ways: the Tunku had hunted the tiger which Lee had tried to tame. Whereas Abdul Rahman had rejected Chin Peng's peace offer in 1955, in 1959 Lee awarded a government position to Lim Chin Siong on his release from detention. Of course, different circumstances called for different strategies; Malaya's shooting war with its communal undertones was not reproduced in Singapore. Nevertheless, remembering the Malayan emergency, the Tunku was predisposed to mass arrests in Singapore, though, it must be said, he was much more sensitive to the political implications of detaining federal citizens.

Lee, too, manipulated detention for political, not simply security, purposes. Thus, the release of detainees in June 1959 was both a gesture of respect to comrades in the struggle against colonialism and an attempt to contain communism. After the PAP rebels had defected to form the Barisan Sosialis, Lee awaited an opportunity to round up political opponents on the grounds of suspected subversion. Because he knew that he would be finished politically if he acted on his own accord, he hoped to use the ISC as a front for unpopular decisions initiated by the Singapore government (33). Selkirk, however, was not readily compliant. After the Tunku had threatened to withdraw from the ISC, Selkirk avoided convening it. Moreover, just as Selkirk had assured Lim Chin Siong and his colleagues at the 'Eden Hall tea-party' in July 1961 that, provided they acted constitutionally, there would be no justification for Britain to suspend the constitution, so the commissioner-general now protested that there was no case for blanket detentions of political activists.

The rise of the Barisan Sosialis called into question the future stability of Singapore. The Malayan prime minister had no wish to be saddled with a turbulent island, but he veered in his reaction from demanding arrests, to offering to accommodate radicals who worked within the constitution, to threatening to abandon merger altogether. Meanwhile, discussions about a security sweep took place between Singapore and Kuala Lumpur without involving Britain or the ISC. In February 1962, in an attempt to induce British co-operation, Abdul Rahman offered to resume participation in the ISC on condition that it authorised arrests. The following month Lee Kuan Yew accepted that those suspected of subversion should be detained before merger but, in order to preserve his nationalist credentials, he urged Britain to take responsibility for what could be presented as a characteristically colonial act. The British, for their part, remained unconvinced that the situation warranted such an operation and in any case refused to assume entire responsibility for it should it later be deemed necessary. While Maudling reassured Lee that 'we have broad backs and are not afraid to carry our share of the burden', he insisted that he 'must…be convinced that the action taken will make things better not worse' (129).

The possibility of a breakdown of internal security in Singapore was addressed at the London Conference in July 1962 when Tunku Abdul Rahman and Harold Macmillan concluded a secret agreement to bring Malaysia into being as soon as practicable 'if the present Government of Singapore fell or appeared to be about to fall' (134–140). Lee and the Tunku then urged a pre-emptive round-up of subversives, but Sandys categorically refused to take unilateral action, arguing that it should be a matter for the ISC (137, 138). Selkirk also hung back; he was not convinced that there was evidence to justify arrests and he maintained that any such operation might be counter-productive by, firstly, making martyrs of the detainees, secondly, strengthening the cause of the opposition and, thirdly, provoking international outcry (144). As Abdul Rahman became more militant, Lee grew nervous; he speculated whether the Tunku would use arrests to disrupt the Barisan, discard the PAP and prepare the way for the restoration of Lim Yew Hock. Indeed, Lansdowne believed that the Tunku wished 'to be quit of Lee at the earliest convenient moment, and replace him with Lim Yew Hock who would, I suppose do what he was told'.[72] It was an unlikely prognosis but their mutual mistrust ran so deep that Lee suspected that the Tunku would take measures to undermine, rather than reinforce, the PAP regime (144).

Selkirk and Sandys accepted that the time had come for action when the Party Rakyat of Malaya and the Barisan came out in public support of the Brunei rising of December 1962. With Macmillan's approval, Selkirk convened the ISC which agreed to mount an operation that was immediately aborted on account of disagreements between Malaya and Singapore regarded the list of suspects (147, 148).[73] In spite of Lee's misgivings regarding the Tunku's intentions, the British were now convinced that such action was the only way to induce the Federation to agree to merger with Singapore. Code-named 'Cold Store', it was authorised on 1 February (156, 158).[74] Some 120 suspected subversives were detained and, as the British had foreseen, the operation resulted in demonstrations in Singapore and international protests. 'Cold Store' was uncannily similar to 'Operation Sunrise' which rounded-up Africans implicated in Nyasaland's so-called 'murder plot' and which marked the beginning of the end of the Central African Federation.[75]

Far from being prepared to join Malaysia at any price, Lee was by no means averse to tough bargaining with the Malayans and subsequently succeeded in improving the terms—or at least the presentation of those terms—on which Singapore would join Malaysia. He was particularly anxious to neutralise his opponents' criticisms of the citizenship provisions and at the London conference in July 1962 he successfully pressed Abdul Rahman and Razak to accept Singapore citizens as citizens of Malaysia, rather than as nationals of Malaysia (137, 140).[76] Lee also tried to improve the financial and commercial arrangements. In 1961 Jacques Rueff, a distinguished French economist and financier, was appointed to lead the World Bank Mission to examine the feasibility of closer economic co-operation between Malaya and Singapore. Rueff recommended a common market but Malaya feared that competition from Singapore would suffocate its infant industries. By mid-June 1963 negotiations between Malaya and Singapore on financial and commercial arrangements had reached deadlock. The sticking points were the terms of their common market, the apportionment of federal revenues arising in Singapore and the extent of financial assistance from Singapore to the Borneo territories. An additional issue was authority over broadcasting and television in Singapore. In his frustration with both Singapore (and also with Brunei), the Tunku proposed a 'Little Malaysia', ie a merger of only Malaya, North Borneo and Sarawak. As we have seen, in order to prevent the project foundering on technical issues Sandys intervened and invited all parties to London for arbitration (182–184, 186–191). Lee led the Singapore side in these sessions, but the Tunku played no part. He relied on Tun Razak and his minister of finance, Tan Siew Sin. But when he arrived in London for the final ceremony, he was prevailed upon by Lee to accept a few more conditions which were scribbled on the back of an envelope for the Tunku to sign before they both hastened to Marlborough House for the formal signing of the Malaysia Agreement at twelve midnight (192, 193).[77] Because little progress had been made either on these issues or with respect to legislation for the tariff board, Lee took advantage of the postponement of Malaysia Day from 31 August to 16 September, first, to declare independence unilaterally and then to insist on a supplementary agreement to the agreement of 9 July relating to specific inter-governmental arrangements between Singapore and Kuala Lumpur. This was not concluded until 11 September,[78] only a few days before the inauguration of Malaysia and even then Kuala Lumpur held up its implementation (209, 215–219, 221, 222).

Lee Kuan Yew entered Malaysia on his fortieth birthday and the prospects were far more favourable than at one time seemed possible. Through hard and persistent negotiation he had improved at least the presentational aspects of the citizenship terms and had achieved agreement to a common market. No matter that the gesture was legally invalid, he had taken the political step to declare independence before Malaysia Day. Now, as the result of merger, Singapore seemed economically secure in its wider hinterland. Most significantly, Lee had recovered his strength at home, as was confirmed by elections to Singapore's Legislative Assembly held five days after Malaysia Day. The results (PAP 37, Barisan Sosialis 13, United People's Party 1) shattered the Tunku's hopes for Alliance control. Instead the PAP was restored to the commanding position which it had lost in July 1961 when, following by-election defeats and the Tunku's Malaysia initiative, dissidents had defected to form the Barisan.

British colonialism in Borneo

> HMG's accepted policy… is that the peoples of North Borneo and Sarawak should, subject to their own wishes, ultimately achieve self-government. Attractive as is the prospect (not least to many of their own inhabitants at present) of their remaining Crown Colonies, experience shows that we must not delude ourselves into thinking that can be a permanent state.
>
> [Sir John Martin (CO) to Sir Denis Allen (Singapore), 18 May 1960 (see 20)]

Britain's responsibilities in Borneo originated in the activities of nineteenth-century freelance imperialists operating at the frontiers of empire and frequently beyond London's control. By the 1890s the sultanate of Brunei, which had once exercised suzerainty over much of coastal Borneo and parts of the Philippines archipelago, had been reduced to two tiny enclaves as the result of territorial concessions to the Brookes of Sarawak and to European traders. Having interceded in a dispute between the sultan's viceroy and Malays and Dayaks of Sarawak, in 1841 James Brooke was appointed the sultan's governor of this district. Two years later the sultan ceded Sarawak in perpetuity to James and his heirs. In 1864 Britain recognised Sarawak as an independent state but in 1888 it became a British protectorate and surrendered control of its external affairs, as did Brunei and North Borneo at the same time. Committed to the eradication of piracy and head-hunting, James (reigned 1841–1868) and his nephew and successor, Charles (reigned 1868–1917), had by 1890 extended the frontier of their kingdom as far as the Limbang river. This last annexation dissected all that remained of the sultanate and caused deep resentment amongst Brunei Malays and their royal family. During the century of Brooke rule, the economy of Sarawak remained undeveloped and, making a virtue of their lack of resources, the Brookes preferred informal methods and personal rule to a structured bureaucracy.[79] In the centenary year of the regime and only three months before the Japanese occupation, the third and last rajah, Charles Vyner (reigned 1917–1946), issued a constitution which contained the Cardinal Principles of Brooke rule. These principles, one of which promised that 'the people of Sarawak shall be entrusted in due course with the governance of themselves', would be incorporated into the constitution of the post-war crown colony. It would be upon the Cardinal Principles that those Sarawakians and old Sarawak hands who objected to Malaysia would build their case.[80]

To the north of the Brookes' domain British, European and American merchants negotiated concessions with the rulers of Brunei and Sulu. One of these treaties, signed with the Sultan of Sulu in January 1878, either ceded or leased (depending on the translation used) in perpetuity much of what later became known as North Borneo. (In this ambivalence lay the origins of the Philippines claim to North Borneo made by Macapagal at the time of the creation of Malaysia and reiterated by subsequent presidents.) These pioneers sold out to a British commercial syndicate which, having received a charter from Gladstone's government in 1881, restructured itself as the British North Borneo Chartered Company and administered the territory until the Japanese occupation in January 1942. Although it retained the outward form of a commercial concern with shareholders and the occasional distribution of dividends, the Company did not itself engage in trade. Managing 'a gambling style of government' in its early days,[81] it later followed many of the norms of British colonial rule but it lacked 'the resources, experience, or international authority to exercise sovereign functions over a backward people'.[82]

In addition to loss of territory,[83] the Sultan of Brunei relinquished control of external relations, when his kingdom became a British protectorate in 1888, and he surrendered power over domestic affairs in 1906, when he accepted a British resident whose advice he agreed to follow in all matters save those relating to religion and custom. Although Brunei's fortunes improved dramatically in 1929 with the discovery of a large oil field at Seria by the British Malayan Petroleum Company (later Brunei Shell), this did nothing to restore its independence. Moreover, the upheaval in the region during and after the Japanese occupation called into question the future viability of this kingdom.

Already regarded as anachronisms by the 1930s, the Brunei sultanate, the Brooke regime and chartered company rule were closely scrutinised by wartime planners in London. None was deemed to be a 'modern form of authority' or capable of meeting the economic, political and international challenges of the post-war world. It was concluded, therefore, that the restoration of pre-war systems would be 'undesirable in the interests of security and of our declared purpose of promoting social, economic and political progress in Colonial territories' which required 'growing participation in the Government by people of all communities in each territory'.[84] As has been seen, the most radical scheme for post-war reconstruction would have subordinated all three Borneo dependencies to direct British rule under a governor-general in Singapore, but in the end only North Borneo and Sarawak became crown colonies in July 1946 while Brunei remained a protected state. It was decided not to tamper with the sultan's sovereignty, in contrast to the treatment meted out to the rulers of the Malay states. Negotiations over the cession of North Borneo went smoothly enough with the company directors, whose principal concern was adequate financial compensation. Any proposal affecting Sarawak's independence required the acquiescence of his people but, although the highly contentious arrangement by which Charles Vyner ceded Sarawak to the Crown was accepted by the Council Negri (state council) during the post-war military administration, virulent Malay opposition continued, reaching a climax in 1949 when Governor Stewart was assassinated. The episode revealed the passions that could be aroused when the autonomy of the Borneo territories was threatened.[85]

As has already been discussed, 'closer association' had been a key feature of the wartime plan for reconstruction and remained a principle of policy over the next two decades. In spite of the fact that the Borneo territories had 'few racial or other affinities' and that 'the basis for closer union between them hardly exists', the British government insisted that 'the promotion of closer union should be a continuing matter of our policy' and expected the governor-general (later commissioner-general) to sponsor 'community of policy and of administrative action'.[86] Although the sovereignty of the Sultan of Brunei remained intact after the war, in May 1948 his government was brought under the control of his former vassal—Sarawak. The governor of Sarawak became ex officio high commissioner of Brunei; the British resident of Brunei now reported to the high commissioner in Kuching; British officers from the Sarawak government were seconded for service in the sultanate. From the time of his accession in 1950, Sultan Omar Ali Saifuddin III was determined to cut this humiliating connection, to regain Limbang from Sarawak (thereby ending the partition of his kingdom), to roll back British control over his domestic affairs without damaging British guarantees of defence, and to obstruct any attempt to bring about the union or federation of the three Borneo territories. When in 1953 he publicly announced his intention to draw up a written constitution, he turned what might have been a constraint into an enhancement of his authority.[87]

After prolonged discussions, including London talks in September 1957 and March 1959, a constitution was promulgated and a new treaty concluded with Britain on 29 September 1959 (4, 9).[88] The treaty guaranteed British protection in defence and external affairs. It also replaced the British resident with a British high commissioner whose advice the Sultan was to accept 'on all matters connected with the government of the state other than matters relating to the Muslim religion and the custom of the Malays'. In practice, however, the high commissioner would refrain from interfering in domestic affairs since the 'advice clause' was qualified by an exchange of letters between the secretary of state and the Sultan specifying the areas for British guidance. Clearly, it was to the Sultan's advantage that the high commissioner had neither a formal role in internal administration nor a connection with the government of Sarawak. It was also to his advantage that, notwithstanding the provision of a partially elected legislature, the constitution invested supreme executive authority (including all appointments) in the Sultan. Hereafter, his highness would be assisted, not by a British officer, but by a Malay mentri besar (chief minister), a state secretary and an executive council with an official majority. As one authority has commented, the constitution of 1959 was 'no victory for parliamentary democracy, but it was a victory for the Sultan. The British had granted internal self-government to the Sultan, not to the people.' [89]

It has been argued that the British devised the 1959 arrangements in order to strengthen the Sultan and Brunei Shell against A M Azahari whose Party Rakyat Brunei opposed colonialism, favoured the democratisation of government and advocated the restoration of Brunei's historic grandeur through merger with North Borneo and Sarawak in a United State of North Kalimantan.[90] The records show, on the contrary, that the British, who had hoped that a written constitution would act as a check on the Sultan, were wrong-footed when Omar Saifuddin used it as a buttress for monarchical authority. They were dismayed by the deep-rooted autocracy of his highness, the incompetence of his courtiers and by the replacement of British expatriates with Malay officers seconded from the Federation of Malaya. Impatient with the lack of progress in the modernisation of government and the liberalisation of the constitution but now debarred from intervening in domestic matters, the high commissioner became 'an impotent onlooker' as 'the affairs of Brunei began to slip slowly but steadily from his control' [91] while his masters in London could do little other than sympathise with him in this 'typically oriental imbroglio'.[92]

As regards the post-war development of North Borneo and Sarawak, administrative and economic reconstruction was the first priority of the new colonial regimes. Of the three Borneo territories, North Borneo had been the most devastated by the war and the new colonial regime launched its first rehabilitation and development plan in 1948 and its second in 1956. Recovery rested largely on the timber industry and, when he arrived as governor in mid-1960, Sir William Goode was 'astonished' by the 'remarkable' progress. 'There is a general air of progress, prosperity and smiling happiness,' he noted. The government was also committed to the extension of social services and the association of the local populace in the work of government. As regards the latter, the 1950 constitution provided for executive and legislative councils while town boards and district councils were set up at local level. Amendments in 1960 introduced an unofficial majority in the Legislative Council and increased the unofficial membership of the Executive Council, the unofficials being nominated by the governor. Although Goode reported at the end of 1960 that there were no political parties and the country's claim 'to have no politics' was still broadly true, he noted that this was unlikely to last much longer in the light of outside influences and growing pressures for closer association with neighbouring countries (31).[93] Goode advocated the development, particularly the education, of the 'happy', 'friendly' yet 'backward' people of North Borneo before their merger with others. After the 'Greater Malaysia' initiative was launched in mid-1961, Goode, like Sir Alexander Waddell in Sarawak, was a champion of the interests of the Borneo peoples and would fervently and consistently warn against a precipitate rush to their merger with Malaya and Singapore.

After the Japanese occupation Sarawak made fewer strides economically than did North Borneo. Constitutionally, however, it advanced more rapidly and its peoples were more politically active.[94] Sir Charles Arden-Clarke (governor, 1946–1949) promoted institutions of local government. Sir Anthony Abell (governor, 1950–1959) introduced in 1956 a constitution providing for a majority of unofficial members on both the Legislative Council (Council Negri) and the Executive Council

(Supreme Council) most of whom were to be elected.[95] The introduction of elections led to the formation of the Sarawak United People's Party (SUPP) in June 1959 and the Party Negara Sarawak (PANAS) in April the following year. Ong Kee Hui and other moderate, English-educated Chinese leaders were the driving force behind the formation of SUPP although it was later infiltrated by radicals from the Clandestine Communist Organisation who largely recruited from amongst the rural poor. PANAS was led by Datu Bandar Abang Haji Mustapha who had supported cession in 1946.[96] Although both parties claimed to be multi-racial, SUPP was almost exclusively associated with the Chinese while PANAS was identified with pro-cession Malays. Neither made much headway with the Dayaks who mistrusted both other communities and largely stayed outside party politics until the launch of 'Greater Malaysia' and the Cobbold enquiry. In contrast to the racial harmony reported from North Borneo by Goode, Tory noted a dangerous racial problem in Sarawak which was 'very similar to that which the Malayans have had to face' in the federation. In Tory's opinion, this tension plus the country's poverty could only delay progress towards self-government. As regards the timing of constitutional change, it was the view of senior officials on the spot that none of the territories would be ready for self-government earlier than 1970 (26), and that they should advance together rather than follow separate courses or adopt different timetables. While 'closer association' and self-government were interrelated, long-term objectives for the Borneo territories, it was axiomatic that the achievement of these goals would depend on the acquiescence of the people and should not be jeopardised by any hasty action.

Britain, Malaya and the Borneo territories: the Cobbold Enquiry

> We are all in favour of Greater Malaysia but it will have to be handled with more finesse than the Tunku is showing.
> [E M West (CO) to Reginald Maudling, 21 Mar 1962 [97]]

The Tunku's ardour for assimilating the Borneo territories contrasted with his aversion to merger with Singapore. He wished to be certain of North Borneo, Sarawak and possibly Brunei too, before tying the knot with Lee Kuan Yew. In many ways an Anglophile, he had no wish to be left 'holding the Singapore baby' (63) for the British or to be cast as their 'running dog' in Borneo. He was, after all, the head of the government of a sovereign state with an international reputation to protect and project. More significant in his calculations than international kudos, however, were the likely domestic repercussions of territorial integration. These hinged on demographic arithmetic and the communal composition of the new state. According to figures used in 1961, Malays accounted for 49.3 per cent of the population of Malaya compared with 37.6 per cent Chinese. The bilateral merger of Malaya and Singapore would have shifted the balance to 45 per cent Chinese and 42.3 per cent Malays. Within 'Greater Malaysia', however, Chinese numbers would have been trimmed as follows: Chinese 42.7 per cent, Malays/Borneo Muslims 39.8 per cent, non-Muslim indigenous peoples of Borneo 5.8 per cent, others (including Indians) 11.7 per cent (73). The Tunku concluded that the non-Chinese communities of Borneo would go some way towards neutralising the Singapore threat to the Malay position. Indeed, to be on the safe side he went so far as to demand Malaya's union with the Borneo territories in advance of that with Singapore (57, 61, 63, 64, 66, 67).

Whether it was out of ignorance of Borneo (for example, several years later he told a Dayak leader 'there is no such thing as the Dayak language')[98] or enthusiasm for *Melayu raya* (the greater Malay world), the Tunku was misled into believing that the peoples of Brunei, North Borneo and Sarawak would welcome his intervention. In fact he soon encountered antagonism from local leaders who were suspicious of a stratagem which threatened to replace one colonial regime with another and to subordinate their rights and interests to those of Kuala Lumpur.

Not long after his speech of 27 May 1961 the Tunku paid a 'goodwill' visit to the Borneo territories. It coincided with a crisis in Kuala Lumpur's relations with Brunei where local resentment had boiled over towards officials seconded from Malaya (91). The Tunku's high-handed response to this issue alienated Bruneians and added to their fear of a Malayan take-over, a fear that spread to North Borneo and Sarawak. As a result Ong Kee Hui (SUPP), Azahari (PRB) and Donald Stephens (Kadazan Association, forerunner of UNKO) joined in a United Front to protest against the Tunku's proposed Malaysia. (SUPP and the PRB would remain opposed to Malaysia, though they would part company from each other, but Donald Stephens was later converted to the project.) Waddell reported from Sarawak that 'the feeling has grown that the Tunku's object is a Greater Malaya, not Greater Malaysia' and he warned that 'if merger is forced by 1963 or at all prematurely there is a real prospect of racial conflict and outright rebellion'.[99] Goode (North Borneo), Waddell (Sarawak), White (Brunei) and CO officials accepted Malaysia as their goal but were perturbed by what they saw as the Tunku's headlong rush towards it. Goode and Waddell insisted that the Borneo colonies were not yet ready for self-government within Malaysia which, they feared, would turn out to be an unequal partnership between the Bornean horse and the Malayan rider. They warned of the dangers of a shot-gun marriage when Selkirk recommended to Macleod and Macmillan a 'crash programme' for merger (55, 58).

No matter the posting or departmental affiliation of individuals, there was general agreement amongst the British that the Tunku's conduct immediately after his speech of 27 May 1961 put the scheme at risk and, at the Anglo–Malayan talks in London in November 1961, the British side insisted that progress towards Malaysia should be conditional upon a favourable report on Borneo opinion. (Britain's other stipulation was, as we have seen, a guarantee for the continued use of the Singapore base.) How opinion was to be ascertained posed a problem that would dog the scheme until the eve of its inauguration. All three territories were as yet 'quite unfitted' to enter Malaysia on the basis of popular representation and Selkirk gave 'Sarawak about ten years and North Borneo at least twenty years before a clear-cut electoral opinion could be given on this subject' (55). In the frequent parallels drawn by policy-makers between Malaysia and the Central African Federation, the position of Borneo was compared with that of Nyasaland in that both were under-populated, undeveloped and, at least to begin with, almost innocent of party politics. At the time of the Tunku's announcement there were few registered parties: SUPP, PANAS and SNAP in Sarawak, Party Rakyat in Brunei, but none yet in North Borneo. Because there was as yet little political awareness with which to fashion political activity, it was decided not to test public feeling at the polls in the first instance. Instead, in the colonies of North Borneo and Sarawak opinion was assessed by an Anglo–Malayan commission of enquiry, while as regards Brunei both London and Kuala Lumpur courted Sultan Omar Saifuddin as the sole spokesman of his people. Critics of

Malaysia condemned the exercise as a smoke-screen behind which British colonialists collaborated with their 'stooges'. Largely because the Tunku suspected that the enquiry was a delaying tactic on the part of the British, however, the Anglo–Malayan Commission was troubled from the outset by the markedly different approaches of the British and Malayan governments to the manner and timetable for territorial integration and transfer of power. In addition, there was considerable divergence of views within British circles: on the one hand, CO officials and colonial administrators emphasised trusteeship obligations and the wisdom of making haste slowly; on the other hand, the CRO, the office of the commissioner-general and increasingly the prime minister himself were worried lest procrastination allowed the Tunku's enthusiasm to cool, Lee's regime to fall and the Malaysia project to fail.

The nomination of members of the commission revealed the differences between London and Kuala Lumpur that would subsequently bring the enquiry to the brink of failure (89). Many were considered for the chairmanship but rejected for one reason or another. Malcolm MacDonald was the British first choice but was discounted by the Tunku for having been too pro-Dayak during his time as commissioner-general.[100] The Tunku, for his part, preferred a man who had assisted Malaya along the road to *Merdeka*, such as Lord Ogmore (formerly David Rees-Williams, whom the British regarded as inappropriate as a consequence of his involvement in the cession of Sarawak to the Crown in 1946),[101] or Lord Boyd (formerly Alan Lennox-Boyd, whom the British rejected as being too political). In the end Lord Cobbold, a former governor of the Bank of England, was accepted by both sides as sufficiently detached from colonial affairs. Since the Tunku suggested Sir David Watherston as one of the British members (in what turned out to be the misplaced belief that as a former chief secretary of the Federation he would be sympathetic to Kuala Lumpur), the British chose the late, popular governor of Sarawak, Sir Anthony Abell, to serve as the other British commissioner. The Malayan commissioners were Dato Wong Pow Nee, chief minister of Penang, and the more dominant Ghazali Shafie, permanent secretary of the Ministry of External Affairs, to whom the Tunku was already accustomed 'to give an unusually wide measure of responsibility'.[102]

In January 1962 Sir John Martin and Ian Wallace reconnoitred the colonies in advance of the enquiry (92). Harking back to Sir Harold MacMichael's disastrous mission to extract fresh treaties from the Malay sultans in 1945, Martin warned the minister of state against rushing the people of Sarawak and North Borneo: 'You will remember the unhappy history of the MacMichael agreements in Malaya. More recently we have the lesson of our failure to reconcile people to federation in Central Africa at the outset. We cannot afford to repeat these mistakes in this sensitive region of the world.'[103] As for Brunei, Wallace reported that the sultan was 'not going to be a push-over for Malaysia'.[104] A fortnight before the British commissioners left London, however, they were heartened to learn that the Malaysia Solidarity Consultative Committee, composed of non-British representatives of the five territories (including observers sent by the Sultan of Brunei) and chaired by North Borneo's Donald Stephens (who had initially attacked the Tunku's proposal), had concluded in favour of the 'concept' of Malaysia.[105]

During their tour of the Borneo colonies, the commissioners worked together 'as well as could be expected' but, Cobbold observed, 'the prospects of unanimous recommendations were extremely dim' (94). Fairly soon into the enquiry, the British reached the view that local mistrust of Kuala Lumpur plus the countries' dependence on expatriate officials required a transitional period during which Britain would transfer control in stages for the sake of administrative continuity. Such gradualism was unacceptable to the Malayan commissioners. When members of the colonial services in Borneo also expressed reservations about Malaysia, Ghazali accused them of old-fashioned paternalism and wilful sabotage. This spat is documented in British archives and vividly recalled by the leading Malayan commissioner in his *Memoir*. Observing the Sarawak river from a window in the Kuching istana (palace), Ghazali mused:—

> The river was tidal. Quite often it did not appear to know which way it was flowing. Even if it did flow it was very slow and with it were drift woods and flotsam creating impediments to boats cruising by. It was almost a grotesque mimicry of the attitude of the colonial expatriates towards the Malaysia Concept! [106]

On another occasion he refers scathingly to 'hard core die-hard colonialists who were living in the past' and 'who thought it was the white man's burden to take care of the noble savages who should remain so for them to patronise and gloat'.[107] Ghazali has presented the Tunku as 'a true democrat and a people's prince',[108] liberating Borneo from the yoke of colonialism while British ministers and officials (with a few exceptions such as Malcolm MacDonald, Harold Macmillan and Duncan Sandys) tried to stop the onward march of freedom. He reported that colonial administrators were apathetic, if not hostile to Malaysia, and suggested that the truculence of Sarawakians was probably the result of having been 'coached' by expatriates.[109] Ghazali himself had been coached at the start of his diplomatic career by Malcolm MacDonald. His 'thrusting self-confidence' had taken him to the top of the tree at an early age with the result that he had 'developed a keen sense of his own importance' which indeed was 'real enough'. He was observed by the British to have 'a certain unscrupulous streak of self-aggrandisement' and, while he conveyed 'a sense of considerable bonhomie', he was 'given to bursts of temper if he feels he has been slighted'.[110] Ghazali did indeed feel slighted during the tour of Borneo and he sent the Tunku reports of 'rude treatment' including an occasion when a British resident allegedly snubbed the Malayan commissioners at a cocktail party 'in full view of everybody' (96).[111] When Tunku Abdul Rahman realised that the enquiry might not endorse Malaysia unequivocally and whole-heartedly, he went on the offensive and publicly accused colonial officials of hampering preparations.

The governor of North Borneo, whose knowledge, ability and experience were widely respected, strenuously denied 'foot-dragging' over Malaysia.[112] William Goode had entered the Malayan Civil Service in 1931 and, apart from four years in Aden, he spent his entire career in Southeast Asia. His experience of internment during the Japanese occupation and his sense of having 'let the people down' in 1941–1942 reinforced an instinctive commitment to trusteeship obligations during the period of decolonisation.[113] In 1961–1963 he was appalled by Malayan insensitivity to Borneo and particularly by the Tunku's ignorance, naivete and indifference to local resistance to Malaysia. While the enmity of many people in North Borneo was 'probably a relic of the old repression by Malays from Brunei', it was nonetheless real in 1962.[114] Goode reminded London that the peoples of North Borneo 'had only been steam-rollered once, by the Japanese, and they exacted a price of heads for that' (100).[115] More than twenty years later he recalled how 'one Native Chief, a Dusun, said to me "If the British are unwilling to stay longer, I'd rather have the Japanese than Malays taking over".' When years later he reflected on the making of Malaysia, it seemed to him that a project which was 'merely a desperate political device to enable KL to deal better with Chinese Singapore under the PAP' was not only 'hopelessly ill-founded and unreal' but also 'most unfair on the happy and friendly peoples of North Borneo'.[116] After the commissioners departed, Goode elaborated his ideas: he accepted Malaysia—even advocating that it should be inaugurated while the iron was hot—but he insisted that, before sovereignty was transferred to Kuala Lumpur, there should be a prolonged transitional period during which expatriate officials would administer the country.

Since the establishment of crown colony rule in 1946, the old ethos of government had been changing in both territories. Development funds, directives from the Colonial Office and the recruitment of cadets or transfers from other colonies meant, as has been written of Sarawak, that the practice of 'the eccentric Brooke officer reigning over his "subjects" in a remote outstation without much interference from the centre of government in Kuching' was no longer acceptable.[117] Nevertheless, in the view of Goode, Waddell and the proponents of progressive colonialism, North Borneo and Sarawak still required both time to prepare for Malaysia and British officials to guide the localisation of administration and the growth of self-governing institutions. Neither was guaranteed. Time was running out; as Philip Rogers noted, 'we may have to try and achieve in perhaps as little as two or three years what we ought to spend at least twenty years in doing'.[118] Moreover, the prospect of a Malayan take-over discouraged expatriates from staying-on. This was a problem affecting other territories, too, and in the early 1960s the terms and conditions of the Oversea Civil Service (HMOCS) were amended to provide not only compensation for loss of employment but also financial inducements to continue in post. While North Borneo and Sarawak shared with dependencies elsewhere the problem of lack of preparedness, the Treasury recognised their 'unique' predicament in that, 'if the expatriates were to go, we should be leaving the inhabitants at the mercy of the Malayans'.[119]

Tunku Abdul Rahman's criticism of colonial officials in March 1962 received wide publicity in the region. It reached the British press and was sufficiently grave to catch the attention of the British prime minister. Any hint of blinkered sentimentalism on the part of the Colonial Office and the overseas colonial service disturbed Macmillan and he requested an explanation from the colonial secretary. Reginald Maudling was advised by CO officials against any tendency to 'bounce Borneo on the basis of the Tunku's thinking',[120] and he strongly defended the colonial service: 'The administration in Borneo are not being paternalistic but realistic. They are entirely with us in wanting to see Malaysia brought about.' (97) The CO felt that a riposte to the Tunku would be in order, pointing out that the success of Malaysia would depend on the continuity of administration provided by British officials. In the CRO, however, it was felt that the Tunku may have had a point. The Commonwealth secretary was impatient; six months previously Sandys had allegedly said that 'we could not allow the susceptibilities of headhunters to wreck the project' [121] and he was now eager to take it in hand. On reading Goode's submissions to Cobbold, in which the governor had stated that 'North Borneo is not ready for Malaysia', one CRO official concluded that they provided 'ample justification for the Tunku's feeling that the N.B. administration have not put their heart in Malaysia. Sir W Goode has pulled no punches and, considering the papers were intended for both the British and Malayan members of the Commission, they are astonishingly frank.'[122] On balance, however, ministers preferred to let the matter drop. To pursue it further would have aggravated tensions between Malaya and the Borneo territories and also between Malayan and colonial officials 'to the point of generating an atmosphere of mistrust, such as had developed in the Central African Federation' (98). When Lansdowne referred to the episode several months later the Tunku took it 'in very good part'. With respect to his remarks about 'the British yoke', he reminded the minister of state, 'with a big twinkle in his eye', that when he was fighting for Malayan independence 'he had used the same tactics to build up a national spirit' (142).

Cobbold returned from Borneo full of foreboding: the commissioners were divided and strife was brewing in the Borneo colonies. Unless the Tunku behaved sensibly and the government seized the initiative to act promptly, he warned, 'there will be some slitting of throats' (101, also 102). The commissioners reconvened in Britain in early May and spent the rest of the month and much of June drafting their report in which Watherston took the lead (106–116). They agreed that there was significant support for Malaysia but serious mistrust of it. Where they differed was over recommendations for a transitional period. Watherston and Abell (with Cobbold largely in support) were concerned that sufficient safeguards (regarding the official language, appointment of state governors and expatriate officials) should be built into the transitional arrangements to meet the special interests of the territories and to ensure continuity of administration. Alarmed by the prospect of the simultaneous withdrawal of British governors and imposition of Malayan government, they suggested a compromise whereby, on the inauguration of Malaysia, sovereignty would be transferred to Kuala Lumpur which would immediately assume responsibility for the defence and external relations of the Borneo territories while the British governors of North Borneo and Sarawak would remain in post to ensure administrative continuity and to supervise the localisation of public services. Since such an arrangement was bound to inflame Malayan opinion, they recommended that the details be worked out after the publication of the report. Ghazali Shafie and Wong Pow Nee were shocked by Watherston's draft, which, in Ghazali's view portrayed a colonial golden age plunged into chaos, and they set about drafting an alternative version. Not surprisingly Ghazali showed no particular tenderness towards Borneo peoples; [123] rather his object was to secure a report that neither fudged issues nor brooked delay in the transfer of complete control to Kuala Lumpur. Anything less would have played into the hands of critics keen to brand the Tunku a 'British lackey'.[124] Tunku Abdul Rahman wanted a unanimous report that supported the Malayan viewpoint and, when he learned of the commissioners' disagreements, he issued instructions to the Malayan commissioners, threatening to recall them for consultations. Although Ghazali was able to reassure him that their return would be unnecessary, Abdul Rahman's intervention in what was supposed to be an independent enquiry upset both sides of the Commission and added to their difficulties.[125] At last, on 21 June Cobbold submitted the report simultaneously to the prime ministers of Britain and Malaya, who agreed to keep it confidential until they had decided a course of action (124).[126] At the same time, Cobbold also sent Macmillan, the Tunku and Maudling a number of letters (including a memorandum by Abell and Watherston) which amplified contentious issues that were not mentioned, or were only partially covered, in the report (118–122). Here he was more explicit in his views regarding transition. In his private and personal letter to Macmillan, for example, Cobbold emphasised that British governors would be 'essential' in North Borneo and Sarawak 'for the next few years' because the government in Kuala Lumpur was both 'fully stretched' and largely ignorant of conditions in Borneo (118).

Securing agreement had been touch and go. The talks had nearly collapsed; Ghazali and Wong Pow Nee had been on the point of returning to Kuala Lumpur; the British and Malayan commissioners had considered submitting separate reports. That none of this happened was because, on the one hand, the commissioners' views tallied on many issues while, on the other hand, the presentation of their disagreements was effectively managed. First of all, they were in broad agreement in their assessments of Borneo opinion: they estimated that about one-third strongly favoured Malaysia, another third favoured it provided that there were adequate safeguards, and the remaining third was divided between those seeking independence in advance of the inauguration of Malaysia and those resisting it outright.[127] Secondly, they were unanimous on a number of major recommendations, for example: that a decision in principle should be taken by governments as soon as possible; that the new state should be called Malaysia; that the constitution of the Federation of Malaya should be adapted for Malaysia, instead of drafting a completely new one; that there should be no right to secede from Malaysia after merger; that Borneanisation of the public services should proceed as quickly as possible and that, in the interim, every effort should be made to encourage British officers to remain in the service; that citizens of North Borneo and Sarawak should become citizens of Malaysia.[128] In general, they concluded that 'a Federation of Malaysia is an attractive and workable project and in the best interests of the Borneo territories'.[129] Thirdly, the British commissioners agreed to eliminate references to the appointment of British governors and to accept an arrangement whereby new governors would be appointed by the Yang di-Pertuan Agong (on the joint nomination of the Agong and the Queen). Fourthly, as regards the areas where they diverged, their differences were set out in separate sections, not in the form of conflicting reports but as an agenda requiring further consideration. Finally, the Commission left the controversial points (including the precise constitutional arrangements for the transition and internal security) to be decided in negotiation between the British and Malayan governments. Cobbold saved the Commission from collapse by remitting to inter-governmental negotiations the 'one big and difficult problem' of the transitional stage (124).

Copied into the communications between London and Kuala Lumpur, the governors of North Borneo and Sarawak picked up on the disputes over drafting without being privy to the full contents of the report (103–105, 116). Tit-bits of news fuelled the fears of the guardians of Bornean interests that the British were prepared to compromise principles and suppress awkward issues in order to appease the Malayans. A forceful telegram from Goode, which reiterated the danger of ignoring popular opinion, 'shocked' the prime minister prompting him to ask the Cabinet secretary: 'Does he [Goode] realise (a) our weakness in Singapore (b) our need to hand over the security problem there. If this is the Colonial Office point of view, we shall fail. What are we to do?' (117). To the embarrassment of the prime minister's private office, a copy of Macmillan's minute was inadvertently sent to the colonial secretary and, not surprisingly, 'it made him—and the Colonial Office—angry'. Tartly rejecting the implication that governors made policy, Maudling replied: 'I have not yet made up my mind what the Colonial Office point of view is to be on the matter. The Governor is fully aware of the importance of Malaysia and I am sure his concern is to see it achieved without serious troubles in Borneo.' Tim Bligh, principal private secretary to the prime minister, managed to persuade Maudling to withhold his paper from Macmillan who remained unconscious of the consternation aroused by his question which he himself was to answer a few weeks later by reshuffling the Cabinet in 'the night of the long knives'.[130]

Britain, Malaya and the Borneo colonies: inter-governmental negotiations

I am afraid that the Tunku still shows little sign openly of understanding the difficulties involved over the accession of the territories to Malaysia. I suspect, however, that he may well understand more than he wishes to disclose. I doubt whether any useful purpose can be served by the *British* emphasising the difficulties. He is a man of great perception and I feel certain that if he is able to have informed talks both with the peoples and the British officers, he will quickly grasp the realities of the situation, though he may well not show that he has done so. [Lord Lansdowne to Sir William Goode, 11 Sept 1962 [131]]

Although the Tunku had authorised the Malayan commissioners to sign the report, he was unhappy with it. He was 'very nervous about the effect of Malaysia on his political position' (123) and about its repercussions on Malaya's relations with Indonesia and the Philippines. Having consulted his Cabinet at the hill resort of Fraser's Hill, the Tunku rejected the report and suggested the postponement of Malaysia until Britain was ready for it (125). In London the Oversea Policy Committee realised the need to avoid repeating the mistake already made in Central Africa where, by hanging on too long to responsibility in Nyasaland and Northern Rhodesia, Britain had contributed to the difficulties of the Central African Federation. Since British ministers had no doubt that 'Malaysia offered the best and possibly the only hope for longer term stability in Singapore', they accepted that, if it were to be achieved, 'it would have to be achieved quickly in view of the deteriorating position of Mr. Lee Kuan Yew's Government' as well as the pending claim of the Philippines to North Borneo. Rather than antagonise Malaya and lose Malaysia, therefore, they concluded that full responsibility for the Borneo territories should be conceded to the federal government on Malaysia Day (126).[132] The immediate priority, however, was to re-engage the Tunku in discussions. Intervening personally, Macmillan reassured the Malayan prime minister that the views of Cobbold and the other British commissioners were not those of the British government, that the British government had no wish to retain authority in the Borneo territories during the transition stage, and that he would approach the report 'with a completely open mind'. Macmillan's diplomacy rescued the Anglo–Malayan talks on Malaysia (127, 128).

There was now less than a fortnight before the talks were due to start in London. As part of the preparations, the inter-departmental Committee on Greater Malaysia completed a comprehensive brief for ministers (129, 130). Notwithstanding an apparent consensus, CO officials feared that safeguards for Borneo would be sacrificed on the altar of Anglo–Malayan partnership. They believed it would be bad tactics to allow Macmillan and the Tunku to meet in private, without officials in attendance and before the formal talks got underway. They accordingly advised their secretary of state to be alert and to stand up to the CRO: 'The Tunku, we fear, is coming over expecting to have everything buttoned up in a week or two. Even if there were no major difficulties such as the transitional period this would not be practicable.'[133] Noting how in 'recent official discussions on Malaysia (and I think also in some of the Ministerial consideration of the subject) there have been signs of a tendency to believe that Malaysia is so desirable that we must be prepared to pay any price which the Tunku demands', Sir John Martin felt that the time had come for his secretary of state to fire a shot across the bows of the Oversea Policy Committee. Martin submitted a draft minute for Maudling to sign and send to his Cabinet colleagues. This stated without equivocation that 'it will be paying too high if we agree to terms for the Borneo territories' admission to Malaysia which could frustrate its successful creation'. By such action, Britain would not only be in breach of its trusteeship obligations, but would also risk 'breakdown in administration', 'economic chaos' and 'bloodshed' which 'would infect Malaysia from the start with a fatal instability'.[134] It would appear that the paper had been drafted with Duncan Sandys in mind, but, before it could be signed and circulated, Maudling had been replaced as secretary of state by Sandys himself.

Within a few days of the dramatic Cabinet reshuffle, the Malaysian talks got underway in London (132). They started on the morning of 17 July with the private meeting between Macmillan and Abdul Rahman, which CO officials had hoped either to avert or to attend, and this was followed at 12 noon by the first plenary session. The Tunku's delegation met with Sandys' team that afternoon and the next morning. Thereafter detailed negotiations were conducted in a steering committee chaired by Lord Lansdowne (minister of state, CO). The Borneo peoples were represented by their governors. Judging by the pencilled notes ('Points for Sandys') which he jotted down on the eve of the talks, it is unlikely that Goode's views would have been warmly welcomed by the new secretary of state: 'Wholly support Malaysia but ... Tunku must avoid "taking over" Borneo territories as Colonies. Any impression of being transferred as Colonies from Britain to Malaya will provoke a Merdeka [independence] Movement against K.L.—potentially irresistible'.[135] The talks went badly. After ten days they were in danger of breaking down altogether. The initial meeting between prime ministers, where Macmillan seems to have encouraged the Tunku to believe that the British government would in the end be willing to achieve agreement at almost any price, had unrealistically raised Malayan expectations. A L M Cary of the Cabinet Office noted that 'unless there is some dramatic change in the situation it looks as though a solution may emerge which will cause serious trouble in Borneo and by repercussion, in this country'.[136] The stumbling blocks were, firstly, the implications of extending the existing federal constitution to North Borneo and Sarawak (particularly with respect to religion, language and education) and, secondly, the crucial question of timing. On the one hand, the sound preparation of the Borneo territories warranted the gradual implementation of a measured programme; on the other hand, instability in Singapore and the Tunku's self-esteem necessitated the swift advance towards an early date. Discussions about Singapore's membership of Malaysia were going on in London at the same time as those regarding Borneo, but, because the Tunku was pessimistic about the chances of synchronising both sets of merger and could not, in any case, accept the staged approach whereby Singapore acceded before the Borneo territories, he threatened to pull out of the talks altogether (133).

Breakdown would have been in nobody's interest, least of all the Tunku's who could not risk returning to Kuala Lumpur empty-handed. In order to get negotiations back on track, Macmillan invited the Tunku to lunch at Chequers on 28 July when Macmillan outlined a formula to enable the establishment of Malaysia (134–137). First of all the governments should jointly declare their intention to conclude a formal agreement which would provide for the transfer of sovereignty to Malaysia by 31 August 1963, safeguards for Singapore and the Borneo territories and also the extension of the existing defence arrangement. Secondly, the prime ministers of Malaya and the UK would exchange secret letters agreeing that 'if the present Government of Singapore fell or appeared to be about to fall, the new Federation of Malaysia should be brought into being as soon as practicable'. This, as has already been discussed in the section on relations between Malaya and Singapore, was a contingency plan in the event of Lee's regime collapsing, but it also had implications for the control of the Borneo territories. If Malaysia was brought into being prematurely (ie before 31 August 1963), the British governors would cease to be responsible to the British government but would continue to exercise executive powers until the appointment by the Yang di-pertuan Agong of new governors with effect from 31 August. Three days after the Chequers lunch an agreement in principle for setting up the Federation of Malaysia by 31 August 1963 was signed by Macmillan and the Tunku, with Lee Kuan Yew in attendance (139). The following day, a joint statement to this effect was made in both Houses at Westminster as well as in the Federal Parliament and the Cobbold Report was published.[137] But the agreement itself was not released, nor were its annex and most of its appendices. The reasons for this secrecy were, firstly, the sensitivity of the Chequers formula allowing pre-emptive action, and, secondly, the likely opposition of the peoples of Borneo to the constitutional structure. As CO officials and governors had always feared would happen, 'the agreement records an acceptance (not achieved by the Malayan members without hard bargaining) of the view of the Malayan members of the [Cobbold] Commission' (140).[138] Indeed, the Tunku's private observation to Goode, made the day after the agreement had been signed, did nothing to reassure the governor: 'The peoples of the territories are good, simple people. They will be easy to handle if ideas are not put in their heads.' [139] Prolonged discussions within the forum of an inter-governmental committee were now required if Borneo leaders were to be persuaded to accept the timetable for merger and the Anglo–Malayan framework for their state constitutions.

The announcement of the early target date came as a great shock to many in British Borneo. It seemed to confirm that Malaysia was to be a Malayan 'take-over'. On 13–14 August Donald Stephens convened a meeting of North Borneo political leaders who drew up a fourteen-point (later twenty-point) programme of minimum demands. These demands went far beyond what the Malayans had conceded at the London talks and gained added weight by attracting support in Sarawak. Although the Legislative Councils of both North Borneo and Sarawak accepted Malaysia in principle in September, they did so on condition that state rights were constitutionally safeguarded. The task of drafting these safeguards had been devolved by the London conference to the Inter-Governmental Committee working in consultation with the two legislatures. Chaired by Lord Lansdowne, with Tun Razak as deputy chairman, the IGC consisted of representatives from Malaya, North Borneo and Sarawak (141–143). Specific topics were handled by five sub-committees, each of which was chaired by Sir John Martin. The IGC's first task was to allay anxieties and secure local co-operation. One of the most intractable problems was the extent of development aid for the Borneo territories (146). This was later dealt with as part of the financial settlement which British ministers discussed with the Malayan government in May 1963 (145, 173–177, 179, 181). With respect to constitutional relations, although they failed to secure an initial seven-year period during which legislative power should remain within the state (rather than being delegated to it), North Borneo and Sarawak did win a number of safeguards which could not be changed by the federal government without the concurrence of the state government. The committee's final report was initialled on 22 January 1963, published on 27 February and adopted by the Council Negri and North Borneo's Legislative Council on 8 and 13 March respectively.[140]

Although local opposition to Malaysia had not evaporated in North Borneo, by now much of it was being channelled through an increasing number of parties which, in response both to the previous practices of colonial rule and to the communal imperatives of Malaysian politics, championed particular ethnic and regional interests. In addition to SUPP and PANAS in Sarawak, by the end of 1962 the following parties had been registered and were active: the Sarawak National Party (SNAP, predominantly Ibans of the Second Division), Barisan Ra'ayat Jati Sarawak (BARJASA, a Malay party in competition with PANAS), Party Pesaka Anak Sarawak (PAPAS or PESAKA, largely Ibans of the Third Division), and the Sarawak Chinese Association (SCA). In November 1962 BARJASA, PANAS, PESAKA, SCA, and SNAP formed the Sarawak Alliance (though PANAS later defected) to fight elections in 1963 as the result of which a pro-Malaysia coalition was formed with Stephen Kalong Ningkan (SNAP) as chief minister designate (198). In Sabah, the formation of Donald Stephens' United National Kadazan Organisation (UNKO) was followed by the United Sabah National Organisation (USNO) led by Dato Mustapha bin Dato Harun (Sabah's first head of state) and a number of other parties (United National Pasok Momogun Organisation, Democratic Party, United Party, Sabah Indian Congress). In various combinations these parties composed the Sabah Alliance that supported Malaysia in elections as the result of which Donald Stephens emerged as chief minister designate of Sabah. The staged electoral process was concluded in North Borneo and Sarawak by July 1963 (Appendix, paras 311–317).

The Malaysia Agreement was signed in London on 9 July 1963.[141] Neither sovereign, nor even self-governing, strictly speaking North Borneo and Sarawak were not of a status to be parties to the formal agreement. It would have been injudicious, however, to have stuck to the letter of the law in this matter. In fact, the British recognised the presentational importance of ensuring that leaders of indigenous peoples of Borneo participated in the signing ceremony alongside representatives of the British, Malayan and Singapore governments (178). Dato Mustapha bin Dato Harun and Donald Stephens were amongst the six signatories for North Borneo. Sarawak's five representatives included Temenggong Jugah (who would be federal minister for Sarawak Affairs), Dato Abang Haji Openg (the future governor) and Dato Abang Haji Mustapha (of PANAS which would shortly split from the Sarawak Alliance), but Stephen Kalong Ningkan was not present. Annexed to the Malaysia Agreement were a number of constitutional instruments. These included: the Malaysia bill to enable the admission to the federation of the three former British dependencies; state constitutions for Sabah (as North Borneo would be called), Sarawak and Singapore; a scheme to compensate officers retiring from government service in North Borneo and Sarawak; terms and conditions by which expatriates would continue to be employed in the public services of Sabah, Sarawak and Singapore.

Legislation ending British jurisdiction in North Borneo, Sarawak and Singapore was enacted at Westminster.[142] It did not provide for the separate independence of the three territories but transferred sovereignty to the new Federation of Malaysia. Since it involved amendments to the constitution of the Federation of Malaya, legislation to set up the Federation of Malaysia was enacted by the Yang di-Pertuan Agong and the Malayan parliament. The state constitutions of Sabah, Sarawak and Singapore were authorised in London by Orders-in-Council, as were arrangements for the compensation of retiring officers. The conditions of service of those officers continuing in the employment of the governments of Sabah, Sarawak and Singapore would later be confirmed by an agreement concluded between the UK and the new Federation of Malaysia.[143] A last-minute dispute between Malayan and Sarawak leaders over the nomination of Sarawak's first head of state was resolved through the personal intervention of Sandys but it did not bode well for future relations between Kuching and Kuala Lumpur (210, 224).

The UN Mission to Borneo

... there is no doubt about the wishes of a sizeable majority of the peoples of these territories to join the Federation of Malaysia.
[U Thant, 13 Sept 1963 (225)]

As preparations for Malaysia proceeded, opponents contested its legitimacy by appeals to the United Nations. Decolonisation through the integration of a non-self-governing territory with an already independent state would be regarded as legitimate provided that, firstly, the acceding territory had 'attained an advanced stage of self-government with free political institutions', and, secondly, its peoples had expressed their wishes through democratic processes based on universal adult suffrage. It was also expected that, notwithstanding constitutional variations between them, the peoples of the acceding territory would enjoy equal rights and status with those of the already independent state (205).[144]

After they lost the debate on Singapore's referendum bill in July 1962, a group of assemblymen led by the Barisan Sosalis and David Marshall sent an appeal to the UN's Committee of Seventeen (the decolonisation committee; later the Committee of Twenty Four). Both the petitioners and Lee Kuan Yew in due course appeared before the committee and Lee's rebuttal of his critics made such an impression that no further action was taken. In September 1962 a joint appeal from the United National Pasok Momogun Organisation (North Borneo), Party Rakyat Brunei and the Sarawak United People's Party requested UN intervention to prevent the transfer of sovereignty without the exercise of self-determination. However, the Brunei revolt broke this alliance; in January 1963 SUPP submitted a petition on its own and in February (after the suppression of the Brunei revolt) Azahari contemplated putting his case to the UN.[145] By this time both the Sabah Alliance and the Sarawak Alliance were preparing cases in favour of Malaysia. The British had carefully monitored all such submissions and mentored Malayan representatives in techniques of lobbying for UN support (159).

The last and potentially most damaging appeal to the UN was submitted following an agreement at the Manila Summit in August 1963. Macapagal, Sukarno and the Tunku met in Manila to discuss ways of improving their relations through international association (Maphilindo) and, in particular, of resolving their differences over Malaysia. Their accords included a request that the UN secretary-general, or his representative, should 'ascertain' the extent of support in the Borneo territories for Malaysia, that observers from all three governments should accompany the UN mission, and that the formation of Malaysia should be postponed until the completion of the UN report. The British were dismayed by this proposal (200). They argued that the legitimacy of Malaysia had already been established; so far as North Borneo and Sarawak were concerned it rested on the Cobbold Enquiry, the report of the IGC, resolutions in the legislatures of the Borneo colonies and recent popular elections. Not fully appreciating the pressure upon the Tunku to maintain a semblance of good relations with his neighbours, they rejected the view that the Manila initiative might actually assist the cause of Malaysia by appeasing Sukarno. On the contrary, believing the Tunku to have surrendered to enemies of the project, Sandys intervened directly in a vain attempt to hold the Malayan prime minister to the agreed timetable (201–203). Ministers and officials were also concerned by the implications of Manila for Britain's use of the Singapore base and its likely impact upon the PAP regime; any delay might force Lee Kuan Yew to hold a general election which could result in a Barisan victory. Furthermore, the British were apprehensive lest the Manila Accord opened up differences between them and the US administration. It was largely to prevent such a deterioration in Anglo–American solidarity that Macmillan allowed himself to be persuaded by Kennedy of the diplomatic value of offering Sukarno the 'fig leaf' of the UN mission (204–208).

Led by Lawrence Michelmore (the American deputy director of the UN Office of Personnel) the mission consisted of Argentinian, Brazilian, Ceylonese, Czech, Ghanaian, Pakistani, Japanese, and Jordanian members of the UN Secretariat. It was accompanied by observers from Indonesia and the Philippines—an arrangement which the British government grudgingly accepted. The mission arrived in Kuching on 16 August and divided into two teams, one for Sarawak and the other for North Borneo. From 24 August to 4 September they held public hearings in widespread locations and reconvened in Kuching on 5 September (the day when Sarawak's newly elected Council Negri endorsed the Malaysia agreement). Meanwhile, under pressure from Sandys, the Malayan government did not wait on the results of the UN enquiry before agreeing a new date for Malaysia Day, but announced that the federation would be inaugurated on 16 September (211–214). The postponement of Malaysia Day did not, however, interfere with the award of internal self-government to North Borneo and Sarawak. On 31 August powers were 'arrogated' and the governors declared that, until the day of Malaysia's inauguration (when they would stand down), they would retain all those powers that would in future be federal powers and that they would act only on the advice of their chief ministers in respect of matters within the province of state government. As we have seen, Lee Kuan Yew unilaterally declared independence on 31 August, an action which caused consternation in Kuala Lumpur but to which the British turned a blind eye.

In case the mission found against Malaysia, Sandys, who remained in the region until the last crises were over, took the precaution of drafting a joint Anglo–Malayan statement setting out the history of consultations with Borneo peoples. In the event this document was not required. The UN report, which was published on 14 September, was generally favourable to Malaysia (223, 225). In his assessment of the mission's findings, U Thant was in no doubt that 'a sizeable majority of the peoples' wished to join Malaysia, although he also rebuked the Malayans for fixing a new Malaysia Day before the mission had completed its work. Even before the survey was finished, however, Indonesia and the Philippines were attempting to discredit it and, on its publication, they rejected the report and refused to be bound by its findings. Nevertheless, the Tunku's tactics had paid off: Malaysia was inaugurated with the ringing endorsement of the United Nations which endowed the federation with the international legitimacy that it might otherwise have lacked.

Brunei [146]

[I] implore whatever gods may be to use everything up to and including thumbscrews to oblige the Sultan to decide to join Malaysia before August 31st,— for his own good, certainly, but more importantly for the good of more important people like ourselves.
[Sir Paul Gore-Booth to Sir Saville Garner, 15 July 1963 [147]]

Whether or not Brunei joined the new federation was a matter for its sovereign ruler to decide. Having vacillated since the inception of Malaysia, his highness delayed his decision to the very last minute when he resolutely refused to join. There has been considerable speculation as to his reasons: oil, status, popular opinion and the repercussions of the Brunei rising have all been suggested. As we have seen, the Sultan of Brunei was jealous of his autonomy and had opposed various forms of closer association since his accession in 1950. His attitude to Malaysia was determined by the terms for entry and also by the likely impact of membership upon his position at home which was challenged, though more indirectly than head-on, by A M Azahari and the Party Rakyat.

Azahari campaigned against union with Malaya, favouring instead a unitary state of Brunei, Sabah and Sarawak. He also advocated further constitutional reform and was equivocal regarding the future role of the monarchy. A mercurial leader whose cause suffered from poor organisation and financial problems, Azahari could mobilise considerable popular support and represented a nationalist threat to the status quo. The Sultan was anxious to restrict his activities; thus, he delayed elections under the 1959 constitution and, when the PRB won control of all the elected seats on the Legislative Council, he put off its first meeting.[148] Frustrated by this postponement and already in self-imposed exile as a protest against the Sultan's apparent predilection for Malaysia, Azahari launched a coup. On 8 December 1962 the PRB's military wing (Tentera Nasional Kalimantan Utara or North Kalimantan National Army) attempted to seize the Sultan and set up the United State of North Kalimantan. Colonial critics hailed the rising as an heroic challenge to a decadent sultan who was conspiring with outsiders to propel his subjects into a federation which they did not seek.[149]

The British immediately sent in troops under the terms of the 1959 treaty and, although Selkirk reckoned it 'came within an inch of being completely successful' (151), the revolt was suppressed within a few weeks. Amongst its consequences were a prolonged state of emergency, the suspension of the constitution and the proscription of the PRB. It also raised questions regarding the aims and objectives of the TNKU, the quality of British intelligence, the effectiveness of the British high commissioner, the extent of popular support, the involvement of Indonesia, the complicity of the sultan, and, not least, Brunei's future prospects. With respect to the last issue, the revolt convinced the British of the necessity to press ahead with modernisation and constitutional reform. They even investigated the possibility of collaborating with Azahari and, when his links with Indonesia ruled out a deal with him,[150] they worked strenuously to rehabilitate key detainees as progressive leaders of the future (153 N). The British soon discovered, however, that their military intervention in defence of the Sultan had consolidated the royal ascendancy. Sultan Omar Ali Saifuddin III emerged from the crisis more determined than ever to thwart liberal measures and loss of autonomy (149–155, 157).

Having incurred financial expense and international embarrassment to protect a discredited autocrat, the British put pressure on his highness to join Malaysia. 'Unless Brunei enters Malaysia soon,' Selkirk signalled on 13 December, 'we may never get her in'.[151] On 28 December he reported that his highness had decided to accept Malaysia in principle and to resume negotiations with the Tunku. In February the Sultan conferred with the Tunku in Kuala Lumpur and working parties were set up to examine constitutional and financial matters. By early March they had drawn up heads of agreement that included favourable conditions for Brunei (165). From this point, however, relations deteriorated as the Malayans whittled down Brunei's privileges. In early April, the Conference of Rulers (ie the rulers of the Malay states) reduced the sultan's chances of being elected the Yang di-Pertuan Agong (or King of Malaysia) by stipulating that his precedence would be determined by the date of Brunei's entry into Malaysia instead of his accession to the throne. In June relations between Brunei and Malaya were transformed by the announcement of the discovery of considerable, off-shore oil resources (190). Notwithstanding Bruneian protests, the Malayans now insisted on oil revenues wholly falling to the federation after ten years as well as on the right to tax any new oil discoveries in the interim (188). When the Tunku issued an ultimatum containing Kuala Lumpur's final offer, his highness withdrew from the negotiations although he did come to London for the final round of talks in early July. Here he asked Sandys to mediate with the Malayans, but on this occasion Sandys' skills failed (184, 188, 190).

Why did the Sultan decide not to join Malaysia? At the time and since, attention focused on the question of the allocation of oil revenue between federal and state governments. Omar Saifuddin stated publicly that he had declined to sign the Malaysia Agreement because the government of Malaya had been unable to give effect to previously agreed terms. In fact, as time ran out the Malayan delegation wooed Omar Ali with substantial concessions, even at the risk of alienating the delegations from North Borneo and Sarawak who were not being so favoured. The Tunku and his Malay colleagues did their utmost not to lose Brunei; after all, as a Malay sultanate it made a better fit with the federation than did the other acceding territories. Furthermore, its revenues would have compensated for the expenditure needed in the development of Malaysia's other Borneo territories. For his part, the Tunku, who was bitterly disappointed by the outcome and later withdrew the hundreds of federal officers and teachers on secondment to Brunei, claimed that his highness's position in the hierarchy of Malay rulers had been the cause of the breakdown. In addition to oil and status, Omar Saifuddin would have been influenced by public opinion in Brunei. It is clear that he emerged from the Brunei revolt in no mood to surrender to democratic demands, but at the same time he 'saw no reason to flout the strong anti-Malaysia feelings revealed by the rising'.[152] Sensing widespread opposition to closer association with Malaya, he was willing to make a popular gesture. The British had long been urging him to appeal to the wishes of his people and it was ironic that he chose to do so by rejecting the centrepiece of their Southeast Asian strategy. On his return from London after the July talks, Omar Ali received a rapturous welcome from the crowd gathered to meet him at the airport. Bruneians were 'particularly grateful to Sultan Omar Ali Saifuddin III for extricating himself from a scheme that was handed down to him almost as a *fait accompli* by both the British and the Malayan Governments'.[153] In this way he avoided the constitutional reforms which membership of Malaysia would have hastened by virtue of the requirement for Brunei to send elected representatives to the Dewan Ra'ayat (house of representatives) in Kuala Lumpur. Perhaps the outcome of the revolt had convinced his highness that he could spin out his special relationship with Britain more or less indefinitely and therefore had no need to subordinate himself to Kuala Lumpur. Whatever his reasons for not joining Malaysia, Angus MacKintosh (British high commissioner) was of the view that 'if all the difficulties raised by the Sultan could have been overcome at the wave of a hand, he would have invented others'.[154]

The British were displeased by the Sultan's decision, but no matter how convincingly ministers argued that 'the best future for Brunei' would be to join the federation (194, also 197, 199) and in spite of Macmillan's advice to Lansdowne that 'ultimately pressure will have to be exerted by the threat that we cannot protect him indefinitely' (195), the Sultan adamantly refused to relinquish his bilateral relationship with Britain. The British were worried by their open-ended commitment to the protection of Brunei since it could make the sultanate a target of Indonesian subversion. Hoping that progress towards complete independence might draw Brunei towards Malaysia, the British continued to press for constitutional reform in Brunei. Their style may have grown harsher and more direct but their options were limited to warnings, such as that issued by Sandys during a four-hour stop-over in Brunei two days before the inauguration of Malaysia: unless constitutional progress was volunteered, the secretary of state might have to instruct the high commissioner to tender formal advice on this matter according to the 1959 treaty. The fact that Britain did not—or could not—coerce the Sultan goes some way to countering the claim that Malaysia was a neo-colonial plot. Indeed, and in keeping with its desire to avoid any appearance of 'recolonising' Brunei, the British government transferred responsibility for the affairs of the sultanate from the Colonial Office to the Commonwealth Relations Office in November 1963.

There are perhaps parallels, although contemporaries were reluctant to draw them, with the treatment of the Indian princes in 1947.[155] One is the disquiet of politicians, both in India and in Malaya, about the potential problems of accommodating autocracies within a democracy. Another is British unease over defence commitments. Just as the British government pressed the princely states to join either India or Pakistan because it would be unable to honour military guarantees to them without offending the successor states, so in 1963 it feared that 'if Brunei did not join Malaysia, there would be an increasing likelihood of political and other troubles, both arising inside Brunei and originating in Indonesia'. In a desperate attempt to change the Sultan's mind, Sandys insisted:—

It simply would not be possible for Britain to deal as effectively as before with internal security problems in Brunei if she did not join Malaysia. Moreover, Britain could not guarantee on future occasions, as had happened in December, 1962, to resist with British troops the demands of the people of Brunei for a larger measure of democracy. In addition, once Britain's defence system in South East Asia had been largely merged with that of Malaysia, it would be more difficult than in the past for Britain to discharge her responsibilities for the protection of the State and Government of Brunei.[156]

Whereas their integration within the successor states extinguished the power and privileges of Indian princes and reduced the Malay sultans to constitutional monarchs, by resisting assimilation within Malaysia the Sultan of Brunei succeeded in retaining the autonomy of his kingdom and kept at bay democratic politics.

*   *   *   *

The 'Grand Design' for Malaysia was central to Britain's post-colonial role in Southeast Asia. It was shaped, however, as much by Britain's declining power and its incapacity to control developments as by a forceful strategy of planned decolonisation. Ministers and officials differed in their priorities while Southeast Asian leaders pursued competing objectives. Recognising their dependence upon the initiative of local leaders and the acquiescence of their peoples, the British at first refrained from forcing the pace and later concentrated on managing conflicts between territories. Constrained by circumstances beyond British control, plans were deflected by events and the outcome fell short of expectations in several respects. As inauguration day drew near, Malaysia was placed in jeopardy by greater or lesser crises: unresolved disputes between Malaya and Singapore; a last-minute hitch in the relations between Malaya and Sarawak; the United Nations mission to Borneo; Indonesian 'Confrontation'; an attempt by Kelantan to win an injunction against the implementation of the Malaysia Act.[157] Indeed, a nation-state had yet to be fashioned from Britain's former dependencies and in the following years resentment of control from Kuala Lumpur would fester in Sabah and Sarawak and force Singapore to secede.

Meanwhile, the benefits of Malaysia to the British looked uncertain. The 'Grand Design' turned out to be trouble, almost more trouble than it was worth. Britain was encumbered with the embarrassing obligation to protect the micro-state of Brunei. Moreover, Singapore's separation in August 1965 seemed a disaster, since the British government had always regarded the merger of Malaya and Singapore as the principal advantage of Malaysia, if not its raison d'être. In addition, the three-year 'Confrontation' with Indonesia aggravated regional instability and damaged Anglo–American relations. It also resulted in untoward military expenditure that would be a major factor leading to the decision to withdraw from Southeast Asia by the end of 1971. It was with these consequences in mind that in 1984 Sir William Goode wondered 'whether if HMG had foreseen the cost of "confrontasi", Harold Macmillan would have agreed so readily to the Tunku's bright idea of forming Malaysia'.[158] As has been seen, in the early 1960s Goode had condemned the scheme as too much too soon for the Borneo territories, yet, reflecting on two decades of progress, he could only conclude that 'North Borneo's decision to join Malaysia in 1963 was right'.[159]

A J Stockwell

Notes to Introduction

1   British Documents on the End of Empire: series B, vol 3, A J Stockwell, ed, *Malaya* (1995), Part 3, 346. Other BDEE volumes cited in this introduction are: series A, vol 4, Ronald Hyam & Wm Roger Louis, eds, *The Conservative government and the end of empire 1957–1964* (2000); series A, vol 5, S R Ashton & Wm Roger Louis, eds, *East of Suez and the Commonwealth 1964–1971* (2004); series B, vol 4, John Kent, *Egypt and the defence of the Middle East* (1998); series B, vol 6, S R Ashton & David Killingray, eds, *The West Indies* (1999); series B, vol 9, Philip Murphy, ed, *Central Africa* (forthcoming)..

2   Stockwell, ed, *Malaya*, especially Part 1, 8, 12, 19, 21, 22, 25, 48, 98, 112, 115, 121; Part 2, 141, 143, 218, 267, 276, 286, 288, 292, 293, 300; Part 3, 324, 344, 346, 348

3   *ibid*, 286, 292, 293 and 300.

4   *ibid*, 267, 276, 324 and 346.

5   B A Hussainmiya , *Sultan Omar Saifuddin III and Britain: the making of Brunei Darussalam* (Kuala Lumpur, 1995) pp 233–240.

6   Sir R Scott to Sir W Goode, 13 Oct 1959, Goode Papers, box 1, file 1, f 13.

7   Martin's letter was distributed widely in Whitehall and some phrases from it later garnished Macleod's memorandum of July 1960 to the Colonial Policy Committee, see 25.

8   Tunku Abdul Rahman Putra Al-Haj, *Looking back: Monday musings and memories* (Kuala Lumpur, 1977) pp 81–82.

9   Since, however, its very lack of specificity avoided 'prejudicing any possible solution to the question', the term was retained until 'Malaysia' acquired greater currency following the Anglo–Malayan talks in November 1961. See minutes by S Martin and R Omerod, 9–14 June 1961, DO 169/25.

10   C C Lucas (Treasury) to W I J Wallace (CO), 21 Aug 1960, DO 169/24.

11   See John Darwin, *Britain and decolonisation* (London, 1988); Wm Roger Louis and Ronald Robinson, 'The imperialism of decolonization', *Journal of Imperial and Commonwealth History* 22, 3 (Sept 1994) 462–511; Ronald Hyam, 'The primacy of geopolitics: the dynamics of British imperial policy, 1763–1963', *JICH*, 27, 2 (May 1999) 27–52.

12   Ministry of External Affairs, Malaysia, *Malaysia's case in the United Nations Security Council. Documents reproduced from the Official Record of the Security Council Proceedings* (Kuala Lumpur, 1964) pp 25 and 27.

13   For a restatement of the radical critique see Greg Poulgrain, *The genesis of konfrontasi: Malaysia, Brunei and Indonesia, 1945–1965* (Bathurst, NSW, and London, 1998).

14   Stockwell, ed, *Malaya*, Part 3, 454.

15   For an examination of relations between business and government in Malaya/Malaysia see Nicholas J White, *Business, government and the end of empire: Malaya, 1942–1957* (Kuala Lumpur, 1997); 'Gentlemanly capitalism and empire in the twentieth century: the "forgotten" case of Malaya, 1914–1965', in R E Dumett, ed, *Gentlemanly capitalism and British imperialism: the new debate on empire* (Harlow, 1999) pp 175–95; 'The business and the politics of decolonization: the British experience in the twentieth century', *Economic History Review* LIII, 2 (2000) pp 544–64; and 'The survival, revival and decline of British economic influence in Malaysia, 1957–70', *Twentieth Century British History*, 14, 3 (2003) pp 222–242. See also A J Stockwell, 'Malaysia: the making of a neo–colony?', *Journal of Imperial and Commonwealth History*, 26, 2 (1998) pp 138–156.

16 CAB 134/1644, DSE(60)2nd meeting, 21 June 1960.

17 DO 189/361 and PREM 11/3421.

18 DO 189/219, no 35.

19 For the 'honeymoon' see DO 189/351; for the pessimism of British business and its declining influence in the 1960s, see chapter 3 of Nicholas J White, *British business in post-colonial Malaysia, 1957–70: 'neo-colonialism' or 'disengagement'?* (London, 2004). I am grateful to Dr White for generously making this work available to me in advance of publication.

20 Poulgrain, *The genesis of konfrontasi*, p 6. See also Malcolm Caldwell, 'From "emergency" to "independence", 1948–57', in Mohamed Amin and Malcolm Caldwell, eds, *Malaya: The making of a neo-colony* (Nottingham, 1977).

21 C C Lucas (Treasury) to W I J Wallace (CO), 29 Aug 1960, W J Smith (CRO) to C C Lucas, 8 Sept 1960, Wallace to Lucas, 8 Sept 1960, DO 169/24, nos 17, 18, 19.

22 Minute by A D Peck, 23 Apr 1963, T 225/2552.

23 Macmillan to the Tunku, 27 Apr 1963, PREM 11/4347.

24 CAB 134/1644, DSE(60)4th meeting, 8 July 1960.

25 For British defence strategy east of Suez, see: Philip Darby, *British defence policy east of Suez 1948–1968* (Oxford, 1973); Saki Dockrill, *Britain's retreat from east of Suez. The choice between Europe and the world?* (Basingstoke, 2002); David Easter, 'British defence policy in South East Asia and Confrontation 1960–66' (University of London, LSE, PhD, 1998); Phuong Pham, 'The end to "east of Suez": the British withdrawal from Malaysia and Singapore, 1964 to 1968' (University of Oxford, DPhil, 2001); S R Ashton & Wm Roger Louis, eds.

26 Selkirk's valedictory despatch as commissioner–general to the prime minister, 3 Sept 1963, CAB 21/4867.

27 East of Suez referred to the Gulf and places further east. The Middle East denoted the area from Suez to West Pakistan, while the region including and stretching east of West Pakistan was referred to as South and Southeast Asia. Strictly speaking Southeast Asia covered the lands and seas between the Indian sub–continent and China (or East Asia), but sometimes Southeast Asia was incorporated with everything east of the Bay of Bengal in the so–called Far East.

28 CAB 134/1929, 7 June 1959, see Hyam & Louis, eds, Part 1, 8, also 17.

29 CAB 134/1929, 1st meeting, 23 March 1960 and FP(60)1, 24 Feb 1960; also at CAB 129/100, C(60)35.

30 See also CAB 134/1644 and 1645.

31 Alistair Horne, *Macmillan, 1957–1986* (London, 1989) p 284.

32 Quoted in John Subritzky, *Confronting Sukarno. British, American, Australian and New Zealand diplomacy in the Malaysian-Indonesian Confrontation, 1961–5* (Basingstoke, 2000) p 39.

33 John Kent, ed, Part 1, lxxviii and Part 3, 377.

34 See Hyam & Louis, eds, Part 1, 263.

35 'Defence implications of an association of the British Borneo territories with the Federation of Malaya and the State of Singapore', report by the Joint Planning Staff, JP(61)57(Final), 21 June 1961, DEFE 4/136.

36   JP(61)57(Revised Final), 17 July 1961, DEFE 4/137.

37   *Federation of Malaysia: Joint Statement by the Governments of the United Kingdom and of the Federation of Malaya* Cmnd 1563 (Nov 1961). For the original, signed version, see DO 118/227. In the original version (which is undated) the signatures of Macmillan and the Tunku appear at the bottom of appendix B, whereas in the printed version (which is dated 22 Nov 1961) they appear before appendix A.

38   *Malaysia: Agreement concluded between the United Kingdom of Great Britain and Northern Ireland, the Federation of Malaya, North Borneo, Sarawak and Singapore* Cmnd 2094 (July 1963); see also CO 968/760, no 86. When on 11 Mar 1963, Commander Kerans MP asked the civil lord of the Admiralty in the House of Commons what guarantee there was that the Singapore base would remain for ever, the CRO referred the Admiralty to the Joint Statement of November 1961. The CRO added in confidence that this commitment would remain in force and separate from the Defence Agreement, ie if the Malayans/Malaysian terminated the Defence Agreement their action would not negate the conditions set out in the Joint Statement, see CO 968/760, no E(ii)72. At the time of the Manila Summit and a month after signing the Malaysia Agreement, the Tunku publicly declared that 'our defence arrangements with Britain are not perpetual or permanent. They can be revoked by either party'. The British view was that it could only be changed with the consent of both parties, but, in the atmosphere of mounting 'Confrontation' with Indonesia, they privately recognised that effective use of the bases would depend on local consent. See Appendix, 'The origins and formation of Malaysia', para 196.

39   For CO views on responsibility for internal security in Singapore and Borneo, see CO 968/761.

40   For the international dimension, see Matthew Jones, *Conflict and Confrontation in South East Asia, 1961–1965: Britain, the United States, Indonesia and the Creation of Malaysia* (Cambridge, 2002) and Subritzky, *Confronting Sukarno*.

41   For the papers presented to this meeting by Thorneycroft, Maudling and Home see CAB 131/28, D(63), 19, 20, 21 and 22. The minutes of this meeting are at CAB 131/28, D8(63)1.

42   Macmillan to Sir N Brook, 5 Apr 1962, CAB 21/4626.

43   C E F Gough (MoD) to E Melville (CO), 17 Feb 1961, DO169/24, no 53.

44   F Warner to Sir A Gilchrist, 13 Aug 1963, FO371/169706, no 244.

45   See S J Ball, 'Selkirk in Singapore', *Twentieth Century British History* 10, 2 (1999) pp 162–191.

46   Their view of Tory is recorded in a minute by Wallace of the CO, 2 Feb 1961, who was anxious lest the views of the CRO became over-influential in shaping the attitude of the prime minister. CO 1030/1083.

47   Alastair Morrison, *Fair land Sarawak: some recollections of an expatriate official* (Ithaca, New York, 1993) p 176.

48   Tan Sri Ghazali Shafie, *Ghazali Shafie's memoir on the formation of Malaysia* (Bangi, Malaysa, 1998) pp 92 and 252.

49   Macmillan to Sandys, 26 March 1962, Sandys Papers, DSND,15/5. See Philip Murphy, ed, *Central Africa*.

50   Quoted in Hyam & Louis, eds, Part 1, liii.

51   On 14 June the Conservative candidate lost his deposit at the West Lothian by-election and on 13 July the Conservatives were at the bottom of the poll in the Leicester North by-election.

52   Horne, *Macmillan, 1957–1986* pp 339–350.

53   Obituary, *The Times*, 27 Nov 1987.

54   Selkirk to Macmillan, 30 Nov 1962, PREM11/3869.

55   De Zulueta to Macmillan, 8 May 1963, PREM11/4347; see also CAB 21/4851.

56   Taking advantage of emergency powers after the Brunei revolt, 'the Special Branch made widespread arrests of anyone suspected of any links, however tenuous, with Sarawak's Clandestine Communist Organisation' including 50 members of SUPP. The effect was to deter SUPP moderates and to encourage radicals and youth members to defect to the CCO, Ong Kee Hui (chairman, SUPP) *Footprints in Sarawak: Memoirs of Tan Sri Datuk (Dr) Ong Kee Hui, 1914–1963* (Kuching, 1998) p 595. See also Sarawak Information Service, *The Danger Within: A History of the Clandestine Communist Organisation in Sarawak* (1963).

57   *Report of the Commission of Enquiry, North Borneo and Sarawak* [Cobbold Report], Cmnd 1794 (Aug 1962) p 78, para 237. See also J P Ongkili, *The Borneo response to Malaysia 1961–1963* (Singapore, 1967) p 67.

58   Joe Garner, *The Commonwealth Office 1925–68* (London, 1978) p 358. See also the obituary by Enoch Powell describing Sandy's working methods, *Independent*, 28 Nov 1987.

59   Lee Kuan Yew, *The Singapore story: memoirs of Lee Kuan Yew* (Singapore, 1998) p 480.

60   Garner, p 357.

61   Obituary, *The Times*, 27 Nov 1987.

62   Sandys to Menzies, teleg 1571, 23 Aug 1963, PREM 11/4349.

63   See also Harold Macmillan, *At the end of the day 1961–63* (London, 1973) p 259. R H C Steed writing in the *Daily Telegraph*, 13 Sept 1963, under the heading 'Malaysia: the uneasy compact', commented: 'Mr Sandys's functions during the critical pre-natal period for Malaysia have been strenuous and varied. He has been a doctor preparing for a difficult delivery, a fireman putting out fires in the natal chamber, a solicitor sorting out disputes between families and a policeman chasing away burglars and small boys throwing stones.'

64   Sir G Tory to Maudling, 18 June 1962, CO 1030/989, no 1260.

65   See Chan Heng Chee, *A sensation of independence. David Marshall: a political biography* (Singapore, 2nd ed 2001); James Low Choon Sai, 'Kept in position: the Labour Front-Alliance government of chief minister David Marshall in Singapore April 1955–June 1956' (National University of Singapore, MA thesis, 2000); and Edwin Lee's forthcoming book, *Singapore, the unexpected nation* in the History of Nation-building series, Institute of Southeast Asian Studies, Singapore.

66   Toh Chin Chye, the first chairman of the PAP, quoted in C M Turnbull, *A history of Singapore 1819–1975* (Singapore, 1985 ed) p 269.

67   Minute on a meeting with the Tunku at the Ritz Hotel on 1 Aug 1962 by Sir William Goode, 2 Aug 1962, Goode Papers, box 3, file 1, f 65.

68   For Malayan political developments see Gordon P Means, *Malaysian politics* (Kuala Lumpur, 1970); Mohamed Noordin Sopiee, *From Malayan Union to Singapore separation* (Kuala Lumpur, 1974); Cheah Boon Kheng, *Malaysia: the making of a nation* (Singapore, 2002).

69   Lee, *Memoirs*, pp 357–361, 364.

70   The retrospective articles, which the Tunku wrote for *The Star* (Penang) about merger and relations with Singapore and which were subsequently published in the collection *Looking back: Monday musings and memories*, are sketchy. The long and detailed memoirs of Ghazali Shafie and Lee Kuan Yew are valuable sources to set against the regular reports on the Tunku's policies and politics which Tory sent to London.

71   *Memorandum setting out the Heads of Agreement for a Merger between the Federation of Malaya and Singapore* Cmd 33 (Singapore, Nov 1961).

72   Lansdowne to Garner, 8 Nov 1962, CO 967/414.

73   For the minutes of the ISC meeting on 13 Dec 1962, see DO 187/16, no 111.

74   For the minutes of the ISC meeting on 1 Feb 1963, see DO 187/16, no 112.

75   For 'Coldstore' see Matthew Jones, 'Creating Malaysia: Singapore security, the Borneo territories and the contours of British policy, 1961–63', *Journal of Imperial and Commonwealth History*, 28, 2 (2000) pp 85–109, and T.N. Harper, 'Lim Chin Siong and the "Singapore Story"', in Tan Jing Quee and Jomo K S eds, *Comet in our sky: Lim Chin Siong in History*, Kuala Lumpur, 2001. For 'Operation Sunrise' see Colin Baker, *State of emergency: crisis in Central Africa, Nyasaland 1959–1960* (London, 1997) pp 40–74, and Philip Murphy, ed, *Central Africa* (BDEEP, forthcoming).

76   Ghazali recalls, however, that the Tunku was at the time distracted by the issue of Singapore's internal security and signed the citizenship amendment without realising that 'the notion of a common citizenship' meant 'nothing could be done if Kuala Lumpur, for some reason later, would want to discriminate against Singaporeans'. Having been reminded of the reason for the original definition he instructed the federal attorney-general, Cecil Sheridan, to redraft his reply. Be that as it may, Lee was satisfied with the letter he received from the Tunku confirming the amendment. Appendix C to the agreement of 31 Aug 1962, stated 'Singapore citizens will be citizens of Malaysia', although it goes on to distinguish between their voting rights. Article 53(3) of the constitution of Singapore annexed to the Malaysia Agreement of 9 July 1963 stated 'every person who is a citizen of Singapore enjoys by virtue of that citizenship and in accordance with the provisions of the Federal Constitution the status of a citizen of Malaysia'. See Lee, *Memoirs* pp 437–440; Ghazali, *Memoir* pp 261–262; Federal Agreement, 9 July, annexe D.

77   Under the headline 'Mac signs at midnight', the London *Evening Standard* of 9 July carried a photograph of the British prime minister, head in hands, after the signing ceremony at Marlborough House. The three-page Malaysia Agreement signed on 9 July 1963 was accompanied by a further 230 pages of eleven annexes. It was presented to parliament as *Malaysia: Agreement concluded between the United Kingdom of Great Britain and Northern Ireland, the Federation of Malaya, North Borneo, Sarawak and Singapore* Cmnd. 2094 (July 1963). One of the original, signed and sealed versions in both English and Malay is at DO 118/258. Article II stated that Malaysia would be brought into operation on 31 Aug. The postponement of Malaysia Day to 16 Sept 1963 required an amendment which was dated 28 Aug and signed by Sandys (UK), Razak (Malaya), Stephens (North Borneo), Sockalingham (Sarawak) and Goh Keng Swee (Singapore).

78   *Supplementary Agreement relating to Malaysia*, Cmnd. 2150 (11 Sept 1963). One of the original, signed versions is at DO 118/265.

79   See Robert Pringle, *Rajahs and rebels: the Ibans of Sarawak under Brooke rule, 1841–1941* (New York, 1970).

80   The Cardinal Principles were appended to the Cobbold Report, *Report of the Commission of Enquiry, North Borneo and Sarawak, 1962* Cmnd 1794 (Aug 1962), appendix C.

81   See Ian Black, *A gambling style of government: the establishment of chartered company rule in Sabah, 1878–1915* (Kuala Lumpur, 1983) and D S Ranjit Singh, *The making of Sabah 1865–1941* (Kuala Lumpur, 2000).

82   See Stockwell, ed, *Malaya*, Part 1, 8, para 36.

83   It measured a mere 2,226 square miles; its population, which in 1947 was only 40,657, had risen to about 85,000 by the early 1960s.

84   See Stockwell, ed, *Malaya*, Part 1, 25, appendix 2.

85   See R H C Reece, *The name of Brooke: the end of white rajah rule in Sarawak* (Kuala Lumpur, 1982).

86   See Stockwell, ed, *Malaya*, Part 1, 25, appendix 2.

87   See Graham Saunders, *A history of Brunei* (London, ed 2002); D S Ranjit Singh, *Brunei 1839–1983: the problems of political survival* (Singapore, 1991); Hussainmiya, *Sultan Omar Ali Saifuddin III* ; A V M Horton, 'British administration in Brunei 1906–1959', *Modern Asian Studies* 20, 2 (1988) pp 353–374. For a fuller discussion of the points raised in this section, see A J Stockwell, 'Britain and Brunei, 1945–1963: imperial retreat and royal ascendancy', *Modern Asian Studies* 38, 4 (2004) pp 785–820.

88   For the constitution and treaty see *Brunei constitutional documents*, Kuala Lumpur, n.d. [1960]. The treaty is also printed in J de V Allen, A J Stockwell and L R Wright, eds, *A collection of treaties and other documents affecting the states of Malaysia 1761–1963* (London, 1981) vol II, p 680. The specified areas for the high commissioner's guidance were: public safety and public order including the efficiency of the police, reinforcement of local security forces, measures for the protection of the state, currency, banking and certain aspects of the Sultan's power of either checking or enforcing legislation.

89   Saunders, *A history of Brunei* pp 137–138.

90   Poulgrain, *The genesis of Konfrontasi* p 206.

91   Hussainmiya, *Sultan Omar Ali Saifuddin* p 207.

92   Melville to White, 5 May 1961, CO 1030/1447, no 20/21.

93   Donald Stephens (Sabah's first chief minister in 1963) founded the Kadazan Society in 1958 which was the basis for the United National Kadazan Organisation (North Borneo's first political party) registered in August 1961.

94   See Michael B Leigh, *The rising moon: political change in Sarawak* (Sydney University Press, 1974); R S Milne and K J Ratnam, *Malaysia—new states in a new nation: political development of Sarawak and Sabah in Malaysia* (London, 1974); Margaret Clark Roff, *The politics of belonging: political change in Sabah and Sarawak* (Kuala Lumpur, 1974).

95   Elections followed a three–stage process: the popular vote returned representatives to district and town councils; these members then elected representatives from their number to serve on divisional councils who in turn elected members to the Council Negri. The elected members of the Council Negri decided which amongst them should fill the seats allocated to elected members on the Supreme Council.

96   Ong Kee Hui, *Footprints in Sarawak*; Bob Reece, *Datu Bandar Abang Haji Mustapha of Sarawak* Sarawak Literary Society (nd).

97   CO 1030/987, no 1146.

98   Tunku Abdul Rahman to Stephen Kalong Ningkan, July 1966, cited in Vernon L. Porritt, *Operation Hammer: enforced resettlement in Sarawak in 1965* (Hull, nd) p 6.

99   Waddell to Tory (Kuala Lumpur), 27 July 1961, CO1030/981; Waddell to Melville (CO), 26 Aug. 1961, CO1030/982.

100   For the appointment of the commission, see CAB 21/4626 and CO 1030/1009 and 1010. Ghazali Shafie, the leading Malayan commissioner, advised the Tunku against the nomination of 'my old and dear

friend Malcolm MacDonald' on the grounds that, firstly, he 'had his own view of the grand design which might contradict the Malaysia plan as we had envisaged', secondly, he 'had a great deal of influence amongst the Iban [Dayak] and Chinese which might work against the interests of the other communities' and, finally and most importantly, since 'all the credit would go to MacDonald... it would be easy for the opponents of Malaysia to brand it as a British design'. *Memoir* p 171.

101 David Rees-Williams visited Sarawak with David Gammans in 1946 to assess whether there was sufficient support for placing the cession bill before the Council Negri.

102 Confidential brief on Mohamed Ghazali bin Shafie, Sept 1961, CAB 130/179.

103 Sir J Martin (Jesselton) to Lord Perth (CO), tel 16, 31 Jan, Goode Papers, box 2, file 1, f 23. Immediately after the Japanese occupation Sir Harold MacMichael was sent from London as special envoy to conclude with the Malay rulers new treaties whereby they surrendered jurisdiction to the crown and enabled the introduction of the Malayan Union which, in dispossessing the sultans, introducing direct British rule and providing for a multi-racial citizenship, provoked a Malay outcry. See Stockwell, ed, *Malaya*, Part 1.

104 Wallace to Eastwood, 17 Jan 1962, CO 1030/1012, no 67.

105 See CO 1030/1000, 1001 and 102. Its 'Memorandum on Malaysia' was submitted to the Cobbold Commission and printed as appendix F of its report.

106 Ghazali Shafie, *Memoir* pp 197–198.

107 ibid, p 242.

108 ibid, p 304.

109 ibid, p 210.

110 Confidential brief on Mohamed Ghazali bin Shafie, Sept 1961, CAB 130/179.

111 Tory to CRO, tel 161, 12 Mar 1962, CO 1030/987 no 1109.

112 Goode to CO, 14 Mar 1962, CO 1030/987, no 1114.

113 cf his testimony in the programme on Malaya in Granada TV's series on 'End of Empire', 1984.

114 Goode to Tory, 14 Mar 1962, CO 1030/987, no 1131.

115 The governor of Sarawak agreed with this view, cf. Waddell to Wallace, 3 May 1962, PREM 11/3866.

116 Goode to Mubin Sheppard, 2 Oct 1984, Goode Papers, box 5, file 5, f 45.

117 Naimah S Talib, *Administrators and their service: the Sarawak Administrative Service under the Brooke rajahs and British colonial rule* (Kuala Lumpur, 1999) p 142.

118 Rogers to Goode and Waddell, 1 Nov 1961, CO 1030/1005, no 4.

119 Sir R Harris (Treasury) to Sir H Poynton (CO), 26 Oct 1962, CO 1030/1064. Having accepted this principle, however, the Treasury refused to make a financial commitment until the scheme had been costed, see 143 and 145.

120 E M West to Maudling, memo in preparation for a meeting of the Cabinet Greater Malaysia Committee on 21 Mar 1962, CO 1030/987, no 1146.

121 As reported by Wallace to West, 29 Sept 1961, CO 1030/983.

122 Goode, 'Timing of Malaysia', 7 Apr 1962, and CRO minute 17 May 1962, DO 187/21. Papers issued by the governments of North Borneo and Sarawak to inform the public about the Malaysia proposal, the

purpose of the commission and the issues on which views would be sought were reproduced as appendix E of the Cobbold Report.

123   See 'Malaysia: Gossip', memo by Sir A Snelling (CRO), 24 May 1961, on which Martin (CO) commented 'very unpleasant', CO 1030/1016, no 74.

124   For an account of the Malayan political developments which largely accounted for the Tunku's changeable attitude to Malaysia, see Tory's despatch no 3 of 18 June 1962 (which was distributed as CRO Confidential Print on 4 July as a background for the London talks), CO1030/989, no 1260.

125   Hall to Wallace, 19 June 1962, PREM 11/3867; minute by Martin, 6 June 1962, CO 1030/1016; Ghazali Shafie, *Memoir* p 240 ff.

126   The report was styled 'interim report' although it did not differ from the version published on 1 Aug 1962 as *Report of the Commission of Enquiry, North Borneo and Sarawak, 1962*, Cmnd 1794.

127   *Report,* chapter 3, paras 141–144.

128   *Report,* chapter 4, section A, paras 145–148.

129   *Report,* para 237.

130   Maudling to Macmillan, 22 June 1962, PM(62)38, but not seen by the prime minister; J H Robertson to Sir N Brook, 22 June; T Bligh to Brook, 22 June; Brook to Bligh, 3 July, CAB 21/4847.

131   CO 967/414, emphasis in the original.

132   On the following day, the Cabinet agreed to proceed with talks for the formation of Malaysia at the earliest possible date on condition that Borneo interests were safeguarded during the transitional period, CAB 128/36 pt.2, CC44(62)1, 5 July 1962.

133   West to Maudling, 11 July 1962, CO 967/407.

134   Martin to Maudling, 11 July 1962, CO 967/407. Goode, who was in London for the conference, also received a copy of this draft minute, Goode Papers, box 3, file 1, f 2.

135   'Points for Sandys', Goode Papers, box 3, file 1, f 6.

136   Cary to Brook, 27 July 1962, CAB 21/4847, and de Zulueta to Macmillan, 27 July 1962, PREM 11/3865.

137   *H of C Debs,* vol 664, cols 584–590, 1 Aug 1962; *H of L Debs,* vol 243, cols 286–292, 1 Aug 1962.

138   Memorandum by the Far Eastern Department, CRO, 29 Oct 1962, DO 169/215.

139   Minute by Goode of a conversation with Tunku Abdul Rahman on 1 Aug 1963 at the Ritz Hotel, 2 Aug 1963, Goode Papers, box 3, file 1, f 89.

140   *Malaysia: Report of the Inter-Governmental Committee, 1962*, Cmnd 1954 (Feb 1963).

141   See note 77 above.

142   For briefing papers see DO 169/329.

143   *Public Officers' Agreement between Her Majesty's Government in the United Kingdom and the Government of Malaysia in respect of Singapore*, Cmnd 2468, … *in respect of Sabah*, Cmnd 2469 and … *in respect of Sarawak*, Cmnd 2670 (1963–1964).

144   The UN General Assembly had defined the process of integration in Resolution 1541 (XV) (Annex) of 15 Dec 1960. Other examples, of decolonisation through integration are Somaliland in Somalia, Togoland in Ghana, the Northern and Southern Cameroons in Nigeria and Cameroun respectively, and Zanzibar in

Tanzania. In theory the integration of the smaller Caribbean islands with Britain would have been a way of completing the decolonisation of the West Indies but was never seriously considered on account of its implications for immigration policy, see Rafael Cox-Alomar, 'Britain's withdrawal from the Eastern Caribbean 1965–67: a reappraisal', *Journal of Imperial and Commonwealth History*, 31, 3 (Sept 2003) pp 84–85 and notes 62–63; also S R Ashton & David Killingray, eds, *The West Indies*.

145   CO 936/839–841; Lee, *Memoirs* pp 434–436.

146   For a fuller discussion of Brunei's decision not to join Malaysia, see Stockwell, 'Britain and Brunei, 1945–1963'.

147   CO 1030/1469, f 20. Gore-Booth had been observing developments from his post as high commissioner in New Delhi.

148   The 1959 constitution provided for a two-tier electoral system: direct elections were held to 55 seats on the District Councils which returned 16 representatives to the 33-member Legislative Council (17 of whom were ex officio, official or nominated members). The PRB won 54 out of the 55 District Council seats and thus secured control of the electable seats on the Legislative Council. In fact 15 PRB representatives were immediately returned to the legislature and a week later the single independent member joined the PRB. Although it did not command an overall majority on the Legislative Council, the PRB had won a sweeping popular mandate which the Sultan would ignore at his peril.

149   eg, R W Sorrenson MP in the *Guardian* 14 Dec 1962.

150   See FO 371/169694, D1071/3, D1071/5 and D1071/12.

151   Selkirk to Colonial Office, tel. 357, CO 1030/1071, no 344.

152   Saunders, *A history of Brunei* pp 157–158.

153   Hussainmiya, *Sultan Omar Ali Saifuddin III and Britain* p 218.

154   The same point was added as a confidential note to a parliamentary brief, which the secretary of state was advised not to use in the House: 'Our view is now that the Sultan never intended to sign the Agreement and would have found some pretext even if his demands on the question of precedence had been fully met.' Brief no 2, Malaysia Bill—Brunei, 16 July 1963, CO 1030/1510, no 137.

155   When, however, Gore-Booth remarked that the 'parallel to the late Maharajah of Kashmir is positively uncanny', Garner retorted: 'I am not sure that I quite understand the parallel which you see. … The Sultan is certainly a very troublesome person, but the sort of trouble he is brewing for us will surely be rather different from that which arose over Kashmir.' Gore-Booth to Garner,15 July 1963 and Garner to Gore-Booth, 30 July, CO 1030/1469. For the Labour government's policy towards the Indian princes, Mountbatten's role and the action of Congress politicians, see Ian Copland, *The princes of India in the endgame of empire 1917–1947* (Cambridge, 1997) p 217 ff.

156   Note of a meeting between Sandys and the Sultan of Brunei, 8 July 1963, CO 1030/1469, f 91.

157   The government of Kelantan (controlled by the PMIP) applied to the High Court in Kuala Lumpur for a declaration that the Malaysia Agreement and the Malaysia Act were 'void and inoperative', or alternatively that they were not binding on Kelantan, and sought an injunction to restrain the Federation government from implementing the Act on Malaysia Day. It argued that the Act would abolish the Federation of Malaya, thereby violating the Federation of Malaya Agreement of 1957; that the proposed changes needed the consent of each state of Malaya and that this had not been obtained; that the Sultan of Kelantan should have been a party to the Malaysia Agreement in the same way as the Malay rulers had been signatories of the Malaya Agreement of 1957; that constitutional convention called for consultation with the rulers of individual Malay states regarding subsequent changes to the constitution; and that the

federal parliament had no power to legislate for Kelantan in this matter. On 14 September the chief justice ruled that both the Malaysia Agreement and the Malaysia Act were constitutional. See Tan Sri Mohamed Suffian bin Hashim, *An introduction to the constitution of Malaysia* (Kuala Lumpur, 1972) pp 13–14; Allen, Stockwell and Wright, eds, *A collection of treaties*, II, p 277; Richard Allen, *Malaysia: prospect and retrospect: the impact and aftermath of colonial rule* (London, 1968) pp 174–175.

158   Goode to Mubin Sheppard, 2 Oct 1984, Goode Papers, box 5, file 5, f 45.

159   Goode to Mubin Sheppard, 16 Nov 1984, ibid, f 48.

Summary of Documents

Chapter 2
Principles for a Federation of Malaysia, June–Dec 1961: internal security of Singapore; the Singapore base and regional defence; obligations to Borneo peoples; the question of timing; London talks and the Anglo–Malayan statement of Nov 1961

Chapter 3
The Cobbold Commission, Dec 1961-July 1962:
the enquiry in North Borneo and Sarawak; drafting the report; Anglo–Malayan differences; London talks and the agreement of 31 July 1962

Chapter 4

Conflict, deadlock and agreement, Aug 1962–July 1963: Lansdowne's Inter-Governmental Committee; the Brunei revolt; operation 'Cold Store' in Singapore; opposition from Indonesia and the Philippines; attitudes of the UN and USA; British financial and military assistance; deadlock in talks between Malaya and Singapore, and between Malaya and Brunei; prospect of 'Little Malaysia'; the Malaysia agreement of 9 July 1963

Chapter 5:
Malaysia postponed, July–Sept 1963:
the future of Brunei; the Manila Summit; Sandys' mission to Kuala Lumpur; Lee Kuan Yew's unilateral declaration of independence; crisis over Sarawak appointments; the UN mission; Malaysia Day

1963

1   CAB 134/1556, CPC(57)34   29 Nov 1957
'Borneo Territories': memorandum for Cabinet Colonial Policy Committee by Mr Lennox Boyd, assessing the possibility of closer association of the Borneo territories

[Despite the separate constitutional development of Malaya, Singapore and the Borneo territories, their eventual closer association was a declared principle of British policy from 1945 onwards. As early as Aug 1942 the FO and CO agreed on the desirability of a union of the Malay States, Straits Settlements and Borneo territories (*BDEE: Malaya*, document 8). Although the final plans for the post-war reoccupation of Southeast Asia fell far short of such a union, the government created a structure for regional co-ordination in the offices of the special commissioner and governor-general (later commissioner-general) and held out the prospect for the closer association of Malaya, Singapore and the three Borneo territories (*BDEE: Malaya*, 293). The post-war separation of Singapore and Malaya was deeply regretted in many quarters, and Malcolm MacDonald encouraged thinking about merger in his governor-general's conferences, the Communities Liaison Committee and local branches of the Commonwealth Parliamentary Association (*BDEE: Malaya*, 112, 115, 121, 141, 143). Senior officials and ministers envisaged parallel developments leading to the merger of Malaya and Singapore, on the one hand, and the merger of the Borneo territories, on the other. It was expected that Malaya and Singapore would complete their process sooner than the Borneo territories, and that merger of the two blocs would take place in the end, although an alternative option might be merger of the five territories at a stroke but only when the time was right (*BDEE: Malaya*, 288). Although territorial mergers were their objective, the British government refrained from forcing the pace. They believed that it would be counter-productive to impose a scheme or to issue a directive, and preferred that the impetus should come from community leaders. Thus, they attempted to stimulate local interest in closer association or in the formation of a territorial conglomerate which MacDonald referred to as a self-governing British dominion of Southeast Asia. Despite declarations of interest and good intentions, however, the pace was slow: Malays mistrusted domination by the Chinese and commercial interests of Singapore; Singaporeans mistrusted subordination as a twelfth state in a Malay-controlled federation; the Sultan of Brunei was on his guard against loss of both sovereignty and oil revenue; Sarawak and North Borneo would be at a disadvantage in any merger with Malaya and Singapore on account of their economic and political backwardness. Momentum towards merger was lost during the worst years of the emergency and there was a danger of drift during which territories moved further apart and separateness became entrenched and underpinned by vested interests. In 1952 Templer and the Chiefs of Staff pressed for a merger between Malaya and Singapore for purposes of defence and internal security with the result that in 1953 the policy for closer association was reviewed and a Joint Co-ordinating Committee established to plan for the merger of island and peninsula (*BDEE: Malaya*, 286, 292, 293, 300). Fresh impetus was also given to the scheme for closer association of the Borneo territories; in April 1953 MacDonald chaired a conference in Kuching which established the Inter-Territorial Conference for the co-ordination of policies and common services in British Borneo. MacDonald was tireless and infinitely optimistic in encouraging closer association of the five dependencies (*BDEE: Malaya*, 267, 276, 324, 346) and on the eve of his departure from Southeast Asia he was looking forward to the eventual realisation of the 'grand design' (as he called it, *BDEE: Malaya*, 346). Meanwhile, politically, economically and constitutionally the Borneo peoples lagged far behind the Singaporeans and Malayans with the result that Malaya achieved independence on its own in 1957 when Singapore was also on course for self-government. Nevertheless, if a 'Greater Malaysia' consisting of the Federation of Malaya, Singapore, Brunei, North Borneo and Sarawak now looked remote, the closer association of the three Borneo territories became more pressing. Anxious about their vulnerability and keen to shape their political development, British officials suggested a fresh initiative. Lennox-Boyd responded cautiously; in recommending to the Colonial Policy Committee that steps be taken to encourage public debate about the territories' future, he reiterated the dangers of forcing the pace and of imposing any specific constitutional model.]

Introductory

1.   A short background note on the three British territories in Borneo, namely, the Colonies of Sarawak and North Borneo and the protected state of Brunei, is at Annex I. A map is also attached.[1]

2.   There is already some degree of co-operation between the three territories in the administrative field. Apart from the secondment of staff from Sarawak to Brunei, there is, for example, successful joint machinery for the Geological Survey, and for the Judiciary and Civil Aviation. But this co-operation cannot be carried much further without the creation of new links, the political implications of which have to be taken into account.

Present state of political opinion

3.   The possibilities of closer association between these three small territories have been canvassed for some years, both locally and in this country. Our line in public statements has been that we support it, but that the form that any political association might take is for the people of the territories themselves in the first instance to discuss and reach a view on. More recently, local opinion in North Borneo and Sarawak has come out openly, if mildly, in favour of some form of closer association and of there being public discussion to explore the idea. The Commissioner-General in South East Asia and the Governors of Sarawak and North Borneo strongly urge that the time has come for us to take an initiative and encourage discussion. If we delay, they say, we shall lose the power we still have of influencing the direction to be taken.

4.   In Brunei the danger lies in the extreme Malay nationalism which already exists and is being encouraged by elements from outside. This might well develop quickly into rabid opposition to the Sultanate and to the British connection, with grave prejudice to the stability of the administration and the security of the oilfield at Seria, which is the largest single oilfield in the Commonwealth.[2] Pressure from Indonesia, Malaya and Singapore and from extremists in the United Malays National Organisation cannot be ruled out.

Sarawak's danger is Communist subversion among the Chinese. There is evidence of Communist infiltration in the Chinese schools. These threats are contained at present. But events outside Borneo (e.g. in Malaya or Singapore) might increase them.

North Borneo is not as yet subject to these threats.

Indonesian irredentism lays claim to all three territories. The Philippines have a dormant claim to North Borneo.

5.   The Sultan of Brunei, whose views I have taken, is naturally suspicious of any plans which might reduce the status of his territory, impinge on his sovereignty or involve a sharing of Brunei's revenues, which come from oil. He has not, however, closed his mind to the idea of public discussion in Brunei of the idea of closer association and I do not think that we should be deterred by his present reluctance to commit himself from exploring the possibilities further.

---

[1] Not printed.
[2] The large oilfield was discovered at Seria in 1929 and was later developed by the Brunei Shell Petroleum Co Ltd.

The political case for closer association

6.   The basic argument in favour of some form of closer political association is that it will be more difficult for each of these small territories individually to resist such externally supported pressures and claims as are mentioned above than it would for the three of them standing together.

7.   In any event, we must envisage progressive moves in each of them towards forms of self-government. All three territories are still politically backward, but nationalist politics have begun in Brunei and will undoubtedly start up in the others. Closer association would provide a larger stage for political leaders. This can have its disadvantages. It might stimulate the growth of nationalist parties and increase the status of their leaders. But it could have the great advantage of reducing the influence of extremists: a Malay nationalist should be of much less importance in the wider area, where Malays would not preponderate, than in Brunei alone; and it might in the long run help to preserve our influence in the area beyond the time which would be possible if separatist policies were allowed to develop in each territory individually. That is certainly the view of our representatives on the spot.

Other considerations

8.   It is less easy at this stage to assess the practical administrative and economic advantages, which might flow from closer association, particularly as we cannot foresee the precise form which it might take. On the administrative side, the Governors have discussed tentative proposals for the creation of an office of High Commissioner for the Borneo territories, possibly in Labuan,[3] together with an Executive Council of representatives of all three territories; for the administrative separation of Brunei and Sarawak; and for the subordination of the Governors of Sarawak and North Borneo to the new High Commission. Such arrangements would clearly not bring any immediate administrative economies, and the extent to which the relative burden of administrative costs could later be reduced (it is at present heavy, particularly in Brunei) would depend on the economic results of the new arrangements which are hard to estimate now. The immediate benefit of closer association to Sarawak and North Borneo would lie in the sharing of Brunei's greater wealth, which is scarcely likely to commend itself to the Sultan. In the longer run, however, the economic strength of the whole area may come to depend more upon the development of the resources of North Borneo and Sarawak, which are more varied and durable than the oil wealth of Brunei. The common planning of economic development which closer association might be expected to achieve would, particularly in relation to communications, the recruitment and exchange of labour and technical staff and the provision of external capital, assist greatly in exploiting the potential wealth of North Borneo and Sarawak to the benefit of all three territories.

Conclusion

9.   While I accept that it is not possible to state now an overwhelming case in favour of closer association, I consider that, taking all the factors together, the political

---

[3] Ceded by the Sultan of Brunei to the British in 1846 as a place where ships might refit, the island of Labuan was administered as a separate colony until 1907 when it was incorporated in the Straits Settlements, becoming a separate settlement in 1911. In 1946 it became part of the crown colony of North Borneo.

balance is in favour of some discreet move in that direction. I am much impressed by the consensus of views amongst our representatives on the spot, including the Commissioner-General for South East Asia, that in such an association, guided by us, there lies a better chance of ultimate preservation of British links than if the territories are treated independently. Closer political association will, of course, take a long time to come about, and there is no question of hurrying it. It is not proposed at present to suggest a political union or even to put forward any cut and dried proposals about the lines along which closer association might develop. And we shall have to have careful regard to our defence needs in the area. The men on the spot say that we must no longer delay initiating public discussion on the subject, ascertaining the views of the people and exploring the possibilities: failure to do this now would in their opinion, lose us the chance of taking the lead in the future.

10.   The purpose of this paper is to tell my colleagues of the lines on which my discussions with our representatives in the area have been proceeding and to say that I propose to authorise the initiation of public discussion in North Borneo and Sarawak and have urged the Sultan of Brunei to give a lead to similar discussion in his own territory. These discussions will be exploratory at this stage. I shall inform my colleagues of the result and will seek their concurrence in any further steps which appear to me to be necessary or desirable thereafter.

2   CAB 134/1555, CPC 14(57)2   4 Dec 1957
'Borneo territories': Cabinet Colonial Policy Committee minutes approving initiation of public discussion of closer association

[Chaired by Lord Kilmuir (lord chancellor) in the absence of the prime minister, the meeting was attended by Home (foreign secretary), Lennox-Boyd (Colonial Office), Lord Hailsham (lord president).]

The Committee had before them a memorandum by the Colonial Secretary (C.P.C. (57) 34)[1] about the possibility of a closer association between the Colonies of Sarawak and North Borneo and the protected state of Brunei.

The Colonial Secretary said that this possibility had already been canvassed for some years both locally and in the United Kingdom. There was already some degree of co-operation between the three territories administratively, and local opinion in North Borneo and Sarawak had recently appeared to favour public discussion of the conception of a closer association. He had felt some hesitation in encouraging such a process, which, by creating a larger political unit, might stimulate the growth of nationalist parties and pressure for independence. He had, however, been impressed by the consensus of view between the Commissioner-General in South East Asia and the Governors of Sarawak and North Borneo that our influence in these territories could best be preserved by encouraging the movement towards closer association. It would therefore be right to take such opportunities as occurred to suggest that the possibility of some form of association between the territories concerned might merit public discussion. This policy should, however, be launched tentatively and we should be prepared to withdraw it if it was not well received. Much, for example, would depend upon the reaction of the Sultan of Brunei.

---

[1] See 1.

In discussion it was suggested that any public discussion of closer association between these territories might merely stimulate the tendency towards nationalism (with possibly serious strategic consequences for the future control of the important oil fields in Brunei). But the danger of separatism was inherent in the present situation, and it was to counter this danger that any federal movement would be designed. Notwithstanding the risks involved, the balance of advantage lay in the initiation of public discussion of the kind proposed.[2] While it would be premature at this stage to envisage the lines upon which a closer association might develop, any federal system might well be administered by a Commissioner for the Borneo Territories (whom it would be important to distinguish from a High Commissioner), together with an Executive Council representative of all three territories.

The Committee:—

Approved the proposals in C.P.C. (57) 34.

---

[2] Public discussion included broadcasts by the governors of North Borneo and Sarawak. Sir Roland Turnbull spoke on Radio Sabah in Feb 1958 (see 3), followed by Sir Anthony Abell on Radio Sarawak in Apr 1958.

3   DO 35/6297, no 70   7 Feb 1958
[Closer association of Borneo territories]: text of an address broadcast by Sir R Turnbull over Radio Sabah

[Turnbull followed up his broadcast with a resolution passed in North Borneo's Legislative Council in March that the three territories discuss their constitutional association but this initiative was blocked by the Sultan of Brunei. In Oct 1959, as he was preparing to leave the post of commissioner-general, Sir Robert Scott came across the text of Turnbull's radio address. He forwarded it to Goode, who was about to take over as governor, North Borneo, with a commentary on developments over the intervening period: 'Since then, our ideas for closer association between the three territories in Borneo have got into the doldrums and made no headway, chiefly because of the opposition of Brunei. . . . But I hope they will not drift too far apart. For practical reasons of geography and administration there must be contacts between the three, and we are trying to keep these contacts alive by the six-monthly (in fact, usually nine-monthly) "Interterritorial Conference" . . .' By this time, however, the British were uncertain whether to let things slide or push ahead with the closer association of North Borneo and Sarawak alone. Scott concluded his letter in the manner of someone who was demob-happy: 'These questions are being left in abeyance for the time being. They will be for you and the new Governor of Sarawak to think about next year' (Scott to Goode, personal, 13 Oct 1959, Goode Papers, box 1, file 1, f 13).]

When I spoke to you on the 9th November on the second anniversary of Radio Sabah, I forecast that this station would in its third year be most concerned with political matters. I suggested that we must now begin to think of the political structures that go to the building of a nation and in that phrase I included the relations of the several communities within North Borneo, each with the others, the association and identification of all the people of the country with its government, and the relations of this country and government with others external to it—particularly with its near neighbours, Brunei and Sarawak. I was not then being prophetic, for I had every reason to believe that at no distant date I would be talking to you, as I do to-night, about a matter of very especial importance to you all, the constitutional future of the three countries of North Borneo, Brunei and Sarawak. Together these countries are commonly spoken of as British Borneo, but the term is of course only one of convenience. Two of them, Sarawak and North Borneo, are indeed British, but Brunei is an Islamic State with its own sovereign head, His Highness the Sultan, who is in treaty relations with Her Majesty the Queen and by that treaty accepts Her Majesty's advice and protection. It is of the utmost importance that that cardinal fact should be kept in mind when thought is given, as I am sure it will be given, to what I am about to say.

The possibility of the closer political association of these three countries is no new subject. Her Majesty's Government in the United Kingdom, through individual Ministers, have several times spoken of the suggestion with favour. From time to time the newspapers of the world have featured articles representing their political association as a natural and seemingly inevitable development, and our failure to bring it about has more than once been criticised. For five years an inter-territorial committee[1] has met at regular intervals in one or other of the countries to consider the application in practice of a policy that has all along been assumed, that the three countries should work together.

The difference to-night is that I, as the responsible head of your Government, am asking you to consider, in all gravity, the merits from the point of view of you, the people of North Borneo, of the proposition that North Borneo should enter into with Brunei and Sarawak, some kind of firm constitutional pact. Whenever Her Majesty's Ministers in the United Kingdom have expressed themselves as being in favour of some kind of political association of these countries, they have always said that the question was ultimately one for the people here to decide for themselves. Permit me to be more precise as to the meaning of that phrase. It means that the Governments of North Borneo and Sarawak must be satisfied both that it is a desirable development and that there exists in their countries bodies of opinion in favour of federation sufficiently substantial to make it workable; in the case of Brunei it would mean that His Highness the Sultan and his Government were convinced that it would be to the advantage of His Highness's country and acceptable to a substantial body of his people.

This is the only sure foundation for such a departure as I now propose. This also explains what may have already occurred to those of my Legislative advisers who are listening to me, why I should have chosen to broach this subject on the radio rather than in the constitutional body which determines your affairs. I did of course give very careful thought to the choice of medium. At first sight the obvious course would have been to address the Legislative Council. But I considered it unfair to do so without due warning, the absence of which would deny to my Councillors the opportunity for consultation and deliberation provided by the course I have in fact adopted. So fundamental a change is not a matter on which any man should be asked to utter at short notice. I have no doubt that many of you have considered it already. But I ask you now to consider it anew. There are advantages and disadvantages, and second thoughts after the event are of immeasurably less value than considered thoughts before it. That does not mean that I have any doubts. It is a subject on which I have pondered for years and there remains no question in my mind that it is to the long term advantage of the peoples of all three countries that they should join together to become as nearly as possible one country as their many differences may permit. But in this matter my opinion is only one opinion.

---

[1] The inter-territorial committee or conference (chaired by the commissioner-general) was initiated by Malcolm MacDonald in Apr 1953.

I shall go, regretfully, perhaps long before this dramatic adventure is embarked on; it is you who will live in the federated country if it is brought about and it is your opinion that, at any rate as far as North Borneo is concerned, must be decisive.

I can describe very readily, and later will describe, what to my mind would be a workable form of association for the three countries. But I think you know me well enough to realise that I never have and never would seek to impose on the people of this country a political structure for which you are not ready. I have many times expressed the hope that North Borneo, which I am quite sure will ultimately emerge as a strong country, would evolve in accordance with its own genius. Anything that I suggest to-night must be accepted as no more than a suggestion, a possible framework which it is for you to consider, and so far at any rate as North Borneo is concerned, to accept, to refuse, or to amend. But whatever opinion you may ultimately arrive at, let there be no doubt in your mind, as there is none in mine, of the advantage of the proposal in theory. The history of the world in recent centuries leaves no room for such doubt. The free association of peoples everywhere results in an accretion of strength far beyond the sum total of their individual capacity. It is not the case where nations are concerned that $1 + 1 + 1$ will make 3; together they make a unit that is much more powerful, more effective, more efficient and more capable of making life better for its members than the sum total of their individual strengths would ever suggest. For instance, it is usual here to speak of England, but in fact England is only one of the four countries that go to make up the United Kingdom. America is the combination of forty-eight States, many of which wrangle between themselves and with their Federal Government, but all of which stand as one where the rest of the world is concerned. Do you suppose for one moment that, if they were separate, those States, the names of all of which I doubt whether some of you even know, could command such a voice in the affairs of the world as they do together in the might of the United States of America. A few years ago the countries of Southern Rhodesia, Northern Rhodesia and Nyasaland joined together—after much controversy, much difficulty, much deliberation—as a Federation.[2] As units, each was relatively unimportant. Together, I believe that in time they may point the way for the whole of an as yet uncertain Africa. A few weeks ago there was created the Federation of the West Indies,[3] and in welcoming that event, Mr. Casey, the Minister for External Affairs in the Commonwealth of Australia, said it was the outcome of 'patient and constructive effort by local leaders working closely with the United Kingdom Government', and he added that 'as we found in Australia, experience in working together builds up habits of co-operation and a sense of nationhood'. But I must point out, here, that the experience, and the nationhood, and indeed the strength, came after the six states of the Commonwealth of Australia had engaged to submerge their differences in the act of faith which made them one. There are so many examples, nearly all of them provided by the British Commonwealth, itself the greatest aggregation of diverse peoples, moved ultimately by a single common love of freedom, that the world has ever known. One instance, closest of all to your own knowledge, is the Federation of Malaya, the emergence of which as an independent

---

[2] For the Central African Federation, 1953–1963 see Murphy, ed, *BDEE: Central Africa* (forthcoming).
[3] For the West Indies Federation, Jan 1958–May 1962 see Ashton and Killingray, eds, *BDEE: The West Indies*.

member of the Commonwealth we so warmly welcomed only a few months ago.[4] The voice of that country will be heard in the councils of the world, as the separate voices of Pahang or Perlis or Negri Sembilan could never have been heard.

In this address I use the word 'federation' as one of convenience to describe the formal political association of two or more separate countries for the furtherance of their joint interests. There are many different kinds of federation, some of them very close, some very loose, and I do not attempt to forecast what particular form of association will emerge as most appropriate for these countries if, in fact, agreement is reached for the creation of any.

But let us accept it, being guided by experience elsewhere, that some form of federation is in principle both desirable and advantageous. That does not mean that you should not look closely to your own interests before changing from principle to practice. Such association has not always proved possible, even between countries where it seemed most likely. The three Scandinavian countries of Sweden, Norway and Denmark, closely related as they are, have always found their local, separate interests more important than their common interests.

Again, close at hand, although the states and settlements of the mainland of Malaya have found it possible to join in a single federation, and although their affairs and those of Singapore are inevitably entwined, it has not been found possible to agree on the inclusion of Singapore in the Federation. It may be that you here in North Borneo, or our neighbours in Brunei or Sarawak, may come to a similar conclusion, albeit—as I think—unwisely, for whereas the geographical proximity of the three countries makes the rest of the world regard them as naturally akin, in truth they are surprisingly different. All I would say about that is this: North Borneo is developing quickly, and developing upon its own lines; so also are Brunei and Sarawak. With time the differences will become greater, and not less, and if you desire to grasp the advantages of federation you should do so soon, for in time the differences could be too great to overcome. But just as one should give sober thought before entering into marriage, so, before entering into a partnership, particularly a permanent partnership, you must give thought not only to what you yourself have to offer but to the merits of your prospective partners. We here can offer a country of great economic potential, which is already growing rapidly, with a record of political stability. In Brunei I see two particular advantages, the wealth it draws from oil and the personality of its present Ruler. The State has, I think, few natural advantages other than oil, but the riches it draws from oil are very great. Let there be no misunderstanding. Federation would not mean that Brunei money would be shared with North Borneo or Sarawak. The money is Brunei's, and would remain Brunei's. In the event of federation being brought about, Brunei would contribute its share of the cost of joint services just as we should. Nevertheless, it would be not unnatural to assume that the Government of Brunei might be prepared to invest some at any rate of its surplus wealth in the territories of its new partners as, indeed, Brunei has already done in a small way. Brunei is also fortunate in having at its head a forward-looking ruler dedicated to the service of his people. There is a Malay proverb which speaks of 'Katak di-bawah tempurong', of a frog beneath a coconut shell which believes that shell to be the whole world. In a small country there is always the danger of the people developing a mentality akin to that of the frog, but His Highness the

---

[4] See Stockwell, ed, *BDEE: Malaya*, part III.

Sultan, on the contrary, is extremely anxious to groom his people for the responsibilities that wealth places on them in a turbulent world. Sarawak is larger, richer and more, populous than North Borneo. But it may not always be richer, perhaps indeed not for so very much longer, and even now it certainly has no revenues to spare. Looking at the other side of the account, the peoples of the three countries are very far from being homogenous, Sarawak has been touched by communism in a way that we here have not,[5] and even Brunei is politically a little yeasty. But it must be admitted that of the three territories, Sarawak with 50,000 square miles and between 6 and 700,000 people, North Borneo with 30,000 square miles and less than 400,000 people, and Brunei with 2,000 odd square miles and some 60,000 people, none is a very considerable country; but with more than 80,000 square miles (much larger than the Federation of Malaya) and well over a million people we might build a country of some importance in South East Asia. And against the larger background, the problems of each would appear so much the smaller.

Formal political association could be secured, of course, only at a price, and that price you must now assess. To enable you to do so, I had best outline the kind of association that I think will be possible. But I must emphasize that these are my ideas and not in any way specific proposals. Clearly, recognising the special position of Brunei, amalgamation of the three countries into one is impracticable even if it were desirable, which I do not think would be the case. Their constitutions apart, the three countries are very individual and their individuality is worthy of retention. On the other hand, if their association is to be effective, they must be clearly identified to the rest of the world as one. The mere superimposition of yet another constitutional body over the three Governments, with limited and begrudged authority, would be extravagant, ineffective and otiose. It would be essential that the three Governments should define those interests that they regard as common, and be prepared to surrender, of their own will, the control of those interests to a central body representative of all of them. Obviously the first of such common interests would be our relations with other countries, for which Her Majesty's Government are in any case responsible. Secondly would come those matters that are already the responsibility of joint departments, although those joint departments must for the present look for their authority to the several separate Governments. To my mind the next most obvious responsibility to be given to the Federation Government would be internal security. We have already helped each other on several occasions, and there is much duplication of effort. Nor is it possible to say that disturbance in Sarawak or Brunei is of no concern to North Borneo. I have not the slightest doubt that in this, as in many other fields, our individual resources when combined could be deployed to the much greater advantage of all. Customs, immigration policy, health, education are all subjects in which we have already sought to secure unanimity but in which, because we are not bound together, local interests have so far won the day. Some or all of them could be made the ultimate responsibility of the central authority. But perhaps I go too far and too fast. These are matters that would necessarily be the subject of much thought

---

[5] Sarawak's first experience of communist terrorism was dated from an incident at Batu Kitang (ten miles from Kuching) in August 1952 perpetrated by members of the Sarawak Peoples Army. The government adopted the term the Clandestine Communist Organisation to embrace all such groups, see Sarawak Information Service, *The Danger Within: A History of the Clandestine Communist Organisation in Sarawak*, 1963.

before agreement could be reached. But of this I am quite sure. That we could all profit very greatly in all these fields by the joint use of the resources that are available to us individually. And I personally would like to see the identity of interests personified in a single Governor and High Commissioner for all three territories who would be advised by counsellors coming from all three.

Economically small countries suffer from their excessive dependence on foreign trade. The economic success of federation would depend largely on the extent to which we are prepared to abandon internal trade barriers and to pool our productive resources. But in this too, we need not go too quickly for, as Mr. Casey said, it is experience in working together that builds up the habit of co-operation and emphasizes its worth.

I think I know you well enough to guess the question that will now be uppermost in your minds. Where, in all this, stands Her Majesty's Government in the United Kingdom? You are all aware that it is the policy of Her Majesty's Government—and this is true of all likely Governments in England—to lead colonial peoples towards self-government. I know that many of you will now think that the proposal for the federation of the three territories denotes the desire of the British Government to transfer responsibility for the three territories to a local Government. I can say in all certainty that that is not true. It is not the case that Her Majesty's Government have any desire to shed responsibility for these countries. I said recently that, although the number of officers from the United Kingdom would inevitably decrease as more local officers became experienced, it was my hope that the association of the United Kingdom Government with North Borneo would subsist as long as sentiment and need demanded. I am certain that Her Majesty's Government would confirm that statement, whether it related to North Borneo alone or to the possible federation of which I am now speaking. Indeed, the Federation would be an association not of three countries, but of four, of Sarawak, Brunei, North Borneo and the United Kingdom, and I am sure that the United Kingdom would not set a term to its interest and its association in advance of the wishes of the people of these countries.

I have given you much to ponder on. Nobody is committed to any decision in the matters of which I have spoken, not Her Majesty's Government, nor His Highness the Sultan nor the Governments of Sarawak and North Borneo. And all four must needs consent before such an association can be brought about. But if it is brought about, it will closely affect your own children and their future. I trust you will think about it soberly and gravely.

4   CO 1030/658, no 11   30 July 1958
[Brunei]: letter from Sir A Abell[1] to W I J Wallace. *Enclosure:* **'A brief appreciation of the political situation in Brunei—June, 1958' by E R Bevington[2]**

[By the end of the nineteenth century Brunei, which had once exercised suzerainty over much of Borneo and parts of the Philippines archipelago, had been reduced to two

---

[1] As governor of Sarawak 1950–1959, Sir Anthony Abell also served as high commissioner of Brunei.
[2] E R Bevington had served in the Gilbert and Ellice Islands and in Fiji before being seconded to Brunei as commissioner for development, 1954–1958, when amongst other tasks he supervised the construction of the National Mosque.

enclaves, as the result of territorial concessions to the Brookes of Sarawak and to European traders (notably the North Borneo Company). In 1888 Brunei became a British protectorate, thereby losing control of external relations, and in 1906 the sultan accepted a British officer, or resident, whose advice he agreed to follow in all matters save those relating to religion and custom. Although the discovery of a large oil field at Seria in 1929 transformed its fortunes, the upheaval of world war and nationalist movements across the region called into question the viability of the tiny state. On 1 May 1948, the government of Brunei was in effect placed under the supervision of Sarawak whose governor acted as high commissioner for the sultanate and whose officials were seconded to its administration. Since Brunei had formerly ruled Sarawak, this measure caused considerable resentment and dampened enthusiasm for any closer association with Sarawak or North Borneo. In 1953 Sultan Omar Ali Saifuddin, who had ascended the throne in 1950, responded to popular demands for political change by preparing a written constitution that, on its promulgation in Sept 1959, would introduce representative government and reduce the role of the British in domestic affairs. The prospect of reform triggered a contest between the conservative 'palace party' of *pengirans* (hereditary nobles) and the radical Party Rakyat Brunei led by Azahari, see 9.]

You may be interested to read the enclosed paper by Mr. E. R. Bevington; it is on the whole, I think, a fair assessment of the present situation in Brunei and I am in general agreement with his views as to the root causes of the present difficulties. There is, however, one other fact which bedevils the present situation and will have a considerable influence on the future course of events. That is the struggle for personal power and position among the principal performers. This struggle has, of course, gone on throughout the history of Brunei and all the refinements of the known methods of liquidation of rivals and removal of obstacles have been practised freely and with considerable originality. I have no doubt at all that if it suited a group who felt sufficiently strong to do so they would without hesitation or regret remove the Sultan from his throne. In fact I have been told by a politically disinterested Malay from Malaya that His Highness would remain but a fortnight on his throne if the British buttress was removed. I think that is an exaggeration because I believe His Highness to be still generally popular. But I would add to Bevington's three main sources of present difficulties in his paragraph one the struggle for personal power. At present the ambitious politician requires His Highness' patronage and until he has satisfied his ambition he must toe the line. There are plums in the future to be picked—various high state appointments, such as Mentri Besar open to commoners. His Highness while hinting that he has candidates for these posts is careful not to tell me or anyone else who they are— hence his reluctance to agree to a period of training. Then the Palace and family group though strongly entrenched do not approve of and distrust His Highness' new friends among the school teachers. The young educated element, who support the M.T.U.,[3] despise and dislike the Palace toadies and the Party Ra'ayat dislike everything to do with the present Government. There are signs that all these antagonistic groups are at present uneasily allied in a common determination to bring the present administration into disrepute and so force out of business the one element which keeps the ring—the British. It is vital in my view that we should remain in the ring as a referee who interprets the rules and we must retain our powers at least until a new constitution with a competent system of popular election is working smoothly.

---

[3] Malay Teachers Union.

Enclosure to 4

The administration has for some few months been faced with great difficulty, not only in obtaining consent to constructive forward moves, but even to the maintenance of normal constructive Government. The difficulty has arisen apparently from three sources:—

The Sultan
A section of State Council (M.T.U.)
The Party Ra'ayat.

Had there been any one underlying motive directing the apparent obstructions, it would have been possible to appreciate it and take steps either to accommodate it or to meet it. Difficulty has arisen because there seems to be no clear motive and generally the actions and reactions of the first two parties mentioned above have been well nigh unpredictable.

After mulling over this problem for some months it seems possible that the motive is obscured because it has three root causes. It is suggested that these are:—

Nationalism-as to approximately 30%
Xenophobia " "   "   20%
fear   " "   "   50%

the proportions must vary according to the party considering any given problem (para. 1 above) and the problem under consideration.

The first two ingredients need little elaboration and are common to nearly all the non-self governing territories to-day. Nationalism in Brunei has its major negative manifestation in an anti-Chinese attitude, an attitude undoubtedly motivated by fear. Brunei nationalism demands that the country shall be governed solely and absolutely by Brunei Malays who are some 50% of the present total population.

The second ingredient—xenophobia—extends to all 'outsiders', whether they are British Indian or even Malaya Malays. Of these the British, so long as they are not in key administrative positions, are the most acceptable: the Bruneis know (but will not admit) that one day the British will go as in India, Ghana, Ceylon, Malaya. Not so the others: they are tropical people who are born, marry or die in this part of the world. The Bruneis fear that they will provide the expertise, technical crafts and ability to make themselves indispensable: they will settle, and one day with their greater drive and initiative they will possess the country. And until then, they will take the best jobs and block promotion for Bruneis.

The third ingredient—fear—is a general fear of the future based on a secret and inward knowledge that the Bruneis are unable to deal with the technological complications of life in the modern world. To technological complications must be added political complications. The Sultan sees the lesser status to which the Malaya Sultans have been reduced. Members of State Council see the political troubles of Singapore and the 'Emergency' in the Federation. Only the leader of the Party Ra'ayat[4] has shown any willingness to grapple with technological and political complications. But even if he came to power he would be held firmly back by his following.

---

[4] A M Azahari, see 9, note 2.

Oddly enough, the first 5 years Development Plan has increased fear. It has gone too fast. The new members of State Council in particular realise that one thing leads to another, that all the time they must bring in outside staff to man the new services, that more and more of the State's funds are pre-empted to pay for the new services. It is possibly not an exaggeration to say that they fear they are on a Gadarene slope being rushed to their doom—or rather to the doom of the dream of a paradisaical Brunei wholly preserved for the Brunei Malays. This explains their resistance to new development projects and even the desire to terminate old ones. In their view the previous decisions of State Council are suspect, and must be revised: those decisions were no more than assent to the advice of an administering authority. They were not the freely expressed will of the people: in their minds the fact that the people had no way of freely expressing their will merely begs the issue. This explains the desire to go back over formerly approved decisions—to try and regain ground that was 'lost' in the past.

None of these factors are new: they have all arisen in other places. But in Brunei the handling of the problem is made much more difficult by the constitutional position which must now be dealt with.

The constitutional position
De jure, Brunei is an autocracy. The Sultan must accept and act on the advice of the British Resident. The administration is a bureaucracy.

De facto, Brunei has a State Council and Legislative body with an overwhelming unofficial majority, and a power of veto in the hands of the Sultan which is exercised almost exclusively against the official advice.

The foregoing two factors are the immediate cause of the present impasse. The administration's advice (and often its day to day actions) can be and are flouted either by the State Council in its executive or legislative capacity (for as at present constituted it is both legislative and executive council) or by the State Council's Finance Committee by refusing supply.

British administration has therefore lost the substance of power while retaining the form. How has this position come about? The process was all too simple, and one which gives hindsight easy wisdom.

From 1906 the British Resident was in fact Administrator of Brunei. Sultans were simple men of little or no education. Following the policy of indirect rule, the desire to train the local people in government, and the obvious wisdom of maintaining the trappings of government known and understood by the people, the old State Council nominated by the Sultan was retained. From 1906 to about 1956 all went well: Sultan and Council were amenable, and were even glad to leave the cares and chores of government to their British advisers. Education, newspapers, the affairs of Singapore and Malaya, and the sheer march of time, have had their cumulative effect. The Sultan became worried about his dynasty, a local political party was formed, and the Malay Teachers Union sought to defend their own position when they saw expatriate teachers necessarily brought in to provide secondary education. These are the three groups cited in the first paragraph.

The Party Ra'ayat being unrepresented in either State Council or the administration has had little more than a nuisance value so far. The first signs of difficulty arose when the Sultan started using a de facto veto power—a power which arose out of the administration's natural reluctance to use its Treaty powers and compel acceptance of advice. These early difficulties were greatly increased when members of the Malay Teachers Union were appointed to State Council. It is they who have brought about the present near-impasse. The administration is faced with the task of obtaining legislative authority and funds for administration from the virtually hostile body.

These are the essential factors which make up the present situation. The future, as always, is less easy to see.

One factor which does seem to be of growing importance is a confluence of the three parties mentioned in paragraph 1. While each may have different motives, one self-preservation, another self-aggrandisement, another political power, there are signs that they are coming to realise that a marriage of convenience would serve their immediate ends—which are absolute control of Brunei by Brunei Malays with all others on suffrance. Once they have that power, their individual manoeuvres for position can be resumed, in an atmosphere free from interference by the British or anyone else.

There is little doubt that the M.T.U. members of State Council are often (although not always) the spokesmen of the Sultan in sessions of State Council. There is evidence that they meet in advance and agree on the action to be taken in Council. There is also evidence that the M.T.U. Members are not unconnected with the Party Ra'ayat and at least compare notes as to possible lines of action in Party Congress or State Council. Xenophobia and Nationalism are probably the amalgam which has brought them together.

Additional difficulty is lent to the situation by the fact that neither the M.T.U. members nor the Party Ra'ayat have responsibility or power (other than negative power). Their influence is therefore wholly destructive and obstructive.

Here are all the ingredients of as knotty a problem as could exist—and the smallness of the State makes it more difficult and parochial rather than the reverse.

It is possible that the only solution lies in finding means of transferring responsibility to Brunei Malays, provided always that those to whom responsibility is transferred have reached their position as responsibly elected representatives of the people, and not by nomination by the Sultan or the administration. The difficulties are immense: there is no one fitted to assume responsibility and the three existing Malay Heads of Department are examples. Undoubtedly there would be a hiatus and a slowing down of advancement coupled with inefficiency in administration. But it is possible that the only alternative may prove to be (one day) the use of force with all the stigma that that carries in a world where information travels literally with the speed of light.

The Brunei Malays wish to build a fence around their country. So long as oil flows they can do that, until they themselves start dismantling the fence. But in those circumstances can the flow of oil be assured—it is doubtful.

5   DO 35/10019, no 12, E/2   18 Dec 1958
[Developments in Brunei]: note by M MacDonald of talks with the Sultan of Brunei on 13–14 December

[Malcolm MacDonald, high commissioner to India, 1955–1958, had promoted the closer association of British dependencies in Southeast Asia during his time as governor-general of Malaya and Borneo, 1946–1948, and commissioner-general in SE Asia, 1948–1955 (see 1, note), so much so that he would be the British government's first choice to lead the commission of enquiry to Borneo in 1962. During a visit to the region in Dec 1958 MacDonald held informal and secret talks with the Sultan of Brunei and Tunku Abdul Rahman and these are reported in documents 5, 6, 7 and 8. Having cleared drafts with local British officials, MacDonald sent copies of the final versions to Sir Gilbert Laithwaite, permanent under-secretary at the CRO, 1955–1959, for circulation to appropriate Whitehall departments whose officials would regularly refer to these reports during the initiation of the 'Grand Design' for 'Greater Malaysia'.]

1.   I visited Brunei on December 13th and 14th, and Kuching on the 15th and 16th. I was very impressed by the developments which have occurred in Brunei since my last visit just over three years ago. Moreover, I noticed a pleasing change in the Sultan himself. Immediately on meeting him I observed that his face reveals a much more mature, self-confident character than before. Nor did I see in his eyes any hint of the madness which one should perhaps look for in a member of the Royal House of Brunei. All my conversations with him confirmed my impression of a responsible and statesmanlike young Ruler. But these are comparatively early days, and heredity may yet catch up with His Highness.

The constitution

2.   I had several talks with him on numerous subjects, and one long, sustained discussion on political affairs. The Resident (Mr. Dennis White) accompanied me, and the Pengiran Bundahara, the Pengiran Pemancha and Data Perdana Mentri were with the Sultan on that occasion.

3.   After various courteous preliminaries and some exchanges on topics of lesser importance, I asked His Highness how he thought affairs were developing in Brunei. Was he satisfied, for example, with the stage of economic, social and educational progress which had so far been reached? Quite a lengthy discussion on these topics followed, the details of which I need not report since they included nothing of particular significance. The Sultan did, however, pay tribute to the soundness of the planning and of the implementation of plans which had occurred in recent years, and by implication expressed gratitude to the British authorities for their guiding part in all this. Mr. Dennis White said this was the first time he had heard the Sultan express any such appreciation.

4.   I then turned the talk to political questions, saying I was glad to know that His Highness intended to press ahead with a new, more democratic Constitution for the State.[1] I remarked that it was wise of him to wish to introduce the Constitution soon, because by doing that he would give some early satisfaction to local Nationalist opinion, retain his influence over the moderate progressive movement, and avoid being forced into a position of making more far-reaching concessions to extremist

---

[1] Following talks in London in late Mar-early Apr 1959, the Sultan proceeded to grant Brunei's first written constitution on 29 Sept 1959. Under its terms, supreme executive authority was vested in the sultan, the old State Council was replaced by an Executive Council and a Legislative Council, and the administration was to be run by the mentri besar (chief minister), state secretary, attorney-general and state financial officer. On the same day he also concluded a new treaty with Britain by which Britain granted self-government but retained control over external affairs, defence and internal security. The post of resident was abolished and a high commissioner was appointed to advise the Sultan. The governor of Sarawak ceased to act as high commissioner (thereby ending administrative ties with Sarawak which had long been a source of resentment in Brunei) and the resident, D C White, was appointed high commissioner.

political leaders. In my view it was of great importance that he himself should move with the times and retain the leadership of his people.

5.   He said he entirely agreed with this conception, and that he favoured a slow, steady constitutional advance in the government of Brunei. In reply to a question from me he said he expects to go to London next March for discussions with the Secretary of State with a view to the details of the new Constitution being finally agreed.

6.   I said that, as he well knew, Mr. Lennox Boyd is a Minister with great experience and wisdom in such matters, who would do his utmost to reach accord, and who would have a conciliatory approach to any difficult problems. If it were possible for the British authorities to make one or two concessions on points of outstanding disagreement, Mr. Lennox Boyd would be inclined to make them. The Sultan replied that he also had great confidence in the friendly and constructive spirit in which the Secretary of State would negotiate.

7.   I remarked that the negotiations would nevertheless fail if he himself did not respond to the Secretary of State's conciliatory spirit by being ready to make concessions himself on points of difficulty. He must be flexible in his approach and meet the British authorities half-way. Only if both sides were so disposed could a settlement be reached. He said that he understood this position, and that he would be ready to reach compromise agreements.

8.   In further discussion he agreed that it might take between nine months and a year after negotiations had been successfully concluded before the new Constitution could be introduced in practice.

Inter-territorial conference

9.   I then raised the question of the Inter-Territorial Conference, pretending ignorance of the present situation concerning it, and expressing a hope that its meetings were as regular and as helpful as they had been in the past. He replied that unfortunately things in the Conference were not going well, and that he was considering whether he should continue his membership of it.

10.   I said I was surprised and sorry to hear this, and asked what the difficulty was. He answered that on one or two occasions recently tentative agreements reached in the Conference had been regarded as firm decisions, and that action implementing them had been taken before he had an opportunity to consult his State Council and have the agreements confirmed. This had put him in an impossible position.

11.   I commented that I thought there must be some misunderstanding, for I felt sure that all the other authorities concerned intended that proposals made in the Conference should not prejudice in any way his and his Government's complete freedom either to adopt or reject agreements tentatively reached there. That was the basis on which we had originally formed the Conference, and I was certain that Sir Robert Scott[2] and the others involved intended no change in that position.

12.   His Highness said that if the Conference had continued to work in that way, there would be no difficulty; but that things had changed. I repeated that I was sure there must be a misunderstanding somewhere, and added that, if His Highness wished, I would have a personal word with Sir Robert or anyone else, to let him know that His

---

[2] Commissioner-general SE Asia, 1955–1959.

Highness was troubled on this point of the implementation of tentative agreements ahead of such agreements being confirmed by the Brunei Government. I said I felt sure that if I reported this, Sir Robert and his British colleagues would at once see that any misunderstandings were removed or unintentional mistakes corrected.

13.   The Sultan thanked me for this suggestion, but said that for the present he would prefer me not to say anything. He was considering the whole position, and if he found that the difficulties which he had mentioned no longer existed, it would be unnecessary for me to speak to anyone. If, on the other hand, the difficulties, continued, he would send me a message, and would be grateful if I would speak informally to others concerned.

14.   I promised to say nothing now, but reiterated that I would be ready to speak if he wished me to do so. I urged him to feel confidence in the Conference, and said I hoped he would attend the next meeting on January the 21st.

Relations with Sarawak and North Borneo
15.   I said I was glad His Highness had established friendly relations between Brunei and Malaya.[3] He smiled and remarked that he had been a bit criticised for this. I said I thought he was wise, and that I hoped he would maintain at least as friendly relations with Sarawak and North Borneo as he had established with Malaya. It would strengthen Brunei's position if she had the most cordial relations with all her neighbours.

16.   He answered that he wished for good relations with all other countries. I remarked that this was right, but that some countries were of particular importance as near neighbours to Brunei. Sarawak and North Borneo were in this special category. He agreed that he should maintain the best possible relations with them.

17.   I would have liked to discuss the point further, and to urge him to give the same generous terms for loans to Sarawak and North Borneo as he had accorded recently to Malaya; but I judged that if I pressed this matter in that conversation, he would suspect that I had been especially briefed by the Colonial Office, that our whole conversation had been officially inspired, and that any good that the talk had done on one or two previous points might be undone. I therefore switched the talk to the innocent question of building a museum in Brunei.

18.   After discussion with Mr. Dennis White, and with Sir Anthony Abell in Kuching on the following day, I decided to write a letter to His Highness mentioning in it not only the point about the Inter-Territorial Conference, but also the matter of the loans to Sarawak and North Borneo. I attach to this Note a copy of the letter which has now been sent to His Highness.[4] Its terms were agreed with Sir Anthony and Mr. White.

19.   It was very pleasing to see the excellent relations which Mr. White has established with the Sultan. His Highness evidently feels entirely at his ease with the Resident, likes him and trusts him, is ready to discuss any question frankly with him, and is beginning to be influenced by Mr. White's opinions on affairs. If I may say so, on his side Mr. White is conducting his personal and official relations with the Ruler with conspicuous tact, skill and wisdom.

---

[3] But relations between Brunei and Malaya deteriorated after the inauguration of the Brunei constitution as a result of the influx of Malay administrative officers seconded from the Federation of Malaya.
[4] See 6.

6   DO 35/10019, no 12, E/1   20 Dec 1958
[Developments in Brunei]: letter from M MacDonald to the Sultan of Brunei

Your Highness,
I very much enjoyed my visit to Your Highness in Brunei. Again, I congratulate you very warmly on your great achievements in the State since I last visited it three years ago. I was delighted with everything that I saw last weekend, much of it obviously the results of your leadership.

I also benefited greatly from my talks with you, and was happy to hear of the progress being made in various directions. I was very sorry to learn, however, that difficulties seem to have arisen in the Inter-Territorial Conference of Brunei, Sarawak and North Borneo. I shall say nothing about this to Sir Robert Scott or others whilst I am here in Singapore; but, as I promised, shall be ready to speak personally later if you send me a message that you would like me to do so. As it happens, I shall be back in Singapore between the 11th and the 17th of January, when I return here for the annual conference of British Ambassadors and other high officers in the Far East. Sir Robert Scott, Sir Anthony Abell and Sir Roland Turnbull will all be here then for that conference, so it will be easy for me to have a word with any or all of them, if you so wish.

However, I hope that the difficulties may be overcome in the meantime. I am sure that the Conference is intended to function in exactly the same way as it did when we started it a few years ago, and that its discussions are therefore not intended to prejudice in any way your and your Government's freedom either to adopt or to reject any suggestions made at the Conference. If action has been taken recently on one or two matters ahead of your being able to consult your State Council about them, I am sure that this is owing to a misunderstanding or a mistake, and that it will not recur. I therefore hope that the consideration which you are at present giving to the problem will result in your being able to attend the next meeting of the Conference, when I am sure that the question can be cleared up to your satisfaction. You are, of course, right in saying that Your Highness's and the Brunei Government's autonomy must be fully preserved.

As I said in our talk, I am glad that you have established such good relations with the leaders in Malaya. This will not only help Brunei as well as Malaya, but also spread good-neighbourliness amongst different Governments in this region. If I may say so, I do hope you will also maintain unimpaired similar friendly relations with your immediate neighbours, Sarawak and North Borneo. Since our talk I have heard that there might be a suggestion of the Brunei Government lending money to Sarawak and North Borneo on terms different from the terms arranged in Malaya's case. I venture to express a hope that Your Highness will not support this suggestion, and that your generous act of friendship will be similar in the cases of all the three countries whom you intend to help. Like other of your admirers, I look forward to seeing your influence increase steadily in this part of the world, and your fame as an enlightened Ruler and statesman grow. I believe that a helpful policy towards all your neighbours will greatly assist in achieving this.

You are always good enough to let me speak with the frankness of true friendship to you, and therefore I venture to write the above. As you know, I have your and your country's well-being very much at heart, and am always ready to do anything I can to help you. I prize Your Highness's and my friendship—which is now more than a dozen years old—very highly.

I greatly look forward to seeing you when you come to Delhi on your way back from your next visit to England. Mr. Nehru[1] will also be happy to meet you, but I can assure you that there will be no formality whatever attached to the visit. You will be my private guest at my house, and the programme will contain nothing that will not be congenial to you. It will be a light programme, and will include visits to the beautiful Taj Mahal and other places of Moghul and Muslim interest. My colleagues and I in Delhi will gladly take care of as many travelling companions as you like to bring with you.

I am writing to the headmaster of Bedales School in England about the admission of your four children and their four young friends to the school in September 1960.[2]

With renewed thanks for all your kindness and hospitality in Brunei, and with warm regards.

---

[1] Jawaharlal Nehru, prime minister of India, 1947–1964.

[2] Sultan Omar Ali Saifuddin was the first ruler of Brunei to have received a modern education. He had attended Malay College, Kuala Kangsar ('the Malay Eton') in the Malay state of Perak. MacDonald recommended his old school, Bedales, for the Sultan's sons. Bedales was a co-educational school in Hampshire. However, the crown prince and his brother were sent to Jalan Gurney School, Kuala Lumpur, to prepare for entry into Victoria Institution, KL, which they attended in 1961–1963. The crown prince then went to Sandhurst. Lord Chalfont, *By God's will: a portrait of the Sultan of Brunei*, London, 1989, pp 53–54.

---

7   DO 35/10019, no 12, E/3   22 Dec 1958
[Closer association of Malaya with Singapore and the Borneo territories]: note by M MacDonald of his talk with Tunku Abdul Rahman on 20 December

When I returned to Singapore from Brunei and Sarawak, I received a message from Tunku Abdul Rahman through a personal friend saying that if possible he would like to talk with me before I returned to India; so I flew to Kuala Lumpur on Saturday, December 20th and spent an hour-and-a-half with him.

2.   He said that this was a purely personal conversation. He had received a verbal message from the British Ambassador in the Philippines, through the Malayan Head of Protocol, who had just visited Manila, warning him that when he arrived in Manila in January either the Filipino authorities or the local pressmen, or both, would raise with him the question of the Philippines Government's claim to North Borneo.[1] The message indicated that they intended to ask him his opinion on the point. The Tunku then said to me that he also anticipated that at some future date the Indonesian

---

[1] The Philippines' claim to North Borneo originated in the 1878 agreement between the Sultan of Sulu and a British commercial syndicate. Indonesia was also demanding West Irian from Holland, and the Tunku's interest in federating with Singapore and the Borneo territories appears to arise from anxiety about the possible territorial ambitions of his neighbours, whereas in 1962–1963 such threats inhibited his enthusiasm for Malaysia. During his visit to Manila in Jan 1959 the Tunku agreed with President Garcia to forge a regional association for economic and cultural co-operation. In due course this would be known as the Association of Southeast Asia (ASA).

Government would make a claim to Sarawak and perhaps Brunei. He was anxious to say the right thing in Manila, and would like my views on this. He would also like to know my ideas about broader future policy concerning the British Borneo territories.

3. I replied that with regard to any possible Indonesian claim to Sarawak or Brunei, I had been gratuitously assured by Indonesian authorities in Djakarta in two or three informal conversations when I was Commissioner-General that they had no intention of making any such claim at any time. My own interpretation of this was that there was at any rate no likelihood of the Indonesians making any claim in the foreseeable future, but that this would not necessarily always remain the position. (The Tunku commented that he accepted this, but that he thought the Indonesians might some day try to subvert Malay and other opinion in Sarawak and Brunei in order to create a local opinion in favour of joining Indonesia.)

With regard to the Filipino claim to North Borneo, I said that this had been put forward periodically in recent years, and was a claim based on some Filipino notions of early ancient history. I added that H.M.G.'s advisers had always assured the Government that the claim had no proper legal basis, and could be resisted without qualification. We invariably adopted that attitude whenever the matter was mentioned. I said I would suggest to Sir Robert Scott on my return to Singapore that he should send the Tunku a brief on the subject, so that he was fully aware of all the facts before he went to Manila. I also suggested that the Tunku should discuss the matter with the Governor of North Borneo when he visits Jesselton in the course of his forthcoming travels.

4. The Tunku said he would be very grateful for a brief from Sir Robert, and that he would also be ready to seek the Governor's authoritative information on the subject in Jesselton. He then asked me again what were my ideas about the more distant future in British Borneo, saying that these would guide him if ever the matter were raised with him. He would not of course quote me or any other British authority, but would be assisted in his own thinking.

5. I answered that I was more than three years out-of-date on Borneo affairs, and that my views were therefore not authoritative or official; nevertheless I would speak to him personally and non-committally on the clear understanding that my remarks had no other significance. I then said that when I was Commissioner-General my British colleagues and I thought tentatively along the following lines:—

(a) Our first long-term task in all the three Borneo territories was to assist the gradual constitutional advance of the local peoples towards self-government in their internal affairs. Those peoples were politically backward and had no particular yearnings for self-government, and therefore this would be a long process.

(b) Ultimately the question of independence for the territories might arise. It seemed to us that the idea of three tiny independent states in British Borneo was rather impractical in the modern world, and therefore we contemplated as one possibility closer association—perhaps a federation—between the three countries. But this could only be if the local governments and peoples wished for such a development. We would not impose any policy against their wills, though if they liked the idea of federation we would in due course encourage and help them to achieve it. It was much too early to formulate precise ideas; indeed, a federation might never be a practical proposition, though we favoured it in principle.

(c) We also considered as a possibility a larger federation: i.e., if the Government of Malaya, the Government of Singapore and the Government of the three Borneo territories thought they would be individually and collectively stronger by joining in some sort of super-federation, this might be a beneficial development for them all. But again, this was looking far ahead, and would depend entirely on the wishes of the governments and peoples concerned. If they all wished to come politically closer together, the British authorities would no doubt give any proper assistance that they could. We had it in mind that this large federated group of lands in South-East Asia would remain a member of the Commonwealth.

6.   I reiterated that these were not only my personal ideas, but also wholly tentative and rather vague, and not necessarily realisable or wise in the circumstances of the future. Nor did I know whether the British Government still contemplated any or all of these possibilities, for circumstances and attitudes might have altered since I was officially concerned with South-East Asian affairs.

7.   The Tunku said he had been thinking of these problems recently, and that his thoughts had become more focused since the warning which he received of the question that might be put to him in Manila. His own ideas were very similar to mine. For one thing, he said, the conception of a larger federation of South-East Asian countries in the Commonwealth would help to settle decisively the problem of relations between the Federation of Malaya and Singapore. He and his Ministerial colleagues could not and would not consider a merger between Malaya and Singapore alone. Even if Singapore came in as an additional State in the Federation, the Malays could not regard with favour the idea of the Singapore Chinese reinforcing the Chinese in Malaya, with the effect of establishing, in due course, a Chinese political predominance. However, if the three Borneo territories could also come into the Federation, the non-Chinese populations in those territories would be a counter-weight to the Singapore Chinese. Such a plan would be acceptable to him. He said that he had not discussed the idea with anyone else, not even Dato Razak yet; but he himself had considered it, and liked it. He thought the Government of the Federation would be ready to contemplate in due course Singapore and the three Borneo territories all becoming units in the Federation.

8.   I said I did not think the proposal for the Borneo territories to become units in the Federation of Malaya would work. That was not my idea. There would be strong opposition to it in all the three Borneo territories. For example, the people of Sarawak were very jealous of their independent entity, and H.M.G. were pledged not to prejudice that. Again, the Brunei authorities would not agree to any plan which involved their wealth being put at the disposal of a central Federal Government in Kuala Lumpur, or anywhere else except Brunei. My conception was therefore rather different. I had thought that the Federation of Malaya, a possible Federation of the three Borneo territories, and Singapore either as a separate State or as part of the Federation of Malaya might all form what I called a 'Super-Federation'. They would have a common government for foreign policy, defence and certain co-operative services, but otherwise would each enjoy complete autonomy in their own internal affairs. I remarked that I agreed with his view that the non-Chinese peoples of the Borneo territories could be an effective counter-weight in such a Super-Federation to any predominance by the Chinese population. In my opinion the Dyaks of Sarawak, for example, would become during the next few decades a quite formidable political force, who would be ready to co-operate well with the Malay peoples in

preventing any undue Chinese domination. They would be ready to accept the Chinese as partners, but not as masters.

9.   I added that my views were not at all dogmatic; it might be that the peoples of the Borneo territories would oppose anything in the nature of a Super-Federation, and wish to remain a separate, independent group on their own. On the other hand someday something along the lines of the closer Federation which he envisaged might prove possible; though I did not think this would be practical politics at any time in the foreseeable future.

10.   The Tunku said that the idea of a Super-Federation was a new conception to him, and that it attracted him. He presumed that in such a set-up Brunei, for example, would be ready to contribute some of its wealth to the common defence, and that he personally would be entirely ready for Brunei and other units in the association to keep as much autonomy over other expenditures as they wished. One of his prime concerns was the defence of the whole area, and Malaya could of course give very effective defence aid to the Borneo territories in case of need.

11.   He observed that his immediate problem was what he should say in Manila, and added that from our conversation it looked as if he might say that the future destiny of the peoples of the three Borneo territories must remain their own choice, but that they were likely to choose eventually to come in with Malaya rather than with some other State. I answered that if he made any such statement it would do more harm than good. If such a pronouncement were published in Sarawak, North Borneo and Brunei, the peoples there might well react against it. They had scarcely begun to consider these long-term problems, being solely concerned at present with their internal economic and political development; and they would resent any suggestion from outside that they might wish to join Malaya.

12.   I added that I thought the Tunku should speak with Sir Robert Scott before he went to Manila. Sir Robert would know much better than I what official policy is, and what line he might properly take in Manila.

13.   The Tunku said he would gladly speak with Sir Robert. He added that he agreed he should not say in Manila what he had just suggested. He thought he might confine himself to saying that the future destiny of the Borneo peoples was entirely a matter for them to decide when the time came—and leave it at that.

14.   I reiterated that he should discuss the matter with Sir Robert Scott before he considered it any further. I also suggested that he might like to ask the Governors of Sarawak and North Borneo what were the ideas of the peoples of their territories on these questions when he met them in Kuching and Jesselton. He replied that he thought he should not talk with the Governors about these matters, but that he would like to discuss them with Sir Robert Scott or (if he could not come to Kuala Lumpur in the near future) with Mr. Angus MacKintosh.[2] I promised to report this to Mr. MacKintosh, in Sir Robert's absence, on my return to Singapore. The Tunku said that I could tell him that he would be ready to see Sir Robert or him at any mutually convenient time in Kuala Lumpur after December 28th.

15.   I remarked that he had told me that he had not yet broached these problems with Dato Razak. Might I suggest that he should not do so at present? It would be better in my view if, following his and my talk, the matter were kept between him, Sir Robert Scott and Mr. MacKintosh. The broad ideas that we had considered could not

---

[2] Deputy commissioner-general, SE Asia, 1956–1960.

be implemented until the rather distant future, if at all; and there was no hurry to start anything but a tentative and even academic consideration of them.

16.   He said he had intended to talk to Dato Razak soon after his talk with me, and that there was a particular reason why he should do so. This is that he intends to take 'a long holiday' after his return from the Philippines, and to hand the conduct of the Government over to Dato Razak for several months. He will not in fact spend his time holidaying, but preparing for the General Elections next year. (I shall dictate a separate note[3] on his plans about this, which might even involve his resigning the Prime Ministership and making Razak Prime Minister in his place at least until after the Elections.) For this reason he thought he must tell Razak of his ideas about Borneo in relation to what might come up in talks in Manila. I repeated that these matters were very tentative and long-term, and that there was nothing that Razak or anybody else need do about them in the near future. The Tunku agreed with this in general, but thought that one or two particular practical matters might arise which could only be settled the right way if those concerned had the longer view of the possible future. I think he will talk with Dato Razak quite soon.

17.   He then said that he understood that the Sultan of Brunei would go to London in March for discussions about a new Constitution for Brunei. He wondered whether it might be useful to H.M.G. for the Federation Government to be represented in that conference, either by a member of the conference or by an observer, as had been the case in the similar discussions about the Singapore Constitution. He said that he only put forward this suggestion to be helpful. I could assure the British authorities that his Government would be willing to assist in any way they properly could regarding developments in the Borneo territories, especially on the defence side.

18.   I said I would report what he had said to Sir Robert Scott and that the Tunku should discuss it with him in the first instance before taking the matter any further.

19.   I then said I was glad that the Sultan of Brunei had established friendly relations with Malaya, but that I personally was concerned lest the Sultan developed closer relations with Malaya at the expense of closer relations with Sarawak and North Borneo. The first need in British Borneo was that the three territories should cultivate the most co-operative neighbourly relations. I hoped that if the Tunku had any opportunity to express to the Sultan the view that he should have at least as good relations with Sarawak and North Borneo as he had with Malaya, he would do so. The Tunku replied that, he wholly agreed with me. He had been impressed with what he saw of development works in Brunei during his recent visit, but wondered whether the Brunei Malays would really be able to take advantage of them. He felt that they were being too much 'pampered', and that instead of strengthening their characters their wealth might weaken them.

20.   The Tunku had met me at the airport on my arrival and insisted on seeing me off at the airport when I left, though I urged that he should not bother to do so. As we drove to the airfield I said that if any newspapers reporters had noted my visit to Kuala Lumpur and asked me questions about it, I would tell them I had come to discuss with him questions concerning the new constitution of the University of Malaya.[4] He laughed and remarked that this would be very prudent. Five minutes later a reporter from the Straits Times accosted us in the V.I.P. room at the airport and asked what was the significance of our meeting. The Tunku smiled blandly and

---

[3] See 8.   [4] MacDonald was chancellor of the University of Malaya, 1949–1961.

replied 'We have spent an hour talking about the new constitution of the University of Malaya'. This fiction was duly reported in the newspapers the next morning.

8   DO 35/10019, no 12, E/4   24 Dec 1958
[Malayan politics]: second note by M MacDonald of his talk with Tunku Abdul Rahman on 20 December about preparations for elections in 1959

1.   As I have mentioned in paragraph 16 of my other Note on my talk with Tunku Abdul Rahman on December 20th,[1] he spoke to me about his plan to take 'a long holiday' soon after his return from the Philippines next month. He said that he is very overworked and tired; he has to spend a lot of time dealing with the tasks of the leader of the Government in Kuala Lumpur and doing all sorts of courtesy duties with visitors and others there, and at the same time must tour the country, keeping in touch with the voters. He finds that he does not get enough time for all this work; and that it is becoming increasingly essential that he personally should spend more time in the constituencies preparing for the General Elections next year. Therefore, he has decided to take the 'long holiday'.

2.   In fact it will not be a holiday at all. He will devote months to travelling throughout the Federation preparing for the Elections. His primary task will not be to organise support amongst the voters, for that already exists in goodly measure. His chief concern—and the chief reason for his rather drastic decision—will be to persuade a number of constituencies dominated by Malay voters to choose Chinese or Indian candidates to champion the Alliance's cause. This has become a serious problem. At the last Elections he took great trouble to induce various constituency branches of UMNO to adopt Chinese candidates, who were subsequently elected.[2] Many of those Chinese have since 'let him and the M.C.A. down badly.' Some had not even visited their constituencies since, and their Malay supporters are thoroughly disgruntled. The Tunku feels it imperative to have proper representation of the Chinese and the Indians, and he will therefore study the position in all the constituencies to see which will be the best for the adoption of Chinese and Indian candidates next year. He will have to examine carefully various local situations, and do a lot of arguing and persuading with UMNO organisations. This job will take several months; hence his decision to abandon his duties as leader of the Government in Kuala Lumpur during that period. He will put Dato Razak in charge of affairs. He told me that he had not yet discussed the matter fully with Razak, but that he would do so in the next few days.

3.   I asked whether this meant that he would cease to be Prime Minister. He replied that he had not absolutely settled this yet, and would not do so until he had talked with Razak; but he thought that he would at least temporarily resign the Premiership. In any case he would take his 'holiday' without pay. Assuming that the Alliance won the Elections, he would probably become Prime Minister again afterwards.

---

[1] See 7.
[2] At the time of the first federal elections in July 1955 the Malays accounted for 84 per cent of the electorate (out of all proportion to their share of the total population) and some UMNO branches were persuaded to adopt non-Malay candidates in order to demonstrate the Alliance's multi-racialism. See *BDEE: Malaya*, 360, 361 and 362.

4.   I asked him when the Elections would be. He answered that no date had yet been settled, but that it would probably be at the beginning of August or even the end of July. He was anxious to get the Elections over as soon as possible. He would not be able to fix a date until he had been in the constituencies for a month or two and studied the situation. He would then let Razak know what date would be most convenient from the Government's point of view, and Razak would announce that date.[3]

---

[3] The Tunku's UMNO suffered setbacks in the east-coast states and the Alliance's majority was reduced in the 1959 federal elections, see 71, n 3.

9   CO 1030/658, no E13   3 Jan 1959
[Political situation in Brunei]: letter from D C White to Sir A Abell reporting on his first six months as British resident

I have now been about six months in Brunei, and it might be of some value if I record my impressions on the political situation as it exists today.

Party Ra'ayat
When I was here in 1956, the Party Ra'ayat was probably at its peak; subscriptions were pouring in, meetings were well attended, and it would not have needed a very large spark to have caused an explosion.[1] There was, I should say, a good deal more anti-British sentiment than there is now. The Party today is in the doldrums; easy money is unobtainable and even keen supporters are no longer gullible enough to provide further funds for the pleasure of a handful of Party leaders. Azahari is almost all the time in Singapore running his Press—it is hard to see where he got the money for it, except by a manipulation of funds from Brunei, and all his interests here are now more or less insolvent.[2]

---

[1] Founded by A M Azahari in Jan and registered in Aug 1956, Party Rakyat (or Ra'ayat) Brunei was modelled on Party Rakyat Malaya, led by Ahmad Boestamam, whom Azahari had met in Malaya in 1955. Attracting considerable Malay support, especially from teachers, PRB held its first congress in Apr 1957. While it opposed colonialism and favoured the democratisation of government, it advocated constitutional methods and was not openly hostile to the position of the sultan. Aspiring to the restoration of Brunei's lost territories through merger with North Borneo and Sarawak ('Kalimantan Utara' or north Kalimantan) and ultimately the creation of 'Melayu raya' (the unity of all Malays), the PRB rejected Anglo-Malayan proposals for Brunei's incorporation within Malaysia.
[2] Sheikh A M Azahari bin Sheikh Mahmoud was born in 1928. His father was of Arab descent and his mother was a Brunei Malay. During the Japanese occupation he was sent to study veterinary science in Indonesia where he later joined the republicans in their struggle against the restoration of Dutch rule. He returned to Brunei in 1952 and organised a party inspired by Indonesian nationalism but was jailed for six months on account of unlawful assembly. After his release and a further period abroad, he came back to Brunei and was involved in a number of unsuccessful business ventures. In Jan 1956 he founded the Party Rakyat Brunei. As a member of Brunei's Legislative Council, in Apr 1962 he failed to secure the passage of a motion seeking to restore Brunei's sovereignty over northern Borneo. He was in Manila at the outbreak of the Brunei revolt in Dec 1962 and it was from there that he proclaimed the 'Unitary State of North Kalimantan', embracing Brunei, North Borneo and Sarawak. On the failure of the revolt he took refuge in the Indonesian embassy in Manila and later moved to Indonesia. In an assessment dated Sep 1961, Dennis White commented: 'His two main personal troubles are money and women; he always has too little of the former and too many of the latter. As Nationalist leaders go, he is now moderate and far from unpleasant to deal with.' See CO 1030/1075, no 620.

Salleh[3] and his clique are now merely strong-arm racketeers. Efforts are being made to whip up more enthusiasm, but cash is not forthcoming. The danger potential lies more in the criminal rather than the political sphere, as there are large numbers (for Brunei) of young men of low educational standards for whom jobs cannot be found, and who might well join Salleh in his activities.

The Sultan

The Sultan himself has matured. In 1956 he was still very much inclined to lean on his British Resident and Gilbert's stock was high.[4] I do not know what caused the deterioration in their relationship, but it is clear that the Sultan encouraged certain Members of State Council to bait the Resident and oppose all his projects, in an attempt, I assume, to get him removed.

As you foretold, my arrival was regarded as a local victory and an unnatural honeymoon has resulted, but on a limited scale! The vociferous Members of State Council have no doubts about their own abilities and have an inflated sense of their own importance. They take a fiendish delight in digging up anything they can find which may further discredit my predecessor.

The Sultan's own views are not easy to assess. He has been lauded to the skies, acclaimed as a gifted and wise Ruler with modern ideas, wooed by Malaya (with excellent results for Malaya), and it is hardly surprising if he is now suffering from 'folie de grandeur'.

Sarawak

The Sultan's hostility to Sarawak is not difficult to assess. In his view, Brunei has become subordinate to what was once a province of his ancestors and which was, to the extent that tribute was paid, still in theory subordinate to him when under the Brookes.[5] This explains his attitude over the outright purchase of Cession Monies.

He is encouraged in his attitude by many of his advisers, not all on State Council, who genuinely think that independence will be accelerated if the connection with a Crown Colony can be broken. I do not think there is anything altruistic in their views. As an independent State, Brunei would be a gold mine for the chosen few and the 'protection' of Malaya, a good deal further away than Sarawak, would leave them more or less unfettered in their handling of Brunei's internal affairs. They do not

---

[3] Salleh bin Masri was deputy president of Party Rakyat Brunei but more militant and confrontational than Azahari.
[4] J O Gilbert, of the Sarawak Civil Service, succeeded J H Barcroft as resident in 1953. In 1958 Abell replaced Gilbert with White in an attempt to break the stalemate in Anglo-Bruneian negotiations over the proposed constitution.
[5] Resentment of Sarawak derived from past territorial losses and current administrative subordination. Rajah Charles Brooke's annexation of Limbang in 1890 had split Brunei into two enclaves and had been made the more galling by the fact that the British government, in allowing the annexation, appeared to have neglected its obligations under the Anglo-Brunei treaty of 1888. Furthermore, in 1948 the administration of Brunei had been attached, if not subordinated, to Sarawak whose governor became high commissioner of Brunei. The British resident of Brunei reported to the governor of Sarawak and Sarawak officers were seconded to the Brunei administration. On the introduction of the Brunei constitution in 1959, the governor of Sarawak ceased to be high commissioner for Brunei and White took over as high commissioner.

seem to realise that Malaya is primarily interested in their money and that a federation with Malaya might well mean an inrush of Malayan Chinese, to the detriment of their own policy of Brunei for the Bruneis.

From what is known of the political aspirations of the Party Ra'ayat, their attitude towards Sarawak and North Borneo is considerably more liberal and realistic, and they apparently would be willing to share most of their revenue. Cynically, it could be observed that they have next to no chance of furthering their own financial interests with independence, whereas the local nobility have every hope and indeed a very good chance of being able to do so.

Constitution

It is not easy to form an appreciation of the Sultan's real feelings over a Constitution. It is a Western concept which he was persuaded to accept and, unless he can so manipulate negotiations that any failure to implement a Constitution can be blamed on the British Government, he is committed to granting one. He is being put under heavy pressure by certain Members of State Council, particularly Chegu Marsal, and to a lesser extent by Pengiran Ali and Pengiran Yusof, and also by a Nationalist element among the Brunei Malay Teachers' Association. Marsal, Ali and Yusof may well have aspirations for advancement, and Yusof is regarded in some quarters as a possible Mentri Besar; though the Sultan's reluctance to mention his choice of Mentri Besar perhaps indicates that he intends to look to Malaya for his man.[6]

The Party Ra'ayat's attitude to the Constitution is considerably more democratic than anyone else in Brunei. They want popular franchise and an elected Government, and would at once deal with the local nobility, though they would retain the Sultan as a Constitutional Head of the State.

The Sultan's continued support of the local nobility and his undercover counter-attack on the Party Ra'ayat (which has been highly successful) will undoubtedly do

---

[6] Brunei's first mentri besar (chief minister) under the 1959 constitution was the Sultan's private secretary, Dato Peduka Haji Ibrahim bin Jafar, who originated from Labuan and had previously served as secretary to the British resident. The Tunku proposed his own private secretary, Wan Ahmed bin Wan Omar, and Ali bin Hassan for the posts of state secretary and attorney-general respectively and both were appointed, despite British misgivings that Wan Ahmed was of 'very limited ability'. In addition, the Tunku offered some forty school-teachers as well as ten Malays for so called 'key posts', including Dr Wan Ahmed (state medical officer) and Mohd Yakim bin Haji Long (state forestry officer). After a year White was reporting a gathering tension in Brunei's administration which reached a crisis in mid-1961: His Highness was acting arbitrarily; the mentri besar was powerless and medically unfit; Malayan officers were unhappy in their posts and resented by Bruneians; the British high commissioner was constitutionally prevented from intervening. In Apr 1961 it was reported that the medical service was about to collapse on account of the incompetence of the state medical officer. Then, in June 1961 Mohd Yakim bin Haji Long (state forestry officer) was assaulted by some Bruneians. This incident provoked, firstly, the seconded officers to demand repatriation to Malaya and, secondly, clumsy intervention from the Tunku. The crisis led to changes of personnel: Haji Ibrahim took sick leave prior to retirement and was succeeded as mentri besar by Marsal bin Maun; Wan Ahmed bin Wan Omar was replaced as acting state secretary by Haji Mohamed Yussof; Dato Abdul Aziz bin Haji Mahomed Zain took over from Ali bin Hassan as attorney-general. The new mentri besar, Marsal bin Maun, had once been close to the PRB but his rapid rise within the 'palace party' ended their association. Dato Abdul Aziz, like his predecessor as attorney-general, was seconded from the federation and, having been selected by the Tunku to supervise the constitutional issues connected with Brunei's prospective membership of Malaysia, he was regarded in some quarters as 'the Tunku's spy'. See CO 1030/529, 533 and 1147; see also documents 52 n 4, 91 and 93.

him and his family harm in the long run. There is already a good deal of discontent amongst the peasantry at the rapacity of some of the Pengirans.[7]

Conclusions
The proposed Constitution will, undoubtedly, help to clip the wings of the local nobility, and an elected element could well introduce a more reasonable attitude in the Legislative Council towards Sarawak and North Borneo, but the danger to relationship with these territories is acute, both here and in Sarawak, where the loan interest rate could well spark off a strong anti-Brunei campaign. It is neither politically desirable nor practical to arrest the pro-Malayan swing and, with Singapore's future uncertain, to say the least of it, probably all three territories would be wise to look to Malaya for help. I feel, therefore, that it is expedient to let the Sultan know as soon as possible that Sarawak would not be averse to relief from the thankless task of trying to staff Brunei, who would then have to face the realities of the staff position, instead of needling Sarawak, but falling back on them for help when they need it.

---

[7] Aristocrats of Brunei.

---

10   DO 35/10019, no 17   [16 Jan] 1959
'Future of the British Borneo territories': CRO brief for Lord Home's visit to the Federation of Malaya

The Tunku has apparently been giving a good deal of thought recently to the future of the British Borneo Territories (North Borneo, Sarawak and Brunei) and their possible association with the Federation. The Tunku discussed this subject with Mr. Malcolm Macdonald [sic] in Kuala Lumpur on 20th December (a copy of Mr. Macdonald's record of and note on the discussion is attached),[1] and he has recently paid flying visits to North Borneo and Sarawak en route to and from the Philippines. The Tunku is, of course, a close friend of the Sultan of Brunei and has recently negotiated a loan of 100 million Malayan dollars from the Sultan on most generous terms.

2.   Since returning from Brunei the Tunku has told Sir G. Tory that he feels that the question of the association of Borneo with the Federation of Malaya may be precipitated within the next few years by claims from either the Philippines or Indonesia or both for one Territory or another, and he hopes that, if this happens, the Territories would indicate that they wished, when politically more advanced, to be free to decide on the question of an association with Malaya. This seems to the Tunku to be a more attractive solution than any alternative. The Tunku realises, however, that the process of bringing the Borneo Territories to political maturity is likely to take from ten to twenty years and that the question of an association with the Federation is a very long term prospect.

3.   The Tunku's thinking may have been stimulated by the idea of a 'super Federation' comprising the Federation and the Borneo Territories, thrown out by Mr. Malcolm Macdonald (paragraphs 5(c) and 8 of Mr. Macdonald's note refer). This suggestion has caused surprise in the Colonial Office because Her Majesty's Government has not given serious consideration to the idea.

---

[1] See 7 and 8.

4.   The possibilities of closer association of the three Borneo Territories have, however, been canvassed for some years. People of the Borneo Territories are backward and there is no intention of hurrying them into a political union. In 1957, however, it was felt that the time had come for Her Majesty's Government to take the initiative and encourage local discussion of proposals for closer association, and in Sarawak and North Borneo there is a desire to explore possibilities further. The Sultan of Brunei has, however, steadfastly refused to join in any discussion on closer association and the Secretary of State for the Colonies feels that for the present it would not be right to press the matter further against his will, although the Colonial Office considers that an association restricted to North Borneo and Sarawak would not be in the best interests of either Brunei or the other Territories.

5.   It is suggested that the Secretary of State should be non-committal if the Tunku raises the subject of future Malaya/Borneo relations. He might point out that the peoples of the Borneo Territories are still politically backward and that it is too early to formulate precise ideas as to their future. These are matters to be decided in the light of the wishes of the Borneo Governments and their peoples.

6.   Paragraph 17 of Mr. Macdonald's record mentioned that the Tunku suggested that it might be helpful to the United Kingdom if the Federation were represented at forthcoming constitutional discussions between the Sultan of Brunei and the Secretary of State for the Colonies in London. The presence of a Malayan representative at these talks would almost certainly give rise to embarrassing speculation, and Sir G. Tory[2] was instructed to ensure that the Tunku did not pursue this idea. Sir G. Tory has reported that the Tunku has accepted our point, apparently with some relief. Sir G. Tory has, however, told the Tunku that we should like to call on his assistance if this seemed desirable during the talks.

---

[2] Sir Geofroy Tory, Britain's high commissioner to independent Malaya, 1957–1963.

11   DO 35/10019, no 21   29 Jan 1959
[The future of the Borneo territories]: letter from Sir R Scott to Mr Lennox-Boyd

[The commissioner-general recognised the benefits of a non-military pact between Malaya, Indonesia and the Philippines, on the one hand, and, on the other, a union of Malaya, Singapore and the Borneo territories. But he argued that the Tunku's exuberant pursuit of both objectives would be counter-productive and that a rushed attempt to incorporate North Borneo and Sarawak within the Federation would antagonise their non-Malay majorities. Commenting on Scott's recommendation that the British continue to work steadily towards the development and closer association of the Borneo territories, the high commissioner in Kuala Lumpur pointed out that the emergence of what looked like a Malaya-Brunei axis was alienating North Borneo and Sarawak, see 14.]

This letter is about the future of the Borneo Territories and is written in the light of some general discussion of the subject during the recent Eden Hall Conference,[1] and

---

[1] Each year, usually in Jan, the commissioner-general held a conference on regional affairs at Eden Hall, his residence in Singapore. It was attended by heads of mission, governors and high commissioners as well as by representatives from Australia and New Zealand and usually by a minister from London.

tailed talk which I had in Kuching last week with Sir Anthony Abell and ..Uiand Turnbull.

2.   These talks were to some extent stimulated by the ideas recently canvassed in public by Tunku Abdul Rahman for some new form of non-military association between the countries of South-East Asia, and by the suggestion which he made privately to Mr. Malcolm MacDonald last month that the Federation of Malaya, Singapore and the Borneo Territories might enter into a political union of some kind.[2] Although these two propositions are no doubt linked—at least, in the Tunku's mind—our interest lies in keeping them separate: indeed, we should discreetly encourage exploration of the former not only because it merits cautious encouragement but also because we may by that means hope to discourage the latter, which at this stage offers no advantage and considerable disadvantage to the Borneo Territories.

3.   The Tunku's motives in using his visit to the Philippines to launch an appeal for a cultural and economic pact between the independent nations of South-East Asia are clearly mixed. Among them are fear of Communist China and suspicion of all overseas Chinese, a consequent desire to align and combine the influences of the Muslim religion and the Malaysian racial group, dislike of the Afro–Asian bloc as such, and the hope, particularly in an election year of cutting a dash in the international arena. Whether he will in fact get very far with this idea in its present form is doubtful, since it has had on the whole a poor reception in Indonesia and does not seem to have evoked much enthusiasm in the Philippines who have been toying with somewhat similar concepts for some time but for quite different motives. Determined to remain a Christian country, there are few developments the Filipinos fear more than an extension of Moslem influence in their direction. Nor are they greatly flattered to be reminded of their Malay racial origins. Nevertheless, the idea of a regional association appeals in principle to them, and indeed they are inclined to wonder how the Tunku has managed to gain credit for an initiative which they imagined was their own. In recent years they have begun to meet their neighbours and to find that they apparently have quite a lot in common—fear of China, chafing at Western assumptions of superiority, sharing many of the social and economic problems of the Philippines and the same administrative weaknesses. In their current anti-American mood the Filipinos, by nature 'joiners' and always ready to take part in any international gathering, are particularly attracted by the idea of a group which will exclude the United States.

4.   At present it looks as though the outcome would at most be a series of bilateral agreements between Malaya and a few other South-East Asian countries. Nevertheless, the Tunku has committed himself pretty deeply to the pursuit of a multilateral agreement and, as I have said, we should in my view give him such support as we safely can, not merely in the interests of relations with Malaya but also because the interests of the free world might well be served by the establishment in South-East Asia of a loose association (without overt Western participation) of independent countries sharing a resolute open aversion from Communism, a watchful but not actively hostile attitude towards the overseas Chinese and

---

[2] The idea of a non-military association stemmed the Tunku's meeting with Garcia (see 7, n 1); for the Tunku's meeting with MacDonald, see 7 and 8.

combining sturdy, even assertive, independence with readiness to co-operate with the West.

5. The Tunku made clear to Mr. MacDonald that his main reason for seeking to incorporate the Borneo Territories in the Federation of Malaya or, failing that, to enter into a federal union with them as a whole, is due mainly to a feeling that the indigenous races and the Malays living in those territories would be an accretion of strength, tipping the racial balance against the Chinese, which might provide a safeguard sufficient to justify the risk of accepting the incorporation of Singapore. No doubt the Tunku is aware also of the relative stability and prosperity of Sarawak and North Borneo, and the oil revenues of Brunei must appear a prize worth much effort to acquire. From the Tunku's point of view this is a natural and sensible line of thought, but it does not suit the present position and interests of the Borneo Territories and it is therefore satisfactory that Sir Anthony Abell and Sir Roland Turnbull appear, for the time being at least, to have persuaded the Tunku that it would not serve even his own purposes to give any immediate, open indication of his aims. I would not by any means rule out the possibility that a union of Malaya, Singapore and the Borneo Territories might at some future date prove advantageous to them all as well as to Britain and the free world, but the Borneo Territories must first both approach much more closely than today to the stage of general development of the others and must also first have determined their relations with each other.

6. Fortunately, neither of the Tunku's two propositions has any substantial appeal to Sarawak and North Borneo today. Both Governors are satisfied that, apart from the Malay communities, the peoples of both territories would react strongly against any suggestion that they should now accept a commitment, however remote and tentative, to future political association with Malaya (and possibly Singapore) or anywhere else. In their view the peoples of the two Colonies recognise clearly that they are as yet in no position to make up their minds on so fundamental an issue, that it will be many years before they reach a degree of political maturity that will enable them to judge it for themselves or justify their being asked to make such a judgement, that they have no desire to force the pace, and that meanwhile they are anxious to continue to enjoy all the help that Britain can give them in prosecuting their political, economic and social development at a rate commensurate with their resources. This attitude is sound and we should do all that we can to encourage it and to preserve the safeguards necessary to maintain it. It may be that as has happened elsewhere the forces of local nationalism will develop faster than we all should like, and that politicians will arise in Sarawak and North Borneo demanding independence before either territory is anywhere near ready for it or their peoples as a whole really want it. But there is so far no sign of this and on present evidence we have a good chance of preventing it if we keep our policies imaginative and flexible, promoting the growth of informed, reasonable public opinion and leading it.

7. Nor is there any general attraction for Sarawak and North Borneo in a racial appeal directed to the Malay communities. It is true that in Sarawak the Malay community amounts to about a third of the population; and to it, of course, such an appeal would undoubtedly be attractive as the position of the Malays has much weakened since the days of the Brooke Rajahs and they are conscious that they have already been outstripped by the Chinese and that the Dyaks will rapidly catch up with

them in the years to come.[3] But these very considerations are bound to strengthen the aversion of the other two-thirds of the population to any political appeal which seemed likely to lead to revival of a Malay hegemony. Such an appeal could therefore have only a disruptive effect in Sarawak and could not command general acceptance. In North Borneo the Malay community is negligible in numbers and influence: there an external appeal to Malay nationalism would be rejected with little or no discussion, although it would disturb the Philippines (which is anxious that North Borneo should develop preferably as a Christian and above all not as a Muslim country) and might produce repercussions in Brunei and Indonesia.

8.   The situation in Brunei is different on both scores. It is an entirely Malay State led by a Sultan devoted to the Muslim Faith and, together with his closest associates, anxious to keep his rich country so far as possible free from non-Malay influence, even if this costs him progress in the social and political fields. It might therefore be expected that the eyes of Brunei should turn with much more favour than those of Sarawak or North Borneo to the possibility of some form of political association with Malaya, and we know that the Sultan at least has of late been looking in that direction. There is, however, reason to believe that by no means all his people share his view and in any case the practical obstacles in the way of an agreement acceptable both to the Sultan of Brunei and to the Government and Council of Rulers in Malaya are so formidable that political association of the two countries cannot be regarded as likely in the near future.

9.   It is not only to the Malays that appeals from outside might be made. There is already some evidence that Chinese leaders in Singapore are ready to work on the Chinese communities in Sarawak and North Borneo. To the extent that their overtures evoked any response at all, the effect would be disruptive and harmful to racial unity.

10.   All this adds up to the need of the Borneo Territories for protection against external influences likely to breed communal tensions and to impede orderly progress. This does not, of course, mean that the territories should be cut off from outside influence of the right kind. To mention only two institutions, the Commonwealth Parliamentary Association[4] and the Colonial Development and Welfare Funds have made notable contributions.[5] But it does mean that at present the principal desideratum for the three territories is that they should look inwards upon themselves and concentrate upon their own internal development and the improvement of relations between them. Sarawak and North Borneo are still encouragingly free from racial conflict and Communist subversion, economically sound and promising for the future, demonstrably capable of a sober approach to political evolution. There seems no reason why, with sustained British guidance and support, they should not maintain a steady rate of progress unimpeded by major

---

[3] Sarawak was ceded in stages to the Brookes, rajahs of Sarawak from 1841 to 1946 (discounting the Japanese occupation); Rajah Charles Vyner ceded the country to the British crown in 1946. For population figures, see 73 appendix B.

[4] While commissioner-general, MacDonald had used the Commonwealth Parliamentary Association as a forum to foster inter-territorial co-operation and it was at its regional conference in Singapore in July 1961 that the Malaysia Solidarity Consultative Committee was set up.

[5] From 1947 to 1964 Colonial Development and Welfare funding provided 19 per cent of Sarawak's capital programme and in the early post-war years most of its development was funded in this way.

upheavals. In Brunei, too, the ground is not fertile either for racialism or for Communist subversion, but the Sultan comes of a notoriously unstable line and has of late been behaving erratically and obstinately. The average Brunei Malay is an indifferent character and revolutionary possibilities already lurk in the wide gulf between the Sultan and his immediate advisers and supporters on the one hand and the mass of the people on the other. Despite the wealth of the State it is still extremely backward and badly needs the moral, administrative and other assistance from its neighbours from which it is at present turning away.

11.   British policy towards the Borneo Territories rests upon four pillars which we should strive to strengthen.

12.   The first is that Britain should make it clear to the Borneo peoples and to the outside world that there is no intention of withdrawing. The more that we can induce the Borneo peoples openly to declare their need and desire for our continued support, the more likely it will be that that support can go on being given so long as the need lasts. This is in the interests not only of the Borneo Territories but also of ourselves and the Commonwealth and the free world, for it is increasingly clear that in the contexts both of Defence and of Commonwealth policy the Borneo Territories have an important role to play.

13.   The second is a steady process of internal development in all fields—economic development, chiefly agricultural, social development with the main emphasis upon education and especially the teaching of English, political development through the creation and extension of local government institutions at a pace and on a scale matching the desires and capacities of the people.

14.   The third pillar is recognition of the vital necessity of achieving an amicable and stable settlement of our relations with Brunei and of hers with her neighbours. Here the first step is agreement upon a constitution for the State and its complete separation from Sarawak under a High Commissioner directly responsible to you, Sir. The talks to be held in London in March will be crucial. It is reasonable to hope that the introduction of a constitution providing the foundations for democratic progress in what has hitherto been essentially an autocratic State will stimulate the normal process of social, economic and political development in which Brunei is today so far behind Sarawak and North Borneo. The attainment of a constitutional settlement should also be considerably facilitated by agreement—which, I understand, you, Sir, have already accepted in principle—to separate Brunei entirely from Sarawak. I need not repeat or elaborate the reasons for this, as they have already been fully set before you, but I reiterate my conviction that this step is essential to satisfactory further progress both internally in Brunei and externally in her relations with Britain and with her neighbours.

15.   Moreover, a settlement with Brunei on these lines should in due course buttress the fourth pillar of British policy, our plans for closer association between the three Borneo Territories. Once more, it is unnecessary for me to recapitulate the arguments already submitted to you at length and in detail for the desirability of closer association. I would say now only that the future holds great promise for the Borneo Territories in conjunction and danger if they fail to unite.

16.   I agree entirely with you, Sir, and with Sir Anthony Abell and Sir Roland Turnbull that no pressure should be put upon the Sultan to drive him in the direction of closer association, but I also think that he should be kept aware how desirable it seems in our eyes and that everything possible should be done to induce

him of his own accord to modify his opposition to it. Once he ceases to feel himself tied in a semi-subordinate position to the apron-strings of Sarawak, I believe there to be a chance that he will adopt a more relaxed and [less] intransigent posture in this context as in others.

17.   Meanwhile, Sarawak and North Borneo should quietly proceed to examine the practical implications of closer association and to formulate considered judgement upon them and upon the concept in principle. In so doing they should continue to take account of Brunei without either literally or figuratively trespassing upon Brunei ground. It is to be hoped that as they do so they will adhere to the view that the participation of Brunei in any form of closer association in British Borneo is at least highly desirable, but I would not regard it as a serious matter if they more and more came to think that union between the two territories would be worth while even if Brunei resolutely refused to join them, and I see no reason to believe that this need necessarily exclude the adhesion of Brunei at a later date, since this development, if it is to take place at all, will (and should) be of slow growth. I foresee, for instance, that the proposed joint mission of representatives of Sarawak and North Borneo which is to visit both territories to test public sentiment on the question of closer association will do the job with very deliberate speed over many months.

18.   I am copying this letter to Sir Anthony Abell and Sir Roland Turnbull.

12   DO 35/10019, no 23   7 March 1959
[Future of North Borneo]: letter from Sir R Turnbull to E Melville on the eve of his departure as governor

When Wallace was here he suggested that I might with advantage tell you rather more of what I saw for the future of this country, and I admitted the soft impeachment. It would seem that Rob Scott has very largely done the job for me in his secret letter of the 29th January to the Secretary of State,[1] with none of the contents of which I would differ except perhaps in matters of minor emphasis.

2.   It may help to record the advantages that this country possesses:—

(i) it is peaceful;

(ii) race relations are good: this is in part a bequest from the Chartered Company,[2] but it is also the consequence of current policies consciously and conscientiously pursued, though without suggestion of complacency. The cultures, the economic and educational standards and, indeed, the ambitions of the Chinese and the indigenous peoples differ so widely that there is always the possibility of strife, but we have the inestimable advantage that racial differences are not here exacerbated by the existence of exclusive religions (as, for instance, Islam in Malaya);

(iii) the overall standards of living are, in the Asian context, good. There are no very rich people, but there is no urban poverty and, except in pockets that can be eliminated, remarkably little rural poverty. It is a country of the middle class.

---

[1] See 11.

[2] Under a charter granted by the British government in 1881, the British North Borneo Company governed the country until it fell to the Japanese in January 1942. In July 1946 North Borneo became a crown colony.

Again by Asian standards, the country and its population are relatively healthy. Much of its soil is very fertile, certainly a great deal more so than has been believed in the past, so that the agricultural potential is great and is in fact in process of realization;

(iv) the discovery of oil is more a probability than a possibility.

3. Against all this must be set one fact, that a country capable of providing a livelihood for millions is populated by less than half a million. There are other relatively vacant spaces in South-East Asia, but none, I think, with the attractions of this country. India, Hong Kong, Singapore, Malaya, the Philippines and Indonesia have all, in recent years, shown interest in North Borneo as a depository for their surplus population. I have written of this elsewhere at length; here it is sufficient to say that I believe, firstly, that if we fail to people the country H.M.G. will in the foreseeable future be subject to many pressures and, secondly, that if such embarrassment is to be avoided we must add to the population people of our own selection who are reasonably acceptable to those already in the country, and that we must pursue its economic development to that end.

4. You will ask what there is for H.M.G. in such an apparently eleemosynary[3] policy. The answer, apart from the long-term economic prospects, which are considerable, lies in defence. I have been beating this drum to little effect for a long time, and I have no wish to arouse any perturbation by exaggerating the interest recently displayed by the defence authorities, but I have no doubt that ultimately it will be Borneo that will prove to be the meeting place of British, American and Australian strategic interests in South-East Asia, and that our influence here will be recognised as vital to the maintenance of British interests in Asia if, as I presume, it is indeed the intention of H.M.G. to remain a power in this part of the world.

5. The corollary is significant. It is that, in her own interest and those of the people of this country, H.M.G. must be prepared to tolerate the stigma of 'colonialism' for many years by their retention of this, or these, countries amidst a welter of independence, some of it less than edifying.

6. Scott is quite right in saying that the Borneo peoples should openly declare themselves in support of the connexion. There will be no difficulty in North Borneo, and I have long had it in mind to secure, before I go, an even more overt and unequivocal declaration than has as yet been given of the local desire for our continued partnership.

7. Despite all that we say about race relations, the indigenous peoples are nervous of the fate that would be theirs, in our absence, at the hands of the Chinese. The Chinese, on the other hand, would take political power only if it were forced on them by us; if they did so, they would have little care for the others. The more intelligent of the 'natives' are very well aware of their deficiences. The Chinese of this country will be satisfied to pursue their economic concerns for a long time; the few who take part in politics, and they for the most part must be persuaded to do so, are with few exceptions those who are relative failures in commerce or those who consider that political influence would further their commercial or professional success; in both cases the economic interest is preponderant. The Chinese are not in

---

[3] Eleemosynary = charitable

the least afraid of the indigenous peoples, and are entirely ready to pay us a reasonable share of their profits in order that we should look after the native peoples and assure to them, the Chinese, the peace and time to pursue their own preoccupations. It is in the interests of both parties (though it is a mistake to speak or think of the native peoples in the singular) that we should remain.

8.   It is in this context that the oft-declared policy of H.M's Government to lead her dependent peoples to self-government must be considered. Nobody would seek to argue with that policy insofar as it is designed to serve a long-term objective, but what is regarded here as the sometimes unseemly haste of its application elsewhere does cause concern. If on some appropriate occasion the reaffirmation of the policy could be associated with the declaration that in such territories as this H.M's Government intend to continue their association as long as it is desired and so long as it can contribute to the welfare of their peoples, fears would be quieted, and the creation of the circumstances that make difficult the continuation of such an association would be forfended.

9.   Meanwhile, of course, as I have written elsewhere, we should continue to educate the people in the management of their own affairs, but should not transfer authority at any level so quickly as to leave the unprepared indigeneous people lagging hopelessly, and fearfully, behind the Chinese.

10.   Finally, I think it most unlikely that this country will offer political difficulty for a long time to come provided always that we can secure for it the economic investment for which it is now ripe. You do not need me to tell you how many expensive political difficulties in other places could have been avoided by relatively minor, but judicious, financial generosity at an earlier stage. North Borneo is a good financial investment; unfortunately, private investors are nowadays inclined to look askance at the whole of South East Asia, without particular discrimination, and it may prove wise to make more public money available at an economic rate.

13   CO 1030/652, no 103   26 June 1959
[People's Action Party government of Singapore]: despatch from Sir W Goode to Mr Lennox-Boyd

[Singapore's first elections were held in 1948 when 6 of 23 Legislative Council members were elected. In 1951 the number of elected members was increased by 3. In 1955 a large measure of responsible government was granted with a Council of Ministers being made collectively responsible to a Legislative Assembly of 32, 25 of whom were elected. Following talks in London in 1957 and 1958, Singapore achieved Statehood in 1959 (see Hyam and Louis, eds, *BDEE: The Conservative Government and the End of Empire 1957–1964*, 256). The new constitution provided Singapore with full internal self-government, a Singapore citizenship scheme and a Cabinet responsible to a wholly elected Legislative Assembly of 51, although internal security was managed by the Internal Security Council of 3 British, 3 Singaporean and one Malayan representatives. Elections were held on 30 May 1959 and the People's Action Party won 43 out of 51 seats and 53.4 per cent of the votes cast by 90 per cent of the electorate. Lee Kuan Yew was sworn in as prime minister on 5 June and Goode stood down as governor to fulfil the joint roles of UK commissioner and head of state (ie the queen's representative) or Yang di-Pertuan Negara. When Goode departed Singapore in early Dec, Yusof bin Ishak became Yang di-Pertuan Negara and Lord Selkirk assumed the duties of UK commissioner in Singapore as well as those of commissioner-general in SE Asia. Goode's despatch of 26 June was subsequently printed for confidential circulation. In his memoirs Lee Kuan Yew refers to Goode's 'dispassionate assessment' of the PAP's first six months in office and

quotes extensively from his despatches of 26 June and 23 Nov, see document 15 below
(see also Lee Kuan Yew's memoirs, *The Singapore story*, Singapore, 1998, pp 337–341).]

I have the honour to submit the following observations on the new People's Action
Party Government of Singapore led by Mr. Lee Kuan Yew.

2.   The new Ministers are intelligent men. They have given much thought to
their political programme which was put to the electorate in carefully prepared
speeches (later published in the two enclosed pamphlets).[1] They are extreme
Socialists by conviction, but they realise the practical limitations imposed by
Singapore's peculiar circumstances as an international trading centre. They also
realise the gravity of the economic problem presented by a rapidly increasing
population expecting a high standard of living in a city which depends for its income
upon winning business against keen competition. Above all else, they are obsessed by
the threat of Communism. They propose to meet this threat not by repressive police
action but by winning the minds of the people of Singapore to democratic socialism,
by fostering loyalty to Singapore and Malaya in the Chinese population, and by
showing that in Singapore's circumstances democratic socialism is effective in
providing a welfare state without the rigours of Communism.

3.   To succeed they must retain the support of the Chinese working and student
classes. In this lies their weakness, since they will be obliged to indulge in popular
gestures which will antagonise the business and commercial class upon whom they
depend for economic progress. Their obsession with the political and ideological
struggle to win the minds of the masses to democratic socialism in preference to
Communism is likely to prejudice a competent approach to the other problems of
making Singapore's economy work.

4.   Like the Marshall Government in 1955,[2] the new Ministers have begun by
trying to show that they are different from the previous Ministers and closer to the
people. They have changed the names of the Ministries; appointed Parliamentary
Secretaries (for whom there is no provision in the Constitution) instead of Assistant
Ministers; and moved the Cabinet Offices from Government House to the City Hall
(which is available since they are abolishing the City Council). The new Government
has been publicly presented as a people's government deriving its strength from the
masses. For public occasions Ministers and P.A.P. Assemblymen have adopted a
uniform of open-necked white shirts and white linen trousers. The Ministers have
also decided to restrict attendance at social functions such as cocktail parties or
garden parties. The general impression which they are trying to foster is that of sober
dignified dedication to the task of governing for the benefit of the masses. They have
immediately carried out easy changes appealing to the puritanical spirit of the
younger Chinese generation such as banning sexy magazines, rock-and-roll and pin-
tables; measures which the previous Government contemplated but abandoned as
likely to provoke opposition.

5.   Their economic and social programme, as set out in their party pamphlet,
contains measures which are common form in democratic, Western countries and

---

[1] Not printed.
[2] David Marshall was the first chief minister of Singapore holding office for 14 months in 1955–1956. It
was a turbulent period and he resigned when talks with the British over self-government broke down; he
was succeeded by Lim Yew Hock.

whilst the pace they are setting themselves may prove to be unduly ambitious, the P.A.P. have shown a complete awareness of the limits which the economic facts of life in Singapore and the Federation must impose on doctrinaire, socialist ideas. Their championing of Malay as the national language of a predominantly Chinese city, their positive discouragement of communal attitudes, their condemnation of 'Chinese chauvinism' and the over-riding importance they attach to winning the confidence of the Federation with a view to merger show admirable political courage and good sense. Mr. Lee Kuan Yew has also made it clear that the P.A.P. stand by the constitutional agreements to which they were a party, and that in their view full independence can only be obtained through merger with the Federation. He has accepted that the British bases, though not desired, will have to remain for the five, ten, fifteen or twenty years that it may take to achieve merger. Even then, he recognises that any change would have to be gradual so that the Government could find alternative work for the many thousands of civilians employed by the Services.

6.   Mr. Lee Kuan Yew stated clearly during the election campaign that the Party would not tolerate subversion from any quarter, whether from left or right. Although Formosa and 'Russian imperialism' were specifically mentioned, the implication that the M.C.P. and China were also included was clear. Moreover, immediately after the Party's victory, Mr. Lee Kuan Yew unequivocally stated that the Party did not intend to be or even appear to be the handmaid of Communism.

7.   On the other hand, the P.A.P. leaders believe that it is no good being anti-Communist in a Chinese city where 'anti-Communist' has come to mean 'pro-Western capitalism and imperialism' and 'anti-Chinese'. They therefore call themselves non-Communist and are at pains to show that they are not puppets of the West. They are sensitive even to praise from the West, since they consider that it damages the popular support of the left-wing Chinese population of Singapore which they must firmly retain against the alternative leadership of the Communists. They are therefore allergic to anything which they think makes them appear to be siding with the West against the East. They believe that to beat the Communists they must offer an alternative socialism that is equally dynamic and equally successful. They also believe in using the Communist technique. In this there are obvious dangers. Their organisation in 'cadres', their discipline, their emphasis on party rule, their doctrinal approach and their ruthless methods are characteristic of Communism and could well prepare the way for the Communists to take over. Their present policy of publicly welcoming the detainees back into the fold has obvious dangers: the detainees[3] have lost no time in re-establishing their contacts with trade unions. Six of the new P.A.P. Assemblymen are Communist suspects. Two, who were previously detained for short periods, have been made Parliamentary Secretaries to the Prime Minister and the Minister for Finance. I am confident, however, that Mr. Lee Kuan Yew sincerely intends to counteract any attempt by such persons to engage in Communist activities inside or outside the Party. He has expressed cautious

---

[3] Riots in Oct 1956 (arising from a crisis in the Chinese middle schools and leaving 13 dead and 123 injured) had resulted in hundreds of arrests. The detainees included leading communists with whom Lee Kuan Yew was closely associated: Lim Chin Siong, Fong Swee Suan, Devan Nair, James Puthucheary, Sidney Woodhull and three others. On winning the election of May 1959, Lee refused to take office until the eight had been released. He then tried to neutralise their influence by appointing some of them to government posts.

optimism that they have had a change of heart or can be controlled. But he may well be over-confident in his estimate of personalities and his ability to beat the Communists at their own game.

8.   The will and ability of the P.A.P. to face and fight the challenge of Communism will obviously be one of the major concerns of the United Kingdom and Federation in the days to come. For the present, however, the auguries are good. The M.C.P. are unlikely for some time to challenge a Government which undoubtedly commands the enthusiastic support of the Chinese-speaking mass of the population. Mr. Lee Kuan Yew himself estimates this period of grace as being probably a year or more. But even if this estimate is correct, the months ahead will present many problems and worries.

9.   The most difficult and dangerous of these is growing unemployment in the face of population pressure. The new Government has promised much. Mr. Ong Eng Guan,[4] in particular, will lose no time in trying to make his mark as Minister for National Development in which capacity he will be responsible for a manifold variety of tasks impinging directly on the daily lives of the people. In doing so, he will no doubt stir up a good deal of dust and he may well give offence to various sections of the community. The patience, understanding and tolerance of the British business community and the English-educated sections of the local population will be severely strained. So far they have shown commendable restraint which I hope will be continued in the future. But the problem of finding employment for the thousands of young people leaving school each year remains to be solved, and as economic and social difficulties prove stubborn or intractable and political pressures mount, the new Government will increasingly find themselves in a dilemma which has been familiar to other governments in Singapore and elsewhere. The temptation to distract discontent and disillusion into more dangerous channels may be strong, particularly as, at that stage, they will undoubtedly be faced with that challenge from the left which their recent manoeuvres were intended to thwart. Their political ideologies and sensitivities throw doubt on the determination of the P.A.P. leaders to do what they know to be right when they judge that it will weaken their popularity.

10.   Much will depend on the political and economic relationship which is developed with the Federation. As is well known, the Federation is not ready to accept merger of Singapore and is likely to remain cool if not hostile to the idea as long as the U.M.N.O.–M.C.A. Alliance provides the ruling party and Government in the Federation. The present Federation Government are suspicious of the true character of the P.A.P. and of the ability of its present leaders to maintain their control against the Communist threat. It will be our constant concern that these feelings of suspicion should not harden into outright hostility which might lead to the Federation refusing to participate in the work of the Internal Security Council[5] and to the Chinese population of Singapore abandoning the aim of merger as impractical and turning back to China for guidance. So far the Federation Ministers have publicly appeared to be friendly to the new Singapore Government and the first

---

[4] Ong Eng Guan was expelled from the PAP in 1960 and won the Hong Lim by-election in April 1961, see 38.
[5] The Federation of Malaya had the right to withdraw from the Internal Security Council on giving six months' notice.

informal meeting between the two Cabinets on June 13th was encouraging; but there are underlying suspicions and prejudices. Whether the Federation will be willing to adopt a more friendly economic policy towards Singapore must depend on the political relations between the two countries. But the Federation Government will in any case be fully stretched in dealing with its own economic difficulties and it can hardly be expected that even with goodwill the Federation will provide any great help towards the solution of Singapore's serious economic problems. If the Singapore Government is to deliver the goods to the people of Singapore, it is difficult to see how they will be able to do so without substantial help from outside Malaya.

11.   In conclusion, therefore, it may be said that while there is cause in recent events for guarded optimism about at least the immediate future, the main battle with Chinese chauvinism, Communism and, above all, with the grave economic problems of Singapore, has not yet been joined.

12.   I am sending a copy of this despatch to the U.K. High Commissioner, Kuala Lumpur, and to the Deputy Commissioner General in Singapore.

14   DO 35/10019, no 26   14 Oct 1959
[Future of the Borneo territories]: letter from Sir G Tory to D W S Hunt[1]

You have asked for our comments on Scott's letter of the 29th January to the Colonial Secretary[2] about the future of the Borneo territories. I have seen Turnbull's views,[3] enclosed with Smith's letter MAL.236/1 of the 6th May to Roland Hunt, and now understand that there are no comments from Sarawak.

I agree with Scott in saying that the two ideas in the Tunku's mind at the time of his Manila visit,[4] (a) the closer association of South East Asian countries, and (b) the political union of the Federation and the Borneo territories, should be kept distinct, the first to be encouraged, the second to be treated with great caution, if not actively discouraged, at least until the territories have reached a much more advanced stage of constitutional development. Since January the two projects have, in fact, gone their separate ways. The scheme for the closer association of South East Asian countries has been regularly aired and has acquired the imposing name of the South East Asia Friendship and Economic Treaty (SEAFET) though little else as yet in the way of positive attributes. Now that the Federation elections are over we may expect a fairly early meeting between the Filipinos and the Malayans to draw up a suitable agreement. The intention is then to invite other S.E. Asian countries to attend a conference with the object of commending the purposes of the agreement to them, and encouraging them to accede to it. The Borneo project, on the other hand, has had no further mention from the Tunku since we discussed it in January (my telegram No. 25). I think he is aware of the fact that association with N. Borneo and Sarawak should be regarded

---

[1] D W S Hunt (later Sir David) was assistant under-secretary at the CRO, 1959–1960, and accompanied Macmillan on his 'wind of change' tour of Africa in Jan–Feb 1960.
[2] See 11.   [3] cf 12.   [4] See 7, n 1.

as a very long term prospect. But the idea is not dead. In particular he fears that the question of the future of these territories may be precipitated by the Philippines or by Indonesia, or both, and thinks that we ought in the meantime at least to clear our own minds about the sort of future we consider best for them in their interests as well as those of the Commonwealth. He is convinced that these interests would ultimately be best served by the Borneo territories joining a wider Federation of Malaya, which could in those conditions include Singapore.

The main theme of Scott's letter is that while association between the Borneo territories and Malaya may be desirable at some point, the time is not yet; that for the present the Borneo territories should be protected from external interference, and from any suggestion that their future may be bound up with a Muslim Malayan Federation; and that they should be encouraged to develop their links with one another. With all this I agree, and if need arises, I shall reiterate our advice of December to the Tunku against ventilating his ambitions. My only comment is that it may not be so easy to provide a long, safe incubation period of the kind Scott envisages. The scene has already changed. Since January, there has been a noticeable strengthening of the links between Brunei and the Federation. Brunei has given the Federation a loan of M$100 million on extremely generous terms. The Sultan has paid an official visit here; he is always made much of and is on close personal terms with the Tunku. The Yang di-Pertuan Agong made a return trip to Brunei in May. The Sultan has also made determined efforts to recruit Malays from the Federation for his civil service. He has, in fact, succeeded in acquiring a Federation State Secretary (formerly the Tunku's Private Secretary), and other appointments are under consideration.[5] Federation Ministers attach considerable importance to placing their Malay officials in influential positions in Brunei, and have disregarded the advice of their Establishment Office in doing so. I doubt if this is solely because of interest in Brunei as a source of future loans. On the Sultan's motives I am not competent to comment. The new Brunei constitution and the separation from Sarawak may, as suggested in paragraph 14 of Scott's letter, open the way to closer connections between Brunei on the one hand and Sarawak and North Borneo on the other. But the present danger seems to be that Brunei may seek her friends elsewhere and develop relations with the Federation to the detriment of those with her immediate neighbours.

If this movement continues, it might eventually result in the demand for some kind of Federation/Brunei union. Given a strong desire on the part of the Sultan of Brunei and of all the Malay rulers here, for such a union, I do not think the practical obstacles to its consummation would be insurmountable. Brunei could readily be incorporated as another state in the Federation; the Constitution (para. 2(a)) provides for just such an event. If the union were one between equal partners, difficulties in the way of negotiation would, of course, be greater, but not insuperable. I agree that from our point of view any movement in this direction would be an undesirable trend, but it is one we may find it hard to counter; and we should not exclude the possibility of Federation/Brunei relations and eventually some form of Federation/Brunei association cutting across our plans for the Borneo territories as a whole.

I am sending copies of this letter to Rob Scott, Turnbull, Abell and also to White in Brunei

---

[5] See 9, n 6.

15 CO 1030/652, no 113   23 Nov 1959

[People's Action Party government of Singapore]: despatch from Sir
W Goode to Mr Macleod, assessing the first six months of the PAP
government

> [This was Goode's valedictory despatch. On 2 Dec he departed Singapore for home leave
> before taking over from Turnbull as governor of North Borneo. There was a general
> stock-taking towards the end of 1959 as Scott prepared to give way to Selkirk, as Abell left
> Sarawak to be succeeded by Waddell, and as (in consequence of Brunei's constitution)
> White assumed the position of high commissioner of Brunei which had formerly been
> filled by the governor of Sarawak (see also 16 and 17).]

I have the honour to refer to your Despatch No.371 about the performance of the
new Government of the State of Singapore, and to submit, as my last general report
before my departure, the following comments on developments since my Despatch
No.7 of 26th June.[1]

2.   It is now nearly six months since the P.A.P. took office, and their record
during that period has in several important respects confirmed earlier favourable
impressions. Thus in the field of subversion and security, their electoral stand as a
democratic, socialist, non-Communist party has been confirmed and reinforced.
They have been frank and unequivocal in the presentation of their position in the
Internal Security Council, where I have been impressed by their patience and
flexibility and by their readiness to meet the difficulties of the Federation
Government. It is particularly encouraging that they have now publicly declared
their attitude on the problem of security in a statement made by the Deputy Prime
Minister in the Legislative Assembly on 14th October, immediately before they
renewed for five years the Preservation of Public Security Ordinance, which provides
the powers of arrest and detention without trial which are essential to deal with
Communist subversion. A copy of this statement is enclosed.[2]

3.   It is unlikely that the present leadership of the P.A.P. will ever commit
themselves publicly as anti-Communist. They are obsessed with the need to persuade
the politically unsophisticated masses that the P.A.P. is 'on their side', and this
involves demonstrating that the P.A.P. is not a friend of the foreigner and the rich
man, nor of the English-educated middle class. Thus while the Government are fully
committed to opposing Chinese chauvinism and other communal attitudes and to
the promotion of a new loyalty towards Malaya, they will continue, within this policy,
to act and speak in a way which may seem equivocal towards Communism and
Communist China and which will often be offensive to Western or English-educated
minds. Indeed, it is possible that the process of fostering a Malayan nationalism may
lead to a real or apparent intensification of hostility towards the 'Colonial' past and
its associations. The Government's attitude towards Communism is, however,
fundamentally sound, and for this fact we have profound cause to be grateful. I
remain convinced that to regard the present P.A.P. leaders as crypto-Communists
would be an entire mistake. To describe them as crypto-anti-Communists would be
much nearer the mark.

---

[1] See 13.   [2] Not Printed.

4.   The P.A.P. Government have also lived up to expectation in their attitude towards the military base. This attitude has of course never been one of warm friendship, but the P.A.P. came into power with the declared policy of abiding by the Constitution and of tolerating British bases in Singapore at least until merger with the Federation had been achieved. Privately the Prime Minister relies on the British military power here as effectively ruling out violence from Communist tactics as well as for its value to the economy. They have since done nothing to belie their declared policy. It is true that public references to the British strategic hold over the island tend, for obvious reasons, to be in somewhat derogatory terms. Inevitably, too, we have had a number of minor administrative difficulties over Service facilities, but these have been amicably resolved. Again, the strong desire of the Government not to be seen to be associated in any way with Western defence policies or with their local manifestations has led to difficulties, notably in connection with visits by allied warships to Singapore harbour. These difficulties, too, have been largely resolved and the Prime Minister has accepted the visit of large numbers of U.S. sailors during a SEATO exercise next spring, subject to any unexpected political development. I have no doubt that particular difficulties will continue to arise, but I think it would be quite mistaken to regard them as evidence of a desire by the Singapore Government to undermine the British strategic position here. On the contrary, the Prime Minister has recently welcomed public reference to the presence of British armed force to remind the people of Singapore that it is part of the essential background to their lives.

5.   Another welcome feature of the P.A.P. Government's performance since they came into power has been their good relationship with myself and with the United Kingdom Commission as a whole. My personal relationship with the Prime Minister remains frank and cordial, and he and his colleagues have been prepared to conduct themselves in a similar way in their dealings with members of my staff. They might so easily have been difficult, touchy and suspicious, but so far they have shown little sign of this in their direct dealings with the Commission. Some trouble has arisen from their tendency to do things first and consider the implications (including the international implications) afterwards; but they have at least been ready to go over the consequential difficulties with us in a frank and objective spirit and even, occasionally, to consult us about their problems. Their unwillingness to accept social invitations remains a bar to close personal relationships, but there are signs that even this is beginning to break down.

6.   Relations with the Federation continue to be polite but cool. Despite the best endeavours of the Singapore Ministers to win acceptance by the Federation Ministers, the attitude of the Federation remains distrustful. The Prime Minister now realises that there can be no hope of merger during the lifetime of the present Federation Government and he also appreciates that public emphasis on merger in Singapore causes political embarrassment and consequent public rebuffs in the Federation. But he is concerned to hold Singapore to its present constitutional modus vivendi, and to keep the aim of merger as the decisive influence on Singapore politics. He rightly believes that it would be disastrous for both Singapore and the Federation if merger became discredited as unattainable and Singapore turned elsewhere for its future. It is of paramount importance to all of us that this should not happen. Meanwhile the maximum co-operation by the Federation is vital in dealing successfully with Singapore's two great problems of providing a living for its

teeming population and stemming Communist subversion. A stable Singapore is essential to the well being of the Federation, and I hope that the Federation Government will come to realise where their true interest lies.

7.   In their external relations the Government have behaved better than I feared they might. The Finance Minister, Dr. Goh Keng Swee, attended the Conference of Commonwealth Finance Ministers in London in September. I think he made a good impression and he was certainly very favourably impressed himself by the spirit of co-operation he found in all discussions. The Deputy Prime Minister, Dr. Toh Chin Chye, represented Singapore at the Colombo Plan Meeting in Indonesia this month, at which Singapore was elected to full membership. He thus met Ministers from many countries and had his outlook broadened. He also followed up in Djakarta personal relations with Indonesian Ministers which he and the Prime Minister have been cultivating at every opportunity in order to build up at least a facade of goodwill towards Singapore. Ministers have also met a number of distinguished visitors passing through Singapore, including the Prime Minister of Australia. I have no doubt that these contacts have been valuable in educating these young men and I hope in breaking down some of their callow prejudices. Although they are anxious to get outside help in money and expertise, they have an immature sensitivity to anything that savours of paternalism, and they are at pains to show themselves Asian and not pro-European. This explains the unfortunate criticisms of Australia made by Dr. Toh Chin Chye at the Colombo Plan Meeting. Psychologically he responded to the allegation of racial discrimination and had no inhibitions about giving offense [sic] himself. The fact remains, however, that Ministers have been readier than I expected to take up Commonwealth associations. The more they do this, the quicker they will acquire a more mature and enlightened understanding of world affairs. But we must beware of seeming to push the Commonwealth at them and we must not be surprised if they redress the balance in their own minds by public emphasis on contacts with Asian nations such as Indonesia, Japan or even China or by petty criticisms of the West.

8.   Against these encouraging features of the P.A.P. Government's performance during the past five months must be set the damage done to the public service. This has mainly been the work of Mr. Ong Eng Guan, the Minister for National Development, but other Ministers have contributed. There have been many resignations of senior staff both local and European, and others, not protected by the Public Service Commission, have been summarily dismissed. The worst damage is in the Singapore Improvement Trust and the Public Works Department, but throughout the public service morale has been badly shaken. I am glad to be able to report that the worst now seems to be over. The Prime Minister, who has always appreciated the folly of wrecking the public service, has at last judged the time to be ripe to intervene. He has removed from the charge of Mr. Ong Eng Guan most of the City Council Departments, including the important public utilities, and has taken charge himself. More pointedly, he has had posted to his own Ministry to administer these departments and the Singapore Harbour Board (transferred from the Minister of Finance) an able European officer, Mr. P. H. Meadows, who had previously been the victim of one of Mr. Ong Eng Guan's worst outbursts of personal animosity.[3] A

---

[3] See Lee's account of Ong Eng Guan's treatment of his deputy secretary, P H ('Val') Meadows, in *The Singapore story*, pp 335–336.

new Ministry has been formed under the Deputy Prime Minister, Dr. Toh Chin Chye, consisting of other departments previously under Mr. Ong Eng Guan and some from the Minister of Finance who was over-burdened. To restore morale generally the Prime Minister has given public assurances to the old City Council staff and has declared in an address at the Staff Training School that Singapore has the best administrative machine in South East Asia and that it is the business of Ministers and Assemblymen to make the machine work at its best. He added that the political leadership must get away from the atmosphere of smear and character assassination. He is encouraging some of those who resigned from the City Council, including three European officers, to continue, and has sharply shattered the personal expectations of a 27 year old Chinese, put in to act as City Treasurer by Mr. Ong Eng Guan, by declaring that a more competent and experienced officer is required to take charge of public accounts amounting to $120 million per annum. There have also been reassuring instances of the Public Service Commission asserting its independence of Ministers.

Nevertheless much damage has been done and it will take time and good behaviour by Ministers and their attendant Assemblymen to restore morale in the public service.

9. It is not yet possible to judge the effectiveness of the Government's efforts to defeat Communist subversion. There has been no real evidence of any extensive underground Communist organisation. Nor has there been any open issue between known Communists and the Government. Most of the detainees released before the P.A.P. took office have been brought into the Government in some way. Only a few are regarded as dangerous. Of these Lim Chin Siong is by far the most capable. He has been appointed Political Secretary to Dr. Goh Keng Swee, the Minister of Finance, but appears to devote his time and energy to trade union organisation. The Singapore General Employees Union shows signs of developing into the powerful mass organisation which the Communists had in the Factory and Shopworkers Union in 1956, and several Communist dominated unions in the building and motor trades are amalgamating into two more powerful groups. It is significant that the Government have had second thoughts about their election policy of creating a unified trade union movement. They have modified their intention of forming a single all-embracing transport union to a much looser federation of unions. They have been much impressed by advice given by the Permanent Secretary of the Australian Ministry of Labour and National Service who has been here on a short visit at their request. They have realised the danger of two or three powerful unions, each covering all the workers in one industry or trade. The Prime Minister has spoken of the need to take the initiative against Lim Chin Siong before his position becomes too strong. At the same time it is likely that Lim will also move cautiously and be careful not to go too far in building a trade union empire which the Government could crush as an obvious threat to its authority. It is most improbable that Lim wishes to provoke an issue with the Government yet. The Prime Minister has also become more cautious about releasing more detainees, despite his repeated assertion that it is politically necessary for him to release all who were detained by the previous Government. He seems well content to shelter behind the Internal Security Council, allowing the impression to be given that he has been overruled. He is worried about Nanyang University which is not only a most awkward claimant for Government finance but a breeding ground for Communists of high quality. Here

again he seeks the help of the Federation which supplies 60% of the students, but which yet appears to be refusing to face the problem they present. The Chinese schools are quiet and healthier.

Over all I think the general position has not changed significantly. The Communists are working hard to gain mass support through trade unions and peasants, but Ministers realise the threat and are less likely to take risks. The position must be watched, but I see no reason for alarm.

10.　Although the Government has on the whole behaved responsibly during the past six months, there is still a distressing stagnation of commerce and industry. Retail trade has been very slack and there is a general atmosphere of waiting to see what will happen. The sudden cut in the pay of the public service undoubtedly seriously affected purchasing power. Precipitate legislation to tax the film business and dramatic (and illegal) increases in assessments for rates frightened businessmen. Now they are waiting for the budget. While this hesitation is understandable, it is bad for Singapore, and I hope very much that businessmen will soon pluck up their courage and get to work to revive the economy. Ministers are learning from their mistakes and Mr. Ong Eng Guan's responsibilities have now been limited. I hope, too, that the budget with a large sum for development expenditure will provide the needed primer. For the economic problem of providing a living for the population must be solved if Singapore is to have stability. The Government can help by firmly following its declared policies of building up a climate of business confidence and industrial peace; and commercial enterprise must not be too sensitive to the comparatively minor gestures the Government feel obliged to make to show their loyalty to the workers. The more pressing need is economic assistance, and I hope that substantial aid will be forthcoming from western sources. This is the best way to help Singapore today.

11.　The picture of this initial period of the P.A.P. stewardship presents bewildering contradictions and often their behaviour is open to both good and bad interpretations. Their concentration on maintaining their political strength is both welcome for its promise of firm and stable government and disturbing for its totalitarian character. P.A.P. Assemblymen and ex-detainees have been brought into the business of governing to commit them to support of Ministers' actions and policies, but inevitably this has led to undue political interference with day to day administration and to suspicion that they are political commissars. Sound measures have been taken in a damaging manner. Public attitudes have been struck for political reasons in apparent conflict with more sober policies. The explanation of these inconsistencies is complex. To a great extent Ministers are the prisoners of the political propaganda they used to win mass support. They therefore wish to present themselves as extremists while carrying out the moderate policies they know to be right for Singapore. Individually, too, several, if not most, of them are emotionally antipathetic to the European and the West, suspicious of the motives of others, and too ready to find evidence to support their own pre-conceived ideas. And as a party they are young, impatient, arrogant and intolerant of the past achievements of others. Even the Prime Minister himself, in spite of the impressive way in which his personality has matured over the past few years, is not yet entirely devoid of these weaknesses. But these defects should not blind us to the main features of this Government: its genuine opposition to Communist subversion, its unceasing drive to inculcate a new loyalty towards Malaya particularly in the Chinese masses of Singapore, its acceptance of the Constitution and British rights here, and the amicable attitude so far adopted in dealing with matters of common concern to the Singapore and United Kingdom Governments. I hope that with time, patience and understanding they will grow out of their disquieting features and come to a better understanding of the art of public administration.

12.   In the Cabinet the outstanding ability of the Prime Minister has firmly established his position as leader. His closest associates are Dr. Goh, the Finance Minister, and Dr. Toh Chin Chye, the Deputy Prime Minister. Dr. Goh has obvious qualities of intelligence and some experience of public administration and the outside world, though in my judgment he falls a long way short of the Prime Minister in general competence. Dr. Toh Chin Chye is an unimpressive little man who appears to me to be small minded and petty in his outlook; but the Prime Minister holds him in high esteem. The outstanding political figure in the Cabinet is Mr. Ong Eng Guan, the Minister for National Development. He commands the mass support of the Chinese speaking population, and has long been regarded by many as likely to oust the more moderate English educated Mr. Lee Kuan Yew from the leadership. I have never been able to find evidence to support this view. Today Mr. Ong Eng Guan's prestige has undoubtedly fallen. His hasty and unsound measures as a Minister have embarrassed his colleagues, and discredited him. He has had to retract dramatic increases in the assessment of business properties because they were illegal, and it is common knowledge that he has been relieved of most of the old City Council responsibilities because of the damage he was doing. With shrewd political judgment the Prime Minister deliberately delayed making this move until it was clearly justified, but he has paid a sad cost in damage to the departments concerned. The Prime Minister still assures me that Mr. Ong Eng Guan is a great asset to the Cabinet for his sure touch with the mass of the electorate. However, for the present at least he does not have the respect of his colleagues and is no danger to Mr. Lee Kuan Yew. In addition to his administrative failure, he recently declined to make the Government's Assembly statement on security and it is accepted by his colleagues that this was because he was frightened.

13.   So the position today is that Mr. Lee Kuan Yew is very much in command of the Cabinet and the Cabinet are impressively united. They have made mistakes, as was to be expected, and with the exception of the Prime Minister I doubt they are as able as they first appeared to be. They are finding it much more difficult to run a government than to organise a successful political party. But on the whole they have made a good start to carry out their declared policies. The Prime Minister tells me to postpone judgment on their competence until they have had a year in office. So far most of what he has said has been proved right.

14.   There is still no sign of any effective opposition party and only Mr. A.P. Rajah of the Assemblymen has made any serious attempt to provide intelligent opposition there.[4] Mr. David Marshall occasionally raises a lone cry in the political wilderness. The only dangerous threat to the present Government is Communism.

15.   Our policy must continue to be to work with the P.A.P. Government and to do all we can to secure their goodwill and confidence. Thus we shall be able to help them to give Singapore a stable and competent government, and only thus shall we overcome the constant minor difficulties and provocations which I am sure we shall

---

[4] A P Rajah was the one independent candidate returned to the Assembly in the elections of May 1959.

encounter. While firmly maintaining our essential rights under the Constitution, we should not be too sensitive on minor details. Experience over the past six months has been that Ministers have responded helpfully to a patient and sympathetic approach, whereas they harden into precipitate action if they consider that they are being opposed by failure to understand their basic political principles. These last are not in themselves incompatible with our basic interests.

16.   I am sending copies of this Despatch to the Acting Commissioner General for South East Asia and to the United Kingdom High Commissioner, Kuala Lumpur.

16   DO 35/10019, no E/195   2 Dec 1959
[Closer association of Borneo territories]: letter from Sir A Abell to F D Jakeway[1]

> [At the end of his governorship Abell noted that, while the need for the closer association of Borneo territories was as great as ever, the practical difficulties were growing. Rather than allow Brunei, North Borneo and Sarawak to drift further apart, he suggested that Iain Macleod should give a lead and issue a policy directive, something which the previous secretary of state had been reluctant to do. Sir D Allen expressed similar impatience two months later, see 18.]

I promised to let you have my views on the closer association of North Borneo, Sarawak and Brunei before I leave South-East Asia. You can of course make what use you wish of this letter.

The case for a form of closer association is as strong to-day as it ever was; the arguments used in its favour are as unassailable as they ever were but the practical difficulties have grown immeasurably and will continue to grow unless we do something about them.

Brunei is now less likely than ever to favour a closer relationship with neighbours and Sarawak and North Borneo continue to drift further apart. The time may shortly be reached when the whole conception may have to be discarded and this I firmly believe would be against the best interests of the three territories and of Her Majesty's Government. In trade, in the development of natural resources, in research, in defence and internal security, in administration, in bargaining power and in international esteem the Borneo territories would be greatly strengthened by a firm partnership, working under joint direction to a common plan. I agree with my colleagues that at the present time there is little that Her Majesty's Government or her local officers can do publicly to encourage closer association but I do believe that it is possible to prevent some of the greater divergencies in policy becoming definite barriers to closer association in the future.

Brunei is now in practice no longer a Colonial Office responsibility. She will go her own way. She may follow an historic xenophobic line or she may move closer to Malaya. She will not favour a closer relationship with any country which has a dominant Chinese community. If she goes on her own independent way she may in time, in her own interests, seek an accommodation with her two neighbours. On the

---

[1] Having served in Nigeria, the Seychelles, the CO (briefly) and British Guiana, F D Jakeway (later Sir Derek), assumed the post of chief secretary of Sarawak in April 1959 and was appointed governor of Fiji on Sarawak's merger with Malaysia.

other hand, if she joins a pan Malayan islamic anti-Chinese Block she will certainly take no part in any scheme for a United Borneo and she may well cause a final and irreparable split between the Malays and the Chinese in Sarawak.

I do not therefore believe it is in the interests of a future which includes plans for uniting Borneo or in the interests of Sarawak that Brunei should become wholly identified with Malaya, nor incidentally do I believe it to be in the best interests of Brunei either. The Chinese are going through a lean time in South-East Asia but I do not believe this phase will last. The Chinese problem in Malaya has yet to be resolved and I do not believe the Malays have it in them to hold down the Chinese politically, or commercially as in Indonesia, for long.

If Brunei were to become the twelfth state of Malaya it would probably become a focus for Malay discontent or Malay irredentism throughout Borneo. We in Sarawak do not wish our considerable Malay population to look to Brunei or Kuala Lumpur for salvation any more than we wish our Chinese to look to Peking. Furthermore, I would deprecate reducing a politically immature community for whose welfare we have been responsible for half a century to the status of a colony of another power.

There is probably little that we can do to influence the course of events in Brunei but I suggest that the High Commissioner should receive clear instructions in the matter so that he can use his influence when it can be applied with effect and without danger to our relations with Malaya. I suggest that these instructions should state that nothing should be done to encourage a closer relationship with Malaya than at present exists.

Sarawak and North Borneo are drifting apart for some of the reasons given by Sir Roland Turnbull in his paper of 21/10/59. Sarawak still adheres to a paternal regime in regard to its native people (and is glad to do so) and its economy is based on the small holder. The native of the country has certain rights in the land and these the Government will protect. Promises have been made by the Rajah and confirmed by the Queen that the policy of the Government will be to prepare the people for self-Government. In Sarawak people are proud to be described by a word[2] which elsewhere is regarded as derogatory because they know that it carries with it promises and guarantees that the resources of Sarawak will be developed for their use and in the interests of the people of Sarawak as a whole. The policy of the Government is to establish a plural society in which all citizens of Sarawak will have equal rights and opportunities. We hope to raise the native races to standards of living and education comparable to the Chinese and to give the Chinese a good title to what land is available for them. A great deal of this may differ radically from the North Borneo policy of an economy based on large-scale capitalist enterprise particularly if that means a dominant Chinese or other foreign community with the native reduced to the state of a landless labourer.

Whether two countries geographically so close together and with so much in common should have been allowed to develop so divergently is another matter. Perhaps it was inevitable. It is certain that Sarawak could not have pursued the policy of North Borneo. North Borneo will undoubtedly get rich quickly but may in doing so inherit some of the problems of East Africa. Sarawak may fail to establish a balanced plural society and have to bow to Chinese domination. Whatever may

---

[2] This reference to 'a word' is not made clear and it puzzled officials in Whitehall.

happen in the future I am convinced that these two countries who are about the same stage of political development would be better to face the future together. It is the outside influences which are most likely to dictate events and they will most certainly not take into account the interests of two small countries whose interests are in fact identical but who have failed to show sufficient foresight to realise the fact.

The difference in policy may appear to be fundamental and such as to give little hope of a successful experiment in closer association but I do not think anything irrevocable has been done as yet and we should strive to ensure that no new barriers to closer association are created. A lead must be given and it can only come from the Secretary of State who if convinced that a form of closer association is in the best interests of these three territories, should instruct the Governors and the High Commissioners that this is Her Majesty's Government's long term policy and while recognising that nothing immediate can be done expects each to keep this ultimate goal in the forefront of his mind and give practical effect to this policy when it is expedient and possible to do so. In questions of immigration, free trade areas, removal of customs barriers and the like no progress can be made unless each country is prepared to make the relatively small sacrifices required now in the interests of the future and without a clear directive from above it seems unlikely that any move will be made. In fact, I would go so far as to suggest that where a difference in policy clearly jeopardises closer association, the question should be referred to the Secretary of State for a directive. The Governors of both territories still have power to influence unofficial opinion.

As Sir Roland Turnbull says, our inter-territorial conference has for obvious reasons deliberately avoided controversial topics, but such matters as the immigration policy of the countries might well be discussed with benefit. There are empty spaces in North Borneo which the Government is anxious to exploit, in Sarawak there are over-population problems in certain districts. In the Second Division there are Ibans with insufficient or exhausted land who should be moved elsewhere. There are Foochows in the Rejang Delta, excellent industrious farmers and good citizens who are very short of land. We have both Iban and Foochows trained as administrative officers who might accompany groups of immigrants. In this way it is possible that North Borneo and Sarawak could be of assistance to each other—at least the possibility should be explored before other arrangements are made.

To sum up, I think it is essential that Her Majesty's Government should have a policy in this matter which her representatives in Borneo should be instructed to follow. If we are allowed to drift further apart we may find, as in the case of Malaya and Singapore that the gulf is too wide to bridge.

17 DO 35/10019, no E193   7 Dec 1959
'Closer association between the British Borneo territories (with special reference to the position of Brunei)': memorandum prepared by the Office of the Commissioner General, Singapore[1]

Closer association between the three British Borneo territories is an ideal which has so far been frustrated by the unco-operative attitude of the Sultan of Brunei. The six-

---

[1] This memorandum was prepared by Sir R Scott, Sir D Allen and other senior officials in Singapore.

monthly Inter-Territorial Conferences, originally aimed at welding into a single compact unit the three territories with their historical, economic and political differences, have in fact been restricted, despite the Sultan's absence, to a lowest common level of non-controversial discussion on administrative matters. This has been done in the hope that the gradual progress made by Sarawak and North Borneo towards closer association would tempt the Sultan of Brunei to join in. He may still do so but there are no signs that he will make such a move in the near future; and so long as the High Commissioner can act as the Sultan's 'observer' at the Inter-Territorial Conferences, Brunei will not miss any important development, even though in his present mood, the Sultan is unlikely to take any step in co-operation with it. The JIC(FE) paper on the 'Outlook in Borneo' (DCC(FE)(59)367) concluded that by 1964 'no major step towards closer association between the three territories will be possible during this period. Some progress will doubtless be achieved.'

2.   Given the new Constitution recently granted to Brunei,[2] the present seems a good moment at which to review (a) the direction in which Brunei is heading and (b) the possibility of making closer association between the other two territories more of a reality.

Position of Brunei

3.   The High Commissioner for Brunei, in his memorandum of October 27, has discussed the development of close links between Brunei and Malaya and pointed out that an identification of interests between Malaya and Brunei could act as a brake on Indonesian designs. Sir Roland Turnbull on the other hand, in his memorandum of October 21, foresees political complications for the British Borneo territories in the event of the identification of Brunei with Malaya. But while problems would certainly arise in such an event, they might well be a lesser evil and more readily solved than those that would confront us if Brunei turned to Indonesia. It is most unlikely that the Sultan himself would turn to Djakarta but if a Malay Nationalist party with left-wing sentiments grew up in opposition to the Sultan it might well turn to Indonesia for sympathy and support. By opening the way to Indonesian penetration of the Borneo territories, this would be a prelude to a far more awkward situation for us than Brunei's identification with Malaya.

4.   Perhaps the Sultan's ideas about getting closer together with Malaya should therefore be regarded, if not with benevolence, at least with equanimity. Moreover, the disparity of interests between the two states is such that closer association between them cannot take place easily or quickly. On the one hand the cold shouldering of the Malayan officials in Brunei, and other local factors to which Mr. White refers, and on the other the Tungku's rather cynical view of Brunei as his banker, will ensure that. The Brunei Constitution though not a good one, seems likely to prove a fair safeguard of the United Kingdom's position for at least about five years, simply because it will be difficult for the Sultan and his advisers and the people of Brunei to agree on how to modify it. The risk that Brunei might become a 'colony' of Malaya is perhaps exaggerated, though we should not exclude the possibility that Brunei—and other territories—might take a proper place in some such looser South-East Asian Federation headed by Malaya, as has been sketched by the Tungku.

---

[2] The Sultan granted the constitution on 29 Sept 1959, see 5, n 1.

Closer association of Sarawak and North Borneo

5.   Even if the idea of a loose South-East Asia Federation on an Indian or Swiss model is a long way ahead, there is much to be said for our taking steps now to ensure that the two territories in the area which are still under direct British control bring their policies, economies and administrations more closely into line with each other, so a viable unit of a reasonable size can contribute to the stability of the region. Each of the Governors is still in a position to control his Executive Council, through it to influence public opinion and thus to impose far-reaching but possibly unpopular policies: though North Borneo may be able to keep this control for a few years longer, Sarawak is likely to have to yield to popular clamour within the next few years and thereafter there is a risk that the territories may develop on narrow parochial lines.

6.   Seen from a distance, the closer association of the two—or even the three— territories seems an obvious development. At closer range the outside observer is struck by the contrast between Sarawak and North Borneo: in the former the poor soil, the Brooke tradition, the smallholder system and consequent land-hunger, and the growing political consciousness of the Malays, Ibans and Singapore-looking Chinese; in the latter the rich soils and valuable timber, the 'Company' tradition, the large plantations with their chronic labour shortage, and the political apathy of the Dusuns, Malays and Hong Kong-looking Chinese. For reasons which flow from this different historical and economic background North Borneo sees no advantage in drawing closer to Sarawak unless Brunei can be brought in too; Sarawak on the other hand sees an outlet for its land-hungry native population in parts of North Borneo which are being made available to Timorese and Bugis labourers drifting in from Indonesia or to Chinese deliberately imported from Hong Kong. Communalism is a danger in Sarawak and, to a lesser extent, in North Borneo: it can be inflamed by poverty and it may be in the longer-term interest of the two territories to share their economic and manpower assets more evenly. Even though North Borneo has greater potential wealth than Sarawak, the latter can contribute a historical tradition and a sturdily native background which may go some way to offset the growing domination of the Chinese in both territories and create a national consciousness.

7.   The internal divergencies of the two territories, though considerable on a close inspection, appear on a wider view to be not such as to outweigh the more numerous points of similarity which should in the long-term bring them together. They are both British colonies, both under-developed, both in Borneo, both with mixed races, both with Indonesian frontier problems, both prizes which Indonesia, China and Japan, will sooner or later try to secure for themselves, both run on similar lines by officers with the same training and traditions, both with the same systems of justice and education and pattern of government, and both having English as the language of government.

8.   Though we should not try to force the pace, there seems much to be gained by not letting the idea of closer association die of inanition or even remain at the level of the non-controversial administrative topics which have made up the agenda of recent Inter-Territorial Conferences. The natural process of economic rationalisation between two friendly administrations will lead easily enough to sharing of experts, etc. but this alone, without a clear policy directive, will not enable the two territories to embark on long-term policies of mutual interdependence and assimilation in more difficult fields such as immigration. It is not too late to start on this course; and

Brunei, when the advantages of closer association between Sarawak and North Borneo become more apparent, may yet perceive where its own best interests lie.

18 DO 35/10019, ff 71–72   5 Feb 1960

[Closer association of the Borneo territories and Brunei-Malaya relations]: letter from Sir D Allen to E Melville

Thank you for your telegram No. 24 of January 16 to the United Kingdom Commission about closer association of the British Borneo Territories and Brunei-Malaya relations. As foreshadowed in my letter R. 1013/102/59G of December 7 to Dennis White, an informal meeting to discuss Borneo problems was held during the course of the Eden Hall Conference, and I enclose a brief summary record.[1] As you will have realised we could not take the discussion very far in the absence of a representative from North Borneo. But one point on which there seemed to be fairly general agreement was that it would be desirable, if possible, to clear our minds about the attitude to be adopted by Her Majesty's Government towards any move by the Sultan of Brunei in the direction of closer association in Malaya, bearing in mind that any such move would be likely to affect not only the problem of closer association between Sarawak and North Borneo but also the eventual possibility of some wider confederation in this part of the world in which Singapore as well might find her place. It might indeed present opportunities as well as dangers.

2. You have no doubt been considering this problem in the Colonial Office. I understand that Dennis White has had some correspondence with you on the subject and I believe that Tory has also written to the Commonwealth Relations Office about it. I have not, I think, seen all the correspondence and will not venture any views from here at this stage. But it seems to me important that we should be as clear in our minds as we can about the probability of such a move by the Sultan and about what our attitude towards it should be if it took place. Such an estimate would help us, for example, in deciding how rapidly we should try to push ahead with a policy of closer association between Sarawak and North Borneo. And in general I confess to some uneasiness whether, if as suggested in your telegram our attitude remained simply one of 'wait and see', we might not find ourselves missing important opportunities when the critical moment came. I know that it is always difficult and often unwise to try to define one's attitude too clearly in advance when so much is bound to depend upon just how and when a particular happening takes place. But in this case it seems important that we should all have at least some idea of the various wider issues that would be involved. I am not sure that we are yet clear about this and it would be very helpful to us here[2] to know of any conclusions that you and the Commonwealth Relations Office may have reached about the longer term direction in which you would like to see the relationships between the various Commonwealth and dependent territories in South-East Asia develop over the coming years. One thing that is pretty clear is that our own ability to influence those relationships is declining fast. Already it is only in North Borneo and to a lesser extent in Sarawak that we can exercise any direct control, and if we wish to use our remaining influence

---

[1] Not printed.   [2] ie, Singapore.

in those territories to steer events in one direction rather than another we ought to
begin soon.

19   DO 35/10035, no 6   23 Feb 1960
'Greater Malaysia': letter from Sir G Tory to Sir A Clutterbuck on possible merger of Borneo territories with Malaya and Singapore

During the last few years there has been talk from time to time about the possibility
that the Borneo Territories might ultimately join the Federation of Malaya and that
the Federation Government might be willing to absorb Singapore into this wider
system. The Tunku discussed this possibility with Malcolm MacDonald[1] and myself in
December, 1958, as you will know from the correspondence ending with my
telegram No. 25 of the 13th January, 1959.

It emerged at that time, however, and subsequently at the Eden Hall conference
last year, when the matter was further ventilated,[2] that the Governors of North
Borneo and Sarawak in particular were most anxious that the Tunku should be
discouraged from saying anything at all about this possibility at the present time lest
this should distract the three Borneo Territories from the immediate aim of
achieving closer integration amongst themselves. It was argued that only Brunei had
a Malay majority and that the prospect of association with a predominantly Malay
Islamic Federation might encourage fissiparous tendencies in the Chinese and Dyak
populations who formed the majority in the other two Territories. The two
Governors did not, however, rule out the possibility that joining the Malayan
Federation might prove in the end to be the correct solution.

When I discussed this matter with the Tunku in December, 1958, he accepted
these points but maintained that whether we liked it or not the question of the future
of the Borneo Territories was almost certain to be precipitated by developments
outside our control in this part of the world—possibly by attempts on the part of
Indonesia to absorb the rest of Borneo, with perhaps counter-claims from the
Philippines—and that we in the Commonwealth ought in the meantime to clear our
minds about the long term policy which would be best likely to serve the interests of
ourselves and of the Commonwealth as a whole. It seemed clear to him that there
could be no doubt that the best ultimate solution would be for these Territories to
attach themselves to the nearest appropriate Commonwealth country, namely, the
Federation of Malaya. Subsequently the Tunku visited the Borneo Territories himself
and when he came back he realised that North Borneo, in particular, was a long way
yet from the stage of self-determination and that if matters were left to themselves
the prospect of North Borneo and Sarawak joining the Federation through normal
constitutional developments was a long term one. He was, however, I think, still left
with the feeling that developments in the area might not allow these constitutional
developments to run their normal course.

In the meantime there has been a very marked drawing together of Brunei and the
Federation (see my letter of the 14th October, 1959, to Hunt).[3] Royal visits have been

---

[1] See 7 and 8.   [2] See 11.   [3] See 14.

exchanged and the Sultan of Brunei, with the reluctant consent of his Advisory Council, has granted the Federation a $100 million loan on uneconomic terms. The Sultan, on the basis of understandings arrived at personally with the Tunku and Razak at the time of his visit here, has since acquired the services of Malayan officials for key appointments in the Brunei administration, and both he and the Tunku show signs of wishing to continue this process despite the manpower strain which this obviously places on the Federation. The Sultan has decided to educate his children in the Federation and is coming here, ostensibly for the purpose of placing them in schools, for a period of several months starting from the end of March.[4] He intends, we are told, to build himself an Istana (palace) in Kuala Lumpur.

Latterly there has been speculation amongst well placed Federation Civil Servants to the effect that the Tunku would like to see the Sultan of Brunei become the next Yang di-Pertuan Agong of the Federation. This could, of course, only happen if Brunei had in the meantime become a part of the Federation and the signs as a whole therefore seem to suggest that we should not rule out the possibility that the U.K. Government may be faced before very long with a request from the Sultan of Brunei, on the one hand, and from the Federation Government on the other, for the incorporation of Brunei into the Federation of Malaya. The fact that the health of the Yang di-Pertuan Agong is very delicate, that he might not survive very long, and that there is no obvious suitable successor amongst the present collection of Sultans, suggests to me that the U.K. Government ought quickly to consider this possibility and to make up their minds what attitude they would adopt.[5]

This matter was discussed again during this year's Eden Hall conference in very general terms and without any very clear recommendation emerging. White, the High Commissioner for Brunei, shared my own feeling that Brunei and the Federation were drawing closer together and did not, for his part, see how we could very well prevent the two from joining each other if they ever wished to do so. As regards the other two Territories, however, the consensus of opinion was that, although federation with Malaya might well be the eventual answer, the territories still had a very long way to go constitutionally before they reached the stage at which they might reasonably be expected to express worthwhile views about their own future. The general feeling seemed to be that we should sit back and await developments with regard to Brunei and the Federation, without interfering in any way, and that North Borneo and Sarawak should continue their efforts to draw closer to each other as an essential preliminary to possible federation with Malaya in the distant future.

I said that although at the time of Independence, and at the time of his talk with Malcolm MacDonald, the Tunku had contemplated the possibility of absorbing Singapore provided that he could at the same time absorb the Borneo Territories, developments in Singapore since then might well have hardened the Tunku against

---

[4] See 6, n 2.
[5] The Yang di-Pertuan Agong was the constitutional monarch of the Federation of Malaya elected every five years by and from among the rulers of the Malay states, see *BDEE: Malaya*, 449, 453, 455 and 459. The first Agong, His Highness Tuanku Abdul Rahman of Negri Sembilan died a few days after Tory's despatch of 23 Feb; he was succeeded as Agong by Hisamuddin Alam Shah of Selangor who himself died on 1 Sept 1960, the day he was due to be installed. Syed Putra of Perlis was the third Agong, 1960–1965. For the Sultan of Brunei's interest in becoming Agong, see 41.

accepting Singapore in any circumstances so long as the present P.A.P. administration continued. He had shown lately very clearly that he believed that we were wrong in allowing the P.A.P. Government to carry out its policy of trying to absorb and contain the Communist elements in Singapore, that the situation was bound to deteriorate to the point at which the Communists would take over, that this was a problem of our own making and that it was up to us to sort it out. In the meantime the Federation would have nothing whatever to do with Singapore, apart from their unwelcome, and I think now much regretted, commitment to play a part in the Internal Security Council.[6] From an informal conversation I have had lately with Razak this impression of mine has been confirmed. Razak said that the Federation would accept Brunei at any time but that they would not want Singapore which should, in their view, continue for a considerable further period as a colony 'like Hong Kong'. This was all in the course of light-hearted banter and not to be quoted against Razak as a statement of his Government's policy, but I am sure it reflected something of his thinking and that of the Tunku.

When Laithwaite[7] paid his visit here I mentioned these matters to him and said that the Governors of North Borneo and Sarawak, and Rob Scott himself, had all expressed the view that I ought some time to pay a visit to the Borneo Territories so as to be able to deal more effectively with the Tunku if necessary when this subject cropped up. I have been waiting for a suitable time for this. Goode, who takes over as Governor of North Borneo in April, has actually invited my wife and myself to visit him after he is settled in and it had been my intention to suggest to you that I might pay a visit of a few days at that time, visiting Sarawak and Brunei as part of the same operation. White, the High Commissioner in Brunei, has however urged me to visit Brunei before the Sultan comes to stay in Kuala Lumpur and the Sultan himself tackled me on the subject during the Coronation celebrations in Johore last week[8]. The Sultan was extremely friendly and made the personal suggestion that my wife and I should visit Brunei during the early part of March before he himself left for the Federation. I understand that the R.A.F. would be able to fly us there in the course of their normal operation on the 8th March, but we should have to return by a commercial service. I should very much like your authority to pay this visit in this way. The journey by air only takes a few hours and we could make a worthwhile visit within the compass of four or five days.

I should be most grateful if you could let me know by telegraph whether you approve.

This would, I am afraid, mean that a visit to [North] Borneo and Sarawak would have to be made at another time, perhaps in May.[9] That again might be done within the period of about a week. I would propose to approach you again about this second visit nearer the time but if you could say now whether the C.R.O. would be content in principle for me to undertake it I should find this very helpful for planning purposes. On that occasion, too, I should expect to be able to fly at least in one direction by R.A.F.

---

[6] See 13, note and n, 5.
[7] Permanent under-secretary of state, CRO, 1955–1959.
[8] This was the coronation of Ismail, former Tunku Mahkota or crown prince of Johore and eldest son of Sultan Ibrahim who had reigned from 1895 to 1959.
[9] Tory visited Sarawak and North Borneo in May, for his report, see 26.

20   CO 1030/1126, no. 5   18 May 1960

[Closer association of Borneo territories and Brunei–Malaya relations]: letter from Sir J Martin to Sir D Allen replying to 18 and summarising interdepartmental discussions in London

[Copies of this correspondence were distributed widely in Whitehall, for example it was reproduced for the committee (chaired by Sir R Scott) examining future developments in SE Asia (CAB 134/1644, DSE(60)6; CO 1030/1078, no 16A/21; DO 169/24, no 1).]

This is in reply to your letter to Melville of the 5th February[1] about closer association of the British Borneo territories and Brunei–Malaya relations, with which you enclosed a brief, but most interesting, note of the side-talk you had on the Borneo territories at the Eden Hall Conference in January. (Melville is still in Cyprus, where he has been with Mr. Amery for the better part of three months)[2].

We took the opportunity of Sir William Goode's presence in this country to discuss these questions with him, not only because of his future interest in North Borneo, but because of his recent experience of the problems of the area as seen from Singapore. The Commonwealth Relations Office and the Foreign Office joined in our discussions. These talks revealed a general agreement and the following paragraphs summarise the views common to us all. In fact MacDermot of the Foreign Office and Hunt of the Commonwealth Relations Office have seen this letter in draft and agree with it. The views here expressed do not purport to be firm policy decisions (we have made no submissions to Ministers) and are of course subject to your comments and those of the others to whom I am sending copies of this letter. But they will give you an idea of how our minds are moving here and, unless any of you have different views, can serve as a general background guide to policy in the Borneo territories.

We took as our starting point H.M.G.'s accepted policy, which is that the peoples of North Borneo and Sarawak should, subject to their own wishes, ultimately achieve self-government. Attractive as is the prospect (not least to many of their own inhabitants at present) of their remaining Crown Colonies, experience shows that we must not delude ourselves into thinking that that can be a permanent state. (I recur to the question of the pace of this change below.) That means that sooner or later we shall move out and they will be left, either each alone, or in association with each other, or (either individually or as a Borneo entity) inside some wider association, to face the South East Asian world without our protection. They are very vulnerable, both because of their geographical position and because of their racial make-up. China, Indonesia, the Philippines all have, or could easily work up, interests of one kind or another. Nor, I suppose, could one exclude the possibility of a revived Japanese interest. It could be a very uncomfortable world for a little North Borneo or Sarawak trying to stand alone and we certainly have no intention of moving out so that someone else should step in. Even an associated North Borneo–Sarawak would

---

[1] See 18.

[2] Julian Amery, parliamentary under-secretary of state for the colonies 1958–1960, was negotiating the final arrangements relating to Cyprus's independence and the extent of the areas to be retained by Britain as military bases (see 59 para 5). As secretary of state for air (1960–1963), Amery argued in Oct 1961 that a Greater Malaysia would weaken Britain's title to the Singapore base, see Hyam and Louis, eds, *BDEE: Conservative government 1957–1964*, 1, 263.

not be a very strong state. With Brunei in also it could be more viable (though the oil won't last for ever). But here we come to our second assumption, namely, that there is no prospect in the foreseeable future of Brunei's joining an association with North Borneo and Sarawak alone. We were led by these paths to the conclusion that, as seen at present (and I must emphasise the 'at present', for most of the circumstances we do not control) the most hopeful ultimate solution would be an association of the Federation of Malaya, Sarawak, North Borneo and Brunei, with, if possible, Singapore in also—MacDonald's 'Grand Design'[3]—which, one might hope, might stay within the Commonwealth. That can be no more than a hope. Some of the difficulties in the way are obvious—not least the present remote prospect of the Federation and Singapore forming an association together. But at least it seems to us the most sensible goal to have before us.

Given this as the goal, we went on to consider what our attitude should be towards a proposal for political association of Brunei and the Federation, if one eventuated. It seemed to us that we should not resist it, since it would be a step towards the ultimate goal. Indeed, we might view it with benevolence. On the other hand, we noted that there might well be opposition to it in Brunei itself and we ought to avoid getting involved in an internal Brunei argument of this kind. (We also noted that an element in the opposition to it within Brunei might be an unpleasing preference for Indonesia, though this doesn't seem a very important factor at present). We also did not forget that a political association of Brunei with the Federation of Malaya might cause the Malays in Sarawak to begin looking the same way. But, given that the 'Grand Design' is accepted as the ultimate aim this would not necessarily be bad in the long term, though in the short term it could of course give rise to difficulties in Sarawak. The likelihood of a sudden movement towards Malaya on the part of the Sultan has possibly been reduced by the recent death of the Agong and the election of a successor for a full five-year period. On the whole, benevolent neutrality, but with 'later rather than sooner' the motto, seems our right policy in this matter.

We next considered the question of closer association between Sarawak and North Borneo alone, Brunei being left aside. Clearly, this would fit in with the general aim, just as closer association between Brunei and the Federation would. And the disadvantages would seem less. There is the risk of pushing Brunei quicker into the arms of Malaya but, for the reasons I have already given, though we don't want to hurry this it would not be disastrous. There need therefore be no doubt here on which side our influence should generally be exercised. But there should be no question of forcing the pace (too enthusiastic expressions of Chinese opinion in

---

[3] MacDonald had used 'grand design' to describe the ultimate federation of Malaya, Singapore and the Borneo territories, see 1, note. By Jan 1961 the phrase would be used as short-hand for the policy of closer association (see, for example, 32). When the CRO opened a file series on the Malaysia project, it was entitled 'Greater Malaysia and the Grand Design' (DO 169/25-43). The committees of officials and ministers dealing with the subject in 1961–1963 were known as 'Greater Malaysia' committees (CAB 134/1949-1953). Although Sandys thought 'grand design' was 'a bad description of the plans for closer association in Malaya and Borneo' since it was 'pretentious and vague', alternative nomenclature proved hard to come by. In the view of officials, the advantage of 'grand design' lay in its very lack of specificity which avoided 'prejudging any possible solution of the question' (minutes by S Martin, 9 June, and R Omerod, 14 June 1961, DO 169/25).

favour of closer association have already tended to frighten off the indigenous races). How progress can best be made is for the two Governors to consider together after they have had time to get the local 'feel', but it certainly seems to us that the closer association of the two territories should be pursued by every reasonable means that offers.

I revert now to the point we started from—that sooner or later self-government must come to Sarawak and North Borneo—and I do this to emphasise that there is no question of H.M.G. wanting to get out in the near future. To do that prematurely would be the exact reverse of helping the territories, where we still have an immense task before us of trying to bring forward the indigenous peoples to a level where, subject to their innate capabilities, they have the opportunity to compete with the Chinese on reasonably equal terms in political and economic life. The indigenous races at present do not want us to leave (this, we think, still includes the Malays in Sarawak) and even the Chinese, except for a section in Sarawak, in the light of the recent treatment of their compatriots in Indonesia, are well content with things as they are. But because we cannot count on things remaining thus we have had to take this look into what is a very hypothetical future and make a rough guess at what looks likely to be the best future for the territories if events, some of which are outside our control, permit it to come to pass.

We should welcome comments on the views in this letter, of which I have sent copies to Goode in North Borneo, Waddell in Sarawak and White in Brunei. I have also sent a copy to Bourdillon.[4]

I have also sent copies (together with spare copies), to MacDermot and Hunt. The former is, I understand, sending copies to Djakarta and Manila, to which posts you copied your letter, and no doubt the latter will wish to send a copy to Tory.

---

[4] H T Bourdillon was seconded from the CO as deputy UK commissioner, Singapore, 1959–1961, see 32, annex A.

21   DO 35/10019, no 42   9 June 1960
'Brief for the minister of state for talk with Tunku Abdul Rahman': CO memorandum for Lord Perth

[The Tunku came to London for the meeting of Commonwealth prime ministers in May. This was the occasion when Eric Louw, the South African foreign minister, opened the question of his country's continuing membership of the Commonwealth by announcing its intention to become a republic (Hyam and Louis, eds. *BDEE: The Conservative Government and the end of empire 1957–1964*, lxxiv-lxxvi and 450). The Tunku stayed on after the Commonwealth conference to discuss with British ministers the situation in SE Asia and the possibility of Malaya's closer association with the Borneo territories. His meeting with Lord Perth, minister of state at the Colonial Office, was scheduled for 11 am, Friday, 10 June, see 22.]

The Tunku has asked for a talk with Lord Perth about the future of Sarawak and North Borneo. He told Lord Home on the 3rd June that we must be ready for 'an Indonesian move' against these territories and he spoke to Miss Vickers, MP,[1] a few

---

[1] Joan Vickers (later Dame Joan), MP for Devonport since 1955, had served in the British Red Cross in SE Asia in 1945–1946 and maintained a strong interest in the region.

days ago about a possible federation between Malaya, North Borneo, Brunei and Sarawak, with, if this came off, a possibility of Singapore then joining with certain safeguards. Presumably he is going to press the desirability of a scheme of this sort with Lord Perth.

2. It so happens that the future of the British Borneo territories has quite recently been considered at official level between the Foreign Office, the Commonwealth Relations Office and ourselves. The upshot is Sir John Martin's letter to Sir Denis Allen of the 18th May—copy attached[2]—and there can be no better brief than that letter.

3. I would add only the following points:—

(a) The Tunku knows very little about the Borneo territories (except Brunei) and almost certainly over-estimates the attractiveness of Malaya to Dayaks, Dusuns, etc., who have memories of past (Brunei) Malay oppression and who want nothing better than a continuance of the present regime.

(b) That cannot last forever, so in due course an association with Malaya would, so far as we can see at present, be the best answer. But we must not rush it. In the long run it is the people of the territories who have got to decide what they want.

(c) At present there is *not* any Indonesian heat turned on our territories. Every now and again an Indonesian does make a noise about them. On the most recent occasion the Indonesian Government commented that they did not claim any territory except that which the Dutch had held. At present Dutch New Guinea entirely occupies their attention.[3] That is not to say that later they may not begin an 'anti-colonial' campaign about our territories and the Tunku may well be inclined to exaggerate the likelihood of this. What is certain is that if *we* or the Tunku start talking about a future association of the territories with Malaya that will set off the rush of other claimants. Let sleeping dogs lie.

(d) We have no intention at all of seeing our territories pass to Indonesia.

4. Lord Home has left a very curious record of what the Tunku said to him about Singapore at the same time as he made his mention of the Borneo territories. It runs as follows:—

---

[2] See 20.

[3] The status of the western half of New Guinea or Irian Jaya had been a matter of dispute since the international recognition of Indonesian independence in 1949. The Dutch insisted on retaining control of the territory while President Sukarno prosecuted the nationalist claim through coercive diplomacy which he called 'Confrontation'. In grappling with the task of welding the vast and diverse archipelago of Indonesia into a nation-state, Sukarno resorted to 'Guided Democracy' from 1957 and foreign adventures. Consequent power struggles culminated in the coup and counter-coup of 1965 which brought the military to power, although Sukarno remained nominal president until 1968. With respect to Irian Jaya, in Aug 1962, following US intervention, Indonesia and Holland concluded an agreement, whereby the territory would be transferred first to the United Nations on 1 Oct 1962 and ultimately to Indonesia on 1 May 1963. It was also stipulated that, with UN assistance, an assessment would be made of the inhabitants' wishes regarding continued Indonesian jurisdiction. Although the enquiry was clearly stage-managed, Irian Jaya was formally incorporated into the republic of Indonesia on 17 Sept 1969. Sukarno's designs upon New Guinea had implications for any plans to merge the Borneo territories with Malaya and the scheme for assessing local wishes in West Irian became the model proposed by Indonesia and the Philippines for the 'ascertainment' of Borneo opinion in 1963.

'The Tunku approved our veto on Russian aid to Singapore. He said he could deal with the Prime Minister of Singapore and had some money with which to help. He felt convinced there was no need for a sum anything like the one named by the Russians.

X 'He thought we must be absolutely firm about Russian aid. It would be seen as a Communist victory and would undo all the good achieved by the defeat of the Communists in Malaya. He asked that he should be consulted at all times on any move in Singapore. He claimed to be on good terms with the Prime Minister.'

The statement at X is incomprehensible, since the Russians have never named any sum or even given the slightest indication that they are prepared to help Singapore in any way at all. (The recent row has simply been about a representative of a Russian state trading organisation who was to come to Singapore on a six-month visit to buy rubber. We saw this as the thin end of the wedge. But there has been absolutely nothing more than this.) It seems just possible that the Tunku is misquoted and what he said was that there was no need for a sum anything like that being put forward by the Singapore Government as necessary outside help towards their development plan. No doubt, for tactical reasons, they are opening their mouths pretty wide. Nevertheless there is no doubt whatever that they do need external assistance in a big way.

5.   We had hoped to take advantage of the Tunku's presence at the Commonwealth Prime Ministers' Conference to have a talk with him about Singapore/Federation relations so as to impress on him that, however much he may innately dislike the present Chinese and left-wing government of Singapore, it was nevertheless the best bet that he and we had of stability in Singapore and that therefore it was to our joint interest to help the Singapore Government and not make things difficult for it. In the event the Tunku declined to talk about Singapore because the Russian rubber buying affair blew up and he was in a bad temper about it. An opportunity may be now presented for Lord Perth to get across some of the points which we had hoped to make earlier. I attach a copy of the brief for the earlier abortive talk.[4]

---

[4] Not printed.

22   CO 1030/1126, no 10   10 June 1960
'Note of my talk with Tunku Abdul Rahman 10 June, 1960': memorandum by Lord Perth recording Tunku Abdul Rahman's proposal for closer association of independent Malaya and British dependencies in SE Asia

[Perth's note was widely circulated and elicited immediate response. Knowing the Tunku's reluctance to contemplate merger with Singapore and conscious of the vulnerability of Singapore without merger, Selkirk urged that the Tunku be encouraged in this initiative (see 23). Macmillan commented: 'All this seems to me rather doubtful but I suppose it is worth considering', and was persuaded by the Commonwealth secretary and Cabinet secretary that it should be followed up (Macmillan to Brook, 19 June 1960, Home to Macmillan, 21 June 1960 and Brook to Macmillan, 27 June 1960, PREM 11/3418). The Colonial Office was concerned about the implications for the Borneo territories and Sir Hilton Poynton requested Sir Norman Brook to refer the matter of closer association to the Colonial Policy Committee (see 24, 25 and 27). CO unease was not alleviated a month later by the report from the British high commissioner in Kuala Lumpur that the Tunku was firmly in favour of the alternative 'solution' developed in his talk with Perth, namely Malaya's merger with the Borneo territories rather than with Singapore (Tory to Hunt, 19 July 1960, CO 1030/977 no E/43).]

After the usual courtesies the Tunku plunged into the purpose of his visit, namely the possibility of federation of Malaya, Singapore, North Borneo, Sarawak and Brunei. He wanted the British Government to know that he would be prepared to face such a happening although it would give him a great number of headaches. I replied that this was something which we hadn't really given a great deal of thought to. It was a comfort to know his willingness as outlined above. I pointed out that Indonesia recently had disclaimed any territorial ambition and that at the moment it seemed wise to let sleeping dogs lie. If there was any hint of a move such as he mentioned I could imagine all sorts of agitation by other potential claimants. I pointed out that politically North Borneo and Sarawak were backward and how it was clearly important that they should learn the art of running themselves before they were asked to face decisions on their ultimate future. I feared that if we pressed the pace too fast it would lead to the predominance of the Chinese because they were the most advanced from an education point of view in both territories. Later on the indigenous people and the Malays would be more able to play their part in deciding the future of their country. This seemed to me another reason to go slowly. I of course mentioned the idea of closer association between the territories (North Borneo, Brunei and Sarawak) which at one time or another had been suggested.

The Tunku then came back again on another tack which was: what would be our attitude if the Sultan of Brunei asked to join the Federation, and he added as an afterthought that the Sultan had shown nervousness himself at this, the Tunku thought because it might cost him money. I would gather from this that the Tunku has in fact at some time pressed him quite hard to be a member of the Federation and that the Sultan has held back, even though there was held in front of him the possibility of his one day being Yang di-Pertuan Agong. I said that this was something which I really had not considered, but offhand it surely had to be something for the people of Brunei themselves to decide and that as they had only just embarked on a new Constitution perhaps it was important to see how that worked out.

The Tunku then tried a slightly new line and suggested Brunei and Sarawak joining the Federation while the British Government remained in North Borneo to develop it economically and to use it as a military base. The people of Sarawak, Dyaks and so forth, were of Malay origin and he felt confident that it would be a good move. I pointed out the real economic difficulties that faced development in Sarawak.

From all the above it seems clear to me that he is really quite keen on getting something more to add to the Federation and I think he felt that the sort of deal—H.M.G. to hang on to North Borneo, he to take over Brunei and Sarawak—would be something which we might be willing to accept. I did what I could to leave him with the feeling that we were neither for nor against the general principle, that it was early times to say anything more, although naturally the linking up of our friends would be a logical course to see followed.

I then took the opportunity of touching once more on relations between Malaya and Singapore and stressed how important it was to try and help Singapore in its economic development. I also told him how I felt that the Security Council had worked well because he and we understood each other and that our firmness at times was probably something equally acceptable to Lee Kuan Yew. On the whole he was not too negative about giving a helping hand and he said that one day he had very much in mind to have a real talk with Lee Kuan Yew, a fellow undergraduate of Cambridge. All the same I think there is a pretty deep-rooted suspicion of all that the present Singapore Government stands for.

23 PREM 11/3418   17 June 1960
[Lord Perth's talk with Tunku Abdul Rahman]: note by Lord Selkirk
for Mr Selwyn Lloyd

I have just seen a note of Lord Perth's discussion with Tunku Abdul Rehman dated June 10[1] in which the Tunku expressed interest in the possibility of an association, perhaps amounting to political federation, between the Federation of Malaya, Singapore, North Borneo, Sarawak and Brunei.

2.   The Tunku has had this in mind before. He has now quite specifically declared his interest in the development of his case and, in the very short time I have been in Singapore, it has become abundantly clear to me that some association of this sort is the only evolution which I could envisage which can give a measure of stability to the area. I must therefore recommend that these proposals be examined very closely and urgently.

3.   I have no doubt that Singapore would readily agree to them, and have little doubt that Brunei would also agree. North Borneo and Sarawak obviously present greater difficulties. Even if at the end of twenty years they would be capable of managing their affairs they could not defend themselves. Moreover, if any difficulties in government arise in Sarawak or North Borneo, which is possible, if not immediately imminent, it would be extremely difficult for us to defend the position without using a considerable measure of force to maintain order. The Tunku would do it far more easily.

4.   In present circumstances the merger of the Federation and Singapore does not seem practical. If she is to be independant for ten years, Singapore will either become viable herself and not wish to join the Federation or, alternatively, she will have to be carried by heavy external subsidies. Accordingly, the opportunity to bring Singapore into a wider Federation may be lost by deferment.

5.   These proposals raise very big questions with regard to the protection of the more primitive people of the Borneo territories, with the possible danger of running into a situation somewhat similar to that in the Central African Federation. But I believe these problems would be much more easily dealt with by a government from Kuala Lumpur than from London.

6.   The proposal also raises problems of defence. In his present mood, the Tunku could not agree to a similar arrangement to that which now exists with Singapore.[2]

---

[1] See 22.
[2] Britain had the constitutional right to use the Singapore base for SEATO purposes, whereas Britain's defence interests in Malaya were determined by AMDA, which, by contrast, was a treaty between sovereign powers and excluded SEATO operations.

On the other hand, he could not possibly take over Singapore and then seek to denude it of the economic advantages of defence installations. But, however that might be, I do not believe that, in the long run, our defence position would be any worse off within a wider federation showing some measure of stability than it is at the present time. The detachment of Labuan from North Borneo, making it at least a useful base with certain specific functions, particularly connected with R.A.F. and Royal Navy, might be necessary.[3]

7.   I have suggested that this should be dealt with urgently because I do not think it can wait indefinitely. The Tunku has still some years to run as Prime Minister[4] but a succeeding Government might not be so willing to take any step to bring the five territories closer together, politically or economically. The forces dividing the territories are likely to become stronger as time passes at the same time as the cohesive factor—the imprint of British rule—becomes less marked.

8.   I shall be visiting North Borneo in August and Sarawak in September.

9.   I am sending copies of this minute to the Secretary of State for the Colonies, the Secretary of State for Commonwealth Relations, the Minister of Defence and the Private Secretary at No. 10.

---

[3] The Chiefs of Staff would continue to consider Labuan (and also Australia) as an alternative to the Singapore base, see COS(61)259, 8 Aug 1961, DO 169/28, no 110A; cf 45, note and para 18, 73 para 32, 74 point (a).

[4] The Tunku's Alliance had won the 1959 elections, albeit with a reduced majority. The next state and federal elections were due in 1964.

24   CO 1030/1126, no 32   30 June 1960
[Lord Perth's talk with Tunku Abdul Rahman]: letter from Sir H Poynton to Sir N Brook requesting that the matter of closer association be referred to the Colonial Policy Committee

You spoke to me the other day about Lord Selkirk's minute of the 17th June commenting on Lord Perth's note of a discussion with Tunku Abdul Rahman on the 10th in which the Tunku expressed interest in the possibility of an association, perhaps amounting to political federation, between the Federation of Malaya, Singapore, North Borneo, Sarawak and Brunei.[1] You asked me to let you have our views on this.

2.   The idea is not a new one. It was, I think, first floated as a future possibility by Malcolm MacDonald when he was High Commissioner [sic] in South East Asia at Singapore ten years or so ago. For some years we have been considering the possibility of a closer association of the three Borneo territories. That has not got very far because local feeling about it in North Borneo and Sarawak while mildly favourable, has not yet developed much enthusiasm and because the Sultan of Brunei has made it quite clear that he is not interested. We have also kept before us the hope that the Federation of [? and] Singapore would one day merge. We have also always had in mind the ultimate possibility of an association of all five territories.

---

[1] See 22 and 23.

3.   On the 18th May, John Martin wrote a letter to Denis Allen in Singapore summarising the agreed thoughts at official level of the Foreign Office, the Commonwealth Relations Office and ourselves about the political future of the Borneo territories, and the possibility of their ultimate association with the Federation and Singapore.[2] I enclose a copy of that letter. It presumably arrived in Singapore after Lord Selkirk had left. (A copy has been sent to him here.) I also enclose a copy of Allen's reply just received[3] (a copy of which has also been sent to Lord Selkirk). You will see that Allen suggests that these questions should be discussed at the October meetings of the Borneo Inter-Territorial Conference and the Joint Advisory Defence Committee (Borneo). These are high-level bodies of very limited membership. The first consists of the Governors of North Borneo and Sarawak and the High Commissioner for Brunei, with senior officials plus an unofficial (local) Executive Council member from each of the two Colonies and, possibly, the Chief Minister from Brunei. The Commissioner General for South East Asia (Lord Selkirk) goes over to Borneo to preside. The second body has the same membership but without the unofficial members and with the addition of one of the Commanders-in-Chief, Far East. It is a 'UK eyes only'[4] body. These bodies, which meet normally twice a year, provide a useful forum for joint discussion (the most valuable part of which sometimes takes place outside the Conference room). The Commissioner General has of course no authority over, or constitutional function in, North Borneo and Sarawak, the Governors of which must speak for them—and, *mutatis mutandis*[5] the High Commissioner in the case of Brunei. But his central and impartial position in Singapore and close connection with the Commanders-in-Chief there enable him to play a co-ordinating role.

4.   A paramount factor is going to be what the heterogeneous people of the Borneo territories will want, and this is not easy to predict. In Sarawak and North Borneo the predominating strong feeling at present is to remain with us. Even in Brunei our latest information is that there would certainly be opposition to any attempt by the Sultan to link up with Malaya. We think that the Tunku is too optimistic about the feelings of the inhabitants of the Borneo territories towards Malaya, and if we want to guide them in that direction we shall be able to do so only gradually. Admittedly our power to influence them will decrease rather than increase, and admittedly the Indonesians might (at least if they got the West New Guinea question out of the way) begin to agitate.[6] But we cannot force Borneo opinion.

5.   As regards Singapore, we should like to see the closest possible co-operation, especially economic, short of political union, between the Federation and the State and ultimately, if and when we no longer need the Singapore base, probably political union. This is a stated objective of the Singapore Government, one of their reasons for wanting it being that they see in it the best way of attaining independence. We recognise that such political union is 'out' for the present anyway, because the Federation don't want it. But from the defence point of view that suits us. Union with

---

[2] See 20.   [3] Not printed.

[4] 'UK eyes only' meant that the records were not distributed to the US government.

[5] 'Mutatis mutandis' means 'with necessary changes' or 'similarly'.

[6] For the New Guinea question, see 21 note 3.

the independent Federation would end our constitutional right to the base in Singapore and we should be dependent on a treaty arrangement. Paragraph 6 of Lord Selkirk's minute recognises this, but I am not sure that it recognises the disadvantages from the defence point of view of *early* termination of the present constitutional arrangements.

6.   Lord Perth got the impression that the Tunku was very much more interested in getting some or all the Borneo territories into the Federation than in a five-territory Federation including Singapore.

7.   I have shown this in draft to the Secretary of State who thinks that before this matter is discussed by the Governors and Lord Selkirk when they meet in the autumn, there should be some Ministerial consideration of the matter. He would therefore like the question to be brought before the C.P.C.—if possible while Lord Selkirk is still in this country. If the Prime Minister agrees, we will prepare a C.P.C. paper.[7] Alternatively an ad hoc meeting could be arranged if the Prime Minister preferred, in which case the Ministers concerned, apart from the Prime Minister himself if he wished to take the Chair, would, I suggest, be the Colonial Secretary, the Commonwealth Secretary, the Foreign Secretary and the Minister of Defence.

8.   I am sending copies of this letter and enclosures to Hoyer Millar, Clutterbuck and Playfair.

---

[7] See 25 for the CPC memorandum and 27 for the CPC meeting with Selkirk.

25   CAB 134/1559, CPC(60)17   15 July 1960
'Possibility of an association of the British Borneo territories with the Federation of Malaya, and Singapore': memorandum by Mr Macleod for Cabinet Colonial Policy Committee

Introduction
The three British territories in Borneo are the Colonies of North Borneo and Sarawak and the Protected State of Brunei. A note on them is at Annex 1.[1]

2.   During his recent visit to London for the Prime Ministers' Conference, Tunku Abdul Rahman, Prime Minister of the Federation of Malaya, raised informally the possibility of a federation of Malaya, Singapore, North Borneo, Sarawak and Brunei. Lord Perth's note of his discussion with the Tunku on this subject is at Annex 2.[2] Lord Selkirk has urged that early consideration should be given to the idea.[3]

Previous consideration of the idea
3.   Ten years or so ago Mr. Malcolm MacDonald, then High Commissioner [sic] in South East Asia, put forward the idea that the most favourable plan for our South East Asia territories might be some sort of association, perhaps amounting to political federation, between the Borneo territories, the Federation of Malaya and Singapore.

4.   In recent years consideration has been given to the possibility of a closer association of the three Borneo territories. This has not got far because local feeling about it in North Borneo and Sarawak, while mildly favourable, has not developed

---

[1] Not printed.   [2] See 22.   [3] See 23.

much enthusiasm and because the Sultan of Brunei is not interested, his eyes being turned towards the Federation of Malaya.

5.   We have always had in mind that Singapore and the Federation of Malaya would one day merge and have publicly blessed this idea on more than one occasion.

The idea from the Borneo angle

6.   Our stated policy for Sarawak and North Borneo is that, subject to their own wishes, the peoples should ultimately achieve self-government. At present many of their inhabitants have no wish other than that the territories should remain with us as Crown Colonies. Experience elsewhere shows that it would be a delusion to think that this state can last for ever. If we move out they will be left, either each alone, or in association with each other, or (either individually or as a Borneo entity) inside some wider association. They are very vulnerable, both because of their geographical position and because of their racial make-up. China, Indonesia and the Philippines all have, or could easily work up, interests of one kind or another. We certainly would not wish to move out so that anyone else might step in. Even an association of North Borneo and Sarawak would not be a very strong state. With Brunei in it could be more viable (though the oil will not last for ever), but it looks unlikely at present that Brunei would join an association with North Borneo and Sarawak alone. An ultimate solution might therefore be an association of the Federation of Malaya, Sarawak, North Borneo and Brunei with, if possible, Singapore in also—which, one might hope, might stay within the Commonwealth. From this point of view the Tunku's idea is not unattractive to us. There are, however, some important further considerations.

7.   The whole idea hangs in any case on what the peoples of the Borneo territories will themselves want. No sign[s] whatever of a wish to link with Indonesia or the Philippines have shown themselves in the territories. The great majority of the peoples of Sarawak and North Borneo undoubtedly are quite content with their present status. There are, however, the beginnings of talk about 'self-government' in Sarawak. Neither of the territories has shown any interest in a closer association with Malaya. In North Borneo the Malays are a very small minority; in Sarawak the Malay minority is larger but even here the above holds. As for Brunei, recent events have shown that, although the Sultan may see his future in the union of his State with Malaya, he may by no means carry his people with him. It now appears that about the time of his talk with Lord Perth, Tunku Abdul Rahman told some Brunei students in London that he was going to sound the Sultan on the possibility of Brunei joining the Federation. This caused a sharp reaction in Brunei when it got back there and the Sultan himself felt obliged to issue a denial that he had had any discussions with the Tunku on this subject. Even in Brunei we cannot count on a wish to join up with Malaya.

8.   The Tunku in his conversation with Lord Perth suggested that he might take over Brunei and Sarawak, ourselves retaining North Borneo for defence purposes. We have a brigade training area in North Borneo at present and consideration is being given to more permanent installations there, in view of the possibility that our use of the base in Singapore may in the future become restricted or be lost. It is true of course that we ought to be able to enjoy a longer peaceful tenure of defence facilities in North Borneo than we can in Singapore. It is true also that North Borneo is behind Sarawak in political development and that, as between the two, we could

expect to retain it peacefully as a Crown Colony for a longer time. I do however, feel very great doubt whether it is realistic to think of our retaining North Borneo as a Crown Colony after Sarawak has either become self-governing on its own or had merged with the Federation of Malaya. From the point of view of the Borneo territories it does not seem to me that we need expect, or hope for, any early move towards an association with Malaya. They are happy as they are and this can go on for quite some time, possibly even a decade. There is one qualification to this, which is that, *if* the West New Guinea question gets settled, Indonesian attention might turn to our Borneo territories; from that point of view a settlement of the future of the territories might be come to with less outside interference if it took place sooner rather than later.

The idea from the Singapore angle

9.   As regards Singapore, we should like to see the closest possible co-operation, especially economic, short of political union, between the Federation and the State and ultimately, if and when we no longer need the Singapore base, probably political union. This is a stated objective of the Singapore Government, one of the reasons for wanting it being that they see in it the best way of attaining independence. We recognise that such a political union is not likely to take place in the near future, because the Federation do not want it. But from the defence point of view that suits us. Union with the independent Federation would end our constitutional right to the base in Singapore and we should become dependent at best on a treaty arrangement. From the defence point of view therefore an early merger with the Federation would not suit us.

Tentative conclusions

10.   There are so many unknowns here, notably the future feelings of the peoples of the Borneo territories, that I feel this is a matter where we ought to go slowly. On balance I incline towards the idea of an association of the five territories as likely to provide the least unsatisfactory future for them and for us which we can at present envisage for the long term, but there are far too many imponderables for us to be certain about this. I think our attitude to the Tunku in this matter should be one of benevolent neutrality. He ought to be left in no doubt that this is a matter where the Borneo peoples have got to have their own say in due course and in which we are not going to try to force them. The result of his recent indiscretion about Brunei may cause him to realise that this is the best possible attitude even from his own point of view.

11.   Before the Tunku made his approach, there had already been some discussion between ourselves and our representatives in the area about the questions dealt with in this paper and we had had it in mind that they should be further discussed between the Governors of North Borneo and Sarawak, the High Commissioner for Brunei and Lord Selkirk when they meet together in Borneo in October for the Borneo Inter-Territorial Conference and the Joint Defence Advisory Committee (Borneo).

12.   I think the best thing would be to let discussions proceed on the basis suggested in the preceding two paragraphs. In particular I would like to have the views of the men on the spot on the likely feasibility of our remaining in North Borneo alone after we have abandoned our position in Sarawak and Brunei.

26   DO 35/6297, no 92   20 July 1960

[Impressions of Sarawak and North Borneo]: report by Sir G Tory of visits to the Borneo territories in May 1960[1]

Sarawak

After my short stay in Sarawak my strongest impression was that it was very backward and that it would be 10 or 15 years before it would be ready for self-government, other things being equal. There is a racial problem there very similar to that which the Malayans have had to face. The Chinese are very far ahead of the other races in education, skill, industry and wealth and would be likely to dominate the country politically and economically if power were transferred within the next decade. The Sea Dyaks, or Ibans, who are the principal indigenous race, could, in my view, be developed to a point at which they might balance the Chinese but they have been neglected for a very long time and serious attempts to educate them both generally and agriculturally have only just been started. They are much more like the Chinese than like the Malays and are promising material. The Malays are few in numbers, indolent and apparently without ambition.

2.   There are two political parties in Sarawak. One is the Party Negri, which is run by a Malay.[2] This is alleged to be multi-racial but it is, in fact, more concerned with the welfare of the Malays than that of the other races. Its policy, I understand, is that Sarawak should hurry slowly towards independence, the obvious reason being that if it hurried quickly the Chinese would dominate the country. The other party, the United People's Party, is run by the Chinese Mayor of Kuching, a very go-ahead Chinese who has extensive commercial interests in Sarawak. This is also multi-racial in theory.[3] The policy is, if I remember rightly, to press for independence sooner than later, for the obvious reasons that the sooner power is transferred the more likely the Chinese will be able to maintain a position of dominance. When the Governor of Sarawak at successive Eden Hall conferences has stated that the people of Sarawak are not interested in independence what he has really meant, I suspect, is that the indigenous peoples are clinging to the protection of H.M.G. against the Chinese.[4]

3.   Economically the country is in a very poor condition and my impression was

---

[1] As high commissioner to Malaya, Tory was responsible to the CRO and not to the CO. Since this report was an account of his impressions of territories under CO jurisdiction, he explicitly requested that it should not be circulated outside the CRO.

[2] Party Negri: this is a reference to Party Negara Sarawak (or PANAS, meaning 'hot'), a right-wing Malay party which was led by Dato Haji Abang Mustapha and was registered in Apr 1960. It would favour Malaysia but withdrew from the Sarawak Alliance in the 1963 elections.

[3] The Sarawak United People's Party (SUPP) was formed in June 1959 and, though it claimed to be multi-racial, was primarily Chinese. SUPP's chairman was Ong Kee Hui. It opposed the formation of Malaysia.

[4] Other parties were later formed in response to the Malaysia proposal and the introduction of elections: Sarawak National Party (SNAP, predominantly Ibans of the Second Division), Apr 1961; Barisan Ra'ayat Jati Sarawak (BARJASA, a Malay party that competed against PANAS, although they merged as Party Bumiputra in 1967), Dec 1961; Party Pesaka Anak Sarawak (PAPAS or PESAKA, largely Ibans of the Third Division), June 1962; Sarawak Chinese Association (SCA, opposed SUPP), June 1962. The Sarawak Alliance, which was formed in Nov 1962 in support of Malaysia, consisted of BARJASA, PANAS, PESAKA, SCA, and SNAP, but PANAS withdrew on account of tensions within the politics of the Malay community dating from the conflict between pro-cessionists and anti-cessionists in 1946. For the elections of June 1963, see 198.

that this was due largely to the fact that the Sea Dyaks had been permitted, and indeed encouraged by the Brooke regime and by our colonial regime since then, to continue their wasteful nomadic system of land tenure. Rather like the aborigines in Malaya they squat on land for a number of years, growing hill paddy and other crops, and then they move on leaving the land behind them to lallang and ruin.[5] Over the years they have, by these peripatetic habits, and in the process of felling timber, acquired rights to land over large areas of Sarawak, which are now protected as native reserves. These lie mostly inland from the banks of the rivers which are mainly occupied by Chinese descended from those Chinese imported by the Brookes to introduce wet paddy techniques amongst the Dayaks. The Dayaks were encouraged to spread themselves in this way as a safeguard against the possibility of further Chinese revolts on the scale of those which took place in Sarawak in earlier years.

4.   As stated above, the Governor of Sarawak has now started seriously to implement a policy of bringing on the Dayaks. The best of the teachers passing out from the Training College are being sent willy-nilly for two years to the Dayak areas and the Agricultural Research Station has started an extension course for teams of two men and one woman from various backward areas with the idea that they should be trained for a year in agricultural techniques which they can then take back and disseminate amongst their own people. The Agricultural Research Station are also developing high grade seeds and fruit stocks for distribution. It will be some years before they develop the best type of rubber clone and in the meantime they depend entirely on Malaya for their supply. Everywhere I went I heard complaints about the recent increase in the export duty on Malaya rubber seeds. The Temenggong, the leader of the Dayaks,[6] even said that it was beyond his comprehension how Malaya could strike this blow at the Sarawak replantation scheme when they had provided the Malayans with the Sarawak Rangers to fight the Communists. This duty looms large in Sarawak and has definitely affected the attitude of the Sea Dayaks towards Malaya.

5.   These measures cannot hope to bring the Sea Dayaks to a position remotely approaching competition with the Chinese for at least a decade in my opinion. It will probably be 15 years before self-government for Sarawak could be on a genuine multi-racial basis.

North Borneo
6.   The situation in North Borneo is very different. Politically it is even more backward than Sarawak and the same interval would be likely to lapse before it was ready for multi-racial self-government. Since Sir Roland Turnbull's Governorship the Government have concentrated on economic development and have not been in a hurry to introduce constitutional reform. There are no elections whatsoever in North Borneo at the present time so far as I remember.

7.   Economically North Borneo is very far ahead of Sarawak thanks to Sir Roland Turnbull's determination to encourage British commercial interests to open up

---

[5] Slash-and-burn methods of growing hill rice embodied Iban rituals and beliefs which the government was committed to uphold, yet shifting cultivation was regarded as uneconomical by developers. 'Lallang' is coarse grass.

[6] In Jan 1955 Jugah anak Barieng became Temenggong or paramount chief, although his letter of appointment did not clarify whether his paramountey covered all the Ibans in Sarawak.

estates there.[7] This is in direct contradistinction to the situation in Sarawak where the Brookes and successive Colonial Governors have adhered to the policy of preserving the native races from outside exploitation. The native system in Sarawak has, so to speak, been deliberately, even artificially, preserved. In North Borneo on the other hand the country has been opened up by companies such as the Bombay Burmah Trading Corporation, which concentrates on timber, and Borneo Abaca Limited, run at present by the Colonial Development Corporation, which grows rubber, hemp and cocoa extremely successfully there, and other companies which develop timber and natural resources of various kinds. Most of the buildings in North Borneo were completely destroyed in the course of the Japanese occupation or withdrawal and most of the Asian middle class were killed off. There has been no replacement of this middle class and this in itself has delayed constitutional and economic progress. Some advance has however been made recently with rebuilding the waterfront at Jesselton and Sandakan.

8.   Here again the Malay element is very small almost to the point of insignificance. The main native ingredient of the population is the Dusuns who are in no way related to the Malays and have no desire to join Malaya. When North Borneo initiated the idea of closer association between the three Borneo territories the people of North Borneo showed that they wanted the British connection to be safeguarded. This again, I assume, is largely due to fear of domination by the Chinese who are here also far ahead of the other Asians in every way. The desire to strengthen the British connection is reflected in the demand for the English language to be developed as the main medium of education in North Borneo. There is in fact at present a swing away from Malay.

9.   Economically there is also no link with Sarawak or Malaya. The Chinese on the east coast at Tawau look to the Philippines, Formosa, Hong Kong, Australia and Japan for their trade whereas Sarawak, i.e. Kuching, looks towards Singapore. In the view of Sir R. Turnbull, the former Governor of North Borneo, if North Borneo were to turn or to be directed towards Singapore and the Federation this would increase the likelihood that the Philippines and Indonesia would close in on North Borneo. Any serious proposal for confederation with Malaya, for example, would, in Sir R. Turnbull's view, be likely to start a separatist movement in the Philippines amongst those inhabitants of the south parts of it who are Muslim. This would, it is argued, be likely to produce some counter-action on the part of the Philippine Government. There is also outstanding a claim by the Sultan of Sulu to a part of North Borneo which is still held from him under a rental agreement; this also might be pursued in an embarrassing way if the question of integration with Malaya were raised. There is a big Christian element amongst the native population in North Borneo and this factor too would militate against any easy merger with Muslim Malaya and might encourage separatist tendencies.

10.   It certainly seems therefore that North Borneo will be unlikely for a long time to welcome any form of integration with the Federation of Malaya. My own feeling is that all three Borneo territories will in the end join the Federation of Malaya, that this is the best possible solution of the problem of their future and that we should, as the Tunku himself advises, start as soon as possible to make this

[7] See 31 for Goode's review of 1960.

integration feasible. In particular it seems nonsensical to me that in this small territory set in Malaya-speaking [sic] Borneo, neighbouring on Malay-speaking Brunei, and Malay and Iban-speaking Sarawak (Iban is closely related to Malay and the Ibans are supposed to have come from Sumatra, the Tunku says the Ibans are the purest of all Malays) the Government should be deliberately turning away from Malay in favour of English. It would seem the merest commonsense to teach Malay equally with English. For example, Malay in the primary schools and Malay and English in the secondary schools as in the Federation of Malaya itself.

11.   The Governor of North Borneo and the Chief Secretary make much of the fact that there is no desire to join Malaya and a continuing wish for the British connection to be maintained. As I said, this is undoubtedly due to fear of the Chinese. When the people of North Borneo come to realise that the British connection cannot be indefinitely prolonged they might, I suppose, regard confederation with Malaya as providing them with a safeguard against the Chinese, which after all the Tunku himself is anxious to achieve by this very process.

12.   Meanwhile the only thing approaching a political movement in North Borneo appears to consist of the activities of a Mr. Stevens [sic],[8] a Eurasian with Dusun blood, who owns the only substantial newspaper there and who has set himself up as the representative of the native races. He is constantly advocating political and economic advancement on an emergency basis lest there should be trouble between the races. He obviously feels that the Government are working in much too low a gear and that history is leaving North Borneo behind.

The attitude of the governors to integration with the Federation
13.   In general the attitude of the two Governors is very much the same. They both feel that in the long term some form of political association between all three territories and the Federation of Malaya, together with Singapore, will probably be the best solution of the future of these three small territories, which cannot hope to survive the strong gravitational influences which will be brought to bear on them once we move out. But they are both very conscious, and justifiably so, of the political and economic backwardness of the indigenous races—apart from the Chinese—and of the danger of prejudicing progress in the shorter term by putting forward the idea of association with Malaya to native people who are not as a whole likely to be attracted by the prospect at the present time and who might in fact react against it, by seeking affiliations and protection elsewhere.

---

[8] Donald Stephens was chairman of the Kadazan Society (1958), founder-president of the first political party (United National Kadazan Organisation, UNKO) from Aug 1961 and Sabah's first chief minister in 1963. Other parties were later formed: United Sabah National Organisation (USNO, led by Dato Mustapha bin Dato Harun), Dec 1961; United National Pasok Momogun Organisation (UNPMO, 'Pasok Momogun' means 'sons of the soil' and the organisation consisted mainly of Muruts), late 1961; Democratic Party (primarily Chinese), 1961; United Party (Chinese), Feb 1962; the small Sabah Indian Congress (SIC). These parties combined in various coalitions: first the Democratic and United Parties came together in the Borneo Utara National Party (BUNAP, later Sabah National Party); towards the end of 1962 UNKO, USNO and BUNAP formed the Sabah Alliance (SABAPA) which favoured Malaysia; finally UNPMO and SIC joined the Sabah Alliance. The Sabah Alliance, which was increasingly dominated by USNO, was unopposed, although its component parties competed against each other in local elections, see 198, note.

27   CAB 134/1559, CPC(60)20   27 July 1960
[Closer association]: Cabinet Colonial Policy Committee minutes of a meeting with Lord Selkirk

[This was an ad hoc, rather than formal, meeting of the CPC held with the dual object of allowing ministers to hear Selkirk's views, especially on Singapore, and to give preliminary consideration to the possibility of merger of Malaya, Singapore and the Borneo territories. It was chaired by Macmillan and attended by Selwyn Lloyd (FO), Home (CRO), Macleod (CO), Watkinson (Ministry of Defence), Selkirk (commissioner-general for SE Asia), and Brook (secretary to the Cabinet). The discussion was informed by Macleod's memorandum (see 25) and shaped the subsequent meeting of Selkirk with governors in Kuching on 20 Oct and the Eden Hall Conference in Jan 1961.]

Lord Selkirk said that, given the intrinsic difficulties of governing a State comprising four different races, the present Government of Singapore had dealt with the situation a good deal more satisfactorily than could have been expected, and it was in our interest to satisfy their natural aspirations, for improved status in the Commonwealth. Although they could not be regarded as an independent country, they were equally no longer a colony, but enjoyed a greater degree of independence than the Federation of Rhodesia and Nyasaland. It was also important that we should try to accommodate them in their current request for financial aid, since our response would be regarded locally as the measure of our confidence in the Singapore administration. It would also be helpful if outlets could be found for migrants from Singapore, where the population was increasing at a rate of 4 per cent per annum.

In discussion the following points were made:—

(a) Since Singapore was not an independent country it would not be appropriate for her Prime Minister to be invited to attend meetings of Commonwealth Prime Ministers. In their report[1] on future constitutional development in the Commonwealth a group of Commonwealth officials had suggested that countries which had reached a similar stage of constitutional development to Singapore might be allowed to improve their status in the Commonwealth by sending in their own right representatives to Commonwealth meetings on specific subjects, e.g. finance and education, instead of, as at present, attending as part of a composite delegation from the Colonies. If this recommendation were to be accepted by Commonwealth Governments it might go a considerable way towards satisfying Singapore aspirations at the present time. The question of which Department in Whitehall should be responsible for relations with Singapore, and with other territories which might attain similar status, raised the wider question of the future arrangements for conducting relations with the Commonwealth, both independent and dependent, as a whole; this would need further careful study.

(b) The possibility of an invitation being extended to the Prime Minister of Singapore to visit London in the course of next year might be considered.

(c) As regards Singapore's request for financial aid, we could offer a total of £7.6

---

[1] An extract from the report is reproduced in Hyam and Louis eds, *BDEE: the Conservative government, 1957–1964*, II, 534.

millions, mostly by way of loan but some in the form of a grant, in response to Singapore's request for £28 millions. It would not be possible for us to offer more than this, but in view of the risk that if Singapore could not obtain sufficient financial assistance from the West she might seek aid from Soviet bloc countries,[2] the United States authorities should be informed of the position before the Singapore Finance Minister made his forthcoming visit to Washington.

(d) It might be suggested to the Prime Minister of the Federation of Malaya that he should consider a loan to the Government of Singapore, and also that Malaya might enter into a closer economic relationship with Singapore, possibly by establishing a free trade area.

(e) As regards Singapore's surplus population it might be suggested to the Singapore Government that they should approach the Government of British Honduras, which had recently notified other Governments of its desire to receive immigrants.

(f) It might not be desirable to seek to include Singapore in a wider Malayan federation since the subsequent emergence of a Communist dominated Government in Singapore would threaten the political situation in the whole of the Federation. On the other hand we might find it easier to maintain our defence facilities in Singapore by means of a defence treaty if Singapore were part of the Federation; Singapore could not be expected to be content with her present relationship with the United Kingdom for more than a few years.

(g) So far as the Borneo territories were concerned our attitude towards their association with the Malayan Federation should be one of benevolent neutrality. It would be useful however if Lord Selkirk were to discuss the matter further at the meetings of the Borneo Inter-territorial Conference and the Joint Defence Advisory Committee (Borneo) to be held in October, 1960. In view of the reactions of the Sultan of Brunei to the Tunku's suggestion that Brunei should join the Federation, it seemed unlikely that the Tunku would for his part wish to press matters further at this stage.

In the course of further discussion it was suggested that there might be advantage in suggesting to a new administration in the United States, that a study might be made of a joint United States/United Kingdom approach to problems in the Far East. It was for consideration whether the maintenance of our base at Singapore should become a S.E.A.T.O. responsibility, in which case some of the cost which we were at present incurring in the area might be more widely shared. We might also wish to conduct a reappraisal of our military commitments to N.A.T.O. and in particular the strength of our armed forces in Germany. Now that a significant military contribution was being made by the Federal German Republic it might, for instance, be desirable for much of our military effort there to be redeployed in areas outside continental Europe.

The Meeting:—

(1) Took note that further consideration would be given to the relationship of Singapore to the Commonwealth in the light of the report of Commonwealth officials on the future constitutional development of the Commonwealth.

(2) Invited the Foreign Secretary to inform the United States Government, in advance of the Singapore Finance Minister's visit to Washington, of our

---

[2] See 21, para 4.

apprehensions lest in the event of Singapore being unable to secure sufficient
financial assistance from the West, she might seek it from the Soviet bloc.
(3) Invited Lord Selkirk:—
   (i) to suggest to the Government of Singapore that they should approach the
   Government of British Honduras regarding the migration of Singapore
   citizens to that Colony;
   (ii) to discuss with the Prime Minister of Malaya the possibility of the
   Federation adopting a policy of closer economic co-operation with Singapore,
   including the granting of a loan for development purposes;
   (iii) to discuss at the forthcoming meetings of the Borneo Inter-territorial
   Conference and the Joint Defence Advisory Committee (Borneo) the possibility
   of the future association of the Borneo territories with a wider Malayan
   federation.

28   CAB 134/1644, DSE(60)15th meeting   29 Sept 1960
[Future developments in SE Asia]: Committee on Future
Developments in SE Asia minutes   [Extract]

[As part of a comprehensive study of Britain's global role during the decade 1960–1970, a
committee of officials chaired by Sir Norman Brook recommended in Feb 1960 that, for
economic reasons, Britain should reduce its forces in SE Asia and plan for the eventuality
of losing the Singapore base. A specialist, inter-departmental committee, the Committee
on Future Developments in SE Asia, was then charged to identify likely developments in
the region over the next ten years as well as Britain's aims, obligations and means for
achieving them (see 'Study of future policy 1960–1970', issued by the Cabinet Office on 9
June 1959, DO 35/8864). Chaired by Sir Robert Scott, who had returned from Singapore
to the post of commandant of the Imperial Defence College, this committee met for the
first time on 13 June 1960 and produced the 'gist' or summary of its report in mid-Oct (see
29). Its final report, which was completed on 3 Nov, consists of 37 pages and 159 paragraphs
and includes the 'gist'. The minutes and some memoranda are open at CAB 134/1644 while
the memoranda and final report held in CAB 134/1645 were released in Sept 2002 (D(60)50,
CAB 131/24; CAB 134/1644; DSE(60)25(Final) and DSE(60)30(Final), CAB 134/1645;
FP(60)1, CAB 134/1929; also Hyam and Louis eds, *BDEE: the Conservative government,
1957–1964*, xxxiv–xxxvi, 4–17).]

Future developments in South East Asia: draft summary of conclusions
The Committee had before them a note by the Secretaries D.S.E. (60) 25 circulating
a draft concluding chapter for the Committee's report.
   In discussion the following points were made:—

(a) It was generally accepted that this chapter would be of more value as a summary
placed at the beginning of the report, and that it should include the military facilities
available in Singapore in order to show more clearly the present position.
(b) It would be helpful to have some form of balance sheet for the area. This presented
some difficulty as there was no material asset in the area essential to our national
economy to compare with, for example, oil in the Middle East. Most of our assets in
East Asia were intangibles, the containment of communism, the Commonwealth,
relations with the United States and our general influence and trade in the area.
Rubber and tin were no longer essential to our balance of payments and we were
spending money in the area for political reasons rather than for any prospect of
financial gain.

(c) Both for financial reasons and for reasons of man-power the size of forces which we could afford to maintain in the area might not be militarily sound. Any sudden change of policy or reduction of our military presence might be taken by the countries of East Asia to be weakness, but this could to some extent be overcome by effecting changes gradually. In the meantime, we should take every opportunity to help with the training of local military and police forces and to train technicians. In this way we could help to ensure stability in the area at the same time reducing our expenditure on defence there. A comprehensive programme would be too great for us to undertake on our own. We should however do as much as we could in this field and encourage others to follow suit. In order to ensure their co-operation we should have early discussions with Australia, New Zealand and America and we should encourage the use of the United Nations in the area.

(d) It was hard to estimate what our security of tenure might be in the Borneo Territories. Once a move for independence was started events were apt to move very quickly. However, it seemed likely that we could enjoy facilities in North Borneo for as long as we remained in Hong Kong, though it would not be necessary for these to be on the same scale as those at present available in Singapore. It would also be worth considering housing the Gurkha Brigade, withdrawn from jungle operations, in Johore rather than in Borneo. Some savings might be possible from this and it might also be possible to sell the accommodation there when we vacated it.

(e) Though India should have a very high priority in any economic programme it would be incorrect to indicate that she should have an overriding priority.

29   CAB 131/24, D(60)50   12 Oct 1960
'Future developments in South East Asia': gist of report by the Committee on Future Developments in SE Asia, circulated to the Cabinet Defence Committee by Sir N Brook

Terms of reference
The Committee was appointed by direction of the Prime Minister with the following terms of reference:—

> 'To study the likely course of developments during the next ten years in South and South East Asia and the Far East; and to review our aims in this area and our means of securing them.'

2.   Subsequently certain questions about the loss of bases and Gurkhas and the deployment of nuclear weapons in the area were remitted to the Committee. Their answers are contained in an earlier report (D.S.E. (60) 26 (Final), circulated to the Defence Committee as D.(60) 46).

3.   The area covered by the following study is bounded by Pakistan on the West, Japan on the East and Indonesia on the South. For convenience the area as a whole is referred to as Eastern Asia.

Assumptions
4.   The Committee adopted the following assumptions:—

(a) In the period under review there will be neither a global war nor a genuine *détente* between the two power blocs.

(b) There will be no major split between Russia and China, but they will be rivals for Communist leadership throughout Asia and Africa and relations between them will at times be strained because of Chinese arrogance and Russian fears.

(c) Among the free countries of South East Asia some progress may be made towards regional association; but national differences will still be strong throughout Eastern Asia, and Asian countries will find it easier to rally together for negative purposes (anti-West, anti-Colonial, anti-China) than for positive ones (a genuine pooling of effort). Policies of non-alignment between East and West are likely to be followed by many of the free countries, and neutralist sentiment will retain some anti-Western bias.

(d) China will, in terms of power, increasingly over-shadow the area. She will seek to expel the West from Formosa, Japan, Korea and Indo-China by all means short of deliberate overt armed aggression, and will generally seek to weaken the West throughout Asia and in Africa and Latin America.

(e) The free countries of the area will be preoccupied by social and economic problems and by the search for external assistance to solve them. Amongst China's immediate neighbours there will be mounting fear of Chinese imperialism and in a few cases an inclination to come to terms with her. Japan will be playing a major political as well as economic role in the area. With the exception of Japan and possibly India the free countries in the area will not have achieved self-sustaining economic growth.

(f) The United States will continue to maintain a considerable capacity for military intervention in the area.

(g) The United Nations will still be in existence, with China as a member and the Formosa issue not yet resolved to China's satisfaction.

(h) Whatever the course of constitutional developments in other dependent territories in the area, Hong Kong will still be a British responsibility.

Forecast

5. The area will continue to be a major scene of conflict in the East/West struggle. There will be no defections of major countries, now free, to the Communist bloc, provided that they continue to receive Western support, including military backing, without which they are unlikely to maintain their independence.

Aims

6. In common with the rest of the Western world the United Kingdom shares certain general aims in the area:—

(a) to contain Communism;
(b) to maintain Western influence;
(c) to preserve peace and strengthen non-Communist societies, especially India;
(d) to foster trade;
(e) to maintain political stability and economic development.

7. The United Kingdom also has certain special obligations in the area:—

(a) as the centre of the Commonwealth and the sterling area;
(b) to her dependent territories, notably responsibility for Hong Kong and prevention of Communist control over Singapore;

(c) as a member of S.E.A.T.O.;

(d) under the Malayan Defence Agreement;

(e) under the Geneva Agreement of 1954;

(f) under the ANZAM Agreement.

8.   Nearly two-thirds of the population of the non-Communist countries of the area are in the Commonwealth (India, Pakistan, Ceylon and Malaya). In addition Australia and New Zealand are vitally interested. It is a major United Kingdom interest to fortify these Commonwealth links, which are a source of strength to us and help us to exercise influence in the area, and to maintain our large stakes and influence in the individual Commonwealth countries.

9.   In Eastern Asia the collapse of sterling would have grave consequences. The United Kingdom shares her interest in maintaining the strength of sterling with the other members of the sterling area, but the main burden falls on the United Kingdom. This places a limit on the amount of United Kingdom expenditure that can safely be incurred in Eastern Asia as in other areas. However desirable it might be for us to play a greater role there in all spheres, the Committee has felt obliged to accept that even the continuance of our present role with consequent increases in Government expenditure would weaken the economic position of this country and sterling. The Committee has therefore sought ways in which our present role might be modified without undue detriment to our interests in Eastern Asia.

10.   The United States must inevitably make the largest single contribution to the pursuit of Western aims in the area, but the United Kingdom must continue by political action, economic aid and military backing to play her part in this process, working as closely as possible with her friends and Allies, and in addition to maintain her own special interests.

Political action

11.   We must clearly maintain and foster our established relationships with the Commonwealth and other free countries of Eastern Asia, if we are to influence developments in the area, including the evolution of United States policy. If, for example, the United States were obliged to retreat from her present China policy in circumstances which looked like a political defeat, this would be a major setback for the whole Western position. We should therefore aim to maintain such influence as we may have on the evolution of American policy in order to reduce the possibility of any such damaging consequences.

12.   Information work, broadcasting and cultural work (especially English language teaching) make an important contribution to the maintenance of United Kingdom and Western influence and the understanding of Western policies, and must continue to play a significant part in countering Communist penetration in the area.

Economic aid and technical assistance

13.   The requirements are:—

(a) for capital loans where they can be used with the best chance of being effective (India is the outstanding example); and

(b) for training—administrative, technical, police, military—throughout the area to promote administrative and technical efficiency and security, and hence political stability and the foundations of economic and social progress.

14.   As a long-term policy the emphasis of our efforts in the area should shift increasingly towards economic and technical aid.

Defence policy
15.   The main roles of British defence forces and facilities at present in the area are:—

(a) internal security and external defence of British dependent territories;
(b) a contribution to the strategic deterrent against China;
(c) a contribution to operations on land (for example, a S.E.A.T.O. operation).

16.   The United Kingdom cannot continue for another decade to play all three roles on present scales and in present forms. Political currents in Malaya and Singapore might turn against the presence of British bases and forces. Direct communications to Singapore from Gan and Australia might be insecure because of uncertainty about the Indonesian attitude in a crisis. The Services' man-power situation is already difficult, and if (as is possible) we have lost the Gurkhas it will become acute. Though these are possibilities and not certainties they must cumulatively cast doubt on the long-term availability or value of the bases in Malaya and Singapore. Furthermore, a future Australian or New Zealand Government might withdraw its component from the Strategic Reserve now in Malaya. Sterling crises might enforce cuts in expenditure, or emergencies elsewhere in the world might require the sudden withdrawal of forces from Eastern Asia.

17.   More decisive and also more certain is the cost factor. At present direct United Kingdom expenditure in the area for defence purposes is about £50 millions annually, and at least twice as much again is incurred in the United Kingdom in connection with it. If this defence effort continues on present lines, defence expenditure for the area is bound to increase. In the light of our present economic and man-power situation any such increase is hard to justify on direct political or economic grounds or in relation to inescapable defence commitments.

18.   A review of present defence roles in the area is therefore needed. The total withdrawal of forces cannot be contemplated, because this would mean abandoning our Colonial responsibilities, our obligations to Malaya and S.E.A.T.O., and the playing of a significant part in containing China and resisting the spread of Communism; it would also damage our relations with Australia and New Zealand to an unacceptable extent and would seriously harm our relations with the United States. For general political reasons—influence with the United States, the Commonwealth connection, and our status as a power with a worldwide stake in stemming Communist expansion—the United Kingdom must continue to make a contribution to the nuclear deterrent against China. In addition, the United Kingdom cannot avoid her special obligations to her dependent territories, notably Hong Kong.

19.   If for the reasons given above some cut must be made in our defence effort in the area, it is only in the third defence role (a contribution to land operations) that we could afford to risk some reduction. To drop it completely during the next ten years would have unacceptable political consequences: it would encourage the Communists, weaken S.E.A.T.O. and the free countries of the area, upset political stability and damage our relations with Australia and New Zealand and also with America. No modification can be made without some adverse effects. However, the

scale of British participation in S.E.A.T.O.-type operations in the area by 1970 might be reduced to our contribution to the Commonwealth Brigade (stationed in Malaya if the base is still available, but otherwise in Australia) and a carrier-borne Royal Marine Commando, with air and naval support but without Gurkhas. In the meanwhile it would be politically acceptable to limit the participation of British ground forces in future limited wars in Eastern Asia to the scale of forces now there for the purpose.

20.   The central problems for British defence policy in the area in the long-term are to determine in detail the scale and form of a reduced contribution to a land campaign on the mainland of Eastern Asia and the timing and manner of progress to that end.

21.   Everything possible should be done in advance to offset the weakening of the defences of the area which will result from the eventual achievement of the restricted scale of British defence effort suggested above. A major drive is needed to promote stability in friendly countries through administrative and technical training, and to strengthen their security forces by police and military training. This would call for action in the area, additional training facilities in the United Kingdom and co-ordination with Commonwealth and Western Powers.

22.   Thus the Committee envisages the following main roles for British defence forces in the area by 1970:—

(a) the security of remaining British territories;
(b) a contribution to the strategic deterrent;
(c) a much reduced contribution to land operations;
(d) training and otherwise strengthening defence forces of friendly countries.

23.   The first is primarily a United Kingdom commitment. The others should be discharged in the closest co-operation with our Allies.

24.   As regards bases, in the long run our strategy in the area must come to depend increasingly on airborne and seaborne forces operating from Australia and New Zealand, the only permanent and reliable Western bases in the Eastern Hemisphere. In addition, some centrally placed cantonment is needed for certain of the ground forces required to discharge our Colonial responsibilities, so long as they exist in the area. This cantonment should be as free as possible from risks of local political blackmail and insecure communications, and these considerations point to North Borneo. Although North Borneo cannot be expected to remain indefinitely free from political pressures, at least for the period under review it is likely to be freer from them than Malaya or Singapore. While nothing should be done which might hasten the loss of facilities in Malaya and Singapore, these factors should be considered in connection with any future programmes for building permanent accommodation for forces in the area.

Conclusions

25.   Western policy in the area, in which the United Kingdom must play her part, must continue to be to maintain peace and to sustain the free countries by political action, economic aid and military backing. In addition, the United Kingdom has certain special interests and obligations as the centre of the Commonwealth and to her dependent territories and as a signatory of various international treaties. She has a further special responsibility for the strength of sterling.

26.   At least throughout the next decade it will be necessary for the United Kingdom to maintain a military presence and capacity to intervene in Eastern Asia. The long-term trend during this period should be towards reducing capacity to intervene in operations on the East Asian mainland with ground and tactical air forces.

27.   The Committee is driven to the concept of a diminished British military presence in the area by 1970, not because interests and obligations will have been reduced but because man-power and financial difficulties, coupled with uncertainties about bases, force this upon the United Kingdom. The Committee further accepts the concept (subject to balance of payment considerations) of more stress on economic programmes. Such changes of role and of emphasis carry political and military risks. It is therefore necessary to do what is possible to lessen these risks by, for example:—

(a) helping the countries of the area to stand on their own feet and so lessen the need for intervention; and

(b) sharing with friends and Allies commitments which in many cases are more vital to them than to us.

28.   A major effort to improve the strength and efficiency of the defence forces of non-Communist countries in the area e.g. by military training would contribute to their stability and security. Our efforts in this direction should be co-ordinated as far as possible with Commonwealth and Western countries.

29.   The Committee believes that Australia should make a bigger effort to provide for her own defence and vital interests, but does not favour putting pressure on Australia to do this. The United Kingdom could, and may have to, put itself in a position where pressure comes from Australia and New Zealand on the United Kingdom rather than vice versa.

30.   There is every reason for the closest consultation with Australia and New Zealand as well as with the United States in formulating United Kingdom defence policy for the area. Our ANZAM obligations to Australia and New Zealand could not be modified without their agreement.

31.   Increased United Nations presence in the area might promote stability and lessen the risks of incidents and hence the need for Western intervention or support. It could take many forms—technical missions, political observers, or even in some circumstances United Nations gendarmerie forces. American views on the advantage of increased United Nations presence, if it connoted neutralism, would be important and probably decisive. It is recommended that possible roles for, and consequences of, United Nations activity in the area be studied.

32.   Finally, the Committee wishes to stress that policy towards Eastern Asia and the scale of the United Kingdom effort there cannot be considered in isolation. They are affected by the political and military situation elsewhere and by the strength or weakness of sterling. For this reason and because the above conclusions flow from assumptions which only time will test, United Kingdom interests in and policy towards the area should be reviewed from time to time.

30   CO 1030/977, no 75   25 Oct 1960

[Prospects for closer association]: despatch from Lord Selkirk to Mr
Macleod reporting his personal views following high-level discussions
in Kuching

On the occasion of the recent meetings in Kuching of the Inter-Territorial
Conference for the Borneo Territories and the Joint Advisory Defence Committee
(Borneo) I took the opportunity to hold a discussion with the Governors of North
Borneo and Sarawak and the High Commissioner for Brunei on the future evolution
of these territories and their relationship with the Federation of Malaya and the State
of Singapore. We were greatly assisted in our consideration of these questions by the
presence of The Right Honourable The Earl of Perth, Minister of State, of Mr. Eugene
Melville of your Department, and of General Sir Richard Hull, Commander-in-Chief,
Far East Land Forces.

2.   A summary record of the discussion is enclosed.[1] The main conclusion which
emerged was that we must now seek endorsement from Ministers in London of
certain broad lines of policy to guide the future shaping of our course in Colonial and
Commonwealth affairs in South-East Asia so as to safeguard as fully and as long as
possible our defence and other interests in this area.

3.   Our first recommendation is that Her Majesty's Government in the United
Kingdom should accept as the ultimate aim of their policy the development of a
political association between Malaya, Singapore and the Borneo territories such as
would enable them to take their place within the Commonwealth as a single entity
strong enough to resist encroachment from their neighbours or from Communist
China. Though the exact form of union, federation or confederation that might
emerge cannot be foreseen at this stage, we consider that some such broad
association provides the only satisfactory evolution which will safeguard in the
longer term not only the security, economic development and welfare of the
territories themselves, but also, on a basis of consent, the United Kingdom's own
essential defence interests consisting of the base in Singapore and the necessary
deployment areas outside it.

4.   We hold it important to avoid any appearance that Her Majesty's Government
are actively pushing such a solution or seeking to impose it upon the peoples
concerned, and we consider that in public, if the need arose, no more should be said
for the present than that a broad association of this kind is among the possible
outcomes to be studied by the peoples concerned and one that Her Majesty's
Government would not themselves regard as excluded from consideration. At the
same time we are sufficiently impressed by the growing interest of all the territories
concerned, despite the very real and obvious differences between them, in some such
eventual solution to their problems, to believe that with discreet encouragement on
our own part a general desire for it might in time arise. And we think that the
moment has come when we should be ready to begin discussing the matter in
confidence as occasion may arise with interested parties such as Tunku Abdul
Rahman, Mr. Lee Kuan Yew and the Sultan of Brunei. In particular, we should use

---

[1] Not printed.

the possibility of some eventual political association as an argument with which meanwhile to resist any retrograde step in the economic field such as the break up of the existing currency union of the five territories or the imposition of new restrictions on trade between them.

5.   In any such discussions we should make it plain that progress towards the ultimate goal must be gradual and adjusted to the rate of political evolution in the Borneo territories. We consider that our first step in such evolution must be the strengthening of existing links between North Borneo and Sarawak with the intention that they might eventually enter the wider association as a single unit. Some further steps in this direction were agreed upon at the recent Twelfth Meeting of the Inter-Territorial Conference in Kuching.

6.   We recommend that this gradual bringing together of the two Borneo colonies should henceforth proceed without expectation of Brunei's participation, but so far as possible without prejudice to her joining in later should it be found possible to bring about any modification of the Sultan's present attitude of opposition.

7.   This despatch has not been agreed textually with the Governors of North Borneo and Sarawak and the High Commissioner for Brunei, but it represents my own interpretation of the sense of our discussions and the agreement emerging from them. They will no doubt send you any further comments they may wish to offer from their own viewpoints. Subject to any such comments, I trust that you will agree to seek the endorsement of Her Majesty's Government for the policy I have outlined.[2]

8.   I am sending copies of this despatch to the Secretaries of State for Commonwealth Relations and Foreign Affairs and the Minister of Defence, to the Governors of North Borneo and Sarawak and the High Commissioner for Brunei, to the United Kingdom High Commissioner in Kuala Lumpur and the United Kingdom Commissioner, Singapore,[3] and to the three Commanders-in-Chief in Singapore.

---

[2] While Selkirk mentioned the need for a gradual approach towards the Borneo territories, the CO noted that his views did not altogether accord with those of governors Goode and Waddell.
[3] This post was also held by Selkirk.

31   CO 1030/1153, no 3   30 Dec 1960
'North Borneo: review of affairs': despatch from Sir W Goode to Mr Macleod, reviewing his first eight months as governor of North Borneo

[This despatch, which was printed for wider circulation on 20 Feb 1961, develops themes to which Goode frequently returns during the planning of Malaysia: North Borneo is 'a happy country' which is 'still content with colonial rule' and should be protected from the political aspirations in neighbouring countries while being assisted in the development of its economic potential and social services (especially education). Although Goode accepts that 'the best future for North Borneo lies in association with its near neighbours and with Malaya' (paragraph 10), he argues that closer association should not be rushed. Sir Alexander Waddell wrote in a similar vein from Sarawak, although he painted a slightly darker picture of a less developed and a more politically aware country where the Chinese-dominated Sarawak United People's Party was active and where, unless there was greater investment particularly in roads and education, economic disparities might be exploited by the Clandestine Communist Organisation to provoke racial clashes (see Waddell to Macleod, 21 Apr, 15 July, 17 Aug and 13 Dec 1960, CO 1030/1154).]

I have the honour to report on conditions and problems in North Borneo as I see them after eight months here.

2.   North Borneo is a strikingly beautiful country of happy, friendly people, busy building and planting for the future, and still content with Colonial rule. On arrival I was astonished to find how much had been done since I last visited North Borneo in 1957. The main towns have now been rebuilt from the ruins of the war; Government offices, hospitals and schools have also been built; and thousands of acres of land are being cleared and planted, mostly for rubber, by native smallholders and Chinese, though two British companies, following the lead given by the Colonial Development Corporation, are developing large areas for cocoa and palm oil. The timber industry flourishes particularly on the east coast and now provides the largest export. It is well founded on two strong British firms, the British Borneo Timber Co. (Harrisons & Crosfield) and the Bombay Burmah Trading Corporation. There is a general air of progress, prosperity and smiling happiness.

3.   Economically 1960 has been a wonderful year. The total value of trade for the year will be over $400 million, some 27 per cent. better than last year, and there will be a favourable trade balance of some $24 million. Much of this is due to the thriving entrepôt or barter trade with Indonesia and the Philippines, based on the import of copra and spices in exchange for cigarettes and other consumer goods. Government revenue this year will also break all previous records: $58 million, as compared to the original estimate of $45 million and $46 million collected in 1959. It has been possible to pay $15 million into the Development Fund and still leave a general revenue balance of $15½ million at the end of the year. It would be unwise to count on repeating this next year, since revenue is much affected by the price of rubber and the volume of the entrepôt trade, both of which can fluctuate for causes outside our control. Given reasonable world conditions, however, there is every reason to expect that North Borneo's national income will increase steadily as increased areas under rubber, cocoa, oil palm and coconuts come into bearing.

4.   Progress over the last few years has been remarkable. There is still much to do. We are only beginning a big programme of road construction; a main road to join Jesselton to Sandakan by crossing the mountains and a series of other roads to provide a continuous road system from Kudat in the north down the west coast to Sipitang in the south. New wharfs are needed at Kudat and elsewhere. At least three hospitals badly need replacing. And schools are needed all over the country. There are still rural areas where the native peoples live in scattered villages along rivers at a bare subsistence level beyond reach of existing services with little to distinguish their conditions to-day from those of the past centuries.

5.   So much has been done during the past few years that the administration generally is now stretched to the utmost. Available funds have rightly been spent on capital investment: reconstruction of war damage and new development; recurrent commitments have been held down. There has been little expansion of the public service and it is too thin on the ground to meet the needs of a rapidly developing country. Land offices are choked with thousands of land applications awaiting survey and settlement; more agricultural officers are needed to advise the thousands of smallholders opening up new land; and rural areas need teachers and doctors. Nor is it only quantity that is lacking; there is also a lack of quality in senior posts. North Borneo is no longer a rustic backwater; it is thriving and stirring and is surrounded by the complex political conditions of South-East Asia. If North Borneo is to hold its

own with its more advanced neighbours in a difficult world, it needs men of real ability, imagination and leadership in the top ranks of its administration to build fast and soundly. Local resources are sadly limited. Less than half of the children get any education at all; only 3,000 were in secondary schools last year, and only 78 achieved a school certificate. Standards of local public servants are inevitably low. Yet already there is the natural pressure to staff the public service with local men and women. Overseas officers have to work with very weak clerical and executive assistance (as emphasised by the critical reports each year from the Director of Audit) and must devote more time than they can spare to training staff. There is no place in North Borneo for the weaker overseas officer.

6.   Not the least of the attractions of this lovely country is its claim to have no politics, no secret societies, no trade unions and no Communist subversion. Broadly, this claim is still true. There is no political party.[1] There is no sign whatsoever of secret societies, incredible though this may be to anyone with experience of the Chinese in Malaya. Nor is there any interest in trade unions. There is a general shortage of labour and there are no large industrial works. The individual still seems to be well able to look after his own interests with occasional assistance from officials of the Labour and Welfare Department. The threat of Communist subversion is as yet negligible, though it needs careful watching.

7.   The North Borneo Chinese are very different from the Chinese communities in Singapore and Malaya. There has been no mass immigration into North Borneo of Chinese labour. The Chinese came here in small family groups, most of them many years ago. They settled on the land, and still to-day most Chinese here have an interest in the land. In the towns there are many small shop-keepers and few wealthy business men. The towns and villages are still small communities where everyone knows everyone else, everyone mixes, and there is a common language, Malay. Interests are parochial: in local events, in personal advancement in a land of opportunity, and in getting more land. The native peoples are mainly pagan or Christian, and this has led to intermarriage with Chinese. There is not the fundamental antipathy found in Malaya between the Muslim Malays and the Chinese, each at heart disliking and despising the other. There are few newspapers and those there are also tend to be mainly interested in parish doings and people. Places and events outside Borneo are a long way away. In so far as the Chinese take an interest in other Chinese, they are probably more interested in Hong Kong, with which they have business and often family ties, or in Formosa than in mainland China. As always the Chinese have provided themselves with schools. One-third of the primary schools are Chinese run by committees of local Chinese. But there is comparatively little Chinese secondary education, most of the children going on from a Chinese primary school to an English secondary school run by one of the many Christian missions. Thus, although primary education fosters Chinese communalism, there is not the menace from the big Chinese middle schools that creates such problems in Malaya, and to some extent in Sarawak. Some attempts have been made by the clandestine Communist organisation in Sarawak to penetrate one or two of the larger Chinese schools in North Borneo, but so far only a handful of boys has been interested in Communist ideas. It would be rash to say that this happy state of affairs will

---

[1] For a summary of the subsequent development of political parties in North Borneo, see 26, n 8.

continue. The Sarawak Communist organisation will exploit every opportunity to organise cells in North Borneo schools. But at present the general tone of the schools is sound; the management committees are on the best terms with the Education Department and are themselves, with a very few exceptions, opposed to their schools going the way of Chinese schools in neighbouring countries. Moreover, there is a most encouraging degree of acceptance of the Government's declared policy of making English the common language of North Borneo and the language of education.

8.   The absence of political parties does not indicate lack of political consciousness. Inevitably there are repercussions here from the constitutional changes and political excitements of nearby territories, particularly Brunei and Sarawak. If it were not for these outside influences, North Borneo would wish to be left alone: to get on with developing the country, each individual working for the betterment of himself and his family; to raise the general level of education, especially in the rural areas; and generally to catch up with conditions in the more advanced territories around before embarking on political and constitutional progress. It is North Borneo's misfortune that it is 30 years behind the rest of South-East Asia, and is unlikely to be given that important 30 years before to-day's troubles invade it. Even if the political leaders of nearby countries would leave North Borneo alone, it just is not possible to exclude outside influences. In Sandakan, the prosperous commercial capital of North Borneo, the wealthy Chinese business man is emerging, flexing his muscles in a small tightly knit Chinese community, conscious of the local power his success in business has given him, and I suspect slightly embarrassed in relation to associates in Sarawak and Singapore, who live in the more up-to-date world of political parties and emancipation from Colonial rule. To a lesser extent the same thing is happening in Tawau and Jesselton. In all the towns there is the usual Chinese Chamber of Commerce, acting as the governing body of the Chinese community, offering a platform for personal advancement and influence, potentially a parallel authority to the Government. As the towns get bigger, they will become more Chinese and there will be less personal mixing of the different races. The more far-seeing of the Chinese leaders are taking heed of what is happening to the Chinese in Sarawak, Indonesia and Malaya, and give thought to their own future. Should they now take control of political developments here, as they so easily can, and ensure their future before the backward native peoples get the education that will enable them to hold the Chinese, as the Malays have done in Malaya? So there are amongst the Chinese those who are inclined to respond to the approaches from the Sarawak United People's Party to start an associated political party in North Borneo.

9.   The native peoples, however, are apprehensive of any extension of Sarawak or Brunei politics to North Borneo. They are conscious of their backwardness. They fear that the formation of political parties here will mean that political power will go to the Chinese. They distrust what they know of recent developments in Sarawak. They would prefer that there should be no political development here until they have had time to catch up, mainly in education, so that they will be able to hold their own. Nor do they have any kindred feelings for Brunei; they inherit resentment from the past domination of North Borneo by the Muslim Malays of Brunei. The leading natives have rejected discreet approaches by Chinese leaders to join in starting a political party, with the warning that any political move by the Chinese will arouse the hostility of the natives and destroy the present happy harmony between the various

communities. I think the majority of politically conscious people here realise the danger of provoking communal tension, and for this reason are in no hurry to start politics in North Borneo. They do not wish to arouse here the tensions they believe to trouble Sarawak, and they are worried by the way politics are developing in Sarawak.

10.   So at present there is virtually no enthusiasm to start political parties here. The question is how long will it be so, or will outside influence allow it to be so? Of one thing I am sure; it will not be long enough. The leaders of political parties in Sarawak and Brunei are already advocating some form of political association between the three Borneo territories; the Sultan of Brunei may well cherish ideas of restoring to his rule the lands ceded by his predecessors to the Brookes and the Chartered Company;[2] and in the Federation Tunku Abdul Rahman has hinted at linking the Borneo territories into the Federation of Malaya. I have no doubt that the best future for North Borneo lies in association with its near neighbours and with Malaya, all having a common heritage from British rule. Given time and the help she needs, North Borneo could join such an association from a position of strength. But to-day the country just is not capable of looking after its own interests.

11.   The greatest and most urgent need is education. Hundreds of schools are needed to give the majority of the population, the natives who live in the rural areas, universal primary education and enough secondary education to produce their fair share of the leaders, merchants, professional men and civil servants, while ensuring that they are not turned into unemployed white-collar workers but remain firmly rooted to the land. This task is only partly a matter of money. The real difficulty is teachers. Teachers to staff teacher training colleges and teachers to set standards in the secondary schools. They can only be found from overseas; and so far our efforts to get them have met with little success. We still have a great opportunity here to avoid one of the most serious mistakes of Malaya; our failure to establish a system of education common to all who live in the country, in which children of every race are taught in the same language the same syllabus using the same text-books, thus producing a united people. It is accepted that the language of education should be English, though no doubt Malay will long remain the *lingua franca* of daily life; and there is acceptance of a common school system. The opportunity will not wait indefinitely, and until we can get the teachers we need from overseas we can make no serious start.

12.   Economically the country is developing soundly and as fast as is practical. Thousands of acres of land are being cleared and planted, mainly with rubber, but if all goes well cocoa and oil palms will soon broaden the agricultural economy. There is plenty of good land available and some exceptionally good land. The limits on agricultural development are set by the capacity of the administration, particularly the Lands and Survey Department, and the supply of labour. Large estates manage with difficulty to get enough labour, much of it supplied by Dusuns and Muruts from the interior who return at intervals to their villages and padi fields. Additional labour comes in from the Philippines and to a greater extent from the Celebes, Timor and Kalimantan in Indonesia. The Indonesians are the main supply. They come because conditions are bad in their own country, and most return home when they have

---

[2] For documents on the Sultan of Brunei's cessions see J de V Allen, A J Stockwell and L R Wright, *A collection of treaties and other documents affecting the states of Malaysia 1761–1963*, volume II (London, 1981).

accumulated some savings. Though many are critical of their own central Government in Djakarta, they are now here in sufficient numbers to present a potential problem for the future, particularly in the Tawau area. For the present, however, they are most useful and the risk must be accepted. For its future supply of labour North Borneo should look to its own people. If the current campaign eradicates malaria and communications can be built into the rural areas, there should be an adequate supply of young people growing up to provide for steady development. It would be unwise to disturb the present racial composition of the country by any mass immigration of Chinese or Indians or other race not akin to the native peoples. Meanwhile the Indonesians meet to-day's needs and those of them who decide to settle permanently should be more readily assimilated than any other race.

13. To sum up my impressions: I find North Borneo a happy country, going ahead fast, with a great potential for the future and as yet untroubled by the problems which bedevil the rest of South-East Asia, but ill-prepared to meet those troubles when they come, as surely they will and sooner than all but a very few here realise. It must be our task to do all we can as quickly as we can to strengthen these warm-hearted friendly people to meet their future. And I urge that their claim upon our resources should not be subordinated to generous but largely futile efforts to rescue others who are incapable of being helped. A tithe of the aid given to Indonesia would build a North Borneo worthy of our tutelage. The most obvious, urgent, task is to bring on the backward native peoples who are three-quarters of the population. For this we need capital works such as roads, wharfs, airfields, and buildings for hospitals, offices and schools. We also need more staff and of high quality for the administration. But most of all we need teachers to educate the people of North Borneo to develop for themselves the resources of their country and to produce men and women to manage their affairs.

32   CO 1030/978, no 119   30 Jan 1961
[The 'Grand Design']: despatch from Lord Selkirk to Mr Macleod following up his despatch of 25 Oct and urging a government statement of policy on the closer association. *Annex* A by H T Bourdillon;[1] *Annex* B by Sir G Tory

[Whereas interest in closer association had hitherto focused on the Borneo territories, from this point the instability of Singapore increasingly became a major factor in British calculations. Selkirk repeatedly argued that, unless Britain responded positively to local interest in merger, Lee Kuan Yew would be challenged, and possibly toppled, by the extreme left, see 33. To counter this threat and also to satisfy the PAP's demand for independence through merger, Selkirk believed that the British government would need to advance the 'grand design' more quickly than the Borneo territories would wish. Moreover, progress with the larger grouping of territories might reduce Malaya's abhorrence of closer association with Singapore.]

In my Despatch No. 3 of the 25th of October[2] I set out my recommendations concerning Her Majesty's Government's policy towards the development of a

---

[1] Deputy UK commissioner in Singapore 1959–1961.   [2] See 30.

political association between Malaya, Singapore and the Borneo Territories. Since that Despatch was written there have been certain changes in the situation which are relevant to the recommendations I made then. I therefore took the opportunity of the Eden Hall Conference to hold a discussion with the Governors of North Borneo and Sarawak, the High Commissioner for Brunei, the United Kingdom High Commissioners from Kuala Lumpur and Canberra, Her Majesty's Ambassador in Djakarta and representatives from the Foreign Office and Commonwealth Relations Office.

2.   Mr. Lee Kuan Yew has recently on more than one occasion talked with me and my staff about the Grand Design, and most recently he discussed it with the Secretary of State for Commonwealth Relations. He has given the clear impression that, since the Peoples' Action Party's declared aim of independence through merger with the Federation is vulnerable to destructive criticism because the Federation's attitude is so unforthcoming, he is keen to explore the idea of a route to independence through a wider political association which would include the Borneo Territories. This would not be an immediate goal but it would come to replace independence through merger with the Federation alone as the ideal to which the Singapore people can eventually aspire.

3.   The reasons behind this new line of thought by Mr. Lee Kuan Yew and some reflections on its implications for Her Majesty's Government are set out in a paper by Mr. Bourdillon which is attached to this Despatch at Annex A. I agree with the arguments and conclusions in this paper.

4.   In Kuala Lumpur, Sir Geofroy Tory has had an interesting discussion which reveals that at any rate one senior Federation Minister is also thinking about the possibility of a Grand Design. I enclose at Annex B a copy of the record of this discussion which has already been given to the Secretary of State for Commonwealth Relations. While it is clear that the ideas of Tun Razak have not yet been discussed with the Tunku, nor their practical implications thought out very far, it is nevertheless possible that they may provide a means of persuading the Tunku to adopt a more conciliatory attitude towards Singapore, through the medium of the Grand Design.

5.   At the discussion of these developments during the Eden Hall Conference everyone present agreed that some form of Grand Design should be our ultimate goal in this area, but that questions of timing were important and the precise form that the Design should take could not be decided at this stage. On timing it was recognised that the Federation and Singapore would be likely to want to move more quickly than North Borneo and possibly Sarawak. It was however clear that there is a distinct possibility that, whatever we do, a proposal for some kind of Grand Design will be launched sooner or later by the Federation or by Singapore. It therefore seemed important to us all that Her Majesty's Government should decide urgently what its attitude should be towards a Grand Design in order to be in a position to influence its shape and character during the formative period. This shape and character will naturally depend on the wishes of the various peoples involved, but this should not preclude us from studying possible alternatives and where advisable discussing them with the interested parties. If, as I hope, we accept it as the best ultimate goal for the area from our point of view, then we were agreed that Her Majesty's Government should in the near future, after consultation with the Governments involved and particularly after discussion with the Federation and

Singapore, (the former because it is the only completely independent country directly concerned, and the latter because its Prime Minister is at present showing such an active interest in the subject), make a statement in whatever manner would be most appropriate. This statement should be on the lines recommended by the Governor of North Borneo in his Despatch No. 766 of the 11th of November, namely that a broad association between the Federation and Singapore and the Borneo Territories has great possibilities for the future of this area, provided it is acceptable to the peoples concerned.

6.   In the light of these developments I feel bound to renew the recommendation made in my Despatch No. 3 of the 25th of October that Her Majesty's Government should reach an early decision on this matter.

7.   In the latter part of Annex A attention is drawn to some of the implications of the concept of the Grand Design from the political, economic and strategic points of view. I would not wish the decision in principle or the resultant action advocated in paragraphs 5 and 6 above to be delayed pending consideration of these implications. On the contrary, I am convinced that this action must be taken soon if we are to retain the initiative and if, in particular, we are to prevent the pressure for separate independence for Singapore, which is accumulating under the surface and by which Mr. Lee Kuan Yew is plainly embarrassed, from becoming unmanageable, with extremely embarrassing effects on our own position here. I think you will agree, however, that it is important that the implications should be spelt out and considered rather than being left to emerge of their own accord. I propose to address you further on this aspect of the matter when I have received, as I hope to do very shortly, your approval for the proposals in paragraphs 5 and 6 of this Despatch.

8.   I am sending copies of this Despatch to the Secretaries of State for Commonwealth Relations and Foreign Affairs and the Minister of Defence, to the Governors of North Borneo and Sarawak, and the High Commissioner for Brunei, to the United Kingdom High Commissioners in Kuala Lumpur, Canberra and Wellington, and the United Kingdom Commissioner, Singapore, to Her Majesty's Ambassador in Djakarta and to the three Commanders-in-Chief in Singapore.

Annex A to 32: by H T Bourdillon

I am becoming more and more convinced that the main policy objective advocated in the Commissioner General's despatch No. 3 of October 25, 1960 to the Colonial Office will be necessary in order to hold the political situation in Singapore as well as from the broader points of view which were considered in Kuching. Most of my reflections on this topic will not be new, but it may be useful if I put them on paper as a basis for further thought and discussion.

2.   Ever since the P.A.P. came into power they have continued to proclaim that independence through merger with the Federation is their objective and that separate independence for Singapore would be a dangerous illusion. That they have hitherto successfully held this line in spite of repeated rebuffs from across the Causeway and in spite of the emotional appeal of 'independence' as a slogan is a testimony to the Prime Minister's consistency of thought, to his moral courage and to his grip on the local situation. At the moment, indeed, he seems to be more firmly entrenched than ever—on the basis of a policy which tells the people of Singapore in

slightly different words that they cannot achieve independence for a long time to come. We have almost come to accept this remarkable phenomenon (doubly remarkable if we consider the helter-skelter rush towards independence which is going on elsewhere in the world) as a permanent feature of the Singapore scene. Nevertheless, I think we must all doubt whether the present situation can last indefinitely. Is not the time coming, perhaps quite soon, when the P.A.P. will have to choose between the alternatives of changing their line on independence or of destroying themselves by adhering to it?

3.   This conclusion would be less compelling if the attitude of the Federation Government were less bleak. Mr. Lee Kuan Yew has repeatedly said that he does not want the Federation leaders to welcome the idea of merger, but only to keep the door ajar and to offer some immediate cooperation in the economic field. At present he is not getting even this minimal measure of assistance. The Tengku's suspicion and dislike of the P.A.P. Government is said to have diminished, and it will probably diminish still further as the latter come out more and more into the open in their struggle against the Communists; but unfortunately the good effect of this improvement is counteracted by another tendency in the Federation which is very strong and which is not fundamentally due to any hostility towards Singapore as such. I refer to the craving for economic self-sufficiency, to the urge on the part of the Federation to have its own separate national institutions under its own undisputed control—its own major port, its own industrial policy, its own rubber market, its own airport, its own stock exchange. This urge is of course mixed up with envious feelings towards Singapore as the big Chinese city which has hitherto provided these amenities, but it is basically a product of nationalist sentiment spurred on by the attainment of independence in 1957. It may well continue even if the attitude towards Singapore goes on improving, and so long as it continues it is bound to make the P.A.P. policy of independence through merger look more and more unrealistic even to P.A.P. supporters.

4.   It is implicit in this P.A.P. policy that it cannot survive indefinitely in static or deteriorating circumstances. In proclaiming independence through merger as their objective the P.A.P. Government have recognised that in their statement of aims the word 'independence' cannot be omitted, or in other words that the demand for independence is an aspiration which must ultimately be met somehow. It follows that if time goes on and independence by the chosen means comes no nearer, the policy will sooner or later collapse. It is very convenient for H.M.G. that the status quo in Singapore should be maintained for the time being by the Singapore Government's habit of forecasting independence in conditions which are not within sight of being realised, but it would be folly to assume that a permanent settlement of Singapore's future can be established on this foundation.

5.   The relevance of all this to the despatch of October 25th is obvious. If we are doubtful whether the policy of independence through merger can be indefinitely maintained, and if on the other hand we share Mr. Lee Kuan Yew's conviction that separate independence for Singapore is a dangerous nonsense, the conclusion that H.M.G. ought to encourage the ultimate participation of both Singapore and the Federation of Malaya in a wider political grouping follows almost automatically. We know moreover that there is at least the possibility that the Tengku might not feel the same repugnance towards association with Singapore in a wider grouping as he feels towards merger in its simple form—though his feelings on this matter seem to

fluctuate a good deal. Finally, it is clear from all our recent conversations with Mr. Lee Kuan Yew himself that he is now strongly attracted by the idea of the larger grouping both as a solution to his own dilemma and as a desirable development in its own right. These considerations seem to me to make the case for the larger grouping, as H.M.G.'s best bet for solving the present and future problem of Singapore, almost unanswerable.

6. If this is accepted, we shall next have to consider what positive steps on our part may be desirable, over and above those already contemplated. First, however, I should like to emphasise certain dangers which it is necessary to avoid:—

(a) We must in no way relax our efforts to improve relations between the Federation and Singapore. There is a temptation to conclude that if from now on we are going to attach increasing importance to the larger grouping, the problem of the bilateral relationship between Singapore and the Federation of Malaya can be put on one side. This would be a dangerous fallacy. In the first place we are not yet entitled to assume that the larger grouping will come off. In the second place the improvement of relations between the Federation and Singapore, particularly on the economic side, is an urgent necessity in its own right, whatever the political future may hold. In the third place the improvement of these relations will be a necessary element in the success of any plans for the larger grouping itself. If the relationship between the Federation and Singapore continues poor or becomes exacerbated, this may tip the scales in the Federation not only against merger with Singapore but also against association with Singapore in a wider group.

(b) Nor must we encourage the Prime Minister of Singapore to switch his line too rapidly from merger to the Grand Design. There is a real danger of his doing this, and in fact we have very recently had to discourage him from coming out in public in favour of the larger grouping in a way which might have caused adverse reactions both in the Federation and in the Borneo territories. In making this point I do not mean that we should urge Mr. Lee Kuan Yew to go on pressing for merger in and out of season. We all know the reaction which this causes in Kuala Lumpur, and in any case H.M.G.'s disinterested attitude towards merger must of course be maintained in everything that we do. On the other hand the Prime Minister will not do himself any good politically if he appears to change horses in mid-stream. Any change on his part must be gradual and must be presented as an expansion rather than an abandonment of previous ideas. Moreover, he cannot afford any more than we can to forget that the improvement of relations between Singapore and the Federation remains his most pressing immediate problem, whatever the long-term objective may be.

(c) Finally, we should not abandon the idea of trying to give Singapore and its Prime Minister a more dignified place in Commonwealth councils, within the framework of the present Constitution. It is tempting to argue that this idea can also be put on one side, but it is in no way incompatible with the ultimate absorption of Singapore into a larger group. Moreover it is bound to be some years before the Grand Design can actually come into being, and in the meanwhile it may be very important to hold the position in Singapore by making the present status of the island as politically palatable as possible.

7. So much for the dangers to be avoided. In my opinion the most important positive step which we should now take in furtherance of the Grand Design is to

examine more closely the implications of the concept from the political, economic and strategic point of view. I have the following comments on these three aspects:—

(a) Politically we are faced with the problem that the Borneo territories will not be ready for independence (even as part of a larger grouping) for a number of years, while on the other hand the whole idea of the larger grouping may lose impetus and be lost if it is held up because of the relative constitutional backwardness of the Borneo territories. It is tempting to believe that one might devise a constitutional framework, on the lines of the Central African Federation, which could include both self-governing and non-self-governing territories, but I am afraid this would not be possible in the present case. Southern Rhodesia, which is the most 'advanced' territory in the Central African Federation, is not a sovereign independent state, and I do not see how it would be possible to include fully independent and dependent territories in the same federation without either trammelling the independence of the former or entirely relinquishing control over the latter. I think, therefore, that progress must be found in the evolution in the first instance of *consultative* institutions which could bring the territories closer together and pave the way for an ultimate constitutional association.

Then again, the composition of the federal legislature in an ultimate federation of the five territories needs to be thought out. The Prime Minister of Singapore at present seems to believe that the legislatures in the individual territories could constitute themselves into a kind of electoral college which would choose the members of the central parliament. This is an attractive idea, since it would emphasise the self-governing status of the individual territories, but the whole concept needs further examination. I am fearful lest in the last resort any federal parliament which is not based on a popular vote may come to be regarded as unrepresentative and therefore to be an object of suspicion and discontent. We may use loose terms like 'confederation', but we cannot blink the fact that in any effective political grouping there must be a real pooling of sovereignty, with all the problems that that involves.

(b) Economically we are faced with the problem (among others) that a customs union is usually regarded as being an indispensable condition of a political federation, however loose. On the other hand the Malayan Government is at present averse even to a limited common market with Singapore. This difficulty is not necessarily fatal, since the Malayan Government might be prepared to look with a more favourable eye on a full customs union with Singapore within a larger grouping which would provide a more capacious home market for the products of both territories. Further examination of the economic implication is, however, clearly required in relation to this problem if to no others.

(c) Strategically we are faced with the problem that if Singapore were to become part of an independent Malaya/Borneo federation, the United Kingdom's strategic position in Singapore could no longer be maintained on the present basis. We should either have to rely on a defence treaty or on territorial enclaves [as] in Cyprus. The latter idea may not be so ridiculous if we consider Singapore as part of an extensive federation as it seems to be when we consider Singapore as a separate political unit. Here again, however, further examination of the implications is needed in the near future if not immediately.

Annex B to 32: by Sir G Tory

Immediately before my departure for the Eden Hall Conference last week I had an interesting talk with Mr Thompson, the Secretary for Defence,[3] which indicated that Tun Razak, the Deputy Prime Minister and Minister of Defence, is modifying his attitude towards the relations between the Federation and Singapore.

I had asked Mr Thompson what he was going to do when he retired in April next but he said there was a chance that he might stay on in Malaya to take charge of planning for some future constitutional association between the Federation and Singapore and also with the Borneo Territories. Tun Razak was, he said, now becoming convinced that the Federation would have to accept responsibility for Singapore in the end. It was of course Tun Razak's view, like that of everyone else in Malaya, that Singapore could not be assimilated without the addition also of non-Chinese peoples from some or all of the Borneo Territories. Malaya had hitherto been working on the assumption that only Sarawak and Brunei could be accepted by the Federation in the foreseeable future but Tun Razak was now reconciled to the fact that a solution on these lines would not be acceptable and that there would have to be a 'package deal'. Tun Razak's present idea was said to be that Mr. Thompson should work out a scheme accordingly.

Mr. Thompson said that the sort of plan he was going to put forward was that the Federation should be prepared to absorb Sarawak and Brunei in three years' time, Singapore in five years, and North Borneo in ten years. This was only a cock-shy but it reflected:—

(a) the inability of the Federation to assimilate too much at once;
(b) the Federation's awareness that North Borneo was still some way behind the others from the political point of view; and
(c) the Federation's hope that in the meantime we should develop North Borneo's defence potentialities.

I reminded Mr. Thompson that Tun Razak had once said to me that if the Federation ever accepted Singapore, even with the addition of the Borneo Territories, it would be impossible for the Federation Government to allow us to keep our base there because one Defence Agreement was all that they could politically sustain. Mr Thompson said at once that he was confident of being able to shift Tun Razak from this point of view. His idea was that the existing Defence Agreement would simply have to be amended to cover the Singapore base also.

Mr. Thompson said that the Tunku was still rigid in his attitude to Singapore and would not, in his present mood, begin to look at a Grand Design on the above lines. But Mr. Thompson thought that Tun Razak would be able in the end to bring him round. He was quite certain that Tun Razak was the only person who could do this and that it would be a mistake for anyone else to tackle the Tunku on the subject in the meantime. The Tunku, as everyone knows, is very stubborn and there is a risk that he would adopt an intransigent position from which he would find it difficult to withdraw if we attacked him too soon.

---

[3] R G K (later Sir Robert) Thompson, former member of the Malayan Civil Service who played a significant role in the counter-insurgency operations of the Malayan emergency, was permanent secretary for defence in the Federation of Malaya, 1959–1961, and head of the British Advisory Mission to Vietnam, 1961–1965.

33   DO 169/18, no 11   17 Mar 1961

'The outlook in Singapore for the next twelve months': report
(DCC(FE)61/90) by the Joint Intelligence Committee (Far East) for
the British Defence Coordinating Committee (Far East)

[This paper, prognosticating that Lee Kuan Yew 'will continue to be faced with potential
opposition from the extreme left but he and his party will maintain their position and
power', was circulated to the Chiefs of Staff as the annex to COS(61)107, 24 Mar 1961.]

Aim
By examining the developments which have taken place since JIC(FE)(59)93(Final)⁺
was written, to assess the Political and Economic outlook in Singapore for the next
12 months.

Internal
    2.   *Political.* The PAP has increasingly emphasised that it is a democratic, socialist,
non-Communist Party. Neither its programme nor its methods are revolutionary or
even extreme, but it frequently employs Communist jargon and techniques in what
are essentially anti-Communist contexts. This tends to make the public picture of the
PAP somewhat equivocal. This equivocal impression is reinforced by dictatorial
tendencies, such as restriction of the freedom of the press and radio and political
indoctrination of the administration. The influence of the right wing opposition
remains negligible. In the industrial field, despite further Communist penetration
among certain trade unions, the Government have for the moment contained the
extreme left by providing for compulsory arbitration in industrial disputes, by holding
back on previous proposals to consolidate trade unions under an all powerful TUC, and
by driving home to the public the paramount importance of industrial peace.
    3.   The relations between the Government and the trade unions will continue to
be a major problem in the next twelve months. Although these improved towards the
end of 1960 as a result of a lull in industrial strife, the unions will continue to press
the Government to approve the constitution of the new TUC and to pass the Trades
Union Bill to consolidate unions under the TUC's control. The Government are,
however, likely to go slow as long as they cannot rely on a majority in the TUC
Secretariat. The danger of the TUC pursuing an independent and aggressive line
comes not from the pro-Communist element alone led by Lim Chin Siong and Fong
Swee Suan, but rather from a combination of this element with other left wing
members of the Secretariat led by Woodhull, Bani, Dominic Puthucheary and Jamit
Singh.¹ The Government is, however, still contemplating sterner measures against
pro-Communist elements in the unions as part of its general drive to defeat the
Communists. A more immediate problem for the Government is the nuisance value
constituted by an impending by-election resulting from Ong Eng Guan's resignation
from the Assembly.² This nuisance value derives from Ong Eng Guan's appeal to anti-

+ DCC(FE)(59)261 (COS(59)237)

---

¹ Together with Lim Chin Siong, Fong Swee Suan and Sidney Woodhull, S T Bani, Dominic Puthucheary
(younger brother of James) and Jamit Singh were the so-called 'Big Six' trade union leaders.
² Having resigned office and membership of the PAP, Ong Eng Guan challenged the PAP candidate at the
Hong Lim by-election in late Apr 1961 and won, see 38.

colonialist feeling in general, and, in particular, his attack on the Internal Security Council and the privileged position of the British Armed Forces in Singapore. The most difficult problem for the Government, however, will be to contain the slowly mounting pressure for independence without merger. This pressure is being applied by a combination of extreme left and Chinese chauvinist elements and builds upon disillusion over the chances of merger with the Federation, distaste for the economic policy of attracting free enterprise investment founded on industrial peace with justice, and impatience with the constitutional limitations in internal security and external affairs. Against this pressure the Government continue to take an aggressive and courageous stand in favour of creating a non-communal pan-Malayan loyalty. Whether the Government succeed will depend on progress made towards industrialisation and on improving relations with the Federation.

Internal Security Council
4.   The Internal Security Council has been working for over a year. It has dealt successfully with the tricky question of the detainees remaining in custody after the leading eight had been released before the Government took office.[3] The Government has now released others and some further detentions have taken place, mostly under the umbrella of the Internal Security Council. The United Kingdom and Federation Governments are willing to bear part of the burden of responsibility, as the Council undoubtedly does have a collective responsibility for its decisions, even though these may be based on initiatives taken by the Singapore Government. If and when the Government proceed, however, with their new policy of detaining Communists in various fields including the trade unions, it will become increasingly difficult to use the Council as a front for unpopular decisions initiated by the Singapore Government. In the long run, this issue of responsibility could assume very serious proportions in event of any disorders involving the use of British troops, since the Prime Minister has indicated that it would finish him politically to assume responsibility for bringing in British troops of his own accord.

Nanyang University and Chinese schools
5.   The Government has been pursuing a policy of opening opportunities in the Civil Service for the Chinese educated. An important part of their programme is to offer equality of treatment between Nanyang and the University to Malaya [sic], and, for this purpose, to make available large sums of money to Nanyang University in return for reforms at Nanyang. The Chinese businessmen who, with Tan Lark Sye, control Nanyang University, are, however, resisting the Government.[4] The Government is proceeding slowly and has gained some support from the students. Its

---

[3] See 13, n 3.
[4] Tan Lark Sye came to Singapore in his youth and became a wealthy rubber merchant and industrialist. In 1953 he proposed the foundation of a Chinese-medium university as a counter to the English-medium University of Malaya. As a result of massive public subscription the Nanyang University opened in 1956 but three years later the Prescott Commission reported adversely on its academic standards. There were protests over lost employment prospects for Nanyang graduates but violence was avoided by a compromise whereby they were admitted to the public services as probationers. After the elections of Sept 1963, Tan Lark Sye's citizenship was revoked and he resigned from the chairmanship of the Nanyang University executive council.

attempts to exercise stricter control over the Chinese Schools have also been proceeding without any open reaction. However, the potential threat of the puritanical and chauvinistic appeal of Communism to Chinese speaking students remains.

Communalism

6.   The dissensions in UMNO, Singapore, are now being patched up, but Malay antipathy to the predominantly Chinese population continues despite constant efforts by the Singapore Government to promote Malay as the national language and to create a pan-Malayan loyalty. This antipathy can be exploited by small, but dangerous groups of political extremists or opportunists as in the case of the abortive ARTIS plot in January, 1961.[5] This plot, which mainly involved elements of Javanese and Boyanese origin, did not have the backing of any reputable Malay organisation, nor did it attract general support among Malays in the island, but the wide-spread fears and rumours engendered by the plot showed the dangerous potentialities of the communal feeling which remains in Singapore.

Police

7.   The police force has recovered from the pay cuts and its relations with the public have improved but it is several hundreds below strength in its present establishment and the Commissioner's request for an increase in the establishment, particularly in the rank and file, is being resisted by the Government, partly on the ground that quantity is less important than quality and partly on financial grounds. Attempts to attract a better class of candidate for various ranks have not, however, been very successful so far. The Police are therefore likely to remain below strength for some time to come, particularly in the rank and file, and this is bound to affect their confidence in their own ability to carry out their tasks. Moreover, their morale has also been adversely affected by Ministerial interference or undue influence upon promotions and disciplinary matters and by the restrictions placed upon them in their handling of strike pickets. In this last aspect the Government have in the very recent past displayed a more satisfactory attitude.

8.   The Gurkha contingent of the Police Force is still reliable but they need an infusion of new recruits. The prospect of obtaining suitable replacements for the two British officers is not promising.

Special Branch

9.   The Government has now decided to train a senior administrative civil servant as Director of Special Branch. Meanwhile, they have asked for and are using two members of the United Kingdom Security Service within the Special Branch for reorganisation and training purposes. The Prime Minister clearly places great value on the Special Branch as the source of expert assistance against the subversive threat and in the process the Special Branch has gained confidence and greater influence on the Government. The burden mainly rests however, on the remaining expatriates (European and Pakistani). Their immediate departure would gravely affect the efficiency of the Branch.

---

[5] ARTIS (Angkatan Revolusi Tentera Islam Singapore or Singapore Islamic Revolutionary Armed Forces) was a Malay militant group that received funds from the Indonesian consulate-general in Singapore. In Jan 1961 the Singapore police uncovered an ARTIS plot to foment Sino-Malay race riots.

External relations

Relations with the Federation
10.   Singapore is no closer to merger with the Federation and the situation is unlikely to alter in the next twelve months. The Federation Government do not approve of the Singapore Government's attempts to 'ride the tiger of Communism' by appointing ex-detainees to be Political Secretaries and members of the TUC instead of keeping them locked up. While they expect the Singapore Government to contain and even attack Communism in Singapore they are most reluctant to co-operate with the Singapore Government on this. Nevertheless, the Tengku, in response to advice from the United Kingdom Government and assiduous personal cultivation by Lee Kuan Yew, has recently made a much more forthcoming statement about Federation/Singapore relations. While still maintaining that merger is not possible at this moment, the Tengku has for the first time said complimentary things about the PAP, and their policy of fostering Malayan consciousness in Singapore. Lee Kuan Yew could not have expected more at this stage.

Relations with the United Kingdom
11.   Relations with the United Kingdom have improved. The Singapore Government has shown itself ready to accept HMG's advice on a number of occasions and has even listened to views on matters which are rightfully within its own competence. Despite goading from Ong Eng Guan it has refrained from agitation against the presence of British forces on large areas of Singapore land. In fact Lee Kuan Yew clearly regards the presence of British forces as the ultimate safeguard against Communist subversion inside Singapore. He also recognises the economic importance of the Services as the largest employers in Singapore. For both these reasons he has in private encouraged HMG to declare that it intends to maintain its bases and forces in Singapore.
12.   The Singapore Government has also resisted the temptation to call for full independence. It has repeatedly stressed that while independence must be its ultimate goal, it can only be obtained through merger with the Federation, and that meanwhile Singapore has full internal self-government under the present Constitution which will be reviewed in 1963.
13.   If Her Majesty's Government were involved in a limited war in South East Asia whether under SEATO auspices or not, opposition from left-wing elements in Singapore would almost certainly be strong. The three bases on the Island are dependent on local civilian labour, and their effective working can be rapidly impaired by a withdrawal of local labour. The attitude of the Government and the consequent likelihood of civil disorder would depend on whether HMG came into direct conflict or was likely to come into direct conflict with Indonesia or China. It is also clear that relations may undergo strain from time to time on external issues which can be exploited by the extreme left, e.g. Algeria and the Congo.

Relations with other countries
14.   In South East Asia Singapore has shown a healthy desire to play a constructive role and to add to her reputation. This has been fostered by her promotion to full membership of the Colombo Plan Consultative Committee and to separate associate membership of the Economic Commission for Asia and the Far East (ECAFE).

15.   Singapore's relations with her two major trading partners, the Federation of Malaya and Indonesia, are the most important. The Federation is dealt with in a separate section (paragraph 10 above). With Indonesia, the economic aspect is all important, since Singapore's exports have declined alarmingly during the past two years and are still declining. Singapore is trying assiduously to improve the economic relationship. A permanent trade and cultural post is to be established and current inter-Governmental trade negotiations seem likely to result in the signing of a trade agreement.

16.   After Malaya and Indonesia, Singapore is probably most interested in the Borneo territories. The Yang di-Pertuan Negara and the Prime Minister were official guests at the Sultan of Brunei's birthday celebrations in September, 1960, and the Prime Minister took the occasion to pay informal visits to Sarawak and North Borneo. The Prime Minister spoke, with commendable tact and restraint, of the need for the smaller countries in the region to hang together and of his hope that Singapore's experience could be of benefit to them in their progress towards independence. Since then the Prime Minister has shown increasing interest in the possibilities of the Grand Design, e.g. some form of Federation between Malaya, Singapore and the Borneo territories, as something above and beyond merger with the Federation through which he can divert the aspirations of the people of Singapore towards an ultimate, constitutional goal.

Economic

The basic problem

17.   Singapore's great problem is to provide employment for her rapidly increasing population. On 30th June, 1960, the population was estimated at 1,634,100 which represents an increase of more than 188,000 since the last census in June, 1957. The rate of increase has recently declined from about 66,000 a year to 44,000, but this decline is due more to population movements than to a slowing down in the rate of natural increase. The movement of population cannot be relied on to continue, and the mounting numbers coming into the age group of maximum fertility will tend to make the natural increase higher rather than lower.

18.   In mid-1960 over 10% of the economically active population of about 500,000 were unemployed, and the Singapore Government have estimated that a further 10,000 will be seeking employment each year until 1962, and nearly 16,000 a year in 1963/64.

Government's economic policy

19.   After a slow start the Government is now facing the economic problem more realistically. A five year development plan has been prepared with two main objects; first to create employment by industrialisation and the development of the entrepot services, and second, to provide social services for the expanding population. The plan includes improvements to harbour and airport facilities and more roads, houses; schools and hospitals. In the industrialisation programme Singapore will rely primarily on private investment, but the Government is prepared to consider limited state participation on an empirical basis. Its aim is to supply the framework for industrialisation by the creation of industrial estates and by the establishment of an Economic Development Board. In suitable cases, new or expanding industries will be

given 'pioneer' status (i.e. relief from income tax for 5 years); a further incentive in some cases (but subject to consideration of Singapore's 'free port' interests) may be a protective tariff. To determine which industries should be encouraged, the Government is seeking advice from the United Nations Technical Assistance Board, who are undertaking a survey and should report in early 1961.

20.   The estimated cost of the plan over the five year period is $968M. Of this, the Government hopes to raise some $685M from local resources. Singapore recently received $43M in loans, together with $22M in grants, from the United Kingdom, and further United Kingdom aid under the Colonial Development and Welfare will be considered in 1963 in the light of Singapore's needs at that time. The Government has had preliminary discussions with the World Bank, and the latter has agreed to consider the request for loans in the light of a survey of Singapore's credit worthiness. The development programme is unlikely to be held up by lack of finance; it is more probable that because of shortage of technical staff, the Government will find difficulty in spending the available money within the time proposed.

Local confidence
21.   Singapore Ministers have to walk a tight rope, between their socialist principles and the need to woo left-wing extremists on the one side, and a realistic appreciation of Singapore's necessary dependence on commerce and on private capital on the other. Recently they have made it clear that they regard thoroughgoing socialism as impracticable in Singapore, at any rate within the foreseeable future. There has been no substantial migration of capital during the period, because a responsible body of opinion in local business circles (though more in the European than in the Chinese section) recognises that the present Government is, from their point of view, the best they can hope for and is thus worthy of support. Apart, however, from a few mildly encouraging moves (e.g. new Shell and Japanese refineries, and some applications for 'pioneer status'), local confidence has not brought about any large scale investment in local industry. There is a fair hope that local confidence will grow during the coming twelve months. It would be greatly strengthened by a closer economic understanding between Singapore and the Federation. The Singapore Government recognises this and has been trying to establish a limited Common Market with the Federation. This has not, however, made much progress and there is already a tendency in the Federation, to reduce the traditional dependence on Singapore by establishing in the Federation, wherever possible, the communications and commercial services in which Singapore specialises. Examples of this are a proposal to create a rubber market in Kuala Lumpur, and competition with Singapore in the development of an international airport and of port facilities. If this trend continues, it is bound in time to prove harmful to Singapore.

External confidence
22.   Although tendencies may develop in other surrounding countries to bypass Singapore as entrepot centre, world trade conditions should be favourable for South East Asia over the next twelve months and Singapore should retain its commercial position and prosperity during the period. It is still regarded as an efficient port and entrepot centre; the volume of traffic at the harbour is as high as ever and shows no signs of contracting. Singapore's geographical position and trade links are an asset, but the cost of labour is about twice as high as in Hong Kong. Various industrialists

and bankers have commented encouragingly during recent months on Singapore's economic situation and potentialities, but there has been no rush to seize whatever advantages it may offer. Even Japan, with its pressing need for economic outlets is hesitant. On the other hand if the various outside missions (UNTAB, World Bank) report favourably, and if some impetus is imparted by the Economic Development Board, then prospects should improve. More generally, there is an indefinite asset in the native wits and resourcefulness of the Singapore Chinese. However, it must be emphasised that any optimism depends on Singapore achieving a fair measure of industrial peace; unless this is done, so far from industrialisation getting under way, existing firms may move out of Singapore.

Prospects of bloc aid[6]

23.   Singapore Ministers are well aware of the menace of Communist China and it is unlikely that it would seek or accept economic aid from this source. Their attitude to the Soviet Union is somewhat different and they have over the past year shown interest in economic aid from Soviet sources. However, HMG has taken a firm line and forbidden any acceptance of Soviet aid and at the same time has brought home to the Singapore Government the serious effect that the encouragement of Soviet connections could have on its relations with the Federation. There is no reason to suppose that Ministers are at present contemplating further approaches to the Soviet Union or that they are in a mood to risk defiance of the UK. Moreover, there has developed over recent months a healthy westward and free world orientation. As against that, however, Singapore Ministers have undoubtedly observed with interest the tactics of the other South East Asian countries which play off one bloc against the other; it would be unwise to rule out any future emulation of these tactics. If there were to be any serious stagnation in industrial development or a major recession in world prices, and if the Russians, perceiving their political opportunity, were to come forward with some attractive offer of aid (e.g. the provision of a factory), Singapore might well have difficulty in turning it down, and a veto by the UK might lead to serious tension. On the whole, however, prospects seem just sufficiently encouraging to make this improbable during the next year.

Conclusions

24.   We conclude that:—

(a) Lee Kuan Yew will continue to be faced with potential opposition from the extreme left but he and his party will maintain their position and power.

(b) The Government's present policy towards the trade unions might lead to an open breach between the Government and the pro-Communist elements, but so long as the Government retains its determination and is supported by the United Kingdom and Federation in the Internal Security Council it is likely to be able to hold its position at the cost of some of its popular support.

(c) Relations with HMG have improved and so long as Lee Kuan Yew's position is not undermined should remain good on basic issues although there may well be strain from time to time on external questions such as the Congo where he has to retain left-wing support.

---

[6] See 21, para 4 and 27, para (c).

(d) In the event of the UK becoming involved in a limited war, the danger of serious interference with the operation of the military bases remains likely.

(e) Relations with the Federation, both political and economic, did not improve during 1960, but 1961 has started out hopefully, with a more forthcoming statement by the Tengku. Nevertheless, the Government will probably pursue its increasing interest in the Grand Design.

(f) Unless there is a major recession in world prices, or unless continued irresponsibility or aggression in trade union tactics frighten off all investments, the economy will not be impaired sufficiently in the next twelve months to weaken the Government's authority. In these circumstances the Government is unlikely to seek aid from the Communist Bloc. Its prestige will, however, suffer if its cherished major industrial projects do not show signs of coming to fruition or if no progress is made in economic co-operation with the Federation.

34   CAB 134/1560, CPC(61)9   14 Apr 1961

'Possibility of an association of the British Borneo territories with the Federation of Malaya and the state of Singapore': memorandum by Mr Macleod for Cabinet Colonial Policy Committee reporting on developments since July 1960

[In his assessment of Selkirk's recommendation publicly to accept closer association, Macleod argued against such a statement of policy but in favour of consultations with Australia and New Zealand followed by confidential discussions with the Tunku and Lee. The prime minister was briefed on this paper but was not present when it was discussed by the Colonial Policy Committee (PREM 11/3418; see 35).]

The problem and previous consideration

At a meeting on the 27th July, 1960, there was discussion of my memorandum (C. P. C. (60)17) on the long term possibility of a political association of the British Borneo territories (the Colonies of North Borneo and Sarawak, and the Protected State of Brunei) with the Federation of Malaya and the State of Singapore.[1] Such an association, which one would hope would remain within the Commonwealth, would provide a possible future home for the small Borneo territories, which, trying to stand alone or even in association together, might find themselves up against heavy pressures from Indonesia, the Philippines and China. It would also seem to offer the best answer to the future problem of Singapore. The conclusion of the meeting was that Lord Selkirk, who was present, should discuss the matter in Borneo. This discussion was held at Kuching, Sarawak, on the 20th October, 1960.[2] In addition to the Governors of Sarawak and North Borneo and the High Commissioner for Brunei, Lord Perth was also present.

Lord Selkirk's recommendations

2.   In accordance with the conclusions of that meeting, and of a further discussion at the time of the Eden Hall Conference in January this year, at which, in

---

[1] See 25 and 27.   [2] See 30.

addition to the two Governors and the High Commissioner for Brunei, our High Commissioners from Kuala Lumpur and Canberra and our Ambassador from Djakarta were also present, Lord Selkirk has submitted recommendations for consideration by Her Majesty's Government.[3] The recommendations, which have the general support of those present at the meetings, may be summarised as follows:—

(a) Her Majesty's Government should accept as the ultimate aim of their policy the development of a political association between Malaya, Singapore and the three Borneo territories;

(b) progress towards this goal must be gradual and adjusted to the rate of political evolution in the Borneo territories; the first step must be the strengthening of existing links between North Borneo and Sarawak with the intention that these two territories might eventually enter the wider association as a single unit; this gradual bringing together of the two Borneo colonies should proceed without expectation of Brunei's participation, but without prejudice to her joining later should this be found possible;

(c) while progress is being made under (b) we should do our best to avoid political or economic developments in the area which would cut across the idea of an ultimate association of the five territories, and, conversely, should encourage any development leading to co-operation between them;

(d) we should be ready to discuss this matter in confidence, as occasion may arise, with interested parties such as Tunku Abdul Rahman, Mr. Lee Kuan Yew and the Sultan of Brunei;

(e) after consultation with the Governments involved Her Majesty's Government should in the near future make a statement in whatever manner would be most appropriate to the effect that a broad association between the Federation and Singapore and the Borneo territories has great possibilities for the future of the area, provided it is acceptable to the peoples concerned.

Timing

3. Lord Selkirk has emphasised that it is important to avoid any appearance that Her Majesty's Government are making the pace in this matter or seeking to impose the idea upon the peoples concerned. I strongly endorse this (though of course some development outside our control might force our hand). If the plan is to be successful, it cannot be rushed. The parties to it must evolve it as their own plan.

4. Nor is it in our interest to rush it. The present situation suits us. The political association of the five territories which we are now considering fits into a future when we can no longer, or need no longer, insist on maintaining our present constitutional defence rights in Singapore and the Borneo territories and can be content to safeguard what defence interests we may still wish to retain, as Lord Selkirk puts it, 'on a basis of consent' by a friendly independent country.

5. In C.P.C. (60) 17, in reference to the Tunku's suggestion made to Lord Perth last June that he might take over Sarawak and Brunei while we retained North Borneo for defence purposes, I said that I felt very great doubt if it was realistic to think of retaining North Borneo as a Crown Colony after Sarawak had either become

---

[3] See 32.

self-governing on its own or had merged with the Federation. This view was confirmed at Lord Selkirk's Kuching meeting and I am sure we should give the Tunku no encouragement on this score. If Brunei alone were to want to join the Federation in advance of the other two, we could not, and need not, object; though here again we should not encourage it. Brunei, the wealthiest and most Malay of the three territories, is the plum from the Tunku's point of view and once he had got it his interest in the rest might decline.

Should Her Majesty's Government make a public statement?

6. Paragraphs 3 and 4 above argue against the desirability of an early statement by Her Majesty's Government. The reason why such a statement has been recommended is the growing pressure in Singapore for 'separate' independence. Mr. Lee Kuan Yew's policy of independence through merger with the Federation of Malaya has come under fire because the Federation's unwillingness to merge in the foreseeable future is only too clear. This remains so even though the Tunku recently made some friendly statements about Singapore. Lord Selkirk thinks it would fortify Mr. Lee and frustrate his and our enemies if the possibility of independence through a wider association were to be produced as an attainable goal. There is clearly much in this. Nevertheless I am not in favour of a public statement by Her Majesty's Government 'in the near future' in advance of evidence of some weight of local opinion in favour of such an association.

Consultation with other governments

7. The interests of Australia and New Zealand are closely involved in the future of the area and I accept the advice of the Commonwealth Relations Office that our next step should be to take these two Governments into our confidence and give them a chance of expressing their views.

Sounding of Tunku Abdul Rahman and others

8. Subject to the result of these consultations we should then, as may seem appropriate, sound confidentially Tunku Abdul Rahman and Mr. Lee Kuan Yew, probably in that order, and possibly also the Sultan of Brunei and, subject to the views of the Governors, selected local notables in Sarawak and North Borneo.

Recommendations

9. I recommend that my colleagues should endorse the recommendations in paragraph 2 above, as modified and expanded in paragraphs 3 to 8.

35 CAB 134/1560, CPC 4(61)1   18 Apr 1961

'The possibility of an association of the British Borneo territories with the Federation of Malaya and the state of Singapore': Cabinet Colonial Policy Committee minutes

[Chaired by Lord Kilmuir (lord chancellor) in the absence of Macmillan, the committee endorsed Macleod's paper, including the recommendation that no public statement of policy should be made for the time being. Selkirk was informed of the outcome by telegram on 21 Apr 1961 (CO 1030/1079, no 1). After the 13th Inter-Territorial

Conference of the Borneo Territories at the end of April, Selkirk wrote to Macleod urging more rapid advance towards closer association (see 36).]

The Committee had before them a memorandum by the Colonial Secretary (C.P.C. (61) 9)[1] on the possibility of an association of the British Borneo Territories with the Federation of Malaya and the State of Singapore.

The Colonial Secretary recalled that Ministers had agreed in July 1960 (C.P.C. (61) 20) that Lord Selkirk, the Commissioner General for South East Asia, should discuss at the Borneo Inter-Territorial Conference at Kuching in October, 1960 the possibility of a political association between the five territories. In the light of this Conference Lord Selkirk had recommended that the Government should adopt the concept of association as an ultimate aim of policy and should work gradually towards it in full consultation with the various local interests concerned. He had also suggested that the Government should make a statement to the effect that association between the territories had great possibilities for the future of the area, provided it was acceptable to the peoples concerned.

He generally endorsed Lord Selkirk's proposals; but, since it was essential that the United Kingdom Government should not appear to be trying to impose a political association and that support for it should be seen to come from those concerned in the area, he was not in favour of a public statement by the Government at the present time. He proposed to give Lord Selkirk appropriate instructions in time for a further meeting which Lord Selkirk was holding on 26th April with the Governors of North Borneo and Sarawak and the High Commission for Brunei. It was also desirable that Australia and New Zealand should be taken into our confidence and given a chance of expressing their views before we come to any final decision. Subsequently consultations might be held with the Prime Ministers of Malaya and Singapore and possibly also with the Sultan of Brunei and selected local notables in the North Borneo territories.

Discussion showed general agreement with these proposals. They were acceptable from a defence point of view, and would need to be taken into account in considering the future defence arrangements and deployment of troops in the area; and they were also to the long-term advantage of Malaya. But the Prime Minister of Malaya, who wished to extend his influence into the North Borneo territories, was at present opposed to a wider federation which included Singapore, since he felt that the Chinese majority there might threaten the political stability of Malaya. On this point however much would depend on the form of political association proposed; it would be necessary to consider at a later stage whether it should take the form of a federation or whether some looser organisation would be more appropriate.

The Committee:—

(1) Agreed that Lord Selkirk should be authorised at the meeting to be held on 26th April to discuss the future of the British Borneo Territories on the lines indicated in paragraphs 2(a) to (c) and 5 of C.P.C. (61) 9.

(2) Agreed to consider the matter further in the light of the discussions referred to at Conclusion (1) above.

(3) Agreed that no statement should meanwhile be made by Her Majesty's Government.

[1] See 34.

36   CO 1030/1079, no 2   2 May 1961
[Closer association of the Borneo territories]: letter from Lord Selkirk
to Mr Macleod, reporting on the 13th Inter-Territorial Conference of
Borneo Territories in Jesselton

[Despite an attempt to present consensus, these discussions revealed significant
differences between the commissioner-general and British representatives in North
Borneo, Sarawak and Brunei. Whereas Selkirk argued that the stability of Singapore and
hence the 'Greater Malaysia' scheme would be jeopardised by delay, Goode, Waddell and
White feared that a precipitate approach to merger would endanger the interests of the
'more backward' Borneo territories to the lasting detriment of the larger project.
Identifying one reason for delay to be the fact that North Borneo was less advanced
educationally and politically than Sarawak, Selkirk recommended the appointment of a
senior officer to co-ordinate the development of the Borneo colonies and assist their
union. This suggestion led to the posting of H P Hall from the CO to Jesselton where his
first task was to follow up the Rampton Report on the economic development of the
Borneo territories (CO 1030/1080). As regards the comment on the political
backwardness of North Borneo compared with Sarawak, it might be noted that on 26 Mar
1961 a decision had been taken in Donald Stephens' house to form the first political
party, United National Kadazan Organisation (UNKO), although the party was not
formally inaugurated until Aug.]

I have just returned from the Thirteenth Inter-Territorial Conference of the Borneo
Territories in Jesselton. The questions we discussed were nearly all related in one
way or another to the central problem of closer association between North Borneo
and Sarawak and I naturally took the opportunity to have a full exchange of views
with the two Governors about it. We did not attempt to formulate joint conclusions,
but it was agreed that it might be useful if I were to let you have my own thoughts
about the position we have now reached.

2.   Some modest progress has been made over the past year towards better
cooperation and coordination between the two Administrations. Exchanges of visits
between unofficial representatives of the two territories are being encouraged. It has
been agreed to aim at bringing the Free Trade Area into being by the beginning of
next year as a first step towards a Customs Union.[1]

3.   But advance is still too slow. It is, I fear, bound to remain slow so long as we
continue to allow the pace to be set by North Borneo's very natural fears of
'contamination' from Sarawak. I believe that we can no longer afford this and that
the time has come when we must give more positive leadership to local opinion and
confront it with firm decisions.

4.   The core of the difficulty is that educationally and politically Sarawak is far
ahead of North Borneo. There can be no question of waiting for North Borneo to
catch up; on the contrary, the gap between the two is bound to increase. This means,
to my mind, that unless we can firmly set the two territories on the road to union
within the next year or so the opportunity will be lost for ever. It will not be easy now
to convince the people of North Borneo that union will not mean subordination to

---

[1] In Oct 1960 it was agreed that the financial secretaries of North Borneo and Sarawak should meet under
the chairmanship of J L Rampton (seconded from the Treasury as financial adviser to the UK high
commissioner in Kuala Lumpur) to study the question of establishing a common market or free trade
area. They reported on 6 Mar 1961 recommending an agreement (largely based on the European Free
Trade Association) which came into force in Jan 1962 (CO 1030/1382, 1383 and 1384).

Sarawak and contamination by its left-wing politics. But this task will grow still harder as time passes and the alternative for North Borneo is isolation and eventual absorption by Indonesia. In North Borneo the people would respond to a clear and firm lead. In Sarawak impatience is growing and the Government is being criticised for not being active enough in the pursuit of closer association. These problems are the more difficult because in each territory the Chinese development is far ahead of that of the indigenous people.

5. I remain convinced that union is the right course for the two territories, whether or not Brunei joins them and whether or not means can eventually be found of bringing them into some broader association with Malaya and Singapore. And I believe, for the reasons I have indicated, that if union is to be achieved Her Majesty's Government must be prepared to announce publicly during the course of the present year that it is their firm policy that North Borneo and Sarawak shall achieve independence as a single unit, preferably in some form of association with Malaya and Singapore.

6. We need not attempt to set a date for independence, though I doubt myself whether we shall be able to delay it beyond about 1970. But we should, in my opinion, decide now that in, say, two years' time a single Governor of the two territories shall be installed, as a first step towards the later merger of the two Administrations and the separate legislatures.

7. The form of eventual union and sequence of constitutional steps to be taken on the road towards it will of course call for careful working out over the years. To this end I believe that a suitable senior officer should be appointed now with the task of considering these problems in the regional context and of stimulating and coordinating the necessary joint studies by the individual Governments.

8. A suitable opportunity for making such an appointment will arise with the creation of the projected joint committee which is to work out the proposed Free Trade Area and later Customs Union. The independent chairman of that committee will have a key role to play in maintaining the drive towards economic unification which will do more than anything else to prepare the way for eventual political union; and he will be well placed to plan the stages of constitutional advance.

9. A key factor in progress towards joint economic development and political unity is the improvement of communications between the two territories. A through road linking Jesselton with Kuching is the most important and urgent single need of the two territories. This work should in my opinion be set in hand at once as a large scale international project with whatever outside assistance can be mobilised from the International Bank and other sources and with the firm resolve to complete it in five years.

10. Finally, very high priority must be given to the improvement of education facilities, especially in North Borneo. A first class secondary school from which leaders can be trained from all races is the immediate requirement for North Borneo. Her Majesty's Government must be prepared to give increased and urgent help in providing teachers and, if need be, money to make possible a rapid expansion.

11. I am aware that these are far reaching proposals, going far beyond the most cautious line indicated in your telegram No. 28 of April 21.[2] But I have not put them forward without careful thought and, while there is of course room for much

---

[2] Not printed but see 35, note.

discussion on individual points, they represent my own firm conviction of the scale of effort and degree of urgency that is now essential if we are to keep pace with events in this fast moving region and enable the Borneo Territories to achieve and maintain their independence in reasonable security and prosperity.

12.   In sum, what I should like to see is:—

(i) An early statement by Her Majesty's Government that union of the two territories is their aim;

(ii) A decision now to appoint a single Governor in about two years;

(iii) Early appointment of an official to coordinate economic economic unification and plan constitutional advance;

(iv) Inauguration of a trunk road project with massive outside aid;

(v) Active help in the field of education.

13.   I am sending copies of this letter to the two Governors, to White in Brunei and to Tory in Kuala Lumpur. A copy is also being put on my United Kingdom Commission files.

37   CO 1030/973, no E203   9 May 1961
['Paper on the future of the Federation of Malaya, Singapore and the Borneo Territories']: memorandum by Lee Kuan Yew for the government of the Federation of Malaya

[In this paper Lee puts the case for independence through merger. The merger he proposes is not simply of Singapore and Malaya but the larger federation embracing the Borneo territories. The background to this paper is as follows. On 24 Apr Lee Kuan Yew informed Selkirk that on the previous day he had spoken to the Tunku for the first time about the Grand Design. Dr Goh Keng Swee, Tun Razak and Dr Ismail bin Abdul Rahman had also been present. At the end of this meeting the Tunku had invited Lee to prepare a paper setting out his ideas on how merger might be achieved. Lee, who later stated that he was encouraged to write the paper by Selkirk and Philip Moore (Selkirk's deputy), discussed the matter with Moore on 28 Apr but insisted that the Tunku should not be told of their meeting. On 9 May Lee showed the final version to Selkirk before giving it to Ismail for transmission to the Tunku and Razak in Kuala Lumpur, without the Malayans being aware that Selkirk had seen it first. Selkirk sent a copy of Lee's paper to London on 10 May. Although they had doubts about its practical value, especially as regards the Borneo territories, senior British officials in Singapore thought the exercise worthwhile if only to persuade Kuala Lumpur of Lee's honourable intentions. Indeed, Lee tried to make palatable the case for an early agreement on merger in principle by stressing that an independent Singapore on its own would be a greater risk than in combination with other territories and by reassuring the federal government that Malay political predominance would not be threatened by Singapore's Chinese. On 11 May, Fang Chuang Pi ('the Plen' of Singapore's communist organisation) set up a secret meeting with Lee to ascertain the likelihood of merger. Lee came away convinced that, if merger did not take place soon, the communists would gain time to foment unrest. On 16 May Selkirk reported to London on a further meeting between Singapore and Federation leaders and noted that Razak was attempting to convince the Tunku of the need for merger (CO 1030/973, nos 132 and 133; also 'The origins and formation of Malaysia', memorandum by the FCO Research Department, 10 July 1970, FCO 51/154, paragraphs 58-61 (the document is reproduced as an Appendix to this volume), and Lee, *Memoirs*, pp 357-361, 364).]

Introduction

1.   These three territories comprise what were the British colonial possessions in South East Asia. Since the end of the Second World War great political and

constitutional changes have taken place in the whole of this region. The Federation of Malaya has become independent, and Singapore an internally self-governing state with defence and foreign affairs in the hands of the British and internal security under the joint control of an Internal Security Council. Constitutional changes have also taken place in Sarawak, Brunei and North Borneo. It is evident that in the next few years even greater and more rapid constitutional changes will take place both in Singapore and the Borneo Territories.

2.   What is to become of all these territories? In the Annex are two tables (Annexes A & B) which show a breakdown of the area and population of each of these territories, and a map of this region (Annex C).[1]

3.   Historically, Singapore has always been much closer to the Federation of Malaya. The Borneo territories, although not altogether different in population composition, have always been a little further away, and the concept of the political unity of these three territories has not been as much in the forefront as the concept of merger between Singapore and the Federation. Therefore, a plan to create a federation of these three territories must be tactfully and gradually introduced into the minds of the peoples of the three territories, and should be presented as a desire of the peoples living in this region, and not initiated by the British.

The alternatives

4.   There are two alternative ways in which political development in these three territories could evolve:—

(A)   Federation of Malaya independent, Singapore independent and the Borneo territories independent in three separate units. If this alternative develops, it means that merger between Singapore and the Federation is abandoned as a political objective, and power in Singapore would pass to a China-minded group with strong cultural and economic links with Communist China.

In the opening phase, it may be that an independent Singapore government may come to some defence treaty arrangements with the British, but being independent these treaty arrangements would be discarded and revoked and replaced by ties with the Chinese mainland. This would ultimately lead to a Chinese Communist base right in the heart of South East Asia with incalculable consequences to all territories of the whole region. Knowing this, it is not unlikely that the British and even the Americans, may go to great pains to prevent an independent Singapore from ever emerging. However, if the desire of the people in Singapore for political independence through merger with the Federation is constantly frustrated and no progress is apparent either in common economic links, let alone political links, then frustration and desperation would drive them to the extremes of Communist policy and help the Communist pay the price in blood if necessary, to secure their political objective of an independent Singapore from which to undermine and subvert the Federation of Malaya.

Recent statements by open front Communist leaders have shown a positive change of line. The long-term M.C.P. policy of a united Singapore and Federation of Malaya is now glossed over. It is likely that knowing the strength of a Malay-based Federation Government, the M.C.P. would strongly resist proposals for

---

[1] Annexes not printed.

merger between Singapore and the Federation, which would leave them at the mercy of a Malay-based Federation Government able to take unpleasant measures against the Communists with electoral impunity.

(B)   A larger federation of the three territories—Federation of Malaya, Singapore, Borneo territories. This is the most satisfactory solution for the peoples of the three territories and also one which the British could accede to. It would also preserve the common economic, social and political ties that have existed between these territories as part of a common Empire in this region. But in working out the constitutional arrangements, care must be taken not to upset the sense of security and stability of the people of the Federation of Malaya, nor to arouse fears among the peoples of the Borneo territories that they are being swamped by more active and sophisticated people from the big cities of Singapore and the Federation.

5.   However, the pace of political changes taking place throughout the whole world and the rate at which pressure is mounting in Singapore, with or without the aid of the M.C.P. makes it imperative that agreement on principle on some constitutional arrangements must be achieved soon, or they may never be achieved at all. In the spring of 1963 the Singapore Government, by agreement recorded in the constitutional discussions with the United Kingdom in 1957,[2] is obliged to re-open talks on the constitutional future. The next step forward from the present constitutional position in Singapore is independence. The alternative is a standstill with minor constitutional re-adjustments of a purely window-dressing nature. If no constitutional advance takes place, the PAP cannot hold the position in Singapore. It will probably be replaced by a pro-M.C.P. and pro-China Singapore Government. It is likely that this Government would be intelligent enough to avoid a direct clash of arms with the British until the international position is such that direct Chinese armed intervention is possible. The effect of a pro-M.C.P. and pro-China Government in Singapore on the Chinese in the Federation will accentuate in the Federation the communal conflicts and dissolve the Chinese will to resist 'Chinese' Communism. This will sooner or later end up in an independent Singapore. A Singapore independent by itself must pander to its 75% Chinese population and will end up with greater appeals to Chinese chauvinism and eventually all talk of Malayan culture, national language, national solidarity and nation-building will disappear with tremendous adverse repercussions on the Chinese in the Federation of Malaya. The consequences are incalculable and would certainly put an and to any hope of building a united community composing of Malay, Chinese, Indian and other races in Malaya. The solution lies in the larger federation, with the strength and stability from the centre. This course of events can only be avoided if Singapore is merged into the larger entity described below, and such tendencies contained.

Alternative (B) or the 'Grand Design'
6.   In broad outline, the scheme is to use the stable Malay-based Federation Government as the sheet anchor of the whole of this region. In grand total population

---

[2] Three all-party delegations went to London for talks about self-government. Marshall demanded too much and came away empty-handed from the first (Apr 1956). Lim Yew Hock was more successful; the framework of the State of Singapore was agreed in Apr 1957, the details were settled in May 1958 and the new constitution was inaugurated following the elections of May 1959.

the Federation of Malaya has 6.82 million people, Singapore 1.63 million people, and the Borneo territories 1.25 million people. How each state is to elect its own government can be left to existing state arrangements and can remain flexible. In the Borneo territories some definite proposals will have to be reached as to how future representation from the Borneo territories in the larger Federation is to take place.

7.   Roughly speaking, the three states of the larger Federation would be entitled to the ratio of 68(Federation of Malaya) : 16(Singapore) : 12(Borneo) seats in the larger Federation Parliament. Representation from each state will be that of the government's side only, i.e. there is no direct election to the government of the larger federation. It will be noted that the population breakdown of the three territories, if we include the indigenous population together with the Malays, would mean that the Malays would constitute the largest ethnic group in the larger federation—4.5 million Malays and indigenous population as against 4.1 million Chinese, 0.9 million Indians and 0.2 million others. But because only the Government side is represented in the larger Federation Government, the effective vote is the 3.4 million Malays in the Federation who can in effect decide the vote of 68 out of 96 seats of the larger federation. Elections will be held in the respective states and each government of the respective states is entitled to nominate from among its members the number of seats agreed in the constitution in proportion to its population. In other words, it means that the Federation of Malaya government would be entitled to 68 out of 96 seats in the Parliament of the larger federation. Thus the government of the Federation of Malaya will automatically control the government of the larger federation.

8.   To protect the susceptibilities of the Borneo people and the present balance of power between Singapore and the Federation of Malaya, provisions will have to be built into the constitution of the larger federation to ensure that voting by citizens of the respective three states can only be done in their own states, e.g. a Singapore citizen can only vote in Singapore, a Federal citizen can only vote in the Federation, and no Singapore or Federal citizen can vote in Borneo. Provision can be made in the constitution for review after 5 or 10 years. This safeguard would prevent upsets in the balance of power.

9.   The powers of the larger federation Government should include defence, foreign affairs, police and security and such matters which like currency and common economic development could be more efficiently discharged by a central Government. A working party of administrative experts should put up a working paper for consideration at a later stage. The cost of running the central Government should be borne by the three states in proportion to their representation in the larger federation parliament.

10.   There are no constitutional problems however novel or difficult which cannot be resolved. The main problem will be how to present the 'Grand Design' politically to the people of the three respective territories. In this informal discussion on the 'Grand Design', both the Federation of Malaya and Singapore can express their own will through their own elected representatives. But the people of the Borneo territories are in that stage of political development where there are no elected representatives who can speak in the name of the Borneo people. Therefore, final arrangements will have to be carefully worked out so that they can be accepted and endorsed by the hereditary, community and the newly elected leaders of local government bodies of the Borneo territories.

11.   In such a framework it is possible to govern Singapore with considerable firmness and success. National identification in a large and powerful federation comprising a grand total of nearly 10 million people with a total of 130,000 square miles as against the Federation's 50,000 and Singapore's 225 square miles would hold the hearts and loyalties of the people. Pride in a more powerful and viable state, which may be called the 'Federation of Malaysia' or the 'United States of Malaysia', would give a boost to nation-building to the mutual advantage of the three territories and would help to stabilise the future of the whole region.

12.   In discussions from time to time with the United Kingdom Commissioner, it would appear that whilst they may go a long way to accede to this larger federation, they would want to have special defence treaty arrangements about their bases in Singapore and the Borneo territories. This is not an insoluble matter.

13.   After discussions on the principle of this paper, it will be useful if a working party of top administrative officials could work out the constitutional arrangements and administrative implications. At the same time a working party of ministers could hammer out the details of presentation and political strategy. If the plan is to succeed, it must be fairly well crystallised and advanced soon, before the position in Singapore hardens against merger and before divergent constitutional developments take the Borneo territories on a separatist path.

38   CO 1030/1149, nos 68–71   19 May 1961

[Political developments in Singapore since June 1959]; despatch from Lord Selkirk to Mr Macleod, surveying developments since the PAP came to power and commenting on the impact of its defeat in the Hong Lim by-election

[Growing opposition to Lee Kuan Yew from the left within his PAP, called into question the long-term political survival of the prime minister as well as prospects for 'Greater Malaysia'. Ong Eng Guan's defeat of the PAP candidate at the Hong Lim by-election at the end of April was a serious reverse for Lee who was by now clearly committed to merger. Selkirk believed that the island's merger with the federation was the best way of reinforcing Lee's position and ensuring Singapore's security. He advised continuing support for the PAP, though not at all costs; if negotiations with Malaya on merger showed signs of foundering, it would be wise to make separate plans for the constitutional development of Singapore which would satisfy aspirations for independence while guaranteeing Britain the 'permanent and effective use of our bases'. CO officials were relieved that Selkirk, who had been a critic of the Singapore constitution, had become far less pessimistic. Selkirk's depatch was subsequently printed for confidential circulation (CO 1030/1150 no 164 and DO 169/18, no 21).]

I have the honour to submit the following brief survey of the main trends of political development since the P.A.P. came into power in June 1959. Although I have myself only been in Singapore since January 1960, the period is, I think, best taken as a whole.

2.   There was much natural apprehension as to what would happen when the Government came in. In the result, a fair amount of capital left the State for Hong Kong and the Federation of Malaya. The Civil Service had their pay docked and the English-speaking Chinese came in for a good deal of criticism. This was relatively mild after the antics of Ong Eng Guan as Mayor of the City Council and it was in their attitudes rather than in their actions that the P.A.P. first revealed their

weakness. What had been noted as self-confidence before the P.A.P. took power soon became touched with arrogance, their energy became aggressive and their party loyalty marked with extreme intolerance of any opposition or criticism. Their discipline was characterised by bullying. I was disappointed that the Opposition had not shown themselves capable of pricking the bubble of the P.A.P.'s claim to omnipotence and omniscience, let alone providing an alternative for the electorate.

3.   After their first errors, however, a number of clear, sound, policies emerged. They have produced a well-founded if slightly ambitious Development Plan. Their budgets have been orthodox and sound. They have maintained wholeheartedly their policy of independence only through merger with the Federation of Malaya even when public opinion seemed to be turning towards complete independence for Singapore on her own. The administrative services have been well maintained. They have up to now behaved with great restraint and understanding in regard to the military establishments and bases in Singapore and have only asked that we should be as reasonably unostentatious in their use as possible. They have shown a surprising willingness to get advice from all kinds of outside authorities, though naturally enough they do not always accept what these bodies say. Of particular value have been the visits of U.N.T.A.B. and I.B.R.D. representatives. Although the responsible conduct of Lee's Government has almost inevitably led to loss of support among more irresponsible elements of the community, he has gained a great deal of sober regard from the business community and generally with the English-speaking Chinese. Dr. Goh's sense of reality has enabled him to state quite frankly 'that nobody owes Singapore a living'; Singapore can only depend on Singapore's own efforts. The P.A.P. political journal 'PETIR'[1] has stated publicly and frankly the economic benefits which Singapore derives from the military base and has said that if the British Services were not here, Singapore would have to create her own army, thus losing $250 million a year and having to expend a further $150 million a year herself.

4.   Throughout this period, the central point of anxiety has been the attitude of the trade unions. It was inevitable that, with a Government which can blandly say that all its legislation is biased in favour of its workers, the trade unions should endeavour to take advantage of the situation. The number of man hours lost in 1960 went up considerably, although in many cases unnecessarily. This was the period in which the new Singapore T.U.C. was building itself up. The T.U.C. Secretariat is nearly half composed of pro-communist or extreme left ex-detainees. The Government had planned to set up a strong Singapore trade union organisation with executive powers. I warned them of the dangers of this type of organisation and they changed their plans when they realised I was right in suggesting that it was likely to be used against the Government itself. At this moment, I believe that they are uncertain of the best way in which to proceed on this problem. Meanwhile, a larger number of individual unions have come to be controlled to a substantial degree by a group under Lim Chin Siong, the leading pro-communist ex-detainee. This group have strengthened their position for future action but at one and the same time have been able to claim that they have reduced the number of strikes. (They have found it more profitable to 'negotiate' concessions from the better-off firms). The

---

[1] Literally 'thunder'.

Government has set up an independent Industrial Arbitration Court which could provide a measure of stability, but has not yet been able to assert itself, largely because of fumbling by the Minister of Labour.

5.   The Internal Security Council has developed in directions that can hardly have been envisaged by those who wrote the Constitution. Only on two subjects has the I.S.C. exercised its constitutional powers of decision: first in regard to the continued detention of agitators held under the P.P.S.O. and secondly in regard to the introduction of a Russian trade mission. In the former, the I.S.C. was advised by Lee Kuan Yew to accept responsibility for the detention of subversives when he did not want to accept it himself. In the second, the United Kingdom and the Federation Government, which holds very strong views on the admission of communist nationals for more than a fortnight at a time, in effect over-rode the Singapore Government. For the rest, the I.S.C. meetings have developed into social occasions which provide the only regular and easy communication between Federation and Singapore Ministers and are largely characterised by convivial entertainment and golf.

6.   The I.S.C. has, however, been the subject of attack on various political platforms by the extreme left. Our agreement that the detailed work should remain confidential has allowed rumours to circulate, some fairly accurate, some without the slightest justification. The Prime Minister has not helped matters by his equivocal approach on certain occasions to the question of responsibility. The future of the I.S.C. in its present form will be in the forefront of the constitutional talks when these take place.

7.   Where, however, the Government have chiefly fallen down is over their complete failure to understand the mechanics of successful democratic government. The outstanding example is the manner in which they handled the case of Ong Eng Guan. Lee Kuan Yew thought he must crush rather than tolerate him and tried to do this by casting reflections on his personal veracity and private life in a series of elaborate enquiries and debates. I warned him nearly three months before the election that all this publicity would inevitably result in Ong Eng Guan's re-election for the Hong Lim Constituency. But in spite of warnings, the Prime Minister insisted on harrying Ong Eng Guan and regarding the election as a test of confidence in his Government and in his own position.

8.   I believe nonetheless that he has acted with honesty and with some courage, and indeed he has sought to denounce the 'lunatic left' as he calls it, or left wing adventurers, on more than one occasion and notably at the last May Day Rally. But I doubt how much this really gets across to the ordinary man in the street. Even Mr. Strachey during a recent visit remarked to him in a kindly vein that he had found his Hong Lim speeches far more intellectual than he would himself ever dare to make to his own constituents.[2]

9.   The P.A.P. have been severely shaken by their heavy defeat in the Hong Lim by-election. Their first reaction was to consider a General Election but commonsense

---

[2] John Strachey, Labour intellectual, MP and secretary of state for war, 1950–1951. He had been secretary of state at the War Office during the lowest point in British fortunes in the Malayan emergency. During the years of parliamentary opposition from 1951, he developed a theoretical position on empire, for example in his book, *The end of empire* (1959). He was briefly shadow Commonwealth secretary in 1963, the year that he died.

prevailed and they are now taking their defeat more calmly. Lee is not so much concerned with the evident, considerable loss of public support, which frankly is not unexpected after the first two years of Government, as with a weakening within his own party which he ascribes primarily to the sapping of Party loyalty inspired by Lim Chin Siong, whom the Prime Minister still regards as his chief opponent. No doubt much of this anxiety is justified. Lim Chin Siong's grip on the Unions, if not the electorate, is strong, and he benefits by, even if he does not at present encourage, Chinese chauvinism which is still fundamental. Mr. Tan Lark Sye, multi-millionaire supporter of Nanyang University, recently told me that it would take a long time for Chinese chauvinism to be replaced by true Malayan loyalty. Anti-colonialist sentiment is the standard of all parties, of the right or left, however jocularly it may be referred to in private. The body of the people are politically uneducated and the more intellectual leaders, such as students, are going through a phase of political ferment. The economic problems of Singapore are very intractable. Any stabilised alternative to the P.A.P. Government is still not in sight. A General Election could well produce a number of smallish groups, none of which would be strong enough to form a stable government. This would probably lead to the formation of a new party to the left of the P.A.P. which would sooner or later win decisive political power in Singapore.

10.   In spite of the uncertainty which I always feel of Lee's reaction to a given circumstance, there is a most interesting long term consistency in his political view. So, today, he continues to look three years ahead. His dilemma is how to maintain political momentum in the face of increasing pressures for constitutional advance, when he believes that major constitutional changes could be dangerous and independence disastrous but is receiving only limited encouragement from the Federation for the cause of 'Grand Design' and Merger. Either he must obtain in the next eighteen months some advance or commitment towards a merger with the Federation of Malaya, or he has to face up to the prospect of going to London for constitutional talks in 1963 where he could ask for virtually no significant changes and lose the General Election or ask for big changes which he does not at present consider to be in Singapore's best interests. This does emphasise, however, that as far as he is concerned, the obvious and immediate goal is advance towards a form of Grand Design in which both the Federation and the Borneo Territories must participate.

11.   In all the circumstances, we should continue to encourage the P.A.P. to pursue a patient and sensible policy until the end of its term, although we should not appear to be ready to keep them in power at all costs. If, however, it appears that the discussions with the Federation on Grand Design are never likely to succeed, then we must begin to think about constitutional developments in Singapore which will satisfy aspirations for independence while guaranteeing permanent and effective use of our bases. Although, in fact, the present Constitution is admirably suited to serve Singapore, it has failed to command the broad measure of support necessary for its continuance beyond 1964, and I doubt now if it ever will before irresponsible elements are likely to gain power.

12.   I am sending copies of this despatch to the Governors in Hong Kong, Jesselton and Kuching on a personal basis; to the United Kingdom High Commissioners in Canberra, Wellington, and Kuala Lumpur; to H.M. Ambassador in Djakarta; and to the High Commissioner for Brunei. I also enclose extra copies for you to pase to the Foreign Secretary, the Commonwealth Secretary and Minister of Defence.

39   PREM 11/3418   26 May 1961

'Grand Design': inward telegram no 382 from Sir G Tory to Mr
Sandys, giving advance notice of Tunku Abdul Rahman's speech to
the Press Club lunch in Singapore on 27 May

[The Tunku's speech marked, not the start of the Malaysia story, but the end of one
chapter and the beginning of the next. The Tunku later described the 'electrifying' effect
of his announcement at the Press Club lunch: 'Suddenly everyone was sitting bolt
upright, hardly believing their ears ... My reference so discreetly but publicly to
"Malaysia" took all the territories by storm.' What was remarkable about the speech was
not the suggestion of merger but its apparent espousal by the Tunku. It provoked mixed
reactions. In Singapore, Selkirk and Lee were encouraged by the Tunku's apparent
change of heart regarding association with Singapore, but the speech triggered a political
crisis culminating in July with Lee's critics leaving the PAP to form the Barisan Sosialis.
In the Federation most Malays were wary of any connection with Chinese-dominated
Singapore, so much so that, to avoid dissent, the Tunku soon shifted his emphasis to the
alternative plan of merging the Federation with the Borneo territories in advance of
union with Singapore. In North Borneo and Sarawak, British officials and community
leaders grew more mistrustful of Malayan 'colonialism', preferring progress towards a
federation of Borneo territories. The Sultan of Brunei, on the other hand, declared an
interest in taking part and the Tunku recalled that, when he returned to Kuala Lumpur
after his speech, 'the first person to come and see me was the Sultan of Brunei. He
showed great excitement over my speech and urged me to carry out the plan for merger
without delay.' In London ministers had hitherto refrained from forcing the pace towards
'Greater Malaysia' and had, instead, awaited a major, local initiative in that direction.
Now, at the Tunku's instigation, the British government addressed the issue of the 'grand
design' and on 20 June the prime minister made a parliamentary statement about it (*H of
C Debs*, vol 642, 1171–1173; see also Tunku Abdul Rahman, *Looking Back*, Kuala
Lumpur, 1977, pp 81–82).]

As you may know Lee Kuan Yew has several times visited Kuala Lumpur recently to
press Grand Design upon Tunku having regard particularly to his need to offer some
evidence of Constitutional advance before Spring 1963 when Singapore Constitution
is due for review.[1] Lee had formed conclusion (I believe correctly) that Razak was
already converted and he has I suspect relied largely on Razak to break down Tunku's
prejudice. Complete break through has in fact now been made.

2.   Tunku told me this morning that in speech to Press Club in Singapore
tomorrow afternoon 27th May at lunch for International correspondents he intends
to include passage on following lines. *Begins*: Malaya cannot stand alone. Sooner or
later she must have an understanding with the Territories of Singapore, North
Borneo, Brunei and Sarawak. It is premature at this stage to say how this could be
brought about but we have got to plan ahead now with this as our objective. *Ends*.

3.   Tunku said that as I knew he had hitherto argued that Federation's interest
would be better served by keeping Singapore independent of it and that it would be
easy for Federation to insulate herself from effects of any political deterioration there
by physical means (e.g. closing the causeway) or by relying on friendly Western
Powers. He had now come to realise that this would only be short term solution at best
and that in Malaya's interests she should find some means of absorbing Singapore
safely and constructively. The Grand Design offered only means of doing this.

4.   He made it clear from his remarks he was thinking of Brunei, Sarawak and
North Borneo being absorbed into Federation of Malaya as integral states with

---

[1] See 37.

Singapore alone enjoying substantial self government. I said present tendency was for North Borneo and Sarawak to draw together and that I thought it likely they would have to be offered considerable measure of self government also if it were to be made worth their while to be associated. He said however that these were all matters that could be thrashed out. He expected that when the time was ripe he would be asked to go to London to enter into negotiations.

5.   I said this was most welcome information. As regards his proposed public conference tomorrow I thought there might be some danger of adverse reaction in North Borneo and Sarawak (or even in Brunei) where public opinion still needed to be conditioned. He said however with a laugh that nothing would happen at all unless someone gave a lead. He was obviously determined to make his statement but he wished to give me opportunity to inform you and others concerned in advance so that you 'would not be taken by surprise'.

6.   I very much hope we can leave Tunku to take this initiative. Given his violent prejudice hitherto this represents almost miraculous change of heart. As suspected, now penny has dropped, he is perhaps moving ahead faster than we were prepared to go but we have more hope of steering him if we go along with him than if we try to restrain him at this juncture.

40   CO 1030/1079, nos 3–6   1 June 1961
[Closer association of North Borneo and Sarawak]: letter from Sir A Waddell to E Melville

[The Tunku's speech of 27 May opened a new phase in policy-making in which the British government addressed the implications of the 'grand design' for the development of the Borneo territories, on the one hand, and for regional security, on the other. Over the next five months, these issues dominated discussions which veered one way and another in response to the growing crisis in Singapore, the Tunku's desire for a quick decision and the anxieties of the Borneo governors. After erratic preparations involving at times tense Anglo–Malayan diplomacy, a conference was held in London where the British and Federation governments agreed two key principles for planning a 'Federation of Malaysia': firstly, the inclusion of the Borneo territories would depend on the views of the peoples of North Borneo and Sarawak as well as the view of the Sultan of Brunei; secondly, the Anglo–Malayan defence arrangement would be extended to the new state. In the first document of this chapter (40), the governor of Sarawak reported a generally favourable response to the Tunku's speech and he advised the British government to take a lead in effecting the closer association of North Borneo and Sarawak in the first instance. But he warned against an over-hasty approach to their unification. In doing so, he compared the predicament of the Borneo territories with that of Northern Rhodesia and Nyasaland within the Central African Federation, whose problems were frequently cited during the planning of Malaysia over the next two years. Melville replied to Waddell on 8 Aug—and sent a similar letter to Goode, governor of North Borneo—stating that the government would appoint a co-ordinator for North Borneo and Sarawak to follow up the Rampton Report on economic development (CO 1030/1079, nos 26/29 and 30).]

The Secretary of State's telegram to the Commissioner-General, No. 36 of 24th May invited comments on the latters [sic] demi-official letter R.1011/49/61 of 2nd May on closer association in Borneo.[1] And all this has been overlaid by the Tunku's speech last Saturday on the Grand Design.[2]

---

[1] See 36.   [2] See 39.

2.   I have little that is new to add but to restate my position which is briefly that we should hasten along with Borneo unification or federation with the longer term aim of association as a reasonably viable and influential unit with Malaya.

3.   While supporting the Commissioner General's emphasis on greater speed I do not quite subscribe to the method described in paragraphs 5 and 6 of his letter, namely that H.M.G. should declare now its firm intention of uniting the Borneo territories (as a prerequisite to self-government) and that in two years time a single Governor should be installed for both territories. Such a shot-gun marriage would I am sure give rise to reactions not entirely unlike those experienced in the Central African Federation. Notwithstanding this I believe that a definite lead from H.M.G. is required and, locally, a declaration of intention as I believe that we have very nearly exhausted the possibilities of closer administrative and departmental association which can profitably be undertaken without clearly stating the final objective. Given a clear objective, ratified by the legislatures and with the fullest backing (including financial) by H.M.G. we can get on with the job. Otherwise we will jog along and be in danger of being picked off singly by Indonesia (or by Malaya, for it seems from paragraph 4 of Tory's telegram No. 382 to C.R.O. of 26th May that the Tungku envisages the absorption of the Borneo territories as integral states without any substantial measure of self-government). Or if that does not occur we will be faced with the problem in due course of Sarawak (pop. 750,000) seeking independence with entry to the Prime Ministers Conference, United Nations and with ambassadorial commitments and the other expenses of independence which she cannot afford—far less its own army for protection. Then H.M.G. will have to pour in money to keep the place going and you can be sure that the bidding from the Communist bloc would push up the stakes. Far better to spend some of that now to build a United Borneo—and here I echo the plea made by Bill Goode in the last paragraph of his despatch No. 876 of 30th December[3] although he was referring to North Borneo alone.

4.   My recommendation is this. That H.M.G. should declare at an early date that it firmly believes that the interests of the people of the Borneo territories will best be served by the creation of a viable unified state or federation and that it is prepared to give all possible assistance to that end. Such assistance would take the form of providing (and paying for) an inter-territorial organisation charged with the responsibility in the first instance of working out for approval by the Governments the details of this common market recommended by the Rampton Report,[4] for the correlation of economic activity and for the promotion of joint departments and of joint activities in the fields of research, communications, training and higher education (and here although we are struggling against time and shortage of funds in the field of primary and secondary education it is in fact time that we were thinking of a University College for even the most modest institution of that kind takes years to create). And to make the organisation effective H.M.G. should be prepared to make substantial *additional* grants for inter-territorial projects, one of which, as Lord Selkirk strongly recommends, would be the inauguration of a trunk road project linking Sarawak with North Borneo (and this means Jesselton to Kuching or such part of this as we have not already built or can build from our own

---

[3] See 31.   [4] See 36, n 1.

resources). The Administrator of this inter-territorial organisation (which partakes of Sir Stephen Luke's West Indian Welfare and Development organisation, East Africa High Commission and the former West Africa Inter-territorial Secretariat)[5] would need to be a man of the highest calibre who, in addition to the tasks indicated above, could as the Commissioner General suggests initiate the studies required for planning constitutional advance towards federation or unification.

5.   In this way we could make quicker progress locally and be in a much better position when we come, as we should, to negotiate terms on the Grand Design.

6.   With these qualifications, which are only of method and approach, I support Lord Selkirk's views. The matter has now of course become more pressing with the Tunku's initiative on the Grand Design. The pointed references to Indonesia in his speech may well provoke increased attention by the latter to the Borneo territories, so the sooner we strengthen our own position the better.

7.   With regard to the Tunku's statement on the Grand Design the local reaction as far as it has had time to be expressed is generally favourable, the Chinese in full support and also seeing it as a means of early self-government for Sarawak, the Malays much more cautious as they do not in fact have much fellow feeling for Malaya, as Malayans incline to look down on our local Malays, as indeed they do from all accounts on Brunei Malays. The Ibans have not yet uttered but their greatest fear as I have said before would be that Sarawak would be swamped with surplus Chinese from Singapore. They and I will need assurances on that.

8.   I enclose the copy of an article from the Sarawak Tribune of Wednesday, 31st May, which gives the official utterances of the parties, and a copy of a cutting from today's issue correcting the last sentence of the PANAS statement.[6] You will note that they agree with me that Borneo federation should come first.

9.   I am sending a copy of this letter to the recipients of the Commissioner General's letter of 2nd May.

---

[5] Sir Stephen Luke was comptroller for development and welfare in the West Indies and British co-chairman of the Caribbean Commission, 1953–1958; commissioner for the preparation of West Indies Federal Organisation, 1956–1958; senior crown agent for overseas governments and administrations, 1959–1965.

[6] Not printed; for PANAS see 26, n 2.

41   PREM 11/3418   3 June 1961

'Grand Design': inward telegram no 399 from Sir G Tory to Mr Sandys, reporting a talk with the Tunku on reactions to his speech of 27 May]

Tunku sent for me this morning to speak of a number of matters but obviously with intention of finding out how United Kingdom Government had reacted to his announcement. He said he had been thinking over what I had told him about North Borneo and Sarawak but was still determined that if Grand Design were to be implemented at all they should be absorbed into existing Federation of Malaya as two member states or as one state if they should merge.

2.   Sultan of Brunei had told him he would be glad to bring Brunei in on same basis. Indeed he would according to Tunku not be prepared to come in otherwise.

Sultan felt that incorporation as a Malayan state would alone give him 'protection' he needed (presumably of his purely Malay way of life and religion). Tunku admitted that another factor weighing with Sultan was prospect which integration would offer him of eventually becoming Yang Di-Pertuan Agong.[1]

3. As regards Singapore Tunku said he was now clear that only possible solution from his standpoint would be on Ulster pattern with Singapore sending a number of representatives to Federal Parliament in Kuala Lumpur. This had at one time been put forward in discussions by Mr. Lee Kuan Yew. He is not prepared to consider a confederation with the Federation of Malaya, Singapore and perhaps a unified North Borneo and Sarawak sending representatives to a higher Parliament with limited responsibility, for example, over Foreign Affairs, Defence and Currency.

4. I again warned Tunku that so far as North Borneo and Sarawak were concerned his proposal might not find ready acceptance. I reminded him that these two states at least seemed likely on present showing to wish to draw together first and pointed out that comment by such political community leaders as there were in Kuching and Jesselton as quoted in Straits Times of 2nd June tended to confirm this. I was, however, expressing my own personal view since there had not yet been time for considered comment from North Borneo and Sarawak or indeed from the United Kingdom.

5. Tunku said he was now working on a memorandum setting out his view and hoped to let me have it within a week. He trusted that when Mr. Macmillan came he and Tunku and Lee Kuan Yew would be able to clinch matters.[2] Again I warned Tunku that I thought he was going too fast for us and that to force the pace to this extent might set up adverse reactions which might fatally prejudice the Design. Tunku, however, made it clear that he was impatient to get on with the plan and that he thought it would become more difficult to implement the longer we delayed.

6. Tunku was obviously anxious to have early reaction from London. I told him he had given us rather large morsel to digest. In any event now that he was going to convey his idea to us in the form of a memorandum it would surely be best for us to defer our observations until this could be studied.[3] He agreed. This will give us a little time. We will telegraph effect of Tunku's memorandum when received.

---

[1] For the Yang di-Pertuan Agong, see 19, n 5.
[2] A visit by Macmillan was mooted at one time but was overtaken by events and replaced by plans for the Tunku to go to London.
[3] The Tunku sent the memorandum with his letter to Macmillan of 26 June, see 46.

42 CO 1030/979, nos 242–247   6 June 1961
'Possibility of an association of British Borneo territories with the Federation of Malaya and the State of Singapore': minute from Mr Macleod to Mr Watkinson

[In this minute Macleod refers to the following documents which are printed in this collection: the meeting of the Colonial Policy Committee on 18 Apr (see 35), Lord Selkirk's reports from Singapore (for example 36 and 38) and Tory's telegram number 399 (41). On reading Macleod's minute on 7 June, Macmillan noted: 'This must go to the Cabinet—or perhaps Defence Committee' (CO 1030/979 and PREM 11/3418). Following Macleod's minute to the minister of defence, the Joint Planning Staff prepared a paper for the Chiefs of Staff Committee (45) which examined the defence implications of the decision taken by the Colonial Policy Committee on 18 Apr 1961.]

This question of the 'Grand Design' was considered at a meeting of the Colonial Policy Committee on the 18th April. As a result, Lord Selkirk and others concerned in the area were told that before coming to a final decision H.M.G. proposed to give the governments of Australia and New Zealand an opportunity of expressing their views and that in the meantime our representatives might be guided by the assumption that H.M.G. accepted the development of a political association between Malaya, Singapore and the three Borneo territories as an ultimate aim of policy.

2.   I understand that it has since been agreed that before the governments of Australia and New Zealand are consulted the Chiefs of Staff should have an opportunity to express their views on the defence implications and that the necessary steps to this end are now being taken.

3.   I should, however, draw your attention to recent developments in the area which make it urgent for us to reach a decision in principle on the desirability or otherwise of this ultimate aim.

4.   First, Lord Selkirk has been reporting recently the anxiety of Mr. Lee Kuan Yew to be in a position to show the people of Singapore some progress towards the achievement of his policy of ultimate merger with the Federation of Malaya and his hope that to this end it might be possible for the Prime Minister on his visit to Singapore to be able to say something favourable about a future association of Singapore and the Borneo territories with the Federation.

5.   Secondly, Tunku Abdul Rahman himself has now come out with a public statement the special importance of which is that for the first time he acknowledges the desirability of a future association between the Federation and Singapore. He said in Singapore on the 26th May:—[1]

> 'Malaya today as a nation realises that she cannot stand alone and in isolation. Outside of international politics the national one must be broad based. Sooner or later she should have an understanding with Britain and the peoples of the territories of Singapore, Borneo, Brunei and Sarawak. It is premature for me to say now how this closer understanding can be brought about but it is inevitable that we should look ahead to this objective and think of a plan whereby these territories can be brought closer together in a political and economic co-operation.'

6.   The Tunku has followed this up with the demarche reported in Sir G. Tory's telegram No.399 to the Commonwealth Relations Office and is preparing a memorandum setting out his views. He is pressing for our reactions.

7.   These developments make it essential that we should reach our own decision in principle on the Grand Design as quickly as possible. Before we can do this we must, as already agreed, consult with the governments of Australia and New Zealand. Assuming that our decision then is that in principle we support the idea, there will then be need for much further consultation with our authorities in the area and with the Prime Ministers of the Federation and of Singapore before September, when Tunku has put us on notice he will want to raise the matter with the Prime Minister during his visit.

---

[1] In fact the Tunku delivered the speech on 27 May, although London was informed of its content on 26 May (see 39).

8. I am sending copies of this minute to the Prime Minister, the Foreign Secretary, the Commonwealth Secretary, the Chancellor of the Exchequer and the President of the Board of Trade.

43 DO 169/25, no 63:   7 June 1961
[Brunei and the 'Grand Design']: letter from D C White to E Melville

The latest report from Geofroy Tory[1] on his talks with Tungku Abdul Rahman in Kuala Lumpur makes it essential that I should receive guidance as a matter of urgency on the line to take with the Sultan when he returns from Malaya, which we now hear will be on the 21st June.

I have never personally doubted that the Sultan himself was ready to consider making Brunei an additional State of the Federation and take his place in the queue for the Agong's job. If the Sultan was honest in his remarks to Lord Selkirk (see para. 4 of Lord Selkirk's telegram to you numbered 183 of 29th May), it is clear from Tory's para. 2 of his telegram of 3rd June that he had no difficulty in making up his mind as to his reply to the Tungku. This is interesting, in view of Tory's remarks in his despatch of 19th July, 1960, when the Tungku reported the Sultan as 'not very keen on integration at the present time because of his fear that Malaya would use Brunei as a milch cow'. He seems to have gained assurance in the face of local opinion.

Sir John Martin, in his letter to Sir Denis Allen of 18th May last year,[2] indicated that we must regard with benevolence any proposal for Brunei to federate with Malaya, and he noted that moves for closer association between Sarawak and North Borneo might push Brunei more quickly into the arms of Malaya. The recent move of the two colonies towards a free trade area, together with the Economist article on 'glittering isolation', may have influenced the Sultan to be more forthcoming with the Tungku, and provided the 'push'.

I entirely agree with Waddell's views in his despatch of the 1st June, 1961,[3] that Borneo federation should come first (if possible), and the remarks of the Datu Bandar of Sarawak, Abang Haji Mustapha, as leader of Party Negara, Sarawak,[4] are most significant and indeed represent in the main the views expressed here by the Party Rakayaat [sic].[5] I expect you have seen the Borneo Bulletin of 3rd June but, in case you have not, I enclose a copy of the relevant articles.[6] The North Borneo News & Sabah Times (Donald Stephens,[7] I assume) remarked that 'history has changed but not to the extent where the three should not be able to get together again and the Royal House of Brunei be given the place it once had in these parts.'

---

[1] See 41.   [2] See 20.   [3] See 40.
[4] Abang Haji Mustapha championed Japanese interests in the occupation but after the Second World War he favoured cession of Sarawak by Rajah Charles Vyner Brooke to the crown. This made him a controversial figure in Sarawak politics, though he was rewarded when the last Rajah designated him Datu Bandar in June 1946. He was leader of the Party Negara Sarawak (PANAS) which was registered as a party on 9 Apr 1960. Modelled on the multi-racial, Malayan Alliance, it became increasingly identified with right-wing Malay causes. Dato Haji Mustapha was later appointed CBE.
[5] But the Party Negara came to support Malaysia (see 26, n 2) while the Party Rakyat opposed it (see 9, n 1).
[6] Not printed.
[7] Stephens was owner, editor and publisher of the *North Borneo News and Sabah Times*.

The Brunei Party Rakayaat has consistently advocated re-unification of the Borneo territories under the Sultan as a Constitutional Ruler and it is difficult to see how re-unification could be achieved without the Sultan taking a prominent part.

While it is probably correct to say that it was preferable for someone other than Her Majesty's Government to take the lead in introducing the Grand Design, there seems every likelihood of the Tungku and Lee Kuan Yew setting far too hot a pace to be comfortable over here. I have always hoped to see some of Brunei's wealth used for the mutual benefit of herself and her neighbours in projects such as the University College that Waddell mentions. Is there enough sugar to coat the pill of accepting the Sultan as a Consitutional Ruler?

I suppose that, if Lee Kuan Yew does not achieve some form of merger or promise of a merger before the next Singapore election, he will fall and the chance of unifying the Federation and Singapore will be lost, perhaps for ever, with the alternative of an extremely left wing, if not openly Communist, City State posing a serious threat to both Malaya and the Borneo Territories. We cannot, therefore, drag our feet without upsetting both the Tengku and Lee. Nevertheless, I hope that the Tengku can be made to realise the weight of popular opinion in the Borneo territories in favour of re-unification in some form and use his influence in this direction with the Sultan.

In the event of integration, as I interpret the Federal Constitution document, grants and sources of revenue assigned to States, Brunei would retain about $70 million per annum at present (over 50% emanating from investment income and much of the rest from the 12¼% ad valorem Royalty on oil) and hand over about $60 million, receiving a capitation grant of $1,550,000/-; North Borneo would hand over about $30 million and retain about $28 million, with a capitation grant of about $4,750,000/-; while Sarawak would hand over about $55 million, retaining about $23 million, with a capitation grant of $7,750,000/-. Brunei's contribution would more than cover the cost of the services which Malaya would have to provide; so would Sarawak's. North Borneo's contribution would probably need a further subsidy. Jointly, about $130 million would be available for development in the three territories.

While Brunei's surplus will decrease if new oil is not found, nevertheless it will decrease mainly in the contribution to the Federation (i.e. the income from Company Tax), as interest from investments is still increasing and the revenue from the 12½% Royalty ad valorem will decrease more slowly than the contribution from the Company's profits. There is the sugar. Should I raise the question of re-unification with the Sultan, in the light of what has been said in the Press?

I am sending copies of this to Lord Selkirk, Waddell, Goode and Tory.

44 CO 1030/1079, no 11   14 June 1961
[North Borneo and the 'Grand Design']: letter from Sir W Goode to E Melville

[Like Waddell and White (40 and 43), Goode expressed reservations about rapid advance towards a federation of Malaya, Singapore and the Borneo territories. Instead, developing a theme introduced in his despatch of 30 Dec 1960 (see 31), he advocated a step-by-step approach. He focused on greater co-operation between North Borneo and Sarawak, although even in this respect he felt that the accelerated union of North Borneo and Sarawak would be unwise given the differences between them. For, while North Borneo was ahead of Sarawak economically, it lagged behind politically.]

I am sorry I have been so long commenting on Lord Selkirk's letter of 2nd May.[1] It has been over-taken by the Tunku's statement on which my telegram No. 117 of 14th June gives the local reactions. I have subsequently received a copy of Nick Waddell's letter of 1st June.[2]

2.   The background to the problem in North Borneo is as follows:—

(i) The end of the war found North Borneo completely devastated and it has taken time to rebuild our towns and ports and to start providing essential requirements such as hospitals, teachers' training colleges and schools. It was inevitable that educationally and politically we should be behind Sarawak, for not only was North Borneo more backward educationally before the war, but also so many of those who had some education were killed during the war. We are taking such steps as we can to catch up, but all the indications are that Sarawak is going ahead equally fast.

(ii) On the economic front the picture is different. Since the war North Borneo has concentrated on economic development. It is now going ahead of Sarawak and all the indications are that its natural advantages in soils, relative ease of communications and geography will put it further and further ahead. Hence there is a distinct feeling that North Borneo should not have to carry a poor and troubled relation.

(iii) It is unfortunate for closer association that the tempo of political development in Sarawak has gone so far ahead of that in North Borneo. For there is not the slightest doubt that this is the main obstacle to closer association, and an obstacle which will become very considerably greater if the member system is introduced in Sarawak. There is in North Borneo a general feeling of apprehension over the way politics have developed in Sarawak and a widespread mistrust of political parties and politicians, especially Chinese. I find reluctance here even to start limited elections at the local government level.

(iv) It follows that in the interest of closer association Sarawak must be prepared to slow down her tempo of political development to suit North Borneo and that any mention of independence should be avoided. The British association is greatly valued in North Borneo and talk of independence will be interpreted locally as surrender to the left wing politicians and political troubles of Sarawak.

(v) The special position of Brunei and the difference in outlook between the Sultan and the Party Raayat are appreciated in North Borneo. Public opinion would welcome Brunei in a Borneo Union or Federation. It is therefore essential that at every stage the door should be seen to be open for Brunei participation.

3.   Against this background, I agree with Lord Selkirk that we cannot wait for North Borneo to catch up, that the task of bringing North Borneo and Sarawak

---

[1] See 36.   [2] See 40.

together will become harder as time passes, and that North Borneo would respond to a clear, firm lead by H.M.G.

4.   But, like Waddell, I consider that the announcement recommended in paragraph 5 of Lord Selkirk's letter, namely that it is H.M.G's firm policy that North Borneo and Sarawak shall achieve independence as a single unit, preferably in some form of association with Malaya and Singapore, goes too far for North Borneo's present thinking. Independence is not yet attractive; it is important not to give the impression that we are about to abandon the loyal and peaceful people of North Borneo to the political parties of Sarawak, Singapore and Malaya; nor must we weaken confidence in our continued acceptance of responsibility for the well-being of North Borneo.

5.   I, therefore, prefer the alternative declaration of policy suggested by Waddell in paragraph 5[3] of his letter, that H.M.G. firmly believes that the interests of the people of the Borneo territories will be best served by the creation of a viable, unified state or federation, and that it is prepared to give all possible assistance to that end.

6.   I believe that if we give the right lead, we shall be able to move forward at an ever increasing speed as public opinion comes to accept the main principle.

7.   I agree with Lord Selkirk that a single Governor for Sarawak and North Borneo would be the most effective administrative step to achieve our purpose (and conversely, that as long as there are two Governors a divergence of views will inevitably seep through both Governments). This step may be politically practical in two or three years; but the time is not yet ripe, and I advise against committing ourselves to it now.

8.   I strongly support Lord Selkirk's proposal in paragraph 7 for the appointment of a suitable senior officer—and he must be of the highest calibre, as Waddell states—to consider the problems of bringing the territories together, not excluding Brunei, and to stimulate and co-ordinate the necessary joint studies by the Governments. I am less confident than Waddell is of the value of an inter-territorial organisation charged primarily with co-ordinating economic policies. As reported separately (my savingram No. 413 of 30th May) I do not think such an organisation is required in the early stages of setting up a free trade area; and I am doubtful whether the precedents of inter-territorial organisations quoted by Waddell are sound. I would rather find the right man and proceed empirically from there. I agree with Waddell that H.M.G. should pay the cost.

9.   I fully agree that H.M.G. must be prepared to make substantial additional grants for inter-territorial projects such as trunk roads. North Borneo has already started work on making a through road from our boundary with Sarawak to Beaufort and thence to Papar and Jesselton, on another road which will join Kudat in the north with Jesselton, and on the first stage of a trunk road between Jesselton and Sandakan. But the rate of construction will be slow and some sections will not be all weather.

10.   I also wholeheartedly endorse Lord Selkirk's view in paragraph 10 of his letter that we must make a much bigger and more vigorous effort to improve education in North Borneo. Our present rate of progress is far too slow to keep pace with events. We are drawing up a new development programme for education of the order of $40 million in capital costs and additional recurrent expenditure of some

---

[3] In fact he is referring to paragraph 4.

$12 million per annum. If this is to be practical, we shall need powerful backing in both staff and finance.

11.   To sum up, I support the five recommendations set out in paragraph 12 of Lord Selkirk's letter, subject only to the comments on points of detail made above.

12.   I have two final comments:—

(a) If we are to make real progress quickly we must be prepared to find the necessary resources; and we must also be prepared to surmount the inevitable misrepresentation of our policy before world opinion by those who seek every opportunity to discredit us. Our prospects for a successful outcome will be greatly prejudiced should our policy become a party issue in the House of Commons.

(b) It will not be easy to bring the Borneo territories together and it will be more difficult to achieve their further association with Malaya and Singapore. But both can be done if we make the necessary effort and get the timing right. Already we have made some progress and there are a number of practical administrative steps such as the free trade area, unifying departments, (for example Posts and Telegraphs, Broadcasting, Customs,) and improving communications, which present no serious political difficulty.

13.   I am copying this letter to Lord Selkirk, Tory, Waddell and White.

45   DEFE 4/136, annex to JP(61)57(Final)   21 June 1961
'Defence implications of an association of the British Borneo territories with the Federation of Malaya and the State of Singapore': report by the Joint Planning Staff for the Chiefs of Staff Committee

[This report was prepared by the Joint Planning Staff (D L Powell-Jones, E B Ashmore, E V M Strickland and D C Stapleton) in accordance with the instructions of the chief of the defence staff following discussions in the Colonial Policy Committee on 18 Apr 1961 (document 35). The planners concluded that the Grand Design would improve Britain's defensive position in the region, save money, allow the re-deployment of forces outside Singapore (which was likely to become unreliable in the long term) and require advance base facilities on the island of Labuan. In their covering note they recommended that, if they approved the report, the chiefs of staff should forward it to the minister of defence. The chiefs of staff discussed the report on 27 June, with Lord Mountbatten in the chair. The COS objected to the speed of change, cast doubt on the advantages of the Grand Design, expressed concern lest the run-down of Singapore would discourage Britain's friends and allies, and instructed the JPS to revise their report. Selkirk, who was invited to attend the COS meeting on 4 July, argued that long-term defence interests would be better served by the Grand Design than by upholding the status quo, although he added the rider that 'our defence facilities would be orientated towards maintaining the stability of the area rather than towards furnishing a base for SEATO or British operations outside this Organisation'. The revised version of the Joint Planners' report made the point that the status quo would provide necessary facilities but, since it was unlikely that the status quo could be preserved for much longer, accepted that the Grand Design 'appears the least harmful of possible developments'. On 3 Aug 1961 the chiefs of staff (with Lt General Sir William Pike in the chair) were still cautious, stating that, while they preferred the status quo, they accepted the possibility of the need for change on political and economic grounds. The chiefs of staff continued to examine the feasibility of establishing a base on Labuan, although it was ruled out by the British Defence Co-ordinating Committee (Far East) (see 47 para 23). For these discussions see COS 40(61)6, 27 June 1961, and COS 42(61)1, 4 July 1961, DEFE 4/136; JP(61)57(Revised Final), 17 July 1961, and COS 50(61)1, 3 Aug 1961, DEFE 4/137; COS 67(61)6, 3 Oct 1961, COS 69(61)3, 10 Oct 1961, DEFE 4/139.]

Introduction
1.   Subject to final political decision after consultation with Australia and New Zealand, Her Majesty's Government may accept as an aim of their policy in South East Asia the development, in step with the wishes of the peoples concerned, of a political Association between the Federation of Malaya, the State of Singapore and the three Borneo territories[s].
2.   We are advised that the alternative in Singapore to the prospect of an Association on the lines of the 'Grand Design' is increasing pressure for separate independence. If this were not granted, we should have to deal with a city a large proportion of whose population would be hostile, and be involved in an internal security situation which might largely nullify the value of the base if not, in fact, make it untenable. If independence were granted, the new government of Singapore would be likely to be orientated towards Communist China and less inclined to grant us satisfactory defence facilities than the government of an Association led by a friendly-disposed Malaya. It would no doubt be possible to hold something like our present position in Borneo for longer than we can in Singapore but the facilities which we could expect to have there would be limited compared to those in Singapore and the period during which we could expect full and unfettered use of them would also be limited eventually by political factors.

Aim
3.   To examine the defence implications of the proposed Association.

Assumptions

Political
4.   We assume for the purpose of this paper that whatever form the Association takes there will be a central government responsible for defence, foreign affairs and internal security. The precise form is uncertain and will no doubt be the subject of prolonged negotiation. It is perhaps unlikely to take the form of a straight federation between the existing units of Singapore and the Federation of Malaya and a possible union of the Borneo Territories, if only because this would involve a triple-tier government in the existing Federation of Malaya, which would be impracticable. Present indications are that a likely form of government would be an extension of the existing Federal Government in Kuala Lumpur to Brunei, with Singapore and possibly North Borneo and Sarawak (the last two perhaps united) joining as additional units on special terms. Whatever the form of the Association we assume that the United Kingdom will wish to relinquish direct responsibility for internal security in it.
5.   Prima facie we may expect that the new Association will seek to have the present Malayan Defence Agreement[1] extended to the whole of the Association. In

---

[s] Colonial Office to Singapore Telegram No. 28

---

[1] At this point in the report the authors refer to a footnote citing the parliamentary paper, Cmnd 263 (Sept 1957). The Anglo–Malayan Defence Agreement was negotiated before Malayan independence but signed in Oct, after Malaya became independent, see *BDEE: Malaya*, lxxvii-lxviii, lxxx, and 402, 407, 408, 410, 414, 417, 431, 432, 441, 462.

short, the new Association would be likely to agree to British bases and the stationing of British forces in their territory but to retain restrictions on their use in a SEATO context. On the other hand we would have bargaining counters in seeking to negotiate arrangements to retain forces in these territories with safeguards to enable their effective use. These are the contribution we could make to external defence, internal stability and prosperity. We discuss these in paragraphs 6–8 below.

6. *External defence*. The present Malayan Government is seriously concerned at the trend of development in the Protocol States[2] and also at the situation which would follow from an invasion of West New Guinea by Indonesia, in which the Tunku expects that international communism would speedily involve itself.[3] Indeed by the time the Association comes about there is a possibility of its having to face other external threats.

7. *Internal stability*. Overseas Commonwealth forces are still being employed against Communist terrorists in the north of Malaya and the need for this may continue for some time.[4] Moreover, in view of the Tunku's motives in now accepting the 'Grand Design' proposals, he is likely to welcome the presence of overseas Commonwealth forces in the new Association as some reassurance against internal trouble even though he would not necessarily wish to ask for the assistance of these forces to put down disturbances except in the last resort. These arguments cannot be applied to Singapore, which is a special internal security risk and will remain so for the new Association.

8. *Economic factors*. The overseas Commonwealth forces in Malaya and Singapore are important employers of labour and providers of external currency. In view of the rapidly increasing population and difficult employment situation in Singapore, the Prime Minister, Mr. Lee Kuan Yew, has let it be known privately that he is anxious to preserve this source of income. This is a consideration which would also weigh with Malaya in negotiations for the new Association.

9. *The attitude of Australia and New Zealand*. Australia and New Zealand have at least as great an interest as ourselves in a satisfactory solution, and we assume that we should carry them with us in our policy on the 'Grand Design'.

Implications of the proposed association on United Kingdom defence arrangements
10. From these political assumptions, and having regard to treaty obligations and conclusions already reached by HM Government, we assume that our defence aims in South East Asia, should the 'Grand Design' come about, would be:—

(a) The external defence and internal security of the remaining British dependent territories, i.e. Hong Kong and the Pacific islands, and the external defence of the Maldives.

---

[2] The Protocol States were South Vietnam, Cambodia and Laos, so called because a protocol to the SE Asia Collective Defence Treaty of 1954 placed them under the SEATO's protection. In 1960 war resumed between communist and non-communist forces in Indochina and an international crisis over Laos was resolved only by agreements in July 1962 for the political unity and neutralisation of the country.
[3] For Indonesia's claims upon West New Guinea, see 21, n 3.
[4] Although the twelve-year Malayan Emergency officially ended on 31 July 1960, sporadic engagements continued on the border with Thailand where remaining communist forces had retreated. The CPM did not abandon the armed struggle until its general secretary signed agreements with the governments of Malaysia and Thailand in Dec 1989.

(b) The ability to provide an independently controlled contribution to the nuclear deterrent against China.

(c) The ability to contribute to land operations in support of SEATO, together with the appropriate naval and air support.

(d) To meet the requirements of any defence agreement with the new Association.

11. We are able to meet our present aims, which include those above, by the stationing of troops in Malaya and Singapore (and, shortly, Borneo) and in particular by the unrestricted use of Singapore as a naval/land/air base for the mounting and support of external operations. The situation has not proved entirely satisfactory in the planning for the ANZAM[5] support of SEATO because of the attitude of the Malayan Government towards the direct use of forces stationed in the Federation. In Singapore, also, we are involved in considerable overheads owing to the need for substantial garrison and reinforcement commitments to maintain internal security; these amount in the worst case to 14 major units plus one equivalent unit from the RAF.

12. It is the availability of Singapore which is above all called in question if the Association is formed.[6] If the Association were to be responsible for the internal security of Singapore, we would not be able to rely on its use as a main base. Provided, however, that a satisfactory agreement could be negotiated with the Association, allowing us freedom of action for our forces in exchange for an undertaking to help in the external defence of the Association, it should be possible for us to continue to meet the defence aims set out in paragraph 10 by relying on our present facilities at Malacca and Butterworth and by establishing elsewhere, free from the special risks of Singapore, the minimum facilities now there which it would be desirable to replace. These would comprise for the Royal Navy a fleet anchorage and for the RAF an airfield. The Army would require new base facilities sufficient to provide forward support to forces deployed in any of the roles described in paragraph 10 above. These facilities would allow us to suspend or discontinue the use of residual installations in Singapore at our convenience. A new defence agreement on these lines should not explicitly exclude and therefore should tacitly safeguard our ability to deploy and maintain nuclear forces in the new Association.

13. On the other hand the new Association, though wishing us to accept responsibility for external defence, may not be prepared to afford us acceptable freedom of action in the use of our forces based in their territory in support of Commonwealth or SEATO interests. While we do not believe that we or the ANZAM powers would stand by and see the Association attacked, it would not be in the United Kingdom's interest to accept a defence agreement which limited us in this way. The aims in paragraph 10 would then have to be met by some other means.

14. There appear to be the following alternatives:—

---

[5] ANZAM a consultative arrangement set up in 1948 through which (from 1950) Australia and New Zealand made contributions for the defence of British Malaya. ANZAM was largely subsumed within the structure of the Anglo–Malayan Defence Agreement.

[6] It was this likelihood that worried Julian Amery, secretary of state for air, see 74.

(a) To secure sovereign areas.

(b) To station ANZAM forces in SEATO countries, possibly under strengthened SEATO organization.

(c) To provide a military force for the area based on Australia.

We consider these in paragraphs 15 to 22 below.

Sovereign areas

15.   The day-to-day operation of Sovereign Areas, especially one including an urban complex, depends to a very large extent on local goodwill over such things as public utilities, particularly water and local labour. The danger always remains that freedom to use Sovereign Areas in support of national policy, e.g. the use of nuclear forces from them, will be inhibited by political pressure. Sovereign Areas must be chosen so that consideration of internal and external defence does not nullify their value as bases.

16.   *Malaya and Singapore.* For political reasons there could, of course, be no hope of securing Sovereign Areas in Malaya, though it might be possible to preserve our position in Malacca, Butterworth and Penang. In Singapore—political objections aside—such areas would be most difficult to delineate and would have to include several different parts of Singapore Island. The maintenance of their security and contact between them would tie down many troops.

17.   *Borneo Territories.* It is in the Borneo area that the possibility of Sovereign Areas and for that matter, leases, appears most promising. We have in mind particularly Labuan where there would be great advantage for the United Kingdom in retaining sovereign control, whether or not a satisfactory defence agreement were reached with the Association.

18.   *Labuan.* Labuan, an island of 35 square miles with a population of approximately 15,000 people, traditionally separate from neighbouring territories, could readily be developed as an advance base with a fine anchorage in Brunei Bay. The airfield would have to be improved but installations on the scale of our facilities in Singapore are not contemplated. It would be especially valuable to us as a refuelling base for strategic nuclear forces based in Australia; on the other hand it could not replace Kota Belud as an army training area and we would therefore wish to retain training facilities in this small area of the North Borneo mainland. Information on Labuan is given at Appendix.[7]

Stationing ANZAM forces in SEATO countries

19.   Another way in which the United Kingdom might be able to fulfil at least part of her SEATO commitments would be by stationing land and air forces in Thailand. It is doubtful, however, if she could obtain the necessary base facilities there. In any case, we are advised that HM Government might not agree to such a course, since the cost in foreign currency would be high, the use of forces in defence of British interests outside SEATO might be prejudiced and the United Kingdom would be committed in advance to operations in South East Asia.

20.   The idea, however, has positive attractions in that it would contribute to a permanent SEATO military presence as a deterrent against further Communist incursion and should obviate delay in mounting operations on the mainland with forces fully

---

[7] Not printed.

equipped and supported with heavy weapons. Indeed, from the military point of view, this is the most satisfactory and timely way of meeting the needs of SEATO military action.

21.   Although the political circumstances are widely different, from the military standpoint the reorganization of the SEATO alliance on NATO lines with, for example, declared forces, common defence responsibilities, a defended frontier and common logistics, offers a far more certain means of ensuring the physical security of the remaining free nations of South East Asia in defence against Communism. We recognize that, apart from the difficulties for the United Kingdom referred to in paragraph 19 above, these South East Asia nations might not be persuaded of the advantages of having SEATO forces on their territory in peace-time. This is a course of action, however, which must depend essentially on political judgement of the chances of success.

Providing a military force based on Australia

22.   This alternative is under separate examination$^{£}$, in which the possible effect of 'Grand Design' will be taken into account.

Strength of United Kingdom forces

23.   At present our initial contribution to external defence of the area under ANZAM and for SEATO purposes consists of the British element of the Commonwealth Brigade Group with naval and air support, reinforced if necessary from the United Kingdom.

24.   In addition we plan* to have available in the Theatre against the internal security threat in Singapore eight army units, one Royal Marine Commando, and one equivalent unit of the RAF. For some of these units internal security is their prime role and a significant reduction could be made if we gave up our internal security responsibilities. There may, however, be some commitments to help with the formation of the Association, but these would have to be studied as negotiation proceeds. Our eventual contribution to internal stability would be implicit in our forces provided in the area for other purposes.

The alternative to 'Grand Design'

25.   A hostile Singapore held down by force, or a separately independent and possibly communistic Singapore, and the weaknesses of the separate Borneo territories, whatever their political status, would seriously extend the defence responsibilities of the United Kingdom and indeed for the ANZAM powers and the West as a whole.

Timing

26.   The problems associated with becoming militarily independent in all essentials of Singapore before it becomes unreliable as a main base are complex. Apart from possible political and economic objections to a precipitate or complete withdrawal, we should not wish, from the military point of view, to lose useful facilities prematurely. Moreover, detailed studies by the Principal Administrative Officers will be required to decide what must be provided elsewhere and when. These studies can hardly be carried out realistically at this stage in the launching of the 'Grand Design', nor until the place of Australia in our plans has been decided. That they will ultimately be essential seems certain.

£ JP(61)67   * COS(61)13

Conclusions

27.   The formation of the 'Grand Design' should in the long term free our forces from substantial internal security commitments. In the short term we may be called upon for some assistance during the formation and development of the Association.

28.   Singapore, in or out of the 'Grand Design', will eventually become unreliable as a main base. The negotiation of the 'Grand Design' offers an opportunity of recognizing this fact and planning the deployment of our forces in the area on a firmer long-term basis.

29.   We should, as part of the 'Grand Design', acquire advanced base facilities in Labuan.

30.   From the military point of view, therefore, the 'Grand Design' would improve our defence position in the Theatre, providing that satisfactory agreements could be reached on the various points discussed above. Moreover, if it comes about and we exploit it to realign our defence arrangements, the longer-term improvement in our defence position in the area as a whole could be substantial.

46   PREM 11/3418   26 June 1961
[The Grand Design]: letter from Tunku Abdul Rahman to Mr Macmillan. *Enclosure*: 'Integration of British North Borneo territories and Singapore with the Federation of Malaya'

[Ghazali Shafie, permanent secretary of the Malayan Ministry of External Affairs, brought this letter from Kuala Lumpur to Selkirk in Singapore for forwarding to Macmillan. The Tunku remained mistrustful of Lee's intentions and ever wary of dissent amongst Malays in the Federation. For these reasons he hoped to minimise the Singapore threat by first securing merger with the Borneo territories. Since the principal attraction of the Grand Design for the British was to ensure the stability of Singapore through integration with the Federation, they did not welcome the Tunku's 'further thoughts'. Selkirk received the letter, just after he had concluded with Goode, Waddell and White the terms of a despatch to Macleod (see 47). In forwarding the Tunku's letter to Macmillan, Selkirk commented: 'The views which the Tunku puts forward are much on the lines anticipated in the despatch and are, in some ways, harder than I had hoped.' Waddell was 'extremely irritated' and told Tory that the feeling had grown in Sarawak that 'the Tunku's object is a Greater Malaya, not Greater Malaysia'. CO officials were alarmed by the Tunku's change of tack, although they were somewhat relieved that Selkirk was becoming more aware of the difficulties emanating from Kuala Lumpur (Selkirk to Macmillan, 27 June 1961, PREM 11/3418; Waddell to Tory, 27 July 1961, CO 1030/981, no 412c; CO 1030/980, no 340). The Tunku's letter and its enclosures were later circulated to the inter-departmental committee of officials which was set up in Sept to prepare for the Anglo–Malayan talks on 'Greater Malaysia' (CAB 134/1949 and also CO 1030/1079, no 4). Macmillan did not reply to the Tunku until 3 Aug and then he evaded the issue of a prior Malaya/Borneo merger by proposing talks for the autumn (see 51). The Tunku and Macmillan corresponded at key moments and particularly when the possibility of Anglo–Malayan differences jeopardised Malaysia, for example, as we shall see below, over the recommendations of the Cobbold Commission in June-July 1962 or the financial settlement in 1963.]

I was gratified to read your encouraging statement in Parliament last week about the proposed association of the Borneo territories, Singapore and the Federation of Malaya.[1] As you may already be aware, I have written to Mr. Sandys regarding this, in

---

[1] *H of C Debs*, vol 642, cols 1171–1173, 20 June 1961.

particular about the future relationship of Brunei and the Federation.[2] I am now forwarding a memorandum giving in some details our further thoughts on the subject, which I hope may serve as a basis for discussions.

Enclosure to 46

Introduction
It is generally agreed that all dependent territories should in due course attain Sovereign and Independent status, an objective over which the United Kingdom and the Federation Government have no differences. Indeed, the Federation Government has followed the policies pursued in various parts of the world by the United Kingdom Government in this regard with appreciation and sympathy, being aware of the delicate balance required between progressive policies and the realities of particular situations. The immediate areas of concern to the Federation Government is Singapore, and further away, however, are the neighbouring territories, namely North Borneo, Brunei and Sarawak. The future must inevitably require careful, longterm and in the present political climate, urgent consideration.

2.   Annexes A and B show a breakdown of the area and population of each of these territories, and a map of this region.[3]

3.   The history of the Federation of Malaya is interrelated with the history of the Sultanate of Brunei which was formerly a powerful state with authority over those other two Borneo territories and territories of the Malay archipelago. There had been trade and political, social and cultural ties between those territories and Malaya from time immemorial. Racially the various indigenous peoples of those territories are related to the Malays, in fact they come of the same stock. The British domination in various degrees in this region during recent history brought about a closer political and administrative connection between the British North Borneo territories and British Malaya. There was established a currency union which still exists in the form of a Currency Agreement and there was interchangeability of the civil, police, educational and technical services, and in the case of the State of Brunei, many Malayan Civil Service, Medical Service and Technical Service officers are serving on secondment with the Brunei Government.

Proposal
4.   Under the Defence Treaty with the United Kingdom, Malaya is committed for the defence of the Borneo territories, Singapore and Hong Kong in the event of external aggression or outbreak of hostilities in these territories. With regard to Singapore the Federation of Malaya is represented in the Internal Security Council. It would not be out of place therefore if these territories were brought into closer ties with the Federation of Malaya. It is proposed therefore as a first step that the territories of Brunei, Borneo and Sarawak be brought into the Federation as units of

---

[2] Sandys was in Central Africa at the time of the Tunku's speech on 27 May, but on his return he sent a message to the Tunku on 5 June welcoming his suggestion and the Tunku replied on 15 June (DO 169/25, nos 45 and 55).

[3] Annexes A and B are not printed. A more accurate population table than that at appendix C is at 73, appendix B.

the Federation, enjoying the same rights and privileges as the States which presently form the Federation of Malaya, namely, Johore, Malacca, Negri Sembilan, Selangor, Pahang, Perak, Kelantan, Trengganu, Kedah, Perlis and Penang. Brunei, being a Sultanate, would have a Sultan as Head of State, the other two territories would be headed by Governors as is done with Penang and Malacca. It would be better of course if Sarawak could be returned to Brunei, at least the northern part of Sarawak, where the population is mainly Malays and Dyaks.

5.   After the merger of these territories with the Federation of Malaya, the next logical step would be to form a greater federation with Singapore. As the present Constitution of Singapore requires to be reviewed in 1963, the most appropriate time for preliminary discussions with Singapore would be before that date. It would be difficult at this stage, to determine the position of Singapore in its relation with the Federation, but it is obvious that once they become part of the greater federation, Singapore would be subject to the influence of the Federation, with rights to determine fully its internal affairs, except with regard to matters of national importance, such as internal security, defence, development finance, immigration, education and internal defence, and so it follows with regard to foreign affairs the Greater Federation Government will assume sole responsibility.

6.   The next matter which will require attention will be the question of British bases in Singapore which are now used as part of SEATO defence. But after the merger of Singapore with the Federation it is obvious that these bases would no longer be at the disposal of SEATO but could be maintained as bases for the defence of the Commonwealth.

7.   The administration of Singapore, Brunei and the Federation presents no difficulties whatsoever because the system of civil administration in these territories follows the same pattern based on British administration. It only remains to maintain the present administrative system, and in the future the officers of these territories would be interchangeable or transferable as they belong to the same service. It is proposed however that Singapore should maintain their own civil service but with rights to claim for secondment of officers from the Federation.

8.   It is proposed that a discussion on this line mentioned above should be held when the Prime Minister of the United Kingdom visits the Federation in September, after which a formal discussion can be arranged with representatives of the Federation Government on one side and the United Kingdom as representing the United Kingdom Government and these other territories on the other side.

9.   There are no Constitutional problems however novel or difficult which cannot be resolved. The main problem will be how to present the plan for Greater Malaysia to the peoples of three respective territories.[4] Singapore can express their own will through their elected representatives, but in view of the political immaturity of the people of Borneo it is not anticipated that they will have politicians who can represent them. It is to be expected therefore that the representation of the United Kingdom Government will include representatives from each of these territories as well. This meeting should decide on the appointment of an independent Commission with terms of reference to work out the Constitutional details of such a federation of

---

[4] Apart from the substitution of 'Greater Malaysia' for 'the "Grand Design"', the first two sentences of para 9 are identical with the beginning of para 10 in Lee Kuan Yew's paper of 9 May (see 37).

territories. It is suggested that this Commission should, if possible, be made up of those members of the Commission who drafted the Constitution of the Federation of Malaya, with the exception of the Chairman, Lord Reid,[5] who it is understood is indisposed. In his place it is proposed that Lord Ogmore[6] who is conversant with affairs in this part of the world should be invited to serve as Chairman.

10. It is a matter for emphasis that such a federation, comprising a grand total of nearly ten million people, in an area of 130,000 square miles, as against a Federation of 50,000 square miles, will have the effect of creating a greater importance in the hearts and minds of the people of these territories and a national pride which would go a long way in building up a feeling of loyalty to the country. The federation of a Greater Malaysia or a Greater Malaya, whichever name may be decided upon, will be powerful and viable and will be able to give greater contribution in the support of the Commonwealth association.

11. It has been suggested in some quarters that the merger of these territories is a matter for a long term objective and should be considered as such. The Federation Government however does not share this view. It is felt that the time is opportune to give immediate consideration to a plan for an early integration of these territories with the Federation of Malaya. A delay will only result in many undesirable consequences. For example, the Federation is one of the participating Governments to the present Currency Agreement. The other four participating Governments are those whose territories are the subject of this proposal. It will be appreciated that this participation in an Agreement which requires unanimity on all major issues derogates materially from the Federation's sovereignty as an independent nation in currency and financial matters. It is therefore natural that continued participation in such an Agreement under such conditions would be unsatisfactory from a long term point of view. The Federation Government is already being subjected to constant criticism by political opponents and the matter has become a live issue in recent election campaigns. In fact the Federation Government is actively considering withdrawing from this Agreement in accordance with the agreed procedure specified therein. At the same time it is felt that it would be a pity to break up an Agreement which has served all concerned so well in the past, but this Government would have no alternative, unless there is a reasonable prospect that all the territories covered by this Agreement will, in the near future, form an integral part of the Federation.

12. It is hoped that the British Government would give favourable consideration to this proposal for a Greater Malaysia. While relationship between the Federation of Malaya and the United Kingdom has been most cordial and the ties of friendship and common interest are inseparable, such a federation of territories as proposed will do much to arrest the spread of Communism in this region of Asia, and this is particularly urgent in view of the recent intensive Communist activities in South East Asia as a result of their success in Laos.

---

[5] Lord Reid chaired the Federation of Malaya Constitutional Commission, 1956–1957, see *BDEE: Malaya*, lii, lxxvii, 401 n 1, 404, 423, 424, 427–430, 438, 439, 443, 448, 453.
[6] Lord Ogmore (formerly David Rees-Williams) had known the Tunku since the 1930s. He had practised law in Penang before the Second World War and had served as parliamentary under-secretary of state, CO, 1947–1950; parliamentary under-secretary of state, CRO, 1950–1951; minister of civil aviation, June–Oct 1951. The Tunku proposed him as chairman of the Borneo commission, see 89, note.

47   CO 1030/980 no 324A   27 June 1961
[The 'Grand Design']: despatch from Lord Selkirk to Mr Macleod
reporting recent developments and urging a decision on policy

[The Tunku's speech of 27 May provoked a confrontation between Lee and the moderates,
on the one hand, and their left-wing critics in the PAP, on the other. Fearing the fall of
Lee's government, Selkirk convened in Singapore a high-level conference of British
representatives who were 'in broad agreement with the terms of this despatch' which was
written in anticipation of the Tunku's memorandum regarding merger (see 46). Selkirk
identified in the Tunku's proposal significant problems regarding the Borneo territories
and regional defence, but he urged the secretary of state to decide on a policy and take
advantage of the Tunku's initiative in order to shape its development. On the same day
Selkirk reinforced his despatch to Macleod with a letter to Macmillan (see 48). Shortly
afterwards, Selkirk flew to London for meetings with Macmillan, Macleod, the chiefs of
staff and Whitehall officials (CO 1030/980, no 340; CO 1030/1079, no 14A; COS 42(61)1, 4
July 1961, DEFE 4/136; draft minutes of Selkirk's meeting with Goode, Waddell, White
and others, DO 169/27, no 37; PREM 11/3418).]

I have the honour to refer to my despatch No. 2 of the 30th January 1961[1] and to
address you on the subject of recent developments on the Grand Design. I held a
meeting in Singapore on the 26th June with Sir William Goode, Sir Alexander
Waddell, Mr. D. C. White and representatives of the United Kingdom High
Commission in Kuala Lumpur and they are in broad agreement with the terms of
this despatch. I had previously had discussions with the Tunku and Tun Razak in
Kuala Lumpur.

British interests
    2.   The United Kingdom has a strong interest in peace and stability in the area.
The United Kingdom Government have a constitutional responsibility for Singapore
and the Borneo territories and for guiding their future as far as practicable in the
direction of the agreed aim for all United Kingdom dependent territories of full self-
Government within the Commonwealth. In the long run the political stability and
prosperity of the area is the best if not the only guarantee against subversion by
Communist movements and against outside aggression. We have political interests
and strategic obligations connected with the defence of Malaya, Australia, New
Zealand and Hong Kong, the protection of our communications with these countries
and our obligations to S.E.A.T.O. The United Kingdom also has important economic
interests in the region.
    3.   Grand Design is the most likely policy to satisfy long-term United Kingdom
interests in the area. The formation of a larger group under the leadership of the
Federation of Malaya would give a greater strength to the territories concerned than
they could hope to achieve individually; this would help them to resist internal and
external pressures. In the long term there are threats to the area from both China
and Indonesia and the Philippines have shadowy claims to North Borneo. Grand
Design would provide a political solution for the territories for which the United
Kingdom Government is at present responsible and would provide an answer to the
pressures which may arise in the United Nations for the grant of early independence
to these territories. Economically Grand Design would be likely to provide a broader

---

[1] See 32.

base for the territories in the area which should help to promote economic development and political stability. If Grand Design were brought about with the goodwill of the United Kingdom Government it seems probable that the United Kingdom economic interests would not be seriously affected—certainly not more so than if we retained political control against the will of the local people—and might even benefit. Arrangements would, however, have to be made to safeguard our strategic obligations.

The Tunku's initiative

4.   On the 27th May, 1961 the Prime Minister of the Federation of Malaya made a speech at a luncheon given in his honour in Singapore by the Foreign Correspondents' Association of South East Asia in which he referred to Grand Design in the following terms:—

> 'Malaya today as a nation realises that she cannot stand alone and in isolation. Outside of international politics the national one must be broad based. Sooner or later she should have an understanding with Britain and the peoples of the territories of Singapore, [North] Borneo, Brunei and Sarawak. It is premature for me to say now how this closer understanding can be brought about but it is inevitable that we should look ahead to this objective and think of a plan whereby these territories can be brought closer together in a political and economic co-operation.'

Reasons for Tunku's change of attitude

5.   This statement indicated a remarkable and welcome change of attitude on the Tunku's part. Among the factors contributing to this were no doubt the talks which the Secretary of State for Commonwealth Relations had with the Tunku in January and the Prime Minister of Singapore's recent representations to him on the subject.[2] Hitherto the Tunku had argued that the interests of the Federation would be best served by keeping Singapore separate and that it would be easy for the Federation to insulate herself from the effects of any political deterioration there by physical means (e.g. closing the Causeway) and by relying on friendly Western powers. He has, however, now, according to his own admission, come to realise that this would only be a short term solution at best and that the Federation's interests would be better served by finding some means of absorbing Singapore. The main difficulty in this was that it would lead to an overall Chinese majority. If, however, the Borneo territories were included as well, the overall proportion of Chinese would be only about 42%. For this reason, in the Tunku's view Grand Design offered the only safe means of absorbing Singapore.

Singapore

6.   For Singapore there is some urgency if Grand Design is the only method by which the Tunku can be persuaded to accept Singapore. Since the P.A.P. came into power in June 1959 they have consistently advocated a policy of 'independence through merger'. But the position of the P.A.P. leadership is weakening and they are being subjected to increasing pressure for outright independence—or for

---

[2] See 37.

independence before merger which might well postpone merger indefinitely. The P.A.P. Government have recently announced that at the 1963 Constitutional Review Talks they will demand independence through merger with the Federation or merger in a larger federation, and they have said to me and to members of my staff, though not in public, that they will stand or fall by this. If the P.A.P. were ousted, it seems likely that the major political force in the State would be the extreme left group, led by the communist or near communist trade union leaders, who have recently urged the abolition, as a first step, of all existing British powers in relation to the internal government of Singapore.

The Borneo territories

7.   The position of the Borneo territories is entirely different. Politically and economically North Borneo and Sarawak are much less developed than Malaya or Singapore and it would be fair to say that North Borneo needed British administration for a number of years before being ready for full self-government which, while it need not depend on direct elections, will only be a reality if the people take a part in the administration. In Sarawak there are elected representatives elected by indirect means but the territory still has a considerable way to go to self-government and will continue to need a strong British element in the administration for some years. There are risks in trying to push the two territories too fast. The first step clearly is for them to be linked with each other and, although it has been slow, there has recently been some progress in this direction.

8.   Up to 1959 Brunei had a Treaty with the United Kingdom Government under which the Sultan agreed that the foreign relations of the territory should be conducted by Her Majesty's Government, who were represented in the territory by a Resident. In 1959 the Sultan promulgated a written constitution which *inter alia* commits him to introduce elections within two years. Under a new Agreement concluded with the Sultan, Her Majesty's Government continues to be responsible for defence and external affairs through a High Commissioner who advises the Sultan on these matters, and by an Exchange of Letters between the Sultan and your predecessor it was agreed that the High Commissioner would not normally be expected to advise on other matters unless the Sultan so wished.

Reactions to the Tunku's statement of 27th May

9.   The Prime Minister of Singapore has welcomed the Tunku's declaration as something that should accelerate the speed of independence through merger for Singapore. In Sarawak and North Borneo, while some association of the Borneo territories with Malaya and Singapore has been welcomed as a long-term aim, it is felt that the first step should be a closer association of the Borneo territories, that time should be allowed for them to evolve their own institutions and that incorporation as an integral part of the Federation of Malaya would not be acceptable today.

10.   The indications are that there may well be adverse reactions from the Indonesians, who themselves have vague aspirations to leadership of the area. The newspaper 'Suluh Indonesia'[3] attacked the Tunku's statement as a 'manifestation of

---

[3] Literally 'torch of Indonesia'.

lack of understanding of the historical development of mankind'. Dr. Subandrio[4] recently passed through Singapore and his attitude to the Tunku's proposal was apparently one of truculence. Dr. Subandrio is reported in the Press as having said that his country was not interested in the plan and that it was a matter for the countries concerned to decide for themselves. The possibility cannot, however, be ignored that developments on Grand Design may antagonise the Indonesian Government and might conceivably lead them to attempt an irredentist movement in the Borneo territories.

Form and timing

11.   A number of suggestions have been put forward as regards the form which Grand Design might take. One suggestion proposed for the Federation and Singapore is an arrangement on what has been termed an Ulster model. Under this the Federation would take over from Singapore external affairs, defence and internal security, including the Police, for which Singapore would pay a financial subvention to Kuala Lumpur. Otherwise Singapore would retain a large measure of self-government—certainly greater than that allowed to the existing States in the Federation. In return for this Singapore would have to agree to send only say five to ten representatives to Parliament in Kuala Lumpur instead of the eighteen to twenty to which she would be entitled by reason of her population. This would not upset the Malay/Chinese equilibrium. Both the Tunku and Lee Kuan Yew appear to consider that something on these lines would be the most practicable solution. Similarly the Ulster model could be applied to the Borneo territories.

12.   A possible alternative to the Ulster model would be some kind of confederation under which each constituent territory had its own elected parliament and nominated members to a confederation parliament in proportion to its population. So long as the Alliance Government were in power in the Federation, this would ensure that the Malays were not swamped by the Chinese. Such an arrangement would however be open to a number of objections. It would lead in effect to three-tier government in Malaya. Unless a strong confederal government were established it would not be able to deal effectively with internal security problems in Singapore.

13.   According to the Tunku, the Sultan of Brunei is anxious to have Brunei incorporated as a State of the Federation as quickly as possible. We know that the Tunku would like this, but there seems to be some doubt what the Sultan actually said and moreover it is far from certain to what extent he is supported by the people of Brunei. An important political factor is the Party Ra'ayat which seeks closer association with Sarawak and has said that it does not want integration with Malaya except in conjunction with the other two Borneo territories. The situation may become clearer as a result of the Tunku's visit.

14.   The Tunku is having a memorandum prepared setting out his views on Grand Design but this has not yet been received.[5] As far as they are known at present, his ideas are somewhat vague but the Federation Government appear to be thinking

---

[4] Dr Subandrio, foreign minister of Indonesia, 1957–1966, directed the radical, leftist foreign policy of Sukarno's 'Guided Democracy'.

[5] See 46. The Tunku's memorandum reached Selkirk after this despatch had been drafted and agreed.

on the following lines. The Borneo territories should associate with Malaya at the same time as Singapore; the Federation Government would not be willing to absorb Singapore in advance of the other territories. They agree that the association with Singapore should come into operation by 1963 but do not see why the Borneo territories should not also be associated within that period. They recognise that the Borneo territories are in a very early stage of political and educational development but are prepared to take over the United Kingdom responsibility for administering them. They accept the need to maintain continuity of administration and would be willing to provide safeguards for the British Administrative Service. They would also consider assuming responsibility for the provision of development finance. They apparently envisage that the territories would be represented in the Federal Parliament by members of the Council Negri in Sarawak and members nominated by the Government of North Borneo. In the interim period, while British administration was still required, some form of condominium between the Federation and the United Kingdom might be feasible and desirable.

15.   These Federation proposals would raise extreme difficulty for the United Kingdom Government. In the first place, the territories could not be joined with Malaya without an opportunity being given to their peoples to indicate whether they had any objections to this course. It would hardly be practicable to consult the people, particularly in North Borneo, until there is a much greater degree of education and self-government. Secondly, North Borneo in particular needs British administration for a number of years yet. Thirdly, the reports that have been received from the Borneo territories indicate that if eventually they are associated with Malaya they would not wish to be absorbed as additional states of the Federation.

16.   The Tunku is still vague on some points. At present he appears to be firmly wedded to the idea that the Borneo territories should join Malaya at the same time as, if not before, Singapore and that the Borneo territories should join as integral states, although he might accept some form of condominium.

17.   There could be many different variations on the theme of an Anglo–Malaya condominium, according to the extent of the responsibilities of the Malayan and United Kingdom Governments. Among the possible advantages of a condominium would be that it would help to reassure the peoples of the territories that the United Kingdom Government were not abdicating their responsibilities towards them. It would also serve to introduce the Federation to the problems of the area. I do not under-estimate the difficulties of operating a condominium but, in the last resort, we might have to consider something on these lines.

18.   An alternative to condominium would be for the United Kingdom to continue to administer the Borneo territories for a period of years on an agency basis on behalf of the Federation Government. This would have the advantage that it would oblige the Federation to cultivate good relations with the territories. If this were done there would have to be some undertaking that after a period of five to ten years the territories would be free to dissociate themselves if they so wished. Both this arrangement and condominium would involve a transfer of sovereignty and any early transfer of sovereignty would be difficult.

19.   Another possible alternative would be the establishment of some consultative and administrative arrangement, not involving transfer of sovereignty, whereby the Federation could be practically associated with the administration of the territories

during an interim period at the end of which the peoples would be asked to approve their inclusion in the Federation.

20. Discussion with the Tunku indicates that he may not yet fully appreciate the need to carry the peoples of the Borneo territories with him in any arrangements made. Moreover, it appears that his knowledge of the Borneo territories is slight. At the moment the impression I have is that the Tunku may feel that we are making difficulties whereas in fact these difficulties are inherent in the situation. The Tunku must make or be given early opportunities to learn of the difficulties from the representatives of the territories themselves, preferably meeting them in the territories, instead of merely from representatives of the United Kingdom Government. If the Borneo territories are to come in, the Tunku must sell the idea to them and the Federation Government must become aware of the realities in these territories.

Defence aspects

21. The Chiefs of Staff are considering the defence aspects in some detail: I have shown this despatch to the Commanders-in-Chief but it has not been formally cleared with the B.D.C.C.

22. Our military aims in the area are to discharge our reponsibilities in ANZAM, SEATO and the Malayan Defence Agreement, to defend Singapore, the Borneo territories and Hong Kong and to protect our communications. In order to fulfil these reponsibilities we need the physical presence of forces in the area and a base from which to sustain them. If these forces are to operate in furtherance of United Kingdom and Commonwealth policy, we must have the ability to operate the base as we require. We recognise, nonetheless, that in the long run we cannot maintain our military presence in the area without the consent of the indigenous peoples who need to be brought to realise that we are not here for repressive purposes. If Commonwealth forces cease to be in the area a strategic vacuum will exist between China, Australia and the Indian Ocean with nothing to prevent the spread of Communism to these areas.

23. One of the Tunku's early ideas was that the United Kingdom bases would be transferred to North Borneo, which would remain indefinitely under British control. This is ruled out however by the lack of skilled labour in North Borneo, the cost of such a move, and the time it would take. In any case by the time the move had been made it might no longer be possible politically to remain in North Borneo. Under any arrangements for Grand Design we should need therefore to keep our bases in Singapore.

24. The Tunku has said in the past that he could not contemplate asking his Parliament to agree to another Defence Agreement. He appears to envisage that the existing Malayan Defence Agreement should merely be extended to cover Singapore. The difficulty about this Agreement is that the United Kingdom Government cannot make major alteration to the character or deployment of their forces based in the Federation without prior consultation with the Federation Government. At the present time the arrangement is that these forces can only be used for SEATO purposes if they are first brought to Singapore. On present indications the Tunku is unlikely to agree to any amendment to the Agreement as regards Singapore, and we should therefore need to reach some prior understanding with him which would enable us to continue to use our forces for SEATO purposes. Any reduction in our

capacity to fulfil our SEATO obligations would adversely affect our relations with our SEATO allies. But in any event it is unlikely that we should be able to use our bases in pursuit of policies greatly out of line with the policies of the Federation Government.

25. There are obvious political difficulties about retaining bases in independent countries and, in the last resort, no base can be used for any length of time if the local population are hostile. The Singapore bases in particular are heavily dependent on local civilian labour, both skilled and unskilled, and on such services as water supplies. In this case, however, there are a number of factors in our favour. The Tunku would not wish to take over Singapore without the bases because they are important to the defence of Malaya and also because they bring considerable economic and employment benefits to Singapore.

The next steps

26. The Tunku's Memorandum will probably include a proposal for a conference to be held in the fairly near future, one of the objects of which might be to draw up terms of reference for a Constitutional Commission of eminent Commonwealth persons, on the lines of the Reid Commission for Malaya. Both the Tunku and Lee Kuan Yew are hoping that Mr. Macmillan's visit in September will lead to significant progress being made.

27. The first essential is for the United Kingdom Government to decide its policy. I remain convinced that the right aim of our policy is Grand Design and that advantage should be taken of the opportunity which the Tunku has now given us to lend encouragement to the scheme. But there are admittedly serious problems to be faced.

28. The two critical questions to be considered are the extent to which we would be prepared to go in meeting the Federation Government's views on (a) the Borneo territories, bearing in mind the need to take into account the wishes of the people, and (b) defence and our strategic requirements. Having formed our conclusions on these matters the next stage, before there could be any question of a conference, would seem to be a round of confidential discussions, mainly with the Tunku, to ascertain whether there was sufficient common ground to enable us to go ahead. I would hope that it might be possible to complete this process before Mr. Macmillan's visit in September,[6] so that some forthcoming statement about the United Kingdom's attitude could then be made. This statement might be to the effect that H.M.G. welcomed the Tunku's proposal provided it led to the establishment of a stable political unit in accordance with the wishes of the people concerned and provided it enabled us to fulfil what we still regarded as our essential defence obligations. The statement could go on to express agreement with the Tunku's suggestion that it would be desirable to hold a conference at which representatives of the territories could express their views.

29. It would be desirable to consult closely with the Australian and New Zealand Governments at all stages.

30. I am sending copies of this despatch to the Secretary of State for Foreign Affairs, the Secretary of State for Commonwealth Relations, the Minister of Defence;

---

[6] CO officials added manuscript comments in the margins of this despatch; here one wrote, 'the heat is now off on this point' for the proposed visit was cancelled.

the Governors of North Borneo and Sarawak, the High Commissioner for Brunei, the United Kingdom High Commissioners in Canberra, Wellington and Kuala Lumpur and Her Majesty's Ambassador in Djakarta. I am also sending a copy to the Private Secretary to the Prime Minister.

48 PREM 11/3418 27 June 1961
[The 'Grand Design']: letter from Lord Selkirk to Mr Macmillan, reinforcing the points made in his despatch to Mr Macleod

I am sending to the Colonial Secretary a despatch about the proposal for a closer association of Malaya, Singapore and the Borneo territories, 'Grand Design',[1] but I thought I ought to put the issues at stake clearly to you personally because:—

(a) they are big and bristle with very real difficulties;
(b) they affect four separate departments—the Foreign Office, the Colonial Office, the Commonwealth Relations Office and the Ministry of Defence;
(c) the Federation hope that you will play an important role in the development of this proposal during your visit next September.

2. The proposals likely to be put to us by the Malayans are as follows:—

(a) The Federation would take over from us the defence, foreign policy and internal security of Singapore. Singapore would remain responsible for the other functions of Government as now.
(b) The Federation would take over responsibility for the administration of the three Borneo territories—North Borneo, Sarawak and Brunei—either united or separately.
(c) The existing defence treaty with the Federation would be extended to Singapore and the Borneo territories with its limitations on the free use of our troops.

3. The difficulties this poses are:—

Firstly, that the Borneo territories are evolving quietly and peacefully. North Borneo and Sarawak are, by and large, well satisfied with the British administrations which hold the ring between the indigenous peoples and the Chinese and Malays. There are virtually no European settlers. Although North Borneo and Sarawak have, on the whole, reacted favourably to the scheme in principle, I would expect them to show very strong opposition if it was rushed too quickly or if it appears that the stabilising force of British rule is likely to be impaired. Memories of what happened in 1946 are still green. Lack of confidence in the administration might well be followed by a reversion to the traditional practice of head hunting. The Sultan of Brunei, with a majority of Malays in the state has, however, long been anxious for closer ties with the Federation of Malaya, although he will have some difficulty in carrying local opinion with him.

Secondly, our defence position would be weakened overtly and, we would not have freedom to deploy our troops from Singapore. This would have far

---

[1] See 47.

reaching effects both in our position in SEATO and in our relations with Australia and New Zealand and would mean something of a shift in the balance of power. There is a risk that this change would be regarded as giving an opportunity for the Communists to pursue a more militant course with better chance of success.

Thirdly, while the continued presence of our forces here would serve to deter any Indonesian designs on the greater Malaysia area covered by this proposal, the additional limitation on their use might lead the Indonesians to conclude that they had less to fear if they embarked on military activity elsewhere.

Fourthly, the new arrangements would isolate Hong Kong a little more and it might not be easy to maintain stability there.

4.   It is not, however, advisable to delay consideration of this matter indefinitely. Singapore is due for constitutional talks in 1963 and there is a growing movement here for immediate independence with full Commonwealth status. Bargaining on the wide questions posed by these proposals can be most advantageously conducted while the present realistic Singapore Government is in power.

5.   Furthermore, the advantages we should gain are considerable. We should be relieved of internal security responsibilities in Singapore and the Federation would take over Singapore's foreign relations before an extreme left wing movement, possibly Communist, can get in.

6.   We have been in various parts of the Borneo territories from 70 to 120 years. We can truthfully say that we have virtually abolished piracy, slavery and head hunting and that both colonies, as well as Brunei, are making steady progress. But it is very hard to say that North Borneo and Sarawak on their own would be able to achieve a viable balance of effective government for many years to come. By their association with the Federation, we should largely be freed from the anti-Colonial pressures of the United Nations and might well maintain our influence on a sounder long term basis. The parallel position of the Dutch in West Irian comes readily to mind. Moreover, in the economic field, the preservation of the Malayan dollar as the common currency will be ensured.

7.   Greater Malaysia would be an independent member of the Commonwealth, as such strictly speaking responsible for its own defence and, in this sense, there would be no direct United Kingdom defence interest.

8.   We should, however, wish to maintain a defence capacity to enable us to continue to play our part in the containment of the overall Communist threat and in promoting stability in the area. Indonesian ambitions, which they do not conceal to local Asian opinion, also have to be kept in check. In addition, we must support our important economic stake in Malaya and Singapore with its significant contribution to the sterling area. We would be remaining in the area militarily at the invitation of the Federation, and with the full support of Australia and New Zealand, in what would come to be regarded as a Commonwealth defence base. It is in any case necessary for us under present arrangements to keep our defence policy in line generally with the outlook on foreign policy of the Federation Government and such new arrangements as might be made are unlikely to be so very far from the present position if we reach agreement soon. We may well, however, be in for some hard negotiation with the Federation in order to obtain a greater freedom in the use of our

troops in the greater Malaysia area than the Tunku allows under the existing defence treaty in the Federation. The basis of our position in South East Asia would be changed but we would be moving in line with current ideas in a manner which would be more acceptable and understandable to most of the Asian nations. In any case, our commitments today are probably greater than our present resources can meet.

9.   Considerable risks are involved which can compare with those taken in 1947 in India, although the number of people involved is, of course much less. Perhaps the biggest risk is to the morale of our own personnel, service and civilian, and of those Asians who are most closely associated with the policies which we support.

10.   These issues will have to be very carefully balanced and we may encounter considerable difficulties over North Borneo and Sarawak, and in the sphere of defence. Negotiating gambits are, however, not all on the side of the Federation. I believe therefore that we would be wise in the long run to try to go forward with this policy:—

> *Firstly*, because it prevents the Communists and others hostile to us shielding their activities behind anti-colonialism.
>
> *Secondly*, because it is the only way to secure the independent future of the countries concerned with a reasonable prospect of survival as members of the free world.
>
> *Thirdly*, because I believe our position would be healthier and our influence in the future stronger if it is clearly seen that we are here with the consent and agreement of the Governments concerned.

11.   Finally, I need hardly say how important it is that these questions are fully and frankly discussed with the Australians and New Zealanders.

49   CO 1030/1149, no 127E   18 July 1961
[The Eden hall tea-party]: note (dated 31 July) by the office of the UK Commissioner-General of a meeting held at Eden Hall at 4.30pm on 18 July of Lord Selkirk and P B C Moore with J Puthucheary, Lim Chin Siong, Fong Swee Suan and S Woodhull

[At the Anson by-election on 15 July, Lim Chin Siong and seven other left-wing PAP assemblymen withheld support from the government's candidate and instead backed David Marshall (former chief minister and currently chairman of the Workers' Party) who stood for immediate independence. Lim Chin Siong's group also protested against Lee Kuan Yew's promotion of merger with Malaya and called for the release of all political detainees. To Lee's embarrassment, David Marshall won. Lee and Goh Keng Swee became, in the words of Selkirk, 'pretty broken men, extremely jumpy and uncertain of their political future'. Selkirk was disappointed that, instead of pressing for merger in the face of communist opposition, Lee proposed to release detainees in order to embarrass the British (Selkirk to Macleod, 17 July, tel nos 263 and 264, DO 169/18, nos 41 and 42). Irritated by Lee's moves to appease the communists and his attempt to blame the British and Malayans for Singapore's unrest, Tunku Abdul Rahman threatened to withdraw the Federation's representative on the Internal Security Council. Meanwhile, Lim Chin Siong and three other dissident members of the PAP—James Puthucheary, Fong Swee Suan and Sidney Woodhull—requested a meeting with Selkirk at his residence, Eden Hall. Their aim was to discover whether he would suspend the constitution and resort to direct rule in the event of Lee being voted out of office and the pro-communists coming to power by constitutional means. The so-called 'Eden Hall tea-party' has acquired notoriety in the eyes of opposing conspiracy theorists: whereas the PAP dissidents suspected Lee of colluding with the British, Lee accused Selkirk of plotting with his opponents. The 'gang of four' tested Selkirk's commitment to constitutionalism. Selkirk appears to have played it straight, informing his guests that his responsibility was to uphold the constitution and that he would intervene only to prevent direct action. Notwithstanding the fact that after the meeting Selkirk informed Lee Kuan Yew what had happened via Special Branch, the prime minister of Singapore publicly condemned the 'Eden Hall tea party' as a plot hatched by the British with the intention either of placing the onus on him to smash the left or of destabilising his government to allow the resumption of direct rule by Britain. Lee tabled a motion of confidence in his government on 20 July which he won at 3.40 in the morning of 21 July by a majority of one (26 votes out of 51) but it precipitated the secession of the rebels. On 29 July they announced the formation of the Barisan Sosialis (Socialist Front) with Dr Lee Siew Choh as chairman and Lim Chin Siong as secretary-general. Document 49, dated 31 July, is an account written in the knowledge of events culminating in the inauguration of the Barisan; document 50 is a telegram composed shortly after the vote of confidence.]

1.   James Puthucheary telephoned Lord Selkirk at Phoenix Park[1] at about noon that day to ask whether he could come to see Lord Selkirk accompanied by two of his friends. He did not state who the friends would be. Lord Selkirk suggested he should come to lunch on Thursday, 20th July, but Puthucheary obviously wanted an earlier meeting and Lord Selkirk therefore suggested 4 p.m. that afternoon. Puthucheary agreed.

2.   Puthucheary explained that his motive in coming to see Lord Selkirk was to seek a re-assurance that in the event of the fall of Lee Kuan Yew's Government, the British would not take over in Singapore. He said the view had been widely put about that the British would never allow the Communists to take over and that if the dissidents in the P.A.P. split the party, the British would take over rather than let anyone else be Prime Minister. Lord Selkirk replied, as he had done on a number of previous occasions to similar questions, that his duty as United Kingdom Commissioner was to see the Constitution of Singapore observed. Provided there was no infringement of the Constitution or resort to direct action and violence, it would be quite improper for him to interfere in the political life of Singapore. Lord Selkirk stressed, however, that if anybody broke the Constitution or incited people in Singapore to industrial unrest and violence, he would not hesitate to take whatever action he considered necessary.

3.   Lord Selkirk emphasised that if Singapore were to survive, she had to solve her economic problems and this could only be achieved if stability were maintained. He asked Lim Chin Siong and Fong Swee Suan whether they were Communists. They seemed to be embarrassed by this question and failed to give a clear reply. Mr. Woodhull, on the other hand, stated categorically that he was not a Communist. Lord Selkirk then asked Lim and Fong whether they were looking to Communist China to dominate Malaya and Singapore and whether they were good Malayans. They all said they were good Malayans. Lord Selkirk then asked whether they intended to resort to industrial unrest in order to achieve their aims. To these questions they gave a clear negative. Lord Selkirk then said that he was certain the future of Singapore lay in becoming part of Malaya and he asked Lim and Fong whether they were in favour of merger. All four said they were in favour of merger but were not prepared to give Lee Kuan Yew a blank cheque. Merger, as previously

---

[1] Phoenix Park was the office of the UK commissioner for Singapore and commissioner-general for SE Asia; Eden Hall was his residence.

understood, meant the straight acceptance of Singapore into the Federation as a further state. It seemed unlikely that the Tengku would agree to this. Lord Selkirk then explained the Ulster model and they said that they would be quite prepared to accept merger on these terms, even if it were with the Tengku's right-wing government. It emerged, however, that they were obviously concerned about what their own position would be if the Federation took over internal security.

4.   Puthucheary explained that one of the reasons he was out of sympathy with the P.A.P. Government was that he felt extremely strongly about the position of the detainees. Lord Selkirk said he was not prepared to discuss this question. Puthucheary also emphasised that the main reason for the split in the P.A.P. was the arrogance of Lee Kuan Yew and his refusal to allow proper consultation within the Party.

5.   Woodhull asked whether the British Government would be prepared to agree to the abolition of the Internal Security Council and full internal self-government. He said that under the Six's programme the British would still have the right of intervention in Singapore if their defence position were threatened by the internal security situation.[2] He stressed that the Six were anxious and willing for the British to maintain their bases in Singapore. Mr. Moore said that new constitutional talks were not due until 1963 and that it was premature at this stage to consider amendments to a constitution which had only run for two years (and very successfully, notwithstanding the trumped up campaign against the Internal Security Council). The Tengku's Greater Malaysia proposal was much wider in scope and more important than the programme put forward by the Six and discussion should be concentrated on this.

6.   Lord Selkirk also said a few words on our concept of multi-racial commonwealth, in which they seemed to show a taciturn interest.

In accordance with his usual practice of informing Lee Kuan Yew about visits made to him by political leaders in Singapore, Lord Selkirk directed Mr. Hughes to inform Singapore Special Branch that the meeting had taken place and of its content. Mr. Hughes gave Mr. Linsell, Director Special Branch, an account of the meeting the following morning. This was the first D.S.B. or Lee Kuan Yew had heard of the meeting. In fact it is doubtful whether they would ever otherwise have known that it had taken place.

---

[2] 'The Six' were six trade union leaders. Lim Chin Siong, Fong Swee Suan, Sidney Woodhull, Jamit Singh, S T Bani and Dominic Puthucheary (brother of James) had issued a statement on 2 June calling for full internal self-government and the abolition of the ISC, and had supported Marshall at Anson.

50   DO 169/18, no 59   21 July 1961
[Singapore's Legislative Assembly: vote of confidence in the PAP government]: inward telegram no 278 from Lord Selkirk to Mr Macleod, commenting on Lee Kuan Yew's allegations during the debate

Lee Kuan Yew gave us no warning that he was going to produce this ridiculous fairy tale.[1] The only point on which I would comment in detail is the visit of Messrs. Lim

---

[1] In his previous telegram to the CO Selkirk reported that, in his speech to the Legislative Assembly, Lee had accused the British of both colluding with the communists (at the Eden Hall tea-party) and of plotting to engineer a collision between the PAP and the communists (DO 169/18, no 58).

Chin Siong, Woodhull and Fong Swee Suan to Eden Hall on 18th July. The facts are that James Puthucheary asked if he could come to see me with one or two of his friends. I agreed to see him and he turned up accompanied by the other three. He explained that his motive in coming was to seek reassurance that in the event of the fall of Lee Kuan Yew's Government, the British would not take over in Singapore. I replied, as I have done on a number of previous occasions to similar questions that my duty was to see the constitution of Singapore observed, and provided there was no infringement of the constitution or resort to direct action, it would be quite improper for me to interfere in the political life of Singapore. A full report of the conversation follows by bag.

2.   Lee's motive is clearly that proposition he put to me on the detainees was designed first to allay suspicions in the party that he had not in fact been pressing for the release of the detainees and secondly to produce a public clash with the British which would present him in an anti-Colonial light. When I rejected his proposition on the detainees, he must have decided that it was necessary to concoct some other form of public clash with the British in order to throw a smoke screen over the grave dissensions within the party. In a telephone conversation this morning he made it clear that he hopes we will publicly answer his allegations so that 'The maximum amount of public antagonism can be created between the Government and the British'.

3.   David Marshall and Lim Yew Hock ridiculed the story which they dismissed as a fairy tale and there will be few if any responsible observers in Singapore who will give it any credence. We have to decide however whether I should make any public comment. In making this decision, we have to consider where this is leading us. Lee has telephoned us twice this morning. He still hopes we will help him to make immediate progress with the Tengku with a view to a quick decision in favour of merger. In the first conversation, however, he envisaged that within a matter of months he would be forced to resign and that the only chance of state government for Singapore would be for British to take over. Later he suggested that if he could obtain merger, he would see the matter through and accept the full consequences. He appears to be in a state of vacillation and I can no longer put any trust in his word.

4.   Lee's speeches in the Assembly, which deliberately eschewed a strong anti-communist line, together with the publication of the I.S.C. paper on the detainees and the announcement of the decision to order the release of the detainees in batches, may well seriously prejudice the prospects of merger. If this proves correct, we must do all we can to avoid Lee manoeuvring us into a position in which we shall be forced to take over the Government of Singapore. I am certain that even if the next Government is much further to the Left or even communist manipulated, we must allow the full democratic processes to work under the Constitution, provided there is no threat to the internal security situation which requires our intervention. It is too early to say what sort of government is likely to emerge from general elections in the event of the fall of Lee Kuan Yew and for the present the best course is to keep down the political temperature. This leads me to the conclusion that we should, if possible, avoid being drawn into making any public comment. Any reply to Press enquiries (corrupt group) saying 'No comment'. I realise, however, that Lee's allegations may attract attention in the U.K. and we may in the next few days be forced to comment. In that event I suggest that our line should be as follows:—The U.K. Commissioner for Singapore wishes to state there is no truth whatsoever in the

allegations made by the Prime Minister of Singapore in the Legislative Assembly on 21st July about a British plot to engineer a collision between the pro-Communists and the P.A.P. Government. The U.K. Commissioner made it clear that his function in Singapore is to carry out his duties under the Singapore Constitution and that he will never attempt in any way to interefere in party politics. Questioned specifically about the visit of Lim and Co. to Eden Hall we should simply confirm that this visit took place at their request.

5. I should be grateful for your comments and information on any publicity this may receive in the U.K.

51 PREM 11/3418 3 Aug 1961

[Proposal to hold talks in London]: letter from Mr Macmillan to Tunku Abdul Rahman, replying to document 46

[Apart from a temporising message from Sandys, the Tunku's letter of 26 June went unanswered for seven weeks. There were two principal reasons for the delay: the first was the need for exploratory discussions in London, with Selkirk and Tory and with the governments of Australia and New Zealand; the second was the deterioration in relations between the Tunku and Lee Kuan Yew prompted by the instability of Singapore's politics. A draft letter (agreed between the CRO, CO, FO and Ministry of Defence) was not ready until the end of July and Sandys advised the prime minister: 'The sooner you can send it, therefore, the better.' He also recommended that Macmillan should restrain the Tunku from 'any further over-exuberant activities' regarding Borneo since his recent visits to Brunei and Sarawak had 'caused some alarm' in all three territories (Sandys to Macmillan, 31 July 1961, PREM 11/3418, f 97; such 'over-exuberant activities' were reported by White in his review of 1961, see 91). Macmillan's reply carefully side-stepped the issues of prior merger of the Borneo territories with Malaya and the future of the Singapore base and, instead, invited the Tunku to talks in London.]

Thank you for your letter of June 26 about the proposed association of Singapore and the Borneo Territories with the Federation of Malaya.

As I said in Parliament on June 20, I had observed with interest the constructive suggestion you made in the course of your speech in Singapore on May 27. The ideas which I know have been developing in your mind for some time, and which you have now put forward, could have an encouraging effect for the political stability of South East Asia; and I warmly welcome the stimulus they have already given to discussion. I was particularly glad to receive from you the secret memorandum enclosed with your letter, setting out your ideas about the form of such an association and the ways in which it might be brought about. I have arranged for the ideas in your memorandum to be examined with all possible expedition. We have already had an opportunity of discussing it with Lord Selkirk and Sir Geofroy Tory while they were over here.

As you know these very important proposals require consideration from a number of different aspects. You will therefore understand that I cannot at this stage commit the British Government on the possibility of a wider association. In particular, there are some points, on defence and on the Borneo Territories, on which they will need to be reassured.

On defence, the question of the continued use of our important bases and facilities in Malaya and the other countries concerned raises very large issues. Certainly the present difficult state of affairs in South East Asia, and the need in all our interests to maintain confidence there, makes it very important that nothing should be said which might cast doubt on the maintenance of British defence capabilities in the area. Our mutual friends in Australia and New Zealand are of course also directly concerned, and we shall wish to consult with them.

As regards the Borneo Territories, I hear that you have just been visiting Brunei and Sarawak yourself. You will thus have been able to form some preliminary impressions about the situation there, and the state of opinion on a wider association of the kind you have in mind. Our impression is that the idea of finding their eventual political future in some kind of link with Malaya is seen to have attractions. This suggests that, if the ground were carefully prepared, and the advantages of any wider association became generally recognised, the Borneo Territories would be ready to come in as free and willing members. I am sure you will agree that it is most important at this initial stage, and in view of the doubts and hesitations which have been expressed publicly in the territories over what close political association would involve for the various races there, that we do not give the impression that we are deciding on their future without regard for their own wishes.

I had been greatly looking forward to discussions about this project with yourself and Mr. Lee Kuan Yew in September. I am most disappointed that I had to postpone my visit to you. I think it is important that we should meet soon to talk these matters over, and since you have been good enough to suggest that you would be prepared to come to London, I am wondering whether you could in fact visit us instead. Several of my colleagues are of course closely involved and our various engagements here would not permit us to meet as early as September. As you know, the international calendar in September and October is at the moment rather uncertain and I may not yet be able to propose a definite date on which we might have talks. I would very much hope, however, that it would be possible to hold these in late October or early November. If this period would be suitable for you in principle perhaps you would let me write again in late September in order to propose a definite date. I believe it would be useful if Mr. Lee could come to London at about the same time so that we could bring him into our discussions. This would I think be a necessary preliminary to any formal conference which might seem appropriate later on, in which of course we should have to include the Borneo Territories.

Would you be good enough to let me know whether my suggestion for a visit appeals to you and whether the sort of dates I have suggested would suit you so that we can sound out Mr. Lee? In the meantime, for this and for a number of other reasons, I should greatly prefer that nothing be said publicly about a possible visit.

52   DO 169/27, no 91   5 Aug 1961
[Proposal to hold talks in London]: letter from Sir G Tory to N Pritchard,[1] reporting Tunku Abdul Rahman's reactions to Mr Macmillan's letter

[On the same day that he wrote this letter, Tory sent a telegram to the CRO recounting the Tunku's response to document 51: 'When I gave Tunku advance copy of Prime

---

[1] N (later Sir Neil) Pritchard, acting deputy under-secretary of state, CRO, 1961; high commissioner in Tanganyika, 1961–1963; deputy under-secretary of state, Commonwealth Office, 1963–1967.

Minister's letter yesterday he begged me to impress on U.K. Government that it would be politically impossible for him to accept any kind of link with Singapore even in a limited field such as that of internal security except on broad lines of greater Malaysia plan. His Malays would never forgive him if he were by connection with Singapore alone to create at any time a Chinese majority in the two territories.' (DO 169/27, no 89, tel no 576) In his reply to Macmillan of 11 August, the Tunku stressed the importance of effecting a merger with Borneo in advance of Singapore because of the communist threat in the latter (see 53). CO officials reckoned that the Tunku was only going through the motions of supporting Lee, since he appeared reconciled to Lee's likely fall and convinced the British would never let the communists gain control of Singapore. They also felt that his determination to merge with the Borneo territories first was alienating their inhabitants and would prove counter-productive (CO 1030/982, nos 486 and E/498A, and minutes by H Nield, 31 Aug and I Wallace, 1 Sept 1961). A week earlier Tory had passed on the views of the US ambassador in Kuala Lumpur who favoured the Grand Design but stressed that timing was crucial so as not to dilute British defence capability in the region. 'It is gratifying', commented Tory, 'to find my American colleague takes this intelligent view of the situation.' (Tory to Pritchard, 28 July 1961, CO 1030/990, no 57).]

As you will have seen from my telegram No. 570, the Tunku was pleased with the Prime Minister's letter of the 3rd August about Greater Malaysia,[2] when I gave him an advance copy of it yesterday. As you will also have seen from one of my two letters of the 28th July, I had prepared the Tunku for the delay and also for our reference to the Borneo Territories and defence as points on which the U.K. Government would need reassurance. He was, therefore, not upset or puzzled at the inclusion of these references in the Prime Minister's letter. He seems to be very keen on going to London in November and is already in his mind planning a sea voyage for most of the way so as to arrive in London at that time.

As regards Lee Kuan Yew, the Tunku was anxious that he should be associated with the talks in London and said he thought he would like to arrange for Lee and himself to travel in the same ship together, so that they could have a good deal of informal contact about Greater Malaysia.[3] The Tunku thought he might fly the last part of the journey so as to be in London a little bit before Lee Kuan Yew. He seems to feel as we did that it might be a good thing if he had an opportunity at some stage of talking to us without Lee Kuan Yew present.

On the Borneo Territories, the Tunku's only comment was in relation to Brunei. He said that the Sultan was standing on the strict constitutional position that it was up to the U.K. Government to make the first move with regard to Brunei's future relationship with Malaya. I said I thought we should shortly be asking the Sultan for his view and the Tunku welcomed this. He said he was convinced that the bulk of the Brunei Malays were well disposed towards Malaya and would gladly follow the Sultan's lead if he were to decide in favour of association with the Federation. The Party Ra'ayat in Brunei, the Tunku said, was very small and completely unrepresentative. Much too much attention was being paid to Azahari, who really should not be allowed to influence Brunei's future. He very much doubted whether Party Ra'ayat were strong enough to start any significant trouble in Brunei. He was sure there was no need to woo the Brunei Malays. I think it possible that he will say

---

[2] See 51.

[3] The parallel is clear (and explicitly drawn in document 63, para 7) between this proposal and the travel arrangements for the independence talks in London (Jan–Feb 1956). Then the Malayan delegation had settled their differences in advance of the conference on board MV *Asia* between Singapore and Karachi after which they had completed the journey by air (*BDEE: Malaya*, document 392). In the end Lee Kuan Yew decided not to attend the London talks in November.

something about this in the reply which he at present intends to send to the Prime Minister's letter.

The Tunku did say that he thought the Sultan of Brunei had been partly responsible for the unpopularity of the seconded Malay civil servants in that he had always shown almost a contempt for his own Brunei Malays.[4] The Tunku had told him that some of the latter could easily be trained up to take over responsibilities in the Administration but the Sultan would have none of it. He had thus created in the minds of the Brunei Malays close to him the impression that he had a very ill opinion of them and did not trust them. This naturally created a bad atmosphere for the Federation Malays. As regards the recent incident and the wish of the Federation Malays to be repatriated, the Sultan had pointed out that coming back to Malaya in present circumstances would be like running away and would cause more loss of face to the Federation Malays than sticking it out where they were. The Tunku thought there might be something in this. He was in any event now going to replace the Federation Malays in Brunei with another batch of civil servants who would as far as possible be more senior and have more experience behind them. He was sending Dato' Abdul Aziz, the Permanent Secretary of his Ministry,[5] to Brunei shortly to go into all this.

On the question of defence the Tunku once again said that we could always station troops in Malaya for Commonwealth purposes. If there were a war, and Commonwealth countries in the area were involved, Malaya would also be dragged in whether she liked it or not. Was this not enough for us? I said it was not enough because, as I had explained on earlier occasions, we had obligations towards SEATO which we might have to discharge in circumstances short of actual war. I sketched out some examples and again referred to the Kuwait operation as an example of the kind of thing we might have to do to stop a war from breaking out.[6] For this purpose, I said, we should need a base and a base we could continue to use. At the present time we were dependent on Singapore. Here was a practical problem to which we must find an answer.

The Tunku then surprised me by saying he wondered whether it would not after all be possible for Malaya, after assuming responsibility for Singapore's defence and

---

[4] The secondment of Malay officers from the Malayan government service was an arrangement made at the time of Brunei's constitution, but their presence became a focus of resentment when the Tunku proposed Malaysia. On 12 June 1961 the state forestry officer seconded from the Federation, Mohd Yakim bin Haji Long, was assaulted by some Bruneians. Immediately ten Malayan officers resigned and some forty school teachers requested repatriation. On 24 June the PRB distributed a pamphlet accusing the Tunku of colonial intent. The Tunku and the Agong paid a goodwill visit to Brunei and Sarawak in early July, but this tour did not dispel mistrust. In fact, the public was antagonised by the Tunku's statement that there was no need for the merger and independence of the Borneo territories in advance of their assimilation within Greater Malaysia. A hastily convened United Front of Ong Kee Hui (SUPP), Azahari (PRB) and Donald Stephens (whose UNKO would be inaugurated in Aug) promptly rejected this approach. The Tunku then attempted to mollify his critics by assuring them that Malaya did not wish to colonise Borneo, but the damage had been done. See 91 for White's report on political developments in Brunei in 1961.
[5] Dato Abdul Aziz bin Haji Abdul Majid had been permanent secretary, Prime Minister's Department, since 1957. He is not to be confused with Dato Abdul Aziz bin Haji Mahomed Zain, also from the Federation, who would replace Wan Ahmed as attorney-general after the crisis in Brunei's administration of June-July 1961.
[6] In June 1961 General Abdul Karim Kassem of Iraq laid claim to Kuwait. Bound by treaty to protect Kuwait, British troops arrived from 1 July and by the end of the month the Iraqi threat dissolved.

external relations, to allow us to go on using it as a base for SEATO purposes on the grounds that it was now available to us for that purpose and that its continued availability for SEATO was a condition of transfer of our sovereignty over Singapore in all other respects. This was something, he said, which he would like to leave to the Singapore Government to negotiate direct with the U.K. Government. It would be up to Singapore to decide whether such an arrangement would be possible from their point of view. Anyway, this was something which he was quite prepared to talk about.

From a conversation I had with Ghazali last night, he seems to be thinking on the same lines as the Tunku about the Singapore base. He says that our genuine need to have a base for SEATO is beginning to be understood by the Tunku. The Malayans could not for political reasons join SEATO,[7] but at any rate some of them realised that, if SEATO did not exist, it would have to be created for the defence of countries like Malaya. I have a feeling that Razak may try to move the Tunku and Ghazali away from this reasonable approach and that we ought not to be too optimistic about the Singapore base in the meantime. It is obvious, however, that the Tunku's mind is not shut on this subject and that he is personally ready to go to considerable limits in trying to satisfy our defence requirements. Whether Lee Kuan Yew would feel able to accept an arrangement of this kind is another matter. His opponents would be only too ready to say that continued use of the Singapore base for SEATO purposes was an obvious derogation from true independence. I should think he would argue that this would play into the hands of the Communists but that is something on which Selkirk is in a better position to comment than I.

I should record here that, as reported more briefly in my telegram No. 576, the Tunku has begged me to impress upon the U.K. Government that it would be politically impossible for him to accept any kind of link with Singapore, even in a limited field, except in accordance with the broad lines of the Greater Malaysia plan. He would, he said, be very much happier without Singapore at all but he had been persuaded now that unless he accepted responsibility for Singapore it would degenerate into Communism and would become a bridgehead of the Communist powers on the Federation's doorstep. His Malays would never forgive him, however, if he were, by connection with Singapore alone, to create at any time a Chinese majority in the two Territories. To press him to agree to some bilateral arrangement with Singapore in the short-term was to invite him to commit political suicide. The Tunku obviously sincerely believes this and I think it would not be productive for us to press him on the subject.

You will have seen, however, from Singapore telegram No. 308 to the Colonial Office that Goh Keng Swee believes that Razak and Ghazali are now convinced that the Federation cannot afford to let Singapore wait for the three Borneo territories and are therefore working for a face-saving compromise under which the Federation would accept control of Singapore on condition that Brunei would be immediately transferred and on the understanding that 'Consultative Committees' would be promised for the other two Borneo Territories. I do not yet know how true this is; Lee and Goh have deceived themselves before about true Malay feelings on crucial matters. At any rate we know, and the Tunku knows, that Lee Kuan Yew will be

---

[7] Sovereign but still closely aligned with Britain, the Malayan government refused to join SEATO in order to avoid further antagonising critics at home and abroad (notably China and Indonesia).

tackling the Tunku himself in the near future on these lines and we shall see what impression he makes. The Tunku is prepared to do a great deal of listening to Lee and he fully understands the delicacy of Lee's political position and his pressing reasons for trying to get some tangible link with Malaya in the very near future. The Tunku is however inclined to think that Lee is exaggerating his difficulties and that he could hold out for quite a long time if he simply went on quietly and firmly, without getting hysterical and without double-crossing his well-wishers. In any event, I know that the Tunku's present intention is to tell Lee plainly that the Federation will have none of Singapore by itself and that it is all of Greater Malaysia or nothing.

I am sending copies of this letter to Selkirk in Singapore and also to the Governors of North Borneo and Sarawak and the High Commissioner in Brunei.

P.S. Since writing the above I have learnt in strictest confidence from an entirely reliable source that both Razak and Ismail are dismayed at the attitude of the Tunku and Ghazali on the subject of Singapore and SEATO and are doing their best to persuade the Tunku that any compromise on this issue would be politically fatal for the Tunku.

53 PREM 11 11/3418   11 Aug 1961
[Proposal to hold talks in London]: letter from Tunku Abdul Rahman to Mr Macmillan

I was very pleased to receive your letter of 3rd August[1] giving your present views about the proposed association of Singapore and the Borneo territories with the Federation of Malaya. Your generous and constructive attitude in this matter is a source of much encouragement to me.

As you know, the question of the integration of Singapore and the Federation is not a new one; indeed since Independence, the idea of 'merger', to give its popular name, has been constantly mooted, but I have stood out against it because of my fear that the communal politics of Singapore based on Chinese chauvinism would upset the balance of political thinking in the Federation, and destroy our hopes for the peace and well-being and harmony of our peoples. The politics of this region, however, would not allow for isolation and the idea of greater co-operation and association between the Borneo territories, Singapore and the Federation has been exercising my mind for some considerable time.

While I agree that the pace for such a development should not be forced, I am at the same time most concerned about the Communist threat in Singapore which becomes more menacing as time goes on, and I feel very strongly that before long the question of the future of Singapore will have to be settled. I am convinced that an independent Singapore will be drawn towards China; unless that is forestalled, it is needless for me to say the Federation, as well as the region, will be exposed to grave dangers.

If we are to take in Singapore, it would be necessary first to strengthen our own position, and we can only do that if the three territories of Borneo join us. This would provide a measure of confidence in our people and would correct the imbalance in the population. The Malays and the Dayaks are of the same racial origin while the

---

[1] See 51.

Chinese in those territories have not as yet been seriously penetrated by Chinese Communist politics. Without the Borneo territories I would find it impossible to contemplate the integration of Singapore and the Federation and to persuade my political colleagues and the country to accept it.

You were right, of course, in emphasizing that the Borneo territories should be associated under the proposed arrangements only as free and willing partners. I have no doubt that once they are persuaded that such a merger would be in their interest, they would be only too happy to join us. The difficulties to which you have referred are no more serious than those which existed in the Federation before independence. They are purely parochial and create no insuperable barrier. These susceptibilities and demands can be met and provided for under the Federation Constitution, and assurances to that effect will, I think, satisfy the territories concerned.

As regards defence, I fully appreciate the points you have raised. Let me hasten to assure you that I am equally concerned that the defence arrangements for this region should not be jeopardized under the proposed arrangements. However, I foresee no difficulty in arriving at some suitable arrangement within the framework of the existing Mutual Defence Agreement between our two countries whereby the various defence requirements may be satisfied. This would, at the same time, remove any possible fears that we are drawn unwittingly into SEATO.

These, however, are matters for more detailed discussions, and I, therefore, warmly welcome your suggestion that we might meet in London, and I propose that early in the New Year would be most suitable for me. I agree with you that it would be useful to bring Mr. Lee Kuan Yew into these discussions.

54   PREM 11/3737   14 Aug 1961
['Greater Malaysia' and Britain's role in SE Asia]: letter from Lord Selkirk to Mr Macmillan

[An argument which Selkirk regularly put forward in favour of 'Greater Malaysia' was that it would enable Britain to reduce military commitments and to adopt a new role assisting nation-states in the containment of communism. An argument which he used in support of speed was Singapore's political fragility. The relevance and costs of Britain's traditional obligations in the region had also been central to the report of the Committee on Future Developments in SE Asia (see 28 and 29). Selkirk returned to this theme on 12 Sept 1961 when he advocated early talks on 'Greater Malaysia' as a way towards, not only economies, but also more realistic regional policies (PREM 11/3418, ff 42–44). Macmillan did not reply until 17 Oct when he commented that SEATO had been originally intended as a temporary expedient to protect the Geneva settlement of 1954 until the region had been stabilised. But, he pointed out, 'the continuation of tension over Laos, with its global repercussions, makes it impossible to lower our guard with safety and re-align our defence objectives' so as to encourage self-reliance on the part of SE Asian governments and reduce British military expenditure. Nevertheless, the prospect of a settlement over Laos and progress towards achieving 'Greater Malaysia' might, he thought, allow a reduction of British commitments, although it would be vital 'to carry the Australians and New Zealanders with us' in any such retrenchment (PREM 11/3737; cf CO 1030/1120)]

I would like to recapitulate the general line of thought which I expressed when you were good enough to let me come and see you in your room in the House of Commons about a month ago.[1]

---

[1] They had met on 27 July, see 47, note.

2.   It seems to me that in this area we are still finding it extremely difficult to get away from the traditions of our past and in particular from what other people expect of us.

3.   From Trafalgar to the Entente Cordiale we were able to maintain peace in almost all parts of the world. Since then we have continued this policy, though with much less success, first in co-operation with the French and more recently in co-operation with the U.S.A. We have done this partly from a sense of duty and partly because of the inherent dependence of our economic position on world trade. But the means at our disposal have become less and less adequate to meet the commitments which we still retain. The result of this is that we are stretched to a point where our strength might snap under the strain, and indeed our present position would be highly perilous were it not for our basic dependence on the U.S.A. This fact does not seem to me to be adequately recognised. It is the more regrettable that we have not been able to achieve the close understanding and pooling of ideas with the Americans over China and the Pacific which we have in a fair measure succeeded in attaining across the Atlantic.

4.   It is, I think, because of a failure to appreciate the gradual changes which have taken place that we are burdened with a number of misconceptions about the role which we can and should play in this part of the world today. We seem still to assume that we are in a position to mount an expedition from Singapore and Malaya as it were from a secure base. This is no longer true. First our lines of communication, both to Europe and Australia, have been rendered very tenuous. Secondly, our ability to act depends far more than was formerly the case on the consent or at least the acquiescence of the peoples of the area. Whether we like it or not we have to recognise that China, both militarily and ideologically, is becoming increasingly the dominant force throughout South East Asia. The only long-term effective answer to Communist China is nationalism, coupled with a recognition by each State that it has an obligation to defend its own territory. I was glad to note recently that this idea seems to be more readily recognised in Washington than it was. We must clearly do everything we can to promote nationalism as a counter to communism and avoid policies (especially those with an imperialistic flavour) which may lead nationalists and communists to join forces against us. In these circumstances to pursue a defence policy for purposes which cannot be identified with the interests of the area and may even be contrary to the wishes of its inhabitants is both militarily hazardous and politically unwise. Our object must rather be to identify our presence in South East Asia with the national aspirations of the area, and at the same time play down and eventually obliterate the concept either that the United Kingdom has a distinctive interest apart from those of the countries in the area or that the United Kingdom proposes to continue to maintain the defence of the countries and stability of the area regardless of the individual policies of the countries concerned.

5.   Such a position might not be too difficult to achieve if the countries with which we are concerned were members of SEATO. Malaya has however refused to join SEATO and there seems little present likelihood of her changing her mind. She cannot therefore associate herself overtly in advance with policies for the support of SEATO. The result is an inevitable conflict between the demands placed on us by our SEATO obligations and the limitations to which we are subject by reason of our position in Singapore and Malaya.

6.   If our contribution to SEATO could be made otherwise than through these

bases, of course, there would be no problem. But excluding this possibility and that of Malaya joining the alliance, the solution which seems to me the only possible one is a gradual redefinition of our position in SEATO which, while identifying us more closely with the defence of Malaya, would make fewer demands on us for other forms of support. This would, of course, involve a considerable re-orientation of our policy, which it would necessarily take some time to carry through. Superficially it could no doubt be taken as a weakening in our contribution to SEATO but the gain in terms both of stability in the Malayan area and of our ability to act effectively even in support of SEATO in given circumstances would, I feel sure, be a solid and lasting benefit. I doubt indeed whether SEATO will be able to continue for long unless it can be identified more closely with specific South East Asian interests and the countries of the area are themselves able to take up a larger proportion of the strain. The change would also have the further advantage of making our policy more acceptable to countries like India.

7.   Such a solution would of course also involve a change in our attitude towards Malaya. If they pressed us to help them to maintain their own defence, we would be willing to assist them to do so and would eventually only be there at their request. The effect would be not only to dispel the notion that we were still engaged in some imperialist plan of our own, but also to give a much greater sense of responsibility to Malay foreign policy. This I believe in the long run would be greatly in the interests of that country itself.

8.   A solution on these lines would, as I say, have to be approached gradually. There would be no question of our abdicating our responsibilities in this area or of any immediate reduction in our defence establishment. Any impression that this was contemplated would indeed be most damaging and should be studiously avoided. Nevertheless, in the long run we could reasonably expect some relaxation of the strain on United Kingdom resources. I do not suggest that this would come soon, but some relief to our forces should be possible in course of time without giving undue encouragement to the Communists. It was no doubt proper that we should carry a disproportionate burden of defence during the early periods of evolution of members of the Commonwealth, but today they continue quite openly to lean on us in a manner which has relatively little relation to the resources which are available in Commonwealth countries outside the United Kingdom. But it does not stop here. For instance, Thailand and the Philippines, whose combined population is about the same as that of the United Kingdom, are repeatedly complaining that we show reluctance to mount an expedition into the jungle of Laos at a distance of some 7,000 miles from the United Kingdom, whilst they themselves are only prepared to declare negligible forces for the same purpose. It seems to me that even if we had the strength to do more, it must still remain our main task to contribute to the objectives of SEATO by maintaining stability in the areas with which we are most closely associated, namely Malaya, Singapore, the Borneo territories and Hong Kong, and to do this by helping the countries in the area to maintain their own defence rather than starting from the premise that we will deal with all defence issues regardless of their wishes. I was interested to see from a recent report from Tory that the American Ambassador in Kuala Lumpur had supported this proposition.[2]

---

[2] See 52, note. Charles F Baldwin was US ambassador in Kuala Lumpur, 1961–1964.

9.   The course I am suggesting will need a good deal of explanation to the United States of America but I believe the present Administration[3] will understand this very much better than its predecessors, and it would, I think, remove something of the false note which exists in our relationship with the United States in this area.

10.   We would also have to be careful to avoid giving any sense of alarm to the Australians. On the other hand, they have been suspecting our motives for so long that I believe it would clarify their minds and in the long run would give less rise to suspicion.

11.   I write this very much in the context of the proposals for a 'Greater Malaysia' which are currently being examined. But one of the reasons which makes the above line of policy attractive to me is that it would fall very much more naturally into any new defence arrangement that would become necessary if the 'Greater Malaysia' scheme should eventuate, as I hope it will and I think should be encouraged to do.

12.   May I recapitulate shortly:—

(1) Our strongest card here against the expansion of communism is nationalism.

(2) To give nationalism the best chance of holding communism in check we should avoid weakening local nationalist governments by pursuing an independent policy not directly related to their countries' interests.

(3) We should rather strengthen them by identifying our aims with theirs and by encouraging them to assume charge of their own defence.

(4) By removing any grounds for the suspicion that we were pursuing imperialistic ends, we should prevent the communists from hiding behind an anti-colonial shield and thus attracting support from many who otherwise would not listen to their doctrines.

(5) Our continued military presence here, even if our freedom of action is restricted, will remain an important element in maintaining stability.

---

[3] J F Kennedy, 35th president of the USA, Jan 1961-Nov 1963, appointed the veteran diplomat, Averell Harriman, as assistant secretary for Far East affairs.

55   CO 1030/982, no 498C   24 Aug 1961
[Crash programme for 'Greater Malaysia']: letter from Lord Selkirk to Mr Macleod, urging 'a crash programme' on merger to ensure survival of Lee Kuan Yew's government

[From this point onwards the question of timing bulked increasingly large. While the CO and CRO were still reluctant to force the pace, Selkirk argued in favour of seizing the opportunity provided by the joint approach of the Tunku and Lee Kuan Yew to merger. Delay might result in Malaya and Singapore once more drawing apart, the collapse of the PAP government and the Borneo territories remaining a British responsibility for the next decade or so. See also 58.]

I think the time has come when it is necessary to consider how far a crash programme for the 'Greater Malaysia' scheme is desirable and practicable.[1] As I see it, the situation is as follows.

---

[1] The phrase 'crash programme' alarmed officials in the Colonial Office and Borneo territories. In his reply Macleod urged caution as regards Borneo (tel no 360, 8 Sept 1961, CO 1030/982, nos 541–544).

2.   Lee Kuan Yew has not been successful in riding the Communist tiger and was in danger of being gobbled up. He has however now broken with the Communists and, if he can obtain merger on reasonable terms, is apparently prepared to take a firm stand.[2] The original Communist concept was to accept merger as a long-term aim in the belief that, on the one hand, it would give them a broader base from which to work for the Communisation of the whole peninsula, and, on the other, that it was unlikely to be achieved in the near future. Meanwhile they would continue in Singapore to undermine the P.A.P. with a view to ultimately taking it over. In these calculations they may not have fully grasped the implications for them of giving the Tunku control of Singapore. At all events it appears that they have now realised that if the Tunku takes over internal security in Singapore, they will be much more directly threatened than they were by the present Internal Security Council.

3.   Lee is now mad keen to achieve merger and indeed sees in it the only possible salvation for his own political future and his party, the P.A.P. If he fails to get merger by the end of the year, he will probably have to face a general election where he would lose to the new left-wing 'Barisan Socialis' manipulated by the Communists. Alternatively, he may try to force us to suspend the Constitution and take over. We have to decide whether it is worth trying to save him. On balance, I think it is, though this opinion might have to be revised in the light of Singapore developments. Certainly, no other Singapore political leader (except Lim Yew Hock) would be likely to fight for merger. The successor to Lee will almost certainly present us with demands for a further measure of independence, if not more. The problem is, however, whether there is any hope of getting the Tunku to move in time.

4.   Tunku Abdul Rahman is quite keen to take over Singapore since he now realises the political danger. But he believes it is politically impossible for him to do this unless he can explain to his Malay electors that he has some counter weight to the large chunk of Chinese who constitute the bulk of the population of Singapore. This means the Borneo territories.

5.   All three Borneo territories are quite unfitted as yet to enter an association of this sort on the basis of popular representation. But they will continue to be so unfitted for many years to come. I should give Sarawak about ten years and North Borneo at least twenty years before a clear-cut electoral opinion could be given on this subject. This means bluntly that if we proceed by normal constitutional methods, and assuming the Tunku will not compromise, merger between the Federation and Singapore is virtually out.

6.   But I believe it may be possible to give the Tunku enough association with the Borneo territories to justify his closer association with Singapore in the eyes of his Malay population. In the sort of picture I have in mind, which is one which I have only tentatively formulated and which I am bound to admit contains many difficulties, Singapore would become a self-governing state of the Federation with much more extensive powers than the other States; something on the lines of Ulster. The Kuala Lumpur Government would, however, be responsible for defence, foreign policy and internal security. The powers of internal security would necessarily require to be fairly extensive to be acceptable to the Federation. The great advantage

---

[2] Selkirk is referring to the vote of confidence which Lee narrowly won on 20–21 July and the subsequent secession from the PAP of rebels to form the Barisan Sosialis on 30 July (see 49, note).

of the Tunku taking over foreign policy is that it would effectively prevent Chinese or Russian missions being set up in Singapore. The Borneo territories would be substantially in the same position, subject to certain safeguards. That is to say, they would send to Kuala Lumpur the same number of representatives as Singapore. If the Singapore representatives were increased, the Borneo territories should be increased. That should reasonably safeguard the parliamentary position. The Borneo representatives would of course have to be nominated, which Tun Razak quite specifically told me he would be perfectly satisfied to accept.

7.   I can see at first sight that such an arrangement might not greatly appeal to the Governors,[3] particularly in so far as it meant their being subordinated in some way to the Kuala Lumpur Government in respect of internal security. It is of course not the ideal for them, but failing some such solution the future of their territories will present an increasing problem to which it is hard to see the ultimate answer. I think in fact that their requirements could be met in fair measure by forming a Borneo Defence Council in Kuala Lumpur on which the U.K. High Commissioner would necessarily sit and which would be specially charged with the problems of defence and internal security of the Borneo territories.

8.   Such a plan does, of course, involve a number of considerable risks. The Borneo territories might very well react violently against it. They have, however, had in Singapore recently a Commonwealth Parliamentary Association conference which has been open to the press.[4] The representatives of the Borneo territories have come a very long way in saying that they support Greater Malaysia in principle, and there have latterly been several further indications that, if handled properly, the local peoples will be prepared to go along with the idea.

9.   It would of course be essential that British staff should remain for some considerable time and should be assured of doing so. I have no doubt that the existing peace and quiet which runs throughout the Borneo territories is entirely due to the quality and manner in which the British staff carry out their duties. The Federation Government appear to be quite willing to give the fullest undertaking in regard to this matter and could be kept up to it through the Borneo Defence Council or some similar organisation in Kuala Lumpur. There would have to be, I do not doubt, a provision enabling any of the territories to opt out within a period of say five years if they should wish to do so. I should have thought something of this sort would be essential to satisfy local sentiment as well as to meet backbench criticism in the House of Commons. In any case I think it is a desirable safeguard.

10.   This leaves the question of defence. On this subject there has been a great deal of discussion and I will not go into details here. But I believe that basically, if we can get the political organisation right, we can fit in defence requirements with the broad agreement of the people concerned. I think it is important that we do so and in

---

[3] ie, of North Borneo and Sarawak.
[4] At its conference in Singapore on 23 July the Commonwealth Parliamentary Association announced the formation of the Greater Malaysia Solidarity Committee (known as the Malaysia Solidarity Consultative Committee). Consisting of representatives from each of the five territories (though Brunei sent observers only) and chaired by Donald Stephens, the MSCC set out to collect views on Malaysia, disseminate information on Malaysia, encourage discussion of Malaysia and foster activities promoting the realisation of Malaysia. It met in Jesselton on 24 Aug, Kuching on 18–20 Dec 1961, Kuala Lumpur on 6–8 Jan and Singapore on 1–3 Feb 1962 when it agreed a memorandum which was submitted to the Cobbold Commission and printed as appendix F of the enquiry (cf CO 1030/1000, 1001, and 1002).

any case, unless the defence arrangements are broadly accepted by the people, they will not be of long duration.

11.   Of course all this is putting tremendous confidence in Tunku Abdul Rahman. We cannot foresee precisely his political life but he seems to be very reasonably established and we have to take a chance on the irresponsible remarks which he makes from time to time.[5] There will be considerable difficulties and the scheme may seem so loose that it hardly constitutes a political unity. These are all risks which I think have got to be run. But I have come to the conclusion that, unless we are prepared to take a chance, we may miss the psychological moment in the tide of the affairs of men which would enable the foundations to be laid for the only stable evolution of these territories which seems to me and most of our advisers to be sound.

12.   There is one further possibility, which has been suggested by Lee Kuan Yew, i.e. that if Brunei by itself were to join the Federation now, the Tunku might agree to early merger for Singapore if offered some prospect of North Borneo and Sarawak being brought in at a later stage and an assurance of our intention to work to this end. A union of Brunei with Malaya would not of course present the same constitutional, social or economic difficulties as exist in the case of the other two territories. It is by no means certain that the Tunku would be prepared to contemplate such a proposal or indeed that it would be acceptable on the Brunei side. But the possibility may be worth exploring.

13.   Some of the above points have been touched upon in Melville's letter FED 59/4/01 of August 11 to the Governors and White, of which I have just seen a copy.[6] It is encouraging to know that the problem is under active study in London. I am not sure however whether Melville's main suggestion of a declaration of intent will go far enough to satisfy the Tunku. It may therefore be worthwhile to consider the admittedly more drastic and far-reaching solution which I have outlined above.

14.   I am sending copies of this letter to Tory, Goode, Waddell and White.

---

[5] See, for example, 52, n 4.
[6] Melville's letter is not printed here but see document 56 for Waddell's reply to it.

56   CO 1030/982, no 506A   26 Aug 1961
'Grand Design': letter from Sir A Waddell to E Melville

[Waddell agreed with Selkirk that the British government should give a lead in planning territorial mergers, but, alarmed by the increasing pace advocated by the commissioner-general and more especially by the Tunku's insensitivity to the Borneo peoples, he argued that premature merger could lead to 'racial conflict and outright rebellion' in Sarawak.]

Your letter FED 59/4/01 of 11th August has just reached me. As I am off at the weekend for a visit to the Fourth Division[1] with Selkirk I had better try to give some assessment of the position now, although as the Grand Design is at the moment in a state of flux, not to say confusion, the present is not ideal for making assessments.

I think that quite frankly we have lost a good deal of the ability we once could have had to guide the Greater Malaysia movement. You will recall that after the I.T.C. last

---

[1] Sarawak was divided into five administrative divisions; Fourth Division, with its headquarters at Miri, shared a border with Brunei.

year and again this year Selkirk advocated taking a definite line on the Grand Design[2] while we in Borneo have consistently asked for a positive lead with regard to the Borneo territories including a commitment by H.M.G. to give all practical (and financial) assistance towards closer association.[3] In the absence of a positive lead Sarawak has been beset by doubts as to British intentions and this has led to internal differences which are as wide as the gulf you mention and perhaps more difficult to bridge. Even our main plank for bridging the gulf, that is, unanimity on the idea of Borneo association, has seemingly disintegrated—first there was the defection of the Datu Bandar during the Tunku's visit and more recently Donald Stephens's reported statement that unification of the Borneo territories is not necessary and that merger with Malaya is possible by 1963. It seems, however, that he has not been fully reported and the most recent news is that Borneo unification would be facilitated within the context of the Grand Design. What this precisely means I am not at present sure but we will know more after the Consultative Committee meeting this week.[4]

In any event the line-up in Sarawak is, S.U.P.P. opposed to the Tunku's plan of integration as states but generally in favour of Greater Malaysia as an ultimate objective after independence has been achieved here. S.U.P.P. is linked with Azahari and the Party Rakyat in this policy and previously with Stephens in the so-called United Front.[5] The Front, however, may not be as united as it seems as they have all reached this policy by different motives. S.U.P.P. believe that they will come out on top in an independent Sarawak and the Chinese element in general and the communist Chinese element in particular feel that this is a much better bet than coming under the Tunku who is known to keep a very firm hand on the Chinese. Moreover their links with Singapore and recently with Boestamam[6] and the Party Rakyat in the Federation which has taken shape in the proposal to call a socialist summit meeting makes it obvious enough that their idea of Greater Malaysia is quite different from the Tunku's. It will be an association of the left and extreme left designed to overthrow the Tunku. It therefore does not matter to them, indeed it is an advantage, if Singapore fails to obtain merger and goes further, if that is possible, to the left. At the same time the Tunku's political position and prestige if he fails in his plan will be undermined and he is known to have staked his political future on the Grand Design. Brunei's Party Rakyat line up with S.U.P.P. was, as I see it, initially fortuitous—they were the only political parties then in the field, both striving for independence and Brunei being rather small to accommodate Azahari's political ambitions. Opposition to the Sultan who has for long desired to join Malaya led quite naturally to opposition to the Tunku and therefore to closer alliance with the left. Hence the Tunku's illogical charge that all who opposed his scheme are communists. All communists certainly oppose it and will no doubt make the most of being in the same camp as the moderates and indeed of the right wing. For the right wing (except some of the Sarawak Malays perhaps) also oppose the Tunku's plan through fear of historical subjugation by Malays but mostly because they feel unprepared

---

[2] See 30, 32, 36, 47 and 55.   [3] See 31, 40 and 44.
[4] For the Consultative Committee, see 55, n 4.   [5] See 52, n 4.
[6] Ahmad Boestamam (Abdullah Sani bin Raja Keehil) was a founder-member of the radical Malay Nationalist Party in 1945; leader of the militant youth movement, API, 1946–1947; detained 1948–1955; first president of the Parti Rakyat Malaya, 1955; federal MP, 1959–1964; detained as part of Operation Cold Store in Feb 1963 and until 1967.

educationally, politically and economically to take their rightful part—there is also an understandable feeling of national pride and some sheer parochialism. By the right wing I of course mean the Ibans, Land Dayaks, Kayans, Kenyahs and other indigenous peoples. So we find some strange bedfellows in the anti-Tunku bed.

In the other bed are some of the Sarawak Malays (and now possibly Stephens and his following in North Borneo) who originally shared the indigenous view above but switched very suddenly. In quick merger the Malays see the only hope of regaining their pristine position of influence and of keeping the Chinese in their place. I may be overrating the influence of the Datu Bandar[7] whose leadership has never been accepted by more than a portion of the Malays but nevertheless the only Malay newspaper has taken up his line and may influence a wider circle. The volte-face by the Datu Bandar has undoubtedly been caused by promises of preferential treatment and the blandishments of the Tunku and Ghazali have been quite open and unashamed. The Tunku clearly hopes to win over the Ibans and others by the same methods and we are being bombarded by invitations to send parties to Malaya to receive 'the treatment' which, one must admit, seems to be temporarily effective even if one cannot admire it. I expect that Tory is doing what is possible to counter the quite outrageous claims that more has been done in the last three years since independence than in the previous century under British rule. I suppose I should welcome the greater interest in the Grand Design but I deplore the methods and motives which have debased a fine concept into a somewhat squalid political intrigue. No doubt it will be elevated in due course but that is how it appears to me now. And it is of course pregnant with racial trouble.

My own view on how things should go remains unchanged—Borneo association first accelerated by considerable practical and financial assistance by H.M.G. to make it a reality (and I warmly welcome the decision to appoint a Co-ordinator[8]). Eventually in the long term political association with Malaya in a confederation with a high degree of self-governing power remaining in Borneo. Meantime, and working to that end, the forging of closer links through joint institutions and joint planning for which, as you say, the economic field affords the most obvious opportunities. The development of consultative machinery would be natural and desirable. We are told by the Tunku that it is is impracticable but I do not see that with trust on both sides it need be. I do not see in what other way it is possible to fulfil our obligations, particularly to the indigenous people, as set out in our constitution (the Nine Principles[9]) and the assurances given in the past (c.f. the Baram petition forwarded under cover of my Saving No. 34 of 14th January 1960, to which your Saving No. 52 of 11th February 1960 was the reply) that our aim is to lead the people of all races to take their full and proportionate part in the conduct of public affairs. This is a subject which is repeatedly brought up as I travel the country and the trust imposed

---

[7] See 43, n 4.   [8] For the decision to appoint H P Hall as co-ordinator, see 36, note.
[9] When the British government annexed Sarawak on 1 July 1946 it assumed the obligation to uphold the Nine Cardinal Principles set out in the preamble to the Rajah's Constitution of Sarawak of 1941. These principles emphasised the rights and interests of the people of Sarawak and were included as appendix C of the report of the Cobbold Commission (Cmnd 1794, Aug 1962). Concerned that the colonial government was deviating from them in its pursuit of Malaysia, the former Rajah and Bertram Brooke also drew Macmillan's attention to these obligations (C V Brooke to Macmillan, 16 July 1962, and B Brooke to Macmillan, 20 Aug and 13 Sep 1963, PREM 11/4345).

in us must be maintained. The constitutional proposals I have put forward are aimed at the same objective as are our educational and development schemes. The pace may well quicken (and the constitutional proposals are a bit ahead of public demand) but that will not matter as long as the proper people are making the running. It may be too that the Tunku's efforts to win over the indigenous people will bear more and better fruit than I suppose, but I doubt it. Behind the attitude of the indigenous people is the feeling that while they themselves (the elders) have not had the chance or the experience or education to compete with the others inside the country (far less with those outside) their sons now in the upper readers [reaches] of the schools will be ready in ten to fifteen years time. With this feeling I have every sympathy. With complete frankness the Ibans have said 'We will not permit the Chinese or Malays to kick the British out, we ourselves will ask them to go when we feel the time has come.'

In consequence of all this I have reached the same conclusion that I have reached many times over recent months that no formula can be produced to cover the positions of Malaya and Sarawak. Unless the Tunku can be persuaded to concede the long term approach I very much fear that the deal is off. If it is off we face more tempestuous winds of change and increased subversive activity. On the other hand if merger is forced by 1963 or at all prematurely there is a real prospect of racial conflict and outright rebellion. If one has to make the choice then I must take the first where the responsibility remains ours.

I fully agree with what Bill Goode says in his letter of the 24th August about the initiative having been left long enough, indeed too long, with the Tunku. It is a most awkward position for a Governor to have all this going on round him, pompous Consultative Committees disposing of all and sundry, without being in a position to do more than utter the authorised platitudes about 'the wishes of the people'. I meet my parishioners daily and they ask point blank what the British Government and I think about Greater Malaysia. This is not now an academic question for back rooms—not here at any rate. I would urge that H.M.G. should give a lead in the following sense, that while Greater Malaysia is a constructive idea no decision has been or will be taken without H.M.G. having fully consulted the peoples of the territories and obtained their agreement on the basis of clear-cut proposals. This is bound to take a considerable time and the present period of informal discussion is helpful in determining some of the difficulties and appreciating some of the advantages. H.M.G.'s responsibilities towards the Borneo territories are not diminished. H.M.G. does not regard the trend towards closer association between Sarawak and North Borneo as in any way prejudicial to some future association with Malaya and is prepared to give all practical assistance to the furtherance of a Bornean association in accordance with the general and particular wishes of these territories for such an association. (And here I repeat my previous plea for increased financial support for joint projects such as are already under consideration and such as the Co-ordinator may be able to develop.)

I regret that I cannot be more helpful at this stage. However, yesterday's report that the Tunku and Lee Kuan Yew have agreed in principle to merger,[10] without mentioning the accession of the Borneo territories as a pre-requisite, gives me some hope that the long term Borneo approach may in the end be accepted.

---

[10] See 59, note.

57   PREM 11/3418   4 Sept 1961
[Proposal for talks in London]: letter from Tunku Abdul Rahman to
Mr Macmillan

[In response to the Tunku's request for a statement of British policy and an early
meeting, Macmillan authorised Sandys to set up an *ad hoc* committee of officials, under
CRO chairmanship, to examine policy on closer association (see 60).]

Since my last letter to you of 11th August[1] about the proposed association of the Borneo
territories, Singapore and the Federation of Malaya, events have been moving very
swiftly and I think, therefore, that I should keep you informed of these developments.

As you probably know, Mr. Lee Kuan Yew and I had a meeting recently at which we
agreed in principle on the question of the integration of Singapore and the
Federation.[2] We were also agreed that the question of Defence, External Affairs and
Security should be the responsibility of the Federal Government while the State of
Singapore would retain Education and Labour. As a result we decided on the
appointment of a Working Party to go into the various implications arising out of the
proposed arrangements.

I am fully convinced that this subject must now be pursued with the utmost
vigour and urgency and I am hoping, therefore, that the Working Party will be able
to meet in the very near future. As you are no doubt aware there are elements in
Singapore owing allegiance beyond these shores who are now working very actively
to arouse chauvinist and anti-merger sentiment as they realised that the real object
of the merger was to combat Communism in this region. For my part I am equally
determined to keep ahead of their moves and my recent meeting with Mr. Lee was
partly designed to keep the issue alive. A respite will only work to their advantage.

In these circumstances, I would like to revise my earlier proposal in response to your
invitation that we might meet early next year. It appears to me to be in the interest of
us all that we should arrange to meet as soon as possible. However, before we meet it
may perhaps be best to settle beforehand the basis for our talks. It is extremely important
that we should do all we can in advance to ensure the success of our discussions as
their failure will be a serious setback of which the Communists will make full use, and
to their advantage. I wonder, therefore, if at this stage, you could say whether the
British Government would agree to relinquishing its sovereignty over the Borneo
territories and Singapore in the immediate future to enable them to become member
States of Malaysia and, if so, the means by which this could be effected. At the same
time, I think it would be important to know whether the British Government would
contemplate the use of the Singapore base within the framework of our Mutual Defence
Agreement including the fulfilment of Commonwealth obligations.

It might perhaps be possible to carry on with the discussion here with
representatives of our three Governments and find agreed basis for the talks in
London. This would save much time as it would help to remove any obstacle there
might be in the way of bringing about a successful merger of these territories with
the Federation. I suggest that only after careful planning and preparation have been
made here should we go to London. If the intention is to meet earlier then we might
meet soon.

---

[1] See 53.   [2] See 59, note.

58   CO 1030/983, no 615   16 Sept 1961
[Crash programme for 'Greater Malaysia']: letter from Lord Selkirk to
Mr Macleod, amplifying the case put in document 55

In my telegram No. 41 I have given a short answer to the point about relinquishment
of sovereignty in your telegram No. 360 on Greater Malaysia. I am now writing to
give you my further comments.

2.   In my letter of August 24,[1] I said that I thought the time had come when it was
necessary to consider a crash programme for 'Greater Malaysia'. I should like first to
recapitulate the various reasons why I consider that such a programme is
necessary:—

(i) We must look at the whole scheme against the background of our overall
policy in the area. In my earlier letters and despatches on the subject I have made
it plain that I believe that 'Greater Malaysia' would be an important factor for
stability in the area and that it would satisfy long-term British and Commonwealth
interests.

(ii) Owing to the speed and manner in which the situation is now developing
there is a serious risk that unless Greater Malaysia can be achieved in the near
future, the opportunity may be lost for good. This is due to a combination of
circumstances in the various territories involved, i.e., notably:—

(a) For the first time we have governments in both the Federation and in
Singapore that are actively in favour of Greater Malaysia; this may never
recur.
(b) The present Singapore Government will almost certainly fall in the next few
months if rapid progress cannot be made. If this happens there will be no
prospect of merger as long as the Tunku remains in power in Kuala Lumpur.
(c) If we do not bring the Borneo territories in now (i.e. by 1963–64) so that the
Greater Malaysia plan fails, the long-term alternatives for them would be
independence or absorption by Indonesia or China. The first of these
alternatives is not likely to be maintained and would probably lead to the
second. Moreover it is certain that if we do not take the opportunity presented
by the Tunku's present initiative, we cannot expect to remain in the Borneo
territories for another ten or twenty years. The Tunku's proposals have already
made their impact on political consciousness there and, whatever happens, we
must expect demands for political change to come forward with much greater
urgency than they have hitherto.
(d) The Tunku has, to a considerable extent, staked his political future and
reputation on the success of his 'Greater Malaysia' proposals. If they fail, it will
be a set-back for him which could be damaging to his position at home.
Moreover failure will be blamed on us, and this would mean a serious blow to
our present good relations with the Tunku. We should be faced with an angry
and resentful Tunku over Singapore and over other problems.
(e) This may be our last chance to prevent Chinese preponderance in the area
which must inevitably involve a serious risk of ultimate Communist domination.

---

[1] See 55.

3. Before I set out my further comments on how the Borneo territories might fit into the Greater Malaysia concept I should like to say this about our own policy there. We must of course continue our efforts to train the peoples of those territories for self-government and to bequeath to them respect for the rule of law. But we have at the same time to face up to the fact that 'one man, one vote' has not been a wild success in South East Asia. In my view therefore our greatest contribution to the future stability of the Borneo territories has been and will be made in the fields of administration and of education and in such economic spheres as communications, land utilization and agriculture.

4. I said in my telegram No. 41 that I thought we could surrender sovereignty in the Borneo territories provided that satisfactory arrangements were made for us to continue making this contribution until such time as the local people are ready to run their own affairs at the State level. We want the Tunku to assume sovereignty over Singapore and it would certainly be logical for him to want the Borneo territories to join a Greater Malaysia on essentially the same basis. Moreover, I doubt if it would be wise to share sovereignty with the Federation even in the unlikely event of our being able to induce the Tunku to do so, lest we lend countenance to the allegation that Greater Malaysia is a plot for the preservation of British imperialism.

5. The basic problem is how to ensure that the constitutional provisions for the Borneo territories are properly worked out, put to the territories for their consent and then enacted in such a way that the people in the territories can be assured that they will in due course be brought into full operation, while at the same time making progress as rapidly as the Tunku and Lee Kuan Yew require. I suggest that the best way of doing this would be to negotiate now State constitutions for the Borneo territories with whatever State powers, financial provisions and so-forth that are desirable. These constitutions would include provision for representative institutions and for the Governors ultimately to be in similar positions to the Governors of Penang and Malacca.[2] The constitutions would, however, come into force in stages and, in this way, the pace of constitutional advance could be suited to the territory. At the same time the important requirement of an assured ultimate constitutional position would be achieved by enacting these constitutions by means of appropriate legislative action in both the United Kingdom and the Federation. This legislation in the Federation would provide that these constitutions would be capable of amendment only in the same way as the Federal constitution itself, thereby entrenching them to the same extent.

6. If the suggestion I have outlined is constitutionally feasible it remains to determine to whom the Governors would be responsible for the administration of the Borneo territories at the State level until they are ready to administer themselves and the full provisions of their State constitutions have been brought into operation. In addition, there must be some means of deciding when each suspended section of the State constitution should become effective. Broadly speaking, there seems to be three possible alternatives.

7. The first of these is to trust the Tunku absolutely. By this I mean that we make the Governors finally responsible to Kuala Lumpur and leave it to the Tunku to

---

[2] For the appointment of governors of Penang and Malacca at the time of Malayan independence see *BDEE: Malaya*, lxxvii and 448 (12), 449, 453, 459, 460.

decide when the State constitution can become fully operative. The difficulty here is that the Tunku does not want to take over colonies and the Borneo territories do not want to become colonies of the Federation (the Ibans for example are not Moslems and do not relish being administered by Moslems). The other obvious disadvantage of this course is that it would probably undermine the morale of the expatriates in the Borneo territories with the result that our further contribution to their future stability would be much reduced.

8.   The second alternative is that the Governors should continue to be responsible to London. In other words, although sovereignty was transferred to the Federation they would agree to derogate from it to the extent of leaving direction of State administration to H.M.G. for a transitional period. This would presumably re-assure the local people and the administrators, but it would hardly appeal to the Tunku. Moreover, I should have thought that H.M.G., on the analogy of the Central African Federation, might not like it either.

9.   Both these alternatives could, of course, be modified by various measures of joint responsibility and consultation. But if this is to be the case, it seems to me worthwhile to think in terms of formal machinery. This might be done by setting up by agreement with the Federation Government a Joint Trust Council for the Borneo territories. There are obviously various possibilities for the membership of this council which I will not go into at this stage, but I think it might well be necessary to give the Federation the chairmanship, at any rate on a rotating basis. The powers of the council would include the ability to give the Governors, who would, I hope, be prepared to continue in office in these circumstances, general guidance on State matters, the future selection and appointment of new Governors and the power to decide on the introduction of successive stages in the State constitutions. The Council would not however meet too frequently and the Governors should be able to conduct day to day affairs without interference from it. As a concomitant of this arrangement it would be essential to include in the constitutional arrangements provision for the establishment immediately of a Public Service Commission with powers to make recommendations only to the Governor and to have it agreed that the Governor would act solely in his discretion in matters affecting the Public Service. I would hope in this way to postpone for some time the need to introduce a scheme of compensation for expatriate officers, though I realise that in due course this would have to come as the pressure increases, as it surely will, for increased Borneonisation.

10.   So far, I have been primarily concerned with the interests of the peoples of the Borneo territories. From H.M.G.'s point of view there is also the need for a satisfactory arrangement on Defence. This I envisage would take the form of an extension of the Malayan Defence Agreement to cover the Borneo territories, as well as Singapore. It must however be on a basis that would make it clear to the Federation Government that they were responsible for their own defence and that we were merely helping them to achieve their objective, probably through some form of Defence Council in Kuala Lumpur. It would also have to be understood that they would be prepared to undertake to co-operate in assuring the Defence and Internal Security of remaining British territories in this area. Such arrangements would necessarily presuppose goodwill and continuous consultation between the two Governments. Such goodwill is fundamental to the whole concept of Greater Malaysia and at this stage we must assume it.

11. I realise that it will not be easy to persuade the Tunku to accept the arrangements I have proposed above even though we are prepared to cede sovereignty over the Borneo territories. The opting out clause for the Borneo territories which I advocated in my letter of August 24 would obviously make the scheme very much easier to put across there, but I am seriously wondering whether, in the light of Tory's telegram No. 651 of September 7 to the Commonwealth Relations Office, there is any chance of getting the Tunku to agree to it. That being so, and since some way must be found of consulting the peoples of the Borneo territories before they are irrevocably committed to Greater Malaysia, the only alternative is some form of consultation within the next year or two. At first sight this may sound impracticable, but we should not forget the speed with which other former colonies at least as underdeveloped as North Borneo and Sarawak have been asked to decide their future. While still without any substantial experience of managing their own affairs, Singapore may hold a referendum towards the end of this year. Obviously, we could not move as quickly as that but popular consultation in the Borneo territories in, say, late 1962 would be a very different proposition. This would mean that the Tunku would have to accept that the inclusion of the Borneo territories was subject to the will of the people there as expressed in 1962, but there would be no provision for opting out once Greater Malaysia had been chosen. Of course the risk of an adverse vote would have to be incurred but if we believe, as I think we do, that the people must be consulted at some stage, this would have to be faced sooner or later. The Tunku may not much like this, but since, as Tory has said in his telegram No. 652 of September 7 to the Commonwealth Relations Office he believes that we could swing public opinion in the Borneo territories in favour of Greater Malaysia, he might be prepared to agree if it comes to the point. There would still be the problem that the Tunku would presumably not finally accept Singapore until the outcome of the Borneo Consultation was known but this also need not be an insuperable difficulty.

12. If we had a crash programme on the lines I have described with such consultations as the Governors think fair in the Borneo territories in about twelve months' time we should clearly have to try to ensure that the result was the one that we and the Tunku wanted. I am quite sure that the influence of the administrations in the Borneo territories is very considerable and that whatever is said about Greater Malaysia by Her Majesty's Government, by the Governors and by their District Officers will carry very great weight with the local people. Conversely silence would be taken as disapproval of the scheme. I recall the criticism in the case of the Central African Federation that there had at the time of its introduction been no firm instructions to District Officers in the protectorate to take a positive line in support of it. I believe this point was commented on in the Monckton Report.[3] It is therefore essential for its success that any Greater Malaysia scheme should have the full support of the local administrations on whom would fall the task of explaining its implications and of setting its practical advantages against the immense problems that would otherwise face the peoples of the Borneo territories when they became

---

[3] Lord Monckton chaired the Advisory Commission on Central Africa whose report was published on 18 Oct 1960, see Hyam and Louis eds, *BDEE: The Conservative Government and the End of Empire*, liv-lv and 495, n 1.

independent. I believe that the Greater Malaysia scheme would be in the long term interests of the Borneo peoples and that we can tell them this in all sincerity.

13.   I realise that there are many other important aspects to be considered that I have not dealt with in this letter. A joint Working Party will clearly have to be set up to produce a detailed plan once the broad heads of agreement have been reached at the top level discussions. I think a scheme on these lines could be worked out and the prospective results merit the risks involved. The Tunku is very keen on this concept and would, I believe, co-operate in the organisational change.

14.   I am copying this to Goode in Jesselton, Waddell in Kuching, White in Brunei, Tory in Kuala Lumpur, Oliver in Canberra and Cumming-Bruce in Wellington.

P.S. I m sending copies to Alec and Duncan.[4]

---

[4] ie, Lord Home and Mr Sandys.

59   PREM 11/3418   18 Sept 1961
'Greater Malaysia': inward telegram no 387 from P B C Moore to Mr Macleod, reporting agreement between Tunku Abdul Rahman and Lee Kuan Yew

[On 24 Aug the Tunku and Lee had reached preliminary agreement on the principle of merger as well as the degree of autonomy to be retained by Singapore. They took this further in Sept and set up a working party to examine details. By the middle of Nov Heads of Agreement were drawn up and presented to the Singapore Legislative Assembly which accepted them on 6 Dec (see 87 note 1). On 20 Sept the Tunku repeated his request for 'some clear indication' of British policy (CAB 134/1949, GM(61)2, annex). Others, too, such as Selkirk and Sandys felt that London could not be seen to dither on the question of closer association. Sandys was anxious to allay the Tunku's misgivings and hold talks sooner rather than later. Thus, although a meeting in late Oct had previously been ruled out by other pressures on the prime minister's diary, Macmillan's private office advised him to accept Sandys' suggestion for a meeting with the Tunku on 23 Oct. This was the date Macmillan offered the Tunku in a message of 23 Sept, attempting at one and the same time to avoid giving a clear indication of British policy on either the Borneo territories or the use of the Singapore base and to steer clear of antagonising the Malayan government. It was now essential for ministers to be briefed on policy options, and the inter-departmental Greater Malaysia (Official) Committee met for the first time on 27 Sept (see 62). Lee had already decided not to accompany the Tunku to the London talks and, for his own domestic reasons, the Tunku now wished to avoid being too obviously associated with the Chinese leader of Singapore. Lee remained in Singapore to prepare for a referendum on merger. As part of his campaign, between 13 Sept and 9 Oct he gave twelve broadcasts, each in three languages, against communism and in favour of merger. These talks were published as *The Battle for Merger* (Government Printing Office, Singapore, 1961).]

Greater Malaysia.

Following is text of communiqué issued in Kuala Lumpur following meeting of the Tunku and Lee Kuan Yew:—

'The Prime Minister of the Federation of Malaya, Tengku Abdul Rahman Putra Al-Haj, and the Prime Minister of Singapore, Mr. Lee Kuan Yew, had talks for three days at the Residency in Kuala Lumpur.

Present at the talks were the Federation Deputy Prime Minister, Tun Abdul Razak bin Dato Hussein, and the Singapore Minister of Culture, Mr. S.

Rajaratnam. Permanent Secretary for External Affairs, Inche Muhammad Ghazali bin Shafie, was also present.

The Prime Ministers of the Federation and Singapore have agreed that the working party should be instructed to work out the details of merger, with a view to bringing about the integration of the two territories and its peoples in or before June 1963.

On the basis of the agreement reached on 23rd August the two Prime Ministers discussed important constitutional and economic problems arising out of merger and broad agreement was reached.

The two Prime Ministers are satisfied that all legitimate local and special interests of the people in the two territories can, and will, be safeguarded, with the merger of Singapore as a State within the Federation.

Much progress has been made as a result of the discussions between the two Prime Ministers. It is decided that the two Prime Ministers will meet from time to time to review the working and decide on the recommendations of the working party.'

2.   Following are main points made by Lee Kuan Yew on arrival in Singapore.

3.   All the main problems of merger had been ironed out and it only remained to settle the details. Singapore was merging with the Federation as a very special State. The Federation recognised its very special position, which was like that of Penang although Singapore was bigger than Penang and was a free port and a big city. If Singapore did not reserve to itself powers on Education and Labour there would be a great deal of misunderstanding and unhappiness amongst Singapore people.

4.   Although every State in the Federation came under the 9th Schedule of the Constitution and customs, excise and income tax powers belonged to the central Government, Singapore would have administrative duties like education, labour, health and social services and would be getting a considerable amount of taxes to discharge those duties. There would therefore have to be an equitable adjustment of representation in the federal Parliament otherwise Singapore would be represented twice over. Representation would be in proportion with the amount of reserve taxes that would be kept for Singapore.

5.   Singapore's status as the twelfth State in the Federation would affect the position of the British in Singapore. The British were at present in Singapore as of right. With merger they could not remain as of right; sovereignty would no longer be with them. This is a matter to be settled between the Tunku, Singapore and the U.K. Government. It would create a considerable amount of difficulty if the British tried to get rights of the nature they had in Cyprus where they were in complete control of certain sections of the island.[1] Singapore was not as large as Cyprus and large parts of the island could not be cut off for the Naval base and the airfields but these problems were not insuperable.

6.   Greater Malaysia could come at the same time or shortly after merger between Singapore and the Federation.

7.   On merger Singapore citizens and federal citizens would become federal nationals. The question of citizenship and other matters would in due course be published in a command paper for public information.

---

[1] When Cyprus became independent in Aug 1960, Britain retained sovereignty over ninety-nine square miles of base-enclaves.

8.   There would have to be constitutional talks with the British Government by 1963. After all the details of merger had been settled he and the Tunku would jointly present the plan to the British Government.

9.   The ideal must be complete integration between Singapore and the Federation. That was not possible now; there was a lot of misunderstanding and unhappiness about Chinese education. If at any time in the future all the difficulties were ironed out and the people agreed to education going to the central Government, then it could be done, but at present the people of Singapore did not want it. The Federation was quite prepared to take charge of all subjects, but he was going to safeguard what he thought were the legitimate rights of Singapore. The P.A.P.'s duty for 1963 was to bring about merger on fair and just conditions. After merger the position could be regularly reviewed and if both the State Government and the central Government agreed to more powers going to the centre there was nothing to prevent it.

60   CAB 134/1949, GM(61)2   25 Sept 1961
'Summary of Malayan proposals and issues to be considered by the British Government': CRO memorandum for the Greater Malaysia (Official) Committee

[This memorandum was discussed at the first meeting of the Greater Malaysia (Official) Committee on 27 Sept. Set up by Macmillan '[t]o examine the proposals by the Prime Minister of the Federation of Malaya for the creation of a "Greater Malaysia" incorporating the Federation of Malaya, Brunei, North Borneo, Sarawak and Singapore, and to make recommendations to Ministers', the committee was chaired first by Sir Alexander Clutterbuck and later by Sir Saville Garner, and included representatives of the CO (either E Melville or Sir J Martin), the FO (generally E Peck), the Ministry of Defence and Treasury. It was dissolved on 22 Oct 1963, five weeks after the inauguration of Malaysia. Its papers are at CAB 134/1949–1951. One of the points raised during the discussion of this paper was the likely reaction of the Americans since 'for political reasons they wanted us to maintain a military presence of significant proportions' (see 62 and also CAB 21/5350).]

The Tunku's proposals and attitude have been described in his messages to the Prime Minister of 26th June, 11th August and 20th September. Copies of these are attached, together with the memorandum enclosed with the message of the 26th June.[1]

2.   The Tunku's original proposals for the status of Singapore after merger have been slightly modified following his discussions with Mr. Lee Kuan Yew.[2]

Malayan proposals
3.   These are now as follows:—

(1) As a first step Brunei, North Borneo and Sarawak should be brought into the Malayan Federation as constituent units on the same basis as the existing states (though he has informed Bornese [sic] leaders that he would be ready to give the Borneo territories a large measure of self-government). He appears to be

---

[1] See 46 for the Tunku's message and memorandum of 26 June and 53 for his message of 11 Aug. His message of 20 Sept is not printed here.
[2] See 59.

convinced that if the British Government gave a firm lead, the Borneo peoples would be happy to come in at a very early date.

(2) Once (1) was secured, Singapore would join the Federation on a special basis retaining powers to administer its own affairs in the fields of education and labour. Singapore would then have proportionately smaller representation in the central Parliament than they could claim on a population basis if they came in on the same footing as the Borneo territories. Internal security would be a federal subject.

(3) The British bases in Singapore would cease to be at the disposal of SEATO but could be maintained as bases for Commonwealth defence.

(4) There would be no administrative changes, but Singapore would maintain its own Civil Service.

(5) After initial talks with the Prime Minister, there should be a more formal discussion in which representatives of all the territories concerned and the United Kingdom would participate. That meeting should decide on the appointment of an independent constitutional commission on the lines of the Reid Commission which drafted the present Constitution of the Federation of Malaya, to work out the Constitution of the new union.

4.   In Malaya the attitude of the opposition parties to these matters is not clear. The initiative remains firmly in the Tunku's hands.

5.   In Singapore Mr. Lee Kuan Yew's fundamental aim is to secure a viable independence for Singapore in a democratic framework. He is fully committed to Singapore achieving 'independence through merger' and his political future depends on securing early progress. The left-wing opposition in Singapore are powerful and anxious to create maximum difficulties for Lee and the Tunku. They are likely to come out in favour of either a programme of complete merger with Malaya or one which left internal security with the Singapore Government. Either, they reason, would frustrate the Tunku's designs against the Chinese. If full merger were completed they would hope to be able to establish a Chinese-dominated government at the centre, while if they retained internal security they could be sure of continued freedom of action in Singapore. They would doubtless prefer a policy of complete independence to the Tunku's proposals.

Issues for examination

6.   To assist the work of the Committee an attempt has been made in the following paragraphs to indicate the issues on which Ministers will require recommendations. As a first step, the Committee may wish to examine these paragraphs with a view to agreeing on a list of the issues to be covered in the Committee's work.

7.   Previous consideration of the idea of Greater Malaysia, at both Ministerial and official level, has indicated general agreement that a closer association between Malaya, Singapore and the Borneo Territories should be accepted as the ultimate aim. In general Ministers will need to reach a conclusion on (a) the importance to British policies and interests of achieving Greater Malaysia and (b) how far the British Government can go at the London meeting to contribute to this end.

8.   The question of *timing* has now become of critical importance. The Tunku and Lee appear to have made considerable progress in defining what kind of relationship between Singapore and the proposed central Government would be

acceptable to both of them. The left-wing opposition in Singapore would no doubt insist on terms unacceptable to the Tunku, and it is in any case highly improbable that the Tunku would be prepared to negotiate with them. Retention of power by Lee in Singapore appears therefore to be essential if the whole idea of a Greater Malaysia is not to founder. If it fails now, the opportunity may be permanently lost.

9.   Lee's position in Singapore is weak. Some immediate and concrete evidence of progress is essential to him to enable him to retain power. He and the Tunku have made it clear that the central issue for the London meeting is whether the British and Malayan Governments can reach a sufficient measure of agreement to provide Lee with the public material necessary to enable him to sustain his position in the Singapore Parliament which meets again on the 30th October. Our representatives on the spot agree with this. It is necessary to define how far the British Government can go at this stage in a *statement of intentions*.

10.   The Tunku's position is that he is not prepared to go any further over a merger between Malaya and Singapore until he can be assured that the Borneo territories will be brought into a federal scheme at least as early as Singapore. In his view this is a fundamental requirement for him in order to enable him to deal with the Chinese and left-wing elements in Singapore. His latest message envisages a 'firm undertaking' on this point by the British Government to be announced at the London meeting. The British Government's position has been that they will not commit the Borneo territories without consultation with their peoples. There will therefore be difficulties in finding a formula which the Tunku will regard as adequate.

11.   It is assumed that we shall wish to maintain *defence facilities* in Singapore and Malaya under conditions which will enable us to use our forces to carry out our SEATO and other defence obligations. Greater Malaysia would involve the loss of our sovereign rights in Singapore and we should have to negotiate an agreement covering our defence facilities and their use. The extension to Singapore of our existing Defence Agreement with Malaya would not be satisfactory unless there could be an agreed modification of the conditions which the Malayan Government have hitherto imposed on the use of our forces for SEATO purposes. The Tunku has made it clear that he could not accept any formal public link between SEATO and our defence facilities. He has however indicated that, subject to this, he wishes to be as helpful as possible over our defence requirements.

12.   These defence matters will require detailed, and no doubt lengthy, negotiation. At the London meeting we should presumably at least aim to bring the Tunku to accept that an agreement covering the effective strategic use of our forces is essential to is [sic], and to agree with him the lines on which further examination of the details should proceed. Any announcement following the London meeting would, from our point of view, need to include some reassuring reference to defence matters.

13.   Consideration of our general Defence Review has been on the basis that, if Greater Malaysia is achieved, the British Government would no longer have any responsibility for *internal security* in the territories concerned and that this would lead to a substantial reduction in our forces. It would seem desirable to confirm with the Tunku that he also envisages that in a Greater Malaysia the British Government would have no internal security responsibilities, direct or indirect.

14.   The Tunku will wish to discuss *the internal situation in Singapore*—in

particular what the attitude of the British Government would be if the Socialist Front were to overthrow Lee, and what we, and the Tunku, might do to help sustain Lee (over and above any general commitments about Greater Malaysia). This ties in with the problem of the Tunku's present attitude to the political detainees in Singapore and the Internal Security Council.

15.   We have told *the Australian and New Zealand Governments* that we will give them considered Ministerial views before the London meeting. They will expect to be given time to comment.

61   PREM 11/3422   26 Sept 1961
'Greater Malaysia': inward telegram no 705 from Sir G Tory to Mr Sandys, reporting the Tunku's reaction to Mr Macmillan's latest message.

Greater Malaysia

Prime Minister's message[1] was delivered to Tunku yesterday and I saw him today about it. He made it clear at the outset that he was hardening still further on question of need to obtain some clear assurance about our relinquishing sovereignty over Borneo territories before going to London. Strange as it may seem he evidently sincerely believed when writing his last two letters to Prime Minister (my telegrams No. 654 and No. 688) that Her Majesty's Government could if they wished commit themselves without reservation at London meeting to transfer of sovereignty over Borneo territories. It was explained in my telegram No. 687 that when Lee Kuan Yew came to inform Singapore Legislative Assembly at end of October, that scheme for Federation/Singapore merger had been agreed, Tunku or his spokesman wished to be able to say for benefit of Malays that all was well because Her Majesty's Government had undertaken to hand over Borneo territories whose populations would balance net addition of Chinese from Singapore. Tunku noted from Prime Minister's message of 23rd September that we could give no early assurance of kind he wished and that we should need more time to study implications. In answer to his question I felt bound to tell him that Her Majesty's Government were unlikely to be able by 23rd October to be in a position to give definite and unqualified undertaking to transfer sovereignty. Tunku said that if that were true, there was no point in his going to London at this stage. For him to go to London and come back empty handed would be undignified and damaging to his position. It was better that Her Majesty's Government should first satisfy themselves by consulting the populations of Borneo territories that they wanted Greater Malaysia so that we should be able if we wished to give undertaking about transfer of sovereignty when Tunku eventually paid his visit. It had never been his intention to go to London to try and persuade us to surrender sovereignty. His object had always been to discuss not the principle but the practical implications of the transfer of power.

2.   I begged Tunku to think again about this reminding him of serious implications of Greater Malaysia for us, of our obligations towards Borneo territories

---

[1] For Macmillan's message of 23 Sept, see document 59, note.

and political impossibility of handing them over without assuring ourselves and Parliament that their wishes had been properly consulted, of our pre-occupation over defence and our need to retain unrestricted facilities in order to discharge our SEATO obligations and so on. Discussion between Prime Ministers would help to clarify these matters. Only by frank discussion at highest level could effective decisions be secured on what were more important questions of Government policy. Tunku remained unmoved.

3.   I got him to see once again that it was necessary for us to consult wishes of Borneo territories before committing them to Greater Malaysia but he professed to believe that this could easily be done at once and the desired answer obtained. I told him that the Governors and all their officers in Borneo and Sarawak had warned us that although opinion was coming round towards Greater Malaysia it was not yet ready to accept it in its present form and to force the pace would be to set up adverse and probably dangerous reactions. Tunku brushed this aside saying that he did not believe there was any significant feeling against Greater Malaysia and that the peoples of the territories if left to make up their own minds and not told what was good for them by the British administration would now opt for Greater Malaysia. The Tunku claimed that in the case of Malaya itself the Colonial administration had proved wrong in their assessment of the will of the people as regards independence. He was speaking as an expert in these matters. Tunku was in his most stubborn mood and I found it impossible to reason with him.

4.   It happens that this morning I was told in confidence by a very senior British officer still in Malayan Government service that he was aware of growing disquiet on the part of the Tunku's Malays about the way in which the Tunku appeared to be committing the Federation to Singapore without adequate safeguards. Ismail in particular the Minister of the Interior and Internal Security was becoming very anxious about the effect of these policies on political support for the Tunku in his own party and I suspect that he and perhaps Razak, too, have at (?last) penetrated the screen which the Tunku and Ghazali have built round themselves lately over Greater Malaysia and have (4 corrupt groups) some of their apprehension.

5.   Tunku recalled an earlier conversation in which he had told me he was not at all anxious to take Singapore or Borneo territories for that matter and that he had only been induced against his better judgment to accept principle of Greater Malaysia because he feared that Communism would otherwise get foothold in Singapore and in Borneo territories too. He said we ought to see matters in same light. It was up to us to decide whether we wanted to stop Communism from engulfing these territories or whether we did not care. In the former event we ought to see that Greater Malaysia offered the only chance of stemming this Communist advance and that there was only very little time.

6.   I said I thought that if Tunku decided not to go to London in October that would be a grave setback for Lee Kuan Yew. Tunku said that was not necessarily so in his view. He was at that moment consulting his friends in the Singapore Alliance on this point.

7.   Tunku expressed regret that it had not proved possible for Prime Minister to come here as originally planned and he suggested that visit by Prime Minister to Federation, Singapore and the Borneo Territories when world situation had quietened down a little would still be most welcome so far as he was concerned and would probably be more fruitful than anything else in advancing Greater Malaysia.

8.   Tunku appears also to have suffered further reaction on question of defence. He is again harping on theme that we could have Singapore for 'Commonwealth defence purposes'. I am afraid that here too we shall have to inform Tunku of our minimum defence requirements and shall have to argue these matters with him in advance of any visit by him to London.

9.   I now expect to receive from Tunku for transmission by telegraph a further message to Prime Minister saying he sees no purpose in coming to London unless we can meantime give assurance on transfer of sovereignty over Borneo territories.

10.   I have never known the Tunku so difficult as he was this morning. I hope to talk things over with Ghazali tomorrow and shall report further then.

62   CAB 134/1949, GM(61) 1st meeting   27 Sept 1961
'Summary of the proposals and of the issues involved': minutes of the Greater Malaysia (Official) Committee relating to document 60

[This meeting marked the first time that Whitehall formally engaged with the proposal to create Malaysia. The following were present: Sir A Clutterbuck (CRO, chair), E H Peck (FO), E Melville (CO), P S Milner-Barry (Treasury), C J Hayes (Treasury), N Pritchard (CRO), R C Omerod (CRO), D G R Bentliff (CRO), C E F Gough (Ministry of Defence) and F A Bishop (Cabinet Office). For the committee's final report, see 73.]

The Committee had before them a memorandum by the Commonwealth Relations Office (G.M. (61) 2) summarising the Malayan proposals and the issues to which they give rise for the British Government,[1] together with Kuala Lumpur telegram no. 705 dated 26th September, 1961,[2] and a note by the Commonwealth Relations Office containing the framework of a report to Ministers in preparation for their prospective discussions with the Malayan Prime Minister, Tunku Abdul Rahman.

The Chairman said that it appeared from Kuala Lumpur telegram no. 705 that the Tunku would be sending a further message to the Prime Minister on the lines indicated by Sir Geofroy Tory. This need not prevent the Prime Minister from insisting that the Tunku should visit London for a first round of general discussion about Greater Malaysia before we could contemplate any commitment going beyond a general welcome for the project. We should be able to prepare a reply to the Tunku in terms which would make it very difficult for him to refuse to come to London without prior commitment on our part. No doubt, because of the weakness of the present position of the Prime Minister of Singapore, Mr. Lee Kuan Yew, we could not afford much delay in coming to grips with the material issues involved in the project but the urgency was not such as to justify the Tunku's demands that we should prejudge any of the vitally important questions to be discussed.

Mr. Melville said that it would be wrong to assume that the question whether Mr. Lee stood or fell depended upon our reaching firm decisions of substance in talks with the Tunku before the end of October. We should aim in those talks at reaching sufficient agreement for it to be worth while for the Tunku to continue his negotiations with Mr. Lee and to enable the latter to argue in public with demonstrable justification that he was making progress towards satisfactory terms of

---

[1] See 60.   [2] See 61.

merger with the Federation of Malaya. But if Mr. Lee did fall a merger might still not be finally lost. His opponents might still decide to play their hand constitutionally (e.g., by avoiding action likely to force the British Government to intervene directly in Singapore); and even if a new Singapore Government made demands which the Tunku could not accept—such as a number of seats in the Federal Legislature in full proportions to population—it was conceivable that they might later resile from such a position so as to allow the possibility of a merger to be reopened. It had, of course, to be recognised that any such developments might turn the Tunku finally away from the idea of bringing Singapore into the Federation, and the crux remained how far we could go towards committing the Borneo Territories. We could not simply commit them unilaterally but if we could satisfy the Tunku about our support for Greater Malaysia in principle and about the extent to which we were prepared to give a lead in that direction to the Borneo Territories, we should have a reasonable chance of keeping the project alive despite any inevitable delays and some deterioration in the situation in Singapore.

In discussion it was agreed that the problem of timing was extremely difficult. It was obviously most desirable to move fast in order to meet the wishes of the Tunku and to anticipate any further weakening of Mr. Lee's position in Singapore. Moreover, we must avoid laying ourselves open to a charge of responsibility through default for preventing the Greater Malaysia project from getting off the ground at all. On the other hand, we badly needed time to try and carry the Borneo Territories along with us without appearing to dragoon them into a Greater Malaysia; we could not afford to take precipitate decisions about our defence interests; and we must be able to engage in adequate consultation with Australia and New Zealand on the project as a whole, and with them and other allies on its defence aspects in particular. Our best course would be to get the Tunku to London for the proposed talks and in them to explore with him in a general way, and against a background of warm welcome for a Greater Malaysia in principle, the various different courses along which we might seek solutions to the problems which it involved. This would no doubt be a task of considerable delicacy but there was no alternative if we were on the one hand to keep the project alive and on the other to avoid committing ourselves too soon on issues of the first magnitude.

Throughout the discussion it was recognised that questions relating to our defence interests in South East Asia and the Far East were crucial to our approach to the Tunku about Greater Malaysia, and these questions were currently under radical examination and that decisions upon them were most unlikely before the end of October.

Mr. Gough said that hitherto the political Departments had quite rightly based their thinking on the assumption that we must insist on maintaining our present defence facilities and rights in Malaya and Singapore more or less unchanged. But this, together with other fundamental assumptions of our defence policy, was today very much under review. On grounds of finance, and because of the pressing need to find additional man-power to fill the serious gaps in our forces in Germany without recourse to some form of National Service, it was imperative and urgent to seek reductions in our commitments and establishments outside Germany, and we must therefore take a new look at our position in South East Asia and the Far East.

There were three major points to consider. First, we could assume that the creation of a Greater Malaysia would relieve us of our responsibilities for internal security in

Singapore and the Borneo Territories. This was of great importance since it would release at least eight major units at present tied down for that purpose. Second, we at present had responsibilities for the external defence of those territories, and of Malaya under our bilateral defence agreement with her. No doubt the Tunku would want us to stand by that agreement but we had to ask ourselves whether we could not and should not find means of extricating ourselves from all these external defence responsibilities. Third, we had up till now assumed that the manner in which we fulfilled our obligations to the South East Asia Treaty Organisation (SEATO) would continue unchanged. If so, then we should certainly still need to keep substantial forces in Malaya and Singapore, but if we decided that we could and should make radical changes in the way of meeting our obligations to SEATO we were at once faced with a totally different situation. It might be possible for us to take with SEATO the line that, on the one hand, we regarded the creation of a Greater Malaysia not only as desirable in itself but also as likely to reinforce the general security of South East Asia but that, on the other hand, it would not be possible for us to retain in a Greater Malaysia the bases necessary for the fulfilment of our SEATO obligations in accordance with existing plans. The other Governments concerned with Greater Malaysia would not agree that we should do so; we could not contemplate continuing our present arrangements for the support of SEATO against the will of those Governments; and it was therefore necessary for us to make other arrangements for meeting our SEATO obligations— e.g. by relying upon long-range air striking power based upon Australia, without substantial ground forces in South East Asia itself. It was difficult to see how we could enter into serious negotiations with the Tunku before such questions were answered, since so to do would inevitably limit the freedom of Ministers in seeking the best answers: but it simply was not possible to have the questions adequately considered in time for talks with the Tunku before the end of October, especially as the British forces which at present relied upon bases in Malaya and Singapore were by no means all United Kingdom forces but contained substantial Australian and New Zealand elements, so that the United Kingdom could not enter unilaterally into firm agreements with the Tunku about the future of the bases and must carry Australia and New Zealand with it in full consultation.

The validity and importance of these considerations were fully recognised in the discussion and the following were the other main points made:—

(a) The present Australian line was that we must make sure in our dealings with the Tunku about Greater Malaysia that its creation would in no way require us to give up the defence facilities which we needed for the proper fulfilment of our existing obligations of all kinds.

(b) The internal security situation in Singapore might gravely deteriorate if Mr. Lee's position was destroyed and we were unable to make any progress on Greater Malaysia. In that case we might be deprived for a considerable time to come of any hope of obtaining the release of the forces committed to internal security duties in Singapore.

(c) We should have to be very careful about the manner and timing of any reduction in the strength of our forces in Singapore since precipitate change would create grave problems of employment and other kinds.

(d) We must not overlook the likely reaction of the Americans to all these matters. For political reasons they wanted us to maintain a military presence of significant proportions. On the other hand it was argued that we might have to get it across to the Americans that, whereas our military presence in South East Asia had hitherto been characterised chiefly by the possession of bases and nuclear power, our liberal approach to the political problems of the area required us to change the form and method of our military contribution to its security and that, while we should continue to make an effective contribution as a nuclear power, we must do so from outside the South East Asian land area.

The Committee:—
(1)   Invited the Ministry of Defence to prepare a statement of the defence problem for inclusion in a draft report to Ministers.
(2)   Invited the Colonial Office to elaborate Part II of the Commonwealth Relations Office draft note, in particular to spell out the broad situation from which arose the urgency of the whole matter and the differences of view between the Tunku and ourselves with regard to the Borneo Territories.
(3)   Invited the Commonwealth Relations Office to set out more fully the premises of our approach to the Great [sic] Malaysia project.
(4)   Invited the Commonwealth Relations Office to co-ordinate the production of a draft report for consideration at a further meeting of 4th October.

63   PREM 11/3422   28 Sept 1961

'Greater Malaysia': inward telegram no 715 from Sir G Tory to Mr Sandys, reporting further on the Tunku's reaction to Mr Macmillan's latest message

Greater Malaysia

My immediately following telegram[1] contains message for Prime Minister from Tunku handed to me this morning under covering letter from Ghazali dated today.

2.   In long discussion with Ghazali yesterday it merged that one of main troubles is the Tunku's persistent suspicion that we still hope that he will be compelled by deteriorating political situation in Singapore to accept responsibility for Singapore before we are able to hand over Borneo Territories and that he will thus be left 'holding the baby'. This suspicion has been reinforced in his mind by Razak. This was confirmed to me today by Thompson[2] (here on his way to Vietnam) who was present yesterday when Razak was trying to curdle Tunku's blood on subject of Singapore. Ismail's contribution lately has been to argue that addition of Borneo Territories is not in fact going to help Tunku in the slightest with additional Chinese problem which he will acquire with Singapore.

3.   Moral of this seems to Ghazali and me to be that a considerable advance would be made by us with Tunku if we were able to assure him that sovereignty over Borneo Territories would only be transferred to Federation simultaneously with that over Singapore.

4.   Tunku still has difficulty in understanding why we insist so much on consulting 'people' of Borneo Territories on question of Greater Malaysia. He recalls

---

[1] See 64.   [2] For Robert Thompson, see 32, n 3.

a number of instances in our recent history when control of Territories has been transferred without waiting for them to reach the stage of full democratic self-Government. Given urgency of need to preserve these Territories from an uncertain and probably unsatisfactory fate why were we not content to consult the Governments they now had. With his ambivalent approach to questions of self-determination Tunku is inclined to attribute our wish to consult these people to our intention to stall rather than to our sense of trusteeship. On this point he is still more inclined to respect our need to satisfy our own Parliament than our obligation to do justice to Borneo peoples.

5.   I have no doubt that if Tunku's visit to London is put off for long Greater Malaysia scheme will suffer serious setback apart altogether from unfortunate effect on Lee's political position. People here who have sincere misgivings about Greater Malaysia will be given time and encouragement to develop their arguments. Ghazali and I think it might be possible still to persuade Tunku to go to London fairly soon if not next month if we could give him assurance on following lines which I have told Ghazali represents absolute limit which could be expected from us at this stage. *Begins*.

(a) H.M.G. accept principle of Greater Malaysia.

(b) They will wholeheartedly commend scheme to peoples of Borneo Territories in hope that Greater Malaysia might be implemented with the consent of these Territories by 1963.

(c) Subject to assurance that Borneo Territories were willing to enter proposed association with Federation of Malaya, H.M.G. undertake that they would transfer sovereignty over Borneo Territories to Federation of Matala [sic] at the same time as or before they transfer sovereignty over Singapore. *Ends*.

6.   Question of defence facilities in Singapore remains. My latest information confirms that Razak has infected Tunku with some of his apprehension about your [sic] retaining unrestricted facilities in Singapore but according to Ghazali, Tunku still thinks it should be possible to devise some formula which would satisfy both him and us. As you will see Tunku says in his message that question of Singapore base is one which will have to be sorted out once position is clear on future of Territories but this problem is not insurmountable. I do not know what decision has been taken in London on this question but I imagine you will wish to consider whether any assurance to Tunku on above lines should include also some reservation on following lines which would not of course be for publication. *Begins*.

It would of course also be necessary for H.M.G. to work out with Federation Government some practical means whereby they could continue to discharge their international defence obligations after the transfer of sovereignty over Singapore. *Ends*.

7.   I am satisfied that in adopting his latest attitude Tunku is genuinely anxious about his ability to sell Greater Malaysia to his Malays. They would never accept any arrangement under which Federation acquired Singapore in isolation. To enable Lee Kuan Yew to play his hand the way he wants it in Singapore, Tunku has gone to the absolute limit in allowing Lee to project idea of Federation/Singapore merger as something separate from transfer of Borneo Territories. Tunku decided recently that for him to go hand in hand with Lee to London to get approval for Federation/Singapore blueprint would deepen suspicion on part of Malays that he was going to

take over Singapore whatever happened. This was why he decided to go alone. Knowing that his Malays are already taking him a great deal on trust over Greater Malaysia and have deep misgiving about it, Tunku has also concluded now that he should not go to London unless he is sure of coming back with some evidence of success. When we first invited Tunku to go to London he saw this visit as the second stage of Merdeka and planned his journey to coincide exactly with original journey to London from which he returned with assurance of independence even to extent of sailing in the very same ship and of breaking his journey at the same point.[3] This may not be an important factor but it helps to illustrate Tunku's attitude to this second 'historic' journey and his wish to be sure of having something significant to bring back.

8.   I very much hope we can give Tunku quickly some such assurance as I have suggested and that we can persuade him to go to London in the near future as we had planned. You will see from my telegram No. 713 that Tunku has told Thompson he proposes to visit Saigon on 19th October for about a week ostensibly as President of Malayan Football Association but really in order to have talks with President Diem[4] about situation in Vietnam. I have no doubt that if we were able to give Tunku quick and satisfactory assurance, London visit would take priority over this especially if in meantime Lee Kuan Yew impressed Tunku with desirability from his standpoint of Tunku adhering to October date. On other hand you may now need a little more time.

---

[3] See 52, n 3.

[4] Ngo Dinh Diem, president of the Republic of (South) Vietnam from its proclamation on 26 Oct 1955 until his assassination on 2 Nov 1963.

64   PREM 11/3422   28 Sept 1961
'Greater Malaysia': inward telegram no 716 from Sir G Tory to Mr Sandys, forwarding a message from Tunku Abdul Rahman to Mr Macmillan

[The Tunku had not yet succumbed to Macmillan's blandishments. On the contrary, determined to get an early decision on the sovereignty of the Borneo territories, he recommended postponing talks until Macmillan had had a chance to come out to SE Asia and gather first-hand information. On seeing the Tunku's message, Sandys was reported to have said that 'we could not allow the susceptibilities of headhunters to wreck this project (or words to that effect)' (Wallace to West, 29 Sept 1961, CO 1030/983). There was no doubt, Tory informed Selkirk, that the Tunku was in a 'dangerous frame of mind'. While he hoped to induce Lee Kuan Yew to dissuade the Tunku from 'any waspish public statement', Tory also urged the CRO to reassure him on the lines set out in document 63 (see Tory to Selkirk, tel no 718, 29 Sept 1961, PREM 11/3422).]

Greater Malaysia
Following is text of Tunku's message to Prime Minister. *Begins*:

My dear Prime Minister,
Thank you for your message of 23rd September, in which you conveyed the wish that we might meet on 23rd October 1961. I observed from your message that you would need time to study the implications of the Malaysia plan before you could give a decision on the matter. I would like to say once again that our concept of Malaysia

implies the integration of the three Borneo territories on the same basis as the other existing states of the Federation of Malaya while Singapore may be merged with certain powers reserved for the state in matters of education and labour. The integration of the Borneo territories with the Federation should be agreed now and take effect before or at least simultaneously with Singapore. The main issue and in fact the only issue therefore is whether the British Government (? would) be ready to relinquish their sovereignty over the Borneo territories before or at least simultaneously with Singapore in favour of Malaysia. Any preliminary discussion between us would serve no useful purpose unless this issue is first settled. From my conversation with Sir Geofroy Tory I had obtained the impression that the British Government would not be able to decide until they are certain that they can get a wholehearted support from Parliament and the people of Borneo territories. I hope it is appreciated that as far as my Government is concerned the main reason for the merger of the Borneo territories is to prevent Singapore from falling into the hands of the Communists, which we are sure would happen if she were to be given independence. With the exception of the Communist elements and their proxies all Singapore politicians realise that in such an event disaster would follow which will affect the rest of South East Asia. I have emphasised that my Government would not be able to carry the idea of merger of Singapore unless the Borneo territories are merged with the Federation as well. Frankly, if we are prone to think in terms of balances, even the Borneo territories would not be an adequate compensation for our trouble in the event of a merger with Singapore. Perhaps I should venture to propose that it would be best if you have a little time after some of the more serious of the world crises had blown over to visit those territories and this part in order that you may gather a first-hand information. If it is not possible for you to come here, then I would suggest that Mr. Lee Kuan Yew and the present leaders or representatives of the Borneo territories be invited to London for a discussion with you. Your visit to this (? area) or a meeting in London with the leaders of Singapore and Borneo territories I think would materially assist you in arriving at your decision. Our meeting should take place only after you are in a position to give a firm commitment of the British Government in favour of Malaysia. The question of the Singapore base within the framework of the mutual Defence Agreement, constitutional procedures and administration arrangements are matters which will naturally have to be sorted out once the position is clear regarding the future of these territories but these, as I have said before, are not insurmountable.

My [sic] Lee Kuan Yew is worried about his position and the future of Singapore but I am afraid I cannot help him much until I have received a firm answer from you about the transfer of the sovereignty over the Borneo territories to the Federation.

65   CAB 134/1929, ff 87–99   29 Sept 1961

'Our foreign and defence policy for the future': memorandum by Mr Macmillan for the Cabinet Committee on Future Policy.   [Extract]

[This comprehensive review provided the context for the high-level thinking on the future of the Singapore base and Britain's role in SE Asia and suggested that 'the concept of Greater Malaysia seems to offer the best hope for the future'. It was discussed on 6 Oct

1961 (see 68). The following extracts have been printed: the prime minister's introductory note; section I paragraphs 1–6 (general issues) and 16–19 (SE Asia); section II paragraphs 23–29. Material on the Mediterranean, Middle East, Africa, Hong Kong, and Europe has been omitted from this volume, as has the annex showing a forecast of local defence expenditure abroad. Since the document is a copy, the original having been retained under section 3(4) of the Public Records Act 1958, there may be other omissions.]

At least two important studies are being made by officials about our future policy. One group (the Future Policy Committee under the chairmanship of Sir Norman Brook) is reviewing our commitments in theatres outside Europe to see what changes of policy might be possible.[1] The military advisers, at the direction of the Minister of Defence, have been examining, for the longer term, the practicability of meeting our overseas commitments by a strategy based on greater air and sea mobility; and, for the shorter term, in what way, consistent with their long-term thinking, the reductions which we need to make in our oversea military expenditure could be obtained. It is naturally proving difficult to relate all this work together—it is not easy to devise the means until we are sure of the ends, and to some extent the ends depend on the means available. Meanwhile, we are under pressure to deal with two separate problems, both of them of great urgency:—

(i) The need to reduce our expenditure overseas, including our military expenditure, to fulfil the declared aims of the Chancellor of the Exchequer.
(ii) The need to decide how to secure the man-power target which we have accepted for our armed forces.

2. I do not think that we shall resolve these problems in time, and keep control over our economic, foreign and defence policies unless we can find some way of reaching agreement quickly on:—

(a) what commitments oversea we must maintain for the next ten years or so;
(b) what principles we should adopt for our defence policy, in order to meet those commitments.

3. If we could reach agreement under both these headings, then the Minister of Defence would be in a position to give the Chiefs of Staff and the military planners a politico-military directive in broad terms, on the basis of which they could recommend an organisation, strategy and deployment of our defence forces for the next decade.

4. In the attached paper. I have accordingly made an attempt to indicate the answers to two questions:—

I. What are the commitments oversea, involving defence forces, which we must maintain during, say, the next decade, having regard to likely political developments affecting our defence agreements, bases, lines of communication, and so on, and having regard also to the undoubted need for economy, both budgetary and in oversea expenditure, which will persist and even increase?
II. How can the limited resources which we can afford for defence purposes best be used to support our oversea commitments in the next decade, bearing in mind the requirement that these resources must also serve the other aims of our

---

[1] cf, the studies of future policy done in 1960, 28 and 29 above.

defence policy e.g., the support of N.A.T.O., and under present policy the strategic nuclear deterrent?

5.   I propose that a small group of Ministers most closely concerned should first discuss Part I. When we see how we get on, we might discuss Part II on a later occasion.

I.

'What are the commitments oversea, involving defence forces, which we must maintain during, say, the next decade, having regard to likely political developments affecting our defence agreements, bases, lines of communication, and so on, and having regard also to the undoubted need for economy, both budgetary and in oversea expenditure, which will persist and even increase?'

General objectives
1.   (i) The general aim of our foreign policy is to prevent further areas of the world from falling under the influence or domination of the Sino-Soviet *bloc*.
(ii) We have also a direct responsibility for maintaining the internal security and effective protection of the remaining colonial territories.
(iii) Our foreign policy must also be directed to protecting our economic interests oversea, notably our oil interests in the Persian Gulf.

2.   To serve primarily the purpose of (i) above, it is a particular aim to support the regional alliances, N.A.T.O., CENTO and SEATO. The Commonwealth connection, though it is much less of a military and more of a political connection than these regional alliances, is also of value for the same purpose.

Political developments
3.   None of these alliances or links is static; all will inevitably suffer adjustment as time passes. It is important to bear this in mind in deciding how far we should rely on military, and how far on political or economic means to secure our aims. The number of allies on whom we can completely rely, in using military means, may well dwindle—the United States, Australia and New Zealand, Canada and (let us hope) most of our N.A.T.O. allies will be almost the only ones.

4.   We are likely to lose, too, the full use of some of our present bases and our overflying rights, partly because other colonial territories will achieve independence, partly because neutral nations will be under increasing pressure not to assist our military operations. We must moreover realise that world opinion will more and more criticise the use of military means. We have nearly reached a position in which we can only exercise our rights under a defence agreement with another country in order to take military action (even if it is only precautionary) if the government (and perhaps the people) of that country are in full support of our action.

5.   The moral is not that we must despair of ever using military means, but that we must plan for their use only on a basis on which we can rely for the next decade (see Part II). In considering what our oversea commitments should be, we must have in mind the need to be realistic in this respect.

Areas of substantial military expenditure
6.   The areas oversea in which we incur substantial military expenditure are set out in the following paragraphs, with some points to suggest what our future

commitments in those areas in the next decade should be. The current annual rate of oversea expenditure for defence in these areas is indicated in each case and forecasts of expenditure up to and including 1966/7, by areas, showing works services and other expenditure separately, on the basis of present plans, are contained at Annex. But of course, important though foreign exchange is, the real issue is the burden which the commitments in each area, and the totality or the burdens in all areas, place on our national resources. A reduction in our commitments, with a consequent saving in man-power and accordingly in weapons and equipment, means a reduction in the total defence budget. . . .

16. *South East Asia* (£45.5 millions)
Our present commitments arise mainly from a mixture of our interest in preventing the expansion of Sino–Soviet influence, particularly in South East Asia, and our responsibility for the internal security and defence of our colonial territories; but, mingled with these aims, there has also been our wish to help in the protection of Australia and New Zealand, and our hope to maintain our standing in this area in the eyes of the United States. We are all conscious that the potential changes in South East Asia may come about very quickly. So any review of our commitments here should be radical and imaginative.

17. Although study of the problem has not been completed, by common consent the concept of a Greater Malaysia seems to offer the best hope for the future. Of course we cannot hope, even so, to keep all our existing facilities or freedom of action; but, correspondingly, we may be able to dispose of some of our obligations, without undue risk.

18. If Greater Malaysia came about, we would presumably give up our responsibility for internal security in Singapore. The present burden of this responsibility is in any case partly due to our need to use the Singapore base for our part in SEATO operations. In a Greater Malaysia, though we might hope that the Tunku would be sympathetic, we could not *rely* on the use of Singapore. This raises the question—how can we play our part (or rather, an acceptable part) in SEATO—and in ANZAM, from the point of view of Australia, New Zealand and the United States—without relying on Singapore? The developing situation (it seems to me) will drive our allies to realise that our role in South East Asia must be reassessed. We should take advantage of that, and try to adjust our agreed role in the way that suits us best, politically as well as financially.

19. Such a reassessment is a major undertaking. Need we provide a *land* contribution at all to SEATO operations? If so, need it be at a forward base, or could it not be in reserve (in Australia)? In either case, can we dispense with permanent large-scale forward bases? Do we need *any* nuclear capability for our forces in this area, either to impress the Australians or to influence (and perhaps restrain) the United States? Might the deployment of some such capability from Australian bases make it easier for our allies to accept a further reduction in our land forces? These questions are perhaps directed more towards means than ends. Politically, our main objective (except for the very short term) should be to play a role in the alliances in the area, which would be acceptable to our partners, particularly the Australians and the United States, and considerably less onerous in military terms than our present commitments. . . .

II.

'How can the limited resources which we can afford for defence purposes best be used to support our oversea commitments in the next decade, bearing in mind the requirement that these resources must also serve the other aims of our defence policy e.g., the support of N.A.T.O., and under present policy the strategic nuclear deterrent?'

23.   Let us assume that, as a result of discussion of Part I, we have succeeded in defining our future (longer-term) commitments in the various main areas in the world. The military advisers will then need some further guidance, if they are to be in a position to make recommendations about the organisation, strategy and disposition of our defence forces, about a number of important issues. I set these issues out in the following paragraphs, with some provisional comments.

24.   *Should we continue our independent contribution to the strategic nuclear deterrent, and if so on what sort of scale and by what sort of means?*
I have indicated in Part I, paragraph 22, the military arguments for maintaining an independent contribution under our national control in the last resort, and there is the political argument—valid by past experience—that our measure of independence in this field enables us to influence United States policy. (Independence in this sense would not be inconsistent with sharing political control for some worthwhile purpose e.g. to help to discourage the emergence of other independent nuclear powers, or as part of an advantageous political bargain.) Although with technical advances our strategic nuclear forces may in the longer-term be a dwindling asset, they are at present of very great significance, and re-equipped with SKYBOLT would remain so for most of this decade. There would be no sense in throwing this asset away. But, for the longer-term, do we need, or could we afford, to replace it, at the end of its useful life, with an entirely new form of strategic nuclear deterrent—such as V.C.10's with SKYBOLT, or POLARIS submarines?

25.   *What man-power should be available for the Services? Will national service, in some form, be reintroduced if necessary to provide a minimum?*
Whether or not national service is to be introduced in the short-term, either in connection with Berlin, or to meet a temporary shortage, is irrelevant to the longer-term issue. For economic reasons, we cannot in any case afford to assign more than (say) 380,000 men to the Services. But if we take a realistic view about the commitments we should accept in the long-term, we may well not need defence forces of this size. In any case, the most efficient and economic use of this manpower can be made if the Services are on an all-Regular basis.

26.   *What facilities under the control of other governments (bases, overflying rights, etc.) can it be assumed will be available for the next decade?*
Should we plan on the basis that we can only rely on facilities in territories where we retain sovereignty and on those provided by a small range of reliable allies, e.g., the United States, Canada, Australia, New Zealand, and perhaps South Africa. Some facilities, e.g. overflying rights, can in practice be enforced in an emergency, e.g. by aircraft flying too high to be intercepted, even against the wish of the country

concerned; but presumably it would be unsound to base our strategy on this fact. Should our strategy therefore be primarily based on freedom of movement in, on or over the high seas?

27. *How far will technological developments in weapons etc. be freely available, having regard to their expense?*
Technological advances will clearly provide our forces with greater power and mobility—if we can foot the bill. This is a very difficult problem of selection and balance. We shall clearly have to rely on the principle of interdependence to keep our expenditure on research and development within reasonable bounds. Even so, the production cost of all equipment is continually rising and we must ensure that the 'forward look' estimates are realistic in this respect.

28. *What will be the future level of expenditure which can be afforded for defence? Can the military planners be given a ceiling?*
This raises serious difficulties. From one point of view, anything necessary for the national defence must be afforded. But if the national economy is to survive, some limit is essential. It is for this reason that we must reduce our objectives and commitments to those that are vital. For purposes of planning defence expenditure, is not the best guide that contained in the repot [sic] by the Treasury on public expenditure and resources 1961/2 to 1965/6?

29. *How can the present organisation for defence be improved in order to secure the most efficient and economic use of the resources available for defence?*
It is quite clear that we shall need to make the fullest use of whatever resources we can afford for defence if we are to realise our objectives and fulfil our commitments over the next years. We cannot afford any slack or waste. In any case, with the prospective loss of some of our oversea bases, a drastic re-casting of defence strategy will be necessary.

These needs are likely to require a re-examination of the functions of the three Services, and they certainly will call for greater flexibility in the use of the various forces in each Service and in inter-Service co-operation. It may be desirable to examine means of facilitating the transfer of man-power between the Services, and the possibilities of integrating common services, in the interests both of efficiency and economy.

It will be desirable to improve the co-ordination of forward planning for defence, including research and development. It may also be desirable to clarify the functions of the Ministry of Defence and the other Departments concerned with defence.

There is also the question of improving the unified control of operational and major administrative policies. This means developing still further the inter-Service character of the machine which the Minister of Defence needs to carry out his wide responsibilities for the central organisation for defence (the 1958 White Paper). In short, far-reaching changes may be necessary, especially in the habit of mind of our defence organisation, and I believe that the staff concerned are ready to help to bring this about.

66   PREM 11/3422, PM(61)75   3 Oct 1961

[Rescuing the London talks]: minute from Mr Macleod to Mr Macmillan

[Following Macleod's advice, a message was drafted for Macmillan to send to the Tunku. Rather than prevaricate further and in order to maintain the momentum of planning, he approved 'Greater Malaysia' in principle (despite the fact that the Cabinet had not yet approved it in principle) and renewed his invitation to talks in London which the Malayan prime minister accepted (see 67 and 69). The first time the proposal for 'Greater Malaysia' went to Cabinet was on 10 Oct when ministers recognised that defence interests might be better served by promoting 'Greater Malaysia' than by allowing Singapore to claim independence as a separate unit and when they approved the invitation for the Tunku to come to London for talks 'in the near future' (CAB 128/35, CC 55(61)5 and CO 1030/984, nos 665 and 680).]

The Official Committee have considered the Tunku's message to you of the 28th September.[1] The Committee have concluded that, if there is not to be grave danger of the whole operation foundering, every effort should be made to persuade the Tunku to accept your proposal for a meeting in London.

It is clear however that the Tunku is in a difficult and dangerous mood, and we shall not succeed with him unless we can very quickly reassure him that we accept in principle the concept of a Greater Malaysia and that, without committing ourselves on form or timing, we will commend it to the Borneo territories.

We have not yet discussed the matter in detail in Cabinet, but I agree with the Committee that we can and should go as far as this. Lord Selkirk and the Governors of the Borneo territories concur. The important thing is to get the Tunku to face up realistically to the very difficult problems involved in achieving what he wants. We shall only be able to do this if we can discuss them with him face to face.

In the absence of the Commonwealth Secretary, who is also very anxious that the proposed meeting should take place, I send you a draft which the Committee accordingly suggest for your reply to the Tunku.[2] I am sure this is the right line.

I also send you the draft of a message for you to send to Mr. Menzies and Mr. Holyoake.[3]

I am sending copies of this to the Chancellor, the Foreign Secretary, the Minister of Defence and the Parliamentary Under-Secretary in the Commonwealth Relations Office.

---

[1] See 64.   [2] Not printed, but see 67.
[3] Not printed, but see 67, note

67   PREM 11/3422   3 Oct 1961

[Rescuing the London talks]: outward telegram no 1478 from Mr Sandys to Sir G Tory, forwarding a message from Mr Macmillan to Tunku Abdul Rahman

[Macmillan also had this message copied to Menzies and Holyoake (prime ministers of Australia and New Zealand) with the following minute: 'It is clear from his latest message to me that the Tunku has worked himself up into rather a difficult frame of mind. We are all agreed that the idea of Greater Malaysia offers the best prospects for the future and that it is in all our interests to give it a fair wind. But the Tunku's inclination towards crash tactics may wreck the whole concept. It is all the more important therefore to get him here as soon as possible for frank and personal discussion. I am sending you a copy of my latest message to him in which I have gone as far as possible at this stage to reassure him and have pressed him to agree to an early meeting' (PREM 11/3422, T 560/61)]

Please pass following message from the Prime Minister to the Tunku. *Begins*:

My dear Prime Minister,
I was most disturbed when I read in your message of 28th September that you might prefer to postpone our proposed meeting in London.[1]

2.   I have as you know taken a close personal interest from the start in your plan for a Greater Malaysia and I was particularly disappointed that I had to cancel my plans for a visit to Malaya in September. I very much wish to have an early opportunity of visiting you, but I fear that this will not be possible for a little time.

3.   Meanwhile the immediate question is how best we can make progress on this very important matter. There is, I believe, already a very wide measure of agreement between us on our aims. Indeed I would not have suggested that you come to London for a meeting unless I had felt confident that we should be able to make useful progress together.

4.   I should make it clear at once that the British Government welcome and accept the concept of a Greater Malaysia which would incorporate Malaya, Singapore and the three Borneo territories.

5.   I fully understand that it is of basic importance to you that the Borneo territories should be included in the plan. Their inclusion is our aim too. Greater Malaysia must be brought about by a concerted operation covering both Singapore and the Borneo territories.

6.   So far as we are concerned, we believe that the best future for the Borneo territories lies in close political association with the Federation and Singapore, and my purpose in suggesting early talks in London was to see how we could best work together with you in attaining this end. There is already a considerable body of opinion in the Borneo territories which accepts Malaysia as the ultimate aim, but there are anxieties, which we cannot ignore, about the form of the association and about timing. We must therefore bend our efforts, in close consultation with you, to bring the peoples of the Borneo territories freely to join with you.

7.   I agree with you that there would be great dangers to stability in the area as a whole and in Singapore in particular if the present opportunity is let slip. It is therefore urgent that you and we should consider jointly what means are best calculated to achieve our objectives as quickly as may be possible.

8.   We have much to plan together. We shall wish to discuss with you what might be the constitutional position of the Borneo territories within a Greater Malaysia and the best means of preparing the ground in them and presenting our ideas to their peoples. Other matters are the economic development of the Borneo territories and administrative arrangements, including the staffing of the public services. It will, as you appreciate, be necessary to ensure that future defence arrangements are on the right lines; the Australian and New Zealand Governments are of course closely concerned in this.

---

[1] See 64.

9.   Imaginative plans of this kind are, I am sure, best examined in the first instance by personal discussion in the tradition of Commonwealth consultation. In this way we can insure against the misunderstandings which are liable to arise from long range correspondence.

10.   I very much hope therefore that, in the light of what I have said as to our attitude and approach to these matters, you will feel assured that a meeting between us will be fruitful. I understand, and agree with, your sense of urgency about the project.

11.   There are real problems to be surmounted in bringing it about, and I am sure that much the best way of making early progress would be for us to meet as soon as possible and talk over together how best to handle them. My colleagues and I are therefore holding ourselves in readiness for a meeting in the week beginning the 23rd October.

12.   If you agree we ought to issue a public statement as soon as possible and I attach a copy of what we would propose to say.[2] As to this I am convinced that it would hinder the attainment of what you and I wish to see come about if any public statements were made prematurely which might lead the Borneo peoples to think that decisions about their future had been taken by others without any consultation with them. The terms of the statement have therefore been most carefully chosen so as to avoid this danger.

Yours very sincerely,
Harold Macmillan   Ends.

My immediately following telegram contains text of Draft Announcement.

---

[2] Not printed.

---

68   CAB 134/1929, FP(61) 1st meeting   6 Oct 1961
'Future foreign and defence policy': Cabinet Future Policy Committee minutes, agreeing to Greater Malaysia in principle

[Extract]

[Chaired by Macmillan, the meeting was attended by the following ministers: Butler (Home Office), Selwyn Lloyd (Treasury), Home (FO), Sandys (CRO), Macleod (CO), Watkinson (Defence). Sir Frederick Hoyer Millar, permanent under-secretary at the FO, was also present. Macleod would be replaced as secretary of state for the colonies by Maudling a few days later, on 9 Oct. The committee adjourned to 10 Oct when it resumed discussion of document 65. The extracts printed here relate to those extracts selected for document 65.]

The Committee had before them a memorandum by the Prime Minister discussing the probable nature of our oversea commitments for the next decade and the means by which it might be possible to meet them.

The Prime Minister said that it would, as a beginning, be convenient to make two separate approaches to this problem. The first would be to divide our overseas bases into two broad classes; Class I would contain those on which we could rely for unrestricted use for any purpose within our own discretion and Class II those where our freedom of action was likely to be hampered by local susceptibilities. Within

Class II there might of course be wide variations in the extent of the restraints to which we were exposed. In most cases, however, we should be able to use bases in this class for total war, when we should be justified in ignoring local susceptibilities, and in many cases we might use them for a once for all limited war operation. The second approach would be to review our probable oversea commitments and objectives overseas during the next decade. The two approaches would provide assessments of the means and the ends of overseas policy; the two were of course to a large extent interdependent and in some theatres we might be compelled, in the face of local political developments, to choose whether we should modify our current policies or whether we should seek new ways of supporting them.

In discussion of the extent to which we could rely on overseas bases for the next decade the following points were made:—

. . .

The Far East
(e) Singapore had so far been regarded as a base of the Class I type, but when it attained independence, either as part of a Greater Malaysia or in isolation, it would certainly be relegated to Class II. Indeed, the Commissioner-General for South East Asia had recently expressed fears that even now an attempt to use troops based on Singapore for certain purposes might be opposed by the local population. For planning purposes, therefore, Singapore should, like Malaya, be placed in Class II. It was unlikely that we could rely on any base within the area of Greater Malaysia, for example, in Borneo, remaining in Class I.

Future policy in the Far East
The Committee then discussed our future commitments and objectives in South East Asia and Hong Kong. The following points were made:—

(f) The most urgent task was to determine our attitude to the proposal for a Greater Malaysia. It was clear that if a Greater Malaysia were established our freedom to use the Singapore base would be restricted; indeed the Tunku had stated publicly that in that event the Singapore Defence Agreement would have to be renegotiated. It also seemed likely that, with the increased proportion of Chinese in the new state, the Tunku might be increasingly compelled to oppose any projects in support of SEATO. Nevertheless, a completely independent Singapore would be more disadvantageous to our interests than a Greater Malaysia. Further, unless the present Prime Minister of Singapore, Mr. Lee Kuan Yew, could demonstrate that his policy for merger with Malaya was proceeding successfully, he might well lose control in the very near future; in that case his Government would almost certainly be replaced by one of the extreme left wing. It was therefore in our general interest to support the project for a Greater Malaysia. The difficulty was that we were not in a position to commit the political future of our Borneo territories without regard to the wishes of their populations, whereas the Tunku would not risk a merger with Singapore alone. Although the territories appeared to favour the concept of Greater Malaysia in principle, they required time in which to attain a higher standard of political development before joining. If decisions in principle were taken now, it might be possible to achieve a Greater Malaysia by 1963. We should therefore support the project, but without prejudicing the ultimate freedom of choice of the Borneo territories.

(g) As part of the new arrangements, we should transfer our responsibility for the internal security of Singapore and the Borneo territories to the new state. We should also seek to negotiate a continuance of our present freedom to use Singapore. We should, however, recognise that in practice it would be extremely difficult to use Singapore as a base if the population was actively hostile. It might be possible to operate from our Naval and air bases which were reasonably self-contained. It would, however, become increasingly difficult to use Singapore as an Army base; it was normally the presence of troops, rather than ships or aircraft which tended to rouse local resentment. It would therefore become progressively more difficult to rely on using for operations in support of SEATO the Commonwealth Brigade Group, which relied on transit facilities in Singapore. It would, however, be imprudent as yet to seek to withdraw it; it provided the first example of a joint Commonwealth force in peace time and its withdrawal would not be welcome to Australia and New Zealand, whom it should be our policy to encourage to bear their full share of responsibility for the defence of the area. We should, however, recognise that in the longer term (certainly not before Greater Malaysia had been established) it might be necessary to withdraw the Commonwealth Brigade Group, possibly to a base in Australia. . . .

69 PREM 11/3422   7 Oct 1961
'Greater Malaysia': inward telegram no 746 from Sir G Tory to Mr Sandys, forwarding a personal message from Tunku Abdul Rahman to Mr Macmillan in reply to document 67

Following is text of personal message from Tunku. *Begins*.

My dear Prime Minister,
Thank you for your personal message of 3rd October.

The constitutional position of the North Borneo Territories in Malaysia outlined in that message would be on the same basis as the other existing States of the Federation of Malaya. It is of course envisaged that there will be transitional and other provisions to meet local requirements. The essential point is the transfer of British sovereignty over North Borneo Territories to Malaya for the Federation of Malaysia and this should be done before or at least simultaneously with the merger of Singapore.

I am deeply appreciative of the personal interest you have taken in what may be regarded as a matter for common endeavour. There are difficulties which we must resolve arising out of anxieties of people of these Territories. However, this is nothing new as we had to go through all these difficulties ourselves before independence. Much of these fears can be removed if the advantages rather than the disadvantages could be emphasised and the British Government would unreservedly commend the proposal of Malaysia to the Borneo Territories. Of course, the ideal way would be to seek the opinions and views of responsible people there but as you have already acknowledged we do not have this much time at our disposal. I am sure you agree that we have to resort to the process of telescoping time by some crash programme. But such bold steps will I am certain prove advantageous.

As you are already aware we have to reckon with the fact that the status of Singapore would be the subject of review in 1963. It cannot be ruled out that Mr. Lee Kuan Yew's Government might not last that time and a general election might perhaps return a Government not so well disposed towards the merger of Singapore with the Federation or vice versa. This therefore makes me feel that we cannot wait for 1963 but that Malaysia should be brought into being as early as reasonably convenient to both our Governments. Hence my anxiety that there should be a firm commitment on the part of the British Government now in the belief that a delay might defeat our common objective. I have committed myself to visiting President Ngo Din [sic] Diem in Saigon from 20th to 26th October and until I can persuade President Ngo Din Diem to a postponement I cannot say if I can come to London on the date proposed. The situation in Vietnam is serious and getting more so every day and the President is most anxious to get my views on certain matters about which he considered I could be of help. I hope you will agree to an alternative date, perhaps during the first week of November in case I am unable to have my visit to Vietnam postponed.

I am bringing a motion on the subject of Malaysia and Singapore merger in Parliament to seek support at the coming session beginning on 16th October. You may already be aware that the Colombo Plan conference will be held in Kuala Lumpur from 30th October to 18th November and I am hoping that I should have an opportunity to entertain the delegates while they are here.

I agree to the release of the text of your draft announcement subject of course to the (? possibility) of the date of the actual visit being altered as suggested above. However, I would like to see a couple of amendments to the text. With reference to the third sentence of the draft text I would like to suggest the following be substituted: 'Her Majesty's Government have welcomed Tunku Abdul Rahman's constructive proposals which would bring the Federation of Malaya, Singapore, Brunei, North Borneo and Sarawak into close political and economic association.' This would remove any ambiguity and thereby avoid misunderstanding and confusion in the public mind on how the matter stands between us. Furthermore I would like to suggest that while I agree that the wishes of the local people should not be ignored the inclusion of your last sentence in the draft statement will over-emphasise the need for consultation with the people of the Borneo Territories who are at this moment not sufficiently advanced in their political outlook to give an unbiased opinion of their own as they are very much under the influence of the British Colonial administrators.

Yours very sincerely,
Tunku Abdul Rahman Putra. *Ends.*

70   CAB 134/1929, FP(61) 2nd meeting   10 Oct 1961

'Future foreign and defence policy': Cabinet Future Policy Committee minutes, regarding Greater Malaysia and regional security   [Extract]

[Present: Macmillan, Butler, Home, Sandys, Watkinson, Perth, and Thorneycroft (Aviation).]

The Committee resumed its discussion of a memorandum by the Prime Minister discussing our oversea defence policy for the next decade.[1]

The Prime Minister recalled that at their previous meeting the Committee had divided overseas bases into two classes: Class I, those of which we might expect to have unrestricted use and Class II, those where our freedom of action might be hampered by local suceptibilities (except in the case of total war or possibly for a once-for-all limited operation).

In discussion of South East Asia, there had been general agreement to four proposals:—

(i) That we should try to take advantage of the Great [sic] Malaysia concept so as to retain Naval and air facilities in Singapore, which would be freely available to us in normal times and might conceivably be used as a forward operating base in war.

(ii) That we should continue to contribute to the Commonwealth Brigade Group, stationed for the time being in Malaya, and forming a contribution to SEATO.

(iii) That for the longer term we should have to reassess, with Australia, New Zealand and the United States, the nature of our role in SEATO.

(iv) That while Hong Kong had no value as a base, we should seek to maintain our position by providing for its internal security and by making its occupation by Communist China impossible without an operation of war.

It was now necessary to consider our policy and commitments in other theatres.

In discussion the following points were made:—

. . .

The Far East

(g) In the forthcoming discussions with the Tunku it should be made clear that we intended, on the establishment of a Greater Malaysia, to hand over our internal security responsibilities, but to seek to retain our defence facilities. Although the Tunku would be unwilling to commit himself publicly to allowing facilities in Greater Malaysia to be used for operations in support of SEATO, it was quite possible that, in a situation which threatened a closer Communist threat to Malaya, he might be willing to acquiesce in operations from his territory, except the direct use of airfields for bombing. Nevertheless, it would be wise to consider, in consultation with Australia and New Zealand, alternative methods of fulfilling our SEATO commitments after Greater Malaysia were established. It should be our general aim to reduce our forces to the Commonwealth Brigade Group stationed near Malacca, and the Naval and air facilities on Singapore Island. . . .

Summing up *The Prime Minister* said that in the light of the discussion he would prepare a directive for a review of our oversea defence policy in the longer term. Meanwhile, it would be advisable for the Minister of Defence to bring to the Defence Committee, after consultation with other Ministers as necessary, any proposals for more immediate savings which might result from the decisions which had been reached. These proposals should include consideration of the possible effects of reductions in troops, for instance demands for compensation from Malta and Cyprus. It was however undesirable to station troops in a country primarily for the purpose of

---

[1] See 65 and 68.

giving it economic assistance; moreover, it could be expected that grants in aid, or other forms of economic assistance, would progressively diminish, whereas the cost of overseas garrisons tended to rise.

In South East Asia we must accept that the best prospect lay in support for the concept of Greater Malaysia, even though this might mean some diminution in our freedom of action in the theatre. In discussions with the Tunku we should seek to retain our present facilities if possible, but for the longer term we would have to be prepared to regard facilities in Greater Malaysia as no more than forward operating bases on the use of which we could not rely in all circumstances. It would be advisable now for him to write to Mr. Menzies and Mr. Holyoake informing them of the lines on which our policy was likely to develop.

It would be necessary at a later stage, as part of the general review of future policy, to consider the future of the deterrent. A suitable time would be early in 1962, when the future of SKYBOLT should be more precisely known.[2]

The Committee:—

(1) Took note that the Prime Minister would issue a directive for a review of defence policy in the longer term.

(2) Took note that the Prime Minister would invite the Minister of Defence to bring to the Defence Committee his proposals for savings in oversea defence expenditure in the short term.

(3) Invited the Commonwealth Secretary, in consultation with the Foreign Secretary and the Minister of Defence, to prepare letters from the Prime Minister to Mr. Menzies and Mr. Holyoake informing them of the probable course of development of our policy in South East Asia.

---

[2] Although Britain possessed independent nuclear weapons, it depended on the USA for the means of their delivery. One possible method was the Skybolt rocket, but, when this was cancelled, Macmillan negotiated with Kennedy at Nassau in Dec 1962 an agreement whereby America would supply Britain with the Polaris-submarine missile-launching system which could be loaded with British weapons, cf 166, note.

71   CO 1030/984, no 786B   12 Oct 1961

[Malayan background to Greater Malaysia]: despatch no 7 from M J Moynihan[1] to Mr Sandys

[This despatch (which was printed for confidential circulation) briefed Whitehall on the Tunku's approach to the forthcoming London talks. The Malayan premier was, Moynihan pointed out, taking a big risk, in going ahead with Greater Malaysia. His attitude was determined, not by greed, but by hostility to communism, Malayan communalism and mistrust of Singapore. Two days later Selkirk wrote to Maudling (the new secretary of state for the colonies) with respect to tactics to be adopted at the London talks in order to restore the Tunku's confidence in British intentions, while the governors of North Borneo and Sarawak sent assessments from the Borneo perspective (CO 1030/984 nos 792 and E/811, CO 1030/985 no 886).]

Tunku Abdul Rahman is shortly coming to London to discuss Greater Malaysia. It may be useful to you to have the following analysis of the political background to this plan so far as Malaya and the Tunku are concerned.

---

[1] M J Moynihan, deputy high commissioner, Kuala Lumpur, 1961–1963.

2.   Out of approximately seven million inhabitants in Malaya nearly half are Malays and there are almost as many Chinese. This racial balance constitutes Malaya's main political problem and its solution is essential if Malaya is to remain stable and free from Communist influences. A successful resolution of these racial forces is the Tunku's principal objective and his pursuit of this objective was exemplified in his formation of the alliance, the Government coalition of the three principal racial parties.[2]

3.   The attempt to turn Malays and Chinese alike into good Malayans involves some sacrifice on the part of each. To understand the reactions which this sacrifice produces it is necessary to remind oneself that the Chinese in general are more skilful, more industrious and better educated than the Malays and that the Malays are permanently conscious of this comparative disability of theirs in free competition with the Chinese. Hitherto the balance has been redressed by artificial means such as the various reservations built into the Constitution in favour of the Malays and a number of other devices which go some small way to hold the Chinese back.

4.   Amongst those Malays who do not understand the longer term issues involved there is a widespread feeling that the Chinese in Malaya are interlopers who have no right to a stake in the control of the country's destinies. To the extent, therefore, that the Tunku in pursuit of his main objective of creating a Malayan nation gives the Chinese a reasonable share in the country's affairs, in rough proportion to the contribution which they make to the economy and to the population, he is causing deep disquiet to a substantial number of the people upon whom he principally relies for his political support. Correspondingly, in his efforts to turn Chinese into Malayans, he is naturally trying to make them in some respects less Chinese.

5.   The Chinese have never been easy to assimilate. It is a matter of piety with them to maintain intact connexions reaching back into their ancient history and every respectable Chinese, including even Ministers in the present Cabinet, spends a part of his day doing reverence to the spirits of his ancestors. The most ignorant Chinese in Kuala Lumpur is for ever trying to appease his ancestors in one way or another or at least taking care not to upset them. It is deeply foreign, therefore, to the Chinese nature deliberately to sever or allow to be weakened any of the links between himself and his ancestry in Mother China.

6.   The acid test of the Tunku's attempt to Malayanise the Chinese is now being made in the imposition upon the Chinese secondary schools of the Government's new education policy, that is, a policy denying Government financial assistance to those Chinese secondary schools which continue in effect to teach in Chinese. To this policy there is still considerable opposition on the part of the Chinese and this is being led amongst others by Mr. Lim Lian Geok, a Chinese schoolmaster, whom the Tunku is at present trying to deprive of his citizenship, with a view to his banishment from Malaya, on the grounds that he is promoting ill will between the races and that this is a grave potential threat to the internal security of Malaya. By our standards these measures are harsh but seen against the Malayan background they appear perfectly logical.

7.   The Tunku has always admitted that the Malays are the only people he trusts in Malaya and that if his attempt to Malayanise the Chinese should fail or should

---

[2] For the Alliance of the United Malays National Organisation, Malayan Chinese Association and Malayan Indian Congress see *BDEE: Malaya*, part III.

result in a serious drain of Malay support from his Government he would not hesitate to fall back upon his Malays, even to the extent of making common cause with his Malay nationalist opponents. In the 1959 general election the two purely Malay States, Kelantan and Trengganu, deserted the Tunku. This desertion was partly attributed to the sense of neglect which the rural Malay felt on the east coast and to the lack of those facilities and amenities which had been promised as one of the dividends of independence. By the Tunku, however, it was also attributed to fears felt by these backwoodsmen of the east coast regarding the extent to which he, the Tunku, was giving power to the Chinese. There, on the east coast, in those two States where hardly a Chinaman is to be seen from one day's end to the next, it was hard for a Malay to understand why the Chinese should have very nearly as much say in the running of Malaya as the Malays. This desertion of Malays to the opposition came as a shock to the Tunku and, since then, despite the fact that the general election gave him more than a two-thirds majority in Parliament, he has been determined not to alienate any more of his Malay support and has been at pains to win back support which he has lost.

8.   In the domestic sphere this determination has shown itself in the prosecution of the Rural Development Plan, a plan directed not only to meet Malaya's urgent need of development in order to absorb the tremendous increase in the working population during the next five years, but also to bring to the rural Malays the concrete benefits which they have hitherto been denied. It is not publicly acknowledged, but simple mathematical analysis will show, that this development plan will, at best, only succeed in holding the overall standard of living where it now is. This, however, will be done by raising the standard of living of the rural Malay and by allowing the standard of living of the Chinese to fall back. It can be argued that the Tunku is also restoring the situation, that is to say, restoring the trust and confidence of his Malays, by taking, at last, the drastic step of implementing, as described above, the Government's long-awaited education policy at the expense of Chinese secondary education: this is an indication to the Malays that the Tunku is prepared to be tough with the Chinese.

9.   The position in Parliament is, as I have said, that the Government enjoy slightly more than a two-thirds majority.[3] The Opposition are divided between Malay nationalists, mostly from Kelantan and Trengganu, and a number of more or less Socialist parties. The key influence in all these Socialist parties is Chinese. The Malayan Communist Party is also virtually completely Chinese. Having lost the open

---

[3] In the 1959 state elections the Pan-Malayan Islamic Party won 17 of the 24 seats in the Trengganu Legislative Assembly and 28 of 30 in Kelantan. This setback for the Alliance caused the Tunku temporarily to resign as prime minister in order to concentrate on the campaign for the federal elections later in the year, see 7 and 8. The federal elections in August 1959 differed significantly from those in 1955 that had shaped the route to independence. The Merdeka (independence) constitution was fully implemented in 1959, doubling the electorate and increasing the number of Chinese voters sevenfold: Malays were now only 57 per cent of the electorate compared with 80 per cent in 1955. The result was that, while the Alliance was victorious, its share of the vote fell from 81.7 per cent in 1955 to 51.5 per cent and its majority dropped from 51 of the 52 electable seats in 1955 to 74 out of 104 places in the now fully elected lower house, although it retained the two-thirds majority necessary to amend the constitution. The PMIP, having won the single opposition seat in 1955, accounted for 13 of the opposition members in the federal parliament of 1959. The others were: the Socialist Front 8 (led by Boestamam, president of Party Rakyat), People's Progressive Party 4, Party Negara 1 and the Malayan Party 1. There were 3 independent members.

battle, the Malayan Communists are now fighting their war underground. They have succeeded to some extent in penetrating the Socialist parties as well as the trade unions, apart from the influence which they already or rather still exercise in the Chinese secondary schools. As a result of the 'united front' policy now being pursued by the Communists, the platform of the Malayan Communist Party's so-called manifesto is virtually the same as the political platform of the Socialist parties. These are important points for an understanding of the Tunku's attitude towards the Chinese. However, the Tunku is not so much worried about this political opposition as he is about maintaining the solidarity of his own Malay support. Something like a third of the Malay population of Malaya is of fairly recent Indonesian origin. The Tunku has often remarked that about the same proportion tend to adopt what might be called Afro–Asian attitudes on important international issues, and it is these same Malays who feel genuine misgivings about the Tunku's policy of defence commitment to Britain and about his firm declaration of identity with the West when it comes to a show-down with the Communists. The support of these Malays is essential to the Tunku if he is to be able to carry out his policy of creating a Malayan nation or, in other words, if he is to preserve Malaya for the free world. It is not too much to say this, because failure of his policy and the emergence of one race as master of the others would inevitably advance the cause of Communism. In particular, alienation of the Chinese would result in their making common cause with their Chinese Socialist friends in Singapore and would strengthen the movement which already exists among many Chinese in favour of a Chinese Socialist take-over throughout the whole Malayan Peninsula.

10.   It is with these considerations in mind that the Tunku from time to time feels bound to adopt attitudes on world issues which diverge from our own and which appear to favour the neutralists. Malay emotions are easily roused. 'Amok' is a Malay word and running *amok* is a Malay habit. When Algerian rebels come here they receive an enthusiastic welcome from the Malays and the Tunku must place himself at the head of the welcoming party if he is not to damage his domestic political position.

11.   Since the day when Singapore received its Constitution and the Peoples Action Party Government with Communist support came into power under Lee Kuan Yew the Tunku has regarded Singapore as a power-house of Communist subversion from which Malaya had to insulate herself. The Tunku consented to take part in the Internal Security Council of Singapore by appointing a Minister to attend its meetings but Malayan participation became increasingly unwilling and the Malayan representative more and more took the line that Singapore was a British responsibility, that *we* should take any of the unpleasant measures necessary to preserve our interests in Singapore and that we should not expect the Malayans to pick our chestnuts out of the fire for us. From the outset the Malayans wanted no responsibility for Singapore and no part in it.

12.   Thus every time Lee Kuan Yew mentioned merger as a possibility, or as a desirable objective, the Tunku was quick to deny that merger was possible in the foreseeable future, and to affirm that Malaya had first to settle her own racial policies. He knew that hopes of merger encouraged the Chinese Socialists in Malaya to dream of their pan Malayan Socialist State, and he knew also that the prospect of merger struck terror into the hearts of his Malays. For these reasons the Tunku shut his ears for a long time to all suggestions about merger or even about a wider

association with Singapore and the Borneo Territories known at an earlier stage as The Grand Design. The idea of this wider association with the Borneo Territories is by no means a new one; it has been current for at least seven years. At one time the Tunku himself was in favour of it. Immediately before independence, he took part in a broadcast on the B.B.C. in London, and said specifically, in answer to questions, that he was favourable to the idea of extending the Malayan Federation to the Borneo Territories if these Territories wanted this. When he visited the Philippines on a State occasion, he thought the Malays there might raise the question of Philippine claims upon North Borneo and he wished, if so, to deal with these by saying that the long-term future of the Borneo Territories obviously lay with Malaya. At that time, however, we poured cold water on these ideas of the Tunku's because we feared they might distract attention from the objective of that closer association of the Borneo Territories amongst themselves which was then our immediate objective in that area. With the coming of the P.A.P. Government into power, a Government whose Ministers the Tunku regarded at first as little better than Communists, the Tunku at once turned cold towards the idea of association with Singapore at any cost. The people of Singapore would, he said, never be the friends of Malaya or become true Malayans in a thousand years.

13.   With the deterioration in Lee Kuan Yew's political position and with growing fears of the eventual loss of Singapore to Communism, merger between the Federation and Singapore, whether by itself or as part of a wider federation embracing the Borneo Territories, began to seem to us to offer the only hope of saving Singapore and of halting a process which if not checked could undermine the freedom and stability of the whole of South-East Asia. The Tunku continued to resist strongly all suggestions that Malayan interests lay in their assuming control over Singapore. Even efforts on the part of Singapore to induce Malaya to develop a limited common market foundered on the Tunku's determination to maintain the virtual insulation of Malaya from Singapore. Singapore was a British responsibility and if necessary the British should stay there for ever and should certainly maintain a position of strength so that they could deal firmly with any nonsense on the part of the Chinese in Singapore. It was argued with the Tunku that it would be unrealistic to imagine that the British could retain control of Singapore for ever; once we had to withdraw Singapore would go Communist, the Communist Powers would move in and Malaya would find a Cuba on her doorstep. Surely it made sense for Malaya to take charge of Singapore before it was too late. To this line of argument the Tunku always replied that it was our fault that Singapore had been separated from Malaya in the first place and since we had let it deteriorate to its present deplorable condition it was up to us to clean it up, or to go on keeping it in order ourselves. As to the risk that the Communist Powers might establish bridgeheads there, the Tunku was confident that any such move would be countered effectively by ourselves or, failing this, by the Americans.

14.   As time went on, however, the Tunku gradually came to the conclusion not only that the British could not be relied on to hold the fort in Singapore indefinitely or to take effective counter-measures if the Communists tried to establish a bridgehead there, but also that the British either would not or could not even keep Singapore Communism in check when it came within the scope of the Internal Security Council. In this way the Tunku came finally to see that if Singapore were to be saved from Communism he and nobody else would have to do it.

15.   Merger between the Federation and Singapore by itself was obviously not to be thought of. This would result in a net addition of approximately a million Chinese of doubtful loyalty to the Chinese population of Malaya, *i.e.*, nearly half of the existing total in the Federation, which already represented a serious headache to the Tunku. His Malays would regard a Federation–Singapore merger as the final surrender of Malay rights to the Chinese. The Tunku appreciated, however, that he would be able to secure support from his Malays for merger with Singapore provided that at the same time he could achieve a balance by taking in the three Borneo Territories, which would contribute a substantial if not an equal number of people at least non-Chinese if not anti-Chinese. In any event if the Borneo States came in, as he intended, as individual States there would be three new non-Chinese States as against one Chinese State. One to three against the Chinese has come to be accepted by the Malays as a minimum safeguard if the Chinese are to be effectively kept down. In order that the Tunku should be able to carry his Malays with him, it was therefore essential not only that the Borneo States should come in as well but also that they should be acquired simultaneously with, if not before, Singapore, so that the racial balance should at no time be thrown into jeopardy. The Tunku made it clear at the outset that this was his basic requirement.

16.   The Tunku also stressed that there was very little time, and that we should be prepared to transfer sovereignty immediately. If we believed, as he did, that association with Malaya was in the best interests of the Borneo Territories in the long term and that failure to bring about this association very quickly would allow time and opportunity for a Communist United Front Government to take over in Singapore we ought surely not to be too delicate about treading on a few toes or about short-circuiting normal processes of consultation. Here was an opportunity not only to save Singapore but also to halt a Communist process which would be bound in the end to spread to Indonesia and the Borneo Territories themselves and to undermine the cause of freedom in all those countries which still remained free south of Communist China. If we were to let this opportunity slip, by insistence on maintaining the slow and measured pace of Whitehall, history would condemn us.

17.   Nevertheless, the Tunku was unreasonable in expecting Her Majesty's Government to sign immediately on the dotted line, having regard to their responsibilities not only to the Borneo Territories but also in the sphere of defence. It has taken some time to bring home to the Tunku that not only would it be fatal to the Greater Malaysia Federation if the Borneo Territories were dragooned into this association without first being convinced that it was genuinely in their interests, but also that this would lay us open to damaging attack in the United Nations, by the Afro–Asian countries, for example, prompted by the Socialists in Malaya and the Borneo Territories themselves. We should also have troubles in our own Parliament, alerted as it already was to the finer points of our colonial policy in relation to Africa.

18.   On defence too it was some time before the Tunku was brought to realise that we had responsibilities which might well have to be discharged in circumstances short of actual warfare. The Tunku's line has always been that when war broke out in this part of the world, Malaya would be with us, provided that he was still in charge, and this meant that we must not expect him to incur politically dangerous liabilities in peacetime. He now realises, however, that even in so-called peacetime there are jobs we may have to do, that for us to be seen to be willingly sacrificing our ability to do these jobs at the present disturbed time in South-East Asia would be damaging to

the cause of peace, and that here is a problem to which we must both try to find a practical solution. It is clear however that, whatever solution is found, it must be one which permits him to continue to put his hand on his heart, if necessary, and say that there is no link between Malaya and SEATO.

19.   This brings us to the situation as it is to-day. The Tunku has agreed to go to London, having received confirmation from us that we accept the concept of Greater Malaysia and, in particular, that we regard the inclusion of the Borneo Territories in a wider association with Malaya as an integral part of the whole arrangement. We have therefore satisfied the Tunku that he need no longer fear that we have the sinister design of delaying the transfer of the Borneo Territories in the hope that the situation in Singapore will deteriorate in the meantime to such an extent that he will be compelled, despite all his scruples, to take control of it by itself.

20.   The Tunku is a man of enthusiasm and vision. Tun Razak his trusted lieutenant and his eventual successor is a more hard-headed, calculating and, let us face it, more intelligent man. The Tunku relies, and has successfully relied so far, on his flair, his personal charm and his prestige. Tun Razak works it all out with his slide rule. The two of them are thus complementary. Experience has shown that success is only assured in any Malayan project if both are agreed upon it. The two of them are now in line.

21.   In dealing with the Tunku in London it, would be natural for us to feel that we were the ones who were being asked to give most away, so to speak, and that he should not come and dictate to us. Here, however, it must be remembered that the Tunku thinks that he is the one who is being called upon to make the real sacrifice. He would prefer to have nothing to do with Singapore and is not particularly interested in acquiring the Borneo Territories with all the trouble they represent for him, in terms of development and education and entirely new racial problems. He is only being driven to this by the deep and passionate need which he feels to fight Communism in this part of the world. Malaya has had 12 years of open warfare with Communists on its own soil and is now continuing the fight against Communism underground. The balance of internal security is still delicate. Anything to do with the Chinese is thought of here in terms of its possible effect upon that balance. In taking on Singapore, the Tunku is taking a very big and a nicely calculated risk. Some of his colleagues have told him that the Borneo Territories will not compensate him for the added problems of Singapore and he already half believes this. Muddled or not, he is therefore actuated by a very strong sense of duty and it would I submit be fatal if we, by our attitude to him, suggested that we thought he was being tiresome or greedy, or that he was some kind of neo-imperialist. Tactically, I suggest, the most effective attitude for us to adopt would be that here are practical problems to which we must both find a practical solution. The Tunku is a man who combines aristocratic standards of conduct with a remarkable political flair. On the subject of the Singapore base he is therefore, I think, less likely to be impressed by arguments on the merits of SEATO than by our showing him that for us to give up our facilities in Singapore would be tantamount to going back on solemn treaty undertakings. As regards the Borneo Territories, the Tunku would not, I fear, be moved by appeals to the rights of man or to the principle of self-determination whereas he would I think show understanding of the need to satisfy Parliament that Her Majesty's Government were not transferring sovereignty over these dependent peoples without due regard to their wishes.

22.   I am sending copies of this despatch to the British Commissioner-General for South-East Asia and Commissioner in Singapore, to the Governors of North Borneo and Sarawak and the High Commissioner for Brunei, to the British High Commissioners in Canberra and Wellington, to Her Majesty's Ambassadors in Bangkok and Djakarta and also to Her Majesty's Ambassador in Washington.

72   CO 1030/986, no 959   18 Oct 1961
'Singapore and merger': letter from P B C Moore to W I J Wallace, assessing the PAP's attitude to 'Greater Malaysia' and the prospect of the Barisan overthrowing Lee's government

Attention has been focussed in recent weeks on the Borneo and Defence aspects of 'Greater Malaysia', especially the need to give the Tunku enough expectation on the Borneo Territories to persuade him to go to London for talks with Mr. Macmillan. The Tunku has now been sufficiently reassured to enable the talks to take place, and in this short breathing space before London, it would perhaps be as well to consider another possible obstacle—will Singapore be a willing party to 'Greater Malaysia'?

2.   Lee Kuan Yew has always been most anxious to achieve merger with the Federation, because he saw quite clearly that in the long term this was his only hope of containing the Chinese chauvinists and Communists in Singapore. For a long time the Tunku was adamant that Merger could not take place, but the logic of the situation was so inescapable to Lee Kuan Yew and us that we never entirely despaired. Martin Moynihan's despatch of 12th October, 1961[1] describes how the Tunku finally came round. There was never, of course, any question of our not being prepared to deal with the problem of the Communists in Singapore in the short term, but we had to persuade the Tunku that he alone, in the present climate of international opinion, could deal with Singapore in the long term. This was not an easy task, since it inevitably involved giving the Tunku the impression that we, his allies, might not be as decisive as he was prepared to be in dealing with Communist penetration. Nevertheless, it was essential to disabuse him of his illusion that Singapore could safely be left to the British on an indefinite basis. When, therefore, it appeared at the end of July that the Barisan Socialis might be going to unseat Lee Kuan Yew, we had to explain to the Federation that, provided the Barisan Socialis behaved in a constitutional manner, there was no question of our preserving Lee Kuan Yew simply by putting the Barisan Socialis leaders in gaol or suspending the Singapore Constitution. This led to some harsh feelings from the Federation, but Ghazali, in particular, was very realistic, and I hope they have gradually come to see some force in our argument, although they probably still feel in their hearts that we have been pusillanimous in our approach to Singapore.

3.   The outcome is that the Tunku appears to be completely convinced that he must take Singapore into the Federation. Unfortunately, he became convinced about a year too late, and the irony of the situation is that whereas a year ago Lee Kuan Yew held 43 seats out of 51 in the Singapore Assembly and could probably have put

---

[1] See 71.

through Merger fairly comfortably, he has now been very nearly out-flanked by the Chinese chauvinists and Communists with whom he tried to maintain a united front. Lee was within an ace of falling on 20th July, and indeed he only survived by a handful of votes.[2] Since then, however, with the Tunku's assistance, he has regained a lot of lost ground. Few people ever believed that Lee could bring off merger between Singapore and the Federation, even though this had always formed the main plank of the P.A.P.'s political platform, and he has undoubtedly won a considerable measure of respect by the success so far of his negotiations with the Tunku. The Chinese are great respecters of power, and Lee has succeeded in giving the impression that Merger is going to come about with the active support and encouragement of the Tunku and the agreement of the British. At the same time, Lee has come right out into the open about the Communists, and in a series of twelve broadcasts[3] has explained that the Communists fear Merger because this will involve internal security passing into the hands of the Tunku in Kuala Lumpur. Opinions are divided about the effectiveness of this move. It has probably had a useful effect with the English-speaking Chinese. There has, however, been a fair amount of cynicism from those who have asked why he accepted the Communists as bed-fellows for so long if they were so dangerous, and also why he has not taken any action against them now. Also, he is giving the impression to many people, particularly among the Chinese-speaking, that he is merely labelling as a Communist anybody who is his political opponent. So much for the background.

4.   The Barisan Socialis' aim is to force Lee Kuan Yew to resign and hold a General Election, since it is commonly thought in Singapore that the P.A.P. would be defeated at a General Election, and that the Barisan Socialis would emerge as the majority party. The P.A.P. have only 26 seats out of 51 seats and on the face of it their position in the Assembly is weak. Three months, however, have passed since the defection of the 13 P.A.P. members, and although there have been rumours of more waverers, no further defections have taken place and the 26 remaining P.A.P. members have publicly re-affirmed their loyalty. It seems, therefore, that while Lee can maintain progress with merger, he will be able to deter any further waverers. In addition, he is reasonably assured that the 7 Alliance members will either abstain or vote with him on merger. The same can probably be said of the one Independent. This leaves 17 members, comprising 13 Barisan Socialis, Ong Eng Guan and his two supporters and David Marshall. Lee's programme is for the Assembly to re-convene on 31st October, and for the debate on Merger to start on 8th November. Toh Chin Chye told me the other day that this would probably last a week. Although there can be no certainty until we see the stand taken by the 51 members after the lapse of over three months, I believe Lee Kuan Yew will emerge from the Assembly debate with a vote of confidence on his plan for merger. Probably only a breakdown in the negotiations between the Tunku and H.M.G. could seriously prejudice this.

5.   Unfortunately, however, a successful vote in the Assembly will not be sufficient. The P.A.P. have already committed themselves to referring the issue of Merger to the people in a Referendum. I am not sure whether this was a wise move,

---

[2] For this debate, see 49, note and 50.
[3] Given between 13 Sept and 9 Oct, the twelve broadcasts were published as *The Battle for Merger* (Government Printing Office, Singapore, 1961).

in view of the known unpopularity of the P.A.P., and it might have been better tactics to depend on Lim Yew Hock's 7 votes to obtain a majority of 33 out of the 51 seats in the Assembly and leave it at that. Merger was in the P.A.P's platform at the General Election in 1959, and they might have claimed that a two-thirds majority of the Assembly was sufficient for the implementation of Merger. On the other hand, the loss of two by-elections,[4] and the defection of a further 13 P.A.P. members was a staggering reverse, and there would no doubt have been considerable criticism in Singapore if Lee had sought to implement Merger solely on the basis of a favourable vote in the Assembly. Be that as it may, the Government are committed to a Referendum, and the question is whether they can win it. Here we come right up against the problem of the P.A.P's general unpopularity in Singapore, which was a considerable factor in their defeats at Hong Lim and Anson. The danger of any appeal to the people at this stage is that votes in a Referendum will be cast not on the merits of Merger, but simply for or against the P.A.P. At long last, I think Lee and his Ministers have realised the extent of their unpopularity in the State, and Lee is therefore anxious not to have to put the Referendum question in the form of, 'Are you in favour of merger with the Federation on the terms agreed by me with the Tunku—yes or no?'. Lee has also been disturbed by the recent Referendum vote in Jamaica, and considers there is too much at stake in a question as important as this to put it to the vote of the people in a straight yes or no form.[5]

6.   Lee has, therefore, been considering whether he can hold a Referendum in which there could be no final defeat for him whichever way the vote goes, on the following lines. All political parties in Singapore have currently stated they want Merger, and therefore there is no need to ask the people of Singapore whether they are in favour of Merger. Everybody wants Merger, and it is just a question of how Merger is to be achieved. He therefore has in mind that the Referendum should ask the people of Singapore whether they want:—

(a) Merger on the terms agreed by the P.A.P. with the Tunku, or
(b) Complete Merger.

Both the Tunku and Lee have already pointed to the drawbacks in complete Merger for Singapore. Not all the 628,000 present Singapore electors will qualify for Federal citizenship and voting rights; labour relations will be in the hands of the Federation and therefore the Trade Unions can expect a much stricter Governmental control than exists in Singapore today; and Singapore may have to accept the full implications of the Federal Government's Chinese education policy. In this way, Lee hopes that Singapore will be persuaded to vote for alternative (a). But a vote in favour of (b) will still be a vote in favour of Merger and in that event Lee would undertake to go back to the Tunku and try to negotiate Merger in a form more acceptable to the people of Singapore. There would be no question of his having suffered an adverse vote demanding resignation of the P.A.P. Government.

---

[4] For the by-elections at Hong Lim and Anson, see 38 and 49, note.
[5] The referendum bill was debated in the Singapore Legislative Assembly from 27 June to 11 July 1962 and the referendum was held on 1 Sept 1962 (see 131). The Jamaican referendum on 19 Sept 1961 returned a 'yes' vote for secession and led to the break-up of the Federation of the West Indies, see Ashton and Killingray, eds, *BDEE: The West Indies*, lxxiii, 158 and 163.

7.   The obvious obstacle to Lee's plan is that the Tunku may feel obliged to say in advance that the Federation could not agree to full Merger. Thompson has already reported that Razak is against Lee's plan, although apparently the Tunku sees the merit in Lee's tactic. Lee has told me that he is doing his utmost to persuade the Tunku to agree to the Referendum being put in this form and that he has already made some progress with Ghazali. I am hoping to go to Kuala Lumpur this week to ask Sir Geofroy Tory whether it might be possible for him to lend some support to Lee's plea. I know the Tunku realises how important it is that Lee should not be toppled, and I think we should, in all fairness, warn him that there might be considerable risk for Lee Kuan Yew putting the Ulster type of merger in a Referendum in the form of a straight, 'Yes or No'.

8.   The Barisan Socialis can counter Lee's plan by advocating voters to tear up the ballot paper. This is not a very satisfactory policy for a political party to adopt at a Referendum, and in the absence of a more constructive attitude from the Opposition, Lee might get a favourable vote for (a). Alternatively, the Barisan Socialis may ask their supporters to vote for (b), but on their interpretation of full Merger, which would give all existing Singapore electors Federal citizenship and voting rights. But whichever way the Barisan Socialis play it, we hope that if Lee does not take up too rigid an attitude, it may yet be open to him to continue in power even if the people in Singapore reject his form of Merger and vote for 'full Merger'. I would hope also that if Singapore indicate clearly that they want a form of full Merger, the Tunku might be prepared to consider this, although it is rather worrying that both the P.P.P. and the Socialist Front have advocated full Merger in the current debate in the House of Representatives in Kuala Lumpur.

9.   So far, I have examined the possibility of the Barisan Socialis bringing down the P.A.P. by constitutional means. If, however, they fail to force the P.A.P. to a General Election, are they likely to resort to direct action? No doubt there will be large-scale demonstrations, and possibly a number of strikes to demonstrate the power of the Barisan Socialis on the industrial front. But on the whole we think it unlikely that they will resort to riots and a general strike, thus giving Lee Kuan Yew the opportunity to arrest them. Once Lim Chin Siong becomes convinced that the people of Singapore are going to support Merger, then I suspect he may well revert to the original long term policy of the M.C.P.—a Socialist Government throughout Malaya. The opportunity of over-throwing Lee Kuan Yew and achieving a Communist-manipulated Government in Singapore seemed, in July, to be so golden that Lim Chin Siong could not resist it. If, however, he comes to the conclusion that this cannot be achieved, I believe he may quite realistically revert to the original plan. He will accept that this may mean gaol for him and his associates at the hands of the Tunku, but he is probably prepared to take a long term view. Even Merger on the terms agreed by Lee with the Tunku will give Singapore 14 seats in the Kuala Lumpur House of Representatives, and one day there will have to be not only a General Election in Singapore for a new State Assembly but also elections to fill the 14 Singapore seats in Kuala Lumpur. Victories in these elections will, in Lim's opinion, bring much closer the ultimate day of 'Socialist Victory' in Malaya. I would not wish to be too dogmatic on this, and it is quite possible that the pressure of events will force the Barisan Socialis to take violent action against Merger. On balance, however, I believe they will, if possible, stick to constitutional means.

10.   Our assessment at this point, therefore, is that the Barisan Socialis will

employ every available means to depose Lee Kuan Yew constitutionally but may well stop short of violent direct action; and that Lee Kuan Yew will win a vote of confidence for his Merger policy from the Assembly but will face a much harder task in winning a Referendum on Merger.

11.   I am sending copies of this letter to Sir Denis Allen, Moynihan in Kuala Lumpur, Jakeway in Kuching, Turner in Jesselton and White in Brunei.

73   CAB 134/1949, GM(61)11(Final)   20 Oct 1961
'Greater Malaysia: report by the chairman of the Official Committee':
report for ministers by Sir A Clutterbuck. *Appendices* **B and C**

[Set up to brief ministers for talks with the Tunku, the Official Committee on Greater Malaysia met for the first time on 27 Sep (see 62), and on 19 Oct the committee agreed their report which was submitted to ministers the following day. It substantiates the case for proceeding with 'Greater Malaysia' and outlines tactics for forthcoming discussions with the Tunku. It starts by identifying the reasons for, and the problems of, bringing about territorial merger. In so doing it assesses the range of local opinion and discusses the dilemma of timing: whereas circumstances in Malaya and Singapore demanded immediate action, those in the Borneo territories called for a gradual approach. Turning to defence, the report points out that 'Greater Malaysia' should relieve Britain of costly commitments although it could curtail its rights to the use of military bases (an issue about which Julian Amery, secretary of state for air, expressed misgivings in a paper considered alongside this report at the Cabinet Defence Committee on 25 Oct). The report therefore advises negotiators to work towards an arrangement whereby Commonwealth forces stationed in 'Greater Malaysia' could fulfil their SEATO obligations while the new state assumed responsibilities for its own internal security. It was the defence aspects of the report (which was presented to the Cabinet Defence Committee with an introductory note by the Cabinet secretary and numbered D(61)62)) that held the attention of ministers at their meeting on 25 Oct (see 74). Following the discussion in the Defence Committee, Macmillan felt that ministers should give further thought to the officials' report, particularly those matters not relating to defence; hence the establishment of the ministerial Greater Malaysia Committee which was first convened on 9 Nov (see 77). On 10 Nov a twelve-page, 43-paragraph summary of the officials' report was despatched to high commissioners in Commonwealth capitals (CAB 134/1949, GM(61) 5th meeting; CAB 131/25, D14(61)3; DO 169/213, no 3; PREM 11/3422).]

Introduction
The Committee was established with the following terms of reference:—

'To examine the proposals by the Prime Minister of the Federation of Malaya for the creation of a "Greater Malaysia" incorporating the Federation of Malaya, Brunei, North Borneo, Sarawak and Singapore, and to make recommendations to Ministers.'

2.   The genesis of these proposals is as follows. The possibility of a political association between Malaya, Singapore and the three British Borneo territories has been under general discussion for many years and the United Kingdom Government have throughout regarded it with favour in principle. It was discussed earlier this year at a meeting of the Commissioner General for the United Kingdom in South East Asia and other United Kingdom representatives in the area and they strongly recommended that the United Kingdom should accept the development of such an association as an *ultimate* goal of Government policy.

3. In the past a major obstacle has been the attitude of the Malayan Government, who were not prepared to run the risk that the Chinese majority in Singapore might join with the Chinese minority in Malaya to the detriment of the interests of the Malays. Recently, however, there has been a complete change of front on the part of the Malayan Government. The Prime Minister, Tunku Abdul Rahman, in a speech on 27th May spoke favourably about the possibility of an association including all five territories. He has followed this up with great vigour and on 26th June sent the Prime Minister a memorandum setting out in some detail his proposals for a Greater Malaysia (Appendix A to this report).[1] The population figures in Annex A to the Tunku's memorandum are in a number of respects inaccurate: the most accurate figures available are given in Appendix B to this report.

4. The Tunku now regards this matter as one of great urgency because the position of the present Prime Minister of Singapore, Mr. Lee Kuan Yew, and his party has of late rapidly deteriorated; and while the Tunku finds it possible to co-operate with Mr. Lee, he sees no prospect of doing so with any other likely Prime Minister of Singapore should Mr. Lee and his Government fall.

5. In Singapore Mr. Lee is committed to a policy of achieving independence through a political merger with Malaya. He and the Tunku have met on several occasions to discuss the Malayan proposals. Mr. Lee has made it clear that these proposals have his full backing and he has agreed with the Tunku on the general arrangements under which Singapore could enter the Federation on special terms. These arrangements would be generally acceptable to us. Mr. Lee believes that his only hope of achieving his aim of 'independence through merger' lies in rapid progress on these proposals. The only major problem which such a merger poses for us—and it is a very serious problem indeed—is the future of our rights in the Singapore bases.

6. On the other hand, it is essential to the Tunku's proposals that the three Borneo territories should be brought into the association in order that their predominantly non-Chinese populations may provide a counter-balance to the Chinese majority in Singapore, and the Tunku is not prepared to contemplate a merger of Malaya and Singapore without the inclusion of the Borneo territories. This faces us with a serious dilemma since the Borneo territories are in almost every way quite unready for effective participation in the proposed union.

7. The succeeding paragraphs of this report deal with the problems presented to the United Kingdom Government by this situation under the following heads:—

Malaya	(paragraphs 8–11)
Singapore	(paragraphs 12–15)
Borneo	(paragraphs 16–23)
Defence	(paragraphs 24–32)
Finance	(paragraphs 33–40)

Thereafter the report sets out the general conclusions of the Committee (paragraphs 41 and 42) and deals with tactics for the discussions with the Tunku which are due to take place early in November (paragraphs 43–53). Finally, there is a summary of our conclusions and recommendations (paragraphs 54–60).

---

[1] See 46.

Malaya

8.   The future of Singapore is of direct and deep concern to Malaya. Economically its separation from the Federation makes nonsense. But the Malay majority in the Federation are deeply concerned at the likely results of a direct merger, since the Chinese population in the combined territories would then be greater than the Malay population, and moreover the Singapore Chinese contain a high proportion of Communist sympathisers. After defeating their own Communists in the long Emergency the last thing that the Malayans want to risk is Communist domination from Singapore.

9.   For a long time the Tunku's view had been that he must keep the Singapore Chinese out. He relied on us to control the situation there and said that in the event of trouble his policy was to seal off Singapore by closing the Johore causeway. It has, however, become apparent to him that the situation in Singapore is changing, and he is aware that a constitutional review is due in Singapore during 1963. As a result, he has now come round to the view that an independent Singapore would be a source of continuous danger and embarrassment to Malaya and that the only alternative is some form of merger between Malaya and Singapore.

10.   But it is vital to Malaya that the terms of the merger with Singapore should contain provisions which will safeguard the Federation as a whole against Chinese domination. To achieve this the Tunku has laid down two essential conditions:—

(a) before being committed to a merger with Singapore he must be absolutely certain that the three Borneo territories with their prodominantly non-Chinese population will be brought into the wider Federation; and

(b) Singapore should have a smaller representation in the central Parliament than they would be entitled to on a population basis: in return for this Singapore would retain much wider powers than the other member states—but not responsibility for internal security.

11.   The Tunku's specific proposals as they now stand are as follows:—

(1) As a first step Brunei, North Borneo and Sarawak should be brought into the Malayan Federation as constituent units on the same basis as the existing States (although he has informed certain Borneo leaders that he would be ready to give the Borneo territories a large measure of self-government). He appears to be convinced that if the British Government gave a firm lead the Borneo peoples would be happy to come in at a very early date.

(2) Once (1) was secured, Singapore would join the Federation on special terms, retaining powers (much beyond those of existing States in the Federation—e.g. in the field of education and labour) to administer its own affairs. Singapore would then have proportionately smaller representation in the central Parliament than it could claim on a population basis if it came in on the same footing as the existing States. Internal security would be a Federal subject.

(3) The British bases in Singapore would cease to be at the disposal of SEATO but could be maintained as bases for Commonwealth defence.

(4) There would be no administrative change in Singapore and it would maintain its own civil service.

(5) After initial talks with United Kingdom Ministers, there should be a formal discussion in which representatives of all the territories concerned and the United

Kingdom would participate. That meeting should decide on the appointment of an independent constitutional commission on the lines of the Reid Commission which drafted the constitution of the Federation of Malaya.

Singapore

12.   All the urgency and one of the two major elements of the problem lie in Singapore, where the present constitutional position is full internal self-government subject to certain controls over internal security, with the United Kingdom responsible for defence and external affairs and enjoying full rights of occupation, control and use of the bases. Singapore is under mounting economic pressures, particularly as a result of an explosive rate of increase in population. Politically, there is a powerful and growing demand for early independence in one form or another. In the absence of any clear design for the future, Singapore's economic and political circumstances alike play directly into the hands of the Communists, whose influence is strong and pervasive. Mr. Lee's relatively moderate Government have recently lost much ground to the extreme left and their hold on power is now tenuous.

13.   We have always had in mind that Singapore and Malaya should one day merge (and have on more than one occasion blessed the idea in public), partly because only in that direction have we been able to see any real hope for Singapore's economy and partly because the political alternative has more and more seemed to be Communist domination of Singapore. Since the proposal before us is that on joining Malaya Singapore should surrender to the Federal Government all responsibility for internal security and external defence, merger with a prosperous Malaya ruled by a resolutely anti-Communist Government should greatly improve the prospects of Singapore's economic and political stability. If we can now agree upon the creation of a Greater Malaysia, Mr. Lee and his Government may survive to see it through. There is, of course, no guarantee that he will win the referendum on the subject which he has undertaken to hold in November, but he will have a far better chance if he can present his electorate with a firm promise of merger with Malaya should the voters so choose. Finally, if a merger of Singapore with Malaya can be achieved we shall not only succeed in extricating ourselves from an increasingly menacing situation in the former, but do so in the one way likely to reinforce rather than undermine the security of South East Asia in general and our own interests in particular.

14.   If, however, the Greater Malaysia project fails, Mr. Lee and his Government will almost certainly fall and be succeeded by another much further to the left and unwilling to contemplate merger with Malaya on terms acceptable to the Tunku. Either of two unpleasant situations could then develop. First, under the new Government the situation in Singapore might so deteriorate that our right under certain conditions to suspend the constitution could and had to be exercised. This would mean assuming direct administration of the island against the background of a hostile population, a public service now containing virtually no British officials, and a brittle economy at least badly shaken. We should then be left for an indefinite period with sole responsibility for a Singapore gone thoroughly bad and requiring (on our present reckoning) considerable reinforcement of the eight major army units at present stationed there to safeguard internal security. In such circumstances the value to us of the Singapore bases would, to say the least, be highly problematical: even as things are it is arguable whether we could operate effectively from the bases

if the Singapore Government set out to frustrate us. Second, the new Government might so conduct themselves as to give us no proper grounds for suspending the constitution, however sure we might feel that a Communist take-over was being prepared behind the scenes. In either situation, any previous default on our part in support of Greater Malaysia would have turned the Tunku almost as antagonistic to ourselves as to Singapore.

15. We are committed to review the existing Singapore constitution in 1963. If Singapore is not by then at least firmly set on the road to independence through merger with Malaya (and assuming that the constitution had not meanwhile been suspended) we shall be faced with a choice no less painful than that set out in the previous paragraph. There will certainly be a demand for separate independence. Should we refuse it we shall be faced by a hostile Singapore, whether or not we have to suspend the constitution: should we accede, we shall establish in the heart of South East Asia a new sovereign state likely to be increasingly influenced by Peking. On the second of these hypotheses it seems inconceivable that the Singapore bases would in any way continue to be available to us, and even on the first they would be of very limited use.

Borneo

16. We have seen that there is no time to lose if we want to bring about a merger of Singapore with Malaya; and we have also seen that that is unacceptable to the Tunku unless the Borneo territories are included. Herein, if we leave aside our defence problem, is our chief dilemma since we are under obligation to the peoples of the Borneo territories to advance them socially, economically and politically until they are able to assume responsibility for their own future—and in the ordinary way that point would take many years to reach as their political, social and economic institutions are still at a relatively early stage of evolution.

17. We have no doubt that inclusion in a Greater Malaysia offers the Borneo territories their best hope for the future in the long term. Individually they are all highly vulnerable on account of their small size and population, their racial composition and their geographical position; and even a union of the three states would by itself be relatively weak. Moreover China, Indonesia and the Philippines have, or could readily work up, interests of one kind or another in them: in particular, Indonesian irredentism is likely to prove an increasingly grave threat to which there may well be no answer except Greater Malaysia. In the light of these circumstances, of Colonial experience elsewhere and of general trends in South East Asia, it seems unlikely that we can foster the political development of the Borneo territories at a pace allowing time to secure their capacity to survive and prosper in independence by themselves: if they are left on their own we shall almost certainly be driven by external pressures to grant independence long before they are ready for it, with all the dangers in which that will involve them. On this analysis our choice lies between guiding them now into a Greater Malaysia which we are satisfied is their most desirable destination, despite the fact that their peoples are not yet themselves really capable of exercising considered judgement on the matter and are not yet ready to stand on their own feet in this wider association, or waiting until they have become so capable and ready, when the opportunity of Greater Malaysia may well have been lost and the alternative prospect of separate independence will be parlous and brief.

18.   The issue is further complicated by the Tunku's apparent conviction that most of the people of the Borneo territories would gladly join with Malaya at an early date and that any reluctance on our part to commit them thereto without delay must be due either to failure to read the situation aright or to a desire to saddle him with Singapore alone. Indeed, any show of reluctance in the Borneo territories to accept the Greater Malaysia project at once will almost certainly be attributed by the Tunku to the influence of British officials. As we see it, however, the state of public opinion (such as it is) in the Borneo territories, although not unfavourable, is generally cautious. Doubts relate rather to the form of association and to timing than to principle: few people like the idea of joining a Greater Malaysia as States on a par with the existing States of the Federation of Malaya (as the Tunku proposes) or feel that they are anything like yet ready to join. Opinion in the individual territories is as follows:—

(a) In *Sarawak* the leading Malays (whose community forms less than a quarter of the whole population) and some of their followers favour early merger with Malaya without closer association of the Borneo territories first. The leftwing Chinese, while not openly opposed to Greater Malaysia as an ultimate aim, want independence in Sarawak first. There are signs that the leaders of the indigenous peoples (Ibans, Land Dayaks, Kayans, Kenyas, etc.) are favourably disposed towards the idea of a Greater Malaysia and have some awareness of a common interest with Malaya in combating Communism. But they do not want to be rushed and would prefer a union with North Borneo first. They do not yet feel ready educationally, economically or politically for a merger and want us to stay and help them until they are stronger. They fear Malay discrimination and have unhappy memories of their relations with the Malays in the past. They are a tough people and would resist, very possibly to the extent of armed insurrection, a premature transfer of sovereignty to which they have not agreed. As the Governor puts it, 'they are interested in the pig, but do not want to buy it in the present poke'.
(b) In *North Borneo* the Malays are a small minority and here, too, are for historical reasons unpopular among the non-Muslim majority (Dusuns, Muruts, etc.). The Chinese generally want to go slow on Greater Malaysia and to work first for self-government for North Borneo and federation with Sarawak (and possibly Brunei). One or two native leaders are in favour of early merger with Malaya. For the rest, opinion seems to be in favour of closer association of the Borneo territories first, although there is some native opinion against any union with Sarawak in view of Communist activity there. The Governor's latest advice is that merger with Malaya cannot be rushed: it must follow a federation of the Borneo territories and then allow for a larger measure of self-government in Borneo. He thinks that the Borneo territories would be well advised to wait and see the sort of Governments in power in Malaya and Singapore in 1964.
(c) In *Brunei*, which is predominantly Malay, the Sultan has for some time been in favour of his State becoming a State of the Federation of Malaya. He has, however, refused to express to our High Commissioner in Brunei even preliminary views on the Tunku's proposals and now seems rather nervous about them, no doubt because of the reactions in his State, where the only political party has come out for elections first and a federation of the Borneo territories before merger with Malaya. It is not certain how far this party could stage an effective revolt against a

move by the Sultan for an early merger with Malaya, but the latest advice from the High Commissioner and Lord Selkirk is that they are probably strong enough to prevent it.

19.   There is thus nothing in the material circumstances or in the general state of opinion of the Borneo territories which need inhibit us in wholeheartedly commending the *principle* of Greater Malaysia to their peoples: indeed, all Her Majesty's representatives there agree that we should do so. On the other hand, we assume that the United Kingdom Government would not commit themselves to hand over sovereignty in Sarawak and North Borneo (we have no sovereignty in Brunei) until they were satisfied that this was substantially in line with local wishes. Any outward indication that we contemplated including the Borneo territories in a Greater Malaysia without local agreement would not only do us damage in the territories and in the eyes of the world but also prejudice the success of the project (an argument which should carry weight with the Tunku). This raises the question to what extent it is in fact possible for us now, or will be in the near future, reasonably to satisfy ourselves—and opinion both within and without the Borneo territories—about local wishes.

20.   In Sarawak the United Kingdom Government are particularly committed by the eighth of the 'Nine Cardinal Principles of the Rule of the English Rajahs'[2], repeated in the constitution of 1946 when the Crown took over from the Brooke Rajahs, and reaffirmed last year in reply to a petition to The Queen which said that the United Kingdom Government would not surrender final responsibility for the development of Sarawak until they were satisfied that the people as a whole were able to play their full part in the government of the country, and that in pursuing this goal sight would not be lost of the best interests and desires of the indigenous communities. It cannot be claimed that, even as a result of a sharply accelerated programme of administrative, political and social development, these conditions could be satisfied within the next few years and the people of Sarawak be able to assume the responsibilities of government as a constituent state in a Greater Malaysia. At present there are still few indigenous civil servants and none of them hold senior positions. British officials might not be willing to stay on in numbers for long if Sarawak entered a Greater Malaysia. In accordance with practice, when the Secretary of State's responsibility for protecting British officials ceases, there would have to be a compensation scheme under which they would have the right to retire. This could be framed so as to put no premium on retirement. Nevertheless, the atmosphere might change so markedly that many might decide to retire. Malays from Malaya (if available, which is doubtful) would be unpopular, as has recently been seen even in Malay Brunei. Sarawak's premature entry into a Greater Malaysia might therefore lead to a breakdown in the administration. On the other hand, the Supreme Council (Executive Council) and the Council Negri (Legislative Council) both have majorities of unofficial members, and these in turn contain majorities of (indirectly) elected members. It thus might not be altogether unreasonable to claim that we could even today ascertain through the two Councils the wishes of the peoples of Sarawak. Further, proposals for constitutional advance in 1963 have been

---

[2] See 56, n 9.

approved in principle and are to be presented to the Council Negri in December. It may be desirable to accelerate some features of these. But in any case it will be the British officials who will have to put across the idea of an early Greater Malaysia to the non-Malay peoples and they will not be able to do this successfully unless they believe that it involves a fair deal for those peoples.

21.   North Borneo is still more backward, both politically and in the share taken by local people in the public service, and even less ready than Sarawak to assume the responsibilities of government. Although the Legislative Council has a majority of unofficial members, there are as yet no elected members; and on the Executive Council official and unofficial members are equal in numbers. It would thus be difficult to argue either that North Borneo is ready for full participation in a Greater Malaysia or that its people are in a position to decide for themselves whether or not to join. In particular, if we wanted at an early date to make an attempt to ascertain the wishes of the peoples of North Borneo in relation to Greater Malaysia, we could hardly claim that the Executive and Legislative Councils were adequate to speak for the whole country and we should have to consider whether the task could be carried out by other means.

22.   Brunei presents less difficulty since it is a Protected State in which the direct internal responsibilities of the United Kingdom Government are limited; the Sultan is believed to favour joining Malaya and the majority of the population is Malay and Muslim. Moreover, although in most ways backward, Brunei enjoys great (although diminishing) oil wealth. Unfortunately, owing to the Sultan's failure to hold promised elections and to clumsy tactics by him and the Tunku on a recent visit by the latter, substantial opposition to merger with Malaya has grown up in Brunei: but the High Commissioner advises that, if the Sultan and the Tunku were to moderate their autocratic attitudes, there would be a good chance that the opposition party could be brought round. There is a petition before the United Kingdom Government from the opposition party complaining of the failure to hold elections and, in the context of this, we could advise the Sultan that his promise to hold elections should be carried out as soon as possible and that the issue of merger should at once be placed before the new legislature, at the same time telling him that we regard merger as desirable in the interests of Brunei. We could tell the Tunku that this seemed to us the best course.

23.   Provided, then, that the Tunku and the Sultan can agree upon mutually satisfactory arrangements for the immediate incorporation of Brunei, we need raise no objection. In Sarawak and North Borneo the Governors believe that, given a firm lead from the United Kingdom Government, they could work out proposals for accession to a Greater Malaysia which would be acceptable in their territories. They think that these would have to include the following:—

(a) Existing British staff must be retained.
(b) Sarawak and North Borneo must have a large measure of internal self-government, including in particular control over:—
   immigration,
   education including language,
   citizenship,
   land development.
(c) Sarawak and North Borneo must retain their revenues, every cent of which is needed for their own development.

(d) There must be freedom to pursue closer association of Sarawak and North Borneo.

(e) The United Kingdom Government must somehow guarantee these provisions for a period at end of which Sarawak and North Borneo would have opportunity to opt out.

To what extent such proposals would be negotiable with the Tunku is very doubtful. (a) is referred to in paragraphs 20 and 21 above and paragraph 49 below. (b) and (c) are in different degrees out of accord with the Tunku's present insistence that the constitutional position of Sarawak and North Borneo in a Greater Malaysia must be that of States in the Federation of Malaya on the same basis as the present States, but it is not clear how far he may be prepared to make concessions on points of this kind. (d) might not be so difficult. There is already a movement towards closer association between Sarawak and North Borneo (for example, a joint Free Trade Area has been agreed on and is likely to be introduced early next year), we have encouraged it and local support is growing. It is a good thing in itself, particularly if Greater Malaysia were not to come off; and, provided that it is pursued without prejudice to the idea of Greater Malaysia, we should continue to encourage it. The Tunku might not like this, regarding it as a pretext for putting off the entry of Sarawak and North Borneo into Greater Malaysia, but it would be incomprehensible to the peoples of the territories why on any consideration of *their* interests we should not continue to support this salutary movement, and their suspicions would be aroused. (e) looks entirely unacceptable to the Tunku.

Defence

24. Ministers have already decided (F.P. (61) 2nd Meeting)[3] that in our forthcoming discussions with the Tunku we should make it clear that we intend, on the establishment of a Greater Malaysia, to hand over our internal security responsibilities in Singapore and the Borneo territories, but to seek to retain our defence facilities in Malaya and Singapore. Our general aim should be to reduce our forces to the Commonwealth Brigade Group stationed near Malacca and our existing naval and air facilities in Malaya and Singapore. Ministers thought that, although the Tunku would be unwilling to commit himself to allow facilities in Greater Malaysia to be used for operations in support of SEATO, it was quite possible that in a situation which involved a closer Communist threat to Malaya, he might be willing to acquiesce in operations from his territory except for the direct use of airfields for bombing. They accepted that we should support the concept of Greater Malaysia even though it might mean some diminution in our freedom of action in the theatre so far as defence goes. In the longer term we should have to be prepared to regard facilities in a Greater Malaysia as no more than forward operating bases on the use of which we could not rely in all circumstances; and we should consider, in consultation with Australia and New Zealand, alternative methods of fulfilling our SEATO commitments after the establishment of a Greater Malaysia.

25.   The background to these decisions is that under our existing constitutional relationships with Singapore and the Borneo territories we have an absolute right to establish and maintain any defence facilities that we require in those territories and

---

[3] See 70.

to use our forces stationed there for any purposes. In Malaya, however, our rights to maintain defence facilities and to use our forces stationed there depend on the terms of our defence agreement with Malaya and on the extent to which the Malayan Government, on local political grounds, feel able to allow our forces free entry and exit (Appendix C to this report). We maintain bases and forces in the area for three main purposes—internal security in Singapore, the Borneo territories, Hong Kong and our Pacific territories; the external defence of these British possessions and of Malaya (under the terms of our defence agreement); and the discharge of international (i.e. SEATO) and Commonwealth obligations.

26.   Eight of our major army units in Malaya and Singapore are on present plans required for internal security in Singapore itself and in our other possessions in the Far East and the Pacific. If Greater Malaysia is not achieved we must expect our commitment to remain indefinitely at no less than at its present level (unless Singapore is granted separate independence). We are anxious, however, on financial and man-power grounds, to reduce our forces in South East Asia as much as we can. It is implied in the Tunku's proposals that we should be relieved of all responsibility for internal security in Singapore and the Borneo territories. We do not know whether the Tunku is really alive to the implications of this. We have no evidence that he has yet considered what arrangements a Greater Malaysia would have to make to ensure that its responsibility for internal security could be effectively carried out from its own resources. We shall have to bring home to him the importance of this issue and the need for him to make concrete plans to meet it. The point may arise early in relation to Brunei if it decides to join in advance of the other territories (see paragraphs 46 and 56).

27.   If Greater Malaysia is not achieved we shall remain indefinitely responsible for the external defence of the Borneo territories, Singapore (unless separate independence is granted to it) and Malaya (under the terms of the Malayan Defence Agreement unless we decided to denounce it). If Greater Malaysia does come about we shall in any case still be responsible for the defence of Hong Kong and the Pacific territories and we shall have to renegotiate the Malayan Defence Agreement to fit the new situation. What commitments we undertake in the process will depend largely on the decisions which we take about the future scale and character of our contributions to SEATO. If we decided that in the long term we should aim to meet our SEATO obligations without maintaining substantial forces on the mainland of South East Asia, we should naturally want to reduce to a minimum any commitment to the defence of Greater Malaysia. On the other hand, the Tunku may well count upon British forces remaining in the area, believing that by their mere presence they will contribute to stability. In any case, as Australia has pointed out, we want the Malayan Government to remain anti-Communist and to be strong enough to control Singapore. It might therefore suit us for the time being to retain certain forces in Malaya and Singapore, whose role would include the external defence of Greater Malaysia.

28.   The essential elements of the defence problem may therefore be summarised as follows:—

(a) In planning our long-term policy and strategy in the Far East we recognise that we shall not be able to rely indefinitely upon the ability to use defence bases freely for all purposes. This is true whether or not Greater Malaysia comes about.

Indeed, it may be that the political realities in Singapore would even now impose great difficulties on our using the bases for SEATO operations in Laos.

(b) In the long term the most that we shall need in Greater Malaysia may be forward operating facilities; but final decisions on this must await the completion of our strategic studies and consultation with Australia, New Zealand and the United States.

(c) Meanwhile we should seek to negotiate terms which would enable us to use our facilities in the area as freely as possible for strategic purposes after Greater Malaysia has been brought about.

(d) The defence aspects of the Greater Malaysia project are of critical concern to Australia and New Zealand. Both Australia and New Zealand have forces in the Malayan area, and they have contributed and are still contributing large sums for the construction of defence facilities there. The Australian Government have emphasised to us the need to secure the best possible terms for the continued presence in the Malayan area of the Commonwealth strategic forces in their primary role of deterring Communist aggression. Both Governments have been informed of the considerations which we shall have in mind in the discussions with the Tunku; and they have been promised full and close consultation throughout.

(e) We expect to achieve a substantial reduction in our land forces there once Greater Malaysia is established, since the new State would take over responsibility for internal security.

(f) The Tunku clearly envisages that our defence facilities in Malaya and Singapore would be retained in a Greater Malaysia. But he seeks to impose conditions on their free use. In his memorandum at Appendix A he states that the bases 'will no longer be at the disposal of SEATO but could be maintained as bases for the defence of the Commonwealth.'

29.   It seems likely that the Tunku is in fact hoping to get the best of both worlds. On the one hand he hopes to be relieved of the very acute political problem of having bases on his territory overtly available for SEATO purposes. On the other hand he appears to be counting on the continued presence of substantial British Commonwealth forces in Greater Malaysia. The following considerations lead us to suppose that he will in fact wish these forces to be retained:—

(a) We would expect him to feel that the presence of British Commonwealth forces was a major contribution to the stability of the area; and this consideration may be particularly important during the early stages of the establishment of Greater Malaysia.

(b) The assumption by Greater Malaysia of responsibility for internal security in Singapore and Borneo will in itself impose a very heavy new burden on its own defence resources.

(c) Mr. Lee has recently emphasised in public how essential are our defence facilities in Singapore for the economy of the island, and has indicated that their removal would be most unwelcome from the economic point of view.

30.   We must recognise that politically it would be extremely difficult for the Tunku to agree to any public formula or agreement which linked our bases in Malaya and Singapore with SEATO by name. But the Tunku for his part must recognise that

we have obligations to SEATO which we cannot abandon. These are in fact in a very real sense 'Commonwealth' obligations because we share them with Australia, New Zealand and Pakistan. Moreover, there can be no doubt that SEATO has contributed to the stability of the area and has played an important part in preventing Communist aggression. Finally, a situation in which there were in a Greater Malaysia substantial British Commonwealth forces which were prevented from playing an effective part in the defence of South East Asia outside Greater Malaysia would be strategic nonsense.

31.   The Tunku appears to contemplate extension to Greater Malaysia of the existing Malayan Defence Agreement. This would not in itself meet the strategic requirements of ourselves, Australia and New Zealand. But the Tunku has indicated that he is concerned that the defence arrangements for the region should not be jeopardised; and he thinks that some suitable arrangement within the framework of the Defence Agreement could be arrived at whereby the various defence requirements may be satisfied. It is on that basis that we want to explore with him the possibility of some arrangement which would not cause unacceptable political difficulties for him but which would meet our essential strategic requirements.

32.   It has been suggested that to avoid relying on Singapore we should negotiate a retention of sovereignty over the island of Labuan off the coast of North Borneo, of which constitutionally it forms part. The success of such negotiations is, however, doubtful and the arrangement, besides involving considerable expense, would probably not prove durable.

Finance

33.   It is not possible at the present stage of our thinking to assess all the financial implications in the defence field of the attainment of a Greater Malaysia. We may reasonably expect to achieve substantial economies in overseas expenditure in the Far East by reduction of those forces stationed in Malaya and Singapore for purposes of internal security. But no substantial budgetary saving would be achieved unless the total strength of the armed forces was reduced by an amount substantially equivalent to the strength of the forces withdrawn; and if there were no such reduction, additional expenditure on the reprovision of accommodation in the United Kingdom or elsewhere might for some years even exceed the savings in running costs which might reasonably be expected from withdrawal.

34.   If in the longer term efforts were made to replace our existing defence facilities, or part of them in Labuan (paragraph 32 above) or in Australia, or through improved facilities for seaborne support, very substantial new expenditure over a period of years would be entailed.

35.   In any case, even if we did not have to agree to a request from the Tunku to keep certain forces in Malaya solely to fill the gap while Malaysian forces were being built up to replace them, we might nevertheless find it difficult to resist pressure to give the Tunku fresh help in money, material or training in expanding his own forces, over and above the substantial assistance (now nearly finished) which he has had from us since independence.

36.   As for financial implications outside the defence field, the United Kingdom Government's present assistance under the Colonial Development and Welfare Acts towards development in Sarawak and North Borneo is of the order of about

£1 million a year. If they remain dependent such aid will no doubt continue. If Greater Malaysia came about it would presumably cease but we should no doubt be expected to give assistance in some other form; we should also look to the Federation of Malaya to give substantial help.

37.   If Sarawak and North Borneo are to be equipped to take their places as part of a Greater Malaysia there will have to be an accelerated programme of training of local public servants; in so far as this is done before Greater Malaysia comes about the United Kingdom Government will be expected to meet most of the cost. Plans for this are now being considered but it is not yet possible to estimate the likely cost.

38.   The cost of compensating members of the Overseas Civil Service in Sarawak and North Borneo for loss of career and commutation of their pensions has been calculated at about £3.2 millions. Of this about £1.3 millions will be payable by the United Kingdom Government under the Overseas Service Aid Scheme. They might also have to assist the two Governments with their share.

39.   No financial implications for the United Kingdom Government would arise from Brunei's entry into a Greater Malaysia.

40.   Questions of accelerated aid for training or of compensation do not arise in Singapore. We are committed to an Exchequer loan in aid of Singapore's development of up to £5 millions in the period to the end of 1962 (although there is a good prospect that this will not be drawn down). We have also stated our intention to make a further contribution after an examination of the need at the beginning of 1963. Thus, even if Greater Malaysia supervenes in 1963, we are likely to be asked to honour this intention.

Conclusions

41.   The foregoing study of the problem leads us to the general conclusion that the earliest possible achievement of Greater Malaysia should be regarded as an aim of British Government policy because:—

(a) It offers the only satisfactory prospect of settling the political problem of Singapore.
(b) It would thereby contribute to the general security of the area and avoid the new threat of a Singapore either contained by British arms or independent under Chinese Communist influence.
(c) It offers the best long term prospect for the Borneo territories.
(d) It would relieve us of a heavy and costly military burden in the field of internal security in the Far East.
(e) It would probably reduce, and certainly could not increase, our commitments to the external defence of the territories concerned.
(f) It is unlikely to increase the difficulties which will in any case confront us in the discharge of our international defence obligations (i.e. SEATO).

42.   At the same time, it is clear from what has already been said that there are wide divergencies, at any rate in the short term, between our aims and interests and those of the Tunku in relation to defence and the Borneo territories. The following paragraphs outline the tactics which we recommend for the forthcoming discussions with the Tunku over the whole field of the Greater Malaysia project and in particular with regard to defence and the Borneo territories.

Tactics for discussions with the Tunku

General

43.   It will be important to win the Tunku's confidence in the United Kingdom Government's aims and intentions. At the moment there is a critical lack of confidence on his part. In the last few weeks, despite the re-assurances in the Prime Minister's messages to him, he seems to have become deeply and unreasonably suspicious of us. He appears to believe that we are deliberately magnifying, if not actually creating, difficulties over the Borneo territories and that it is our object to manoeuvre him into a position where Singapore and all its problems are left for him to deal with on his own. His reference in a speech on 16th October to the unavailability of Singapore as a SEATO base may have been intended by him as a reminder to us that we cannot take him for granted.

44.   If we are to create an atmosphere favourable to realistic and frank discussions it will be necessary to convince the Tunku of our wholehearted support for the Greater Malaysia project in principle, of our desire to see it achieved as soon as possible and of our willingness to give a warm public lead in its favour. But we must also make it clear to him that we cannot at this stage commit ourselves to definite dates for the accession of Sarawak and North Borneo; and also that arrangements will be necessary to enable our forces to continue to carry out their essential strategic role of deterring Communist aggression.

Singapore

45.   No difficulty arises here. The terms on which the Tunku and Mr. Lee are planning the merger of Singapore and Malaya are acceptable to us and we can so inform the Tunku.

Brunei

46.   We should approach the Tunku on the basis that Brunei is a Malaya [sic] and Muslim Protected State and that, so far as the United Kingdom Government are concerned, there is no objection at all to its joining the Federation of Malaya now. We should remind him that there is, however, strong (Malay) opposition to this in Brunei and tell him that our advice to the Sultan would be as suggested in paragraph 22 above, to carry out his promise to hold elections as soon as possible, and to put the issue of merger before the Legislature. We should be prepared to tell the Sultan that we regard merger as being in the interests of Brunei. We should invite the Tunku to give the Sultan similar advice. The Tunku may well say to this that we ought not to bother about the opposition or about elections, but ought just to advise the Sultan to announce that he is going to take his State into Malaya and be prepared to treat the opposition rough if they object. The Tunku makes light of the strength of this opposition. Our information both from our High Commissioner and the Shell Company is that it cannot be ignored. There are therefore three very good reasons why we should not agree if the Tunku takes the above line:—

(a) So long as our present Treaty with Brunei stands, we are ultimately responsible for security there and liable to be involved if disorder broke out. If it were serious we might even have to bring over troops from Singapore; and if that happened both parties would put the blame on us—indeed, the Sultan's cagey attitude over merger with Malaya is almost certainly calculated to make it possible for him to blame the United Kingdom Government for anything that might go wrong.

(b) Disorder might threaten the Shell oil installations in Brunei, which might make the need to introduce troops more cogent.

(c) The example of Brunei Malays (and this argument should appeal to the Tunku) resisting a merger with Malaya would be damning to the Tunku in Sarawak and North Borneo.

It must be made clear to the Tunku that it is for the Sultan and himself to sell the idea of a Greater Malaysia to the Brunei Malays. We cannot do it for them and we will not give the Sultan advice which we believe might lead to violence.

Sarawak and North Borneo

47. We should explain to the Tunku frankly what our difficulties are—the dangers of breakdown in the administration; our pledges to Sarawak; the need which we have to show publicly (not least in Parliament here) that we are not handing over Colonial peoples without due regard to their own wishes; and the matters to which we believe many of them will attach importance, including the continuation of the movement towards closer association between Sarawak and North Borneo (paragraph 23 above).

48. The best result would be if we could get the Tunku to accept the accession of Singapore without insisting upon the simultaneous accession of Sarawak and North Borneo, and instead to co-operate with us in planning for the accession of Sarawak only after, say, three or four years, and of North Borneo some years later still. No doubt any such plan would require us to undertake a very special effort to accelerate development of all kinds, particularly the training of public servants, in Sarawak and North Borneo—which would inevitably cost a good deal of money—but we might at the same time be able without much delay to obtain provisional agreement from Sarawak and North Borneo to enter a Greater Malaysia and we might expect that, with careful handling, they would more and more look towards that as a settled goal. We might also as an earnest of our intentions set up joint consultative councils, both official and unofficial, on which the Federation and the Borneo territories would be represented. And we could tell the Tunku that we propose (as we already have in mind) to appoint a senior officer on the staff of the Commissioner General to help further the plan. But we must face the fact that even in the first round of talks the Tunku seems unlikely to be satisfied with anything less than a firm undertaking on our part to get the Borneo territories into Greater Malaysia somehow and at some stage.

49. We have considered various means whereby responsibility for the administration of Sarawak and North Borneo might for a period of years be shared between Malaya and the United Kingdom. However they are dressed up, all such schemes, involving two sovereign countries, amount to a kind of condominium. A condominium over these two territories is probably incompatible with their incorporation in the Federation. Indeed, the incorporation of these two territories, subject to such a condominium, might even be considered to have an adverse effect on the international standing of the Federation. For example, the United Kingdom Government have in the past taken the view that 'dominion status' or full

membership of the Commonwealth is not possible for the Federation of Rhodesia and Nyasaland so long as the United Kingdom retains control of Northern Rhodesia and Nyasaland. However this might be, the possibilities of friction would obviously be immense and a condominium is in any case not likely to be acceptable to the Tunku. He is, however, understood not to object to British staff staying on, Malay Governors taking the place of British. Such a substitution of Governors would destroy the confidence of the non-Malays. But it seems just conceivable that an arrangement could be worked out whereby sovereignty was surrendered but the United Kingdom Government continued for a time to provide the staff to run the territories, including the Governors. The Governors would have to be appointed by, and responsible to, the Yang di-Pertuan Agong (King) of Malaya, but it might be possible to have an agreement that such appointments would be made on the advice of the United Kingdom Government. It might, perhaps, also be possible to agree that on non-Federal matters the Governors would have access to advice from this country: but this might prove to be a very difficult concept if such advice were to include 'political' advice as well as 'technical' advice. Such arrangements might, however, be acceptable neither to the Tunku nor to the territories, and the possibilities of friction in practice are nearly, although not quite, as great as in a condominium. In any case, a solution on those lines would be so complicated and so dependent for its successful adoption on agreement in the territories that it would be best not to mention it to the Tunku at this stage.

50.   The most hopeful line with the Tunku would seem to be to take up his own suggestion of an independent Commission. As he put it forward, such a Commission would result from a conference of representatives of the territories to be called in the near future and would be charged with the task of working out the constitutional details of a federation of the territories. Given the political immaturity of the territories it might be better not to have a conference at this stage and instead to let a Commission sound local opinion, consider what particular safeguards and other special arrangements would be needed for Sarawak and North Borneo if they entered a Greater Malaysia in their present state of unreadiness and propose constitutional arrangements to meet these. A conference could then follow the Commission with something practical to bite upon. (We are, however, in consultation with the Governors on the Tunku's suggestion and cannot give firm advice until their views are available.) It would seem quite unnecessary for such a Commission to cover Singapore, where a continuation of direct negotiation between the Tunku and Mr. Lee seems all that is necessary (although the Commission would, of course, need to know what the plans for Singapore were). Whether it should cover Brunei or not would need discussion with the Tunku and the Sultan.

Defence

51.   In accordance with the Ministerial decisions on the handling of defence aspects of the discussions, we should say to the Tunku that, as he appreciates, the formation of Greater Malaysia creates defence problems for us in the context of our international obligations and our joint responsibilities with Australia and New Zealand. We understand the Tunku's political difficulties over any specific commitment to SEATO. We want to explore with him ways and means whereby defence requirements do not become an obstacle to the creation of a Greater Malaysia. We should tell him that we should expect a Greater Malaysia to assume

military responsibility for its own internal security and that consequently we should make a substantial reduction in the land forces which we at present maintain in Malaya and Singapore. We should tell him that we should want to continue to have unfettered use of our defence facilities in Singapore and that, for as far as we can at present see, we should like, together with Australia and New Zealand, to continue to station the Commonwealth Strategic Brigade in Malaya on the understanding that we could if necessary commit it to SEATO operations; we should also like to retain the use of Butterworth airfield indefinitely. The Tunku on his side may say that he would like us to consider maintaining land forces in a Greater Malaysia over and above our contribution to the Commonwealth Strategic Brigade in order to assist the new country in its external defence. Also, he may say that a Greater Malaysia could not allow us either the use of facilities in Singapore and Malaya, or the stationing of the Commonwealth Strategic Brigade in Malacca if these were to be used for SEATO operations. If such a stage is reached in the negotiations we should take the line that this exchange of views has served as a valuable confrontation of his and our aims and difficulties and that we suggest that the next stage should be for both sides to do some re-thinking but that we are confident that, given mutual goodwill, these problems can be solved in such a way that, on the one hand, we can continue to fulfil our defence obligations and, on the other hand, defence problems need not in themselves constitute an obstacle to the formation of a Greater Malaysia.

52.   It is our aim to reduce as much as possible the forces stationed in Malaya and Singapore for internal security purposes. When we propose their reduction to the Tunku he may react by saying that the Malaysian Government will need assistance to build up its forces to replace those of ours which are leaving. The Federation of Malaya has had considerable defence aid from us since independence but it is very nearly finished and it is quite possible that the Tunku may press us for more. It would not be necessary for Ministers to answer such a request at once. The right tactics would probably be to remit the question for consideration by officials on the same basis as the financial talks of 1959.

53.   With regard to Labuan, referred to in paragraph 32 above, we should, at this stage, make no mention to the Tunku of the possibility of our wishing to retain sovereignty. We must, however, accept in consequence that if we get involved in a campaign to persuade the Borneo territories to accept the rapid achievement of Greater Malaysia before we have decided on our defence requirements, it may later become difficult to mention for the first time our desire to negotiate the retention of sovereignty over Labuan.

Summary of conclusions and recommendations

54.   We should accept the earliest practicable creation of Greater Malaysia as an aim of Government policy. We can tell the Tunku that we wholeheartedly welcome the idea of Greater Malaysia in principle and that we are prepared to give a warm public lead in its favour. We must make clear to him the importance of our working out together satisfactory defence arrangements. But the most pressing problem is one of timing, particularly in relation to the Borneo territories.

55.   We fully understand the urgency of the situation in Singapore. We also fully understand the strength of the Tunku's desire that the incorporation of Singapore and of the Borneo territories in a Greater Malaysia should be a concerted operation. It is, however, essential, if the operation is to be carried through successfully, that

Greater Malaysia should not be arbitrarily imposed on the inhabitants of the Borneo territories. We fully agree that their incorporation in a Greater Malaysia is to their best advantage in the long term; and we are anxious to press ahead as fast as possible. But time will be needed to ensure that the population as a whole are demonstrably in favour of this solution, and time will also be needed to develop the apparatus of Government and administration so that the territories are competent to carry out their functions as parts of a Greater Malaysia. We cannot, therefore, at this stage commit ourselves to firm dates for the accession of Sarawak and North Borneo. But we shall do everything that we can on the following lines to ensure that no time is lost.

56.   We are prepared to use our influence towards the early accession of Brunei to Greater Malaysia on such terms as the Tunku and the Sultan can agree between themselves and succeed in getting accepted in Brunei. But care will be needed in the handling of the opposition in Brunei and much harm would be done if the issue were to be so forced as to cause serious disorders.

57.   As regards Sarawak and North Borneo, we welcome the Tunku's suggestion for a Commission with the two-fold task of assessing the state of opinion about Greater Malaysia and of making recommendations on the manner in which the two territories might be associated in a Greater Malaysia (including any necessary safeguards for their special interests) and on the timing of their entry. We should be glad to discuss the composition and terms of reference of the Commission with the Tunku.

58.   We can go on to assure the Tunku that we are already pressing ahead with three different developments designed to expedite the participation of Sarawak and North Borneo in a Greater Malaysia—the appointment on the staff of the Commissioner-General of a senior officer to co-ordinate action in this context;[4] measures to accelerate the training of local people for their own public services; and advance in the constitutional and political field. As the Tunku knows, there is already a movement towards closer association between the two territories and we think it right to encourage this provided that it is proved without prejudice to the concept of Greater Malaysia.

59.   On defence we should do our best to make the Tunku realise the importance to himself and Greater Malaysia as well as to us of our continued ability to discharge our international, Commonwealth and other obligations, and consequently of our need to retain unfettered use of our existing defence facilities in the area. If we fail to reach agreement with him along that line, we should tell him that the exchange of views has been a valuable preparation for the further thought which is clearly necessary, adding that meanwhile we are sure that it would be right to assume that agreement can and will be reached and that we therefore need not delay such action as can be taken in other ways to promote the realisation of the Greater Malaysia concept.

60.   As regards Singapore, apart from the defence aspect, the arrangements which the Tunku has been discussing with Mr. Lee Kuan Yew do not raise any major problems for us, though the detailed arrangements will require consultation at a later stage.

---

[4] In Feb 1962 H P Hall, who was seconded from the CO to the commissioner-general's office, was posted to the Jesselton as co-ordinator for North Borneo and Sarawak.

Appendix B to 73: Population figures of the territories in the proposed Greater Malaysia

(Figures based on 1957 census in Singapore and Malaya and 1960 census in Borneo with adjustments estimated according to known rate of increase.)

Estimated population 1961

Malaya
Malays	3,500,000	49.3%
Chinese	2,675,000	37.6%
Indians	795,000	9.8%
Others	125,000	3.3%
	7,095,000	100%

Singapore
Malays	227,500	13.3%
Chinese	1,289,600	75.7%
Indians	145,100	8.7%
Others	45,100	2.3%
	1,707,300	100%

Combined Singapore/Malaya Population
Malays	3,727,500	42.3%
Chinese	3,964,600	45.0%
Indians	940,100	10.7%
Others	170,100	2.0%
	8,802,300	100%

British North Borneo
Indigenous ⎰ Non-Muslim	233,081	49.9%
Muslim ⎰ Brajaus, Bruneis	72,804	15.6%
Chinese	116,016	24.8%
Others (Indians, Pakistanis, Indonesians, etc.)	45,099	9.7%
	467,000	100%

Sarawak
Indigenous ⎰ Non-Muslim	353,130	44.7%
Muslim (Melanus)	47,400	6.0%
Chinese	243,320	30.8%
Malays	137,460	17.4%
Others (Indians, Asians, etc)	8,690	1.1%
	790,000	100%

Brunei

Indigenous	Muslim	(Kedayans)	14,450	17.0%
	Non-Muslim	(Dusuns, Dyaks, etc.)	9,350	11.0%
Chinese			16,150	19.0%
Malays			41,650	49.0%
Indians and Others			3,400	4.0%
			85,000	100%

Estimated Population of the Borneo Territories
(N. Borneo, Sarawak, and Brunei)

Indigenous	Muslim	134,654	10.0%
	Non-Muslim	595,561	44.4%
Chinese		375,486	28.0%
Malays		179,110	13.3%
Others		57,189	4.3%
		1,342,000	100%

Greater Malaysia (Population by territories)

Malaya	7,095,000	69.8%
Singapore	1,707,300	16.8%
N. Borneo	467,000	4.6%
Sarawak	790,000	7.1%
Brunei	85,000	1.7%
	10,144,300	100%

Greater Malaysia (Population by races)

Malays		3,906,610	38.5%
Indigenous	Muslim (Borneo)	134,654	1.3%
	Non Muslim (Borneo)	595,561	5.8%
Chinese		4,340,086	42.7%
Others (including Indians)		1,167,389	11.7%
		10,144,300	100%

Appendix C to 73: The Malayan defence agreement[5]

1. Our rights to maintain defence facilities in the Federation of Malaya and to use our forces stationed there depend on the terms of our defence agreement with the Malayan Government.

2. Under this Agreement:—

---

[5] For the negotiation of this agreement see *BDEE: Malaya*, lxxvii–lxviii, lxxx and 402, 407, 408, 410, 414, 417, 431, 432, 441, 462; for the text of the agreement see *Parliamentary Papers*, Cmnd 264, Sept 1957 and J de V Allen, A J Stockwell and L R Wright, *A collection of treaties and other documents affecting the states of Malaysia, 1763–1963* (London, 1981) vol II, 264–268.

(a) The United Kingdom Government undertake to afford Malaya 'such assistance as the Government of Malaya may require for the external defence of its territory'.

(b) The Government of Malaya afford to us the right to maintain in the Federation such naval, land and air forces as are agreed between the two Governments to be necessary for the external defence of Malaya and for the fulfilment of Commonwealth and international obligations. The Government of Malaya agree to the United Kingdom Government maintaining and using bases and facilities for these purposes. The United Kingdom Government undertake to consult the Government of Malaya when major changes in the character or deployment of their forces in the Federation are contemplated.

(c) In the event of an armed attack against Malaya or any British territories in the Far East, the two Governments undertake to co-operate with each other and to take such action as each considers necessary.

(d) In the event of a threat to peace or hostilities not covered by (c), the United Kingdom Government are committed to obtaining the prior agreement of the Malayan Government before committing their forces to active operations involving the use of bases in Malaya; but this does not affect the right of the United Kingdom Government to withdraw forces from the Federation.

3. The terms of the Malayan Defence Agreement have in practice placed restrictions on the use for SEATO purposes of our forces (including Australian and New Zealand forces). The Malayan position has been that our defence facilities in Malaya must not be used directly for SEATO purposes. It was, however, agreed with them that British forces stationed in Malaya could take part in SEATO exercises and return to Malaya provided that they were staged through Singapore. When consulted last March about the possibility of British forces in Malaya taking part in an operation in Laos, the Tunku stated that he would not object to the despatch of British troops from Malaya direct to the scene of hostilities provided that this country was not used as a base for military operations—in other words, a once for all withdrawal.

74   CAB 131/25, D 14(61)6   25 Oct 1961
'Greater Malaysia': Cabinet Defence Committee minutes

[The Committee reached the provisional conclusion that in the first round of talks with the Tunku, 'Greater Malaysia' should be welcomed in principle but the impression should be avoided that the British government was prepared to implement it forthwith and at all costs. Ministerial caution was expressed by Macmillan in his summing-up: 'the matter was one of great difficulty since it seemed likely that we should be faced with grave problems whether or not Greater Malaysia were achieved'. This document is also printed in Hyam and Louis, eds, *BDEE: Conservative government 1957–1964*, 1, 264.]

The Committee had before them notes by the Secretary of the Cabinet covering a report by the Official Committee on Greater Malaysia (D. (61) 62)[1] and a memorandum on Greater Malaysia by the Secretary of State for Air (D. (61) 66).[2]

---

[1] For the report of the Official Committee on Greater Malaysia, see 73.

[2] As secretary of state for Air (1960–1963), Amery expressed misgivings over the Greater Malaysia project which, he argued, would weaken Britain's title to the Singapore base. His memorandum is printed in Hyam and Louis, eds, *BDEE: Conservative government 1957–1964*, I, 263.

They also had before them a directive from the Prime Minister to the Minister of Defence on defence policy and strategy (D. (61) 65).[3]

The Commonwealth Secretary said that the present proposals by Tunku Abdul Rahman, the Prime Minister of the Federation of Malaya, for a Greater Malaysia comprising Malaya, Singapore and the three British Borneo territories represented a striking change of mind since he had in January of this year discussed with the Tunku the possibility of a merger of Singapore with Malaya. The Tunku was then utterly opposed to such a merger despite pressure for it from Mr. Lee Kuan Yew, the Prime Minister of Singapore. In the meantime, however, the shift of political strength in Singapore away from Mr. Lee towards the extreme Left had evidently persuaded the Tunku that he must as a matter of urgency incorporate Singapore while it still had a Government with which he could agree terms acceptable to Malaya, the alternative being an increase in Singapore of Chinese Communist influence which he did not trust the British to control. At the same time, the Tunku was not prepared to take Singapore into the Federation of Malaya unless by then he could also incorporate the three British Borneo territories, in order that their predominantly non-Chinese populations should be available to counter-balance the overwhelmingly Chinese population of Singapore. This presented the British Government with a difficult problem of timing as the Borneo territories were far from ready for such an association: in the last analysis we must do what we thought right about that and not simply abide by local opinion in Borneo, but it would be important to carry local opinion with us and the Tunku must be made to understand the need to do so. At present he over-rated the strength of Malaya's attraction in the Borneo territories. More difficult still was the problem of our bases in Singapore. The Tunku clearly aimed at getting all the military and economic advantages of a major British military presence in Malaya and Singapore while subjecting to his veto our operational use of our bases and other facilities.

We could agree to the creation of a Greater Malaysia subject to reasonable arrangements for the Borneo territories and satisfaction of our defence requirements, but we should exercise great caution in the conduct of our first round of talks with the Tunku next month. He was now so bent upon achieving a Greater Malaysia that we could afford to insist that our needs, particularly in the field of defence, must be adequately met. These talks should be regarded as an exploratory operation, and we should be ready to reserve our position for further consideration at a later stage if the Tunku's initial attitude proved intransigent and uncompromising. The situation in Singapore certainly imparted an element of urgency to the matter but was not itself immediately decisive.

The Secretary of State for Air said that the issue turned on whether we should be prepared to maintain our military position in Singapore, and whether we could in fact do so. In his view our whole position the Far East, and our ability to exert any influence with our allies—especially the United States, Australia and New Zealand—depended upon the retention of nothing less than our present rights in both Malaya (where they were limited) and Singapore (where they were quite unfettered). It was an illusion to think that, if we withdrew our forces from their internal security role in Singapore, the Tunku could still safeguard internal security with his own forces.

---

[3] *ibid*, document 66.

In a Greater Malaysia the influence of the Chinese was bound to increase and in due course to prevail. It was asking too much of the Tunku to leave this problem with him; and if we did so we should find ourselves having to move back again in difficult circumstances, such as those now facing the United States in South Vietnam. On the other hand, if we made the pivot of our policy a determination to stand firm in Singapore we could succeed in safeguarding our essential interests. The Tunku's confidence in us would be restored; non-Communist opinion everywhere would support us; and in Singapore itself we could count on the advantages of the local economic importance of our bases and the fact that the Singapore Chinese were an isolated community surrounded by hostile neighbours in Malaya, Indonesia and other countries.

In discussion the general feeling of the Committee supported the view of the Commonwealth Secretary that in the first round of talks with the Tunku we should adopt a favourable attitude towards the principle of Greater Malaysia but avoid giving any impression that we were prepared to implement it forthwith at all costs. We should bring out into the open all the very real difficulties for us attending the project, notably the necessity for great care in dealing with the Borneo territories (where too forceful an approach could not only wreck the whole enterprise but turn local eyes dangerously in the direction of Indonesia) and the vital importance which we attached to agreement upon defence arrangements fully adequate to our needs.

The other main points made in discussion were:—

(a) In the long-term we could not afford to go on defending Commonwealth countries which did not co-operate with us to the full. As was pointed out in the Prime Minister's minute of 23rd October to the Minister of Defence,[4] and as was clear from the Tunku's declaration that in a Greater Malaysia our Singapore bases would not be available for SEATO purposes, we could not assume that our defence facilities in Malaya and Singapore would indefinitely offer a balance of advantage to us. We must therefore in any case reconsider our long-term position there but we must also make every effort to ensure that our present position was not meanwhile further weakened. In this connexion *the Chief of the Defence Staff*[5] said that the island of Labuan had an airfield, a good anchorage, and only some 10,000 inhabitants; if necessary, Labuan might be to Singapore what Gan was to Ceylon. The island had been a gift to Queen Victoria, and recently had been administered by North Borneo purely as a matter of administrative convenience. The Official Committee's report had recommended that no mention be made at present of the possibility of our wishing to retain sovereignty, although this might make it difficult to mention it for the first time at a later stage. This seemed to be a somewhat unrealistic approach.

(b) In the short term it was very desirable that we should be able to reduce our heavy commitment to maintain internal security in Singapore; and we should remember that, if that responsibility passed to the Tunku, he could be expected to find it much easier than it would be for us to take and sustain repressive measures. For that reason he could afford to rely upon smaller forces than we had to earmark for internal security. We needed to obtain this reduction in Singapore for two main reasons. One was the pressing requirement for the savings which it would

---

[4] *ibid.*   [5] Lord Mountbatten.

represent in men and money. If we had indefinitely to keep forces in Singapore for internal security purposes on the present scale the whole balance of our long-term plans for the Services would be upset as regards both finance and man-power. The other reason was the urgent demand in other theatres for the forces thus tied up in Singapore. On these grounds the achievement of Greater Malaysia—if we assumed that it would relieve us of responsibility for internal security—would be most welcome. Moreover, if Greater Malaysia was not in sight before the review of the Singapore Constitution due in 1963 we were likely to encounter trouble there (as we could even earlier if Mr. Lee and his Government fell). In that case we should probably have to suspend the Constitution, perhaps for an indefinite period. Whether or not we suspended the Constitution we should be very ill-placed in Singapore (or Malaya) if we had to maintain our position in circumstances of local hostility. No doubt, as experience elsewhere had shown, we could hold the bases for some time—perhaps quite a long time—against the will of the local Governments and peoples, but this would inevitably make it extremely difficult to operate effectively from the bases. We should be in a particular quandary in Singapore since, although the Army could possibly be moved from the city into the naval and air bases, the bases themselves were so placed that reorganisation into a relatively compact and easily defensible pattern was impracticable. The idea of retaining sovereign areas in Singapore had its attractions, but an arrangement of that kind might not be of great help in practice.

(c) The paragraphs in the officials' report dealing with finance were as fair a statement of this issue as was possible at this stage, and there appeared to be no decisive financial objection to the Greater Malaysia project.

Summing up the discussion *the Prime Minister* said that the matter was one of great difficulty since it seemed likely that we should be faced with grave problems whether or not Greater Malaysia were achieved. Further consideration by Ministers would be necessary before the discussions with the Tunku took place.[6]

---

[6] See 77 and 78.

75 CO 1030/985, no 828   30 Oct 1961

[Preparations for the London talks]: letter from Sir J Martin to Sir A Waddell, responding to issues raised by governors of North Borneo and Sarawak in connection with the proposal for 'Greater Malaysia'
[Extract]

[In preparation for the London talks, Sir John Martin sent more or less identical letters to Waddell and Goode, passing on points from the report of the Official Committee (see 73) about the special position of the Borneo territories and inviting the governors' views on the tactics to be adopted during discussions with the Tunku. He noted, for example, the need for a commission of enquiry to assess Borneo opinion, safeguards for Borneo interests, retention of expatriate administrators during a transitional stage and the training of local staff. As regards the last point, P Rogers of the CO commented: 'we may have to try to achieve in perhaps as little as two or three years what we ought to spend at least twenty years in doing.' (Rogers to Goode and Waddell, 1 Nov 1961, CO 1030/1005, no 4).]

... 3.   The dilemma facing us all is clear. Unless we can clinch a plan for Greater Malaysia in the near future with the Tunku, the opportunity may pass for ever. The Tunku wants an assurance that Sarawak and North Borneo will join at least not later than Singapore. The Singapore situation sets 1963 as the deadline there. Yet, apart from the difficulty of ascertaining the real wishes of the majority of a population such as that of Sarawak and North Borneo, we know that, whatever steps we may take to hasten political advance, the training of local public servents (we shall be writing to you and Goode separately about this) and so on, the peoples cannot be ready by so near a date to support by any reasonable standards governments of their own within a Greater Malaysia.

4.   In the Commissioner General's telegram No. 46 of the 30th September, which gave his, your and Goode's agreed views, it was stated that you were agreed that Greater Malaysia offers the best future for the territories and that our basic policy should be to achieve it and that, if given a firm lead, you thought you could work out proposals which would be acceptable in Borneo. Paragraph 6 of that telegram then listed what you thought the Borneo requirements would be. These were as follows:—

(a) Retention of existing British staff.
(b) Borneo territories must have large measure of internal self-government, including in particular control over:—
      immigration,
      education including language,
      citizenship,
      land development.
(c) Borneo territories retain their revenues every cent of which is needed for their own development.
(d) Freedom to pursue closer association of Borneo territories.
(e) Somehow Her Majesty's Government must guarantee these provisions for a period at end of which Borneo territories would have opportunity to opt out.

There have been indications that (a) might not be entirely unacceptable to the Tunku, though it raises great difficulties (I recur to this question below). From what he has said to various Borneo visitors and from what he said in his speech on the 16th October in Parliament in Kuala Lumpur there seems to be room for negotiation on the question of the division of powers between the Federal Government and the 'State Governments' in Sarawak and North Borneo ((b) and (c) above). (d) also might be negotiable. But the requirement of a right to opt out at the end of a period seems to us frankly on present form an insuperable difficulty.

5.   Since local men to administer the territories cannot be trained in a year or two, however drastically one accelerates training and the giving of responsibility, and since Malays from the peninsula would be unlikely either to be available or acceptable (witness recent events in Brunei), the need to retain British staff as long as possible is clear. Apart from our obligations to the peoples, the absence of an adequate administration would carry the risk, as you have warned us, of racial strife and that in turn might lead to Indonesia fishing in troubled waters and a state of instability the exact opposite of what we would hope to achieve by the bringing about of Greater Malaysia.

6.   We have therefore given much thought to various means of sharing for a period of years responsibility for the administration of Sarawak and North Borneo

between the United Kingdom and the Federation Governments. Lord Selkirk's letters to which I have referred have been most helpful in this connection. But the fact is that, however such schemes are dressed up, all of them, involving two sovereign states, amount to a kind of condominium. The legal view is that a condominium over these two territories is probably incompatible with their incorporation in the Federation. Indeed, the incorporation of these two territories, subject to such a condominium, might even be considered to have an adverse effect on the international standing of the Federation. For example, the United Kingdom Government have in the past taken the view that 'dominion status' or full membership of the Commonwealth is not possible for the Federation of Rhodesia and Nyasaland so long as the United Kingdom retains control of Northern Rhodesia and Nyasaland. However this might be, the possibilities of friction would obviously be immense and a condominium is in any case not likely to be acceptable to the Tunku. He is, however, understood not to object to British staff staying on, Malay Governors taking the place of British. Such a substitution of Governors would destroy the confidence of the non-Malays. But it seems just conceivable that an arrangement could be worked out whereby sovereignty was surrendered but the United Kingdom Government continued for a time to provide the staff to run the territories, including the Governors. The Governors would have to be appointed by, and responsible to, the Yang di-Pertuan Agong of Malaya, but it might be possible to have an agreement that such appointments would be made on the advice of the United Kingdom Government. It might, perhaps, also be possible to agree that on non-Federal matters the Governors would have access to advice from this country; but this might prove to be a very difficult concept if such advice were to include 'political' advice as well as 'technical' advice. Such arrangements might, however, be acceptable neither to the Tunku nor to the territories, and the possibilities of friction in practice are nearly, although not quite, as great as in a condominium. (There would of course have to be a compensation scheme for officers, under which they would have the right to retire, this being framed, as in the more recent schemes elsewhere, so as not to put a premium on retirement.) We should be glad to have your comments on the above.

7.   Our general conclusion here is that the right course is to try to convince the Tunku that we—and you too—are with him in believing Greater Malaysia to be the best answer for Sarawak and North Borneo and that, because we really do believe it to be in the best interests of the territories, we do intend to do our best to persuade the territories to this view. But we should then try to get him to see, in his own interest and that of the Greater Malaysia plan, that, if this operation is to be carried through successfully, it is essential that Greater Malaysia should not be arbitrarily imposed on the inhabitants of the Borneo territories. We would tell him that we fully agree that their incorporation in a Greater Malaysia is to their best advantage in the long term; and that we are anxious to press ahead as fast as possible. But time will be needed to ensure that the population as a whole are demonstrably in favour of this solution, and time will also be needed to develop the apparatus of Government and administration so that the territories are competent to carry out their functions as parts of a Greater Malaysia. We cannot, therefore, we should have to make clear, at this stage commit ourselves to firm dates for the accession of Sarawak and North Borneo. We should, for preference, avoid discussion with the Tunku of the difficult and complicated concepts of shared sovereignties or that referred to in paragraph 6

above and should put forward the suggestion of an independent Commission of Enquiry with the two-fold task of assessing the state of opinion about Greater Malaysia and of making recommendations on the manner in which the two territories might be associated in a Greater Malaysia (including any necessary safeguards for their special interests) and on the timing of their entry. We have had some exchanges of view with you as to whether a Conference should precede such a Commission or not. The state of the game on this at the moment is that North Borneo would on balance like a Conference first (North Borneo telegram No. 207). Sarawak would on the whole now perhaps favour a Commission without a Conference (Sarawak telegram No. C.219)—and this is still, I think, our own preference—but nobody feels uncompromisingly on this point. It may be that we should wait and see how the Tunku feels on it before making up our own minds. At the same time as we proposed a Commission of Enquiry (with or without a Conference) we would assure the Tunku that we are already pressing ahead with three different developments designed to expedite the participation of Sarawak and North Borneo in a Greater Malaysia—the appointment on the staff of the Commissioner General of a senior officer to co-ordinate action in this context (if we reach agreement with the Tunku this appointment will of course have to take on the appearance and, indeed, the actuality of a Greater Malaysia co-ordinator rather than simply a Sarawak/North Borneo co-ordinator; we have just received Treasury agreement to such a post and shall soon be writing separately about this); measures to accelerate the training of local people for their own public services (we are writing separately about this also); and advance in the constitutional and political field (this also is being pursued in separate correspondence). We would also say that, as the Tunku knows, there is already a movement towards closer association between the two territories and we think it right to encourage this provided that it is done without prejudice to the concept of Greater Malaysia. We should have to see how he took this. It might be difficult to press it if he came out strongly against it; on the other hand it might be difficult to explain to the territories why in a consideration of *their* interests H.M.G. no longer thought it a good idea.

8.   I should welcome your early views on these suggestions. In addition, I should like to know whether you endorse Goode's suggestion in his telegram No. 202 that the Tunku and his close advisers should be encouraged to visit the territories to assess conditions and views for themselves.

9.   I should be grateful if in these coming weeks you would keep us very closely in touch with any local expressions of opinion on this issue (with your comments where appropriate on the importance to be attached to these).

10.   I am sending copies of this letter to Lord Selkirk, White and Tory. . . .

76   CO 1030/985, no 892   8 Nov 1961

[Preparations for the London talks]: letter from P B C Moore to W I J Wallace giving advice on how to counter Tunku Abdul Rahman's likely criticism of British policy towards Singapore

I mentioned in my telegram No. 466 that I would be commenting on two recent remarks made to the Press by the Tunku. I think we should consider these both for the reason that the Tunku may revert to them in London and because one has a close bearing upon the merger issue in Singapore. What the Tunku said was:—

(a) that the Singapore officials and trade union leaders have been given too much rope; that the British have not been firm enough and have tried to please everyone;

(b) that if Merger did not come about then in all probability the British would in 1963 give Singapore a constitution that made them independent and thus lead to a communist threat on the doorstep of the Federation.

2. As to the first point, one might hope that the Tunku would not feel any useful purpose would be served by going over with us the rights and wrongs as he sees them of our handling of political and constitutional developments in Singapore during the past two or three years. I suspect, however, that he may well do so, at any rate in private conversation with Ministers, and I think we must be prepared to deal in a general way with his charge of weakness.

3. If the question is whether we were right in giving Singapore its present Constitution, the answer is surely that this was inevitable given our general Colonial policy and the pace of progress in other territories. The Tunku himself must see that having granted independence to the Federation in 1957, when merger with Singapore was not a starter, H.M.G. were bound to go some way towards meeting the wishes of the people of Singapore for a greater measure of self-government. The Constitution was an attempt to do this while not divesting ourselves of the powers needed to maintain internal security and to protect our military base facilities. The Tunku may counter that even so there was no call for us when the Constitution came into force to agree to the release of the leading political detainees, some of whom we must have suspected to be communists. The answer is that we had to take this risk in order to induce the P.A.P. leaders to undertake the responsibilities under the Constitution. Only thus could we open the way for the development of a strong, stable local government that might be prepared to stand up publicly and clearly for the things in which it believed and to resist the efforts of a communist minority to lead the people astray. The Tunku must know that we have missed no opportunity of encouraging Lee Kuan Yew to take such a stand: the pity is that he has left it so late.

4. I think that we must also be prepared to deal with the further question whether H.M.G. themselves, through the U.K. Commissioner and using his powers under the Constitution, should not have taken firmer action themselves over the past two years to deal with the communists in Singapore. It is not easy to deal with this shortly: the fact is that having granted the Constitution we had to give it a fair trial and there has been no obvious instance in which we failed to use our powers in the I.S.C. or otherwise. Indeed, in the cases of Soviet economic aid and Gazov, we used them to good effect.[1] The Tunku may allude to the 'Eden Hall tea party' and question the wisdom of our telling Lim Chin Siong & Co. that our task was to see that the Constitution was worked properly.[2] I need not go into all this again. The short answer is that, having given Singapore its Constitution, we had to make it clear that we would abide by it. The undermining of the P.A.P. was partly inevitable but largely the fault of Lee Kuan Yew. We were not responsible.

---

[1] For British concern about Singapore's interest in Soviet aid, see 33, para 23.   [2] See 49.

5.   This brings us to the second of the Tunku's points—that H.M.G. will, failing Merger, give Singapore independence in 1963. There are I think two questions arising from his public statement to this effect; first, whether we should make any public statement in reply and, second, what in any event we should say to the Tunku if he raises in London the question of H.M.G's policy for Singapore if Merger fails to come about.

6.   As regards a possible public statement, I have already reported in our telegram No. 465 Lee Kuan Yew's view that it is essential that H.M.G. should publicly contradict the Tunku's assertion and say that Singapore belongs to Malaya, historically, politically, economically and geographically and is in effect a West Irian to which the Tunku can lay an unassailable claim.[3] At a later meeting he put forward a somewhat different suggestion to the effect that H.M.G. should say that if there were ever any question of relinquishing their sovereignty over Singapore it could, for historical, economic and geographical reasons, only be relinquished—with the consent of the people of Singapore—to the Federation of Malaya. In devising these formulas Lee Kuan Yew has of course in mind the need to indicate to the people of Singapore before the referendum that if they vote against Merger there is no prospect of independence for the Island alone. As reported, I told Lee that it is very unlikely that we would be prepared to say anything on the lines of his first formula, although it might be that we should want to say something to dispel the idea put out by the Tunku that complete independence would in all probability be given to Singapore in 1963. The sort of statement I had in mind was on the lines that the question of what H.M.G. might do as a result of constitutional review for Singapore in 1963 is premature; that at the present juncture both H.M.G. and the people of Singapore are considering the fundamental and more immediate question of whether or not the State should merge with the Federation of Malaya; and that it is quite impossible at this time for H.M.G. to commit themselves in any way on the hypothetical question of what might be done in 1963 if Merger did not take place. I imagine that we could fairly readily agree to make such a statement and it would go some way towards meeting Lee Kuan Yew's point by leaving quite open the question of Singapore's political future if they go it alone. However, I doubt whether Lee Kuan Yew would be satisfied and we need to consider whether it would be possible for H.M.G. to go further and make a statement on the lines of the second formula that he has suggested.

7.   That formula contains in effect three propositions:—

(i)   that independence will not be granted to Singapore alone;
(ii)   that independence will only be granted through merger with the Federation of Malaya;
(iii)   that merger with Malaya will not be effected except at the wish of the people of Singapore.

So far as (iii) is concerned no difficulty arises. It was stated in 1956 (see last para. of Appendix 5 to Report of Singapore Constitutional Conference—Cmd. 9777) that Merger would not be forced. It was also stated in Parliament in 1958 by the then

---

[3] That is to say, Singapore was to be regarded as much an extension of Malaya as Dutch West Irian was of Indonesia.

Secretary of State that a decision on Merger was for the peoples of the two countries alone to take and I do not think we would hesitate to reaffirm this if necessary. The other two points are, however, very much more difficult. I suppose it is not impossible that H.M.G. should declare in effect that they do not have any intention of transferring sovereignty over Singapore to any other country than the Federation of Malaya. But there is no point in making such a statement except in conjunction with the further proposition that we have no intention of relinquishing sovereignty to the people of the Island itself. In other words, that Singapore cannot become independent alone.

8.   There is in fact quite a lot of material bearing on this question in the Report of the 1956 Singapore Constitutional Conference mentioned above. The Singapore delegation put forward a closely reasoned case for saying that Singapore could become a fully independent state within the Commonwealth and arguments against this on grounds of non-viability, risk of communist subversion and Commonwealth strategic requirements were all dismissed. In equally closely reasoned rebuttal of the proposition H.M.G. did not go so far as to make a flat statement that independence for Singapore was ruled out. The general remarks at the end of Appendix 5 in Cmd. 9777 summed up the case against independence in the circumstances then prevailing but indicated that the position of Singapore would have to be reviewed if it became clear that the road to full independence through Merger, which H.M.G. favoured, was closed. In the light of this and of the development in other Colonial territories since 1956—Cyprus springs naturally to mind—I do not see how it would be possible for H.M.G. to say categorically that they would never grant independence to Singapore alone. The conclusion, I suggest, is therefore that we cannot make a statement on the lines of either of the formulas suggested by Lee Kuan Yew and that if a statement is to be made it will have to be of the kind I have suggested earlier.

9.   There remains the related but separate question of what we should say to the Tunku in confidential discussions if he asks how H.M.G. foresee events panning out over the period up to 1963, and thereafter, if in fact Merger is rejected and Singapore is left for us to deal with. So far as the short term is concerned, the question is one to which we have given much thought in the Commission. Our judgement is that if Lee Kuan Yew is defeated on the Merger issue his position will crumble rapidly. Unless his fall is accompanied by disturbances in which we are forced to re-assume direct responsibility for the government of Singapore, the ordinary processes of the Constitution will operate and there will be a general election. The likelihood in that event is that the Barisan Socialis will form the new government and the question that the Tunku may well put to H.M.G. is whether they intend to let this happen or whether they have any plan for preventing either the party or certain of its individual leaders from assuming political office. The answer to this is not easy and there are some who judge that H.M.G. would be well advised to take 'firm action' at the very start and put a number of people in detention. I am satisfied however that, always assuming that there is no resort to direct action and that the Barisan Socialis play their cards strictly constitutionally, it would be impossible for H.M.G. to advocate the taking of purely preventive action against the party or any of its leaders. Such action would in any case be a confession of failure and would lead us down a blind alley from which it would be difficult to extricate ourselves. We cannot know for certain how the political forces within the party would work out over any period in which the Barisan Socialis were in office and it must surely be our hope that, as with the P.A.P.

so with the Barisan Socialis, the extremist leaders would not in the event prove so extreme and a communist take-over in Singapore would be averted.

10.   I doubt whether any forecast of events working out satisfactorily on this course would convince the Tunku or prevent his asking the obvious question—'What if you discover after Barisan Socialis come to power, that there are no leaders of consequence within the party other than the communist leaders, and that they are following the classical communist procedure of subverting the organs and processes of democratic government from within?' This is of course the most difficult question and one that cannot be answered in detail in advance. The point to be made to the Tunku however is that H.M.G. are not blind to the risk, that they will certainly watch very carefully the way things are going in Singapore and will be prepared to take such action as they deem necessary to forestall communist subversion of democratic government in the Island. The point can be put convincingly that we should not be so foolish as to allow a communist take-over in the very place where we were basing the forces charged with the task of resisting communist expansion in the rest of S.E. Asia.

11.   Finally we should perhaps consider what we would say if the Tunku asked bluntly how long we thought we should continue to require substantial defence facilities in Singapore and whether there was any risk of our abdicating our responsibilities here once our strategic interest had disappeared. In the nature of things these questions are unanswerable but presumably H.M.G. will in the general defence discussions with the Tunku make it clear that in the short to medium run they will need and intend to retain their defence bases in Singapore. I would only add that one of the ways in which we have brought the Tunku to contemplate Merger is by bringing home to him the possible long term threat of Singapore to the Federation. We must not at this stage run any risk of persuading him that Merger is not necessary after all!

12.   To sum up, I suggest:—

(a) that if the Tunku should revert to his charge that the British have given the politicians and Trade Union leaders here 'too much rope' we should, as far as possible, forego detailed rebuttal and content ourselves by making the general point that Britain has in Singapore, as in many other Colonial territories, had no option but to take quite considerable risks in pursuing the broad policy of advancing the Colonies as rapidly as possible towards self-government. The Tunku must know as well as any other Commonwealth leader that in the second half of the twentieth century, a bold policy of this sort is the only one open to us, and that there is no need to equate it with weakness towards communism.

(b) that if H.M.G. felt obliged to make a public statement about the constitutional prospects for Singapore in 1963 should Merger not come about, we should say that it is premature to consider such a hypothetical question at this stage; Merger with the Federation is the immediate and fundamental question on which we are concentrating our attention.

(c) that, if pressed by the Tunku to say how we envisage dealing with the immediate situation if the P.A.P. Government should fall, we should re-assure him privately that even if the Barisan Socialis come to power we shall watch developments closely and will take determined action as necessary if we see communists in the party working successfully towards a gradual take-over of the

democratic institutions in this Island; but that we should be careful not to reassure him too completely lest he should decide that Merger is, after all,
unnecessary.

13.   I am sending a copy of this letter to Martin Moynihan.

77   CAB 130/179, GEN 754/1st meeting   **9 Nov 1961**
**[Preparations for the London talks]: minutes of the first meeting of
the Cabinet Greater Malaysia Committee**

[Set up primarily to consider matters other than defence and chaired by the prime
minister, the Greater Malaysia Committee met three times: 9 Nov, 15 Nov 1961 (see 78)
and 21 March 1962 (see 98). The day before the first meeting, Brook briefed Macmillan on
the Tunku's suspicion that 'we want to unload Singapore upon Malaya while keeping the
Borneo territories in our own possession'. Sir Norman Brook stressed that it 'is essential
for us to reassure him about this' (Brook to Macmillan, 8 Nov 1961, PREM 11/3422). The
meeting on 9 Nov was attended by Macmillan, Butler (Home), Home (FO), Watkinson
(Defence), Maudling (CO), Carrington (first lord of the Admiralty) and the Duke of
Devonshire (joint parliamentary under-secretary of state, CRO). Sir A Clutterbuck, chair
of the official committee, was also present. Notwithstanding its object to consider 'those
aspects of the problem which did not relate to defence', the meeting reverted to defence
and the future of Singapore bases bulked large in Macmillan's summing up.]

1. Visit by the first lord of the Admiralty to Canberra and Wellington
The Meeting considered a telegram from the United Kingdom High Commissioner in
Canberra to the Commonwealth Relations Office (No. 996 of 9th November) saying
that the Prime Minister of Australia would be replying personally to the Prime
Minister's message but that he had reluctantly decided that, as the Australian
election campaign had already begun, it was not practicable for him or other
Australian Ministers to receive the First Lord properly in the time available.[1] Mr.
Menzies also said that it could be embarrassing for him if the First Lord were to visit
New Zealand but not Australia.

In discussion the Meeting agreed that in these circumstances the proposed visit by
the First Lord to Canberra and Wellington should not now take place. This was
regrettable and it would be worth while to bear in mind the possibility of a meeting
of Ministers from Australia, Malaya, New Zealand and the United Kingdom after the
first round of talks with the Tunku if it had not resulted in agreement upon
arrangements for defence fully adequate to our needs.

The Meeting:—

Invited the Joint Parliamentary Under-Secretary of State for Commonwealth
Relations[2] to arrange for a telegram to be sent to the United Kingdom High
Commissioner in Wellington telling him that the First Lord's visit would not

---

[1] Australia and New Zealand were partners with Britain in the defence of Malaya and Singapore, and on 20
Oct Macmillan warned their prime ministers (Sir Robert Menzies and Keith Holyoake) of the likelihood of
Britain losing its full freedom over the Singapore base. Lord Carrington, first lord of the Admiralty, was
then lined up for a goodwill mission to Canberra and Wellington, but the visit was called off because of the
Australian election campaign. Menzies' Liberal-Country Party was returned to power on 9 Dec.
[2] The Duke of Devonshire was the nephew of Macmillan's wife and was promoted to minister of state, CRO,
in Sept 1962.

now be taking place but that no further communication on the subject would be sent to the Prime Minister of New Zealand until the Prime Minister had had the promised telegram from the Prime Minister of Australia.

2. Greater Malaysia

The Prime Minister said that the object of the meeting was to consider primarily those aspects of the problem which did not relate to defence. The Defence Committee had considered the defence aspects of the officials' report on Greater Malaysia (D. (61) 62) on 25th October[3] and had reached the provisional conclusion that in the first round of talks with the Tunku we should adopt a favourable attitude towards the principle of Greater Malaysia, but avoid giving the impression that we were prepared to give effect to it at once or at all costs. We should bring out with the Tunku the difficulties with which the project presented us, notably the necessity for great care in dealing with the Borneo territories and the vital importance which we attached to agreement on defence arrangements fully adequate to our needs. The Chief Secretary to the Treasury[4] had already expressed the view that there appeared to be no decisive financial objection to Greater Malaysia, and we were thus left to consider its political implications.

The Tunku was at present deeply suspicious of our attitude towards Greater Malaysia, believing that we wanted to make Malaya assume our responsibilities for Singapore while we retained possession of the Borneo territories. We must seek to remove this suspicion without committing ourselves too hastily or deeply over the Borneo territories. We need not greatly concern ourselves about arrangements for Singapore (apart from the problem of the bases) or for Brunei: so long as the Tunku could reach agreement with the Government of Singapore and the Sultan of Brunei on arrangements for closer association acceptable in all three territories, those arrangements would almost certainly be acceptable to us. But there were real difficulties about North Borneo and Sarawak. The Tunku was wrongly convinced that the non-Chinese majorities of their populations were Malays of a sort and that, left to themselves, they would at once accept immediate incorporation in Greater Malaysia. This was untrue: not only were these peoples not of Malay stock but, for historical and other reasons, they regarded the Malays with some suspicion; and such public opinion on the subject as existed in the two territories, although cautiously favouring Greater Malaysia in principle, did not favour entry into it at an early date or on a par with the present States of the Federation of Malaya. We were deeply pledged (particularly in relation to Sarawak) to retain responsibility for both territories until their peoples were themselves ready to take over from us. Since by ordinary standards this would not come about for many years, a rigid interpretation of our obligations would involve a lengthy postponement of the idea of a Greater Malaysia. On the other hand, substantial delay was likely not only to lead to grave trouble in Singapore but also to increase the difficulty of bringing the Borneo territories into Greater Malaysia at all (and we were satisfied that membership of Greater Malaysia offered them the best prospects in the long-term). In this dilemma we must seek to persuade the Tunku that we sincerely desire to get the Borneo territories into Greater Malaysia but that we must also make a genuine effort to establish the

---

[3] See 74.   [4] Henry Brooke.

willingness of their peoples to come in, if only because any attempt to dragoon them without at least proper consultation could stir up such trouble in the territories as seriously to damage, and perhaps altogether to destroy, any prospect of success.

In discussion the following points were made:—

(a) The political situation in Singapore was precarious and gave rise to the question whether, even supposing that Mr. Lee won his referendum, he and his party might not, before Greater Malaysia could be brought into existence, be replaced by a different government which would repudiate any agreement already reached with the Tunku. The general feeling was that that risk has to be taken but that it imparted additional importance to the awkward differences which had lately arisen between Mr. Lee and the Tunku about the form of the Singapore referendum. The Tunku wanted it to pose a single question relating to a form of merger which would associate Singapore with the Federation in much the same way as Northern Ireland is associated with Great Britain. Mr. Lee wanted to avoid the risk of outright defeat on a single question by adding a second choice of full merger between the two territories, but this was quite unacceptable to the Tunku. Every effort was being made locally to resolve these differences and there was nothing that we could do about them. It seemed reasonable to hope that Mr. Lee's position would be stronger once he had won his referendum and that he would not be forced into a general election before one became due in the ordinary way in 1963. This would allow some time in which to make progress in North Borneo and Sarawak.

(b) The United Kingdom representatives in those territories thought that we could get them into Greater Malaysia if we avoided undue haste. The best way of setting about the problem might be, as the Tunku had himself proposed, the appointment of a Commission to examine the matter on the spot. But whereas the Tunku wanted a Commission only to work out constitutional arrangements for the incorporation of the Borneo territories in Greater Malaysia, it seemed essential that it should also be given the task of assessing local opinion on the project. The Commission might take any one of various forms. The Tunku's idea appeared to be an independent chairman together with two Malayan and two British representatives. But it might be better to have a Commission which was wholly independent in the sense that it contained no direct representatives of any of the Governments concerned. Another possibility was a one-man Commission, and in that case Mr. Malcolm MacDonald might be a suitable and generally acceptable choice if his services could be obtained. The Meeting agreed that the only practicable means, first of reassuring the Tunku about our willingness in principle to bring North Borneo and Sarawak into Greater Malaysia, and second, of carrying opinion both in the two territories and outside with us in any such attempt, was the appointment of a suitable Commission of some kind, with terms of reference and membership satisfactory to the four Governments concerned. Its tasks would be to establish the general state of local opinion about Greater Malaysia and to recommend the constitutional and other terms on which North Borneo and Sarawak might enter the wider association, including any special arrangements which might be necessary to safeguard their interests until they reached a stage of development on a par with the existing status of the Federation of Malaya.

In further discussion the Meeting reverted to the defence aspects of the problem and the following were the main points made:—

(c) It was impossible in advance of the forthcoming talks with the Tunku to define the defence problem more precisely than had been done in the officials' report, or to determine our approach to it more exactly than the general conclusion of the Defence Committee on 25th October, 1961. We must probe the Tunku very hard about it in order to discover to the greatest possible extent what he really had in mind, but without giving any indication at this stage that we might be able to accept any derogation from our present rights in the Singapore bases. It would be very damaging if we made any substantial concession before engaging in thorough consultation with our Australian, New Zealand and American allies, all of whom wanted us to retain our existing rights and facilities in Singapore. It might be, however, that we ought in any case to begin planning a radical change in our military presence in the Far East, switching from a pattern of cantonments in Malaya and Singapore to a main base in Western Australia (possibly with a forward operating base in e.g. Labuan) and relying upon an air-borne and sea-borne capacity to intervene in South East Asia. On that calculation, if the Tunku refused to allow us freedom in the use of our facilities in Singapore within a Greater Malaysia, our best course might be simply to live it out in Singapore for some years while we made our new arrangements. During that time, despite all the local difficulties which would beset us, we could probably count upon being able at least to mount a 'once for all' operation from Singapore if necessary.

(d) The question was largely one of presentation. The Tunku's attitude to our difficulties over Laos had not been unreasonable and he might be willing to enter into private agreements with us which would meet our material requirements. But no private agreement would fully serve our ends, if our public position involved a ban (or even a veto) by a Greater Malaysian Government on our use of the Singapore bases for SEATO purposes. A possible compromise might be to develop the ANZAM arrangement, bringing Greater Malaysia more fully into it and turning our defence agreement with Malaya into a quadripartite treaty between Australia, New Zealand, Greater Malaysia and the United Kingdom. This would accord with the Tunku's present willingness to allow us free use of the Malayan and Singapore bases for Commonwealth defence, although not for SEATO; and the New Zealand Government had in fact made such a suggestion. If it were adopted, the Tunku might be prepared to agree publicly not only that we should have complete freedom of action for Commonwealth defence, but also that we could use the bases operationally for other (i.e. in fact, SEATO) purposes also, subject to consultation, at the same time undertaking privately not to make difficulties for us in any such consultation.

(e) We had several useful cards to play in our talks with the Tunku—his own enthusiasm for Greater Malaysia, enhanced the general value of the part which we could and must play if it were to be achieved; we could offer him material co-operation in getting the Borneo territories in, or at least committed; he almost certainly wanted us to maintain a substantial military presence in South East Asia; and it would be in his interest to ensure that the merger did not entail a reduction in the massive employment which our forces provided in Singapore.

Summing up *the Prime Minister* said that we could support the Greater Malaysia project in relation to Singapore (subject to satisfactory arrangements about the bases) or Brunei, and that we could give it our blessing in principle in relation to North Borneo and Sarawak, while insisting upon fair treatment for their peoples. But in the last analysis our attitude must be determined by our ability or inability to obtain satisfaction of our defence requirements: any agreement with the Tunku about them must be not only adequate in effect but also defensible in public.

The Meeting:—

(1) Took note of the Prime Minister's summing up.

(2) Agreed to discuss the Greater Malaysia project further the following week.

78   CAB 130/179, GEN 754/2nd meeting   15 Nov 1961
[Preparations for the London talks]: minutes of the second meeting of the Cabinet Greater Malaysia Committee

[The attendance at the second meeting of the committee differed from that on 9 Nov: Macmillan, Kilmuir (lord chancellor), Home, Hailsham (lord president and minister of science), Sandys, Watkinson, and Maudling.]

1. Discussions with the Tunku

The Prime Minister said that discussions with the Prime Minister of Malaya (Tunku Abdul Rahman) about Greater Malaysia were due to start on 20th November. The Malayan delegation would be small, consisting of four Ministers and two senior officials, and it seemed desirable to avoid confronting them with too large a United Kingdom team.[1] The nature of the talks themselves, which would be largely exploratory, also made it desirable to keep the meetings relatively intimate and informal. Our aim should therefore be to limit regular attendance at the meetings to the Ministers most directly concerned (the Commonwealth Secretary, the Colonial Secretary and the Minister of Defence), each being accompanied by preferably not more than one official adviser. It did not seem necessary to trouble the Chancellor of the Exchequer or the Foreign Secretary to attend these meetings as a matter of course, but it would be helpful if they could be available to attend a particular meeting if that seemed desirable. In these circumstances it also seemed desirable to dispense with any full, formal record of the proceedings for agreement between the two sides. No doubt each side would want to take their own notes and we should certainly keep an adequate record ourselves: for the rest, we should aim at the end of the talks to agree with the Malayans upon a summary of the conclusions reached.

He suggested that he should preside at an opening meeting at 11 a.m. on Monday, 20th November, and a closing meeting at 4 p.m. on Thursday, 23rd November, although it would be possible for him if necessary, to take the closing meeting at 11 a.m. on Friday, 24th November. These meetings would be held at Admiralty House. The intervening meetings should be conducted by the Commonwealth Secretary at the Commonwealth Relations Office.

He would open the first meeting by giving a general welcome to the idea of Greater Malaysia and then ask the Tunku to give his own views at length on the subject. He would then wind up by describing the United Kingdom's general attitude to the concept, including a statement of the main problems as we saw them—how to deal with the Borneo territories; the future of the Singapore bases; and by what practical means we might seek to make progress in bringing Greater Malaysia into being.

---

[1] See 79, note, for the composition of the negotiating teams.

The Meeting:—

(1) Took note of the Prime Minister's statement.

(2) Instructed the Secretaries to arrange for the Official Committee on Greater Malaysia to consider detailed preparations for the discussions in accordance with that statement.

2. Proposal for a commission of enquiry

The Meeting considered a brief on this subject (GEN. 754/2, Annex A) prepared by officials for use in the discussions with the Tunku.[2]

The Prime Minister said that the Tunku had suggested that a commission should be appointed to work out the constitutional details of a Greater Malaysia on the model of the commission under Lord Reid which had drafted the constitution of the Federation of Malaya.[3] But officials, while supporting the idea of a commission, had recommended that its task should be rather different and two-fold—to ascertain the views of the peoples of North Borneo and Sarawak on Greater Malaysia, and then, in the light of those views, to make recommendations about the manner and timing under which such an association might be achieved and the safeguards which might be necessary for the two Borneo territories. Arrangements for the merger of Singapore with Malaya were already far advanced separately and there seemed no reason for the proposed commission to cover Singapore; and this was probably also true of Brunei since it was in a different position from the other two Borneo territories as a predominantly Malay and Muslim Protected State over which we had no sovereignty. Ministers had already agreed that we could almost certainly accept any arrangements which the Tunku might reach with the Government of Singapore and the Sultan of Brunei for closer association acceptable to all three territories. We had, however, to consider whether there should be separate commissions to assess opinion in North Borneo and Sarawak about Greater Malaysia and to make constitutional recommendations about their incorporation, or whether one commission could undertake both tasks. We had also to consider whether there should be conferences between the Governments concerned before or after any such commission had done its work, or both. Officials recommended that we should aim in our discussions with the Tunku to get agreement on a single commission with terms of reference on the lines which he had mentioned, and that in the light of its report there should be a conference representing all the territories of Greater Malaysia and the United Kingdom at which formal decisions might be taken on the creation of Greater Malaysia.

In discussion the following points were made:—

(a) There seemed advantage in having one commission and not two since it would be difficult to examine the state of local opinion in Borneo about Greater Malaysia without at the same time considering what might be the form of the Greater Malaysia which was the subject of that opinion.

(b) Because the work of the commission would be focussed upon North Borneo and Sarawak it was arguable that it should consist entirely of members appointed by the United Kingdom Government. A suitable team might consist of Mr. Malcolm MacDonald as chairman (he was known to be favourable to the concept of Great [sic]

---

[2] Not printed.   [3] See 46, n 5; for the selection of the commission's chairman see 89, note.

Malaysia, he enjoyed wide confidence in the Borneo territories and he was likely to be acceptable to the Tunku), together with a suitable lawyer and a third member with appropriate experience in colonial administration.[4]

(c) We had to recognise that, unless we could bring Greater Malaysia into being fairly quickly, we might lose the opportunity for all time. If, therefore, as Ministers had already agreed, we thought Greater Malaysia desirable in the interests of all the territories concerned, we might have to press North Borneo and Sarawak into it more urgently than we should ideally want. For this reason, it was important to retain flexibility in our position with relation to the views of the local peoples, and the proposed commission should not be unduly formal in its constitution.

(d) The best plan might be for any commission to report to a conference representing the Governments of all the territories concerned, including the United Kingdom. If that conference then decided that Greater Malaysia should be created, it could agree how the necessary constitutional arrangements could be made. A further commission could be appointed to carry out this task (like the Reid Commission in Malaya) but there might be advantage in the work being done by direct negotiation between Governments without recourse to 'independent' legal aid.

Summing up *the Prime Minister* said that the general feeling of the Meeting seemed to favour a small United Kingdom commission which would both assess opinion in North Borneo and Sarawak and make general recommendations about arrangements for their incorporation in Greater Malaysia, including safeguards to meet the needs of their special circumstances. It would be possible for the commission also to consider the position of Singapore and Brunei in relation to Greater Malaysia, but this might not be necessary. It would also be possible to consider the appointment of a Malayan member to the commission: on the whole, that perhaps would be better avoided but the point could be left for discussion with the Tunku. It seemed unnecessary to have an inter-governmental conference before the commission went to work—the right occasion for a conference would be to consider the commission's report and decide how to proceed from that point.

Although Ministers had now considered the Greater Malaysia problem on a number of occasions it had not yet been raised in the Cabinet and it was desirable that the Commonwealth Secretary should mention it in Cabinet on the following day.[5]

The Meeting:—

(1) Took note of the Prime Minister's summing up on the subject of the proposed commission of enquiry.

(2) Invited the Commonwealth Secretary to make an oral report to the Cabinet on the following day about the way in which the talks with the Tunku were to be handled.

---

[4] The Reid Commission, however, had not been entirely appointed by the British government; it had been a commission of Commonwealth jurists and had reported to both the Crown and Their Highnesses the Malay rulers. Ministers soon came round to the view that the Borneo enquiry should be conducted by a joint Anglo–Malayan Commission, see 80.

[5] In fact Cabinet had already agreed (10 Oct) that talks should go ahead with the Tunku about 'Greater Malaysia' (CAB 128/35, CC 55(61)5, 10 Oct 1961 and document 66 N). On 16 Nov Sandys notified Cabinet that 'exploratory discussions' were due to start on 20 Nov (CAB 128/35/2, CC 63(61)6) which is printed in Hyam and Louis, eds, *BDEE: Conservative government 1957–1964*, I, 265).]

79   CAB 134/1953, GMD(B)61/1st meeting   20 Nov 1961
[London talks]: minutes of the first meeting held at Admiralty House at 11 am with Mr Macmillan in the chair

[The Anglo–Malayan talks of Nov 1961 were the first of four Greater Malaysia conferences held in London; the others took place in July 1962, May 1963 and June–July 1963. The talks of Nov 1961 consisted of six formal sessions (see 79–84). The first and last were chaired by Macmillan at Admiralty House (the prime minister's base during renovations to 10 Downing Street from the summer of 1960 to the summer of 1963) and the other three by Sandys at the CRO. The Malayan delegation was led by the Tunku (prime minister and minister for external affairs), Abdul Razak (Defence) and Tan Siew Sin (Finance). Federal officials in attendance included Ghazali Shafie (External Affairs), Abdul Kadir bin Shamsudin (Defence) and the Malayan high commissioner in London. The British ministerial team was Sandys, Maudling, Watkinson and Perth (for one meeting only), and it was supported by Sir R Scott, Sir J Martin, Sir G Tory, P B C Moore, G P Hampshire (assistant under-secretary, CRO) and E H Peck (assistant under-secretary, FO). At the conclusion of the talks a brief, joint statement was published and Selkirk was notified of the outcome by telegram. The next day, Sandys reported to Cabinet that it had been agreed, firstly, to appoint a commission to ascertain the views of Borneo peoples and, secondly, to extend the Anglo–Malayan Defence Agreement of 1957 to the other territories. On 28 Nov Sandys informed the House of Commons and a joint Anglo-Malayan statement was published at the same time. Particular care was taken with the wording of the formula governing the use of Singapore bases so as neither to constrain Britain's fulfilment of regional defence obligations nor to impair Malayan/Malaysian sovereignty. The published statement permitted the United Kingdom to use the facilities of Singapore as it 'may consider necessary for the purpose of assisting in the defence of Malaya, and for Commonwealth defence and for the preservation of peace in South East Asia'. Each side sought to avoid embarrassment—the British with their allies, the Malayans with their electorate—but it proved very difficult to reconcile differences in an unequivocal, public statement. To the consternation of Sandys and Watkinson, the Tunku and Razak were soon tempted to reassure their public that Britain's continued use of the bases would be subject to a Malaysian veto (see 85 and 86). See *Federation of Malaysia. Joint Statement by the Governments of the United Kingdom and of the Federation of Malaya* (Cmnd 1563); *H of C Debs*, vol 650, cols 242–248, 28 Nov 1961; CAB 129/107/2, C(61)190, 22 Nov 1961; CAB 128/35/2, CC 65(61)4; CAB 134/1953; DO 169/213; DO 169/307, nos 20A, 33A and 63A; PREM 11/3420.]

Greater Malaysia discussions: opening meeting

The Prime Minister, after extending a welcome to Tunku Abdul Rahman and the members of his Delegation, expressed the British Government's whole-hearted acceptance of the concept of Greater Malaysia. Britain recognised that there were compelling reasons for bringing about this association while the present opportunity lasted. Time was not on our side in view of the precariousness of the situation in Singapore. It was necessary, therefore, to examine urgently practical ways and means of advancing towards the common objectives.

    The best way of proceeding might be for the discussions to be continued by a small and informal group, with the Commonwealth Secretary leading on the British side, supported by the Colonial Secretary and the Minister of Defence, the Chancellor of the Exchequer and the Foreign Secretary being available if required. It would be convenient for the subsequent meetings to be held in the Commonwealth Secretary's room at the Commonwealth Relations Office. In order to preserve the informality and flexibility in the discussions, there would be a minimum of officials on the British side. For the same reason it might be desirable to have no formal agreed minutes of the meetings although at their conclusion an agreed statement might be desirable. He suggested that the first meeting should be at 3.00 p.m. on Monday afternoon and subsequent meetings at 10.30 a.m. and 3.00 p.m. on Tuesday. Later in the week, perhaps on Thursday, discussion might be resumed at Admiralty House under his own chairmanship.

Singapore

The Prime Minister went on to say that although the British Government had already had a clear explanation from Tunku Abdul Rahman himself of his plan for Greater Malaysia, that was some little time ago. There would now be more recent developments to report. It would be helpful, for instance, if the Tunku could say something about the understanding which he had recently arrived at with the Prime Minister of Singapore.

Tunku Abdul Rahman said that for a long time he had hesitated to agree to the proposals of the Prime Minister of Singapore, Mr. Lee Kuan Yew, for a merger between the Federation and Singapore. Mr. Lee Kuan Yew had, however, succeeded in convincing him of the danger to which the Federation would be exposed if Singapore became separately independent and, as was probable in that event, came under communist control. This, and the renewal of communist aggression in the countries to the north of Malaya, had satisfied him that he ought to come to some arrangement with Mr. Lee. As a result they had agreed upon the principle of a merger between their two countries, and a working party had been set up to work out the way in which this might be arranged. The conclusions of the working party, which had been agreed to by both Mr. Lee and himself, were embodied in a White Paper which had been published in Singapore within the last few days.[1] Briefly, what was proposed was as follows:—

(i) Singapore would be a State within the Federation but on special conditions and with a larger measure of local automony than the other States forming the Federation. Defence, external affairs and internal security would be Federal subjects: education and labour would be State subjects.

(ii) The fundamental liberties and the special position of the Malays in Singapore would be preserved.

(iii) The present Singapore Legislative Assembly would continue as a State Legislature, with reduced powers.

(iv) The existing Singapore civil service would be retained as a State civil service.

(v) The present Singapore Judicial and Legal Services would become a separate branch of the Federal Judicial and Legal Services. The ultimate control of the Judiciary would rest with the Federal Chief Justice in Kuala Lumpur.

(vi) The present separate Singapore citizenship and voting rights would be retained, but in other respects Singapore citizens would enjoy the same national rights and have the same passport as Federal citizens.

(vii) If Singapore were to join the Federation on a par with the existing member States it would be entitled to about twenty-five seats in the Federal Legislature by virtue of the size of its electorate. In view, however, of the greater autonomy which Singapore would enjoy in comparison with the existing States, it had been agreed

---

[1] The Singapore White Paper, *Memorandum Setting out the Heads of Agreement for a Merger Between the Federation of Malaya and Singapore* (Cmd 33), was the product of negotiations that had been going on since Aug and was adopted by Singapore's legislative assembly on 6 Dec 1961 (see 59, note and 87 n 1).

that the number of Singapore representatives should in practice be limited to fifteen.

It had also been agreed (though this was not stated in the White Paper) to consider further a proposal that, as a territorial measure pending merger, the Singapore Government should be invited to appoint fifteen representatives, on an all-party basis, from the Singapore Legislative Assembly to join the Federation of Malaya House of Representatives.

It had originally been Mr. Lee Kuan Yew's intention, to hold a referendum in Singapore on the subject of merger. Mr. Lee had come to feel, however, that there was a real risk that the outcome of such a referendum might be unfavourable, and he seemed now inclined to look upon a majority vote in the Singapore Legislature as a sufficient indication of the country's support for the proposed change.[2]

The Borneo territories

The Meeting then went on to give initial consideration to the position of the Borneo territories in relation to Greater Malaysia.

The Prime Minister said that, as the Tunku was already aware and had publicly acknowledged, before the British Government could transfer sovereignty over the Borneo territories they would have to satisfy themselves, and the world at large, that this change was being made with the consent of those territories. Some form of consultation with them was therefore essential, and one of the important problems which now had to be decided was how this could most expeditiously be carried out.

Tunku Abdul Rahman said that his Government fully understood the British Government's feelings about this aspect of the matter. On the other hand, preparation of the Borneo territories for entry into Greater Malaysia was a matter of urgency. If it were delayed, the opponents of Greater Malaysia would be given time to foster opposition to the idea. He hoped that the position of the Borneo territories would not in fact be found to cause any great difficulty. The efficiency of their administration after a hand-over of sovereignty could be preserved if the present British civil servants there could be retained as others were in the Federation of Malaya after the country became independent. In general, the change of sovereignty need have little effect on the lives of the peoples of the Borneo territories. They would enter the proposed new association on the same basis as the existing States of the Federation with broadly the same limited amount of local autonomy. He recognised, however, their fears that amalgamation with Malaya might lead to an influx of Chinese immigrants, and that it might, therefore, be necessary to make special provision for local control over immigration.

The Sultan of Brunei would have exactly the same position in Greater Malaysia as the Rulers of the Malay States now have in the Federation of Malaya: this he fully understood.

Defence and internal security

The Meeting then turned to the questions of defence and internal security and the Prime Minister invited Tunku Abdul Rahman to give his views.

Tunku Abdul Rahman said that the main issue in relation to defence was the South East Asia Treaty Organisation (SEATO). He fully recognised that the purpose

---

[2] In fact Lee went ahead with the referendum which was held on 1 Sept 1962.

of SEATO was to provide for the defence of South East Asia against communism—but that, after all, was also the object of the Malayan Defence Agreement between Britain and Malaya. SEATO was not popular in South East Asia, partly because only two of the South East Asian countries were members. Because Malaya was not a member of SEATO and SEATO was unpopular in Malaya, it was impossible for his Government to agree that in Greater Malaysia the SEATO label should continue to be attached to the British bases in Singapore. Nevertheless, if trouble with communism came to a head and war broke out, Britain would, of course, be able to make full use of all her facilities in Malaya as well as the Singapore bases: indeed, the Singapore bases would be less useful than the others in war because their situation made them more vulnerable. He therefore thought that they ought to be put on the same footing as the bases in the Federation of Malaya, and he believed that it should be possible to work out arrangements which would satisfy Britain's real needs, including those relating to SEATO. When preparations were being made for the last SEATO exercise he had told the British to go ahead with those preparations which involved the use of our bases in Malaya, but had asked us not to insist upon a formal, written agreement. That should perhaps be the approach to the problem of the Singapore bases.

On internal security he said that the communist threat in South East Asia was grave and widespread. Things were going badly in South Viet Nam and if the communists succeeded in taking over that country they would undoubtedly step up their activities in Singapore. He would have much preferred to leave Singapore well alone as hitherto and concentrate on keeping Malaya free from communism, as at present: but he could not help fearing that, when the Singapore constitution came under review in 1963, Britain might feel obliged to grant separate independence. This would inevitably lead to Singapore becoming a communist state and he had decided that the only way of avoiding that danger was to accept the merger of Singapore with the Federation of Malaya. He believed that he would be able to deal successfully with the internal security situation in Singapore after merger, even though that might mean increasing his armed forces and police. All these forces would be under central control from Kuala Lumpur, and it was his intention to set up an Inspectorate General of Police with responsibility for internal security throughout the whole of Greater Malaysia.

The Prime Minister said that the problem of the Singapore bases was one of great importance for us. He repeated that we fully shared the Tunku's desire to bring Greater Malaysia into being but it would be very difficult for us to accept defence arrangements which imposed fresh restrictions upon our freedom to use our bases and other facilities in Malaya and Singapore. We were under firm obligations to SEATO and we could not contemplate going back on them: moreover, the vast effort in men and money which we had put and were still putting into our bases would be wasted if we did not continue to enjoy freedom of operation in time of need.

The Minister of Defence said that we would naturally very much welcome being relieved of our present responsibilities for internal security in the Greater Malaysia territories. As the Tunku had himself said, it would inevitably do harm both to the local Governments and to ourselves if British troops had in fact to be used in support of the civil power. On the other hand, the problem of the use of our bases for external defence was much more difficult: they were of value to us only if we could say openly that we should be in a position to carry out our obligations in full when occasion arose. He asked whether it might help if the Malayan Defence Agreement were extended to become a Commonwealth agreement rather than a bilateral agreement between Malaya and the United Kingdom (with which Australia and New Zealand were associated). But the real issue for us was our need to enjoy unfettered use of our bases and facilities in Singapore.

The Tunku said that he thought that talks on defence between all the Commonwealth countries directly interested in South East Asia were desirable as a matter of urgency, but that they should be pursued as a separate issue from the question of the merger of Singapore and the Federation of Malaya. The aim of the present discussions should be to work out a satisfactory agreement over the Singapore bases.

The Commonwealth Secretary said that the morning's discussion had been most helpful in clarifying the issues at stake. It was clear that far and away the two most important questions were those of consultation with North Borneo and Sarawak and the Singapore bases. As the Prime Minister had stressed, Britain sincerely wanted to achieve Greater Malaysia in principle because she thought it the right answer to the long-term problems of all the territories concerned: he shared the Tunku's anxieties about Singapore and agreed that independence there would mean Chinese communist control; and he also agreed that the Borneo territories had little hope of a decent future in separation from one another or from Malaya. But the questions of consultation and timing were crucial since we must not only do what we thought right, but also ensure that what we did could properly be represented as meeting the broad wishes of the Borneo peoples. He had been very glad to hear the Tunku recognise that the aims of SEATO—predominantly to combat communism in South East Asia—were in fact helpful to Malaya. He had no doubt that if SEATO military operations became necessary the Tunku would agree to the use of our bases for that purpose, but the main object of SEATO was not so much to fight a war against communism as to provide a deterrent which would make war unnecessary by establishing general confidence that aggression would be resisted if it took place. Because of this, secret agreements about the operational use of our bases were not really enough: we must be able to demonstrate to our allies and the world that we could use our bases and their facilities for SEATO purposes if necessary. It was clear from the discussion that both the Malayans and ourselves recognised each other's difficulties in this connection and our joint aim must be to work out a practical solution satisfactory to both sides.

The Meeting:—
Agreed to resume its business in the Commonwealth Secretary's room in the Commonwealth Relations Office at 3 p.m. that afternoon.

80 CAB 134/1953, GMD(B)61/2nd meeting	20 Nov 1961
[London talks]: minutes of the second meeting held at the Commonwealth Relations Office at 3 pm with Mr Sandys in the chair

Greater Malaysia discussions

Singapore
The Commonwealth Secretary asked about the significance of the word 'transitional' which had been used in describing the proposed arrangements for merger between

the Federation of Malaya and Singapore, as set out in the White Paper presented to the Singapore Legislative Assembly.

In discussion it emerged that they were not intended to be temporary, although they could be described as 'provisional' until they had been approved by the authorities concerned. Once the Singapore Legislative Assembly had approved them they would be submitted for approval by the British Government and by the Parliament of the Federation as part of arrangements for Greater Malaysia as a whole. Thereafter they would be subject to alteration only by agreement between the Malaysian and Singapore Governments.

The Commonwealth Secretary also asked what would happen to the proposals for merger between Singapore and the Federation if the present Government of Singapore were to fall: there was some danger of this as they had a majority of only one in the Legislative Assembly.

Tunku Abdul Rahman felt that, with the support of his own Alliance Party representatives and of the Singapore Peoples Alliance, the present Singapore Government might be able to hold on until the next general elections due in 1963. But there was no certainty that they could do so, and it would be fatal to the prospects of Greater Malaysia if they failed. It was therefore essential to press ahead with Greater Malaysia as quickly as possible.

Problems of the Borneo Territories

The Commonwealth Secretary stressed that we believed Greater Malaysia to be in the best interests of all the countries concerned; and that we recognised the inclusion of the Borneo territories in Greater Malaysia to be an indispensible part of the Federation's plans. Before the Borneo territories could be included, however, certain problems had to be settled: in mentioning these we did so in a constructive spirit and with no desire to delay the achievement of Greater Malaysia.

The Colonial Secretary said that we were ready to advise the Sultan of Brunei to join Greater Malaysia, although we should not want him to do so in any way that might risk provoking opposition among his own people. If, as was possible, such opposition resulted in civil disturbance, the effect would be not only to damage the prospects of Brunei joining Greater Malaysia, but also to raise doubts among the peoples of North Borneo and Sarawak about the wisdom of their joining.

Before decisions could be taken whether or not North Borneo and Sarawak should join Greater Malaysia we must ascertain the views of their peoples in principle and we must be certain of administrative arrangements ensuring that their own Governments could fulfil the functions which would be required of them after merger. To meet these requisites we suggested the appointment of a commission of enquiry with two roles. The first would be to find out what were the views of the local peoples, the second to recommend arrangements for merger, including any special provisions necessitated by the particular circumstances of the two territories. A constitutional conference of representatives of the British, Malayan and both Borneo Governments would in due course be required, but that should be held after the commission had done its work. The proposed commission might perhaps consist of a British chairman together with four other members, two appointed by the British and two by the Malayan Governments. The chairman should be a man of wide general experience rather than a constitutional expert but one of the British members would in all probability be a suitably qualified lawyer.

The Meeting then considered the possible terms of reference set out in G.M.D.(61) 2:—

> 'Taking into account the expressed agreement of the Governments of Britain and the Federation of Malaya that a closer association between Singapore, North Borneo, Brunei, Sarawak and the Federation of Malaya is a desirable aim in the interests of the people of the territories concerned,
>
> (a) to examine and ascertain the views of the peoples of North Borneo and Sarawak on the possibility of a closer association of the five territories;
> (b) in the light of their assessment of these views to make recommendations regarding the conditions and timing under which association with the Federation of Malaya might be achieved and the safeguards for North Borneo and Sarawak which might be necessary.'

In discussion the Malayan representatives made the following points:—

(a) It was possible to be too cautious over consulting the Borneo territories. In 1957 Penang and Malacca had been included in an independent Federation of Malaya without special consultation; and the Brookes had ceded Sarawak to Britain on their own personal authority immediately after the war.

(b) The terms of reference of the proposed commission should leave no doubt that full merger of the Borneo territories in Greater Malaysia was intended. The present mention of 'closer association', coupled with a reference to Singapore in the preamble, implied something less than full merger of the Borneo territories; and the point was important presentationally in Malaya, where full merger of the Borneo territories was regarded as essential if the Federation was to take in Singapore.

(c) There need be no difficulty over Brunei as the Sultan was very keen on merger. Although there was some local opposition to it from the only political party, that did not amount to very much and the people would follow the lead given them by the Sultan. There was no natural basis for the growth of party politics in Brunei as the people shared in the general prosperity which the Sultan derived from his oil revenues and were content with things as they were.

(d) Lord Ogmore[1] would be a very suitable chairman for the commission.

On the British side the following points were made:—

(e) There were essential differences between Penang and Malacca joining the Federation and the Borneo territories joining Greater Malaysia. Sarawak's coming under British administration had special features: in particular assurances had been given by us in effect not to transfer sovereignty ourselves without consulting the people of Sarawak. It was essential to show the British Parliament and the world generally that we had done as much as was reasonably possible to consult local opinion, and that would be one of the main functions of the proposed commission, which would not only consult the Legislative Councils of North Borneo and Sarawak but also sound opinion at large in both territories.

(f) It was important to provide safeguards which would satisfy the two

---

[1] Lord Ogmore (formerly David Rees-Williams) had Malayan experience and was a friend of the Tunku, see 46, n 6.

territories that the terms on which they joined Greater Malays [sic] could not be altered against their will. It would not, therefore, be enough to have those safeguards protected by provision in the Federal constitution that they could not be altered except by a two-thirds majority in the Federal Parliament: it would be necessary to provide that any change required the agreement of the territorial Legislatures.

(g) Full merger was the aim of the consultations which the commission would have in the Borneo territories—we understood the importance of this presentationally in Malaya. Nevertheless while the commission should put over the case for Greater Malaysia to the peoples of the territories, they could not be expected in their recommendations to insist on the territories necessarily joining on the same terms as the existing States of the Federation of Malaya. There would have to be room for meeting the special needs of the territories, particularly over immigration: not to allow this might prejudice the chances of securing the territories' agreement.

Broad general agreement emerged as follows:—

(i) Consultation in the Borneo territories was necessary before they could be committed to joining Greater Malaysia. The best approach to this would be a commission composed of a British chairman with two members drawn from the Federation of Malaya and two from Britain. The terms of reference proposed in G.M.D.(61)2 were discussed and revised in order to include a note of urgency and to give more of a lead in favour of Greater Malaysia, while avoiding the impression that its achievement was regarded as a *fait accompli*. The Secretaries were instructed to re-issue G.M.D.(61)2 thus revised and the Malayan representatives would give the matter further thought with a view to discussing it again next day. In any case the proposed commission should be set up as soon as possible and asked to complete its work with all speed, preferably within three months.

(ii) When the commission had completed its work there should be a constitutional conference to consider its recommendations and reach agreement for arrangements to achieve Greater Malaysia.

(iii) There might be need to ensure that the terms on which the Borneo territories entered Greater Malaysia could not subsequently be altered without their individual agreement.

(iv) There would be no objection to Brunei's being covered by the commission if the Sultan so wished: indeed, that might be a safer course than submitting the issue to a Brunei Legislature after elections had been held, since the only existing political party at present professed opposition to Greater Malaysia. The British Government would seek the Sultan's views. While there was no objection to discussion between Brunei and the Federation of Malaya about merger, agreement on the inclusion of Brunei required careful timing: it was important that no final or public agreement should be reached between Brunei and the Federation without prior consultation with the British Government.

The Meeting:—

Agreed to resume its discussion at 10.30 a.m. on the following day.

81   CAB 134/1953, GMD(B)61/3rd meeting   21 Nov 1961
[London talks]: minutes of the third meeting held at the
Commonwealth Relations Office at 10.30 am with Mr Sandys in the
chair

Greater Malaysia discussions

Defence

The Meeting discussed the extent to which the defence bases in Singapore would continue to be available for use by Britain and her SEATO allies after the achievement of Greater Malaysia.

The Commonwealth Secretary said that there did not seem to be any basic disagreement on this matter between the Federation and British Governments. The latter had been given reason to believe that, whatever interpretation was to be put on the terms of the Malayan Defence Agreement, the Federation Government would not in practice put any obstacles in the way of use of the existing bases in the Federation by British forces and the forces of other SEATO countries if those forces became required for defensive operations within the region. It was also their understanding (which Tunku Abdul Rahman now confirmed) that the Federation Government were prepared to apply the same understanding to the use of the Singapore bases after a Federation/Singapore merger. The British Government recognised that the state of public opinion in the Federation did not allow the Federation to accept any proposals which publicly associated them with SEATO, or to pass through their Legislature any measures which would have the effect of increasing the Federation's present undertakings about the use of Commonwealth forces stationed on Malayan territory. The British Government certainly had no wish to try to involve the Federation Government in SEATO against their wishes. On the other hand, the Federation Government must recognise that Britain had to remain free, and be seen to remain free, to discharge the international obligations which they had undertaken under the Manila Treaty.

The following points were made in discussion:—

(a)   From the point of view of the Federation Government it would be sufficient if an understanding between them and the British Government over the use of the Singapore bases after the establishment of Greater Malaysia were recorded in a secret agreement. This would not, however, meet the British Government's needs. It was essential to them that there should be a public indication which would satisfy the British Parliament and Britain's allies of their continued ability to honour their SEATO obligations. Only in this way could the main function of SEATO as a deterrent remain unimpaired. That this should be so was in the interest of the Federation as well as of Britain and her SEATO allies.

(b)   Agreed arrangements about the future use of the bases in Greater Malaysia might be recorded in either of two ways: there could be a new Defence Agreement altogether, or the existing Malayan Defence Agreement could be extended and adapted to meet the changed circumstances. From the point of view of presentation in both the Federation and Britain, the latter course was preferable. If necessary the extension of the present Malayan Defence Agreement might be accompanied by a public exchange of letters to indicate the interpretation which the two Governments had agreed to put upon it.

(c)   It would meet the British Government's requirement if the amended Agreement, or the accompanying exchange of letters of interpretation, could show, in substance, that the Government of the future Federation of Malaysia would permit unrestricted use of the British bases within the Federation for the purposes of the defence of Malaya and other Commonwealth territories; and that it was accepted in this connection that the defence of Malaya was best achieved, and the interests of Malaya best served, by the preservation of peace within the whole area of South East Asia.

(d)   The present Malayan Defence Agreement did not stipulate whether Britain and her allies were entitled to deploy forces direct from the bases in the Federation for use on SEATO exercises, and it had become the practice for forces embarking on such exercises to be removed in the first place from the Federation to Singapore, which then became the 'jumping-off' point. It was necessary from the British Government's view-point that an amended Defence Agreement should not adversely affect the use of the Singapore bases in this way.

(e)   One solution of the problem of reconciling the British Government's requirements with the difficulties in which the Federation Government were placed domestically might be for the Singapore bases in a Greater Malaysia to be leased to Britain, whose responsibility it would then be to decide the uses to which they were put.

(f)   After a mutually acceptable arrangement had been arrived at between the Federation and British Governments for the future use of the Singapore bases, care would have to be taken on each side not to make any public statements which would compromise the public position of the other.

The Meeting:—

(1) Agreed that although the British and Federation Governments had somewhat conflicting requirements over the public presentation of matters affecting the future use of the Singapore bases in Greater Malaysia, the Federation Government would in practice not wish to impede the full use of the bases by British and allied forces in the event of their being required for defence operations in the region.

(2) Agreed that the use to which those bases in a Greater Malaysia could be put would best be defined by an agreed amendment of the existing Malayan Defence Agreement, accompanied, if found necessary, by a public exchange of letters between the two Governments.

The Borneo territories

The Meeting then considered the draft terms of reference for the proposed commission of enquiry into the inclusion of North Borneo and Sarawak in Greater Malaysia as revised in accordance with discussion at the meeting on the previous afternoon (G.M.D. (61) 2 (Revise)).

In discussion the revised draft was agreed subject to a number of amendments, and the following points were made:—

(g)   There would be no mention of Brunei in the terms of reference unless and until the Sultan, in response to an enquiry on our part, asked for the commission to cover his State.

(h)   The commission should begin its task as soon as possible and the earliest practicable date would probably be January, 1962.

(i)   It would be of great assistance in carrying the Borneo territories with us over merger to have representatives of their peoples associated at all stages with the arrangements for the achievement of Greater Malaysia. However, it was impossible at this stage to decide exactly who should participate in discussions on the commission's recommendations: a decision could be taken only when it was known what those recommendations were. It was therefore agreed that the commission should submit its recommendations to the Governments of Britain and the Federation, whose responsibility it would then be to agree what further steps should be taken.

(j)   The Malayan representatives agreed that there was no objection to administrative measures, such as the forthcoming introduction of a free trade area between the two territories, designed to promote closer association between Sarawak and North Borneo: but it was also agreed that the Greater Malaysia project took precedence over any proposals for closer political association between the two territories.

The Singapore Internal Security Council

The Colonial Secretary raised the question of the Federation's decision to withdraw their representative from the Council. They had given notice of this last August and their decision would take effect next February. The Federation's withdrawal would be a serious matter as the Council would then have only a consultative role and there would be no possible check on the Government of Singapore in the field of internal security except through the suspension of the constitution.

Tunku Abdul Rahman explained that his Government, after due consideration, had felt it necessary to take the decision in order to show their displeasure at the Singapore Government's policy over releasing communist detainees. The Malayan decision had proved effective in making the Singapore Government more careful over releasing further detainees. The Singapore Government had agreed to give no publicity to the Federation's action because they realised that once publicity had been given there was no chance of the Federation's reconsidering their decision. It was possible that the Federation might reconsider their decision in the light of the new atmosphere that now existed between the Federation and the Singapore Governments. He would be glad to discuss the problem separately with the Colonial Secretary.

The Meeting:—
(3) Agreed that a draft statement of understanding between the two Governments on the interpretation of their mutual Defence Agreement in relation to Greater Malaysia should be prepared for further discussion at 3 p.m. that afternoon.

82   CAB 134/1953, GMD(B)61/4th meeting   21 Nov 1961
[London talks]: minutes of the fourth meeting held at the Commonwealth Relations Office at 3 pm with Mr Sandys in the chair

Greater Malaysia discussions

Defence
The Meeting had before them a draft statement of understanding between the British and Federation Governments on the interpretion of the existing Defence Agreement

between the two countries as extended to cover the proposed Federation of Malaysia (G.M.D. (61) 3). Tunku Abdul Rahman indicated that the draft in its present form was unacceptable politically to the Malayans because it could be interpreted in the Federation as a commitment on the use of the Singapore bases for SEATO purposes.

The Commonwealth Secretary suggested that a possible solution might be a lease to cover the use of the Singapore bases: it might be on the lines of leases for bases elsewhere—for example, the United States' bases in the West Indies—which were not subject to unilateral revocation by either of the Government concerned.

In discussion the draft statement was amended to read as follows:—

> 'The Government of the United Kingdom and the Government of the Federation of Malaya have agreed, on the formation of the proposed Federation of Malaysia, as follows:—
>
> (a) The Agreement on External Defence and Mutual Assistance of 1957 and its Annexes shall be extended to apply to all the territories of the Federation of Malaysia, and any references in that Agreement to the Federation of Malaya shall be deemed to apply to the Federation of Malaysia.
>
> (b) The Agreement and Annexes shall, in respect of Singapore, be interpreted to mean that the Government of the Federation of Malaysia will afford to the Government of the United Kingdom the right to continue to maintain the bases and other facilities at present occupied by their Service authorities within the State of Singapore, and will permit the United Kingdom Government to make such use of these bases and facilities as they consider necessary for the protection of the territories of Malaysia and other Commonwealth countries, and the preservation of peace in South East Asia.'

In arriving at this agreed text the following points were taken into consideration:—

(a) A statement of understanding was a better solution to the problem of Singapore than a lease because a lease would involve complicated drafting, with the need to spell out in considerable detail provisions to cover all possible eventualities: it would in effect amount to a separate defence agreement for Singapore.

(b) In the special arrangement for Singapore set out in sub-paragraph (b) reference to 'unrestricted' use of the bases and other facilities would have raised serious political difficulties for the Federation Government because of the SEATO implications. The words 'exclusive right' were also politically objectionable to the Federation. These words had been employed so as to ensure that only Britain and no other country would be given rights over the bases but it was agreed to omit 'exclusive' as the point was academic since the Federation of Malaysia would never in fact want to give such rights to a third country. The description in the agreed text of how the bases might be used would enable Britian to employ them for all likely purposes, including that of meeting her SEATO obligations (both operationally and for exercises) and the use of the bases by her allies. There was no reference in the statement to the consent of the Federation Government being required for the use of the Singapore bases as was necessary under a similar clause of the existing Defence Agreement. On the use of the Singapore bases for purposes strictly outside South East Asia it was felt that the reference to the protection of the territories of 'other Commonwealth countries' provided adequate cover.

(c) The statement of understanding would extend the existing Defence

Agreement to the Borneo territories. Precise arrangements for British defence facilities there were not yet settled and we must reserve our position in that respect. We might, for example, want to continue to use the territories for SEATO exercises; and in any case they were valuable for training purposes. We were also interested in the possible use of Labuan for defence purposes. We felt, however, that it should be possible in the event to agree satisfactory arrangements for the Borneo territories within the ambit of the Defence Agreement.

(d)   In reply to a Malayan inquiry about the British attitude in the event of an attack upon Australian territory in New Guinea it was made clear that we must be free to use the Singapore bases to help the Australians.

Press communique
The Commonwealth Secretary suggested that some preliminary consideration should be given to the terms of the communique which should be issued at the conclusion of the present talks. It was also desirable to agree upon what should be said publicly in reply to enquiries from the press and others about the extent to which the use of the bases in Singapore would be affected by the creation of Greater Malaysia. Since the statements about the terms of reference of the commission of enquiry and about future defence arrangements which the meeting had considered were to be published, the communique itself could incorporate them verbatim, and its preparation should not therefore, present any difficulty. A draft would be prepared for consideration at a later meeting. In the meantime the British Government would inform the Prime Ministers of Australia and New Zealand at once of the contents of the two statements which had been proposed. In doing so, they would have in mind that, although the meeting had agreed broadly on the terms of the statement about future defence arrangements, the exact text was still subject to further consideration by the Federation representatives.

Federation/Singapore merger arrangements
The Colonial Secretary invited the Malayan representatives to clarify the statement which they had made on the previous day to the effect that the arrangements for a Federation/Singapore merger described in the White Paper presented to the Singapore Legislative Assembly were 'transitional'.

Enche Ghazali explained that, although the term 'transitional' did not appear in the White Paper itself, it was the one used by the Federation Government to describe the means by which a merger of Singapore with the Federation could be achieved at short notice without running into constitutional difficulties. Under the existing Federal Constitution new States could join the Federation only on the same terms as the existing member States. The Constitution would have to be amended in considerable detail to provide for the entry of Singapore into the Federation on the intended special terms. This could not be done at all quickly. In order, therefore, that the merger might be effected at short notice, if necessary, it was the intention to introduce a new provision into the Federal Constitution which would allow for a new State to join the Federation on special terms in anticipation of the later full amendment of the Constitution. There was no intention of changing the 'transitional' arrangements embodied in the White Paper before they were finally enshrined in the Federal Constitution; and the agreement of the Government of Singapore would be necessary before any such changes could be made.

It was suggested by the British representatives that this arrangement was liable to lead to misunderstandings and trouble in Singapore. It would be possible for ill-disposed persons to argue that the published arrangements whereby Singapore would join the Federation on special terms were not as permanent as they seemed. The Federation Government, they felt, would do well to go ahead as quickly as possible with preparations for the necessary fuller amendment of the Constitution with a view to completing it, if at all possible, before the merger of Singapore with the Federation took place.

The Minister of Defence informed the meeting that Tunku [sic] Abdul Razak and he had arranged to meet on Monday, 27th November to discuss what help, if any, the Federation Government would need from Britain in preparing to assume responsibility for internal security in Singapore after merger was effected.

The Meeting:—
Agreed to resume their discussion at 10.00 a.m. on the following day.

83   CAB 134/1953, GMD(B)61/5th meeting   22 Nov 1961
[London talks]: minutes of the fifth meeting held at the Commonwealth Relations Office at 10 am with Mr Sandys in the chair

Greater Malaysia discussions

Press communique
The Meeting considered a draft press communique (G.M.D.(61)4) announcing the outcome of the discussions. Annexed to the communique were draft statements on the terms of reference of the commission of enquiry for North Borneo and Sarawak, and on the agreed arrangements on defence.

Defence arrangements
The Commonwealth Secretary observed that it was essential that any statement about the future defence arrangements should leave no doubt that Britain would continue to be able to despatch forces, and especially naval forces, from Singapore for activities outside South East Asia without the prior consent of the Federation Government, even though the Federation Government would in practice normally be informed of such movements.

Tunku Abdul Rahman said that the Malayans for their part could not agree to any arrangement which could be said to be inconsistent with the future sovereignty of the Federation over Singapore. The sort of movements envisaged by the British representatives could, however, be interpreted as 'withdrawals' of forces from Malaya and so would be acceptable.

The Meeting:—
(1) Agreed that the draft statement of agreed arrangements on defence (Annex B)[1] should be amended so as to make it clear that after the formation of Greater Malaysia, Britain would remain free to make such use of the bases and facilities in

---

[1] Not printed.

Singapore as she might consider necessary for the purpose of assisting in the defence of Malaysia, and for Commonwealth defence and for the preservation of peace in South East Asia.

(2) Agreed that the main text of the draft communique should also be amended accordingly.

Press enquiries

The Meeting went on to consider what should be said by the British and Federation representatives in reply to press and other enquiries about the outcome of the discussions.

The Meeting:—

(3) Agreed that the following guidance should be observed in answering enquiries about defence arrangements:

'(a) The bases at Singapore will be British bases and will not be transferred to the control of SEATO or to any other nation or group of nations.

(b) The new arrangement does not prevent Britain carrying out her international and Commonwealth obligations.

(c) Neither of our Governments shall make any public statement which conflicts with the provisions of paragraphs (a) and (b) above.'

Constitution of the commission of enquiry

The Meeting:—

(4) Agreed that, as regards the proposed commission of enquiry no forecasts should be made of how soon it would begin and finish its work. It would be sufficient to say that the commission would be set up, and would report, as soon as possible.

(5) Agreed that the choice of a chairman and other members for the commission of enquiry should be discussed before the Federation representatives left London.

Historical documents

Tun Abdul Razak asked if it would be possible for the Federation Government to obtain copies of certain past records which were no longer available in Malaya but, it was hoped, could be found in London. The Commonwealth Secretary undertook that they would be given every assistance in this.

General

The Commonwealth Secretary expressed appreciation of the frank and cordial atmosphere in which the talks had taken place and of the contribution made by the Federation Prime Minister and his colleagues to their successful and speedy outcome.

Tunku Abdul Rahman expressed similar appreciation. The satisfactory result of the talks was indicative of the common aims and outlook of the British and Federation Governments.

The Meeting:—

(6) Agreed to conclude the discussions at an immediately following meeting under the chairmanship of the British Prime Minister.

84   CAB 134/1953, GMD(B)61/6th meeting   22 Nov 1961
[London talks]: minutes of the sixth meeting held at Admiralty House at 12 noon with Mr Macmillan in the chair

Greater Malaysia discussions
The Meeting had before them a joint statement by the Governments of the United Kingdom and the Federation of Malaya on the outcome of the talks about Greater Malaysia.[1]

North Borneo and Sarawak
The Prime Minister said that he assumed that the report of the Commission of Enquiry would be published. He was sure that this would in fact prove necessary and he therefore thought that the Commission should be so informed before they started work as the knowledge was bound to have some influence on the manner in which their report was drawn up. He regarded it as important that the Commission should complete their task with all reasonable speed. They should be able to make rapid progress as there seemed no need for their report exhaustively to cover all possible constitutional arrangements for the entry of the two territories into Greater Malaysia. It would be very important to make the right choice of Chairman: he understood that Tunku Abdul Rahman and the Colonial Secretary had already had some discussion on the matter and that it would be considered further while the Malayan representatives were still in London.

The Commission would have to take into account the special needs of the two territories in recommending the terms on which they might join Greater Malaysia. These terms might well be different from those on which the existing States of Malaya were members of the Federation, although some at least of the differences might be of a temporary nature. Land would no doubt have to be a State subject (as, indeed, it was under the existing Constitution of the Federation of Malaya); and it might be necessary, for example, that education should be a State subject in North Borneo and Sarawak although it was a Federal subject in Malaya.

Tunku Abdul Rahman said that he thought it important that, although the special circumstances of Singapore justified leaving education as a State subject there, it should be a Federal subject in North Borneo and Sarawak. This was desirable as his most effective means of developing a sense of Malaysian nationhood and of binding the peoples concerned into a practical, working unity. The task would be facilitated by the fact that the Malay language and the languages of the non-Chinese peoples of Borneo had a common basis.

He agreed that, in order to avoid a breakdown in the local administrations, it was essential to retain the services of British officials until local people were ready to take their places. This would require careful presentation but the problem had been handled successfully in Malaya and he had no doubt that that could also be done in the Borneo territories. Meanwhile, his Government could help by sending officials to

---

[1] Published as *Federation of Malaysia. Joint Statement by the Governments of the United Kingdom and of the Federation of Malaya* (Cmnd 1563).

help in Borneo (although experience in Brunei had shewn the need for great care over any such arrangement) and by taking local officials from Borneo to Malaya for training.

The Colonial Secretary said that a British Act of Parliament would be necessary for the transfer to Greater Malaysia of Sovereignty over North Borneo and Sarawak (and Singapore), but not in relation to Brunei, where sovereignty was vested in the Sultan. Whatever might be the timing of entry into Greater Malaysia by North Borneo and Sarawak, he saw no reason why the British Government should object to Brunei going in at once provided that the transition could be arranged on terms acceptable to all concerned.

Defence

The Prime Minister said that it was gratifying to find that agreement had been reached over defence arrangements, and in particular that a satisfactory formula had been found to meet the presentational needs of the British and Federation Governments in relation to the Singapore bases. His line with his own Parliament would be that Singapore had never been, and would not be, a SEATO base: it had always been, and would remain, a United Kingdom base, although it was available to enable us to fulfil our international (including SEATO) obligations.

Singapore

The Prime Minister felt that the outcome of the present talks should encourage and strengthen moderate opinion in Singapore.

Tunku Abdul Rahman added that the outcome would also be particularly welcome to businessmen and especially to foreign business whose capital investment in Singapore was so vital.

Communique

The Meeting:—

(1) Agreed that neither we nor the Malayan representatives should make any separate statement to the press about the talks; the communique should be allowed to speak for itself. It would be released in the Federation and in Britain in time for the following day's morning newspapers.

(2) Agreed that the Sultan of Brunei should be informed as soon as possible of the agreement reached in the present talks: otherwise he might feel that decisions of importance to Brunei were being taken over his head. It would be necessary at the same time, or as soon after as was possible, to sound him on the question whether or not the Commission should cover Brunei.

Concluding remarks

Both *the Prime Minister* and *Tunku Abdul Rahman* expressed their satisfaction at the outcome of the talks, in which results that met the needs of both sides had been quickly reached in the frank and cordial atmosphere appropriate to discussions between Commonwealth countries.

85   DO 169/307, no 63A   27 Nov 1961
[Anglo–Malayan differences over defence]: note by C Benwell[1] of a discussion between Mr Watkinson and Tun Abdul Razak

The Minister saw Tun Abdul Razak privately after the official meeting this morning. The Secretary, Enche Abdul Kadir and myself were also present.

2.   Tun Abdul Razak said that he had sought an opportunity of seeing the Minister alone because he was worried about the questions that would be put to his Government in connection with the joint statement on Defence issued on November 23rd. He felt that in public his Government would be bound to take up the position that the Singapore base could only be used in support of SEATO with the permission of the Federation. In practice, it would of course be sufficient if the Federation Government were simply informed of what the United Kingdom intended to do, e.g. by way of exercises or troop movements.

3.   The Minister said that he must make plain that if it were publicly stated that the use of the Singapore base by H.M.G. was subject to a Malayan veto, he would be bound to deny it. If there were in fact a right of veto, the base would be of little further use and H.M.G. would stop spending money on it. He pointed out to Tun Abdul Razak that it was in the clear interest both of the Federation and of the United Kingdom to encourage the United States to maintain a presence in S.E. Asia and this they would not do if there were doubt about the United Kingdom's capacity or will to do likewise. He also drew attention to a possible Commonwealth solution to the problem—namely an agreement drawing in India, Pakistan, Australia, New Zealand, the Federation and the United Kingdom.

4.   Tun Abdul Razak appeared to agree with both the last two points.

5.   In conclusion, both Ministers accepted that there was a genuine difficulty about reconciling the different attitudes of the two Governments when it came to public interpretation of the statement on defence; but that it was best not to try to bridge the gap at this stage by any form of words. Though there would be difficulties and embarrassment, the best line was for each Government to stand by the agreed principles governing public statements, and refrain from interpretations inconsistent with those made by the other.

---

[1] C W R Benwell, private secretary to Mr Watkinson, minister of defence, 1959–1962.

86   DO 169/213, no 42:   2 Dec 1961
[Anglo-Malayan differences over defence]: outward telegram no 1719 from Mr Sandys to Sir G Tory, reporting his conversation with the Tunku on 1 Dec

I saw the Tunku tonight and told him that I had heard that Razak on his return to Malaya had said to the press that the Singapore base would not be used for S.E.A.T.O purposes and that the British could not make use of it without consulting the Malayans.

2.   I warned the Tunku very firmly that the entire value of our recent agreement

would be destroyed if he and his Ministers continued to put an interpretation upon it which the text could not by any stretch of the imagination justify.

3. He assured me once again that he fully accepted that the base could be used for S.E.A.T.O purposes without the agreement of the Government of Malaysia but that he and Lee Kuan Yew had political difficulties in presenting this to their own peoples.

4. I said that we fully appreciated his position but that a private understanding was not enough. It was quite impossible for us to go on speaking with two contradictory voices on a vital aspect of the agreement. This was bound to lead to a misunderstanding which would become acute when the time came to embody the agreement in a formal treaty. I added that unless he could clear up the doubts which he and his Ministers had created we would have to consider carefully whether it was right to proceed with the Commission of Enquiry.

5. He said that he was very worried about the reactions to the agreement particularly in Singapore and that he was afraid that Lee Kuan Yew might lose his slender majority and be replaced by a near Communist Government. He would not know how serious the situation was until he got back on Monday but he would consult his Cabinet and Lee Kuan Yew at once and communicate with us.

6. In the circumstances he thought his Cabinet might decide that they would prefer the Commission to be composed wholly of British Government representatives.

7. I told him that if he had originally made this proposal we could probably have accepted it without difficulty but that having announced that the Commission would be a joint one the withdrawal of the Malayan representatives would certainly be interpreted as implying disagreement between us.

8. I got the general impression that the Tunku was thoroughly rattled. He felt that he had agreed in London to more than he could carry with his own people and with the people of Singapore. He seemed genuinely afraid that the pressure of public opinion might force him to withdraw from the agreement and renounce the idea of Greater Malaysia.

9. If he returns to Malaya in this depressed and despairing mood I'm afraid he may not put up much fight and may be disposed to throw in his hand.[1]

10. In the light of the above please telegraph urgently your assessment of the state of opinion in Kuala Lumpur/Singapore and if possible obtain the views of Razak/Lee Kuan Yew.

11. I should like to receive your reply in time for me to talk further with the Tunku on Saturday evening before his departure on Sunday morning.

---

[1] This is the first indication of Sandys' impatience with the Tunku which reached a crescendo in Aug–Sept 1963. The British official who saw him off at the airport gained a very different impression of the Malayan premier and reassured Sandys on 4 Dec that he was 'certainly not in a "depressed mood" then; he seemed relaxed and cheerful and spoke kindly of you'. Indeed, he seemed to be optimistic about the Greater Malaysia project and he arrived back in Malaya to a rousing welcome.

87   PREM 11/3866   2 Dec 1961

[Role of commissioner-general in Anglo–Malayan defence
arrangements]: letter from Lord Selkirk to Mr Macmillan, proposing
formal machinery for Anglo–Malayan defence co-operation and the
extension of his term as commissioner-general

The speed with which the discussions with Tunku Abdul Rahman were completed
have made a considerable impression here although curiously enough, there has
been absolutely no comment here from any of the political figures in Singapore.[1] I
was glad to see from the recent telegram from the Ministry of Defence (COSSEA 41)
that they fully appreciate the importance of avoiding any wordy discussion between
Kuala Lumpur and Whitehall. Indeed, it must be, I think, quite obvious that when
the Federation has sole charge of internal security in Malaya and Singapore, it will be
fully within their power to prevent us from doing things which they do not want us
to do. I have, therefore, no doubt that the effect of the agreement is that we can do
anything we like provided the Tunku agrees. But, if the Tunku is prepared to oppose
us, our sphere of activity will be severely curtailed.

In these circumstances, I consider it of first class importance to establish proper
joint machinery in Kuala Lumpur for the purpose of carrying out the three common
objectives promoted under the defence agreement: that is, the defence of Malaya, the
defence of Commonwealth interests and the maintenance of peace in South East
Asia. Such arrangements would not only serve to educate the Malays but would also
give them reasonable assurance and confidence that they know what we are doing.
They would also provide a formal link between the Malayan armed forces and the
Commonwealth armed forces in Malayan territory. Their exact form would need
careful examination and eventually discussion with the Malayan Government but I
have no doubt that something of this character is necessary.

The second point I want to make concerns timing. It is already clear that the
interim period before Greater Malaysia is achieved should not be prolonged a day
longer than is absolutely necessary. All decisions on policy, investment and
appointments are already tending to be deferred. Lee is just holding his own in
Singapore, but with some difficulty, and could well be destroyed at any time by
further defections in his party. As the Tunku said yesterday, if the present
Government fell, the whole idea of merger would collapse. I believe, therefore, we
should not only be ready to bring Malaysia into being next year but we should bend
all our efforts to achieve that objective. I believe the earliest date this might be
possible is August which conveniently coincides with Merdeka Day in the Federation.

This overriding aim will, I hope, be clearly before the Borneo Commission when it
proceeds with its work. It will, I hope, also be in our minds when considering the
setting up of new organisation both in Singapore and in Kuala Lumpur to operate
the new arrangement. By the same criterion, I also think it would be unwise for me
to leave as at present suggested in April as this will mean the establishment of an

---

[1] On 5 Dec, however, the Sultan of Brunei publicly expressed approval of the outcome of the London talks
and on 6 Dec Singapore's Legislative Assembly voted 33 to 0 (with 18 Barisan supporters absenting
themselves) in favour of the Heads of Agreement on merger with Malaya, cf 59, note and 79, n 1.

interim organisation at precisely the time when these matters are being brought to fruition. My replacement by a 'U.K. Commissioner for Singapore' will leave no one with an oversight covering the whole area. It will seem as if we are withdrawing before the job is properly completed.

I realise this new suggestion may run counter to our short term financial policy but what we are trying to do is to achieve a sounder evolution of this area. In the long run this will mean not only a reduced British liability generally but peaceful progress in a manner which would serve not only our interests but also the best interests of South East Asia as a whole. I must, therefore, suggest to you that my removal from this position be deferred until, say, August to see whether it is not possible to get these arrangements through by that date. By then, even if it was not completed, we should be able to have a clearer picture of the manner in which it can be completed. I have no doubt that though we have surmounted a big hurdle, one or two quite difficult fences lie ahead of us.

88 PREM 11/3866   19 Dec 1961
[Role of commissioner-general in Anglo–Malayan defence arrangements]: letter from Mr Macmillan to Lord Selkirk

[In his reply, Macmillan took into account the views of the foreign secretary and argued 'that it would be a mistake to create formal consultative machinery too soon' while the need for economies warranted immediate retrenchment in the commissioner-general's office. He concluded, therefore, that 'we should stick to our present plans' rather than prolong Selkirk's term to the inauguration of Malaysia, although he was later persuaded to extend (see 90). On the same day, the chiefs of staff discussed British strategy in the 1960s and noted that projected defence expenditure still did not come within budget (COS 85(61)3, DEFE 4/141; see also CAB 21/4626 and D1(62)1, 12 Jan 1962, CAB 131/27).]

Thank you for your letter of December 2[1] about some of the problems arising from the Greater Malaysia project. The two particular suggestions which you have made— on consultation with the Malayans about defence and on the timing of changes in the United Kingdom organisation in Singapore—raise important questions and I am grateful to you for writing to me about them.

Assuming that Greater Malaysia comes into being, I agree that in practice our ability to use our bases in Malaya and Singapore as we want will largely depend upon good relations with the Malaysian Government, and that we should therefore without delay do everything possible to develop with the present Malayan Government a habit of close and frank consultation. Harold Watkinson had some discussion about this with Abdul Razak and Kadir when the Malayans were over here recently,[2] and all of us concerned with the problem have since been giving it further careful thought, as a result of which we find ourselves in accord with your views except on one point of some importance.

We do not differ from you on objectives (particularly the necessity to educate the Malayans in the problems relating to the defence of Malaya, the defence of Commonwealth interests and the maintenance of peace in South-East Asia, and to

---

¹ See 87.   ² See 85.

give them reasonable confidence that they know what we are doing), and we also agree, as I have already indicated, that the way to attain these objectives lies through the development of regular and effective consultation. But we think that it would be a mistake to create formal consultative machinery too soon. Instead I feel that we should begin by encouraging informal and increasingly frequent exchanges of views and information without the publicity and rigidity which would inevitably attend a more formal approach.

There are several reasons for this. It seemed clear from the attitude of the Tunku and Razak when they were here last month that they would prefer both Governments to approach defence problems flexibly and pragmatically without too constant an eye to the exact interpretation of written agreements. Again, we are already, under the Malayan Defence Agreement, virtually committed in principle to discuss problems relating to the defence of Malaya and of the Commonwealth; and formal machinery for discussing the maintenance of peace in South East Asia might embarrass both sides, ourselves because it could lead to arguments about our freedom of action which we could otherwise avoid, and the Malayans because it might involve them in matters which they would prefer quietly to leave to us alone. Moreover, experience in ANZAM suggests that we might find difficulty in providing enough material for worthwhile discussion at regular meetings of a formal character; and if the agenda tended to be on the thin side we might well arouse in the Malayan mind a suspicion that we were not serious about consultation and were deliberately withholding our confidence from them.

On the other hand, as I have said, we are fully aware of the desirability of bringing the Malayans, both in the Services and in Government, to a better understanding of the relevance to Malaya of the general defence problems of South East Asia, and of the particular issues to which they give rise for the United Kingdom. One of the difficulties hitherto has been that because the broader aspects of defence have been handled by British officers, seconded to Malayan service, there has been little opportunity for Malay officers to extend their horizons. The Chiefs of Staff are considering this problem now and will be consulting the Commanders-in-Chief in Singapore about the best means of dealing with it. Our present view is that we should begin by increasing the regular supply of general information, especially in the field of intelligence, and move on to a more liberal exchange of planning information when the educational process is well established and showing good results. That would seem to be the stage at which we might hope to instill in the Malayans a better appreciation of the nature and value of SEATO. At the same time, we also think that we should develop more extensive and frequent contacts with Ministers and senior officials of the Malayan Government—again, informally to start with. The Commonwealth Relations Office will be getting in touch with Tory about this. We think that at first exchanges of both kinds should be bilateral, but we are anxious to draw Australia and New Zealand into this pattern of informal consultation and shall be consulting their Governments about the best means and timing for doing so. We feel sure that they will want such an association and we have no doubt that it would be in our interests. It may well prove in due course that informal consultation could with advantage be replaced by more formal arrangements but, for the reasons which I have given, we think it desirable that that should happen, if at all, as a result of general agreement arising from experience.

Your second suggestion related to the timing of the Greater Malaysia project. I agree that we want to achieve it as quickly as possible, but we have to recognise just what the possibilities are. It seems to me that it might well be fatal to the whole project if we appeared to be rushing our fences, particularly in relation to the Borneo territories. You will have seen that Goode and Waddell believe that, if the Commission of Enquiry is to do a satisfactory job, time must first be allowed for the peoples of North Borneo and Sarawak to gain at any rate some general understanding of what is proposed, and that even then the Commission will require something like three months on the ground. That may be asking too much but by any standard it seems unlikely that the Commission can submit its report before the end of April at the earliest. Time will than be required for the report to be considered separately by the Governments concerned before the proposed inter-governmental conference is held; and we know from our experience of Malaya itself and other territories that months of hard detailed preparatory work are likely to be required between agreement on principles and the actual establishment of a Greater Malaysia. We therefore think it unrealistic to hope that we could achieve a Great [sic] Malaysian 'Merdeka Day' by August 1962, and that it would be dangerous to let any such impression gain currency. That being so, although I share your sense of urgency and see the attractions of deferring changes in your organisation—above all, your own departure—at any rate until August, 1962. I believe that we should stick to our present plans. Things may go smoothly but I think that we should be unwise to entertain too lively expectations on that score. One element in the situation which we cannot overlook is our very real need to obtain as soon as possible the substantial economies which we can achieve by the proposed changes in your organisation and I have come to the conclusion that, taking everything into account, we must adhere to our existing programme.

89 CAB 21/4626   29 Dec 1961
'Malaysia commission': outward telegram no 1829 from Mr Sandys to Sir G Tory, forwarding a personal message from Mr Macmillan to Tunku Abdul Rahman about the selection of the chairman

[The commission of enquiry was set up to ascertain the views of the peoples of North Borneo and Sarawak on the proposed Federation of Malaysia and to make recommendations. Its remit included neither Brunei (because it was not a colony) nor Singapore (since it was internally self-governing with institutions and machinery for assessing public opinion). The British and Malayan governments each nominated two members while the chairman was appointed by the British prime minister with the concurrence of the Malayan prime minister. It was not until 16 Jan 1962 that the commissioners were announced and not until 3 February that Lord Cobbold received his formal instructions from Macmillan. From the outset the British favoured Malcolm MacDonald as chairman on the grounds of, firstly, his reputation as a skilled arbitrator, secondly his earlier advocacy of 'Greater Malaysia' and, thirdly, his knowledge of British Borneo and sympathy with its peoples. It was probably on account of the last factor, as well as unspecified 'personal difficulties', that the Tunku rejected his nomination. Ghazali Shafie has recalled advising the Tunku against 'my old and dear friend Malcolm MacDonald' as chairman principally because 'all the credit would go to MacDonald and that it would be easy for the opponents of [the] Malaysia plan to brand it as a British design'. In any case, MacDonald was ruled out on account of his duties as co-chairman of the International Conference on Laos, 1961–1963. The Tunku pressed for Lord Ogmore (formerly David Rees-Williams), a friend who had been a useful ally in London during the negotiations for Malayan independence. The Colonial Office, however, felt that Ogmore's role in the cession of Sarawak to the Crown in 1946 would make him unacceptable to many Sarawakians. There followed a succession of vain suggestions: Lord Boyd (A Lennox Boyd)—too political; Sir J Robertson, Sir J Macpherson and Lord Shawcross—unavailable; Sir S Caine—not interested; Lord Radcliffe; Lord Tweedsmuir; and so on. Sir H Poynton remarked on 8 Jan 1962: 'The situation keeps changing almost from hour to hour & we can't keep pace with it on a sheet of paper.' He wryly suggested that Proteus (the old man of Greek legend who had the power to assume different shapes at will) might make a good chairman. On 12 Jan Macmillan put forward Lord Cobbold, Lord Tweedsmuir and Field Marshal Sir Francis Festig, from whom the Tunku chose Cobbold, a former governor of the Bank of England. The British accepted the Tunku's suggestion that Sir David Watherston (formerly chief secretary of Malaya) should serve on the commission, and, in order to ensure that the commission was not too 'Malayan', they selected Sir Anthony Abell as the other British commissioner. The Malayan representatives were Ghazali Shafie, permanent secretary of the Ministry of External Affairs, and Dato Wong Pow Nee, chief minister of Penang. I H Harris, a principal in the CO, was seconded as the commission's secretary. The commission toured Sarawak and North Borneo between mid-February and mid-April and reassembled in Britain to write up the report in May and June. The report was then scrutinised by Whitehall's inter-departmental Greater Malaysia (Official) Committee. For the appointment of the commission see CAB 21/4626, CO 1030/1009 and 1010 and Tan Sri Ghazali Shafie, *Ghazali Shafie's memoir on the formation of Malaysia*, Bangi, Malaysia, 1998, p 171. The tour is covered in CO 1030/1011–1014 and files on the commission's hearings, deliberations and recommendations are at CO 947. CO 947 consists of 61 pieces, as follows: 1 chairman's papers; 2 briefing papers for British members; 3 minutes and hearings (including notes of meetings in England during May–June); 4 policy and report (April–May); 5 legal advice; 6 political parties; 7 draft approved report; 8–12 Malaysia Solidarity Consultative Committee; 13–31 North Borneo papers; 32–61 Sarawak papers. The report was published in Aug 1962 as *Report of the Commission of Enquiry, North Borneo and Sarawak, 1962* (Cmnd 1794).]

Please see Tunku yourself as soon as possible after his return to Malaya and deliver following personal message from Mr. Macmillan. *Begins.*

'My dear Tunku,

Since I received your letter of 7th December about the Commission for the Borneo territories, we have been doing our utmost to find a suitable chairman in whom both of us would have full confidence. I am sure it is of the utmost importance that the Federal Government should be represented on the Commission. Moreover, a failure to agree on this matter would create a most unfortunate impression.

We have tried hard to persuade Alan Boyd to take it on. He was obviously attracted and I think would have done it well. But he felt that more time would be required to do it properly than he himself would be able to give, so we have had to look around again.

As we see it, there are two all-important qualifications for this job. First, the man concerned must be fully convinced that the objective of a Greater Malaysia is right. Secondly, he should be someone who is trusted by the people of the Borneo territories, so that they will listen to his advice.

For this reason, I venture to ask whether you would not reconsider your earlier doubts about Malcolm MacDonald. He certainly shares our belief that a Greater Malaysia is right; and nobody is better qualified to sell the idea to the peoples of Borneo. I understand your misgivings about his personal difficulties, but I still feel that he is much the best man for this job. I hope therefore that you will give this further consideration.

Of other names that have occurred to us, those of Sir Donald MacGillivray[1] and

---

[1] The last British high commissioner of Malaya, 1954–1957; he retired to Kenya and served as vice-chairman of the Monckton Commission on the Central African Federation, 1960.

Lord McCorquodale[2] seem possible. We have not, however, put the idea to either of them, and we think it doubtful whether MacGillivray would be willing to leave Kenya where he is now settled. McCorquodale is one of a number of people we have considered; but he has no detailed local knowledge. If therefore we appointed him, one would think it desirable to include in the team someone like Tony Abell, who is familiar with the area.

I have thought a great deal about Ogmore. I am, however, convinced that this would not be a wise appointment. It might indeed do great harm to our cause. His part in the recent history of Sarawak has left the people there with a prejudice against him, and, however baseless this may be, it is bound to operate against the efforts of the Commission to secure the trust and confidence of the population.

Perhaps you would let me know your thoughts on all this as soon as you can. If there are any further names which you may wish to suggest, I shall naturally be most happy to consider them.

Best wishes for 1962.

Yours ever,

Harold Macmillan'. *Ends*.

---

[2] A former Conservative MP and businessman, including the chairmanship of McCorquodale & Co Ltd and other printing companies.

90   PREM 11/3866   30 Dec 1961
[Role of the commissioner-general in Anglo–Malayan defence arrangements]: letter from Lord Selkirk to Mr Macmillan

[In this document Selkirk reiterates his request to remain commissioner-general in order to see Malaysia through to inauguration. Having conferred with the foreign secretary and others. Macmillan replied to Selkirk on 5 Jan agreeing to extend his term of office until Aug 1962 'by which time I would hope that we should see our way clearer on Greater Malaysia'. At the same time he urged Selkirk to continue the reorganisation of his headquarters at Phoenix Park 'in the interests of economy'. There was, therefore, no need for Selkirk to return to London for consultations in advance of his Eden Hall Conference in January on which he reported to the prime minister and from which Macmillan drew the conclusion: 'Our limited resources and our growing commitments elsewhere make it essential that we should gradually reduce our military and colonial responsibilities in South East Asia. This will clearly be a long and difficult process and will have to be conducted with great care, if we are to avoid the creation of a partial power vacuum in the area.' See Macmillan to Selkirk, 5 Jan 1962, PREM 11/3866; Selkirk to Macmillan, 24 Jan 1962, and Macmillan to Selkirk, 12 Mar 1962, CO1030/1084; and also CAB 21/4626.]

I have your letter of December 19[1] which you signed just before you left for the talks in Bermuda.[2]

2.   You were good enough to say that the points I raised in my letter of December 2 are important. I must regard them as fundamental.

3.   During my two years here it has become apparent to me that we would have to lighten the load of our commitments in this area. To this end I have sought to reach a posture when this would gradually become possible. We now, however, seem to be

---

[1] See 88.   [2] Macmillan met Kennedy at Bermuda just before Christmas for talks about nuclear tests.

pursuing two separate policies: first to maintain freedom of military action in the area generally and in Singapore in particular without consulting the Government of Malaya, and secondly substantially to reduce our forces in this area.

4.   These two policies cannot be reconciled and we will have to decide which we consider to be the more important. In practice I have little doubt that reasons of economy will compel us to accept the latter. Indeed, the Ministry of Defence are already considering ways and means to transfer responsibility for internal security to the Malayans, thereby reducing our obligation to maintain a substantial number of British troops in this area. With this aim in view, what you suggest in your letter does not seem to me to go far enough. I accept that the habit of close and frank consultation with the Malayan Government must be developed gradually. But this must be based on some machinery from the outset which would reassure the Malayans that we really are prepared to discuss common problems. In any case they are now tentatively asking for some sort of joint committee. If we have to pour cold water on such a suggestion, their natural sense of suspicion will be incurred.

5.   At the present time there is no formal contact between the British Services in this area and the Malayan Government. No joint planning of any kind has taken place and indeed our personnel have not hitherto been authorised to hold any discussions except on a purely personal and inevitably restricted basis. They can of course communicate through the High Commissioner in Kuala Lumpur on specific points but I do not think this is enough. The Malayans want us to stay, they want to talk to us and it is essential that we should be forthcoming if we are to regain their confidence on which alone our continued presence in this area depends. The steady process of consultations can, I believe, bring them a long way towards an understanding of our approach to the problems of this area.

6.   I must leave you in no doubt that I do not think without the concurrence of the Malayans that we are free to mount operations from Singapore except in the most circumscribed manner. To do so would be to run the risk of our being forced to leave this area completely at a much earlier date. It may be necessary to take such steps but we should do so with our eyes wide open.

7.   As regards the second point in your letter, it appears to me that, unlike some other places in this area, we have for some time been ahead of public opinion in proposing a constructive solution to the problem of the remaining British territories in South East Asia. We have already made some progress leading this opinion along right paths and it is important that we should continue to keep up the momentum if we are to thwart communist aspirations.

8.   I am of course fully aware of the dangers of rushing the Borneo Territories and it may well be that August next year will prove too soon. But I do not think we should exclude it as a possibility. It is really not correct to say that the people are not apprised of what it is all about. There has been an unceasing flow of information on the radio, in the press, in speeches and in meetings held in Singapore, Kuching, Jesselton and elsewhere, almost without a break over the last six months. If it goes on too long doubts and suspicions will increase and a sense of disenchantment prevail. Parties are forming fairly rapidly in the Borneo Territories and those with communist affiliations are striving to strengthen and consolidate their positions for the purpose of blocking Malaysia.

9.   I do not suggest that we should disclose that we are prepared to consider reaching an agreement by August nor allow it to become clear that we are ahead of

public opinion. Our object should be to maintain the momentum by means of objective comments and explanations. This would of course be done substantially under the direction of the Governors of Sarawak and North Borneo. A recent telegram to Kuching has now initiated this approach. Even so, it is not practical to expect that we will ever get unanimous support for Malaysia from the Borneo Territories; but I believe it is possible to achieve in the next twelve months a wide measure of support which would permit us to overrule opposition. The opposition however is likely to gain rather than lose in strength unless we can keep our plans moving steadily forward.

10.   Nor should we exclude the possibility, remote as it may be, that the Tunku would be willing to take on Singapore before the Borneo Territories are in fact ready to transfer sovereignty. This will, however, only be likely if he is satisfied that real progress has been made and that we are fully supporting his plans.

11.   You are asking me to come away from here with these developments little more than half finished. There are many ways of course in which they could go wrong and I am anxious that these points should be kept at least to a minimum. The manifold problems which are before you to-day are all too apparent and it would be wrong for this one to be added if it can be avoided. I would therefore like to come and see you if you would be good enough to give me a date, if possible before the Eden Hall Conference which is being held from January 17 to 20.

91   CO 1030/1447, no 101   15 Jan 1962
[Brunei: political developments during 1961]: despatch from Sir D White to Mr Maudling

[On 22 Nov the Sultan of Brunei had written to Maudling welcoming the prospect of 'Greater Malaysia' and expressing his willingness to take part in negotiations with the Federation and Britain and he had made a further statement of support after the conclusion of the London talks (CO1030/1012, nos E48 and 49). This despondent report by the British high commissioner, however, revealed British anxiety about the sultan's apparent capriciousness towards the project. White's assessment was shared by two senior CO officials (Sir John Martin and Ian Wallace) who at this time were touring the region in advance of the Cobbold commission. Following a discussion with His Highness and his ministers at the Istana (palace) on 15 Jan, Wallace noted: 'Brunei is not going to be a push-over for Malaysia' (Wallace to Eastwod, 17 Jan 1962, CO 1030/1012, no 67). It was in order to stiffen the Sultan's resolve that Maudling spelled out the advantages of Malaysia for Brunei in a letter of 9 Mar 1962 (see 95).]

I have the honour to submit a report on political developments in the State during the second full year of what is virtually internal self-government, under the new constitution.

2.   The political situation in 1961 was dominated by three main issues, the breakdown of the administration, the Sultan's attitude on closer association with Malaya, and the question of elections.

3.   The breakdown of the administration was largely due to the Sultan's interference in its every aspect. The Mentri Besar[1], as ex-Private Secretary to the Sultan, was not tough enough mentally or physically to cope with the Sultan and he

---

[1] For the appointment of Brunei's first mentri besar (chief minister) under the 1959 constitution see 9, n 6.

was further handicapped, in his new capacity, by the increasingly obvious incompetence of several of the Malayan officers seconded to Brunei. As the public concern at the delays in handling Government business increased, so the Mentri Besar's acceptability to the Sultan decreased, and it became obvious that his days were numbered.

4.   The Malayan officers admittedly faced a difficult situation. The fact that they were Malays, sharing a language and a religion, replacing British officials at the Sultan's request, was not sufficient to guarantee them a welcome from the suspicious Brunei Malays. In common with every other foreigner, acceptance by the Bruneis has to be won. The Malayans took it for granted and when it was withheld, retired into an expatriate clique and ignored the locals. This was also resented and they became increasingly unpopular. Senior Brunei officials in the Public Service, especially those nominated to the Councils as unofficial members, missed no opportunity of thwarting them and, although they were in Brunei at the Sultan's request, neither he nor the Mentri Besar gave them adequate backing; frustrated officially and ostracised socially, they were determined to get back to Malaya by hook or by crook. The opportunity came when the State Forest Officer was assaulted. This relatively trivial but unpleasant incident provided an opportunity of which they took the maximum advantage.[2]

5.   This assault took place shortly before the State Visit of His Majesty the Yang di-Pertuan Agong, and a well-meaning but misguided attempt to settle the incident quietly out of court was, perhaps deliberately, misconstrued by the Malayan Prime Minister. Without any adequate inquiry into the facts, the Tungku flew to the support of his officers; criticised the Brunei Government, particularly the Senior Police Officers, publicly attacked the Party Rakyat, who were only concerned to the extent that Azahari, their President, was the brother of the attacker, and delivered an ultimatum to the Sultan which was deeply resented.

6.   The Tungku probably hoped that the threat to withdraw his officers would force the Sultan's hand over Malaysia; instead, the Sultan went cold on the project.

7.   The Party Rakyat had already declared their stand on Malaysia—reunification of the Borneo Territories as a first step, after elections, and then independence and perhaps Malaysia later. The Tungku's public utterances in Brunei, and elsewhere, were calamitous. Apart from gravely embarrassing the Sultan and infuriating the Party Rakyat, they underlined what was already widely suspected, that the Bruneis were regarded as a backward people, who should be honoured to accept an invitation to join Malaya.

8.   Apart from stimulating opposition to the Malaysia plan, the Tungku's remarks also gave rise to strong suspicion, not without justification, that he was advising against elections for Brunei. The failure to hold the elections by the agreed date was certainly to some small extent due to the dilatory way in which the Attorney General performed his duties, but the Sultan himself was obviously concerned at the prospect of elections with only the Party Rakyat in the field, and indulged in attempts to form a new party and intrigue against the Party Rakyat.

9.   The result was that by the end of July the situation was extremely tense; the Party Rakyat were more active and more threatening than ever before—they had

---

[2] See 52, n 4.

gained both support from and control over the labour organisation and were ready to use any cudgel, including 'sit-in' strikes, to force the Government to get on with the elections, get rid of the Malayan officers, and reorganise, even, if necessary, by recruiting more British officers.

10.   The Sultan was, for the first time, genuinely alarmed. He seemed to realise at last the dangers of becoming too closely involved in the administration. Personally, he probably favoured steam-roller tactics, putting the Malaysia scheme through the Executive Council and having a show-down with the Party Rakyat and, if necessary, arresting the leaders. Wiser councils prevailed; the Mentri Besar retired more or less permanently to hospital, the Attorney General and the State Secretary left for Malaya, the latter without authorisation, and the Sultan left for a dental operation in Malaya, after formally announcing that the elections would have to be postponed to a date not later than October, 1962.

11.   The attitude of the Brunei Malays is often unpredictable—so it was again. The undignified retreat of the Attorney General and the State Secretary to the safety of Kuala Lumpur was welcomed. The Sultan's announcement of the postponement of the elections, and a reasoned explanation of why this was necessary, occasioned strong protest, but it was obvious to all that postponement was now inevitable and there was little point in striking to enforce a date that was no longer within reach. Furthermore, the Sultan appointed Marsal bin Maun as Deputy Mentri Besar, acting as Mentri Besar while the substantive holder was permitted to take all leave due to him. Pengiran Yussof was appointed Deputy State Secretary, acting as State Secretary, after the departure of the substantive holder. The Party Rakyat became increasingly anxious to avoid the clash with Government which a sit-in strike would have precipitated and chose the demonstration and petition to the Secretary of State as a way out.

12.   At any time up to a few months ago, it would have been impossible to view the appointments of Marsal and Pengiran Yussof with anything but the gravest apprehension. They, together with Pengiran Ali, now head of the Religious Affairs Department, were the three members of the Brunei Malay Teachers Association who had been specially selected by the Sultan in 1956 as the spearhead of the attack on the British Resident's entrenched position.[3] Ardent nationalists, they all had close contact with the Party Rakyat.

13.   From the beginning, the Sultan made it clear that he intended to allow the new Mentri Besar to lead the Government and he continues to refer to 'his Government' on all occasions to eliminate as far as possible the criticism that was mounting against him personally. Marsal and Yussof started, with exemplary diligence, to clear up the enormous back-log of business, including some 600 files in the State Secretary's office awaiting attention. The speed with which they achieved this, in spite of Marsal's complete lack of English, was commendable. A new Attorney General arrived from Malaya, a vast improvement on his predecessor. Tactfully he gained the confidence of his local colleagues and the Sultan, and Council meetings proceeded with efficiency and dispatch, instead of wrangling and interminable loquacity.

---

[3] One way of reducing British control in his kingdom had been for the Sultan to embark on constitutional reform which he did in the mid-1950s with the support of the PRB.

14.   The rigidity of Marsal's attitude to administration leads to some inequity, but, after the impartiality[4] and lack of sense of responsibility by the Malayan officers, discipline in the service was at a low ebb and a firm hand was needed. Once he has established his authority and, if, as seems likely, he is confirmed in office, he should be able to adopt a more reasonable approach. It is only fair to say that he and Yussof have done extraordinarily well so far.

15.   The Party Rakyat, in the meantime, have remained quiet, ostensibly awaiting the reply to their petition. Azahari has been ill and away in Malaya and Indonesia and several of the leading members of the Committee have also been to Indonesia. It seems likely that they were apprehensive of the attitude Marshal would adopt. They are not anxious for martyrdom and are known to have had ideas on seeking political asylum if a clash had occurred.

16.   On the advice of the new Attorney General, Dato' Abdul Aziz, supported by Marsal, Pengiran Yussof and Pengiran Ali, the Sultan has welcomed Malaysia in his speech from the throne at the budget meeting of Council, but has undertaken to consult the people first. A firm assurance was also given on the holding of elections and, indeed, much of the enabling legislation and regulations made thereunder were tabled at the meeting, after some hard work by the Attorney General to get them ready. Furthermore, attempts have been made to conciliate the Party Rakyat, as well as attempts to split its unity. One of the more violent members has been made State Welfare Officer! Azahari has been invited to serve under Marsal on an all races Committee to study the Malaysia idea and he probably had some sympathetic treatment in his business difficulties. He now owes some $120,000 to Government.

17.   It remains to be seen whether the Sultan and Marsal can swing public opinion over to Malaysia. If they fail, the onus will lie on Tunku Abdul Rahman. Much of the opposition to the scheme stems from dislike and distrust of him. He must bear the responsibility for seconding officers to Brunei without adequate experience and without briefing on the role of expatriate officers in a foreign State. The notoriety attached to the lamentable performance of some of the seconded officers has spread to Sarawak and North Borneo, who clearly share now Brunei's reluctance to have Malayans in high office. There seems little likelihood that Brunei will now hurry into Malaysia; if they go at all, it will be on their own terms and not the Tunku's and the terms will be a large degree of local autonomy.

18.   Recent events have to some extent relieved the pressure on the High Commission. The Sultan has made it clear that the High Commissioner is responsible for External Affairs and Defence and that his Government is responsible for internal affairs. Marsal has made it clear that the High Commissioner is an adviser to the Sultan only and not to him and, while courteous and socially friendly, avoids official contact except by correspondence. This reduces the danger of Her Majesty's Government becoming entangled, as seemed likely at one time, in a struggle between the Sultan and the Party Rakyat, though it is a rather liberal interpretation of the Agreement and the Constitution.

19.   I am copying this despatch to the Commissioner General for South East Asia and the Governors of Sarawak and North Borneo. I also enclose copies for onward transmission to the Commonwealth Relations Office, for High Commissioners in Kuala Lumpur, Canberra and Wellington.

---

[4] 'Impartiality' is a mistake; White clearly means 'partiality'.

92   CO 1030/1011, no E/280(iii)   16 Jan 1962
[Sir J Martin's mission]: note of a meeting of British officials with Lee
Kuan Yew

[Martin and Wallace toured the region in advance of the Cobbold enquiry to assess the
prospects for, and administrative requirements of, the proposed Federation. Telegraphing
Lord Perth from Jesselton, Martin reported that the 'advice from those to whom we have
spoken of all races is unanimous that people in Sarawak and North Borneo feel they are
being rushed'. Urging that the commission heed the objections of the Borneo peoples and
work out safeguards to meet them, he reminded Lord Perth of 'the unhappy history of the
MacMichael agreements in Malaya' in 1945 and 'the lesson of our failure to reconcile
people to federation in Central Africa at the outset' (31 Jan 1962 Goode Papers, box 2, file
1, f 23). Having visited Sarawak and Brunei, they met Lee Kuan Yew and his minister of
culture, Sinnathamby Rajaratnam. Before they discussed the political problems of
Singapore and the dangers inherent in delaying merger, Martin reported his impressions
of opinion in Borneo but Lee was inclined to dismiss Bornean reservations about 'Greater
Malaysia'. See also Lee, *Memoirs*, pp 415–416 and Michael Jackson (ed by Janet Jackson),
A Scottish Life: Sir John Martin, Churchill and Empire (London, 1999, pp 208–212).]

The Prime Minister, Mr. Lee Kuan Yew, and Mr. Rajaratnam, Minister of Culture,
met Sir John Martin, Mr. Wallace, Mr. Moore and myself[1] at Sri Temasek at 9.30 p.m.
on Tuesday, 16th January, for a general discussion on Greater Malaysia.

2.   Sir John Martin summarised the general state of opinion about Greater
Malaysia as he and Mr. Wallace had found it during their recent visit to Sarawak and
Brunei.[2] Their general impression, contrary to that given by the statements made at
meetings of the Malaysia Solidarity Consultative Committee,[3] was of hesitation on
almost all sides. The unsophisticated people up the rivers knew as yet very little of
the implications for them of Greater Malaysia and they would need time to think
about it. The Chinese too were hesitant knowing the policy of the Federal
Government of ensuring that the Chinese in Malaya were kept in their place. In
Brunei, Azahari, who had considerable support from the young Malays, was firmly
opposed to Brunei joining Greater Malaysia and thought that the aim should be an
independent federation of the three Borneo territories. Sir John Martin said that they
had had a long discussion with the Sultan of Brunei who had asked what were the
advantages of Greater Malaysia for his state. They had explained to him why HMG
considered this the best policy for the Borneo territories and in fact had put the case
just as the Tunku himself would have done. They had agreed however that it was
right for Brunei to seek special terms and told the Sultan that the Secretary of State
was sending a letter agreeing that he should enter into direct negotiations with the
Federal Government.

3.   Sir John Martin said that although they could not yet speak for North Borneo
their visit to Sarawak and Brunei had given them the clear impression that more
time would be needed before the territories could be satisfied that it would be in their
interests to join Greater Malaysia. This was particularly surprising in Brunei which
they had thought would, as an Islamic Malay State, be naturally attracted to
partnership with the Federation.

---

[1] This note is unsigned but is presumed to have been written by an official of the UK Commission,
Singapore.
[2] See 91, note.
[3] On 4 Feb 1962 the Malaysia Solidarity Consultative Committee produced a report broadly favourable to
merger, see 55, n 4.

4. Sir John Martin said that he had been impressed too by the administrative difficulties of moving quickly to Greater Malaysia. It would be necessary, as in all other territories approaching independence, to give expatriate officers the option of leaving the Service with compensation. The latest form of compansation scheme was designed to encourage officers to stay on but in the nature of things a considerable number of officers would decide to go. It would be some years before local officers could be trained to take over nor could the Federal Government spare qualified Malayan officers. In any case, the last thing the local people wanted was to see the jobs handed over to Malays; there was also the difficulty that the first people available locally would be the Chinese and not the indigenous people whose education was very backward. Clearly this was a long term problem but a pause of two to three years would enable something to be done to ease the administrative strain at handover.

5. Mr. Lee Kuan Yew said that the doubts and hesitations that people had confided in Sir John Martin and Mr. Wallace should not be taken too seriously. The leaders and spokesmen in the Borneo territories were people who respected authority and who believed in getting themselves as close as they could to its ultimate source. They saw that with Greater Malaysia the Tunku would be that ultimate source and they were beginning to accommodate themselves to this fact. Nevertheless, it was natural for them to hanker for the alternative of separate independence, with the prospect of their playing a larger part on the smaller stage, and this would explain the difference between the views given to senior officials of the British Government and those expressed at the Consultative Committee meetings. The important thing with people such as these was to give a strong lead and let them understand that HMG's support for Greater Malaysia was a settled matter.

6. Mr. Lee Kuan Yew said that he had no doubt that the Sultan of Brunei realised the advantages for him of close association with like-minded Muslim rulers in the other States within a strong Federation. Although he would want special terms for Brunei he would come in all right. Possibly Azahari's opposition to Greater Malaysia was genuine but he must know that he could not resist it if the Sultan agreed and he would settle on the best terms he could get. As for the Chinese, they were realists, mostly engaged in commerce and they would decide on the basis of what was best for business. They had wide contacts with other countries in this part of the world, and knew about conditions facing Chinese in Indonesia and elsewhere. They realised that although in Malaya Chinese did not have full political rights the conditions were on the whole better than elsewhere and they would acquiesce in Greater Malaysia. There remained the indigenous tribes who were simple people and understood little of the issues involved. Mr. Lee Kuan Yew said that he knew that there could be serious trouble if these people opposed Greater Malaysia and he stressed the importance of the Commission of Enquiry including someone whom they knew and trusted who would tell them it was a good plan. This was why he had suggested Sir Anthony Abell as a man who was remembered in Sarawak with affection and whose advice the people would accept.

7. The discussion then turned to the particular problems in Singapore. Mr. Lee Kuan Yew explained, as he had on previous occasions, the difficulty of keeping up the momentum and maintaining his position in Singapore during the period that would elapse before Greater Malaysia could be effected. He said that the Tunku believed it could all be accomplished by August, 1962; Jakeway in Sarawak thought they could be ready by September; on the other hand, Sir William Goode had mentioned June,

1963 as the more probable date. Meanwhile in Singapore the Barisan Socialis would continue harrying the Government in the hope of finding some issue on which it could be brought down. On the merger issue itself, they had not taken the line of bold opposition but had made the tactical blunder of declaring themselves in favour of complete merger and opposed only to various features of the White Paper proposals. This was a difficult line to sustain and it had not prevented the loss of all Malay support for the Barisan Socialis. (This was shown at their recent rally on West Irian which was attended mostly by Chinese and by only a few hundred Malays). In these circumstances, since no one opposed merger in principle, it was legitimate and logical for Government in the referendum to ask a series of questions directed at the particular objections to their White Paper. Mr. Lee Kuan Yew said that the Barisan Socialis would then see that they could not win and they would decide that the balance of advantage lay in staging wide-spread disorders rather than in accepting quietly the implementation of merger and their removal from the scene. They would argue that it would be better to go down fighting and so, as a result of police and military action, create bitterness on which they could build again. Mr. Lee Kuan Yew explained again why he could not take responsibility for the use of British troops to deal with such disorders and why in consequence interim arrangements must be made for the Tunku to take over responsibility for law and order before trouble came.

8.   Sir John Martin said he understood Mr. Lee Kuan Yew's difficulties in Singapore though he did not altogether see the need to hold a referendum now that the Assembly had endorsed the merger plan.[4] The major point was that however fast we might move in the Borneo territories the Tunku did not seem willing to consider taking Singapore into the Federation before the others. Mr. Lee Kuan Yew agreed that this was so and said that the Tunku's attitude had hardened because he had come to believe that HMG were trying to foist Singapore upon him without committing themselves about the Borneo territories. This was why the Tunku had lost confidence in the good faith of HMG and the first essential was to win back that confidence. If that could be done it was possible that the Tunku might be prepared to move a little from his firm position. Sir John Martin suggested the possibility that if all went well in the Borneo territories and the Commission of Enquiry recommended a plan that was endorsed at a conference of all the territories, the Tunku might then agree to take in Singapore at once on the basis of a firm commitment by HMG that sovereignty over the Borneo territories would be transferred at some later date that would leave time for the necessary administrative preparations to be made. Mr. Lee Kuan Yew agreed that this was a possibility, but only if confidence had been restored between the Tunku and HMG.

9.   Sir John Martin thanked Mr. Lee Kuan Yew for the opportunity of a full and frank discussion on Greater Malaysia. So far as the Borneo territories were concerned, it was clear that the most important thing was for the people to be given a firm lead by HMG and this was now happening. His impression was that the people there would come to accept the plan provided the Tunku was wise enough to grant the reasonable safeguards that they wanted. It did appear however that more time would be wanted to make the necessary preparations and to ensure that the administration did not collapse after sovereignty was transferred. On the other hand,

---

[4] On 6 Dec 1961 the Legislative Assembly had voted in favour of merger. For British views on the referendum, see 72 and 131.

it was also clear from Singapore's standpoint delay meant danger and the major problem was to reconcile these different requirements. The discussion had been useful in pointing the way to possible answers on this and the first task seemed to be the re-establishment of complete confidence with the Tunku. The hope must be that he would then be willing to accept some special arrangements that would enable the position in Singapore to be secured.

93   CO 1030/1011, no 305   20 Feb 1962
[Attitude of Sultan of Brunei to Cobbold Commission]: letter from Sir D White to C G Eastwood, reporting the Sultan's dilemma

You will have seen my telegram of 18th February, reporting the Sultan's inability to receive Lord Cobbold on Sunday, 25th February, as proposed.[1]

I asked the Sultan if he could not possibly fit in even a brief call, but he said that he would be praying and could not receive any more afternoon visitors while the fast was on. He would be pleased to receive Lord Cobbold after the fast was over. It may well be a genuine excuse; the fast is a trying time and the Sultan looks tired and strained. There may, however, be a political 'nuance'. The Sultan is obviously under pressure from Kuala Lumpur to make up his mind on Malaysia and it is equally obvious that the Tunku either cannot or will not believe the strength of the opposition here. The Sultan may, therefore, feel that Lord Cobbold would, somewhat naturally, wish to know how his mind is working; he may also wish to see how things go in Sarawak and North Borneo before he talks to Lord Cobbold.

I discussed the position with the Mentri Besar and Dato' Pengiran Ali and with the Malayan State Secretary and Attorney General, all of whom dined with me on Saturday night. The general opinion seems to be that the whole Commission should call later on, after Hari Raya.[2] I will meet the Commission at the airport en route to Jesselton on the 25th February and see what they think.

Meanwhile, I sense an increase in tension. There is strong criticism from the Party Rakyat over the signing of the Consultative Committee Memorandum by the Brunei overservers[3] and over their public utterances. Pengiran Ali, the leader, has had threatening letters. The Malayan Attorney General, whose mission it is to achieve merger, is talking of proscribing Party Rakyat; their reported application to join the Afro–Asian Solidarity Group is a breach of the Societies Enactment, I admit, and some of the speeches by Party members have come close to treason. Nevertheless, I can see no valid case for proscription and the suppression of a political party at this juncture would be construed as an obvious move to facilitate merger. I have made it clear to the Attorney General that I should be bound to oppose any action to suppress the Party which could not be clearly justified in open open court, and I pointed out that the Police might well prove unreliable if called upon to deal with trouble

---

[1] The sultan later relented and in March agreed to a courtesy call from Cobbold. He continued to take a keen interest in the commission and its report but quoted to British officials the Malay proverb: 'Travel slowly, and arrive safely' (White to Wallace, 12 June 1962, PREM 11/3867).

[2] The holiday that follows the fasting month of Ramadan.

[3] 'Overservers' in this sentence is probably a misprint for 'observers'. For the MSCC's memorandum, see 55, n 4.

emanating from such an action. H.M. Government would find it gravely embarrassing to be called upon to restore order, if the trouble was caused by unjustifiable repression. Furthermore, it is more than possible that the Police Forces of Sarawak and North Borneo would not be available to assist the Brunei Force whilst Malaysia is a 'hot' issue in the territories.

I have a great deal of sympathy with the Sultan in his dilemma. I do not think that I should be guilty of over-emphasis if I stated that the situation posed a threat to the dynasty. Her Majesty's Government have not only welcomed the Malaysia concept, they have advised the Sultan to merge on conditions to be negotiated. It would not, therefore, be appropriate for us to bring any further pressure to bear on the Sultan, though it is for further consideration whether anything more can be done to ease the pressure on him, either in London or in Kuala Lumpur.

I still believe that a gesture by the Tunku to the Party Rakyat would have a value, but I understand that the Brunei Attorney General has also failed to persuade the Tunku to accept this view, hence his new approach, which I believe to be ill-advised. I am well aware that the Tunku is convinced that the Party Rakyat is Communist impregnated; I do not share his view and, indeed, there is no evidence whatsoever of it, but I do think that the Party is swinging further left, partly as a result of the Tunku's attitude, and I hope that this can be brought to his attention.

If I were the Tunku, I should now write a sympathetic letter to the Sultan, expressing regret at the dilemma in which he is placed and adding that it seems clear that there must be many misunderstandings to be cleared up, as the Brunei Malays, i.e. Party Rakyat, seem the only Malay organisation in the Borneo territories who have not welcomed Malaysia, and that it seems incomprehensible that they should seem prepared to throw in their lot with the Chinese Communist Barisan Socialis of Singapore and the predominantly Chinese left-wing S.U.P.P. of Sarawak. I should then suggest a goodwill delegation from Malaya to go round amongst the Brunei Malays and talk to them. This should not be a political delegation, but should consist of someone like Dato' Osman,[4] who is a personal friend of the Sultan and liked here, I think, and is now Chairman of the Central Electricity Board, with a well-known religious leader (dangerous, I know, to mix religion with politics but the situation is already dangerous), and perhaps someone from the U.M.N.O. Youth Movement. They should be briefed not to attack the Party Rakyat, but to talk to them and reason with them. They should know how far the Tunku is prepared to go in the way of concessions.

It is already becoming obvious that the Attorney General has compromised his official position by his advocacy of Malaysia, and his usefulness will rapidly become limited in this sphere.[5]

Of course, it would be inappropriate for me to make the suggestion from here, nor should it be traceable back to me, but, if there is any merit in the idea, it might be possible to ask Sir Geofroy Tory to throw out the idea on some suitable occasion. Will

---

[4] Dato Osman bin Talib, entered the MAS in 1926, transferred to the MCS in 1929, was appointed state secretary of Perlis in 1948, state secretary of Perak in 1949, deputy mentri besar of Perak in 1953, and chief minister of Malacca in 1957.
[5] For changes in administrative personnel made in 1961 and the role of Dato Abdul Aziz, the attorney-general, see 9, n 6.

you give this your urgent consideration, and also let me know if you think I am taking the right line on the possible proscription of the Party Rakyat.

I am copying this to Lord Selkirk, Sir William Goode, Sir Alexander Waddell and Sir Geofroy Tory.

94   CO 1030/987, no E/1128   6 Mar 1962
[Progress report on Cobbold Commission]: letter from Lord Cobbold to Mr Maudling. *Enclosure*: note by Lord Cobbold

[Cobbold wrote this letter while staying at the British high commissioner's residence in Kuala Lumpur on the eve of the Hari Raya public holiday (at the end of the Ramadan fasting month) and at a point when the commissioners had made preliminary visits to a few, principal centres in Borneo. In spite of his request to keep it out of official files, Cobbold's paper was considered formally by Macmillan and his ministers after the Tunku's allegations regarding British attitudes to Borneo threatened the completion of the enquiry (see 97 and 98).]

I enclose a private note for yourself and other Ministers who may be interested (I should be grateful if you would keep the Prime Minister informed). Please regard it as personal and 'thinking on paper' and not for any official files—we have only just started and I may change my views completely as we go along.

I have seen a good deal of Selkirk, Goode, Waddell and Tory who have all been most helpful and co-operative.

I have also had pleasant private talks with the Prime Minister of Singapore in Selkirk's house, and, as I say in the note, with the Tunku and Razak.

We are all well so far, but the pace is hot. Interest in the Commission throughout the area is enormous and somewhat alarming. I have kept no copy of this note.

Enclosure to 94

My present thoughts, quite preliminary since we have a long way to go, are on the following lines.

1. The whole position is even more difficult, and certainly more dangerous, than it appeared in London.

2. Whatever decision emerges there will be a period, certainly of months and perhaps of years, when strong and tactful handling will be necessary if serious racial trouble and possibly bloodshed are to be avoided.

3. There are possibilities of a sensible and constructive solution on Malaysia lines, but only if the Malayan Government are prepared to move quite a long way from their present detailed thinking.

4. I see five main essentials if a success is to be made of the Malaysia idea:—

(a) The first step should be taken quickly and decisively as soon as possible after our report is published. A long period of uncertainty at that stage would be dangerous in the extreme. You would be wise to envisage a Governmental conference not more than two months after our report, which I hope to get out before the end of May.

(b) The first step must however be a very limited one, leaving the present local

Governments very much in their present shape, with no weakening either in appearance or reality of their authority on all matters of administration of the territories—i.e. the immediate change should not go beyond e.g. sovereignty, external affairs, defence and some combination of federal and local authority on internal security.

(c) There must be a considerable interval before more complete integration can be effected. It would be silly and dangerous to force the pace on this until local politicians have grown up and local support and co-operation can be assured. At present the main attitude, except for the Sarawak Malays and some others who think they would do better under Malaysia, varies from a dislike of change and fear of the unknown to positive hostility and dislike of the Malays. It just is not true that these people feel themselves blood-brothers to the Malays—the marriage would have to be one of convenience, and, if it is to survive, of mutual convenience.

(d) The Civil Service must be kept going by British officers for a number of years. This will mean encouragement and financial inducement from H.M.G. and also adequate assurance that a competent and uncorrupt Government can be maintained in the territories.

(e) A carrot will have to be provided both by the Malayan Government and for some years by H.M.G., e.g. by contribution to a Development Fund, to persuade the territories that they are better with Malaysia than without it.

5. I had a long and friendly talk with the Tunku and Razak yesterday, in which I gave him some idea of these feelings (in more general terms). He will doubtless be difficult to shift from his ideas of a fairly rapid integration into something very like the existing Federation, though he did not seem wholly unwilling to contemplate a 2-stage operation.

6. In spite of all the difficulties I believe that Malaysia could with wisdom and moderation be the right solution for the territories. Although they are at present happy with their existing Government, the forces of nationalism and communist influence are on the march in Sarawak and imminent in North Borneo—even without external pressures I would not judge that happy Colonial Government would have a life of many years. Whether Malaysia can be achieved will depend, in my present judgment, on whether the Tunku is keen enough on it—or can be pushed hard enough at the later stages by H.M.G.—to accept the facts of life far enough to make the plan workable and acceptable to the territories.

7. The Commission get on well together personally and work together as well as could be expected. I would think, however, that the prospects of unanimous recommendations on the controversial points are extremely dim. The most I would hope for is some meeting of minds and some appreciation of the facts of life, leaving some thorny fundamental issues to be argued out between Governments. Constitution-drafting is a long way away. We have provisionally agreed to meet in England early in May to consider and write our report—I have invited the Malays to stay at Knebworth. We feel no need for legal advice until we get to the drafting stage.

8. I repeat, and emphasise, that the position is difficult and dangerous. Quite apart from Singapore, on which Ministers will be as well or better informed than I am, things could blow up very quickly in several different ways. All I can ask at the moment is that Ministers should be warned that difficult situations may have to be

faced urgently and should be ready to take early and decisive action as soon as we are able to produce a report. If the decision of Governments goes in favour of Malaysia the plan will at that stage have to be sold, and sold hard, to the territories on the basis that it will give them material benefits and not only on the basis of protection against communism or aggression.

95   CAB 21/4849   9 Mar 1962
[Brunei's future within Malaysia]: letter from Mr Maudling to the Sultan of Brunei, setting out the advantages of merger

I have received a report from Sir John Martin of the interesting discussion about the Malaysia proposal that he had with Your Highness recently in Brunei.[1] I readily confirm that, after most careful consideration, Her Majesty's Government think it right to advise Your Highness to accede to Tunku Abdul Rahman's proposal that Brunei should enter Malaysia, upon such terms and under such conditions as Your Highness might, after having consulted public opinion, agree with the Tunku. With this end in view, I wrote to Your Highness on the 8th January suggesting that informal discussions might well take place between the two Governments, if Your Highness so wished.

As Your Highness knows, it is the policy of Her Majesty's Government to work for the independence of the territories either directly or indirectly under Her Majesty's control, within, it is always hoped, the Commonwealth. Her Majesty's Government therefore welcomed the great constitutional advance which Brunei achieved as a result of the 1959 talks in London. I know that my predecessor greatly appreciated the friendly and co-operative spirit in which the talks took place, and which indeed further underlined the long and happy relationship which has existed between Brunei and Great Britain.

During these talks, Your Highness indicated a desire that Malayan officers should be considered for appointment to Brunei. Lord Boyd[2] unhesitatingly agreed to Your Highness's proposal, well knowing the long-standing bonds of friendship between Malaya and Brunei, and fully understanding and appreciating the advantages of employing officers sharing a religion, language and culture with Your Highness and Your Highness's people.

It was, therefore, with a full understanding of Your Highness's policy in this respect that Mr. Macmillan agreed with Tunku Abdul Rahman in welcoming the Malaysia concept and in seeking Your Highness's views. Indeed, as Your Highness may know, the Tunku specifically asked whether Her Majesty's Government would raise any objection to Brunei's joining Malaysia at an early date, if that was Your Highness's wish. Naturally, the Prime Minister replied that, if Your Highness decided on merger, Her Majesty's Government would agree to any date acceptable to Brunei and Malaya.

---

[1] See 91, note. Maudling's letter arose from the concern expressed by White and Martin and was based on a draft by White which was revised after consultation with Selkirk, Tory, Waddell and officials in the CRO and FO.
[2] As Mr Lennox-Boyd, secretary of state for the colonies, 1954–1959.

Apart from our understanding of the close ties between Brunei and Malaya, there are other important factors which persuaded Her Majesty's Government that the Malaysia plan would be of benefit to Brunei.

Malaya, with massive Commonwealth aid, was the first country to defeat armed Communist insurrection. The Communist effort in Malaya has continued underground in the form of subversion, but this too has been brought and kept under control thanks to the dynamic and decisive policies of Malayan leaders. In looking to the future, apart from the internal threat of Communist subversion, we have also had to take into consideration the possible threat of hostile action in Asia, particularly against small countries. Communist pressure is increasing in a number of places in South East Asia and there is a continuing risk of war which might involve the whole Peninsula and constitute a direct threat to the integrity ultimately of Brunei. Again, besides possible threats from Communism, both internal and external, there is always the possibility that a small but wealthy country like Brunei may appear a tempting prey to a more powerful neighbour. If Brunei were a part of Malaysia her position would be strengthened. She would enjoy the protection of the forces of Malaysia, together with those of the United Kingdom based there by agreement. We recognise the right of Brunei to independence, whenever the difficulties can be resolved to Your Highness's satisfaction, but we believe in all sincerity that the best hope of long-term peace and security for the State is to be sought within the framework of some wider association with neighbours of goodwill with, preferably, cultural, religious and language ties.

On the economic side, we have heard of Your Highness's wise decision to draw up a plan of economic development for Brunei. We understand that this includes industrial development with the aim of providing full employment for Your Highness's people, but we believe that this can only logically take place in an atmosphere of stability and with guaranteed markets such as we hope Malaysia would afford.

We fully recognise, furthermore, the importance of the throne to the people of Brunei and their desire for the security of the dynasty. In the changing world in which we live, it had occurred to us here that there would be greater security for the Brunei dynasty within the Federal Constitution, which contains effective safeguards for the position of the Rulers.

There is, as Your Highness knows, heavy pressure on what are called 'Colonial Powers' to disengage from their colonial responsibilities. We regard not with sorrow but with pride our achievements in this field, a pride that, with independence, friendship remains. We wish, therefore, independence to come to the territories under our protection, peacefully and without bitterness. We wish it to bring permanent prosperity and peace. The prospects of an independent Brunei standing alone must be uncertain; the future of a Brunei forming part of a greater Malaysia will be much better assured. Malaysia will not sever the link between Brunei and Britain—it will perpetuate that link in a different but more enduring form as members of our great family of Commonwealth countries.

I apologise for writing to Your Highness at such length. We are, of course, awaiting Your Highness's views on this important matter and will be ready at all times to enter into any discussions or negotiations which Your Highness might wish.

96   CO 1030/987, no 1108   12 Mar 1962

[Crisis over the Cobbold Commission]: inward telegram no 160 from Sir G Tory to Mr Sandys reporting the Tunku's public allegation that British officials in the Borneo territories were obstructing Malaysia

[The Tunku's accusations that British colonial servants in Borneo were hampering preparations for Malaysia, were printed in the *Straits Times* and reached the British press too. In a follow-up telegram on the same day, Tory informed the CRO that the Tunku was 'unrepentant' while Wong Pow Nee and Ghazali (the Malayan members of the Cobbold Commission) were complaining of 'rude treatment in North Borneo'. In asking the secretary of state for an explanation, Macmillan wondered whether the attack was 'really a manoeuvre by the Tunku to forestall Communist criticism' (Macmillan to Maudling, 12 Mar 1962, CO 1030/987, no 1112). Drawing upon material written at the time, Ghazali Shafie has described warm receptions in Sarawak and North Borneo and attributed such 'rudeness' there was on the part of local people to their coaching by die-hard British expatriates, see *Memoir*, pp 197–229.]

Today's Straits Times publishes following front page report of interview with Tunku 11th March under banner headlines 'British Civil Servants in Borneo territories hampering Malaysia' 'Tengku accuses' 'Resident snubs Ghazali, Wong'.

Begins

Tengku Abdul Rahman today accused British civil servants in Borneo territories of hampering Malaysia. Tenku said 'British civil servants in Borneo territories can do a lot to influence people, especially natives, because of their high position. 'However, they are very antagonistic towards Malaysia. They have now been persuaded not to take an active part in opposing Malaysia. Instead, they have adopted an apathetic attitude' he stressed that 'opinion' of British civil servants in Borneo territories did not count as far as he was concerned as he had already obtained agreement of the British Government to Malaysia concept 'I do realise necessity that they (British civil servants) should not be allowed to influence natives, like Malays and Dyaks.' 'The British civil servants in their position can do a lot of harm,' he said. Tengku said that a British resident in North Borneo had snubbed Malayan members of Cobbold Commission at a cocktail party 'in full view of everybody'. He said 'So bitter was the British civil servants opposition to Malaysia that when Wong Pow Nee and Ghazali were leaving the party, the British resident involved did not have courtesy or politeness, as one would expect from a British official in high position, to stand up and bid guests farewell'. Tengku added 'When matter was reported to me personally by Dato Wong and Inche Ghazali on their return to Kuala Lumpur last week, I was really very annoyed at this complete lack of courtesy, politeness and good manners on part of the host'. He would bring this to notice of Governor. Tunku said that, beside British civil servants, people in Borneo territories opposing Malaysia were Chinese people and businessmen, and British merchants.

He recalled that various Chinese millionaires were opposed to Merdeka[1] fearing chaos and disaster but no single Chinese in Malaya did not agree with Malayan independence now. Look at their wealth.

Regarding British businessmen in Borneo territories opposing Malaysia, Tengku said he could not understand their attitude 'these people merely want to cling to their possessions without due regard for changing situation'. North Borneo had not

---

[1] Independence.

been an easy place to push forward concept of Malaysia but it had dedicated people like Donald Stephens[2] and Dato Mustapha[3] who believed in Malaysia. Danger facing Borneo territories was 'clear enough for everyone to see'.

'I don't have to repeat it time and again. We can all see threat of Communists. If I did not see this danger I would not be bothered with other territories like Singapore, Sarawak, Brunei and North Borneo.

'Why should I really bother with these territories, if I did not see the danger ahead for us and for them. I am happy to have Malaya which is rich, prosperous and enjoying peace and security.'

Dealing with Singapore, which might require 'some special attention' he said he was certain that Singapore could not become an independent country. 'Singapore finds it a bit hard to accept merger terms because it has always regarded itself as a little China' he said. *Ends*

---

[2] Founder-president of UNKO, 1961; chairman of the MSCC, 1961–1962; first chief minister of Sabah, 1963.
[3] Founder of USNO, 1961; leader of Sabah's delegation to the MSCC, 1961–1962; first head of state of Sabah, 1963.

97 CO 1030/987, no 1128   19 Mar 1962
[Crisis over the Cobbold commission]: minute (PM(62)22) from Mr Maudling to Mr Macmillan, rejecting the Tunku's allegations contained in document 96

[CO officials drafted for the secretary of state a long rejection of the Tunku's allegations which was eventually submitted to the prime minister in an abbreviated form. They argued that the Tunku's conduct was dangerously unacceptable and, in his brief for ministerial discussions of this, Maudling's private secretary pointed out: 'we cannot bounce Borneo on the basis of the Tunku's present thinking; these are not just a bunch of head-hunters who have no ideas at all, or whose views can be ignored; we are all in favour of Greater Malaysia but it will have to be handled with more finesse than the Tunku is showing' (CO 1030/987, no 1146) While CO officials pressed for a strong ministerial riposte, however, the CRO was inclined to let the matter drop, and following discussion in the Cabinet Greater Malaysia Committee on 21 Mar, it was decided to take the matter no further with the Tunku (see 98).]

I promised you my comments on the Tunku's attack on Borneo civil servants and also to send you Cobbold's note of his preliminary impressions of the prospects for Malaysia. I enclose a copy of his note.[1]

2.   The Tunku's accusation that British officials in North Borneo are sabotaging our plans for Malaysia and are at most apathetic is quite unjustified. We have this from the Governor,[2] there has been the statement by the President of the North

---

[1] See 94.
[2] In a telegram to the CO on 14 Mar, Goode strenuously denied 'foot-dragging' and stated: 'We have done our best to give warnings of problems which the Tunku has preferred to ignore' (CO 1030/987, no 1114) On the same day Goode wrote to Tory: 'A Dusun Native Chief on the West Coast has told one of my officers that he expressed very strong views to the Commission on Malay supremacy. In that conversation he described Ghazalie as "kulit hitam" [black skin], and he may well have used this phrase in the hearing. The story has reached Sandakan [North Borneo's second principal town] that Ghazalie was referred to as a "black man" by a local native. As I reported many months ago, there are many people in North Borneo who dislike and distrust Malays, probably a relic of the old repression by Malays from Brunei. Ghazalie has probably sensed this ill-feeling in some of the witnesses appearing before the Commission' (*ibid*, no 1131) For Ghazali Shafie's own account based on material compiled at the time, see his *Memoir*, pp. 197–229.]

Borneo Civil Servants' Association of which I attach a copy,[3] and I have personal confirmation of what they say from Sir John Martin, who spent most of January in Borneo and made it his particular business to talk to as many British officials as he could meet.[4] All this is now confirmed in unequivocal terms by Cobbold in his two telegrams C.67 and C.68,[5] the background to which is in his note.

3. The administrations in Borneo are not being paternalistic but realistic. They are entirely with us in wanting to see Malaysia brought about. But, as Cobbold says, the people do not feel themselves blood brothers to the Malays and, if there is to be a marriage, and it is to survive, it will have to be one of mutual convenience. That means that the terms will have to be acceptable to the peoples in Borneo.

4. There is in fact no hope of an early and successful Greater Malaysia without British Officials. That is a particular reason why the Tunku's outburst is so unfortunate. The officers will stay on when the territories cease to be British colonies only if they want to stay. Some will go anyway—this always happens—but the urge to go will be greatly increased if it is made clear by this sort of public attack that they are not trusted by their future Prime Minister.

5. We have got to get the points in the two preceding paragraphs across to the Tunku if there is to be hope of Malaysia. My first thought is that this could best be done in a message from you to the Tunku. A draft is being prepared which will be available for our discussion on Wednesday.

6. I am not commenting here in any detail on Cobbold's note—as he says he may change his views completely. In general it contains no real surprises. A transitional stage, as he suggests, with sovereignty handed over, but much responsibility remaining with us, is a possibility we have thought of, but it would of course be very difficult to work in practice. I see Cobbold does not feel the need for legal advice yet—he will certainly need it on this sort of thing when the Commission come to write their report.

7. The only other point I would comment on here is his suggestion that there should be a Governmental conference not more than two months after his report, which he hopes to get out before the end of May (that would mean the end of July or August for the conference). I very much doubt if two months would be long enough for printing, translation and dissemination in the territories and debates in their legislatures and for our own and the Malayan Government's consideration. I would think September a more likely time.

8. I am sending copies of this minute and its enclosure to the Lord Chancellor, the Foreign Secretary, the Commonwealth Secretary and Minister of Defence.

---

[3] The president of the North Borneo Civil Servants' Association was Roland Smith, assistant director of agriculture since 1959. The statement, which was published in *The Times* on 14 Mar, is not printed in this collection.

[4] Martin minuted on 13 Mar: 'I fear that Ghazali has prepared the Tunku for the possibility of an adverse report by the majority of the Cobbold Commission & [sic] the Tunku, who seems to be a bit rattled, is in turn preparing to blame the British and Chinese' (CO 1030/987, no 1113).

[5] In a telegram of 16 Mar, Cobbold suggested that the Tunku had reacted in 'a fit of temper' when told by Ghazali of opposition in Borneo to his blue-print. Although the allegations were unjustified, Cobbold accepted that they had amounted to a set-back for the commission (*ibid*, no 1126).

98   CAB 130/179, GEN 754/3rd meeting   21 Mar 1962
['Commission of enquiry, North Borneo and Sarawak']: Cabinet Greater Malaysia Committee minutes

[This meeting was chaired by Macmillan and attended by Sandys (CRO), Maudling (CO), Peter Thomas (joint parliamentary under-secretary, FO) and Brook (Cabinet secretary). The Tunku's allegation brought home to ministers the dangerous tension between the territories. It also revealed differences of approach between Whitehall departments and between local officials rooting for one or another of the 'Malaysian' territories. Ministers noted ominous similarities here with the Central African Federation. Immediately after this committee meeting, Sandys asked Macmillan for sole charge of the Greater Malaysia scheme and its implementation, instead of sharing it with the CO. Although Macmillan was sympathetic to the proposal—accepting that 'we must do all we can to avoid a repetition of the Federation of Rhodesia and Nyasaland'—he felt that any reallocation of responsibilities should follow, rather than precede, the Cobbold Report. He therefore asked Sandys not to press him further for the time being. Yet even Macmillan's patience was wearing thin. Additional evidence of dysfunctional policy-making, provoked him to protest: 'This kind of telegram shows how impossible the present system is. It is Rhodesia all over again. Can we really wait for Cobbold?' But Brook reined him back: 'The time to make any change is when we have finally decided to put our money on a Greater Malaysia.' (Macmillan to Sandys, M86/62, 26 Mar; Macmillan to Brook, 5 Apr; Brook to Macmillan, 10 Apr 1962, CAB 21/4626; see also *BDEE: The Conservative government and the end of empire*, 266). On the other hand, those imbued with the Colonial Service tradition were deeply suspicious of the CRO which, they felt, was ill-equipped for the task of coping with the Borneo territories (see 104, para 8). The Cabinet reshuffle of 12–13 July 1962 ('the night of the long knives', see 130, note), as a result of which Sandys added the CO to his portfolio, provided him with the opportunity to assume control over the Malaysian project. Even so, however, diffusion and fragmentation of policy and its implementation continued into 1963 (see 164).]

The Meeting had before them a letter from Lord Cobbold to the Colonial Secretary dated 6th March, 1962 on the work and programme of the Commission of Enquiry; and telegrams from the Governor of North Borneo, the British High Commissioner in Malaya, and Lord Cobbold, about the Malayan reaction to reports of hostility to the Commission on the part of British officials in North Borneo.[1]

In discussion the following points were made:—

(a) It would probably be thought best, when the Commission's report was received about the end of May, to publish at least the substance of it, but it would be wrong to enter into any commitment to publish it in any form until Ministers had had an opportunity of discussing its contents.

(b) The difficulties and dangers to which Lord Cobbold referred in his letter were chiefly evident in the case of Singapore. The most important feature of the project of Greater Malaysia, from the point of view of this country, was that it seemed to offer the only reasonable prospect of maintaining the integrity of Singapore and preserving the British position there.

(c) In the event of Greater Malaysia being generally accepted, it would still be necessary to make provision for the continuance of the services of British officials for a considerable time thereafter, especially in the less-developed territories.

Summing up this part of the discussion *The Prime Minister* said that if we were successful in achieving Greater Malaysia this would relieve the British Government

---

[1] See 94, 96 and 97.

of its most invidious and burdensome responsibilities in the area. If we failed, the problem of Singapore would be the most urgent: at the next elections a situation might arise in which most of the British forces in the Island would be required to defend their own bases. In regard to North Borneo, Sarawak and Brunei, there was also the special factor of a possible irredentist threat from Indonesia.

In further discussion of the unfortunate Malayan reaction to reports of discourtesy towards the Malayan members of the Commission in North Borneo, it was pointed out that the British High Commissioner had talked this matter over with the Tunku, who appeared to recognise that he had been ill-advised. It might now be better to regard the incident as closed, in the expectation that no more would be heard of it.

Nevertheless, the episode pointed to the possibility of a serious danger, namely that the Tunku's advisers in Kuala Lumpur and the British Colonial Service officials in North Borneo might be suspicious of each other's aims and motives, to the point of generating an atmosphere of mistrust, such as had developed in the Central African Federation. If the Government, having considered the report of the Commission of Enquiry, should conclude that Greater Malaysia would be in the best interests of the peoples of North Borneo and Sarawak, it might be necessary to take special steps to ensure that the British Colonial Service officials in the territories fully appreciated the convictions underlying the Government's policy and could conscientiously devote themselves to its fulfilment.

The Meeting:—
(1) Took note of the points made in discussion.
(2) Invited the Colonial Secretary to arrange for a reply to be sent to Lord Cobbold, informing him of Sir Geofroy Tory's discussion with the Tunku and explaining that no further action would be taken about the latter's complaint.

99   PREM 11/3866   31 Mar 1962
[Sarawakian suspicions of 'Greater Malaysia']: letter from Lord Cobbold to Mr Maudling

Thank you for your telegram in reply to mine about the Tunku's outburst. I sincerely hope he will keep quiet about these territories, though his recent threats to Singapore all strengthen the opposition to Malaysia here.

This is our last day in Sarawak and we have been glad of three days here to pause and recoup. We have not had any formal hearings in Kuching this time but have been doing some individual coffee-housing, and I have been talking with some of the senior officials, Chief Justice, Bishops etc.[1]

Ghazali has gone to K.L. for the week-end, ostensibly to see his wife who is not well—but he will doubtless be reporting to The Tunku at the same time.

---

[1] Muslims accounted for only about 23 per cent of the population of Sarawak (and 38 per cent in North Borneo) and Christian and other non-Muslim communities were insistent that there should be complete religious freedom in the Borneo territories. Mission schools (Anglican, Roman Catholic, non-conformist, Seventh-Day Adventist) played a major role in Sarawak's education. The commissioners differed over religious provisions, see 124, appendix B and 129, appendix A.

I have little to add to what I said in my earlier letter. It is quite clear that, apart from the Malays, who think Malaysia would make life easier for them, and the younger nationalist and/or communist Chinese, who are shouting 'independence in 1963', the bulk of the population would prefer to see continuation of British rule.

I still think that something acceptable to the majority could be devised if they can be satisfied (a) that Malaysia is a partnership in a joint enterprise and does not mean Sarawak being handed over to rule by Malays. (b) that things will be taken gradually and a lot of local autonomy left to the State Government so that there will not be much change too quickly. (c) that they can get, in some early and practical form, some advantages from Malaysia e.g. in education and development.

Unfortunately almost every utterance from Malaya tends to confirm suspicions here that the Malayan Government intends to gobble up Sarawak quickly and on their own terms, and that H.M.G. have agreed, or are about to agree, to this process.

I remain convinced that if the Malayan Government persist in this sort of attitude and are not prepared to be accommodating in the matters of safeguards, timing and local autonomy (and generous in the matter of carrots), Malaysia will not be acceptable to these territories. I am afraid that the project may well founder on these sort of rocks. But I may be (I trust I am) underrating the Tunku's wisdom when it comes to the point. His handling of these territories has certainly been inept so far.

I confirm what I said earlier about the risks of serious disorder if the period of uncertainty goes on for long after we report. Indeed, whatever the outcome of the Malaysia proposals, I fear that there is bound to be a period of great trouble, and I still rate the maintenance of a strong and stable local Government here as a prime necessity in any circumstances—K.L. seems almost as far away from here as London.

None of this changes my belief that Malaysia is the best solution if only the Tunku will be sensible enough to make it possible.

Please treat this on the same basis as my previous note (no copy kept).[2]

---

[2] In spite of his request to the contrary, Cobbold's letter was placed on file (as was that of 6 Mar, see 94).

100   CO 1030/1016, no 23   19 Apr 1962
[Transitional arrangements for Borneo territories]: letter from Sir W Goode to W I J Wallace on the preparation of the Cobbold Report

[In this letter (whose importance Macmillan acknowledged) Goode pointed to a fundamental dilemma facing the planners of the new federation: the effective merger of North Borneo within Malaysia required lengthy preparation, yet it was unrealistic to expect the Tunku to wait several years for its completion. He stressed the need for both a firm acceptance of 'the principles of Malaysia' and safeguards for North Borneo, and he urged the adoption of a transitional period during which the special interests of North Borneo would be protected. Accepting that a transitional period during which British officials exercised power raised problems of sovereignty, he argued that a compromise between the Malayan and Bornean viewpoints should be worked out by experts in London while the commissioners were writing their report. To allow the commissioners to submit conflicting recommendations and to leave the resolution of differences until after the publication of the report would be, 'if not disastrous, extremely dangerous'. Waddell agreed with Goode's approach to the enquiry (Waddell to Wallace, 3 May, PREM 11/3866). In his correspondence with the CO, Goode became more and more explicit about the need to retain British staff and to counter the Tunku's approach to the Borneo territories (see 104 and 105 and also CAB 21/4626 and PREM 11/3866.)]

Under cover of a separate letter I have sent you copies of the memoranda which we put in to the Cobbold Commission while they were here. You will see from the memorandum on the machinery of government and process to self-government within Malaysia that in my view North Borneo cannot become a self-governing member State of a Federation of Malaysia for several years. To be successful, Malaysia must give a large measure of local self-government to North Borneo. This means that North Borneo must have a State Government capable of handling the State responsibilities before Malaysia can be achieved, and I cannot see how we can produce such a Government today. It must take us several years to produce a local Government in which we can have reasonable confidence that it will be able to undertake its responsibilities. We have two essential steps to take: introduction of elections, and the emergence of Ministers of minimum competence recognised as elected by the people and responsible to them. I cannot see how we can achieve this position before 1967 at the earliest. Meanwhile it is not possible to hand over to the local people full responsibility for State affairs.

2.   But I think it is unrealistic to expect the Tunku to wait the several years which North Borneo needs. We must therefore try to work out a plan which will give the Tunku a form of Malaysia at the latest next year and yet can be made to work in North Borneo.

3.   We must go for some arrangement whereby:—

(a) the British Government accepts today the principles of Malaysia;

(b) we reach quick agreement with the Malayans on the division of powers between the State and Federal Governments;

(c) some important powers, such as external relations, defence, internal security, judiciary and others are transferred within a few months to the new Federal Government of Malaysia; and

(d) North Borneo gets the safeguards it needs and retains a large measure of self-government.

4.   I think such a solution would be generally acceptable in North Borneo. It would have the advantage of securing Malaysia now while the opportunity offers. The division of State and Federal powers could, given the co-operation of the Malayan Government, be so agreed as to remove most of the objections raised here to Malaysia. Inevitably serving British officers would have to be given the option of retiring with compensation and some will go. My own assessment is that the greater the measure of self-government given to North Borneo, the fewer will leave. This is the solution I hope the Commission will recommend.

5.   But the crucial difficulty in this solution is to devise some way in which, while giving the Tunku his side of Malaysia, we can retain our ability to help and in effect control the North Borneo State Government until such time as it is capable of discharging its responsibilities and holding its appropriate place in Malaysia in relation to the other Governments thereof. This raises the bogey of sovereignty. Malaysia requires that sovereignty over North Borneo now vested in the British Government (pace the Filipinos) shall pass partly to the Federal Government of Malaysia in respect of the Federal subjects, and partly to the North Borneo Government in respect of State subjects. But we cannot in conscience transfer their measure of sovereignty to the North Borneo Government until they are reasonably capable of undertaking the responsibility involved. The problem is to devise some

form of constitutional arrangement or inter-governmental agreement which will make it possible for British officials to retain sufficient power to look after North Borneo until such time as it can look after itself.

6. I cannot myself devise a scheme to achieve this. I wish I could. To me this has always been the key problem of Malaysia, and I can only hope that it is not beyond the ingenuity of experts in London somehow to devise a solution to it. (Compare our telegrams from Kuching last year, Nos. 46 of 30th September and No. 47 of 1st October).

7. I get the impression from Lord Cobbold that he is not optimistic about solving this constitutional problem, always assuming that Tunku Abdul Rahman will be prepared to accept such a form of Malaysia. And on this too Lord Cobbold seemed doubtful. Unless we can solve the constitutional problem, and the Tunku will accept such a form of Malaysia, then it seems to me that Malaysia is off.

8. I hope that the report and recommendations of the Cobbold Commission will both solve the constitutional problem and sell the resulting form of Malaysia to the Tunku. But I am not optimistic that it will. The constitutional problem must be a matter for the best brains we can find in London. The sooner they get at it the better, for we have no time to lose before we shall have to take big decisions. Any constitutional lawyer will probably say that it is not legally possible to solve the problem. Personally I would not accept this answer: the problem is somehow to achieve what the constitutional lawyer believes is legally impossible, and I cannot believe that, with all our experience of peculiar constitutional arrangements which at any given time would have been ruled out as legally impossible, it is beyond us to devise a solution. If necessary we must make new constitutional precedents; we've done this before.

9. The Tunku's co-operation is essential. He must be persuaded to accept a compromise solution; and if we can give him a fair measure of what he needs to claim that he has achieved Malaysia, I think he could be persuaded. This is an issue between London and Kuala Lumpur which may have to be finally settled between Prime Ministers. But it is no good securing the Tunku's agreement, unless we are reasonably confident that we can solve the constitutional problem and deliver the goods. Conversely, it will be a waste of time racking our brains over the constitutional problem, if there is no prospect at all that the Tunku will accept such a solution.

10. I do not know what the Cobbold Commission will recommend. Lord Cobbold told me that he hoped to be able to present his report by the end of May. We shall then be under immediate pressure to publish the report, and it will have to be published. Any delay between publication and announcement of firm decisions on the main issues will be, if not disastrous, extremely dangerous. Any indication of indecision or of dissension between the British and Malayan Governments will be exploited to the full by all factions, both pro- and anti-Malaysia. Unless Nick Waddell and I are in a position to make clear, firm statements about the future, we could well find ourselves faced with serious threats to public security and we shall probably lose our ability to control events. It is vital, therefore, that we should know what we are going to do and have taken our major decisions before we publish the Cobbold report. I do not think we should sit back hoping that the Commission will solve the problem of Malaysia for us. We should anticipate the issues that are likely to face us in the report and tackle them now.

11.   If the Commission is able to produce unanimous recommendations for a form of Malaysia which will give the Tunku the substance of what he needs and will also give North Borneo a large measure of self-government, particularly in respect of those matters on which there are strong feelings here, we shall have no great difficulty over the Commission's report. For I assume that:—

(i)   Ghazalie will not agree to recommendations which will be unacceptable to the Tunku; and Waddell and I will probably be able to accept what the British members recommend as satisfactory for Sarawak and North Borneo; and

(ii)   the Commission will have satisfied themselves that the form of Malaysia they recommend is both practically workable having regard to conditions in Borneo, and constitutionally sound.

12.   There will no doubt be arguments over details and legal drafting to be settled at a subsequent inter-governmental conference, but we should be able to accept the main recommendations very soon after the report is received.

13.   If, however, the Commission is unable to produce a unanimous report, we shall have to make very difficult decisions, and make them quickly.

14.   The simplest decision will be that Malaysia is not practical at present, because the Commission's report shows that there are difficulties which cannot be overcome.

15.   A much more difficult, but more constructive course will be to make a last determined effort on the basis of the report to find a compromise solution which will produce Malaysia. We can assume that the division in the Commission will be between the British members with one view and the Malayans with another. A compromise solution will mean requiring Waddell and me to consider to what extent we can go further than the British members of the Commission in meeting the Malayan view without unacceptable risk; and seeking to persuade the Tunku to make more concessions to Borneo needs in order to get Malaysia and avoid a deadlock.

16.   I foresee the greatest difficulty in achieving any compromise solution after the report has been put in; even greater once it has been published. Delay in publication will be ascribed to deadlock of some sort, and publication of divergent views of the British and Malayan members will cause acute controversy here and might produce a situation where we can no longer control developments. Unless we have been able to agree upon a solution to the problem before the report is published, I believe we shall find that we cannot achieve Malaysia.

17.   We must therefore make every effort to reach a solution acceptable to both the British and the Malayan Governments *before* the report is published. We shall have little time between presentation of the report and its publication. Moreover, if a solution to the problem is possible, it should be put forward in the report. It will then have the authority of the Commission behind it and so will have the best prospects of popular acceptance; whereas it will be very difficult to recover from the effect of a divided report which will provide authority for rejecting any compromise.

18.   When he left Lord Cobbold was not optimistic about getting a unanimous report. It will, therefore, be prudent to anticipate that the Commission will not be able to produce an agreed plan. We have only a few weeks left in which to make a decisive effort to achieve Malaysia. I urge that we must do all we can to assist the Commission to reach agreement, working on the basis that unless they do, Malaysia is off.

19.   The Commission will be in London. Lord Cobbold will be able to consult the Colonial Office and Ministers. Waddell is also in England, and if necessary I will fly

back for consultations. But my hunch is that the Tunku will be the key person. If Ghazalie cannot be persuaded to bridge the gap, then it seems to me that Lord Cobbold may have to return to Kuala Lumpur, since this will be less difficult than getting the Tunku to London.

20.   My main point is that if we do not solve the problem now while the report is being written, I do not think we ever shall. It is no good waiting for the report, hoping that we shall somehow find a solution after we have received the report.

21.   Of course, if Lord Cobbold is able to reassure you that he will be able to produce a workable solution backed unanimously by the Commission, then things will be much easier. I shall be vastly relieved.

22.   My worry is that:—

(a) the Tunku still does not appreciate how great is the gap between his idea of Malaysia and what we can accept as right for the Borneo territories;
(b) the Commission will fail to work out a plan to bridge the gap between what the Tunku wants and what will work in Borneo;
(c) the Commission will not do enough to persuade the Tunku to accept such a plan;
(d) if these things are not done before the Commission reports, it will be too late.

23.   To sum up this far too long letter:—

(i) We have got to devise some way in which we can support the North Borneo Government so that it can manage its State affairs in the type of Malaysia that conditions in Borneo require.
(ii) We have got to persuade the Tunku to accept the resulting form of Malaysia.
(iii) If the Cobbold Commission does both these things, we shall have only minor difficulties in following up the Cobbold Report.
(iv) But if the Commission fails to produce a unanimous report, I see little prospect of achieving Malaysia in the near future. Delay in deciding what we are going to do will be dangerous.
(v) The only way to achieve Malaysia is to find an acceptable solution of the problem before the report is completed and get it incorporated in the report.
(vi) If we cannot get an acceptable solution into the report, then we should be ready to announce when the report is published that Malaysia has proved impracticable at present.

24.   I am copying this letter to Jakeway, White, Tory and Lord Selkirk.

101   CO 1030/1016, no 20   **19 Apr 1962**
[Cobbold's views on the prospects for Malaysia]: minute by C G Eastwood to E M West[1]

[At the conclusion of their tour of North Borneo and Sarawak, the commissioners dispersed. Watherston and Ghazali went to talk with the Tunku in Kuala Lumpur and Cobbold returned to London. He was debriefed on the prospects for Greater Malaysia in a series of Whitehall meetings before the commissioners reassembled in early May at Knebworth House, Hertfordshire, Cobbold's country home which he had acquired through his wife, the elder daughter of the second Earl of Lytton. Throughout May and

---

[1] E M West private secretary to secretary of state, CO, 1961; private secretary to minister of state, CO, 1962.

much of June they drafted the report, mostly at Knebworth though also in London (CO 947/3, CO 947/4 and CO 947/7; see also Ghazali Shafie, *Memoir*, p 230 ff).]

The Secretary of State may like to know that Lord Cobbold arrived safely back this morning. I met him at London Airport. He had a trying journey back with six hours in the middle of the night at Calcutta airport.

He is confident that there can be a scheme for Greater Malaysia which is both practicable and acceptable *if* the Governments are sensible. The 'if' is of course a big one as regards the Tunku. The general shape of his ideas has not altered much since his last letter to the Secretary of State: they have still to work out their plan in detail. Meanwhile he has sent Sir David Watherston to Kuala Lumpur with Ghazali to talk to the Tunku: he thought it wiser not to go himself.

The Commission meet again at Knebworth about the 5th May to write the report. They hope to complete it by about the end of the month.

Lord Cobbold would like to come and see the Secretary of State some time, probably during the first week of May and will have a word with Sir John Martin probably on Wednesday next.[2] The point he principally wants to make is that the period immediately after the publication of their report will be one of great tension in North Borneo and Sarawak. He is anxious that Governments should make up their minds on the report quickly; otherwise he fears there will be some slitting of throats. I said that we had had somewhat unfortunate experience of rushing people into federations without giving them time to make up their minds: our idea had been that there ought to be full discussion of the report in all the legislatures followed probably by a conference. Lord Cobbold did not at all disagree with this: what I really think he has in mind is that we, and I suppose the Government of Malaya too, should give an early indication of the way in which the band-wagon is likely to go in order that those who are hesitating may be given an opportunity of jumping on it. In other words we should say something to the effect that the plan in the report seems a reasonable one: H.M.G. in the U.K. will not make up their minds about it until it has been fully discussed locally but it would seem to them to provide a practicable solution to a difficult problem.

He said that the Tunku was fully prepared to come himself to London in June or July. He did not want to wait until the Prime Ministers' Conference in September.[3]

If the report is presented about the end of May it would, I suppose, be published about the middle of June. He did not think that it would be necessary to have full translations into any other language though I suppose the summary and the texts of important parts would have to be translated locally into local languages.

---

[2] See 102.
[3] ie, the meeting of Commonwealth prime ministers where they would endorse Britain's resumed negotiations to enter the Common Market.

102   CO 1030/1016, no 22   25 Apr 1962
[Cobbold's views on the prospects for Malaysia]: minute by Sir J Martin to C G Eastwood

Lord Cobbold called this afternoon on his return from Borneo. He said that he was quite satisfied that Greater Malaysia was the right policy for the Borneo territories, provided however that it was on the right conditions and not in the form which the

Tunku seems hitherto to have contemplated. Merger on the Tunku's original terms would be quite unacceptable for Borneo and its imposition would have the most serious consequences. Lord Cobbold seems to have no hope of a unanimous report, since he evidently does not expect the Malayan members to go along with his views. He hopes however to avoid the appearance of majority and minority reports, so that there would be a single report saying on points of difference some members thought this and some thought that. He fears that the Tunku is still woefully ignorant of conditions in the Borneo territories and is pessimistic about the chances of obtaining his agreement to acceptable terms of merger. On the other hand it is of great importance to the Tunku that Malaysia should come off: failure would mean great loss of face for him and it is even more in his interests than in that of H.M.G. to ensure that things go well in Singapore. Lord Cobbold therefore thinks there may be a 50/50 chance of persuading him. Unfortunately Ghazali is not an independent Commissioner and will do as the Tunku tells him.

2.   Lord Cobbold says that he contemplates quite a short report, though it will indicate clearly the terms on which merger is proposed. The descriptive part has already been drafted by Sir David Watherston and, since he does not think that the members could argue for more than about a fortnight about their conclusions, Lord Cobbold hopes that the report may be completed by as early as the 20th May or at any rate before the end of the month. Thereafter he urges that we should go into action as quickly as possible and that the report should not be published without some indication of H.M.G.'s views. This will rally all the many people who wait to climb on the band waggon, while its absence would encourage the growth of opposition and dissension. He assumes that before any such statement could be issued we would try to come to some agreement with the Tunku and the Tunku had spoken of the possibility of coming to London in the summer. Lord Cobbold agreed that there should be some consultation with the B. territories (eg by debates in legislatures) and possibly a Conference.

3.   Lord Cobbold did not go into detail about the content of the recommendations he envisages, beyond indicating that he believed in a two-stage approach. It was essential that, if Malaysia was to come at all, it should be introduced very quickly, but the transfer of many powers would not come till a few years later and he evidently contemplates work for a number of commissions or working-parties in determining the details of this transfer during the intermediate period. He seems to contemplate immediate transfer of sovereignty accompanied by temporary delegation, but this is no doubt the subject which he wishes to discuss with Mr. McPetrie,[1] whom he is to see on Friday at 10 a.m.

4.   I raised the question of legal advice.[2] Lord Cobbold indicated that he did not at present envisage the need for a legal adviser attached to the Commission while drafting their report, but that he had certain questions which he wished to put to the Legal Adviser. I suggested that it might be found helpful to consult Professor Kenneth Wheare.[3] I said how important it was that the Commission should not

---

[1] J C (later Sir James) McPetrie, legal adviser, CO, 1960; legal adviser for Commonwealth Office, 1966, and FCO, 1968.
[2] See Goode's recommendation, 100, para 8.
[3] Rector of Exeter College Oxford. The CO frequently consulted Wheare on constitutional issues, including those of Malaya in the early 1950s.

recommend anything which it was found afterwards did not stand up legally. Lord Cobbold fully takes this point.

5.   Lord Cobbold subsequently looked in on the Secretary of State for a few minutes and also on the Minister of State. The Secretary of State has minuted about this to the Prime Minister.

6.   Lord Cobbold asked me to keep to myself what he had told me, but did not object when I said that I would like to inform one or two others in the Office. This minute (which I am afraid has had to be prepared rather hurriedly) should be registered for record after Mr. Wallace has seen, but please do not circulate outside the Office.

7.   It is convenient to add here that Sir Anthony Abell, whom I also saw earlier in the day, gave as his opinion that not more than about 50% of the expatriate Service would remain after the introduction of Malaysia.

103   CO 1030/1016, nos 52–59   23 May 1962
[Transitional arrangements for Borneo territories]: letter from C G Eastwood to Sir W Goode

I am writing further, in Ian Wallace's absence on leave, about your most valuable letter of the 19th April on Malaysia.[1]

2.   At the moment, we think it not impossible that the Commission will be able to agree on a general solution which would meet a good deal of what you say (in paragraph 3) we must have (with which we agree). But they may not be unanimous on some issues. In that case, we do not see any real hope of ensuring that the differences are removed from the report before it is published. For one thing, Lord Cobbold is not a person amenable to pressure from Government, nor would he, I think, be prepared to fly to Kuala Lumpur again to talk to the Tunku (nor indeed should we think it a wise thing for him to do). He has emphasised since his return that he does not regard negotiation with the Tunku as his function. So, if the Commission cannot agree among themselves, Governmental intervention would not persuade them to do so.

3.   A report containing some differences of opinion would be a pity but it might not be disastrous, at any rate if—as it is possible to hope—any differences are over 'subjects' rather than constitutional fundamentals, since there might be room for settlement of these points between Governments.

4.   I gather that both you and Jakeway[2] (whose letter to Ian of the 3rd May has just been received) assume that, in the event of immediate transfer of sovereignty, a compensation scheme would have to be introduced at once and that of course involves the risk of an exodus of expatriate officers sufficient (in Jakeway's words) 'at any rate to make the task of bringing the country to orderly and competent self-government immensely more difficult'. In that connection you should know that we understand that a possible solution has been under consideration which, although unique in our constitutional experience, might be feasible, viz. for the United

---

[1] See 100.   [2] Chief secretary, Sarawak, 1959–1963.

Kingdom to cede North Borneo and Sarawak at once to the new Federation of Malaysia but to provide by an immediately effective agreement between the United Kingdom and the new Federation that during a prescribed transitional period the internal government of the two territories would remain the responsibility of the British Government, who would have the power to make laws.

5.   Under such a plan the Public Service would not immediately be entitled to claim compensation, since during the transitional period it would still be the responsibility of the Secretary of State. Compensation schemes have hitherto been introduced when the Secretary of State's responsibility has been handed over to an executive Public Service Commission at the stage either of self-government or of independence, i.e. when British sovereignty was relinquished. The compensation is appropriate because from then on the Secretary of State is no longer in a position to carry out his responsibilities to the Service, i.e. there is a change of master. So far, we have not unnaturally been more or less assuming that transfer of sovereignty to Malaysia would inevitably mean the end of the Secretary of State's responsibility i.e. that the two things would happen simultaneously. But, if a unique constitutional solution was found on the above lines, the two events would not be simultaneous and there would not be a case in logic, and certainly not in expediency, for a compensation scheme with immediate effect. Of course, there would have to be immediate agreement that a compensation scheme would start as soon as the Secretary of State lost control and/or the transtitional arrangements came to an end; and there might be room for flexibility in introducing compensation even before then, say if the situation were seriously to deteriorate.

6.   I should however emphasise that this is entirely hypothetical, since we do not know if the Commission will in the end come up with a solution on these lines. Obviously any solution of this kind would require very careful presentation to the Service and we should have to be very careful to ensure that the Secretary of State's responsibility was effectively preserved; that officers were saved from interference in performing their duties properly and that the agreement for compensation at the end of the transitional period was fully satisfactory.

7.   Although, as I say, all this is hypothetical, we should nevertheless be glad to have your comments, particularly on the likely attitude of expatriate officers.

8.   To come back, however, to the question of how to handle the Report, we entirely agree with you (and so, we know, does Cobbold) that any delay between publication and the announcement of pretty firm decisions of principle by the U.K. and Malayan Governments would be most dangerous. If the Governments can give a general blessing to the report, then waverers will know which is the band wagon on to which they should jump. But of course the U.K. Government's blessing must be expressed in a way which leaves freedom to local opinion, and particularly the local legislatures, in North Borneo and Sarawak to express their views. It would be fatal to give the impression that we had pre-judged the issue completely before there had been any opportunity for local opinion to express itself.

9.   We think the best course will be to hold back publication while we try to iron out a common line of policy with the Tunku. We think we ought to be able to delay publication for this purpose for three or four weeks after we receive the report. As you know, a telegram has already gone to the Tunku asking him to come here for about a week some time after the middle of June when he has had time to study it. As soon as they are available, we would propose to send copies to you, to Waddell here

and to Jakeway, White, Allen[3] and Moore for confidential discussions with senior advisers but not with unofficials. We are grateful to you for your suggestion that you might fly back here for discussions and we should like to take advantage of it. We hope you could come here to join Waddell in discussions a little before the Tunku arrives. We would then hope to be able to settle at least some of any differences with the Tunku and to issue perhaps a joint statement simultaneously with publication of the Report, giving a general blessing to it, subject to such provisos as may be agreed and also subject of course to the result of discussions in local legislatures and perhaps of a subsequent intergovernmental conference.

10. We can only hope that such a programme will not lead to the confusion and opposition in Borneo referred to in para. 16 of your letter, although there can obviously be no doubt that the less the Commission disagree, the easier acceptance of Malaysia will be, and *vice versa*. Much will, of course, depend not only on what the Commission recommend but also on what they may leave for subsequent agreement, for which it may be necessary to appoint *ad hoc* inter-governmental committees or working parties.

11. The next step would presumably be discussion of the Report locally ending with a vote on it in the local legislatures. Following on that there may have to be an intergovernmental Conference. If there has to be such a Conference it would probably best be held in London, though we would not rule out somewhere in the Far East altogether.

12. Singapore will of course be very much concerned with the Report. If it recommends a more attractive position for the Borneo Territories than Singapore will have under Lee Kuan Yew's agreement with the Tunku, then the implications of this for Singapore will be considerable. As at present advised Lord Selkirk considers that the discussions in June should only be between the U.K. Government (with of course your advice and that of Waddell) and the Tunku. But we shall no doubt have to tell Lee what is in the Report as soon as we get copies of it and it might be necessary to think again about this when we know what his reactions to it are. Certainly if there is a subsequent inter-governmental conference, the Singapore Government should be represented at it.

13. If there is such an intergovernmental conference we shall have to settle the correct basis of representation at it. Normally, at our 'independence' conferences, we insist on having all parties in the Legislative Assembly represented. The Tunku, however, for obvious reasons does not want to involve his Opposition. He and his colleagues could speak for and commit his Government, as could Lee Kuan Yew his. Whether or not it would be desirable to exclude these Oppositions from the opportunity of having their say, we are left in an apparent difficulty about the representation of N. Borneo and Sarawak. Do you think you could represent N. Borneo on your own (I imagine not) or with one or two members of your Executive Council, or would you expect all the unofficial members of it to attend or even a cross-section of your Legislative Council? This question would possibly present less difficulties in North Borneo than in Sarawak, where the leader of the SUPP is a member of Executive Council. (And who would represent Brunei?) It is premature to form conclusions on this, but it would be useful to have your comments.

---

[3] Deputy commissioner-general, SE Asia, 1959–1962.

14.   There would obviously be a rather uneasy period between publication of the Report, even with a general blessing from the U.K. and Malayan Governments, and final decisions on it and this ought to be as short as is consistent with giving time for the proper consideration of so important a matter. It would clearly be necessary, if we were all going for Greater Malaysia, to do all we could during that period to guide public opinion along the right lines, to reassure the public against fears and perplexities, and to keep up the morale of the Public Service.

15.   In this connection there is just a possibility (I would put it no higher) that the Secretary of State might be able to fit in a short visit to the two Borneo territories in July. He would have liked to see them before now, but that has not been possible. I do not know if he can manage it at all, and if he could, he would only be able to spend three or four days at the most in N. Borneo and three or four in Sarawak. I imagine, however, that even in that time much could be done to discuss with you local reactions to the Report and to put over H.M.G.'s views to the British officials and community leaders. The timing of such a visit would clearly be affected by the content of the Report and by the outcome of the discussions with the Tunku and Waddell and yourself in London. In principle, however, it seems to us that a visit could be most useful and we assume you would welcome it similarly. We will let you know as soon as there is anything more definite to report.[4]

16.   Meanwhile we should be glad if you would confirm that you would be ready to come here in June, once we have all had a chance to study the report and before it is published. We should also, of course, be glad to have your comments on the other points in this letter.

17.   I am giving Lord Selkirk a copy of this letter. We are also giving the C.R.O. a copy for Tory and I am sending copies to Waddell and to Jakeway, White, Allen and Moore. We shall be grateful for any comments any of them like to make. I also enclose an extra copy which perhaps, if you see no objection, you would kindly hand on to Henry Hall.

---

[4] The secretary of state did not go to Borneo in July. Agreement on the Cobbold Report was not reached until 31 July by which time Sandys had succeeded Maudling at the CO while the idea of a visit by the secretary of state had been overtaken by the proposal for an inter-governmental committee chaired by Lansdowne (minister of state), see 141, note.

104   PREM 11/3866   4 June 1962

[Transitional arrangements for Borneo territories]: letter from Sir W Goode to C G Eastwood, replying to document 103 on the need to retain British officers

Your long letter of May 23rd was most welcome for the encouraging possibilities suggested in paragraphs 4 and 5.

2.   The solution you suggest is what I was asking for in paragraphs 5 to 6 of my letter of April 19th to Wallace, with the addition of postponement of entitlement to compensation.

3.   This additional point is of paramount importance. You will recall that in Selkirk's telegram No. 46 of 30th September last year, drafted in Kuching, we put

retention of the British staff as our first requirement; and in my telegram No. 224 of 15th November I recommended that the Secretary of State should retain responsibility for overseas officers and thus avoid the necessity for a compensation scheme, at least for some years.

4.   In recent months, however, I formed the impression that the view in London was quite inflexible about this: that a compensation scheme must be introduced immediately Malaysia was accepted, and there could be no departure from this principle, cost what it might in loss of serving officers. This is why I had come, albeit most reluctantly, to assume, as you rightly state in paragraph 4 of your letter, that we must accept an immediate compensation scheme as inevitable. I am immensely relieved to learn now from your letter that consideration is being given to an arrangement which will make it possible to postpone entitlement to compensation, and so postpone also loss of British officers.

5.   So my immediate comment on the possible solution in your paragraphs 4 and 5 is to welcome it with relief and full support.

6.   The difficulties and risks involved in such a plan are formidable. But I urge that we should not let them put us off it. In any solution to this problem of Malaysia there will be difficulties and risks just as formidable, if not more so. The important thing is to go for a solution which is sound. I would rather accept failure now than agree to arrangements which have no prospect of enduring, and so will bring much greater troubles in the future.

7.   I see particular difficulty in drafting the agreement giving the British Government responsibility during the transition period. It must be as explicit as possible in order to provide a clear division of powers between the British and Malaysian Governments, and yet avoid impugning the Tunku's achievement of Malaysia. And there will be all sorts of possibilities of friction between Jesselton/Kuching and Kuala Lumpur in working the transition period. But given mutual goodwill and co-operation I think the plan is practical.

8.   I am sure that if the plan is to work, it should be the Colonial Office, not the C.R.O., which retains responsibility for the two Borneo territories during the transition period. The C.R.O. is not fitted for the work involved, and transfer from the Colonial Office to the C.R.O. would undermine confidence in North Borneo in one of the two main purposes of the plan, namely that we will continue to safeguard the interests of North Borneo in those matters which are not transferred to the Federation of Malaysia.[1]

9.   As regards the second main purpose, the retention of British officers, postponement of entitlement to compensation would certainly postpone any exodus. It is difficult to forecast the likely attitude of expatriate officers.

10.   During his visit early this year John Martin, in talking to a delegation of expatriate officers, was careful not to go beyond saying that it seemed probable that the date for introducing a compensation scheme would be the date of transfer of sovereignty (again the bogey of sovereignty), in qualification of his earlier remark that it was H.M.G.'s accepted policy that there should be a compensation scheme in a territory when the Civil Service passed outside the control and protection of the

---

[1] As regards problems arising from the division of responsibilities between the CO and CRO, see 98, note. Despite Goode's criticism of the CRO in this paragraph, his despatch was given interdepartmental circulation.

Secretary of State. If in fact the Secretary of State, under the terms of the agreement, retains responsibility for the Service, officers would have to accept that conditions had not arisen which entitled them to compensation. They might, however, put up a claim based on transfer of sovereignty.

11.   I am advised, however, that a number of officers has probably assumed that if Malaysia is effected, a compensation scheme will be introduced simultaneously. They are likely to be disgruntled if they find that we have produced a device to secure Malaysia without giving them a compensation scheme. The more convincingly the Tunku is able to claim that he has achieved Malaysia, the stronger will be the feeling that the expatriate officers have been denied their expected entitlement.

12.   It will no doubt also be argued that the difficulties of working under elected Ministers justify a compensation scheme. I do not regard this argument as acceptable. It will be some time before we have elected Ministers, and in any case it is the surrender of control over the public service by the Secretary of State which is the operative change, not the preliminary progress towards self-government. Nevertheless, as elections and political parties increasingly dominate the administration of the country, conditions become disagreeable to some officers.

13.   It will be necessary to safeguard those officers who are in departments which are to become federal under Malaysia. Presumably the Secretary of State would retain authority over them in Service matters. But as long as they serve in federal departments, they will be under policy direction from the Ministers of the Federal Government in Kuala Lumpur. Unfortunately the recent public outburst by the Tunku, in which he unjustly accused expatriate officers here, has made a lasting unfavourable impression on many officers, including some of the most senior. I think they have been too sensitive, but unless the Tunku can regain their confidence they will continue to regard service under Malayan Ministers as distasteful.

14.   So there will be difficulties over postponing a compensation scheme. But I hope they are not insurmountable. It would be essential that we get down immediately to negotiating a compensation scheme to become operative in agreed circumstances. These negotiations themselves should provide an outlet for disgruntled feelings, and perhaps some fears could be met. As I have written before, a great deal will depend upon the extent of self-government given to North Borneo under Malaysia.

15.   We have a high proportion of older officers in the Service here. 10 out of 34 in the Administrative Service and 9 out of 20 in the Police are already over 45 years of age and so can opt to retire. We also have many officers on contract who can give notice at any time and will not be influenced by compensation prospects.

16.   I agree generally with the points made in paragraphs 8 to 12 of your letter and have no further comment at this stage.

17.   If we have an inter-governmental conference later, and I think this will be necessary, I could not represent North Borneo alone. I should have to bring with me the Unofficial Members of my Executive Council who are also leaders of the four main parties here:—

Datu Mustapha	U.S.N.O.
Donald Stephens	U.N.K.O.
Khoo Siak Chiew	United Party
G.S. Sundang	Pasok Momogun

I think I could keep the representation down to these four.

18.   A visit by the Secretary of State, however brief, would be most welcome. He would be able to establish personal contacts with the community leaders and with British officials. I am sure that in this way he would be able to do a great deal to restore confidence in British intentions and to win acceptance for whatever plan has by then emerged for Malaysia. John Martin will be able to advise from his personal experience this year how best to use whatever time the Secretary of State could give to North Borneo. The longer this can be, the better.

19.   To revert in conclusion to the beginning of your letter, I think it is a great pity that Lord Cobbold was not willing to do more to try to get the Tunku and others of us to accept whatever recommendations he thinks would best achieve Malaysia. I fear that this will be much more difficult after the report has been presented, when each of us will probably be able to find in it support for his particular view. We failed to bring the problems home to the Tunku last year. I hoped the Commission would get him thinking about the compromises needed to bridge the gap between his ideas and what is practical. The prospect of success is much less now at this late stage. However, we must do the best we can.

20.   I am copying this letter to Jakeway, White, Allen, Moore and Tory, and send you an extra copy for Waddell.

105   CO 1030/17, no 168   5 June 1962
[Transitional arrangements for Borneo territories]: letter from Sir W Goode to C G Eastwood on the need for the Tunku to make concessions

Geofroy Tory's letter of May 29th to Hampshire is a cold douche to hopes raised by your letter of May 23rd.

2.   If the Tunku is not able to make a substantial contribution to solving the two related problems of helping North Borneo to run its State Government and of retaining British officers, until such time as North Borneo can look after its own interests, then in my view we shall not get Malaysia.

3.   The Tunku may be able to take a firm line with his Malays and the Malayan Chinese—they elected him—, but I don't think this will work with my Muruts and Dusuns, strengthened by the Chinese, a thousand miles away from Kuala Lumpur, who start with a dislike for Malays and Muslims. They have only been steam-rollered once, by the Japanese, and they exacted a price of heads for that.

4.   Nor do I see how we could in conscience hand these people over to be disciplined by the Tunku.

5.   I do not recall hearing before about the arrangement mentioned by Tory in his third paragraph. Its acceptability here would depend on several points:—

(a) the extent of the powers to pass ultimately to the centre;
(b) the safeguards in the special agreement against subsequent alteration by Kuala Lumpur, c.f. recent amendments of the Malayan constitution;
(c) the constitution of the 'fully representative working party': it would command no confidence here if it were under the control of the Malays;
(d) whether or not the British Government would guarantee or somehow ensure that the Borneo territories got a fair deal during the transition period.

6. Nor do I see much hope that Tory's suggestion in his fourth paragraph would hold the British officers. If they are not to get immediate right to retire with compensation, they will have to have something more formal and reliable than an understanding that in practice the Federal Establishment Officer would agree to act on the advice of the Colonial Secretary. State Services, of course, are nothing to do with the Federal Establishment Officer. I see great difficulty in persuading British officers that although we are bringing in Malaysia, and although the Federal Establishment Officer will take over from me responsibility for their appointments etc., the time has not yet come to give them the right to retire with compensation. I fear this would arouse strong resentment.

7. If we grant the right to retire with compensation, too many will go too soon. The Tunku must appreciate that unless enough British officers can be persuaded to stay, Malaysia so far as North Borneo is concerned is impractical.

8. I hope that Tory will be able to get the Tunku to realise before he comes to London that if he is to get Malaysia he is going to have to make substantial concessions to meet our common problems, even though these concessions will cause him political difficulty at home.

9. I am copying this to Tory, Jakeway, White and Allen.

P.S. Tory's telegram No. 323 to the C.R.O. has now arrived. If the Tunku persists in his refusal to compromise, Malaysia must be off.[1]

---

[1] Commenting percipiently on this postscript, a CO official wrote in the margin of Goode's letter: 'Tunku will withdraw Malayan members of Commission, etc.' See 111, para 8.

106   PREM 11/3866   8 June 1962
[Commissioners' differences over their report]: letter from Lord Cobbold to Mr Sandys

[A start on drafting the report had been made by Watherston before the commissioners reassembled at Knebworth in early May. Thereafter, however, they made heavy weather of it. Ghazali arrived from Kuala Lumpur no better disposed than before to Bornean feelings, and in early June the Tunku intervened at a distance, threatening to withdraw the Malayan members. While the commissioners were in agreement on integration through 'Greater Malaysia' and also on the need for the Borneo territories to pass through a transition period, they differed over the nature of that transition. On the one hand, Abell and Watherston (with Cobbold in support) argued for a continuing British role to ensure effective administration and prepare for the 'localisation' of public services, although they tried to avoid confrontation with the Malayans by proposing that the details be worked out on a government-to-government basis after the publication of the report. On the other hand, Ghazali and Wong Pow Nee were under pressure from the Tunku to ensure that the report spelled out transitional arrangements and eliminated the retention of British governors or anything else which would open him to the charge of being an 'imperialist stooge'. Cobbold worked against the clock to avoid a break-down or the presentation of alternative reports (CO 947/3, and CO 1030/1016 and 1017).]

I do not think I can properly send you copies of sections of the Report, which, though provisionally agreed, are subject to final agreement and to the dangers of a general explosion of which you know.

I think, however, that in the special circumstances I can properly send you, subject to all reserve, drafts of a letter which I have it in mind to send to both Prime

Ministers[1] if the Report is signed more or less in its present shape, and of a private letter which I have it in mind to send to Admiralty House.

The Malayans will press at every stage for a complete handover of powers at once. They might come as far as 'British Governors' and delegating a number of Federal powers to the State Government for a period—but in fact they see themselves as running the whole thing from Kuala Lumpur right away. I do not think you should give way to this.

On the long-term we have reached a lot of agreement except, as I warned you, in the area of religion and language—you will have trouble with religion, where there are strong emotional feelings all round, with both Catholic and Protestant churches firmly entrenched.

There will be a strong unanimous recommendation that in the early years both H.M. Government and the Federal Government should provide generous help, both financial and technical, for development.

I enclose two copies of this letter and enclosures,[2] for the P.M. and Reggie.[3] But I must please ask you to keep it very close indeed because the whole thing may blow up or I may have to make changes.

---

[1] The Cobbold enquiry was set up as an independent commission charged with reporting to the prime ministers of Britain and Malaya.
[2] Not printed.   [3] Maudling.

107 PREM 11/3866   11 June 1962
[Commissioners' differences over their final report]: minute from Lord Cobbold to Mr Sandys

Two things have happened since I sent you privately some papers on Friday.[1]

I have had a redraft of the piece which the Malayan members are putting in, in which they go strongly (and rather offensively) against the idea of British Governors for a transitional period.

Secondly I have heard from all members of the Commission that they are prepared to 'go to Press' on the present drafts.

I am holding a meeting of the Commission at 3 p.m. on Tuesday.[2] I propose at that meeting to attempt to get specific references to retention of British Governors for a transitional period removed from both British and Malayan versions of the formal Report and included instead in a confidential letter to Prime Ministers.

If I fail, as I probably shall, I will arrange for the report to be prepared for signature in its present form, but should ask you to accept from me, and convey to the Tunku, the following message:—

(1) Final drafts of the Report have now been agreed and copies are being produced for signature later in the week.

(2) I would, however, ask Prime Ministers to consider one point.

(3) In accordance with strong representations from the Malayan side, British

---

[1] See 106.   [2] ie, 12 June, see 109.

members and I myself have refrained from any recommendation in the Report in favour of the retention of a measure of British sovereignty in the territories for a transitional period.

(4) I am, however, as Chairman, worried by the inclusion in the present drafts of strong conflicting views about possible retention of British Governors for a transitional period. I believe that these specific references may make Governmental negotiation more difficult.

(5) I should therefore be grateful if Prime Ministers would consider suggesting to the members nominated by their respective Governments that these specific references to British Governors should be deleted from the formal Report before signature and included instead in confidential letters.

108   PREM 11/3866   12 June 1962

'Greater Malaysia': note and supplementary note by Sir S Garner for ministers on commissioners' differences

[When Clutterbuck retired as permanent under-secretary, CRO, he was succeeded by Saville Garner who also took over the chairmanship of the Greater Malaysia (Official) Committee. These notes briefed Macmillan, Sandys and Maudling for their meeting later that day, by which time Garner expected to have heard the latest position from Cobbold.]

The background is set out in the report of the Committee on Greater Malaysia.[1]

There have since been the following further developments:—

(1) Lord Cobbold hopes to complete his report this week. He has, in the meantime, drafted letters which he has it in mind to address to the two Prime Ministers, together with a private and personal letter to the British Prime Minister.[2]

(2) The Tunku has now made a public announcement that he is planning to leave Malaya for London on the 29th June to discuss the Malaysia plan with Mr. Macmillan.

(3) The report is near completion and fortunately appears to reach unanimity on the main aim of a Greater Malaysia. The sole major difficulty is the presentation of proposals for the transitional arrangements, which both sides recognise will be necessary before the plan can be implemented in full. At one time the Tunku threatened to withdraw the Malayan members if other members insisted on recommending a division of responsibility during this period. This point has now been conceded by the British members of the Commission, though Lord Cobbold intends to make it clear in his confidential letter to Prime Ministers that he, himself, favoured a solution under which the territories would be ceded to the new Federation subject to an agreement that a number of powers would, for some years, continue to be exercised in the territories by the British Government. No problem arises on this major issue now, and it is hoped that the report will recommend that it should be left to the Governments to decide on the exact solution.

---

[1] See 73.   [2] For the final versions, see 118–121.

(4)   The immediate problem centres on the question of the retention or otherwise of 'British Governors' during the transitional period.

Lord Cobbold is seeking to leave all details, including the position of British Governors for discussion between Governments and not to refer to them in the report. The British members of the Commission were prepared to accept this. But Ghazali has made it clear that he must insist on his own version and has apparently forwarded some draft paragraphs to Lord Cobbold which are phrased in somewhat offensive terms. If Ghazali insists on the inclusion of his paragraphs, the British members will equally, and no doubt rightly, insist on the retention of their statement that it is essential to retain the British Governors.

Lord Cobbold feels – and this seems right – that if extreme positions are taken up in the report, and subsequently made public, it will be difficult for either side to make any concessions, and particularly for the Malayans to draw back. He aims, therefore, at the meeting of the Commission which will be held this afternoon, to secure the omission of both paragraphs and will, if necessary, tell the members of the Commission that he is proposing to refer this point to the two Prime Ministers. If he is not successful this afternoon in his aim, he plans to invite the British Prime Minister to receive a message from him and to pass it on to the Tunku (see his minute to the Commonwealth Secretary of the 11th June).[3]

Lord Cobbold has undertaken to report the upshot of his meeting before the Ministerial talk at 5 p.m. and the result will be reported orally.[4]

Supplementary Note to 108

Greater Malaysia
The following sets out what is believed to be the general view of Lord Cobbold:—

(1)   The Greater Malaysia plan is right in principle and the Commission proposes to say so unanimously in their report.
(2)   The Government of the Federation of Malaya have therefore got what they want and should be content. They are making a great mistake in cavilling over details.
(3)   In view of the backward state of the Borneo territories and the lack of indigenous administration, there is a most serious threat to law and order and the gravest risk of a breakdown in the administration and of anarchy if the British personnel are withdrawn too soon. It is not in the interests of the Federation that this should happen and they would be unable by themselves to hold the position.
(4)   Nevertheless, Lord Cobbold and the British members of the Commission are prepared to recommend that sovereignty should be ceded and that there should be no division in responsibility. But they are not prepared to recommend that the British Governors should be withdrawn for the following reasons:—
    (a) It is vital that a British officer should be in control and should be seen to be in control.

---

[3] See 107.
[4] The commissioners met at 3 pm and Cobbold telephoned the result to Garner in time for the ministerial meeting at 5.15 pm, see 109 and 110.

(b) It would not be understood locally if someone were placed over their heads as a nominal Head of State and lived in Government House. Symbols are important.
(c) The retention of British Governors is also vital to the retention of British expatriate officers generally, and might provide a way of getting over the difficulty of offering compensation.

Lord Cobbold considers that the main reason why the Tunku is pressing this issue is that he has already offered the top positions to his local supporters.
(5)   Lord Cobbold also wishes to draw attention to the very awkward situation that may arise over religion. Under the existing Constitution in the Federation, the religion of the State is declared to be Moslem, but if this were to be applied to Borneo and Sarawak, where the majority is not Moslem this would not only give rise to intense local difficulties, but also, he considers, to violent protests from the Church of England and the Church of Rome.
(6)   Lord Cobbold is prepared to amend his draft letter to the two Prime Ministers so as not to refer in it in detail to the compromise solution.

109   PREM 11/3866   12 June 1962
[Commissioners' differences over their report]: note by Sir S Garner of a telephone conversation with Lord Cobbold

Lord Cobbold has telephoned me to say that he had a rather difficult time at the session of the Malaysia Commission this afternoon, and that the Malayan members were particularly difficult. He was, however, as firm as he could be with them and insisted on reaching agreement, as far as possible, on the existing drafts, and pressed both sides to agree to the omission of any reference to British Governors in the formal report. The British members said that they would agree to this, but the Malayan members asked for three further days in order to consider this among themselves.

Lord Cobbold felt bound to agree to this and will therefore not be able to report further progress until Friday, but he secured confirmation that, subject to this point, the report in its present form could be regarded as agreed by all the members.

In the circumstances, Lord Cobbold does not wish to send any messages to the Prime Ministers at this stage; he will let us know the outcome of the meeting on Friday.

110   PREM 11/3866   12 June 1962
[Commissioners' differences over their report]: note by T J Bligh of a ministerial meeting at Admiralty House

[This meeting attended by Macmillan, Sandys, Maudling, Garner and Bligh started at 5.15 pm and lasted fifteen minutes.]

Sir Saville Garner said that Lord Cobbold had had his meeting with the Malayan members of his Commission earlier in the afternoon. He had put to them that they should be prepared to agree to any passage about British Governors being left out of the Report. They had asked for three days to consider their position on this. For the rest the Report was now broadly agreed.

The Prime Minister thought it would be entirely right that the Report should stick to the main proposal, namely to set up Greater Malaysia and to leave it to a matter of negotiation between the Governments concerned as to how any transitional arrangements might be reached.

It was agreed that if the Malayan members should on Friday say that they wished their paragraphs about British Governors to be included in the Report, we should in our turn ask for a further three days and should then be prepared to put pressure on the Tunku to admit [?omit]¹ these paragraphs.

Ministers then looked at the draft letter which Lord Cobbold had prepared to send to the two Prime Ministers. It was generally agreed that this was on the right lines. The Commonwealth Secretary prepared a revised ante-penultimate paragraph which the Prime Minister thought suitable.

The meeting adjourned at 5.30 p.m.

---

¹ Ministers shared Cobbold's strong preference to omit from the report any reference to British governors rather than include commissioners' conflicting views on the transitional period.

111   PREM 11/3867   13 June 1962
[Commissioners' differences over their report]: inward telegram no 349 from Sir G Tory to Mr Sandys, reporting the reasons for the Tunku's decision to recall Ghazali for consultations

Tunku has ordered Ghazali back to Kuala Lumpur immediately for consultations before he signs report. Tunku assures me Ghazali is not being withdrawn from Commission and that he will return. This move has been prompted by Ghazali's report of latest position of British and Malayan teams, particularly on transitional period. The basic differences seem now to be as follows:—

2.   Malayan view:—

(a) With transfer of sovereignty there should be simultaneous transfer of legislative and executive authority in all agreed Federal matters to the Central Government. Because danger of administrative breakdown if drastic change were made too quickly Federal functions should be delegated back by Central Government to respective States for a transitional period (compare paragraph 3 of my letter to Hampshire of 29th May). But the constitution would show the final position from the outset.

(b) Existing State laws would continue in force subject to their becoming Federal laws on Federal matters until repealed or amended by the Central Government notwithstanding any conflict with the constitution.

(c) Joint working party for each of territories should be set up with equal representation from the territory and the Central Government 'to examine and make recommendations on measure and timing of integration into Federal system of laws and practices relating to subject in the Federal list'. Similar working parties on finance and economic matters and also on education and legal and judicial services.

(d) British officials must be retained, but retention of British Government 'was not requested by British officers as a condition for their staying on was overwhelmingly against wishes of the people and was contrary to the concept of Malaysia'. First Head of State for each Borneo territory as an interim measure should, however, be appointed by the Agong on the 'joint nomination of His Majesty and The Queen'.

3.   British view:—

(a) For a transitional period of 5 years adjustable by 2 years either way there should be following provisions:—

(i) External Affairs and anti-subversive aspects of internal security would pass to the Central Government.

(ii) Some representation from Borneo to Central Legislature elected from unofficial member of State Legislatures.

(iii) Governor with present executive powers to remain and 'to be expatriate'.

(iv) Constitutional development in the Borneo territories leading to full ministerial and electoral system.

(v) Appointment of joint working party of representatives of Central Government and Borneo territories to recommend on timing and measure of integration into the Federal system of the laws and practices and of those departments due eventually to become Federal.

(vi) Basis of employment of expatriate officers to remain unchanged.

(b) To bring this about Britain would surrender sovereignty over Borneo territories, Federal Government would assume responsibility for external affairs and anti-subversion, by agreement all other powers relating to both Federal and non-current matters would remain with the states and by agreement also States would be administered by British Governor appointed jointly by Agong and Queen.

4.   Tunku and his Cabinet are unalterably opposed to British proposals in two respects:—

(a) They would leave the Borneo [territories] from 3 to 7 years in constitutional possession of State powers comparable, if not superior, to those to be enjoyed by Singapore under the Ulster arrangement. This the Tunku could, he says, never justify to the existing States of the Federation or internationally. It would also make it impossible to 'get away with' the special arrangements for Singapore. He could only accept Singapore on a basis of restricted citizenship and representation at the centre. These limitations were at present justified because Singapore expected to enjoy a greater measure of State autonomy than the other States of Malaysia. If under constitutional arrangements applying when Malaysia came into being Borneo territories were to enjoy equal or even greater State powers than Singapore, the Singapore arrangement already under very strong political attack both in Singapore and Malaya, would become utterly indefensible.

(b) The retention of Governors exactly as at present would make it impossible for the Tunku to refute the accusations of his enemies and even more serious of his friends and neighbours (Indonesia in particular) that he was lending himself to the continuation of the Imperialist regime under cover of a bogus transfer of sovereignty.

5.   Goode in his letter of 5th June says Tunku must make some concessions to meet common problems.[1] Tunku thinks that he would be making a very great concession indeed if he were to agree to delegate Federal functions back to the States for a period to be determined by an impartial working party and this is surely true.

6.   Difficulty of denying British officers their right to retire with compensation unless the British administration continues is understood, but this problem ought to be capable of solution in some other way. If we are prepared to go to the extraordinary length of accepting a condominium arrangement (Eastwood letter of 23rd May)[2] we ought to be able to stretch a point when it comes to compensation terms, in any event there has never been a transfer of power to a formerly dependent territory without some loss of administrative efficiency.

7.   As regards paragraph 5 of Goode's letter, the extent of the powers to pass ultimately to the centre has been already agreed between the British and Malayan teams I understand, and the working party would contain equal numbers of Central and State representatives. As to his paragraph 6 about safeguards for British officers, I have no doubt there would be some Treaty guarantee of conditions of service of expatriates like the Public Officers Agreement in the case of Malaya. For the rest we shall have to trust the Tunku to play fair as he has done in Malaya. After all the whole scheme is an act of faith.

8.   At the end of his letter Goode says that if the Tunku persists in refusing to compromise, Malaysia must be off. I feel certain Tunku will not compromise on basic issues mentioned in paragraph 4 above and there is indeed a great danger that if we do not yield on those Tunku himself will call Malaysia off. Several times lately he has repeated his earlier remark to me that if we really believe people in Borneo territories are so full of mistrust then we must retain sovereignty until we feel that this mistrust has been removed. He still says, however, that he believes this will prove to be our last chance of pulling off Malaysia and that political deterioration in Singapore will make it impossible for Malaya again to contemplate taking this enormous calculated risk. He is surrounded by Ministers who are already persuading [sic] that Malaysia will be bad for Malaya. Razak and Ismail are openly saying they believe there is now no hope of achieving Malaysia and their satisfaction is ill-concealed. The only man of influence, apart from the Tunku, who has his own clear vision of Malaysia as being Malaya's best interests, is Ghazali and however tiresome the further delay may be I think it will not be a bad thing on balance if Ghazali comes home now to clear the Tunku's mind.

9.   I have re-emphasised to Tunku your assurances that we are determined to proceed towards realisation of Malaysia in agreement with him and he is pinning his hopes to this. He said earlier he would find it impossible even to discuss the Cobbold Report if it contained completely unacceptable recommendations on vital matters, but I got him to agree yesterday that inclusion of some impossible recommendation in Report need not preclude discussion between us provided that two Governments agreed to reject it and to take joint responsibility in public for doing so.

---

[1] See 105.   [2] See 103.

112　PREM 11/3867　　　　　　　　　　　13 June 1962

[Commissioner's differences over their report]: outward telegram no 553 from Sir S Garner to Sir G Tory, reporting attempts to achieve agreement

You should know that latest position is that Cobbold Report can now be regarded as 'agreed' by all members but is still unsigned for following reasons.

2.　British members have agreed to Cobbold's suggestion that Report should include no recommendation about division of responsibility in transitional period and should recommend that the precise arrangements to govern transitional period should be discussed between Governments. However in forwarding Report to both Prime Ministers Cobbold intends to state in confidential letter that he and British members favoured solution under which Borneo Territories would be ceded to new Federation subject to agreement that certain powers in Territories would be exercised by H.M.G. for some years.

3.　Remaining outstanding point is that Ghazali is pressing for inclusion of paragraphs (said to be offensively phrased) stating Malayan views on question of 'British Governors' during transitional period; if he insists, British members will equally insist on stating their views. Cobbold has urged that these conflicting views should also be omitted from Report but suggests they could be embodied in confidential letters. Malayan members have asked for three days to consider this and Cobbold hopes to report further on Friday 15th. Failing agreement he intends to ask Prime Minister to accept and pass on to Tunku message from him asking Prime Ministers to suggest to members nominated by them that specific references to 'British Governors' should be deleted.

4.　We strongly agree with Cobbold since statement of strong conflicting views in Report would inevitably make subsequent Ministerial negotiation more difficult.

113　PREM 11/3867　　　　　　　　　　　15 June 1962

[Commissioners' differences over their report]: inward telegram no 354 from Sir G Tory to Mr Sandys, reporting the Tunku's authorisation of Ghazali and Wong Pow Nee to sign the report

Tunku has cancelled Ghazali's order to return on receipt of message summarised in my immediately following telegram.[1] In light of this message he has authorised Ghazali and Wong Pow Nee to sign report subject to following conditions. *Begins*:

Since it is a main condition of Tunku's Malaysia plan that external affairs, defence and all matters affecting security should be wholly Federal, the Malayan members should not agree to British proposal that only the anti-subversive aspect of security should be Federal. In addition they should not, repeat not, commit Malaya to the delegation to States of 'matters essentially Federal particularly finance'. Subject to this and if their conscience is clear they are authorised to sign. *Ends*.

---

[1] See 114.

I understand report is now likely to be signed early next week.[2]

2.   Tunku is still determined not to leave Kuala Lumpur[3] until all important questions have been settled between British and Federation Governments. It seems now that with acceptance of Malayan view on appointment of Governors, main issue outstanding is constitutional basis of transitional period. Tunku confirmed that his Government are opposed to British recommendations on this for reasons explained in paragraph 4(a) of my telegram No. 349 amongst others.[4] But he did not want to pursue question further with me until Ghazali's return and he had studied report as a whole. We cannot possibly therefore hope to get to grips here until end of next week at earliest.

3.   I hope you will let me have your observations in the meantime so that I shall be ready for Ghazali when he gets back.

4.   My second immediately following telegram[5] relates to other matters outstanding on which it would be helpful to have your views by the middle of next week.

---

[2] On the same day, Cobbold telephoned Maudling with the news that he expected the commissioners to sign 'next Thursday', 21 June, on which Macmillan commented: 'Good news so far.' In fact they did sign on 21 June.
[3] ie in order to attend talks in London.   [4] See 111.   [5] See 115.

114   PREM 11/3867   15 June 1962

[Commissioners' differences over their report]: inward telegram no 355 from Sir G Tory to Mr Sandys, summarising Ghazali's recommendation to the Tunku that the report be signed

[Ghazali Shafie has recalled how he persuaded the Tunku to accept a report containing separate recommendations from the British and Malayan members rather than strive for agreement at this stage: 'I reminded the Tunku that we were dealing with hard core die-hard colonialists who were living in the past. They had a special feeling for the natives as we had had a few of them in Malaya who thought that it was the white man's burden to take care of the noble savages who should remain so for them to patronise and gloat' (*Memoir*, p 242).]

Summary of Ghazali's message to Tunku dated 13th June. *Begins.*

British have agreed to withdraw all reference to appointment of British Governor and also agree to first Governor being appointed by Agong on joint nomination by Agong and Queen. Disagreement over transitional arrangements is therefore now limited to executive powers of first Governor.

2.   Malayans propose Governor should be constitutional Head and should appoint Chief Minister with confidence of legislature. State Government would have all powers in accordance with State List and Chief Minister should have certain additional functions (not powers) of the central authority delegated to him in order not to cause sudden changes in administration. Joint working party should be formed to work out integration of what have hitherto been state matters into Federal system.

3.   British side feel that Borneo territories are not yet ready for such an arrangement and the Governor should be given full executive authority as he has to-day, subject only to transfer of responsibility to the Agong. Governor should not only have full powers in all the state matters but also should have delegated to him, for

transitional period, powers and functions of Central Government except External Affairs, Defence and anti-subversive aspects of security. British recommend transitional period should be from 3 to 7 years.

4.   British views are being presented not as condition for merger 'in a pack it or leave it attitude' but as proposals for serious consideration. In circumstances Ghazali thinks way is now open for negotiation between two Governments on constitutional issue and that there is no longer any ground for not signing report. *Ends.*

115 PREM 11/3867   15 June 1962
[Commissioners' differences over their report]: inward telegram no 356 from Sir G Tory to Mr Sandys, identifying outstanding issues

Other outstanding issues.

Ghazali has reported agreement with British team on following matters need for early decision. 'Constitutional basis for Malaysia' (this presumably under Federal and State Lists). Appointment of Agong. Name 'Malaysia'. Immigration. No repeat no right of secession. North Borneonisation of public services as soon as possible. Encouragement of British officers to remain until replaced by qualified Borneo people. Citizenship.

2.   Two sides have disagreed on:—

(a) Religion. Chairman and British members recommend specific provision regarding freedom of religion in state constitution and that present Malayan provisions regarding Islam should not apply to Borneo and Sarawak. Malayans for their part recommend Islam as national religion for Malaysia.

(b) National and official language. British members are opposed to Malay as national language whereas Chairman and both Malayan members agree that Malay should be national language. As regards official languages Chairman and British members recommend Malay and English as official languages in Borneo territories with no time limit, whereas Malayan members recommend English as official language for ten years or until such time as Central Government in consultation with State Government provide otherwise. Similarly with languages at present used in legislatures.

116 PREM 11/3867   19 June 1962
[Borneo interests and the commissioners' recommendations]: inward telegram no 104 from Sir W Goode to Mr Maudling, commenting on document 111

[Goode found the Tunku's intransigence and the British preparedness to compromise 'all most disturbing'. In telegram number 99, despatched on 17 June, he had argued: 'If we suppress views of the British members on vital issues such as transitional period we shall mislead ourselves and misinform the public on publication. This is the way to disaster . . . Tunku seems to be outmanoeuvring us . . . I cannot agree to any watering-down of views of British members until I have seen the whole report.' H P Hall, co-ordinator of Borneo territories in Jesselton, similarly lamented that Ghazali's methods together with 'the

Tunku's pressure, via the C.R.O., on the Cobbold Commission seems to be paying off'. Hall reported popular support in North Borneo for the British governors and he also defended British officials against charges of obstructionism (Hall to Wallace, 19 June 1962, PREM 11/3867). Recalling the ministerial meeting on 12 June (see 110), Macmillan felt that Goode's telegram of 17 June 'shows how right it is for *Governments* to reach a decision in *principle*', but he was dismayed by his telegram of 19 June (Macmillan to Brook, 19 June, PREM 11/3867, and document 117).]

It is difficult to comment without knowing the terms of the Cobbold Report as Kuala Lumpur telegram is based on information provided by Ghazali only.

2. I must repeat my view that if Tunku persists in refusing to compromise, Malaysia must be off. All our information is that Malaysia will only be acceptable here with safeguards written into the Constitution, and the suggestion that the only guarantee should be trust of Tunku ties of good faith (paragraph 7) would be viewed with cynicism by large section of the community, particularly in view of the recent amendments to Malayan Constitution on citizenship.

3. I also view with dismay the suggestion in paragraph 9 that Governments may agree to reject the Cobbold Report. I agree with the view expressed by the Tunku as reported in paragraph 3 of Kuala Lumpur telegram No. 323 to C.R.O. that Governments could not possibly override or disregard the Cobbold Commission recommendations. I assume that H.M.G. still accept the principle of self-determination. So far, the only self-determination emphasized has been that carried out by the Cobbold Commission who were asked to ascertain the views of the Borneo peoples about Malaysia. If views as expressed to the Commission are now disregarded, how will H.M.G. decide that any alternative proposals are acceptable to Borneo peoples? After all, although Singapore has an elected Legislature, the decision on Malaysia is still to be subject to a referendum.

4. Cobbold Commission is already being subjected to Government pressure at the instigation of the Tunku. Malaysia without a real measure of popular consent is fraught with danger and the attitude of Razak and Ismail reported in paragraph 8 of Kuala Lumpur telegram is also hardly reassuring that the idea is popular in Malaya itself either. The Borneo peoples are not so backward that they do not know the lack of success in attempting to establish federations in other parts of the world e.g. West Indies, Central Africa and United Arab Republic. They hope to go into Malaysia on some basis of partnership and will expect H.M.G. to support them on this. Singapore Government negotiated on its own terms with Malaya, and Borneo Territories had no say in those negotiations. Similarly Borneo Territories should be allowed to go in on terms which are acceptable to Borneo peoples and not forced to accept conditions agreed in Singapore/Malaya negotiations to which they were not a party. If this was H.M.G.'s intention, then this should have been part of the terms of reference of the Cobbold Commission and the views of the people here ascertained on that plan.

117 PREM 11/3867, M161/62   21 June 1962

[Colonial attitudes to the Cobbold commission]: minute from Mr Macmillan to Sir N Brook, commenting on document 116

[A copy of the prime minister's minute was inadvertently sent to the secretary of state for the colonies. 'It made him—and the Colonial Office—angry', J H Robertson of the

Cabinet Office informed Brook. Indeed, Maudling immediately wrote a reply to Macmillan rejecting the implication that governors made policy: 'I have not yet made up my mind what the Colonial Office point of view is to be on the matter. The Governor is fully aware of the importance of Malaysia and I am sure his concern is to see it achieved without serious troubles in Borneo.' Tim Bligh of the prime minister's Private Office pacified Maudling and managed to secure his 'willing agreement' not to pass his paper to Macmillan who remained oblivious of the consternation. A few days later, Brook discussed with Macmillan the general point about 'the attitude of colonial administrators in the Borneo Territories towards the concept of Greater Malaysia' and, 'suggested that certain organisational changes . . . would help to meet this difficulty'. He may have been referring here to the plan for Duncan Sandys to add the Colonial Office to his ministerial portfolio which took effect from 13 July. See CAB 21/4847.]

I am rather shocked by telegram No.104 from North Borneo and the attitude it reveals. Does he realise (a) our weakness in Singapore, and (b) our urgent need to hand over the security problem there? The whole mood is based on a false assessment of our power. If this is the Colonial Office point of view, we shall fail. What are we to do?

118 CO 1030/1028, no 1   21 June 1962
[Submission of the Cobbold Report]: private and personal letter from Lord Cobbold to Mr Macmillan, explaining the difficulties encountered in writing the report

[All the commissioners having signed the report, on 21 June Cobbold submitted it to the prime ministers of Britain and Malaya who agreed to keep it confidential until they had decided a course of action. It was published in early Aug 1962 as *Report of the Commission of Enquiry, North Borneo and Sarawak, 1962* (Cmnd 1794). As regards the first of their two tasks (ascertaining the views of Borneo peoples), the commissioners noted that the opinions of the inhabitants of North Borneo and Sarawak varied, tending to run on racial and communal lines, but that about one-third strongly favoured Malaysia, another third favoured it provided that there were adequate safeguards, and the remaining third was divided between those seeking independence in advance of the inauguration of Malaysia and those resisting it outright (*Report*, chapter 3, paras 141–144). As regards recommendations (their second task), the commissioners were unanimous on a number of major issues, for example: that a decision in principle should be taken by governments as soon as possible; that the new state should be called Malaysia; that the constitution of the Federation of Malaya should be adapted for Malaysia, instead of drafting a completely new one; that there should be no right to secede from Malaysia after merger; that Borneanisation of the public services should proceed as quickly as possible and that, in the interim, every effort should be made to encourage British officers to remain in the service; that (in contrast to the terms for Singapore already agreed with Malaya) there should not be a separate citizenship for the Borneo territories carrying with it the nationality of Malaysia but that citizens of North Borneo should become citizens of Malaysia (*Report*, chapter 4, section A, paras 145–148). In general, they concluded that 'a Federation of Malaysia is an attractive and workable project and is in the best interests of the Borneo territories', a view that Cobbold strongly endorsed on the assumption that Singapore would also join (*Report*, para 237). The commissioners differed, however, over the constitutional provision for religion and language, and, most notably, over the transitional arrangements. The views of Abell and Watherston were set out in section B of chapter 4, those of Ghazali and Wong Pow Nee in section C, while Cobbold summarised and commented on them in section D. Although Cobbold shared the approach of the British members, he felt that the precise constitutional arrangements for the transition and internal security should be referred for inter-governmental discussion (*Report*, para 238). Cobbold also sent Macmillan, the Tunku and Maudling a series of letters (including a memorandum by Abell and Watherston) which amplified issues that were not mentioned or only partially covered in the report, principally on account of disagreement between the British and Malayan commissioners (see 118–122). Here he was more explicit in his views regarding transition. In his private and personal letter to Macmillan (see 118), for example, Cobbold insisted that British governors would be 'essential' in North Borneo and Sarawak 'for the next few years' because the government in Kuala Lumpur was both 'fully stretched' and largely ignorant of conditions in Borneo. Since they were all written on the same day, the letters are presented here in the order in which they were filed by the CO and exceptionally their security classification (eg private and personal, personal and confidential) has been included in the headings to assist in distinguishing between them. The letters were later copied to the Cabinet Oversea Policy Committee which considered the Cobbold Report on 4 July, see 126 (PREM 11/3867, CAB 21/4848, and OP(62)3, 2 July 1962, CAB 134/2370).]

Dear Prime Minister,

I write this letter on a private and personal basis and not as Chairman of the Commission.

I am sorry about the inordinate length and repetitiveness of the Report. I have had great difficulty with two quite different approaches. We have had to write almost everything at least twice over, but I have tried, as far as I could, to bring it together at the end.

The only essential reading is:—

Chapter III—Assessment
Chapter IV—A. Recommendations on Certain General Matters
                B. Recommendations by British Members
                C. Recommendations by Malayan Members (to glance through)
                D. My summary of B. and C. and comments, and also my two letters
and the memorandum by British members enclosed in a third letter.

The best solution for the transitional period would in my view be the creation of Malaysia in two definite stages, leaving all powers other than External Affairs, Defence and the 'anti-subversive' side of Internal Security with the British Government for 3, 5 or 7 years.

I have no doubt that this is what would suit the Borneo territories best, what would fulfil H.M. Government's obligations best, and that would make the whole thing work best if the Malayans would play. But they evidently would not—as you know, the Tunku instructed the Malayan members to withdraw from the Commission if this recommendation were made. To avoid a breakdown I have reluctantly dropped this specific recommendation from the Report and have, instead, dealt with this subject in a personal and confidential letter to yourself and the Tunku.

If H.M. Government conclude that, for the sake of getting Malaysia, they can properly agree to the British Government as such stepping out of the picture (not an easy conclusion in view of the very definite commitments, including the 1960 reply to the Baram petition to the Queen),[1] I would see a tolerable compromise on the following lines.

I regard British Governors for the next few years (three years might suffice) as

---

[1] Commitments were enshrined in the Nine Cardinal Principles of 1941 which had been reiterated on the annexation of Sarawak in 1946, included in the first schedule of the Sarawak (Constitution) Order in Council of 1956 and appended to the Cobbold Report. The Baram district was in Sarawak's Fourth Division and the lower Baram river formed the border with Brunei. The commissioners met one group of Baram Ibans who, clearly mindful of rule by Brunei Malays in the past, 'hotly opposed' Malaysia and insisted that, if the decision went against them, safeguards should be built into the scheme (see *Report*, paras 46 and 48, and appendix C: also document 56, n 9).

essential, and H.M. Government will have to make some arrangements which will keep the great majority of British officers there and fill the gaps (already alarming) by getting contract officers.

The British Governors could then be left to get on with it, with as much support as they could get from local legislative assemblies. It might help a solution if British officers were employed by the Secretary of State but seconded to the State Government. I should not myself be happy to see any powers handed over at once to the Federation other than External Affairs, Defence and the anti-subversive side of Internal Security (the last to be administered by delegation to the Governor). All other powers should, I suggest, remain with the State Governments during the transitional period. I think Kuala Lumpur already has enough on its hands: they have done well in Malaya, but they are fully stretched and few of their top people know anything about Borneo or have ever been there. I think they might make a mess of the Borneo territories in the early years. One has to remember three things: there is a lot of personal ambition and empire-building in Kuala Lumpur; the Malayans have promised top jobs to several quite unripe Borneo politicians in order to get their support for Malaysia; and, last but not least, many of the local head-hunting tribes are backward and fearless and would revert with pleasure to their former pastimes.

One other point. I have supported Malaysia in the Report 'on the assumption that Singapore also joins in'. I do not wish to say anything more specific on this subject for publication, as I thought it might be damaging. But I should feel bound to advise H.M. Government that, if Singapore were to drop out, a federation between Malaya and the Borneo territories without Singapore would have few attractions.

If a solution emerges which in my view does not take sufficient account of all these things, I must reserve the right to say so in the House of Lords.

I should be grateful if you would restrict circulation of this letter to a close circle in Whitehall.

119 CO 1030/1028, no 3   21 June 1962
[Submission of the Cobbold Report]: personal and confidential letter from Lord Cobbold to Mr Macmillan (also to Tunku Abdul Rahman), giving his views on transitional arrangements

Dear Prime Minister,

I write with reference to the Report of the Commission of Enquiry on Malaysia in order to put before yourself and Tunku Abdul Rahman certain personal views of my own.

I am, as I have stated in the Report, a firm supporter of Malaysia, and I have endeavoured, in Chapter IV, Section D, to bring the views of members of the Commission as far as possible together and to stress the high degree of unanimity which exists in the Commission's thinking.[1]

In a reference in the Report (paragraph 238) to the problems of the years

---

[1] Chapter 4, section D was the chairman's summary of the differing views of British and Malayan members, as set out in B and C respectively, see 118, note.

immediately following Federation, I have suggested that the precise constitutional and other arrangements to govern a transitional period are matters for discussion between Governments.

In the same paragraph I have used the words:—

'I urge most strongly that any arrangements made for the early years after Federation should provide for continuity of administration in the Borneo territories and should not result in any weakening, either real or apparent, of authority in Kuching and Jesselton.'

The points which I have in mind, stated in more specific terms, are these. The present stage of political development in the territories is some way behind that of other parts of the proposed Federation, and qualified local candidates to take the place of British officers are not available in sufficient numbers. Nor would it be wise, or generally acceptable in the territories, to fill vacancies by the appointment of officers from Malaya or Singapore, even if they were available. I therefore judge it necessary that for the next few years the highest posts (those of Governor and Chief Secretary or their equivalents) should be held by expatriate officers, that these officers should retain their present authority over domestic affairs (excepting only that, in the anti-subversive aspects of Internal Security, they should be subject to the overriding authority of the Federal Government), and that a high proportion of expatriate officers should remain in the service. Whilst the precise arrangements to cover Internal Security would have to be worked out by experts, I feel strongly that, in this first period, the police should be under the control of the Governor and Chief Secretary (or their equivalents) who should exercise their authority in matters relating to subversion by delegation from the Federal Government and under the Federal Government's responsibility. I regard these as essential requirements for the proper administration of the territories and for the maintenance of law and order. I feel moreover that, considering the novelty of this project for the Borneo territories, their political immaturity as compared with Malaya, and their distance from the Federal centre, arrangements on these lines would be a positive benefit both to the Borneo territories and to the new Federation.

I have myself favoured a solution under which the territories would be ceded to the new Federation subject to an agreement that powers, other than those over External Affairs, Defence, and the anti-subversive aspects of Internal Security, would for some years continue to be exercised in the territories by the British Government. I have felt that, from the practical point of view, this is the solution which would suit the Borneo territories best and would give the best start to the new Federation of Malaysia. But in order to meet strong representations made to me by the Malayan members, I have omitted from the Report, as have the British members, any recommendation to this effect, and I have instead, set out my views on these subjects in this confidential letter.

I wish to add my personal opinion on one other question, which is a matter of individual judgement and on which members of the Commission hold divergent views. On my own assessment, if any offer of compensation were to be introduced at an early stage, but otherwise the Public Services were to enjoy conditions of service similar to those now in force with a British Governor at their head, between 30% and 50% of expatriate officers would be likely to leave the service in the next year or two: if a compensation offer were made and the services of British Governors were dispensed with, I should expect to see the percentage of resignation go materially above 50%. Loss of between a third and a half of the expatriate officers would put an almost intolerable strain on the administration. Loss of more than half could easily lead to a breakdown of the administration and be a serious prejudice to law and order. I do not feel that in the interests of the territories themselves or in the interests of the British Government or the Government of the Federation of Malaya these risks could properly be run.

I trust that the Report, and the suggestions made in this letter, may be of some assistance to you in laying the foundations for the new Federation, to which I have devoted much time and thought, and in the future of which I profoundly believe.

I have written in the same terms to Tunku Abdul Rahman.

120   CO 1030/1028, no 4   21 June 1962
[Submission of the Cobbold Report]: memorandum[1] to Lord Cobbold on transitional arrangements by Sir A Abell and Sir D Watherston

As the British members of the Malaysia Commission we would wish to place on record certain factors which emerged during the later stages of the Commission's deliberations and which have materially affected our recommendations in Chapter IV (Section B) of the Report, on the arrangements to be made during the transitional period.

When it became apparent that there was a serious divergence of view between the Malayan and British members of the Commission over these arrangements, it was agreed that each side should prepare its own recommendations. Our firm conviction was—and still is—that it is essential that a British Governor should remain in effective control of the administration both in Sarawak and North Borneo during this difficult period. With this in mind the first recommendation that we drafted was to the effect that Sovereignty over the two territories should be transferred to the new Federation, but that this should be subject to an Agreement under which the Federation Government would, for a period of three to seven years, be responsible only for External Affairs, Defence, and the anti-subversive aspects of internal security; and the British Government would be responsible for the government of the two territories in all its other aspects. This responsibility would be exercised through a Governor appointed by the Queen. By this arrangement ultimate control of the staff would continue to lie with the Secretary of State for the Colonies and there would be no change in the basis of their employment and no question of retirement and the payment of compensation. Thus the continuity and stability which we regard as essential would be provided during the 'running in' period of the new Federation.

When this proposal became known to our Malayan colleagues (and was, we understand, reported by them to their Government) we were informed that no form of dual sovereignty would be acceptable to Malaya and that if we persisted in this recommendation the Malayan members of the Commission would be withdrawn.

We accordingly amended our recommendation to provide for complete sovereignty to pass to the new Federation at once, but we reiterated our view that the first Head of State in both territories should be a British Governor appointed jointly

---

[1] Enclosed in Lord Cobbold's confidential letter to the prime minister, 21 June 1962.

by H.M. The Queen and H.M. The Yang di-Pertuan Agong. As you are aware,[2] this led to the inclusion in the section of Chapter IV of the Report which was being drafted by our Malayan colleagues, of passages setting out their views as to why there should not be a British Governor, even in the initial stages. You pointed out that these two opposing views would clearly increase the difficulties of the subsequent negotiations between the Governments and might even make agreement on Malaysia impossible. Both we and our Malayan colleagues therefore agreed to your request that the passages in question should be omitted.

We have recorded those events because the final form of our recommendations in the Commission's report may not sufficiently clearly convey the strong conviction that we feel that it is quite vital that there should be a period of firm and experienced leadership during the first few years of difficult adjustments, not only for the Governments but for the peoples of Sarawak and North Borneo. This is of the first importance if the Federal Government is to allay the fears of many of the people and to win their good-will.

We understand that our Malayan colleagues hold the view that the retention of the Chief Secretaries of each of the present Governments in Borneo as State Secretaries under the new regime will ensure continuity and stability of administration. We do not agree with this view. The officers concerned would in our opinion be placed in an intolerable position of great responsibility but without any real authority, under a new and inexperienced Chief Minister and a native Head of State also without any knowledge of the snares which would inevitably beset his path.

We appreciate the difficulties of our Malayan colleagues and we recognise too the dangers of including recommendations in the Report which might adversely affect the future negotiations which must take place between the British and Malayan Governments. Nevertheless the fact remains that we have yielded a number of points of the first importance under pressure. We were greatly concerned by the reluctance of our Malayan colleagues, apparently supported by their Government, to make any concessions in favour of non-Muslim susceptibilities and national pride. We believe therefore that it is imperative that it should be brought home to the Prime Minister of Malaya that if he wants to see a happy and united Malaysia in the next few years, he must show that he will pay sympathetic attention to the strong feelings held by the majority of people in the Borneo territories on such matters as the eligibility of their Heads of State to become Head of the Federation, national religion, and language.

---

[2] ie, Lord Cobbold.

121 CO 1030/1028, no 5   21 June 1962

[Submission of the Cobbold Report]: confidential letter from Lord Cobbold to Mr Macmillan (also to Tunku Abdul Rahman), mentioning certain points (notably racial tension in Sarawak) not suitable for inclusion in the report

Dear Prime Minister,

I write on behalf of the Commission of Enquiry on Malaysia to mention certain points which we desire to bring to your notice but do not regard as suitable for inclusion in a Report destined for publication.

We wish first to lay stress on the dangerous position which we believe exists in Sarawak and which might easily spread to North Borneo. The happy relationship between different races which was until recently a notable feature of both territories has largely disappeared in recent months in Sarawak, and is under strain in North Borneo, mainly because of strong feelings about the Malaysia proposals. Sarawak has become divided on racial lines, and communal feelings are being whipped up by well-organised Communist cells. Feelings were running high in Sarawak at the time of our visit, and, but for the obvious presence of strong police and field force detachments, there might well have been incidents at several places.

We believe that there will, in any event, be a period of tension and difficulty which will need firm and careful handling if law and order are to be maintained. If the issue of Malaysia should remain long in doubt, we should regard the outlook with foreboding.

This leads us to suggest that the British and Malayan Governments should take a decision of principle as early as possible after they receive our Report, certainly not later than early July, and that this decision should be made known at the same time as, or very shortly after, the Report is published. Active steps should then be taken to disseminate the Report and Governmental decisions of principle throughout the territories, with a view to debate in the local legislative assemblies in the early autumn, and (if thought desirable) an inter-governmental conference with official and unofficial representatives of the two territories shortly thereafter.

There are obvious arguments for delaying a concrete step until after the Sarawak elections, which are timed for next June but could, we understand, be advanced by some months. But, in our judgement, these arguments are overridden by the risks that, if action were delayed until a new legislature had been elected and had settled down, the communal situation would have greatly deteriorated.

Next I should wish to mention a question relating to citizenship and immigration. The recommendations of the Commission on these matters are based on the assumption that present practice will generally be followed by the Governments of North Borneo and Sarawak between now and the creation of Malaysia.

I am writing in the same terms to Tunku Abdul Rahman.

122 CO 1030/1028, no 6   21 June 1962
[Submission of the Cobbold Report]: letter from Lord Cobbold to Mr Maudling, mentioning certain points on the public services not suitable for inclusion in the report

[The Oversea Civil Service was established in May 1956 although this was followed by further protracted planning, see D Goldsworthy, ed, *BDEE: The Conservative government and the end of empire 1951–1957*, part II, 219–242 and Hyam and Louis, eds, *BDEE: The conservative government and the end of empire 1957–1964*, part I, 82–87. For the localisation of the public service of Malaya and provision for expatriate officers to apply for positions in it, see *BDEE: Malaya* part III, 394 (17–20), 416, 418–420. See also A H M Kirk-Greene, *Britain's imperial administrators, 1858–1966* (Basingstoke, 2000) pp 263–267 and *On crown service: a history of HM colonial and overseas civil services 1837–1997* (London, 1999) pp 62–91.]

I am asked by the Commission of Enquiry on Malaysia to bring to your notice certain points about the Public Services which, for various reasons, they did not think it appropriate to mention in a Report destined for publication.

We refer in many places in the Report to the high regard in which British officers are held and to the necessity that they should be encouraged to stay on. We refer specifically to the need to maintain the Service at full strength and fill existing vacancies: we urge that H.M. Government should give immediate attention to this point.

The other matters to which the Commission wish to draw your attention are as follows:—

1. Both in Sarawak and North Borneo the Commission were able to meet delegations from the Associations and Unions which represent the majority of officers in the senior and junior branches of Government service. We also had opportunities of discussing with senior officials the problems of staffing and organisation which might arise if Malaysia came into being in the near future.

2. The senior staff associations in both territories (almost entirely composed of expatriate officers) represented about 70% of the Grade I and Grade II officers in the Government service. They told the Commission that they expected compensation to be payable to their members when a change of sovereignty took place. They also expected to be given the option either of resigning from their present employment with compensation and pension and with the opportunity of taking up a contract appointment in the country, or of continuing on permanent and pensionable terms for the remainder of their service. Both associations considered that the Malayan scheme for lump sum compensation was more likely to retain officers than an instalment scheme as approved for Tanganyika. The North Borneo delegation said that their members would be less likely to remain in the country if they were made liable for service outside North Borneo.

3. The junior branches of the Civil Service (composed of locally recruited officers) were represented by the North Borneo Civil Service Union and the Sarawak Government Asian Officers Union. They were chiefly concerned with the acceleration of the training programme and more rapid promotion in the service. Neither delegation considered there would be many, if any, resignations in the junior branches of the service on account of a change in sovereignty, provided the terms and conditions of service were not changed for the worse. Some anxiety was expressed lest many of the Federal posts in the Borneo territories would be filled by persons from Malaya. They also expressed the hope that European officers would remain until local personnel were qualified to fill their places.

4. Both at Jesselton and Labuan the Commission saw representatives of a number of officers of the North Borneo Government who had been recruited onto the permanent establishment from Burma, Ceylon and Hong Kong. These people were worried that their future in the service and their promotion prospects might be adversely affected by a change of sovereignty and the rapid Borneanisation of the service. The Commission, while unable to give any assurance on this matter, expressed the view that the shortage of trained and experienced officers and the expansion of services appeared to offer good prospects of future employment and security.

5. We were much impressed and encouraged by the responsible and reasonable attitude of these delegations. Although they were primarily interested in the prospects and treatment of the Government staff, this did not conceal their real concern for the future welfare of the people of the Borneo territories.

123   DO 169/214, no 95   28 June 1962

'The Tunku and Malaysia': memorandum by Sir G Tory, enlarging on the implications of Malaysia for the Tunku's political position

[Tory sent this 'hurriedly dictated note' to Garner on 28 June, 'in case you need some ammunition'. He had reported on Malayan politics in a more measured way two weeks earlier, in a despatch which was later printed by the CRO for confidential circulation (Tory to Sandys, 18 June, CO 1030/989, no 1260).]

The Tunku is very nervous about the effect of Malaysia on his political position. He knows that he will have to deal with many new and difficult problems in the field both of politics and of internal security and he would be glad to be able to avoid this responsibility if he could do this without hurt to his conscience. He is driven on purely and simply by his belief that Singapore left to us, or to itself, will deteriorate into Communism very rapidly and that the contamination will spread both to the Malayan peninsula and through Indonesia to the Borneo Territories themselves. This is the premise on which his whole approach to Malaysia is based and his attitude must be judged against this background.

The basis of the Tunku's assumption is that Lee Kuan Yew's Government cannot survive more than a few months more and that it will be replaced by the Barisan Sosialis, a United Front dominated and manipulated by expert and devoted Communists with the object of taking over Singapore for Communism. Lee Kuan Yew himself has told me that he cannot hold the political position in Singapore for more than four months or so, that is, until he has to go to the Legislative Assembly for more money, unless merger has in the meantime been assured. His whole survival is now based, and deliberately based, on the inevitability of Malaysia and if any setback occurs he believes his position will collapse.

If the Tunku could rely on Britain to remain in charge in Singapore for as long as the Communist threat remained he would never have agreed to merger even within the context of Greater Malaysia. He believes in fact that H.M.G. will not be able, or willing, to resist for long Singapore's demand for independence. Nor does he think us likely to render the leading Communists harmless before we leave Singapore to its own devices. His object, therefore, is to take over Singapore before Lee Kuan Yew's Government falls, in the hope that in the meantime we shall join with the Tunku and Lee Kuan Yew (under cover of the anonymity which the I.S.C. provides) in immobilising the Communist leaders, but in the certainty that in the last resort he will himself undertake the job.

The Tunku states categorically that he will not accept merger with Singapore once the Barisan Sosialis, with its present Communist leadership, has come to power there. This is because he knows that with Malaysia the Communists who are the hard core of the Barisan Sosialis would become leaders of an important section of the political Opposition in the new Federal Parliament and that it would then be impossible for him to proceed against them in the absence of obviously illegal activity on their part without arousing dangerous communal emotions throughout Malaysia, and without drawing trouble down on his head in the United Nations. At that stage, according to the Tunku's estimate, any repressive measures would be regarded as anti-Chinese rather than anti-Communist. The movement for Greater Malaysia has already sharpened communal feeling to a considerable extent and the Tunku fears Malaysia will fail if this situation is aggravated.

There are important persons on the British side who do not share the Tunku's view that all would be lost if Lee Kuan Yew's Government were displaced by a Communist-dominated Barisan Sosialis either before or after the implementation of Malaysia. The Communists in the Barisan Sosialis must, they argue, be left to make their mistakes, to commit illegal acts and so to allow themselves to be eliminated by legal methods consistent with the principles of democracy; otherwise we play into their hands. The Tunku, however, is certain that the Barisan Sosialis represents a significant stage, what Mao Tse-Tung calls the 'minimum programme', of a deliberate Communist conspiracy to take over Singapore and that the longer these Communist leaders are left to build up their support the more likely they are to succeed. The whole basis of the United Front technique, as the Tunku well knows, is that it employs legal methods for illegal ends and that it remains invulnerable to normal police action until it switches to the 'maximum programme' and takes over openly for Communism.[1] The people on our side who do not share the Tunku's view argue that Lee Kuan Yew's Government was also a United Front and yet this is, so to speak, the Tunku's instrument. (In fact, of course, he has no choice.) The Tunku would say to this that in Lee Kuan Yew's Government the Communists, the very same who now strongly influence the Barisan Sosialis, were in a subordinate position and Lee Kuan Yew always realised, and reckoned with, the fact that one day he would have to have a show-down with them. With the Barisan Sosialis it is a very different matter since the Communists already dominate it.

The Tunku's decision to go ahead with Malaysia was taken despite the serious doubts of his ministerial colleagues and the disquiet of his Malay supporters. These saw, as the Tunku does also, that Malaysia would greatly increase the strength of the Chinese component in the Federation and the consequent risk of inter-communal trouble and successful Communist subversion. The Tunku accordingly believes it is essential that with Malaysia power in both the political and internal security fields should be concentrated, and should be seen to be concentrated, in Kuala Lumpur. Now that the people of the Borneo Territories have become suddenly aware of politics, they have become vulnerable to subversion by the Communists, who are already noticeably active in Sarawak, presumably with the object of frustrating Malaysia. The Tunku argues therefore that the longer we delay the visible transfer of power to the centre the more time the Communists will have to do their mischief. (This point was made on a number of occasions to the Cobbold Commission by people in the Borneo Territories who were generally in favour of Malaysia.)

The Tunku has also to reckon with criticism from his Asian friends to the effect that he is lending himself to a British Imperialist manoeuvre designed to perpetuate British political, military and economic influence in this area despite Britain's involuntary retreat before the forces of anti-colonialism. An alternative charge which he fears is that he is a 'neo-colonialist' seeking to build up a colonial empire of his own. For these reasons he considers it to be politically impossible for him to allow the present British Governors to stay once Malaysia is established, or to allow the control of Administration in the Borneo Territories to continue exactly along

---

[1] A major example of the Tunku's experience of this communist strategy is the attempt by Chin Peng of the MCP to gain political recognition at the Baling talks in Dec 1955, see *BDEE: Malaya* part III, 350–353, 378–382, 391.

colonial lines. If he is to be able to meet criticism from the Afro–Asian bloc, for example, in the United Nations, criticism which the Communist-penetrated Socialists in Malaya and the Borneo Territories are only too ready to stimulate, he must also be able to say that there is an element of 'liberation' in the creation of Malaysia, that Malaysia will bring some constitutional advance, as well as independence from Britain.

For these reasons the Tunku insists that the British Governors should be replaced and that with their replacement there should be some form of responsible government, however rudimentary. The Government must henceforward be seen to be a constitutional government and the functions of government must be vested in a Chief Minister responsible to a Legislature.

The Governors argue that a sudden transition of this kind will lead to the breakdown of government and public order. The Tunku cannot believe that this is so. He says that there never was a Colonial Governor who did not sincerely fear such a breakdown of administration at the actual moment of transfer of power, who did not argue that independence was coming too soon. He says this is what people said in 1956 and 1957 with regard to Penang and Malacca; these two dependencies even sent missions to London to appeal against the 'premature' transfer of power,[2] but circumstances showed that good government continued in Penang and Malacca despite the fact that Governors entirely new to governing were introduced and Chief Ministers appointed with no experience other than that which they had gained in their political parties. The Tunku would probably admit that people in Penang and Malacca were more advanced politically and educationally than those in the Borneo Territories but he would argue that this was only a matter of degree, that there were in fact a number of potential leaders in the Borneo Territories. He is confident that at least two competent persons can be found to undertake the constitutional role of Governor and he is not convinced that two others cannot be found in the two Territories concerned who are competent to undertake the role of Chief Minister. He says that with the retention of the existing Chief Secretaries and also of the bulk of the British officers in the subordinate ranks of the Administration, good government and public order can in fact be maintained. He speaks (optimistically) of being able to lay his hands on a number of British officers, either recently retired or about to retire from the Federation, who might well accept a contract posting in the Borneo Territories, but he would not in fact deny that the majority of the existing British officers would have to stay on if there were not to be a dangerous slowing down of Administration.

This is the essence of the Tunku's case. He is at present quite unshakable and it is doubtful whether his Ministers will even try to shake him. He considers that he will have conceded as much as he dare if he agrees to the suggestion of the Malayan members of the Cobbold Commission that most of the State functions should be delegated to the new Chief Ministers until a joint Working Party decides they may be permanently transferred to the Centre. He may give way on some of the other minor points at issue but on the constitutional basis of the transitional administration in the Borneo Territories under Malaysia he is adamant.

Mr. Lee Kuan Yew has told me that he recently suggested to the Tunku that he

---

[2] See *BDEE: Malaya* part III, 451 and 452.

might at least be prepared to accept a compromise under which the present Governor-type administration would continue for a short period, say a year or 18 months, but Lee says the Tunku would have none of this. The Tunku has himself told me that if H.M.G. are really persuaded by the Governors that there will be a dangerous breakdown in administration and public order if Malaysia on his terms is accepted at once, then there is no alternative to our retaining sovereignty over the Territories until we have brought them to a point at which we are prepared to hand them over on the Tunku's terms.[3] When asked what would happen if Lee Kuan Yew's Government failed in the meantime and the Barisan Sosialis got in, the Tunku says he would not, in these circumstances, contemplate merger with Singapore on any terms. The implication is always that if we wanted the Tunku to take on Singapore with the Borneo Territories at some later stage, it would be up to us meanwhile either to see that the Barisan Sosialis did not get into power or to render its Communist leaders harmless. There is no doubt that in his heart the Tunku would regard Malaysia as dead if the transfer of sovereignty were in fact put off for more than a very short time and if the Barisan Sosialis were during this time to displace the P.A.P.

It will be seen from the foregoing paragraphs that the Tunku regards the neutralisation of the Communist leadership in Singapore as an essential condition of merger. He will be taking with him to London Dato' Dr. Ismail, the Minister of Internal Security, and also the Commissioner or Police, Dato' Fenner[4], to support him in this part of his mission. On this question of internal security in Singapore and the extent of the danger from the Communists (Lim Chin Siong, Fong Swee Suan, etc.) now in the Barisan Sosialis, there is a considerable difference between the current view of the British Commission in Singapore and the view of the Malayans. On the British side it is said that the evidence that these men are Communists is now very stale and that there has been no recent proof of Communist activity or allegiance on their part. The Tunku and his advisers for their part, and also Lee Kuan Yew and the British police officers serving him, believe that Lim Chin Siong and his friends are committed to a deliberate Communist conspiracy, the nature of which has required them to sever their active links with the Communist movement. The Malayans' analysis of their activities in recent years shows that they were active Communists at an earlier date (there is no argument about this question of fact), that they cut themselves off from their Communist contacts at the time when they became engaged in Trade Union and political work, but that in these latter years their activities have fitted exactly into the pattern laid down for Communist United Front programmes by Mao Tse-Tung in his own elaboration of Lenin's doctrines. The Malayans maintain that skilful exposure of this conspiracy would be enough to justify police action against the identified Communists, and it is likely that this will be the main argument put forward by the Malayans in the forthcoming London talks when

---

[3] This was what the Tunku proposed when he formally rejected the Cobbold recommendations a few days later, see 125.
[4] Dato Claude Fenner (later Tan Sri Sir Claude) entered the FMS police in 1936; senior assistant commissioner of police, Federation of Malaya, 1954; deputy secretary (security and intelligence), Prime Minister's Department, Malaya, 1958; director of police affairs, Malaya, 1962; inspector-general of police, Malaysia, 1963–1966.

they press us to share responsibility with them and Singapore in the I.S.C. for repressive action against the Communists.[5]

There is also a radical disagreement about the probable effect of repressive action on relatively uncommitted Chinese opinion in Singapore and it is on a correct assessment of this effect and on the implications for Malaysia that justification of police action must depend. The Communists themselves believe that repressive action against them at the 'minimum programme' stage, when they are using legal methods, will consolidate nationalist opinion behind them. This is also the argument of the British Commissioner in Singapore and his Security officers. The Malayans for their part believe, on the basis of their own long experience in dealing with the Chinese and with Communist subversion in this peninsula, that once the existence of a Communist conspiracy has been effectively revealed, firm and determined action against the Communists will bring the uncommitted Chinese into line with the Government rather than to the support of the Communists who are the object of police action. This was conclusively demonstrated during the Emergency. The Malayans affirm that the Chinese in this part of the world are for the most part concerned only with their material advancement and will accommodate themselves with whichever party has shown itself to be able to provide firm and effective government. If the show-down were merely between Lee Kuan Yew and Lim Chin Siong, the support would go to Lim Chin Siong. But the show-down is really now between Lim Chin Siong on the one hand and on the other Lee Kuan Yew, with the Tunku standing over him, and it is the Tunku/Lee Kuan Yew combination which is clearly going to win.

---

[5] See 129, appendix C for Singapore's internal security and 132–140 for the London talks in July; the issue of mass arrests came to a head in Dec and again in Jan-Feb 1963, see 144, 147, 148, 156, and 158.

124   CAB 134/1951, GM(62)15   2 July 1962
'The Cobbold Commission Report. Interim Report by the Committee on Greater Malaysia'. *Annex* A: 'Main points of agreement between British and Malayan sides of the Cobbold commission'; *Annex* B: 'Main points of difference between British and Malayan sides of the Cobbold commission'

[The interdepartmental Committee (Official) on Greater Malaysia, prepared this analysis of the Cobbold Report, identifying the problems of transitional arrangements and suggesting tactics that might be adopted in the next round of Anglo–Malayan negotiations which were due to resume in London during the week beginning 16 July. Before the Cabinet Oversea Policy Committee met to discuss this paper on 4 July (see 126), the Tunku announced his rejection of the Cobbold Report (see 125). The references to numbered paragraphs are precisely those in the *Report of the Commission of Enquiry* as later published (see also 118, note).]

Introductory
The Greater Malaysia project is of vital concern to British policy, since, if successfully established, it offers the promise of a new stabilising factor in South East Asia, of an arrangement for Singapore which would ensure the maintenance of our defence position there, and of being able to forestall claims on the Borneo Territories which might be made if they retain colonial status.

2. It is therefore very satisfactory that the Cobbold Commission is unanimously in favour of the project and also considers it as being in the interests of the Borneo Territories.

3. Nevertheless, while the Report is unanimous on this main issue and on many other matters, it has left one big and difficult problem to be settled in negotiation between the British and Malayan Governments. This is the problem of what should be the nature of the arrangements for governing and administering the Territories during the transitional phase which must precede their full integration into the new Federation.

Main points of agreement within commission
4. These are listed in Annex A. It is very satisfactory that there is apparently full agreement on the following:—

(a) Degree of support for Malaysia in territories.

(b) Malaysia a workable attractive project which would be in best interests of territories.

(c) Early decision in principle should be taken and announced by Governments. This and Report should be published in territories and debated in territorial legislatures. Subject to results, Malaysia should be set up within twelve months from the date of the decision in principle.

(d) On the creation of Malaysia sovereignty over the two territories should be surrendered to the new Federation.

(e) Malaysian Constitution to be modelled on existing Malayan Federal Constitution i.e. strong Central Government with States enjoying a measure of autonomy; but in view of special circumstances of Borneo Territories certain additional special safeguards should apply to them and be unalterable except with positive concurrence of State Government.

N.B. No important differences are recorded about the nature of these safeguards and in particular there seems to be full agreement on immigration.

(f) No right of secession of States.

(g) Some form of transitional period during which it is essential to retain the services of the present British staff and to institute no change in administrative arrangements so far as they affect the 'ordinary lives of the people'.

(h) Citizenship proposals. N.B. These raise a difficulty, since they allow Federation citizenship to classes of persons who would not get it under the proposals already agreed for Singapore. There is however also a recommendation of the Malayan members (paragraph 190(g)) that persons normally resident in either of the Borneo Territories should not be allowed to vote or stand for election outside their own territory. If this were applied *mutatis mutandis* to Singapore it might enable the Federation to agree to the wider citizenship proposals for Singapore. Mr. Lee Kuan Yew is going to take this up with the Tunku.

(i) Method of appointing first Head of State in each territory.

In brief, there is virtually no disagreement on the *ultimate* position. Greater precision on the division of powers is however necessary before a final decision could be taken on the actual setting up of Malaysia.

The only really important points of disagreement, all inter-related, are over the *transitional period*.

Main points of disagreement

5.   These are listed in Annex B. Briefly, the Malayan members think it possible, on Malaysia Day, to anticipate by several years the constitutional evolution that would be normal in such backward territories by giving immediately a large measure of local political control to elected Bornean Ministers under a constitutional Head of State. The British members think this quite unrealistic and propose a clearly marked transitional period of three to seven years at the beginning of which, though sovereignty would have been transferred to Malaysia at the outset, the administration would be carried on exactly as now i.e. a British Governor with full executive powers; this system to evolve as speedily as possible towards a full ministerial set-up during the transitional phase. As shown in the separate letters,[1] the British members would prefer Her Majesty's Government to continue, by delegation from the Federation, to have full authority for all aspects of administration other than external affairs, defence and anti-subversive measures during this phase.

The position of the Malayan members of the commission

6.

(i) The arrangements must be defensible by the Tunku against charges from the Afro-Asians, the Communists and his own public opinion of 'neo-colonialism' and 'imperialist stooge'.

(ii) The arrangements must not be such as to exacerbate dissatisfaction in Singapore with the terms of the provisional agreement on merger concluded between Malaya and Singapore.

(iii) Integration of the Territories in the new Federation as soon as possible is necessary to prevent racial strife, to forestall Communist mischief-making and to enable an energetic start to be made with essential development plans.

(iv) As an independent country, the Federation could not accept that it should share jurisdiction with Britain in a part of its territory.

The position of the British members of the commission

7.

(a) It is essential to retain effective administration during the transitional phase. Otherwise there will be a break-down of law and order, and civil strife.

(b) It will be some time before the Territories can produce a trained personnel to man an effective administration of their own. Meanwhile administration must depend on ex-patriate officers.

(c) It is not fair or reasonable to expect ex-patriate officers to stay on unless in some way British control of the Executive is maintained—in fact it would amount simply to transferring these officers to the service of a foreign government if British control was not maintained.

(d) Moreover if there is no British control of the Executive ex-patriate officers would regard themselves under the normal rules as having a legitimate claim to retire with compensation; and if this had to be granted at least half of them would go.

---

[1] See 118–122.

Difficulties for Her Majesty's Government of Malayan proposals

8.   Briefly these are:—

(a) Our belief that they would be contrary to the wishes and interests of the Bornean peoples (they would almost certainly be regarded as a breach of our formal assurances in Sarawak).

(b) They might not ensure reasonable and stable Government and might even lead to a breakdown of administration.

(c) They would involve transferring to another Government the services of the HMOCS officers,[2] whom all agree should stay at their posts and on whose retention most Borneans are insistent. To do this compulsorily would cause very great difficulties with the staff and might not even succeed in retaining them. On the other hand if the right to retire with compensation is offered, (according to precedent elsewhere) it is virtually certain that so many would prefer to go that administration might break-down completely possibly with serious disorders and bloodshed.

Negotiations with the Tunku

9.   The crux of the negotiations with the Tunku will, therefore be to secure his agreement to a form of administration for the transitional period which will ensure stability and enable us to retain willing British administrators in Borneo until effective Bornean replacements can be trained. (N.B. Malays even if they were available would not be acceptable to the Borneans while Chinese, who form at present the great majority of potential local senior civil servants, would not be acceptable to the Malay Government either.)

10.   Our tactics with the Tunku should no doubt be to start negotiating from the most favourable position from our point of view. But we must recognise that final success depends on the Tunku accepting and working whatever arrangements can be agreed upon and some concessions to meet him will not doubt have to be made.

11.   We are preparing a paper which looks at all the possible alternatives, and we shall be having talks with the Governors and with the British High Commissioner in the next few days, after which we shall be in a position to make concrete proposals for the handling of the negotiations with the Tunku.

12.   *Summary of Conclusions*

(1) It is very satisfactory that there should be such a wide area of agreement in the Commission's Report. It seems likely that we and the Malayans should be able to endorse without difficulty most of the agreed recommendations.

(2) The main difference of view thrown up by the Report is over the transitional arrangements. This will be the main subject of the forthcoming negotiations with the Tunku. We may expect the initial Malayan negotiating position to be at least the recommendations made by the Malayan members of the Commission for the transitional period.

(3) We must seek a negotiable compromise between these Malayan recommendations and the recommendations of the British members of the Commission which would protect our own main *desiderata* while at the same time

---

[2] 122, note.

avoiding the difficulties the Tunku would foresee in accepting the recommendations of the British members.

(4) Urgent and detailed study is being given to what precise shape such a compromise might take and a further report on this will be submitted to Ministers as soon as possible.

Annex A to 124

Subject	View of Commission	Paragraph Reference
1. Feeling in territories	Approximately a third unreservedly in favour; another third in favour subject to conditions and safeguards; remaining third against—hard-core of opposition perhaps 20 per cent.	144
2. Interests of territories	A Federation of Malaysia is in the best interests of both territories.	237
3. Next steps	Decision in principle should be taken as soon as possible by British and Malayan Governments. Report and these decisions of principle then to be disseminated throughout the territories with a view to debate in local legislative assemblies.	151 Lord Cobbold's letter of 21st June on behalf of Commission to both Prime Ministers
4. Sovereignty	On the creation of Malaysia, sovereignty over the two territories should be surrendered to the new Federation	153 188
5. Form of Constitution	Existing Constitution of Federation of Malaya should be taken as basis of Constitution of the new Federation, subject to amendments and safeguards. Present Federation of Malaya would then cease to exist and Sarawak and North Borneo would join new Federation as States. No amendments in any special safeguard should be made by Central Government without positive concurrence of Government of State. Power of amending Constitution of each State to belong exclusively to the peoples of each State.	148(b)
6. Name	'Malaysia' all right, but should have, a Malay translation which does not mean 'Great Malaya'.	148(d)
7. Head of Federation	Cannot see any way of meeting local wish that Head of State should be eligible for appointment as Head of Federation	148(c)

Subject	View of Commission	Paragraph Reference
8. Legislative Lists	Federal, State and Concurrent Lists should broadly follow lines of existing Federal Constitution	236(b)(iv)
9. Representation in Federal Parliament	Should take account of size as well as population	236(a)(i)
10. Special position of indigenous races	Native races in territories should be placed in position analogous to that of Malays in Federation of Malaya Constitution	236(a)(ii)
11. Secession	Right of secession not recommended	148(h)
12. State Constitution	Should be on lines of those of Penang and Malacca	153
13. Head of State	In first instance appointment by Yang di-Pertuan Agong on joint recommendation of The Queen and the Yang di-Pertuan Agong	236(b)(ii)
14. Electoral system	Present electoral college system should be retained in Sarawak and introduced in North Borneo	194
15. Development	Urgent attention should be given to this in fields of rural improvement, education, medical and other social services, and training for administrative and technical posts	170 220–228 236(a)(iii)
16. Public Service	Essential that expatriates should remain until locals can take their place. (Malayan members 'reluctant to advocate secondment from Malaya or Singapore unless there is a very definite request from Borneo territories.')	151(d) 231–233
17. Immigration	Entry into Sarawak and North Borneo, even from other parts of Malaysia, should require approval of State Government	148(g)
18. Citizenship	Agreed proposals (of some complexity) put forward	148(k)
19. Transitional period	There is wide difference of view about this (see Annex B), but there is agreement that 'at least in the early years there should be no change in administrative arrangements in so far as they affect the ordinary lives of the people'.	236(a)(v)

Annex B to 124

Subject	Malayan View	British View*
1. *Transitional Period*		
(a) General	Both sides envisage a comparatively early transfer of sovereignty—the Malayans say 'within the next twelve months' (paragraph 188)—and both say that there should be a transitional period thereafter, but their respective concepts of this transitional period are basically different. The Malayans want over-all power to pass at once to the Federation; they say this is essential if they are to produce rapid advance in economic and social development.	The British think that the best guarantee of success and avoidance of racial conflict and disorder would be for Her Majesty's Government to remain in effective control *in* the territories for a period of three-seven years. Both sides, much more particularly the British, have watered down their views in the Report so as to avoid open contradiction on these matters. The British views are therefore to be obtained from Lord Cobbold's letter of the 21st June to both Prime Ministers and from the Memorandum of the two British members of the Commission of the same date which Lord Cobbold submitted to our Prime Minister. This fundamental difference of approach comes out, but only in 7a suppressed form, in Chapter VI of the Report. It comes out much more clearly in the accompanying letters.
(b) Governor and Administration	The Governor should be a constitutional ruler and there is no need for him to be British. He would appoint a Chief Minister	The Governor should be British and be an executive Head with the same powers as now. A full Ministerial system should develop

---

* Except where otherwise specified 'British View' includes Lord Cobbold's own view.

Subject	Malayan View	British View
(b) Governor and Administration *contd*	who had the confidence of the Legislature and act on his advice, i.e. a full Ministerial system could be set up straight away in each State.	but would take some years.
(c) State and Federal Powers	Essential that not only defence and external affairs but all aspects of internal security (not just anti-subversion) be Federal subjects from the start. All subjects that are eventually to be Federal should also be handed over to the new Federation at once although the Federation would delegate to the Chief Ministers of the respective States the exercise of as many functions as may be necessary for the maintenance of good administration. Malayans do not want to delegate back Finance but seem to regard this point as negotiable.	The real British view is that, after the transfer of sovereignty, there would be an agreement between the new Federation and Her Majesty's Government that powers other than those over External Affairs, Defence and the anti-subversive aspects of Internal Security would for some years continue to be exercised in the territories by the British Government (Lord Cobbold's letter of 21st June on behalf of Commission to both Prime Ministers.) This is watered down in the Report. Since the Report leaves out the idea that these powers should be exercised by Her Majesty's Government, it appears that the proposal would be for them to be exercised by the Governor as the Head of State Government. The State Government would have policy control and legislative powers, not merely 'executive functions'. (Paragraph 153)
(d) Expatriate Staff	Malayans agree that British staff should be retained but offer no solution to problem of avoiding an offer of early retirement with compensation.	Governor to be as at (b) above, with Secretary of State for Colonies still exercising ultimate control over staff; basis of their employment would be unchanged and thus no question of immediate retirement would arise.
2. *Ultimate Position*		
(a) Religion (para.148(e))	Islam should be the National Religion of Malaysia as in the present Federation. (Article 3(1) of the Federal Constitution says 'Islam is the religion of the Federation: but other religions may be practised in peace and harmony in any part of the Federation.'). They note that	Specific provisions about freedom of religion should be written into 'State Constitution.' Present provision in the Malayan Constitution about Islam should not apply to North Borneo and Sarawak. (NOTE: These make the Ruler of a State, other than Malacca and Penang, the Head of

Subject	Malayan View	British View
(a) Religion *contd*	under present federal constitution certain public expenditure may be incurred for Islamic purposes and that this may be considered objectionable in Borneo, but they make no recommendation about this.	the Muslim religion in his State. In Malacca and Penang the State Constitutions are required to provide that the Agong is Head of the Muslim religion in those States.)
(b) Language (para. 148(f))	Lord Cobbold and Malayan members of the Commission think Malay should be the national language. (NOTE: Presumably as in present Federal Constitution.) Malay members think English should remain official language for ten years or until Central Government decides otherwise 'in consultation with' State Government	British members of Commission think that question whether Malay should be the national language should be decided by Borneo peoples themselves when fully elected representative bodies have been constituted. Lord Cobbold and they consider Malay and English should be official languages without time limit, until and unless State Government decides otherwise.

Possible differences that might be inferred from correspondence about completing the Cobbold Commission's Report

(a) Ultimate Constitutional Position	The Malayans want the ultimate position of North Borneo and Sarawak in Malaysia to be made clear from the start.	There is nothing to show that the British members or Lord Cobbold disagree with this but they have not specifically agreed.
(b) Length of Transitional Period	Malayans have not specifically disagreed with this but may in the event differ with us over the length of the period (they have apparently not agreed to any length but prefer this should be left to joint working parties of Central and State Governments.)	British members and Lord Cobbold have proposed the period should be, three, five or seven years.

125 PREM 11/3867   4 July 1962

[The Tunku's rejection of the Cobbold Report]: letter from Tunku Yaacob to Mr Macmillan, forwarding a message from Tunku Abdul Rahman rejecting the Cobbold Report

[A committee of the Malayan Cabinet considered the report at Fraser's Hill, a hill station north of Kuala Lumpur, and rejected the proposal to retain British governors and British expatriate officers until they were replaced by Borneans to the exclusion of Malayans. Although it was not immediately clear to the British from his message whether the Tunku was proposing the postponement of Malaysia until the British government could certify that the Borneo territories were ready for merger, by calling off his visit to London he put 'the whole subject ... back in the melting pot' (de Zulueta to Macmillan, 4 July 1962, PREM 11/3867; see also CO 1030/1024).]

I am forwarding herewith a message which I have received from the Prime Minister of the Federation of Malaya for submission to you.

'My colleagues and I have studied the Report of the Cobbold Commission and we have come to the conclusion that we cannot accept the recommendations of the Chairman and the British Members. In particular we feel it is impossible for us to agree:—

(a) that on transfer of sovereignty, only External Affairs, Defence and anti-subversive aspects of internal security are to be transferred to the Central Government;
(b) to a situation whereby British Governors and Chief Secretaries (or their equivalents) are not only retained but will continue to exercise full authority over other domestic matters; and
(c) to a situation whereby all expatriate officers are not only retained but until they are replaced by Borneo officers to exclusion of officers from Malaya but are to be replaced by other expatriate officers should they leave before Borneo officers are ready to take their places.

It will be apparent from above recommendations that it is not intended to have any merger of these territories with the Federation. Although Report recommends immediate transfer of sovereignty to the Federation, power will still rest with Britain and the British officials during transitional period. It will clearly be impossible for me to accept such a situation without losing face with our own people. I would accordingly suggest that during transitional period as recommended in the Report, Britain retains her sovereignty over these territories and implements recommendations of the Commission. At the end of this period, when U.K. Government has decided that these territories are ready for merger, I would be happy to discuss creation of Malaysia with you.

Tunku Abdul Rahman Putra.'

This message was received early this morning.

126   CAB 134/2370, OP(62)2nd meeting   4 July 1962
'Malaysia: report of the Cobbold Commission': Cabinet Oversea Policy Committee minutes

[The Oversea Policy Committee was set up at the end of June. Its membership was: prime minister (chair), lord chancellor, foreign secretary, chief secretary to the Treasury and paymaster general, commonwealth secretary, minister of defence, and colonial secretary. It succeeded the Colonial Policy Committee and its terms of reference were to consider questions of oversea policy (other than defence policy and external economic policy) which concerned more than one department. Its second meeting was attended by Macmillan, Henry Brooke (chief secretary), Sandys, Watkinson, Maudling and the Earl of Dundee (minister of state, FO). Norman Brook and Saville Garner were also present. The entire meeting was devoted to the Cobbold Report and the officials' analysis (see 124) was put in a different light by the Tunku's bombshell (see 125). The committee agreed that the prime minister should send a conciliatory message to the Tunku (see 127 and 128) and noted his intention to inform the full Cabinet of developments the following day. CO officials, however, took a dim view of appeasing the Tunku. Thus, on 11 July, John Martin wrote to Maudling: 'In recent official discussions on Malaysia (and I think also in some of the Ministerial consideration of the subject) there have been signs of a tendency to believe that Malaysia is so desirable that we must be prepared to pay any price which the Tunku demands. This, I believe, is a dangerous thought . . .' (CO 967/407).]

The Committee had before them a note by the Secretaries (O.P.(62)4) covering an interim report by the Committee on Greater Malaysia,[1] and a note by the Secretaries (O.P.(62)6) circulating a copy of a message to the Prime Minister from the Prime Minister of the Federation of Malaya (Tunku Abdul Rahman).[2]

The Prime Minister said that the Tunku's message appeared to be based on a misunderstanding. It suggested that since it would be impossible for Malayan Ministers to accept the view of Lord Cobbold that British Governors and Chief Secretaries should continue to exercise authority in the Borneo territories during the transitional period, no point would be served in coming to London for negotiations. The Tunku had clearly made the mistake of assuming that the views of Lord Cobbold and of the British members of his Commission were in fact the views of the British Government. This was not of course the case; the main disadvantage of independent commissions was that they were independent. It would be necessary to send an immediate reply to the Tunku, pointing out that the British Government did not wish to retain authority in the Borneo territories during the transitional period, that they were not in any way committed to the views of Lord Cobbold, and that they would be prepared, on the Tunku's arrival in London, to discuss with him with a completely open mind any proposals which he might wish to put forward.

In discussion the following points were made:—

(a)   There had been a very substantial measure of agreement between the Malayan and British members of the Cobbold Commission. They were both agreed that Malaysia would be in the interest of the Borneo territories, that it would be necessary to retain British expatriate officers during the transitional period and that on the creation of Malaysia, sovereignty over the territories should be surrendered to the new Federation. The points of disagreement centred on the transitional period.

(b)   Malaysia offered the best and possibly the only hope for longer term stability in Singapore. If it was to be achieved it would have to be achieved quickly in view of the deteriorating position of Mr. Lee Kuan Yew's Government. A further defection from his party had just been reported. The Tunku's suggestion that discussions on the Federation should be deferred until the end of the transitional period, in fact amounted to an abandonment of Malaysia and he must have known this himself.

(c)   A further reason for setting up Malaysia as soon as possible was that the Philippine claim to North Borneo[3] might be taken to the United Nations and might attract considerable support, even though it had no merit. There was also the possibility of a similar claim from Indonesia.

---

[1] See 124.   [2] See 125.

[3] Following a resolution adopted by the Philippines House of Representatives in April 1962, on 22 June Diasdado Macapagal (president of the Philippines 1961–1965) made a formal claim to North Borneo. The claim was based on the status of the concession of land made by the Sultan of Sulu (later part of the Philippines) to the precursors of the North Borneo Company whose rights had passed to the Crown in 1946. The British government had long been aware of these claims and the CO had prepared a paper on them in Feb 1962, 'Sovereignty over North Borneo' (CAB 21/4626). Meeting Dean Rusk on 25 June, Lord Home had assured the US secretary of state that 'the Filipino claim was without foundation' although he accepted that Indonesia might turn its attention to North Borneo once the question of New Guinea had been resolved (D1071/83 in PREM 11/3867; see also document 129, appendix B).

(d)   The balance of advantage lay in arranging for the full and complete transfer of responsibility for the Borneo territories to the Federal Government when the Federation itself was established. Great difficulties would be created if the British Government were to retain some responsibility for the Borneo territories and to be answerable to them in Parliament at a time when a large measure of overall responsibility had passed to the Federal Government. This was the kind of situation which had caused so much difficulty with the Federation of Rhodesia and Nyasaland. Since both sides accepted the need to retain the administrative services of British expatriate officers, the problem resolved itself into devising suitable terms of service.

(e)   The right to retire with compensation had hitherto been offered to British expatriate officers when the Colonial Secretary's control over them was withdrawn; experience showed that many did in fact retire. One way of retaining the British officials under satisfactory conditions might be for them to be taken into the direct employ of the British Government and lent back to the local government; such an arrangement would have some similarity to the secondment of service officers to assist ex-colonial territories.

The Prime Minister summing up said that he proposed to bring the question before the Cabinet on the following day and to seek their agreement to the transfer of full responsibility for the Borneo territories to the Federal Government when the Federation itself was established. It should on this basis be possible to reach early agreement with the Tunku on principles. Further study would be needed of the terms under which British officers would continue to serve in the transitional period.

The Committee:—

Took note that the Prime Minister would bring the question of Malaysia before the Cabinet on the lines indicated in his summing up.[4]

---

[4] On 5 July Cabinet considered a note from Macmillan enclosing the officials' interim report. It endorsed his proposal that negotiations should be pursued with the Tunku to bring about Malaysia as soon as possible (while safeguarding the interests of the Borneo territories) and noted that he would press the Tunku to visit London as planned (CAB 129/110, C(62)106 and CAB 128/36/2, CC 44(62)7).

127   PREM 11/3867, T335/62   4 July 1962
[Resumption of talks with the Tunku]: outward telegram no 641 from Mr Sandys to Sir G Tory

My immediately following telegram contains Prime Minister's reply to Tunku's message received this morning via Malayan High Commissioner in London.

2.   In handing the Prime Minister's reply to the Tunku you should emphasise that the Prime Minister is very anxious that the Tunku should come here and discuss everything perfectly freely. You may be able to impress discreetly upon the Tunku that once we have appointed Commissioners we are powerless to influence them, and therefore the views of the British members of the Commission are entirely their own, and not in any way inspired by the British Government. If you like to make a jocular reference, you could say that we have had a very tiresome example in a matter of great domestic interest with regard to broadcasting, where, once having let the Commission loose, it has made a report entirely unsatisfactory

to the Government.¹ This is what happens with respectable men once you appoint
them to an independent Commission.

---

¹ The Committee on Broadcasting (chaired by Sir Harry Pilkington) was appointed in July 1960 and
reported two years later. On the whole it praised the output of the BBC but criticised 'trivialisation' of
programmes on independent TV, thus rekindling the political controversy over the relative merits of
public service and commercial broadcasting. *Report of the Committee on Broadcasting*, Cmnd 1753
(1962).

128   PREM 11/3867   4 July 1962
[Resumption of talks with the Tunku]: outward telegram no 642 from
Mr Sandys to Sir G Tory, enclosing Mr Macmillan's reply to the
Tunku's message (document 125)

Please deliver following reply to Tunku from Mr. Macmillan. *Begins*.

I have just received your message and I feel that there is some misunderstanding.
We both agreed that it would be a good thing to have an independent Commission to
ascertain the views of the Borneo territories and make recommendations.

2.   There are always dangers in these independent Commissions for the very
reason that they are independent and I can assure you that I have had many examples
of this. I regard the situation to be as follows: both of us are anxious to get Greater
Malaysia created as soon as possible and agree that there should be a transfer of
Sovereignty to the new Federal State. There will be of course, as in every Federation,
problems as to the respective rights and duties of the central Government and of the
local governments. But these are matters for settlement between us.

3.   The British Government has not the slightest desire to maintain its authority
during the transitional period over the Borneo territories. We are not of course in
any way bound by the recommendations of the Commission or of any of its members.
I hope, therefore, that you will come to London this month as planned in the full
knowledge that we will be completely open for free discussion on all the points and
any proposals which you may wish to make with a view to an early settlement which
I believe to be equally in the interests of your Government and ours. *Ends*.

129   CAB 134/2370, OP(62)7   10 July 1962
'Discussions with the prime minister of the Federation of Malaya on
Greater Malaysia. Report by the chairman of the Official Committee':
report from Sir S Garner for the Cabinet Oversea Policy Committee.
Appendices: A–E

[This paper offered answers to questions raised in the officials' interim report of 2 July
(see 124). As regards the vexed issue of transitional arrangements, the officials suggested
five alternative models: 1) 'Cobbold's confidential letter' (see 121); 2) 'Sudan type'; 3)
'special council scheme'; 4) 'local head of state and British chief executive'; 5) 'the
Malayan proposals'. In his brief for the prime minister, Brook ruled out the first on the
ground that the Tunku would reject it and that it would in any case give Britain 'the worst
of both worlds', ie responsibility for the internal administration of the Borneo territories
after they had joined the Federation. He also advised against the fourth model which was

a compromise that would satisfy neither the Malayan government nor the people of Borneo and would be unlikely to attract expatriate officers. Of the five alternatives, Brook preferred the third ('special council scheme') which he saw as an improved variant of the 'Sudan type'. In their report the officials themselves raised objections to the last option ('the Malayan proposals'), but Brook felt that one tactic in the negotiations might be to start with these proposals with the intention of bringing them more closely into line with British aims. Another ploy would be to build on the Tunku's known acceptance of the need to retain expatriate officers for the transitional period, by making their employment more palatable both to Kuala Lumpur and to the expatriates themselves. The Oversea Policy Committee, which considered the options on 12 July, felt that the order of preference declined from the first to the fifth scheme and that the British side should argue the case downwards from as high up the list as possible, though it accepted that it was 'unlikely that we should achieve anything better than Arrangement 3' (see 130). In his brief Brook also drew Macmillan's attention to the importance of consulting the local legislatures in order 'to avoid giving any public impression that the United Kingdom and Malayan Governments intend to force North Borneo and Sarawak into the new Federation willy-nilly' (Brook to Macmillan, 12 July 1962, PREM 11/3868).]

Introduction

1.   The aim of the discussions is to reach agreement in principle on the creation of a new Federation of Malaysia, including the territories of North Borneo and Sarawak, with a view to a joint declaration by the British and Malayan Governments.

2.   Thereafter, before the new Federation can be established, there will be much consequential work to be done, including securing the agreement of the Legislatures of North Borneo and Sarawak and working out detailed constitutional proposals in joint working parties and inter-governmental conferences. Legislation will also be required both here and in Malaya; and we estimate that, with the best will in the world, these processes will require a year from now before the new Federation can come into being.

3.   We start with the following advantages in seeking to reach agreement in principle:—

(a) Both Governments are committed to the concept of Greater Malaysia and both have strong reasons for wishing to bring it about.

(b) The Cobbold Commission have unanimously reported in its favour.

(c) On appropriate conditions there would be majority support for it in North Borneo and Sarawak.

4.   But the application of the principle is difficult:—

(a) On the one hand, the Tunku will insist that the United Kingdom must from the outset not retain power in the two territories; otherwise he will lose face.

(b) On the other hand, we have a duty to see that the interests of the peoples of the two territories are safeguarded; and we are convinced that this can be achieved only if effective administrations are maintained in them, and that this requires the retention during the first few years of a substantial body of British officers.

5.   The major points to put to the Malayan Government are:—

(i) We are determined to make a success of Greater Malaysia.

(ii) We have no desire whatever to retain any authority on the part of the British Government after the transfer of sovereignty.

(iii) But in both our interests, and to ensure future stability in the territories, it is essential that the transfer takes place in an orderly fashion with the consent of the people.

(iv) It is agreed on all sides that to achieve this expatriate officers must remain.

(v) We are anxious to play our part but must look to the Tunku to help create an atmosphere and provide conditions under which expatriate officers will be willing to remain.

(vi) In particular, we want to avoid having to offer expatriate officers an option to retire with compensation, since past experience shows that this would lead to the departure of a large number (possibly more than 50 per cent).

Transitional arrangements

6. The Cobbold Commission unanimously recommend early transfer of sovereignty (i.e., within twelve months). This means that The Queen under Act of Parliament would relinquish sovereignty over the two territories to the new Federation of Malaysia, and they would accordingly cease to be part of Her Majesty's dominions.

7. As stated above, we need to preserve stable government in North Borneo and Sarawak while quickly bringing on the inhabitants to a state of self-government in accordance with previous assurances to the peoples; and to ensure this we need the continued presence of the majority of the expatriate civil servants. What we seek is an arrangement whereby, after sovereignty has been transferred and during the transitional period, there is an administration which can exercise real control over the internal government and of such a nature that expatriate civil servants can be expected to serve without being given the right to retire immediately on compensation. The problem is how to secure this in a way which the Prime Minister of Malaya, Tunku Abdul Rahman, can be persuaded to accept and which will prevent friction between the British Government and the Government of the new Federation.

8. We examine below a number of alternative constitutional arrangements. All of them start from the assumption that sovereignty has been transferred and that the new Federal Government will have full control of defence, external affairs and at least the 'anti-subversion' aspects of internal security.

Arrangement 1 (Cobbold's confidential letter)

9. Lord Cobbold's proposal in his confidential letter to the two Prime Ministers is that the territories should be ceded to the new Federation subject to agreement that powers other than those for external affairs, defence and the anti-subversive aspects of internal security continue for some years to be exercised in the territories by the British Government.[1] At the outset the Governors would exercise the same powers as at present but changes leading up to full self-government in State matters would be introduced as quickly as possible. There would also be a gradual transfer back to the centre of Federal subjects by agreement.

Comment. This course would most effectively enable us to resist any claim from the expatriate staff to retire with compensation, but it is ruled out because we know that it would be unacceptable to the Malayan Government and would in any case be inconsistent with the assurance which has been given to the Tunku that the British Government have no desire to maintain their authority during the transitional period.

---

[1] See 119.

Arrangement 2 ('Sudan Type')[2]

10.   This is broadly the scheme recommended by the British members of the Cobbold Commission in the Report itself—although it is clear from the confidential letters that they would prefer Arrangement 1. Under such a scheme the Heads of State of the two territories would be appointed by the Agong (Federal Head of State). By agreement they would be the present Governors and for the rest of the transitional period any successor would be appointed on the nomination of the British Government. The Federation would at the outset delegate to the States (not to the British Government) Federal powers and functions other than for the three subjects excluded under Arrangement 1. Changes leading up to full self-government in State matters would be introduced as quickly as possible and there would be a gradual transfer back to the centre of Federal subjects. Under this scheme the Governors would be responsible neither to the Federal Government nor to the British Government, except that in relation to conditions of service for expatriate officers they would be under the ultimate authority of the British Government.

Comment. This course would leave the Governors in an exposed position but it would still enable us to resist any claim from the expatriate officers to retire with compensation. Nevertheless, it is unlikely to be acceptable to the Tunku because it provides for the sharing of jurisdiction for the States between the Federal Government and independent British Governors.

Arrangement 3 (Special Council Scheme)

11.   It would be possible to mitigate the independence of the Governors' position in Arrangement 2 by the creation of a Special Council. The Federation would delegate to the States at the outset Federal powers and functions as under Arrangement 2. The Governors, as at present, would at the outset have full discretion over the whole field though in practice they would increasingly act in accordance with the advice of their Executive Councils. Changes leading up to full internal self-government would be introduced as quickly as possible but up to that stage the Governors would still have reserve powers. A special Council would, however, be set up, to be presided over by the Governor and consisting of, say, four members—perhaps two nominated by the Federation and two by the Governor himself (possibly, one being the leading local politician and the other the Chief Secretary). If, while he still had discretion over the whole field, the Governor wished to act against the advice of his Executive Council, or in later stages wished to exercise his reserve powers, he would be able to do so only if the Special Council agreed. The Public Service would, however, remain his personal responsibility subject, as under Arrangement 2, to the ultimate authority of the British Government. The Special Council would drop out at the end of the transitional period.

Comment. The practical difficulties of such a complicated arrangement are obvious but it might help to make the retention during the transitional period of the British Governor and the delegation of Federal powers to the States slightly less

---

[2] Sudan had been administered as an Anglo–Egyptian condominium from 1899 to the end of 1955. As Sudan's advance to self-government had accelerated in the early 1950s British officials attempted to prevent the sacrifice of Sudanese interests for the appeasement of Egypt and also to provide the south with constitutional safeguards against northern domination by allowing for the retention of British administrative staff later than elsewhere in the Sudan. See Douglas H Johnson, ed, *BDEE: Sudan*.

difficult for the Tunku. The advantage from our point of view is that it would still, we think, be possible to avoid allowing retirement with compensation.

Arrangement 4 (Local Head of State and British Chief Executive)

12.   Under this Arrangement there would be a local Head of State appointed by the Agong with the agreement of the British Government, who would have the functions of a Constitutional Monarch. The Federation would at the outset delegate to the States Federal powers and functions as under Arrangement 2. The effective head of the administration would be a Chief Executive who would be a British officer appointed by the local Head of State on the nomination of the British Government. The Public Service would be his personal responsibility, subject, as under Arrangement 2, to the ultimate authority of the British Government. The Head of State would act in accordance with the advice of the Executive Council except where that advice differed from that of the Chief Executive, in which case he would act in accordance with the advice of the latter. The Chief Executive would preside in Executive Council. As and when a Ministerial system was introduced, the Chief Executive's power to advise the Head of State contrary to the views of the Executive Council would be progressively restricted. A further variant would be to introduce a Special Council as in Arrangement 3, to which the Chief Executive would have to refer in the event of a difference of view between himself and his Executive Council.

Comment. This proposal should dispose of some of the Malayan objections but it would not be attractive politically in the States, where the embryo political leaders, while willing enough to be guided by a Governor seen to be the top man, would not relish a position of inferiority to a Chief Executive. Further, the Colonial Office, the Department of Technical Co-operation and the Governors all feel strongly that the change in the circumstances would be so great that expatriate officers would have to be given the right to go with compensation.

Arrangement 5 ('The Malayan Proposals')

13.   Under the Malayan proposals the Governor would be a constitutional ruler and he would not be British (although this is not explicitly stated either in the Cobbold Report or in the accompanying letters). He would appoint a local Chief Minister who had the confidence of the Legislature, and would act on his advice. The Central Government, having been legally and constitutionally vested with the Federal powers simultaneously with the transfer of sovereignty, should immediately delegate to the Chief Minister the exercise of as many executive functions as might be necessary for the maintenance of good administration. What the Malayans have in mind on this point is not fully clear. The administration would function under a State Secretary subordinate to the Chief Minister, and this officer would be the present British Chief Secretary.

Comment. This is the proposal which the Tunku is likely to press since it is the minimum which clearly puts undivided jurisdiction in Malayan hands. On the other hand the objections to this arrangement are:—

(i) The Territories are not yet ready for a Ministerial system of this kind.
(ii) The sudden transfer and retention of power in Kuala Lumpur would be resented.

(iii) It would be a major change in policy for the British Government to refuse to expatriate officers the right to go with compensation.

Public Service

14.   The British Government are committed by Col. 306[3] to the principle that when the Secretary of State for the Colonies ceases to have responsibility for a Public Service overseas, pensionable officers should be entitled to retire with compensation for a broken career. With the transfer of sovereignty, the responsibility of the British Government in any form would normally cease and the right to retire with compensation would therefore follow.

15.   But if this right is given, experience shows that, however carefully a compensation scheme is framed to minimise the inducement to go, at least one-third of the entitled officers will leave within a year; and in North Borneo and Sarawak we are advised it might be as many as 50 per cent—and in the vital 35 to 40 age group, possibly even higher. Many of them, particularly the administrative and police officers, could not effectively be replaced.

16.   It may be thought strange that, of a devoted Service, so large a proportion should be ready to leave, but the drawbacks of staying are from the officers' point of view great. None but the oldest of them can see the prospect of completing their careers in the territories; they probably have growing family responsibilities and feel that they must be assured of an income for the rest of their working lives; and so they wish to start off in a new career as soon as they can before it is too late. Moreover, if they stay on they fear that they will be subjected to pressure to do things against their conscience. The conclusion is inescapable that if officers have the right to retire at the outset with compensation, the whole effectiveness of the administration will be in danger.

17.   How then, in order to meet the need to retain expatriate officers, can we devise arrangements which will not necessitate giving them the right to immediate retirement with compensation? It must be remembered that any scheme proposed must be one which officers will accept and work: otherwise it will fail in its purpose. Much will depend on whether they consider that the constitutional arrangements proposed are fair to the people of the territories. We have explored three possible lines of action which, singly or in combination, might meet the case:—

(i) A satisfactory constitutional arrangement.

(ii) An agreement with the new Federation or with the State Governments guaranteeing their terms of service.

(iii) The British Government might take these officers into their service and second them to the Federation or to the State Governments.

18.   We have covered (i) in the paragraphs above on constitutional arrangements.

19.   As regards (ii), the British Government are already committed to the protection of conditions of service of all officers in Her Majesty's Overseas Civil Service at the time of self-government, by a Public Officers Agreement. Such an Agreement in this case would not, therefore, be anything new. In the past the British

---

[3] Col No 306, *Reorganisation of the Colonial Service*, 1954, provided for the creation of HMOCS (Her Majesty's Oversea Civil Service), cf 122, note.

Government have held that such agreements are sufficient only if accompanied by the right to retire with compensation, because, although terms of service are thereby protected, officers are still exposed to the risk of being required to perform duties which they cannot conscientiously carry out. These considerations apply with particular force in the Borneo territories, where overseas officers fill almost all the senior posts and bear the brunt of administration. Even if an agreement were concluded with the new Federation in this case, the Colonial Office and the Department of Technical Co-operation feel that it would still be essential to grant the right to retire with compensation if the nature of the constitutional arrangements were such as to involve the transfer of the officers to, in effect, another government. Both Departments fear that if, contrary to past policy, the right to retire with compensation were to be withheld in these circumstances, the confidence of the Overseas Service generally in the British Government would be severely shaken and morale in the Borneo territories would be broken.

20.   (iii) above has the advantage, by bringing officers directly under the British Government for the payment of salary and pensions and for other terms of service, of appearing to give them additional protection. On the other hand, it leaves the officers as exposed as under (ii) to being made the servants of another government whose policies they might not be able conscientiously to carry out. Moreover, the question whether officers taken directly into the service of the British Government in this way should be granted compensation at any stage has still to be considered. There would be strong objection in the Overseas Service to being brought under such a scheme without the option of retirement with compensation. (iii) has the additional disadvantage that the British Government would be blamed for any shortcomings in the discharge of the officers' duties. Any appeal by the officers would put the British Government in the position of arbiter on local policy.

21.   Our objective in the talks with the Tunku must be to secure constitutional arrangements under which we are satisfied that there is no need to offer the right to retire with compensation. (This would be possible under Arrangement 2 and, perhaps, Arrangement 3: the Colonial Office and the Department of Technical Co-operation do not think that it would be possible under Arrangement 4).

22.   If arrangements were agreed under which the offer to retire with compensation would have to be given there are a number of steps which could be taken to encourage British officers to remain. Among these are:—

(i) Persuasion by the British Government—e.g., on the occasion of a Ministerial visit.
(ii) Creation of a better atmosphere by the Tunku in addition to any Governmental agreement.
(iii) Financial inducements.
(iv) The form of the compensation scheme.

23.   The British High Commissioner in Kuala Lumpur believes that Arrangement 5 is the one which the Tunku is likely to press. The Tunku has said that it would be politically impossible for him to accept any arrangements which placed effective control in the hands of a British officer even for a limited period, or would be different in kind from the standard pattern for the existing Malayan States. The Tunku believes that more expatriate officers would stay than we appear to think; and in any case he also believes that he could recruit enough volunteers from among

ex-officers of the Malayan Civil Service to fill any significant gaps in the administration. His attitude is based upon his own assessment that anything short of Arrangement 5 would weaken his political position to a point at which Malaya's interests would be better served without Malaysia. He is also certain (as is Mr. Lee), that failing Malaysia, Singapore will in a few months' time be lost to a Communist-controlled government, with which the Tunku would not accept merger and which, it is known, would not want merger on terms acceptable to him. The Causeway would then be closed and Singapore sealed off.

Other matters

24. We think that, subject to agreement on satisfactory arrangements for the transitional period, Ministers can generally accept those recommendations of the Cobbold Commission which are unanimous, although a number of these will require detailed study by working parties or other means before final agreement can be reached upon the exact form of the new Federation. Meanwhile, we make the following comments upon some of the more important of these matters:—

(a) *Citizenship*

The Prime Minister of Singapore, Mr. Lee Kwan Yew, is understood to be writing to the Colonial Secretary seeking his support in representations to the Tunku, to the effect that the arrangements for citizenship in relation to North Borneo and Sarawak should not be more generous than those already worked out for Singapore. But even the unanimous recommendations of the Cobbold Commission will in any case come under criticism in North Borneo and Sarawak, and we therefore recommend that, should it be decided to try and meet Mr. Lee's wishes in relation to citizenship, this should not be done by varying the recommendations of the Cobbold Commission to the disadvantage of North Borneo and Sarawak.

(b) *Finance and development*

We do not think that Ministers need engage in detailed discussion with the Tunku on matters relating to finance and development but we suggest that he should be told that fiscal and financial arrangements relating to North Borneo and Sarawak will need a great deal of further elaboration by a working party or parties: some independent examination may even be called for. He should in our view also be told that it will be necessary for the British and Malayan Governments at an early date to examine between themselves the joint planning and co-ordination of development which will undoubtedly be required both before and after the Federation of Malaysia is established.

(c) *Courts*

We suggest that Ministers should accept the two unanimous recommendations of the Cobbold Commission together with one of the recommendations by the Malayan members. These three recommendations are:—

(i) There should be a Federal Supreme Court having appellate jurisdiction throughout the Federation.

(ii) There should be a separate High Court for the Borneo territories from which appeals would lie to the Federal Supreme Court.

(iii) The Federal Supreme Court should have exclusive original jurisdiction in cases between States or between a State and the Central Government.

We further suggest that Ministers should inform the Tunku that they would like to see effect given to these recommendations from the date of the establishment of the Federation of Malaysia but that there are many other matters which will require further examination by a working party before that date.

(d)   *Miscellaneous Public Service matters*

Various matters in this category will require examination by a working party before the Federation of Malaysia is established but we do not think that, beyond making that point, Ministers need raise any of them in discussion with the Tunku.

(e)   *Education*

We recommend that Ministers should remind the Tunku that this subject closely engages the concern of every parent in North Borneo and Sarawak and that there will be strong pressure for a measure of local autonomy. Apart from this, we do not think that Ministers need go into the matter with the Tunku, although he should again be told that it requires examination by a working party before the Federation of Malaysia comes into being.

(f)   *Language*

The question of national and official language is an emotional matter in North Borneo and Sarawak, and we recommend that Ministers should not enter into any commitment with the Tunku before the peoples of the territories have had a further opportunity of expressing themselves through their legislatures. Subject to this important proviso, we believe that it should be possible to accept Malay as the national language, provided that, as recommended by the Chairman and British members of the Cobbold Commission, English remains one of the official languages unless or until the State legislatures decide otherwise. The matter of an official language has practical importance in relation to the language of laws and other official documents, the language of debates in the legislatures and the language of proceedings in the Courts. The retention of English as an official language has a bearing on education, and the Chairman and British members of the Cobbold Commission have stressed the importance of maintaining existing policies regarding the use of English as a medium of instruction.

Religion

25.   One important subject on which agreement was not reached by the Cobbold Commission is religion. This is a highly emotional issue in North Borneo and Sarawak and a note on the subject is at Appendix A to this Report. We recommend that Ministers should urge the Tunku to accept the conclusions in paragraph 6 of that note.

General Matters not covered by the Cobbold Report

26.   We make the following comments upon a number of these matters:—

(a)   *Entry of Brunei and Singapore into the Federation of Malaysia*

The terms of Singapore's entry into the Federation of Malaysia have already been agreed between the Governments of Singapore and the Federation of Malaya, but negotiations for the entry of Brunei have not yet begun between the Sultan of Brunei and the Malayan Government. We recommend that Ministers should tell the Tunku that it will be necessary at a later stage to ensure that North Borneo and Sarawak enter the new Federation on terms generally not less favourable than those agreed for Brunei.

(b)   *Indonesian and Philippine claims to part of North Borneo*

We recommend that Ministers should raise these questions with the Tunku and in so doing take the line indicated in paragraph 7 of the note on this subject at Appendix B to this Report.

(c)   *Internal Security in Singapore before the state's merger with Malaya*

A note on this subject is at Appendix C to this Report. If the Tunku raises the matter, we recommend that Ministers should take the line set out in paragraph 9 of that note.

(d)   *Defence aspects*

We do not think that Ministers need raise any defence points during discussions with the Tunku of the Cobbold Commission's recommendations, but a note on the defence aspects of the problem is at Appendix D to this Report and the Minister of Defence will no doubt want to discuss with Malayan Ministers the progress of the joint defence talks which have been going on in Kuala Lumpur. In so doing he might in particular refer to the question of the level of British forces to be retained in Malaysia (paragraphs 2 to 4 of the attached note) and to the position regarding the use of British forces on active internal security operations in Singapore after the formation of the Federation of Malaysia (paragraphs 5 to 7 of the attached note).

(e)   *Situation in South East Asia*

In case Ministers should have occasion to discuss this subject generally with the Tunku a note upon it is attached at Appendix E to this Report.

Conclusions

27.   The precise picture can emerge only in the course of negotiations, and Ministers will wish to decide on the tactics to be employed.

28.   The crux of the problem is the need to retain the expatriate officers and to devise arrangements which will ensure this. The Tunku does not yet appreciate either the need or the extent of the difficulties and he will need a good deal of convincing.

29.   Although Arrangement 2 would be inconsistent with everything that the Tunku has so far said, there is something to be said at least for starting with this. It is not necessary to contemplate this Arrangement lasting for the whole transitional period. We could suggest that it should be limited to three years, two years or, in the last resort, even one year from the establishment of the new Federation in order to ensure smooth transition before passing over to one of the other Arrangements.

30.   It should be brought home to the Tunku, that if he insists on something which goes beyond Arrangement 3, this at once raises the problem of the need for us to offer expatriate officers the option of retirement with compensation. In that case we must reckon with the possibility that half of them would go. This would be a serious matter for all of us, which we must seek to avoid. If, therefore, we have to offer the option of retiring with compensation, we must do all that we can to encourage officers to stay, both by the terms of the compensation scheme and,

perhaps, even more by constitutional arrangements which they will think fair to the people. If the atmosphere is right, then there will be a much better chance of many staying on. We are entitled to look to the Tunku to make some concessions in order to reach a reasonable compromise which will ensure that the Greater Malaysia project is successfully launched.

Appendix A to 129: Religion

Introduction

There was a difference of opinion in the Cobbold Commission on this subject. The relevant paragraph of the Report is 148(e).

2.   The Chairman and British members:—

(i) *Recommend* that the State constitution of each of the Borneo territories should contain a provision to the effect that there shall be 'complete religious freedom as to worship, education and propagation'.

(ii) *Consider* that it is for the Borneo territories to decide for themselves, once they have fully elected representative bodies, whether the provisions of the existing Federal constitution that Islam is the national religion and that certain public expenditure may be incurred for the maintenance of Muslim institutions or instruction in the Muslim religion should extend to the Borneo territories.

(iii) *Recommend* that these provisions should not extend to the Borneo territories in the meantime.

3.   The Malayan members:—

(i) *Recommend* that Islam should be the national religion of the new Federation (thereby implying that clause (1) of Article 3 of the existing Federal constitution should extend to the Borneo territories as well as to the other parts of the Federation).

(ii) *Without making any recommendation*, direct attention to the fact that under the present Federal constitution certain public expenditure may be incurred for Islamic purposes, and that this may be considered objectionable in certain quarters so far as the Borneo territories are concerned.

4.   The relevant Articles of the existing Federal constitution are 3, 11 and 12.

Article 3

5.   The first part of clause (1) provides that Islam is the religion of the Federation. Clause (2) relates to the States of Muslim Rulers and is therefore irrelevant to the Borneo territories. Clause (3) requires the constitutions of the States of Malacca and Penang to confer the position of Head of the Muslim Religion in each of those States on the Yang di-Pertuan Agong.

6.   It does not appear that clause (1)—or indeed the Article as a whole—has any practical effect in constitutional terms except to set the background for the other provisions of the constitution which do give certain practical advantages to the Muslim religion. It also provides justification for the inclusion in the Yang di-Pertuan Agong's oath (Fourth Schedule to the constitution) of an undertaking to protect the Muslim religion.

7. The Malayan members would leave clause (1) unqualified so that it would extend to the Borneo territories, and would presumably also wish to see clause (3) expressly applied to those territories. The Chairman and British members consider that whether Islam should be the national religion of the Borneo territories is a matter for the territories themselves to decide when they have fully elected institutions. They consequently recommend that clause (1) should not apply in relation to the Borneo territories. It is not clear whether this recommendation also extends to clause (3). It would be possible to provide that clause (1) shall not apply in relation to the Borneo territories. This would, of course, look rather odd, for clause (1) would then in effect provide that Islam shall be the religion of part of the Federation—a rather untidy proposition which might be thought not to be entirely consistent with the terms of the oath of the Yang di-Pertuan Agong. Whether clause (1) does or does not apply to the Borneo territories makes no practical difference in constitutional terms to the inhabitants of the territories. If clause (1) were not applied to the territories it would be difficult to justify the application to them of Article 11(4) and, perhaps, the second half of Article 12(2), which are referred to below, but they could be excepted from the application of these last two provisions even though clause (1) of Article 3 did apply to them. Clause (3) of Article 3 could be applied to the Borneo territories even if clause (1) were not, and the Muslims of North Borneo and Sarawak might wish to see the Yang di-Pertuan Agong constitutionally recognised as Head of the Muslim Religion in their States.

Article 11

8. Clause (1) contains a general guarantee of the right to profess, practise and propagate one's religion. This is qualified by clause (4), which provides that a State law may control or restrict the propagation of any religious doctrine or belief among Muslims, and clause (5), which stipulates that the Article does not authorise acts contrary to any general law relating to public order, public health or morality.

9. The guarantee in clause (1) is in terms which are binding upon the authorities of a State as well as the Federal authorities. Consequently, there is no need in law to repeat this guarantee in the constitution of a State as the Chairman and the British members recommend. It might, however, be politically desirable to include such a guarantee in the State constitutions of the Borneo territories even though, as a provision of a State constitution, it would not be binding upon the Federal authorities.

10. Clause (4) of Article 11 could scarcely operate to the prejudice of non-Muslims in States such as the Borneo territories, where Muslims did not command a majority in the legislature. Nevertheless, the clause would in theory allow Muslims to be treated as a special case under the law of the Borneo territories: this would give offence locally and it would be quite easy to provide that the clause shall not apply in relation to the Borneo territories.

Article 12

11. The general effect of this Article is to prohibit discrimination in the field of education and religious instruction. The provision that is directly relevant to the recommendation of the Commission is the second half of clause (2) which, as an exception to the general proposition that there shall be no discrimination on ground only of religion in any law relating to institutions for the education of children,

permits Federal law to provide special financial aid for the establishment or maintenance of Muslim institutions or instruction in the Muslim religion of persons professing that religion. Such aid would have to come out of Federal funds since Federal law could not make provision for the appropriation of State funds. There is thus no question of the revenues of a State itself being used in a discriminatory way under this provision. Nor, in view of Article 11(2), could the provision be invoked to justify the application to non-Muslims of any special Federal tax designed to support Muslim institutions or instruction in the Muslim religion. Nevertheless, the provision would permit special allocations to be made for those purposes out of the general revenues of the Federation; and since the Federal revenues of Malaysia would in part be derived from the Borneo territories, its application in relation to the Borneo territories might be considered objectionable, as the Malay members of the Commission themselves recognise. The Chairman and British members recommend that the provision should not apply in relation to the Borneo territories. There would appear to be two ways of dealing with the point. Article 12(2) could be amended so that the provision in question did not apply in relation to Muslim institutions established in, or Muslim religious instruction given in, North Borneo and Sarawak. If this were done, then Federal law could not provide special financial aid for Muslim institutions or instruction in the Muslim religion in the two territories in excess of anything which it provided for non-Muslim institutions or instruction in other religions there. It would still, however, be open to the Federal Legislature to appropriate Federal revenues, which had been derived from the Borneo territories, in aid of Muslim institutions elsewhere in Malaysia. The alternative way of dealing with the matter, which would obviate this objection, would be to amend Article 12(2) in such a way as to remove from the Federal Legislature the power to give special financial aid to Muslim institutions and instruction in the Muslim religion, whether in the Borneo territories, or elsewhere, and to vest such a power in State Legislatures.

Conclusions

12.   The possible application to North Borneo and Sarawak of the provisions of the Federal constitution relating to Islam is a highly emotional issue with non-Muslims in those territories. It is suggested that the following recommendations should be made to Ministers:—

(i) The provision of Article 3(1) of the Federal constitution that Islam is the religion of the Federation should not extend to North Borneo and Sarawak.

(ii) References to North Borneo and Sarawak should be included in Article 3(3) of the Federal constitution so that the constitutions of each of those States would be required to confer on the Yang di-Pertuan Agong the position of Head of the Muslim religion in the State.

(iii) Article 11(4) of the Federal constitution, which permits a State law to control or restrict the propagation of any religious doctrine or belief among persons professing the Muslim religion, should not apply to State laws of North Borneo or Sarawak.

(iv) The State constitutions of North Borneo and Sarawak should contain guarantees of religious freedom.

(v) Article 12(2) of the Federal constitution should be amended by removing from the Federal Legislature the power to provide special financial aid for Muslim institutions and instruction in the Muslim religion and transferring this power to State Legislatures.

Appendix B to 129: Indonesian and Philippine claims to the Borneo Territories

In the long run the most likely alternative to Greater Malaysia is Greater Indonesia. No Asian Government would consider that either independence or continued Colonial rule could offer a lasting third choice for the Borneo territories in their present form. If these are not absorbed by Malaysia, they are likely to be swallowed up, sooner or later, by Indonesia or the Philippines or, just possibly, to be turned into outposts of Communist China.

2.   Indonesia, as the immediate neighbour of the Borneo territories, offers by far the most serious potential challenge to Malaysia. Indonesia's resources and her population of 90 million greatly exceed those of the Philippines; and the Indonesians have closer affinities (religious, racial, etc.) with the people of the Borneo territories. So far, however, Indonesia has made no official claim, though one of the politicians who, while out of office advocated the 'liberation' of the British Borneo territories, is now a member of the Indonesian Government. Apart from tactical considerations arising out of the Indonesian claim to New Guinea, the main reason for this abstention is probably Indonesia's own political disunity. The fundamental conflict between the Javanese and non-Javanese races of Indonesia has produced a strong Federalist movement in Indonesia which, in a crisis, might develop in the direction of separatism. The Indonesian Government must accordingly realise that, in a head on clash with Malaysia, parts at least of the outer islands might find Kuala Lumpur quite as attractive as Djakarta. Although Indonesia's leaders can not welcome the creation of Malaysia, they are unlikely to interfere with the process or to advance claims to the Borneo territories until they feel their own internal position to be a good deal stronger than it is today. Indeed, they have denied any such intentions publicly. On the other hand, if the Indonesians come to regard Malaysia as unlikely to be achieved, they would find it difficult to leave the Philippines as the only challenger to British rule and would probably put forward a claim themselves. As the progress of the New Guinea dispute has shown, such a claim would be a serious menace.

3.   In itself the claim officially advanced by the Philippine Government in June, 1962, has little more than nuisance value. It has given rise to great resentment in North Borneo itself, where there is no public support for the Philippine claim. It concerns only that part of North Borneo originally under the sovereignty of the Sultan of Sulu, and the Philippine Government have not specifically demanded more than discussion on the status and sovereignty of North Borneo. Indeed, their intention is probably limited to extracting substantial financial compensation instead of the annual payments (5,300 Malayan dollars) made to the heirs of the Sultan of Sulu in respect of the original cession (or, as the Filipinos contend, lease). The Philippine Government may conceivably have the Indonesian danger at the back of their minds, but their main reason, apart from considerations of internal politics, for raising this issue now, is that they would find it much easier to bring pressure to bear on the British Government as a 'Colonialist' power, than on a purely Asian Malaysian

Government. Not only would the Philippine Government themselves be reluctant to quarrel with the Malayans, but they would receive less sympathy from the Afro–Asian bloc, the United Nations and international opinion than they would in a straight forward (as they would represent it) anti-Colonialist issue. The Philippine Government must accordingly be expected to apply pressure in support of their claim during the coming months (perhaps even taking the issue to the United Nations or the International Court of Justice) and to maintain this as long as the British Government remain responsible for the Borneo territories. The longer it takes the British Government to divest themselves of such responsibility, the greater the risks, not only of damage to Anglo–Philippine relations, but also of arousing so much emotion in the Philippines that the Philippine Government will be unable, even if they so wished, to abandon their claim without obtaining satisfaction, even after the establishment of Malaysia. Moreover, the harder the Philippine Government press their claim, the more the Indonesian Government will be tempted to advance their own.

4.   Apart from an actual offer to buy them off (the only figure so far mentioned is the £10 million demanded in 1958 by the Filipino lawyer who originally fomented the present agitation) the only argument likely to influence the Philippine Government would be that their claim would be seriously embarrassing to the Government of Malaya, as potential inheritor of Her Majesty's Government's responsibilities in North Borneo. Unfortunately, the attitude of the Malayan Government, apart from an early and somewhat half-hearted attempt to dissuade the Philippine Government from putting forward the claim, has been unhelpful. On 27th June, for instance, the Tunku told the press that the Philippine claim was a matter between the British and Philippine Governments, in which Malaya was in no way involved. The claim would not, he said, affect the relationship between the A.S.A. countries (Association of South East Asia, to which Malaya, the Philippines and Thailand belong[4]). But, if the British Government asked A.S.A. to help find a solution, he would gladly consider this.

5.   If the Tunku's reference to assistance from A.S.A. implies mediation by that organisation, this would not be welcome. It would virtually mean mediation by Thailand (the only disinterested member) which would certainly favour the Philippines at British expense, and any influence the Malayans might be able to exert would not, for instance, prevent the Thais recommending some large British payment to the Philippines. The outcome might thus be much more unsatisfactory than that of direct bargaining with the Philippine Government.

6.   On the other hand, the Tunku is most unlikely to reverse his attitude now and to join us in whole-hearted opposition to the Philippine claim. Even if he did, the Philippine Government have by now committed themselves too far to be much influenced by such a belated conversion. The most we can expect from the Tunku is that he might exert a moderating influence on the Philippine Government and try to persuade them to proceed a little more discreetly. If the Philippine Government

---

[4] The Association of South-East Asia (ASA) was an experiment in regional co-operation between Malaya, the Philippines and Thailand. Established on 31 July 1961, ASA was intended to offer an alternative to SEATO. It foundered on the Philippines' claim to North Borneo and was superseded by the formation of ASEAN (Association of SE Asian Nations) in 1967. On the Philippines' claim, see 126, n 3.

made an outright demand for the annexation of North Borneo, the Tunku's attitude might change. The trouble is that the Tunku would probably like the dispute with the Philippines to come to a head as soon as possible. He wants it to be settled to the satisfaction of the Philippine Government before Greater Malaysia comes into being, so that he inherits North Borneo with a clean title unencumbered by prior claims. He may, therefore, at some stage, urge us to buy the Filipinos off.

Arguments for use with the Tunku

7.   If a decision is reached with the Tunku to go ahead with Malaysia at the forthcoming talks we are to have with him in London it is suggested Ministers take the opportunity of raising with him the following points:—

(a) The Malayan Government are better placed than anyone else to exercise a moderating influence on the Government of the Philippines over North Borneo.

(b) Without this, the Philippine Government are likely to work themselves and their public opinion into an inconveniently emotional attitude.

(c) If this happens, it would disturb North Borneo and increase Malayan problems after the establishment of Malaysia.

(d) It could also make it impossible for the Philippine Government to abandon the claim even after the establishment of Malaysia.

(e) It could also provoke the Indonesians into putting forward a much more dangerous claim of their own. For all these reasons it is as much in the interests of the Malayan Government as of the British Government that the Tunku should do what he can to induce the Philippine Government to adopt a more reasonable attitude.

(f) The British Government cannot possibly compromise their entire case (that sovereignty over North Borneo is settled and not open to dispute) by agreeing to open negotiations with the Philippines on this issue or accepting outside mediation.

Appendix C to 129: Internal security in Singapore before the state's merger with Malaysia

Under the present constitution of Singapore the maintenance of internal security is a matter for the Singapore Government; but the Internal Security Council, on which Malaya, Singapore and Britain are all represented, has power to take decisions which are then binding on the Singapore Government.

2.   There has for some time been a difference of opinion as to whether anything needs to be done to suppress the Communists and their sympathisers in Singapore, who are opposed to the merger of Singapore with Malaya on the terms which have been agreed between the Tunku and Mr. Lee. The focus of this opposition is the Barisan Socialis party and, in particular, its Secretary-General, Mr. Lim Chin Siong.

3.   The Malayan feeling is that the leaders of the Barisan Socialis party should be arrested and detained in advance of merger. This could, in their view, be put over to the Singapore public for what it is, action against Communists who are planning to take over Singapore by constitutional means in accordance with classic Chinese Communist doctrine. The Chinese of Singapore would then, they feel, climb on to

the Lee/Tunku bandwagon and merger would go through peaceably. The Tunku is reluctant to mark Malaysia's birth by action against the Barisan Socialis after merger. Lord Selkirk, on the other hand, as British Commissioner in Singapore, advises us that such action might have the very opposite effect to that for which the Malayans wish, by providing the opposition with opportunities to exploit the situation—e.g., by giving them the chance to pose as martyrs. On this view the better hope of achieving merger successfully probably lies in keeping down the local political temperature.

4.   Because of this disagreement, the Malayans have threatened to withdraw their representative from the Internal Security Council (paragraph 1 above). The effect of withdrawal would be to deprive the Council of its powers of decision; and the Chairman (Lord Selkirk) is not for the time being calling any meetings.

5.   An *ad hoc* committee of police and security officers was recently set up by the Malayan and Singapore Governments to examine and make recommendations for a phased plan of action against Communists and Communist sympathisers in Singapore before merger. (The British Government were invited to participate in the committee but declined on the grounds that its terms of reference prejudged the issue.) The committee has now recommended the following course of action:—

> *Phase 1* (action to be taken immediately)—Control of selected organs of the Press and restriction of political activity on the part of trade unions.

> *Phase 2* (action to be taken after the proposed referendum in Singapore* but before merger)—Searches of suspect organisations, detention of a short list of established Communists (in particular Mr. Lim Chin Siong) and restrictions upon the movements and activities of others.

These proposals have been accepted by the Malayan and Singapore Governments. A start has already been made with Phase 1 by way of pressure upon certain publications and banning of some meetings and processions.

6.   The proposed action lies within the Singapore Government's own field of responsibility, and in theory it might be possible for the British Government to allow it to be taken without their having to declare their own attitude. The Malayan and Singapore Governments, however, will probably try to associate the British Government with the responsibility for at any rate Phase 2 of the plan, perhaps through the medium of the Internal Security Council, and in practice it would be difficult to avoid sharing this responsibility. Even if we were to oppose the plan in the Internal Security Council, we should still be implicated in the public eye by reason of our membership of the Council.

7.   Although constitutionally the British Government's power to intervene in this matter is somewhat limited, we have the ultimate responsibility for Singapore up to the time of merger, and it is British troops which will in the last resort be needed to restore order if the situation gets out of hand. Also, it is to the British Government that any international criticism (e.g. in the International Labour Organisation) of the proposed action will be directed. Moreover, serious disturbances in Singapore might affect the ability of the British Government to discharge their defence commitments in South East Asia.

*The date of the referendum in Singapore is still undecided. It is expected to be during the next few months and, according to the latest report, may be as early as August.

8.   When Mr. Lee was in London in May[5] he was told by the Colonial Secretary, in discussion of this question, that 'we have broad backs and are not afraid to carry our share of the burden. I must, however, be convinced that the action taken will make things better and not worse'. After his return to Singapore, Mr. Lee, for reasons not apparent, deliberately gave the Tunku reason to understand that he had secured from Ministers here unqualified approval of the plan; but the record has since been put straight with the Tunku through the British High Commissioner, who has told him that it will be up to him in London to persuade British Ministers that, as both he and Mr. Lee believe, these measures will on balance be good for Singapore and Malaysia.

9.   The Tunku is expected to press the question while he is in London. If he does so, it is suggested that Ministers might take the following line:—

(a) We cannot ignore the possibility that the proposed repressive measures might exacerbate rather than improve the situation.

(b) We should accordingly still prefer to postpone a decision until nearer the time when it is suggested that the main action will be needed, viz., following the referendum in Singapore, when the situation may be clearer.

(c) Even then we should feel at liberty to disagree with the Tunku as long as we have the ultimate responsibility and Malaya is not unavoidably committed to taking over Singapore.

(d) Our hesitation is due to a genuine uncertainty as to whether what is proposed is the best way of handling the situation in Singapore, and not to any reluctance to share with the Malayan and Singapore Governments whatever unpopularity the measures may evoke.

Appendix D to 129: Defence aspects

General position

1.   The main defence aspects of the formation of Malaysia were covered at the meetings with Malayan Ministers in November, 1961. It was then agreed that the Malayan Defence Agreement and its annexes should be extended to all territories of the Federation of Malaysia, subject to the proviso that Britain should have the right to continue to maintain the Singapore bases and to make such use of these as Britain might consider necessary for the purpose of assisting in the defence of Malaysia, for Commonwealth defence and for the preservation of peace in South East Asia (Cmnd. 1563 Annex B).[6] Subsequently the Minister of Defence agreed with the Malayan Minister of Defence that a joint examination should be carried out in Malaya of the more detailed defence questions that would arise from merger between Malaya and Singapore. The report of the joint defence talks which have since taken place is now under examination in London. The agreement reached last November represents a very satisfactory arrangement and it is neither necessary nor desirable to reopen this question during the forthcoming talks. A number of minor points arising from the application of the Agreement to Singapore will have to be jointly examined shortly, but there are no issues of principle in the defence field to be settled at the forthcoming talks.

---

[5] He flew to London via meetings with Nehru (New Delhi), Nasser (Cairo) and Tito (Belgrade).
[6] Cmnd 1563 was the joint Anglo–Malayan statement issued after the London talks in Nov 1961, see 79–84.

Strength of British forces in Malaysia

2.   By assuming responsibility for internal security in Singapore the new Federation would in due course relieve Britain of a considerable responsibility, for which a number of major units of the British army (including Gurkhas) are at present stationed in Malaya and Singapore. To meet requirements other than internal security we plan to keep certain forces in the area. As a result of the joint examination in Malaya, proposals have been made for handing over internal security commitments in Singapore to the Federation Government, and these are now being studied in London.

3.   Following rumours in the local press about reductions in the Brigade of Gurkhas, the Malayan Minister of Defence asked Her Majesty's Government that no decision to remove forces from Malaya and Singapore should be taken without consultation with the Federation Government because of the needs of external defence which had yet to be examined. Ministers agreed that the Malayan Minister of Defence should be told that the subject might be discussed during the Malayan Prime Minister's visit. In the same reply it has also been confirmed that it is Her Majesty's Government's intention to have the question jointly examined on the spot, and that no reduction in the strength of British forces in the area would be made without consultation. Attention was also drawn in the reply to the Secretary of State for War's statement of 30th May explaining that no decision on the future of the Brigade of Gurkhas would be taken until next year.

4.   The Malayan views on force levels for external defence have yet to be considered through joint machinery for combined military planning. Proposals for this machinery have been agreed at the joint defence talks and are now under examination by both Governments. It will therefore be necessary at a suitable stage in the forthcoming talks for the Minister of Defence to reassure the Malayan Prime Minister that it is our intention to have external defence questions examined locally as soon as the necessary machinery has been set up, and in the light of such examination, to consult the Federation Government before withdrawing any forces no longer required for internal security commitments in Singapore.

British Assistance to Malaysia for internal security

5.   The agreed terms of reference for the joint defence talks referred to 'a phased plan for the assumption by the Federation Government of all internal security commitments in Singapore and the Borneo territories' taking into account the rate of build-up of the Federation armed forces. Britain normally regards internal security in an independent Commonwealth country as the responsibility of the Government concerned, and units of British forces would not normally be employed on internal security duties in a sovereign state. However, the report from the joint defence talks suggests that Britain should have a continuing commitment to help with internal security problems in Singapore until the end of 1964, by when the Federation would have built up adequate forces for internal security.

6.   We imagine that Malaysian Ministers would have to approve an actual request to call in British help and British Ministers would similarly require to be consulted. Until the report on the defence talks has been examined in detail by officials it will be difficult to weigh up at all accurately the implications of allowing British troops to be used after merger in active internal security operations. In order to meet commitments, more detailed plans would have to be considered for the part which British forces might have to play until Malaysian forces were able to assume all

commitments, and these plans would have to take into account the legal position as well as the possibility of not committing British forces, except in the last resort, to the more active roles such as operations in the streets of Singapore.

7. The Malayan Government are alive to these considerations. The Malayan Minister of Defence has already told our High Commissioner that his Government would be most reluctant for their own political reasons to call on British forces for active internal security operations, and would only do so in the direst emergency. They would however consider it necessary to be assured that our forces would in fact be available in those extreme circumstances. The Minister of Defence will no doubt wish to discuss this matter with his Malayan colleague.

Appendix E to 129: Situation in South East Asia

Laos
The formation of the Coalition Government and the resumption of the Geneva Conference[7] are very welcome, but they are only a beginning. It will be a long and difficult job to build up a genuinely neutral, independent and stable Laos. We hope the Tunku will do what he can to cultivate closer relations with the new Laotian Government. They could do with some friendly advice from an Asian Government of a more balanced and disinterested character than the immediate neighbours of Laos.

Vietnam
2. The situation in South Vietnam remains very difficult. The Tunku has already given valuable assistance over the despatch of the Thompson Mission to South Vietnam and by supplying arms, advice and training facilities.[8] We should welcome any further suggestions which he likes to put to us. The immediate problem is to help the Saigon Government to re-establish their authority themselves, and to defeat the insurrection organised from Hanoi, without the need for assistance from foreign combatant troops. Meanwhile, we do not think that international negotiations could possibly help, since South Vietnam would be at such a disadvantage in them until the military situation is restored. The success of the Geneva Conference on Laos offers no precedent for a similar conference on Vietnam.

New Guinea
3. The British Government are seriously concerned by the attitude of the Indonesian Government. Dutch acceptance of the Bunker formula[9] (which had been endorsed by the British Government and the United States Government, as well as by U Thant) does not seem to have satisfied them. The Indonesian demand for further

---

[7] On 23 July 1962 the Geneva Conference on Laos, which had convened in May the previous year, reached international agreement on the political unity and neutralisation of the country.
[8] This was the British Advisory Mission to South Vietnam, 1961–1965, under Robert Thompson.
[9] Ellsworth Bunker was a US diplomat acting as a UN moderator in the West Irian dispute; the Bunker formula called for the Netherlands to transfer West Irian to UN administration for a period of a maximum of two years during which the UN and Indonesia would test indigenous opinion and Indonesia might prepare for the assumption of control. It was on this basis that the dispute was resolved.

clarification suggests that they really want additional concessions. It may even be that President Sukarno does not really want a negotiated settlement, even on his own terms, but is intent on humiliating the Dutch militarily, so that they have to come to the conference table to sue for an armistice. This could create a very dangerous situation.

Association of South East Asia (A.S.A.)

4. The British Government welcomed the Tunku's initiative in founding this association of Malaya, the Philippines and Thailand last year. They would be glad to see it become the nucleus of a wider association of South East Asian states. The British Government have, however, deliberately avoided giving any public encouragements to such ideas. Overt Western sponsorship might, in their view, only frighten off such neutralist states as Burma. The British Government would welcome the Tunku's own ideas on the subject. Has he any plans for expansion? In particular, has he considered the idea of sounding out the new Burmese Government?[10]

---

[10] It was led by General Ne Win who overthrew the government of U Nu in a military coup in Mar 1962.

130 CAB 134/2370, OP(62)3rd meeting   12 July 1962
'Greater Malaysia': Cabinet Oversea Policy Committee minutes

[This meeting was attended by Macmillan (chair), Kilmuir, Home, Sandys, Watkinson, Maudling, and Anthony Barber (economic secretary, Treasury). The following senior civil servants were present: Brook, Garner and Martin. It may be wondered how much ministerial attention was paid to 'Greater Malaysia' at that afternoon's meeting since a major and clumsy Cabinet reshuffle was in the offing: the morning had seen what Macmillan's biographer has described as 'a thoroughly unhappy Cabinet' and by the next day, after the so-called 'night of the long knives', Macmillan had sacked one third of his Cabinet in 'an act of carnage unprecedented in British political history' (Alistair Horne, *Macmillan*, vol II, pp 343–348). As regards overseas responsibilities, Butler (who became deputy prime minister) was given charge of Central Africa, Thorneycroft succeeded Watkinson as minister of defence, and, as anticipated a few months earlier (see 98, note), Sandys took over the CO from Maudling (who replaced Selwyn Lloyd as chancellor of the Exchequer). Sandys was now secretary of state at both the CO and CRO, although the two departments remained separate until they combined as the Commonwealth Office in 1966.]

The Committee had before them a Note by the Secretaries (O.P. (62) 7) covering a Report by the Chairman of the Official Committee on Greater Malaysia[1] on the conduct of the forthcoming discussions with the Prime Minister of the Federation of Malaya, Tunku Abdul Rahman, about the proposed new Federation of Malaysia.

The Prime Minister said that during the transitional period following the establishment of the new Federation it would be necessary to preserve stable government in North Borneo and Sarawak while at the same time bringing the inhabitants to a stage at which they could themselves manage their own local affairs. It was generally accepted that this required the retention for a number of years of the bulk of the British expatriate officers now serving in the two territories; and the main question was how to reach agreement with the Tunku on arrangements which would

---

[1] See 129.

secure this without appearing to derogate from the sovereignty of the new Federation over North Borneo and Singapore.

Officials had examined five different possible arrangements. Arrangement 1, which had been proposed by Lord Cobbold, was clearly ruled out since under it the United Kingdom would retain direct authority in the Borneo territories: this, as he (the Prime Minister) had assured the Tunku, they did not desire to do. Arrangement 2, which had been proposed by the British members of the Cobbold Commission, copied the Sudan model. Although under it the Governors would not be responsible to the United Kingdom Government, the Tunku might not be willing to accept as Governors British officers who would not be responsible to the new Federal Government either. Arrangement 3 was a modification of Arrangement 2 whereby the independence of the Governors would be to some extent qualified. Arrangement 4 provided for a local Head of State but the effective head of the administration would remain a British officer, appointed on the nomination of the United Kingdom Government, who would retain personal responsibility for the public service. This would no doubt be more attractive to the Tunku in that the Head of State would be a Malaysian. Arrangement 5 was that proposed by the Malayan members of the Cobbold Commission and still further reduced the British element in the administration. From our point of view the order of preference was reversed. The less control we retained over his administration, the harder it would be to retain staff.

The Commonwealth Secretary said that the Prime Minister's preliminary talk with the Tunku would be of vital importance. In his view the aim of the talk should be to reassure the Tunku that we had no wish to retain British authority in the Territories, to seek broad agreement on the essential practical requirements of the situation, but not to determine in any detail how those requirements might be met. No concessions should be offered at this stage, and the main issue of the transitional arrangements should not be brought to the crunch until later in the discussions, when the outstanding points of lesser importance had been settled.

The Colonial Secretary said that it would be best to deal first with the long-term issues such as education and religion: it should then be easier to agree the transitional arrangements in the knowledge that Malaysia was attainable.

Transitional arrangements
In discussion of the five possible Arrangements for the transitional period which the Prime Minister had outlined, the general feeling of the Committee was as follows. Our order of preference declined from Arrangement 1 to Arrangement 5, and we should argue the case downwards from as high up the list as possible. Arrangement 1 was clearly ruled out. Arrangement 2 was very doubtful. It was in practice unlikely that we should achieve anything better than Arrangement 3, and even that might be difficult as it involved retention of British officers rather than the appointment of Malaysians as Governors and Heads of State in the two territories. If the Tunku proved adamant we might have to make our main stand on a determined effort to close for Arrangement 4: in that case, to have any hope at all (and it would in any case be slight) of avoiding the grant to expatriate officers of a right to retire with compensation, it would be essential to obtain firm agreement that the British Chief Executive would retain effective responsibility for the public service. We might in the end have no option but to negotiate on the basis of Arrangement 5. We could not accept it as it stood but it was, perhaps, capable of amendment to an acceptable form: for example, we might

insist—and there was precedent for it—that the first Chief Ministers should be British officers and that the initial delegation of Federal powers should include, as under the other proposed Arrangements, all powers other than those relating to external affairs, defence and the anti-subversive aspects of internal security. Finally, it might be possible to obtain agreement upon the division of the transitional period into an initial phase under one Arrangement and a later phase under another.

In further discussion the following were the main points made:—

Internal security

(a)   It might be possible to obtain some advantage from the Tunku's recent request that United Kingdom forces should in the last resort be available to help in an internal security role in Singapore or the Borneo territories between the establishment of Malaysia and the time (estimated at 1964) when his own local forces would have been built up sufficiently to undertake that role unaided. He might recognise that our agreement to this request would make it the more incumbent upon him to agree with us upon suitable transitional arrangements for the Borneo territories, although it would be unwise to link the two transitional periods directly together.

Public service

(b)   On the vital questions of the need, and the means, to retain expatriate officers, we had the advantage of knowing that the Tunku agreed with us on the need; and it should therefore be possible to persuade him to be reasonable about the means even though he was understood at present not to share our view of the likely scale on which expatriate officers would leave should it be necessary to grant them a right to retire with compensation, and to believe that he could in any case fill the gaps from other sources. The best approach would be to impress upon him with all possible force, first, the damaging consequences which we think would flow from a major exodus of expatriate officers, and second, our conviction that such an exodus would be difficult to avoid if a right to retire with compensation had to be granted. It might thus be possible to bring him to see the wisdom of generosity to North Borneo and Sarawak over such long-term matters as religion, education and language, both of which would have a vital influence upon the attitude of expatriate officers towards further service in the two territories.

(c)   Of the 700 or so expatriate officers in the two territories, some 300 really mattered, although the number holding key posts (mainly in the administrations and the police) was, of course, a good deal smaller. Professional officers might find it possible to stay on and could perhaps be replaced if they went: but the loss of administrative and police officers would be much likely and more damaging, and their replacement almost impossible. What weighed with them all was not merely their material interests in terms of conditions of service or career-prospects, but the nature of the work they would be called upon to undertake. They were afraid that they might be called upon to execute policies laid down by Malayans who had inadequate regard for the Borneo peoples and pursued courses of action inimical to the interests of those peoples. They also feared that they might become the unwilling instruments of nepotism and corruption.

(d)   One solution would be for the United Kingdom Government to take these expatriate officers into their employment and second them to the two Borneo Governments: this would not cost more than a compensation scheme.

(e)   In seeking any solution to the problem of retaining expatriate officers a factor of great importance would be consultation with their own Staff Associations: if we could secure a reasonable accommodation with the Tunku it should be possible through such consultations to ensure the retention of expatriate officers in satisfactory numbers whether or not it proved necessary to grant a right to retire with compensation—although it would, of course, be preferable by agreement to avoid that. Alternatively, it might be possible to work out an acceptably modified compensation scheme whereby, for example, a limited measure of compensation was granted to those who chose to retire early but proportionately larger amounts at a later date to any who agreed to serve on.

(f)   One difficulty was that compensation on the scale which had been paid elsewhere (it averaged £7,000) was a powerful inducement to retire; and if it were by any method increased as an inducement to serve on, a dangerous precedent would be set—in Kenya, for instance, where there would soon be an equally grave problem of the same kind, 16,000 officers were involved.

Local consultation

(g)   It would be necessary at a number of stages in the progress to the establishment of Malaysia to consult the Legislatures in North Borneo and Sarawak. This had an important bearing in two respects on the discussions with the Tunku. First, we must persuade him of the need (which he had dangerously overlooked in the past) to avoid making public statements suggesting that the United Kingdom and Malayan Governments already regarded the Malaysia project as a settled affair in relation to which only their views were significant; and second, we must make it clear in the statement to be published at the close of the discussions that any agreements which the two Governments might have reached about North Borneo and Sarawak, were subject to consultation with the local Legislatures.

Outstanding long-term issues

(h)   The recommendations of the Cobbold Commission on citizenship were unanimous and acceptable but there were several other long-term issues to be settled which to a greater or lesser degree aroused strong emotions in North Borneo and Sarawak. The most important of these were religion, education and language (especially in relation to education, since the Borneo territories set great store both upon education and upon English as the medium of instruction). Religion was a highly emotional issue as the majority of the Borneo peoples were not Muslims and disliked the idea of Islam as their national religion. On language the Cobbold Commission had made the useful suggestion that, if Malay were accepted as the national language, provision should be made for North Borneo and Sarawak to retain English as an official language for as long as they wanted. Generally, it was very desirable to persuade the Tunku of the solid material advantages to be gained for Malaysia by understanding of local feelings on all these matters in the two Borneo territories, and by corresponding magnanimity in the practical arrangements to be made in relation to them. Failure in these respects would be needlessly damaging to the prospects of Malaysia.

Summing up *the Prime Minister* said that in his first private talk with the Tunku he would begin by repeating that the United Kingdom Government were just as anxious as the Tunku to ensure that the proposed Federation of Malaysia came into being. He would then reiterate the assurance which he had already given to the Tunku that the United Kingdom Government had no desire after the establishment of the new Federation to retain over North Borneo and Sarawak either sovereignty or any direct authority. He would emphasise that the other matters which remained to be settled were practical questions to which the United Kingdom and Malayan Governments, sharing the same essential concern for the successful future of Malaysia, should be able in their forthcoming discussions to find answers acceptable both to themselves and to the peoples of the two Borneo territories.

As the Tunku himself had recognised, the retention of the largest possible number of the British expatriate officers—particularly administrative and police officers—now serving in the two Borneo territories was crucial, and this required that, during the transitional period, because the United Kingdom Government would no longer have any direct authority in North Borneo and Sarawak, the United Kingdom and Malayan Governments must agree upon arrangements calculated to encourage expatriate officers to remain in their posts. This heightened the need to work out terms for the entry of North Borneo and Sarawak into Malaysia which fully satisfied the special requirements of their peoples, particularly in such matters as religion, education and language, which were highly emotional issues in the two territories. Success in this would be a powerful inducement for the expatriate officers to remain at their posts.

Generally, he would in this talk enter into no new commitment to the Tunku and would not engage in argument about the precise arrangements for the transitional period.

He would conclude by seeking the Tunku's agreement that the right order of procedure would be to take, first, all those matters on which the recommendations of the Cobbold Commission were unanimous; second, the long-term issues which had not been agreed in the Cobbold Commission but must be settled; and finally, against the background of agreement upon the long-term arrangements, the arrangements to be made for the transitional period.

He would also take an opportunity at a suitable point in his talk with the Tunku to emphasise the need both for adequate consultation with the Legislatures in North Borneo and Sarawak and to avoid meanwhile giving any public impression that the United Kingdom and Malayan Governments intended to dragoon the two territories into Malaysia willy-nilly.

The Committee:—
(1) Took note of the Prime Minister's summing-up.
(2) Invited the Commonwealth Secretary, in consultation with the Colonial Secretary, to prepare, on the lines indicated by the Prime Minister, a draft programme for the main discussions which the Prime Minister could agree with the Tunku during their private talk.

131 CO 1030/1150, no 183   12 July 1962
[Political developments in Singapore since the Tunku's speech of 27 May 1961]: despatch from P B C Moore to Mr Maudling on the chances of Lee winning the battle for merger

[Moore was acting UK commissioner, Singapore, in place of Selkirk at this time. By the time the despatch reached the CO, Sandys had replaced Maudling as secretary of state.

This document was later printed for confidential circulation and was also considered by the Cabinet (Official) Committee on Greater Malaysia (CO 1030/1150, no 187 and DO 169/19, no 173A; see also CAB 134/1951, GM(62)36, 17 July 1962).]

I have the honour to submit a brief review on political developments in Singapore since May last year when the Tunku first responded to the promptings of the British and Lee Kuan Yew and spoke out in favour of closer association of the Federation of Malaya, Singapore and the Borneo Territories. The Tunku's bold initiative set in train events which will climax shortly in the discussions on the Cobbold Commission's Report in London and in the hotly debated referendum in Singapore.

2.   Experience of three years of the Singapore Constitution suggests that we have been fortunate in having Lee Kuan Yew as Prime Minister.[1] It would have been only too easy for the Singapore Prime Minister to have maintained widespread popular support by pressing for a greater measure of independence for Singapore on her own when it seemed that the Tunku was unalterably opposed to Merger between Singapore and the Federation. Instead, Lee took the far harder course of telling the Singapore Chinese that their independence could only come through merging with the Malay dominated Federation. Lee's tactics, however, have not always matched up to the quality of his overall policy and the road he has trod to Merger has been even more stony than it need have been.

3.   The outlook for the P.A.P. following their defeat by Ong Eng Guan at the Hong Lim bye-election [sic] in April 1961 was not good. After two years of office the Party had lost considerable public support and was faced with another bye-election in the Anson division. Lee had persisted in his attempt to keep the left wing extremists within the Government and Party instead of looking for increased support from moderate opinion. As a result the Party and the T.U.C. had been badly weakened by the internal sapping of Lim Chin Siong and his colleagues. Progress along the Party's main policy line of Merger with the Federation seemed to be blocked indefinitely and political momentum was taking Singapore towards what Lee believed was the disastrous goal of an independent Chinese city state. Then came the Tunku's speech and the situation changed fundamentally.

4.   Lee lost no time in welcoming the initiative towards Merger in his speech on National Day[2] and open conflict in the P.A.P. at once ensued. The left wing of the Party, led by Lim Chin Siong and supported by eight P.A.P. Assemblymen and a large section of the trade union movement, reacted instinctively against the prospect of control by the right wing Federation Government and made it a condition of their support for the P.A.P. candidate in the Anson bye-election that the Party should work for full internal self-government. Lee stood firm, the bye-election was lost to David Marshall (Singapore's first Chief Minister and new leader of the Workers' Party) five more P.A.P. Assemblymen defected and the struggle within the P.A.P. culminated in a debate on a motion of confidence in the Assembly on 20th/21st July.[3]

5.   The Government were left with a majority of only one in the Assembly, but they reaffirmed their belief in Merger and survived. During the debate Lee launched a

---

[1] See 13, 15 and 38 for previous assessments by the UK commissioner of political developments in Singapore.
[2] 3 June 1961, the second anniversary of the inauguration of the constitution for self-governing Singapore; later replaced by 9 Aug, commemorating Singapore's separation from Malaysia in 1965.
[3] See 50.

sudden attack on the British in an attempt to cast a smoke screen over the disaster which had befallen the Government as a result of allowing the extremists to undermine them in the Party. He suggested that there had been a Machiavellian ploy by the United Kingdom Commission (culminating in the so-called Eden Hall tea party) to encourage the extremists into open conflict with the P.A.P. leadership and thus to force the leadership to take repressive action against them.[4] The truth was that the extremists, faced with the threat of Merger, thought that their best course was a swift attempt to overthrow the leadership and to assume control of the Government; their visit to Eden Hall was that of prudent men who wanted to know whether the British would allow them to take office in the ordinary constitutional way. Their narrow failure to defeat the Government must have been a great disappointment but they rapidly adjusted themselves to the role of militant opposition. A new party—Barisan Sosialis—was formed, with Lim Chin Siong as the Secretary General, thirteen members in the Assembly and the greater part of the P.A.P. constituency apparatus under their control. A parallel development in the trade union field led to the dissolution of the T.U.C. into two groups of unions, the one that supported Barisan Sosialis having about forty members, including the powerful Singapore General Employees Union and many smaller industrial unions.

6.   From this point on, the story is essentially one of the P.A.P.'s 'Battle for Merger' as Lee himself termed it in the published version of a series of twelve broadcast talks that he gave in the Autumn.[5] It was clear that the Government could not face a general election and that their only course was to seize the initiative offered by the Tunku. This Lee did with characteristic skill and determination and by late August he had succeeded in hammering out with the Tunku a practical basis for Merger whereby the Federation would control Defence, External Affairs and Internal Security, while Singapore would keep control of Education and Labour. The scheme was worked out in more detail over the next two months and by the middle of November Lee was able to publish a White Paper containing a formal Exchange of Letters between the two Prime Ministers and a memorandum setting out the agreed proposals. The essence of the scheme, which we originally suggested to Lee and was at first called the 'Ulster Model', was that the Federation should have complete constitutional safeguards against any possibility of the Singapore Chinese upsetting the political dominance of the Malays in the Kuala Lumpur House of Representatives. To this end it was agreed that Singapore should only have 15 seats in the House of Representatives instead of the 25 to which she was entitled by reason of her population and that Singapore citizens should not become Federation citizens on Merger although they would be given Malaysian nationality and passports.

7.   During this time the Merger issue was widely debated in the Press and on the radio, and opposition parties tried hard to persuade the Government to associate them in the negotiations. At an early stage, Barisan Sosialis concluded (whether wisely or not still remains to be seen) that they could not oppose Merger absolutely even though in their hearts the last thing they wanted was for Internal Security of Singapore to come under the control of the right wing Federation Government. Accordingly, they adopted the tactic of declaring themselves in favour of full and complete Merger, with proportionate representation for Singapore in the Federation

---

[4] See 49, note.   [5] See 59, note.

Parliament and with automatic Federation citizenship for all its citizens; for good measure, they also demanded general elections in Singapore before Merger and Pan-Malayan general elections after it. All other opposition parties accepted the principle of Merger too, but only the Alliance was ready to support the White Paper proposals as the best way for the present of making progress towards full Merger. By the time of the debate on the White Paper in the Assembly towards the end of November, criticism of the Government's Merger proposals was clearly centred on the twin questions of representation in the Federation Parliament and citizenship. On the first point, the debate on the whole went in favour of the Government who justified less than proportionate representation for Singapore on the grounds that the State was being given greater local powers. On the question of citizenship, the Government argued that full Merger would mean the application of Federation rules of citizenship to Singapore, and that under these rules those not born in Singapore would have to re-register for citizenship. The Government estimated that this would result in several hundred thousand citizens being disenfranchised, and on this ground they justified the special provisions of the White Paper whereby Singapore citizens retained their separate citizenship and automatically became 'Federal Nationals'. Barisan Sosialis firmly rejected this argument and maintained that a reasonable and fair application of the Federation citizenship rules to Singapore should mean that all existing Singapore citizens would automatically become Federation citizens on Merger.

8. The debate in the Assembly concluded on the 6th December with a vote of thirty-three to nil in favour of the White Paper, all opposition parties except the Alliance having walked out before the division. In general, Lee was entitled at this point to considerable satisfaction with the progress he had made since near disaster in July. His series of broadcasts in which he argued the case for merger and exposed the whole history of Communist united front tactics had perhaps not made the impact he had hoped but he still held the initiative and the essential margin of support in the Assembly. He himself was playing a constructive part in the meetings of the Malaysia Solidarity Consultative Committee which was devoting itself to the essential task of bringing the Borneo Territories around to Malaysia. There had been a satisfactory outcome to the Defence talks with the Tunku in London and H.M.G. had both expressed their general support for Malaysia and had taken note of the Singapore White Paper. There remained one serious obstacle. The Tunku was not willing to take Singapore unless he could have the Borneo territories at the same time. Singapore was therefore faced with the prospect of a long wait, probably until 1963.

9. Faced with this delay, Lee Kuan Yew made a major mistake, which may yet be his undoing, in pledging the Government to submit their Merger proposals for endorsement by the people at a referendum. At the time this no doubt seemed a good way of relieving pressure on the Government for general elections but it is now proving a tremendous millstone around their necks. Given the P.A.P's firm stand in favour of Merger at the previous general election and the approval of their White Paper proposals by almost two thirds of the members of the Assembly, it would have been quite reasonable for the Government to proceed with Merger without more ado. Certainly H.M.G. for their part would have seen no difficulty in transferring sovereignty to the Federation on the strength of the vote in the Assembly. The risk in any referendum, as the Government soon saw, was that their White Paper proposals

would be rejected, not on their merits, but merely to show dissatisfaction with the Government itself. Lee therefore decided to make the people choose between the White Paper proposals and full Merger as urged by Barisan Sosialis and other opposition parties, with the clear implication that full Merger would mean loss of citizenship for many people in Singapore. The Opposition were soon aware of the trap being laid for them and countered by threatening to frustrate the referendum by telling their supporters to cast blank ballots. The Government were thus forced step by step to tighten up the provisions of the Referendum Bill and it now provides for blank ballots to be construed as support for the White Paper, and for the number of such ballots to be declared only if the Government see fit. The result is that Government have no hope of any sort of credit for holding a referendum and it is generally regarded as a dishonest manoeuvre.

10.   Meanwhile, behind the public debate on Merger during the last six months there have been secret discussions on the question whether the left wing extremists should be arrested before Singapore is handed over to the Federation.[6] These discussions were initiated by the Federal Government who feel strongly that firm action should be taken against the extreme left wing while the British are still in charge. At first Lee shared the British view that it would be dangerous to take such action in the months leading up to Merger, and that the overriding need was for a calm political position in Singapore. Subsequently, however, partly to appease the Tunku but also no doubt to some extent to suit his own political needs, he changed his stand and agreed to a programme of action that provides in its first phase for the intensification of measures to harrass and provoke the extreme left wing, followed in the second phase by the arrests of its leaders. How far Lee intends to go on his own responsibility and whether the initial phase will succeed in its intention of provoking unconstitutional action by the extremists remain to be seen.

11.   Thus, on the eve of the discussions in London on the Cobbold Commission's Report which it is hoped will put the Borneo piece of the Malaysia jigsaw firmly into position, Singapore remains the doubtful quantity. In the last weeks, the debate on the Referendum Bill has reached a new pitch of intensity and, although the Government can rely upon the support of the Alliance to force it through, the strain on their own supporters is very great. Already, this has resulted in the defection of one back-bencher and the outlook for the Government is uncertain.[7] If it should fall, this would mean the end of Malaysia for the time being and the opening of a period of great difficulty for the British in Singapore. On balance, however, I should judge

---

[6] For the detention of subversives, see references at 123, n 5.
[7] Hoe Puay Choo defected from the PAP, thereby reducing the PAP to 25 out of the 51 seats. Nonetheless, it carried the vote on the referendum by 29 to 17 with the support of Lim Yew Hock's SPA and UMNO. Lee regained his majority of one on 4 Aug. Lee now had the authority to run a referendum on merger. He would do so on the following terms. Three alternatives would be presented: A (in support of the government's proposals); B (in favour of Singapore becoming a state within the federation); C (in favour of merger on terms no less favourable than those offered to the Borneo territories). It was also laid down that all blank or spoiled ballot papers would be counted as supporting 'A'. Two days after losing the vote on the referendum bill, the Barisan sent an appeal to the UN protesting against the terms of the referendum. Lee also went to New York to rebut the charges. He then travelled to London for the Malaysia talks, arriving on 27 July and moving immediately into a round of meetings. The referendum on merger was held on 1 Sept and the result was as follows: A 71.1 per cent; B 1.7 per cent; C 1.4 per cent; blank 25.8 per cent.

that, with luck and the continuing determination of Lee Kuan Yew, the Government may succeed in 'winning' the referendum and holding on until H.M.G. and the Federation together can implement the whole Malaysia plan. But time is very short and the transfer of sovereignty must take place at the earliest possible moment.

12.   I am sending copies of this despatch to the Governors in Hong Kong, Jesselton and Kuching on a personal basis; to the United Kingdom High Commissioners in Canberra, Wellington, and Kuala Lumpur; to H.M. Ambassador in Djakarta; and to the High Commissioner for Brunei.

132   CO 1030/1024, no E/90   20 July 1962

[Anglo–Malayan talks in London]: minute from Mr Sandys to Lord Lansdowne recording his lunchtime conversation with the Tunku about a staged transfer of power

[The Tunku arrived in London in mid-July and established his court at the Ritz Hotel. 'The Tunku is like a Spanish grandee. That's his world', Macmillan once remarked to Lee Kuan Yew. The Malayan delegation included Razak, Tan Siew Sin, Abdul Aziz bin Haji Abdul Majid (permanent secretary, Prime Minister's Department), Abdul Kadir bin Shamsudin (Defence), Shariff bin Hassan, C M Sheridan (attorney-general) and C Fenner (director, police affairs). At 12 noon on 17 July, after a brief meeting between prime ministers, the talks got underway with a plenary session in Admiralty House which was followed by meetings in the CRO between the Tunku and Sandys that afternoon and the next morning. The detailed negotiations were left to a steering committee, where Lansdowne took over from Sandys as leader of the British side. The plenary session reconvened on 23 July, with Sandys in the chair, to consider a summary of the committee's proceedings (for the record of meetings see DO 169/273 and DO 189/221). North Borneo and Sarawak were represented at the London talks by Goode and Waddell. Agreement was reached on a number of points but after ten days the talks were in danger of breaking down. The stumbling blocks were, firstly, the implications of extending the existing federal constitution to North Borneo and Sarawak (particularly with respect to religion, language and education) and, secondly and most significantly, the timing of merger (see 134). On the one hand, further preparation of the Borneo territories warranted a later date; on the other hand, instability in Singapore necessitated an earlier date. The Tunku was anxious that Malaya's merger with Singapore should synchronise with, and certainly not precede, its merger with the Borneo territories. Lee Kuan Yew, who reached London on 27 July after a mission to the UN to refute the Barisan's charges regarding Singapore's prospective referendum, brought demands of his own; he wished the British government to detain or restrict up to 150 subversives and opponents and the Malayan government to make concessions on citizenship. Because he was afraid that he might be left 'holding the Singapore baby' without the countervailing support of the Borneo peoples, the Tunku threatened to pull out of the talks (see 133). Breakdown would have been in nobody's interest, least of all the Tunku's, since to return to Kuala Lumpur empty-handed would have damaged his political reputation. In order to get negotiations back on track, Macmillan, who had in any case been intending to offer the Malayan premier some hospitality for he sensed that he had been somewhat neglected socially, invited the Tunku to lunch at Chequers on 28 July. Here a significant, secret formula was proposed (see 135 and 136).]

1.   The Prime Minister of Malaya lunched alone with me to-day and we discussed the setting up of Malaysia.

2.   I stressed the importance we attached to a smooth transfer of power in a way which would not alarm the local population or lead to the premature withdrawal of the British officials. I suggested that it would be desirable to retain the British Governors for another two or three years, whilst indigenous Ministers were being trained on to take over responsibility.

3.   The Tunku was vehemently opposed to the idea of British Governors in any form within the new Federation. However, after some discussion he said he thought there would be no objection to delaying the incorporation of North Borneo and Sarawak into the new Federation for a year or two. I pointed out that the merger with Singapore could obviously not be similarly delayed.

4.   After examining various possible courses, we agreed to consider a solution on the following lines:—

(a) At the end of the present talks, the British and Malayan Governments would announce their decision (subject to working out detailed arrangements) to set up the new Federation of Malaysia, comprising Malaya, Singapore, North Borneo, Sarawak and Brunei.

(b) The actual transfer of sovereignty in respect of each territory would be left over for determination by the two Governments, subject to a maximum time limit of two or three years.

(c) The transfer of sovereignty in respect of Singapore and Brunei would be effected as quickly as possible during the next few months.

(d) The transfer of sovereignty in respect of North Borneo and Sarawak would be effected at such time as the British Government thought right, subject to the maximum time limit of two or three years, at the end of which we would be irrevocably committed to merge the territories in the new Federation.

(e) During the transitional period, the Federal Government could begin to initiate development schemes in Sarawak and North Borneo with the consent and co-operation of the British authorities.

133   PREM 11/3868   26 July 1962
[Anglo–Malayan talks in London]: letter from Tunku Abdul Rahman to Mr Sandys, announcing his intention to break off the talks

I have given most careful thought to your proposal for the creation of Malaysia which envisages the possibility of the admission of Singapore into the Federation prior to the Borneo territories but found it unacceptable.

The mandates which I have obtained from Parliament, from the Alliance Party, and from my own Party, have at all times been most emphatic that the merger with Singapore must be done simultaneously with the Borneo territories. The reason is obvious, for, the admission of Singapore into the Federation earlier than the Borneo territories would tip the balance of population in favour of the non-Malay population by 869,000.

There is a very real apprehension of the people of the Federation, in particular the Malays, of the danger of the preponderance of Chinese population which would affect the trend of our politics, for the majority of them are inclined to Chinese chauvinism and communism. This is the problem of Singapore of which both our Governments are most concerned.

I have been able to win the support of the people of the Federation to the Malaysia proposal on the assurance that the balance of population would be made up by the simultaneous admission of the other territories. You might say that these measures are purely temporary in that the Borneo territories would merge in the next few months. That might be so, but the psychological effect in the minds of the Malay people would be one of suspicion, and fear—suspicion in that I have gone back on my promise to them and likely to do so again, and fear that I have been weak enough to allow myself to be used as an instrument of British interest in order to perpetuate British Imperialism. If therefore Malaysia is created in the way you envisage, I fear that I shall lose the trust which has been reposed in me. For this reason, my colleagues and I suggested a package deal.

The question of having British governors in Malaysia after the transfer of sovereignty for a period which you suggested would open myself to very severe attack and criticism from my own people and would indeed provide the communists with the best opportunity to create dissension in our ranks. With that, my standing in the eyes of my people would suffer a severe set-back, and I would be of no further use both to my country and to our friends in the Commonwealth.

In the circumstances, if we are not able to arrive at some agreement, my colleagues and I feel that we would rather remain as we are, and should Malaya be faced with the threat of Communist aggression I am sure with the help of God and the determination of our people we should be able to resist it.

I have, therefore, decided to return home but before I do so I would very much like to meet the Prime Minister to say goodbye as well as to explain to him my position regarding these matters.

134 DO 169/273, no 11B   26 July 1962
'Progress report on Anglo–Malayan talks': CRO memorandum on behalf of Mr Sandys and forwarded by W I McIndoe to P de Zulueta for Mr Macmillan's information

[The Anglo–Malayan talks went badly. Officials regretted that in their initial meeting on 17 July Macmillan had encouraged the Tunku to believe that the British government would in the end be willing to achieve agreement at almost any price. In the view of A M R Cary of the Cabinet Office, 'unless there is some dramatic change in the situation it looks as though a solution may emerge which will cause serious trouble in Borneo and by repercussion, in this country'. The invitation to Chequers was intended to avert such a crisis. De Zulueta requested this report from McIndoe (Sandys' private secretary) in order to brief the prime minister for his forthcoming lunch with the Tunku (see Cary to Brook, 27 July 1962, CAB 21/4847, and de Zulueta to Macmillan, 27 July 1962, PREM 11/3865).]

Long term arrangements
1. On a large number of points agreement has been reached, the most important being that the ultimate constitutions for North Borneo and Sarawak in Malaysia should be based on those for Penang and Malacca with additional safeguards, the details of which have yet to be settled. On some points, e.g. religion, agreement has still to be reached.[1]

---

[1] The main issues outstanding as regards the Borneo territories were religion, language and compensation for expatriate officers; for Singapore the principal matter was citizenship. The Tunku wanted Islam to be the state religion for the whole federation to which the non-Muslim communities of Borneo objected. With respect to language, Cobbold had recommended that English should remain the official language unless local legislatures proposed otherwise, whereas the Tunku wished to control the date of change. In any case, it was accepted that the practical details of these and other matters would have to be worked out on the spot, hence the subsequent appointment of the Inter-Governmental Committee chaired by Lansdowne.

The transition

2.   The main questions which have still to be resolved are: when sovereignty should be transferred and whether Singapore should enter Malaysia earlier than or at the same time as the other territories.

3.   For internal political reasons the Tunku wants all the territories to join the Federation simultaneously. What we require is a little time to effect the transfer smoothly and without losing the confidence of the inhabitants. The Tunku would be quite prepared for the transfer of all territories to take place on any date that suits us, i.e. in eighteen months or two years time. But the political situation in Singapore makes a long delay impossible in practice. The present minority government may easily collapse before the end of this year.

4.   To meet this difficulty Mr. Sandys has proposed that the two Governments should announce:—

(a) that the transfer of all territories should take place on 31st December, 1963,[2] subject to the proviso that by agreement all or any of the territories may be incorporated into the Federation at an earlier dates; and
(b) that the two Governments should secretly agree that if, in the interval, Lee Kuan Yew's Government appears at any time to be on the point of collapse, Singapore and Brunei will be incorporated into the Federation in advance of Sarawak and North Borneo.[3]

5.   The Tunku, in a private talk with Mr. Sandys, accepted this arrangement. But later after talking to Tun Razak, he changed his mind.

6.   The position now is that the Malayans have been asked to consider the matter further. It is important that they should not think that the British Government are prepared to make further concessions beyond those already offered by Mr. Sandys, which go a great deal further than Lord Cobbold recommended.

7.   It would be politically most damaging for the Tunku to return to Malaya empty-handed and without achieving agreement on the creation of Malaysia. There is, therefore, reasonable hope that to avoid this he will be willing to make some move in our direction. In the last resort it may be possible for us to make some small further concession of a presentational nature to him. But Mr. Sandys does not wish to play this remaining card just yet.

General

8.   Assuming that agreement is reached in the next few days with the Malayans, it is envisaged that a joint announcement would be made, the Cobbold Report would be published, joint inter-governmental committees would then be set up to meet in the Far East and Lord Landowne and a Malayan Minister would visit the Borneo Territories quickly to expound and win approval for the arrangements proposed.

---

[2] The Tunku had proposed that sovereignty over the Borneo territories should be transferred on 8 Feb 1963, his birthday.
[3] This became the nub of the Chequers' formula (see 136) and was the reason why the agreement of 31 July remained secret apart from the joint public statement (see 140).

135   DO 169/273, no 12   28 July 1962

'Record of a Meeting at Chequers at 12.15 pm on Saturday, July 28, 1962': minutes by P F de Zulueta of a meeting attended by Mr Macmillan, Tunku Abdul Rahman and Tun Razak

[The Chequers' lunch-time meeting was orchestrated as follows: Sandys arrived first and briefed Macmillan on a formula which he should suggest to the Tunku and which he later sent him in writing (document 136). Sandys withdrew before the arrival of the Tunku and Tun Razak who had a half-hour's discussion with Macmillan. Sandys then joined the meeting, appearing to have just arrived at Chequers. Finally, Home joined the party which then went into lunch. Macmillan reported the Chequers' meeting to Cabinet on 3 Aug (CAB 128/36/2, CC 53(62)2); see also CO 1030/1025, no E107A; PREM 11/3868).]

The Prime Minister began by expressing his regret that his other engagements had prevented his taking a very active part in the discussions which had been going on. *The Tunku* expressed his complete understanding. He said that he had just been having a good discussion with Lee Kuan Yew which had turned largely on the date at which Malaysia could be brought into effect. Lee Kuan Yew was not sure how long he could hold on and February, 1963, seemed about the latest safe date. The Commonwealth Secretary however had talked about December 31. The Government of Malaya would not mind how long they waited for Malaysia, were it not for the dangers in Singapore which seemed imminent.

The Prime Minister asked if Lee Kuan Yew and the Tunku had now agreed about the Citizenship question. *The Tunku* agreed that there had been some misunderstanding on this point but said that the legal advisers were now working on the formula and he hoped that it would be acceptable to Lee Kuan Yew.

The Prime Minister said that he would like to speak very frankly to the Tunku. Although most people in the United Kingdom were in favour of the idea of Greater Malaysia the Bill giving effect to it would not have quite as easy a passage as had the Bills, for example, for the Independence of Tanganyika.[1] There would be a certain amount of discussion, particularly from those on both sides of the House who were particularly concerned with the traditional British tenderness for minority groups. This would be true both in the House of Commons and in the House of Lords. It would be a great help in the passage of any Bill if a clear declaration of intent had been made to cover the interests of the inhabitants of the Borneo territories. He quite understood the Federal Government did not in fact intend to change the way of life of these people but detailed declarations of this intention could be very important. It would also be helpful if the question of dangerous communists in Singapore could be deferred until after the Parliamentary discussions. Granted these points, the Prime Minister quite saw the difficulties of timing to which the Tunku had referred. He assumed that in fact agreement could be reached about safeguards for the Borneo peoples and about the defence arrangements. If all that could be agreed then he wondered whether a formula might not be found which would allow the formal date for Malaysia to be fixed as August 31, 1963. There could be a declaration in principle now to that effect. Even this would be quite difficult because the Cobbold Report had spoken of a much longer transitional period. The Prime

---

[1] For the decolonisation of Tanganyika, which became independent in Dec 1961, see Hyam and Louis eds, *BDEE: The Conservative government*, I, 140–156.

Minister then spoke from a formula which he subsequently sent to the Tunku, stating that this was a personal idea. He explained that in any Bill to establish Greater Malaysia a formula must be used which would allow the Federation to be established on August 31, 1963 or on such earlier date as might be laid down by Order of Council. It would be privately agreed between the Governments of the United Kingdom and of the Federation of Malaya that if an earlier date than August 31 proved necessary owing to the position in Singapore then the British Governors would continue to exercise executive authority in the Borneo territories under the Agong until the latter appointed new Governors on August 31, 1963. *The Tunku* said that this was an interesting idea. He thought that the formula should provide that the formal agreement between the Governments concerned should be reached by February 8, 1963. *The Prime Minister* agreed that this might be possible and said that he would send the Tunku a copy of his personal idea for him to study.

136   DO 169/273, no 12   28 July 1962
[The Chequers' formula]: letter from Mr Macmillan to Tunku Abdul Rahman. *Enclosure*: 'Suggested plan for Malaysia'

My dear Prime Minister,

As I promised, I enclose a copy of the suggestion which I outlined to you today as a possible plan for the establishment of Malaysia. I believe that something on these lines might provide a solution.

It was a great pleasure to entertain you and the Deputy Prime Minister to luncheon today.

Yours very sincerely,
HAROLD MACMILLAN

Enclosure to 136

1.   At the end of the present talks, a public announcement would be made that the British and Malayan Governments had decided in principle that the proposed Federation of Malaysia should be brought into being on 31st August, 1963.

2.   At the same time the two Governments would declare their intention (after the referendum in Singapore and after consultation with the legislatures of North Borneo and Sarawak but not later than January 1963) to conclude a formal agreement which would provide for:—

(i) the transfer of sovereignty on 31st August, 1963;
(ii) safeguards for the special interests of North Borneo and Sarawak; and
(iii) defence arrangements on the lines already agreed.

3.   In addition, the two Governments would, by an unpublished exchange of letters, agree:—

(a) that, if the present Government of Singapore fell or appeared to be about to fall, the new Federation of Malaysia should be brought into being as soon as practicable; and

(b) that, in that event, the British Governors of North Borneo and Sarawak, while ceasing to be responsible to the British Government, would continue, as an interim measure, to exercise their present executive powers until the appointment of new Governors by the Agong on 31st August, 1963.[1]

---

[1] The secret agreement of 31 July reproduced this formula more or less word for word, see 140.

137 PREM 11/3868   30 July 1962

[London talks on merger between Malaya and Singapore]: minute from P F de Zulueta to Mr Macmillan, reporting discussions between Mr Sandys, Tun Razak and Lee Kuan Yew on 29 July about citizenship and internal security

> [The Singapore and Malayan leaders used the London talks not only to conduct business but also to improve their working relationship. Following the Chequers' lunch, the Tunku had tea with Lee Kuan Yew at the Ritz and the next morning (Sunday, 29 July) they were joined by Razak and Goh Keng Swee for golf at Swindon. That afternoon Lee and Razak discussed citizenship and internal security with Sandys at the CRO. As regards citizenship, Lee pressed for Singapore's citizens to be known as citizens, rather than nationals, of Malaysia—nomenclature which he felt sure would meet his critics' grievances. Razak conceded the point on Sunday and the Tunku endorsed it on Monday morning (30 July) when they met at the Ritz. Lee immediately returned to his base at the Hyde Park Hotel to commit to paper the new scheme (which would necessitate an amendment to paragraph 14 of the Singapore white paper, Cmd 33 of 1961, agreed by the Singapore Assembly on 6 Dec 1961). The prime ministers of Singapore and Malaya then confirmed their agreement by an exchange of letters. For the final wording of these arrangements see 140, appendix C. As regards Singapore's internal security, both Lee and the Tunku pressed for a round-up of subversives before merger and hoped to shift onto the British the responsibility for such an operation. Sandys categorically refused to take the initiative in, or sole responsibility for, the matter and argued that it would be a matter for the Internal Security Council, which was composed of British, Singaporean and Malayan representatives (see 138; cf CO 1030/1029 and Lee, *Memoirs*, pp 437–440).]

At the talks between the Commonwealth Secretary, Tun Razak and Lee Kwan Yew on July 29 they discussed Singapore's citizenship and security.

On citizenship Lee Kwan Yew said that he had now reached agreement with the Tunku that Singapore's citizens should be described as citizens of the Federation of Malaysia. This meets his point. He was, however, rather vague about the rights which Singapore citizens would have and agreed, at Mr. Sandy's request, to send a document setting out the position which would be agreed also with the Malayans. Mr. Sandys pointed out that he would have to consider the position in relation to the rights which would be enjoyed by the inhabitants of the Borneo territories.

As regards security in Singapore, Lee Kwan Yew argued strongly for an operation against known Communists to take place after the referendum in Singapore but before merger. He was supported by the Malayans. He apparently had in mind the arrest of some 25 people and the restriction of another 150.

Lee Kwan Yew said that when this happened he could not express enthusiasm for political reasons but would say that this action was a regrettable necessity. He suggested that the Malayan Government should be known to have taken the initiative in pressing this action. There was considerable discussion about this because neither we nor the Malayans could understand why Lee Kwan Yew could not take this action on his own responsibility. Lee Kwan Yew explained his political difficulties and Mr. Sandys undertook to consider an operation such as was suggested. He said, however, that before taking a decision he would like to see some specific case histories of the people who would be detained.

On the main question of dates and the rights of the Borneo people, the Commonwealth Secretary is working to get a draft announcement ready for issue on the evening of July 31 when some of the Malayans will go home. This may or may not spell everything out in detail. There is another meeting at 10.00 p.m. tonight and presumably further meetings tomorrow.

138   DO 169/273, no 14   31 July 1962
[London talks on merger between Malaya and Singapore]: note by the Far Eastern Department of the CO of certain points discussed at a meeting between Mr Sandys, the Tunku and Lee Kuan Yew[1]

1.   *Singapore: citizenship*

Mr. Lee Kuan Yew said that he did not wish the agreement which he had reached with the Tunku on Citizenship to be published yet.

It was agreed, however, that in reply to questions Mr. Sandys should be at liberty to say publicly that an agreement had been reached between the Governments of Malaya and Singapore, that he was satisfied that its terms were reasonable, and that it was for the Governments of Malaya and Singapore to decide the question of publication.[2]

2.   *Singapore: internal security*

Mr. Sandys said that:—

(a) He could not allow himself to be put in a position where he could be said to have agreed in advance, even in principle, to a series of arrests in Singapore without having had an opportunity to consider the cases of the individuals concerned. He categorically refused to give any such agreement.

(b) If the Internal Security Council decided on security grounds that arrests were necessary, he would not seek to intervene or to resist such a decision on political grounds. A reasonable case for the arrests must, however, be presented: each individual case must be made out and examined on its merits. It was not for the British Government to initiate action in this matter, nor was he (Mr. Sandys) prepared to put anything in writing at this stage.

(c) If everyone else concerned showed that they were prepared take their share of responsibility the British Government would not shirk theirs and would not let the others down.[3]

---

[1] This meeting took place in the CRO at 7 pm; they then moved to Admiralty House where they met with Macmillan at 7.35 pm, see 139.

[2] Having recovered his majority of one in the Singapore Assembly on 4 Aug, on 14 Aug Lee announced the terms of the citizen provisions and that the long-promised referendum would be held on 1 Sept.

[3] Ghazali Shafie, who attended the meeting as secretary to the Malayan delegation, has recalled: 'The Ministerial Meeting mostly dealt with the question whether the British authorities would take internal security action in Singapore before the merger. Sandys refused to budge an inch and requested the Tunku not to push too hard. He however conceded that if the situation demanded it, UK government would act. The Tunku said Selkirk might not go along with that to which he replied that he would deal with the situation in his own way. Turning to me Sandys said that I should not record his words but that we should take his words in good faith. The Tunku acknowledged the assurance given' (*Memoir*, p 260).

139   CO 1030/1025, no 111A   31 July 1962
[Signing the joint agreement]: note of a meeting of Mr Macmillan and
Mr Sandys with Tunku Abdul Rahman, Tan Siew Sin and Lee Kuan
Yew

The Tunku accompanied by Mr. Tan Siew Sin, Mr. Lee Kuan Yew, the High
Commissioner and others called to see the Prime Minister at 7.35 p.m. on Tuesday,
July 31. The Prime Minister was accompanied by the Commonwealth Secretary, and
I[1] was present.

After an exchange of courtesies two copies of the joint agreement between the
United Kingdom and the Government of Malaya were signed by both sides.[2] There
was some reference made to the draft joint statement[3] and the *Prime Minister*
thought there might be some discussion in the House of Commons on this. It could
not, therefore, be regarded as a formality but the statement made it clear that the
interests of all concerned had been properly looked after. In particular paragraphs
five and six would help to counter any criticisms that the United Kingdom had too
rapidly abandoned its responsibilities. It was hoped that the announcement would
help to stabilise opinion in the Territories. *The Tunku* agreed and said it was
important to get the referendum completed during the dry season. *Mr. Lee* also
agreed.

There was some reference to the position of the Philippines. *The Tunku* said that
the jurisdiction lay in the hands of the United Kingdom and he would not, therefore,
of his own accord have discussions with the Philippine Government. The
Commonwealth Secretary said that no formal claim had been made to the United
Kingdom Government. *The Tunku* added that the Philippines were friendly with
Malaya and there would be no serious embarrassment with them. He thought the
Philippine Government were seeking a way back into a wholly oriental sphere but he
was sure they would listen to him and he would emphasise that Malaysia was based
on self-determination. The *Prime Minister* added that this made it all the more
important that local legislatures should be consulted.

It was agreed that it would be right to tell the Press that evening no more than
that the talks had come to an end, that agreement had been reached and that a joint
statement would be made in the House of Commons[4] and simultaneously in Kuala
Lumpur the following day. There was a further exchange of courtesies in which the
Tunku and *Mr. Lee* expressed their satisfaction at the way in which the talks had been
conducted, at the hospitality they had received in London and at the opportunity the
new arrangements gave them both to confront the common enemy who still pressed
from all sides.

The meeting adjourned at 8.10 p.m.

---

[1] T J (Sir Timothy) Bligh, one of the prime minister's private secretaries.   [2] See 140.
[3] *ibid.*, appendix D.   [4] In fact both Sandys and Lansdowne made parliamentary statements.

140   DO 169/273, no 16A   31 July 1962
'Agreement on the setting up of the Federation of Malaysia':
agreement in principle signed at Admiralty House by Mr Macmillan
and Tunku Abdul Rahman. *Annex* and *Appendices:* A 'Framework of
initial state constitutions of Sarawak and North Borneo'; B
'Citizenship'; C 'Singapore citizenship'; D 'Joint public statement'

[This document, commented H G Turner of the CRO (formerly of the MCS), 'seems likely
to become a basic historical document in the formation of the Federation of Malaysia'
(Turner to Sir Charles Dixon, 8 Aug 1962, DO 169/273). For this reason it was printed and
circulated, but on a highly restricted basis. Indeed, unlike the Cobbold Report which was
published on 1 Aug in its entirety, most of the provisions of the agreement, annex and
appendices remained secret. Three of the five clauses of the agreement itself were
reproduced from the Chequers' formula with only minor variations (see 136). The only
part to be published on 1 Aug and announced in both Houses at Westminster as well as in
the Federal Parliament was the joint statement (appendix D). The reasons for secrecy
were twofold. The first sensitive issue was encapsulated in the provisions set out in
paragraph 3, and confirmed by an exchange of letters between the two governments, for
the inauguration of Malaysia before 31 Aug 1963 'if for any reason it appeared desirable'.
The justification for such action had been spelled out in the Chequers' formula, namely 'if
the present Government of Singapore fell or appeared to be about to fall'. The agreement
was kept secret, secondly, so as not to antagonise the peoples of Borneo; in the view of the
CRO, 'the agreement records an acceptance (not achieved by the Malayan members
without hard bargaining) of the view of the Malayan members of the [Cobbold]
Commission' (memorandum by the Far Eastern Department, CRO, 29 Oct 1962, DO
169/215).]

1.   The British and Malayan Governments have decided in principle that the
proposed Federation of Malaysia shall be brought into being by 31st August, 1963.

2.   The two Governments declare their intention to conclude, within the next six
months, a formal agreement, which among other things will provide for:—

(a) the transfer of sovereignty over Singapore, North Borneo and Sarawak by 31st
August, 1963;
(b) detailed constitutional arrangements including safeguards for the special
interests of North Borneo and Sarawak, to be drawn up after consultation with the
legislatures of the two territories;
(c) defence arrangements, as set out in the joint statement by the Governments of
the United Kingdom and of the Federation of Malaya dated 22nd November, 1961
(Cmnd. 1563).

3.   In addition, the two Governments will, by an unpublished exchange of letters,
agree:—

(a) that, if for any reason it appeared desirable, the new Federation of Malaysia
could, by agreement between the two Governments, be brought into being on a
date earlier than 31st August, 1963;
(b) that, in that event, the British Governors of North Borneo and Sarawak, while
ceasing to be responsible to the British Government, would be confirmed in their
positions by His Majesty The Yang di-Pertuan Agong and would continue, as an
interim measure, to exercise all their present powers by the authority of His
Majesty until the appointment of new Governors by His Majesty on 31st August,
1963.

4.   The two Governments have agreed upon the matters contained in the attached *Annex*. Except where otherwise expressly stated this relates to North Borneo and Sarawak only.

5.   Facilities will be offered to His Highness the Sultan of Brunei to arrange for Brunei to enter the new Federation should His Highness so desire.

For the British Government
HAROLD MACMILLAN
For the Malayan Government
TUNKU ABDUL RAHMAN PUTRA.
LONDON, 31ST JULY, 1962

Annex

1.   *Title of Federation*. 'Malaysia' will be the official title of the Federation.

2.   *Sovereignty*. On the creation of Malaysia, sovereignty over Singapore, North Borneo and Sarawak will be transferred simultaneously by Britain to the new Federation of Malaysia.

3.   *Transitional period*. In the early years after the merger as few changes as possible will be made in the administrative arrangements of North Borneo and Sarawak affecting the day-to-day lives of the people. During this period certain Federal powers will be delegated to the State Governments. This will be a matter for discussion by an Intergovernmental Committee.

4.   *Constitution*

(a) The Constitution of the new Federation of Malaysia will be based on the present Constitution of Malaya.

(b) There will be safeguards for the special interests of North Borneo and Sarawak which will not be capable of amendment without the concurrence of the Government of the territory concerned.

(c) The Constitutions of Sarawak and North Borneo will in the first instance be on the lines indicated in *Appendix A*.

5.   *Amendment of Constitution*

(a) The Constitutions of the two territories will be required to be brought into conformity with the provisions of the Eighth Schedule of the existing Constitution of Malaya within a maximum period of years to be recommended by an Intergovernmental Committee. The Legislatures of each territory will be empowered to effect this change at an earlier date, if they think fit.

(b) Subject to the above, the States will have the exclusive right to amend their own Constitutions.

6.   *Head of State*. The Heads of State in North Borneo and Sarawak will be appointed by His Majesty The Yang di-Pertuan Agong acting in his discretion but after consultation with the Chief Minister. However, in the case of the first appointments the Malayan Government will consult the British Government before tendering advice to His Majesty.

7.   *Secession*. The States of the new Federation of Malaysia will not have any right of secession.

8. *Representation in the Federal Parliament*

(a) Representation in the Federal Parliament for the territories will be in accordance with the principles laid down in the Thirteenth Schedule of the Malayan Constitution with additional weightage to take account of the particular circumstances of the territories.

(b) Representatives of North Borneo and Sarawak in the Federal House of Representatives will, until the system of direct elections is introduced, be elected by their respective legislatures.

(c) The independent Federal Election Commission, which is responsible for delimiting constituencies throughout the Federation and which is now composed of a Chairman and two Malayan members, will be enlarged by the addition of one member from the Borneo territories.

9. *Electoral system*. The present electoral college system in Sarawak will be retained and a similar electoral system will be introduced in North Borneo as soon as practicable and without awaiting the establishment of Malaysia.

10. *Legislative Lists*. The Federal, State and Concurrent Lists in North Borneo and Sarawak will follow the Constitution of the existing Federation of Malaya, except where otherwise agreed between the Malayan and British Governments. An Intergovernmental Committee will consider what exceptions should be made other than those specified.

11. *Judiciary*

(a) There will be a Federal Supreme Court having appellate jurisdiction throughout the Federation.

(b) There will be a High Court in the Borneo territories from which appeals would lie to the Federal Supreme Court.

(c) The Federal Supreme Court will have exclusive original jurisdiction in cases between States or between a State and the central Government.

(d) Other matters relating to the Judiciary will be studied by an Intergovernmental Committee.

12. *Citizenship*. The provisions governing citizenship will be drafted by the legal representatives of the two Governments on the lines set out in *Appendix B* and approved by an Intergovernmental Committee.

13. *Religion*

(a) Complete freedom of religion will be guaranteed in accordance with the Constitution.

(b) An Intergovernmental Committee will consider how best to reassure the peoples of North Borneo and Sarawak on this matter, which is of primary importance to the territories.

14. *Language*

(a) The national language will be Malay.

(b) For all purposes in North Borneo and Sarawak the use of indigenous languages will continue as at present.

(c) So long as the State Government so desires, English will continue to be an official language in North Borneo and Sarawak.

15. *Immigration into North Borneo and Sarawak from other parts of Malaysia*

(a) There will be certain constitutional safeguards with regard to the entry of persons into North Borneo and Sarawak from other parts of Malaysia.
(b) These safeguards will take the following form:—

(i) The existing Federal Constitution will be amended to enable the Federal Parliament to legislate to empower the State Governments to control the movement, otherwise than on the grounds specified in Article 9 (2), of persons from other parts of Malaysia into North Borneo or Sarawak, and to provide that any such legislation may not be repealed or amended without the concurrence of the Government of the State concerned.

(ii) The Government of the Federation would give a solemn undertaking to pass, simultaneously with the admission of the Borneo territories into Malaysia, a law conferring upon each of the States of North Borneo and Sarawak power to control the entry into the State of persons from other parts of Malaysia, subject to provisions designed to secure that a person or class of persons should be admitted or refused admission into the State if the Federal Government considers that this is necessary or expedient in the interests of defence, internal security, external affairs, or in order to enable the Federation Government to carry out its other constitutional and administrative responsibilities.

(iii) The detailed provisions of the law referred to in sub-paragraph (ii) above will be worked out by an Intergovernmental Committee.

16. *Immigration into North Borneo and Sarawak from outside Malaysia*

(a) Whilst it is accepted that the control of immigration from outside Malaysia will be a Federal matter, it is agreed that North Borneo and Sarawak will be given under the Constitution a measure of control over the admission of persons into those States from outside Malaysia.
(b) This will take the form of amending the existing Federal Constitution so as to provide without prejudice to Article 9(1):—

(i) that the Government of North Borneo or Sarawak may request the Federal Government to deny admission to the State to any particular person or class of persons from outside Malaysia other than members or officers of the Federal Government.

(ii) The Federal Government will comply with such a request unless in its opinion the admission of that person or class of persons is necessary or expedient in the interests of defence, internal security, or external affairs or in order to enable the Federal Government to carry out its other constitutional and administrative responsibilities.

17. *Education*. Education will be in the Federal List. An Intergovernmental Committee will consider:—

(a) the form of assurances to be given regarding the continued use of English or other languages of instruction in North Borneo and Sarawak;
(b) the question of the delegation by the Federal Government of functions in regard to education to State or local education bodies.

18. *Tariffs*

(a) Tariffs will be on the Federal List.

(b) The alignment of the present tariffs in North Borneo and Sarawak with those of the rest of the Federation will be effected by stages.

(c) The detailed arrangements will be worked out by an Intergovernmental Committee.

19. *Indigenous Races.* Members of indigenous races in North Borneo and Sarawak (as defined in the Interpretation (Definition of Native) Ordinance, 1952, as amended by the Interpretation (Definition of Native) (Amendment) Ordinance, 1958, of North Borneo, and in the Interpretation Ordinance, 1953, of Sarawak) who are citizens of Malaysia will enjoy a special position analogous to that at present enjoyed by Malays in Malaya under the Constitution of the Federation of Malaya. This provision, the details of which will be worked out by an Intergovernmental Committee, will be embodied in the Constitution of the Federation of Malaysia.

20. *Shipping and Navigation.* Shipping and Navigation will be in the Federal List but the extent to which jetties and small installations (coastal or riverine) should be in the Concurrent List will be considered by an Intergovernmental Committee.

21. *Fisheries.* Fisheries will be in the Federal List, but an Intergovernmental Committee will consider how exclusive rights should be defined and protected.

22. *Labour and Social Security*

(a) Labour and Social Security will be in the Federal List.

(b) Charities will be in the Concurrent List to the extent necessary to give the States power to legislate for local charities.

23. *Regionalisation of Federal Services.* Such Federal Services in North Borneo and Sarawak as may be agreed by an Intergovernmental Committee will be administered on a regional basis.

24. *British Officials*

(a) The two Governments are agreed upon the importance of retaining as many as possible of the British and other expatriate officials.

(b) An appropriate scheme for inducement and compensation will be worked out, in consultation with the representatives of the officers concerned.

25. *Report of Cobbold Commission.* The Cobbold Report will be published simultaneously with the announcement of the present decisions reached by the two Governments.

26. *Brunei.* His Highness the Sultan of Brunei will be consulted regarding the application where appropriate of the above decisions to Brunei.

27. *Intergovernmental Committee*

(a) The Intergovernmental Committee referred to in preceding paragraphs will consist of representatives of the Governments of the United Kingdom, Malaya, North Borneo and Sarawak, under a Chairman to be nominated by the British Government.

(b) The precise composition of the Committee will be decided by agreement between the British and Malayan representatives.

(c) Representatives from Brunei may be invited to attend meetings of the Committee if this is considered desirable.

28. *Singapore Citizenship*. The arrangements for citizenship for the inhabitants of Singapore will be in the form agreed between the Governments of Malaya and Singapore as set out in paragraph 14 of Singapore White Paper Cmd. 33 of 1961, as amended in regard to nomenclature and franchise in the terms of *Appendix C*.

29. *Public Statement*. A joint public statement in the terms of *Appendix D* will be issued on Wednesday, August 1st, at about 14.30 hours G.M.T.

Appendix A: Framework of initial state constitutions of Sarawak and North Borneo

The Governor

1. There will be a *Governor* of each State with powers similar to those possessed by the Governors of Malacca and Penang, i.e. he will be a constitutional Head of State.

2. The Governor in each State will be appointed by H.M. The Yang di-Pertuan Agong acting in his discretion but after consultation with the Chief Minister of the State concerned. However, in the case of the first appointment, the Malayan Government will consult the British Government before tendering advice to His Majesty.

The Executive

3. The executive authority of the State will be formally vested in the Governor. But he will normally be obliged to act on the advice of an *Executive Council* (see below). Thus the general direction and control of the State Governments will be exercised by the Executive Council. The Governor will, however, act in his discretion in:—

(a) the appointment of a Chief Minister (see below) and
(b) the withholding of consent to a request for the dissolution of the Legislative Assembly.

4. The Executive Council in each State will be appointed as follows:—

(a) The Governor will first appoint as *Chief Minister* to preside over the Executive Council a member of the Legislative Assembly (see below) who in his view is likely to command the confidence of a majority of the members of the Assembly.
(b) The Governor will then, on the Advice of the Chief Minister, appoint other members from among the members of the Legislative Assembly. Until such time as the Legislative Assembly is fully elected these will include the State Secretary, the State Legal Adviser and the State Financial Officer (see below) as *ex officio* members.

5. The Executive Council will be collectively responsible to the Legislative Assembly.

The Legislature

6. The Legislature in each State will consist of the Governor and a Legislative Assembly.

7. Initially, the existing State Legislatures will continue in being as the State Legislative Assemblies. Until each Assembly is fully elected, a Speaker will be

appointed by the Governor, and the State Secretary, the State Legal Adviser and the State Financial Officer (see below) will be members *ex officio*, and the practice of nominating members will also continue.

8. Fully elected membership for the Legislative Assemblies would be introduced as soon as practicable. In the first instance election will be effected through the electoral college system.

Administrative Structure

9. The principal officer in charge of administrative affairs in the State will be styled *State Secretary*.

He will be the channel through whom instructions pass from the Executive Council to the civil service.

10. Other principal officers will be the *State Legal Adviser* and the *State Financial Officer*.

11. Below these, government will be effected through departments, each in the charge of a *Head of Department*.

12. The Federal Government will establish a Department charged with general responsibility for the administrative integration of the new States into the Federation. The staff of the Department will include officers with specialized knowledge and experience of the territories.

Appendix B: Citizenship

(a) A citizen of the United Kingdom and Colonies born in Sarawak or North Borneo or naturalized in either territory before the date on which Malaysia comes into effect shall by operation of law become a citizen of the Federation of Malaysia. Included in this category are persons who were born in either of the territories before the dates on which they became British colonies. There is, however, one qualification that needs to be made. Some persons in this category might have severed all connexion with Borneo and the other territories that will form Malaysia. There needs to be evidence of permanent residence and a person in this category shall accordingly be deemed to be permanently resident in a territory if he has resided in either territory (or partly in the one and partly in the other) for a continuous period of five years immediately before the formation of Malaysia. It is important that there should be the minimum of formality in establishing such permanent residence. Periods of absence which are not inconsistent with essential continuity of residence should not be regarded as a break in continuous residence.

(b) A person resident in Sarawak or North Borneo on the date on which Malaysia comes into being should be eligible to apply for registration as a citizen of Malaysia at any time during the first eight years after that date if:—

(i) he has resided before Malaysia in either territory (or partly the one and partly the other) or after Malaysia in any of the territories of the Federation for periods amounting to 8 out of 12 years preceding his application and which include the 12 months immediately preceding his application; and

(ii) he intends to reside permanently in the Federation; and

(iii) he is of good character.

Again, as with the previous category, the formalities for obtaining citizenship should be reduced to the minimum so that as few difficulties as possible are put in the way of people who have made their homes in the Borneo territories and who wish to remain in Malaysia as citizens. During the period of the application of these arrangements the existing provision in Sarawak and North Borneo regarding a language test should apply. There should also be a waiver of the language test where application for registration is made within two years after the creation of Malaysia and the applicant has attained the age of 45 years at the date of the application. Such an applicant should take the citizenship oath in the form prescribed in the existing Constitution of the Federation of Malaya.

If a person obtains a certificate of citizenship under this arrangement it should be possible for him to apply, at the same time that he obtains his own certificate, for the grant of a certificate of citizenship in respect of any of his minor children born before that date and ordinarily resident with him in Malaysia.

(c)   The citizenship provisions recommended above shall be subject to the special guarantee that no amendment, modification or withdrawal shall be made by the Federal Government without the positive concurrence of the Government of the State concerned.

(d)   Subject to the above points, after Malaysia is established, the existing provisions of the Constitution of the Federation of Malaya relating to the acquisition and termination of citizenship shall apply *mutatis mutandis*.

This will mean, *inter alia*, that all persons born in the Borneo territories after Malaysia will be citizens of Malaysia by operation of law, provided that one of their parents is a citizen, or is a permanent resident of the Federation. Adequate publicity should be given to this point in order to dispel doubts about the position of non-natives. The provisions of the Constitution of the Federation of Malaysia relating to citizenship shall be not less favourable for the inhabitants of North Borneo and Sarawak than the provisions governing the citizenship of the inhabitants of any part of the Federation of Malaysia other than Singapore or (in the event of special arrangements being made for citizenship in that territory) Brunei.

Appendix C: Singapore citizenship

Arrangements agreed between Governments of Malaya and Singapore
Singapore citizens will be citizens of Malaysia. As the Federation of Malaya will cease to be a separate State it will not be possible to have a separate citizenship of the Federation of Malaya. There will therefore be only two citizenships:—

(i)   citizenship of Malaysia;
(ii) citizenship of Singapore.

The existing State nationalities of the Malay States will, of course, continue.
2.   There will be reciprocal restrictions on franchise rights so that:—

(a) only citizens of Singapore will be allowed to vote or stand as candidates for election in Singapore; and
(b) citizens of Singapore will not be allowed to vote or stand as candidates for election in any part of Malaysia outside Singapore.

3.   There will have to be constitutional machinery for this. This can be done, it is suggested, by amending the Federal Constitution:—

(a) to prevent a citizen of Malaysia, who is also a citizen of Singapore, from voting or standing for election in any part of the Federation outside Singapore; and

(b) to prevent a citizen of Malaysia, who is not a citizen of Singapore, from voting or standing for election in Singapore.

4.   In order not to disenfranchise a citizen of Singapore permanently in the Federation outside Singapore, it will be necessary to provide machinery to enable a citizen of Malaysia who is also a citizen of Singapore to exercise his franchise rights in the Federation outside Singapore. This can be done by enabling a person who satisfies the residence and other qualifications for citizenship under the Federal law to qualify for a registration as a voter in the Federation outside Singapore. So long as he is registered in the Federation, his name will be deleted from the electoral roll of Singapore.

30TH JULY, 1962

Appendix D: Joint public statement

1.   The British and Malayan Governments have received and studied the Report of the Commission under the chairmanship of Lord Cobbold which visited North Borneo and Sarawak earlier this year to ascertain the views of the inhabitants on the proposal to create a Federation of Malaysia embracing Malaya, Singapore, Sarawak, North Borneo and Brunei. The Report is being published today.

2.   The two Governments are most grateful to the Commission for their valuable Report and have accepted almost all the recommendations on which the Commission were unanimous. The two Governments have noted in particular that the Commission were unanimously agreed that a Federation of Malaysia is in the best interests of North Borneo and Sarawak and that an early decision in principle should be reached.

3.   In the light of this Report and of the agreement reached between the Government of Malaya and the Government of Singapore, the British and Malayan Governments have now decided in principle that, subject to the necessary legislation, the proposed Federation of Malaysia should be brought into being by 31st August, 1963.

4.   To give effect to this decision, the two Governments intend to conclude, within the next six months, a formal agreement which, among other things, will provide for:—

(a) the transfer of sovereignty in North Borneo, Sarawak and Singapore by 31st August, 1963;

(b) provisions governing the relationship between Singapore and the new Federation, as agreed between the Governments of Malaya and Singapore;

(c) defence arrangements as set out in the joint statement by the British and Malayan Governments dated 22nd November, 1961; and

(d) detailed constitutional arrangements, including safeguards for the special interests of North Borneo and Sarawak, to be drawn up after consultation with the Legislatures of the two territories.

5.   These safeguards will cover such matters as religious freedom, education, representation in the Federal Parliament, the position of the indigenous races, control of immigration, citizenship and the State constitutions.

6.   In order that the introduction of the new Federal system may be effected as smoothly as possible and with the least disturbance to existing administrative arrangements, there will be, after the transfer of sovereignty, a transition period, during which a number of the Federal constitutional powers will be delegated temporarily to the State Governments.

7.   An Inter-Governmental Committee will be established as soon as possible, on which the British, Malayan, North Borneo and Sarawak Governments will be represented. Its task will be to work out the future constitutional arrangements and the form of the necessary safeguards.

8.   The Minister of State for the Colonies, Lord Lansdowne, who will be the Chairman of this Committee, and the Deputy Prime Minister of the Federation of Malaya, Tun Abdul Razak, will proceed shortly to Sarawak and North Borneo to conduct discussions.

9.   In order to maintain the efficiency of the administration, the British and Malayan Governments are agreed on the importance of retaining the services of as many of the expatriate officials as possible. The Minister of State will discuss with the Governments of the territories and with the Staff Associations how this best can be done.

10.   The British and Malayan Governments have informed the Sultan of Brunei of the agreement they have reached and have made it clear that they would welcome the inclusion of the State of Brunei in the new Federation.

141   CAB 134/1951, GM(62)42   10 Sept 1962
'Report on visit to North Borneo, Sarawak and Brunei by the minister of state for colonial affairs from 14 August to 30 August, 1962': report by Lord Lansdowne on preparations to implement Malaysia through the Inter-Governmental Committee

[The agreement of 31 July 1962 (see 140), to bring about a Federation of Malaysia by 31 Aug 1963, required an Inter-Governmental Committee to work out the future constitutional arrangements and necessary safeguards for North Borneo and Sarawak. As Lansdowne reports here, however, the London announcement came 'as a great shock' to North Borneo. On 13–14 Aug Donald Stephens convened a meeting of political leaders who drew up a fourteen-point (later twenty-point) programme of minimum demands. These Twenty Points gained weight by attracting support in Sarawak and went far beyond what the Malayans had conceded at the London talks in July. Although North Borneo's Legislative Council and Sarawak's Council Negri agreed to the principle of Malaysia (on 12 and 26 Sept respectively), they did so on condition that state rights were safeguarded. The IGC was chaired by Lord Lansdowne, with Tun Razak as deputy chairman, and had representatives from Malaya, North Borneo and Sarawak. There were no members from Singapore while Brunei sent observers. Lansdowne and Razak visited Borneo in Aug (as reported in this document) and at a preparatory meeting of the IGC in Jesselton on 30 Aug five sub-committees were set up. The sub-committees (all chaired by Sir John Martin) covered constitutional, fiscal, legal and judicial matters, public service, and departmental organisation. H P Hall and T J O'Brien, who was seconded from the British high commission in KL, serviced the IGC. The first sub-committee met on 8 Oct and plenary sessions were held on 22–24 Oct, 23–26 Nov and 18–20 Dec after which remaining points of detail were remitted to an ad hoc committee of specialists. Deadlock almost occurred over financial issues and development aid but these matters were eventually resolved. As regards constitutional relations, although they failed to secure an initial seven-year period during which legislative power should remain within the state (rather than being delegated to it), North Borneo and Sarawak won a number of safeguards which could not be changed by the federal government without the concurrence of the state government. To prevent amendment of the federal constitution, however, they would require a two-thirds majority in the federal house of representatives which they could achieve only by voting together and also in concert with Singapore. Lansdowne's interim reports went to the Greater Malaysia (Official) Committee, see 146. The final report was initialled on 22 Jan 1963 and published on 27 Feb as *Malaysia: Report of the Inter-Governmental Committee, 1962* (Cmnd 1954). The Council Negri of Sarawak adopted its recommendations on 8 Mar and North Borneo's Legislative Council followed suit on 13 Mar (CO 1030/1032; CO 1030/1050; CO1030/1052, no 73; CO 1030/1053–1057, 1065–1067; GM(62)44 and GM(62)46, CAB 134/1951; DO 189/259; FO 371/169694, nos 10 and 11).]

On 1st August, it was announced in Parliament that the British and Malayan Governments had decided in principle that the proposed Federation of Malaysia should be brought into being by 31st August, 1963. It was also announced that detailed constitutional arrangements, including safeguards for the special interests of North Borneo and Sarawak, would be drawn up after consultation with the legislatures of the two territories. An Intergovernmental Committee was to be established as soon as possible on which the British, Malayan, North Borneo and Sarawak Governments would be represented. The task of the Intergovernmental Committee, of which I was to be Chairman, would be to work out the future constitutional arrangements and the form of the necessary safeguards for the two territories.

2. I arrived in Jesselton on 14th August and was joined at Kuching on 18th August by Tun Abdul Razak, the Deputy Prime Minister of the Federation of Malaya.

3. The primary purpose of our visit was to set up the Intergovernmental Committee, but first it was necessary to promote acceptance of the early date for Malaysia and also to attempt to allay the anxieties, both of the people and of the British officers, over what appeared to many of them as a Malayan 'take-over'. We therefore travelled the territories extensively and with our Malayan colleagues met as many of the leaders of the people as possible and talked also with the expatriate and locally employed officers. At our meetings we explained the concept of Malaysia and described how the Intergovernmental Committee would work. We listened to a great number of opinions on special safeguards for the territories. We emphasized that we were not a repeat order of the Cobbold Commission and explained that it was the responsibility of the representatives of the four Governments in the Intergovernmental Committee to work out the form of the necessary safeguards.

4. Mr. Philip Rogers[1] in my party was specifically charged with the task of discussing a compensation scheme with the British expatriate officers.

5. At the London talks, the territories were represented by the Governor of North Borneo, Sir William Goode and the Governor of Sarawak, Sir Alexander Waddell. Unfortunately, Sir Alexander Waddell had to remain in London owing to illness. Sir William Goode returned to North Borneo on 3rd August and was able to do a lot to take the edge off the consternation caused by the London decision. Nevertheless,

---

[1] Philip Rogers, formerly of the CO, was under-secretary, Department of Technical Co-operation, 1961–1964. For discussions about compensation for expatriate officers see, for example, 143, paras 3 and 4.

when we arrived in Jesselton, it was still clear that the London announcement had come as a great shock.

6.   In our numerous meetings, all our conversations were directed towards correcting the basic misconception that Her Majesty's Government was about to sanction a Malayan 'take-over' and that the progress and happiness of the peoples of the territories were being sacrificed to world politics. Although much had been done by British officers to popularize the concept of Malaysia, even amongst people who were in favour of it there were grave misgivings about the speed with which it was being brought about. As our tour proceeded, and with the help of good publicity, there was a general improvement in attitude. Both the concept of Malaysia and its early date gained more general acceptance. But this acceptance was conditional upon the Intergovernmental Committee agreeing constitutional arrangements which would meet the anxieties and aspirations of the territories.

7.   The improvement in the political climate could not have been brought about without the consistent help and tactful guidance of Sir William Goode and Mr. Jakeway, the Officer Administering the Government of Sarawak. Equally our mission could have achieved no success without the co-operation of Tun Razak and his colleagues. Although this British–Malayan mission has helped to restore confidence, it is my opinion that the negotiations in the Intergovernmental Committee will require the most careful handling.

8.   The main problems with which the Intergovernmental Committee will have to deal are:—

(a) Freedom of religion.
(b) English as an official language and medium of instruction.
(c) Heads of the States and their eligibility for Headship of the Federation.
(d) Representation in Federal legislature.
(e) Division of financial control between Federal and State legislatures.
(f) Funds for development.
(g) Control of immigration.
(h) Citizenship.
(i) Degree of State autonomy within the Federation.
(j) Safeguards against future amendment to Federation and State constitutions.

Views were expressed both orally and in memoranda on all these subjects, and by the end of our tour the North Borneo political parties had agreed a joint memorandum outlining their views. It seems likely that the political parties in Sarawak will also attempt to reach an agreed line. The only *organized* political opposition to the concept of Malaysia is from the Communist controlled left-wing of the S.U.P.P. in Sarawak.

9.   I had a two hours private talk with the Sultan of Brunei in the middle of our tour. The Sultan wished to know how the Intergovernmental Committee would work and all his questions on Malaysia were directed towards ascertaining how we thought he would fit into the picture. As I stonewalled, he asked whether I thought he should put up proposals to the Malayan Government. I reminded him that Sir John Martin had suggested this in March.[2] (The Sultan had in fact already set up a Committee, of

---

[2] Martin had visited the Sultan in Jan, and in Mar 1962 Maudling had set out the advantages of merger in a letter, see 91 and 95.

which the High Commissioner, Sir Denis White, is a member, to study the situation and to formulate proposals. I understood that this Committee was to meet shortly after our visit.)

I am convinced that the main attraction of Malaysia to the Sultan is in the hope of protecting his own position by joining the Sultan's [sic] Club. He also wishes to be Agong of the Federation and has been offered this carrot by the Malayans.

He will certainly fight hard for the maximum control of State revenues. Whatever he does will closely affect the Bornean discussions.

Tun Razak who visited the Sultan earlier last month had tentatively agreed to the Sultan sending observers to the Intergovernmental Committee. As I thought this might strengthen our position, I accepted Tun Razak's suggestion and formally invited the Sultan to send observers. This he agreed to do at the first plenary session in October.

10.   We held a preparatory meeting of the Intergovernmental Committee in Jesselton on 30th August and agreed that the following Sub-Committees should be set up:—

Constitutional.
Fiscal.
Public Service.
Legal and Judicial.
Departmental Organization.

The first plenary meeting of the Intergovernmental Committee will be held at its headquarters in Jesselton in the middle of October and will be attended by Tun Razak and myself. Meanwhile, under the supervision of permanent representatives of the four governments, the work of the Sub-Committee is proceeding. I have reserved the right of Chairmanship of all committees to the British.

11.   The joint submission of the North Borneo political parties goes well beyond what the Malayans appeared to be prepared to concede in London. Throughout the London talks, the Malayans consistently under-estimated the difficulties involved in the accession of the territories to Malaysia. Thanks, however, to the frank and forceful way in which the Borneans expressed their views throughout our tour, the Malayans accepted the reality of the difficulties. Dato Aziz[3] even went so far as to acknowledge to Sir William Goode that whereas in London he had considered the Governors' attitude obstructive, he now realized that they had only been representing the true views of the people. He repeated this admission in the presence of a number of colleagues in Kuala Lumpur. I believe that our Malayan colleagues now realize that British concern over the form of Malaysia is directed solely towards the determination to create a federation which will stick.

12.   Our tour enabled our Malayan colleagues to obtain a more realistic appreciation of the situation in the territories. Much will depend, however, upon the impression formed by the Tunku himself after his visit to the territories this month. If *agreed* solutions are to be reached in the Intergovernmental Committee, the Malayans will have to make concessions. There are as yet only very slight indications that they may be prepared to do so.

13.   It is impossible to forecast how many of the British officers will remain. The chief factors upon which they will make their decision are:—

---

[3] Dato Abdul Aziz bin Haji Abdul Majid, permanent secretary, Prime Minister's Office.

(1) The constitutional arrangements and safeguards agreed by the Intergovernmental Committee.

(2) Terms of compensation and inducement.

(3) The length of service to which they may look forward.

(4) Personal considerations.

In my opinion it is most important that the British officers should know the terms of compensation and inducement by the end of this year.

I have requested the Governments of the territories to work out as quickly as possible the probable rate of Borneanization of the Service.

The form of Malaysia and the role which the British officers will be called upon to play will be quite as important to them as any financial consideration.

14.   It was suggested to us that the Malayans, in claiming that Malaysia would bring about an accelerated rate of development in the territories, were offering a 'false prospectus'. It was argued that if the price of rubber continued to fall and if British Colonial and Development Welfare aid were no longer forthcoming, the rate of Bornean development must inevitably be retarded.

The view was expressed both by Bornean and British speakers that the idea of Malaysia was accepted because the British who were responsible for the territories recommended it. If the territories suffered thereby, the British would be to blame.

Not only was the wish that the British officers should remain repeatedly expressed, but also the fervent hope that British financial aid should not be withdrawn.

I am bound to say that in view of the fact that Her Majesty's Government is giving up its responsibility for the territories before they are ready to achieve independence on their own, we have a continuing obligation to help them. I consider that we cannot honourably discharge this obligation to the peoples of the territories whom we are persuading to accept Malaysia, unless we maintain our assistance after Federation at a level not lower than the existing Colonial Development and Welfare grants. This should not include the cost of any compensation scheme.

If Malaysia is to fulfil the hopes we have for it, it must be demonstrably successful and successful from the start and this will cost money.

15.   I would like to record my gratitude to the first-class team which accompanied me and with them to express our thanks to the Governors, the High Commissioner and the officers throughout the territories for the invaluable assistance and co-operation which they gave to us and our Malayan colleagues. Despite short notice, all the arrangements made for our travel and meetings were admirably organized.

142 CO 1030/1031, no E32   11 Sept 1962
[Tunku Abdul Rahman and the Borneo territories]: record by Lord Lansdowne of his conversations with Tunku Abdul Rahman and Tun Razak in Kuala Lumpur on 1 Sept 1962

Before calling on the Tunku, I had a few minutes conversation with Tun Razak. I repeated to him the importance which I attached to his accompanying the Tunku on his visit to the territories. Wallace and I both emphasised that his visit had created confidence and we considered that by his accompanying the Tunku the Malayans would be building on success.

2.   I told Tun Razak that I hoped Ghazalie would not accompany the Tunku as it was my impression that he was on the wrong wavelength and gave the impression of being supercilious. Tun Razak appeared to take the point (he did not bring Ghazalie with him on the second leg of his visit to the territories). I told him that both Dato Abdul Aziz and Dato Nik Daud in his party, had made a good impression.

3.   Tun Razak said that as he had been asked to deputise for the Tunku at the [Commonwealth] Prime Ministers' Conference, he thought it would be difficult for him to accompany the Tunku to the territories in September. Tun Razak told us that the Tunku was due to visit India and Pakistan in October and he himself had to go to Korea in early November. I then suggested that if the Tunku could visit the territories during the last week of September, perhaps Tun Razak could be absent for three days which would enable him to start the tour off on the right foot at Jesselton. Tun Razak said that he thought that would be possible.

The Tunku had reserved from 11.0 a.m. onwards for a talk. I arranged with Tun Razak to see him alone at first, explaining that I thought it would be less embarrassing if I could privately point out the difficulties in which the Tunku had put us by some of his utterances to the Press. Tun Razak agreed to this and I spent about half an hour alone with the Tunku.

2.   I told the Tunku that although H.M.G. was one hundred per cent behind him in wishing to bring about Malaysia I felt it only fair to say that it was [of] vital importance that the territories should be brought in in the right way, if Malaysia was to endure.

3.   I showed him Press reports of his statement on March 12th, with banner headlines 'Tengku accuses' British Civil Servants in the Borneo territories of hampering Malaysia.[1] I also drew his attention to an article in the Straits Times of August 21st which quoted him as saying 'we will be helping (the territories) to throw off the British yoke and attain independence for themselves'. I then recalled a paragraph from his speech in Parliament on the 15th August, in which he referred to the importance of retaining the British Officers. I told him that I had not been aware of this statement during our tour in the territories and much regretted that it had not been given more publicity. I had of course reported at all our meetings what he had said in London about the importance of retaining British Officers, but what had been carried by the Press to which I had referred had made a deep impression.

4.   The Tunku took all this in very good part. As to his statements in March he said quite bluntly that it was then his opinion that the British officers were against Malaysia and 'I therefore had to attack them'. I told him that I was quite satisfied that they were not against Malaysia and indeed were working actively for it. I did think however that the early date was too much of a shock for some of the older members of the Service and I suspected that they would probably leave. As to his remarks about the British yoke, with a big twinkle in his eye, he reminded me that when he was fighting for Merdeka in Malaya, he had used the same tactics to build up a national spirit. Of course, he had always looked upon the British as his best friends and he still did. I told him that I quite understood these tactics, but this sort of thing did make it extremely difficult for us with the British officers on whom he had said himself he very much relied.

---

[1] See 96, 97 and 98.

5. I reminded the Tunku that he had referred in London to a number of expatriate officers who had volunteered to serve in the territories. I asked him if he could remember how many had applied. He said that to the best of his recollection it was about seventeen, all of whom were first class men and had served in Malaya. I told him that when asked at our meetings by the Borneans what would happen if a large number of British officers left and if, as they had been assured, replacements were not available from Malaya, I had said it would be necessary to recruit from outside. The Tunku said that it had been suggested to him that he might recruit exclusively from the U.K. but he doubted the wisdom of this.

6. Tun Razak then joined us and we talked of the political consciousness of the peoples in the territories. The Tunku expressed the view that no one other than the Malays had any political views at all. I decided not to dispute this misconception as I thought it better for the Tunku to learn by his experience on visiting the territories. I did, however, say that it seemed to us that there was a danger of the Malays in Sarawak thinking that they would automatically get all the best posts. The Tunku said at once that I need not worry about that as there has been an exact parallel in the Federation and he had seen to it that there was no preferential treatment. I did not comment on this obvious inaccuracy.

7. The Tunku said that all his information was to the effect that the S.U.P.P. were highly organised and had close links with Communist cells in Singapore. I told him that my impression was that the S.U.P.P. was in considerable state of disarray and with clever handling it might be possible to disengage the Chairman Mr. Ong Kee Hui and thereby to create a separate group of moderates and expose the extremists in their true colours. Tun Razak appeared to accept this possibility and agreed that Ong Kee Hui was one of the most able politicians in the territory.

8. I referred to the anxiety which I believed to exist in the minds of many of the people that they would be dominated by Malaya and that they remembered the unhappy history of Brunei Malays in Sarawak. The Tunku laughed at this and said that of course they couldn't remember as all this took place before the Rajahs and this phobia was something that had been generated by the British. He added that the people from the territories had told him that the British had said that after Malaysia they would be taken over by the Malays.

9. I asked Tun Razak whether he thought we ought to say something to the Tunku about the religious problem. Rather reluctantly Tun Razak agreed that we might, which made me think that he was hoping to handle this matter himself. I told the Tunku that the people wanted more than just freedom of worship i.e. freedom of religion which included freedom to propagate. Tun Razak muttered something about the Tunku having agreed in principle so I decided to leave the subject. I have the impression that we may be edging towards something acceptable.

10. I reminded the Tunku that when I saw him off from the London Airport[2] I had suggested that an early visit to the territories would be very valuable. I repeated this suggestion and the Tunku at once agreed.[3] I told him that I hoped it would be possible for him to take Tun Razak with him and that he might go this month. He said that he would like to meet the people informally. I suggested that he should meet the British officers informally too and to this he readily agreed.

---

[2] On 8 Aug after the Malaysia agreement had been signed on 31 July.   [3] He went in November.

11.   He then went off on a rather rambling talk about the peoples of the territories being good, honest but very unsophisticated people. The Dayaks were suddenly becoming full of self-importance as they were being wooed on all sides and if they were wooed too much they would ask for too much. They should be told what to do. The trouble was that with the exception of Donald Stephens there were no political leaders in the territories.

12.   I asked the Tunku what ideas he had about the Head of each State. From what I had heard there appeared to be no obvious candidates. He said that there seemed to be odd ideas in the territories that a Yang di-Pertuan Negara could be created, but this was ridiculous as there were no hereditary rulers in the territories. I again asked what he had in mind. Without hesitation he replied Datu Bandar for Head of State in Sarawak, though he knew his health was very poor, and a Dayak District Officer as Chief Minister. In North Borneo Datu Mustapha for Head of State and Donald Stephens as his Chief Minister. Tun Razak said that this would work very well as Stephens and Mustapha were good friends and Mustapha was senior to him on the Executive Council. He then spoke vaguely of appointing a Minister from the territories to the Federal Government at an early date.[4] To my surprise he added that if necessary, the Governors could stay on for a few months.

13.   I got the impression that the Tunku was still determined to minimize the difficulties involved. 'Let them come here and see how happy everybody is together.' I said that this would certainly be useful but it was equally important in my opinion for Malays to visit the territories. He said that I could rest assured that he would arrange this.

14.   I told the Tunku that on a number of occasions Borneans who accepted Malaysia in principle had suggested that they would prefer sovereignty to be transferred to them in the first instance, even if only for a day. I also told him that I had discussed this suggestion with Tun Razak and that we were both of the opinion that provided this could be properly buttoned up beforehand it might well have advantages. Apart from the political advantages which might accrue both to H.M.G. and to the Government of the Federation of Malaya (voluntary merger rather than transfer, merger rather than absorption) there might also be advantage over the Filipino claim. U.N. interest in the Filipino claim might be reduced if North Borneo could be shown to be an independent State before joining Malaysia. The Tunku thought this idea was worth thinking about provided there were no risk of a slip between independence and Malaysia. The Philippines being indirectly raised in this context, I was able to ask the Tunku to keep his Government in close touch with H.M.G. so as to avoid conflicting public statements over the Filipino claim. The Tunku said that he had made it clear that his Government was not involved but he had had to 'play about' with the Filipinos. I said that I hoped he would not play about with them too much and that we could maintain close liaison.

15.   I asked Tun Razak whether he had explained the position over the secret London Agreement[5] insofar as negotiations in Borneo were concerned. As he said

---

[4] The appointments of Datu Mustapha as head of state and Donald Stephens as chief minister were uncontested, unlike the nominations for Sarawak. In addition a minister would be appointed from Sarawak and another from Sabah (but none from Singapore) to sit in the federal Cabinet. See 210 and 224.
[5] See 140.

that he had not, I told the Tunku that in my opinion it was necessary in our discussions with the Borneans to start from scratch. This did not, however, of course, mean any retreat from the points already agreed. I told him that I had discussed this with Tun Razak and explained it to Dato Aziz. Although the Tunku did not look particularly pleased he evidently accepted that it was necessary.

143   CAB 134/1951, GM(62)43   28 Sept 1962
'Financial questions': note by the CRO for a meeting of the Greater Malaysia (Official) Committee

A fairly long list of financial questions will need to be settled in connection with the creation of Malaysia.[1] It seems useful at the present stage for the Committee to take stock of these questions, to consider what work needs to be done before answers to them can be suggested, and in due course to submit proposals on certain of them to Ministers. The Committee may also find it useful to examine the timetable for consideration of these questions.

2.   Broadly the financial questions fall into three categories:—

(a) The compensation-incentive scheme for expatriate personnel in North Borneo and Sarawak;
(b) The scale of British assistance to the projected expansion of the Malaysian armed forces;
(c) The question of a British contribution to development expenditure in Malaysia.

These three categories are considered in turn below.

3.   *The compensation-incentive scheme.* Proposals have been submitted to the Treasury by the Colonial Office for a compensation-inducement scheme for expatriate officers in the Borneo Territories. The scheme would cost up to £3½ m. over 5 years.[2] Of this one-half, according to precedent, would be borne by Her Majesty's Government under the Overseas Services Aid Scheme and one half by the Territories.

4.   This is the most urgent financial question from the British point of view. If we are to have a smooth transfer of power, without serious danger of trouble and perhaps bloodshed in the Territories, as many as possible of the expatriates must be induced to stay on and a prerequisite of this is that they should know where they

---

[1] Financial questions were considered by the committee on 2 Oct (GM(62)8th meeting, CAB 134/1950).

[2] See correspondence between Sir H Poynton (permanent, under-secretary, CO) and Sir R Harris (third secretary, Treasury) at CO 1030/1064. In his letter of 26 Oct, Harris accepted in principle the CO's case that inducements should be offered to expatriates to stay on: 'the situation in [North] Borneo and Sarawak is unique, not simply because in HMG's view the local inhabitants are not fully ready for independence (this could be the situation elsewhere and yet we might have had to move to independence for wider reasons of policy) but in addition we are leaving the local inhabitants in a position in which their future may be at risk if non-indigenous authorities get a grip on them before they can look after themselves. To put it bluntly, if the expatriates were to go, we should be leaving the inhabitants at the mercy of the Malayans; this may or may not be to their advantage; but we have a special and unique obligations [sic] to hold the ring with expatriate officers for as long as we can while the inhabitants are being trained to take over.' That said, however, the Treasury refused to agree any financial commitment until the scheme had been costed, see 145.

stand on compensation (with its built in inducements to stay). It will be highly desirable to be able to have a scheme agreed by all concerned by about the end of the year. Before that the scheme has first to be approved in principle by the Treasury, discussed with the Colonial Governments, cleared with the Malayans and put to the officers concerned. Mr. Sandys and Lord Lansdowne attach the utmost importance to rapid progress being made on this subject. This seems to be possible only if the compensation-inducement scheme can be considered on its own straight away, without being held up until some sort of finality can be reached on questions of defence aid and development aid. But a complication will arise if the Territories object to paying their half of compensation; normally we should only consider assistance for this as part of a financial settlement.

5. *Defence Aid.* This is the question to which the Malayans attach most urgency. Joint defence talks have taken place in Kuala Lumpur culminating in a report which envisages a ten-year expansion of Malayan forces at a capital cost estimated by the Malayans at over £50 m. and current costs reaching a peak of £20 m. in 1970. The Malayan Minister of Finance in discussions with the Ministry of Defence in July and with the Economic Secretary to the Treasury in September, has been pressing us to state what contribution we can make towards the cost of this plan. He also hopes to secure contributions from other friendly Governments, e.g. Australia, New Zealand, India, Pakistan and the United States.

6. The Ministry of Defence are assessing the recommendations in the Kuala Lumpur report from the point of view of the desirability of the plan, its cost and the possible extent of British assistance. At the special request of the Malayans, the Ministry of Defence have already given, without commitment, a provisional estimate of the availability and cost of certain items in the plan which the Malayans regard as urgent. These amount to just over £2 million. The Malayans are pressing us to give some advance indication of our willingness to meet the cost of these items in order to enable them to get on with their own planning.[3]

7. *Economic Aid.* The Malayans have asked us, as a minimum, to maintain and if possible to increase our present level of assistance to North Borneo and Sarawak. Mr. Tan Siew Sin pointed out the need to ensure that development in these territories should continue to expand in the early years of Malaysia and specifically asked for continuation of development assistance at present given as Colonial Development and Welfare grants at a level of about £2 million a year and for a continuance of C.D.C. investment in the Territories until 1968. He also asked about the prospect of Malaya being able to float a £4–£5 million loan on the London Market.

8. There is already an I.B.R.D. Team working on a revision of the Malayan Development Plan and the I.B.R.D. have agreed to send a further mission (under Professor Rueff[4]) to study the economic implications of Malaysia. A new Development Plan for

---

[3] Defence talks, initiated by Watkinson (minister of defence) during a visit to Kuala Lumpur and Singapore in late Mar 1962, resulted in a joint Anglo–Malayan report in June. Subsequently the Ministry of Defence set up a working party, chaired by J A Drew, to examine the formation of the Malaysian armed forces.

[4] Jacques Rueff, a distinguished French economist and financier who was judge of the Court of the European Communities 1958–1962, was appointed in 1961 to lead the World Bank Mission to examine the feasibility of closer economic co-operation between Malaya and Singapore. When it was decided in principle to establish Malaysia by Aug 1963, the scope of the Rueff mission was extended to cover the economic aspects of closer association of Malaya, Singapore and the Borneo territories.

Malaya/Singapore is not however expected to be ready before 1st January, 1964. Tun Razak has proposed to Lord Lansdowne the setting up of a Development Sub-Committee of the Intergovernmental Committee. Before a full I.B.R.D. Report is available, it will be necessary for us to have agreed with the Malayans what contributions we are to make to development for the first few years of Malaysia; though we may have by the end of this year some idea of what adjustment of plans over the next two years the I.B.R.D. think will be necessary. The Borneo Territories in any case will shortly have to be told what resources they can count on after the present C.D. and W. period (March 1964) if they are to enter into commitments necessary to keep development moving. It will, therefore, be important that at least an interim financial settlement should be reached at the same time as an agreement on constitutional and other Intergovernmental Committee matters.

9. *Procedure*. If the view is accepted that we should aim first at settling the terms of the compensation-inducement scheme, the main question then is what steps need to be taken before we will be ready to make known our views to the Malayan Government on defence aid and development aid.

10. Mr. Sandys does not wish any offers to be made on defence aid and development aid for the time being, in the belief that it would be desirable to hold back any offers we might be prepared to make until the Inter-Governmental Committee has made some progress, so that we could, if necessary, offer some financial inducement at the appropriate moment to overcome difficulties which might arise in that Committee.

11. In accordance with this line, a brief has been prepared (B.F. (62)44 of the 7th September) for the British delegation to the IMF/IBRD meeting, containing the recommendation that the delegation should listen and assure the Malayans that their requests will be fully considered when the constitutional and financial position has been investigated, when defence needs have been examined, and in the light of our own position at the time.

12. Meanwhile, the Malayans are likely to continue to press for an indication of the likely magnitude of our defence aid in particular. It would be helpful to know from the Ministry of Defence by what date they expect to have completed their examination of the Malayan defence question. If that examination is likely to be left until January, it might be desirable for us to inform the Malayans now that we shall not be able to give them a final answer before then (though we should perhaps avoid debarring ourselves from making offers on particular items earlier if this would be useful in order to secure concessions from the Malayans in the Intergovernmental Committee). The question also needs consideration whether we should aim at dealing with development aid and defence aid piece-meal with the Malayans or whether we should plan for a grand financial discussion with them in the New Year aiming at settling all financial questions apart from the compensation-inducement scheme which will, it is hoped, have been settled earlier.

144 CO 1030/1036, no 152   5 Oct 1962

[Arrest of opposition activists]: despatch from Lord Selkirk to Mr Sandys, reporting an improvement in Lee Kuan Yew's political position and recommending non-compliance with the Tunku's demand for the arrest of members of Barisan Sosialis

[During the London talks in July, British, Malayan and Singaporean ministers had considered the detention of opposition activists in the event of a deterioration of

Singapore's internal security. Sandys had refused to agree either in principle or in advance to such a course, arguing that he would have to examine individual cases. He had also made it clear that the British government could neither initiate nor take sole responsibility for such arrests. Moreover, Sandys and Selkirk reckoned that the detention of Lee Kuan Yew's political opponents would be counter-productive, aggravating radical opposition in Singapore and embarrassing Britain internationally. Nonetheless, as Selkirk reported in this despatch, the Tunku and his ministers now regarded the elimination of Barisan leaders to be an essential precondition of merger. In Selkirk's view, they wished not only to destroy the Barisan Sosialis but also to help the restoration of Lim Yew Hock to power. The Brunei rising two months later reinforced the case for mass arrests with the result that the British gave way; on 12 Dec Sandys approved Selkirk's recommendation for action to be taken through the Internal Security Council (see 138 and 147; also CO 1030/1150).]

I have the honour to address you on the subject of political and security policy in Singapore. When in 1960 it became clear that the next constitutional step for Singapore should, if possible, be a merger with the Federation of Malaya, the problem was to convince the Federation Government that such a merger would not enable the combined Chinese of the peninsula to obtain political control in Kuala Lumpur. A scheme of merger was therefore devised under which the Malays would be assured of lasting protection against Chinese political domination through two safeguards. First, the number of Singapore seats in the Kuala Lumpur House of Representatives would be restricted to 15 instead of the 25 which would be justified by reason of population, and secondly Singapore citizens would not be allowed to vote in the Federation. These safeguards were not, however, in themselves sufficient for the Federation who proposed that at the same time Britain should transfer to Malaya sovereignty over her territories in Borneo in the expectation that a majority of the Borneo representatives would always support the Malays in the Kuala Lumpur House of Representatives. From this it will be seen that the problem in Malay minds was the threat to their political position, not the maintenance of internal security which would in any case be safely in the hands of Kuala Lumpur under any scheme of merger.

2. It also has to be remembered that at the time when the Tunku was formulating his Malaysia proposal, Lee Kuan Yew held a commanding majority in the Singapore Assembly and seemed to be in an unassailable political position. In the first part of the Malaysia discussion, therefore, we heard nothing from the Federation about internal security action in Singapore being a precondition of merger. A few months later, however, in July 1961, Lee Kuan Yew's Government suffered a shattering upheaval from which he emerged with a majority of only one in the Assembly. Furthermore, the defectors from the Government quickly formed themselves into a new party, the Barisan Sosialis, with an effective organisation throughout Singapore. This was a great shock to the Federation, who had expected that Lee Kuan Yew would be able to guide Singapore comfortably into merger. They were now faced with the prospect that he might not even survive until merger, and that the Barisan Sosialis, who included in prominent positions such ex-detainees as Lim Chin Siong, Fong Swee Suan, and Woodhull, might well win the next elections in Singapore. Accordingly the Federation began to consider the possibility of arresting the ex-detainees in the Barisan Sosialis with a view to hamstringing the party as an effective political force. By this action they hoped to clear the way in Singapore for a return to power by Lim Yew Hock as leader of a branch of their own Alliance party. This idea seemed to formulate in their minds towards the end of 1961

and by early 1962 they were strongly urging upon Lee Kuan Yew and HMG the need to make arrests before merger. To show they were in earnest, they declined after February, 1962 to take any part in Internal Security Council meetings unless HMG previously agreed to seek the Council's approval for the arrests. Meanwhile, although Lee was supported temporarily in the Assembly by the Alliance party, his political position remained very uncertain and he appeared to have taken a further unwarrantable risk by pledging himself to hold a referendum on merger. This caused the Federation to redouble their pressure on Lee Kuan Yew and in March, 1962 he accepted in principle the Malay view that arrests would have to take place before merger.

3.   To what extent Lee really believes in this policy is not yet certain. He is probably very much attracted by the idea of destroying his political opponents. It should also be remembered that there is behind all this a very personal aspect. Lim Chin Siong, Woodhull, Fong Swee Suan and James Puthucheary who were arrested by Lim Yew Hock in 1956 following riots were members of Lee's party. Five members of the Executive Committee of the party were also among those arrested by Lim Yew Hock in 1957 and this was always assumed publicly to have been done at Lee Kuan Yew's direct request. The leading detainees were let out by us in 1959 because Lee made this a condition of his taking office and they all held positions in his Government.[1] Twelve months ago Lee was pretending that he also wanted to release the remaining political detainees; now he claims he wishes to put back in detention the very people who were released at his insistence—people who are intimate acquaintances, who have served in his Government, and with whom there is a keen sense of personal rivalry which transcends ideological differences.

4.   In all this the Malay motives have remained primarily political. Singapore has in fact been quiet during all this period and there is no immediate threat to internal security. The police and military are probably better prepared today in Singapore than they ever have been in the history of the Colonial empire. I have found in all my conversations with Federation ministers and officials that while they stress the conspiratorial and subversive aspects of the activities of Lim Chin Siong and his colleagues, their real and understandable fear is that the Barisan Sosialis will gain political control in Singapore which will then become a base for undermining the Federation and eventually winning political control in Kuala Lumpur. For this reason I have all along been urging the need for a proper assessment of the threat before any action is decided and I was glad to have it agreed at the last I.S.C. Meeting that the paper being prepared by the Federation and Singapore Special Branches should try to do this.

5.   I have been unwilling to agree to the Malay proposals for arrests in Singapore for two reasons. First, satisfactory evidence has not yet been produced to show that the persons concerned have been involved in any unlawful activity since they were released from detention by HMG in 1959. A number of them are now leaders of one of the main political parties in Singapore and their arrest without justification would,

---

[1] As part of a campaign to counter subversion, in Sept 1956 Lim Yew Hock's government outlawed a number of communist-front organisations and ordered the police to clear Chinese schools of protesting students. The disturbances, which caused thirteen deaths and more than one hundred other casualties, were quelled only with the assistance of police and troops brought in from the Federation. The principal figures amongst the detainees were released in June 1959, following the PAP's electoral victory, see 13.

in my opinion, have serious repercussions for all three Governments concerned and also for Malaysia. It is one thing to try to control the trade unions and to keep industrial action within reasonable proportions. I myself constantly urged this upon Lee Kuan Yew. It is, however, another matter to arrest politicians who have kept within constitutional limits and we should be hard put to it to defend such action in the House of Commons and in the United Nations where the Barisan Sosialis have already appeared. Secondly, I believe that repressive action against the leaders of a party which draws its support very largely from the Chinese speaking people—who are some 60% of the electorate—and which includes many who are in it simply because they dislike Lee Kuan Yew personally, would tend to strengthen the United Front rather than to divide it. In short, the Malay policy may well succeed in consolidating under United Front leadership all those Chinese who have vague socialist ideas and who feel the emotion of Chinese chauvinism in their blood.

6.   The Malays remain unconvinced and are saying that these arrests are an absolute precondition of merger taking place. They have now returned to the Internal Security Council to pursue their case there. We recently held a valuable meeting of the Council in which I again established to my satisfaction that the Malays' fears are almost wholly political. I have considerable sympathy for them. They remember their own struggles with the Communists, in which twelve thousand of their people were killed, and they are determined that the Communists should not come to power in Singapore by constitutional United Front tactics, riding on the backs of the Chinese. I am anxious, however, that they should not take repressive action that may result in the very thing they fear happening. The successful outcome of the referendum on merger has been a most important development, the full effects of which still remain to be seen.[2] It has been a resounding victory for Lee Kuan Yew. By this I do not mean that the P.A.P. will necessarily win the 1964 elections in Singapore. This is in any case too far ahead to forecast. I do think, however, that the referendum has shown that Lee Kuan Yew and the P.A.P. are still a considerable political force in Singapore and also that there is no other alternative party, likely to obtain a significant number of seats in the 1964 elections, which could govern Singapore better in the general interests of Malaysia. So far as I can judge, the Tunku still thinks in terms of disrupting the Barisan Sosialis by arrests, discarding Lee Kuan Yew and the P.A.P. as a spent political force and enabling the Alliance under Lim Yew Hock's leadership to emerge as the Government of Singapore. This is an unrealistic policy likely to drive the Chinese speaking people into following anti-Malaysia leaders, one of whom—Ong Eng Guan of the United People's Party—we know to be an irresponsible demagogue who is waiting quietly in the wings to step in when the moment suits him. In the Federation the Tunku can rely on the support of his Malays. In Singapore Lim Yew Hock has no such solid foundation on which to build and he is generally regarded as discredited. Anyone who wishes to govern Singapore must be able to make an appeal to the left centre and to the Chinese speaking people, and be able to retain their confidence while weaning them gradually from their Chinese chauvinism. So far, Lee Kuan Yew is the only political leader who is prepared to work for Malaysia who has shown himself competent to do this.

---

[2] Having recovered his majority of one in the Singapore Assembly on 4 Aug, on 14 Aug Lee announced that the long-promised referendum would be held on 1 Sept. The government's proposal won the support of 71.1 per cent of votes.

7.   The Tunku would therefore be much better advised to plan on the basis that Lee Kuan Yew is at present his best instrument for governing Singapore. I know only too well that there are serious differences of ideology and temperament between these two men which at times create a yawning gulf. It is, however, in the interests of us all that they should try to work together. I realise this will not be easy. Lee Kuan Yew, in the glow of his referendum victory, is posturing as a neutralist Afro–Asian leader in a way which is bound to anger the Tunku. His current visit to Moscow is only one example.[3] There is also the problem of Lim Yew Hock. We have a number of times tried to persuade Lee Kuan Yew to form a political alliance with Lim Yew Hock since this would ensure that one party commanded the support of centre and right-wing opinion. I am sure such an alliance could win the Singapore elections. Although, however, Lee Kuan Yew is only too glad to benefit from Lim Yew Hock's support in the Assembly, he has steadfastly refused to contemplate any political alliance. One solution would be for Lim Yew Hock to bow out of politics but I do not see this happening. Perhaps the most we can hope for is an electoral pact between Lee Kuan Yew and Lim Yew Hock when the Singapore elections take place. Only with the Tunku's backing is this remotely possible.

8.   I am very glad to see from the minute of your meeting with Razak and Lee Kuan Yew on 17th September, 1962 that you have deferred any question of arrests.[4] If the Barisan Sosialis resort to direct action in Singapore, then the arrests will be justified and must take place. If, however, the situation remains quiet, then I believe this matter of arrests will become less important by comparison with the political relationship between the Tunku and Lee Kuan Yew. I recommend, therefore, that in the months before Malaysia we must try to work for an effective alliance between the two Prime Ministers. If this can be achieved, I believe many of the Tunku's fears about the political future of Singapore may prove unfounded.

9.   I am sending copies of this despatch to the British High Commissioners in Kuala Lumpur, Canberra and Wellington; to the Governors of North Borneo and Sarawak; and to the High Commissioner for Brunei.

---

[3] To the disapproval of the Tunku, Lee returned from the Commonwealth Conference in London via Moscow.
[4] Sandys met Razak and Lee on 17 Sept while they were in London for the Commonwealth conference which, much to Lee's unease, endorsed Britain's bid to join the European Economic Community.

145   CO 1030/994, no E/134   22 Nov 1962
[British financial assistance for Malaysia]: letter from A A Golds[1] to Sir G Tory, discussing Malayan expectations and Whitehall's response to them. *Enclosure*: 'Notes on progress towards a Malaysian financial assessment'

I think that we owe you some explanation, even though it can only be for your own private information, of what we are trying to do here in Whitehall to meet the Malayans' expectations of British financial assistance for Malaysia; and of when we are likely to be able to give them some kind of answer to their various requests.

---

[1] A A Golds, counsellor in the CRO and FO, 1962–1965; head of the joint Malaysia/Indonesia Department, 1964–1965.

2.   What follows is a wholly private account of the story so far. It has not been cleared with any other department in London. However if you should wish to send us any comments on any of the issues with which the letter deals I should be very glad to have them, especially as Crosthwait[2] and I are members of a Working Party of the Cabinet Official Oversea Co-ordinating Committee which, as mentioned below, is now seized with the problem of a Malaysian 'financial settlement'.[3] (I should perhaps at once add that my use of this term of art has no official authorisation but we are in fact considering the question of British assistance for Malaysia as being in the nature of a 'financial settlement'.)

3.   As you know the Malayans have already put in specific bids for defence aid and development aid of a total magnitude greater than anything we are likely to be able to wring out of the Treasury. So far, British Ministers and officials have carefully avoided giving any commitment to the Malayans but have promised to consider their requests against the whole background of Malaysia's requirements and of our own resources and commitments. This process of consideration has now at last got properly under way. However it is still presenting departments in Whitehall with a difficult 'cart and horse' or 'wood and trees' problem. No one has yet been able to quote to the Treasury even a very approximate figure of the scale of assistance which we should offer to Malaysia. Meanwhile the Treasury have made it clear that before they will even admit that any aid at all must be given and certainly before they will agree to talk of hard figures, they went to know *inter alia* the following:—

(a) Exactly how great a burden the Malayan economy will be assuming as a result of taking over our existing responsibilities in Singapore and the Borneo territories.
(b) How far this will be off-set by the enhanced resources of the new Federation.
(c) What economies to H.M.G. will result from the transfer of our responsibilities.
(d) How much of the Malaysian defence expansion programme is both realistic and essential and what the cost of this portion would be.
(e) What economic development in Borneo (or elsewhere in Malaysia) it is necessary for us to support whether for economic or political reasons.
(f) What help for Malaysia can be expected from other sources than H.M.G. (e.g. Americans, Australians, World Bank etc.).

The Treasury want the Colonial Office, Foreign Office, Department of Technical Co-operation, Ministry of Defence, Service Departments and ourselves to furnish them with all possible data on these points and also, on the basis of the answers to (c) (d) and (f) above (and our assessment of all relevant political and strategic factors) to name the sum which the British tax payer should be called upon to pay as the financial price of Malaysia.

4.   To many of us this does not seem a very realistic sort of exercise and, as you may imagine there are a number of 'carts and horses' mixed up in it. The Ministry of

---

[2] T L Crosthwait, assistant secretary, CRO, 1961–1963.
[3] Set up in July 1962 'to consider questions of oversea policy (other than defence policy) which concern more than one of the oversea Departments', this committee first discussed British financial aid for Malaysia in Nov 1962 and in the light of other investigations, such as the Lintott mission to Kuala Lumpur. It submitted a report to ministers in time for talks with a Malayan delegation in May. See 170, 173–176 and also CAB 134/2276–2278 and 2281.

Defence for example maintain that they cannot answer (d) above *in vacuo*. They argue that they must always have some idea of the total money likely to be available before they can say whether any defence plan is sound (e.g. the one outlined in the Steering Committee's Report)[4] or whether they should aim at something less. Similarly it seems unlikely that we (C.R.O. or F.O.) shall be able to give any answer to (f) until the Malayans themselves make a move, which we assume they are unlikely to do until we have given them a firm indication of the probable limits of our own assistance.

5. The whole question has recently been submitted, after discussion in the Greater Malaysia Committee under the P.U.S's Chairmanship, to the Cabinet Official Oversea Co-ordinating Committee whose function is to examine and make recommendations on all questions involving financial assistance before they go to Ministers. This Committee, on which we and the other departments concerned are represented, has now undertaken to produce recommendations for Ministers early in the New Year. The intention is that Ministers should be in a position to tell the Malayans, by the time that the formal agreement on Malaysia is due to be negotiated, how much financial aid they can confidently expect from us. So far we have been expecting the formal agreement to be concluded in early February but I understand that following Lord Lansdowne's latest private discussions with Tun Razak, it seems now most improbable that the Malayans themselves will be able to keep to this timing. However, we certainly hope that we shall at any rate have been able to clear our own minds about the financial limits of our assistance well before the last lap of the negotiations for formal agreement begins. Meanwhile we hope, for tactical reasons, not to have to enter into advance commitments.

6. The main 'ingredients' of any financial settlement as we see them will be:—

(a) The cost of the Compensation/Inducement Scheme for the expatriate officers in Borneo.
(b) Our contributions to the Malaysian Defence expansion programme.
(c) Our contribution to Malaysian development on account of the Borneo Territories.

(I enclose a wholly informal memorandum summarising the present position reached under each of these heads, as seen in this Department.) As you know only too well the Malayans have been pressing us for some time now to show something of our hand on (b) while both the Malayans and the Borneans are pressing our representatives in the Intergovernmental Committee on (c). It may be that we shall have to give them further interim answers on both. So far as (c) is concerned you may know that Lord Lansdowne himself is convinced that we should not offer less, over the first five years of Malaysia, than the equivalent of what we are at present giving the Borneo territories by way of C.D. and W. aid.[5] This is also what Tan Siew Sin asked for. However, present form is that the Treasury will certainly not agree to make any commitments for economic aid until they know what our commitments under (a) and (b) above are going to be. It was only with the greatest reluctance that

---

[4] ie, the steering committee that dealt with the detailed matters identified during the Anglo–Malayan talks in July 1962, see 132, note.
[5] See 141, para 14 and repeated at 146, para 14.

they agreed even to authorise Lord Lansdowne to promise at this month's plenary session of the Intergovernmental Committee, to make available the unexpired portion of the C.D. and W. allocation which in any case comes to an end in March, 1964. On (b) we have been trying hard to get all the 'internal security' items on the Malayans' 'priority list' agreed in advance of the financial settlement and we hope to be able very soon to let you know definitely about this. (a) has to be given priority, although the question of the other 50% of its total cost (£3½ m. over 5 years) will probably be deferred until the eventual 'financial settlement'. Everything else must however still be regarded as in the melting pot though as I have said our present hope is to have poured something out of it by early next year.

7.   I apologise for the length of this letter, which for obvious reasons I am not copying elsewhere.[6]

Enclosure to 145

The compensation-inducement scheme
The scheme, which has been cast in the light of experience gained in other territories and after consultation with representatives of the men concerned, is estimated to cost some £3½ million over 5 years. According to precedent H.M.G. would pay half of this and it would be up to the Territories (or 'Malaysia') to pay the remaining half. The two Governors have, however, reacted strongly against putting this suggestion to their Governments.

2.   This is the most urgent financial question from the British point of view. If we are to have a smooth transfer of power, without serious danger of trouble, as many as possible of the expatriate officers must be induced to stay on and it is important that they know by the end of the year, if possible, what effect the compensation scheme will have (with its built-in inducements to stay). The various departments here are agreed on the form of the scheme which is being sent now to the Borneo Governments. Later it will go to the Malayan Government but the problem of who is to pay for the cost normally borne locally still remains.

3.   It is recognised that the question of the incidence of local cost is complicated in the circumstances of Malaysia because the fiscal arrangements between the Federal Government and the States are not yet determined and in due course there has to be a general settlement of the financial matters arising out of the establishment of Malaysia. Meanwhile, we have no intention of holding up the application of the compensation scheme itself as it is important to induce as many expatriate officers as possible to stay on.

Defence aid
4.   Conclusion (n.n.) of the Malayan/British Steering Committee's Report stated the Malayan view of the form which financial aid should take was as follows:—

(a) Malayans to pay all seconded personnel at their own (lower) rates with the expatriate element paid by supplying Government.

---

[6] Despite this request, a copy passed out of the CRO to reach this CO file.

(b) Training facilities at concessional rates.

(c) A lease/lend agreement in respect of ships and aircraft.

(d) Free transfer of accommodation and land.

(e) Direct financial assistance towards the increased annual recurrent charges in the initial stages of the programme.

With regard to (a) above, a scheme has been drafted in Whitehall for the subsidisation of the costs of seconded personnel in all Commonwealth countries that might be concerned. This has not yet been approved by Ministers and we do not yet know what particular method of subsidisation will be adopted. If the method of subsidisation recommended in the scheme were adopted, the cost in respect of Malaysia for 1963/4 would be approximately £1 million. This will, no doubt, be taken into account when the general settlement is made.

5.   Points (b) to (e) above will also be taken into account in the general financial settlement but it is unlikely that help will be forthcoming towards annually recurrent expenditure except in respect of specific projects like training or secondment.

6.   Even if it is accepted that in the light of the SEATO forces available the joint Steering Committee's plan provides a suitable basis for military planning it is by no means clear that it has been accepted by the Malayans as a practicable plan for Malaysia without outside financial assistance. Tan Siew Sin in his meeting with the Minister of Defence in July said that his Government could not afford any money towards the capital costs (£50m.) of the expansion programme and he admitted that the Steering Committee had set 'high targets'. In a letter dated 23rd July to the Secretary of State, in commenting on the Committee's recommendations, he used the words 'if implemented in full' which suggests that he has doubts whether it will be fully implemented. The Malayans, therefore, would presumably accept the proposition that a plan is not realistic if it cannot be afforded even if there are sound military reasons in favour of it. It seems likely that such financial aid as is forthcoming from Britain will be limited to certain aspects of the plan particularly those which are directly relevant to our continuing interests and commitments in the area. This need not preclude defence aid from other sources, (e.g. U.S. and Australia), but we have no information about the extent to which aid might be forthcoming from such sources.

7.   We have to consider Malayan requirements in the light of our obligations under the Anglo–Malayan Defence Agreement—which it is proposed to extend to Malaysia—to afford Malaya such assistance as she may require for her external defence. These obligations will, of course, be much in the minds of the Malayans during the Combined Planning discussions which have now started. We are hoping, in the course of these talks, to persuade the Malayans that the forces which we were in any case planning to retain in Malaya to meet our S.E.A.T.O. obligations will be adequate to meet our obligation to assist in the external defence of Malaysia.

8.   Apart from the general problem of Defence Aid there is the more immediate problem of the priority shopping list which the Malayans have produced of barracks, ships, aircraft, etc., which they want us to hand over to them right away as an interim measure without prejudice to a final settlement on defence aid of all kinds. These items have been costed and the total is approximately £3.4 million (this includes the cost of two Heron aircraft. Kuala Lumpur telegram No.830 refers). It

has proved difficult in practice to deal with the financing of these advance items before the whole financial picture is clear. However, it is now proposed that certain essential installations required by Malaysia to implement the internal security plan by M-Day should be handed over without prejudice to the final financial arrangements made in respect of them. An exception is also under consideration with regard to the four helicopters required for internal security.

9.   To sum up the question of Defence Aid this will be considered on a general basis by the end of next January at the earliest and apart from the exceptions referred to in paragraph 8 the Malayans can expect no firm decisions until then.

10.   *Development aid*
The Malayans have asked that, in order to ensure expanding development in North Borneo and Sarawak during the early years of Malaysia, we should undertake to continue to provide assistance at about the present level of Colonial Development and Welfare grants, which now amount to some £2 million a year. The view of Ministers is that, since development aid is a principal card in the hands of British negotiators if there should be difficulty in reaching agreement, no commitment in relation to it should be given until the intergovernmental talks are well advanced. However, Lord Lansdowne, has recently been authorised to give (if necessary) a guarded indication of our intentions at the plenary meeting on 23rd November and an assurance that an amount equivalent to any outstanding Colonial Development and Welfare allocation for the present quinquennium (estimated at something less than £1 million by 31st August, 1963) would be made available to the new Federal Government for the development of North Borneo and Sarawak. Any further aid we give for development will have to be considered with other forms of aid in the context of the financial settlement for Malaysia as a whole.

11.   The Malayans have also asked about the prospect of floating a £4 or £5 million loan on the London market. At present it seems likely that they will be told that they could have access to the market but only to the extent of some £2 million.

146   CO 1030/1032, no 106   6 Dec 1962
'Malaysia: progress report by the minister of state for colonial affairs': report by Lord Lansdowne on the Inter-Governmental Committee, urging British financial assistance to the Borneo territories after the formation of Malaysia

[This report was printed for confidential circulation. For the context of the IGC see document 141, note.]

The Inter-Governmental Committee held four more Plenary sessions in Jesselton between the 23rd–26th November, at which most of the outstanding major points of principle were agreed. Provided some remaining financial questions can now be answered, the Committee should finish its work by the end of the year.

2.   North Borneo finally dropped their demand for fiscal autonomy under the Constitution of Malaysia which at last removed the major obstacle to a satisfactory division of legislative powers on the lines agreed in the London talks.

3.   Citizenship, Education, Religion and Immigration (except for the important

question of the State's right to refuse entry for employment in industry for federal purposes) were agreed. Concessions were made both by the Federation and by the Borneo territories. At the outset of his visit to Borneo which immediately preceded these Plenary sessions, the Tunku announced that he proposed that North Borneo and Sarawak should have 40 seats in the Malaysia House of Representatives.

4. A summary of the main points of agreement reached in the Inter-Governmental Committee is set out in Annex I. A list of outstanding points for settlement by the Inter-Governmental Committee is set out in Annex II.[1]

5. I called for further meetings of Sub-Committees between 6th–8th December, to deal with outstanding questions, and arranged to hold in Kuala Lumpur between 18th–20th what should be the final Plenary sessions. In so far as it can be prepared in advance of final decisions, the first draft report of the Inter-Governmental Committee will be considered at the Kuala Lumpur meetings. The aim will be to complete the report by 31st December. How far this can be achieved will depend largely on the progress of discussions on financial arrangements for Malaysia.

6. In my first report, dated 10th September, I said that we had a continuing obligation to help the Borneo territories and that:—

> 'If Malaysia is to fulfil the hopes we have for it, it must be demonstrably successful and successful from the start and this will cost money.'

After three further months of negotiations, I am more than ever convinced of these propositions.

7. Sarawak's attitude to the negotiations has been constructive and helpful, but it has been coupled with a determination to obtain guaranteed sums for its future development.

8. We would have reached deadlock at the November meetings in Jesselton, if the North Borneo delegation had not at last been persuaded to drop its demand for fiscal autonomy. The undertaking which I was authorised to give—that Her Majesty's Government were prepared to make available to the Government of Malaysia an amount equivalent to any outstanding C.D. and W. allocation for the present quinquennium and to consider helping thereafter for the development of North Borneo and Sarawak—was of some assistance in achieving this change of attitude. But it was made abundantly clear that this 'concession' by North Borneo was subject to the working out of the detailed financial arrangements and on the understanding that development would continue at an increased rate.

9. Neither territory will be satisfied with general assurances. Each will require guarantees of hard cash before they will finally commit themselves to Malaysia.

10. The Malayans made the mistake of overselling Malaysia to the territories with promises of rapidly expanding development. The present expectations of the territories are consequently pitched high. The Malayans are now saying that the financial position of the Federation is not as comfortable as the statistics suggest and that despite a heavy reduction in their own development expenditure they may be faced by the end of 1965 with a large fall in reserves. The Federation is certainly looking to the United Kingdom for continuing assistance in the development programmes of North Borneo and Sarawak.

---

[1] The annexes are not printed.

11.   I agreed that at the outset of these negotiations we should not show our hand on finance and that our future development assistance for the territories should be considered in relation to the extent of our financial arrangements for Malaysia as a whole and that we should reserve our position for comprehensive discussions with the Federation which would include defence and compensation for British officers. In my November report, I agreed that we should still not yet show our full hand on finance.

12.   I consider that the time has now come for us to declare our position on development. In our laborious negotiations we have so far through compromise and concession been able to achieve satisfactory agreements over safeguards for North Borneo and Sarawak. I believe this success will be worthless if we are now hesitant or ungenerous on finance.

13.   We have still to obtain North Borneo's acceptance of detailed arrangements for the handling of their finances and Sarawak's agreement hinges on the guarantee of a development fund. We have already achieved progress beyond what at times seemed possible. I am confident that I can bring the work of the Inter-Governmental Committee to a successful conclusion this month if I am authorised to say at the Plenary meeting in December that subject to the financial arrangements for Malaysia as a whole, Her Majesty's Government will be prepared to provide the new Malaysian Government for five years after Malaysia with aid at a rate *not less* than at present provided for North Borneo and Sarawak for the continued development and welfare of these two territories. Unless we do this, I see little chance of the North Borneo and Sarawak delegations signing the report of the Inter-Governmental Committee and of obtaining a successful vote on it in the two territorial legislatures in January.

14.   In conclusion, I repeat my strongly held personal opinion that in view of the fact that Her Majesty's Government is giving up its responsibility for the territories before they are ready to achieve independence on their own, we have a continuing obligation to help them and we cannot honourably discharge this obligation to the peoples of the territories whom we are persuading to accept Malaysia unless we maintain our assistance after Malaysia at a level not lower than existing C.D. and W. grants, not including the cost of any compensation scheme.

147   CO 1030/1160, no 46   12 Dec 1962
[Singapore arrests]: outward telegram no 546 from Mr Sandys to Lord Selkirk, approving action

[In the aftermath of the Brunei revolt (see 149, note) and in the light of evidence of communist penetration of the Barisan, Selkirk faced heavy pressure to drop his previous resistance to the arrests of 'subversive elements' in Singapore. His inward telegram no 573 of 11 Dec has been retained under section 3(4) of the Public Records Act 1958, but the minute by C S Roberts of the CO reveals that in it Selkirk requested authorisation to concur on behalf of the British government in the immediate arrest of leading communists and communist sympathisers. Macmillan, who was on the distribution list for communications of such significance, responded immediately: 'I would like to have Mr Sandys' view. I must be consulted *before* [sic] reply.' Having obtained prime ministerial approval, Sandys despatched outward telegram no 546. The secretary of state then left London for a tour of the West Indies to examine policy for Britain's remaining dependencies now that Jamaica and Trinidad had achieved independence. Lansdowne, who was in SE Asia on the business of the Inter-Governmental Committee, kept Sandys informed of developments in Singapore reassuring him that he had 'taken great pains to

avoid HMG being driven into the position of appearing to take the initiative over arrests'
(Lansdowne to Sandys, CROSOS no 155, 17 Dec 1962, Sandys Papers, 8/1.]

Personal from Colonial Secretary.

Your telegrams Nos.573 and 575.

As you know I have all along been reluctant to give blanket approval in advance for arrests of subversive elements in Singapore. But if we are to avoid a dangerous disagreement with the Malayan Government we shall have to take some action of this kind before merger.

2.   I am quite sure that the insurrection in Brunei provides the best possible background against which to take this action. I consider therefore that we should move at once, before the atmosphere of emergency evaporates, as it quickly will when active fighting in Brunei ceases.

3.   I have no doubt that the Police and the Army would like to have longer to perfect their plans, but I am inclined to think that the advantages to be gained by delay will be more than offset by:—

(a) the greater difficulty in explaining the need for this action to the world; and
(b) the risk of leakage of information resulting in the flight of some of the birds you most want to catch.

4.   My conclusions are, therefore, as follows:—

(a) Before merger, sooner or later, arrests will have to be made.
(b) This is the best moment to do it.
(c) The emergency justifies a substantial number of arrests of persons who in one way or another constitute a danger to public safety.
(d) If the Internal Security Council so decide, I consider that the sooner the arrests are carried out the better and I shall be content for you to give your consent without detailed reference back to me.

5.   We must of course identify ourselves with this decision. But the public announcement must make it clear that the Malayan and Singapore Governments share equally with us in the decision.

148   CO 1030/1160, no 56   14 Dec 1962
[Singapore arrests]: inward telegram no 582 from Lord Selkirk to Mr Sandys, reporting the decision of the ISC on 13 Dec

[The ISC authorised sweeping arrests for which the British, Malayan and Singaporean governments agreed to take joint responsibility. Action was scheduled for 16 Dec. The operation was aborted, however, because the governments of Malaya and Singapore fell out over the list of detainees. Lee Kuan Yew added political opponents to Special Branch's list. The Tunku strongly objected to this abuse of the operation, probably fearing also that it would inflame his own opponents in the federation. This disagreement prompted Dr Ismail bin Dato Haji Abdul Rahman (minister of internal security and interior) to withdraw from the ISC and much mutual recrimination ensued. The operation was revived in Feb, code-named 'Coldstore' (see 156 and 158).]

The Internal Security Council met in Singapore last night.

2.   We first considered the joint security assessment by the Special Branches. This was a much better paper than had previously been available and contained a great deal

of valuable information about communist activities in Singapore. The paper was only produced yesterday and we did not have time to examine it thoroughly before the meeting. However we recorded our agreement with the broad terms of the paper.

3.   I then asked Ismail to state why the Federation had asked for an emergency meeting. He said the Federation view had always been that strict security measures should be taken in the Federation and Singapore while at the same time every attempt was made to improve the standard of living of the people. The Federation Government had been very concerned at the security situation in Singapore and would not be able to proceed with Malaysia if the communists in Singapore were not arrested.

4.   Lee Kuan Yew said he agreed with Ismail that action must now be taken. The perfect opportunity had been presented by the Brunei revolt and this must not be missed.

5.   I said I had recognised all along that a threat was presented by the communists in Singapore. I had not however previously been convinced that a large number of arrests was necessary to counter this threat. Recently, however, new evidence had been produced about the extent of the communist control of the Barisan Socialis and also there had been indications that the communists might resort to violence if the opportunity occurred. Recent statements by the Barisan Socialis and Party Rakyat supporting the revolt in Brunei confirmed this. Accordingly H.M.G. were prepared to see action taken in Singapore provided:—

(a) it was made clear publicly that all three Governments accepted joint responsibility and
(b) the action was taken very quickly.

6.   Lee Kuan Yew said the Singapore Government agreed that there must be joint responsibility for the action and his public line would be that action was most regrettable but most necessary. I asked Lee to confirm that his Cabinet shared his views. He said that for security reasons he had only been able to consult those who were members of the Council but he thought the others would agree. He went on to explain that previously he had thought that if the action had to be in a cold situation it would be necessary for the British colonial power to accept the main responsibility. In view however of the revolt in Brunei and the evidence of foreign participation, the action could now be presented as taken by the Nationalist Governments of the Federation and Singapore against anti-nationalists who had threatened the security of Malaysia. It would however be essential for the Federation Government to take the initiative publicly and to make it clear that they had pressed for the action. The Singapore Government would support them and the British should remain in the background as much as possible. At Lee's suggestion Ismail agreed to the [omission?] Federation and Singapore Governments would co-ordinate their public statements.

7.   This was highly satisfactory from our point of view except perhaps that we would not wish to place so much emphasis on the threat to Malaysia since this might suggest that the action was political rather than security. In view however of the Federation acceptance of Lee's line, I decided it would be wrong to raise any objections.

8.   The Council approved the terms of the public statement to be issued immediately after the action is taken. This is contained in my immediately following telegram.[1] The statement was signed by Ismail, Lee Kuan Yew and myself. You will

---

[1] This statement was not issued because the operation was aborted.

see that the statement makes it clear that all members of the Council share jointly in the responsibility for the action.

9.   We then considered the extent of the action to be taken and the timing and reached the following conclusions:—

(a) The operation should be sufficiently comprehensive to cripple the communist effort in Singapore. A preliminary assessment by Singapore Special Branch indicated that about 180 persons would be detained in the first instance.

(b) The list of names should if possible be finalised today by the two Special Branches and the S.L.O. and agreed out of Council. The Council will then meet secretly in Kuala Lumpur tomorrow Saturday 15th December at 22.15 hours to record their formal approval of the list.

(c) The operation would commence at 02.00 hours Singapore time on Sunday 16th December.

(d) The Barisan Socialis Party should be banned but it was not decided whether the Party Rakyat S.A.T.U. and the S.G.E.U. should also be banned.

(e) It was agreed that the list ought to include certain Barisan Socialis assemblymen, but Lee thought it most desirable that the Federation should at the same time arrest at least one of their Parliament known to be a communist or communist sympathiser e.g. Lim Kean Siew or Boestamam.[2] Ismail promised to get a decision from the Tunku and we have now received his concurrence.

(f) All the communist publications including 'Plebian' and 'Barisan' should be banned.

(g) It was noted that action had already been taken in Sarawak. Lee hoped there would be more than the 31 arrests so far ordered in Sarawak but I pointed out that this was a matter for the Governor. I also explained that the Governor would not want to ban S.U.P.P. at this stage since there was a distinct possibility of S.U.P.P. breaking up following Ong Kee Hui's condemnation of the Brunei revolt. Today's papers report defections.

(h) At Lee's suggestion the Federation agreed that they should simultaneously mount an operation which would involve the arrest of a substantial number of people in order to show that action was being taken on a Pan Malaysian basis.

(i) The Council statement would be released on Sunday following the completion of the operation.

(j) The Federation Government would make a statement in Parliament on Monday and this would be followed by a statement by Lee Kuan Yew on the Singapore radio.

(k) The U.K. Commission would make no comment in Singapore beyond the statement by the Council, but I explained that you would no doubt have to make a statement in the House of Commons.

10.   Please let me know if there is any further background you require for the House of Commons. I will try to let you have texts of the Federation and Singapore statements before Monday afternoon your time. I suggest your broad line should be to follow the terms of the Council's statement as amplified by the Federation and Singapore statements.

11.   I will report further developments tomorrow.

---

[2] Lim Kean Siew (Labour Party) and Ahmad Boestamam (Party Rakyat Malaya) were leaders of the Socialist Front in the federal parliament of Malaya.

149   CO 1030/1466, ff 103–105   15 Dec 1962

'Political appreciation of the revolt': memorandum on the Brunei rising by Sir D White for Lord Selkirk and others attending a meeting at Labuan on 17 Dec

[At 2 am on 8 Dec—coinciding exactly, although probably not intentionally, with the time and date of the Japanese attack on Malaya in 1941—the Tentera Nasional Kalimantan Utara (TNKU), or National Army of North Borneo launched co-ordinated attacks on key centres. Their forces quickly overran the oilfields at Seria as well as much of Brunei Town and the rest of the state. They moved into parts of the Fourth and Fifth Divisions of Sarawak, including Limbang, that tongue of territory splitting the sultanate into two parts which had been annexed by Sarawak in 1890 and remained a continuing source of acrimony between Brunei and Sarawak. There were also disturbances across the border in North Borneo. Acting under the Anglo–Brunei treaty of 1959, the British sent in Gurkhas, Royal Marines and other military units. By midday on 11 Dec some 1,600 troops had arrived and most important centres had been recovered. Despite widespread support amongst the people of Brunei, TNKU resistance swiftly collapsed. By 18 Dec all hostages had been released and by the end of the month 2,700 rebels (estimated by the British as all but a handful of the TNKU) had been captured or had surrendered. The last few dissidents had been rounded up in mid-May 1963 by which time many original detainees had been released. Following the revolt the constitution was suspended, the PRB was proscribed and a state of emergency was declared. The high commissioner, Sir Dennis White, was in the UK at the time of the outbreak and Selkirk took direct charge. White returned to Brunei on 10 Dec and his subsequent reports breathe the guilt and embarrassment, the defensiveness and frustration of a man during whose watch a crisis had occurred. In addition to streams of situation reports on operations, the files are full of papers addressing the causes and likely consequences of the rising, the aims of the leaders and the extent of their support and, finally, the future course of British policy towards Brunei and the region more widely. Questions were asked, firstly, about the causes and outbreak: Had there been a failure of British intelligence? Had the local administration been complacent? Had British representatives been caught napping? What were the objectives and role of Azahari who was in Manila at the time of the revolt? What was the precise relationship between the PRB and the TNKU? To what extent was the Sultan implicated in the rising? How far was the revolt an attempt to democratise Brunei? Had the PRB been provoked into action by the postponement of the new Legislative Council on which it had won control of all 16 electable seats in the elections of Aug 1962? Was the rebels' primary objective to restore Brunei to its former glory by uniting the Borneo territories in opposition to 'Greater Malaysia'? How widespread was local support for the rebels? Secondly, there were questions about the revolt's repercussions in the region: How much support had the TNKU received from the Philippines and especially Indonesia? What links were there between the TNKU and Sarawak's Clandestine Communist Organisation? In what ways might the revolt exacerbate Singapore's problems of internal security? Thirdly, there were questions concerning Britain's future policy: Did the revolt provide the opportunity for sweeping reform of Brunei's government? Had Britain's intervention and successful suppression of the rising enhanced or diminished its relationship with the Sultan? Should they adopt Azahari as a 'progressive nationalist' in preference to the Sultan and his court? Might they persuade some PRB detainees to espouse the cause of 'Greater Malaysia'? What impact would the incident have on Britain's international relations and reputation? Would the rising improve or impair British attempts to persuade Brunei to join Malaysia? For example, on 20 Dec both White in a despatch to Sandys (see 150) and Selkirk in a letter to Macmillan (see 151) criticised the ineptitude of the Brunei government, and White recommended that Britain should take advantage of the Sultan's weakness to insist on his immediate acceptance of Malaysia (see also 154 and 155). For the course of the rising, see CO 1030/1068–1076; PREM 11/3869 and 4346. For the aftermath of revolt and assessments of the prospects of Brunei joining Malaysia see CO 1030/1466–1470, 1489–1491, 1493; FO 371/169694 and 169702; PREM 11/4347. For the views of Chiefs of Staff, see COS 78(62) and COS 83(62)1, DEFE 4/150; COS 3(63)1, DEFE 4/151; COS 9(63)1, DEFE 4/152. See also the subsequent narrative prepared by the FCO's Research Department, 'The origins and formation of Malaysia', paras 204–218, reproduced as an appendix to this volume.]

Causes

The people of Brunei entertain a long-standing and deeply-felt dislike of the local nobility and ruling clique, of whom the most prominent, the Mentri Besar, Deputy Mentri Besar, and Deputy State Secretary, were at one time associated with Party Rakyat.

Furthermore, the Sultan's own personal interference in the administration of the country, favouritism and out and out nepotism, have brought down upon himself some of the discredit well earned by a dilatory, inept and not particularly honest administration.

I feel that the main purpose of the revolt was to overthrow the present Government, and that reunification of the Borneo Territories and anti-Malaysia were added inducements, the former to attract persons with Brunei connections in Sarawak and North Borneo, and the latter to attract dissident elements in the component parts of the proposed Malaysia.

Outside connections

There is no direct evidence of outside connections. It is equally certain that the rebels expected Indonesian assistance by air; hence the removal of obstructions from the Anduki Airfield by the rebels and the incident at Berkenu when the rebels saluted a British aircraft in mistake for an Indonesian one.

There seems little doubt that both S.U.P.P. and Barisan Socialis were fully in the picture as to Azahari's intentions, and may even have promised support.

Otherwise, the revolt is confined to Brunei Malays and Kedayans within the State, or in Sarawak and North Borneo, and others, who may have joined in for the fun of some Pengiran shooting, to settle some personal grievance, or through intimidation.

The insurrection

I find it impossible to believe that the Sultan and his Government had not had prior knowledge of the way the situation was developing. They share, with the people of Brunei, the deeply felt desire to re-establish their former position as Rulers of a large part of Sarawak and a part of North Borneo. I suspect that the Sultan, with his usual dislike of committing himself, kept his own Government in ignorance of his real views an Azahari's plan for reunification of the territories; I have little doubt that he discussed it with Azahari, and Azahari discussed it with the Tunku.

At the very last moment, the Sultan decided to ask for British help. A day or two before that, the ruling clique started feeding scraps of information to the Police.

The rebels were clearly, in general, not anti-British. Lives and property were, in Brunei, largely respected. There was a more vicious element in the oilfields, and in Limbang.

The future

There is no doubt, in my mind, that if British Military presence were to be withdrawn, or seriously weakened, the rebels would strike again, and this time the Sultan, the nobility and the administration would be butchered.

The outlawing and defeat of the Party Rakyat have created a political vacuum. The Civil Service, at no time a strong organisation, has been decimated by Party Rakyat infiltration and many of its members are under arrest or on the run.

There is no confidence in the Mentri Besar amongst the British, Malayan or other senior Civil Servants, or amongst the population.

The loyalty of the people to the Sultan as Head of the State and Supreme Executive Authority seems to have been virtually destroyed. His position as Religious Head cannot, at present, be assessed.

There are two alternative for the Sultan; abdication in favour of the Crown Prince with a Council of Regency, or an urgent announcement of his intention to become a purely Constitutional Ruler, as soon as the situation permits.

The Mentri Besar should resign or be dismissed, and a figurehead Mentri Besar appointed, possibly the previous man, with, preferably, a Malayan or a British Adviser, in fact administering the territory, with a team of Malayan and British administrators running the State.

The Police Force should be strengthened by at least 6 retired or other Police Officers with a knowledge of Malay.

Special Branch should concentrate urgently on the preparation of a list of key men in the rebellion who should be put on trial as soon as time permits.

The great majority of the prisoners should be released on parole, under restricted residence conditions, as soon as Military operations permit, and employed on useful work at living wages.

The doubtful prisoners should remain in custody at present.

An Economic Development Committee, with executive and financial power, should start, as soon as possible, rural and other development programmes. The United Nations Economic Adviser, an American, might preside; a local Committee would achieve nothing.

Malaysia

Brunei either enters Malaysia now, or as soon as it can be established that the rebellion is largely anti-Government.

Failing this, there seems little chance of achieving the aim, and Brunei remains indefinitely a dangerous source of infection for Sarawak and North Borneo, and an untidy, if not insupportable, defence commitment for Her Majesty's Government.

150 CO 1030/1076, no 6   20 Dec 1962
[Brunei revolt]: despatch from Sir D White to Mr Sandys, providing an account of the disturbances and a preliminary assessment of its causes and political impact

I have the honour to inform you that I returned to Brunei on Monday, December 10th, and resumed duty forthwith.

2.   Until interrogation of prisoners is complete, and there has been a thorough investigation of captured documents, and the information so obtained collated, it is not possible to formulate authoritative conclusions as to the causes and origin of the revolt, and my views must remain tentative.

3.   The position in November when I returned to the U.K. was that the Party Rakyat, having successfully won all seats in the District Council elections, had been

returned to all 16 elected members' seats in Legislative Council.[1] There had been no business meeting of Council, merely a formal session to swear in the new Council and to listen to an address from the throne.

4.   The Sultan, on the advice of the Mentri Besar, nominated six of the elected members of Legislative Council to Executive Council. Some trouble occurred about this, as Party Rakyat wished to say who should be appointed, though the Constitution reserves the right of the Sultan to nominate as he thinks fit. The Party eventually withdrew their opposition; the Sultan's nominees took their seats and their attitude at subsequent meetings was not unduly aggressive.

5.   The information available to me at this time indicated that the Party Rakyat would endeavour to obtain recognition as the successful Political Party by Constitutional means, if possible; there would be a resolution to amend the Constitution, and to demand independence in 1963.

6.   On the Malaysian front, the Sultan had reserved his position, in spite of the unanimous advice of the Palace clique to reject the invitation to join, after the rebuff to the Brunei delegation in Kuala Lumpur. This advice was undoubtedly known to the Party Rakyat, whose leader Azahari and some of his colleagues had been in touch with Tun Razak and the Malayans. Azahari had indicated that if he was recognised as the leader of Brunei, he would 'bend' his Party to accept Malaysia.

The Malayans seemed to have accepted the inevitable and to have reconciled themselves to the fact that Azahari was practically certain to be the next Mentri Besar; indeed, they invited him to lead a delegation to visit Malaya and all arrangements were made for the visit.

The delegates cancelled the visit or postponed it on the morning I left Brunei en route for the U.K.

7.   The Sultan, after many months of investigation and research, had decided to make a formal request to Her Majesty's Government for the return of the Limbang District to his rule.[2] I had discussed the matter with him, and had agreed to take a letter to the Secretary of State from him and to explain his view. I was, myself, well aware of the strength of the feeling in Brunei on the Limbang 'corridor'. The feelings of the Limbang people were thought by the Sarawak Government to be against the proposal, in the case of the majority of the population, and that the agitation in favour of return was confined to a number of Malays and Kedayans of Brunei origin, egged on by Party Rakyat and S.U.P.P.

8.   Brunei has, since time immemorial, been a hot bed of rumour, lies and intrigue. Reports over the last few months have been received of parties of Brunei youths proceeding through Sarawak to Indonesian territory for some form of military training, but investigation failed to substantiate the rumours, either in Sarawak or in Brunei.

---

[1] The 1959 constitution provided for a two-tier electoral system. Direct elections were held to 55 seats on the district councils which returned 16 representatives to the 33-member Legislative Council. The majority of 17 on the Legislative Council were ex officio, official or nominated members. During July and Aug 1962 the PRB, which was the only organised party, won 54 out of the 55 district council seats thereby ensuring that its candidates would secure control of the electable seats on the Legislative Council and could claim to represent popular feeling. The first meeting of the Legislative Council was postponed as a result of the revolt, after which the councils and constitution were suspended and the PRB was banned.

[2] The loss of Limbang to Sarawak was deeply resented in Brunei (see 9, n 5). Not surprisingly the TNKU attempted to reclaim it for Brunei in the rising.

Azahari, however, and his leading colleagues, were paying visits to Djakarta far too frequently for our peace of mind, in view of Azahari's long connection with the successful Army of Liberation leaders in Indonesia, during the Japanese occupation, and during the struggle against the Dutch.

It must also be remembered that Azahari had been imprisoned in 1955 for unlawful assembly (I think) and while in prison had been involved in a scatterbrained plot to overthrow the Government.

9.   I was concerned at this time at the lack of Special Branch information coming in, but it was ascribed to the lull in political activity. I was convinced that the real battle ahead lay between the people of Brunei and the ruling clique, i.e. local nobility and a few elevated commoners, and that the only safe course for the Sultan to pursue was to become a genuinely Constitutional ruler, and grant power to the Party Rakyat, even at the price of letting down the ruling clique. As I have already stated in para 6 above, I believed that Tun Razak had also accepted this view.

10.   A few days before the revolt, arrests were made in the Lawas district of the Vth Division[3] of men with the Tenteraman Nacional [sic] Kalimantan Utara uniform and insignia; one uniform was found in the Temburong enclave, which is part of the State of Brunei. No arrests were made. Special Branch officers of the three territories met in Limbang but their conclusions indicated that there was no immediate danger.

11.   Two or three days before the revolt started, Dato Pengiran Ali, Deputy Mentri Besar and the Sultan's confidant, started to feed reports to the Police of the storing of uniforms and arms in the villages. Police search failed to confirm this. It should be noted here that before this the Malayan Attorney General in Brunei had reported the serious state of events to the Tunku, and a verbal report was also made to the Tunku by a Malayan member of the Staff of Radio Brunei.[4] I have been informed that the Attorney General did not pass the information to the Commissioner of Police or Special Branch in Brunei, surprising as this may be.

12.   On Friday at about mid-day, Mr. Parks, my A.D.C., was informed on the 'safe' telephone by Mr. Linton, the Shell Managing Director in Seria, that the Resident, Miri,[5] Mr. Fisher, had received what he regarded as reliable information that a revolt was timed to start in the early hours of Saturday morning.

This information was conveyed to the Earl of Selkirk, who was in Brunei on a visit of enquiry. The information was also conveyed to the Sultan and Mentri Besar, and Police precautions were taken, resulting in a strong concentration of forces in the Brunei Town Police Station.

13.   About 2 a.m., a heavy attack was launched on the Brunei Police Station. The personal gallantry and leadership of the Commissioner of Police, Mr. Alan Outram, drove off the attack with some casualties to the rebels, and the situation eased

---

[3] In Sarawak, abutting the eastern border of Brunei.

[4] On 1 Dec the Tunku informed Tory that he had received clear evidence from Brunei's attorney-general (who had been seconded from the Federation) that an insurrection was imminent. Noting the warning, Macmillan commented, 'If this is true, it is serious', but Sandys reassured the prime minister that the 'reports received by the Tunku are greatly exaggerated and there is no reason at present to expect an emergency' (CO 1030/1068, nos 1, 4 and 5). After the outbreak of the rising, the Tunku criticised the British for failing to act on information and he issued a questionnaire that provoked White to tender his resignation, see 153. For Selkirk's assessment of the role of the intelligence services, see 151, para 6.

[5] Seria was the centre of Brunei's oil industry; Miri was an oil town and the administrative headquarters of Sarawak's Fourth Division, south-west of Seria.

temporarily. Later the attack was resumed and it was necessary to open fire again. The Power Station had been taken and the power cut off.

14.　A party of rebels went to my house at about 3.15 a.m. and arrested and tied up Mr. Parks. They were not particularly aggressive, and appear to have been looking for me, though it is difficult to understand why it was not known that I was out of the country.

At about 9 a.m. Mr. Outram, with Mr. Glass, an officer of Her Majesty's Overseas Service, and a party of police came up to my house; the rebels surrendered and Mr. Parks was released.

It is interesting to record that Miss Petrie, my confidential secretary, drove unmolested through bands of rebels in uniform to the house, was allowed to talk to Mr. Parks, who was tied up, and to go away again.

I must record here my appreciation of the courage and good sense of Mr. Parks throughout a difficult and dangerous period.

15.　Some rebels in the early morning went up to the Palace but withdrew after an exchange of shots. It can hardly be considered more than a token attack. Two Party Rakyat leaders on Saturday morning drove up to the Palace to see the Sultan; they were refused admission and arrested.

The house of the Mentri Besar was also attacked by the rebels but, again, it does not seem to have been a very determined assault.

16.　No European or other houses were attacked or molested. There was no looting.

17.　A message was received through the Mentri Besar saying that the Sultan wished to invoke the protection of Her Majesty's Forces, as provided for in the Agreement; this message was got through to Lord Selkirk.

18.　In the meantime, the attack on the oilfields had already taken place.

Shell personnel on early morning duty, who were unfortunate enough to encounter rebel bands, were arrested and others who were still in their houses were not molested and, in fact, remained in their quarters throughout the period during which the area was in rebel hands.

The Police, under the leadership of the Malayan Police Officer on secondment, seemed to have retired to the Panaga Police Station at Seria and the one at Kuala Belait, both of which were held in strength. It is impossible to escape the conclusion that more aggressive action could have probably dispersed the rebels.

There was little damage to installations in the oilfield, though there was some looting in Kuala Belait.

The rebel attack on the main Police Station in Seria, at Panaga, was mounted behind the shield of captured Shell employees. One was killed, several wounded, some escaped and found their way back home. The remainder were incarcerated in Seria Town Police Station which had been captured by the rebels without much, if any, resistance.

19.　Police stations elsewhere in the State surrendered to the rebels without known opposition. A considerable quantity of arms and ammunition thus became available to the rebels.

20.　At mid-day on the Saturday, a detachment of North Borneo Police arrived, and played an invaluable part in holding Brunei Airport which up till then had been guarded by British and Malayan civil servants only. Unfortunately, the North Borneo detachment ran into rebel opposition at the Power Station and suffered one fatality. I would record here my deep appreciation of the speed with which His Excellency the

Governor, Sir William Goode, despatched help and of the courage and discipline of the detachment. The importance of holding Brunei Airport till help arrived is self-evident.

21.   Limbang, headquarters of the Vth Division of Sarawak, was also attacked and, after some police opposition, taken, and the Resident and his wife and other Europeans captured and imprisoned.

22.   The situation on Saturday evening, when the first British troops arrived, the 1/2 Gurkhas, was that with the exception of the Brunei Town Police Station and adjacent areas, the Airport, the Panaga Police Station at Seria, and the Kuala Belait Police Station (which eventually surrendered for no satisfactory reason after holding out for three days), the whole of Brunei was in rebel hands, as well as Limbang. One cannot overemphasise the value of the Gurkhas, and the part they played, with their limited forces, in holding essential points till further reinforcements arrived. They are splendid troops.

23.   This is not the time to attempt a detailed account of the history of the military intervention. The operation to relieve the situation was mounted with exemplary speed and efficiency; the co-operation between the services was of the highest order, and the military operations have from the outset been conducted with courage and humanity. The Force Commander, Brigadier Glennie, deserves the gratitude of us all.

24.   The rebel opposition appears to have become more determined and aggressive after the arrival of reinforcements and the 1/2 Gurkhas suffered casualties both in the town area of Brunei and on the road to the oilfields, at Tutong, where heavy opposition made a return to Brunei inevitable.

As reinforcements arrived, immediate relief operations were mounted. All were carried out with speed, courage and efficiency. I must here record our gratitude to the Queen's Own Highlanders whose recapture of the Seria Town Police Station and release of the prisoners, held as hostages, was admirably conceived and executed.

25.   The relief of Limbang was entrusted to the Marine Commandos almost immediately on arrival and, in spite of some of the heaviest opposition encountered, the town was quickly captured and the hostages released. I deeply regret the losses suffered by the Marines, whose courage and efficiency were of a high order.

26.   Reports were received of rebel forces operating near Sibuti in the IVth Division of Sarawak and an immediate and successful operation was mounted by the Greenjackets.

27.   The situation at the date of this Despatch is that all urban or semi-urban areas of Brunei are in our hands. Hard core rebels are still in bands of varying sizes spread over the State of Brunei, and the Vth Division of Sarawak, and perhaps still in the Sibuti area of the IVth Division. Many will, I think, get rid of guns and uniforms, and attempt to infiltrate back into their villages. There then remains a mopping-up commitment in the jungle areas, and a police-cum-military search of all villages and towns in the State, with Special Branch screening of the population.

28.   As I have already said, it is not yet possible to form definite conclusions as to the motives behind the revolt. Indeed, they probably vary according to the areas and races involved.

There is so far no direct evidence of Indonesian or other foreign involvement; nevertheless, I am convinced that the rebels themselves were certain that Indonesian assistance would be forthcoming. I find it hard to believe that the rebel leaders would have attacked Limbang, with the certainty of British reprisals, if they had not felt sure of outside aid.

The manifesto, outlining the Party Rakyat policy, now in our hands, states that the reunification of the three Territories was the main objective, under Brunei leadership. Azahari was almost certainly to be the Prime Minister, and the Sultan of Brunei was to be the first Head of State.

The manifesto is anti-Colonialist, but not anti-British or pro-Communist, and states clearly that, if British forces did not intervene, there was to be no injury to British personnel or damage to property. If British forces were to intervene, the rebels were to resort to guerrilla warfare and sabotage.

29.   It may be helpful to give you some preliminary thoughts of my own on the events, and also my suspicions and guesses.

I find it difficult to acquit the Sultan and the ruling clique of some pre-knowledge of what was going on. I think it possible that the coup d'etat was planned for later this month, perhaps Christmas Day, and that the revolt may have been accelerated by the progress of Special Branch investigations, and perhaps the visit of Lord Selkirk. I suspect that the Indonesians encouraged and perhaps even promised assistance to the rebels, as a means to wreck Malaysia. I suspect that the rebels in Brunei expected little resistance other than that of the British led Police, because they had been told that the Sultan himself was well-disposed to the plans and, indeed, would head the new Federation. With the widespread Brunei irredentism in respect of their lost territories, it is not beyond possibility that the Sultan himself and his ruling clique have indeed entertained from time to time dreams of restoring Brunei's sovereignty over the lost areas. Was he tempted? Did he procrastinate and temporise to the last moment, as he does on issues great and small? We know that Azahari had told the Tunku of his plan to reunite the Borneo Territories under the Sultan and then take them into Malaysia. I suspect, in fact I am almost sure, that Azahari discussed this with the Sultan.

Whether or not the Sultan was attracted and had promised to consider the proposal, but thought he had more time to procrastinate than he had, in fact, got, I have little doubt that the rebels thought the Sultan was with them. The comparatively civil attitude to the British, and the hardening of the rebel resistance with the arrival of outside forces, is in accordance with the manifesto.

30.   Had a coup d'etat taken place in Brunei with the Sultan's secret concurrence, without bloodshed and without interference with foreign lives and property, there could hardly have been British intervention but, once the High Commission was attacked, and Europeans used as a human shield, once Limbang (Sarawak territory) was attacked, the Brunei rebels must have known that H.M.G. would be forced to intervene.

The certainty of intervention appears to indicate the rebels' confidence in outside support, and the only likely sources are Indonesian or Communist.

31.   It is interesting to note that the Kedayans, one time slaves of the Brunei nobility, have played such an active part, both in the Limbang district, in Sibuti and Berkenu, as well as in Brunei. I believe that their hostility was directed against the nobility of Brunei, who have spent the whole period holed up in the Palace with their wives and children.

With the Party Rakyat in control, they could hope for a happier future, freed for ever from the rapacious nobility.

32.   Though I myself am at present inclined to think that Brunei irredentism and the hatred of the people for the local nobility were important internal causes, and the

Indonesian dislike of Malaysia, and the Communist policy of aiding disaffection important external causes, and however equivocal the conduct of the Sultan and his closest advisers may have been, we have no choice but publicly to accept the Sultan's version of events, i.e. that the ringleaders have staged a revolt against his Government and made an attempt on his life.

In supporting his version, we appear to be forced to restore, revitalise, and succour a Government which has been so inept and dilatory that it has to some extent brought about a rebellion which seems to have been supported by a large proportion of the Sultan's subjects. We clearly do not wish to highlight the anti-Malaysian factor in the rebellion.

33.   If I am right in my deductions or guesses, we are faced with the question of whether the public are going to believe the Sultan's story that the Party Rakyat leaders have deliberately misled them into believing that the Sultan himself was to lead the crusade for the 'liberation' of Brunei's lost territories, that there would be little or no serious opposition in Brunei, and that Indonesian aid would be forthcoming, or whether they will believe Azahari, and decide against the Sultan.

There may be a token acceptance of the Sultan's version while the military presence is still here, but I have little doubt that the moment an opportunity presents itself, they will rise again against him and his nobility, and blood will flow.

34.   We have written his speeches for him, drafted his appeals to his people to lay down their arms, persuaded him to adopt a policy of reconciliation, and the maximum degree of clemency subject to security, in spite of his predilection for oriental revenge, pressed for immediate relief of the dependants of the casualties on the rebel side, and of the prisoners, pressed for rural development, land reform, and as massive as possible a programme of relief work, and the immediate formation of an Emergency Executive Committee, with myself or my representative included, and in all this, I am much indebted to Lord Selkirk who pressed, with success, these points, with the help of Sir Geofroy Tory. Nevertheless, it must be remembered that the burden will fall on an inept and inexperienced Civil Service, badly shaken by defection and panic, with our role limited to that of persuasion and cajolery.

35.   The Sultan himself is still vaccilating [sic]. He may want to join Malaysia, but harps on 'benefits' for his people from entry. He is clearly most concerned for his own safety and security of tenure and is thinking in terms of independence with a British garrison. He shows no sign of appreciating our own position in the area, defensively or politically. The Mentri Besar, basically anti-British, and isolationist, as his confidence revives, will be more difficult to persuade or cajole into decisive action.

36.   Three choices appear open to us:—

(1) to support, as we are doing, a discredited Government;
(2) to repudiate the Treaty, in spite of our Shell interest, in view of the distastefulness of our present position; or
(3) to insist, in conjunction with the Government in Kuala Lumpur, on immediate acceptance of Malaysia.

Of these, I favour the last.

37.   I can only conclude this gloomy tale with an expression of gratitude to Her Majesty's Forces, the North Borneo Government, the Malayan Government, and the Governments of Sarawak and Singapore for their assistance, co-operation and support.

38.   I am sending copies of this despatch to the Earl of Selkirk, the Commander in Chief, Sir Geofroy Tory, Sir William Goode, and to Sir Alexander Waddell, with the hope that if copies are required by other posts they will be supplied by your office.

151   T 225/2551   20 Dec 1962

[Brunei revolt]: letter from Lord Selkirk to Mr Macmillan, affirming Indonesian support for the uprising, the near success of the revolt and the decadence of the sultanate

[In the absence of White until 10 Dec, Selkirk took charge at the start of the crisis. On 7 Dec he visited Brunei where he found 'a general air of complacency' (CO 1030/1068, no 17). On Sunday 9 Dec, Sandys telephoned Selkirk both during and immediately after a crisis meeting which the secretary of state had called in London and they agreed that Selkirk should return to Brunei the next day (*ibid*, no 162). Macmillan insisted on being kept informed of events by telegram while he was in the Bahamas tensely negotiating with President Kennedy what came to be known as the Nassau Agreement on nuclear weapons. The Treasury copy of Selkirk's letter is preferred to the version in the Prime Minister's files, since paragraph 6 of the latter has been excised under 3(4) of the Public Records Act 1958, see PREM 11/4346.]

Dear Prime Minister,

I have your letter of December 12 and the following is a note on the position to date in Brunei.

2.   I am writing on the morning following Soekarno's announcement of support for the Brunei revolt in which he says that 'any Indonesian would be a traitor who did not do so'. His words seem to me to echo some of the bouncing threats which we had to listen to from Hitler in the latter thirties, and with the introduction of Russian arms and military preparations for West Irian, he is now a formidable military power who clearly shows signs of wanting to flex his muscles. The border between British and Indonesian Borneo is some 1,000 miles in length. It is an open frontier and would be impossible to guard or even to demarcate except in very limited places. The rugged border area takes a long time to traverse but it could be crossed almost anywhere by tough guerrillas. Frankly, if Soekarno wants to start guerrilla warfare in the jungles of Borneo, I can see no end to it so long as he supports it. Moreover, we do know he wants to kill Malaysia.

3.   In Brunei the revolution came within an inch of being completely successful. Some arrests were made in Sarawak and this probably precipitated the operation by at least a fortnight or perhaps longer. Warning had come the day before the revolt started which enabled police stations to be alerted; otherwise airfields would have been taken, the Sultan captured and we would have had to fight our way ashore from landing craft in an open coast in the north-east monsoon. Although association with the revolt was widespread throughout the entire population, there was not much fire and most rebels were ready to surrender as soon as the police appeared.

4.   Whilst I have no proof, it is felt by many, including the High Commissioner, that the plot was not completely unknown to the Sultan. It may have been that my visit to him the day before the revolt just swung him against it.

5.   The objects of the rebellion, like all these things, seem to be complex. The incompetence and unpopularity of the ancient Brunei Sultanate was basically the reason why Rajah Brooke was asked by the Sultan of Brunei to take over increasing

portions of Sarawak in order to restore peace and this is what the Rajahs achieved. This revolt was in some measure a continuation of the same process—a revolt against the decadent remnants of a feudal society, even though the Sultan is the representative of Allah on earth and is still held in regard by the people. But to this motive, others were added such as the glory of a greater Brunei extending the whole length of the three territories; a certain dislike of the Malays; a good many sheer pecuniary rewards and a general disrespect for the organs of Government which had certainly deteriorated since 1959 when we ceased to carry any direct responsibility. I do not put anti-Malaysia very high among the most important motives because quite clearly no decision had been made on the point and the Sultan remains rather equivocal about it.

6.   I have naturally examined whether we had been let down by our Intelligence Services. In fact, there was a lot of stuff which had not been properly assessed and also a certain supineness on the ground. There are three separate Special Branches for the three territories and my staff maintain the division of M.I.5. and M.I.6., which is a most serious handicap in an area such as this.[1] Moreover, you will recall that the staff here[2] has been heavily cut both in Intelligence and on the Chancery side in the last twelve months. I have also been inhibited from holding the normal Joint Defence Advisory Council meetings of the three territories because of the pressure of investigation and discussion going on about Malaysia. Nevertheless, if we had acted strongly on such evidence as we had, it might well have led to the movement being pushed underground with more serious long-term results instead of boiling over as it has. We have also been unduly trustful in not keeping one single soldier in the Borneo Territories.

7.   My chief concern is to get some life and vigour into the Sultan's Government. Two days ago I preached him a sermon on radical reform, but it is his Government and we must be very careful not to appear to be taking it over; at the moment he is very willing to co-operate. I am therefore seeking to strengthen the High Commissioner's staff so that they are in a position to advise and help in getting the Government going properly. This is the only way we can safely do it without too obviously being accused of making the Sultan our pawn.

8.   North Borneo has been wonderfully steady and indeed carried out local elections only three days ago in which the people appear to have supported overwhelmingly the parties who favour Malaysia. On the whole, Sarawak too has been steady, although they have a potentially dangerous clandestine communist organisation mostly run by Chinese.

9.   My next concern now, however, is what Indonesia is going to do. I have been pressing the Foreign Office to make the strongest protests before Soekarno starts down the slippery path—it may well be that it is too late now. The Tunku in Kuala Lumpur has been rather over-excited about Indonesian complicity and has made a number of provocative remarks. Here we must draw the lesson that if he provokes the Indonesians, it is we who are in the firing line. However, he has been extremely helpful in sending police, interpreters and interrogation officers to Brunei. Even the

---

[1] In a meeting with Macmillan on 25 Apr 1963, Selkirk drew attention to deficiencies in local intelligence organisation as revealed by the Brunei revolt, a matter which the secretary to the Cabinet referred to 'C' and Roger Hollis (Trend to Garner, 29 Apr 1963, DO 169/226, no 67).
[2] ie, commissioner-general's headquarters.

Singapore Government have secretly sent some interrogation officers to help deal with the prisoners in Brunei. I am a little worried about the Singapore Government for although all their feelings are antagonistic to Indonesia, which they regard with contempt, and sympathetic towards the Malays, I can never be quite certain which way they will jump if public opinion swings one way or the other.

10.   I find it hard to believe we will not have to ask you to send military reinforcements here; if our overflying rights in Indonesia are cut and anything goes wrong with the Maldives,[3] we are extremely isolated.

---

[3] Britain's joint strategy with the US in the Indian Ocean depended on island bases, notably Gan in the Maldives, see 221, n 3.

---

152   CO 1030/1466, ff 106–109   29 Dec 1962

[Brunei revolt]: note on future policy by Sir D White for Lord Selkirk and others attending a meeting in Jesselton on 1 Jan 1963

Assuming that there is no change in our policy of steering Brunei towards Malaysia, it is imperative that decisions are taken both as to the methods to be employed and as to timing.

2.   The Tunku not only advocates, but is actively instigating, a 'shotgun' wedding; H.M.G. has so far not issued any directive on this, but the consensus of opinion seems in favour of a more cautious approach, with banns and orange blossom.

3.   In my view, the shotgun wedding was only possible in the heat of battle; it is no longer a feasible solution—it would be damaging both to H.M.G. and the Tunku, and a risky provocation to Soekarno.

If this view is agreed, it is essential that the Tunku should be persuaded to accept it.

4.   Special Branch investigations confirm most of the preliminary views I had formed and circulated in a note at our previous meeting.[1] We are supporting a Government without merit and without backing in the State, whose dilatory methods, lack of integrity and inaccessibility were a contributory factor in the revolt.

If we continue much longer to give our support to the present Government, we shall be committed irrevocably.

In seeking a decision on policy here, I must add that the present Mentri Besar and his Deputy are co-operating with us fully, and both seem to have accepted the principle of the Federation of Malaysia.

5.   The Sultan is believed by the TNKU to have been privy to the rebellion and to have accepted the idea of reunification of the three territories with himself as Ruler. I suspect that, as is his custom, he equivocated; he shares the long-standing and deeply-ingrained irredentism of the Brunei Malays and would have been attracted by the idea of reunification. I imagine that Lord Selkirk's talk with him awoke him to the dangers of his position, and he called for British support. I doubt if he had given his confidence to the Mentri Besar about his intrigue with the TNKU.

I consider it desirable that the Tunku should be informed of the result of Special

---

[1] See 149. For an account of the meeting on 1 Jan, at which White's second note (152) was tabled, see 155.

Branch interrogations on this matter. I doubt if he would withdraw his support of the Sultan, but he might hear of the information through his Malayan officer who was present at the interrogation of our informant.

I do not think that H.M.G. can withdraw their support from the Sultan in consequence of our knowledge; nevertheless I have serious doubts as to whether I should continue to represent H.M.G. in Brunei. My role in Brunei has been conciliatory; my brief was to re-establish friendly relations with the Sultan and his leading Government executives. I am inclined to feel that a tougher approach is needed and that this is more important than proficiency in Malay and a reputation as a sympathetic conciliator. This is for H.M.G.'s decision, and I shall make no difficulties, but my resignation might have a salutary effect on the Sultan and his advisers.[2]

6.   Interrogations so far complete indicate that the Party Rakyat had a political wing which does not appear to have been actively concerned with the revolt. The revolutionary wing led locally by Yassin Affendy in Azahari's calculated absence must be destroyed, but there does seem a reasonable chance of using the 'political' wing, led by Awang Hafidz (now under interrogation) to bring the non-TNKU element, i.e. the majority of the native people of Brunei, to accept the idea of independence within Malaysia.[3]

7.   The following action proposals are tabled for discussion:—

(1) A statement by the Sultan that the revolution has in no way altered his determination to press on with his plans to become a Constitutional Head of State with a fully elected popular Government.

(2) That talks take place in the near future between H.M.G. and Brunei to determine the future of the State in accord with H.M.G.'s expressed determination to grant independence to all her Colonial and quasi-Colonial territories.

(3) In the light of the discussions with H.M.G., His Highness should appoint an interim Executive Council, containing members of Party Rakyat (who had not been members of TNKU), members of the Brunei Malay Teachers' Association, Kedayan representatives (if any can be absolved from participation in the revolt), and representatives of other minority groups. The ruling clique should have the minimum representation.

This Council should be invited to endorse the decisions reached in talks with H.M.G. Offstage discussions would have to take place with selected members prior to their appointment to ensure as far as possible their pre-acceptance of proposals.

(4) The Malayans should undertake a programme of religious and cultural propaganda to overcome the antipathy of the Bruneis to them, an antipathy which has been reported to have slackened as a result of the revolt.

(5) Initiation of a campaign of political education by British or Malayan lecturers, or possibly by both.

N.B. (4) and (5) are the results of Mr. Bennett's[4] talks with Malayan and Brunei Information staff.

---

[2] See 153.   [3] For attempts to 'turn' leaders of the PRB, see 153, note.
[4] John Still Bennett (not to be confused with John Sloman Bennett of the CO) was regional information officer, Singapore and Bangkok, 1959–1963. For the publicity drive from early 1963 onwards to present Malaysia positively to SE Asia and the wider world, see FO 953/2128–2132.

(6) Pressure should be brought on the Sultan to dispense with the services of at least some of the holders of top posts in his Government, even if this has to be achieved by the distribution of honours and financial compensation, and to appoint more generally acceptable persons, including possibly one or two from Party Rakyat political wing, on a temporary basis, pending Malaysia.

(7) Assurances will be needed from H.M.G., even if not given publicity, to the Sultan, the nobility, the ruling clique, Shell and other British commercial interests, as well as to remaining British Government officials, that British troops will remain in Brunei until such time as it can be safely assumed that the threat to internal security is removed. Shell might lose up to 50% of their staff if British troops were prematurely withdrawn. The Tunku, no doubt, has views on this point.

(8) LIMBANG: This is not, perhaps, an immediate problem, nor is it my business, but as much advice has been tendered (and gratefully received) on what should be done in Brunei, I may be excused from expressing the view that Party Rakyat intrigues in the area found a such readier response and were on a far larger scale than were estimated by the authorities.

I do not imagine that the people of Limbang would welcome transfer to Brunei under its present Government in spite of financial and other attractions; nevertheless, I imagine that the Tunku will wish this issue to be resolved before Malaysia.

153 CO 1030/1466, f 112   31 Dec 1962
[Resignation of high commissioner of Brunei]: letter from Sir D White to Mr Sandys

[In addition to the reasons given in this letter to Sandys, White informed Wallace, 'I consider that the Tunku's questionnaire (which Lord Selkirk forwarded to you with my notes) is about the most offensive document that a Commonwealth Prime Minister could send to Her Majesty's representative. Lord Selkirk told the Tunku of his views in no uncertain terms, but no one else seems to think it necessary to protest' (CO 1030/1466, f 102). The Tunku's questionnaire, which was released in June 2003, accused the British of gross neglect regarding security (CO 1030/1493, no 1/E). Although they recognised the difficulties with which White had been contending since the inauguration of Brunei's constitution in 1959 and defended him against the Tunku's charges, Selkirk and Lansdowne were determined that he should be replaced (CO 1030/1493). So, too, was Macmillan who had written to Sandys about this as early as 12 Dec (CO 967/419). Sandys accepted White's request to retire but did so on health grounds alone; his reply was a generous tribute to White's sense of duty and, in focusing exclusively on his medical circumstances, the secretary of state sealed British ranks against charges of mismanagement of the Brunei crisis (Sandys to White, personal, 10 Jan 1963, CO 1030/1493; cf Lansdowne to Selkirk, 21 Jan 1963, CO 967/417). White did not leave immediately and in March 1963 was interviewing PRB detainees (notably Awang Hafidz Laksamana, Awang Tengah and Pengiran Matusin) in an attempt to turn them into organisers of a Brunei Alliance that would actively campaign to secure the people's acceptance of Brunei's entry into Malaysia. Angus MacKintosh, who had been deputy commissioner-general, SE Asia, from 1956 to 1960, served as high commissioner from Apr to Dec 1963 when he was transferred to the Ministry of Defence and replaced by E O Laird.]

Now that the more active phase of the Brunei rebellion seems to be under control, I have the honour to address you upon my own problems as British High Commissioner.

2. As you are aware, I accepted appointment with the proviso that I should be permitted to retire after three years instead of the usual five years in office. I have from time to time raised the question of my retirement with the permanent officials of the Colonial Office and, indeed, in November, had expressed the opinion that a change was desirable in view of the overwhelming success of the Party Rakyat at the polls,[1] and the obvious difficulty that I would face, not only in working with them, but also in persuading the Sultan and the Palace party, with whom I had for so long been closely associated, that recognition of the Party Rakyat was inevitable, though distasteful to them. No suitable relief seemed available at the time.

3. I had also come to the conclusion that a tougher line was needed with the Sultan, if we were to overcome his inability to make up his mind, and had discussed, without solution, how to achieve this, though, here again, I had expressed doubts as to my own suitability to implement a tougher policy.

4. It is obvious that I underestimated both the gravity and the imminence of the threat to the security of the State, and had been inclined to accept Azahari's assurances that he intended to employ Constitutional methods to attain his ends.

5. A decision on the future of this unhappy little State is a matter of urgency, but the political implications of any decision are now of international concern. Under the circumstances, and after careful and anxious consideration, I have come to the conclusion that I should offer you my resignation, and this I now do, with the assurance that I shall accept loyally whatever decision you may care to make.

---

[1] See 150, n 1.

---

154 CO 1030/1466, no E/7, GM(63)1, annex A   nd [Jan] 1963
[Brunei's political future]: draft telegram from Mr Sandys to Lord Selkirk

[On 28 Dec Selkirk reported (inward telegram no 96) that the Sultan of Brunei had decided to accept the principle of Malaysia and to negotiate terms with the Tunku. Selkirk went on to suggest tactics for fostering the process. The draft reply, which was considered by the Greater Malaysia (Official) Committee, was later cut on the instructions of the prime minister. On 2 Jan the secretary of state despatched the abbreviated version. The draft is printed here, however, since it provides a fuller account of London's views on the importance of bringing Brunei into Malaysia and on how to effect the merger.]

Your telegram No. 96.

Brunei
Your telegram has now been considered by Ministers who agree that the policy must be to persuade, but not to force, the Sultan into Malaysia. Other alternatives, i.e. independence outside Malaysia, or continuation of status quo, would be most unsatisfactory both from our point of view and that of the future Government of Malaysia, and, in the long term, for Brunei itself.

2. The problem is to convince the Sultan of this so that there will be no question of his reopening negotiations with the Malayan Government under the impression that, if he cannot get the terms he wants, he has nevertheless two satisfactory fall-back positions. It would be very awkward if negotiations, once reopened, were not to succeed.

3.   We suggest, therefore, that when you see the Tunku you should set out, as we see them, the disadvantages of the alternatives to Malaysia, and discuss with him whether there would be advantage in a preliminary softening up by us (as you had suggested in your telegram No. 86). The arguments for and against the two alternatives to Malaysia seem to be as follows:—

(a) *Independence*. Mr. Maudling in his letter of the 9th March, 1962 to the Sultan (copies of which went to Allen, Goode and Tory) set out the objections to both independence and the status quo, but nevertheless recognised the right of Brunei to independence 'whenever difficulties can be resolved to your Highness's satisfaction'.[1] The Sultan may well feel that there are attractions in independence, particularly if this were guaranteed either by the U.N., by Indonesia or the Philippines, or both, or by a Defence Treaty with the U.K. or with Malaysia (which would in fact exclude the U.K.). From our point of view, of course, the objection to independence is that we should be unable to protect the oilfields except by invitation. An independent Brunei would be a focus for subversive operations against Malaysia in general, and its Borneo components in particular. From the Sultan's point of view no guarantees of external protection could help him against subversive activity which the weakness and wealth of his State would invite.

(b) *Status quo*. It would not be legally possible for H.M.G. to terminate the 1959 Agreement unilaterally. We should therefore have to seek to persuade the Sultan (as was done in Mr. Maudling's letter) that continuation of the Agreement will become increasingly inappropriate after the independence of the neighbouring territories. H.M.G. would be prepared to put their reluctance to continue the 1959 Agreement after Malaysia in the strongest terms to the Sultan on the ground that the advent of Malaysia had radically changed the situation, and that there was now a much more satisfactory alternative for safeguarding the security of Brunei. We could emphasise that it would of course be more difficult for the U.K. to assist in the internal security of Brunei. But in the last resort the Sultan could hold us to the Agreement and he no doubt realises that we could not afford to leave the oilfields unprotected.

4.   In your telegram No. 86 you suggest that the Secretary of State should have discussions with the Sultan, but the Sultan's decision to seek to reopen negotiations with Malaya seems to have removed any immediate necessity for this. Nevertheless some softening up may be desirable before negotiations start, and if you think it would be helpful for you yourself to undertake this, I am sure that White would be grateful for this supplement of the efforts he has already made (your telegram No. 85 and 86). It might be best if whoever saw the Sultan were to bear a letter from the Secretary of State.

5.   Despite our efforts, however, it may be difficult to persuade the Sultan that there is no real alternative to Malaysia, and if he finds the terms unattractive he may well reject it. It may assist in making the Tunku more amenable if you set out to him also the position as we see it.

6.   As regards terms for Brunei to enter Malaysia, we note from paragraph 3 of your telegram No. 86 that you have already moved the Tunku to concede that some

---

[1] See 95.

special financial arrangement with Brunei would be justifiable. We certainly regard some financial concessions as essential, and there may also be other concessions which could be made which would not have the effect of causing Sarawak and North Borneo to reopen the Agreements on the Inter Governmental Committee.

7.   In our telegram Personal No. 211 to Brunei we asked White whether there was any possibility of broadening the base of the Brunei Government. We are impressed with Waddell's and Goode's views about the danger of negotiating with the discredited and unpopular Palace party. While we appreciate the willingness of the Tunku to negotiate with Marsal,[2] this is bound to cause considerable criticism and, unless the Sultan can come to terms with his people, (your telegram Brief No. 55), any agreement reached might be difficult to carry through. We agree, however, that, even if it is not immediately possible for the Sultan to appeal to popular support, the importance of getting Brunei into Malaysia is such that negotiations with Marsal should go ahead faute de mieux.

8.   As regards any statement by the Sultan, we feel strongly that this should avoid suggesting that there are any practicable alternatives to Malaysia.

---

[2] Dato Marsal, the Sultan's chief minister.

155   PREM 11/4346   4 Jan 1963
[Brunei's political future]: letter from Lord Selkirk to W I J Wallace, reporting a meeting held at Jesselton on 1 Jan[1]

I held a meeting on January 1 in Jesselton, at which the Governors of North Borneo and Sarawak, the High Commissioner, Brunei, the Commander-in-Chief, Far East, the Commander-in-Chief, Far East Land Forces, the Director of Military Operations, the three Commissioners of Police and others were present. We discussed the military and political situation and outlook in various aspects.

2.   The discussion on the political future of Brunei took place against the following background:—

(a) there is no immediate alternative to government by the Sultan through Dato Marsal;

(b) there is no existing political organisation other than the Party Rakyat;

(c) Azahari cannot in present circumstances be brought back into the body politic;[2]

(d) unless Azahari has been finally and effectively discredited in Brunei eyes, the Party Rakyat cannot safely be brought back into the body politic under secondary leaders and another name;

---

[1] The letter was signed by a member of Selkirk's staff in his absence.
[2] Azahari played no part in the revolt, but, being in the Philippines at the time, he took refuge in the Indonesian embassy in Manila and later moved to Indonesia. There had been some talk in British circles of grooming him for government office and, after the revolt, Sir Leslie Fry (British ambassador in Jakarta) suggested overtures to Azahari. Although de Zulueta felt that 'there might well be something to be said for getting Azahari committed to joining Malaysia and then letting him overturn the Sultan who has evidently not been conspicuously loyal', he feared that 'Azahari is too drugged with the idea of becoming an independent Sultan to see the true dangers of his position if our protection was withdrawn' (de Zulueta to Macmillan, 27 Dec 1962, PREM 11/4346; see also, FO 371/169694, nos 3, 5 and 12.).

(e) conditions do not yet exist in which an alternative political party could be formed and flourish;

(f) the Tunku appears still anxious to have Brunei in Malaysia;

(g) Malaysia will be less stable without Brunei, whether Brunei is independent or under British protection;

(h) Brunei would not be able to maintain an acceptable form of independence outside Malaysia;

(i) effective British protection, even if politically acceptable, would be more difficult after Malaysia.

3.   Each of the above propositions is arguable, but I myself believe that they must all be accepted.

4.   There is no doubt that we must do all we can, in concert with the Tunku, to get Brunei into Malaysia. The question is whether the operation is to be a 'shotgun' marriage, a long and seemly courtship, or something between the two.

5.   A shotgun marriage—that is to say a decision by the Sultan, taken and announced in the very near future, that he will join Malaysia—would certainly be offensive to large sections of world opinion. It might also, though I am less sure of this, increase tension or at least bitterness within Brunei. Further, I doubt whether we could induce the Sultan to agree, even if we were prepared explicitly to threaten abrogation of our agreement.

6.   A long courtship is in my view impracticable. Insofar as the Sultan's administration improves, it will make him more confident in his ability to sit on the fence. If it does not improve, the courtship will not prosper. Further, I do not believe that the Tunku will be prepared to wait for very long; and the conditions for Brunei's accession will probably become stiffer and less acceptable as time goes by. Lastly, I am frankly doubtful whether, in the foreseeable future, the Sultan will be able to so popularise the idea of Malaysia in advance of the realisation as to be able to achieve a convincing popular endorsement of it.

7.   The solution, in my view, and I think also in that of most of those present at the meeting, seems to be to concert with the Tunku and the Sultan a programme on the following lines:—

(a) Tunku and Sultan to make contact and satisfy themselves and H.M. Government—H.M. Government acting in an intermediary rôle if necessary— that agreement can and will be reached on terms for Brunei's accession to Malaysia.

(b) Sultan to make (but not announce) irrevocable decision to carry negotiations on accession through to a conclusion.

(c) Sultan to announce that he is entering into these negotiations.

(d) H.M. Government to welcome this announcement, while emphasising that the final decision is for the Sultan and the Tunku.

(e) Sultan to institute a careful programme of propaganda and projection covering the following points:—

(i) within Malaysia, inevitable return to representative Government;

(ii) pending Malaysia, amnesty or clemency, relief, rehabilitation, development, administrative vigour;

(iii) outside Malaysia, inability of Brunei to survive alone indefinitely.

In this connexion, Meadows[3] has made a most impressive start in revivifying the administration, and if the momentum which he is generating can be kept up, I do not by any means exclude the possibility of a real reconciliation between the people of Brunei and their Government.

8. I hope to discuss a programme on the foregoing lines with Tun Razak on January 4. The Federation Government must at all costs accept that negotiations must succeed; there can be no third attempt. Further, they must see that their Malayans in Brunei do their very best to support the Sultan's efforts to popularise Malaysia. If you have any qualifications or comments to make, I hope that you will make them very soon, before it is too late.

9. I am sending copies of this letter to the High Commissioner in Brunei, the Governors of North Borneo and Sarawak, the High Commissioner, Kuala Lumpur and our Ambassadors in Djakarta and Manila.

---

[3] P H Meadows joined the MCS in 1948 and served in Singapore from 1951. An expatriate officer in Lee Kuan Yew's government, he was on the point of resigning following victimisation by Ong Eng Guan when Lee transferred him to the Prime Minister's office as deputy permanent secretary (see 15, n 3). He later left the public for the private sector in Singapore. Immediately after the Brunei revolt, Selkirk sought experienced officers for special tasks in Brunei on a short-term basis and Meadows was appointed deputy high commissioner. Working on a plan for administrative reform in consultation with the Sultan, he made an immediate impact and, had his firm been willing to extend his secondment, he would have been considered as a replacement for White. See CO 1030/1450; H P Hall to Selkirk, 24 Dec 1962, CO 1030/1466; Selkirk to Wallace, 8 Jan 1963, CO 1030/1489.

156   PREM 11/4346   5 Jan 1963
[Singapore arrests]: inward telegram no 13 from Lord Selkirk to Mr Sandys

[Several times after mid-Dec, Moore spoke with Lee about reviving the plan to arrest suspected subversives. The British believed that this was the only way to induce the Tunku to accept merger with Singapore, whereas Lee feared the Tunku would abandon Malaysia once the threat of subversion had been eliminated. On 1 Feb the ISC decided to go ahead with operation 'Cold Store', see 148 and 158.]

Moore saw Lee Kuan Yew again yesterday. Lee is still extremely worried lest, after the arrests have been made in Singapore, the Tunku may eventually decide either not to go through with Malaysia at all or to leave out Singapore. His reasons are as follows. First, he argues that the Tunku may feel that, having eventually persuaded Lee Kuan Yew and the British to take action against the Communists in Singapore, he need no longer fear Singapore as a subversive threat to the Federation. In these circumstances the Tunku might think it would be better after all to leave Singapore to the British to handle. Secondly, Lee is concerned about the possibility of the Tunku's nerve failing altogether on Malaysia, especially if Indonesian intervention and pressure persists and grows. He contrasts the Tunku's initial strong reactions to Indonesia with his more recent statements which seem to indicate weakness. He quoted the following two passages from speeches by the Tunku reported in the 'Straits Times' on the 2nd and 4th January respectively:—

'So far Indonesia has been attacking us with words' he said 'and so long as words are used against us we will return the compliments in full measure.

But if it comes to a hot war in which guns and bullets are used we are helpless'.

'We have neither war planes nor war ships and not even firearms to fight with any country'.

Lee is beginning to wonder whether, in the light of these statements, he can have any confidence that the Tunku would persist with Malaysia in the face of serious Indonesian 'volunteer' intervention in Borneo.

2.   Lee went on to say that, while he would like the arrests to take place, he would much prefer to get beforehand a written assurance from the Tunku that, if the arrests were made, Malaysia, including Singapore, would definitely come into being on the 31st August 1963. Moore pointed out again, however, that it hardly seemed practical politics to ask the Tunku for such a written assurance since we cannot seem to bargain the arrests against Malaysia. If the arrests are justified, they should be made irrespectively of Malaysia. Lee's answer to this is that he has always said it is not possible to arrest the Communists in Singapore except as part of the merger arrangement under which Kuala Lumpur takes over responsibility for Singapore's internal security and that he could never make the arrests on his own. While it is true that Lee has always been consistent on this point, I am sure we cannot hope to extract such a written undertaking from the Tunku and that it would be bad tactics to try. The Tunku has said he will accept Singapore into Malaysia provided two conditions are met. First that the Borneo territories must enter at the same time and, secondly, that the arrests should be made in Singapore. With this I think we must be content. Lee appeared reluctantly to accept that a written undertaking was not feasible but he may return to the idea.

3.   Having explored this possibility, Lee then said that he would go through with the arrests provided the British were prepared to assure him that there was no likelihood of the Tunku going back on Malaysia. Moore reiterated what he said in the previous conversation, namely, that he had no reason to suppose that the Tunku would go back on Malaysia provided his two conditions in regard to the Borneo territories and the arrests were met. He undertook, however, to report these views to you and to give Lee an answer early next week.

4.   After speaking to Razak yesterday, I do not share Lee's apprehension about the Tunku's resolution. We are, however, advised by Tory, and I see no reason to question his advice, that there is a real risk the Tunku will try to drop Singapore from Malaysia if the arrests are not carried out. Furthermore, Lee is apparently prepared to accept his share of the public responsibility if the arrests are made and it would be a very considerable achievement with important long term implications to have Lee publicly committed to the arrest of Communists and their sympathisers in Singapore. I think, therefore, our policy must be to assume that the Tunku will go through with Malaysia and to try to strengthen his resolve by dealing with the security situation in Singapore in the way he has always wanted.

5.   I should be grateful, however, if Tory could let you have his views on (a) the likelihood of the Tunku dropping Singapore from Malaysia if the arrests are not carried out fairly soon; and (b) the possibility of the Tunku dropping Malaysia altogether in the face of Indonesian opposition and possible intervention.

6.   Subject to any contrary views Tory may have, I would recommend that we tell Lee at once that we have no reason to suppose that the Tunku will fail to go through

with Malaysia, including Singapore, provided the arrests are made and Lee does not thereafter try to shirk his responsibility. I hope Lee will be satisfied with this answer and will be prepared to proceed. He mentioned that he was now in favour again of a large-scale operation involving the arrest of some 180 people including members of the Singapore Assembly and the banning of the Barisan Socialis. He realises that there is no question of similar action in the Federation.

157   PREM 11/4346   17 Jan 1963
[Indonesian subversion of the Borneo territories and the future defence of Malaysia]: letter from Lord Selkirk to Mr Macmillan

[A week after Selkirk's letter to Macmillan, the foreign secretary informed Cabinet of 'continuing indications of an attempt by Indonesia to subvert the Borneo Territories by gradual infiltration' and of British consultations with the US, Australia and New Zealand about 'the possibility of promoting joint measures to restrain the Indonesian Government'. He added that it would be necessary 'to seek to dissuade the Government of the Philippines from supporting Indonesian policies in this area'. Accepting that 'it might well be necessary to take further measures' to prevent the renewal of Indonesian aggression, Cabinet approved the attempt to work out a joint policy with other governments so that Indonesia should be left in no doubt that, 'unless they abandoned their intentions in relation to Borneo, they would be liable to meet concerted resistance'. Cabinet returned to the subject a week later when the foreign secretary reported continuing military activity by Indonesia that had resulted in some troops in the UK being placed on 72-hour alert. He also mentioned the possibility of the Philippines making common cause with Indonesia. On 7 Feb the foreign secretary reported, though with little conviction, Indonesia's denial of aggressive intent towards the Borneo territories (CC 6(63)2, 24 Jan; CC 9(63)4, 31 Jan; CC 10(63)2, 7 Feb 1963, CAB 128/37).]

Since my letter of December 20[1] on the revolt in Brunei, later information has on the whole served to underline what I said at that time. But it has become clear that, although the revolt was not communist inspired, the communists are using, and will continue to use, it and its aftermath to achieve their aim of preventing the formation of Malaysia or of disrupting it when formed.

2.   Recent events, however, have somewhat altered the image of Malaysia. Brunei, who one would have thought would be the easiest candidate to bring into Malaysia both from the historic and the ethnical associations, may now prove to be the most difficult. Although Brunei does not represent more than about seven per cent of the total population of the Borneo territories it constitutes a focal point on which Indonesia can concentrate her designs to infiltrate with the resources amply available to her for the purpose. To this must be added the deterioration of Indonesian/Malayan relations which have never been good. We are thus presented with bigger problems to face both in the formation of Malaysia and in the maintenance of its security and stability when it comes into existence. Not that the new image is altogether gloomy. Far from it. Indonesian interference in the Borneo territories has swung opinion in North Borneo and Sarawak firmly in favour of Malaysia and has convinced many of the Chinese in Singapore that while a merger under the Malays may not be ideal, it is infinitely preferable to being absorbed by an expansionist Indonesia. These developments serve, however, to underline the

---

[1] See 151.

importance of attaining Malaysia if we are to hope to maintain any stability in this area where, to the north we have a desperate war in Vietnam and in the south there is Indonesia, well armed and highly unstable.

3.   The resultant position is a clear need to increase the defensive capacity of Malaysia, to which I do not doubt we will have to make a greater contribution than we had perhaps originally thought necessary. In other words, we will have to recognise that our military assistance to Malaysia during the formative stage may have to be larger and last longer than we had previously thought would be the case. This will be further complicated by the inevitable overlap of two tasks, the maintenance of internal security and of security against external aggression; it is now clear how very difficult it will be to distinguish between these roles and to restrict our obligations. The military aspect of these problems is now being examined by the Commander-in-Chief's military planners. This may mean an increase in our burden in this area; but I am sure our Malaysia policy is right and has been amply justified by events.[2]

---

[2] The document is incomplete: paragraph 4 has been deleted and retained under 3(4) of the Public Records Act.

158   CO 1030/1577, no E/99   [1 Feb] 1963
'The communist conspiracy': paper authorised by the Internal Security Council of Singapore, accounting for operation 'Cold Store'

[Meeting in Kuala Lumpur on 1 Feb, the ISC decided to proceed in the early hours of the next day with what was code-named operation 'Cold Store'. They authorised 169 arrests of which about 120 were made, including those of Ahmad Boestamam, James Puthucheary, Sidney Woodhull and Lim Chin Siong. Boestamam was detained on account of his links with Indonesia and alleged involvement in the Brunei rising. Lim Chin Siong went into captivity having refused Lee Kuan Yew's offer of a safe passage out of Singapore. At the same time the ISC approved a public statement to which was annexed an explanatory paper, 'The communist conspiracy', which security and intelligence officers had drafted at Lee Kuan Yew's request. 'Cold Store' provoked protests in Singapore and internationally. A team of British Labour MPs visited Singapore in May to find 35 persons still in solitary detention and Amnesty International campaigned on their behalf.]

The Communist Party of Malaya is a pan-Malayan Party and has claimed that it never recognised the 'false' separation of the two Malayan territories. The aim of the Communist Party of Malaya is to establish in the Federation and Singapore a Communist State of Malaya.

2.   In 1951 the Party foiled in its attempt to establish such a state by armed revolution in Malaya, switched its tactics to the familiar Communist methods of the 'United Front' and the 'peaceful constitutional struggle'. Significantly, however, the Party did not disband the defeated remnant of its terriorist force, but kept it in being both as a symbol of resistance and as a potential nucleus for a revival of the 'armed struggle' at any time when conditions appear favourable.

3.   Deriving its inspiration from the revolutionary experience of the Chinese Communist Party, the Communist Party of Malaya is at present in the stage of development described by the CCP as the 'minimum programme'. 'Anti-imperialism' is the keynote of this stage. The United Front, described by the Malayan Communists themselves as 'not an organisation but a sort of struggle strategy', is the principal instrument of the minimum programme.

4. The 'United Front' is an auxiliary unit of the C.P.M. terriorist force. It comprises all those organisations which are either controlled or penetrated by members of the Communist Party of Malaya and, pretending to be independent, endeavour to attract non-Communists to them so as to appear 'respectable'. Its purpose is to advance the cause of Communism in Malaya and Singapore and its main tasks are:—

(i) To recruit adherents to Communism and once recruited to train them into cadres and open front workers.

(ii) To join whenever expedient with non-Communist organisations in pursuing a common objective which is to the ultimate advantage of the Communist Party.

(iii) To provide cover for secret Communists.

5. The Communists in Singapore began to implement this new United Front policy in 1955. Their leaders, trained as underground CPM cadres in numerous cells in the trade unions, schools and rural organisations, first attempted to gain power through winning key positions in the socialist and non-Communist Peoples Action Party. They hoped to use the P.A.P. as the main instrument by which the United Front would capture political power in Singapore. During the years 1955 to 1959, making use of the organisation, skill and experience they had accumulated over a period of more than 30 years, the Communists heavily infiltrated the P.A.P. but never succeeded in exploiting it as a subservient and effective instrument of the United Front. As part of their United Front tactics they began penetrating the trade union movement and by 1956 had made considerable progress in gaining control of it.

6. In 1955/56 the Communists, at the same time as attempting to achieve a dominant influence in the PAP, made considerable progress in gaining control of the bulk of the trade union movement. The militant policy of the Communist-led unions provoked a series of strikes and industrial disputes designed to inflame the workers against the 'foreign capitalists'. The CPM drew upon the extensive student organisations which it had recruited during the previous five years to provide militant support for the strikers. The unrest culminated in the widespread rioting and mass arrests of 1956 and 1957.

7. The Communists acknowledged the tactical mistakes of 1956/57 which caused the loss of many valuable party cadres and the disruption of United Front work. The CPM circulated a pamphlet of self-criticism entitled 'Summary of Experiences of the Anti-Persecution Struggle' for the training of Communist cadres in United Front work in future. Attributing the setbacks of 1956/57 to incorrect tactical guidance arising from the 'left-wing adventurist policy' of the open leaders of the United Front, the document called for a fundamental policy in future to 'conceal the best cadres and conserve our strength'. To implement this policy the CPM in Singapore tightened its security measures, withdrawing valuable cadres to safe areas and disbanding its subsidiary organisation, the Anti-British League.

8. The period 1959 to 1961 marked the final attempt by the Communists to dominate the P.A.P. after the P.A.P. took office following the 1959 elections. *Lim Ching Siong, Fong Swee Suan* and other experienced Communist cadres released from detention established themselves and their followers in key posts in the trade union movement. They quickly dominated the already Communist dominated Singapore General Employees' Union and used it as a base from which to extend their penetration to other unions. They established a similar grip on organisations of

rural dwellers, and thereby hoped to secure their 'mass base', in accordance with Communist doctrine, in the 'workers-peasant alliance'. By drawing individual unions together into federations under their control and establishing a similar grip on organisations of rural dwellers, they hoped to secure their 'mass base', in accordance with Communist doctrine, in the 'workers-peasants alliance'.

9.   The open break with the P.A.P. came with the announcement of joint support for the Malaysia Plan by the Prime Ministers of the Federation of Malaya and Singapore. The achievement of Malaysia should have accorded with the Communists' own proclaimed aims of national unity and independence, but their calculations had in fact been based on the premise of an isolated Singapore where they could make a bid for political control at the next elections and secure self-government with the Internal Security Council abolished. With merger and Malaysia internal security would be in the hands of a central government which could not be captured from Singapore alone. Moreover, a central government of an independent nation could deal more effectively with Communist subversion. The Communists would not then be able to raise a successful counter-attack to rally people on the basis that action against them was colonialist oppression in a non-independent Singapore for the benefit of British military and economic interests. Therefore although committed to the principle of merger, the Communists were obliged to oppose its achievement by every possible means and thereby to expose the fact that the only Malaysia they wanted was one under Communist domination. After a final unsuccessful bid in July 1961 to capture the Government they established their own front party, the Barisan Sosialis, which has since become the principal vehicle of their United Front strategy.

10.   Entrenched in the key positions in the C.E.C., particularly those of Secretary-General and Organising Secretary, the Communists have absolute control of the Barisan Sosialis. The United Front has now become identifiable and exposed by the dominant influence which these same Communists in the Barisan Sosialis have established over their own mass organisations in the trade union, rural organisation and educational fields. Communist leaders of the Barisan Sosialis are at the same time advisers to important trade unions, members of the Executive Council of the 'Singapore Association of Trade Unions' and organisers behind the scenes of Communist activity by their puppet rural organisations and student action committees.

11.   The past year-and-a-half since the formation of the Barisan Sosialis have provided a series of examples of the Communists' mobilization and engagement of the United Front to exploit any issue to foment bitterness, frustration and hatred amongst the people so that Barisan Sosialis can increase their following and the Communists increase their influence amongst the masses. In each case the technique was the same. Students were invited to oppose the Government and go against their parents on the pretext of defending Chinese education. Rural dwellers were incited to obstruct and damage Government's rural development projects designed to improve conditions on the grounds that the compensation they received for resettlement was inadequate. Workers were told that merger with the Federation of Malaya would lead to their suppression and the de-registration of their unions. In each case the Communists took an issue on which a section of the public could be made dissatisfied and by irresponsible propaganda exploited it to prevent the government from resolving the issue. They used the various newspapers and publications of the United Front to distort the facts and whip up public feeling. In

addition various components of the United Front were brought out in support by the issuing of public statements, resolutions, memoranda, circulars, pamphlets, etc., to convey to the public an impression of massive support for their issue. And all the time the Communist manipulators sheltered behind the cover of lawfully registered organisations.

12.   The outstanding example of this mobilization of the various components of the United Front occurred in the National Referendum campaign. A 'Referendum Working Committee' was set up under the chairmanship of *Fong Swee Suan*. Under its direction Barisan Sosialis branches appointed their own working committees to conduct the anti-Referendum campaign in the various constituencies. All the main components gave the public an impression of mass support for the issue. And all the time the Communists sheltered behind the cover of the legally constituted organisation.

13.   These local working committees comprised representations of all component organisations of the United Front in that constituency, which had a significant following in the locality concerned. Thus in a rural constituency the leading part in the local working committees was played by the local officials of the Communist-controlled S.R.R.A. and S.C.P.A. assisted by the local branch officials of the B.S.S. and members of the Communist-dominated O.B.A. or one or more trade unions. In the urban districts the strongest S.A.T.U. controlled trade unions in the constituency concerned was represented on the local working committees, again together with the local Barisan branch officials and members of teachers and O.B.A.

14.   The working committees established in the way were responsible, in accordance with central direction from the Communist leaders on the National Referendum Working Committee, for the massive propaganda campaign all over the island for blank votes in the Referendum involving local mass rallies, banners and posters, house-to-house canvassers, and other demonstrations of 'the peoples' hostility to the phoney Merger'. The National Working Committee also involved another component of the United Front, the N.U.S.U., in their campaign and at its instigation the students organised so-called gallup polls in two constituencies on the following pretext of it being 'for academic research'.

15.   In the left-wing trade union field, the United Front tactics were most clearly demonstrated when the Communists, having failed to capture the Singapore Trade Union Congress, set up in June 1962, a 'Singapore Trade Unions Working Committee'. The Committee served as a central body for the direction of Communist activity within left-wing trade unions and for the co-ordination of the United Front activity with its other components. *Hussein Jahidin* was Chairman with *S. Ghouse*, Secretary of the Naval Base Labour Union as Secretary-General, *Tan Teck Wah*, President of the Singapore General Employees' Union, and *Dominic Puthucheary*, Vice President of the S.G.E.U. and member of Barisan Sosialis Executive Committee. This Committee invited representatives from over 100 civil organisations to two meetings at the Singapore Motor Workshop Employees' Union premises to oppose the Referendum Bill. Both meetings were banned by the Government.

16.   The similarity of this Committee to the 1956 Civil Rights Convention Committee whose meetings led to the riots of October 1956 was quite obvious. The Civil Rights Convention Committee of 1956 was sponsored and organised by the so-called '95 Trade Union Working Committee'. The activities of the 1962 Singapore Trade Unions Working Committee were specifically designed to mobilize mass

support for a Communist-inspired political issue and were of the same pattern as in 1956. They were in no way connected with legitimate industrial grievances. If these activities had been allowed to continue they would have led to a similar situation as in the 1956, resulting in bloodshed and rioting.

17.   As a result of the exposure the Communist directors of the S.T.U.W.C. allowed this organisation to lapse and revived the activities of SATU as a cover for their political objectives. *Fong Swee Suan* has taken direct charge of SATU and its organisation has been strengthened to provide firmer control by its leaders over its 40 affiliated unions.

18.   The Communists have used their domination of the Singapore Rural Residents and Country Peoples Associations and the Hawkers' Union to incite the rural population to oppose government development projects to improve their living conditions. Many of the leading officials of these organisations, headed by *Fong Beng Boo* and *Lim Woon Chye*, Paid Secretaries of the S.R.R.A., have had considerable experience of United Front activity in former banned Communist-controlled organisations such as the Singapore Chinese Middle School Students' Union and the Singapore Farmers' Association. Under their leadership the S.R.R.A., S.C.P.A. and Hawkers' Union participated in the B.S. Referendum and anti-Merger campaigns. They also instigated local dwellers to obstruct government development work such as the canal construction in the Kampong Ang Teng area in October 1962. When these tactics were exposed by the Government, the S.R.R.A. leaders taking their direction from *Lim Ching Siong*, called off their obstruction campaign. Now their new tactics are to attempt to claim credit amongst the people for forcing Government to carry out improvements on their behalf.

19.   The same United Front has been mobilized for the campaign to create an issue over Chinese education. A Chinese Middle School Students' Action Committee was set up to boycott the Government Secondary IV Examinations in November 1961 and its agitation amongst the students was given extensive and seditious publicity in the United Front publications. The agitation was resumed in November 1962. However they failed to win sufficient support and the United Front leadership not daring to risk failure in conducting a further boycott campaign abandoned its plans. Communists and their sympathisers in influential positions in the Nanyang Guild of Graduates, the 33 Chinese School Old Boys' Associations and the Nanyang University Students' Union have concerted to mount a politically-inspired campaign to create an issue over Chinese education. They are currently engaged in attempting to organise a 'torch campaign' for this purpose. This also is receiving United Front and Barisan Sosialis support.

20.   What has been described so far is the way the Communists have used organisations under their control for United Front activity. In contrast to this is the way the Communists have formed temporary alliances with non-Communist and even anti-Communists elements to exploit an issue and to extend their influence over the masses. A particular example was the participation of the Barisan Sosialis in the Council of Joint Action formed, organised by the Liberal Socialist Party and supported by the Singapore Workers' Party to oppose the Merger proposals and the National Referendum. However, people generally recognised that the Communists were only using these persons and organisations for their own ends and that their propaganda concerning 'second class citizenship' was false. The electorate firmly endorsed the merger proposals. But although unsuccessful in using the Council of

Joint Action to mobilise public support for their stand against Merger at the Referendum, they nevertheless succeeded in isolating the Chairman of the Singapore Workers' Party as a prelude to his eventual ousting from that party and its capture by the pro-Communist faction.

21. *Lim Ching Siong*'s admission of the Referendum result as a 'minor and temporary setback' indicated Communist recognition of the defeat of their campaign against Merger. A new phase of the struggle opened, its basis to be broadened to include all the racial communities of the future Malaysia. For this purpose the Communists had already established an instrument under their own control in the form of a 'Liaison Secretariat' of the 'Malaysian Socialist Conference' at Barisan Sosialis Headquarters in Singapore with *Dr. Poh Soo Kai*, the Assistant Secretary-General of the Barisan Sosialis as its Executive Secretary. *Lim Ching Siong* told his followers that they must take heed of any favourable conditions offered to the Malayan 'socialist' forces in future, extend their activities outside Singapore and make the best use of all methods available, seeking co-operation from the left-wing and anti-colonial forces in Malaya and the Borneo territories.

22. After the Referendum results, the Communists re-appraised the situation and on 12.9.62 *Lim Ching Siong* announced the policy along which the United Front was to operate for the immediate future. *Lim Ching Siong*'s admission of the Referendum result as a 'minor and temporary setback' indicated Communist recognition of the defeat of their campaign against Merger. *Lim* laid down three principles for the future struggle:—

(i) To persist in the exploitation of 'constitutional struggle' so long as the administration allowed the conditions for it;

(ii) To strengthen national unity by facing the problems of plural communities throughout Malaysia, and thereby broadening the basis of the struggle; and, in particular to include the Malays;

(iii) On the mass foundation of the workers and peasants to work for a united majority by drawing in the bourgeoisie and petty bourgeoisie.

Lim Ching Siong finally told his followers that they must take heed of any favourable conditions offered to them in future, extend their activities outside Singapore and make the best use of all methods available, seeking co-operation from the left-wing and anti-colonial forces in Malaya and the Borneo territories.

23. The Communists have evidently been in some doubt as to the best methods for implementing this policy. The 'peaceful constitutional struggle' was shown by the Referendum results not to be paying all the dividends they had hoped. The experience of Communist parties elsewhere showed that the armed struggle was also necessary to achieve the complete revolution. The Communists were reminded by *Lim Ching Siong* in his veiled New Year message on 1.1.63 to appreciate the teaching of Lenin, as quoted in the Statement of 81 Parties adopted at the Moscow Conference in 1960, that 'the ruling classes never relinquished power voluntarily'. For this reason the founders of Communism laid down that the armed struggle would always have to be co-ordinated with the constitutional method and that the success of the revolution would depend on how well prepared the Communist parties were for any swift and sudden replacement of one form of struggle by another.

24. These problems and the implementation in Singapore of Communist theory were discussed at a series of cadre training meetings held by the Barisan Sosialis

SGEU and other components of the United Front in the months after the Referendum. In all cases the policy and tactics advocated by *Lim Ching Siong* on 12th September, 1962, in his re-appraisal of the situation after the Referendum setback, were accepted as the fixed party line for the future. His speech on that occasion, his Annual Report as Secretary-General of the Barisan Sosialis and *Fong Swee Suan*'s Annual Report of SATU were circulated for study and purposes of 'political education' to the various component organisations of the United Front in the trade unions, rural associations, cultural associations and student clubs.

25.   The outbreak of the revolt in Brunei on 8.12.62 provided the Communists in the United Front with the type of situation which *Lim Ching Siong* had described in his policy speech. On the night of 9.12.62 the Barisan Sosialis issued a statement supporting the revolt. They organised a mass rally on 23.12.62 and instigated Singapore Partai Rakyat leaders to come out in open support of the Brunei revolt. The leaders of the Barisan Sosialis were also instrumental in causing the Communist controlled SATU and SGEU to bring out all pro-Communist trade unions in Singapore in support of the revolt.

26.   It has also been known that long before the Brunei revolt, *Lim Ching Siong* had been in regular secret contact with *A.M. Azahari*, the leader of the revolt. Their meetings had been arranged by *Said Zahari*,[1] a close associate of *Lim Ching Siong* and other Communist United Front leaders. On all the visits of *A.M. Azahari* to Singapore during the past year, *Said Zahari*, was his closest associate and confidant in Singapore. On two occasions they held clandestine meetings arranged on both occasions by *Said Zahari*. One took place at 2315 hours on 4.3.62 at No.118 Tembeling Road. On the occasion of his last visit to Singapore between 29.11.62 and 7.12.62, *Said Zahari* arranged a meeting between *A.M. Azahari* and *Lim Ching Siong* at the Tiong Hwa Restaurant in Prinsep Street at 1240 hours on 3.12.62. Three days later he fled to Manila.

27.   It will be seen therefore that whilst the Communist conspiracy in Singapore is still a 'peaceful' and an open one it contains within itself the seeds of violence. The United Front must always be regarded as one of the two prongs of the Communist revolution. The other is militant terrorism. There can be no doubt that the hard core organisers and their collaborators of the Communist conspiracy in Singapore believe that the armed struggle remains a weapon to be employed when even [ever?] the opportunity arises. In the meantime the instrument to be used to further the Communist cause is a 'constitutional socialist party' leading the United Front by controlling registered 'legal' organisations of workers, peasants and students and allied with carefully placed cadres in other political parties. By means of this 'United Front', the Communists are conspiring to win power in Singapore and ultimately throughout Malaysia. The Communists in the United Front, which has now consolidated its strength, are trying their utmost to prevent the State of Singapore from attaining complete independence through Merger with the Federation of Malaya. The Merger proposals have been endorsed by an overwhelming majority of the people of Singapore at the National Referendum. It is evident that their intention

---

[1] Said Zahari, editor of *Utusan Melayu* until that newspaper was brought under UMNO control and he was exiled to Singapore in Aug 1961, has recorded his arrest at dawn on 2 Feb 1963 and the subsequent 17 years of detention in *Dark clouds at dawn: a political memoir* (Kuala Lumpur, 2001).

is to set up a Communist controlled Singapore to use it as a base, to capture the Governments of the other territories of Malaysia. The Communist pose a serious security threat to the future peace, prosperity and independence of Singapore and the other territories of Malaysia.

159 FO 371/169695, no 35   7 Feb 1963
[Malaysia and the UN]: letter from Sir P Dean[1] to A D Wilson[2]

[Writing to the FO from New York as head of the UK Mission to the UN, Dean noted the increased interest now taken in Malaysia as a result of lobbying by parties from Singapore and Sarawak as well as the Philippine claim to North Borneo. Conscious that the success of British policy would hinge on support from America (as well as Australia and New Zealand), he noted growing US concern about the implications of Malaysia for international relations in the region. As the subsequent quadripartite talks revealed, Britain's allies were reluctant to participate in concerted action to prevent Indonesian interference in the Borneo territories, see 160–162. Replying on behalf of the FO on 18 Feb, Peck asked Dean to assess the likelihood of UN support for a plebiscite in the Borneo territories, since, despite their objections to it, the British might have to resort to that option as a way of fending off the Philippine claim to North Borneo.]

Adlai Stevenson[3] has recently expressed some concern to me about the Malaysia project, and this, I am sure, reflects a general unease amongst the Americans on the possibility of having to take sides once more in a colonial dispute. Stevenson's chief point was that time is of the essence, and that the sooner Malaysia can become a *fait accompli* the better for all concerned.

2. I have explained to him the position as I understand it, which is that a conference will shortly be held, probably in March, between the British and Malayan governments, at which a formal agreement will be signed providing for the transfer of sovereignty in North Borneo, Sarawak and Singapore by August 31, 1963. However, I was unable to tell Stevenson exactly when the conference would be held, what other steps (apart from an Act of the United Kingdom Parliament) would have to take place thereafter and what the prospects were of Malaysia coming into effect before August 31, 1963. Another point raised by Stevenson, and which I could not answer, was whether the three territories would in fact have a brief moment of independence (a few days or even a few hours) before union with Malaya takes place (as happened with British Somaliland and Somalia).[4]

3. We were much heartened by the decision to bring forward the date of the Aden Federation from March 1 to mid-January, as I think this will put us in a stronger position when the Committee of Twentyfour[5] begins, and if the establishment of Malaysia could similarly be brought forward to (say) mid-June, this (as indeed any advancement) would be welcomed by the Americans and our other friends here and make our task considerably easier. If the advancement of the date could be kept

---

[1] The letter was signed by Alan Campbell in Dean's absence.
[2] A D Wilson, assistant under-secretary, FO, 1960–1964.
[3] Adlai Stevenson, US delegate to the UN, 1961–1965.
[4] The FO firmly discounted this suggestion which had been considered and rejected some time before.
[5] UN Committee of Twenty-Four (formerly Committee of Seventeen) was responsible for overseeing colonialism and was generally critical of British colonial policy.

secret so that our critics believe that August 31 remains the target date, so much the better.

4.   I realise that those concerned with this project are anxious to bring it into being as soon as possible and that a great deal has already been accomplished in a relatively short time to meet this end. However, there has been, as you know, a great increase in interest here at the United Nations in Malaysia in the past weeks, and pressures for some form of U.N. intervention may well build up in the coming months. The Indonesians and the Filipinos look bent on stirring up trouble in one form or another. I suggest, therefore, that our own interests in the United Nations and the need to retain American confidence and support, are added reasons for bringing Malaysia into being at the earliest possible date.

5.   I hope that you will be able to let me have your comments on this question before too long, as I have promised Stevenson that I will give him further information as soon as possible. I am sending a copy of this letter to Greenhill[6] in Washington and am enclosing additional copies of this letter in case you wish to pass them on to the Colonial Office and the Commonwealth Relations Office.

---

[6] Denis Greenhill (later Lord Greenhill) was minister at the British Embassy, Washington, 1962–1964.

160   FO 371/169695, no 21   11 Feb 1963

[Quadripartite talks in Washington]: inward telegram no 471 from Sir D Ormsby-Gore to Lord Home, reporting the views on Malaysia of Australia, New Zealand and the USA

[The support of the USA, Australia and New Zealand was regarded as essential for the success of the Malaysia project. The British hoped to obtain diplomatic and possibly military assistance in their growing confrontation with Indonesia. The quadripartite talks took place while the Cabinet continued to engage with future defence policy. Two days before the meeting in Washington, the Cabinet Defence Committee had addressed the scope of British commitments in the Far East (see 166, note; also DO 169/234–236 and FO 371/169888).]

First meeting between Ambassadors and Mr. Harriman[1] this afternoon was restricted to a general discussion on Malaysia. The following were the main points of interest. A full record follows by bag.

2.   There was general approval for the creation of Malaysia though the other delegations pointed out that this was entirely a British responsibility.

3.   Concern was expressed about the situation after August 31. I explained our intentions and commitments under the extended defence agreement and spoke on the lines of your telegram under reference. Mr. Harriman stated that the United States Government might conceivably consider itself obliged to take action in the event of overt aggression against Malaysia, particularly if Malaysia had become a member of the United Nations. On the other hand they could not contemplate any military commitment to deal with covert warfare arising from Indonesian infiltration. This would be for the British. The Australians and New Zealanders took

---

[1] Averell Harriman was a staunch Democrat and veteran diplomat whom Kennedy had brought back into foreign relations as assistant secretary for Far Eastern Affairs, 1961–1965.

the line that their own participation in countering subversion would depend upon the circumstances at the time. The Australian and New Zealand Governments would have to take into account the action being taken by the British and would reach a decision on the merits of the case. As a general proposition, Australian troops were maintained in South East Asia for strategic purposes and were not normally available to deal with the preservation of civil order or the countering of subversion. Nevertheless they had considered the emergency in Malaya to have been akin to external aggression and had taken part in the fighting. The New Zealanders also pointed out that they had provided aircraft for the Brunei operation. The possibility, therefore, of Australian and New Zealand participation was by no means excluded.

4.   I suggested that the other Governments might wish to consider entering into bilateral defence arrangements with the new Malaysia. Sir Arthur Tange[2] said that this would be a matter for consideration by his Government after the Washington talks; at their Cabinet meeting last week the Australian Government had been aware of this problem.

5.   The other delegations were insistent that we should prepare for trouble in the United Nations between now and the formation of Malaysia. In particular they were anxious that we should be able to show some consultation of the popular will in Brunei and asked whether we could consider action to improve the position. They also asked us to prepare a paper setting out tactics in the United Nations and explaining the steps already taken to consult public opinion in North Borneo and Sarawak.

6.   The Australians mentioned the need to try and improve relations with the Indonesians and reassure them about Malaysia.

7.   In general the other delegations were reasonably sympathetic and anxious to hear our plans. I made it clear that the principal requirement was to show no weakening of our intention to bring Malaysia into being.

8.   Talks will be resumed tomorrow morning and it has been agreed that I should then propose our specific measures for deterring the Indonesians or for offering them some inducement to accept our plans.

---

[2] Sir Arthur Tange, secretary, Department of External Affairs, Canberra, 1954–1965.

161   FO 371/169695, no 23   12 Feb 1963
[Quadripartite talks in Washington]: inward telegram no 482 from Sir D Ormsby-Gore to Lord Home

At today's discussions I put forward the various inducements which we might offer the Indonesians to take a more understanding view of our policies. These included the non-aggression pact, a proposal for a free trade area, common defence arrangements, joint measures to deal with piracy and smuggling, frontier demilitarization in Borneo, and political consultation with the Indonesians and Filipinos. I also asked for the cooperation of other Governments in restraints such as a joint warning to the Indonesians of the military consequences of intervention in Borneo, a united front in face of the Indonesians so as to make it clear that the British would not be subject to pressure to give way as were the Dutch in West New

Guinea, and the possibility of concerted troop movements to frighten off the Indonesians if the situation deteriorated.

2. During discussion both in the morning and afternoon, the following positions were reached:—

(i) So long as Sukarno remained in control of Indonesia we must expect trouble. In the next month or so this would almost certainly take the form of infiltration into the Borneo territories.

(ii) In the event of infiltration the United States would not wish to give military assistance. Their commitment to resist subversion in Viet Nam (and formerly in Laos) was sufficient, and other Powers should take the load in Malaysia. Under pressure from Sir Howard Beale[1] and myself, Mr. Harriman admitted that a point might be reached at which Indonesian infiltration would amount to open aggression against Malaysia and that his Government might then reconsider its attitude, but he would not be moved beyond this.

(iii) The Americans, Australians and New Zealanders, while admitting that the Tunku's recent outbursts had usually been provoked by the Indonesians, felt that the Tunku must be asked to restrain his language during the present difficult period. More than this, they would want him to make some statesmanlike gesture such as resuming discussions with President Macapagal about a Philippine/Malaysia federation or reopening contact with Sukarno so as to discuss with him future Indonesian/Malaysia cooperation.

(iv) Of the measures which I had proposed (paragraph 1 above), the other delegations were strongly opposed to any six-Power or other joint warning to the Indonesians. They felt this would be received as imperialist ganging-up, and that any warnings to be given to the Indonesians should be secret and individual. They were also much opposed to the suggestion made by the Filipinos during their talks with us in London for a six-Power conference.

(v) The other suggestions I had made were matters which the British Government might wish to pursue in the first place bilaterally with the Indonesians. Should we need the cooperation of our allies later on in any of these matters, we should ask for it and they would do their best to help. They hoped that we should not delay an approach to the Indonesians. I said that we must first await Dr. Subandrio's reply to your message sent to him before Christmas. When this had been received and studied we might possibly be in a position to suggest a meeting with him or to put forward explanations or proposals in writing.

(vi) Throughout, the Americans, Australians and New Zealanders stressed the long-term need to preserve good relations with Indonesia, and to try and avoid any final rupture in defence of our immediate objectives.

3. The general impression left by our two days' discussions is that our allies are fearful of impending trouble. The Australians and New Zealanders see themselves as gradually being drawn in to any fighting necessary to keep the Indonesians out. They would be less anxious about this if they were sure that the Americans would be involved also, but the United States Government is determined to try and get the Commonwealth countries to shoulder this burden alone while they themselves concentrate on Viet Nam.

---

[1] Sir Howard Beale, Australian ambassador to the US, 1958–1964.

4. We accepted that there should be no formal agreed conclusions or recommendations, but that our Governments would take up separately the action required. I shall be reporting on the discussions by despatch and will include a list of the various tasks which fall to us. I shall also be reporting in a separate telegram on the question of informing the Tunku of our discussions.

162 FO 371/169908, no 18:   15 Feb 1963
[Quadripartite talks in Washington]: despatch from Sir D Ormsby-Gore to Lord Home. *Annex*: 'Quadripartite talks: lines of action which it was agreed to pursue'

I was instructed by the Permanent Under Secretary[1] in his letter of the 9th of January to express to the United States Administration your serious concern about the expansionist ambitions of President Sukarno and in particular the growing indications that he was actively opposed to the formation of Malaysia. Similar approaches were made to the Australian Government in Canberra. After some delay, mainly caused by the Australian need for further preparation, quadripartite talks were held here at Ambassadorial level on the 11th and 12th of February. The New Zealand Government had meanwhile expressed a wish to participate. Mr. Averell Harriman represented the United States Government.

2.   Our main aims in these talks were first of all to make sure that there was no weakening of American, Australian and New Zealand support for the formation of Malaysia and that this should be made publicly known. From there we hoped to concert measures to prevent the Indonesians from intervening in the British Borneo territories, or alternatively to make sure, that if they did intervene, we received the maximum support from the Americans, Australians and New Zealanders in trying to expel them. In addition we agreed to discuss measures to be taken in regard to the likelihood of an Indonesian attack on Portuguese Timor and in general the policy to be pursued towards Indonesia.

3.   Before the talks began, we had been able to agree at the official level an assessment of the Indonesian threat. This was reported in my Saving telegram No. 65 of the 7th of February. While there were differences of degree in our assessments, it was common ground that the power of Indonesia and the unpredictability of its ruler constituted a serious problem for the West which must be concerned both with the security of the region itself and its relation to the defence of the South East Asia Treaty Organisation, while presenting a continuing opportunity for the Soviet Union, which was actively exploiting the situation. The present focus of attention of the Indonesian leaders was the forthcoming creation of Malaysia whose emergence they saw as a challenge to their interests. We had in this to take into account the claim of the Philippines Government to North Borneo which had now grown to be of primary importance in Philippines politics. We had no difficulty in agreeing that Indonesia certainly intended eventually to take over Portuguese Timor and that this too would result in an embarrassing situation particularly for the United States and the United Kingdom.

---

[1] Sir Harold (later Baron) Caccia, permanent under-secretary of state, FO, 1962–1965.

4. At the outset of the talks it was evident that both the Americans and Australians had recently reviewed the whole situation in the South West Pacific, regarding which they took a very serious view. Mr. Harriman affirmed that American support for the conception of Malaysia remained staunch though he repeatedly said that the concept was the responsibility of the United Kingdom in conjunction with the Government of Malaya. My Australian colleague and Sir Arthur Tange, who flew from Canberra for this exercise, showed that Australian thinking had come out likewise in renewed support for the efforts of Her Majesty's Government to bring Malaysia into being. Nevertheless it was apparent that serious doubts existed about the best way to proceed. Both the Americans and Australians expressed criticism of the hasty statements by the Prime Minister of Malaya, even though they recognised that in most cases these had been provoked by aggressive pronouncements by the Indonesian leaders. The view was taken that if we were to resist political action in the United Nations designed to postpone Malaysia Day beyond the 31st of August and to disrupt the operation altogether, we and the Malayans would require to conduct a considerable preparatory operation. There was more than a little concern about the lack of evidence, for easy consumption by public opinion in the countries concerned and by United Nations Delegations, of the extent to which the population of the Borneo territories had been and would be consulted about their future. It was recognised that the revolt in Brunei had shown that the elected representatives in that territory were against Malaysia, and that this impression would stick unless we could produce clear evidence to the contrary.

5. I had the feeling that both the Americans and the Australians, and to a lesser extent the New Zealanders, thought that we were at fault in not having adequately prepared the ground in their countries for the request for support which we were now making. I am not in a position to comment as to how far this complaint is justified. From the outset the Americans have, at all levels, kept on repeating that Malaysia is primarily a British matter. They have therefore perhaps been less curious about the details than they would have been if they had realised from the start the extent to which their support would be required. However that may be, in their recent re-assessment of the situation, they have become acutely aware of the possible conflict between support for us and their accepted policy of keeping Indonesia neutral and maintaining their alliance with the Philippines, upon which among other things their use of the two bases in the Philippines depends.[2] The Australians have apparently been driven to a similar awareness of a possible conflict of aims, though in their case the situation is further complicated by the proximity of Indonesia, by the precarious political position of the Government and by their desire to undertake no commitments appreciably ahead of those undertaken by the Americans.

6. In consequence I must conclude that we were not entirely successful in obtaining assurances from our allies either on measures for preventing Indonesian intervention in the Borneo territories prior to Malaysia Day, or in meeting the somewhat different problems which will arise once Malaysia is established and we are no longer directly responsible for those territories. As recorded in my telegram No. 481, Sir Howard Beale and Sir Arthur Tange reflected the decision of the Australian cabinet last week to accept the creation of Malaysia as the best solution for the countries concerned, and apparently for the action we had so far taken, but they were

---

[2] The US occupied Clark Air Base and Subic Bay Naval Base until 1992.

set against the prospect of the new Federation having to be supported indefinitely by the Western powers not only against Communist China, but also against its non-communist neighbours, Indonesia and the Philippines. They were under instructions to make the stipulation, which they must have known to be an impossible one, that the acquiescence of Indonesia and the Philippines be obtained and also that due respect should be paid to the genuine fears of these nations. On the American side Mr. Harriman emphasised that the main American leverage on the Indonesian leaders would be reserved for the principal American aims of countering the strong influence within Indonesia of the Indonesian communist party, and to prevent a situation in which Indonesia became tied, hand and foot, to the Soviet Union.

7.   This being so we were pressed hard to explain the extent of our commitment to defend the Borneo territories, particularly after Malaysia Day. On the basis of the instructions in your telegram No. 1665, I explained that if the Indonesians tried to overthrow the Malayan regime in the Borneo territories, and Malayan forces were unable to deal with the situation, we would regard this as a matter of external defence under which Article I of our Defence Agreement with Malaya would become operative; that sufficient British forces would in fact be kept in South East Asia to deal with such commitments; and that combined planning with the Malayans, taking into account the build-up of the Malaysian forces was at present being undertaken. The suppression of the Brunei revolt had shown that forces stationed in the area could be brought in within as little as twelve hours, and it was our intention to retain training facilities in North Borneo which might allow the rotation of some forces there and provide evidence to the Indonesians of a continuing British presence.

8.   I had the uncomfortable feeling that although neither the Americans nor the Australians said so in the meetings, there were considerable misgivings about the will and capacity of Her Majesty's Government to devote the financial and material resources to maintain this commitment for any length of time, and in consequence also apprehension that they themselves might be called upon to undertake counter-guerilla activities against the Indonesians in addition to their existing commitments in Indo–China and elsewhere in South East Asia. This apprehension came out more clearly in private discussion than in the talks themselves. It is however an element which I submit must be taken into account in our future assessments of the situation.

9.   We had to review in some detail the possible inducements to the Indonesians to, as the Australians put it, 'acquiesce' in Malaysia. These included proposals for a Non-Aggression Pact, common defence arrangements, joint measures to deal with piracy and smuggling, a proposal for a free trade area, provision for political consultation and frontier demarcation. We had to conclude that none of these measures would remove the probability that infiltration could begin perhaps as early as next month, and that as long as Sukarno remained in control we must expect trouble. My colleagues felt that the most urgent necessity was to prevail upon the Tunku to restrain his language during the present difficult period, and even to encourage him to resume his discussions with the President of the Philippines, and to re-open contact with the President of Indonesia. They appreciated that we must await a reply from the Indonesian Foreign Minister to your message sent before Christmas, before pursuing any further top level direct approach to the Indonesians ourselves.

10.   We also reviewed the possibilities of deterrent action. All were agreed that any attempt to involve SEATO in the Indonesian situation would be fatal and that the end result would be far worse than the situation we were trying to meet. They were

equally opposed to any joint warning to the Indonesians and to the suggestion, made by the Filipinos during their talks in London, for a Six Power Conference excluding the Americans. The most that I could get from Mr. Harriman, who seemed to be reflecting a prepared position of the United States administration, was that while American support for Malaysia would continue to be reaffirmed in Djakarta and elsewhere and their position in the event of an overt aggression, particularly after Malaysia was properly constituted as an independent state within the United Nations, would be unequivocal, no commitment could be entered into at this stage in regard to Indonesian infiltration. Both my Australian colleague and I pressed him to define his attitude more clearly on this, Sir Howard Beale pointing out that the Australians had regarded their original commitments to Malaya as operative during the emergency caused by Communist insurgency. Under pressure Mr. Harriman did admit that a point might be reached at which Indonesian infiltration would amount to open aggression and that his Government might then reconsider its attitude, but he would not be budged beyond that point. Clearly the extension of existing defence agreements to cover the whole of Malaysia is going to be given consideration in Canberra and Wellington and the stage of commitment to cover the contingencies now in prospect has not yet been reached.

11.   Contingency planning for political action in the United Nations, both in respect of the Borneo territories and Portuguese Timor, is something which we all felt should be undertaken forthwith. This is something which will be pursued later this week by Mr. Warner and Mr. Golds, the officials who came out from the Foreign Office and the Commonwealth Relations Office to take part in these talks, while they are in New York. In any case we agreed to set up a Standing Committee representing our four countries in Washington to keep under continual review the position in regard to Timor.

12.   Among the deterrent measures which you asked me to consider was the possibility of the threat of stopping American aid. Mr. Harriman would make no firm commitment on this, because, as I have set out above, of the Administration's main goals of countering Soviet influence and keeping the Indonesian communists out of power within the country. However the Americans have pointed out to the Indonesians and will continue to do so, that their hopes of obtaining Congressional approval of aid will depend largely on Indonesian good behaviour. In this respect Mr. Harriman set out in some detail the types of aid which the United States expected to be in a position to give, if his proposals find acceptance by Congress. It is highly relevant to consideration of this situation that the State Department must present a picture of Indonesia which does not show any strong probability of the country falling completely into the communist camp or being over-run by the P.K.I. Unless they can do this, there is no chance of getting any aid bill through Congress, and if that fails they will have no leverage at all. I do not suggest that, for this reason, Mr. Harriman regards the actual situation as any less serious than we have represented it. Nevertheless, like all our Governments, the Americans are highly conscious of the need to present the position suitably to their own public opinion.

13.   Although we agreed that there should be no formal conclusions or recommendations resulting from our talks I enclose a list of headings under which we agreed to recommend future action by our Governments. These are all, in my view, clear evidence of the seriousness and the sense of urgency which have now been imparted and they provide the means for continuing close consultation.

I am sending copies of this despatch to Her Majesty's representatives in Djakarta, Kuala Lumpur, Canberra, Wellington, Manila, Bangkok and New York, and to the Commissioner General for the United Kingdom in South East Asia in Singapore.

Annex to 162

Lines of action which it was agreed to pursue:—
(1)   An approach to the Prime Minister of Malaya. Draft instructions to the United Kingdom High Commissioner in Kuala Lumpur, for clearance in Washington, Canberra and Wellington were put forward in my telegrams Nos. 494 and 495.
(2)   Further consultation on the development of relations with Indonesia. United Kingdom initiative on this will hinge upon Indonesian Foreign Minister's reply to Secretary of State's message.
(3)   Further consultation on relations with the Philippines, particularly any follow-up of the London talks, e.g. the Parliamentary Under Secretary's visit to Manila in March.
(4)   Preparation of a paper by the United Kingdom Government, with co-operation from Malaya, on the exercise of self-determination in the Borneo territories. It was emphasised that such a document was essential for background use in the United Nations and with public opinion elsewhere.
(5)   Consideration by the United Kingdom of any possible further measures to consult public opinion in the Borneo territories.
(6)   Joint consultation in New York on the situation in the United Nations and the possibilities open to Indonesia and the Philippines for political action there. Consultations should include exploration of the ways in which the Secretary General might exercise a beneficial influence.
(7)   Study by the four governments concerned of the effect upon SEATO and their respective defence commitments towards SEATO of developments in the Borneo territories before and after Malaysia Day. This includes study of the effect upon Singapore and the Borneo territories of these territories ceasing to be the territory of a member state by reason of the formation of Malaysia, and the status of each of the Commonwealth armed forces now in Malaysia after Malaysia Day.
(8)   The active study, both in the United Nations context and otherwise of the threat to Portuguese Timor and the setting up of a Standing Committee in Washington representing the four countries to keep Timor under continual review.

163   FO 371/169695, no 32   16 Feb 1963
[Malaysia and the UN]: letter from F A Warner[1] to E H Peck,[2] reporting steps being taken to neutralise opposition at the UN

Although I shall be seeing you before you receive this letter I thought you might like to have a record on paper of the various talks which we have had, both in Washington and New York about the United Nations aspect of the Malayan problem.

---

[1] This letter was written by Warner, on secondment to the UK Mission to the United Nations, and signed by another official in his absence.
[2] E H (later Sir Edward) Peck, assistant under-secretary, FO, 1960–1964.

2.   Everybody agrees that this matter will come up first in the Committee of Twenty-four. The Committee has already received petitions addressed to it by Azahari, by the North Borneo parties and by the S.U.P.P. in Sarawak. As you know, the Committee meets at the end of this month and will be well into its business by the beginning of March. Fortunately, there are other problems on its plate. For instance, the Arabs want to discuss Aden whilst the Africans will be hot on Rhodesia. Our item might therefore be pushed lower down on the agenda. Of course, the Indonesians will want it taken as soon as possible and we gather that they have been receiving some support in this from the Russians. But the experts on our own Delegation and amongst the Americans, Australians and New Zealanders say that they think it unlikely that Malaysia will go to the top of the list. It seems that there is a slight danger that the Committee of Twenty-four might split up into sub-committees so that Aden, Rhodesia, Malaysia etc. could all be taken simultaneously. The Americans, however, who are members of the Committee, do not believe that there is any great danger of this since it would be difficult to reach agreement amongst the members of this dreadful and quarrelsome body as to who would sit on which sub-committee.

3.   This means that there is a reasonable chance that the Committee of Twenty-four will not be able to tackle our problem until after the Inter-Governmental Agreement has been finalised and discussed by the Borneo legislatures. The Delegation feel that this is to our advantage and that we should resist any suggestion that the item should come forward until a later stage, though our means of doing this are obviously limited.

4.   When the item arises, the Indonesians and their supporters are likely to argue principally on the basis of self-determination. They will take the line that the inhabitants of British Borneo territories were inadequately consulted as to their own future. They might suggest that the British should be required to give these people complete self-determination. They might ask that the formation of Malaysia be delayed meanwhile. We know that their principal aim is to prevent Malaysia coming into being on August 31; if they could get a postponement the whole matter could then be brought up at the 18th Assembly in the autumn, by which time the Indonesians would hope to have brought about widespread disturbances in the Borneo territories. A Motion of the Committee of Twenty-four asking for postponement might satisfy them or they might add to it a rider asking for plebiscites in all three territories concerned. The latter would be more effective since a demand for mere postponement would amount to a request for the continuation of 'imperialist' rule. If, on the other hand, the postponement were designed to lead up to the exercise of self-determination through plebiscites many of the members of the Committee of Twenty-four would be attracted towards it.

5.   I should note that everyone here thought (with reference to Kuala Lumpur telegram No. 246 to the C.R.O.) that it was now unrealistic to hope that debate in the Committee could be confined to Brunei. I, also, do not believe for a moment that this would be possible. You will have seen the Delegation's comments in their telegram No. 208 sent off yesterday afternoon.

6.   When Malaysia is debated in the Committee of Twenty-four we can certainly not expect a rousing victory. The general opinion seems to be that the best we could hope for would be a general feeling that this is not a very good anti-colonialist case. The Afro–Asian members might be put off by the fact that the quarrel is largely

between two members of their own group—Malaya and Indonesia. They might feel that there was something to be said on the Malayan side, that there had been a barely acceptable minimum of consultation of the populations concerned, that there were much better anti-colonial issues waiting to be debated, and that therefore they really could not be bothered to take this matter beyond expressing a general hope that it would not break out into general hostilities and that principles of self-determination would be observed. In other words a rather confused and unenthusiastic response might perhaps be achieved. Our own Delegation are reasonably optimistic about this without being too sure of the matter. The Americans, Australians and New Zealanders on the other hand feel that we ought to try to do more to smooth the way. They definitely do not think that the arguments in paragraph 4 of Foreign Office telegram No. 690 are sufficient, particularly in respect of Brunei. In their heart of hearts they would obviously like us to hold plebescites if we could get away with it, and I see from Singapore telegram No. 81 that this is also the view of Lord Selkirk for North Borneo. We have explained how difficult this would be and have blown very cold upon the suggestion.

6.   The next best thing to plebiscites would be to make the maximum fuss of parliamentary procedures in North Borneo and Sarawak and to give them as much publicity as possible. It will be even more important to have adequate presence at United Nations debates of the political parties in North Borneo and Sarawak who are favourable to Malaysia. I note that the C.R.O. and Colonial Office have this very much in mind and will be looking for the right men. The real difficulty is Brunei, and we have been constantly questioned about this. Perhaps we might leave this for discussion in London with the other departments. There is perhaps a ray of hope in the report that steps are being taken to form an Alliance Party in Brunei. Goodness knows that political parties grow at a fantastic speed in those tropical climates, and we might perhaps hope for some plausibly representative Brunei spokesmen to be sent here to defend the Malaysian cause within a few weeks.

7.   To sum up the whole position about the Committee of Twenty-four, we ought to be considering the following propositions. The Committee is thoroughly hostile to us. The Americans and Australians who are much more gloomy about the outlook than we, will do the best they can for us as members, but they are in a difficult position and want us to make their task as easy as possible. This means polishing up all the representative side of our programme and producing good spokesmen. It also means that the Malayans must take as much responsibility as possible (though we must remember that they themselves are not members of the Committee). If all this is done we might get a fairly harmless result. In the last resort, we can disregard any resolution of the Committee; we have done so before on many occasions.

8.   The Committee might, of course, ask the Secretary-General to intervene. If he had already taken action there would be nothing new or additionally dangerous about this. The general feeling is that we ought to play along with the Secretary-General, particularly since Narasimhan[3] has shown himself well disposed. We might be able to keep discussions with the Secretary-General going on for a long time until we were well out of the danger area. I fancy that the Americans and Australians

---

[3] Chakravarthi V Narasimhan, under-secretary, UN Secretary-General's Office.

might become difficult if they thought that we were unwilling to co-operate with the Secretariat or were refusing them a chance to use their good offices.

9.   Now we come to the less serious problem of a Special Assembly. It is just possible, though rather unlikely, that the Committee of Twenty-four would recommend a Special Assembly. The Indonesians might also ask for it if they could create a really troublesome situation in our Borneo territories which would enable them to argue that there was a definite threat to peace in the area. I am glad to say that nobody here believes that such a move would be successful. An absolute majority is required (56 votes) and it would apparently be very difficult to get this. An alternative would be for the Indonesians to ask the Special Spring Session, which will meet probably in early May, to add Malaysia to its Agenda, but under rules 16 to 19 this is even more difficult as it requires a two-thirds majority. The Assembly might set aside these rules (a dirty trick which has been used on another previous occasion) but even then a majority of those present and voting would be needed, and this would probably not be forthcoming. We are not therefore expected to take too seriously this possibility.

10.   A third possibility is an appeal by Indonesia to the Security Council. We are told that this is unlikely to appeal to the Indonesians because the membership of that body is reasonably satisfactory from our point of view. There is little likelihood that we should need to use our veto. On the other hand, we might be able to make use of this body ourselves if the Indonesians press their military intervention too blatantly. In any case we should keep the Security Council on our side. It was agreed here that if we are obliged to make any major troop moves there would be advantage in letting the Security Council know what we are doing by sending them a letter without asking for a meeting. Apparently this is considered good United Nations manners and would put us in a favourable tactical position. We should have to make it clear that our troop movements were taken in face of a threat of interference from Indonesia, since we do not admit the right of the United Nations to show any interest in troop movements made to deal with purely internal matters.

11.   In all these United Nations maneouvres we have one favourable factor. It seems that many of the members here are rather fed up with the Indonesians and are suspicious of their motives. But while we can take advantage of this we must remember that anti-colonialism is so powerful an emotion that the factors which are favourable to our case are only secondary.

12.   Now we come to the dispositions of the various delegations. A key point is whether we can count on Indian support. It is good to know that the Indians have again decided that they are in favour of Malaysia. We hope that they will be prepared to say so in New York. No-one has much faith in this because the Indians have let us down on certain previous occasions, even when they were theoretically on our side. But we surely stand a better chance now that the Indian attitudes have been so deeply affected by events on the China border and that Krishna Menon has disappeared from the scene.[4] Even if the Indians won't actively help to rally support, we can get other delegations to go and consult them. We shall no doubt be discussing with the C.R.O. whether anything further can be done to strengthen Indian

---

[4] Krishna Menon, India's minister of defence, 1957–1962, was dismissed as a result of India's defeat in the war with China.

resolution, since it is bound to have a tremendous effect here. Tony Golds has also suggested that we ought to have another look at the position of the Pakistanis.

13.   The really important people are the Malayans. We must make this look like an inter-Asian quarrel. It is the Malayans who must do most of the effective lobbying.[5] They have made a good start at this end. They are systematically going round other Delegations here on a personal basis making the best of their case. They have shown enterprise in producing an excellent paper which they are giving to each Delegation as they canvass it. It has been suggested, however, that there are additional measures which the Malayan Government could take. First (and the Americans and Australians are most serious about this) the Tunku should be careful about his public statements; although they are made in response to Indonesian attacks they could be made to look aggressive if produced as evidence in debates here. Secondly, he might make more use of the support for Malaysia expressed at the last meeting of Commonwealth Prime Ministers. It would be a good thing if the Tunku would write to all the Commonwealth Prime Ministers reminding them of this, asking for their support, and making sure that they follow up by writing to their delegations in New York. Tony Golds has already suggested this to the Malayan Delegation here and will ask the C.R.O. to tell Sir Geoffrey [sic] Tory so that he can follow it up if necessary. The New Zealanders also suggested that the Malayans might send a Delegation round to all the Commonwealth capitals to follow up the Tunku's letters—a good idea. Thirdly, we must make sure that the Malayan Delegation here is properly staffed. There is a danger that Zakaria,[6] the admirable First Secretary who is doing most of the work at present may be withdrawn within the next week or two and we should see if we can get this stopped. There might even be a case for strengthening his team. Fourthly, we must do our best to make sure that the Malayans take the lead in debate. Although they are not members of the Committee of Twenty-four it is quite possible that both Indonesia and Malaya will be invited by the Committee to attend for this item. Sir Patrick Dean says that at the moment they are reluctant to do this and would like us to make the running. We must try to reassure them that if they take the lead we will back them up and not leave them isolated.[7]

14.   This has been a very long letter. Let me sum up the many suggestions which have been made:—

(i) We should have another look at the opportunities which have been given for consultations of the Borneo populations on their future. We should see if there is any wider form of consultation we can devise. If this is not possible we should give all the publicity we can to those constitutional processes which have already taken place or which may follow in the next few months.

---

[5] The Malayan delegation at the UN was led by Dato Ong Yoke Lin. Ong, who had been appointed minister of Labour and Social Welfare when Malaya achieved independence, was also ambassador in Washington.

[6] Zakaria bin Haji Mohd Ali was a member of the Malaysian delegation to the UN in Sept 1964 when the Security Council examined Malaysia's charges against Indonesia under article 39 on the UN Charter. He was permanent representative at the UN, 1970–1974.

[7] Patrick Dean emphasised the points set out in this paragraph in his letter to Peck of 18 Feb, ie the need for the Malayan delegation to make a concerted effort to lobby at the UN, in Commonwealth capitals and in the capitals of those countries of the Committee of Twenty-Four; also at FO 371/169695, no 32.

(ii) We should ensure the best possible representation of all three Borneo territories at any United Nations debate in which their respective affairs may be discussed. We should also think of getting Lee Kuan Yew here; he was terrifically effective last summer.

(iii) Both we and the Tunku should try to appear as aggrieved and long-suffering parties and should avoid any statements which might appear to prove the Indonesian case that Malaysia will be hostile to Indonesia.

(iv) Whenever we are forced to take strong action, such as the movement of troops, we should consider notifying the Security Council and friendly Delegations.

(v) We should encourage the Malayans to continue their present excellent work of lobbying and to extend it by personal letters from the Tunku to other Commonwealth Prime Ministers, perhaps with the despatch of a Malayan Delegation.

(vi) We should consider whether we or the Malayans should make a major effort at lobbying in the capitals of all non-Communist members of the Committee of Twenty-four and of the Security Council.

(vii) We should see that the Malayan Delegation here is not weakened by the transfer of key personnel at this delicate stage and that it is reinforced if necessary.

15.   I am writing you a separate letter about future Malaysian membership of the United Nations. I have also excluded from this letter the questions of Timor and of the Philippines claim to N. Borneo as they are not strictly relevant. I can discuss these on my return.

16.   I am sending copies of this letter to Fry in Djakarta, Pumphrey in Singapore, Ledward in Washington, Fisher in Bangkok and Campbell in New York, and I enclose ten extra copies for distribution in London as necessary.

164   PREM 11/4347   20 Feb 1963
[Co-ordinating policy]: minute from P F de Zulueta to Mr Macmillan, proposing changes in Whitehall for the conduct of Malaysian policy

I find this a disquieting telegram[1] and indeed the whole Malaysian situation looks to me to be getting out of hand. I think that the Americans are now becoming luke warm about Malaysia because they do not wish to be involved with the Indonesians. The same applies to some extent to Australia and New Zealand. I do not believe that U Thant[2] has been manifesting his interests in the area without some American prompting.

---

[1] This refers to a report in the *Manila Bulletin* that President Macapagal was thinking of an alternative to Malaysia. His idea was a confederation incorporating the Philippines, Malaya and Indonesia and possibly Thailand, with Brunei, Sarawak and North Borneo to be jointly administered by the Philippines, Malaya and Indonesia on behalf of the United Nations, until a referendum or plebiscite could ascertain the wishes of their inhabitants. The US and Britain would be asked to guarantee the security of the territories during the transitory period.
[2] Burmese diplomat and UN secretary-general, 1961–1971.

One of the troubles in Whitehall is that there are so many Departments involved—C.R.O./C.O., Foreign Office and Ministry of Defence. There is already a Greater Malaysia Committee consisting of a group of senior Ministers with yourself as Chairman but this seldom meets and is in any case a deliberative and not an executive body. Then of course there is an official body working under Lord Lansdowne in the Colonial Office to deal with the details of the actual establishment of Malaysia but this body does not deal with the wider issues, such as relations with Indonesia and the Philippines, or rarely defence questions. I am not sure that the time has not come for the establishment of an Executive Commitee under a powerful and effective Minister to see that decisions are promptly taken and executed and that the various aspects of policy are co-ordinated all the time. Much the best would be a Committee under Mr. Heath's chairmanship.[3] Its object would be to use all possible means to bring off the Malaysia project and to be sufficiently alert to recognise if this project finally seems likely not to work and to develop alternative policies in time.

If you agree with this idea perhaps I might speak to Sir Burke Trend about it and ask him to take some soundings.[4]

---

[3] Edward Heath was lord privy seal with FO responsibilities, 1960–1963.
[4] Sir Burke Trend, having been deputy Cabinet secretary in 1956–1959, took over from Sir Norman Brook in Jan 1963. Trend's view was that better co-ordination would be achieved by an executive committee of officials since it would be difficult to put any minister in charge other than the Commonwealth secretary. Macmillan approved and a body, known as the Executive Working Group, was set up under the chairmanship of N J Abercrombie (under-secretary, Cabinet Office, 1962–1963, and a scholar of French literature who later became secretary-general of the Arts Council of Great Britain). It consisted of representatives from the overseas departments, the Ministry of Defence, and the Treasury. Its remit did not include policy issues which remained the concern of the official and ministerial Greater Malaysia Committees. Rather its purpose was to take prompt, day-to-day action. It met for the first time on 5 Mar 1963 and thereafter on an almost daily basis. Missions overseas were informed that all telegrams requiring departmental action in London should carry the prefix OCULAR (CAB 21/4851).]

---

165   DO 189/222   6–8 Mar 1963

[Brunei: terms of entry into Malaysia]: minutes by Sir A Snelling and A A Golds (CRO)

[In Feb 1963 the Tunku and Sultan conferred on the terms of Brunei's entry into Malaysia and drew up Heads of Agreement that included the favourable financial conditions for Brunei which are discussed by Snelling and Golds below. Thereafter, however, the Malayans whittled down Brunei's privileges: in early Apr the Conference of Rulers reduced the Sultan's chances of becoming the Yang di-Pertuan Agong or King of Malaysia by insisting that his precedence would be set at the date of Brunei's entry into Malaysia instead of his accession to the throne. The high commissioner in Brunei, who felt that the Rulers' decision was 'shabby', reported that the Sultan was 'taking his rebuff calmly' though his advisers were 'furious' (MacKintosh to Sandys, tel no 77, 5 Apr 1963, DO 189/222). Crisis point was reached in June when the Malayans rejected a number of the Heads of Agreement, including the favourable financial terms, see 182 and 188.]

Mr. Golds

The attached paper[1] which has just arrived from the Colonial Office, about the financial and economic position of Brunei is the first statement I have seen showing

---

[1] Not printed.

just how rich Brunei is with foreign investments at the end of 1961 totalling nearly £100 m.[2]

To my way of thinking this entirely alters the way in which we ought to approach the problem of the extent to which we are to subsidise the defence of Malaysia. I have talked to Mr. Mark[3] in the Treasury and understand from him that the economist, Ross,[4] will soon be back and that this is one of the points he was asked to look into. Mr. Mark also tells me that Sir Maurice Parsons[5] of the Bank of England has recently circulated a memorandum which deals in part with Malaysian finance and no doubt a copy of it has gone to the economic side.

Please keep me in touch with any discussions with Mr. Ross upon his return. Broadly my simple-minded thought is that, if Brunei does become part of Malaysia, this £100 m. must become part of the external assets of Malaysia as a whole and vastly increases Malaysia's ability to buy defence equipment etc.[6] It ought therefore to relieve greatly the legitimate calls that can be made on us to subsidise the cost of Malaysian defence.

A.W.S.

6.3.63

Sir Arthur Snelling

Brunei

As requested, I will keep you in touch with the discussions which we expect to have, probably in the Overseas Co-ordinating Committee, with Mr. Ross later this month.[7]

2.   Meanwhile I thought I should comment that although Brunei is certainly a rich state (per capita) it is by no means certain that the new Federation of Malaysia will obtain the kind of benefits from Brunei's accession which your minute suggests. This is because:—

(a) In order to obtain Brunei's accession, Malaya has had to offer special terms.

(b) Brunei is apparently to keep all her existing investments and the income from them. Only future investments will be 'subject to consultation' with the Federation authorities.

---

[2] Golds corrected this figure to £87 m.

[3] James Mark, Treasury 1948–1964, was appointed under-secretary, Ministry of Overseas Development, in 1965.

[4] In response to a request from the Malayan government for an expert financial adviser, C R Ross visited Kuala Lumpur between 21 Feb and 6 Mar 1963. Ross had until recently been a lecturer in economics at Oxford University and was about to take up the chair in economics at the University of East Anglia. He had some experience of working for the Treasury and had acted in a consultative capacity in Asia and Africa.

[5] Sir Maurice Parsons entered the Bank of England in 1928 rising to deputy governor in 1966; in 1970 he became chairman of the Bank of London and South America.

[6] Amending the figure of £100 m to £87 m, Golds wrote in the margin against this sentence: 'This seems very doubtful. See minute below.'

[7] Ross reported on 8 Mar and his paper was considered by the Oversea Co-ordinating Committee of officials on 12 Mar. Wary that his invitation from the Malayan minister of finance to visit Kuala Lumpur might have been a ploy to soften up the British government in advance of negotiations over the financial settlement for Malaysia, Ross nonetheless concluded that, while Malaya currently enjoyed prosperity, the prospects for future export earnings were less favourable. 'The Malayans', he wrote, 'are seriously afraid that they are being asked to take on more than they can manage, and they are afraid that the United Kingdom may not appreciate the scale of their difficulties when it comes to a negotiation.' The Oversea Co-ordinating Committee agreed to recommend that a British negotiating team be sent to Kuala Lumpur as soon as possible. This resulted in the mission led by Sir Henry Lintott, 6–14 Apr. (OC(O)(63)4, 8 Mar and OC(O)(63)3rd meeting, 12 Mar, CAB 134/2277; DO 189/275; see also 170, note and 173).

(c) Brunei will also keep her oil revenues and will be exempt from most federal taxation.

(d) She will make a fixed annual payment to the Federation of $40 million (i.e. about £5 million). However, out of this the Federation will obviously have to meet the cost of the various federal services, including defence and internal security, for which K.L. will be responsible in Brunei.

(e) Brunei already lends money to the Federation and contributes her quota towards the currency backing. It is not clear that her accession on the terms envisaged for her will bring about any striking increase in this respect.

(f) Brunei's oil is, as appended figures show,[8] a wasting asset. Production is expected to decline pretty steeply after this year.[9]

(g) Brunei has an ambitious scheme of social welfare costing about £1 million a year which it would scarcely be practical politics for her to abandon, but which it will probably be difficult for her to finance in a few years' time.

A.A.G.
7.3.63

Mr. Golds

Thank you for pointing out all these arguments that may be advanced for saying that we must subsidise Malayan defence heavily even when Malaysia absorbs rich Brunei. You will since have seen a note of some facts Mr. Peck of the Foreign Office gave me about the contribution we obtained from Kuwait towards the cost of our defence of her. This at least is some sort of precedent.[10]

The burden of the arguments you advance is that we have no influence on the financial arrangements between the Tunku and the Sultan and that if the Tunku is kind to the Sultan the Tunku will, therefore, remain poor and we must pay out a lot of money to help defend Malaya. This is obviously not a position we can accept. One possibility would be that in our financial negotiations with the Tunku we should stipulate that we intend to take into account the accretion of wealth to Malaya as a result of the absorption of rich Brunei and that the size of our aid must necessarily depend upon proof of Malaysia's need which can only be assessed after adding up the assets of all component parts of the Federation.

A.W.S.
8.3.63

---

[8] These figures are not printed.

[9] Off-shore prospecting resulted in a dramatic improvement in forecasts in early June, see 190.

[10] Referring to this sentence and alluding to the despatch of British troops to protect Kuwait in June-Aug 1961, Golds wrote in the margin: 'It is a precedent for asking the Sultan to pay for the [current?] rescue operation; but I doubt if it will help us when the Federation takes over responsibility for Defence.'

166   CAB 134/2277, OC(O)(63)7   19 Mar 1963
'Defence in the Far East about 1970': memorandum by Sir A Snelling for the Official Oversea Co-ordinating Committee. *Annexes* A & B

[The Nassau Agreement of Dec 1962, whereby the Americans consented to provide Britain with Polaris in place of Skybolt, established the strategic parameters of defence policy-making. Meeting at Chequers on 9 Feb, the Cabinet Defence Committee reviewed the scope and costs of defence commitments in the context of Nassau as well as in the light of financial constraints and economic difficulties. As regards the Far East, Singapore posed a dilemma. Originally valued as an adjunct to India, it had acquired a role of its own, indeed four roles: in Malaysia, in SEATO, in the containment of Indonesia, and in the reinforcement of Hong Kong. 'Our commitment in Singapore had originally derived, like our commitment in the Middle East, from the need to safeguard our position in India. But, now that the total cost of maintaining our forces east of Suez was rising towards some £600 million a year, we should consider realistically the economic and political consequences of withdrawal.' It was accepted that economies could not be made without a corresponding reduction of political commitments in the region. In addition, ministers felt that the withdrawal of forces from the Far East 'would be regarded as a major political defeat and, quite apart from its serious effect on Australia, New Zealand and the United States, would encourage the spread of Communism'. The question of how to carry out effective retrenchment was referred to the Official Oversea Co-ordinating Committee to which Sir Arthur Snelling, deputy under-secretary at the CRO, submitted this memorandum. For the purposes of this collection the value of Snelling's paper lies in its comprehensive review of the many issues with which ministers and officials grappled throughout the planning and implementation of the Malaysia project. In the first part, Snelling identifies British objectives, commitments and deployment in the region. Secondly, he examines the division of opinion over future policy brought about by the discrepancy between the few economic advantages which Britain derived from SE Asia and its heavy expenditure there, and he summarises the political and military arguments (including the nuclear dimension) for and against withdrawal. Thirdly, he assesses the extent to which non-military methods (for example, diplomacy and aid) and a more effective redistribution of the load between allies might achieve British objectives or at least secure relief of current burdens. He concludes, in the fourth part, that few of Britain's current objectives could be achieved by entirely non-military methods. At its meeting on 22 Mar, the committee accepted that marginal adjustments would result in savings and that this would be conveyed to the Group of Permanent Secretaries chaired by the secretary to the Cabinet. Reporting the committee's discussion to Sir Harold Caccia, permanent under-secretary at the FO, E Peck emphasised that Britain could not reduce its forces while Indonesia posed a threat and that a reduction of contributions would jeopardise British influence with the US. He urged a 'softening up' of Australia and New Zealand with a view to increasing their involvement in the defence of their 'near North' and also suggested a streamlining of the military presence in Singapore. A robust response to Snelling's paper was completed by the FO on 9 Apr in a memorandum for the Oversea Co-ordinating Committee, entitled 'Future policy in the Far East'. The Cabinet Defence Committee reviewed the question of Britain's regional role in the wider context of future defence policy on 19 June, see 180 (D(63)3rd meeting, 9 Feb 1963, CAB 131/28; CAB 134/2277; OC(O)(63)18, CAB 134/2278; FO 371/173493, no 65.]

This paper is written in response to a request from the Official Oversea Co-ordinating Committee for a study of the implications of the withdrawal of United Kingdom Forces from the Far East. In accordance with the wishes of the Committee, statements are included of Western interests, of United Kingdom commitments and of the possibility of protecting these interests and of carrying out these commitments by other arrangements than at present. The Committee directed that the examination of the implications of changes in United Kingdom deployment should be based on achieving some savings from 1964 onwards with substantial savings in the years 1968–75. The views expressed in this paper are personal and not to be taken as committing the C.R.O.

I. *The present situation and planning*

Objectives, commitments and deployment

2. Until the Second World War few people questioned the need for Britain to maintain a large military presence in and around the Indian Ocean, Singapore and the South-Western Pacific. Our developing commercial interests in the area from the

sixteenth century onwards led us to assume larger political and military responsibilities. For 200 years from the mid-eighteenth to mid-twentieth centuries our interests in Eastern Asia centred upon the maintenance and defence of the Indian Empire. During the last two or three decades of this period the main function of Singapore was to prevent the incursion of Japan into the Indian Ocean.

3.   But since 1945 the relative decline in the power and resources of Britain and the growth of the Communist threat has forced us to re-define our objectives both globally and regionally. Globally, we now need to identify our interests with those of our Western allies. The Western objectives have been described in the Foreign Office as:—

(i) the maintenance of as many countries as possible outside the Communist camp, either as allies or uncommitted;

(ii) the preservation and development of Western deterrent power;

(iii) the avoidance of nuclear war;

(iv) the safeguarding of Western prosperity.

4.   Regionally, our principal objectives in the Far East were defined by the Prime Minister in 1961 as being:—

(i) to prevent Communist, particularly Chinese Communist, expansion throughout the area by support of SEATO and Malaya and by other means;

(ii) to preserve our links with Australia and New Zealand and to contribute to their forward defence.

Other secondary, but obviously important objectives of policy in the area may be summarised as being:—

(iii) to protect Hong Kong and other British Colonies in the area;

(iv) to safeguard our income from exports and investments in the Far East, as in other parts of the world.

5.   In pursuit of these objectives we have entered into the following regional commitments of a multilateral or bilateral character.

(a) In SEATO we, the United States, France, Australia and New Zealand have in effect undertaken to co-operate with Thailand, the Philippines and Pakistan in defending their territories, and also (if requested) the territories of Cambodia, Laos and Vietnam, against aggression or the threat of aggression. Detailed SEATO plans exist and to enable them to be carried out forces have been 'declared'.

(b) We have a Treaty obligation, for a period of undefined duration, to assist Malaya with her external defence. In common with Australia and New Zealand, we station forces in Malaya and Singapore for this purpose. We have undertaken to support the creation of Malaysia, and when it comes into being our Treaty obligation will be to help defend the whole of Malaysian territory. We have explicitly restated this commitment to the U.S. in February 1963.

(c) Our commitment to contribute to the forward defence of Australia and New Zealand is a moral and not a written one and is not defined with any precision. It arises under ANZAM which is a consultative body of which the U.K., Australia and New Zealand, but not Malaya, are members. The three Commonwealth countries aim to contribute to the external defence of Malaya, Hong Kong and the South

West Pacific. In practice the result of ANZAM has been the creation of the Commonwealth Strategic Reserve. This consists of the Commonwealth Brigade and the allocation to the command of C.-in-C. F.E. of Australian and New Zealand naval and air forces.

(d) We share with fifteen other nations (including the U.S., Canada, Australia and New Zealand) a continuing obligation to the U.N. (expressed in a U.N. resolution) 'to bring about by peaceful means the establishment of a unified independent and democratic Korea under a representative form of Government.' The present situation is technically only an armistice. If war starts again in Korea we shall be formally committed to pursue the aim expressed in the U.N. resolution.

6.   In addition, to complete the list of purposes for which we deploy forces in the Far East, there are certain unilateral obligations.

(e) Although not required to do so by treaty, we station troops in Malaya to combat terrorism and thus to help her maintain internal security. Some time after Singapore and the Borneo Territories become part of Malaysia, we hope that our responsibility for their internal security will be taken over by Malaysia (whilst our external responsibility remains in effect unchanged under (b) above).

(f) There will still remain our obligations to defend and maintain internal security in Hong Kong, Fiji and our other Colonies in the Pacific.

(g) We make our traditional naval contribution to the maintenance of freedom of the seas and the suppression of piracy.

7.   The forces we now deploy in the Far East to achieve these objectives and fulfil these commitments can be summarised as follows:—

Ground Forces. We have 20 major units in the area, at present divided roughly equally between Malaya (including Singapore), Hong Kong and Borneo. This represents about 15 per cent of the strength of the British Army.

Naval Forces. For Naval purposes the Far East and the Middle East must be regarded as a single theatre, as most of the Naval forces East of Suez are based on Singapore. About 50 per cent of the operational strength of the Royal Navy is East of Suez.

Air Forces. There are 16 squadrons and 5 R.A.F. bases in the Far East, of which one squadron and one base are in Hong Kong and the rest in Singapore and Malaya. This represents about 10 per cent of the operational strength of the R.A.F.

The economics of Far Eastern defence

8.   At Annex A is a collection of such estimates and statistics as are readily available bearing on the economics of Far Eastern defence, including data on the cost of our regional defence effort, our income from exports and investments, our aid to Malaya, Singapore and the Borneo Territories, the probable external assets of Malaysia etc.

9.   Until recently the only figures relating to the cost of our forces overseas were of the expenditure in foreign exchange to which their deployment gave rise. The figure for the Far East most frequently quoted on this basis was £50m. a year. It is still not possible to obtain completely accurate statistics of the total cost of our forces in the Far East, but the Treasury estimate that defence in the whole area East of Suez at present involves us in expenditure of nearly £500m. a year, inclusive of the

necessary backing in Britain. This amounts to about one-third of our total defence expenditure (excluding research and development). Very tentatively the Treasury believe it would be reasonable to attribute one quarter of this £500m. to the Middle East and three-quarters, or say £375m. a year to the Far East. The foreign exchange element in the £500m. is some £120m. a year of which about £35m. is incurred in the Middle East. Our annual defence expenditure at present in respect of the Far East can thus be cautiously estimated at about £290m. in sterling plus £85m. in foreign exchange, and amounts in all to about one-quarter of the cost of our total defence effort.

10.   The economic value of South East Asia to the West in general and to Britain in particular is nothing like one-quarter of that of all allied and uncommitted countries. The resources of the area, especially rubber, oil and tin, are considerable but not indispensable. British trade with South East Asia is only about 3 per cent of our total trade. The foreign exchange we earn from our investments in all countries in Asia between West Pakistan and Japan is smaller than the foreign exchange we disperse for defence purposes in the same area. The conclusion is inescapable that our defence expenditure in the Far East is now out of all proportion to our economic stake there.

11.   Yet present plans provide not for a reduction but for an increase in the cost of our defence effort East of Suez. The Chiefs of Staff paper on British Strategy in the Sixties* envisages an expansion in both our naval and air deployment East of Suez. It looks as though the total cost of defence East of Suez will rise in the next decade something as follows:—

	£ millions	
	1962/3	1972/3
Navy	216	290
Army	160	160
Air Force	110	155
	486	605

These rough estimates assume constant prices; if the purchasing power of the pound continues to decline at the rate of 2½ per cent per annum, the actual cost of defence East of Suez will be 1972/3 reach over £750m. The biggest increase on present plans will be in naval expenditure. Already the Royal Navy is the costliest service East of Suez. The prospect is that by the early seventies we shall be spending in respect of that area almost as much money on the Royal Navy as on the British Army and the Royal Air Force put together.

II.   The division of opinion about future policy

The questioning attitude

12.   Faced with this situation, the purpose, value and essentiality of maintaining a military presence in the region is being called in question. At Annex B is a list of some of the Whitehall reports and papers during the last three years bearing wholly or partly on this issue and a collection of quotations from a few of them.

* COS (62)1

13.   In these memoranda strong doubts have been expressed by the Prime Minister, Ministers and officials about the whole scale of our defence effort in the Far East in relation to our resources, our obligations elsewhere, the size of our interests in the region and the efforts of some of our Allies. The need has been questioned for us to make any land contribution at all towards SEATO. Similar doubts have been cast upon the necessity for us to maintain an independent nuclear capacity in the Far East. Doubts have been expressed about the need to retain our base at Singapore and the wisdom of assuming that we shall still be able to keep it in the 1970s. Nevertheless military planning continues to proceed upon the assumptions that our total expenditure on defence in the Far East can be allowed to go on rising during the next decade; that we shall continue to provide a land contribution to SEATO; that we shall retain and develop a nuclear capability in the Far East; that it is essential for us to keep a multi-service base in Singapore; and that we shall still be able to use it in the mid-1970s. In fact there is no identity of view in Whitehall at present upon the need for us to contemplate a large and continued military presence in the Far East. The political and military arguments are examined separately below.

The political argument
14.   The political case in favour of a strong British deployment in the Far East rests upon the following arguments:—

(i) The consequences of the loss of South East Asia to the Communists would be that confidence in the West in other areas would be gravely weakened, that the less staunch among the allies would slip into neutralism or satellite status, that China would be encouraged to adopt aggressive policies more generally, that India and Pakistan would be exposed to increased Chinese pressure and that the Russians might be tempted to a dangerous course elsewhere in the belief that the West was on the run. These results would follow to a greater or less degree whether the Communists achieved their aims by military action or by subversion, and whether the area collapsed quickly or by slow stages.

(ii) The political consequences would be almost as serious in the event of Indonesian territorial aggrandisement at the expense of Malaysia. The threat from Indonesia is new and is not yet fully taken into account in our long-term military planning. There is no acceptable alternative to Malaysia, and if the Indonesians broke it up the blow to the British position in the area would be particularly great.

(iii) As Britain is manifestly unable by herself to contain both China and Indonesia, it is necessary to seek strength in alliances—e.g. SEATO and the Malayan Defence Treaty. But if we hope to benefit from these alliances, we must contribute to them on a scale sufficient to convince our allies that we are sincere and pulling our weight.

(iv) Only by our contributions to SEATO and to the defence of Malaysia and by maintaining our base in Singapore are we able to exert influence on U.S. policy in the area. This is important to us in the nuclear field. And for domestic political reasons the U.S. Government, in order to maintain their own military effort in the region, must be able to show that we are sharing the load and honouring our commitments.

(v) Military withdrawal from the Far East would mean the abandonment of Malaya and of our contribution to the forward defence of Australia and New Zealand.

Politically and eventually economically Australia and New Zealand would be forced to leave the British and enter the American orbit. We have a major moral obligation to Australia and New Zealand if only on account of the way they rallied to our defence in two World Wars.

15. On the other hand there are political arguments against the retention of a large British military presence in the Far East.

(i) Without questioning the consequences of the loss of all or large parts of South East Asia to the Communists of Indonesia, it is possible to doubt whether the scale of the military effort we can muster is big enough to exert a decisive political influence. Certainly a retreat by the United States or a decline in her military effort in the area would bring about dire political results. But would these follow if we quit and the U.S. remained? Would the United States, in her own interest, leave a power vacuum? Would Laos, Cambodia, South Vietnam, Thailand, Malaya or the Philippines really go neutralist or worse if only we and not the Americans departed?

(ii) For us to be able to exert influence on U.S. policy in the Far East may be useful without being vital. It is difficult to see what major British interest would suffer from loss of that influence, which could never amount to a veto. In the nuclear field, are the U.S. Government so irresponsible that if we cannot restrain them they will be inclined to embark on rash and possibly escalatory adventures? Is the influence we do exert on U.S. policy commensurate with the cost of our defence effort in the Far East?

(iii) Our position and influence will not decline so much if we quit Singapore voluntarily as if we wait till we are forced out. The political arguments in favour of a voluntary and total withdrawal are that military bases present a challenge to strident nationalism (e.g. among the young Chinese in Singapore); that they attract the enmity of neighbours (?Indonesia); that military alliances expose regional governments to criticism as neo-colonialist stooges (which is why the Tunku refuses to allow Malaya to join SEATO or to take part in ANZAM planning); and that we get involved in the support of governments which have no popular support (South Vietnam, Laos, Thailand and Brunei). On the other hand there is no more democratic ruler in South East Asia than the Tunku. The inference is drawn that the interests of the West would be better served if we abandoned our policy of military bases and alliances and instead supported local nationalist, democratic movements.

(iv) The voluntary abandonment of Singapore would admittedly do drastic harm to our relations with Australia and New Zealand. But these relations are not healthy if they are dependent upon our contributing over 7 per cent of our Gross National Product to defence whilst they contribute 3.1 per cent and 1.7 per cent respectively of theirs. They can and should carry a bigger share of the load of Far Eastern defence.

(v) Our politico-military thinking over Singapore in relation to Malaysia and SEATO involves some circular reasoning and is creating unforeseen difficulties for us. The circular reasoning arises in respect of every overseas base; we cannot retain a base in an independent country without undertaking to defend that country; one of the purposes of the base then becomes the defence of the country in which it is located in order to permit the base to be retained. Thus we accepted our obligations in the defence treaty with Malaya partly to enable us to keep Singapore, and we needed Singapore partly to be able to defend Malaya. Then we decided that, given the attitude of the Tunku towards Singapore, the best prospect of keeping our base was to support the creation of Malaysia. But unforeseen Indonesian hostility to the Malaysia project is at present adding to the military threat in the area and so obliging us to contemplate adding to our military deployment based on Singapore. So a costly game of politico-military leap-frog proceeds. Meanwhile, of course, our military presence in Singapore enables us also to discharge our obligations under SEATO. But the only safe assumption to make is that long before 1970 we shall be able to go on using Singapore for SEATO purposes only to the extent that the Government of Malaysia agrees with those purposes and is willing to let us use the base for them. And Malaya is not a member of SEATO. For so long as the Tunku stays in power we shall probably be able to retain our Singapore base, but when he goes our tenure of it may become insecure.

The military argument

16.   The military arguments for maintaining a large military presence in the Far East are familiar and can therefore be listed briefly.

(i) Our current commitments in the area cannot be fulfilled with anything less than the forces we now plan to deploy there. Indeed these forces are probably a good deal too small for the job they are meant to be doing, and it is only by a certain amount of sleight-of-hand (e.g. the 'double-pledging' of the same British battalion to meet our obligations under SEATO and the Malayan Defence Treaty) that we can get by.

(ii) Since the last military examination of our long-term plans for the Far East,* the Indonesia threat has grown. It now faces us with the possibility of a commitment either to engage in a long struggle in the Borneo jungles or deal with Indonesia by some other military method e.g. by bombing Jakarta.

(iii) The retention of a base at Singapore is absolutely vital to the discharge of the obligations listed in paragraph 5 and 6 above. The only partially satisfactory alternative would be the establishment, virtually from scratch, of a multi-service base or bases in Australia, which would be vastly more costly than the retention of Singapore.

(iv) While the U.S. have sufficient military power, in depth, to deal adequately with the South-East Asian portion of the Asian continent, they cannot easily get round the corner to deal with Burma or the Indian sub-continent. There is in fact a gap in the U.S. military presence from the Philippines to the Mediterranean and the South Atlantic. Only we can fill it at present. Even if, under pressure, we found that we needed to call upon American help, the U.S. forces would be handicapped if they could not use British bases and staging facilities in Singapore and points to the West. We must therefore retain those facilities unless we are prepared to see the whole of the Indian Ocean area become a power vacuum.

17.   The arguments which can be advanced against the need for the present planned deployment in the Far East can only take the form of questioning some of

---

* COS (62)1

the military assumptions. This can most conveniently be done by treating the general military arguments first and the nuclear issues second.

(i) The land and air forces we could contribute in a war with the Communists on the mainland of South-East Asia probably add little to the strength the U.S. could muster. It is virtually impossible to envisage circumstances in which the Chinese, when contemplating aggression, would be restrained by the British rather than the American armed strength they would have to face. Our total contribution looks marginal. Our Army contribution is not very significant on military as distinct from political grounds. There is scope for Anglo–American discussion at political and service (e.g. between Commanders-in-Chief) levels on the overlap of military deployment in the Far East.

(ii) The Minister of Defence appears to doubt whether we could ever use all the forces we now have in the Far East, including our biggest Naval concentration. The Chiefs of Staff* have recognised that overlapping between the three Services may exist and have envisaged the need for closer definition of their respective roles and responsibilities. The Far East seems a particularly suitable theatre for an examination of this kind.

(iii) A politico-military re-assessment might reveal that the need for stationing forces in the Far East on the scale at present planned could be reduced if fresh assumptions were made. E.g. upon the acceptability of a longer time for reinforcement (which might permit greater dependence upon the Strategic Reserve) and upon the conditions necessary before greater reliance could be placed upon the West-about reinforcement route to avoid the Middle East air barrier (as for instance by arrangements to use long-range U.S. transport aircraft when needed).

(iv) The purpose of two battalions in Hong Kong and at least part of the land forces which are in the Singapore/Borneo area is said to be to enable the 'identification of aggression' to take place. This ought not to be a job solely for our troops even in a British Colony. For ten years a U.N. Observer Corps has been watching both sides of the cease-fire line in Kashmir. Can we not press urgently for this precedent to be followed elsewhere in Asia? The knowledge that a U.N. presence would enable any aggression to be instantly identified might do more to deter Indonesia than all the British troops in Borneo.

(v) It seems paradoxical that such a large and increasing proportion of the cost of Far Eastern defence should be on naval account when the threat in the Pacific from China, unlike the former threat from Japan, is mainly by land and air, and when whatever naval force China could despatch would meet the U.S. Fleet long before it reached Singapore.

(vi) Rejection of the suggestion that we should move our base in Singapore to Australia rests on the assumption that any base or bases there would have to be multi-service and would need to be built wholly or mainly at our expense. Although the Chiefs of Staff have set out in broad terms our possible future requirements for base facilities in Australia† on a multi-service basis, these have not been costed. But need such facilities be multi-service? Can we ever hope to

---

* C.O.S. (62)1, paragraph 117   † COS (61)197.

provide a significant land force contribution to the close defence of Australia without re-imposing conscription? Would not any attack on the mainland of Australia automatically involve global nuclear war? Could not our contribution to the defence of Australia, and even of areas further north, be provided by nuclear means alone? Luckily the Indonesian threat is now provoking Australia into the realisation that she must spend a good deal more money on defence. We should try to ensure that some of it is devoted to the provision of facilities which we could use—in case we lose Singapore—to enable us to help defend Australia. The time is becoming ripe for us to raise these questions with her. We have a card of entry in the desultory exchanges of messages which have been taking place between the Prime Minister and Sir R. Menzies and Mr. Holyoake since 1961 in which we have been gradually getting them to face up to the consequence if we lost Singapore. This correspondence at the moment leaves the ball in our court.

The nuclear issue

18.   The Americans have a nuclear capability in the Far East. So have we. Is ours necessary? The answer must be yes if, but only if, either the American capability is inadequate or if we deem it essential to maintain our nuclear independence in that area.

19.   As to the adequacy of the U.S. capability, the only reasonable assumption to make is that, in the Far East as elsewhere, it is big enough for all conceivable purposes.

20.   The need for British nuclear independence has not been examined with the Americans in a specifically Far Eastern context. The Prime Minister insisted at Nassau that we must retain our nuclear independence and that when the V bombers are replaced by British Polaris missiles we must be free to withdraw the latter from the multi-national force and use them independently when 'supreme national interests' are at stake. But virtually all the discussion at Nassau centred around NATO. Do we conceive it possible that our supreme national interests should be at stake in the Far East to such an extent as to necessitate the unilateral usage of nuclear weapons in that area?

21.   If it is argued that we might wish to preserve an independent nuclear capacity in the Far East for the close defence of Australia or New Zealand if for no other purpose, the following answers might be given:—

(a) it is virtually inconceivable that we should have to act independently of the United States in that situation:

(b) we can be confident that Australia will before long be willing to accept nuclear weapons and to permit us to station nuclear forces of our own in her territory:

(c) it may therefore be unnecessary for us to maintain an independent nuclear capacity 'at large' in the Far East.

22.   Discussions with the United States would obviously be essential before we abandoned our regional nuclear capability. However unwelcome the argument would be to the Americans, it would be possible, in the light of the opposition President Kennedy displayed at Nassau to British nuclear independence, for us to represent the regional abandonment of that independence as a concession to their viewpoint! The opportunity should also be taken to ascertain what U.S. policy is on some fundamental nuclear questions in the region. Do the Americans think that

nuclear weapons in fact deter the Chinese? Does the U.S. intend to use such weapons in the event of Chinese aggression, or is she restrained by the thought of possible Russian support of China? Is the U.S. prepared to contemplate using these weapons against a Far Eastern enemy other than China, e.g. Indonesia?

23.   If for any reason the view is taken that we must maintain an independent nuclear capacity at large in the Far East, the following questions may still be asked about the appropriate methods of ensuring that capacity.

(i) The decision that we need to undertake deployment both by sea and by air was directed primarily to methods of moving our forces, rather than to methods of delivering nuclear weapons.* Is it in fact necessary that in the Far East we should provide for the delivery of nuclear weapons both by V bombers and carrier-borne aircraft?

(ii) The discussion at Nassau was based on the assumption that the V bomber would not provide a credible deterrent after 1970 against Russia. But must we assume that in the first half of the 1970s the V bomber will no longer provide a credible deterrent against China? Could we retain V bombers in the Far East after we had ceased to employ them in the NATO area?

(iii) What is the future of the sea-borne nuclear weapon in the Far East? Do we envisage the deployment of Polaris submarines East of Suez or will all four or five of them be needed nearer home? If we are to have a Polaris capability in the Far East, will there be any need for a carrier-borne nuclear capability in that area in the 1970s?

The summing-up

24.   If we accept the argument that the forces to be deployed under present plans in the Far East are the absolute minimum necessary to enable us to discharge our existing commitments, we must view our military presence there on an 'all-or-nothing' basis; and economic circumstances may then force us to contemplate total withdrawal. We ought if we conceivably can [?try] to avoid total withdrawal. At present it would not be regarded as voluntary but as a retreat in the face of Indonesian threats and a major defeat for the West in general and ourselves in particular. Voluntary withdrawal would involve the abandonment of our moral obligations to Australia, New Zealand and Malaya and would be disastrous to our relations with them. It would also gravely impair our relations with the United States, and impair our position in the Indian sub-continent.

25.   But, as suggested at several points above, there does seem to be a prima facie case for thinking that our deployment could be reduced without abandoning Singapore and without serious damage to our objectives or relations with our allies. Moreover in present circumstances there is a case for examining the feasibility of leaving the U.S. to confront China whilst we concentrate upon confronting Indonesia. We should of course also allow the U.S. to use our facilities, e.g. at Singapore, for purposes connected with the containment of China. And our continued presence in Singapore would permit us to discharge our obligations towards Malaysia, Australia and New Zealand. This would not be an easy matter to negotiate with the Americans, but if economic pressure compels us to envisage large

* COS (62)1: Appendix A

economies in our defence expenditure in the Far East, it may be the least undesirable way of proceeding. Alternatively if we are able to persuade the Americans that we are over-committed in Europe, and so can achieve major defence economies there, we might offer to maintain the contribution to Far Eastern defence which we should otherwise be obliged to curtail.

III. *Non-military methods of achieving our objectives*

26.   The question has been raised whether by diplomatic, economic or other non-military methods we could achieve our major objectives in South East Asia. The quick answer can only be that aggression cannot be deterred or combatted by non-military means. But subversion can. The first question must therefore be whether the Communists, the Indonesians and any other potential enemies in the Far East are likely to have recourse mainly to military or to subversive means in order to gain their ends.

27.   The Chinese mood is uncertain and potentially dangerous. On the one hand her recent dealings with countries on her southern border, other than India, have been generally correct and in some cases conciliatory. On the other hand her dealings with India since last October have shown a new and alarming willingness to achieve political and limited territorial objectives by the use of open and large scale military operations. The latter have hitherto been so limited as to stop far short of anything that would involve a physical confrontation with the Western powers. Avoidance of such a confrontation is likely to continue to be one of the dominant considerations in Chinese external policy wherever both Chinese and Western forces can be brought to bear directly. Though in consequence the threat of direct Chinese military aggression may be extremely limited in territorial terms, nevertheless there is ample evidence that Chinese intentions in terms of subversion and revolution are very great. Prosecution of these intentiors with greater vigour would be consistent with the line China has taken in her quarrel with Moscow, and also with the renewed atmosphere of confidence and arrogance in Peking since the Chinese economy took a turn for the better last year. The threat of Chinese-supported revolution and subversion in South East Asia is greatly exacerbated by the existence of the overseas Chinese communities in the area, and also by the fundamental insecurity of many of the governments. The danger from subversion throughout the area is likely to increase as the power and confidence of Communist China grow.

28.   Similarly Indonesia, whose appetite has been whetted by her success in Dutch New Guinea, is likely to become more aggressive. She too, by her appeals on racial lines to her fellow Malays in other countries may be able to build up an effective fifth column.

29.   What could we achieve by giving or receiving more aid? Neither China nor Indonesia can be bought off by the receipt of Danegeld.[1] The scope for useful aid—whether civil or military—is therefore confined to the allied and uncommitted countries. It is probably desirable for us on political grounds to give a little aid to every undeveloped non-enemy tropical country; otherwise we tend to turn forgotten children into juvenile delinquents. There are at present a multiplicity of aid schemes for the countries in South East Asia, including United Nations schemes, Colombo

---

[1] A tribute paid by the Saxon kings to the Vikings in eleventh-century England; appeasement by bribery.

Plan, American, German and Italian aid schemes, etc. To the countries in and near the front line especially Laos, South Vietnam, Cambodia and Thailand, the Americans have been the biggest benefactors. But the results of American aid have not been impressive and their value had led to questioning in Washington. There seems no reason why we should aim to give more than token aid to these countries. To Malaya, Singapore and the Borneo Territories we have given a certain amount of economic aid but in the near future our principal contribution seems likely to be the provision of help to enable them to build up their own armed forces. Negotiations about our military aid to Malaysia have yet to take place but the cost to us may be up to £30m. in the next few years. It seems right that our aid to Malaysia should principally take this form. One suggestion worth examining might be to accelerate the build-up of Malayan armed forces by transferring to them some of the Gurkhas we shall no longer need; the agreement of the Governments of Nepal and India would be required before such arrangements could be made.

30.   Our burdens in the area would of course be lightened if there could be some more 'inward aid' from other countries in the area. The prospects have already been examined (paragraph 17(vi)) of securing increased defence contributions to the area from Australia. As regards Malaysia the fact stands out that she will be born with a sterling silver spoon in her mouth to the value of over £600m. This is the total of the external assets of the sum of the parts of Malaysia, but not all of it will be at the disposal of the Government in Kuala Lumpur. Nevertheless it is difficult to believe that Malaysia cannot afford to make a larger contribution to its own defence.

31.   Political and diplomatic action to ease our defence burdens in the Far East must be directed primarily towards increasing the share of them which is borne by our Western allies. Suggestions have been made for 'generalising' these burdens, e.g. by a concerted policy within NATO in regard to a mutual defence pact between the countries of South East Asia, under-written by the peace-keeping machinery of the United Nations. If successful such efforts would mean that our European allies would foot part of the bill for containing Communism in the Far East; the French contribution to SEATO has dropped away to virtually nothing and the West Germans have never contributed significantly in that area. However there are arguments against using the NATO forum for this purpose. To ex-Colonial territories NATO often seems to be an organisation of former Colonial powers, and it might do more harm than good to the cause of the West to put a NATO label upon any Western defence activities in the Far East. Close consultation with our representatives in the area would therefore seem desirable before launching any such initiative. Such consultation might take place at the next Eden Hall Conference.

32.   There is scope for securing some relief to our burdens through the greater use of United Nations machinery. One particular suggestion to this end is made in paragraph 17(iv) above.

IV. *Conclusions*

33.

(a) Our present defence responsibilities in the Far East are largely residual from our imperial past.

(b) Our political objectives are now to help contain China and to contribute to the forward defence of Malaysia [sic], Australia and New Zealand.

(c) For this purpose we have entered into a series of specific commitments of which the chief are to contribute to the defence of our SEATO allies and Malaya. Australia and New Zealand are our partners and with them we have formed the Commonwealth Strategic Reserve. We also still retain certain Colonial and naval responsibilities.

(d) We deploy about 15 per cent of the British Army and 10 per cent of the R.A.F. in the Far East, and roughly 50 per cent of the Royal Navy in the Middle and Far East together.

(e) The cost of this deployment in the Far East is about one quarter of our total defence bill and is out of proportion to our economic stake in the area. But on current plans the real cost will rise during the next decade, by the end of which naval expenditure will be nearly half of total defence expenditure East of Suez.

(f) This state of affairs is attracting criticism. Strong arguments are advanced for and against the need for such a British military presence on this scale.

(g) The general case for retaining it is:—

> *politically*, that abandonment of any of our present commitments would have disastrous effects upon the position of the West both locally and further afield, upon our own prestige and interests, and upon our relations with our American and Australasian allies;
>
> *militarily*, that our deployment is the minimum necessary to fulfil our commitments, that it is likely to increase because of the Indonesia threat, that a Singapore base is vital, and that if we quit there will be a power vacuum, which the U.S. will be unable to fill, from the Mediterranean to the Philippines.

(h) The general arguments on the other side are that politically and militarily the value of our presence in the Far East is marginal compared with that of the U.S.; that politically the influence we exert with the U.S. and the loss of prestige if we quit can be over-estimated; that there are political disadvantages in having bases and military alliances; and that our relations with Australia and New Zealand must have regard to the fact that they are not pulling their weight over defence.

(i) An independent British nuclear capacity in the Far East looks unnecessary, but if it must be preserved we may nevertheless be able to economise on the means of delivery.

(j) Total British military withdrawal from the Far East would have disastrous political and military effects, particularly in the face of Indonesian pressure.

(k) But we might be able to achieve a reduction in our regional military commitment as a result of further examination of the possibilities of:—

> reducing the overlap between our and U.S. forces (paragraph 17(i));
>
> reducing the overlap between our own three Services (paragraph 17(ii));
>
> re-examining the military assumptions about timing and routeing of reinforcements (paragraph 17(iii));
>
> working for the setting up of U.N. Observer Corps to identify aggression (paragraph 17(iv));
>
> re-examining the need for the naval deployment envisaged (paragraph 17(v));
>
> abandoning an independent British nuclear capacity in the Far East (paragraphs 18–22);
>
> or alternatively re-examining the need for retaining both land-based and sea-borne methods of delivering nuclear weapons (paragraph 23).

(l) The feasibility should be examined of dividing responsibilities in the Far East between the Americans and ourselves on the basis that they will contain China whilst we contain Indonesia.

(m) Alternatively, we might persuade the Americans that we shall be able to carry our present load in the Far East only if our load in Europe is drastically reduced.

(n) Few of our present objectives in the Far East could be achieved by entirely non-military methods, e.g. aid or diplomacy.

Annex A to 166: Some financial and economic statistics

Cost of British defence effort

The following are rough estimates produced in the Treasury of the cost of the British defence effort east of Suez.

£ millions

	1962/3[1]	Rough Estimate for 1972/3[2]
Navy	216	290
Army	160	160
Air Force	110	155
	486[3]	605[4]

Notes: (1) Includes elements for U.K. backing and apportionment of Strategic Reserve. Excludes any element for research and development.
(2) Assumes constant prices.
(3) Of which roughly £120m. may be for the Middle East.
(4) Of which roughly £150m. may be for the Middle East.

British income

Exports from the U.K. in 1962

To:—	£ millions
Federation of Malaya	40.7
Singapore	38.2
North Borneo	2.8
Sarawak	2.3
Brunei	.4
	84.4

Interest, Profits and Dividends according to U.K. Residents in 1961

From:—	£ millions
Malaysia	22
Hong Kong	4
Indonesia	1
India	38
Pakistan	5
Ceylon	4
Japan	2
Other countries in the Far East	—
	76

Notes: (1) Excludes income from oil.
      (2) Includes income from direct as well as portfolio investment.
      (3) U.S. income from the same area probably does not exceed £40 million; Australian income may
          be up to £3 million; New Zealand income negligible.
      (4) Source: Central Statistical Office.

Aid

Air to Malaysian territories
(expressed as an annual figure)

		£ millions
Federation of Malaya		
1957 Great in Aid for Defence Expenditure (61–62)		2.9
'Fringe benefits' (for British seconded officers)		.081
Singapore		
C.D. & W. (ave.)	.25	
Defence (ave.)	.51	.76
North Borneo		
C.D. & W. (ave.) over		
5 year plan		.6
Sarawak		
C.D. & W. (ave.) over		
5 year plan		.75
		5.091

External Assets

External Reserves of Malaysian Territories

	£ millions
Federation of Malaya (includes private reserves and share of currency fund).	328
Singapore (excludes private reserves other than banks).	140
Sarawak and North Borneo	58
Brunei	90
	616

Annex B to 166: Source material

1.   The following is a list, by no means exhaustive, of some of the major reports and memoranda of the last three years concerned wholly or partly with politico-military policy in the Far East.

    F.P. (60) 1 of 24th February, 1960. Future Policy Study 1960–70. This is a report of a committee of Permanent Secretaries and Chiefs of Staff presided over by Sir N. Brook.

    D.S.E. (60) 30(Final) of 3rd November, 1960. Future Developments in South East Asia. A report by a committee of officials under the chairmanship of Sir R. Scott.[2]

---

[2] cf 28 and 29.

C.O.S. (61) 197 of 22nd June, 1961. Base Facilities in Australia. A short note by the Chiefs of Staff.

Our Foreign and Defence Policy in the Future. Memorandum by the Prime Minister dated 2nd October, 1961.[3]

Directives by the Prime Minister of 23rd October, 1961, on future defence policy and the future cost of defence.

C.O.S. (61)1 of 9th January, 1962. British Strategy in the Sixties. A full study by the Chiefs of Staff.

C.O.S. (62) 415 of 26th October, 1962. Comparative Assessment of Westabout and Eastabout routes.

Defence in the Longer Term. Memorandum by the Minister of Defence dated 28th November, 1962.

C.O.S. (62) 456 of 28th November, 1962. Directive to the C. in C. Far East.

C.O.S. 14/63 of 10th January, 1963. Strategy after 1970—Australia and New Zealand.

Strategy East of Suez. Memorandum by Mr. Cary dated 23rd February, 1963.

Selected quotations

The scale and cost of our defence effort East of Suez

2.   In February 1960 *Sir Norman Brook* wrote:[a] 'there is danger that in future the effort involved in maintaining our position in Singapore may be out of proportion to our interests in doing so, particularly if political developments in Singapore or Malaya were to lead to serious restrictions on the full use of the base facilities. Before the end of the decade we may have to abandon it as a base.' Elsewhere in the same report[b] it is stated that 'as regards our own resources there is a danger that by spreading them too thickly and too widely, we may fail to preserve our most important interests.' The report recommended that[c] 'we should not plan on the assumption that we may have to engage by ourselves in any military action (except conceivably in Hong Kong) but should maintain no greater an effort than is necessary to encourage our Allies, maintain the cohesion of the Commonwealth and make the United States feel both that we are taking a fair share and that we have a right to be consulted on policy in the area.'

3.   In November 1960 *Sir Robert Scott* wrote[d] that the main role of British defence forces and facilities at present in the area was (a) internal security and external defence of British dependent territories; (b) a contribution to the strategic deterrent against China; (c) a contribution to operations on land (for example a SEATO operation). He continued: 'the United Kingdom cannot continue for another decade to play all three roles on present scales and in present forms. . . . The U.K. must continue to make a contribution to the nuclear deterrent against China. In addition the U.K. cannot avoid her special obligations to her dependent territories,

[a] F.P. (60)1, part III, paragraph 85.   [b] F.P. (60)1, part I, paragraph 45(d).
[c] F.P. (60)1, part III, paragraph 72.   [d] D.S.E. (60)30, paragraph 17 et seq.

[3] This would appear to be a reference to the prime minister's memorandum 'Our foreign and defence policy for the future', 29 Sept 1961, printed in this collection as document 65.

notably Hong Kong. . . . It is only in the third defence role (a contribution to land operations) that we could afford to risk some reduction'. Later in the same report he wrote: 'If we are to continue to meet these commitments [i.e. in Eastern Asia] as at present, military expenditure must increase. Such an increase is hard to justify on direct political or economic grounds or in relation to inecapable defence commitments elsewhere.'

4.   In 1961 *the Prime Minister* wrote:[e] 'the developing situation (it seems to me) will drive our Allies to realise that our role in South East Asia must be re-assessed. We should take advantage of that and try to adjust our agreed role in the way that suits us best, politically as well as financially.'

5.   Questions have also been asked about the size of our defence effort in the Far East in relation to that of our Allies. Thus the *Brook Report* contained the following passage:[f] 'Australia and New Zealand benefit more directly than we do from our defence expenditure in the area and they should contribute more. Australia's interests in Asia are growing but she has not yet assumed commensurate responsibilities. . . . But if we are to be realistic we must recognise that it would be difficult to persuade the Australians or even the Americans to do more. . . . It seems unlikely that we shall be able to make substantial economies in our own expenditure without abandoning our major interests or undertaking a radical revision of the means by which we protect them.'

The nature of our Far Eastern defence effort

6.   The view of *Sir R. Scott*[g] was that 'a reduction in the British military presence in Eastern Asia is inevitable. No modification can be made without some adverse effects, and it is only in our contribution to land operations in the area that we can afford to risk a cut.'

7.   In his memorandum of 2nd October, 1961 the *Prime Minister* asked the following questions: 'Need we provide a *land* contribution at all to SEATO operations? If so, need it be at a forward base, or could it not be in reserve (in Australia)? In either case, can we dispense with permanent large-scale forward bases? Do we need *any* nuclear capability for our forces in this area, either to impress the Australians or to influence (and perhaps restrain) the United States? Might the deployment of some such capability from Australian bases make it easier for our allies to accept a further reduction in our land forces? These questions are perhaps directed more towards means than ends. Politically, our main objective (except for the very short term) should be to play a role in the alliances in the area, which would be acceptable to our partners, particularly the Australians and the United States, and considerably less onerous in military terms than our present commitments.'

8.   Subsequently the *Minister of Defence*[h] wrote: 'these forces (i.e in Singapore and Malaya) can operate at the request of Malaya in Malaya and perhaps in Greater Malaysia and make a contribution to operations of a wider character in the area, e.g. the sending of a Hunter squadron to Thailand. They cannot do much more'. The

[e] Memorandum of 2nd October, 1961.   [f] F.P. (60)1, part III, paragraph 72.
[g] D.S.E. (60)30, paragraph 108.   [h] Memorandum of 28th November, 1962, paragraph 9(iv).

Minister of Defence in the same paper also questioned the assumption that we should plan to take independent action in the Far East, and suggested that 'we should assume as at present that in the Far East we should not take part in any major operation without partners or allies'.

The Singapore base

9.   In many papers there has been a questioning attitude towards the wisdom of assuming that we shall be able to stay in Singapore. Thus in the *Brook Report* there is a passage reading:ⁱ 'it is possible that the United Kingdom will be able to retain bases there until 1970 but it would be unwise to base policy for the end of the period (i.e. the 1960s) upon this assumption.' Nevertheless military planning has continued to proceed upon the assumption that we shall continue to be able to use Singapore in the foreseeable future. Thus the *Chiefs of Staff* in their paper on British strategy in the 1960s, arguedʲ that, although they had been told to assume that Singapore would be available only until 1970, the lack of provision for alternative bases during the 1960s would mean that, if we had to abandon Singapore before the middle 1970s, the results would be 'particularly crippling'. The latest paper on strategy after 1970ᵏ contains among its conclusion the statements that: 'the continued basing of United Kingdom forces in Malaysia would be the best military contribution we could make to the maintenance after 1970 of the Western position in the Far East' and that 'unless there is a change in British policy in the Far East area we can foresee no likelihood of any reduction in planned force levels of the United Kingdom contribution to the defence of Australasia after 1970'.

ⁱ F.P. (60)1, part I, paragraph 34.   ʲ COS(62)1, paragraph 121.
ᵏ COS 14/63, paragraph 26.

167   CAB 131/28, D(63)10   25 Mar 1963

'Use of British forces in active internal security roles in Singapore after merger in the Federation of Malaysia': memorandum by Mr Thorneycroft for the Cabinet Defence Committee

[In briefing Macmillan on this subject preparatory to its discussion at the Defence Committee, Trend produced a balanced argument. On the one hand, he cited the following reasons for countenancing a British role in Singapore's internal security: Britain would respond only to the request of an independent government; it was vital that Malaysia should succeed; the internal security of Singapore was crucial to the British base and commerce; British assistance would not require additions to forces already present in Singapore. On the other hand, he pointed out that British involvement risked accusations of 'neo-colonialism', complex political and legal difficulties and unknown financial implications. The Defence Committee considered Thorneycroft's paper on 1 Apr and agreed that: a) in principle British troops could be used for the internal security of Singapore under Malaysia; b) the minister of defence and secretary of state for war would, in consultation with the Malayan government, prepare a scheme setting out the tasks and duties of British forces; c) steps should be taken to indemnify British personnel against possible consequences of their actions when employed on internal security duties on behalf of sovereign Malaysia (Trend to Macmillan, 29 Mar 1963, PREM 11/4347; COS 22(63), 29 Mar 1963, DEFE 4/153; D 5(63)3, 1 Apr 1963, CAB 131/28; CO 968/761).]

Introduction
This paper deals only with internal security requirements in Singapore after merger. The possible requirement for British assistance in the Borneo territories after their merger with Malaysia would arise more from external threats, and this matter has yet to be examined with the Malayan authorities.

Malayan plans
2.   The Federation of Malaysia will assume responsibility for its own internal security on its formation (not later than 31st August, 1963). A local joint examination has been made of certain of the defence arrangements that will then be necessary, including the build-up of Malaysian forces required for internal security. This has shown that Malaysian forces will not be entirely adequate to meet internal security situations between the formation of Malaysia and January, 1965, at the earliest. The Federation of Malaya have pointed out that the latter date depends on a favourable decision by us on financial aid for the expansion of their forces.

3.   The latest assessment of the likely requirement for British military assistance in this interim period is as follows:—

Up to about December, 1963
(a) One company for use from the outset of trouble.
(b) Helicopter and light aircraft for reconnaissance and voice control from the outset, and possibly later in a more active role.
(c) Administrative support, particularly transport and medical, and recovery facilities.
(d) One major unit for use only in the last resort, if trouble occurs simultaneously in Malaya and Singapore.

Up to January, 1965 at earliest
(a) One major unit for use only in the last resort, if trouble occurs simultaneously in Malaya and Singapore.

4.   The Malayan authorities have also indicated that they may like to approach the Commander-in-Chief, Far East, for volunteers from civilian personnel of the Service Departments stationed in Singapore to assist the authorities there in the maintenance of essential services during civil disturbances. There would seem to be no reason why such assistance could not be given provided the Government of Malaysia were prepared to meet all costs and to agree to idemnification and compensation at the normal rates applying under the conditions of service of the United Kingdom Departments concerned.

British interest
5.   Following the inter-Governmental discussions on the proposal to form Malaysia in November, 1961 my predecessor told the Malayan Minister of Defence that we should wish to withdraw us soon as possible those of our forces which were in the theatre primarily for internal security purposes.[1] It was agreed that a phased plan should be worked out for the taking over of internal security responsibilities by

---

[1] Harold Watkinson, minister of defence 1959–1962, negotiated with Tun Razak at the London talks in Nov 1961 and visited Kuala Lumpur in Mar 1962.

Malaysian forces, for the build-up of these forces, and for the run-down of our forces. We are anxious to do everything possible to contribute to the smooth formation of Malaysia and we must therefore give the Government of the new Federation all the help we can in maintaining law and order in Singapore during the period while Malaysian forces are building up. We also have to consider the security of our bases and the safety of the large British community in Singapore. In the worst case of serious trouble there we should almost inevitably become involved.

British forces

6. To meet the requirement set out in paragraph 3 above we would not need to station in Singapore, or elsewhere in the area, more units than we now plan to do for other reasons. As regards forces which could be used in an internal security role, our long-term plan is to retain in Singapore and Malaya the equivalent of 7 major Army units, 2 Royal Marine Commandos, and probably some Gurkhas. Forces for internal security duties in an emergency could, if necessary, be found from these units. The rate of run-down to our planned long-term strength would therefore not be affected by such a commitment.

Political and legal factors

7. Internal security in an independent Commonwealth country is of course the responsibility of the Government concerned, and units of British forces would not normally be employed on internal security duties in a sovereign state. Indeed, I am not aware of a case where British units under British command have been used in this way before. Operations against communist terrorists in Malaya were warlike in nature. Some internal security tasks after merger, particularly those in the streets of Singapore, may be unpalatable. British participation might incur international criticism. We should also have to defend our action in Parliament. There are legal problems in the use of British forces for such tasks. These are complex and may take time to work out. As a first step we are assessing what the position would be under present legislation in Singapore and Malaya and how this would apply under Malaysia. Our aim would be to ensure adequate safeguards for our forces and we should insist on these as part of any agreement to help the Malaysian forces.

8. My predecessor discussed the general question with the Malayan Minister of Defence who made it clear that his Government would be embarrassed if they had to call on British forces, and that the Malayan Government, for their part, are most anxious not to do so if it can be avoided since this would be damaging politically to the new Federation.

9. To a limited extent internal security plans for Singapore can be adjusted to ensure that British forces are allocated to more passive roles such as the guarding of checkpoints and the maintenance of essential services. However, in the event of a complete breakdown in public order and assuming that the Malaysian forces cannot deal with the situation it would be virtually impossible to avoid contact between British forces and the Singapore population.

Finance

10. Since the use of British forces in this way in a sovereign state would be unique, there are no financial precedents to guide us in considering what costs the Malaysian Government should be asked to meet. The Treasury view is that there is no reason why the Malaysian Government should not bear the full costs of the services they require

including pay and upkeep of the forces concerned and an element for compensation in case of injury to or death of personnel and damage on loss of equipment. My own view is that it would be reasonable to expect the Malaysian Government to meet our out of pocket expenses and the cost of compensation for personnel and equipment where this was necessary. I am not convinced that it would be either practicable or in our long term interest to press the Malayans to accept a commitment in advance to pay for the normal upkeep of British forces so used, i.e. the full rather than the extra cost. I should welcome the views of my colleagues on this point.

Conclusions

11.   I consider that in the circumstances I have described we should accept in principle the commitment to help Malaysian forces for an interim period in dealing with serious trouble in Singapore. Agreement to do so should be conditional upon:—

(a) prior political approval being given by both sides in each case;
(b) the highest priority being given by the Malayan Government to the build-up of Malaysian police and military forces for internal security roles;
(c) so far as it is possible, adjustment of internal security plans for Singapore in order to allocate to British forces the most passive roles;
(d) satisfactory agreement on financial questions such as scales of payments for compensation, disability etc., where these might arise from the use of British forces and their civilian component in internal security operations;
(e) the enactment, if required, of legislation by Malaya and Singapore and subsequently by Malaysia, or the signing of bi-lateral agreements, which will confer on British forces and their U.K. civilian component sufficient protection and indemnification.

For our part we should do all we can to help and encourage the build-up of Malaysian forces and in particular by making available the accommodation for which they ask, subject, of course, to agreement on financial arrangements. To accede to requests of this kind may not always be convenient for us, but I consider the need to speed the build-up of Malaysian forces for internal security tasks overrides the inconvenience.

12.   I accordingly invite ny colleagues to agree that:—

(a) We should accept in principle the commitment to help the Malaysian authorities for an interim period in maintaining law and order in Singapore (as described in paragraph 3 and 4).
(b) The Malayan Government should be so informed and that discussions with their representatives on the financial and legal aspects should be arranged.

168   FO 371/169734, no 13   3 Apr 1963
'South East Asia': minute (M 131/63) from Mr Macmillan to Lord Home, expressing anxiety about regional defence after the formation of Malaysia

I am rather uneasy about our position in this area of the world. We are committed to bring Malaysia into existence not later than August 31; and there can, of course, be no question of our not honouring that undertaking. But I am not sure that we have really sized up the subsequent problem of defending her (or helping her to defend herself) against attack, whether overt or covert, by Indonesia and possibly the Philippines. I do not get a great deal of comfort from the record of the recent quadripartite talks in Washington;[1] and I have a feeling that both the Americans and the Australians, while not convinced that we can really protect this new child of ours, are not at all anxious to help us to do so. And I believe that the real reason for their hesitation is the fact that they are not sure that it really makes sense to think simply in terms of defending Malaysia; and they suspect that we are not giving sufficient consideration to the logically prior problem of keeping Indonesia and the Philippines neutral. If they are right, we are indeed taking on a formidable liability, as becomes clear if you look at the map and see how Malaysia will be more or less encircled by Indonesia on the west and south, by the Philippines to the east and by the dubiously neutral structure in Indo–China to the north. I doubt whether this is a situation which, if it really got out of control, we could deal with single handed; nor do I see why we should be expected to do so.

Selkirk will be here over Easter; and I think that we should take the opportunity to review the position with him. But as a preliminary we might consider—perhaps at a meeting of the O.P.C. next week—the nature and extent of the threat to Malaysia and the means of coping with it. For this purpose it would be helpful if you would circulate a memorandum on the political situation in that area of the world, as it is at the moment and as you see it developing over the next year or so, and on the political means at our disposal for neutralising Indonesia and the Philippines. Perhaps the Minister of Defence and the Commonwealth Secretary, to whom I am sending copies of this minute, would also circulate memoranda, dealing respectively with our military capacity to deal with a significant threat to Malaysia, whether overt or covert, and with the possibility of securing from Australia and New Zealand a greater contribution to the defence of South East Asia, in political as well as military terms, than they have been prepared to make hitherto.

I am also sending a copy of this minute to the Chancellor of the Exchequer.

---

[1] See 160–162.

169   PREM 11/4347   16 Apr 1963
'Future defence of Malaysia': minute (PM/63/56) from Lord Home to Mr Macmillan, replying to document 168. *Enclosure*: 'The future defence of Malaysia'

[Home argued that there was no alternative to Malaysia and that its defence against Indonesia and the Philippines would require assistance from Australia and New Zealand. It was clear from the record of Home's meeting with Dean Rusk (US secretary of state, 1961–1969) on 7 Apr that the US expected Britain to handle the problem in co-operation with Australia and New Zealand, 'leaving the United States to take a back seat'. Home's memorandum was circulated to the Oversea Policy Committee for which Macmillan was briefed by Trend who felt that it was 'disappointingly negative'. It was 'disappointingly cautious' particularly as regards, firstly, the value of an association of Malaysia with the Philippines and Indonesia and, secondly, the possibility of sharing costs with Australia and New Zealand. At the Oversea Policy Committee on 24 Apr ministers recognised that there was little prospect of reducing the scale of military commitments to Malaysia in the short term but concluded: 'It would be important not to enter into any commitment to provide any specified level of military assistance to Malaysia in the longer term. Ministers would shortly be undertaking a major review of our Far Eastern strategy and the scope of that examination should not be limited in advance by the acceptance of fresh or more definite commitments' (OP(63)6 and OP 4(63)1, CAB 134/2371; FO 371/169734; PREM 11/4183)]

In your minute of April 3 about South East Asia (M 131/63) you asked for the views or the Foreign Office, Commonwealth Relations Office and the Ministry of Defence, on the implications of our policy on Malaysia, for circulation to the Overseas Policy Committee. I enclose a copy of a memorandum which has been prepared in consultation with the other Departments. A separate memorandum on 'Defence in the Far East' is also being prepared as part of our present review of defence commitments and this will cover the long-term implications of Malaysia. The enclosed memorandum therefore deals with certain immediate questions which you have raised about the rightness of our Malaysia policy. You may care to use it as a brief for your talk with Lord Selkirk on April 25 and I also propose to circulate it as an Overseas Policy Committee paper.

2.   I am copying this minute to the Chancellor of the Exchequer, the Minister of Defence and the Commonwealth Secretary.

Enclosure to 169

Hitherto the Western Powers in South East Asia have been concerned chiefly with the Communist threat. We have been trying to prevent the North Vietnamese Communists from thrusting into South Vietnam and Laos. We have also, by our membership of SEATO, tried to persuade our friends in the area that we are prepared to help to defend them against any future menace from China. In the last two years, however, we have been faced with a 'second front' from Indonesia. Warfare was only narrowly avoided over West New Guinea; there is a continuous threat to Portuguese Timor and the Indonesians now want to prevent the formation of Malaysia.

2.   Indonesian opposition to Malaysia comes partly from their desire one day to seize Sarawak, Brunei and North Borneo for themselves. It also comes from envy and dislike of a prosperous Malaya. Sukarno has had much difficulty in holding together his island empire; he feels that Malaya is a rival attraction for the Sumatrans, and that its economic and political stability show up his own failures. Therefore, to prevent the creation of Malaysia, he has adopted a menacing attitude in an attempt to frighten the Tunku out of going ahead with the plan. The result however has been to stiffen the Tunku and there is little fear that he will be put off Malaysia.

3.   A complication is the Philippines claim to North Borneo. This had led the Filipinos and Indonesians into trying to make common cause and it could damage the Philippines alignment with the Western Powers and threaten American bases. There is, however, little likelihood of any military threat from the Philippines.

4.   It is unlikely that major Indonesian operations against the Borneo territories could be launched without a considerable and protracted build up, which we would be bound to detect and of which there is no evidence at present. In practice, however, the Indonesians are more likely to infiltrate numerous small parties, which they could with little or no warning. The Chiefs of Staff consider that adequate British forces are available in the theatre to meet such infiltration, but it would be necessary

to send replacement forces to Singapore from the United Kingdom. A major overt attack, however, would require further reinforcements, including V bombers from the United Kingdom.

5.   In February we discussed with the Americans, Australians and New Zealanders in Washington what we should do in these circumstances. All four governments felt that Malaysia was the only solution to the problems of Singapore and the future of the Borneo Territories. All four governments agreed to make their position known publicly in order to deter the Indonesians from adopting more dangerous methods. This has been carried out and does seem to have had a sobering effect on the Indonesians. We recognised in Washington, however, that at some stage the Indonesians might step up their attacks and try to produce local rebellions in the Borneo Territories by infiltrating agents and supporting armed insurgency. We explained our position in the case of overt aggression: that the Anglo/Malayan Defence Agreement would extend to the Borneo Territories after Malaysia. In response to a question from the Americans we agreed:—

(a) that should the Indonesians endeavour to overthrow the Malaysian regime in the Borneo territories by heavy infiltration, we should regard this as a case where the Malaysians would be entitled to ask for assistance in the external defence of their territory under the Anglo/Malayan Defence Agreement as extended to cover Malaysia;

(b) that we should keep a sufficient capability in South East Asia to deal with this commitment.

6.   The United States Government said that in the event of overt aggression by Indonesia against Malaysia they might feel obliged to take appropriate action. Subversive activities were a different matter, however, and it would be primarily a Commonwealth responsibility to deal with them. The Americans were too deeply committed in Vietnam to wish to take on a second case of the same kind. They agreed, however, that Indonesia's subversive activities might be carried to the stage where they more or less amounted to outside aggression and that in that case they might have to reconsider their attitude. The Australians and New Zealanders also did not commit themselves but they agreed that they would have to reach some decision in the fairly near future once Malaysia exists and our own defence arrangements are final.

7.   On April 7, during the SEATO meeting in Paris, Mr. Rusk reverted to the subject and said that he wanted to make the position of the United States Government quite clear in regard to any threat to the territory from Indonesian Borneo. So long as the threat remained one of subversion to be countered by police action the United States Government hoped that Her Majesty's Government together with the other Commonwealth countries in the area would handle it by themselves leaving the United States to take a back seat. They had enough problems of their own in that part of the world anyhow and did not want one more. If, however, the problem blew up into greater dimensions than that of police action that would be a new situation and the United States attitude of reserve would no longer apply.

8.   Malaysia will be entirely responsible for internal security in the Borneo territories. But the Malaysian Government might ask for our help in meeting a threat to internal security, which they considered to be beyond their own resources. It would then be for Her Majesty's Government to decide whether to agree. We are not

formally committed in any way (as we are, for a time, at least, in Singapore). Nevertheless, the Americans, at least, would expect H.M.G. to help the Malaysian Government to deal with any subversive threat beyond the capacity of purely Malaysian resources.

9.   Meanwhile the Americans, Australians and New Zealanders are concerned that nothing should be done to aggravate the situation. They recognise that Indonesia and the Philippines cannot be brought to approve of the creation of Malaysia but hope that the process can be handled so tactfully as to avoid clashes. The following steps are being taken to meet these wishes.

(a) *Malaya*
We have on several occasions asked the Tunku to be statesmanlike in his reaction to Indonesian attacks. We have had some success, but Malayan public opinion makes it difficult for the Tunku to be as conciliatory as we would wish.

On the other hand he has agreed to tripartite discussions with the Indonesians and Filipinos, provided they are not aimed at delaying Malaysia. His attitude is that the formation of Malaysia is a domestic concern, but that he is quite prepared to discuss Malaysia's future external relations with her neighbours. Plans are also in hand for building up Malaysian forces, including the Borneo battalions, with training and other assistance from ourselves. These will gradually reduce the likelihood of the Malaysian Government seeking our help in the preservation of public order, but will not free us from the obligation to assist in the external defence of Malaysia.

(b) *Indonesia*
Nothing will make the present Indonesian Government accept the idea of Malaysia sincerely. We can only deter them from interfering by resolute but unprovocative support for Malaysia and hope for a more reasonable Indonesian attitude after Sukarno disappears. To show that we can be conciliatory on anything not incompatible with the essentials of our policy, the Foreign Secretary is maintaining a correspondence with the Indonesian Foreign Minister and has offered to discuss differences and to help in any way to smooth out Malay–Indonesian differences.

(c) *Philippines*
The Philippines have not finally made their choice between Malaysia and Indonesia. Our policy towards the Philippine claim—unlimited polite discussion but no negotiation—has prevented any open breach or any headway with the claim. The Filipinos are now reluctant to press this in the International Court or the United Nations, particularly as they are not receiving full support from the Indonesians, who covet North Borneo for themselves. Meanwhile the Malayans are wooing the Filipinos and having some success in keeping them out of Indonesian arms. Continuation of these British and Malayan policies offers some prospect of eventual Philippine acceptance of Malaysia.

(d) *The United States*
The Americans now seem more satisfied that everything possible is being done to avoid offence to the Indonesians and the Filipinos. The Americans have given good public support to the early creation of Malaysia. So long as their present heavy commitments remain there is no chance of getting them to go beyond what they said

in Washington. The President is having considerable difficulties in getting money for his aid programme and Senator Mansfield's[1] Committee have strongly advised against assuming new commitments in South East Asia.

(e) *The Australians and New Zealanders*

The Australian Government are now publicly committed to political support for not only the Malaysia project but its timing. Sir Garfield Barwick[2] has been taking a robust line with the Indonesians and the Filipinos and has even made it clear to the Indonesians that Australia recognises that her support for Malaysia may well have military implications. All of this has had good effect. The Australian Government have not decided on the form any military arrangements will take and with their present slender majority they have to proceed very carefully before accepting new defence commitments. New Zealand's misgivings over Malaysia have never been so acute as those of the Australians.

We certainly hope to secure from both Australia and New Zealand a larger contribution to the Western military effort in South East Asia. However, the timing of any pressure we shall exert to this end needs careful consideration. They have fought down their recent hesitations about pursuing the Malaysian project in the light of Indonesian opposition. But these could easily be revived if they got the impression that we wished to reduce our own military contribution and were asking them to take up commitments that we were going to lay down. In short it is probably wiser to wait until after Malaysia Day before applying a great deal of extra pressure on them.

(f) *The United Nations*

It is important that we satisfy the United Nations as far as possible. The Colonial Office are doing what they can to ensure that the will of the people in the three Borneo territories is not only consulted but is seen to be consulted, with good results in North Borneo and Sarawak. Special information machinery has been set up. We have accepted the help of the Secretary General through Mr. Narasimhan to iron out differences between Malaya and the Philippines and Indonesia. United Nations debate is unlikely to take place in the near future.

10. *Conclusions*

(i) There is no alternative to the formation of Malaysia.

(ii) We should not delay the original programme for its creation by August 31.

(iii) While it is impossible to predict the course of events, the chances of averting any major showdown with the Indonesians or Filipinos before August 31 appear to be improving.

(iv) But even if we get over this hurdle the future Malaysia will probably be exposed to attempts by Indonesia to overthrow its authority in the Borneo Territories.

---

[1] Mike Mansfield, Democrat majority leader in the Senate, led a Congressional group to Southeast Asia in late 1962. Their report, which sparked fresh debate on US policy in Feb 1963, recommended a thorough revision of military assistance programmes and looked towards the contraction, rather than expansion, of American involvement especially in the Vietnam war, see Appendix to this volume, para 294.

[2] Leader of the Australian delegation at the UN, 1962–1964.

(v) We have a continuing military commitment to help the Malaysia Government against external aggression, and might be asked for help against a serious internal threat.

(vi) The Americans are not willing to commit themselves to dealing with anything except overt aggression. We are unlikely to be able to change their view at this time, though in the long run it is hard to see how they could escape some involvement.

(vii) We must seek to ensure that the Australians and New Zealanders share with us to the fullest possible extent responsibility for the defence of Malaysia. But a successful approach can best be made later.

(viii) We must continue to treat the Indonesians and Filipinos both with firmness and with great care and courtesy. We must maintain our efforts to get the Tunku to do the same.

170 CAB 131/28, D(63)18, Annex C 20 Apr 1963
'Federation of Malaya: financing the defence programme': despatch from Sir G Tory to Mr Sandys

[In Apr 1963 Sir Henry Lintott led a mission to Kuala Lumpur to examine what financial assistance might be offered by Britain towards the Malayan defence programme on the establishment of Malaysia. Lintott was deputy under-secretary at the CRO, 1956–1963, and had previously served in Customs and Excise, the Board of Trade and as secretary-general of the OEEC. In the CRO he had been involved in planning post-independence financial aid for Ghana and Nigeria as well as discussions to mount a Colombo-type plan for Africa (Hyam and Louis, eds, *BDEE: The Conservative Government, 1957–1964*, part II, 327, 332 and 336, and Lynn, ed, *BDEE: Nigeria*, part II, 488). On 28 Mar, before the Lintott delegation departed for Malaya, the Tunku wrote to Macmillan, referring to Britain's financial settlement for Malaya on independence in 1957 and pointing out that the current situation was now 'rather more serious'. This was the result of commitments under the Five-Year Plan plus a sharp drop in the price of rubber, deterioration in the balance of payments and the demands of defence and internal security. The Tunku insisted that the financial settlement should be agreed before the final round of Malaysia talks in London. Macmillan delayed replying to the Tunku until 27 Apr when he sent a brief, generally sympathetic but non-committal letter: 'We are anxious to do what we can, within the limits of our capabilities, to help you with the kind of difficulties which you foresee'. The report of the Lintott mission and Tory's despatch on the subject were considered by the Cabinet Defence Committee on 10 May (see 173; also Tunku to Macmillan, 28 Mar and Macmillan to Tunku, 27 Apr 1963, PREM 11/4347).]

The mission, under the chairmanship of Sir Henry Lintott, which visited Kuala Lumpur from 6th–14th April, 1963, to look into the requirements of finance for Malaya's expanded defence programme, have established to their satisfaction that the Defence Plan is modest and that even so the Malayan Government have no hope of meeting either its capital or recurrent cost, given their present financial commitments. The clear implication is that, to the extent that we cannot help financially to meet the bill, the Malayans must cut down either their Defence Plan or their Development Plan or both. I have the honour to submit the following observations on this situation.

2. Against the background of the Brunei revolt, the threat of subversion in Sarawak and the continuing menace of Indonesian confrontation, the Malayan Defence Plan is most unlikely to be cut. Indeed, it would scarcely be in our interests

if it were. Our military staffs have agreed with the Malayans upon the level of forces needed in Malaysia over the next few years and we shall be obliged, in the discharge of our defence obligations and of our implicit undertaking to see Malaysia through safely, to continue to provide forces to fill the gap between the agreed level and what Malaysia can contribute. It is clearly to our advantage that Malaya should find, or be given, means to implement her present Defence Plan.

3. The Defence Agreement we have with Malaya has, during the first five years of independence, been justified politically by the argument that Malaya needs British military assistance to hold the ring whilst permanently effective barriers to Communism are built up in the form of a landed peasantry and a steady standard of living at a fairly high level. The Tunku looks at the map of South-East Asia—at Communist China, Vietnam, Laos, Cambodia and Indonesia—and rightly concludes that the dyke builders must hasten before the flood runs in. He has always said that the first 10 years would settle Malaya's fate and this does not seem to me to be an exaggeration.

4. The Malayan Government regard their Development Plan as a vital contribution to Malayan security. Compared with other newly independent countries Malaya was born in easy economic circumstances. Her standard of living is said to be the highest in Asia and her reserves are the envy of much larger nations. But she is running into difficulty. Natural rubber, at the mercy of world prices beyond Malaya's control, brings 60 per cent of her export earnings and provides 30 per cent of employment. With growing competition from synthetic rubber there is a downward trend in natural rubber prices and throughout the '60s it will be a struggle for Malaya to maintain her export earnings at their present level.

5. At the same time she is faced with a veritable population 'explosion'. Her natural increase of 3.3 per cent per annum is exceptionally high. An economy that provides adequately for 6.9 million people in 1960 will be strained to the utmost to feed 9.6 million in 1970. In these circumstances Malaya must run very fast in order to stand still economically. To provide for this increasing population and to meet the growing unemployment problem she has embarked upon a vigorous development programme. This will only be enough to keep national income per head at the present level and it brings its own problems in the form of increased demand for imports and capital goods. With the import bill rising and export earnings static Malaya's reserves, though ample at the moment, will come under very severe pressure, particularly as in Malaya foreign trade represents three times as great a share in the national economy as it does in even such a trading nation as Britain.

6. Britain's own interests are very much identified with the continuance of Malaya's prosperity. So long as Malaya is well off and can still be led by a Conservative Government which encourages foreign capital, our own substantial assets in Malaya are safe. We estimate our private capital investment in Malaya as about £400 million. This compares, for example, with £335 million for India and £108 million for Pakistan. Our exports to Malaya are of the order of £60 million per annum. We have, therefore, a very big financial stake in Malaya and a considerable vested interest in the maintenance of a stable and prosperous Malayan economy. Knowing how closely this condition is linked to development we ought not lightly to recommend that the shortfall in defence finance should be made good by economies in development expenditure.

7.   These are practical considerations. There are also strong moral arguments in favour of generosity on our part. The Tunku is attracted by the prospect of building up a bigger stable unit in this troubled region but he dreads the problems which Malaysia will bring. He was only persuaded to take on Singapore because he realised that we should have to contract out and to give Singapore its independence. He foresaw an independent Singapore rapidly sinking into Communism and Malaya falling a prey to Communist attack on two fronts. Taking over Singapore is undoubtedly an act of self-preservation on Malaya's part but it is being undertaken with regret and misgiving because—in the Tunku's estimation—we are not tough enough to maintain our position there indefinitely. The Borneo Territories are being taken in as a balance of non-Chinese population to the net million or so Chinese in Singapore whom the Tunku regards as politically unreliable at the least. The Tunku considers, therefore, that we are shedding our responsibilities in this region and that Malaya, which has already had 12 years of emergency and three more of struggle against subversion, is now taking over from us a new front in the battle against Communism in South-East Asia. He thinks this entitles him to a good deal of assistance from us and his other anti-Communist friends.

8.   At the first talks on Malaysia defence in London, Tun Razak made it clear that, to the extent that we could not supply needed financial assistance, the Malayans would look to other Commonwealth Governments, Australia, New Zealand and Canada, and also to America, to fill the gap. Australia and New Zealand regard Malaysia as their first line of defence and there are strong reasons why both should make some contribution to the Malaysian defence programme. The Australian Government have been sensitive lately on the score of Indonesia but now seem to be taking a more robust line and I hope that we shall not feel precluded from urging both them and the New Zealand Government to live up to their responsibilities. Canadian concern with Malaysia is obviously not so great but Tun Razak, who is visiting Ottawa from 28th–30th April, has some hope of persuading them to supply certain items of military equipment.

9.   The Americans have lately shown clearly that they regard the successful launching and early support of Malaysia as a Commonwealth and primarily British responsibility and that they will be unwilling to make any contributions unless convinced that the British and other Commonwealth countries have first 'scraped the barrel'. If the Malayans are to get worthwhile help from America, and it is surely in our interests that they should, we must at least appear to be making a substantial offer.

10.   Whatever we may say about the comparative wealth of the Malayans, we are agreed that the main requirement now is for foreign exchange which they themselves can do little about. I believe that if we were to offer to meet the whole of the outstanding foreign exchange element in the Malaysia defence bill for capital expenditure up to 1965, estimated by us at about £18.7 million, and to undertake a review early that year, as recommended by Sir Henry Lintott's mission, the Malayans would realise we had done all we could. Certainly the Malayans are hoping that the British offer, together with whatever Australia and New Zealand can be persuaded to give, will cover this foreign exchange element. A British offer of anything less than £10 million would, in my view, cause resentment and would have an adverse effect on our political relations with Malaya. I hope, therefore, that

Ministers, on reflection, will feel able to come to a generous conclusion on the basis of the very cogent analysis of Malaya's financial need as submitted by Sir Henry Lintott.

11.   I am sending copies of this despatch to the Commissioner-General for South-East Asia in Singapore, the High Commissioners in Canberra, Wellington and Ottawa, Her Britannic Majesty's Ambassadors in Washington, Djakarta, Manila and Bangkok, the Governors of North Borneo and Sarawak and the High Commissioner for Brunei.

## 171 DO 169/226					25 Apr 1963
[British representation in the region after the inauguration of Malaysia]: minute by Sir S Garner, recording a discussion with Sir B Trend, Sir H Caccia and Lord Selkirk

[Selkirk was anxious that Britain's presence in Southeast Asia should be led by a political representative rather than the military head of a unified command and he argued in favour of the appointment of a high commissioner who, in addition to his normal functions in Kuala Lumpur, would have a wider regional role, co-ordinating British interests and enjoying some responsibility over the unified commander. Selkirk put these points directly to Macmillan on 25 Apr. Although the office of commissioner-general lapsed on the inauguration of Malaysia, the appointment of Lord Head (a former minister of Defence and Britain's first high commissioner to independent Nigeria) as high commissioner to Malaysia indicated the significance of the post and went a long way to meet Selkirk's concerns. Indeed, when Sandys first approached Head about the position, he stressed that it would be greatly enhanced compared with the high commissioner's status between 1957 and 1963, see Sandys to Head, 25 Mar 1963, Sandys Papers, 8/13. For the directive relating to the functions of the British high commissioner as from 16 Sept 1963, see DO 169/226 no 140; for Head's first impressions as high commissioner of Malaysia, see DO 169/231.]

Sir Burke Trend, Sir Harold Caccia and I had a general discussion with Lord Selkirk about the post-Malaysia set up earlier this week.

Today Lord Selkirk called on me for a further talk, in the course of which he reiterated the following points:—

(1) He thought that it was vital that there should be continuity in the staffing of our various posts in Malaysia after the 31st August.

(2) He insisted on the importance of the High Commissioner in the new set up being completely in the picture as far as any action taken by the United Commander was concerned, which could cause any repercussions in Malaysia; and on Lord Selkirk's definition, virtually any step could possibly have implications for Malaysia.

On the first point Lord Selkirk emphasised how primitive the Borneo Territories were, and how utterly inadequate the Malayan administrative machine. If Malaysia were to succeed it was vital that we should be able to exert our influence and help things along, but this could only be done if we had people in the key posts of the right stature and of the right experience, particularly after the Governors departed from Kuching and Jesselton. It would be most important that our Deputy High Commissioners should be people who gained the confidence of the local inhabitants and were able tactfully to guide things in the right direction (see further note attached about staff).[1]

On (2) Lord Selkirk emphasised his anxiety that our presence in South East Asia should be seen primarily as a political, and not as a military, one, and his concern that the Unified Commander should not be in a position to initiate any military action unless it had the approval of the High Commissioner who, Lord Selkirk thought, must have the responsibility for viewing the problem of the area as a whole.

I suggested to Lord Selkirk that there were two requirements which we somehow had to reconcile:—

(a) The High Commissioner was the British Government's representative to the Malaysian Government, and it would be incorrect to saddle him publicly and formally with responsibilities of relations with the Unified Commander, or otherwise, which took him into the field of SEATO, or of relations with other foreign countries in the area.
(b) At the same time, it was vitally important that the High Commissioner should be fully aware of all that was going on, and in a position to make his views known to the Unified Commander.

Lord Selkirk accepted these two propositions, and I commented that I did not think it would be impossible to take care of the position, though in the last resort everything depended on the relationship which the individuals concerned work out. Lord Selkirk said that we must be very careful not to put too great a strain on human frailties, and that he would prefer to see matters written out with the greatest precision; (so far as I am aware, Lord Selkirk did not know at that time the name of the proposed new High Commissioner).[2]

I concluded by saying that in working out the arrangements I would, of course, bear very carefully in mind what Lord Selkirk had said, but that I thought myself we could probably adequately meet the situation:—

(a) by writing into the charter of the Unified Commander an instruction that he was required to consult the High Commissioner on all matters likely to affect Malaysia; and
(b) ensuring that any instructions to the Political Adviser sent from the Foreign Office should be repeated to the High Commissioner, so that he would have an opportunity of putting his oar in if he wanted to.

---

[1] Not printed.   [2] Garner later added at this point in his minute: 'in fact he did apparently'.

172 PREM 11/4347   26 Apr 1963
[Indonesian opposition to Malaysia]: letter from T E Bridges[1] to P F de Zulueta, explaining the FO's apparent appeasement of Indonesia

[In the opinion of the new British ambassador in Jakarta, Andrew Gilchrist, so determined was Sukarno to block Malaysia that Britain, in its efforts to keep the peace,

---

[1] T E Bridges, son of Sir Edward (Lord) Bridges (former secretary to the Cabinet) and assistant private secretary to the Foreign Secretary.

was liable to lose control over its policy. 'We misunderstand this at our peril', he had added. Macmillan saw Gilchrist's telegram and asked de Zulueta to seek clarification of the FO's policy towards Indonesia. On reading this letter from Bridges, Macmillan noted, 'it is now all quite clear to me'. Meanwhile, the foreign secretary, who recalling the ineffectiveness of Dutch complaints about Indonesian activities in West Irian felt that any public protest might aggravate Sukarno's hostility and 'alarm our friends', arranged for 'a dossier of our evidence to be collected, so that we shall be ready for a fully documented denunciation of the Indonesians if this later seems advisable' (Home to Sandys, 14 May 1963, FS/63/43 in PREM 11/4348).]

You mentioned to me the Prime Minister's interest in Djakarta telegram No. 327 of April 22 about Indonesian opposition to Malaysia. What obviously worries the Ambassador is that elaborate diplomatic efforts are being made (notably by tripartite talks with the Malayan and Philippine Governments and through the mediation of Mr. Narasimhan of the United Nations) to persuade the Indonesians to accept the idea of Malaysia. Mr. Gilchrist is sceptical about these efforts since he considers, with good reason, that there is no hope of persuading President Sukarno to support a project bound to frustrate Indonesian territorial ambitions.

In fact, however, we are not trying to convert the Indonesians, but to justify ourselves in the eyes of our friends, particularly of the Americans and Australians, whose wholehearted support will be essential to the long-term viability of Malaysia. At the Quadripartite talks in Washington in February, for instance, both the Americans and Australians expressed the view that we had made insufficient effort to explain Malaysia to the Indonesians and to answer all the apprehensions and objections raised (however insincerely) by the Indonesians. It was in return for promises of American and Australian political support (whose public manifestation has been most valuable to us) that we undertook to do what we could to reduce tension between Malaya and Indonesia by encouraging all the diplomatic manoeuvres now in progress.

It is also quite true, as the Ambassador says, that the British Government are taking a back seat in the more public aspects of these diplomatic manoeuvres and are leaving the lime-light to the Malayans. This is deliberate. One of the main objects of the whole Malaysia project is to transfer political responsibility from ourselves to the Malayans. Not only do we want them to make more and more of the running as Malaysia Day comes nearer, but the main Indonesian argument against Malaysia is that we intend to retain effective power as the 'neo-colonialist' ruler of a puppet federation.

We are explaining all this to the Ambassador and telling him that, for the present, we do not want a public show-down with Indonesia of the kind he suggests, though we shall continue to make clear to the Indonesians in private, as we have repeatedly done in the past, our determination to see Malaysia through at all costs.

173   CAB 131/28, D(63)18   7 May 1963
'Malaysia: British financial aid': memorandum by Mr Sandys.
Appendix: 'Malaysia—British financial aid. Report and recommendations of British official delegation'

[In briefing Macmillan on Sandys' memorandum, Trend suggested that consideration should be given to ways of extracting contributions from Australia and New Zealand and of levering some compensating concession from Malaya. The Cabinet Defence Committee considered this paper on 10 May and accepted its recommendations. The subsequent Anglo-Malayan ministerial discussions, however, proved inconclusive (see 174–176; Trend to Macmillan 9 May 1963, PREM 11/4347; COS 31(63)6, DEFE 4/154; CO 1030/1509.]

An official delegation led by Sir Henry Lintott of the Commonwealth Relations Office visited Malaya from 8th to 11th April, 1963, to examine what financial assistance might be offered by Britain towards the cost of the Malayan defence programme on the establishment of Malaysia.

2.   The delegation's report is attached. Their conclusion is that defence aid to Malaysia should be limited to the capital element of the defence programme for the period 1963 to 1965 with agreement to hold a review in 1965. They recommend that Britain's contribution on this basis should be £12½ million but that in negotiating a settlement we should make an opening bid of £10 million; they consider that Malayan Ministers would reject an offer of less than £10 million as totally inadequate.

3.   I am in agreement with these recommendations and hope the Committee will approve them.

4.   Tun Razak, the Malayan Minister of Defence, will be in London for financial talks on Monday, 13th May, and a decision is therefore urgently needed.

Appendix to 173

There has never been any doubt that there are strong political arguments in favour of our giving generous financial assistance to Malaysia, particularly for defence. The difficulty so far has been to satisfy ourselves that there is any *prima facie* need for such assistance, given the apparent health of the Malayan economy.

2.   The Mission's purpose was, therefore, to establish the degree of financial need; to ascertain what economies could be made in the Malaysian defence programme without damage to its effectiveness and to assess the ability of the Malayans to pay, having regard to their budgetary and balance of payments prospects. The Mission was instructed to concentrate in its examination of the Defence Programme on the first three years (i.e. 1963–1965 inclusive) on the assumption that any British offer of assistance would be related to these first three years, with a review in 1965. The Mission accordingly discussed the Defence Programme with the Malayans on this basis. But the financial and economic background was considered in terms of the five year period 1963–1967, which was the basis on which the Malayans had prepared their estimates.

3.   The memoranda at Annexes A and B contain the Mission's findings on (Annex A) the Defence Plan itself, and the possibility of economies in it and (Annex B) the financial and economic prospects of Malaysia.[1] The salient features of these findings are as follows.

4.   *Defence plan*

(a) The Malayans accept that any assistance given to the expansion of their defence forces can be of limited duration only, and that the Malaysians must

---

[1] Annexes A and B are not printed.

themselves maintain these forces at the level to which they are built up. They do not, however, yet accept that aid should be limited to capital costs only during this period of build-up.

(b) The capital cost over the first three years, 1963–1965, is estimated at £26.7 m.. This would generate recurrent costs totalling about £23 m. in this period. The foreign exchange element of these figures is estimated at about £20 m. capital, and about £11.5 m. recurrent.

(c) The detailed capital costings show, however, that on the one hand the Malayans have *under estimated* costs to the extent of approximately 10 per cent, and on the other hand experience suggests that they will probably fail to achieve the programme in these first three years to the extent of about 20 per cent. Probable expenditure during this period is therefore £24.5 m. capital and £21 m. recurrent. The foreign exchange content of these figures is approximately £18.5 m. capital and about £11 m. recurrent.

(d) Given the substantial new commitments in respect of internal security throughout Malaysia that the new Federation will be undertaking, the plan is a modest one. Its implementation is also frugally conceived. We could find no grounds for questioning the standard of provisioning. Any reduction by slowing down the programme would presumably slow down the rate at which British forces can expect to shed responsibility for internal security.

Financial and economic prospects

5.   Any future estimate of financial and economic prospects must be subject to wide margins of uncertainty. This is particularly true of the future Federation of Malaysia which does not yet exist, and will derive most of its earnings from rubber, tin and forest products, the prices of which are very volatile. (A change of 10 cents in the price of rubber would mean a difference of over £20 m. in exports earnings in 1963.) It seems clear, however, that the future Federation will have substantial deficits, both in its budget and in its balance of payments for a number of years: these arise mainly from the cost of development and partly from the increased costs of defence.

6.   On the assumption that any further aid given by the United Kingdom will have regard to the problem of foreign exchange and will not be given to finance domestic expenditure, it is the balance of payments deficit which falls to be considered.

(a) The figures for the balance of payments show a foreign exchange deficit of £427 m..

(b) The expenditure attributable to defence is discussed in paragraph 4 above.

(c) The expenditure on development is large. It is argued, however, that this is necessary:—

(i) in order to maintain and perhaps to increase slightly the income per head in Malaya and Singapore, in view of the rise in population.

(ii) To cover increased development in North Borneo and Sarawak which was offered as the main inducement to these territories to join the future Federation.

7.   On the question of bridging the foreign exchange gap, the following considerations are relevant:—

(a) If expenditure on development and defence are not reduced and the deficit remains at £427 m. this might be reduced, on the Malayan Government's (possibly rather optimistic) estimates by an estimated inflow of £95 m. of private capital and of £65 m. of Government borrowing (including our outstanding loan aid to Singapore). This would leave £267 m. to be found: of this it is suggested by the Malayan Government that a maximum amount of £175 m. would be found by running down the existing external reserves (at present estimated by them at £565 m.); the remaining £92 m. is represented by the external cost of the defence programme (£37 m.) and a residual figure (£55 m.) representing what is needed in foreign grant aid.

(b) The only contribution at present in sight towards this figure of £92 m. is our promised contribution of £7.5 m. to the development expenditure of the Borneo territories. The Malayan Government intend to approach other friendly countries besides Britain—especially Australia and New Zealand—for aid but it is a matter of conjecture how much they will get.

(c) The Malayan Government is anxious to keep substantial reserves because of the great importance of external trade to the Federation, because of the fluctuations in export earnings, and in order to maintain confidence in the Malayan dollar, which is vital as a medium of exchange for the area as a whole. The Bank of England emphasises also the need to maintain its standing as a borrower. Moreover, a considerable part of these holdings belongs to individual territories and the Federal Government's access to them is likely in practice to be restricted. The Malayans have, nevertheless, included in their estimates a much larger possible running-down of reserves than those suggested by Mr. Ross[2] (£100 m.) or the International Bank (£80 m.). The Bank of England would consider a running-down by £175 m. as exceeding very considerably the limits of prudence. The Malayan Finance Minister has himself expressed the view that the reserves could not be run down by more than £100 m.. He might well, however, come under pressure to expose the external financial position to more serious risks in order to maintain the standard of living. The conflict of arguments is not unfamiliar in this country.

Conclusions and recommendations

8.   Whatever the uncertainties of the estimate referred to above, it seems clear that Malaysia will experience severe budgetary and balance of payments problems at least for a number of years. The Malayans estimate their foreign exchange gap (after making what is certainly the maximum possible allowance for running down reserves for private investment and for Government borrowing) at £92 m. over the five year period 1963–1967; we cannot say that this order of magnitude is exaggerated.

9.   In so far as this gap cannot be closed by foreign assistance the Malaysian Government is likely to be faced at some stage with difficult decisions about whether to cut defence, development, or both. As indicated above we accept that the defence programme is reasonable to meet the commitments of Malaysia. But the Malayans feel strongly that development is equally essential as a bulwark against Communism;

---

[2] See 165, n 4 and n 7.

their programme is designed to provide no more than a maintenance of the existing standard of living for a rapidly rising population. If they were forced to make cuts now, it might well be that the Malayans would choose to reduce defence rather than development.

10. Malayan Ministers will measure whatever financial assistance we offer against this estimated gap of £92 m. This of course is not entirely reasonable, since if Malaysia were not created the existing Federation would be faced with substantial payments difficulties. But they can reasonably claim that a substantial part of the deficit (and notably that attributable to the defence programme) is the result of their taking over from Britain military and economic commitments in respect of Singapore and the Borneo territories.

11. It can of course be contended that with Britain's limited capacity to give overseas aid, Malaya as a relatively rich country should be at the end of the queue. Against this it can be argued that the relative prosperity of the Federation of Malaya is a principal cause of her political stability, and that in any case if she were less prosperous she could not be expected to shoulder the new burdens which the creation of Malaysia will involve for her even after any contribution which we may make.

12. Our immediate interest is to ensure that Malaysia is established in conditions in which her security and stability can be maintained. An essential element in this is that the Malaysian defence programme should go ahead as planned; if it does not, the date when we can finally shed our responsibility for internal security for Malaysia will be retarded.

13. The more general political considerations which must be borne in mind in considering this problem are set out in the British High Commissioner's Despatch No. 4 (reproduced at Annex C).[3] This despatch also calls attention to the large financial stake represented by British investment in Malaya.

14. In the light of the above considerations our conclusions are as follows:—

(a) We continue to think that it is right to limit our present offer to the period 1963–65, with agreement to hold a review in 1965, in the light of which any further financial contribution would be determined.

(b) We also continue to think it right that (although Malayans' hopes will be much more ambitious) any offer should be related to the capital element of the defence programme in that period; this type of aid will provide the best encouragement to the Malayans to get ahead with the defence programme. We now estimate this capital cost in 1963–65 as about £24.2 m. of which the foreign exchange component might be about £18.5 m.

(c) We agree with the High Commissioner's assessment that an offer of less than £10 m. would be rejected by the Malayans as totally inadequate and would cause resentment; but we think that Ministers might make an opening bid of £10 m. Malayan Ministers will certainly argue strongly for a much larger figure; we would hope that agreement might be reached at about £12½ m. (which was the figure which we recommended that we should be authorised to offer for a quick settlement in Kuala Lumpur).

---

[3] See 170.

(d) The Malayan Government have asked us to support them in an approach to Australia and New Zealand for contributions by those countries to the Malaysian defence programme, and we should agree to do so.

174 CO 1030/1509, no 13 13 May 1963
'Financial and defence talks with Malayan ministers': minutes of the first meeting

[Chaired by Sandys, the meeting was attended by Thorneycroft (minister of Defence), John Boyd-Carpenter (chief secretary to the Treasury), Lord Lansdowne, Sir H Lintott and other officials on the British side. The Malayan delegation consisted of Tun Razak, Tan Siew Sin, the Malayan high commissioner and officials from the Malayan Treasury and Ministry of Defence. No British officials were present from SE Asian postings.]

The Commonwealth Secretary welcomed the Malayan Delegation on behalf of his colleagues and himself. He was sure this meeting of Ministers was the best way to follow up the Lintott Mission[1] and to get the problem of Defence Aid out of the way so as to move on to certain more difficult matters involved in setting up Malaysia, such as the discussions between Singapore and Malaya.

The British Government had already agreed to give aid of up to £5.78 m. to Singapore; development aid to North Borneo and Sarawak of £7½ m.; for the compensation scheme for expatriates in North Borneo and Sarawak, £3½ m.; and the scheme for subsidised secondment and training of military personnel would cost us about £3 m. over the first three years. All this could total nearly £20 m.

The object of the present talks was to decide what aid could be given to help the Malaysians over the build up of the defence forces needed to enable them to meet their internal security and external responsibilities. The Lintott Mission had agreed with the Malayans to concentrate on the first three years of the Defence Expansion Programme, i.e. the calendar years of 1963–65 inclusive. It was not quite clear how quickly the expansion programme would be implemented as the execution of Defence programmes rarely came up to the expectations of the planners. Moreover, other factors such as the rate of implementation of the development programme and the availability of foreign exchange were difficult to foresee over a longer period. Hence the British side thought it more profitable to concentrate these discussions on the period 1963–65 with a review of the situation in 1965. They also considered that British help should be related to the capital costs of building up forces rather than the recurrent costs, and assumed that as the Malayan forces were already supplied with British equipment, a substantial portion of the Malayan expenditure would be on further British equipment.

Tun Razak said that the Malayans were hoping for somewhat more than this. In 1957 when Malaya became independent and inherited an Emergency, Britain had given her £30 m. in aid.[2] Malaysia would now inherit an emergency situation in Brunei, in Sarawak and on the Indonesian border.

---

[1] See 170 and 173.   [2] See *BDEE: Malaya*, lxxviii-lxxix and part III, 440 and 441.

Mr. Tan Siew Sin observed that the Malayans were facing in Malaysia the following problems:—

(i)   Sarawak could not balance her budget;
(ii) while North Borneo could, she could not provide the money required for her own development;
(iii) Brunei had reserves, but was unwilling to make them available;
(iv) Singapore had her own well known problems.

The Commonwealth Secretary said that the British Government could help with the capital costs but could not give budgetary aid. The former was a more appropriate form of assistance to independent sovereign countries. He understood officials had agreed that the capital costs up to the end of 1965 could be about £24.2 m. (approximately $205 m.). The original estimate of $229 m. produced by the Malayans had been agreed with the Lintott Mission to be probably under-costed by about 10 per cent, but did not take account of a probable slippage of 20 per cent.

Malaya was a richer country than many in the Commonwealth, but he recognised that foreign exchange was likely to be a major problem in the early years of Malaysia. The foreign exchange element of the $205 m. was likely to be some $157 m. (£18½ m.). He suggested that this was the figure on which the talks should concentrate, and he proposed that this cost should be shared equally between Britain and Malaya, i.e. Britain should contribute £9¼ m.[3]

The Malayan Ministers said that Malaya would have been in difficulties even if she had not taken on Malaysia. Her reserves were being run down owing firstly to the lowering of the price of rubber, and secondly to the increased expenditure on development. In the years 1961–62 there was an adverse swing of nearly £60 m. in her foreign exchange earnings. With Malaysia they estimated there would be increased expenditure of $100 m. a year because of Brunei and Sarawak and the Indonesian confrontation. However, it was their opinion that once the teething troubles of the first few years were over, the situation would improve.

The Minister of Defence said that Malaysia could call on Britain to help under the Defence Agreement if she became involved in external aggression from Indonesia. Britain had to incur very heavy expenditure in keeping her forces east of Aden for contingencies such as these.

Mr. Tan Siew Sin said that the Malayans, while agreeing that the figure of £18 m. was the important one, hoped that Britain would meet all of it. Malaya's political stability depended on economic expansion and the development programme; defence and internal security had been pared down to a minimum to pay for development, but now under Malaysia Defence and Internal Security forces would have to be built up from scratch. Development aid and economic expansion must nonetheless continue, and all the more so in the new States.

The Chief Secretary said that Britain had enormous demands on her from the Commonwealth; Malaya after all was a rich country. She had big reserves. Even if

---

[3] This sum was smaller than the opening bid of £10 million agreed by the Cabinet Defence Committee on 10 May.

they were not all within the control of the Central Government (e.g. those with the Banks) they could nevertheless be mobilised for development purposes as indeed they were in Britain.

The Commonwealth Secretary said it would be easier for Britain to help with equipment than with cash. Some of the equipment might already be available, and more could probably be provided from industries which the British Government wanted to assist, i.e. those with surplus capacity. He suggested, therefore, that the officials of both sides meet to establish what equipment needed by the Malayans was already available from existing stocks and what would involve new production. He then suggested that Ministers should try to narrow the remaining gap at a meeting next day.

Mr. Tan Siew Sin said, however, that there were two further 'gaps'. Malaysia needed a 'launching ground' of development aid. Within the Commonwealth, Cyprus, even though much richer in per capita income than Malaya, had been much better treated in terms of aid. There was also a third gap. Malaysia had now run into difficulties, as a result of the Brunei revolt, the Indonesian confrontation policy and the opposition of the Communists in Sarawak. If she were simultaneously faced with a revolt in Sarawak and Indonesian infiltration, she would just go bankrupt. When Malaysia was first planned, the idea had been to have only a couple of companies in the Borneo States, but now three battalions were going to be necessary. In Singapore the British had five battalions in an Internal Security role, Malaysia would only be able to provide three. Suppose there had been no Malaysia, Britain would have had to pay far more than now was being suggested in the Malaysia settlement. The Malayans were already committed to making available to the Borneo Territories a very large figure, some $500 m., for development aid and Britain had agreed only to provide some $64 m.

The Commonwealth Secretary said that he thought it was agreed that these talks were concerned only with Defence. Mr. Tan Siew Sin by speaking of development appeared to be reopening questions which he thought were already settled.

Mr. Tan Siew Sin said that he certainly did not wish to reopen any questions already settled but he had thought that these talks were to discuss all aspects of financial aid; not just defence aid. If, however, they were confined to defence he must ask that they take account of the need to meet recurrent expenditure on defence; for example even though Britain had agreed to meet the extra cost involved in the secondment scheme, the Malayans still had to provide a very large sum. Even internal expenditure had a large import content to it. However, *Tun Razak* added they were glad to be offered equipment and in particular were looking forward to obtaining Patrol Craft.

Conclusions

It was agreed that the officials on both sides should meet later that evening and the next day to discuss what equipment could be available to the Malayans (i) out of stock, (ii) by new production, and what the Malayan requirments were. Ministers would then meet again.

175 CO 1030/1509, no 20   15 May 1963

'Malaysia financial discussions': minutes of the third and final formal meeting at which Tun Razak and Tan Siew Sin reported their reactions to the British offer

The purpose of the third and last formal meeting of Ministers in these discussions was for the Malayan delegation to report their reactions to the offer of assistance by the British Government which the Commonwealth Secretary had made at the previous meeting.[1]

2. *Tun Razak* said that, after careful consideration, he had come to the conclusion that he must report personally to the Tunku on the offer which the British Government had made. It was not, of course, sufficient to enable the defence programme to be carried out, although he had not expected that the British Government would be able to fulfil the requests which had been made. He was pleased that the Commonwealth Secretary had been able, at their previous meeting, to undertake to approach the Australian, Canadian and United States Governments about their providing assistance. The *Commonwealth Secretary* said that he fully accepted that the British Government's offer had not fully met the Malayan Government's requirements, but he hoped that Tun Razak would not lead the Tunku to expect that we could increase our offer beyond the level discussed. He did not think it would be helpful to give the Tunku the impression that there was now much elasticity in the amount of aid which could be provided. He had not yet sought the Chancellor of the Exchequer's approval to offer £15 m., but he was prepared to make out a case for improving upon the offer of £12.35 million which would be put to the Tunku. His personal view was that the Malayan Government might be advised to settle for £15 million and to rely upon approaches to other Governments to meet the gap in financing their defence programme. It would not, however, be useful to make such approaches until the amount of financial assistance to be given by the British Government had been financially decided. *Tan Siew Sin* said that he felt it necessary to repeat that the position about financing the defence programme had been made worse, since, as a result of the Brunei revolt and the Indonesian threat, it would not be possible to spread out expenditure evenly over a long period, but large sums would have to be spent immediately. The limited taxing powers of the Federal Government over the Borneo Territories (accepted on the British Government's advice) also made it much more necessary to have external assistance to finance the defence programme. The British Government's total offer—about £30 million including all forms of aid for Malaysia—fell far short of meeting the cost of the defence programme. The *Commonwealth Secretary* pointed out that it was to the Federal Government's advantage to have the Borneo Territories as willing members of Malaysia and that, if this could only have been achieved by coming to financial arrangements already agreed, that seemed a fair price to pay.

---

[1] On 10 May the Cabinet Defence Committee had authorised an upper limit of £12.5 million (see 173). On 14 May Sandys offered the Malayans £12.35 million but agreed to make a case for £15 million to the chancellor.

3. The *Minister of State* said that the offer of aid which we had originally had in mind had been revised in the light of the Brunei revolt. *Sir Henry Lintott*, referring to what Tan Siew Sin had said about the inadequacy of the British Government's offer, considered that the agreement to a review of their financial assistance after three years was important.

Press communique

4. The following points were agreed in considering the terms of a Press communique:—

(1) that it should not refer to the figures of financial assistance which had been discussed;
(2) that it should avoid giving the impression that there was an opportunity for much more bargaining about the proposals which had been discussed;
(3) that it should reiterate that the Anglo–Malayan Defence Agreement was to be extended to cover the whole of Malaysia;
(4) that it should indicate that certain proposals had been made in the discussions which were now to be referred to the Malayan and British Governments.

5. It was accepted that the Malayan delegation, in dealing with press enquiries about the discussions, might have to say that the offer of assistance made by the British Government did not meet the Malayan Government's requests.

6. The Commonwealth Secretary then had to leave the meeting and the Minister of State secured the meeting's approval to the attached communique.[2] It was agreed that this should be available to the press before Tun Razak held his Press Conference on the following day, 16th May.

---

[2] Not printed.

176 CAB 128/37, CC 34(63)8   23 May 1963
[Malaysia financial discussions]: Cabinet conclusions

[Chaired by R A Butler for this agenda item, a thinly-attended Cabinet heard a report from Sandys on the inconclusive Anglo–Malayan discussions and a statement of the Treasury view from the chief secretary, Boyd-Carpenter. Stalemate in London on the financial issue was matched locally by lack of progress in negotiations between the Tunku and the Sultan of Brunei, on the one hand, and, on the other, in the attempts by the Malayan and Singapore governments to resolve outstanding constitutional and economic questions. Consequently, on 27 May Lansdowne departed for Kuala Lumpur on a mission to arbitrate between the various parties.]

The Commonwealth Secretary said that the recent discussions with the Government of Malaya about the level of defence aid to be provided by the United Kingdom had been inconclusive. With the agreement of the Chief Secretary, Treasury, he had offered a contribution of £15 million towards the capital expenses of the Malayan defence programme up to 1996; but the Malayan Government had not accepted this offer, which they claimed was insufficient to enable them to provide for the defence of the Borneo Territories after their forthcoming incorporation in Malaysia. They were unwilling to contemplate the alternative course of curtailing their development programme; and the United Kingdom therefore faced the choice of either accepting a greater liability for the defence of Malaysia or offering more generous defence aid. The Malayan Prime Minister would probably expect to discuss the matter further with the Minister of State, Colonial Office, who would be visiting Malaya in the near future.

The Chief Secretary, Treasury, said that the offer of £15 million, which exceeded the £12½ million authorised by the Cabinet, covered the whole of the foreign exchange element in the Malayan defence programme so far as purchases to be made in the United Kingdom were concerned. The Malayan Government intended to spend a further £3 million on purchases of defence equipment from other countries; but there was no reason why the United Kingdom should assume this additional liability. Malaya was the richest country in South-East Asia; and any increase in our present offer of aid would be liable to have serious repercussions elsewhere, particularly in India.

In discussion it was suggested that it might become essential to offer some further measure of defence aid to Malaya. The military threat which would face Malaysia, on its creation, would be liable to be more grave than had been foreseen when the financial implications of this constitutional change had been first considered. Moreover, under present plans United Kingdom forces in Singapore would be reduced as a result of the transfer to the Government of Malaysia of responsibility for internal security; but, if the local forces were not built up to the necessary level, these reductions might not be secured. On the other hand, it would be premature to commit ourselves, without further consideration, to any specific amount of additional defence aid to be offered to Malaya; and, in so far as such aid might eventually be given, it might be desirable to consider how far it should be related to additional purchases in the United Kingdom.

The Cabinet:—
Invited the Commonwealth Secretary and the Chief Secretary, Treasury, to consider further, in the light of their discussion, the extent of any additional defence aid that might be offered to the Government of Malaya and to arrange for the Minister of State for Colonial Affairs, during his forthcoming visit to Malaya, to ascertain, without commitment, the scope for further negotiation with the Government of Malaya on this subject.[1]

---

[1] Later the same day Sandys wrote to Boyd-Carpenter suggesting either a little more defence aid directly connected with the raising of the Borneo battalions or development aid in North Borneo and Sarawak (over and above the £7.5 million already committed), possibly in the form of a £5 million Commonwealth assistance loan. Sandys Papers, 8/13, 23 May 1963.

177   CAB 134/2371, OP(63)11, annex A   29 May 1963
'Financial assistance for Malaysia': inward telegram no 929 from Sir G Tory to Mr Sandys, forwarding a message from Tunku Abdul Rahman to Mr Macmillan

[The Tunku ensured that Tory and Lansdowne (who had now arrived in Kuala Lumpur) were given a copy of his letter to Macmillan before he left for Tokyo on 30 May for a meeting with Sukarno (see 181, n 4 and 200, note). The signed version of the letter not only arrived in London later than this telegram but was also given the later date of 31 May (PREM 11/4348). In his next telegram, Lansdowne advised Sandys that the Malayans sought £30 million for the three years, 1963–1965, and he requested authority to raise the offer to a grant of £16 million plus a loan of £5 million. Although this fell far short of Malayan expectations, Lansdowne thought it had 'a chance of enabling us to reach a friendly settlement', particularly when other factors were taken into account such as the review promised for 1965, possible contributions from other Commonwealth countries and British commitments to development aid for North Borneo, Sarawak and Singapore (Lansdowne to Sandys, tel no 930, 30 May 1963, CAB 134/2371, OP(63)11 annex C). Ministers next discussed this question on 17 June, see 179 and 181.]

Following is text of letter which Tunku has sent today to the Prime Minister. *Begins*:

I am writing to you on the subject of financial assistance from the United Kingdom Government for Malaysia.

Recently my Deputy Prime Minister and Minister of Finance had talks with your colleagues in London on the subject of British financial aid for Malaysia. They unfortunately did not come to an agreement because the offer made by your Government fell far short of our requirements. I have no doubt that your colleagues have briefed you fully on the position. However I enclose herewith an *aide memoire* for your information.[1]

If I may put it briefly the new Federation will have to spend something of the order of dollars 430 to 460 million per annum on defence and internal security. Of this figure at least dollars 200 million is directly attributable to the four States of Singapore, Sarawak, North Borneo and Brunei. Over a 3-year period, i.e. 1963 to 1965 which is the period agreed upon as the period for which financial aid should be determined in the first instance (herein after referred to as 'the agreed period') the total figure directly attributable to the four newly joining States of Malaysia will therefore be approximately dollars 600 million or £70 million. Your Government has offered us a total of about £15 million for this 3-year period all of it in equipment which will be either obtained or purchased in Britain.

In the field of economic development the report of the Inter-Governmental Committee on Sarawak and North Borneo had specified a figure of dollars 100 million per annum as essential for the two territories.[2] Even if we take only two years of the agreed period viz 1964 and 1965 the amount required would be dollars 200 million or £23.3 million. The British Government has offered £1 and a half million per annum for 5 years as its contribution towards this total. For a 2-year period the British contribution would therefore be £3 million.

It will be seen that the needs of the newly joining territories of Malaysia in the sphere of defence, internal security and economic development in Sarawak and North Borneo would be £93.3 million for the agreed period against the total suggested British contribution of £18 million. The reason for this unusually large outlay on defence is that we are inheriting an emergency in these new territories particularly in Sarawak where there are growing indications of the Communist activities within the territory and in the Sarawak Indonesian border.

---

[1] Not printed.

[2] *Malaysia. Report of the Inter-Governmental Committee, 1962* (Cmnd 1954, Feb 1963); see also 141 and 146.

On the other hand the financial position of the present Federation of Malaya is much weaker than is generally believed and in the circumstances we can see no way of closing this gap from our own available resources. I should add that the assessment and figures given by me above have not been disputed by your Government. The only point at issue lies in the quantum of aid. Without the assurance of a reasonable amount of financial aid from the United Kingdom Government we would have no alternative but to ask you to continue and bear full financial responsibility for the defence forces of Sarawak and North Borneo even after Malaysia is formed or until such time as we are able to take over this responsibility ourselves. This would include the cost of maintaining the 2 infantry battalions which are now being raised there on our behalf and for which we have been asked to pay.

It will therefore be seen that Malaysia could be a grave financial liability to the existing Federation of Malaya. Our burden is aggravated further by the fact that whilst it is the intention that the level of Federal taxation in the Borneo States should be brought to the Federation of Malaya levels in graduated stages over a period of years political expediency would likely dictate that the taxation level could only be significantly raised when the result of greater expenditure is apparent. Our effort to carry out economic development on which our political stability largely depends would be severly jeopardise and Malaysia would have the end result of defeating the very objectives of political and economic stability which it was designed to establish.

In the circumstances I request Britain to give far greater aid during at least the first few critical years of the new nation's existence than she appears disposed to give at the moment. I would therefore be grateful if you could intervene personally and cause a reappraisal to be made of your present offer. *Ends.*

178   CO 1030/1505, no 40   30 May 1963
'Formal agreement relating to Malaysia': minute from Sir J Martin to Mr Sandys

[The formal agreement signed on 9 July would consist of eleven articles running to just over two printed pages plus eleven annexes totalling some 230 pages, see 192, note. In this minute Martin draws the secretary of state's attention to five key points in the draft agreement which require a further gloss here:

a) On the assumption that all three Borneo territories would join Malaysia, there had been discussion over whether North Borneo and Sarawak (not being sovereign) could be parties to the agreement, and whether Brunei should be. For their part, North Borneo and Sarawak did not wish the Sultan to be given undue prominence in the formal agreement. Although the British government was empowered by the 1959 treaty to act for the Sultan in external affairs, to do so would have been completely contrary to the frequently-made declaration that Brunei's entry into Malaysia was a matter for the Sultan's government. For similar, presentational reasons, it was vital that the leaders of indigenous peoples should be signatories for North Borneo and Sarawak.

b) While it was essential to avoid the impression that Malaysia was the product of Malayan expansionism, the British wished to establish Malaysia by amending the constitution of the Federation of Malaya rather than by creating a wholly new state. One reason for this was to escape the requirement of election to UN membership and thus reduce the risk of rejection by the international community. Instead, they hoped to get away with a simple notification of change of title and boundaries.

c) The FO was anxious not to weaken Britain's legal position in the dispute with the Philippines and had even suggested the retention of sovereignty in Borneo which, of course, would be impossible after Malaysia Day.

d) & e) Sandys had article 5 redrafted in order to avoid making British tenure of the Singapore bases directly dependent on the Malayan Defence Agreement and to safeguard Britain's right to dispose of surplus property in Singapore at the market rate. The issue of whether certain crown lands were surplus to military requirements and how they might be released to the government of Singapore government was settled on 7 July and the agreed scheme was adopted as annex F (not G as referred to here) to the final version of the formal agreement.]

Your approval is sought to transmit to the Malayan Government (and the other governments concerned) the attached draft Formal Agreement on Malaysia. A full explanatory note is also attached.[1] Briefly, the points of which you should be aware are:—

(a) The Sultan of Brunei is made a party to the main Agreement. Opinion in Borneo may not welcome this, but we can see no satisfactory way round. The important thing presentationally from the Borneo point of view is that their representatives will initial the Formal Agreement at a public ceremony. The actual signature will be by plenipotentiaries of the British, Malayan and Brunei Governments and will take place in relative obscurity (probably in Kuala Lumpur).

(b) Article I has been drafted to establish that Malaysia is in law an expansion of the present Federation, while at the same time it avoids wording which might make North Borneo, Sarawak and Singapore feel that they were being handed over to Malaya.

(c) Article I(1) of the draft refers to the establishment of Malaysia on 31st August 1963 or such other day as the two governments agree. There would be advantage in fixing the 31st August without qualification, but the Foreign Office feel that so long as there is a possibility of the Philippine Government obtaining an interim injunction from the International Court it is better to retain the flexible wording. I hope that, if it came to the pinch, Foreign Office Ministers would agree to disregard such an injunction. It would probably be better not to put the point to Foreign Office Ministers until the Law Officers' advice on the merits of the claim and the jurisdiction of the International Court, which is now being sought, has been received. For the time being I think we can accept the present wording.

(d) Article V deals with the extension to Malaysia of the Anglo–Malayan Defence Agreement. The Ministry of Defence, Commonwealth Relations Office and Foreign Office consider that it would be imprudent to elaborate on this wording, which reproduces that in the Joint Statement of November 1961, even though it does not cover all contingencies. The matter is described in more detail in paragraph 7 of the note. A submission is being made on this point to the Minister of Defence.

(e) Ministry of Defence, Treasury and Treasury Solicitor are anxious to safeguard our present rights in Singapore to dispose of surplus land at market value. The Colonial Office and C.R.O. would prefer to make no reference to this in the draft Agreement (it is dealt with at Annex G) and to negotiate the matter in parallel with the Malayans and Singapore. We do not want to run the risk of complicating the negotiation of the Formal Agreement by introducing what may be a contentious

---

[1] Not printed.

issue. The form of words in Annex G may well not be negotiable and the views of Sir Geofroy Tory and Lord Selkirk on the point are being sought. The Ministry of Defence recognise that we may have to drop the point. Subject, however, to any strong objections from Sir Geofroy Tory and Lord Selkirk I think we can acquiesce in the present draft.

179   CAB 134/2371, OP(63)11   11 June 1963
'Malaysia: British financial aid': memorandum by Mr Sandys for Cabinet Oversea Policy Committee

[The pressure upon the British government to cultivate Malayan goodwill by improving its financial offer was increasing since two sets of negotiations—between Malaya and Singapore, and between Malaya and Brunei—were in deadlock. Another disturbing development was the recent joint proposal of the foreign ministers of Indonesia, Malaysia and the Philippines to appoint an assessor charged with 'ascertaining' the wishes of the peoples of Singapore and the Borneo territories. One way out of his defence dilemma might have been for the Tunku to cut his costs by entering a confederation with Indonesia and the Philippines. Most British officials deplored such a suggestion, though some saw the case for encouraging a démarche which might enable Britain to reduce its defence commitments as a result of 'some accommodation between Malaysia and Indonesia (for both are Malay peoples) against their common Chinese enemy' (A L M Cary to Mr Butler, 14 June, PREM 11/4348).]

Existing British offer
Since the Chief Secretary and I last discussed with our colleagues, on 23rd May,[1] the question of British financial aid for Malaysian defence, the Tunku has sent to the Prime Minister a message (copy attached at Annex A)[2] requesting his personal intervention to secure a reappraisal of our latest offer. This was a contribution of £15 m. towards the capital expenses of the Malaysian defence expansion programme (details of which are in Annex A of D. (63) 18)[3] up to the end of 1965, with a review in that year. We also offered to pay certain costs of British seconded service personnel, a commitment estimated at about £3 m. In addition we have already offered assistance outside the Defence field which might total as much as £16 m. in loans and grants over the next five years. This (except for £3 m. representing the cost of the compensation scheme in the Borneo territories) broadly reflects what we should probably have spent had Malaysia not been contemplated. Details of non-military aid offered to Malaysia are attached at Annex B.[4]

2.   The £15 m. which we have already offered would cover all the defence orders which the Malayans propose to place in Britain, and also the buildings etc. in Malaya and Singapore which we have already agreed to transfer to the Malayans.

---

[1] See 176.   [2] See 177.
[3] D(63)18 has been printed without its annexes as document 173.
[4] Not printed. There were three non-military commitments: aid to Singapore; development aid to North Borneo and Sarawak; compensation for expatriate officers in North Borneo and Sarawak.

Malayan expectations

3. Although the Tunku's message contains no specific bid, there is good reason to think that the Malayans hope we shall give them about double what we have so far offered for Defence.

Lord Landowne's recommendations

4. My colleagues asked me to arrange for Lord Lansdowne, during his recent visit to Malaya, to ascertain, without commitment, the scope for further negotiation with the Government of Malaya on this subject. He reported (Kuala Lumpur telegram No. 930 attached at Annex C[5]) that he believed that an obvious attempt by us to get away with the minimum will only provoke lack of confidence and illwill in the States concerned, and will call our resolution in question not only by the enemies of Malaysia, but also by those who we hope will support it. He did not recommend that we should go to the length which the Malayans wanted, but he was convinced that an appreciable addition to our present offer is necessary to help Malaysia through its difficult early years. He recommended that our further assistance should take the form of aid over the raising of the two extra battalions which are planned in Borneo, and a Section 3 loan for development in Borneo.

5. I agree with Lord Lansdowne's assessment, and in general accept his recommendations, although it will be seen from paragraph 7 below that I propose a different formula for assistance in financing the Borneo Battalions from that which he has suggested. There are still a number of difficult hurdles to be surmounted in the very near future if Malaysia is to be achieved by 31st August, notably in the Malayans' negotiations with Singapore and Brunei. Against this background, it is in my view, urgently necessary to return a quick and forthcoming reply to the Tunku.

Borneo battalions

6. The Tunku's most telling argument in favour of a greater British contribution is the extra cost of what he chooses to call the Borneo emergency. It is certainly in our interest, as the Malayans are well aware, to ensure that they are able to take over our existing responsibilities for internal security in the Borneo territories as well as in Singapore after Malaysia. Otherwise we shall be left with a most uncomfortable commitment, unprecedented in an independent country, for an indefinite period. We are having, in any case, to plan on the assumption that British forces will be required in support of Malaysian security forces in Borneo until the end of 1965. If this situation is not to be further prolonged, the Malayans must be enabled to raise the multi-racial battalions which they want in Borneo but which they now say they cannot afford.

7. Part of the cost of equipping these battalions is already covered by our £15 m. offer. The remaining costs, which are so much worrying the Malayans, are almost wholly local. Nevertheless, I recommend that we should, in this special case, increase our present offer by agreeing to pay the cost of raising, training and equipping these units ourselves on behalf of the Malaysian Government, meeting all costs for two years, except for the cost of permanent accommodation in Borneo. In practice these units would largely be under training by our own forces in Malaya during this period.

---

[5] Not printed, but see document 177, note.

8.   The extra cost to us of such an arrangement would, I understand, be unlikely to exceed £1½ m., i.e. the current costs of training and maintenance for two years. The cost of initial equipment is estimated at £½ m. but this is largely covered already in our present £15 m. offer. (These costs account for £2 m. of the £3½ m. referred to in paragraph 5 of Lord Lansdowne's telegram as the total cost of raising the Borneo Battalions; the remaining £1½ m. represents the capital cost of permanent accommodation, which need not fall within the period 1963–65). However, we could hope to gain more credit with the Malayans by avoiding putting a monetary value on our offer.

Development in Borneo Territories
9.   In addition to the argument in paragraph 6 above, the Tunku has drawn attention in his message to what he regards as the low level of British assistance towards development in Borneo. The development programmes of North Borneo and Sarawak over the next five years provide for expenditure totalling £58.4 m. towards which we have already promised a £7.5 m. grant. The probable sources are as follows:—

British grant	£7.5
British technical assistance, say	1.4
Federal assistance/expenditure (based on an indication given last year of what they would try to make available)	11.5
Local budgetary sources including reserves	23.5
Loans (local and external)	7.5
Total	51.4

£7 m. remains therefore to be found, or the programmes will remain 12 per cent uncompleted.
10.   The Federation are committed to supporting a programme of this order, and they have sold the Malaysia concept to the Borneo Territories largely by the promise of greatly enhanced development. It is important that their promises should be translated into performance, and that there should be the least possible friction over development finance between the new States and the Federal Government during the early years of Malaysia.
11.   Although Singapore is likely to offer substantial assistance to Borneo development, the Federation is going to have great difficulty in finding the money to enable the £51.4 m. programme to be carried out.

12.   *Recommendations*
What I recommend, therefore, is that in replying to the Tunku we should offer the following further assistance.

(i) *Borneo battalions.* We should undertake to make a free gift of the following items in the Malaysian defence expansion programme in so far as it is implemented in the three years 1963–65 inclusive:—

(a) All the arms and equipment etc. to be supplied from British sources.

(b) All the buildings and facilities which we have undertaken to make available in Singapore and Malaya.

(c) The extra cost of Service seconded personnel in the scheme already offered to the Malayans.

(d) The whole cost of raising, equipping and training the two Borneo battalions (but not their permanent accommodation in Borneo).

The cost of (a) and (b) would be approximately £15 m., and the cost of (c) about £3 m.; they are in fact our existing offer, and these figures could be announced. The extra cost of (d) would probably not exceed £1½ m. but this figure should not be revealed, at least for the present.

(ii) *Development loan.* In addition, as recommended by Lord Lansdowne, we should offer to make available a loan of up to £5 m. for development in Borneo. Although the import content of the Development Plans of the territories has not yet been fully worked out, I understand that there is a good prospect that a Section 3 loan (tied to British goods and services) could be used.

13. I invite my colleagues' concurrence in these recommendations.

180 CAB 131/28, D(63)19   14 June 1963
'Future defence policy': note by Sir B Trend for Cabinet Defence Committee. *Annex:* **'Future defence policy', memorandum by Sir B Trend, 14 June**   **[Extract]**

[Trend's memorandum was followed by papers from Thorneycroft (D(63)20, 14 June), Maudling (D(63)21, 17 June) and Home (D(63)22, 17 June). Thorneycoft's 'broad view' was that Britain's military role should be: '(1) Taking a proper share in the defence of Western Europe. (2) Providing what is necessary for defence of our own overseas territories. (3) Providing for some assistance to our friends and allies as far as we can afford it.' He pointed out, however, that defence costs were rising faster than the GNP. Maudling was 'sure that it is not realistic to form our defence plans for the next 5–10 years on a scale of resources which cannot be comfortably accommodated within a rate of growth of GNP on which we can prudently rely, year by year'. He warned: 'If we try to persuade ourselves that we can do more, all that will happen is that there will be more economic failure—and we all know that this does much more harm to our international position and influence than any technical weakness in defence.' While Home recognised the need to 'set some limit' to defence expenditure, he warned against being dogmatic on the exact percentage of the GNP to be allocated to defence and reminded his colleagues that they had rejected the idea of choosing between Europe and a world role: 'We have world wide interests and must therefore have available a world wide presence to protect them. Our recent commitments to India and Malaysia are cases in point.' Although he found it 'hard to conceive any foreseeable circumstances in which we should, in the 1970's, and entirely on our own, want to land forces in the Middle East or Far East against entrenched opposition', he argued that reduction of 'our forces in the Middle or Far East in an attempt to anticipate events' would 'encourage our enemies, dismay our allies and precipitate the disorder we are anxious to avoid'. The Defence Committee considered all these papers on 19 June and, as regards the Far East, concluded that commitments to Malaysia meant that there could be no question of an early or major withdrawal from Singapore during the remainder of the 1960s. Macmillan, however, felt that reliance on British forces in the defence of Malaysia might be mitigated by drawing further on the support of Australia and New Zealand and also by negotiating a political understanding with Indonesia (CAB 131/28, D(63)8th meeting.]

By direction of the Prime Minister I circulate the attached memorandum on Future Defence Policy.

This memorandum has been prepared as the result of discussions which I have had with the Permanent Secretaries of the Departments mainly concerned and of the Chief of the Defence Staff, in the light of the decision of the Committee at their meeting on 9th February, 1963 (D. (63) 3rd Meeting). But, while it takes account of points which have been raised during those discussions, it does not commit any Department and has been prepared simply as a basis for Ministerial discussion of some of the main issues involved.

Annex to 180

The cost of defence

1.   At their meeting at Chequers on 9th February (D.(63) 3rd Meeting)[1] the Defence Committee agreed that defence expenditure should, if possible, be contained within a limit of 7 per cent of the Gross National Product (G.N.P.); and, in order to test the realism of this hypothesis, they commissioned studies on:—

(i) the cost of maintaining our base at Aden in relation to the value and importance of the interests which it is designed to protect;
(ii) the political and economic consequences of a withdrawal or substantial reduction of the forces at present deployed in the Far East, particularly at Hong Kong and Singapore.

2.   Since the discussion at Chequers, the revised forward costings for defence have become available. These indicate that defence expenditure in 1965–66 will exceed the target for that year (agreed by the Defence Committee in April 1962 at £1,850 million) by about £170 million at current prices. Beyond that date the forecast is speculative; but the costings suggest that, by 1970, expenditure may rise to a level between £2,200–£2,400 million (again at 1963 prices). These figures assume that present strategy and weapons programmes continue unchanged; but they make no allowance for any new defence programmes—e.g. participation in a mixed-manned NATO nuclear force or the development of a space capability, even if only for purposes of military reconnaissance and communications. Even without these potential additions, however, the lowest of the two figures for 1970 would be likely to be well above 7 per cent of G.N.P. on any reasonable estimate of the way in which things are likely to develop.

3.   In the light of the prospect disclosed by the forward costings we have thought it best to translate the Defence Committee's original remit into a rather wider enquiry, extending over the whole range of defence expenditure, in an attempt to ascertain where we should seek to secure economies if the total outlay is not to exceed 7 per cent of G.N.P.

4.   Any enquiry of this kind raises both military and political issues; and,

---

[1] See 166, note.

although these can be discussed separately, they are closely connected. Geographically, our capability in one theatre reinforces, and is reinforced by, our capability in other theatres; and the weapons systems in any one theatre are themselves interdependent. Any economy must therefore be considered in terms of its indirect, as well as its direct, consequences. Moreover, we have always sought hitherto to maintain balanced forces—i.e. forces which are reasonably self-contained and are capable, if necessary, of some degree of independent action. Insofar as we have succeeded in this purpose, any substantial economy which we may effect may result in 'unbalancing' our forces and may therefore reduce disproportionately our ability to intervene, single-handed, in certain types of situation in which we regard our interests as threatened. This capacity for independent action lies near the root of the problem of the cost of defence; and the possibility of effecting defence economies on any significant scale depends largely on our willingness to forego it to a greater extent than at present.

5.   There is one further dilemma—of timescale. A precipitate withdrawal, from any of our positions overseas, would be liable to increase the danger of attack; and it would certainly undermine the confidence of our allies. It would inevitably be some time, therefore, before the effect of any economies decided now could become apparent. Nevertheless, unless they are decided now and implemented gradually thereafter and unless we are prepared to accept the additional risks which will inevitably arise during this period in which our forces are being run down, it will be too late to effect any worthwhile saving.

The military choice

6.   In terms of forces and weapons systems, the scope for substantial economies appears to be confined to:—

(a) the Polaris programme;
(b) Army man-power, primarily in Germany;
(c) the TSR.2, i.e. the replacement for the Canberra;
(d) the naval carrier programme, with which is linked the P.1154, i.e. the replacement of the R.A.F's Hunter and the Fleet Air Arm's Sea Vixen.

In practice even this limited range of choice may not really be open to us. . . .

The political choice

7.   An alternative approach to the problems outlined above would analyse them by reference not to the weapons systems involved but to the political and geographical assumptions on which any military strategy must rest. From this point of view, there are two ways of seeking economies in our defence expenditure:—

(a) We could reduce our forces without purporting to disavow any of our obligations or to abandon any of our interests.
(b) We could explicitly shed our obligations and interests in some parts of the world and tailor our defence effort accordingly.

8.   The first course is hardly practicable. We could not conceal for long the reduction in our military strength; and the implications of a decision to this effect— in terms of orders cancelled or not placed and troops withdrawn or not reinforced—

would become evident, to both our friends and our enemies, relatively quickly. If we claimed to be able still to protect interests that we could no longer in fact defend, we should merely invite the attack which our defence policy must be designed to avert. We must not create a vacuum without arranging for it to be filled by some other means.

9.   If we adopt the second course and seek, by the exercise of a deliberate choice, to eliminate some of our obligations and to reduce some of our existing military capacity to safeguard our interests, we are bound to assume—for the reasons briefly indicated above—that we cannot afford, politically, to curtail our effort in Europe. The field of possible economy is therefore limited to the Middle East and the Far East. What are our main interests in those areas? And how far is it realistic to assume that a continuation of our present strategy will suffice to protect them, and to enable us to discharge obligations related to them, in the political circumstances which may have developed by the mid 1970s?

The Middle East
    10.   Here our interests are:—

(a) to ensure the maintenance of our oil supplies on favourable terms by defending the independence of the rulers of the oil states, particularly Kuwait;
(b) to contain the southward expansion of the Soviet Union by our participation in CENTO and by our support for Iran; and to continue to support Jordan.
(c) to protect, so far as possible the white populations in Africa, particularly in Kenya and Rhodesia; and to discharge our commitments to the High Commission Territories.
(d) to keep open if possible, the direct sea route to the Far East. . . .

14. Nevertheless, it would be wise to contemplate the possibility that we may not be able to retain our base at Aden indefinitely; that, even if we do retain it, we may find ourselves debarred by local political circumstances from using it effectively for the purposes for which it was designed, i.e. mainly the defence of our interests in the Gulf; and that, in any event, we may be unable for more than a relatively short time to support the continued existence of the Gulf sheikhdoms against the rising force of Arab nationalism. A military policy which has to be planned five-ten years ahead must take account of these possible political developments during the same period. But are they only possible? Or are they probable? And, if the latter, what changes in our strategic policy do they suggest?

The Far East
    15.   Here our interests are:—

(a) To contain the expansion of Communism (Chinese as well as Russian), particularly in relation to India, Pakistan and Malaysia, partly by participating in SEATO and partly by retaining the capability to take independent military action, if necessary. Essentially, such action would consist, in the Far East as in the Middle East, of landing troops in the face of opposition, probably in the Malaysia/Indonesia theatre.

(b) To maintain our links with Australia and New Zealand and to contribute to their defence.

(c) To secure a stable and independent Malaysia.

(d) To protect Hong Kong and our Pacific colonies.

16.   The cost of the military effort involved is of the order of £300 million a year, which is likely to rise by 1970 to £400 million. Here, as in the Middle East, it would be unrealistic and misleading to try to measure this expenditure quantitatively against the value of the interests which it is designed to protect. But it is relevant that, although those interests comprise, as in the Middle East, a wide range of commercial connections, they do not include any single economic interest of the same importance as the oil of the Middle East. Our expenditure in the Far East, at a level more than twice that of our expenditure in the Middle East, is therefore devoted primarily to maintaining a politico-military position, based on Singapore.

17.   The consequences of withdrawing from that position, or of reducing our expenditure on maintaining it, cannot be forecast in any detail. But they can be summed up in the single word 'instability', with all that that might imply for the future of Malaysia, and the older members of the Commonwealth. Against this imponderable risk, however, we have to set the same doubt as applied to Aden. We are thinking in terms of the 1970's, some ten years ahead. Can we assume that at that date we shall still be able not only to hold and to control Singapore but also to use it as a base from which to conduct military operations anywhere in the Far East? And can we assume—again, looking ten years ahead—that we shall still need, and be able, to land a brigade group in the Far East in the face of opposition? . . .

20.   . . . But the issues involved are, in fact, both political and military simultaneously; and any questions which attempt to reflect this fact are bound to appear to do less than justice to arguments that can properly be advanced from the point of view of individual Departments—if only because they must try to address themselves to the one central issue, i.e. the future military role of the United Kingdom in world affairs. It is this issue which we must seek to clarify first,—not the individual questions, which it would be premature, in some cases, to try to answer without further examination of the alternative policies or alternative weapons systems which we might adopt.

21.   The central issue can perhaps be summarised thus. So long as we try to discharge the full range of our existing commitments, by means of a strategic policy which includes maintaining some degree of single-handed and independent military capability, there appears to be no escape from the fact that the defence budget will absorb more than 7 per cent of the G.N.P.—and, indeed, that, in the light of the increasing cost of sophisticated weapons system and the associated programmes of research and development, the excess over 7 per cent will itself continue to rise. There is no means of significantly arresting this process without reducing our capabilities to some extent; and a reduction in capabilities implies abandoning some options, without which some types of operation cannot be mounted. Which options, if any, should we abandon?

181   CAB 134/2371, OP(63)6th meeting   17 June 1963
'Malaysia: British financial aid': Cabinet Oversea Policy Committee minutes[1]

The Committee had before them a memorandum by the Commonwealth Secretary (O.P.(63) 11) on British financial aid for Malaysia.[2]

The Commonwealth Secretary said that on 29th May the Prime Minister of Malaya had written to the Prime Minister asking for his personal intervention to secure an increase in the aid which the United Kingdom had previously offered to Malaysia.[3] The negotiations for setting up Malaysia were entering a critical phase and it was still possible that the Prime Minister of Malaya, Tunku Abdul Rahman, might abandon the attempt to establish it by 31st August; this in turn might involve the progressive abandonment of the whole project. The Tunku was known to have discussed alternative solutions with President Sukarno at their recent meeting.[4] The Malayans were particularly concerned with the cost of defence and development of the Borneo Territories, where it was greatly in the British interest that they should relieve us of our defence responsibilities as soon as possible. For this purpose, it would be necessary for the Malayans to raise, equip and train two Borneo battalions. Part of the cost of equipping these battalions was already covered by our offer of £15 million for the equipment of the Malayan forces. The additional cost of raising, training and maintaining the Borneo battalions until the end of 1965 would be unlikely to exceed a further £1½ million. The Tunku had also drawn the Prime Minister's attention to the low level of British assistance towards development in Borneo. Although it was hoped that Singapore would provide a substantial sum of money for this purpose, there was some doubt whether it would be as much as the Malayans expected and the Federation would have great difficulty in finding elsewhere the money for their present ambitious programme. On his return from a recent visit to Malaya the Minister of State for Colonial Affairs had recommended that the United Kingdom should offer a loan, tied to British goods and services, of up to £5 million for development in Borneo.

The following points were made in discussion:—

(a) £1½ million was not an excessive extra sum to pay if it enabled the Malayans to take over present United Kingdom defence responsibilities in Borneo. However, for tactical reasons it would be unwise to make this further offer until the Malayan Government had come forward with a total figure of their own on which further negotiations could be based.

---

[1] The meeting was chaired by Butler and attended by Home, Maudling, Sandys, Boyd-Carpenter, Lansdowne, and James Ramsden (parliamentary undersecretary and financial secretary, War Office).
[2] See 179.   [3] See 177.
[4] While in Tokyo (31 May–1 June) Sukarno had asked the Tunku whether 31 Aug could be varied or postponed as the date for Malaysia Day. The Tunku had replied that change would be undesirable to which Sukarno was not reported to have objected. They issued a joint statement and reaffirmed a desire to settle differences and to meet together with Macapagal in Manila. But alternative proposals, such as the appointment of an assessor of Borneo opinion, were revealed at the tripartite meeting of foreign ministers in Manila, 7–11 June, when the agenda for a meeting of heads of government acquired a firmer shape, see 200, note.

(b) It would be necessary to avoid at this stage any commitment beyond the end of 1965 when the Defence Aid Programme was to be reviewed.

(c) It was not envisaged that the United Kingdom should incur any expenditure on the provision of accommodation for the Borneo battalions.

(d) It was unfortunate that the British team which had advised the Malayan Government on their defence programme should have recommended the purchase of foreign military equipment, including aircraft.

(e) The cost of raising, training and equipping the Borneo battalions would be considered as part of the aid programme and would not fall on Defence Votes.

The Committee:—

Took note, with approval, of the statement by the Commonwealth Secretary and invited him to resume negotiations with the Malayan Government on the lines set out in O.P. (63) 11 and in the light of their discussion.

182   DO 169/221, no 2   19 June 1963
[Deadlock in Malaya's negotiations with Singapore and Brunei]: inward telegram no 1095 from Lord Selkirk to Mr Sandys

[Frustrated by the stalemate in negotiations, the Tunku decided to issue ultimatums to Singapore (see 183) and Brunei. The Sultan took offence and left Kuala Lumpur on 21 June. Lee replied moderately (see 185) but the following matters remained unresolved: Singapore's request for a Malaysian common market; the apportionment of federal revenues arising in Singapore; control of broadcasting and television in Singapore; financial assistance by Singapore to the Borneo territories. Sandys decided to intervene and invited both heads of government for arbitration in London (see 184). Lee agreed and left for London on 25 June. A Malayan delegation also departed for London on 25 June and was led by Tun Razak, Tan Siew Sin and Dr Lim Swee Aun (minister of Commerce). The Sultan followed a few days later. Nevertheless, the Tunku insisted that only North Borneo and Sarawak would be in a position to join Malaysia by 31 Aug and informed Macmillan that the Malayan delegation would be coming to London only in order to discuss terms for the later entry of Singapore and Brunei (see 186).]

With Tory I saw Tunku, Razak and Tan Siew Sin, who attended Malay [sic] Cabinet today which had resolved with firm determination to bring to a close the prolonged and irritating negotiations with Lee Kuan Yew and the Sultan of Brunei whom Tunku described respectively as a snake and an old woman.

2.   The Cabinet decided to present ultimatums both to Singapore and Brunei. I persuaded him to defer the one to Brunei until I had had a further talk with Sultan.

3.   Tunku intimated that he would be requesting the agreement of H.M.G. to proceed with Malaysia on a basis of Sarawak and North Borneo only, and it is his firm belief that both Singapore and Brunei would be asking to come in in a matter of months. I told him that I did not believe that this was the case, and that Lee would go back to Singapore and stir up as much trouble as he could and possibly put himself at the head of a United Socialist front.

4.   Tunku however was adamant and he said in his opinion both territories would come to heel in the not too distant future. He would of course be very willing to come to London if necessary with Lee Kuan Yew at Mr. Macmillan's invitation. I believe it would also be the wish of the Sultan of Brunei to come too. It is possible

that press statements on the at least partial collapse of Malaysia may be expected shortly.

5. The points at issue are trivial in the case of Brunei and in the case of Singapore Federation are choosing in the Common Market a bad subject on which to present an ultimatum. Singapore proposals are basically sensible. But the Federation refuse to consider enshrining them in the Constitution and insist on giving the Rueff Report a very much slower examination.

6. My telegram No. 1094 contains gist of announcement by Tunku.

183 CO 1030/1515, no 3   20 June 1963
[Financial arrangements for merger with Singapore]: letter from Tunku Abdul Rahman to Lee Kuan Yew, making a final offer on terms

The Cabinet at its meeting this morning agreed to offer the following terms to Singapore:—

'(1) The two Governments having agreed in principle to the establishment of a common market, an advisory Tariff Board will be established by Malaysia Day under a Chairman to be nominated jointly by the two Governments. The Chairman is to be appointed as early as possible and official discussion on the terms of the common market will commence under his chairmanship.

(2) Authority in respect of the collection of Customs and Excise duties and income tax in Singapore will be conferred upon the Singapore Government in accordance with Article 80(4) of the Federal Constitution subject to the reservation of certain powers specified in the Annexure to the Federal Government. This authority will not extend to customs duties and other charges collected in Singapore on goods exported from or to be imported into Malaysia outside Singapore.

(3)(a) All taxes collected in Singapore, other than those specified below, will be paid into a separate fund and the fund would be divided annually between the two Governments, or more frequently by agreement between the two Governments in the proportion of 60% to the Singapore Government and 40% to the Federal Government:—

(i) taxes specified in Part III of the Tenth Schedule to the Federal Constitution;

(ii) customs duties and other charges collected in Singapore on goods exported from or to be imported into Malaysia outside Singapore;

(iii) income tax collected in Singapore and attributable to income derived from the Federation of Malaya; such tax will be paid into the Treasury of the Federal Government.

(b) Income Tax attributable to income derived from Singapore and collected in the Federation of Malaya; with respect to such tax 40% should be retained by the Federal Government and 60% should be paid into the Treasury of the Singapore Government.

(c) Income tax attributable to income derived from Singapore and collected by an Agent in the United Kingdom; such tax, upon receipt in Singapore, will be paid into the separate fund referred to in (a) above.

(d) When Part VII of the Federal Constitution is applied to any Borneo State the application of sub-head (a)(iii) and sub-head (b) shall be extended as if for references to the Federation of Malaya there were included references to that State.

(4) The Singapore Government will pay to the Federal Government the cost of capital development of Federal projects in Singapore other than projects for Defence and Internal Security.

(5) The Singapore Government will make available to the Federal Government by way of grant during the first five years of Malaysia, a sum of $50 million for development expenditure of the underdeveloped states of Malaysia.

(6) The financial arrangements specified in paragraphs (1) to (4) above will come into operation on the 1st September, 1963, and will be subject to review by agreement in respect of the period commencing 1st January, 1965, and thereafter in respect of each subsequent period of two years. In default of agreement, review will be by an independent assessor appointed jointly by the two Governments and his recommendations will be binding on both.'

2. The Annexure referred to above is attached herewith.[1]

3. I am to inform you and your Government that these represent our final terms and the Federation Government will not find itself able to make any further concessions. Therefore, I hope to have your reply within the next 48 hours. In case you are unable to accept them within the period specified above, our Government would feel free to withdraw these terms.

4. Finally, I should add that Cabinet has considered the whole question carefully and has come to the conclusion that it cannot go beyond what was offered on 4th June last, as our Government has been very generous in the terms offered to you in an endeavour to reach agreement. In regard to the proposed grant of $50 million for development expenditure of the underdeveloped states of Malaysia for five years I wish to emphasise that this sum is an extremely small contribution on the part of a State having the financial strength of Singapore, and bearing in mind, as stated by the World Bank, that 'even allowing for increased taxation and also for domestic borrowing possibilities, the further slide in rubber prices assumed here may mean a gap during 1963–1965 between spending requirements and domestic resources of $900 or $1,000 million, above and beyond funds which may be expected for special defence financing and private foreign investment'.

5. I hope you will be able to accept these terms so that Singapore can come into Malaysia on 31st August next.

---

[1] Not printed.

184 DO 169/221, ff 4–5   21 June 1963

[Deadlock in Malaya's negotiations with Singapore and with Brunei]: minute from D F Milton to A A Golds, recording a meeting held by Mr Sandys on 21 June[1]

The Secretary of State held a meeting this morning to discuss what action should be taken on Kuala Lumpur telegram No. 1102, reporting that there would be almost certain deadlock in the Malaysia negotiations and suggesting that the Tunku and Mr. Lee Kwan Kew should be invited to London in order to seek to resolve it.

The Secretary of State thought that if it was not possible to bring about agreement between Malaya and Singapore, three alternative courses would present themselves; to force Singapore to join Malaysia against its will, to abandon the Malaysia project, and to allow North Borneo and Sarawak to join a reduced Malaysia, leaving the door open to subsequent membership by Singapore. The Secretary of State thought it would probably be necessary to threaten the Tunku with separate independence for Singapore and it was agreed that this might force the Tunku to reach agreement with Singapore since without her the Malaya Defence Agreement would not continue for long and our free use of the Singapore base would soon be put in jeopardy.

If we decide to abandon Malaysia or to allow it to be formed without Singapore, it was pointed out that we should have to consult the North Borneo territories since they had now come to expect that Malaysia would be formed and that Singapore would form part of it. At the same time it was also pointed out that it would still be to our advantage to have North Borneo and Sarawak (if the outcome of the forthcoming elections confirmed that she would still be a starter) join Malaysia since it would be increasingly difficult to deal with Indonesian subversion, especially if we were unable to retain our base in Singapore.

There was, however, some slight evidence that the Tunku was possibly thinking that if he developed more friendly relations with Indonesia that would serve him better in combating the Chinese influence in Singapore than would the establishment of Malaysia.

As a result of discussion the Secretary of State directed that the Department should work out what we should do in the event of various situations arising e.g. that there was a Sarawak Government opposed to joining Malaysia, that Sarawak and North Borneo only would join Malaysia (either 31st August or later), that there was an immediate demand for independence by Singapore etc. He also wanted reconsidered the question of whether we should force Singapore and possibly Sarawak to join Malaysia against their wishes especially if the points in their disagreement were very slight. After the Secretary of State had spoken to Mr. Bligh (Admiralty House)[2] it was agreed that a telegram should be sent to the High Commissioner in Kuala Lumpur asking him on behalf of the Secretary of State and

---

[1] This minute by D F Milton, assistant private secretary to Sandys 1962–1964, is quoted at some length in Lee Kuan Yew's *Memoirs*, p 479. Lee was not privy to this internal departmental document in 1963 but was provided with PRO material by the research team assisting the preparation of his memoirs.

[2] T J (later Sir Timothy) Bligh, one of the prime minister's private secretaries.

the Prime Minister to invite the Tunku to visit London in order to resolve the disagreement between Malaya and Singapore. It should be made clear to the Tunku that we were not prepared to see him on the basis that Malaysia should be formed without Singapore and he should be told that we would also invite Mr. Lee to London. The Tunku should also be told that we should want to invite the Sultan of Brunei to London but that he should arrive a few days after the Tunku. The Tunku should also be asked to bring Tun Razak with him. The High Commissioner should be asked to speak immediately to the Tunku in this sense provided that the situation reported in his telegram No. 1102 had not changed. (It was noted that Mr. Lee Kwan Yew had today said in public that the establishment of Malaysia without Singapore was unthinkable).

It was agreed that no further action should be taken on the question of defence aid for Malaysia until the Tunku's visit when it would be desirable to try to find out more exactly what the Malayans wanted.

185   CO 1030/1515, no 4   22 June 1963
[Financial arrangements for merger with Malaya]: letter from Lee Kuan Yew to Tunku Abdul Rahman. *Enclosure*: 'Paragraph to paragraph reply [to] federation government's proposals'

I discussed the letter of the Federation Government dated 20th June[1] with my colleagues on my return to Singapore on the 21st June. We met again today the 22nd, and carefully considered again all the points made in the letter.

I append hereto a reply to the six proposals made in the first paragraph of the letter.

As a government my colleagues and I feel obliged to make a detailed reply to each point. But in my personal capacity I would like to add that so little divides us. We are in broad agreement with you on all the major points. Only the details remain to be resolved and spelt out. The percentage is not important because as the Federation Cabinet has stated, there will be periodic reviews and no doubt justice will be done in the reviews.

It is very difficult for any Prime Minister elected by the people of Singapore, to explain how we are to give away $50 million to the Federal Government, when the Federation Government in the Inter-Governmental Committee Report for North Borneo and Sarawak has made no such commitment for themselves as stated in paragraphs 10 and 11. The Federation Government with much larger resources have not promised any grants for development expenditure. But it is only fair that we should be prepared to assist in the development of Malaysia. And loans from Singapore for North Borneo and Sarawak's development up to $150 million will give a greater impetus on their economic growth.

Singapore being what it is, a little island of thrifty workers, shop-keepers and merchants, my colleagues and I would find ourselves in an invidious position if I committed Singapore in Malaysia without constitutional safeguards embodying the terms for a common market in return for which we have agreed to give 39% of our

---

[1] See 183.

national taxes. I am sure that with good faith on both sides, as there has been for so long, we can reduce the Rueff Recommendations to simple forms, and present them as a complete whole before 31st August.[2]

I am sure the important thing to remember is that our enemies are the Communists, the abiding source of mischief, and that these small differences will be forgotten as we combine forces to keep Singapore stable, secure and prosperous, in a happy and peaceful Malaysia.

Two to three years after Malaysia, when unity has been established, and men's minds focussed on the broader horizons of a bigger nation, all these present problems will be dwarfed into insignificance as we forge ahead, united and free, to higher goals which Malaysia's enormous human and natural resources make possible for all of us.

Enclosure to 185

1. The Singapore Government welcomes the decision of the Federation Government in agreeing to the establishment of a Common Market and an Advisory Tariff Board by Malaysia Day under a Chairman to be nominated jointly by the two Governments. However, in order to allay the anxiety of the Government and the fears of the people of Singapore about the future of the entrepot trade, it is felt that constitutional amendments consequential upon Malaysia should embody agreements covering the establishment of a Common Market and the powers and functions of a Tariff Board. A proposed first draft of such agreements, based mainly on the Rueff recommendations, is attached at Annex A.[3] It is proposed that officials from both Governments should immediately examine this draft and complete their work in time for it to be promulgated together with the constitution on the 31st August, 1963. Copies of this draft have been made available to the Federation since 18th June.

2. The Singapore Government agrees in principle with the proposal to delegate authority in respect of the collection of Customs and Excise duty and Income Tax to the Singapore Government in accordance with Article 80(4) of the Federal Constitution. However, this delegation of authority should be stated in the Constitution that such delegation of authority shall not be revocable except by mutual agreement. The details in the annexures attached to the proposals of the Federation Government could be discussed and agreed by the official teams.

3. (a) The Singapore Government working on papers submitted to the Inter-Governmental Committee has arrived at a figure of 34.3% of 1964 estimated yield of national taxes as adequate to cover the cost of Federal Services in Singapore and inside and outside of Malaysia. In the computations enclosed in the letter TRY.Y. 9041/111 of 6.6.63, the Federation has arrived at an estimate of 40.4%. The position can be summarised as follows:—

---

[2] For the appointment of the Rueff mission, see 143, n 4. Rueff recommended a common market but Malaya feared competition from Singapore. Eventually a common market was agreed subject to safeguards and concessions on aid to the Borneo territories, see 191. See also IBRD, *Report on the Economic Aspects of Malaysia* (Kuala Lumpur, July 1963).

[3] Not printed.

	Singapore Estimates	Federation Estimates
1964 Yield of National taxes	$311.6 m	$303.6 m
Expenditure		
Defence & Internal Security	75.0	75.0
External Affairs, Parliament, etc.	5.0	7.5
Federal Departments in Singapore	36.9	50.0
	$116.9 m	$132.5 m
Less Currency Profits	10.0	10.0
	$106.9 m	$122.5 m
	34.3%	40.4%

(b) The Singapore Government's view is that estimated expenditure on Defence and Internal Security is unlikely to be realised in practice. The figure of $75 million is based on two assumptions, an annually recurrent expenditure of $57 million and a development expenditure of $18 million. These figures are based on an expansion programme of the Malaysian armed forces and the police which is estimated to attain the following targets:—

Defence—recurrent	$176.6 m in 1964 rising to
	$224.9 m in 1970
Defence—capital	$328.4 m for 4 years
Internal Security— recurrent	$149.4 m in 1963 rising to $164.0 m in 1967
Internal Security— capital	$97.5 m for 4 years.

These figures are estimates submitted by the Federation Government to the Inter-Governmental Committee[4] on the 18th March, 1963. The figure of $75 million has been accepted by the Singapore Government as its share of the expenditure should this sum be actually spent and subject also to deduction for British Defence contributions. This has been agreed as subject to subsequent review provided for in paragraph (6) of the Federation Government letter of 20th June, 1963 so any errors or omissions on either side can be corrected at the end of the 1st, 3rd and 5th years, as originally proposed by the Federation Government.

(c) As regards the other major item of expenditure on Federal Departments in Singapore, the Federation estimate of $50 million, we believe is an over-estimate. This, however, can be looked after in the review.

(d) As the matter stood before the 11th June, 1963, there is a difference of some 6% between the estimates of the Singapore and Federation Governments. The Singapore

---

[4] ie, a committee of representatives from the Malayan and Singapore governments, not to be confused with Lansdowne's Inter-Governmental Committee on North Borneo and Sarawak that reported in Feb 1963.

Prime Minister in his letter to the Federation Prime Minister on 11th June, 1963 proposed that the difference be split, i.e. a percentage of 37% be agreed upon.

(e) It is understood that our proposal is not acceptable to the Federation Government. In a sincere attempt to reach agreement, the Singapore Government is now prepared to accept 39%, the additional 2% to represent the 'prosperity element' consequent upon the Federation Government agreeing to a Malaysian Common Market.

(f) However, since Singapore's future economic growth depends on satisfactory terms of the Common Market, such as those recommended in the Rueff Report, this offer is conditional on agreement on the Common Market terms referred to in paragraph 1 above.

4.   The Singapore Government agrees that it will bear the cost of the expenditure in respect of development projects of Federal Departments in Singapore which have already been entered in the Singapore development plan and which have been approved by the Singapore Treasury or projects already in progress. The Fiscal Sub-Committee agreed that in regard to the Public Debt, the Federal Government should service outstanding liabilities in respect of those Singapore assets taken over by the Federal Government on merger. These include, inter alia, the Airport development scheme and the round-the-world Commonwealth Cable scheme all of which will involve a total expenditure of more than $20 million. The Singapore Government agrees that the loans already incurred in connection with these items of capital expenditure need not be a charge on the Federal Government. After the completion of these projects, the Singapore Government agrees to bear the cost of future development expenditure in Singapore (other than Defence and Internal Security development expenditure) up to a maximum of $3 million or about 1% of taxes of a national character collected in any one year. Any expenditure above this amount should be with prior agreement of the Singapore Government.

5.   The Singapore Government is required to make available a grant of $50 million during the first five years to the Federal Government. This proposal developed out of discussions as to how the development expenditure of Sarawak and North Borneo can be financed as their internal resources are likely to prove inadequate to their needs, estimated at $300 million and $200 million respectively for the first five years of Malaysia. The Singapore Government is unable to agree to the payment of a grant but is prepared to enter into an undertaking on the same lines as that given by the Malayan Government in paragraphs 10 and 11 of the Report of the Inter-Governmental Committee on Malaysia. In these paragraphs the Malayan Government, subject to certain conditions, 'undertook to use its best endeavours to enable this amount ($300 million) of development expenditure to be achieved'. Similarly the Malayan delegation recognised that additional funds from outside North Borneo would be required. There is no firm commitment in these paragraphs to extend grants to the Borneo territories. The Singapore Government considers that it is inequitable that an undertaking should be asked of the Singapore Government which the Federal Government itself was not prepared to give.

6.   The Singapore Government agrees that the financial arrangements should be subject to review by agreement and in default of agreement by an independent assessor appointed jointly by the two governments. This review should take place at the intervals originally proposed by the Federation Government, that is after the 1st, 3rd and 5th years. It proposes that a list of assessors be agreed as soon as possible before 31st August, 1963.

186   PREM 11/4348   24 June 1963
['Little Malaysia']: letter from Tunku Yaacob to Mr Macmillan, enclosing a personal message from Tunku Abdul Rahman

I have been asked by my Government to convey to you the following personal message from the Hon'ble Tunku Abdul Rahman Putra, our Prime Minister:—

'My dear Prime Minister,

Thank you for your kind invitation which was conveyed to me by Sir Geofroy Tory to come to London early this week.

It is clear that it will not be possible to reach agreement with Singapore and Brunei on a number of basic issues in regard to terms of their entry into Malaysia on 31st August. The Cabinet therefore decided that agreement of British Government should be sought to go ahead with Malaysia with North Borneo and Sarawak only and on scheduled day.

The terms for entry of Singapore and Brunei at a later stage could be discussed in London. For this purpose a Federation Delegation led by Deputy Prime Minister consisting of Minister of Finance and Minister of Commerce and Industry will meet representatives of British Government in London. If this is agreeable to you Delegation will leave immediately. So far prepared to come myself as soon as I receive advice from my delegation.

Yours sincerely,

TUNKU ABDUL RAHMAN PUTRA.'

Please accept, Mr. Prime Minister, the assurance of my highest respect.

187   DO 169/221, no 15, FS/63/58   24 June 1963
['Little Malaysia']: minute from Lord Home to Mr Sandys

You must be very concerned at the difficulties which have arisen between Malaya and Singapore over the negotiations for Malaysia, and also with the deadlock over Brunei. I see that it has been suggested that the Prime Minister should invite the Tunku, Lee Kuan Yew and the Sultan of Brunei to London, and you are no doubt considering what should be said to them, and in particular how we should handle the Tunku's suggestion that, in the last resort, Malaysia might be formed on August 31 without Singapore and Brunei. I presume that you will be strongly opposed to this, but I thought it might be helpful if I were to summarise the foreign policy implications of any solution of this sort. They would also apply to a decision to allow Malaya, North Borneo and Sarawak to federate temporarily while pursuing the negotiations with Singapore and Brunei with a view to bringing the whole of Malaysia into being later on:—

(i) If Singapore fails to get into Malaysia, now or at a later date, there is a strong likelihood that any arrangements for the continued use of our base there would fairly soon become unworkable. This would undermine our relationship with the Americans in the area and our ability to carry out our obligations to SEATO, and would greatly weaken our whole position in South East Asia.

(ii) The failure of our policy would lead the Indonesians and Filipinos to abandon any restraint and to go all out for their own territorial ambitions in Borneo. I do not know what our defence commitments would be towards a lesser Malaysia of this kind, but I would doubt whether we should be justified in getting involved in serious military operations with the Indonesians in defence of a Malaysia which did not include our base at Singapore.

(iii) While the Americans and Australians have made it clear that in the last resort they would be prepared to help us to defend Malaysia, I am not at all sure that they would wish to do so if it no longer served the purpose of giving a stable and permanent future to Singapore.

(iv) The idea of Malaysia is by no means popular with the uncommitted countries, but if it comes into existence rapidly and as now planned I think it will be widely accepted and will be received by the United Nations. But a lesser Malaysia would risk being considered a trick to terminate our own difficulties and would leave so many problems unresolved that neutral opinion might swing sharply against it, and I can foresee a very difficult time in the United Nations.

4. I am sending copies of this minute to the Prime Minister, the Minister of Defence and the Chancellor of the Exchequer.

188 CO 1030/1469, no 360   25 June 1963
[Obduracy of the Sultan of Brunei]: inward telegram no 182 OCULAR[1] from A M MacKintosh to Mr Sandys

Sultan had Marsal and Ali with him.

2. On behalf of Prime Minister and Secretary of State I invited Sultan to visit London at once in a final effort, with help of U.K. Ministers, to reach agreement with Malayans, adding that, even if agreement on Malaysia were not reached, visit would be useful opportunity to discuss Brunei's future outside Malaysia. I explained that Malayan and Singapore delegations were going to London in similar effort, and outlined time-table now envisaged.

3. I said that Brunei and Malaya appeared at present to have adopted rigid positions from which, although little of real substance divided them, neither looked like departing unaided. The only hope of agreement in the time available was further discussion in London with U.K. help.

4. I have never known Sultan more obdurate. He said categorically that he would concede nothing and stood absolutely firm on his own terms. Malayans had gone back on terms previously agreed and had vouchsafed no explanation for so doing. He had already twice visited Kuala Lumpur in vain search for agreement: he had been more than once bitten and was now more than twice shy. He saw no object in visiting London now without prior assurance from both Malayans and H.M.G. that his terms had been accepted unchanged. He did not believe that Malayan delegation would

---

[1] For the significance of OCULAR see 164, n 4.

listen to advice of U.K. Ministers if it were favourable to Brunei or that they would have authority to accept his terms even if, so advised, they wanted to do so.

5.   He was willing to send delegation to London at once in order to explain Brunei stand to U.K. Ministers in hope latter might bring Malays round. But in reply to Ali (who throughout long discussion gave me full support, whereas Marsal, for once vocal, consistently opposed me) he refused to give delegation any authority to consider compromise, saying that, even if U.K. Ministers produced new solutions which in substance met Brunei's demands they would be unacceptable because mere fact that they were new would imply Brunei had given way to some extent.

6.   He made it clear that he regarded Lawson[2] as indispensable in any discussion in London of Brunei affairs.

7.   He said that, if Brunei did not join Malaysia now, he would like to visit London for discussion of Treaty, either before or after Parliament's Summer Recess, in either case at convenience of U.K. Ministers.

8.   In short, prospects for Brunei's entry into Malaysia now seem nil unless Malayans surrender. I am about to discuss Razak's letter to Sultan of 21st June with Attorney-General and State Financial Officer. If I have anything helpful to add as a result I will telegraph again.

9.   Meanwhile, only hope of getting Sultan to London in time (and it is slight) seems to me personal appeal in message from Prime Minister which I could hand over as such. Sultan and Marsal are clearly much offended by what they regard as Malayan outrage of dignity of former and his state. If we are to get anywhere with Brunei over Malaysia the best U.K. butter will have to be applied without stint both here and in London (if we do after all contrive to bring Sultan there).

10.   Without Sultan, I doubt whether visit to London by a Brunei delegation would achieve anything but in this desperate situation we cannot afford to neglect any expedient, however unhopeful. If therefore, we fail to get Sultan to London at once I should still be grateful for request from U.K. Ministers that he should at least send delegation and be ready to follow it without delay if solid prospect of agreement with Malayans were reported back.

11.   I see no point in my coming to London unless Sultan does.[3]

---

[2] Neil Lawson QC was constitutional adviser to the Sultan; he had acted as rulers' representative during the Reid Commission to Malaya, 1956–1957, see *BDEE: Malaya*, part 3, 442.

[3] In fact the Sultan did come to London and on 3 July entrusted Sandys with the task of reactivating negotiations with the Malayans (CO 1030/1469, no 387 and CO 1030/1516, no 9).

189   DO 169/221, no 31, COS 235/63, Annex   27 June 1963

'Military implications of establishing Malaysia without Singapore and possibly Brunei': minute from Lord Mountbatten[1] to Mr Thorneycroft

[J D Higham, assistant secretary at the Colonial Office, attended the meeting of the Chiefs of Staff on 27 June when he speculated as follows on the future of Singapore: 'It was impossible at this stage to forecast what line the Prime Minister of Singapore would take

---

[1] Mountbatten was chief of the defence staff and chairman of the Chiefs of Staff Committee, 1959–1965.

if a solution was not found. He might demand independence for Singapore, or he might resign and request us to include Singapore in Malaysia by executive action. In the former case, Singapore could not remain self-supporting and would inevitably come under the influence of Communist China. In the latter case, it was possible that there might be so much trouble in Singapore that Lee Kuan Yew could return as Prime Minister in which case he might be in a stronger position to ensure that Singapore's position in Malaysia was arranged on terms more favourable to him.' (COS 42(63)1, DO 169/221; see also DEFE 4/156)]

In view of the threat by the Prime Minister of Malaya that, if necessary, he would be prepared to form Malaysia without Singapore or Brunei, the Colonial Office, at the request of the Colonial Secretary, asked the Ministry of Defence for an early assessment of the military implications of establishing Malaysia without Singapore or possibly without Brunei.

2.   At their meeting to-day, the Chiefs of Staff approved the attached Note on this subject.[2]

3.   The Chiefs of Staff concluded that:—

(a) Whether or not Singapore became independent immediately, its exclusion from Malaysia would make its use as a United Kingdom base uncertain in the short term and probably impossible in the long term.

(b) There is no practicable alternative to Singapore as a United Kingdom base, if we are to meet our existing commitments; it is unlikely that adequate facilities could be established elsewhere, even if we were prepared to meet the cost. Despite doubts about the security of the United Kingdom base in an independent Singapore, we should therefore try to remain there as long as it was productive to do so because of its supreme military importance in the area.

(c) If the United Kingdom was forced to leave Singapore, we would:—

(i) Suffer a general reverse to our military standing in the Far East.

(ii) If our commitments elsewhere remained unchanged, have to establish forward operating points north of Indonesia. The provision of these facilities would be very expensive, difficult to negotiate and might well prove impossible.

(iii) Have to re-arrange at great cost our back-up facilities for the area, in Australia and/or the United Kingdom.

(d) If Brunei were excluded from Malaysia and the United Kingdom remained responsible for her external defence and internal security, a United Kingdom garrison would be required there, but the establishment of forward operating facilities would be subject to the Sultan's continuing goodwill.

(e) It is unlikely that we shall be able to extricate our forces from Sarawak, North Borneo, and Brunei for some time to come whether or not Singapore or Brunei is excluded from Malaysia.

4.   We have not considered the military implications of a compromise solution whereby Malaya, North Borneo and Sarawak form a 'Little Malaysia' on 31st August, with discussions proceeding with Singapore and Brunei with a view to resolving the differences and their joining Malaysia at some later date. In view of the uncertainties that surround such a course, we should need further political advice, before we could assume that the military difficulties shown in the paper would not equally apply.

---

[2] Not printed.

190   CO 1030/1469   28 June 1963

[Oil discovery off Brunei coast]: minute from J D Higham to W I J Wallace and Sir J Martin

[The major issue in the negotiations between Brunei and Malaya was Brunei's revenues (especially from oil) and the federal government's right to their taxation. Just before the June talks began, Brunei Shell announced the discovery of considerable, off-shore oil resources.]

1.   Mr. Mackintosh[1] [sic] of Shell called yesterday and saw Mr. Harris and myself. He thought that it would be helpful if he gave us some more information about the possible effects of the new oil discovery 7 miles off the Brunei coast.

2.   He explained that it might be as much as a year before they were able to say whether oil was present in commercially exploitable quantities. So far, only one well had been drilled, and it would be necessary to drill 3 or 4 more before they were able to give any firm estimate of the probable size of the field.

3.   If this proved to be a 200 million barrel field (and Mr. Mackintosh thought this was a maximum estimate) increased revenue to the Brunei Government during the latter part of the first 10-year period would compensate for the decline in revenue from the present field. During the first few years, however, when there would be heavy capital investment, there might even be a net reduction in revenue to Brunei. After the 10-year period it could be expected that there would be a steady increase of revenue, assuming the oilfield was still productive.

4.   Mr. Mackintosh had it in mind that the $M.40 million contribution from the Brunei Government to the Federal Government had been worked out as a fixed percentage of Brunei's revenue from investments and oil. He thought that it might be possible to apply a similar percentage to the revenue from the new field, and to agree this in advance. We explained that the $M.40 million had not been worked out on any such basis.

5.   It is a little difficult to see what the effect of this possible new field on the financial negotiations is going to be. Whether oil is discovered in exploitable quantities or not, Shell obviously intend to go ahead with large scale exploration which will be a very expensive business, and this in itself will have an adverse effect on Brunei's revenue.[2] Mr. Mackintosh has promised to let me have early next week their best assessment of this.

6.   The Federation are insisting that if new sources of revenue (including oil) become available in [? any] time after the first five years, Brunei should accept a binding obligation to pay the tax equivalent to Federal revenues. Brunei have agreed to a review during the 10-year period at the request of the Federal Government, with a view to raising the level of annual payment. There is no question of the payment being less than $M.40 million even if the financial forecasts are worse than expected.

7.   At the end of the 10-year period the Malayans are asking for a review and in default of agreement that the arrangements then subsisting would continue until

---

[1] Charles Macintosh represented the SE Asia department of the London office of Shell International Petroleum Co Ltd; P M Linton was general manager of Brunei Shell in Seria.
[2] Wallace minuted at this point in the margin: 'Mr Lawson [the Sultan's constitutional adviser] made this point this morning.'

agreement is reached. Brunei advisers are prepared to advise the Sultan to agree to this, but not to the further Malayan condition that Brunei should have accepted the Federal case on new oil revenues.

8.   Until Mr. Mackintosh's figures are available it is difficult to see how this new oil situation may affect the attitude of both territories. It would seem that we should stress to the Malayans that the further capital expenditure that will be incurred over the next few years (whether or not large scale exploitation is possible) may well lead to a decline in Brunei revenue. As far as the revenue from new oil is concerned, if it is shown to exist in commercially exploitable quantities, the Bruneis will no doubt argue that the review formula (with a view to an increase) will take care of that. But if the field proves to be a rich one, and Brunei's oil revenue is maintained at its current level of over $M.100 million a year instead of declining to less than half that amount by the end of the 10-year period, the Malayans have a strong case, in equity, for insisting that they should have a firm assurance that at least a proportion of the revenue from the new field should be automatically available for Federal purposes.[3] I wonder if it would be worth trying to persuade both territories that such a percentage should be fixed now.

9.   I am a little surprised that the Bruneis should be willing to agree that, if there is failure to agree at the 10-year review, the present arrangements should continue. This had been their line before the possible new oil field had broken, and I should have thought that it was risky for Brunei to accept the possibility of having to continue to pay $M.40 million a year when it was almost certain that her revenue from oil would be declining steeply, at that time—a decline that could scarcely be offset by an increase in investment income.[4]

---

[3] Wallace minuted at this point in the margin: 'As already agreed, they will have control of its investment, so that it can be used for Federation purposes.'

[4] Having considered this minute Sir John Martin advised Lansdowne that the CO should investigate further the financial terms being negotiated between Malaya and Brunei on the ground that, 'We have a responsibility to see that Brunei gets a square deal and it is not at all easy to judge what this should be.' 'The basic difficulty', as A N Galsworthy pointed out to the secretary of state, 'is that the Sultan is absolutely determined that the ultimate decision as to what shall happen about revenue from oil and oilfields shall always lie with the Brunei Government', whereas the 'Malayans now maintain that if new sources of revenue (ie from new oilfields) become available after five years, Brunei should pay a tax equivalent to the Federal Government.' Galsworthy continued: 'The argument turns around the Malayans' desire to get a right of taxation over oil revenues in Brunei after not more than ten years, and the Sultan's refusal to concede any such right, unless the Government of Brunei so agrees at the time' (Galsworthy to Sandys, 5 July 1963, CO 1030/1470, no 422).

191   CO 1030/1515, no 80   4–5 July 1963
'Talks on Malaya/Singapore financial negotiations': CRO minutes of all-night discussions. Annex: 'Draft agreement between the governments of the Federation of Malaya and Singapore on common market and financial arrangements'

[The Malaysia project nearly foundered over the common market recommended by the Rueff mission and favoured by Lee Kuan Yew. The apportionment of revenues arising in Singapore proved highly contentious and the talks oscillated between hard-fought negotiations and deadlock. Sandys frequently adopted the ploy of late-night meetings to drive participants into compromise and force agreement. That of 4–5 July was the longest, starting at 9.30 pm and ending at 8 am. 'It was', recalled Lee Kuan Yew, 'his method of dealing with stubborn parties' and 'not unlike what the communists did to us at committee meetings' (*Memoirs*, p 480). On the Malayan side, Razak and his colleagues later spoke 'with awe' of their experience and joked with Tory back in Kuala Lumpur that Tan Siew Sin would 'never be the same again' (Tory to Sandys, 19 July 1963, Sandys Papers, 8/14). When they adjourned for breakfast on 5 July, the delegates agreed to reconvene for another two hours at 11 am and they met again that evening at 7 pm. Two days later the evening session got underway at 10.15 pm and lasted until 4.15 the next morning. For the meeting on 4–5 July the British team was led by Sandys and Lansdowne, supported by Garner, Lintott, Tory, Moore, Higham, Golds, H P Hall and six others. The Malayan team was led by Tun Razak, Tan Siew Sin and Dr Lim Swee Aun, supported by eight officials (including the expatriate attorney-general, C M Sheridan). The Singapore team was led by Lee Kuan Yew and Dr Goh Keng Swee, supported by six officials. When the session was over, Sandys informed Selkirk that agreement had been reached on most of the major issues, the crisis point having been reached at about four in the morning when he 'finally managed to bridge the gap between Lee and Razak'. On 10 June the banner headline of the *Straits Budget* ran, 'Malaysia is on and Singapore is part of it'. The paper's London correspondent, Leslie Hoffman, reported Sandys' patience when caught in the cross-fire as well as his capacity to 'give as good as he got' in 'some of the fiery exchanges'. The agreement on common market and financial arrangements became Annex J of the Malaysia document signed on 9 July. Even so, differences rumbled on, requiring the intervention of Sandys in Sept and culminating in a supplementary agreement to the Agreement of 9 July, see 220, note. In addition to the protracted negotiations over the common market and finance, an all-night session was needed to finalise arrangements for service lands in Singapore, see Annex F to the Agreement of 9 July and *Release of Crown Lands made available to the Armed Services in Singapore* (Cmnd 2117) also CO 968/761]

Consideration was given to a further revised draft of the Agreement on Common Market and financial arrangements prepared by the British side after discussions with the Malayan and Singapore sides separately.

2. The draft was considered paragraph by paragraph. A number of separate meetings were held between the British and the Malayan and Singapore sides respectively on points of particular difficulty, and agreement between the Malayan and Singapore sides was finally reached on the revised draft annexed,[1] in which the following matters (paragraphs (i) and (ix) below) remain unresolved:—

(i) *Paragraph 4(3)—concurrence of Singapore government to imposition of new revenue duties*
3. It was noted that the Singapore side wished to add at the end of this paragraph the words: 'on [?or] trade with the rest of the Federation'.

(ii) *Paragraph 4(4)—Singapore veto on the imposition of revenue duties*
4. A compromise providing that this veto would cease to have effect after the end of 1975 was considered. The Singapore side felt it would be impossible to defend in Singapore the ultimate abolition of their power of veto, which the Rueff Report had envisaged as perpetual, and the increase in the cost of living which would ensue. The Malayan side emphasised that the entrepot trade would not be affected and observed that for their part they would find it politically difficult to defend an arrangement insulating Singapore from duties affecting the cost of living.

---

[1] The revised draft records what had been agreed by the close of the all-night session of 4–5 July.

(iii) *Paragraph 8—financial review*

5.   The Singapore side proposed a revision which would define in more detail the matters to be considered at these reviews, and in particular would mention the revenue estimates put forward by the Malayans during the abortive negotiations in the Interdepartmental Committee about the apportionment of Federal revenue in Singapore.

(iv) *Paragraph 9—finance for Borneo development*

6.   *Mr. Lee* said that if it was necessary to import skilled temporary labour into Borneo to erect works, e.g. schools, financed from the loans offered by Singapore, the labour should be from Singapore. He considered this would be a necessary selling point for the arrangement in Singapore. *The Secretary of State* said it was assumed that this would not be a condition of the loan: it could be covered separately in an exchange of letters between the two Governments.

(v) *Annex Part I. Customs and excise (4)*[2]

7.   The Singapore side considered that the grounds on which the Federation's power to prohibit imports and exports should be specified, e.g. trading with the enemy, etc., since they could otherwise, contrary to the 1961 White Paper,[3] encroach on the free port status of Singapore.

(vi) *Annex I (6)*

8.   The Singapore side considered that since executive authority rested with Singapore it would be inconsistent to reserve to the Federal Government the power to determine appeals from decisions of the Controller of Customs.

(vii) *Annex part II. Income tax—section 92(2)*

9.   The Singapore side felt that the proposed recognition of the right of the Federal Minister to issue directions was sufficient to cover the question of remission of tax.

(viii) *Annex Part II. Section 19(2)*

10.   The Singapore side were concerned at the possibility that income tax allowances affecting capital investment might be immediately brought in line with the Malaya scale.

(ix) *Annex Part II. Sections 95(3) and 96(3)*

11.   The Singapore side objected to the proposal to transfer to the Comptroller-General the Comptroller's powers to compound any offence for fraudulent or incorrect returns.

12.   *The Secretary of State* requested the Malayan side to consider whether it was essential to take Federal powers in all the matters included in the annex, and asked the two sides to reach a settlement on these points.

---

[2] The annex to the draft agreement is not printed here.
[3] *Memorandum setting out the Heads of Agreement for a Merger between the Federation of Malaya and Singapore* (Cmd 33) adopted by Singapore's Legislative Assembly on 6 Dec 1961.

13.   Attention was drawn to a paper by the Singapore side on outstanding points in connection with the Malaysia Bill to be introduced in the Federation Parliament. The Secretary of State said he was planning that the Malaysia Agreement would be signed on Monday, 8th July—he would be leaving for British Guiana on 9th July[4]—and hoped that meanwhile the Malayan and Singapore sides would reach agreement on issues outstanding. The Singapore side confirmed that they had no other points to raise.

14.   It was agreed that the three sides would meet again at 11 a.m. on 5th July.

15.   The discussions were adjourned at 8 a.m.

Annex to 191

Common Market

1(1).   The Federal Government, in order to facilitate the maximum practicable degree of economic integration of the territories of Malaysia, while taking account of the interests of the entrepot trade of Singapore, Penang and Labuan and those of existing industries in Malaysia, and the need to ensure a balanced development of these territories, shall progressively establish a common market in Malaysia for all goods or products produced, manufactured or assembled in significant quantities in Malaysia, with the exception of goods and products of which the principal terminal markets lie outside Malaysia.

1(2).   Where the same protective duties or revenue duties are applicable throughout Malaysia in the case of any class of goods or products, then no tariff or trade barrier or trade restriction or discrimination shall be applied to such goods or products in regard to their circulation throughout Malaysia.

1(3).   The provisions of the preceding sub-paragraph shall not be construed to prevent the imposition of:—

(a) any special production tax on producers in a low-tariff State which would offset the cost inequalities arising from the differential import duties; or
(b) any export duty or export restriction on primary products where the principal terminal market lies outside Malaysia.

Tariff Advisory Board

2(1).   The Malayan Government shall take steps to establish by law before Malaysia Day a Tariff Advisory Board[5] to advise the Federal Government generally on the establishment of the common market as defined in paragraph 1 above, including the establishment and maintenance of a common external tariff for the protection (where required) of goods for which there is to be a common market.

2(2).   Appointments to the Board shall be made by the Federal Government but until five years from Malaysia Day the appointment of the Chairman shall require the

---

[4] British Guiana had been discussed at the meeting between Macmillan and President Kennedy at Birch Grove (Macmillan's home) on 30 June. The US were adamant that Cheddi Jagan's left-wing government should be removed before Britain granted independence. See Ashton and Killingray eds, *BDEE: The West Indies*, lxxvii, 215.

[5] For its appointment see 220, note.

concurrence of the Singapore Government; the first Chairman shall be appointed as soon as possible after the conclusion of this Agreement. During the first five years, there shall be three Deputy Chairmen, one of whom shall be nominated by the Singapore Government. In appointing members of the Board regard shall be had to the areas and interests involved.

2(3).   The Board shall sit in public to receive evidence except where the Board deems it necessary to receive evidence *in camera*. Within six months after their receipt the Federal Government shall publish the reports and recommendations of the Board other than those of which publication is not in the public interest.

Protective duties

3(1).   For the purposes of this Agreement a protective duty shall be defined as a duty which is levied in respect of a class of goods or products which are or are to be produced, manufactured, assembled or prepared and used or consumed in the Federation in significant quantities, or which are used or consumed in the production, manufacture, assembly or preparation in the Federation of goods or products of such a class or which are of a description providing a substitute for or alternative to goods or products of such a class. All other duties shall be defined as revenue duties. A duty shall be regarded as imposed in Singapore, if it is imposed on goods imported into Singapore for use or consumption there and not otherwise.

3(2).   Except in cases where it deems preventive action to be urgently necessary, the Federal Government shall not in Singapore make any class of goods or products subject to a protective duty or vary any protective duty before receiving the advice of the Tariff Advisory Board. In cases where a duty has been imposed or varied without prior reference to the Tariff Advisory Board, the Federal Government shall seek the advice of the Board thereon as soon as practicable thereafter.

3(3).   For a period of 5 years from Malaysia Day the Singapore Government shall have the right to require a delay not exceeding 12 months in the imposition in Singapore of any protective duty on the grounds that the duty would significantly prejudice the entrepot trade. In any enquiry by the Tariff Advisory Board on a proposal to impose such a duty, the Singapore Government shall inform the Board of any item on which it may wish, in the interests of the entrepot trade, to avail itself of this option. In regard to such items, the Tariff Advisory Board shall consider the possibility of anticipatory action in Singapore and shall, if necessary, include in its recommendations proposals to prevent such action. During the period of delay, the Singapore Government shall not grant any licence, concession or inducement to any industry which may be affected by the proposed protective duty without the concurrence of the Federal Government.

3(4).   The Tariff Advisory Board shall be required within six months after Malaysia Day to make its first report as to what protective duties should be imposed. For this purpose it shall consider any proposals made to it by the Federal Government or a State Government.

Revenue duties

4(1).   In formulating its policy relating to the harmonisation of revenue duties, the Federal Government shall pay due regard to any representations made by the Singapore Government on the economic, financial and social implications of such harmonisation.

4(2).   Revenue duties in force in Singapore on 1st July, 1963, and the corresponding duties in force in the Federation of Malaya shall be harmonised as soon as practicable.

4(3).   Until the end of 1968, no revenue duty shall, except at the request and with the consent of the Singapore Government, be imposed in Singapore by the Federal Government in respect of any class of goods or products not chargeable with such a duty on the 1st July, 1963. Such consent shall not be withheld except on the grounds that the duty would significantly prejudice the entrepot trade of Singapore (or trade with the rest of the Federation.)[6]

4(4).   Before 31st December 1968, the Tariff Advisory Board shall review the revenue duties in force at that time in Singapore and in the remainder of Malaysia and shall make recommendations regarding the amendment of such duties or the imposition of additional duties. As from 1st January 1969, the Singapore Government shall be entitled to withhold its consent to the amendment or imposition in Singapore of any revenue duty for any period up to 31st December 1975, on the grounds that it would significantly prejudice the entrepot trade, provided that the Singapore Government shall pay to the Federal Government annually compensation equal to the loss of revenue suffered by the Federal Government as a result of the withholding of such consent.[7]

4(5).   For the purposes of this Agreement, the entrepot trade of Singapore means trade in goods and products imported into Singapore from outside Malaysia and primary products imported into Singapore from other parts of Malaysia, which goods or products, whether further processed or not, are subsequently re-exported from Singapore to destinations outside Malaysia.

Tax collection

5.   Subject to the provisions of the Annex to this Agreement, executive authority in respect of the collection in Singapore of customs duties and excise and income tax shall be delegated to the Singapore Government. The Federal Government may revoke this authority if the Singapore Government fails to comply with any direction properly given to them by the Federal Government for the collection or protection of these taxes or shows itself unwilling or unable to discharge these functions efficiently. This authority may extend to customs duties and other charges collected in Singapore on goods exported from or to be imported into Malaysia outside Singapore.

Division of revenue

6(1).   All revenues collected in Singapore, with the exceptions specified below, shall be paid into a separate fund in a branch of the Central Bank to be established in Singapore and the fund shall be divided between the two Governments and paid to them at least once in every year, in the proportion of 60% to the Singapore Government and 40% to the Federal Government. The exceptions are:—

(a) the revenues specified in Part III of the Tenth Schedule to the Federal Constitution, including property tax in lieu of rates, (to be paid into the State Consolidated Fund);

---

[6] This matter remained unresolved at the closure of this all-night session.   [7] *idem.*

(b) customs duties and other charges (including excise not in force at the date of this Agreement and any production tax imposed in respect of goods to which a protective duty is applicable) collected in Singapore on goods to be exported from or imported into Malaysia outside Singapore (to be paid into the Federal Consolidated Fund);

(c) income tax collected in Singapore and attributable to income derived from the States of Malaya (to be paid into the Federal Consolidated Fund).

6(2)   60% of income tax collected in the States of Malaya but attributable to income derived from Singapore shall be paid to the Singapore Government.

6(3)   Income tax attributable to income derived from Singapore and collected by an Agent outside Malaysia shall be paid into the separate fund referred to in paragraph 6(1) above.

6(4)   From the beginning of 1964 paragraphs 6(1)(c) and 6(2) shall apply as if references to the States of Malaya included references to the Borneo States.

6(5)   The provisions of Article 109 and Clauses (3), (3A) and (4) of Article 110 of the Federal Constitution shall not apply in relation to Singapore.

Federal projects in Singapore

7.   The Singapore Government shall pay to the Federal Government the cost of capital development of Federal projects in Singapore other than projects for defence and internal security. The two Governments shall agree together on projects to be covered by this paragraph which do not provide predominantly local services.

Financial review

8.   The arrangements specified in paragraphs 6 and 7 above shall remain in operation until 31st December 1964. The two Governments shall then review these arrangements and shall decide upon any amendments to be made to them in respect of the two year period commencing 1st January 1965. There shall be a similar review in respect of each subsequent period of two years. In default of agreement between the two Governments, any issue in dispute shall be referred to an independent assessor appointed jointly by the two Governments. In default of agreement between the two Governments on the choice of an assessor, the Lord President of the Federal Court, after considering the views of both governments, shall appoint an assessor from among persons recommended by the International Bank for Reconstruction and Development as being persons enjoying an international reputation in finance. The recommendations of the assessor shall be binding on both governments. Such reviews shall have regard to changes in the relation between Federal revenue accruing in Singapore, State revenue and the revenue of the Federation as a whole, to any relevant changes in Federal or State expenditure, and to the progress made in establishing the common market as defined in paragraph 1 above, and to any considerations which either government may wish to have taken into account.[8]

Finance for Borneo territories

9.   To assist development in the Borneo territories the Singapore Government shall make available to the Federal Government:—

---

[8] *idem.*

(a) a 15-year loan of $100 million, bearing interest at current market rates in the Federation, subject to the proviso that the loan shall be free of interest during the first 5 years and that if, having regard to the economic growth in Singapore, it is so recommended in the financial review under paragraph 8 above, the loan shall be free of interest for a second period of 5 years; and

(b) a 15-year loan of $50 million bearing interest at current market rates in the Federation.

The above loans shall be drawn in equal annual instalments over a period of 5 years, commencing in 1964.[9]

Disputes as to interpretation or application of this agreement

10. Any dispute between the Federal Government and the Singapore Government as to the interpretation or application of this Agreement may be referred by either Government to the Federal Court for determination by that Court in exercise of the jurisdiction conferred upon it by Article 128 of the Federal Constitution.

---

[9] *idem.*

192 CO 1030/1511, no 170   8 July 1963
[Agreement at the Ritz Hotel]: Lee Kuan Yew's notes signed by Tunku Abdul Rahman

[The Tunku played no part in the haggling over trade and finances; he relied on Tun Razak and Tan Siew Sin for that. He chose not to arrive in London until a few days before the signing ceremony which was scheduled for the evening of 8 July. There still remained, however, a few matters which Lee Kuan Yew wished to clarify with the Malayan premier and he did so at the Ritz Hotel just before the ceremony at Marlborough House. Lee scribbled these points on the back of an envelope, which the Tunku then signed but dated incorrectly as 7 July (see 192). Lee provided the British government with a photostat of the envelope and on 10 July confirmed the agreement in a fuller note (see 193) which the Singapore government published later in the month. The last-minute bargaining at the Ritz, dinner with Macmillan and speeches at Marlborough House meant that it was not until after mid-night on 8–9 July that the Malaysia agreement was signed by representatives of the United Kingdom, Federation of Malaya, North Borneo, Sarawak and Singapore. The agreement and its eleven annexes provided for: the end of British sovereignty and jurisdiction in North Borneo, Sarawak and Singapore; a Malaysia Bill to be enacted by the parliament of the Federation of Malaya; constitutions (including transitional provisions) for Sabah, Sarawak and Singapore to be enforced by Britain through orders in council; the extension of Malaya's immigration ordinance to the whole of Malaysia; the extension of the Anglo–Malayan defence agreement of 1957 to the whole of Malaysia; continuing British rights to bases, facilities and Service lands in Singapore; compensation and benefits for British officers retiring from public service in North Borneo and Sarawak; terms and conditions of expatriate officers continuing in the public service of Sabah, Sarawak and Singapore; agreement between Malaya and Singapore on common market and financial arrangements; arrangements with respect to broadcasting and television in Singapore. Macmillan, who was pictured in London's *Evening Standard* of 9 July with head in hand above the caption 'Mac signs at midnight', reported the event to the Oversea Policy Committee later that day and the agreement and annexes were then published as a parliamentary paper (OP 8(63)2, CAB 134/2371; FO tel no 385 to oversea diplomatic representatives, 9 July 1963, CO 1030/1507, no 212; *Malaysia. Agreement concluded between the United Kingdom of Great Britain and Northern Ireland, the Federation of Malaya, North Borneo, Sarawak and Singapore*, Cmnd 2094, July 1963).]

Ritz Hotel   8.7.63
    Loan: Labourers—none outside Malaysia—50% S'pore
    S'pore L. Assemblyman: resignation or expulsion—vacate seat so long as does not
                conflict with Parliamentary practice
    Immigration: restriction Order movement reciprocal
    Gangsters Ordinance: detention delegate to us in S'pore
    Last part out—Inter-Governmental-Committee

                                         Sgd. Tunku Abdul Rahman
                                                  7.7.63

193   CO 1030/1511, no 170   10 July 1963
[Agreement at the Ritz Hotel]: letter from Lee Kuan Yew to Tunku Abdul Rahman

[A note prepared by the CO's Far Eastern Department on 25 July commented on the 'envelope agreement' which was concluded at the Ritz Hotel on 8 July and confirmed by Lee Kuan Yew two days later. Whereas the third and fourth points appeared uncontentious so far as the British were concerned, the others were controversial. Political leaders of North Borneo were anxious about the first proposal, regarding the labour force for the development of the Borneo territories, which had not been raised in previous discussions with the secretary of state. The second point was 'quite contrary to British practice' and would in any case require an amendment to the draft Singapore constitution at annex D of the Malaysia agreement. If point 2 were to be included in the order in council containing the constitutions of Sabah, Sarawak and Singapore, Lee and the Tunku would need to approve the revised formulation by about 10 Aug. Because no progress had been made by the end of Aug, Lee made his agreement to the postponement of Malaysia Day to 16 Sept conditional upon the written acceptance of, amongst other things, points 2, 3 and 4 of the 'envelope agreement' (see 215 and 216).]

I refer to our discussion on the evening of 8th July at the Ritz Hotel as a result of which we agreed:—

(i) in respect of the loan for the development of the Borneo States, no labourers will be engaged from outside Malaysia for the development projects and that 50% of such labourers shall be supplied from Singapore;

(ii) that the Federation will not object to the amendment of the Singapore Constitution so that where a member of the Legislative Assembly resigns or is expelled from the political party for which he stood as a member, he shall vacate his seat, so long as this does not conflict with Parliamentary practice;

(iii) that where the Federation enacts any law restricting movement or residence such order shall be reciprocal as between Singapore and the States of Malaya; and

(iv) that the power of detention under the Criminal Law (Temporary Provisions) Ordinance be delegated to Singapore.

I attach a photostat copy of the notes of the agreement which you signed.

194   PREM 11/4349   11 July 1963
[Brunei: future policy]: minute from Lord Lansdowne to Mr Macmillan, providing a brief for the prime minister's meeting with the Sultan

[Although the Sultan of Brunei had been persuaded to attend the final round of talks in early July (see 188), when the Malayan delegation had wooed him with substantial concessions, in the end he declined to sign the Malaysia agreement. He issued a statement regretting the government of Malaya's refusal to give effect to previously agreed terms. The Tunku's view was that negotiations had broken down purely over the question of precedence. Whether the prime concern of His Highness was his status in the hierarchy of rulers, or control of oil revenues, or popular hostility in Brunei to merger with Malaya, Angus MacKintosh was of the view that 'if all the difficulties raised by the Sultan could have been overcome at the wave of a hand, he would have invented others'. I H Harris of the CO's Far Eastern Department also concluded that he 'would have found some pretext or other for refusing' (see 197). This point was added as a confidential note to a parliamentary brief, which the secretary of state was advised not to use in the House: 'Our view is now that the Sultan never intended to sign the Agreement and would have found some pretext even if his demands on the question of precedence had been fully met' (CO 1030/1510, no 137, 16 July 1963). Similarly, P M Linton, general manager of Brunei Shell in Seria, commented in mid-Sept, 'everyone here now accepts that the Sultan had no intention in July of joining Malaysia and pitched his demands at a level which he believed would never be conceded. When they were conceded he fell back on the precedence issue; had that been conceded he intended to insist on a Malay translation of the documents to be signed!' Observing developments from New Delhi, Sir Paul Gore-Booth was prompted 'to implore whatever gods may be to use everything up to and including thumbscrews to oblige the Sultan to decide to join Malaysia before August 31st,—for his own good, certainly, but more importantly for the good of more important people like ourselves'. Sir Saville Garner replied that it was 'a little difficult for us to adopt your excellent suggestion of using thumbscrews' on account of the fact that the Sultan had 'succeeded in getting public opinion in Brunei behind him as a result of his refusal to join Malaysia'. Therefore, he continued, 'a lesser but more lingering form of treatment will be necessary to induce him to enter Malaysia'. This meant further talks, during which the British grew increasingly impatient with His Highness's complacent belief that Brunei's treaty relationship with Britain would continue indefinitely. During a four-hour stop-over in Brunei on 14 Sept Sandys warned the Sultan that, unless constitutional progress was volunteered, he might have to instruct the high commissioner to tender formal advice under the 1959 treaty. The fear was that continued British 'protection' would make Brunei a target of Indonesian subversion; the hope was that progress towards independence might draw Brunei into Malaysia. Determined to resist any temptation to 'recolonise' Brunei, the British government transferred responsibility for the sultanate from the CO to the CRO in Nov 1963. See 195, 197 and 199, and also CO 1030/1457, 1469, 1470 and 1530.]

Talking points

  1. H.M.G. continues to be convinced that the best future for Brunei (and for the Sultan's dynasty which dates from the 16th century) is to join Malaysia.

  2. It is unfortunate that the recent negotiations should have broken down primarily on a question of precedence.[1] It is our belief that the Sultan may have

---

[1] The question of precedence hinged on whether the Sultan's seniority dated from his accession to the throne of Brunei or from Brunei's membership of Malaysia. The Sultan's legal adviser, Neil Lawson, provided Landowne with notes on the discussions between Brunei and Malaya on the question of precedence and the place of the Sultan on the election list for Yang di-Pertuan Agong, see CO 1030/1470, no 426 and also 165, note.

misunderstood the position as he was asking the Tunku for agreement on a matter which has to be referred to the Malayan Conference of Rulers.

3.   We understand that the Sultan wishes to leave the door open for a resumption of negotiations and it is, therefore, of great importance that there should be no recriminations which might be damaging to good relations between Brunei and Malaya.

4.   With the formation of Malaysia, British colonial rule will be ended in this area. Our continued protection of Brunei will, therefore, attract considerable attention and will be regarded, not only in the world outside, but also in Brunei itself, as a form of colonialism.

5.   If we are to continue our protection, there will have to be constitutional reform at an early date. We could not again use British troops to suppress a revolt against an unpopular and autocratic regime.

6.   The position of the Sultans in the Federation of Malaya is secured by the Constitution. By joining Malaysia His Highness would fortify his own position and ensure the succession of his heirs.

195   PREM 11/4349, M246/63   12 July 1963
[Brunei: future policy]: minute from Mr Macmillan to Lord Lansdowne

I spoke to His Highness the Sultan of Brunei on the lines of your talking points,[1] including the problem of Brunei as a relic of colonialisation after the formation of Malaysia. He said that he regarded the negotiations as closed. I asked if they could not be reopened? He said that would depend on whether there was an agreement or not, and I said there could not be an agreement without the reopening of negotiations. He did not seem very impressed by this argument. He is coming back to see the Colonial Office but I would judge that he would be pretty obstinate and ultimately pressure will have to be exerted by the threat that we cannot protect him indefinitely.

---

[1] See 194.

196   PREM 11/4349   12 July 1963
[Financial assistance for Malaysia]: letter from Mr Macmillan to Tunku Abdul Rahman

We have been considering here the letter which you wrote to me on May 29[1] about British financial assistance for Malaysia. I have delayed my reply while the other financial questions arising out of Singapore's future membership of the Federation have been under discussion.

---

[1] 177.

I understand your concern over the financial problems which the new Federation of Malaysia will have to face. I hope that you for your part will appreciate the limitations on our ability to help. As you may know, the claims on Britain for overseas aid and the total of that aid are increasing very significantly. Nor, I am afraid, can we count on savings in defence expenditure as a result of the establishment of Malaysia. In fact, welcome as the increase in Malaya's own forces will be to us and to our friends, it will not reduce, at least during the next few years, the very heavy burden on the British taxpayer of the defence effort which we maintain as our contribution to the security of South-East Asia, including, of course, our obligations under the Defence Agreement as extended to Malaysia.

I had certainly thought that the offer which we made to your Deputy Prime Minister and Finance Minister last May, which was the outcome of careful and sympathetic study by my colleagues and myself, was a reasonably generous one. The main figure mentioned was £15 million in capital aid for defence up to the end of 1965, with provision for review before that time. We had already offered aid towards the employment of service personel seconded from this country, which would amount to £3 million during the agreed period.

In effect, under the arrangements for defence aid, we should be covering the whole cost of the arms and equipment supplied from British sources; we should be transferring free of charge the buildings and other installations which we have been asked to make available to your forces in Singapore and Malaya; and we should be meeting more than half the emoluments of the British service personnel you require.

To this we must add aid for development in Singapore of nearly £6 million which we had already promised, and aid for development in North Borneo and Sarawak of £7.5 million which we had offered during the negotiations for the establishment of Malaysia. We have also offered to pay the cost of compensation for expatriate officers in North Borneo and Sarawak (£3 million), half of which would in the normal course have fallen to the two territories. These three items will add a further charge on the British Exchequer of perhaps as much as £16½ million during the next five years or so. Thus you will see that we have already undertaken to help the new Federation to the tune of over £34 million.

We have, nevertheless, considered, in the light of your letter, what more we can do to assist. We are prepared to do so in two ways:—

(i) In order to help with the raising of the two new battalions in the Borneo territories, we would be willing to meet all the costs of raising, maintaining and training these units up to the end of 1965 by which time they should be ready for active duty. The only cost which would fall upon you (and this, I understand, would not happen until after the end of 1965) would be the cost of their permanent accommodation in the Borneo territories.

(ii) We should also be prepared to make available over the next five years a loan, under Section 3 of the Export Guarantees Act, of up to £5 million for the purchase of goods from Britain to assist the economic development of Malaysia as a whole. Alternatively, if you should prefer it, we would be prepared to increase to £10 million the grant of £7.5 million which we have already agreed to make to assist the development of North Borneo and Sarawak during that period.

Perhaps you would let me know which of these two alternatives you would prefer.[2]

As you know, we have agreed to review the position before the end of 1965 and to consider in the light of that review whether we could give further aid for the defence programme.

I hope that this additional help, together with what we have already offered and the contribution from Singapore, will go a long way to solve the two problems which you particularly mention in your letter, namely the financing of your additional defence programme and development in North Borneo and Sarawak.

---

[2] The Tunku replied from the Ritz Hotel on the same day stating a preference for the second alternative, although he pointed out that his minister of finance (Tan Siew Sin) had advised that the additional grant should have been £5 million instead of £2.5 million.

197   FO 371/169691, no 38   18 July 1963
'Brunei: future policy': notes by I H Harris in preparation for Mr Sandys' meeting with the Sultan of Brunei

[Sandys was briefed at a meeting with CO officials and Angus MacKintosh, High Commissioner of Brunei, on the afternoon of 24 July before talks with the Sultan and his party on 29 July, see 199. While it recommended British dis-engagement from Brunei, the CO's Far Eastern Department pointed out the military and political risks of immediate withdrawal. In accepting that Britain should continue to work for Brunei's membership of Malaysia, officials recognised that this could take some years to achieve, that threatening the Sultan would be of limited value and that the democratisation of Brunei's government might strengthen rather than weaken local opposition to Malaysia.]

Present position
Our view is that the Sultan came to London without any intention of signing the Malaysia agreement, and that he would have found some pretext or other for refusing. Public statements by the Sultan since he returned to Brunei suggest that he has no thought of re-opening the negotiations, which he regards as closed, and that he intends to wait and see how Malaysia shapes before re-considering the question of joining. This may take a long time. The Sultan's attitude is reported to have shaken the most convinced adherents of Malaysia in Brunei. There is thus no early prospect either of the Sultan carrying his people into Malaysia, or of the people sweeping the Sultan in.

Factors
2.   Once Malaysia is formed Brunei will be an embarrassment to Britain and Malaysia. Its external defence ought to be undertaken as part of the external defence of Malaysia. Its internal security will be of great concern to surrounding Malaysian territory and ought to be a Malaysian responsibility. Brunei will be an obvious target for Indonesian intrigue and a potential source of subversive activity where Malaysia is most vulnerable. Its quasi-dependent status will be an anachronism and increasingly difficult to justify to world opinion. Britain cannot remain committed to protect the Sultan's autocratic and inefficient regime indefinitely.

Basic policy

3. The potential political and military embarrassment for Britain in continuing to protect Brunei after Malaysia is formed points clearly to a basic policy of disengagement.

4. We must also take account of the interests of Malaysia, both because we shall be militarily involved and because from an international point of view we want Malaysia to be stable and successful. Malaysia's best interests will be served if Brunei joined the Federation. There is no obvious advantage to Malaysia in Brunei remaining outside, whilst there are real difficulties and dangers.

5. Our basic policy should therefore be, in co-operation with the Government of Malaysia, to end our present bilateral relationship with Brunei and to steer the latter into Malaysia. This is, of course, a continuation, in changed circumstances, of the policy which we have been pursuing for the last two years.

6. It will not be politically possible for us to wait indefinitely for Brunei to join Malaysia. If the Sultan remained obdurate, or too content with British protection, or if popular opinion in Brunei hardened permanently against Malaysia, we might have to consider pulling out and leaving Brunei to her own devices.

Action to implement policy

7. By words, and increasingly by deeds, we should aim to convince the Sultan that the days of British protection are numbered and that he must soon choose between joining Malaysia and taking his chance outside, on his own. His most sensitive point may be his concern for his own future and that of his dynasty. He needs to be persuaded that his best, if not only, chance of survival is by joining Malaysia, and that he must cease toying with any unrealistic idea which he may still entertain of riding to power over 'Northern Borneo' with the support of Indonesia and 'rebel' elements in Brunei, North Borneo and Sarawak.

8. We should tell the Sultan now that, whilst we are prepared to continue external protection for the time being, he cannot count on British aid in future in an internal security situation.

9. We should put pressure on the Sultan to democratise Brunei but should allow an opportunity for the 'right' party (preferably pro-Malaysia) to develop before pushing him into a fully elected Legislature. If the 'right' party does not emerge, it may be necessary to insist on full responsible Government, thus either frightening the Sultan into Malaysia or providing a setting in which Britain could pull out entirely.

10. We should persuade the Tunku that his suggested policy of 'freezing out' the Sultan is wrong and would prejudice any remaining chance there may be of getting Brunei into Malaysia. We should also express the hope that the Tunku will not withdraw his Malayan officers from Brunei at least for the time being.[1]

11. The Sultan is likely to press H.M.G. for professional and technical assistance and other help. His main idea is probably to show how well Brunei can get on without Malaysia. This would not further our basic aims and we should not allow ourselves to become an instrument of the Sultan's policy. On the other hand, it would be difficult for us to refuse all assistance.

---

[1] In fact the Tunku requested their return in Oct 1963.

Questions

12. In pursuing paragraphs 5 and 7–8 above, should we attempt to amend the Brunei Agreement or should we merely tell the Sultan how we propose to interpret and implement it in future?

13. Is it realistic for us to distinguish between external defence and internal security in the circumstances of Brunei today? Can we avoid being involved in internal security if we wish to retain control over the Special Branch?

14. What are our responsibilities towards Shell and how are these to be discharged now and in the long term?

15. Is the policy discussed in this paper too uncertain of success and difficult to execute? Should we perhaps, despite the possible dangers, end our present relationship with Brunei now or within a specified period, e.g. one year?

198 CO 1030/1494, no 50A   20 July 1963
'Sarawak elections': inward telegram C362 OCULAR from Sir A Waddell to Mr Sandys

[Elections were crucial both to the validation of Malaysia and the preparation of North Borneo and Sarawak for independence within Malaysia. North Borneo's first elections were held in late 1962 and early 1963. There were direct, popular elections to local councils which chose electoral colleges that in turn voted for legislative councillors. The Sabah Alliance, consisting of USNO, UNKO, BUNAP, UNPMO, and SIC, campaigned for Malaysia (see 26, n 8). Since the Alliance was returned unopposed, it was a foregone conclusion that Dato Mustapha (leader of USNO) and Donald Stephens (leader of UNKO) would be designated respectively the first governor and the first chief minister of Sabah, as North Borneo was now to be called. In Sarawak, by contrast, there was a contest for control of the legislature and over the nomination of the governor. The Sarawak elections were held between Apr and July. As in North Borneo, there was a three-tiered electoral process, with direct elections to district councils and thereafter indirect elections from district to divisional councils and from divisional councils to the Council Negri (legislature). There had been elections in 1959; the principal innovation in 1963 was a ministerial system. Thus the Supreme Council (Executive Council) would be led by a chief minister chosen by a majority of the elected members of the Council Negri. Six parties contested the elections: a four-party Alliance (of BARJASA, PESAKA, SCA, and SNAP, see 26, n 4) favoured Malaysia which was opposed by a marriage of convenience between SUPP (socialist and largely Chinese) and PANAS (right-wing and largely Malay). PANAS had recently defected from the Alliance, partly as a result of historic enmity with Malays of BARJASA. After complicated manoeuvres, which focused on wooing independent members, the Sarawak Alliance won control of the Council Negri. Although neither a charismatic leader, nor an experienced administrator, nor a deft politician, Stephen Kalong Ningkan emerged as Sarawak's chief minister, as Waddell explains in this telegram to Sandys. The selection of Sarawak's post-colonial governor, however, would provoke a crisis, see 210 and 224.]

With adhesion of four independent members from Fourth Division, Alliance now has 23 seats in Council Negri out of 36.

2. Alliance caucus met Tuesday in Sibu with Malayans in attendance. I sent emissary to summon them to Kuching and at the same time to stress importance of forming a broad based government including independents and indeed moderate leaders of non Alliance parties in interests of national unity, efficient administration and security. I had in mind James Wong[1] as Chief Minister and ministerial

---

[1] James Wong Kim Ming was from the Fifth Division and leader of the Sarawak Chinese Association; he became deputy chief minister.

representation of S.U.P.P./PANAS in hope of breaking communist grip on S.U.P.P. and avoiding split in Malays through leaving PANAS out.

3.   I started preliminary discussions with Alliance delegation today and deployed arguments in support of above. The Malayan influence, however, was evident and I was informed that at no price would they have dealings with S.U.P.P./PANAS, as this would compromise their principles, give communists a Trojan horse, confuse the native electorate who hated S.U.P.P. and dissuade bulk of moderate Chinese from supporting Alliance. I do not expect any change from this position. They are, however, having discussions with independents [?of] Fifth Division and James Wong is coming to Kuching.

4.   Delegation unanimously recommended for my approval appointment of Stephen Kalong Ningkan as Chief Minister. Meeting adjourned until tomorrow, when rest of Alliance recommendations will be mentioned. I understand they have in mind Temonggong Jugah for Governor. These two appointments are clearly linked and represent compromise between Second and Third Division Ibans. Rejection of either would, I fear, put Alliance back in melting pot.

5.   Kalong Ningkan, who has some slight history of collaboration with Japanese, is strongly Iban nationalistic and previously inclined to brashness and swollen head. Light-weight intellectually, he is personable and could get by if supported by adequate ministerial team. In any case, there is no choice.

6.   There is uneasiness amongst Chinese in Third Division who fear a pogrom after 31st August and some tenseness is reported in Kuching with Barjasa/PANAS incidents and apprehension of rule by inexperienced natives. We can no doubt expect more of this in situation where Kuching is centre of opposition and with no responsibility.

7.   I have as yet made no appointments.

199   CO 1030/1470, no 433   29 July 1963
[Brunei: future policy]: note of a meeting between Mr Sandys and the Sultan of Brunei

[Sandys' team consisted of Sir J Martin, W I J Wallace, A M MacKintosh, J D Higham, R F A Shegog and I H Harris. The Sultan was accompanied by Dato Setia Marsal bin Maun (chief minister), Pangiran Kerma Indra (director of telecommunications), Dato Setia Pengiran Haji Yussof (deputy state secretary), Mohd Taib bin Awang Besar (establishment officer), Isa bin Ibrahim (deputy public prosecutor, acting as interpreter), Pehin Abbas bin Ibrahim (ADC), Neil Lawson (constitutional adviser) and Idris Talog Davies (attorney general).]

The Secretary of State said that he understood that the Sultan wished to raise certain matters with him.

Mr. Lawson referred to the paper circulated by the Brunei delegation. The paper was divided into two parts, the first part dealing mainly with requests for staff and the second part dealing with constitutional and other matters. Mr. Lawson said that the Sultan was relying on the 1959 Agreement which placed obligations on Her Majesty's Government to assist Brunei in filling key posts and other posts if required. Mr. Lawson asked the Secretary of State to authorise action at departmental level on

Brunei's requests for staff. Brunei also wished H.M.G. to tie up arrangements with the Malayan Government regarding the Police and the Brunei Regiment.

The Secretary of State expressed the hope that Brunei would maintain good relations with the Malaysian Government and thus secure their co-operation in filling vacant posts. It was also necessary to make Malaysian officers feel welcomed in Brunei. Anti-Malayan or anti-Malaysian incidents would make this more difficult.

The Sultan said that it had been his intention since 1959 to look to Malaya for officers.[1] In present circumstances, however, he believed that Malaysia would not be able to spare officers for Brunei.

The Secretary of State said that Britain would discharge its responsibilities to Brunei but must look to Brunei to go on trying to obtain officials from Malaya to the maximum extent possible. As far as H.M.G. knew the Malayans were still prepared to supply officials and he would seek confirmation from them that this was so. The Sultan must not be surprised if, in view of his decision not to join Malaysia, the Malayans sent their best people to Malaysia.

The Sultan said that he understood this. The Brunei Government would have to review the position of Malayan officers already in Brunei but he intended to retain those who were sufficiently experienced.

The Secretary of State warned the Sultan that H.M.G. could not undertake to replace Malayan officers whom the Sultan pushed out of Brunei.

The Sultan said that he had no intention of declaring all Malayan officers to be unsatisfactory. He had come to seek help in accordance with the 1959 Agreement and in the light of the Secretary of State's own undertaking to him that H.M.G. would do everything it could to help Brunei.

The Secretary of State emphasised that the first duty of Brunei was to obtain help from the Malayans.

The Sultan said that if he was satisfied that Malayan experts were genuinely ready to help Brunei, then Brunei would not refuse them. On the other hand experience since 1959 had shown the need for officers other than Malayans.

The Secretary of State said that after its rejection of Malaysia Brunei could not be too choosy about Malayan officers. H.M.G. could not provide experts on an increased scale with the implication that we were increasing the scale of colonial administration in Brunei. The Secretary of State suggested that Brunei's detailed requirements as set out in the Brunei delegation's paper should be studied at departmental level by the Colonial Office and the Department of Technical Co-operation.

The Sultan said that his decision not to join Malaysia would not affect Brunei's friendly relations with Malaya or Malaysia. Brunei merely wanted expert assistance to enable her to advance economically and constitutionally.

Mr. Lawson thought that it was unrealistic for Brunei to look to Malaya for persons of the calibre she needed. The Sultan was taking his stand on the 1959 Agreement.

The Secretary of State said that Britain must be the judge whether experts could be found from sources other than Malaya.

---

[1] See, for example, 52, n 4 and 91.

The Secretary of State referred to the Sultan's insistence on H.M.G.'s obligations under the 1959 Agreement and reminded the Sultan that he too had obligations under the Agreement. One such obligation was to accept H.M.G.'s advice on the good government of his country.

The Sultan agreed.

The Secretary of State said that as a result of not joining Malaysia Brunei was likely to be subjected to subversion from Indonesia which was determined to break up Malaysia. Brunei was an obvious bridgehead into Malaysia. It was therefore of the utmost importance that His Highness should command the fullest loyalty of his people. If he did not there would be internal political discontent and subversion from outside and a situation might well develop which neither the Sultan nor H.M.G. could handle. The Secretary of State might therefore find it necessary to advise the Sultan formally under the Agreement that the rate of constitutional progress proposed in his paper was totally inadequate. The Secretary of State said that he was not giving formal advice now. This was a warning and he wished to give the matter further consideration. He would, however, like to hear the Sultan's views on the whole problem of political advance in Brunei.

The Sultan said that it was his intention to remove the sources of discontent.

The Secretary of State said that it was his impression that Brunei would have to go a lot faster than was contemplated in the paper.

The Sultan said that he desired advice on an increased rate of progress.

Mr. Lawson thought that premature elections would produce an anti-Malaysia Government.

The Secretary of State remarked that this could hardly be more anti-Malaysia than His Highness The Sultan. After so many concessions had been made to the Sultan by the Malayans the only explanation he could find for the Sultan's rejection of Malaysia was that he had come to London with his mind made up not to join.[2]

The Sultan said that this was not the case.

The Secretary of State said that he did not wish to conduct a post-mortem on what H.M.G. believed was a very grave mistake.

The Secretary of State said that with regard to the political situation in Brunei it would be difficult for Brunei to lag behind North Borneo and Sarawak.

The Sultan said that he was not fully conversant with politics in Brunei. Political questions rarely reached him. Perhaps the Brunei Government might know more about the political situation.

The Secretary of State said that it would be easier for H.M.G. to help Brunei to deal with Indonesian subversion than to put down purely internal disturbances arising from the denial of political rights.

The Sultan said that he appreciated the position. He believed that progress would remove discontent and he looked to H.M.G. for help.

The Secretary of State said that he wanted time to consider this. Brunei must keep abreast of her neighbours politically. Politics went with economics and Brunei had great economic strength (relatively few people and plenty of money). It would help to give the people a very good standard of living. This was one of the best safeguards against discontent. If Brunei could not go fast politically it was more than ever

---

[2] Compare the first sentence of the notes provided by Harris, 197.

necessary to go fast economically. His Highness should not think that material benefits alone would long be accepted in Brunei as a substitute for a share in the political management of the country.

The Sultan indicated assent.

The Secretary of State said that he himself wished to think about all this in the light of the present talks and of the Brunei paper. He would like to speak to the Sultan again and suggested that he might call at Brunei perhaps for a night at the end of August when he would be going to Malaysia for the celebrations.[3] Meanwhile he agreed that there should be detailed discussion on the Brunei paper with the Colonial Office and the Department of Technical Co-operation.

The Sultan welcomed the Secretary of State's intention to visit Brunei. The Sultan added that he wished again to make it clear that he had come for help from H.M.G. to enable Brunei to implement its development plans and to remove the sources of discontent.

Mr. Lawson referred to a letter which the Sultan had sent to the Secretary of State asking for the return of the Limbang district of Sarawak.

The Secretary of State stated that H.M.G. could not consider this request. Limbang was part of Sarawak and would shortly become part of Malaysia. Any claim respecting Limbang would have to go to the Government of Malaysia. The Secretary of State added that he was not encouraging the Sultan to make a claim; he merely wished to make it clear that if any such claim were to be made then it should be addressed to the Government of Malaysia and not to H.M.G.

The Sultan and *Mr. Lawson* said that in fact the letter constituted a claim.

The Secretary of State said that he would pass the correspondence on to Kuala Lumpur.[4]

---

[3] In fact Sandys visited the Sultan on 14 Sept, two days before Malaysia Day.

[4] The Sultan had written to Sandys about the Limbang claim on 27 July, two days before this meeting. Sandys replied on 14 Aug, referring to the discussion on 29 July and informing the Sultan that he would send the correspondence to the government of Malaya. Sandys Papers, 8/14.

200 CAB 128/37, CC 51(63)4   1 Aug 1963
[Manila summit]: Cabinet conclusions

[The Manila summit of Macapagal, Sukarno and the Tunku took place between 30 July and 5 Aug. A series of meetings had paved the way for it: tripartite talks at sub-ministerial level in Manila, 9–17 Apr; encounters between the Tunku and Macapagal in early April and between the Tunku and Sukarno in Tokyo, 31 May–1 June; a conference of foreign ministers in Manila, 7–11 June. Their stated aim was to improve relations through closer association (to be known as Maphilindo) and, in particular, the resolution of problems arising from the Malaysia project and the international status of North Borneo. The British government followed these developments closely and, while opinion was divided on the value of the Maphilindo concept, there was no sympathy for the proposal to re-examine the Malaysia question by holding a UN-sponsored referendum, or plebiscite, or any independent assessment of the wishes of Borneo peoples. The British argued that the legitimacy of Malaysia had already been established; it rested on the Cobbold enquiry, the report of the IGC, the Singapore referendum, resolutions in the legislatures of the territories involved and recent elections in North Borneo and Sarawak. While the Tunku accepted this, he claimed that the results of the Manila summit (ie the Manila Accord of 31 July, the joint statement of 5 Aug and the joint declaration of 5 Aug) were far more favourable to the cause of Malaysia than the British suggested. Indeed, the outcome could have been much worse since Sukarno was incensed at the speed of developments and alleged that the Tunku had reneged on a promise made at Tokyo not to bring about Malaysia until the three leaders had met to discuss it. Nevertheless, the British Cabinet saw Manila as a serious threat to the inauguration of Malaysia and Sandys, who did not disguise his view that the Tunku had lost his nerve, tried to prevent the Malayan government from agreeing to the postponement of Malaysia Day (see 201–203). As a later FCO survey put it, the Manila summit was accompanied, 'by some anxious back seat driving' from the British in an attempt 'to stiffen the Tunku' ('The origins and formation of Malaysia', 10 July 1970, FCO 51/154; see the appendix to this volume, para 259). Sandys' anxiety was aggravated by a report from Selkirk that any substantial change in the timetable might force Lee Kuan Yew to hold a general election which could result in a Barisan victory and the end to hopes of merger between Singapore and Malaya. In fact, Lee responded to the delay in the inauguration of Malaysia by declaring independence unilaterally and arrogating powers on 31 Aug (see 209, 215–221; also Selkirk to Sandys, telegram OCULAR 541, 2 Aug 1963, DO 169/222, no 4). In addition, the Manila Accord threatened to drive a wedge between the British and American governments, and it was to prevent this that Macmillan was persuaded to accept a UN mission to North Borneo and Sarawak (see 204–208).]

The Prime Minister of Malaya, Tunku Abdul Rahman, had apparently been persuaded by the Prime Minister of the Philippines, Mr. Macapagal, and the President of Indonesia, Dr. Sukarno, to ask the Secretary-General of the United Nations how long it would take him to ascertain the attitude of the inhabitants of the North Borneo territories towards Malaysia. He had also indicated that, if some enquiry for this purpose could be conducted under United Nations auspices in the immediate future, he might be prepared to postpone for a short period the establishment of Malaysia, at present fixed for 31st August.

In discussion it was agreed that any postponement of the creation of Malaysia at this stage would be more likely to lead to an indefinite postponement of the project than to promote an early resolution of the current differences between Malaya and Indonesia. Moreover, a survey under United Nations auspices would not only be liable to take a considerable time but would also merely confirm that the inhabitants of North Borneo endorsed the concept of Malaysia. We should therefore impress on the Prime Minister of Malaya the importance of adhering to 31st August as the date for the formation of Malaysia and warn him of the dangers implicit in any further delay.

201   FO 371/169724, no 26   2 Aug 1963
[Manila summit]: outward telegram OCULAR 1002 from Lord Home to T Peters,[1] giving instructions regarding Mr Sandys' personal message for Tunku Abdul Rahman

My immediately following telegram contains the text of a further personal message from Mr Sandys to the Tunku which you should deliver as soon as possible. In doing so please draw attention to the third paragraph and say that a plebiscite would not only arouse political doubts in Borneo, but that we also cannot foresee

---

[1] Theophilus Peters, head of chancery at the British embassy in Manila, was at the time acting for the ambassador, J (later Sir John) Pilcher.

what the result of it would be if it were conducted in this atmosphere. We should have great difficulty in reaching agreement on a satisfactory wording of the question to be put to the local populations, the Indonesians would interfere in every possible way with propaganda and subversion, and we should be faced with many unacceptable demands such as perhaps the withdrawal of British troops during the voting, complete freedom for Azahari to organise opposition, freedom to vote for the alien Indonesian population in North Borneo etc. We should be involved in every sort of dispute and the result might conceivably be different from the recent free elections.

2.   Under no circumstances should you commit the above views to writing. . . .

202   FO 371/169724, no 26   2 Aug 1963

[Manila summit]: outward telegram OCULAR 1003 from Lord Home to T Peters, forwarding a personal message from Mr Sandys for Tunku Abdul Rahman

My immediately preceding telegram.[1]

Please pass following further personal message to Tunku from Commonwealth Secretary.

Begins: I was glad to learn from the report which you asked our Chargé d'Affaires to send us this morning that you are standing firm against Indonesian pressure for a pre-Malaysia plebiscite.

2.   As you know, we are much concerned about the possible effects of postponing Malaysia. If you feel it necessary to agree to a representative of the United Nations Secretary-General visiting North Borneo and Sarawak before 31st August, we would concur even though you and we would naturally not regard any such perfunctory assessment of opinion as more reliable than the clear results of the recent elections in both territories.

3.   However, if Malaysia Day were postponed for the sake of a plebiscite, it would create doubts and uncertainty throughout the area and would encourage everyone to have second thoughts.

4.   No amount of plebiscites will alter Sukarno's basic hostility to Malaysia. His ultimate objective is clearly to round off his empire by absorbing into it the three North Borneo territories. He sees in Malaysia a serious obstacle to his ambitions and, whatever he may say, he will continue to try and undermine it. Therefore it seems to us that for the sake of papering over the cracks in a conference communiqué it would be unwise to run the risk of unsettling and possibly upsetting altogether the new association which we have negotiated with such difficulty.

5.   If as a result of your stand, your relations with Indonesia become more difficult you know you can count on us to back you

With all good wishes,
DUNCAN SANDYS *Ends*.

---

[1] See 201.

203   FO 371/169724, no 26   3 Aug 1963
[Manila summit]: inward telegram OCULAR 593 from T Peters
to Lord Home forwarding Tunku Abdul Rahman's reply to
Mr Sandys

Your telegram No. 1003.

I gave the Tunku Mr. Sandys' personal message this morning, and following is text of his personal reply to Mr. Sandys.

Begins. I agree with you that his motive is not sincere and I think he is being forced into obstructing our Malaysia plan by Communist followers in his country. I am just trying to manoeuvre in the hope of reaching a compromise. I realize only too well that any postponement of Malaysia would be tantamount to a surrender, which will be used to advantage by the Communists. Now that I am assured of your support, I will know what steps to take at the next meeting of heads of State. You can rest assured that Malaysia will be announced on the 31st of August as scheduled. *Ends*.

204   PREM 11/4349, T430/63   4 Aug 1963
[Manila summit]: outward telegram no 7462 from the FO to
Washington Embassy, forwarding a personal message from President
Kennedy to Mr Macmillan

Following message received by Prime Minister from President Kennedy early morning August 4.[1]

Begins. 'I am quite concerned that hopefully successful Manila summit will be torpedoed unless 31 August date for Malaysia can be postponed briefly to give Sukarno a fig leaf. If in fact the Tunku is willing, and if there is a good chance Sukarno can be bought this cheaply, we would urge you give this an urgent look. I well realize that kowtowing to Sukarno is a risky enterprise, but a little give now may be worth the risk, especially if the likely alternative is a further step-up of subversive pressures. This is your show, but I feel we ought to place our worries frankly before you.'

2.   Draft reply to President is being submitted to Prime Minister at Chatsworth[2] this afternoon.

---

[1] It was despatched on 3 Aug and is also printed in *Foreign Relations of the United States, 1961–1963*, XXIII (Washington, 1994), doc 333, p 725.

[2] Chatsworth House was the seat of the Cavendish family into which Macmillan had married.

205   PREM 11/4349, T432/63   4 Aug 1963
[Manila summit]: inward telegram no 1742 from Lord Home to Mr Macmillan

Following for Prime Minister from Foreign Secretary.[1]
Malaysia.
I have read the President's message to you.[2]
2.   I think we should assume the worst of Sukarno, and should not agree to a delay over Malaysia on his account. There are, however, two points which you may wish to take into consideration. Sukarno will cause us trouble after Malaysia, but if we agree to a small postponement to meet American wishes, we are more likely to obtain full American support afterwards. There is also the subsidiary point that we should not let the Tunku shuffle the blame on to us for any possible failure to agree at the Manila Summit now and for subsequent trouble with Indonesia.
3.   U Thant will be here in Moscow for the next day or two. Please let me know if there is anything you think I could usefully say to him. I do not myself see why he should not send Narisimhan [sic] to make his investigation before August 31.

---

[1] Home was in Moscow, negotiating the nuclear test ban treaty signed by Britain, USA and USSR on 5 Aug.
[2] See 204.

206   PREM 11/4349, T434/63   4 Aug 1963
[Manila summit]: outward telegram no 2459 from the FO to Lord Home, forwarding Mr Macmillan's message to President Kennedy

My immediately preceding telegram [of August 4].
Following for Secretary of State.
Following is text of personal message sent by Prime Minister to President Kennedy tonight in reply to latter's message about Malaysia in my telegram No. 7462 to Washington.[1]
2.   *Begins.*[2] 'Many thanks for your message about Malaysia.
If the three Heads of State were to agree on a proposal of the kind you mention and were to put this to us, we should certainly give it careful consideration. So far, however, the Tunku (who has been in close touch with us) has not put such a proposal to us and we have no reason to suppose that he now favours it. We should not think it right to advise him to do so.
I too share your concern about the outcome of this Manila meeting, but I do not believe that Sukarno can be bought off with a fig leaf. He would need something much bigger to cover him effectively. A slight postponement in the date of August 31 may seem an attractive face saver if we were dealing with a man of good faith but poses considerable difficulties for us in that the original date was agreed not only with the Tunku, but also with the North Borneo, Sarawak and Singapore leaders. Moreover, a delay in bringing about what has been so painstakingly prepared could

---

[1] See 204.   [2] This is also printed in *FRUS, 1961–1963*, XXIII, doc 333, p 725n.

sew just that confusion which Sukarno would like to see. There is an old French saying—what is postponed is lost.

The Tunku is well aware of the risks involved. He is battling hard and tells us he is working for a compromise but will not make any major concessions liable to affect the future of Malaysia. We must let him play the hand in Manila.

Incidentally, our information from Manila indicates that the latest Indonesian move reveals that Sukarno's real intention is to obtain a veto on use of our bases. This is very dangerous for us all. It would make nonsense of all our defence arrangements east of Suez and is intended to prevent us fulfilling our S.E.A.T.O. obligations.' *Ends*.

207 PREM 11/4349, T443B/63   5 Aug 1963
[Manila summit]: outward telegram no 2488 from Mr Macmillan to Lord Home

Following from Prime Minister for Foreign Secretary.

Having now studied the terms of the agreement reached at Manila I consider that we should accept a visit by the Secretary-General's representative of the kind proposed in Manila telegram No. 608 on the following assumptions:—

(a) That the Secretary-General can complete this task in time to permit the establishment of Malaysia on August 31;
(b) That the Secretary-General's report shall not be subject to confirmation by the United Nations or by the Governments of Malaya, Indonesia and the Philippines.[1]

2.   The Manila agreement has many vexatious and disagreeable features, particularly the proposal for Indonesian and Philippine observers in paragraph 7 and the reference to foreign bases in paragraph 11.[2] I think we should try to resist the first, though we need not perhaps make it a breaking point. We are not called on to accept the second, though we should seek assurances from the Tunku that he will so interpret it as to enable us to discharge defence commitments in South East Asia.

3.   Nevertheless in view of President Kennedy's message and the considerations set out in your own message to me (Moscow telegram No. 1742)[3] I do not think we should risk forfeiting future American support against Indonesia (which we shall certainly need notwithstanding this agreement) by adopting an intransigent attitude.

4.   I should be grateful if you would take the opportunity of explaining our initial reactions (our formal reply must await the approach from the Tunku envisaged in paragraph 6 of Manila telegram No. 608) to U Thant and seek his views on our two conditions.

[1] On 6 Aug, Home reported that U Thant saw no difficulty with assumption (b) but that it would be highly unlikely that the enquiry would be over in time to inaugurate Malaysia on 31 Aug.
[2] The Manila joint statement, one of the three documents issued at the summit, proposed a UN mission to assess the wishes of the Borneo peoples regarding Malaysia. Paragraph 7 proposed that observers from the Philippines and Indonesia should accompany the UN mission. Paragraph 11 stated: 'The three Heads of

Government further agreed that foreign bases—temporary in nature—should not be allowed to be used directly or indirectly to subvert the national independence of any of the three countries. In accordance with the principle enunciated in the Bandung Declaration, the three countries will abstain from the use of arrangements of collective defence to serve the particular interests of any of the big powers.'
³ See 204 and 205.

208 PREM 11/4349, T442/63   6 Aug 1963
[Manila summit]: outward telegram 7525 from Mr Macmillan to President Kennedy   [Extract]

[This telegram, which Macmillan addressed to his 'Dear Friend', was largely devoted to the nuclear test ban treaty. The extract printed here refers to Malaysia and picks up the reference to the fig leaf made in documents 204 and 206.]

... We are still not quite clear what has happened about Malaysia but it looks as if you may have been right about Sukarno's fig leaf. However, it may all have turned out for the best. The Tunku does seem to have made some concession, but I still feel it better that he should have done this on his own rather than at our instance. If anything had gone wrong he could certainly have put the blame on us: now we can hold his hand. There are some rather dubious phrases about foreign bases which I don't like. For that means Singapore and Singapore is of course vital to both our interests in the Far East. However, we are covered by our Treaty with Malaya. ...

209 DO 169/222, no 17   9 Aug 1963
[Lee Kuan Yew's proposal to declare independence on 31 Aug]: inward telegram OCULAR 554 from Lord Selkirk to Mr Sandys

I saw Lee Kuan Yew again last night just before his departure for Kuala Lumpur and he elaborated on the idea contained in paragraph 2(2) of my above quoted telegram. He suggested that Stephens, Ningkan and himself should at once publicly declare their intention to proceed with their own independence on the 31st August with a view to joining Malaysia as soon as the Tunku was ready to accept them. The three of them would then fly to New York to make their views known to U Thant. Thence to Moscow, where Lee thought they would be able to confirm that Khruschev [sic] would not oppose Malaysia, and finally to London where he would hope to get the agreement of the British Government. His whole theme was that it was vital to stand up to Soekarno and that this expression of self-determination by the territories concerned would be a slap in the eye for the Indonesians. Lee hoped that he would be allowed later to visit Sarawak where he was quite sure that he could destroy the influence of S.U.P.P.

2. I agreed with Lee that it was valuable at this stage to give the maximum impression of support for Malaysia and determination to see it through by the Prime Minister and Chief Ministers of the three territories concerned. I pointed out, however, that:—

(a) it would not be possible for Britain to agree to the independence of Singapore, Sabah[1] and Sarawak on 31st August except as part of Malaysia; and

(b) that there was not time for Stephens and Ningkan to make the length of tour proposed by Lee, since they would have to be in Borneo for the visit by U Thant's representative.

3.   I believe there is a great deal in what Lee is saying. Soekarno has tarnished (possibly irretrievably) Tunku's image by making Tunku bend to Soekarno's will before all the world, The obvious deduction which will be made is that Soekarno could do it again whenever he so desires. The Chinese particularly are worried that Tunku's weakness may eventually hand them over to Indonesia. Our armed forces now preserving the independence of Malaysia cannot do that indefinitely unless there is strong national unity and leadership. The Malays are not providing it. I hope, therefore, we shall not find it necessary to clamp down on any expression of nationalism and desire for self-determination shown by Lee, Stephens and Ningkan. While it may be necessary for us to play a fairly passive part publicly, there seems to be every advantage in the national leaders of the territories concerned taking a forceful line. Indeed, we can hardly expect them to be passive while Soekarno is actively trying to wreck Malaysia.

4.   I have asked Lee to discuss his ideas with Tory when he is in Kuala Lumpur today. When he returns to Singapore tomorrow, I should like to be able to tell him that while it would not be possible to implement the independence of Singapore, Sabah and Sarawak outside Malaysia on 31st August, we privately welcomed the general line he is taking. I see from Governor North Borneo's telegrams Nos. 424 and 426 that Sabah is taking a similar line. I would also suggest that serious consideration is given to Lee's suggestion of a visit by the three leaders to New York and London to make their views known to U Thant and yourself although I doubt whether the visit to Moscow is practicable in the circumstances. It is only by allowing the three leaders of the territories concerned to speak for themselves that we can hope to persuade U Thant to complete his task by 31st August.

---

[1] The pre-colonial name of Sabah had been applied to the area in an English-language document of 29 Dec 1877 when a group of European traders won concessions from the Sultan of Brunei. The Sultan granted to Baron Gustav von Overbeck a number of specific territories and appointed him 'Maharajah of Sabah and Rajah of Gaya and Sandakan'. Thereafter the term 'North Borneo' was used in British documents. When North Borneo acquired de facto self-government on 31 Aug 1963 (sixteen days before the inauguration of Malaysia) it was officially re-named Sabah. See Allen, Stockwell and Wright, *A collection of treaties*, II, p 434; D S Ranjit Singh, *The making of Sabah 1865–1941* (Kuala Lumpur, 2000) pp 3–5; and CO 1030/1453.

210   CO 1030/1494, no 66   9 Aug 1963
[Sarawak's head of state]: telegram OCULAR C400 from Sir A Waddell to Mr Sandys

[The new constitutions for North Borneo and Sarawak provided for a head of state. The office holder was to be recommended jointly by the Queen and the Agong but appointed by the Agong alone. Dato Mustapha had for some time been lined up as Sabah's head of state, but the selection of Sarawak's post-colonial governor proved controversial.

Although Temenggong Jugah, the paramount chief of the Ibans, was the front-runner, the Tunku insisted on a Malay and favoured Dato Haji Openg. Sandys responded to Waddell's telegram by urging the Tunku to accept Jugah so as not to risk losing Iban support for Malaysia and thereby jeopardising the outcome of the UN mission to Sarawak (Sandys to Tory, tel 1976, 12 Aug 1963, DO 189/219, no 179). The problem was not resolved until 13 Sept when Sandys brokered a compromise whereby Openg became the governor while Jugah was appointed federal minister for Sarawak Affairs with a seat in the federal Cabinet (see 224).]

There is no hope of budging me on this either. I repeat that my advice has been tendered after full consideration of all factors involved including repeated intelligence reports which indicate the possible trouble if Jugah not appointed. This is not a matter of personal pique or agitation by Jugah but is deep seated spontaneous feeling amongst Ibans who are now thoroughly awake politically, particularly after success at elections. They are, after all, largest racial block and only race which has voted unanimously and unequivocally for Malaysia. It should also not be forgotten that there are two millions of them on the other side of the border.

2.   It is nonsense to say that Malays are most politically conscious community here. They are the most politically tortuous and divided, and Malayans[1] have not helped matters by vehement denunciation of Datu Bandar and Panas during elections.[2] Appointment of Malay Governor would certainly be ascribed to Barjasa intrigue (which is doubly deplorable as Barjasa part of Alliance which unanimously recommended Jugah) and people here are well aware that Abdul Rahman Yakub[3] has remained on in Kuala Lumpur no doubt for this purpose. Such appointment would (a) divide Malays even more (b) wreck the Alliance (c) turn Ibans anti-Malaysia and (d) give rise to internal and external security situation of utmost gravity which could involve H.M.G. in the most distasteful security action in history. And Malay troops even if available would make matters worse. I am sure strength of Iban feeling well appreciated by Lord Lansdowne and the Cobbold Commission.

3.   Against this Jugah's comparative illiteracy is of no account and was certainly no apparent bar to his being strenuously courted by Malays when the Ibans were being won over.

4.   It is quite unrealistic for Tunku to force a nominee not supported by Alliance. This I am not able or willing to do. I can only suggest invitation to Alliance to visit Kuala Lumpur but see my telegram No. C67 on last occasion. Time is now desperately short before arrival of U.N. Mission. Failure to reach decision could be fatal to Malaysia and to Sarawak.

---

[1] ie, those in the Federation of Malaya.
[2] This refers to disputes within Sarawak's Malay community which, while dating back to the cession crisis of the late 1940s, came to a head in the 1963 elections when PANAS (led by Dato Bandar) defected from the pro-Malaysia Sarawak Alliance.
[3] Dato Abdul Rahman Yakub was the leader of BARJASA, the Malay party that favoured Malaysia and was a member of the Sarawak Alliance.

211   PREM 11/4349   9 Aug 1963
[UN mission and the postponement of Malaysia Day]: inward telegram
no 1503 from Sir G Tory to Mr Sandys, reporting the Tunku's attitude

Your telegram No. 1926:

U Thant and Malaysia
Spoke accordingly to Tunku this morning.

2.   Tunku recognises that postponement of Malaysia day requires agreement of
all signatories. He authorised me to convey his absolutely firm undertaking 'that he
will go ahead with Malaysia on whatever later date may now be agreed between the
signatories. For his part, and subject to agreement of others concerned, he would
like this date to be 16th September irrespective of nature of the Secretary-General
report'. He also accepts that should Secretary-General's report be unfavourable any
further ascertainment of Bornean wishes would then be his responsibility and would
not take place until after establishment of Malaysia. He would be prepared to face the
consequences provided that we stood by him.

3.   Tunku understands that admission of Secretary-General's representatives may
create dangerous precedent for us. He says however that it is already absolutely clear
that if we receive teams we do so at special request of Malayan Government in order
to help them. This carries with it other implications you mention i.e. we should not
ourselves be associated with the request or with the report. The report would not be
addressed to us and we should not be committed to recognising the validity of its
findings. For obvious reasons the Tunku would not wish us to say anything publicly
at this stage about not accepting the validity of U Thant's report.

4.   As regards observers Tunku believes this would be a breaking point for the
Indonesians and that if we do not concede this the Indonesians will repudiate the
Manila Agreement.[1] Subandrio begged Tunku to accept request for observers to
enable Soekarno to placate the Indonesian Army who were becoming extremely
tough in their determination to destroy Malaysia.

5.   Tunku firmly believes that if Indonesians repudiate Manila Agreement there is
serious danger that the Indonesian Army will get out of hand and that there will be
major military incursions into Borneo Territories. He says Army are discontented
because they are not paid regularly and have been stirred up into emotional and
aggressive frame of mind towards Borneo Territories. Nasution[2] is making openly
hostile statements which are bound to make Army even more difficult to restrain.
Over all is Soekarno whom the Tunku found to be more unbalanced, irresponsible
and ill informed than he had feared and who could easily set off aggression by angry
and intemperate reaction to anything he chose to interpret as departure from
understandings at Manila. If real trouble started in Borneo Territories British Forces
would have to bear the blunt [? brunt] of dealing with it.

---

[1] Indonesia and the Philippines wished to send observers to accompany the UN mission. The British
government at first opposed, but later conceded, this request.
[2] General Abdul Harris Nasution was minister co-ordinator for defence and security and deputy
commander-in-chief of Indonesian armed forces; he narrowly avoided assassination during the abortive
coup of Oct 1965 and then supported General Suharto.

6. Tunku is distressed that his friends do not seem to understand his difficulties or his achievements at Manila. He went there to show he was prepared to do anything for peace in this region not really believing that there would be any genuine change of heart in Indonesia but hoping that if they could be brought to accept and endorse the Manila Agreement this would at least make it more difficult for them openly to pursue their aggressive designs against Malaysia. If we are intransigent about observers or about the date he believes Summit Agreement will be destroyed and that, [sic] the situation will then be far worse then if the Summit conference had never taken place. He hopes that we and the other Governments concerned will be able to see matters in this perspective as he does himself. Tunku denies that he is appeasing Indonesians. He is simply playing them along quietly in the hope that the fires will die down.

7. There is a further important point which Tunku did not make on this occasion, that about one third of the Malays have close ties and considerable sympathy with Indonesia and that for his own domestic political reasons he must demonstrate to these people that he is doing his best to get along with Indonesia and that he is not just being a British stooge.

8. As regards statement on bases see my telegram No. 1504.

212 PREM 11/4349 10 Aug 1963
[UN mission and the postponement of Malaysia Day]: outward telegram no 1946 from Mr Sandys to Sir G Tory, replying to document 211 and enclosing a message for the Tunku

Your interview with Tunku is reassuring. It is, however, important to have written confirmation of Tunku's undertakings in paragraph 2 of your telegram under reference.

2. Please therefore send following letter immediately to Tunku:—

> *Begins*: 'I have communicated to the Commonwealth Secretary the assurances which you gave me at our conversation yesterday, in the following terms: I reported that you asked me to convey your absolutely firm assurance that irrespective of the nature of the Secretary-General's report, you will inaugurate the Federation of Malaysia on whatever later date may now be agreed between the signatories. I informed Mr. Sandys that you suggested the revised date should be 16th September. I have reported that you have also assured me that should the Secretary-General's report be unfavourable it would be entirely your responsibility to decide whether there should be any further ascertainment of Bornean wishes and that any such ascertainment would not take place until after the establishment of Malaysia.
>
> I should be grateful if you would now confirm that I have correctly reported the assurances which you gave me orally.
>
> I have been authorised to give you the firm assurance that, if the undertakings set out above are confirmed by you, the British Government, for their part, will give you their full support in the implementation of this policy.' *Ends*.

3.   Please telegraph emergency when you have Tunku's written confirmation of his undertakings.

4.   You should inform Tunku that you require this written assurance most urgently since the action authorised in my three immediately following telegrams cannot be taken until you receive it.[1]

---

[1] Before Sandys' telegram 1946 reached Tory, the high commissioner had informed the Tunku of Sandys' views (as conveyed in the secretary of state's telegram 1926 of 8 Aug) with which the Tunku had concurred in writing. Assuming that this exchange met Sandys' more recent requirement, Tory did not pass on the message enclosed in telegram 1946 but communicated to London the text of his own letter to the Tunku (see 213 and also DO 169/222, no 11 and FO 371/169713, no 99).

213   DO 169/222, no 23   10 Aug 1963

[UN mission and the postponement of Malaysia Day]: inward telegram no 1515 from Sir G Tory to Mr Sandys, enclosing the text of Tory's letter to the Tunku and the notes from which he spoke at his meeting with the Tunku on 9 Aug

Text of letter dated 9th August from British High Commissioner Kuala Lumpur to Prime Minister of Malaya.

Begins: As agreed I enclose the notes from which I spoke this morning in conveying to you the various points which Mr. Duncan Sandys had instructed me to make in a telegram which I had just received from him. I have sent a telegram to Mr. Sandys reporting your observations as follows.

As regards postponement of M Day I said you had authorised me to convey your firm undertaking that you would go ahead with Malaysia on whatever later date might now be agreed between the signatories irrespective of the Secretary-General's report. This was on the understanding that the British Government stood by the Federation Government whatever the consequences. I added that you accepted that any further consultation in the Borneo Territories if the Secretary-General's report should prove to be unfavourable would then be your responsibility after the establishment of Malaysia.

I said you regarded it as already absolutely clear that if we received teams from the United Nations in the Borneo Territories we should be doing so only at the special request of your Government in order to help you.

I went on to say that you also confirmed that this would mean that the British Government would not themselves be associated with a request for an enquiry or with the eventual report. This report would not be addressed to them and they would not be committed to recognising the validity of its findings. I said here that for obvious reasons you would not wish the British Government at this stage to say anything about not recognising the validity of the Secretary-General's report.

As regards observers I reported your view that the Indonesians would be likely to repudiate the Manila Agreement if they and the Filipinos were not allowed to send observers. I explained that Dr. Subandrio had particularly asked you to accept this provision for purposes of presenting the Manila Agreement to the Indonesian Army who were being increasingly tough in their opposition to Malaysia.

I then quoted you as saying that the Manila Agreement represented an achievement which should not be lightly thrown away. You had gone to Manila to show your determination to do everything within reason to secure peace in this area. You had not been very sanguine about any genuine change of heart on the part of Indonesia's leaders but felt that the very fact of their subscribing to the Manila Declaration would inevitably have the effect of putting some restraint on their efforts to subvert Malaysia and would at least make it more difficult for them to pursue any sinister objectives in an open manner.

On the Indonesian army I said you thought they were in a very dangerous frame of mind, underpaid, over-excited, and egged on by General Nasution and that if President Soekarno were to repudiate the Manila Agreement in a fit of temper at what he chose to regard as some departure from understandings with you at Manila this might easily touch off a conflagration which it would be difficult to put out. You were not appeasing the Indonesians but rather playing them along quietly in the hope that the fires would die down.

I hope that this accurately represented what was in your mind.[1]

As regards the Singapore base and the Defence Agreement I enclose also the gist of what Mr. Sandys said in his telegram about the statement which he intended to issue to the press. I simply informed Mr. Sandys that you would not object to this. *Ends*.

2.   Following is full text of enclosure.

Begins: Tunku's message of the 3rd August said that Malaysia would be announced on the 31st August as scheduled. The date of M Day is in the Malaysia Agreement and alteration needs the consent of all signatories.

Before British Government can consider any question of postponement they need an absolutely firm undertaking from the Tunku that he will go ahead with Malaysia on whatever later date may now be agreed between the signatories irrespective of the Secretary-General's report. Any further ascertainment of Bornean wishes if the report were unfavourable would then be the Tunku's responsibility after establishment of Malaysia (cf. West Irian after interval of three years). In any event we could not agree to the postponement of merger between Malaya and Singapore beyond a date in September.

The British Government do not recognise that the Manila Conference or anyone else has the right to invite U Thant's representatives into territories for which we are still responsible. This is most important because of the danger of precedents elsewhere notably British Guiana and British Honduras. If we receive teams it must be absolutely clear that we do so only at the special request of the Malayan Government in order to help them.

This means that the British Government do not wish themselves to be associated with the request for an enquiry or with the eventual report. They do not wish the Secretary-General's decision on the report to be addressed to them nor do they wish to be committed to recognising the validity of its findings.

---

[1] The Tunku confirmed this in writing.

As regards observers the British Government see serious objection to accepting Indonesian and Philippine observers in North Borneo and Sarawak:—

> (a) neither Indonesia nor the Philippines has any status in these territories;
> (b) the admission of observers would increase the danger of delay and subversion;
> (c) the North Borneo Government have already objected strongly to this proposal;
> (d) the Manila communique only says the observers are 'desirable' not a condition of the enquiry.

The British Government have sent the following message to Sir Patrick Dean the British Representative on the United Nations on this question of observers: 'You are not authorised to tell U Thant that we are prepared to agree to observers. We regret that there should have been a request for observers to supervise the Secretary-General's task and you should use all your influence to persuade him not to accept this himself. It is clear that the Malayan Government do not like the idea of observers and strong objection has been expressed to them in North Borneo. We have experience of Indonesian subversive operations and have recently been obliged to expel two Indonesian Consuls from North Borneo. We do not accept that the Indonesians or Filipinos have any status in the Borneo Territories. It is only at the special request of the Government of the Federation of Malaya that we are prepared to agree to the enquiry being carried out.'

Bases: Mr. Duncan Sandys proposes to issue a statement to the press that the Malaysia agreement which includes the arrangements about the Singapore Base can be terminated or amended only with the consent of both parties and that we have confirmed this with the Tunku. As stated by the Tunku the joint declaration would not limit the use of British bases and our defence arrangements are therefore in no way affected. [*Ends*.]

214   DO 169/216, no 176   27 Aug 1963

[Sandys' mission to SE Asia]: inward telegram SOSLON 62 from Mr Sandys to CRO, reporting developments since his arrival in Kuala Lumpur

[On 16 Aug, the day when the UN mission of enquiry arrived in Kuching, Sandys spoke with Macmillan who was pessimistic about the prospects for Malaysia. Opinion in the region veered this way and that; while the Tunku appeared to waver over the inauguration of Malaysia, leaders in the Borneo territories and Singapore were reluctant to accept delay. On 22 Aug Donald Stephens and Stephen Kalong Ningkan flew to Kuala Lumpur to lobby for the original date. Sandys, too, felt the need to apply direct pressure on the Malayan prime minister. On 23 Aug he departed London for Kuala Lumpur in order, as he put it to the Australian prime minister, to 'hold the Tunku's hand'. A few days after his arrival, the Malayan Cabinet agreed to fix 16 Sept as Malaysia Day which the Yang di-Pertuan Agong formally proclaimed on 29 Aug. Macmillan thanked Sandys for 'stiffening the resolution of the Malayans at this critical point' and left him to decide 'how best to play the hand' with respect to the UN mission. By 30 Aug Sandys seemed confident that the 'pieces of the Malaysian jigsaw puzzle now seem to be falling into place', but then a fresh crisis flared up over Singapore (see 215–221 and also PREM 11/4349).]

2.   On my arrival on Saturday, I had a meeting with Malayan Prime Minister. After preliminary cordialities I told Tunku very frankly that we considered that we had not been properly consulted over the Manila Agreement and that this was the cause of most of the subsequent difficulties. I reminded him that we heartily disliked the idea of a United Nations enquiry in a British territory, which was without precedent. Nevertheless, since he had committed himself we had reluctantly agreed to accept the enquiry and a reasonable number of observers.

3.   The Tunku did not attempt to reply to my complaint about lack of consultation, but murmured something about wanting peace with his neighbours. On the question of observers, he said we had made too much fuss about this. It did not really matter how many there were.

4.   I said that we took a different view. At a moment when Indonesia was actively conducting subversive activities and border raids we should not permit a large number of agents to be introduced into the two territories under the cloak of observers. Nor could we allow military aircraft to overfly the two territories, take photographs, possibly drop supplies to dissident elements and no doubt fly low over primitive villages to demonstrate Indonesian presence. I emphasised that we had no intention of making any further concessions. Having agreed a formula with the Secretary General we were on firm ground and we did not intend to move off it.

5.   He then discussed the steps to be taken to establish Malaysia. The Tunku reaffirmed that he intended to bring in Malaysia irrespective of what the Secretary General's report might say. I told him that I had been informed that he had told the Representatives from North Borneo and Sarawak only a few hours earlier that if the report was unfavourable Malaysia would have to be abandoned. He seemed a little embarrassed and said they must have misunderstood him. But I have no doubt that this is what he did say to them since they all told me that this had greatly disturbed them.

6.   On the question of the date he said that the Malayan Government had in mind to issue a proclamation to fix the date in accordance with a flexible formula i.e. a date between 16th September and 30th September.

7.   I emphasised to the Tunku that any apparent wavering about the date would create serious uncertainty in the two territories and would lead the inhabitants to think that he was having second thoughts about Malaysia. If they were led to fear that Malaysia might be abandoned their natural inclination would be to try and reinsure with the Indonesians. I stressed that this might have a most damaging effect on morale in both territories.

8.   At the end of our talk the Tunku said that he would consider dropping the idea of a flexible date and settle instead firmly on September 16th. However the way he said it left me with the impression that he was still wavering on this point.

9.   The Tunku was occupied the whole of Sunday with his Party Conference. But I saw him again on Monday (26th August). This was the most difficult meeting I ever had with him. He was throughout in a highly emotional and touchy state.

10.   He pointed out that under the Malayan–Indonesian Treaty of Friendship which had been reaffirmed in Tokyo in May the two countries were obliged to discuss

together any possible cause of misunderstanding.[1] He had therefore decided to send a telegram to Subandrio the Indonesian Foreign Minister inviting him to come to Singapore in a day or two to review the situation with him.

11.   I pointed out that unless a firm date for Malaysia Day were fixed beforehand a meeting between him and Subandrïo would lead the people in the North Borneo territories to feel that he was appeasing Indonesia and that possibly he was contemplating abandoning Malaysia altogether. If the people of the two territories thought that Malaysia might after all not go through they would be anxious not to get on the wrong side of the Indonesians and this might affect their evidence before the Secretary General's teams. The Ministers of Singapore, Sarawak and North Borneo would in any case view a meeting between him, and Subandrio with great suspicion unless a firm date for Malaysia had been announced beforehand.

12.   The Tunku was very intractable and said he must be allowed to conduct his relations with Indonesia in his own way. This was *his* 'cold war' which he must handle as he thought best. If things went wrong there would be a 'hot war' which *we* would have to deal with. He went so far as to say that it was no concern of the British what he said to Subandrio.

13.   I took strong exception to this language and made it clear that as parties to the Malaysia Agreement and as the Sovereign power in the three territories we expected to be fully consulted about any further moves. The fact (?that, as) he said, we had joint military responsibilities for the defence of the area made it more than ever necessary that he should coordinate his action with us.

14.   He said that all the anxiety in the Borneo territories merely showed the silliness of the local inhabitants who were very immature; and that they should trust him.

15.   On the question of the date he reverted to the idea of a flexible formula which he had put to me on Saturday. I re-emphasised the dangers of creating any uncertainty about our intention to establish Malaysia and urged him strongly to announce September 16th as a firm date.

16.   I said it would of course be necessary to show the Secretary General beforehand the text of any announcement that was to be made and to consider any comments that he might wish to make.

17.   I said that if the Tunku felt it necessary to see Subandrio I could not object but I emphasised that it was essential that before they met a date for Malaysia should have been irrevocably agreed between the five Governments who had signed the London Agreement.

---

[1] The Treaty of Friendship was signed in Kuala Lumpur in Apr 1959 and (after the Anglo–Malayan Defence Arrangement of 1957) was the first international treaty concluded by independent Malaya. Article 4 was explicit on the resolution of disputes: 'The two High Contracting Parties agree that in case any dispute on matters directly and exclusively affecting them should arise they shall endeavour to settle such dispute through usual diplomatic channels in a true spirit of friendship and goodwill. If a settlement cannot be found through such channels within a reasonable time, they shall endeavour to settle them by other ways and means in accordance with the United Nations Charter and the principles enunciated at the Asia–African Conference in Bandung in 1955.' Government of Malaysia, *Malaya/Indonesia Relations, 31st August, 1957 to 15th September, 1963*, 1963, appendix II, p 29.

18.   The Tunku would not give me any assurance on this point but said that he would call a special Cabinet at once to consider what I had said.

19.   He was in a very nervy state and finished by saying 'I have reached the end of my tether and I do not want to discuss anything further with anybody'.

20.   I was accompanied at this talk by the High Commissioner and Warner.[2] We all got the impression that the Tunku realised that at Manila and since he had been guilty of failure to consult us as he should have and that he knew quite well that his efforts to appease Indonesia had lost him a good deal of respect inside and outside his country.

21.   It seemed to us that as Malaysia Day approaches the Tunku is getting increasingly aware of the magnitude of the new responsibilities he is taking on. He realises that Malaysia is a very small fish compared with Indonesia and he is worried about the prospect of living alongside a powerful and aggressive neighbour who has designs upon his territory.

22.   At the Cabinet meeting it seems that the Tunku was stiffened up by some of his colleagues and events took a decided turn for the better.

23.   As reported in my telegrams referred to above it was decided:—

(a) that the Deputy Prime Minister Tun Razak who is much more dependable, and not the Tunku should offer to see Subandrio at Singapore not later than Wednesday;

(b) that the purpose of the talk would be strictly confined to explaining to Subandrio the Malayan Government's position about the observers which was that they considered the formula agreed between the British Government and the Secretary General as reasonable and to inform the Indonesian Government in advance of a public announcement that Malaysia would be established definitely on September 16th;

(c) that the text of the public announcement should be telegraphed to New York and shown at once to the Secretary General;

(d) that the new date of September 16th should be agreed at once with the British Government and the Governments of the three territories (i.e. that the date should be firmly fixed before any meeting with Subandrio) and

(e) that the proclamation announcing the date should be issued on Thursday and published on Friday.

24.   Together with Razak I informed the Ministers of North Borneo and Sarawak who were much relieved to hear this news. Lee Kuan Yew is arriving from Singapore today and the (?position) will be explained to him.

25.   Now that all the other signatory Governments have been officially notified that Malaysia is to be (?established) on September 16th I think it will be very hard for the Malayan Government to engage in any last minute backsliding. Nevertheless, I will keep in close touch with them to see that nothing goes wrong until the new date is officially proclaimed.

---

[2] F A Warner, head of the SE Asia Department, FO, 1960–1964.

215 PREM 11/4349 30 Aug 1963

[Unilateral declaration of independence by Singapore]: inward
telegram OCULAR 612 from Lord Selkirk to the CO forwarding the
text of Lee Kuan Yew's letter of 29 Aug to Mr Sandys

[The postponement of Malaysia Day to 16 Sept 1963 required a short supplementary
agreement by the governments of Britain, Malaya and Singapore to the agreement of 9
July which had provided for the establishment of Malaysia by 31 Aug. Not only would this
measure regularise the delay, but Sandys felt it was also 'necessary in order to get the
Malayans completely tied down to the new arrangements'. Lee Kuan Yew, however, used
the need for a supplementary agreement as an opportunity to press home some last
demands. Amongst his conditions were points from the 'Ritz Hotel agreement' of 8 July
(see 192 and 193). Meanwhile, he went ahead with a ceremony for Singapore's
independence which he declared at a rally outside the City Hall: 'Our act follows the
traditions of the great anti-colonial revolutions in Asia. The only difference is, I hope, that
unlike the French, or worse, the Dutch, the British are a more pragmatic people. So they
concede the inexorable, and hope that by withdrawing from an already untenable
position, they can become friends with those over whom they once were masters. Let us
not deceive ourselves, and believe that they do this for reasons of altruistic charity. But
their enlightened self-interest makes our transition to freedom that much easier.' A few
days later, he dissolved the Legislative Assembly in order to hold elections, fixing
nomination day for 12 Sept. It became clear that, if Lee had not achieved satisfaction on
outstanding issues with Malaya by 12 Sept, he would go to the polls on a programme for
Singapore's independence. At the eleventh hour, the whole Malaysia project appeared to
be on the point of collapse. It should be noted in the case of documents 215–219 that the
standard form of address – 'inward telegram to the secretary of state for the colonies'—is
misleading since Sandys was in Singapore, not London, and using Selkirk's channel of
communication to maintain contact with the CO.]

Following is text of Lee's letter of 29th August to Secretary of State.

'Dear Secretary of State,

After our meeting last night you assured me over the telephone that the sum of $10
million which you, on behalf of the British Government, agreed to pay to the
Singapore Government will be paid to us without deductions before 16th September
1963. I should like to place this assurance of yours on the record.

I refer to my draft letter of today's date[1] in which I have set out the conditions
precedent on which I have agreed to initial the supplementary agreement amending
the Malaysia Agreement signed in London on 9th July 1963. I should like to receive
your assurance that, in the event that the conditions set out in that letter are not
accepted by any of the other parties to the Agreement, the British Government will
ensure that the State of Singapore is not forced into joining the Federation on terms
which are at variance with what has been agreed with the Federation Government
and accepted by the Government, the Legislature and the people of Singapore.

I expect that you personally will be present at the Malaysia celebrations in
Singapore on the 31st August 1963.

On receiving your confirmation of the matters referred to in this letter I shall hand
you the supplementary agreement initialled subject to ratification by me within one
week on receipt of the written acceptance of the conditions by the other parties to
the Malaysia Agreement.

Yours sincerely,
Lee Kuan Yew.'

---

[1] See 216.

216   PREM 11/4349   30 Aug 1963

[Unilateral declaration of independence by Singapore]: inward telegram OCULAR 613 from Lord Selkirk to the CO, forwarding a draft letter that accompanied document 215

Following is text of enclosure to Lee's letter.

'Dear Sir,

I should like to state and to place it on the record that my agreement to the amendment to Article II of the Agreement relating to Malaysia[1] is conditional on the written acceptance of the conditions set out in this letter. My signature to the agreement for the amendment should therefore be regarded as a conditional initialling to be ratified by me within one week of the date of such initially [?initialling] on being satisfied that the conditions precedent for the Agreement have been fulfilled.

2. The conditions on which I have agreed to such amendment to Article II are as follows:—

(a) That Section 7 of the Tariff Advisory Board Act of the Federation will be amended to be in accordance with the Malaysia Agreement signed in London on the 9th July, 1963: formation of the Board as a revision of revenue duties at end of 1968.

7. (1) It shall be the duty of the Board before the end of the year 1968 to review the revenue duties in force in Malaysia at the end of that year and as soon as may be after the end of that year the Board shall make recommendations for the amendment or removal of such duties or the imposition of additional revenue duties.

(2) The recommendations of the Board under this Section may include provision for revenue duties to be imposed or altered or removed after an interval or progressively.

(b) That Article 30 of the Draft Singapore Constitution will be amended by the addition to Clause (2) of the following:—

(b) If, in the case of a member other than the present members elected to the Legislative Assembly established by the Singapore (Constitution) Order in Council, 1958, he ceases to be a member of or is expelled or resigns from the political Party for which he stood in the elections.

(c) That the Malaysia Act will be amended to provide:—

(I) That the Singapore Government will exercise legislative and executive powers under the Criminal Law (Temporary Provisions) Ordinance 1955 and that the powers given to the Singapore Government under this provision will not be revoked without the consent of the Singapore Government;

(II) That any restriction on the right of movement implied under Article 9(3) of the Federal Constitution will be reciprocal. (Drafts of these amendments are attached.)[2]

---

[1] Article 2 of the agreement of 9 July stipulated that legislation enacting Malaysia be 'brought into operation on 31st August, 1963'.

[2] Not printed.

(d) That the date agreed for Malaysia Day, that is the 16th September 1963 will be final and irrevocable.

(e) That Singapore will celebrate Malaysia Day on the 31st August 1963 when a proclamation of *de facto* acceptance of Malaysia will be read by me, in the presence of the United Kingdom Secretary of State for Commonwealth and Colonies and the Deputy Prime Minister of the Federation.

3.   The Singapore Government desires to receive written acceptance of the conditions set out in this letter before the agreement is ratified by me. It is also the view of the Singapore Government that the signing of the supplementary agreement by the Singapore Government should be a public occasion as was the signing of the Malaysia agreement in London. The Secretary of State should be present to attest his signature to the document.

Section 39 – insert immediately after subsection (2) the following new subsection:—

'(3) (a) The Yang di-Pertuan Agong shall by order to be made before Malaysia Day make provision:—

(I) For authorising the legislature of the State of Singapore to make amendments to the Criminal Law (temporary provisions) Ordinance 1955 of Singapore;

(II) For extending the executive authority of the state so as to enable the Government of Singapore to administer the provisions of the Criminal Law (temporary provisions) Ordinance 1955 of Singapore.

(b) Clause (3) of Article 76A shall apply in relation to an order made under paragraph (a) (I) of subsection (1) of this section as it applies in relation to an Act of Parliament.

(c) The order of The Yang di-Pertuan Agong made under this subsection shall be laid before each House of Parliament.

(d) The order made under this subsection shall take effect on Malaysia Day and shall not be revoked without the concurrence of the Governor'.

Section 60(1) – insert immediately after the word 'Malaya' appearing at the end thereof the words 'and any such restriction shall apply reciprocally to the States of Malaya and the State of Singapore'.

217   PREM 11/4349   30 Aug 1963

[Unilateral declaration of independence by Singapore]: inward telegram OCULAR 614 from Lord Selkirk to the CO, forwarding Sandys' reply of 29 Aug to document 215

Following is text of S. of S.'s reply of 29th August to Lee Kuan Yew.

'Thank you for your letter of 29th.

Last night I left with you copies of the agreement regarding the postponement of Malaysia until 16th September which had been signed at different times during the day by the representatives of the Governments of Malaya, North Borneo and Sarawak and by myself on behalf of the British Government. You told me that by 10 o'clock this morning you would be sending me a copy of this document signed by yourself, accompanied by a letter setting out certain matters which your Government required to have settled before Malaysia Day.

When I explained to you that, in view of the timing of the interview between the Malayan representative and the Indonesian Foreign Minister in Djakarta, and an announcement could not be delayed beyond 11 a.m., you told me that, if I did not receive your signature in time, you would have no objection to it being said that the change of date for Malaysia had been decided 'with the concurrence of all the Governments concerned'. I informed the Malayan Government accordingly and a statement to this effect was duly issued at about noon, by which time I had not as yet received your letter.

With regard to the first paragraph of your letter of today's date, I am asking U.K. Commissioner to make arrangements which will ensure that your Government receives the sum of $10 million referred to in my letter of 8th July without deduction, before the entry of Singapore into Malaysia.

With regard to the second paragraph of your letter, I have naturally not had time to study the detailed points contained in the draft of the letter which you propose to send to all the signatories of the London Agreement; but when we receive it, it will be given most careful attention. In the meantime I fully understand that you reserve your position in the event of the non-fulfilment of the Agreement.

With regard to the third paragraph of your letter you will remember that when I said that I would be willing to attend a meeting which you were planning to celebrate Malaysia, you told me that this would take place on Friday evening. In order to make myself free, I cancelled plans which the Commissioner-General had made for me and made arrangements to leave Singapore that evening after your meeting. As I explained to you last night, my programme requires me to leave Singapore at the latest on Saturday morning and I should find it very difficult to rearrange things at this late stage.[1] I should, however, in any case be interested to see the precise terms of the proclamation which you have it in mind to read out to the assembled people. Perhaps you would care to send it to me.

(Signed) Duncan Sandys'

---

[1] Sandys was spared the embarrassment of being present at the declaration of Singapore's independence by a prior engagement: a four-day cruise with his wife aboard *Mutiara* (pearl), a former British mine-sweeper left to the Malayan navy at the time of independence. He explained to Macmillan: 'I am very much in need of a rest and am spending a long weekend on a yacht which has been lent to me by the Malayan Government. It has radio equipment and Royal Navy Cypher Officer, so I shall be able to keep in touch' (Sandys to Macmillan, 30 Aug, PREM 11/4349).

218 PREM 11/4349   30 Aug 1963
[Unilateral declaration of independence by Singapore]: inward telegram OCULAR 618 from Lord Selkirk to the CO, forwarding Lee Kuan Yew's reply to document 217

Text of further letter to Secretary of State for [?from] Lee Kuan Yew received at noon today, 30th August, is as follows:—

My dear S. of S.

I received your letter dated 29th instant at 5.30 p.m. yesterday. From this letter it is not clear whether you have in fact received a copy of the draft letter[1] I proposed sending you on receiving a satisfactory reply to my letter of yesterday's date. I handed the letter and the draft letter to the Deputy U.K. Commissioner at 12.10 p.m. yesterday. In view of the inconclusiveness of your reply, I have to make the position of my Government absolutely clear.

We discussed many things on Wednesday night. The important matters that we had discussed I set out in note form to you. What I told you about the proposed announcement was that you could proceed without specifically naming the Singapore Government. But the news which was announced at 1.30 p.m. yesterday quite erroneously reported that the Singapore Government had concurred. I have no desire at this stage to upset the show of unity amongst the partners of Malaysia by making it known that my Government has not, as Federation of Malaya Government announced, agreed to the postponement of the date for Malaysia, until the matters set out in the draft letter have been settled.

After careful consideration, my colleagues and I have decided that on the evening of the 31st August at 5 p.m. we shall celebrate another milestone in Singapore's history towards independence, an independence within Malaysia if we are able to agree, but outside Malaysia if there is no choice.

In any event I must ask you to agree that tomorrow, 31st August, I will announce that H.M.G. has delegated to my Government powers in matters of foreign relations to the extent and in order that my Government can, between the 31st August and 16th September, settle the question of the nature and substance of the Japanese gesture of atonement for atrocities committed during Japanese occupation.

It has been the policy of my Government to have this independence within Malaysia. But the relationship between State and the Federal Government must be one in accord with the Malaysia Agreement signed by Government of Singapore in London on 9th July. The lighthearted manner in which solemn agreements in writing have been set aside under one pretext or another is most disturbing. I cannot believe that it can be in the interest of the Federation of Malaya, or of the Federation of Malaysia, if these solemn agreements were to be abandoned unilaterally by one of the parties.

I am obliged to inform you that if I do not receive a clear and categorical assurance from you that Singapore will not be forced into Malaysia unless the terms set out in my draft letter of the 29th August are settled by Monday, 2nd September, it is the intention of my Government to resign and seek a new mandate from the people.

Needless to say in the general election these issues could well become the crucial points on which the people of Singapore will make a stand.

It would be difficult then to conceal the fact that Singapore had not concurred to join Malaysia on 16th September. The position would then be wide open.

Whilst I had proposed a weeks time for a settlement of these matters set out in my draft letter (another copy herewith enclosed), the tenor of your reply makes it necessary that these matters be clarified before your proposed departure.

---

[1] See 216.

The nature of the proclamation on Saturday night will depend on the nature of your reply to this letter.

Yours sincerely,
Lee Kuan Yew

219   CO 1030/1465, no 372   1 Sept 1963
[Unilateral declaration of independence by Singapore]: inward telegram OCULAR 130 from Lord Selkirk to the CO, forwarding a message from Mr Sandys

From Colonial Secretary.

I have just heard over radio Lee's announcement that all Federal powers (including defence and external affairs) have been transferred to the Head of State of Singapore. Since Singapore Government already possesses all other powers, this amounts to a unilateral declaration of independence.

2.   As you know, Lee assured me (when I dined with him) that he would drop this idea and would give today's ceremonies the character of a demonstration of Malaysian solidarity. Furthermore, on the telephone on Friday, Lee promised 'to play it cool' and to do nothing which would exaggerate feelings and make it more difficult for me secure a satisfactory settlement of the outstanding difficulties between Singapore and Kuala Lumpur.

3.   In the last remaining fortnight of British rule, I have no wish to spoil relations with the Government and people of Singapore. Nevertheless, I assume that we will be able [?unable] to avoid answering questions in Singapore and in London as to the significance of Lee's announcement.

4.   Subject to what you may already have said, I think it would be best to confine ourselves to a simple statement of facts, namely:—

(a) That a grant of independence to a territory under British sovereignty requires an act of Parliament at Westminster.

(b) That the British Malaysia Act (which comes into force on 16th September) provides for the transfer of British sovereignty over Singapore, Sabah and Sarawak to the new Federation of Malaysia but does not provide for the separate independence of these territories.

(c) That the announcement made by the Prime Minister of Singapore that future Federal powers (including external affairs and defence) have been transferred from Britain to the Government of Singapore has no legal validity.

(d) That the British Government regard Lee Kuan Yew's statement as in the nature of symbolic expression of spontaneous enthusiasm for Malaysian solidarity intended for internal consumption only.

(e) That the division of responsibilities between the British Government and the Government of Singapore up to Malaysia will, of course, remain unaffected.[1]

5.   Please repeat the above to London and Kuala Lumpur.

---

[1] As regards North Borneo and Sarawak, the colonial governors had announced on the authority of the secretary of state that, from 31 Aug to 16 Sept, they would act only on the advice of their chief ministers

with respect to matters which would be within the province of the state government after the inauguration of Malaysia. All those existing powers in the two territories which would be federal powers in the future would continue to be retained by the respective governors until Malaysia Day. In other words, there had been no legal change. On 2 Sept the Tunku protested to Macmillan about the arrogation of powers on 31 Aug by North Borneo, Sarawak and Singapore and called for the repudiation of any changes in the status of these states prior to the establishment of Malaysia (CO 1030/1514, no 9; cf DO 169/249).

220 CO 1030/1465, no 398   5 Sept 1963

[Unilateral declaration of independence by Singapore]: inward telegram OCULAR 651 from Lord Selkirk to Mr Sandys, assessing the aims and tactics of Lee Kuan Yew

[Selkirk sent this telegram to the CO and repeated it to Sandys who was en route to Colombo. Alarmed by deterioration in relations between Singapore and Malaya, the secretary of state cancelled a planned visit to Aden and returned to Kuala Lumpur in order to see Malaysia through to inauguration (see 221). On 11 Sept he reported that 'after several days of hard argument' Malaya and Singapore had settled their differences. A supplement to the Agreement of 9 July was signed by Sandys, Razak, Ismail and Goh Keng Swee and later published in Singapore and in Britain (see *Agreement concluded between the Federation of Malaya, the United Kingdom Government of Great Britain and Northern Ireland and Singapore Supplementary to the Agreement relating to Malaysia of 9th July 1963, between the United Kingdom of Great Britain and Northern Ireland, the Federation of Malaya, North Borneo, Sarawak and Singapore*, Cmnd 2150). It dealt with the tariff advisory board bill, reciprocity of immigration restrictions and the delegation to Singapore of powers of detention under the criminal law (temporary provisions) ordinance of 1955. Sandys now felt 'reasonably confident' that Singapore would join Malaysia on 16 Sept. As regards the common market, Kuala Lumpur dragged its feet; for example, it was not until Dec 1963 that the government was ready to appoint a chairman of the tariff board that was to advise on its establishment which never materialised. See Sandys to Macmillan, 11 Sept 1963, SOSLON 139, PREM 11/4350; see also CAB 21/5520; CAB 128/37, 52(63)1; DO 169/249; DO 189/122.]

My preliminary comments on my conversation with Lee yesterday are as follows.

2.   I consider he is now playing a supreme act of brinkmanship. He believes his position is inviolable. He believes that either he comes into Malaysia on his own terms or he declares independence and can make any terms he likes with us because he is satisfied we would under no circumstances give up our military position in Singapore. He believes, probably rightly that he could win an election on the slogan of independence interspersed with bitter comments on the Malays[1] and ourselves who he will say are seeking to destroy the hard won position of advantage of the Chinese in Singapore. The electorate would be confused and it is not easy to be certain what would happen.

3.   I believe he still basically wants to come into Malaysia. We should therefore press the Malays to meet him fully on the relatively small points still outstanding. Once he is in, the police and army come under Federation control.

4.   We should by all means we can play this whole subject on a low key. If no one answers Lee, his remarks lose much of their sensational value. His speech on Saturday passed practically unnoticed in Singapore until the Malayan protest came in. I hope B.B.C. will comply.

---

[1] ie, Malay ministers in the Malayan government.

5.   We must, I think, almost at all costs avoid suspending the constitution. We could do it but the operation would mean virtually a military reoccupation of Singapore and once accomplished the accusations of neo-colonialism would be so strong that in the end our whole position here would be undermined.

6.   Our course should be to let 16th September dawn as quietly as possible when control of the forces passes to Kuala Lumpur and then base our subsequent action on the clear opinion already expressed in Singapore:—

(a) by referendum,

(b) by decisions of the Singapore Assembly,

(c) by the signature of the Prime Minister on the Malaysia Agreement,

(d) by Singapore's concurrence with the Agong's announcement of 16th September,

(e) by Lee's speech on 31st August when he said that 16th September was an 'irrevocable date',

(f) by the Order in Council, of which Lee has been informed and has made no comment.

7.   Lee cannot call the Assembly together because it is dissolved. In the circumstances, therefore, we could not break our undertaking now fully substantiated by constitutional processes, on the grounds that the Singapore Government had changed their minds, revoked all previous solemn undertakings and resorted to measures unsupported by any constitutional law.

8.   This procedure will, of course, depend on the full co-operation of the Malayans. If their nerves give way we will, I believe, have no alternative but to negotiate with Lee on the basis of the independence.

221   PREM 11/4350, T470/63   5 Sept 1963
[Unilateral declaration of independence by Singapore]: inward telegram SOSLON 109 from Mr Sandys to Mr Macmillan

For Prime Minister from Commonwealth Secretary.

Situation in Singapore

As you will have seen, a potentially explosive situation is developing in Singapore.

2.   Lee Kuan Yew (Prime Minister of Singapore) is unashamely [sic] exploiting the delay in the establishment of Malaysia to further his personal ambitions. Political blackmail or 'brinkmanship' (as he described it to me himself) is his normal method of achieving his ends. While expressing enthusiasm for Malaysia, his objective is to show up the Tunku as feeble and wooly [sic] minded and to build up his own reputation as a tough, clear sighted leader whose will it would be dangerous for anyone to oppose. He speaks freely about his wish to get rid of the Tunku within the next two or three years when his usefulness has been exhausted. Although he professes to believe that a Chinaman could not become Prime Minister of Malaysia, I have little doubt that is his goal.

3.   It is against this background that we must view his recent unilateral declaration that he had taken over Britain's remaining powers in Singapore.

4.   He realises that his declaration has no legal validity and that the British Government would not tolerate any attempt by him actually to exercise powers which he purports to have assumed. On the other hand, this act of public defiance towards Britain and Malaya has no doubt helped to strengthen the public image of himself which he wishes to create.

5.   I naturally considered with Selkirk the advisability of immediately denouncing Lee Kuan Yew's arrogant statement. But whilst it was very tempting to cut him down to size we felt that the all important thing was to get over the remaining fortnight before Malaysia Day without an open clash with Lee.

6.   He is not a man who climbs down. Once he has committed himself to a definite course and has accepted a carefully calculated risk, he is likely to go through with it, for better or worse. Therefore if we were to humiliate him publicly, he would, I believe, retaliate with further acts of defiance of one kind or another and we might very quickly be forced to suspend the constitution.

7.   If the transfer to Malaysia of sovereignty over Singapore were to take place at a time when the constitution was suspended we would be accused throughout the world of handing over the people of Singapore against their will. Thus it seemed to me that, even at the risk of appearing feeble, it was in our interest to do everything possible to avoid that situation.

8.   That is why I did not immediately react in any way to Lee Kuan Yew's declaration.

9.   Unfortunately, the Malayan Government did not feel able likewise to lie quiet. As you know, without consulting me, they issued a public protest in which they asked the British Government to clarify the position. In the joint statement subsequently issued by Tun Razak (Deputy Prime Minister of Malaya) and myself, I was able to avoid any direct reference to Lee's declaration and to confine myself to a factual statement of the constitutional position which without saying so showed that Lee's assumption of powers had no legal effect. (See telegram No. 1825 from Kuala Lumpur).

10.   Now that the immediate excitement has subsided, I am sending Lee a letter which will put briefly on the record that we do not recognise that his declaration has any validity. This letter would not be published unless further developments made it necessary.

11.   So much for past events. More serious difficulties lie ahead.

12.   Lee's declaration of 31st August is only the first round we have several more rounds to get through before Malaysia Day.

13.   In recent weeks Lee threatened that, if the Malayan Government did not give him what he demanded, he would hold elections and seek a vote of confidence from the people. Now he has done it. The Singapore Parliament has been dissolved. Nomination day has been fixed for September 12th. Polling day will probably be about ten days later (i.e. after Malaysia Day).[1]

14.   Lee has so far not announced the issues on which he will fight the election. But he is threatening that, unless the Malayan Government give him satisfaction on

---

[1] Elections to Singapore's Legislative Assembly were held on 21 Sept, five days after the inauguration of Malaysia. The results (PAP 37, Barisan Sosialis 13, United People's Party 1) shattered the Tunku's hopes for Alliance control and restored the PAP to the commanding position which it had lost in July 1961 when rebels defected to form the Barisan Sosialis, see 49, note.

various points connected with the Malaysia Agreement, he will declare independence on September 12th and will ask the electors of Singapore to endorse this with their votes.

15.   His line would probably be:—

(a) That he is still whole heartedly in favour of Malaysia, but that he wishes to ensure that Singapore is given a fair deal.

(b) That since the date of 31st August contained in the London agreement, was not adhered to, he does not consider himself any longer bound by the agreement;

(c) that, as head of an independent sovereign nation, he will renegotiate the terms on which Singapore will enter Malaysia.

16.   If he were to do this, we would be faced with most awkward situation. His declaration of independence would of course, be just as invalid as his recent declaration about the transfer of powers, and it is probable, though not certain, that between September 12th and September 16th (Malaysia Day) he would take no physical action to flout British authority in Singapore. We would have to settle publicly that his unilateral declaration was legally meaningless. But it might not be possible to stop there. If he were openly inciting the populace to rebellion, we might find it extremely difficult not to arrest him and suspend the constitution.

17.   However in my opinion Lee will not wish to provoke the British Government into suspending the constitution before Malaysia Day and that, while behaving in an insolent fashion, he will try and avoid action which would force us to take this step.

18.   The real difficulty is more likely to arise on Malaysia Day itself, when the Kuala Lumpur authorities come in to take over those functions which, under the Malaysia constitution, would be the responsibility of the Federal Government. These include the control of the police, and it's quite possible that Lee will tell his police not to take orders from the Chief Commissioner in Kuala Lumpur. He would doubtless give the same instructions to Civil Servants in those Government Departments which are due to be taken over by the Federation.

19.   As from Malaysia Day, it would of course be for the Government in Kuala Lumpur to deal with this ugly situation. Unless they were prepared to capitulate, they would have no option but to declare a state of emergency, and remove Lee's administration from office and probably arrest him. There would no doubt be disorders among the Chinese population, the seriousness of which would depend upon how far the police, who are mainly Malays, would obey Lee's instructions to defy the Federal authority. In any case it is more than likely that British troops would be needed to help the civil power in maintaining law and order.

20.   I discussed this possibility frankly with Tun Razak yesterday. He agreed with my suggestion that the Malayan Security authorities and the British authorities from Singapore should concert plans to deal with this eventuality. A first meeting is taking place today.

21.   Tun Razak assured me that the Malayan Government were irrevocably committed to Malaysia, and that they would go through with it whatever happened. I believe that he speaks for most of the Ministers but I am not so completely confident about the attitude of the Tunku himself. As I told you in an earlier telegram he is suffering seriously from cold feet and although I think it unlikely, it is just possible that at the last moment he might refuse to take over Singapore. This would obviously

face us with a most awkward dilemma which I will not discuss now.

22. With these uncomfortable possibilities in mind, it is of the utmost importance to avoid if at all possible a head-on collision with Lee between now and September 16th. I have therefore strongly urged the Malayan Government to concede as far as they possibly can the demands which Lee has made regarding the Malaysia Constitution. Most of them are not unreasonable and are based upon rather loosely worded undertakings given by the Tunku to Lee in London, though admittedly Lee is trying to interpret these undertakings in a manner excessively favourable to himself.

23. With this in view I have helped the Malayan Government to draft a letter to Lee in a placatory tone, and to meet him on as many points as possible, they will no doubt argue these points by correspondence during the next few days. At the end I hope we shall reach the position where the Malayan Government have succeeded in reducing Lee's unsatisfied requirements to one or two points on which his demands can be seen to be unreasonable and which would not justify him in taking so drastic a step as a declaration of independence.

24. But even if he gets his way on all points I do not put it past Lee to think up a new set of demands. Think therefore that it is wise to assume that we are going to have trouble and to prepare for the worst.

25. I am dictating this on my way from Kuala Lumpur to Colombo where I shall be spending two days to try and impress upon Mrs. Bandaranaike[2] the short sightedness of her policy towards British commercial interests in Ceylon. I am then going on to the Maldives to try and settle our differences with the Sultan.[3] After that I was due to go to Aden. But in view of the critical situation created by Lee Kuan Yew I have cancelled my visit to Aden and am instead returning to Kuala Lumpur on Monday.

26. The concessions which I hope to persuade the Malayan Government to make may induce Lee to go into Malaysia quietly. But unless I mistake his character, he will bluff, bully and blackmail up to the eleventh hour. In these circumstances it seems to me essential that I should remain on the spot. This will I hope enable me:—

(a) To restrain the Malayan Government from adopting a provocative or overintransigent attitude towards Lee.

(b) To try and help the two of them reach agreement, and

(c) To stiffen the Tunku's resolve to go through with Malaysia if he should show signs of wavering. It would seem silly for the sake of a few days not to do everything in my power to save Malaysia from the possibility of collapse, with all that that would imply.

---

[2] Mrs Sirimavo R D Bandaranaike, leader of Sri Lanka Freedom Party after assassination of her husband, Solomon W R D Bandaranaike, in 1959; prime minister, 1960–1965, 1970–1977—the world's first woman prime minister.

[3] The development of a joint strategy with the US in the Indian Ocean depended on the island bases, notably Gan in the Maldives, see Hyam and Louis, eds, *BDEE: The Conservative government, 1957–1964*, xliv and document 60. The purpose of Sandys' visit was to restore the authority of the Maldives government over Addu Atoll where Gan was situated.

27.   Consequently, if you approve, I propose to remain in this area until we have put Singapore safely in the bag on 16th September. In that case I could stay on the extra two days for the Malaysia celebrations. This would make it unnecessary to find another Cabinet Colleague to take this on.[4]

---

[4] Macmillan approved Sandys' request to return to Kuala Lumpur and reported developments to Cabinet on 12 Sept (CAB 128/37, CC 52(63)1).

222   PREM 11/4440   5 Sept 1963
[Difficulties with Malaysia]: letter from Mr Macmillan to HM the Queen   [Extract]

[Macmillan recounted the difficulties in a letter in which he also commented on his recent visit to Finland and Sweden, the prospects for an improvement in East-West relations in the aftermath of the test ban treaty, Lord Denning's imminent report on the security aspects of the Profumo affair, the future leadership of the Conservative Party, the life of the present parliament, and the state of the economy.]

. . . Malaysia

Your majesty will have been following the complicated story of Malaysia. Our immediate difficulties began with the Tunku's acceptance at the Manila meeting, which was attended by the Malayans, Philippinos and Indonesians, of the idea of a United Nations supervised plebiscite with 'observers' from the three Manila countries. I am not entirely clear why the Tunku accepted this plan but it seems to have been an attempt to gain greater international support for the view that the Indonesians were being unreasonable. However, the result was to cause doubt about the possibility of achieving Malaysia at all and certainly about the date on which it should start. The Commonwealth Secretary, with his usual energy and decisiveness, went out to the area. He has, I feel, been remarkably successful, first in securing general agreement to the date of September 16 for the establishment of Malaysia, and secondly in keeping the rather difficult constituent parts of Malaysia more or less together. The Tunku seems to have behaved in his characteristically impulsive way; Mr. Lee Kwan Yew has tried to exploit the difficulties to his own advantage. The Indonesians were particularly unreasonable in trying to bring more 'observers' in than had been agreed and in trying to insert into their party a majority of intelligence officers with a view to causing as much mischief as they could. However, the Commonwealth Secretary was very successful in preventing this and the Indonesians have finally accepted something not too different from the original proposal. Meanwhile the United Nations team have been doing their work and ought to submit their report in a few more days. We hope that it will be favourable to Malaysia, although the Indonesians will of course say that the enquiry was not properly conducted or was hampered by British colonial rule. However, I trust that Malaysia will in fact come into being on the new date. Since the Commonwealth Secretary proposes to come back before then it may be necessary to ask Your Majesty's permission for another Cabinet Minister to go out to represent Your Majesty's Government at the celebrations.[1] . . .

---

[1] On the same day, however, Sandys reported a 'potentially explosive situation' requiring him to remain in the area until the successful inauguration of Malaysia, see 221.

223   PREM 11/4350   12 Sept 1963
[Report of UN mission to Malaysia]: inward telegram OCULAR 1431
from Sir P Dean to Lord Home

[Led by Lawrence Michelmore (the American deputy director of the UN Office of Personnel) the mission consisted of Czech, Argentinian, Ceylonese, Ghanaian, Pakistani, Japanese, Jordanian and Brazilian members of the UN Secretariat. It was accompanied by observers from Indonesia and the Philippines. The mission arrived in Kuching on 16 Aug and divided into two teams, one for Sarawak and the other for Sabah. From 24 Aug to 4 Sept they conducted formal hearings for the 'ascertainment' (as it was called) of the wishes of Borneo peoples. In case the mission found against Malaysia, Sandys supervised the drafting of a joint Anglo–Malayan statement setting out the history of consultations. In the event, it was not required: the report and U Thant's assessment of it were in general highly favourable to Malaysia (see 225). The parties concerned were given copies of the ascertainment before publication day on 14 Sept. While Macmillan regarded it as 'satisfactory, if pedantic', the Philippines and Indonesia attacked the report, and Indonesia went so far as to criticise the UN itself. For the UN mission see FO 371/169712–169719.]

I saw the Secretary-General this afternoon. He had had a very rough time with the representatives of the three Manila Powers in the afternoon and was rather depressed.

2.   The Indonesians and Filipinos had not submitted written views. Lopez[1] had complained about the delay in issuing visas to observers. The Secretary-General had replied that this was none of his business and did not relate to Michelmore's report. Lopez went on to complain about the announcement of September 16 as the date for Malaysia, which he represented as a slight to the Secretary-General, and he made a great thing of contrasting a British-sponsored Malaysia with a Malaysia born of the goodwill of the three countries in the area. Lopez had hoped that Michelmore's report would enable Malaysia to take the latter form, but this was not now to be.

3.   The Indonesians echoed Lopez's points. In addition they said Michelmore's team had been too small and the time too short for thorough ascertainment. The Manila joint statement[2] had asked for a fresh approach. Michelmore had clearly not adopted such an approach and simply confined himself to rubber-stamping the actions of the imperialists. At this point doubts were cast on Michelmore's impartiality.

4.   Both Lopez and the Indonesians made it clear that they resented the categorical tone of the report, a tone which could not be justified in the light of the superficial approach adopted by the team. The Indonesians said that they would have accepted U Thant's findings if a comprehensive ascertainment had been made, since they would then have been able to persuade their population that Malaysia did represent the will of the people of the Borneo territories. Michelmore had frustrated this ambition by conducting such a haphazard investigation.

5.   The Indonesians and Filipinos were united in blaming the British as the villains of the piece. If the Malayans had been left alone an accommodation between them and the Indonesians and Filipinos would have been easily reached.

6.   The Indonesians and Filipinos asked for a further meeting with the Secretary-General tomorrow. He told them that this was impossible and said that if they had any further views they should put them in writing by 10.30 tomorrow morning.

---

[1] Salvador P Lopez, foreign secretary of the Philippines, 1963, and representative at the UN, 1964.
[2] See 200, note.

7.   The Filipino and Indonesian observers left written *aide-mémoires* with the Secretary-General which he has not yet read, incorporating their comments on the ascertainment team's activities. The Secretary-General is wondering whether to append these *aide-mémoires* to the report when published. I discouraged him.

8.   I asked the Secretary-General whether, in his view, the Indonesians and Filipinos intended to reject his conclusions and to continue stirring up trouble in the area. He was inclined to think that this would be the case, although he thought it possible that their fire and fury was directed to trying to influence the form and content of his conclusions and that when these were out they would acquiesce in Malaysia's formation. He is not optimistic, however. I took the opportunity to stress again that a short categorical report from him would be the best way to persuade the Indonesians and Filipinos that there was no profit for them in continuing to make a fuss about Malaysia.

224   PREM 11/4350   13 Sept 1963
[Sarawak's head of state]: inward telegram SOSLON 152 from Mr Sandys for Mr Macmillan, reporting resolution of the crisis

I much appreciated your message in LONGSOS [LONSOS] No. 209.[1] I have delivered your letter to the Tunku.[2] This came at a timely moment and he was most gratified by your good wishes and support on the eve of his assumption of new and rather frightening responsibilities.

2.   Now that the Secretary General's report has given us a completely clean bill of health I think we are entitled to ask the Americans to use their influence to the full at Djakarta and at the United Nations to deter the Indonesians from further intervention.[3]

3.   If after Malaysia Day the Indonesians repeat their accusation that British or Malaysian troops are carrying out raids across their border I think we should consider urging the New Malaysian Government to propose to the Indonesians that they should jointly request the United Nations to establish observers on both sides of

---

[1] Macmillan congratulated Sandys on having 'done wonders' in bringing about agreement between Malaya and Singapore, see 220, note.

[2] Macmillan's letter was to soothe the Tunku's feelings. De Zulueta informed the prime minister that 'Mr Sandys' victory has been rather a Pyrric [sic] one' because the Tunku 'was rubbed up the wrong way by the Commonwealth Secretary'. As a result of rough treatment, the Tunku 'apparently indicated that he would do whatever the British wanted but that he washed his hands of the results. In other words, he no longer feels personally responsible for Malaysia and if he can do a deal with the Indonesians by himself, he will'. Addressing the Tunku as 'Dear Friend', Macmillan credited him with inspiring 'the conception of Malaysia' and expressed great admiration for 'your subtlety and your courage in pursuing the main aim while seeking so far as possible to disarm the opponents of Malaysia and deprive them of good propaganda positions'. Notwithstanding Macmillan's cordial message, Sandys' conduct rankled and four months later the Tunku recalled in a conversation with Robert Kennedy how 'Sandys came as a friend and became a nuisance' (de Zulueta to Macmillan, 11 Sept; Macmillan to Sandys, 11 Sept; Macmillan to the Tunku, 12 Sept, PREM 11/4350; DO 169/266; Matthew Jones, *Conflict and confrontation in South East Asia, 1961–1965*, Cambridge, 2002, p 252).

[3] Howard P Jones, US ambassador in Jakarta since 1958, was central to American efforts to cultivate the Sukarno regime, and Britain's ambassador in Jakarta, Andrew Gilchrist, blamed him for America's coolness towards the Malaysia project, see FO 371/169888.

the Sarawak border so that mutual accusations may be verified and the facts made known to the world. The Indonesians would no doubt refuse but this would show that they had something to hide and put them in a bad light.

4. You will have seen that we have been through a short but really explosive crisis over the choice of the new Head of State for Sarawak (to be known as 'Governor').[4]

5. Under the London agreement the first Governor has to be nominated jointly by The Queen and the King of Malaya (Agong).

6. Although the Government party in Kuching which has a large majority unanimously urged the appointment of the Dyak leader Jugah the Tunku adamantly opposed it and insisted upon the appointment of a Malay. His party has been becoming increasingly nervous about the prospect of other races securing a position of undue influence in the new Federation. In fact an emergency meeting of the Executive was held yesterday at which it was made clear that the party would not support the Tunku in any further concessions to non-Malay interest.

7. The Malayan Cabinet also had a special meeting to discuss this matter. Afterwards the Tunku told me that the situation had got to the point where his Government would collapse if a Malay did not get the job in Sarawak. The Cabinet had decided that unless a Malay was appointed Governor they would have to go ahead without Sarawak or alternatively if we would not agree to that Malaysia would have to be abandoned altogether.

8. I said I could not seriously believe he would throw everything overboard at the last moment on account of party political pressures and that he ought to lead his party and not follow it. I instanced the leadership which you had given to the Conservative Party over the Common Market and at the same time I made it clear that we would not be prepared to allow Malaysia to go forward without Sarawak.

9. However, it was clear to me that the Tunku was seriously afraid of being overthrown by his party executive that very day and that the other Ministers present shared this fear. There was therefore no hope of his giving way.

10. For my part I was not prepared to make a recommendation to The Queen which ran directly counter to the wishes of the Dyaks upon whom our troops are so dependent for information about Indonesian movements and for guidance through the jungle. Thus it was evident that the only way out was to try and persuade the Dyaks to change their mind. I therefore got the governor to fly over to Kuala Lumpur with a strong delegation of 15 Sarawak leaders including the Chief Minister and Jugah.

11. After a variety of meetings and many rough (? words) on all sides the matter was finally settled on the basis of a compromise which I suggested namely:—

(a) that a Malay should be appointed as first Governor for two years;[5]
(b) that it should be clearly understood that the Agong would appoint as his successor whomsoever the Chief Minister of Sarawak recommended (i.e. a Dyak) and
(c) that in return Jugah should be appointed Minister of Sarawak Affairs resident in Sarawak with a seat in the new Malaysian Federal Cabinet (on the lines of our own wartime pattern).[6]

---

[4] See 210.   [5] Dato Abang Haji Openg was appointed.
[6] In addition, Peter Lo was made minister for Sabah Affairs in the federal Cabinet, but Singapore was not represented in this way. The 'wartime pattern' refers to Churchill's appointment of, for example, Macmillan as minister resident in North Africa.

12. This arrangement has just been confirmed at a signing ceremony with speeches of mutual congratulation and the Dyaks are returning to Sarawak in a smiling mood.[7]

13. I obtained The Queen's approval during the night and the appointment of a respected Malay personality, Openg, will be announced later today.

14. Now that (touch wood) all outstanding questions seem to have been resolved I have decided to pay a three day farewell visit to the Borneo Territories. I am leaving today Friday for Jesselton. On Saturday I shall fly to Kuching stopping off for a few hours in Brunei to talk to the Sultan. I will spend Sunday in the jungle in Sarawak visiting our troops with the Commander in Chief. On Monday morning (Malaysia Day) I will attend the flag raising ceremony in Kuching. Then I will fly on to Singapore and attend the Malaysia Day rally in the afternoon, returning to Kuala Lumpur in the evening for the Federal celebrations on Tuesday and Wednesday.

15. I plan to arrive back in London on Friday just in time to open the Zanzibar Independence Conference that morning.[8]

---

[7] The agreement, dated 13 Sept 1963, was presented as a 'Joint Statement' and signed by the Tunku, Sandys, Dr Sockalingham (speaker of the Council Negri or state legislative assembly) and Temenggong Jugah. The British, signed copy is at DO 118/266. The statement runs as follows:—

'The London Agreement on Malaysia provides that the first Governor of Sarawak shall be appointed on the nomination of the Queen and the Yang di-Pertuan Agong.

'The Malayan Government have maintained that since the Chief Minister in Sarawak is an Iban, the first Governor should be a Malay. For the sake of unity and goodwill on the eve of the formation of Malaysia, Temeggong Jugah has generously asked that his name should not be considered for the first Governorship. This has enabled general consent to be given to the appointment of a Malay, it being understood that, when the term of office of the first Governor expires, the Yang di-Pertuan Agong will be graciously pleased to give favourable consideration to the appointment as Governor of the person whom the Chief Minister may recommend.

'Meanwhile, recognising the outstanding position which he holds in the life of Sarawak, the Prime Minister, Tunku Abdul Rahman Putra, has offered Temenggong Jugah a post in the Federal Malaysian Cabinet as Minister for Sarawak Affairs resident in Sarawak, which he has been pleased to accept.'

A photostat of the statement in the papers of Sir Alexander Waddell is accompanied by the following unsigned and undated explanation in Waddell's hand:—

'On the eve of Malaysia deadlock was reached over the question of the Governorship of Sarawak— due to insistence by Tungku Abdul Rahman that a Malay should be Governor, and equal determination in Sarawak that an Iban (Sea Dayak) should be. Duncan Sandys summoned all to Kuala Lumpur for 3 days of gruelling negotiation.

'Temenggong Jugah, leader of the Ibans, withdrew in order to save Malaysia.

'This paper was signed by Tungku Abdul Rahman, Duncan Sandys, Dr Sockalingham (Speaker Sarawak) & the Temenggong.'

See Waddell Papers, file 7, ff 150–151.

[8] See Hyam and Louis, eds, *BDEE: The Conservative government, 1957–1964*, part I, 137.

225 PREM 11/4350 13 Sept 1963
[Report of UN mission to Malaysia]: inward telegram OCULAR 1441 from Sir P Dean to Lord Home, forwarding the text of U Thant's final conclusions

Following is text of the Secretary General's final conclusions:—[1]

Begins: In response to the request made by the Governments of the Federation of Malaya, the Republic of Indonesia, and the Republic of the Philippines, on 5 August 1963, I agreed to ascertain, prior to the establishment of the Federation of Malaysia, the wishes of the people of Sabah (North Borneo) and Sarawak. As foreseen in my communication of 8 August 1963, a mission was established, comprising two teams, one for Sarawak and the other for Sabah (North Borneo), working under the supervision of my personal representative. The mission has now completed the inquiry assigned to it, and has reported to me.

I wish, first of all, to express my gratitude to the three Governments for the confidence they placed in me by requesting that I should undertake the task of ascertaining the wishes of the population of Sarawak and North Borneo (Sabah) prior to the establishment of Malaysia. I also wish to express my appreciation to the Government of the United Kingdom and of the authorities of the two territories for having given their agreement to the inquiry and their full cooperation to the mission.

It was always understood that the ascertainment would be completed within a limited period of time, and my communication of 8 August noted that every effort would be made to complete the task as quickly as possible. I later informed the Governments concerned that I would endeavour to report my conclusions by 14 September. During the course of the enquiry, the date of 16 September 1963 was announced by the Government of the Federation of Malaya with the concurrence of the British Government, the Singapore Government and the Governments of Sabah and Sarawak, for the establishment of the Federation of Malaysia. This has led to misunderstanding, confusion and even resentment among other parties to the Manila agreement, which could have been avoided if the date could have been fixed after my conclusions had been reached and made known.

There was no reference to a referendum or plebiscite in the request which was addressed to me. I was asked to ascertain the wishes of the people 'within the context of General Assembly resolution 1541 (xv), principle ix of the annex, by a fresh approach' which in my opinion was necessary 'to ensure complete compliance with the principle of self determination within the requirements embodied in principle ix', taking into consideration certain questions relating to the recent elections. The mission accordingly arranged for consultations with the population through the elected representatives of the people, leaders of political parties and other groups and organisations, and with all persons who were willing to express their views, and every

---

[1] These conclusion were printed as the preface of the mission's report which was published on 14 Sept. The UN report was the first publication of Malaysia's Department of Information which produced it as a pamphlet for wide circulation on Malaysia Day itself.

effort was made to ascertain the wishes of the special groups (political detainees and absentees) mentioned in the Manila joint statement. The mission gathered and studied all available documents, reports and other material on the governmental institutions, political organisation, electoral processes in the two territories, and other matters relevant to its terms of reference.

Federation of Malaya, the Republic of Indonesia and the Republic of the Philippines deemed it desirable to send observers to witness the carrying out of the task, and the Government of the United Kingdom decided that it also wished the same facility. Although I did not consider the arrangements for observers to be part of the Secretary General's responsibility, I endeavoured to help the Governments concerned to reach agreement, and I am pleased that an understanding was finally arrived at so that observers of all the Governments concerned could be present during at least part of the enquiry. It is a matter for regret that this understanding could not have been reached earlier, so that all observers could have been present in the territories for the entire period of the enquiries, and that questions of detail pertaining to the status of the observers unnecessarily delayed even further their arrival. A more congenial atmosphere would have been achieved if the necessary facilities had been granted more promptly by the administering authority. The mission, however, made its records, including tape recordings of all its hearings, available for the use of the observer teams to enable them to inform themselves as fully as possible of what had occurred before their arrival.

The basic assessment which I was asked to make has broader implications than the specific questions enumerated in the request addressed to me by the three Governments. As mentioned previously, I was asked to 'ascertain, prior to the establishment of the Federation of Malaysia, the wishes of the people of Sabah (North Borneo) and Sarawak within the context of General Assembly resolution 1541 (xv), principle ix of the annex, by a fresh approach which in the opinion of the Secretary General is necessary to ensure complete compliance with the principle of self determination within the requirements embodied in principle ix.'

Concerning the integration of a non-self-governing territory with an already independent State, principle ix provides:—

'Integration should have come about in the following circumstances:—

(a) The integrating territory should have attained an advanced stage of self government with free political institutions, so that its peoples would have the capacity to make a responsible choice through informed and democratic processes.
(b) The integration should be the result of the freely expressed wishes of the territory's peoples acting with full knowledge of the change in their status, their wishes having been expressed through informed and democratic processes, conducted and based on universal adult suffrage. The United Nations could, when it deems it necessary, supervise these processes'.

I have given consideration to the circumstances in which the proposals for the Federation of Malaysia have been developed and discussed, and the possibility that people progressing through the stages of self government may be less able to consider in an entirely free context the implications of such changes in their status, than a society which has already experienced full self government and the determination of its own affairs. I have also been aware that the peoples of the territories are still striving for a more adequate level of educational development.

Having reflected fully on these considerations, and taking into account the framework within which the mission's task was performed, I have come to the conclusion that the majority of the peoples of Sabah (North Borneo) and of Sarawak, have given serious and thoughtful consideration to their future, and to the implications for them of participation in a Federation of Malaysia. I believe that the majority of them have concluded that they wish to bring their dependent status to an end and to realize their independence through freely chosen association with other peoples in their region with whom they feel ties of ethnic association, heritage, language, religion, culture, economic relationship, and ideals and objectives. Not all of these considerations are present in equal weight in all minds, but it is my conclusion that the majority of the peoples of the two territories having taken them into account, wish to engage, with the peoples of the Federation of Malaya and Singapore, in an enlarged Federation of Malaysia, through which they can strive together to realize the fulfilment of their destiny.

With regard to the more specific questions referred to me, my conclusions, after the examination and verification reported by the mission, are:—

(a) Malaysia has been the subject of wide-spread and intensive public debate and was a major issue in the recent elections in the two territories.

(b) Electoral registers were properly compiled.

(c) The elections took place in an atmosphere free enough to enable the candidates and political parties to put their case before the electorate, and the people were able to express themselves freely by casting their votes in a polling system which provided the basic safeguards for secret balloting, and measures for the prevention and correction of abuses.

(d) The votes were properly polled and counted.

(e) Persons otherwise eligible to vote but who were unable to do so because of detention for political activities or imprisonment for political offences numbered somewhat less than 100 in Sarawak, and even less in Sabah (North Borneo) at the time of the elections. Testimony given by this group, especially in Sarawak, indicated that they would have opposed the Federation of Malaysia if they had participated in the election. The actual votes of this group would not have been sufficient to have had a material effect on the result. The mission has given much attention to the possible effect which the absence of these persons, some of whom were officials of the anti-Malaysia party, might have had on the campaign. The mission considered the similar question concerning some 164 persons whose activity was restricted to some extent, but who retained the right to vote. Noting that the anti-Malaysia party scored convincing electoral victories in many of the areas to which these persons belonged, I accept the mission's conclusion that a substantial limitation of the campaigning potential of the group opposed to the Federation of Malaysia has not occurred, so as seriously and significantly to have affected the result of the election.

(f) The mission made special efforts to obtain reliable information regarding persons who were absent from the territories at the time of the election, particularly as a result of possible political or other intimidation. The evidence available indicated that the number of such persons, other wishes [?otherwise] qualified to vote, did not exceed a few hundred, and that their number could not have affected the results of the election. I note that the principal officials of the Sarawak United Peoples Party, which is opposed to the Federation of Malaysia, agree with this assessment, and I accept it.

Bearing in mind the fundamental agreement of the three participating Governments in the Manila meetings, and the statement by the Republic of Indonesia and the Republic of the Philippines that they would welcome the formation of Malaysia provided that the support of the people of the territories was ascertained by me and that, in my opinion, complete compliance with the principle of self determination within the requirements of General Assembly resolution 1541 (xv), principle ix of the annex, was ensured, my conclusions, based on the findings of the mission, is that on both of these counts there is no doubt about the wishes of a sizable majority of the peoples of these territories to join in the Federation of Malaysia.

In reaching my conclusions, I have taken account of the concern expressed with regard to the political factors resulting from the constitutional status of the territories, and about influences from outside the area on the promotion of the proposed Federation. Giving these considerations their due weight, in relation to the responsibilities and obligations established in article 73 and General Assembly resolution 1541 (xv) in respect of the territories, I am satisified that the conclusions set forth above take cognizance of the requirements set forth in the request addressed to me on 5 August 1963 by the Foreign Ministers of the Republic of Indonesia, the Federation of Malaya and the Republic of the Philippines.

Before concluding, I would like to pay a tribute to my personal representative, Mr. L. Michelmore, my deputy representative, Mr. G. Janecek,[2] and to all the members of the United Nations Malaysia mission who accomplished a sensitive and difficult task in a relatively short period, but at the same time in a thorough and wholly adequate manner. In a sense, it was a pity that the work of the mission had to be accomplished within certain deadlines. But I do feel that, while more time might have enabled the mission to obtain more copious documentation and other evidence, it would not have affected the conclusions to any significant extent.

From the beginning of this year I have been observing the rising tension in South East Asia on account of the differences of opinion among the countries most directly interested in the Malaysia issue. It was in the hope that some form of United Nations involvement might help to reduce tension that I agreed to respond positively to the request made by the three Manila Powers. I would hope that the exercise in which my colleagues and I have been involved in this regard will have this effect, and that the coming into being of Malaysia will not prove to be a continuing source of friction and tension in the area.

The emergence of dependent territories by a process of self-determination to the status of self government, either as independent sovereign States or as autonomous components of larger units, has always been one of the purposes of the Charter and the objectives of the United Nations.

Whatever the origins of the proposal of Malaysia may have been, it seems to me in

---

[2] Michelmore led the mission, assisted by Janecek of Czechoslovakia.

the light of actual events, including the present exercise, that we have witnessed in
Sarawak and North Borneo the same process leading to self government. I fervently
hope that the people of these territories will achieve progress and prosperity and find
their fulfilment as component States of Malaysia. *Ends*.

226 DO 169/223, no 31   18 Sept 1963
'Britain's gift to Malaysia': inward telegram no 2011 from Sir G Tory to the CRO, forwarding the text of Mr Sandys' message to Tunku Abdul Rahman on the inauguration of Malaysia

[Governors Waddell and Goode departed Borneo on the eve of Malaysia Day. On Malaysia
Day itself, 16 Sept 1963, Sandys attended the flag-raising ceremony in Kuching in the
morning, flew to Singapore for a rally in the afternoon and returned to Kuala Lumpur for
the federal celebrations on 17–18 Sept. Alastair Morrison, Sarawak's information officer,
has recalled that the new era for Sarawak 'did not get off to a very auspicious start. The
new Governor, Datu Abang Haji Openg, almost collapsed during the inauguration
ceremony. It was understandable. He was not in strong health; it was a moment of great
emotional stress for him; and he was a very religious man who had been occupied with
his devotions for most of the previous night.' Duncan Sandys, however, was a 'satisfied
spectator' who 'looked like a well-pleased midwife who has brought a difficult
accouchement to a successful conclusion', although he did comment privately that 'after
agreement had been reached with such pain, I did not bargain for the new Governor
collapsing at his inauguration!' (Alastair Morrison, *Fair land Sarawak. Some
recollections of an expatriate official*, New York, 1993, p149; Sandys to Waddell, 20 Sept
1963, Sandys Papers, 8/14). Later that day, Sandys and Ismail (representing Malaysia)
stood on the steps of City Hall, Singapore, alongside Lee Kuan Yew who celebrated both
the fulfilment of a political ambition to achieve independence through merger and his
fortieth birthday (Lee Kuan Yew, *The Singapore story*, pp 504–505). The following day
Lee joined Sandys, Lansdowne and Selkirk (making his last appearance as commissioner-
general for SE Asia) in celebrations in Merdeka Stadium, Kuala Lumpur, where six years
and sixteen days previously the Tunku had proclaimed Malayan independence.
Meanwhile, Indonesia refused to recognise the new state and on 18 Sept the British
embassy in Jakarta was looted and burned in the climax to several days of demonstrations
against Malaysia.]

In making the presentation to the Prime Minister of Malaysia the Commonwealth
Secretary read the following message:—

Begins: 'I have pleasure in presenting to you this gift from the British
Government to the Government of Malaysia. This piece of modern silver specially
designed by British craftsmen for the occasion brings with it the greetings of the
people of Britain.

In your person we salute the man who conceived the inspiring idea of Malaysia and
who possessed the skill and determination to bring it to fruition. Her Majesty The
Queen has transferred to His Majesty the Agong Her Sovereignty over Singapore,
Sabah and Sarawak in the knowledge that this is the clear wish of their peoples. The
inhabitants of these three territories have freely decided to achieve their
independence as self-governing states in the Federation of Malaysia. I am sure that
they have chosen wisely and that Malaysia will offer to them and all its citizens
widening opportunities for progress and prosperity.

We have all admired the patient efforts which you have made to explain and justify
Malaysia to other nations and to remove doubts and fears in the minds of your

neighbours. We are glad that you have been rewarded by the congratulations and good wishes of almost the entire world. If there are one or two exceptions the fault certainly does not lie with you.

For a number of years Britain and Malaya have worked constructively for peace and progress and when necessary we have stood firmly together in the defence of freedom. As it was with Malaya so it will be with the enlarged Federation of Malaysia. Insofar as you need it Britain will be ready to help in any way she can to defend Malaysia's independence and integrity.

As members of the Commonwealth Malaysia and Britain will maintain a continuous and intimate contact with one another; through this multi-racial fellowship of free nations Britain and Malaysia will together play their part in promoting understanding between the nations and in strengthening the cause of freedom and peace throughout the world.

The friendship and confidence between us have been further cemented by the common efforts we have made to build Malaysia. On behalf of the British Government and the British people I express to the Government and people of Malaysia our warm good wishes for the future.

227 DO 169/223, no 32 19 Sept 1963

'Britain's gift to Malaysia': inward telegram no 2026 from Sir G Tory to the CRO, forwarding the text of Tunku Abdul Rahman's reply to Mr Sandys

Following is text of Tunku's reply to Commonwealth Secretary's presentation speech.

'I can assure you that I am most grateful for this message.[1] Expressed in most sincere and beautiful terms it touches the bottom of my heart. I can assure you that we will stand together linked as we have been over past years. You can rest assured that as far as we are concerned we have always expressed ourselves in the terms that we sink or float together.

I am grateful for the confidence of Her Majesty's Government in passing their rights over the Territories (Singapore Sarawak and Sabah) to us. We shall do everything possible to justify the trust you have placed in us.

This gift will enjoy a special place in our Parliament House where it will be on show for all men for all time. We reiterate our stand with you that we will co-operate with you within the Commonwealth to the best of our ability'. The Tunku then presented Mr. Sandys and the Marquess of Lansdowne each with a silver mounted ivory handled kris asking in return a coin so that Malay custom could be honoured the custom being that one never gives an outright gift of a weapon to a friend. Both Mr. Sandys and Lord Lansdowne paid the tribute.

---

[1] See 226.

Appendix

The Origins and Formation of Malaysia

FCO Research Department Memorandum
(FCO 51/154, no 15, 10 July 1970, see Introduction, xxxvii)

A. *Introduction*

A. Introduction

I. *The background*

Pre-war Administration

The British Malayan and Borneo Territories before the Second World War displayed a wide variety of constitutional arrangements. The Straits Settlements, including Singapore, Penang, Malacca and Labuan, were directly ruled as Crown Colonies. The four Federated Malay States were protectorates, but with a substantial degree of administrative unity and direct British control. The Unfederated Malay States, of which Brunei was one, were individually and separately required to accept the advice of British residents, except on matters of religion and Malay custom, but their Rulers retained greater control over the direction of government. The senior British representative in both Federated and Unfederated Malay States, the High Commissioner, was also Governor of the Straits Settlements. Sarawak was a protected State ruled by a rajah of the Brooke family without direct British advice, except on questions of foreign relations. North Borneo was in a similar position, but was governed by a chartered company.

Wartime planning and the Malayan Union proposals

2.   During the war, while all the territories were under Japanese control, it was decided in London to take the opportunity of reoccupation to try to tidy up this confusion of régimes. As Mr. Arthur Creech Jones, who was Parliamentary Under-Secretary of State in 1945 and thereafter until 1950 Secretary of State for the Colonies, subsequently remarked, it was 'ardently desired' to create a unified administrative structure. So far as the peninsular Malay States were concerned this had indeed been an aim of British policy for many years before the war. There was also some feeling that the Chinese in the Malay States and Straits Settlements, who had certainly been more active in resisting the Japanese than the Malays, deserved an improved political position. Before the war the States had been treated as purely Malay kingdoms. The Chinese and the Indians, though overall more than half the population and more active economically, were, unlike Indonesian immigrants, considered intruders of inferior political standing who could only hope for political advance if they could come to terms with the Malay Rulers.

3.   The outcome of this wartime planning was the proposal, announced in October 1945, for a Malayan Union which would unify and centralise the administration of the nine peninsular Malay States together with the Straits Settlements of Penang and Malacca. In the Malay States sovereignty was to be transferred from the Rulers to the Crown. It was expected that the Union would, by its citizenship arrangements, give the Chinese much greater political power. None of the Borneo Territories was included in this arrangement, while provision was made for Singapore, with its great base installations, to remain as a Crown Colony. This initial decision to exclude Singapore from the Malayan Union had substantial political as well as economic consequences. Not only would the communal balance in Malaya have been very different if Singapore had been included, but it might have been unnecessary to rush the Borneo Territories quite so rapidly into Federation in 1963.

Malay reactions and the formation of UMNO

4.   The Malayan Union proposals were brusquely presented to the Malay Rulers individually in an attempt to press them through in the aftermath of war before opposition could develop. They came into effect on 1 April, 1946. They had already however aroused bitter criticism amongst Malay supporters in London and this was paralleled by a great increase of political consciousness amongst the Malays themselves. This in turn led early in 1946 to the formation of the United Malays National Organisation (UMNO) which subsequently became the dominant partner in the ruling Alliance in Malaya. Mr. Creech Jones believed that if he had had the support of any substantial body of Chinese for the Malayan Union proposals, it would have been possible to maintain them. But the Left-wing Chinese, led by the Malayan Communist Party (MCP), were preoccupied with preparations for the violent seizure of power which they attempted in 1948 and the Right wing with re-establishing the economy and their dominance within it. Both at this time were equally indifferent to constitutional progress, while those few Chinese and Indians who did interest themselves in constitutional advance, rejected the Union proposals as insufficiently liberal. The Malays on the other hand were terrified that the granting of citizenship, and so political equality, to the Chinese would rapidly reduce their own people to a subordinate position in a Chinese-run State—this fear was, and is, probably well justified.

The Federation of Malaya

5.   Since they were the only community really engaged in the debate, the Malays succeeded in securing the replacement of the Union on 1 February, 1948, by the Federation of Malaya. This arrangement entrenched the political pre-eminence of the Malays and this is the basis on which Malaya has since been ruled. Maintenance of this position is an issue on which no Malay leader can easily compromise—the founder and first president of UMNO, Dato Onn bin Ja'afar, was in 1951 cast permanently from leadership because he took too liberal a view of the Chinese place in Malayan society. His successor as leader of UMNO was Tunku Abdul Rahman, a brother of the Sultan of Kedah and a relatively unknown barrister before he became president of UMNO, who subsequently became the first Chief Minister and, on independence in 1957, the first Prime Minister. The lesson of Dato Onn's sudden fall has certainly not been lost on the Tunku.

Citizenship and Singapore

6.   The debate on the form of the Federation in 1946–47 centred around questions of citizenship—in effect on the numbers of Chinese who could be excluded from political rights. The Malay anxiety to reduce the numbers of Chinese eligible for citizenship, Singapore's own wish to maintain its free port status, and the British belief that it would be necessary to maintain long-term control of the Singapore bases, led to the city, which had already been divided from the other Straits Settlements under the Malayan Union proposals, being once again left as a separate colony.

The Grand Design

7.   A desire ultimately to unite the territories remained however a continuing facet of British intentions towards the area. In 1949 and 1950, for instance, Mr.

Malcolm MacDonald, then United Kingdom Commissioner-General for South–East Asia, did not conceal his enthusiasm for a 'Grand Design' which should eventually bring together all the British Malayan and Bornean Territories. Efforts were also made to unify the Bornean Territories. North Borneo and Sarawak had come under direct British rule after the war and during the 1950s proposals were made for a closer association of these two territories with Brunei, a tiny protected State with very large per capita revenues originating from oil, of which in 1948 the Governor of Sarawak had become High Commissioner in place of the High Commissioner for the Malay States. Brunei, characteristically, proved reluctant to make any change, but the first steps were taken to draw the Administrations of the other two territories together.

Chinese attitudes

8.   Throughout the 1940s and 1950s the position of the Chinese community was weakened by its own lack of homogeneity. There were long-standing divisions between the English-speaking 'Straits Chinese' and the more recent Chinese-speaking immigrant groups, which were in turn subdivided by dialect. Moreover the Communist insurrection, the 'Emergency', which was not formally ended until August 1960, was primarily conducted by Chinese, while the local forces of law and order were primarily Malay. Traditionally Chinese had come to Malaya seeking economic opportunities—it used to be said with only slight exaggeration before the war that the Chinese did not care who held the cow so long as they could milk it. But in Chinese tradition the status of the official has always been greatly superior to that of the merchant and inevitably many younger Chinese had begun to take the economic opportunities for granted and to resent the advantages given to Malays in the public services, so that there was also something of a division between age groups.

9.   These divisions amongst the non-Communist Chinese were marked by differences of view in regard to the place of their community in a Malayan State. Some wished to press on to a situation of real equality, in which of course the more competitive training and outlook of the Chinese would give them an immense advantage. This group came latterly to be principally represented by the People's Action Party (PAP) in Singapore, led by Mr. Lee Kuan Yew. Mr. Lee had secured a double first in law at Cambridge and had worked closely with the trade union movement on his return to Singapore in 1950; he founded the PAP in 1954. Even within the much more conservative Malayan Chinese Association (MCA) however there was increasing challenge to the Malay political predominance. In the spring of 1958 this led to division within the MCA and in the summer of 1959 to a crisis within the ruling Alliance between UMNO and the MCA over the allocation of Parliamentary seats and the use of the Chinese language in examinations. As a result of this conflict the President of the MCA, Dr. Lim Chong Eu, and the Secretary-General, Mr. Too Joon Hing, resigned; in April 1962 they were prominent in the formation of the United Democratic Party which at the end of the 1960s formed a constituent of the Gerakan Ra'ayat Malaysia.

10.   A majority of the MCA held to the more traditional view that the overriding Chinese concern should be with the maintenance of their economic position. This group considered that the Malay leadership could not be expected to surrender overriding political predominance while Malays were economically so weak. They were also anxious to do nothing which might revive the intercommunal violence

which had occurred in the aftermath of the Japanese occupation. They were concerned therefore to achieve a working relationship which would leave the Malays feeling politically secure and the Chinese free to expand the economy to the benefit of both Chinese and Malays. This viewpoint came to be represented in Malaya by Mr. Tan Siew Sin and in Singapore by Mr. Lim Yew Hock, who was Chief Minister from June 1956 until defeated in the elections at the end of May 1959. It should be said that, of the more radical Chinese groups, the PAP at least did not envisage an overtly Chinese State. Mr. Lim, as Chief Minister, had called for the building up of a Malayan consciousness in Singapore and laid some stress on the learning of the Malay language. When they secured power the PAP followed up and intensified this line.

Economic interests

11. The separation of Singapore gave Mr. Tan's group an increased interest also in developing the economy of the peninsula and in reducing the overwhelming economic dominance hitherto enjoyed by Singapore. This was an issue on which the interests of the Tan group of peninsular Chinese and of the Malays appeared to coincide and it has proved one of the most intractable sources of difference between Singapore and Malaya. Already at the end of 1958 Mr. Tan opposed, unsuccessfully, a proposal to include eventual merger with Singapore as one of its objects in the draft constitution of the MCA—on the ground that this would lead to a clash with UMNO.

12. The Malayan Central Bank started operations in January 1959 and efforts to attract existing companies and new investment to the Federation from Singapore were by then beginning to take effect. During 1959 Mr. Tan also opposed proposals, which originated in Singapore and were at the end of the year mentioned in Dr. Goh Keng Swee's Budget speech, for a common market or free trade area between Singapore and Malaya. Throughout the following years, as discussion on merger with Singapore accelerated, action to disentangle the economies nevertheless continued and in this Mr. Tan and his group were usually prominently in the lead. A continuing example of this has been the effort to build up Port Swettenham in place of Singapore—the contract for the first North Klang Straits development of the port was awarded in January 1960.

II. *Attitudes to merger up to 1960*

The Tunku and Singapore

13. The Tunku was widely said in the late 1950s to be consistently and adamantly opposed to any prospect of merger with Singapore. The record however suggests that the Tunku's opposition was either not so absolute or not so consistent as was supposed. Merger with Singapore alone he regularly excluded in the short term and his attitude became stiffer after the success of the PAP in the City Council elections in February 1958 had made it seem probable that he would have to deal with Mr. Lee Kuan Yew rather than Mr. Lim Yew Hock. By the end of 1958 he was telling the Press that merger was out of the question and a year later that there could be no merger in the foreseeable future because Singapore had a Left-wing Government and Malaya a Right-wing one. In June 1959, as soon as he had formed a Government in Singapore, Mr. Lee took some of his Ministers to Kuala Lumpur for talks with Malayan Ministers led by Tun Razak, then temporarily Prime Minister while the Tunku devoted himself to organising the Alliance electoral effort.

14.   Despite these efforts to foster contact between the two Governments and to develop a Malayan spirit in Singapore, the Tunku undoubtedly himself remained from the outset suspicious of Mr. Lee's intentions. These suspicions were excited later in June 1959 by the PAP decision to release four Communists from detention without prior consultation with the Singapore Internal Security Council, of which Britain and Malaya were the other members. The Tunku must also have been under constant pressure from those Malays within UMNO, later commonly referred to as the 'ultras', who did not wish the Government to take any step which would in any way strengthen the position of Chinese within the Federation. Singapore is overwhelmingly Chinese in population and its connection with the Federation, however hedged about, could not fail to do this.

15.   Singapore within a wider grouping seems however to have been thought less indigestible. The Tunku told Mr. Malcolm MacDonald in 1958 that 'he would readily agree' to merger with Singapore 'if the three Borneo Territories came into a super Federation at the same time' and he expressed much the same view to Sir Geofroy Tory, the British High Commissioner, who was however briefed to persuade him that to ventilate this proposal would be damaging to the constitutional development of the Borneo Territories. This may in consequence have left the impression that the Grand Design was not then well regarded in London.

The Tunku's view of Borneo

16.   Mr. MacDonald, in the course of his conversation with the Tunku in 1958, had delivered the, possibly mistaken, judgment that 'not only the Malays but also most of the other non-Chinese peoples in the Borneo Territories would generally be more sympathetic to Malay than to Chinese opinion in various political matters.' This assessment the Tunku seems to have translated, at least for the benefit of his Malay supporters if not in his own mind, into a conviction that the Ibans, Dusuns and other non-Chinese peoples in Borneo were virtually Malays and could be counted as such in calculations of communal balance within a wider federation.

17.   At the same time the prospect of acquiring Brunei oil and investment revenues and the income from the North Borneo timber exports, which had begun to rise rapidly by the middle of 1960, must have had some attraction. From the sometimes misleading vantage point of hindsight, it is possible to wonder if acquisition of the three Borneo territories without Singapore may not have been in the Tunku's mind, if only subconsciously, throughout. The fact that possession of Sarawak and North Borneo (Sabah) proved a political and military and, initially, an economic burden, and that Brunei, which would have been financially the most attractive acquisition, declined to join the Federation, were matters he clearly did not foresee in 1960.

Economic and defence considerations for Malaya

18.   By the beginning of 1960 some of the initial euphoria in Malayan Government circles following independence had begun to evaporate. The success of the Pan-Malayan Islamic Party (PMIP) in the state elections in Kelantan and Trengganu in June 1959 had served warning on the Tunku and UMNO of the danger of seeming to neglect the Malay peasant on whom their political position was based and a new emergency plan to attack rural poverty was started. This was significant in relation to proposals for merger with Singapore, since there was an obvious prospect

of conflict between an economic policy of achieving maximum growth, which would involve allowing the largely Chinese towns, and above all Singapore if merger had taken place, to form growing points, and the political need to assure the rural Malays, not merely that their economic lot was improving, but that the gap between their conditions and those of the Chinese was narrowing. The consciousness of poverty is relative, not absolute.

19.   This too was at a time when the development of stereo-regular synthetics had begun to make the growth prospects for natural rubber and so for the Malayan economy as a whole, and especially for the agricultural economy, much less encouraging. Moreover independence had not yet led to a significant growth in the Malay stake in the economy. A report on Malay participation in business in Malaya had shown that they owned less than 10 per cent of the number of businesses registered and these were mostly small concerns—Malays owned only 1 per cent of the total capital invested. In consequence in October 1960 a special secretariat was established to help Malays in commerce. In the communal field the language and education issues were beginning to build up, though the Singapore Government, by its stress on the need to learn Malay, was doing something to prevent this being an issue in the event of merger. Both issues, as in India and Ceylon, are of course related to questions of economic opportunity.

20.   In the external field merger was seen to involve the issue of British use of the Singapore bases for SEATO or similar purposes. The existing defence agreement between the United Kingdom and Malaya limited British use of bases in Malaya to Commonwealth defence. Even so the agreement at that time attracted little popular backing in Malaya, was openly attacked by the opposition and was regarded as suspect in UMNO itself. There seemed therefore substantial reasons for the Tunku to be reluctant to take on Singapore.

Singapore's need for merger

21.   The Singapore Government on the other hand had at the beginning of 1960 good reasons for wishing to merge. The city was faced with increasing economic problems. The population was expanding rapidly, while the traditional entrepôt trade seemed to be faced with rapid decline; that with Indonesia had already dropped substantially and the Malayans were considering plans to divert their trade from its traditional channels. The city had begun to try to offset this decline by developing local industry beyond the processing trades; but this in turn demanded markets and there were already signs that investors would wait to see if the Malayan market would be open to industries based in Singapore. The Grand Design may also have suggested to the Singapore leaders a prospect of attracting some North Borneo trade away from Hong Kong.

22.   Mr. Lee and his Government had moreover what seemed pressing political reasons for merger with Malaya. It might be the quickest way to reach full independence and so would help to blunt the challenge of the extreme Left, still at this stage within the PAP. And after merger it could be expected that the staunchly anti-Communist Malayan Government would take firm steps to prevent any extreme Leftist take-over—the need to be able to do this was indeed later believed to be one of the main motives which induced the Tunku to consider taking Singapore on. Mr. Lee and his colleagues were by no means sure of their position—the short history of democratic elections in Singapore suggested that each successful Left-wing group

would, on allowing its views and policies to be moderated by the responsibilities of office, then be trumped from further to the Left. Another problem was that the British bases, which provided a substantial proportion of the national income, were thought at the time to be difficult, if not impossible, to defend politically.

The Borneo Territories in 1960

23.   The Borneo Territories were still in 1960 well back along both the economic and political roads. The boom in North Borneo induced by the Japanese demand for timber was however beginning and the territory in consequence suffered from a labour shortage which led to immigrant labour being attracted from Indonesia, the Philippines, Sarawak and Hong Kong. Sarawak's economy was stagnant and the low quality of its surplus labour inhibited emigration even to North Borneo; trade, hitherto very largely with or through Singapore, was beginning to be a little more diversified, if only by going directly to Thailand, Hong Kong and Japan. Brunei had oil, though the on-shore fields were declining and those off-shore had not yet been proved; but much of the earlier revenues had been invested and the level of the joint income from oil royalties and investment permitted consideration of heavy expenditure on development and social services.

24.   Political awareness was at last stirring in all three territories. A group officially described as the Clandestine Communist Organisation (CCO) existed in Sarawak and the Sarawak United People's Party (SUPP), was formed in the middle of 1959. SUPP was largely Chinese in membership and some of its members certainly had CCO connections. It was in 1959 supposed by outside observers, erroneously as it turned out, to be capable of commanding general popular support. The first elections were held in Sarawak at the end of 1959 on a multi-tier system and SUPP did much less well than had been expected. Sarawak had by 1960 an executive council, known as the Supreme Council, and a legislative council, known as the Council Negri, each with an unofficial majority, the majority of which in turn was composed of members elected by a process of indirect election.

25.   There was by 1960 some evidence of unsuccessful CCO attempts to penetrate North Borneo, where no parties as yet existed, but even here political debate was beginning. There were no elected members in either the Executive Council or the Legislative Council, but there was an unofficial majority in the Legislative Council and an equal balance between officials and others was about to be introduced in the Executive Council. Some co-operation was developing with the parallel Government departments in Sarawak, though slowly.

Brunei

26.   The Sultan of Brunei signed a new agreement with the United Kingdom on 29 September, 1959, and at the same time promulgated a written Constitution. The agreement continued, in form at least, to give the British Government complete control over external affairs and defence, including in effect internal security, and control over appointments to 'key posts', while the Sultan agreed to accept the advice of the High Commissioner on all matters of state except the Muslim religion and the customs of the Malays. The Administrations of Brunei and Sarawak were divorced, and a separate High Commissioner for Brunei was appointed instead of this being a combined post with that of Governor of Sarawak. The Sultan had the right to be consulted on the appointment of the High Commissioner, who was financially

dependent on the Brunei Government. This and the Constitution, with its apparatus of Privy Council, Executive Council and Legislative Council, greatly reduced in practice the degree of control which could be exercised by the High Commissioner. The mandatory advice clause has in consequence proved to be a dead letter.

27. The Legislative Council had a large elected element and was presided over by a Mentri Besar, or Chief Minister, appointed by the Sultan, while some elected members of the Legislative Council served on the Executive Council. Under the new system the Mentri Besar in effect replaced the former British Resident, who had been in charge of the general administration of the State. British civil servants of the Sarawak service were also replaced by seconded Malayan civil servants; this in due course proved inimical to membership of Malaysia, since the Brunei Malays did not find the peninsular Malay officials congenial and complained that they had exchanged experienced for inexperienced expatriates. The Parti Ra'ayat, led by Sheikh A. M. Azahari, which held its first congress in April 1957, had something of a monopoly of political activity in Brunei. The party congress early in 1960, which was attended by SUPP and PMIP representatives, proved to be primarily concerned with proposals for 'Borneo unity' to be followed by 'pan-Malayan federation' of the vague kind advocated by the PMIP and designed to include Indonesia as well as Malaya.

28. Generally however there was little popular interest in the Borneo Territories in the idea of federation, whether with Malaya or with other Borneo Territories, and there was some distaste for such ideas. In Brunei there was a dislike of the prospect of sharing the oil revenues—an income which could provide a high level of free welfare for the State's population of about 60,000 would certainly not do so if some of it were to be diverted to the needs of other territories. The Sultan himself had to balance the prospect of becoming Agong of Malaya against the loss of income and independence. In Sarawak and North Borneo there was the fear that unity and a rapid 'localisation' of Government posts would result in Chinese or Malays getting most of them.

The state of British policy in 1960

29. In January 1960 the process of reducing or eliminating British colonial and defence commitments all over the world was rapidly gathering momentum—the Prime Minister, Mr. Macmillan, launched his 'wind of change' theme in Ghana on 9 January, 1960, and repeated it in Cape Town on 3 February, when it effectively caught public attention. It was already accepted policy for the Borneo Territories that they should ultimately achieve independence, subject within limits to their own wishes. At the same time they were being gently pushed towards federation with each other.

30. The real British interest in the future of Singapore was less easy to decide. Under the existing situation the United Kingdom held naval, air and military facilities in the territory by sovereign right, but to attempt to maintain a colonial status in face of increasingly Left-wing and extreme local political leadership might well result in the Singapore base becoming an albatross. In an independent federation with Malaya on the other hand the bases would be held only by treaty and there had already been some indication of the limitations this might impose on their use. The possibility of developing a base in North Borneo and even of stationing a brigade there was under discussion, but did not arouse great enthusiasm. There was in January 1960 as yet no thought of avoiding this dilemma by a complete

withdrawal, although by June 1963 views at official level had changed enough for it to be asserted without challenge, in an exchange of minutes between two Foreign Office departments, that: 'Everyone in Whitehall would like us to adopt a foreign policy of abandoning our Far East commitments and running down Singapore.'

31.   On 23 January, 1960, an informal meeting of British Foreign, Commonwealth Relations, Colonial and Armed Service representatives from the surrounding countries and territories was held at Phoenix Park, Singapore, to discuss problems in Borneo. Sir Denis Allen, who was in the chair, raised the related problems of the prospect of Brunei joining the Federation of Malaya, which at that point seemed very probable, of the programme of closer association between Sarawak and North Borneo, and of the Grand Design. Objections to the Grand Design, especially the relative backwardness of the Borneo Territories and the fears and ambitions of Indonesia and the Philippines, were raised, but the general conclusions reached were that the Grand Design might have advantages, that in any case it was dangerous merely to await developments, and that consideration should be given to policy on this issue, especially in relation to the prospect of Brunei seeking to join the Federation.

32.   This discussion stimulated consideration of the issues in London and by May 1960, though no submission had been made to Ministers, the general trend of official thinking was that, however much they might wish to be left as Crown Colonies, Sarawak and North Borneo must in due course become self-governing. This they were too weak to sustain individually or even jointly, and so the most hopeful ultimate solution would be in a grouping of the Federation of Malaya and all three Borneo Territories, together if possible with Singapore. This view was expressed in a letter of 18 May, 1960, from Sir John Martin to Sir Denis Allen [see document 20]. It was generally welcomed by British officials in the area, on the explicit assumption however that progress towards the Grand Design would be deliberate in view of the considerable political leeway to be made up by the Borneo Territories.

B. *Preliminary discussions and agreement in principle*

III. *The Tunku's first initiative, June 1960*

The Tunku's visit to Lord Perth, 10 June, 1960

33.   On 10 June, 1960, the Tunku paid a visit to the Minister of State, Lord Perth, at the Colonial Office. His stated purpose was that the British Government should know that he was prepared to face the possibility of a Federation of Malaya, Singapore, North Borneo, Sarawak and Brunei—in other words the full Grand Design. Lord Perth's reaction was to say that the matter had not been given 'a great deal of thought' by his Government and to recite the difficulties, and in particular the unwisdom of haste. In face of this damping reception the Tunku enquired how Her Majesty's Government would view the prospect of Brunei joining the Federation; Lord Perth replied that this must be a matter for the people of Brunei themselves to decide and that it was important first to see how the new Constitution worked out [see 21 and 22].

34.   The Tunku then tried the suggestion that Brunei and Sarawak might join the Federation, while the British remained in North Borneo to develop it economically and to use it as a military base. Lord Perth 'pointed out the real economic difficulties that faced development in Sarawak' and tried to indicate that the British

Government was 'neither for nor against the general principle, that it was early times to say anything more, although naturally the linking up of our friends would be a logical course to see followed.' On 19 July, 1960, Sir Geofroy Tory reported that since his return from London the Tunku had twice raised the general issue, was now firmly in favour of his last alternative, and had stressed the advantages of a British base in North Borneo.

British assessments of the Tunku's intentions

35.   Lord Home, the Commonwealth Secretary, commenting on the original interview in a minute of 21 June, 1960, to the Foreign Secretary, had doubted if the Tunku was 'seriously thinking of Singapore as a partner in a Federation', but had thought that he might do so 'if through it he could mobilise enough Malays to be an effective counter-weight to the Chinese in Singapore.' In his letter of 19 July, however, Sir Geofroy Tory concluded that the Tunku had abandoned his earlier view, expressed to Mr. MacDonald and himself, that the acquisition of the Borneo Territories would enable him to receive Singapore also, and 'that the Tunku's mind is still closed on the subject of closer association with Singapore under its present régime.'

36.   A minute of 16 August, 1960, by Mr. F. A. Warner suggested that Sir Geofroy Tory's letter showed that the Tunku had no real intention of absorbing Singapore 'and merely mentioned it in the first place to make his idea of gobbling up the Borneo Territories seem more attractive.' In an earlier minute, of 26 July, Mr. Warner had expressed the fear 'that what he means to do is to commit us to giving him the Borneo Territories and that he will then refuse to absorb Singapore, which he will leave on our hands.' Within a few weeks of the interview with Lord Perth British official despatches and minutes were unanimous in taking the view that the Tunku was immovable on the issue of merger with Singapore, whether alone or in combination with other territories.

37.   In his letter of 19 July, 1960, Sir Geofroy Tory, however, had mentioned that the Tunku had 'twice lately gone close to admitting to me by implication that he does not rule out eventual merger', and expressed a fear that 'he has necessarily been left with the impression that we are cool about the Grand Design'. It remains at least possible that the Tunku had genuinely intended to take up the Grand Design in full, had once again met with an, as he thought, discouraging British response and had reacted to this by putting on a show of having never contemplated a merger involving Singapore. The split in the PAP from the middle of June, and the prospect of an even more Left-wing Government in Singapore, may also have temporarily induced greater caution. By May 1961, when the Tunku next mentioned his interest in the Grand Design, this time publicly, British official opinion was so convinced that he was adamant on the subject of Singapore that the new initiative was greeted with astonishment.

The initial British reaction: 'Benevolent neutrality'

38.   Whatever the Tunku's intentions, his 1960 initiative had the effect of greatly stimulating British official discussion of the issue. Lord Selkirk, the recently appointed Commissioner-General in South-East Asia, who was visiting London, in a minute of 17 June, 1960 [see 23], to Mr. Selwyn Lloyd, the Foreign Secretary, argued that a direct merger between Malaya and Singapore did not seem practical and that

the full Grand Design Federation was the only development which might give some stability to the area. He recommended therefore 'that these proposals be examined very closely and urgently'. In the course of his argument he met the objection that there would be a loss of defence facilities by claiming that the Tunku 'could not possibly take over Singapore and then seek to denude it of the economic advantages of defence installations', though he agreed that it might be necessary to detach Labuan from North Borneo as a British naval and air base for certain specific functions.

39.   The Colonial Office argued that the wishes of the peoples of the Borneo Territories must be 'a paramount factor' in any consideration of the issue and that 'we cannot force Borneo opinion'. In a Cabinet Colonial Policy Committee memorandum of 15 July, 1960, [see 25] therefore Mr. Macleod, the Colonial Secretary, expressed a feeling that 'we ought to go slowly'. He suggested taking up an attitude to the Tunku of 'benevolent neutrality' and awaiting the outcome of informed discussions amongst the Governors and other British officials concerned at the time of the meeting of the Borneo Inter-Territorial Conference and the Joint Advisory Defence Committee (Borneo) in Kuching in October. The Foreign Secretary also had doubts about the wisdom of disturbing convenient defence arrangements.

40.   Lord Selkirk, however, in a letter of 22 July, 1960, to the Prime Minister, stressed the urgency of action if the position in Singapore was to be held even for five years. He expressed the view that Mr. Lee's was the best Government of Singapore that could be expected from the British point of view, that Mr. Lee himself recognised the necessity of the bases to Singapore for security as well as economic reasons, and that it was essential to help the PAP Government maintain its position by providing both adequate economic assistance and apparent constitutional advance. At a meeting in London on 27 July, 1960, [see 27] between Lord Selkirk and the Prime Minister and other senior Ministers it was also noted that Singapore could not be expected to be content with the existing constitutional position for long and that it might be easier to maintain British defence facilities under a defence treaty if Singapore were to be federated with Malaya. This meeting nevertheless went no further than to agree to adopt an attitude of benevolent neutrality towards any suggestion of association of the Borneo Territories with Malaya and to await further discussion of the issue in Kuching in October.

Tariff protection and common market proposals

41.   Some concern was however expressed at this Ministerial meeting in London about problems of surplus population in Singapore and at the possibility that the Singapore Government might, in view of the United Kingdom's inability to meet its full demands for economic aid, seek assistance from Soviet *bloc* countries. Lord Selkirk was therefore invited to discuss with the Tunku the possibility of Malaya adopting a policy of closer economic co-operation with Singapore.

42.   Malayan and Singapore officials had already been meeting to consider proposals for common market arrangements since 10 June, 1960. These meetings were however adjourned *sine die* on 25 August. On 21 September the Singapore Assembly passed a revised Customs Ordinance permitting the provision of tariff protection for local industries against outside, including Malayan, producers. It was thought that the Malayan attitude towards a limited common market then became even less forthcoming in consequence of action under this ordinance. Certainly Mr.

Tan's Budget in November raised the tariff wall for a number of local industries and, although he denied that this marked the beginning of a tariff war, one import tax was a clear response to tariff action in Singapore.

The Kuching meeting, October 1960

43.   The informal meeting between the Commissioner-General, the Governors of Sarawak and North Borneo and the High Commissioner for Brunei, which the Ministerial meeting in July had asked to discuss the possibility of future association of the Borneo Territories with a wider Malayan Federation, took place in Kuching on 20 October, 1960. Lord Perth and General Sir Richard Hull, Commander-in-Chief Far East Land Forces, together with officials of the Colonial Office and Commission General, were also present.

44.   It was agreed to recommend to Her Majesty's Government that the Grand Design should be the ultimate goal of British policy in the area, and that closer association of North Borneo, Sarawak and possibly Brunei should be a first step in this direction. The Grand Design was thought to provide the only real prospect of safeguarding the security and welfare of the territories themselves and British defence interests. Discussion in confidence should be begun with the Tunku, Mr. Lee, the Sultan of Brunei and other interested parties as occasion offered and the prospect of the Grand Design should be used as an argument with them to resist any further movement towards the disintegration of the economic unity of the area. In such discussions it should be made plain that progress towards the ultimate goal must be gradual and adjusted to the rate of political evolution in the Borneo Territories.

45.   It was suggested in the course of the discussion that a major process of education would be needed in North Borneo and Sarawak before the necessity for such an association could be widely appreciated and that any public impression that Her Majesty's Government were 'actively pushing such a solution or seeking to impose it upon the peoples concerned' should be avoided. If the matter had to be mentioned in public at all no more should be said than that a broad association was one possible outcome which Her Majesty's Government 'would not themselves regard as excluded from consideration'.

46.   Sir William Goode, then Governor of North Borneo and a former Governor of Singapore, in commenting, in a despatch of 11 November, 1960, on Lord Selkirk's despatch of 25 October [see 30] reporting these conclusions, suggested that this proposed public posture was too negative and would be interpreted as discouraging—he suggested that any public statement should be on the lines that the Grand Design 'has great possibilities for the future provided it is acceptable to the peoples concerned'. In the event no decision was taken even to open the subject in confidence with the Tunku before he broached it publicly himself in May 1961. In consequence the impression that Her Majesty's Government did not favour the project could only be dispelled to the satisfaction of the Tunku by abandoning the insistence on gradual progress for the Borneo Territories.

Improved relations between the Malay leaders and Mr. Lee

47.   Meanwhile the movement towards economic autarky continued unchecked. The personal relations between the Malay leaders and Mr. Lee and his colleagues had however begun to improve somewhat. On 7 October, 1960, the Singapore Internal

Security Council met in the Cameron Highlands and provided opportunities for Mr. Lee to improve his standing with the Tunku and to persuade him that for Malaya, as well as for Britain, any probable alternative Government of Singapore would be much less attractive. Mr. Lee and Dr. Goh Keng Swee also spent the Christmas week-end in Kuala Lumpur playing golf with Malayan Ministers and it became clear that Mr. Lee was becoming increasingly interested in the Grand Design as a means of resolving many of his political and economic problems. It was also reported by Sir Geofroy Tory that the Malayan Deputy Prime Minister and Defence Minister, Tun Razak, was thought to be coming to the conclusion that Malaya would have to accept responsibility for Singapore with the Borneo Territories as a counterweight.

48. Mr. Lee's cultivation of the Malayan Government bore public fruit on 30 January, 1961, when, in a Press interview, the Tunku stated that the Singapore Government was 'as good a Malayan Government as mine is'. He did so while explaining that merger would have to wait for 'some' time and that 'we cannot have merger with them at this moment . . ., because certain elements among Chinese there are China minded'; meanwhile the Federation believed in close co-operation with Singapore without effecting actual merger. It was also noted that the workings of the Internal Security Council had become much smoother.

Continued British caution, January–May 1961

49. On 30 January, 1961, in the light of these developments and of a further discussion with the Governors, High Commissioners and Ambassadors in the area, Lord Selkirk sent a despatch to Mr. Macleod [see 32], the Colonial Secretary. In this he pointed out that there was a distinct possibility that some kind of Grand Design would sooner or later be launched by the Federation or by Singapore and again pressed for urgent consideration by the Government of its attitude to a Grand Design 'in order to be in a position to influence its shape and character during the formative period'. He suggested that the British Government should 'in the near future, after consultation with the Governments involved', make a public statement of policy on the issue, on the lines favoured by Sir William Goode. One reason for urgency was 'to prevent the pressure for separate independence for Singapore, which is accumulating under the surface and by which Mr. Lee Kuan Yew is plainly embarrassed, from becoming unmanageable.'

50. Sir Geofroy Tory still thought that the Tunku had 'a closed mind on the subject of Singapore', having been told 'firmly' by Tun Razak that the Tunku's remarks at the Press interview on 30 January, 1961, did not represent any change in attitude towards merger with Singapore alone. Nevertheless Sir Geofroy believed that 'There is a lot to be said for gaining and keeping the initiative in this matter. I can see some risk that, once the penny drops with the Tunku, he will want to go galloping ahead in all sorts of impossible directions, and far faster than we wish.' A draft Cabinet paper prepared in the Colonial Office before receipt of Lord Selkirk's January despatch, followed his and Sir William Goode's proposals, except that it was thought desirable to avoid if possible making any public statement at all. The draft did however suggest broaching the matter with the Tunku during March, when he would be in London for a Commonwealth Prime Ministers' Conference.

51. Mr. Macleod however saw reasons for caution. He was already under fire for his policy of pressing on with the grant of independence to the British colonial territories in Africa and did not wish to increase his difficulties over that policy by

announcing an intention to liquidate the remaining British colonial commitments in South-East Asia. On 10 March, 1961, he therefore sent an informal letter to Lord Selkirk saying that he had decided to postpone putting proposals to the Cabinet until April and that he was not convinced of the need for a public statement.

52.   This letter drew a reply of 23 March, 1961, from Lord Selkirk expressing the hope that some instructions could be issued in time for the Borneo Inter-Territorial Conference in the last week of April and that at least confidential discussions with the Tunku and Mr. Lee, and possibly also with the Sultan of Brunei and local notables in Sarawak and North Borneo, should be authorised. Lord Selkirk concluded that 'If we are to attempt any steering at all we must at least know what our eventual goal is and be authorised to tell our partners what course we propose to set in company with them. Our ability to influence the course of events declines with the passage of time.'

53.   Interim instructions were issued to Lord Selkirk on 21 April, 1961, following a discussion in the Colonial Policy Committee of the Cabinet on 18 April [see 35]. These permitted him to be guided by the assumption that the ultimate aim of British policy was the gradual 'development of a political association between Malaya, Singapore and the three Borneo territories'. But this was to be subject to a final decision which would not be taken until the Governments of Australia and New Zealand had been given an opportunity of expressing their views; pending this 'we should not volunteer discussion on the subject with other parties'. Nor did Her Majesty's Government 'contemplate making any public statement for the present since it is essential that we should avoid all appearance of trying to impose a political association'. On 9 May, 1961, despite the length of time the matter had been under discussion, the Ministry of Defence asked that consultation even with Australia and New Zealand should be held back until the Chiefs of Staff had considered and expressed their views on the defence implications of the Grand Design—the Chief of the Defence Staff had only now instructed the Joint Planning Staff to prepare a report for the Chiefs of Staff Committee.

Political difficulties in Singapore

54.   Throughout this period the internal position of the Government of Singapore appeared to weaken. The split in the PAP in the previous summer was led by Mr. Ong Eng Guan who wanted more 'anti-colonialism' and as Mayor of Singapore had been responsible for some striking gestures against established society. Mr. Ong and two supporters were expelled from the party on 28 July, 1960, and on 29 December he resigned his seat in the Legislative Assembly. This resulted in a by-election in the Hong Lim constituency which Mr. Ong won on 29 April, 1961, with 7,747 votes to the PAP candidate's 2,820 votes. It was assumed at the time that this would set back the prospects of merger by revealing the strength of Leftist opinion in Singapore, but it may in fact have had the opposite effect on the Tunku.

55.   When asked why he had been so forthcoming on 30 January, 1961, about Mr. Lee, the Tunku was reported by Sir Geofroy Tory to have said: 'Poor man, he has so many troubles. I thought he needed a little assistance. These fellows are not so bad,' Mr. Macleod, in explaining to the British Cabinet why Lord Selkirk wanted an early public statement, stated that 'Mr. Lee Kuan Yew's policy of independence through merger with the Federation of Malaya has come under fire because the Federation's unwillingness to merge in the foreseeable future is only too clear . . . Lord Selkirk

thinks it would fortify Mr. Lee and frustrate his and our enemies if the possibility of independence through a wider association were to be produced as an attainable goal.' [See 34.] It seems probable that the Tunku had in the preceding months become increasingly accustomed to Mr. Lee and confident of his intentions and therefore correspondingly less willing to see him displaced by a much more extreme group.

Political developments in Borneo

56.   The situation with regard to Borneo had also changed. In the Cabinet Mr. Macleod came down firmly against holding on to North Borneo while allowing Sarawak to be merged with Malaya. In North Borneo itself Mr. Donald Stephens, proprietor and editor of the *Sabah Times* and Chairman of the Kadazan Society, had, in the Legislative Council on 7 December, 1960, urged the need for federation with Sarawak and later possibly Brunei, and had discussed the probability that political parties would soon be formed in the territory as they had already been in Sarawak. He had also in private conversation with the Governor mentioned the possibility of association with Malaya. The decision to form the United National Kadazan Organisation (UNKO) was taken at a meeting at Mr. Stephens' house on 26 March, 1961, though the party was not formally inaugurated until August.

57.   In Brunei the Sultan, while still inclined to accept a link with Malaya, was becoming more aware of the arguments against, and of opposition to, the proposal. At the same time the Parti Ra'ayat was trying to arouse enthusiasm for closer association amongst the Borneo Territories themselves. By the beginning of 1961 there was also increasing ill-feeling between the seconded Malay police and the local Brunei Malays. The prospects of Malaya getting the 'plum' of Brunei without the other territories was therefore receding.

Mr. Lee's proposals for a Grand Design, 9 May, 1961

58.   On 24 April, 1961, Mr. Lee told Lord Selkirk that on the previous day he had, for the first time, had a talk with the Tunku on a Grand Design. Dr. Goh, Tun Razak and Tun Ismail had also been present at this meeting which had taken place in Kuala Lumpur. At the end of the meeting the Tunku had invited him to prepare a paper setting out his ideas on the way in which a Grand Design could be achieved. On 28 April Mr. Lee discussed the shape of his proposed paper with Mr. P. B. C. Moore. He insisted that the fact that he had told British officials of these talks should be kept from the Tunku. Mr. Lee showed his paper [see 37] in confidence to Lord Selkirk on 9 May before giving it to Tun Ismail on the same day for transmission to Tun Razak and the Tunku.

59.   In his paper Mr. Lee laid great stress on the danger that without merger Singapore would pass into the hands of a China-minded group and become a Communist Chinese base. He mentioned the need for care not to arouse fears in the Borneo Territories that they would be 'swamped by more active and sophisticated people', but stressed that an early agreement in principle was essential if the position in Singapore was to be held. On the question of racial balance the paper included the indigenous population of the Borneo Territories with the Malays making a total of 4,480,900, as against 4,108,000 Chinese, 904,800 Indians and 213,000 'others'.

60.   Mr. Lee's constitutional suggestions were designed to persuade the Malay leaders that there need be no threat to the Malay political predominance in a wider 'Federation of Malaysia', despite the large increase in the numbers of Chinese. He

proposed that there should be indirect elections to the Federal Parliament, with 68 seats for Malaya, 16 for Singapore and 12 for Borneo. He claimed that with indirect election, so that the majority group in each territory could take all its Federal seats, the Malays could always be sure of control of at least 68 out of the total of 96 seats. He also proposed that citizens should only be able to vote in their own state, so preventing the Singapore Chinese from swamping the indigenous majority in either Malaya or the Borneo Territories. In Malaya, on his figures, 'Malays and Indigenous' were already fractionally fewer than half the total population, but this point was not brought out in the paper. Mr. Lee suggested that the powers of the Federation should include defence, foreign affairs, police and security and matters such as currency and common economic development.

61. In his letter of 10 May, 1961, covering Mr. Lee's paper, and in a letter of 16 May reporting a further meeting between Singapore and Malayan leaders, Lord Selkirk expressed the view that the readiness of the Tunku to discuss the Grand Design was a very considerable advance, but doubted if any very concrete progress was being made, despite the belief, held by Mr. Lee, that Tun Razak was himself convinced of the necessity of the Grand Design and was pushing the Tunku towards acceptance of it. At the second meeting in particular the Tunku, according to Mr. Lee, kept harking back to the proposal that the Sultan of Brunei should take over Sarawak and then join Malaya, which would in turn then consider the arrangements to be made with Singapore.

IV. *The Tunku's second initiative, May 1961*

The Tunku's speech of 27 May, 1961

62. On 26 May, 1961, however, the Tunku informed Sir Geofroy Tory that 'he had now come to realise that . . . in Malaya's interests she should find some means of absorbing Singapore safely and constructively'. [See 39.] The Grand Design seemed to offer the only means of doing this and he proposed to include a passage in a speech to the Press Club in Singapore on the following day indicating this. He made it clear that he was thinking of absorbing the Borneo Territories into the Federation of Malaya as integral States, with Singapore alone enjoying substantial self-government, and Sir Geofroy told him that he thought that the Federation would have to give North Borneo and Sarawak as well a considerable measure of self-government. Sir Geofroy also suggested that there might be some danger of adverse reaction to the speech in North Borneo and Sarawak 'where public opinion still needed to be conditioned', and this drew from the Tunku the retort 'that nothing would happen at all unless someone gave a lead.'

Reactions in Borneo

63. The lead given by this speech of 27 May, 1961, produced immediate and widespread effects. It was widely welcomed in Sarawak, subject to prior unity with North Borneo, but, opinion in the Borneo Territories, as Sir Geofroy Tory had predicted to the Tunku, rapidly hardened against absorption in the Federation with the same status as the existing States. This view was strengthened by a disastrous visit to Borneo by the Tunku early in July during which he quite misjudged the temper of the Territories, spoke as if all non-Chinese in Borneo were Malays, and took an over-bearing and uncompromising stance which alarmed opinion in North

Borneo and Sarawak and may well have finally convinced both the Sultan and his people in Brunei that they should stay out of the Federation.

Reactions in Singapore: The founding of the Barisan Sosialis

64. In Singapore the speech immediately precipitated a fierce political struggle. So long as merger had seemed remote the Left wing of the PAP had paid lip service to it; but the Tunku's support made it a genuine prospect and they had therefore to come out in open opposition to it. On 3 June, 1961, six trade unionists, all PAP members and led by Mr. Lim Chin Siong, issued a statement strongly attacking the substitution of projects for merger in place of the earlier demand for 'full and complete self-government by 1963'. They stated that they would not support the PAP candidate in the imminent Anson by-election unless the Government undertook to demand complete internal self-government in the constitutional talks which had been promised for 1963. They subsequently followed this up with demands which included the release of all detainees.

65. On 14 July, 1961, eight PAP members of the Assembly, led by Dr. Lee Siew Choh, issued a public declaration supporting the stand of these trade union leaders and demanding that a party conference be held to discuss the whole issue. They were supported in this by a number of PAP branches. On 21 July there was a vote of confidence in the Assembly. 26 PAP members and 1 independent voted for the Government, 8 Opposition members voted against it, and 13 PAP members and the 3 members of Mr. Ong Eng Guan's United People's Party abstained. Dissident PAP members were then dismissed from the party and on 29 July they announced the formation of a new party, the Barisan Sosialis, or Socialist Front, with Dr. Lee Siew Choh as Chairman.

66. Mr. Lee's political position now became precarious in the extreme and remained so for over a year. For a short period in the summer of 1962 indeed the Government lost its majority in the Assembly. On 14 July, 1961, the PAP lost the Anson by-election to Mr. David Marshall of the Workers Party, a former Chief Minister, though by a smaller margin than most observers had expected, given the split in the PAP. Nevertheless, on 30 January, 1962, the Legislative Assembly passed by 35 votes to 13 a motion moved by Mr. Lee declaring its support in principle for the Tunku's proposed plan for a Federation of Malaysia, with the Barisan Sosialis isolated in opposition.

Irritants in the relationship between Malaya and Singapore

67. The Anson by-election was marked by the intervention of an Alliance candidate. The Singapore Alliance had been formed in June 1961 by the Singapore UMNO, MCA and MIC with the open support of the Tunku and under the leadership of Mr. Lim Yew Hock. The Tunku's support foreshadowed the uneasy record of political intervention by both the Tunku and Mr. Lee in the other's bailiwick which helped to destroy confidence between them and was in the end a principal cause of the break-up of Malaysia.

68.' Confidence between the Malayan and Singapore Governments was also damaged by Mr. Lee's efforts to transfer the odium for the continued detention of a number of leaders of the Left wing in Singapore to the British and Malayan Governments. He informed Lord Selkirk on 19 July, 1961, that he proposed on the following day to publish a confidential memorandum to the Internal Security

Council of 12 August, 1959, in which he had recommended the release of 30 detainees. He also proposed to advise the Head of State to make orders for the release of these detainees in batches. Mr. Lee's decision to break the rules under which the Internal Security Council was run greatly annoyed the Tunku, who was well aware that Mr. Lee wanted detention to continue, but did not wish himself to take responsibility for this, though he was the chief beneficiary. On 8 August therefore the Malayan Government gave formal notice to withdraw from the ISC in six months' time, though this intention was not in the end carried out. Lord Selkirk was also 'becoming increasingly disturbed by Lee Kuan Yew's irresponsibility' and thought it 'clear that he is seriously considering the possibility of forcing a constitutional crisis, in which I should have to suspend the Constitution rather than allow the Government of Singapore to pass into the hands of people whom he believes will be Communist-manipulated.'

Reactions in Malaya: The Alliance recovers support

69.   At the time of the Tunku's speech Malaya had been in the middle of town council elections. These had gone well for the Alliance in the Malay areas and the speech followed encouraging results from Kelantan, the main stronghold of the PMIP. After the speech the Alliance was if anything even more successful in the town council elections in Trengganu, the other state in which the PMIP had earlier had substantial support. Over Malaya as a whole the Alliance won 423 seats against only 17 won by the PMIP and, although it did less well in the bigger, largely Chinese, towns against other groups, the elections suggested that it had recovered a firm hold on the loyalties of the Malays. Public comment in Malaya on the Grand Design proposal after the speech was cautious but not hostile.

The British response

70.   Having publicly launched the Grand Design proposal, the Tunku, as Sir Geofroy Tory had expected, proved anxious to hurry on with it urgently. In view of the fragility of his political position, Mr. Lee also had reason for haste. North Borneo and Sarawak, however, had some considerable way to go before they would be ready for full self-government or able to stand up for their own interests in a federation. Nor did the British Chiefs of Staff show any wish to see an early change in the existing defence pattern in the area. The four British Departments of State involved all therefore took the view that it was desirable to restrain the impetuosity of the Tunku somewhat and the initial British response, while positive, was distinctly cautious.

71.   The Prime Minister, Mr. Macmillan, in answer to questions in the Commons on 20 June, 1961, said that 'I have observed with interest the recent constructive suggestion of the Prime Minister of the Federation of Malaya' and that Her Majesty's Government would wish to take Bornean 'reactions into account in their own consideration of the suggestion'. He concluded his answers to supplementary questions by remarking that 'There are . . . very widely differing stages of political and economic development, and obviously there are great problems in going too rapidly to what might not be a successful conclusion of any discussions.' In answer to a message from the Tunku of 17 June, the Commonwealth Secretary, Mr. Sandys, sent a reply which drew attention to Mr. Macmillan's answers and stated that 'The British Government are indeed interested, and are going into the whole subject', but also emphasised the British 'anxiety not to seem to be putting pressure on the people of the Borneo Territories'.

72.   At a dinner on 20 June, 1961, Lord Selkirk enquired of the Tunku whether he was prepared to administer the Borneo Territories as a sort of colony, to accept the defence of the whole area, and to provide the necessary financial assistance. It was clear that these were issues which the Tunku had not as yet fully considered or preferred to ignore. In a meeting with Tun Razak on the following day Lord Selkirk mentioned a period of 10 to 15 years for the scheme to mature. This led Tun Razak to remark that Malaya would be unwilling to contemplate confederation with Singapore, which he accepted would have to come into operation by 1963, without confederation with the Borneo Territories at the same time.

V. *Initial ideas on a Grand Design*

The Tunku's memorandum on a Grand Design, June 1961

73.   On 26 June, 1961, the Tunku sent Mr. Macmillan a memorandum outlining his ideas on the Grand Design. [See 46.] This suggested that the Borneo Territories should first merge as States of the existing Federation and only then should 'a greater federation' be formed with Singapore. The Tunku envisaged Singapore as having a unique status and its own Civil Service within an otherwise homogeneous federation— Ulster's position within the United Kingdom seems to have been in his mind. The Tunku urged that these arrangements should be brought into operation 'in the near future' and mentioned the Currency Agreement as an example of existing unified arrangements which Malaya could not accept much longer without political unification. Attached to this memorandum was a 'Breakdown of Population Figures' with the same figures quoted earlier by Mr. Lee, but with the 'Malays and Indigenous' column simply headed 'Malays' qualified only by a footnote stating that ' "Malays" here includes the Dayaks, Dusuns, etc.'.

Influences making for a less cautious British approach

74.   Mr. Macmillan replied to the Tunku's letter covering this memorandum on 3 August, 1961 [see 51]. He said that the Tunku's ideas 'could have an encouraging effect for the political stability of South-East Asia' and warmly welcomed the stimulus they had given to discussion. But he went on to say that 'I cannot at this stage commit the British Government on the possibility of a wider association. In particular, there are some points, on defence and on the Borneo Territories, on which they will need to be reassured.' He concluded by proposing that the Tunku and Mr. Lee should visit London at the end of October or early in November to talk these matters over as a preliminary to a formal conference at a later date at which the Borneo Territories would be included.

75.   Despite its cautious tone, by the time this letter was sent a number of influences had combined to induce or permit a greater willingness to accept more rapid progress. At the end of July 1961 Mr. Selwyn Lloyd, by now Chancellor of the Exchequer, introduced an interim Budget and made a statement on the balance of payments situation in which he insisted that it was imperative for the United Kingdom to secure substantial savings in overseas expenditure, in the short term as well as in the long term. In Singapore there was a pressing need to do everything possible to strengthen the hand of the Government in its struggle to retain popular support in face of the bid for power by the Barisan Sosialis. Meanwhile it seemed increasingly probable that the later the Grand Design was introduced the easier and more tempting it would be for the Indonesians to resist it.

The Malaysia Solidarity Consultative Committee

76. At the same time one of the two chief arguments against haste, the fear that the interests of the peoples of Borneo would be virtually ignored and their case go by default, was mitigated a little. A Commonwealth Parliamentary Association regional conference in Singapore from 21 to 26 July, 1961, provided an opportunity to remedy the impression left by the Tunku's visit to Borneo and to enable representatives from North Borneo and Sarawak to convince Malayan and Singapore Ministers that the Tunku's original proposals had been ungenerous. At the meeting Mr. Donald Stephens proposed that a consultative committee of representatives from all five territories should continue informal discussions and make recommendations to their respective Governments on steps to be taken to achieve an acceptable Grand Design. The first meeting of this Malaysia Solidarity Consultative Committee was held in Jesselton on 24 August. It met again in Kuching on 18 December and in Kuala Lumpur on 6 January, 1962. Its fourth and final meeting was held in Singapore on 1 February, 1962. The meetings, if they achieved nothing else, stimulated the crystallisation of ideas on federation in the Borneo Territories.

Greater political awareness in Borneo

77. The Federation was also able during this period to impress on delegations from Borneo the real or apparent advantages merger might have both for the peoples of the territories as a whole and for leading individuals in them and so to generate some enthusiasm for the idea. Within North Borneo, which had been well behind Sarawak, political organisations began to proliferate following the inauguration of UNKO in August 1961. In October Datu Mustapha announced the intention of forming the United Sabah National Organisation (USNO) which should be open to all natives of the territory, though the leadership was predominantly Muslim—the nature of party leadership in Borneo is perhaps illuminated by the 1962 accounts of USNO, which showed an income of M$65,000 and a loan of over M$34,000 to Datu Mustapha. Other groups formed were the United National Pasok Momogun Organisation (UNPMO) in the Interior Residency, the Democratic Party and the Social Democratic Party, which later changed its name to the United Party. The Democratic and United Parties were primarily Chinese in composition. A North Borneo Chinese Association, which claimed to be non-political, was also formed.

78. The Governors of North Borneo and Sarawak, Sir William Goode and Sir Alexander Waddell, were already pressing for greater safeguards for the territories in any federation than the Tunku had originally proposed. The Tunku himself had begun to move a little from his earlier view that the Borneo Territories should be incorporated into the Federation on exactly the same footing as the existing States and by 16 October, 1961, when speaking on Malaysia in the Malayan Parliament, he had come to accept that they should have special powers on immigration, customs, Borneanisation and control of state franchise rights. In mid-November delegates from the two territories to a Colombo Plan meeting were said to have spoken 'very bluntly' to the Tunku and Mr. Lee and to have made some impression on the Tunku, although on 22 November, in London, he still seemed determined to make education a federal subject in Borneo.

Further influences in reducing British caution

79. By the end of August 1961 the influences operating on Her Majesty's Government which made greater haste more acceptable had increased. In a letter of 24 August [see 55] Lord Selkirk argued strongly for 'a crash programme for the "Greater Malaysia" scheme' on the twin premises that Mr. Lee would certainly be overthrown unless merger were to be agreed rapidly and that it was impossible to wait for association of the Borneo Territories on the basis of popular representation, since this would take 10 years in the case of Sarawak and 20 in the case of North Borneo— Lord Selkirk was of course based in Singapore and therefore, despite his wider responsibilities, perhaps tended to give special weight to the problems of the city.

80. Lord Selkirk repeated these views at greater length in a letter of 16 September, 1961, [see 58] stressing *inter alia* the need to make it clear to the Federation Government that they would be responsible for the defence of the Borneo Territories. Meanwhile on 26 August the Tunku stated publicly in Kuala Lumpur that Britain would have to be allowed continued use of her bases in Singapore in the event of merger and that so far as the problem of the use of the bases for SEATO purposes by Britain was concerned 'things will have to be worked out'. On 19 August he had told the Chinese Chamber of Commerce in Singapore that merger between Singapore and Malaya was inevitable because their economies were inseparable.

The Malaya–Singapore discussions, August/September 1961

81. On 25 July, 1961, it was announced that the Tunku had invited Mr. Lee to start preliminary discussions on the future constitutional relationship of Malaya and Singapore. The two countries also agreed to seek the services of two international experts to advise on problems involved in establishing a common market. A common market which included Singapore never in fact materialised and failure to introduce one was a major source of frustration for Mr. Lee's Government while part of Malaysia. But a constitutional relationship proved easier to agree, largely because Mr. Lee, who believed himself to be under the necessity of achieving the apparent political triumph represented by union with Malaya if he was to retain control, was willing to make important political concessions.

82. Mr. Lee and Dr. Goh met the Tunku and Tun Razak, together with the Permanent Secretary of the Malayan Ministry of External Affairs, Enche Mohamed Ghazali bin Shafie, in Kuala Lumpur on 24 August, 1961,[1] and agreed in principle that the new Federation should be responsible for defence, external affairs and security, but that Singapore should retain local autonomy, especially on matters of education and labour. They also agreed to set up a working party to go into financial and related arrangements. The Tunku and Mr. Lee met again for three days in Kuala Lumpur in September and announced that the working party would be instructed 'to work out the details of a merger with a view to bringing about integration of the two Territories and its people in or before June 1963'.

Malaya and Singapore: The proposed basis for merger

83. On 22 September, 1961, Mr. Lee gave the United Kingdom Acting Commissioner in Singapore for information a paper setting out the proposed basis for agreement. This provided for the existing Federal Constitution to be amended to

---

[1] 23 Aug, according to the Cobbold Report, para 3.

permit the Federal Parliament to admit States on such terms and conditions as it thought fit. Elections to the Singapore Legislative Assembly and for Singapore representation in the Federal Parliament were to be based on Singapore citizenship and election laws, but only to be about two-thirds of the number the proportion of the population would have warranted in view of the greater degree of retention of powers and revenues as compared with other States. Both Singapore and Federation citizens were to be Federal nationals with a common passport.

84. Suggested modifications of the Federal Legislative List were to give Singapore exclusive powers over civil and criminal law and the administration of justice, prisons, national registration, Singapore citizenship in relation to electoral rights in Singapore, conduct of elections in Singapore, public utilities, education, medicine and health, labour and social security; and concurrent, but subordinate, powers on a number of other items on the Federal list, including banking, trade, commerce and industry. The Federation was to have exclusive control of taxes of a national character, but the proceeds of both Federal and State taxation would accrue to Singapore which would then make a contribution to the Federation towards defence and other expenditure.

Malayan insistence on simultaneous transfer

85. The Tunku had already claimed, in a letter to Mr. Macmillan of 11 August, 1961, [see 53] that his ability to convince his own people of the wisdom of merger with Singapore depended on his gaining the Borneo Territories at the same time. He therefore now began to insist on full and simultaneous transfer of sovereignty over the Borneo Territories as a condition for accepting merger with Singapore. He declined to attend a London meeting with Mr. Lee for fear this should commit him to merger before he could assure his supporters that he would get the Borneo. Territories as well.

86. On 4 September, 1961, he sent a message to Mr. Macmillan asking 'whether the British Government would agree to relinquishing its sovereignty over the Borneo Territories and Singapore in the immediate future to enable them to become member States of Malaysia' [see 57]. He also asked 'whether the British Government would contemplate the use of the Singapore base within the framework of our mutual defence agreement'. A further message sent on 20 September stressed the need for 'some clear indication on the part of the British Government' on the Borneo Territories and the difficulty of proceeding 'without some such commitment'. Enche Ghazali, in passing on this message to Sir Geofroy Tory, indicated that unless Her Majesty's Government would commit the Borneo Territories without reservation to Malaysia the Malayan Government would abandon the whole idea and leave Britain to cope with a Communist Singapore.

87. Mr. Macmillan's reply of 23 September, 1961, to these messages was still too cautious to satisfy the Tunku. The British view was that the Grand Design would prove 'an important factor for stability in the area' and Lord Selkirk expressed the fear, in a letter of 16 September, that 'there is a serious risk that unless Greater Malaysia can be achieved in the near future, the opportunity may be lost for good' [see 58]. It was nevertheless thought that, although, by raising the issue publicly, the Tunku had stimulated political expectations and activity in Borneo and had thereby made maintenance of the existing slow and steady rate of constitutional progress slightly less attractive, a deliberate rate of advance remained in the best interests of

the peoples of these territories. It was in any event considered that the United Kingdom could not properly promise transfer of sovereignty over the heads of the inhabitants. It was believed moreover that excessive haste in Sarawak might even produce an insurrection by the Ibans who had historical reasons for being suspicious of their prospects under Malay rule.

88.   On balance the danger of missing the opportunity of achieving the Grand Design was thought to be the greater, but British policy was if possible, in discussion with the Tunku, to achieve a compromise which should secure the Tunku the counterbalance he sought for the Chinese of Singapore, but should give the Borneo Territories time to find their feet. Various proposals therefore began to be considered, first for some sort of condominium and then, when that was abandoned as impracticable, for schemes by which sovereignty should be transferred, but British Administrators should be retained for a time. Mr. Macmillan therefore agreed that the Tunku's questions 'about our possible early relinquishment of sovereignty over the Borneo Territories and Singapore and about including Singapore within the framework of the Malayan Defence Agreement are, of course, fundamental to the whole issue', but went on to say that further study was needed before Her Majesty's Government could give its views on them and that only at a meeting between the Tunku and himself could there be hope of making any real progress on these questions.

89.   The Tunku, in a sharp reply received in London on 28 September, 1961, [see 64] insisted that the only issue was whether the British Government would relinquish sovereignty over the Borneo Territories 'before or at least simultaneously with Singapore in favour of Malaysia' and that 'Any preliminary discussion between us would serve no useful purpose unless this issue is first settled.' His Government 'would not be able to carry the idea of merger of Singapore unless the Borneo Territories are merged . . . as well' and 'in terms of balances, even the Borneo Territories would not be an adequate compensation for our trouble.' Questions such as the future of the bases, constitutional procedures and administrative arrangements he regarded as subsidiary and 'not insurmountable.'

90.   This reaction by the Tunku was read in London and amongst British representatives in the area as reflecting a fear that the British intention was to get him to commit Malaya to merger with Singapore by using the lure of the Borneo Territories and then to withhold the prize. A further message from Mr. Macmillan, designed to restore his confidence, was therefore sent on 4 October, 1961 [see 67, dated 3 Oct]. In this Mr. Macmillan stated that 'the British Government welcome and accept the concept of a Greater Malaysia which would incorporate . . . the three Borneo Territories' and that 'we believe that the best future for the Borneo Territories lies in close political association with the Federation and Singapore.' There were however in the Territories 'anxieties, which we cannot ignore, about the form of the association and about timing. We must therefore bend our efforts, in close consultation with you, to bring the peoples of the Borneo Territories freely to join with you.' He added that he wished to discuss with the Tunku the constitutional position, economic development and administrative arrangements, including the staffing of the public services, in the Territories.

The defence issue

91.   Mr Macmillan added that 'It will, as you appreciate, be necessary to ensure that future defence arrangements are on the right lines.' Defence issues had not

hitherto caused difficulty in discussions on the Grand Design between Britain and Malaya. In a broadcast on 2 October, 1961, Tun Razak explained the need for the stationing of British and Commonwealth troops in Malaya for 'the defence of this country and the United Kingdom territories in the Far East', while on 11 October Mr. Lee expressed the hope, in a Press conference, that if the bases were to be run down this would be done slowly over '10, 15, or 20 years'. Earlier, in his letter of 11 August, the Tunku had assured Mr. Macmillan 'that I am equally concerned that the defence arrangements of this region should not be jeopardised', but had foreseen 'no difficulty in arriving at some suitable arrangement within the framework of the existing Mutual Defence Agreement' which 'would, at the same time, remove any possible fears that we are drawn unwittingly into SEATO'. This proviso on SEATO was the point which subsequently caused difficulty.

92.   On 30 September, 1961, however Mr. Lee, for reasons apparently connected with his internal political situation, tried publicly to suggest that any delay in merger talks would be due to British determination to retain the *status quo* in the bases. In fact the British Ministry of Defence was already considering the possible advantages of withdrawing all direct commitments in South-East Asia, even in the short term, since this had begun to seem inevitable in the long term, and were therefore reluctant to engage in early concrete discussions on the defence facilities the United Kingdom might want in Malaysia. It was certainly hoped that British forces would no longer have to be maintained in the area for internal security purposes and Ministers had yet to decide whether they 'were prepared to continue to assist in the external defence of Greater Malaysia'.

The Tunku's attitude to the Borneo peoples

93.   Mr. Macmillan's message of 4 October, 1961, to the Tunku had included a proposed public announcement in which Her Majesty's Government 'welcomed' the Tunku's proposals and finished with a sentence stating that 'The wishes of the peoples concerned must be taken fully into account' and that they would be consulted on 'any commitment affecting their future'. In his message of 7 October accepting the invitation to visit London, the Tunku suggested that this sentence should be omitted. It would, he thought, 'over-emphasise the need for consultation with the people of the Borneo Territories who are at this moment not sufficiently advanced in their political outlook to give an unbiased opinion of their own as they are very much under the influence of the British Colonial administrators' [see 69].

94.   This attitude, which became evident also in his public utterances, lent a certain appearance of substance to Indonesian claims that the transfer of sovereignty lacked the consent of the peoples of the territories and led to difficulties with the emerging local political leaders when the territories became part of Malaysia. It even began to seem possible that the Ibans and other indigenous peoples, far from acting as a counter-weight to the Singapore Chinese, might actually support them, as against the Malays, in pressing for political and constitutional change. The reference to colonial administrators in the message foreshadowed a line of explanation for political difficulties in the territories which was subsequently a source of some tension in relations between Britain and Malaysia.

95.   In the Borneo Territories themselves steps were being taken to speed up constitutional advance. Public statements by the Sultan of Brunei still gave the impression of favouring federation, but he showed increasing caution in face of local

opposition to the proposal; the extent of this opposition had already led the Colonial Office to think that there might be a prospect of disturbances in the State if the decision was taken to join Malaysia. Among British officials concerned with Borneo there was discussion of the possibility of a commission to ascertain the views of the local people and Sir William Goode urged that the Tunku or his close advisers, including some Chinese, should pay a longer visit to North Borneo and Sarawak so that he could be brought to appreciate the anxieties of the local people.

96.   On 30 September, 1961, Lord Selkirk had reported that he and the Governors were agreed that 'Greater Malaysia offers the best future for the Borneo Territories'—indeed in a letter of 3 November Sir Alexander Waddell urged that the idea should be pursued even if Singapore did not come in. But Lord Selkirk and the Governors were convinced that in order to secure acceptance of federation in Borneo it was desirable to provide for the retention of existing British staff, for a large measure of internal self-government, including control over immigration, education, language, citizenship and land development, for retention of all local revenues, for freedom to pursue closer association amongst themselves and for some form of British guarantee for a period after which the territories could opt out of federation. They recognise that some compromise on these desiderata might be necessary; the last in particular can never have been acceptable to the Tunku. Considerable thought was nevertheless given to forms of condominium or treaty commitment; apart from Malayan objections these all presented the danger that the United Kingdom might be left in an anomalous position similar to that in the Central African Federation.

The Singapore White Paper, November 1961

97.   Meanwhile Mr. Lee and Malayan leaders had been haggling over the content and provenance of a White Paper on the proposed terms for the merger of Singapore, which Mr. Lee wished to issue with the Tunku's agreement, and over the alternatives to be put to the Singapore electorate in a referendum to which the PAP were by now publicly committed. Mr. Lee believed that his chances of securing a majority in this referendum for an Ulster-type solution would be greatly strengthened if he could include as another choice complete merger as a State of the Federation. The Tunku had privately made it clear that in practice this would be unacceptable to the Federal Government, but it seemed at first that he might nevertheless be willing to see it voted on; Tun Razak however was entirely opposed to its inclusion as an apparent alternative. On the details of the proposed terms Mr. Lee had conceded to the Federation complete control of the Singapore Police Force, but resisted Tun Razak's desire to reduce the State's representation in the Federal Parliament still further to 12 seats, while there were substantial unresolved differences between Mr. Tan Siew Sin's views of the powers required by the Federation in the financial field and those held by the Singapore Government.

98.   The White Paper, as finally agreed and issued in November 1961, proposed that defence, external affairs and internal security should be Federal subjects, with the Singapore Judicial and Legal Services becoming a separate branch of the Federal Services under the ultimate control of the Federal Chief Justice. Education and labour would be State subjects. The Singapore Legislative Assembly would continue as a State Legislature and the Civil Service as a State Civil Service. The existing separate Singapore citizenship and voting rights would be retained, but, in view of its

greater autonomy as against the founder States, Singapore would only be entitled to 15 members of the Federal Legislature instead of the 25 the numbers of its electorate would otherwise warrant. In other respects Singapore citizens would enjoy the same rights and have the same passport as Federal citizens.

VI. *The London talks, November 1961*

The Tunku's mandate to negotiate

99.   The announcement of the Tunku's proposed visit to London was made on Friday, 13 October, 1961. The last sentence originally proposed in Mr. Macmillan's message of 4 October was omitted and replaced by a phrase designed to retain its substance while toning down the degree of emphasis on consultation. On 16 October the Tunku moved a resolution in the House of Representatives in Kuala Lumpur agreeing with the concept of Malaysia in principle; this was carried on 18 October. The PMIP opposed the Tunku's proposals in the debate, on the ground that they would jeopardise the special position of the Malays, but a weakening of their influence was demonstrated on 30 October when the PMIP Government of Trengganu was defeated on a vote of confidence and was replaced by an Alliance Government. On 4 November an extraordinary General Assembly of UMNO also discussed the Grand Design and, although fears were expressed about the Malay position, the Tunku was given a mandate to negotiate the formation of Malaysia.

100.   The precaution was nevertheless subsequently taken of introducing a constitutional amendment to make it more difficult for non-Malays to acquire citizenship and to give much heavier weighting to the rural electorate. This was passed by the Malayan House of Representatives on 31 January, 1962, by 80 votes to 11.

British preparations and policy

101.   On 24 October, 1961, a report by an official committee on Greater Malaysia [see 73] was circulated to the Cabinet in preparation for the talks with the Tunku. Much of this was concerned with the dilemma that, while there was a clear obligation to the peoples of Borneo, reaffirmed as recently as 1960 in the case of Sarawak, to advance them socially, economically and politically until they were able to take full responsibility for their own future, amalgamation into Malaysia appeared the only way to secure their future viability and the Federation could not wait until they were ready. They were therefore in danger of exchanging a temporary colonial status under the British for a potentially much more permanent colonial status under the Malayans. This dilemma was accentuated by the Tunku's bland inability to realise that there might be genuine reasons for hesitation on the part of the Bornean peoples.

102.   The official committee recommended that 'the earliest possible achievement of Greater Malaysia should be regarded as an aim of British Government policy', but the Government should not commit itself to firm dates for the accession of Sarawak and North Borneo. It should welcome the Tunku's suggestion in his memorandum of 26 June, 1961, for a commission to work out the constitutional details of the new Federation; the functions of this commission should however be extended so that it could both assess the state of opinion in Borneo on the Grand Design and make recommendations on the manner and timing of the association between the territories and Malaysia.

Defence issues

103. The committee also discussed defence issues. Ministers had already decided that it should be made clear to the Tunku that it was intended to hand over all internal security responsibilities in Malaysia, but to seek to retain defence facilities. The general aim was to be to reduce British forces to the Commonwealth Strategic Reserve, including the Commonwealth Brigade Group stationed near Malacca, and existing naval and air facilities. Two questions arose—whether the Tunku was fully alive to the implications of taking over responsibility for internal security in Singapore and the Borneo Territories, and whether he would accept use of the bases for SEATO purposes. On the latter question there was some evidence that he had been influenced by the arguments for unfettered use and was preparing Malayan public opinion to accept this, despite a public remark on 24 October, 1961, to the effect that Singapore could never be used as a base in war because of the danger to the civilian population and a statement by Tun Razak to the UMNO Assembly on 4 November that the bases 'should not be used for SEATO purposes'. The committee however did not think it necessary to press for immediate agreement on this point; general policy was still undetermined, a new addition to the possibilities under consideration being a suggestion by Mr. Holyoake for a quadripartite defence agreement between the United Kingdom, Australia, New Zealand and Malaysia.

The November 1961 discussions and joint statement

104. A meeting of British Ministers on 15 November, 1961 [see 78], agreed, in the light of this official committee's report, on the way in which the talks with the Tunku should be handled and, in particular, to press for the setting up of the proposed commission on the Borneo Territories. These decisions were reported to the Cabinet on 16 November. The discussions with the Tunku began in London on 20 November [see 79–84]. The Tunku at once stated that the change of sovereignty need have little effect on the lives of the peoples of the Borneo Territories and that the present British civil servants could be retained. He still envisaged however a status and degree of autonomy similar to that of the founder States, except for special provision for local control over immigration. The Colonial Secretary, Mr. Maudling, proposed the setting up of a commission composed of a British Chairman, two members appointed by the British Government and two members appointed by the Malayan Government and this was agreed to.

105. The Malayan representatives left no doubt however that they wished the deliberations of this commission to be little more than a formality and the terms of reference originally proposed were revised 'in order to include a note of urgency and to give more of a lead in favour of Greater Malaysia'. In the process reference to 'safeguards' for North Borneo and Sarawak and, in a later version, to 'an acceptable plan' for merger were omitted. British representatives nevertheless pressed the point that there might be a need to ensure that the terms on which the Borneo Territories entered Federation could not be altered without the agreement of their Legislatures. A joint statement issued on 22 November, 1961, stated that both Governments were convinced that Malaysia was 'a desirable aim', that 'Before coming to any final decision it is necessary to ascertain the views of the peoples of North Borneo and Sarawak' and that a commission would be set up to do this and to make recommendations.

The agreement on defence

106.   On defence the Tunku accepted that in the event of war Britain must have full use of her bases in both Malaya and Singapore; but he did not want a formal written agreement which related the bases in any way to SEATO. The point was made by the British Minister of Defence, Mr. Watkinson, however, that the bases were of value to Britain only if it could be said openly that they could be used freely and this point was stressed by other British Ministers. It appears, from the British minutes of the discussions, that it was agreed at the third meeting, on 21 November, 1961 [see 81] that 'the Federation Government would in practice not wish to impede the full use of the bases by British and allied forces in the event of their being required for defence operations in the region'.

107.   The minutes of the fourth meeting, [see 82] when dealing with the joint statement on defence which was to be issued on 22 November, 1961, express the understanding that 'The description in the agreed text of how the bases might be used would enable Britain to employ them for all likely purposes, including that of meeting her SEATO obligations (both operationally and for exercises) and the use of the bases by her allies. There was no reference in the statement to the consent of the Federation Government being required for the use of the Singapore bases as was necessary under a similar clause of the existing Defence Agreement. On the use of the Singapore bases for purposes strictly outside South-East Asia it was felt that the reference to the protection of the territories of "other Commonwealth countries" provided adequate cover.' It was also thought that the statement would permit satisfactory use of the Borneo Territories for defence purposes. Within the Foreign Office the view continued to be expressed that it would have been wiser to have taken the opportunity to remove British forces to Australia, while Lord Selkirk suggested on 25 November that 'The reality of the matter is that, whatever the words of any agreement might say, we should only be able to use the bases on one occasion for purposes which did not carry the consent of the Government and people of the new independent Malaysia . . .'; in other words that after one such use it would be impossible to maintain the agreement.

108.   The statement itself recorded that the two Governments had agreed that the 1957 Agreement should be extended to the whole of Malaysia 'subject to the proviso that the Government of the Federation of Malaysia will afford to the Government of the United Kingdom the right to continue to maintain the bases and other facilities at present occupied by their Service authorities within the State of Singapore and will permit the United Kingdom to make such use of these bases and facilities as the United Kingdom may consider necessary for the purpose of assisting in the defence of Malaysia, and for Commonwealth defence and for the preservation of peace in South-East Asia.' It is perhaps worth noting in this connection that the Tunku had been reported in the *Straits Times* of 26 October, 1961, as having said during his visit to Saigon that 'I have always regarded Viet-Nam as a first line of defence for Malaya.' At the fifth meeting [see 83] it was agreed to state in answer to Press enquiries that the bases at Singapore would be British bases and would not be transferred to the control of SEATO or to any other nation or group of nations and that the new arrangement would not prevent Britain carrying out her international and Commonwealth obligations.

109.   It was also agreed at the fifth meeting that neither Government should make any public statement which might conflict with this position. In the following

days however both the Tunku and Tun Razak in public statements suggested that the United Kingdom could not use the bases without the agreement of the Federation, which would only give permission for use for SEATO purposes if its own interests were involved. On 1 December, 1961, Mr. Sandys felt compelled to warn the Tunku 'very firmly' that such interpretations would destroy the entire value of the agreement [see 86]. In consequence in January 1962, following his return to Malaya, the Tunku made it clear, in a series of answers to questions in Parliament, that the United Kingdom had the right to use the Singapore bases without the consent of the Government of Malaysia; he would nevertheless expect consultation but would not oppose use of the bases 'for SEATO purposes for the maintenance of security in this area', that is South-East Asia.

VII. *The Cobbold Commission, 1962*

Membership and programme

110.   Agreement on the membership of the commission to assess opinion in Borneo and to recommend the manner and timing of association was reached by mid-January 1962. The Chairman was Lord Cobbold, a former Governor of the Bank of England. The British members were Sir Anthony Abell, Governor of Sarawak and High Commissioner in Brunei until 1959, and Sir David Watherston, Chief Secretary of the Federation of Malaya until 1957. The Malayan members were Enche Ghazali and Dato Wong Pow Nee, Chief Minister of Penang. Lord Cobbold flew straight to Borneo by way of Singapore, where he met the other members on 18 February. The Commission arrived in Sarawak on 19 February and reached North Borneo on 25 February; Brunei did not come within the Commission's purview, but its members paid a courtesy call on the Sultan on 11 March. Lord Cobbold returned to London on 19 April and reconvened the Commission at Knebworth early in May to write its report, which was signed on 21 June, 1962.

Opinion in Borneo

111.   The immediate effect of the Commission's work was to reveal to the Tunku, through Enche Ghazali and Dato Wong, the deep doubts and fears which existed in Borneo at the prospect of Malayan rule, based on a widespread dislike and distrust of Malays. He reacted on 11 March, 1962, by accusing British civil servants of discourtesy to the Malayan members of the Commission and of apathy towards Malaysia [see 96]. Later, on 27 March, in a speech to the Chinese Chamber of Commerce in Singapore, he accepted that the Borneo Territories thought of the Federation as having a purely Malay Government, with other races bullied into submission and no freedom of speech, worship or social intercourse. Lord Cobbold's own initial reaction was that, if the territories were to be persuaded that Malaysia would be in their own interest, the Malayans would have to move a long way on constitutional detail and that they and Her Majesty's Government would have to provide funds to ensure that economic conditions improved under the new arrangements.

112.   In practice, in Sarawak and North Borneo, although many people were still very hesitant about the prospect, others were coming round to the view that the Grand Design was inevitable and that what mattered was to secure the best possible position for the territories in Malaysia. In its report the Commission suggested that

perhaps a third of the people of the territories were in favour of Malaysia without too much concern about terms and conditions, that another third would accept it subject to safeguards of various kinds and that the remaining third either wanted independence first or the continuation of colonial rule. The Commission thought that about 20 per cent in Sarawak and somewhat less in North Borneo were opposed to federation on any terms, unless preceded by independence and self-government— the Tunku in a speech on 9 August, managed to translate this into the assertion that 80 per cent agreed with the concept of Malaysia.

Opposition to merger in Brunei

113.   In Brunei, on the other hand, opinion was crystallising against association. So far as his public statements went the Sultan still appeared to be attracted by the idea of an arrangement with the Federation. In November 1961, however, he had instructed his Government to study proposals for association and to canvass popular opinion on the subject. There seems little doubt that by the beginning of 1962 the incompetence of the Malay officials sent earlier to the State and the overbearing tactics adopted by the Tunku had already cooled any enthusiasm the Sultan may earlier have had for co-operation with the Federation.

114.   The Colonial Office view, both at this time and in 1963, was that from January to April 1962 Sheikh A. M. Azahari did not regard the Malaysia proposal as incompatible with his aim of unifying the three Borneo territories under the Sultan as constitutional ruler. The Colonial Office believed that, having met the Tunku in April 1962, he was on the point of convening a meeting with others from North Borneo and Sarawak to consider entering Malaysia as a single constitutionally-governed unit, when, in May, the Brunei Government foreclosed on its loans to him; he then left the State and only returned briefly in October before going to Manila. His opposition to Malaysia was believed to be due to the fear that it might perpetuate the autocratic and inept rule under the Sultan of the Pengirans, rather than to disapproval of the concept itself.

115.   There seems however considerable evidence that the Parti Ra'ayat and popular opinion had already been alienated by the Tunku and that the party was in consequence becoming increasingly favourable to Indonesian claims. Certainly by March 1962 its leaders were reported to have been paying frequent visits to Indonesia for some months. A Reuter report of 31 January, 1962, quoted 'reliable sources' in Brunei as saying that the State's official commission canvassing popular reaction had found stiff and virtually unanimous opposition to association. The Parti Ra'ayat was already active in stirring-up opposition to Malaysia in January and by 24 March the High Commissioner, Sir Dennis White, was envisaging the possibility of 'a situation arising, beyond the ability of the Brunei Police Force to control', if a decision to join Malaysia seemed in prospect. During March the Sultan asked the Malayan Government to postpone the departure of the Malayan police detachment until the end of the year.

116.   Despite these indications of widespread opposition, on 18 July, 1962, the last meeting of the old Legislative Council passed by 22 votes to 4 a motion supporting the principle of participation in the proposed Federation and negotiation with Malaya and Britain on terms 'which will bring benefits to the State of Brunei but not diminish the status of Brunei as a constitutional State'—a formulation which cannot have been welcome to the Malayan Government. Both the Sultan and

others in Brunei also began to raise again the long-standing claim to the Limbang area, annexed by Sarawak in 1890.

Malaya and Singapore: security and political and economic co-operation

117.   The British Minister of Defence, Mr. Watkinson, visited Kuala Lumpur on 22 March, 1962, and then Singapore for talks on the transfer of responsibility for internal security in Singapore and the Borneo Territories and subsequent external defence—these talks were concluded in June 1962 and focused attention on the need to expand the Malayan defence forces and on the cost of expansion. On 25 March, 1962, and again on 30 March, the Tunku spoke of closing the causeway between Singapore and Johore if extremists caused trouble in Singapore and emphasised the economic damage this would do to Singapore. Mr. Tan, on 4 April, explained that the Tunku had had principally in mind immigration controls, but that if the security situation deteriorated other controls would have to be considered, including exchange control.

118.   Lord Selkirk suggested that this attitude indicated that the Tunku was experiencing some qualms about taking on the internal security problem in Singapore—Sir Geofroy Tory had expressed a similar view on 19 February, 1962. Throughout the first half of 1962 the Tunku and Mr. Lee tried to persuade the British Government that it should place leading Barisan Sosialis leaders under preventive arrest, but this they declined to do. By the summer however the PAP at least was recovering its confidence. The Tunku had also been disconcerted by Mr. Lee's failure to dovetail his policies generally with those of the Federal Government—he was particularly incensed by a proposal by Mr. Lee to visit Moscow and Peking. These proposed visits, which Mr. Lee abandoned for the time being in view of the Tunku's attitude, were arranged as part of an international tour which Mr. Lee made in April and May 1962 to gain support for the idea of Malaysia.

119.   Meanwhile the difficult issue of a common market was also under discussion; during April 1962 Tun Razak had asked the United Nations to suggest a team to look into the issue. In Singapore, hitherto a free port, a Bill was introduced to provide for a Tariff Advisory Commission and to permit the imposition of tariffs on selected imports to protect local industries.

The Cobbold Commission and the transitional period

120.   The main difference of opinion within the Cobbold Commission related to the view held by the British members that there should be a transitional period during which responsibility should be shared. The British members thought it essential that there should be continuity of administration if local confidence was to be retained and in particular that there should initially be British Governors, if necessary appointed by the Agong on the nomination of the Agong and The Queen, in order to make it easier to retain the services of expatriate officers, which all were agreed was essential; these Governors should continue to have executive powers. The Malayan members wanted authority to be in the hands of Chief Ministers with the confidence of the Legislatures, but with expatriate State Secretaries.

121.   On 3 June, 1962, the Tunku told Sir Geofroy Tory that he had instructed the Malayan members to withdraw from the Commission if the other members insisted on recommending a division of responsibility. In a separate memorandum recording these differences the British members said that they 'were greatly concerned by the reluctance of our Malayan colleagues, apparently supported by their Government, to

make any concessions in favour of non-Muslim susceptibilities and national pride' [see 120].

122.   In its report the Commission recommended that the formation of Malaysia should be welcomed and made a number of agreed recommendations on terms. Particular proposals recommended were that the existing Constitution of Malaya should be adapted to the new Federation instead of being replaced; that it should provide for a strong central Government, but with additional autonomous powers and safeguards for the new Borneo States and some form of guarantee to prevent amendment, modification or withdrawal of these special powers and safeguards without the positive concurrence of the State Government concerned; and that the power of amending the Constitution of each State should belong exclusively to the people in that State. The Commission however left the contentious issues to be decided in negotiation between the British and Malayan Governments. It also privately urged on both Governments the need for swift action in the light of the emergence in Sarawak of some communal feeling.

123.   On 4 July, 1962, having studied the report, the Tunku sent a message to Mr. Macmillan stating that any proposal for maintenance of a degree of British authority during a transitional period was unacceptable and that in the circumstances it would be best to put the whole question into abeyance until the British Government had decided that the territories were ready for merger [see 125]. This aspect of the issue was at once settled, following a meeting of the Overseas Policy Committee of the British Cabinet [see 126], by a reply from Mr. Macmillan, sent the same day, in which he stated flatly that 'The British Government has not the slightest desire to maintain its authority during the transitional period over the Borneo Territories' and that it was in no way bound by the recommendations of the Commission or of any of its members [see 128].

124.   On 5 July, 1962, Mr. Macmillan reported on the issue to the full Cabinet. He took the view that it was important that the United Kingdom Government should not retain responsibility for the administration of the Borneo Territories if a Federation was established, since, if it did, it would then be answerable for events without having effective control over them. The Cabinet then agreed that negotiations should be urgently pursued during July with the aim of bringing Malaysia into being at the earliest practicable date and agreeing on solutions of the transitional problems which would protect the interests of the peoples of the Borneo Territories.

VIII. *Agreement in principle 1962*

The London talks and joint statement, July 1962

125.   The Tunku arrived in London on 16 July, 1962. Substantive discussions between British and Malayan Ministers began on 17 July, 1962, and were concluded on 31 July, while Mr. Lee joined the discussions on 29 July. On 1 August, 1962, a joint statement was issued by the British and Malayan Governments [see 140, appendix D].

126.   The statement announced that the two Governments had decided in principle that Malaysia should come into being by 31 August, 1963, and that a formal agreement should be concluded during the following six months. This agreement should provide for the transfer of sovereignty over North Borneo, Sarawak and Singapore to the new Federation by the set date; for the terms of the relationship between Singapore and the new Federation as agreed between the Governments of

Malaya and Singapore; for defence arrangements as set out in the joint statement of 22 November, 1961; and for detailed constitutional arrangements, including safeguards for such matters as religious freedom, education, representation in the Federal Parliament, the position of the indigenous races, control of immigration, citizenship and the State Constitutions in relation to North Borneo and Sarawak, to be drawn up after consultation with the Legislatures of the two territories.

127.   It was also stated that during a transitional period a number of the Federal constitutional powers would be delegated temporarily to the State Governments in Borneo and that an Inter-Governmental Committee, on which the Governments of Britain, Malaya, North Borneo and Sarawak would be represented, would be set up to work out the necessary constitutional arrangements and safeguards. The Minister of State for the Colonies, Lord Lansdowne, as Chairman of this Committee, and Tun Razak would go to Borneo to conduct these discussions and to consider how best the services of as many expatriate officials as possible could be retained.

128.   Amongst other points agreed, though not publicly announced, were that under Federation North Borneo and Sarawak should each have a constitutional Governor; that the Governor should appoint as Chief Minister to preside over the Executive Council a person likely to enjoy majority support in the Assembly; and that, until the Assembly was fully elected, the State Secretary, Legal Adviser and Financial Officer, all for some years probably expatriates, should *ex officio* be members of both the Legislative Assembly and the Executive Council. It was also agreed that there should be no right of secession; that representation in the Federal Parliament should be weighted to take account of size of territory as well as population; that there should be freedom of religion; that English should continue as an official language in North Borneo and Sarawak for as long as the territories wished; and that the two States should have special powers to control immigration both from abroad and from other parts of Malaysia. Borneans would be citizens of Malaysia; citizens of Singapore would also be automatically 'citizens'—and not just 'nationals'—of Malaysia, though there would be reciprocal restrictions on franchise rights as between Singaporean and other Malaysian citizens.[2]

129.   On 18 July, 1962, the North Borneo Executive Council had unanimously agreed that there should be detailed discussions and agreement on terms and safeguards amongst all the parties concerned before a final decision to transfer sovereignty was taken and that the Constitution should provide for substantial State powers. The two Governors in a joint Note of 26 July had taken a similar view and had insisted that there must be 'a genuine willingness by the Malayans to treat the Borneo Territories differently from existing States of the Federation'. Several of the points agreed in London represented new concessions by the Malayan delegation to the needs of the Borneo Territories, while other points were left open for discussion in the Inter-Governmental Committee which now became the centre of activity.

The referendum in Singapore

130.   Mr. Lee, who had already made his bargain, gained an improvement in London in the wording of the citizenship provisions by an exchange of letters with the Tunku on 30 and 31 July, 1962 [see 137, note]. On 4 August he recovered his majority

---

[2] This account omits reference to the secret agreement providing for Malaysia's inauguration earlier than 31 Aug 1963 'if for any reason it appeared desirable', see 140, para 3.

of one in the Singapore Assembly and on 14 August he announced the terms of the citizenship arrangement and that the long-promised referendum would be held on 1 September. This resulted in a resounding endorsement of the proposals set out in the Singapore Government's White Paper of November 1961, with 71 per cent of the votes cast in favour. There were two alternative choices on the ballot paper—complete merger with the same status as the existing States of the Federation and merger on terms no less favourable than those for the Borneo Territories. The Opposition however, apart from the Alliance, called on their supporters not to mark their ballot papers and 26 per cent of the ballots cast were blank. This result considerably eased the internal political pressure on the Singapore Government and by extension the urgency of the negotiations for Malaysia, but these had now acquired a momentum which was not dependent on fears for security in Singapore.

C. The interests of Indonesia and the Philippines

IX. Indonesian reactions

Early objections to the Grand Design

131.   There were arguments for urgency in events elsewhere. Indonesian intentions had been a matter of concern for some time. In an article published in March 1965 Dr. Mohammad Hatta, one of the most moderate and sensible of Indonesian leaders, has stated that as early as November 1949 he had told Mr. MacDonald, who had mentioned the Grand Design to him, that, if unified, the British territories would inevitably become a second China, probably in complicity with mainland China, and that this would be dangerous for Indonesia. He claimed that, when Prime Minister, he had issued instructions that objections to these territories being united 'should be considered as one of the most important aspects of our Government's foreign policy'.

Malaya and Indonesia

132.   Relations between Malaya and Indonesia were subject to strain from the first. Some expressions of Indonesian national claims in the 1940s included Malaya in their scope and within weeks of Malaya becoming independent in 1957 there was strong criticism in Indonesia when Malaya abstained in the United Nations General Assembly on the West Irian issue. There were Indonesian complaints about the barter trade between the Outer Islands and Malaya, and suspicion that Malaya might prove attractive to Sumatra. There was also dislike of Malayan proposals for regional arrangements in South-East Asia and indeed for any initiative by other countries in what Indonesians regarded as their sphere of influence. A Treaty of Friendship was signed in 1959 and finally ratified on 30 April, 1960, but relations remained uneasy and the Tunku's offers of mediation on the West Irian issue in the autumn of 1960 were not well received.

Indonesia and British Borneo

133.   On the specific issue of the British Borneo Territories the public Indonesian position, so long as the West Irian issue remained unresolved, was that Indonesian claims were limited to territory formerly part of the Netherlands East Indies. Nevertheless the Phoenix Park meeting in January 1960 was well aware that, although the Indonesians might have their hands full for the moment, should pan-Malaysian sentiment develop, Indonesian suspicions might grow, if only because a prosperous

and expanding Malayan Federation would have obvious attractions for those, especially in Sumatra, who had reasons for wishing to break away from Javanese control.

134. Concern was reinforced when Professor Mohamed Yamin, Indonesian Minister for Special Affairs and Chairman of the National Planning Council, who had it was true made similar claims before and been repudiated by his Government, in a speech on 18 February, 1960, suggested 'eliminating the enclaves in Portuguese Timor and British North Borneo which were still not free'. Commenting to the Press on 10 March, 1960, on Professor Yamin's remarks, Dr. Subandrio said that 'Indonesia would definitely not put forward a claim to foreign territories adjacent to the Indonesian archipelago' and that 'the current geographical *status quo* must be recognised as the basis for establishing firm national boundaries'. He added that 'It is a law laid down by history that every colonised territory will gain emancipation, but this does not mean that it will become part of Indonesia.' The significant passage here was probably not the disclaimer, but the insistence on maintenance of the geographical *status quo*—the Indonesian Government had no objection to a number of small weak independent States as neighbours which it could dominate.

135. The British official view of the Indonesian interest in the summer of 1960 was that it reinforced arguments for haste—the longer the Grand Design was delayed the more likely Indonesia was to work up opposition to it. The increasing Indonesian bellicosity towards the Dutch in the latter part of 1960, and their action in securing massive arms supplies from the USSR, strengthened this view. In North Borneo itself most opinion at this time was still in favour of retaining the existing separate colonial status. Mr. Stephens, however, had begun to be worried that on its own the territory would be vulnerable. He told the Governor in December 1960 that Dr. Subandrio had asked him when North Borneo would get self-government and if it would then join Indonesia. By February 1961, in a draft Commonwealth Relations Office brief for the forthcoming Prime Ministers' Conference, increased Indonesian interest in the Borneo Territories was the only reason cited for greater urgency. Nevertheless, though the possibility of Indonesian reaction was always listed as a problem in early British discussions of the Grand Design, it was never given great prominence.

Attacks on the Tunku's speech of 27 May, 1961

136. Dr. Subandrio, passing through Singapore on 13 June, 1961, was reported as having said sourly, with reference to the Tunku's proposal for a form of the Grand Design, that 'so long as no Indonesian territory is involved, and there is no conflict of interest, we are not-concerned with it'. Early in August he told Lord Selkirk and Sir Leslie Fry that the project was entirely a matter for the territories concerned to decide upon and that Indonesia had no claim on any of them. Sir Leslie, however, doubted if the proposal was welcome to the Indonesian Government and reported his Malayan colleague as being quite clear that it was not. Left-wing Indonesian papers such as *Suluh Indonesia* attacked the speech and the June issue of the Communist *Malayan Monitor* launched the view, later taken up by the Indonesian Communist paper *Harian Rakjat*, the Afro–Asian People's Solidarity Organisation (AAPSO), the Barisan Sosialis in Singapore and other similar journals and bodies, that the Grand Design would mean 'the physical encirclement of Indonesia'.

137. When in January 1962 the Singapore Legislative Assembly passed a motion approving Malaysia in principle opposition came entirely from the Barisan Sosialis.

In winding up the debate Mr. Lee claimed that this was because they took their orders from the Communist Party—the PKI—in Indonesia. The Barisan had good reasons of their own to oppose the incorporation of Singapore into Malaysia, but their attitude was no doubt stiffened by a resolution passed by the PKI at the end of December 1961 condemning Malaysia as 'a form of neo-colonialism'.

The influence of the West Irian issue

138.   The official Indonesian attitude remained more cautious. On 20 November, 1961, Dr. Subandrio told the General Assembly of the United Nations that though 'ethnologically and geographically speaking, this British part is closer to Indonesia than to Malaya'. Indonesia had 'told Malaya that we have no objections to such a merger based upon the will for freedom of the peoples concerned'. At this stage of course the Indonesian Government was still preoccupied with its efforts to secure West New Guinea—in December 1961 Dr. Sukarno called for the liberation of West Irian in 1962.

139.   By the beginning of 1962, however, the Indonesians were said to be enrolling volunteers in Malaysia 'for the liberation of West Irian'; this may well really have been with a view to action against Malaysia, as may preparations to open a consulate in Jesselton. Mr. Macmillan mentioned a possible irredentist threat from Indonesia to a Ministerial Meeting on 21 March, 1962, [see 98] and by May there were even Press reports that an Indonesian-led 'Borneo Liberation Army' was present in the area of the border between the Fifth Division of Sarawak and Indonesian Kalimantan. In April Dr. Hatta, who some weeks earlier had in Singapore publicly described the Grand Design as 'a sound idea', told the Tunku that the Indonesians were becoming very afraid of the gravitational attraction of the Federation of Malaya for the Sumatrans. Mr. Lee subsequently expressed the view to Lord Home that the Indonesians might lay claim to the Borneo Territories.

140.   The Foreign Office view by the summer of 1962 was that this threat was a distinct future possibility if not immediately pressing, and a successful effort was made to have a favourable reference to the progress being made towards the formation of Malaysia in the final communiqué of the Commonwealth Prime Ministers' Meeting in September 1962. Already by August 1962, however, it had begun to seem that there was prospect of a peaceful transfer of West Irian to Indonesia and therefore that that country might soon be in a position to turn its attention to Borneo and Malaya.

X. The Filipino claim

The Sulu inheritance

141.   The claims of the Philippines in Borneo were based on those of the heirs to the Sultans of Sulu to parts of the coast of North Borneo and of adjoining areas of Indonesian Borneo or Kalimantan. These claims were mentioned at the Phoenix Park meeting in January 1960, but as late as May 1961 it was thought that the Philippine Government would welcome the Grand Design and, in the words of a minute by Mr. E. H. Peck, 'will not press the doubtful claim of the Sultan of Sulu to parts of North Borneo, provided we keep the Indonesians out'.[3]

---

[3] At this point in para 141, approximately two and half lines of text have been removed and retained under section 3(4) of the Public Records Act, 1958.

As for the Malayan Government, it seemed determined to ignore the possible existence of either Indonesian or Filipino interest in the Borneo Territories.

Filipino assertion of the claim and the British response

142.   By the beginning of 1962 however a public campaign on the Sulu claim was developing in the Philippines. In the course of 1962 the claim was implicitly extended from the areas on the east and north-east coasts over which former Sultans had had some authority for a time to the whole modern territory of North Borneo, despite a disclaimer by the Acting Secretary of Foreign Affairs, Salvador P. Lopez, in a Press interview in October. On 24 April, 1962, the Philippines House of Representatives unanimously adopted a resolution urging the President 'to take the necessary steps . . . for the recovery of a certain portion . . . of Borneo and adjacent islands which appertain to the Philippines'. On 24 May, 1962, therefore the Philippine Ambassador in London was handed an *aide-mémoire* which asserted undisputed British sovereignty over North Borneo and made it plain that it was the British intention to support the formation of a Federation of Malaysia of which North Borneo would be a part.

143.   Nevertheless in June 1962 President Macapagal, who had been personally concerned with the matter at an earlier stage in his career, took up the claim publicly and on 22 June Mr. Lopez addressed a note to the British Ambassador, Mr. John Pilcher, stating that 'it is clear . . . that there is a dispute between the Sultanate of Sulu and the Philippine Government on the one side and Her Majesty's Government on the other regarding the ownership and sovereignty over North Borneo', and asking for conversations on the subject. A reply to this Note dated 3 August, 1962, pointed out that 'in so far as this refers to a dispute with the "Sultanate of Sulu", Her Majesty's Government had understood that the existence of the Sultanate of Sulu had not been recognised by the Government of the Philippines for many years and that even the residual spiritual authority enjoyed by Sultan Jamalul Kiram had lapsed with his death in 1936.' The Philippines' reply of 12 September spoke of establishing the Sultanate's status in conversations and of 'other documents whose contents will be revealed at the proper time' and called again for such conversations.

Reactions in Malaya and North Borneo

144.   The Tunku's first reaction to these exchanges was to say that Malaya was in no way involved in Filipino claims, which were in his view a matter between the Philippines and the United Kingdom. The reaction in Borneo to the claim was hostile and did much to swing opinion to an acceptance of the need for Malaysia. These developments helped also both to make the Tunku more conscious of the possible disadvantages and difficulties inherent in the Grand Design and the British Government more anxious to have Malaysia well launched before Indonesia was free to turn its attention away from West Irian.

145.   On 4 August, 1962, the Philippine Government sent an *aide-mémoire* to the Federation Government insisting that North Borneo was held only on lease and could not be transferred by the United Kingdom to another party. On 10 August, during a discussion with the Vice-President and Foreign Minister of the Philippines, Dr. Pelaez, Dr. Subandrio seems to have encouraged the Philippine Government to pursue the issue with Malaya.

146.   The Malayan reply to the Philippine *aide-mémoire*, sent on 3 October, 1962, stated that 'At present North Borneo is under effective and direct rule of the British Government and to the British Government the question of sovereignty over North Borneo has at no time been in doubt'. It went on to say that the Malayan Government accepted this as sufficient to justify acceptance of transfer. On 1 October, however, the Tunku, at a Press conference on his departure for a visit to Ceylon, had spoken in approving terms of a Philippine proposal that the people of North Borneo should decide their future by referendum. These remarks and the initial Malayan attempt to remain uninvolved to some extent undermined the hitherto apparently firm legal position.

XI. *Opposition to Malaysia*

Petitions to the United Nations

147.   Opponents of the Grand Design had meanwhile begun to appeal to a wider audience. The United Nations 'Committee of Seventeen' had in July 1962 questioned a number of petitioners from Singapore who opposed merger, as well as Mr. Lee, but had taken no action. On 9 September the Chairman of UNPMO had joined the Chairmen of SUPP and of the Brunei Parti Ra'ayat in sending the United Nations a joint petition seeking intervention to prevent the transfer of sovereignty without the exercise of the right of self-determination. Other leading members of UNPMO repudiated its Chairman's action and reaction in North Borneo to the Filipino claim was in general sharply hostile—indeed in October 1962 the leaders of all parties, including UNPMO, sent a joint letter to the President of the Philippines rejecting the claim.

148.   In January 1963 SUPP also repudiated the joint petition, but submitted a separate one of its own asking for a referendum before merger, while in September 1962 Mr. Lee submitted a petition reporting the results of the Singapore referendum and the fact that Mr. David Marshall, one of the earlier opposition petitioners, had come to support the Anglo–Malayan Agreement. Nevertheless the Tunku's reference to a referendum and the petitions opposing federation made it somewhat less easy to resist demands for some form of popular consultation and to refute Indonesian arguments that rights of self-determination were being overridden.

Indonesia and Brunei

149.   The Indonesian arguments were fortified by events in Brunei. During July and August 1962 the Parti Ra'ayat, the only organised party, won 54 out of the 55 District Council seats, so gaining control of all the District Councils and ensuring that its candidates would secure the 16 Legislative Council seats elected by the District Councils. The party, though not in a majority in the Legislative Council, since there were 17 *ex officio*, official and nominated members, could therefore well lay claim to represent popular feeling. It advocated unity amongst the three Borneo Territories under the constitutional rule of the Sultan and opposed merger into Malaysia, though it seems to have been prepared to bargain with the Malayans. By September 1962 the Mentri Besar, Dato Marsal, was also hostile to merger. In discussions with a Malayan delegation led by Tun Razak, the official Brunei representatives proposed a form of association, instead of incorporation in a federation; they also insisted that Brunei should suffer no loss of sovereignty. This

was summarily rejected by the Malayans and the discussions ended, though the Sultan himself avoided a complete break by reserving his own position.

150.   Meanwhile evidence was accumulating that Bruneis had received training in Indonesia and that Indonesian officials had for some time in all these territories been urging Indonesian claims and the rejection of proposals to join Malaysia. On 24 September, 1962, the Tunku reacted sharply to reports that Dr. Ali Sastroamidjojo, Chairman of the Indonesian Nationalist Party (PNI), who was not at the time a member of the Indonesian Government, had suggested that the country should be 'vigilant' towards Malaysia and that areas bordering on Indonesia 'might be used for military bases'. Dr. Subandrio, who was passing through Kuala Lumpur on 25 September, said that Indonesia had not made any territorial claims on Malaysia, but, since she had a common frontier with the constituent territories, it was natural that she should not remain indifferent. On 26 September in Singapore he was less restrained—'If Malaysia should permit a military base to be established then we are certain to take counter-action. . . . We have made repeated statements that West Irian was the only territory which we would claim as ours. . . . But if our neighbours continue to provoke us and to doubt our sincerity, then things may change. . . . I am not prepared to commit myself or my Government.'

D. Negotiation of the agreement

XII. *The Inter-Governmental (Lansdowne) Committee*

Membership and organisation

151.   It was against this background that Lord Lansdowne and Tun Razak started their consultations with political and community leaders and representatives of civil servants' associations in Sarawak and North Borneo in the middle of August 1962 and subsequently began the work of the Inter-Governmental Committee. A preparatory meeting of the Committee was held in Jesselton on 30 August, 1962. The Committee and its sub-committees were composed of delegations from Sarawak and North Borneo, as well as from Malaya and the United Kingdom, while the Sultan of Brunei accepted an invitation to send observers. Although the delegations from Sarawak and North Borneo were widely representative in character most of the actual negotiation to secure arrangements acceptable to the unofficials from these territories was conducted by the British officials on the two delegations. The Chairmen of all sub-committees were drawn from the United Kingdom delegation. Constitutional, Fiscal, Public Service, Legal and Judicial, and Departmental Organisation Sub-Committees were set up and it was agreed that a plenary session of the full Committee should be held in Jesselton in the middle of October.

152.   Tun Razak subsequently suggested that a sub-committee to consider and co-ordinate future plans for economic development should be added, though he admitted that this was not strictly within the terms of reference of the Lansdowne Committee. Lord Lansdowne's response to this proposal was non-committal, but in a report to the Cabinet on his visit to Borneo, dated 10 September, 1962, [see 141] he expressed the view that since 'Her Majesty's Government is giving up its responsibility for the territories before they are ready to achieve independence on their own, we have a continuing obligation to help them. I consider that we cannot honourably discharge this obligation to the peoples of the territories whom we are persuading to accept Malaysia, unless we maintain our assistance after federation at a

level not lower than the existing Colonial and Welfare Grants. This should not include the cost of any compensation scheme'. Tun Razak's proposal was however resisted in London on the grounds that the Lansdowne Committee was not equipped to undertake a study of development aid and that in any case the question of British financial support for Malaysia in both the development and defence fields was deliberately being left open to be used if necessary to provide some financial inducement to overcome difficulties which might arise in the Committee's main discussions.

Malayan attitudes to the Borneo peoples

153. Having set the work of the Committee in motion—though the first sub-committee did not meet until 8 October, 1962—Lord Lansdowne visited the Tunku in Kuala Lumpur to emphasise that if Malaysia was to endure it must start off with the support of the local people and to persuade him to visit Borneo himself [see 142]. He also pressed Tun Razak to accompany the Tunku, initially at least, on this visit and not to take Enche Ghazali, whose attitude he thought unhelpful. Enche Ghazali, when on the Cobbold Commission, had presumably been responsible for the Tunku's outburst in March 1962 about British civil servants in the territories and had evidently been offended rather than impressed by the doubts of the local people.

154. Tun Razak and the Malay officials with him on the other hand seemed to have been convinced during their tour in August 1962 that there were real difficulties in merger. One of them, Dato Abdul Aziz bin Haji Abdul Majid, Permanent Secretary of the Prime Minister's Department, even told Sir William Goode that, whereas in London he had thought the Governors' attitude obstructive, he now realised that they had only been representing the true views of the people. He later repeated this assessment in Kuala Lumpur. Lord Lansdowne, in reporting this, said that he believed that the Malayans on the Committee 'now realise that British concern over the form of Malaysia is directed solely towards the determination to create a federation which will stick'. But it remained to convince the Tunku of the realities of the situation.

Reactions in North Borneo and the Twenty Points

155. In North Borneo, in the words of Lord Lansdowne, 'the London announcement had come as a great shock' and had caused 'consternation'. On 13 and 14 August, 1962, Mr. Stephens convened a meeting in Jesselton which was attended by the leading representatives of UNKO, USNO, the Democratic and United Parties and of UNPMO, except its Chairman, who was hostile to the Malaysia proposals. These representatives drew up a fourteen-point programme of minimum safeguards which should be met before North Borneo joined Malaysia. The list was extended at a later meeting to twenty points and a memorandum incorporating these points and signed by three representatives of each of the five parties was presented to Lord Lansdowne and Tun Razak when they visited Borneo. These Twenty Points, which gained weight by attracting general support also in Sarawak, went well beyond what the Malayans had appeared to be prepared to concede in London.

156. The more important of the Twenty Points provided in essence: (1) that while Islam might be the national religion of Malaysia there should be no State religion in North Borneo and that the provisions in the Malayan Constitution relating to Islam should not apply in North Borneo; (2) that English should be an

official language of North Borneo for all purposes without time limit; (3) that the Malaysian Constitution should be a completely new document even if based on the existing Malayan Constitution; (6) that North Borneo should have unfettered control of immigration into the State, except for those the Federal Government itself employed or wished to exclude on strictly security grounds; (7) that there should be no right of secession; (8) that Borneanisation of the public service should proceed as quickly as possible; (9) that British officers should be encouraged to remain until they could be suitably replaced by Borneans; (11) that North Borneo should retain control of its own finance, development and tariff and the right to raise loans and should be compensated for the loss of Colonial Development and Welfare Grants; (13) that a proper Ministerial system should be introduced in North Borneo; (14) that during a seven-year transitional period legislative power should remain with the State and not merely be delegated; (15) that the existing educational system in North Borneo should be maintained and remain under State control; (16) that no amendment, modification or withdrawal of any special safeguard relating to North Borneo should be made without the positive concurrence of the Government of the State and that the power of amending the State Constitution should rest exclusively with the people of the State; and (17) that representation in the Federal Parliament should take account of North Borneo's size and potentialities and should not be less than that for Singapore. Point 19 proposed the adoption of the ancient name of Sabah for the State in place of North Borneo.

Formation of an alliance and elections in North Borneo

157.   The North Borneo Legislative Council passed unanimously on 12 September, 1962, a resolution welcoming Malaysia in principle 'provided that the terms of participation and the constitutional arrangements will safeguard the special interests of North Borneo'. On the following day the Council also adopted a resolution calling for the introduction of a Member System by the end of the year, in order to give members more knowledge and experience of administration in preparation for entry into Malaysia.

158.   Meanwhile, on 4 September, 1962, USNO and UNKO had agreed to the formation, on the Malayan model, of a Sabah Alliance Party with provision for other groups to join. By the middle of October, the United and Democratic parties, which had decided to merge, were jointly linked with this proposal and the Chairman of UNPMO had announced that that group had withdrawn its support of the joint petition to the United Nations and also wished to join the proposed Alliance. UNPMO was admitted to membership of the Alliance in November 1962, but was allocated only 5 seats on the National Council as against 12 each for the other three parties and 2 seats as against 5 each on the Executive Council of the Alliance. The tiny Sabah Indian Congress was also admitted in November and given 1 seat on the National Council.

159.   Nominations for elections to 4 Town Boards and 11 District Councils in North Borneo were completed on 26 November, 1962. 53 seats were uncontested and there was no valid nomination for 1 seat where the election had in consequence to be postponed into January. The remaining 65 seats were contested amongst the members of the Alliance and by independents. The elections took place on 16 December, except in Tawau, where all the seats were uncontested; in Sipitang district, where it was necessary to postpone the election to 3 March, 1963, owing to

preoccupation with the aftermath of events in Brunei; and in three rural districts where it had been impossible to prepare rolls in time.

160.   Of those successful in December 1962, 57 represented the Alliance as a whole, 21 UNKO, 13 USNO and 4 UNPMO. 15 seats were secured by independents, most of whom aligned themselves with parties in the Alliance. Overall USNO secured the largest number of seats. 75 per cent of the adult population were on the electoral rolls and these 80 per cent voted, with only 3 per cent of spoilt papers. Two independents known to be affiliated to the Brunei Parti Ra'ayat, who stood in Labuan, were heavily defeated. These local elections were significant since seats were contested on national issues and the new councils were also to perform the function of electoral colleges for the Legislative Assembly. The elections postponed to March 1963, if anything, accentuated the display of popular support for the Malaysia concept.

Reactions in Sarawak and the Tunku's visit to Borneo

161.   In Sarawak the Council Negri, on 26 September, 1962, passed a resolution welcoming Malaysia in principle 'on the understanding that the special interests of Sarawak will be safeguarded'. The issue had previously been discussed in the five Divisional Advisory Councils. In the Council Negri one SUPP member spoke, but did not vote, against the motion and the Chairman of SUPP, a moderate, managed to support both the motion and the joint petition to the United Nations. But, although no vote was cast against the motion, the view that the whole issue was being unduly rushed was widely expressed, as was a feeling that the Council was being presented with a *fait accompli*.

162.   All communities in Sarawak seem by this time to have accepted the inevitability of merger but there still remained general support for safeguards on the lines of the Twenty Points and, especially amongst the Sea Dyaks, or Ibans, a deep-seated fear that Malaysia would mean domination by the Malays. Some groups who had been entirely opposed at the time of the Cobbold Commission enquiry, however, had been impressed by the economic benefits promised for the rural areas by the Malayans and had come to favour merger. The Chinese moderates within SUPP probably accepted merger, but the Left wing remained entirely opposed and the party now began to lose its Malay and Dyak members and some moderate Chinese. On 23 October, 1962, the five other political parties in Sarawak formed a united front to support Malaysia.

163.   A visit by the Tunku to both Sarawak and North Borneo in the second half of November 1962 helped to consolidate support for merger in both territories. His reception amongst the Malay and other Muslim communities was, however, noticeably warmer than amongst the bulk of the population in both Sarawak and North Borneo, while his incautious statement that they would together have 40 seats in the Federal Parliament certainly caused some embarrassment to the Government of Singapore and probably to his own colleagues.

XIII. Inter-territorial negotiations, winter and spring, 1962–63

The Lansdowne Committee Report

164.   Throughout the winter negotiations on the final form of merger continued unchecked in the Lansdowne Committee and its sub-committees. There were

plenary meetings of the full Committee from 22–24 October, 1962, from 23–26 November and again, despite the Brunei revolt, from 18–20 December. The last major points at issue were agreed at the plenary meetings in December and the remaining points of detail were left to an *ad hoc* committee of specialists to resolve. The draft report was initialled on 22 January, 1963, and, after some discussion of amendments, arising largely from the Federation Cabinet's anxiety over the deterioration in the security situation, the report was published on 27 February. That agreement was reached, in the words of Lord Lansdowne, 'owed much to the wisdom and tact of Tun Abdul Razak . . . who always showed himself ready to consider reasonable concessions . . .'; indeed he came to be known in the Committee as 'Tuan Bersetuju' or 'Mr. Agreement'.

165.   Early in December 1962 a deadlock seemed to have been reached on financial issues. The representatives of North Borneo demanded that the State 'should retain control of its own finance, development and tariff, and should have the rights to work up its own taxation and to raise loans on its own credit.' Sarawak had accepted that taxes and tariffs must be Federal matters, but had secured Malayan acceptance of a formula which should enable the State to meet its current expenditures and provide for steady growth in these. Mr. Tan Siew Sin seems to have been convinced that the United Kingdom would compel the territories to accept agreement and so saw no reason to compromise. With the help of a British promise of £1,500,000 a year for five years for development in the territories, which had been held back earlier to be used in case it should be needed to resolve just such a deadlock, agreement was reached on the basis of Malayan proposals which assigned additional items of revenue to the territories; these included the assignment to North Borneo of 40 per cent of any increase in the Federal share of revenue derived from the State.

166.   In general the territories secured the essence of almost all the requirements laid down in the Twenty Points, including provisions for fiscal growth, subject to review by an independent assessor before the sixth and eleventh anniversaries of Malaysia Day, and the right to raise internal loans. They did not, however, secure their proposal that, for an initial seven-year period, legislative power should remain within the State and not merely be delegated to it. They did secure a number of safeguards and the provision that these should not be changed without the concurrence of the Government of the State. North Borneo was conceded an initial allocation of 16 seats in the Federal House of Representatives and Sarawak 24 seats, as against 15 for Singapore, and only 104 for Malaya itself. The estimated populations at the end of 1963 were North Borneo 498,031, Sarawak 809,737, Singapore 1,799,400 and Malaya 7,703,520—population numbers in relation to each Federal seat were therefore roughly North Borneo 31,000, Sarawak, 34,000, Singapore 120,000 and Malaya 74,000. These seat allocations gave the three new States together just sufficient votes to enable them in concert to prevent amendment of the Federal Constitution.

Reactions to the Lansdowne Report in Borneo

167.   In Sarawak the increasing loss by the Communists of non-Chinese support, and even of some Chinese support, had made both political and armed struggle more difficult, while most of the constitutional political parties had managed, for the moment at least, to combine in the Sarawak Alliance, which strongly supported the

Malaysia concept. On 8 March, 1963, the Council Negri, which had 24 elected members out of a total of 43, passed a motion adopting the recommendations of the Lansdowne Committee Report and welcoming the creation of Malaysia by 31 August, 1963. No vote was cast against the motion and most of the very few abstentions seem to have been due to doubts on the language issue and about the continuation of full religious freedom after merger. On 9 March the Council unanimously passed a resolution calling for a Ministerial system and providing for the next Council Negri to be composed of a Speaker, 36 elected members, 3 *ex officio* members, 1 life member and up to 3 nominated members following elections. These arrangements were brought into force during the summer of 1963.

168.   The North Borneo Legislative Council carried a unanimous motion adopting the Lansdowne Committee Report on 13 March, 1963, and the Member System was brought into operation on 25 March. Earlier, following a meeting in Jesselton, North Borneo, on 16 and 17 February, representatives of political parties in all five potential partners in Malaysia had unanimously passed a resolution condemning the Brunei revolt, rejecting the Filipino claim to Sabah and expressing the determination to see Malaysia established by 31 August. A similar convention was held in Kuala Lumpur on 30 and 31 March and proposed the setting up of a 'Grand Alliance Party' for the whole of Malaysia after merger.

Renewed Malayan negotiations with Brunei, January–May 1963

169.   This convention was attended by representatives from Brunei and for a time following the revolt it seemed that the prospect of the Sultanate joining the Federation had if anything improved. In a public statement in December 1962 the Sultan had made it clear that, although the Legislative Council had accepted the concept in principle in July, he had as yet taken no final decision since terms had not been agreed. It was still British policy to persuade and not force Brunei into Malaysia and therefore to persuade the Tunku to offer acceptable terms. Early in January Tun Razak told Sir Geofroy Tory that he assumed these terms would be at least as favourable as those for Sarawak and North Borneo and might possibly even provide for financial autonomy. On 21 January the Sultan, in a statement, described Malaysia as a sound and attractive proposal and on 27 January the Brunei Government announced that discussions on merger would be resumed in Kuala Lumpur.

170.   On 28 January, 1963, the High Commissioner, Sir Dennis White, reported that he thought that the Sultan was convinced that entry into Malaysia was inevitable, but was in no hurry. The Sultan himself arrived in Kuala Lumpur on 31 January, an Inter-Government Committee was set up and on 7 February he announced that he was satisfied that the future prospects of Brunei would best be advanced by joining Malaysia on terms to be negotiated. By 4 March Heads of Agreement on terms had been drawn up, which provided for Brunei to retain control of oil revenues and its existing investments at least for the initial 10-year period, and it was being reported publicly that agreement had virtually been reached. The initialling was however then held up, ostensibly by failure to agree on the amount of the annual 'voluntary donation' to be paid by Brunei to the Federal Government, though this was subsequently fixed as M$45 million for the first year and M$40 million thereafter.

171.   The Sultan returned to Brunei on 24 March, 1963, with the outstanding financial issues still unresolved. These now included the taxation of revenues from and control of any future discoveries of oil or 'other products of the soil of Brunei', the

automatic right of the Federation to receive full Federal rates of taxation or their equivalent after five years on new sources of revenue and, in respect of existing sources of revenue, a continuation of the annual 'donation' or 'contribution' after the first 10 years if a new arrangement had not been agreed upon. The Sultan's advisers took the view that the Malayans had reopened issues, notably disposal of future revenues from oil, already settled, while the Brunei proposal that other mineral rights should be, like oil, free of Federal taxation also seems to have been a new point.

172.   A difference of view also developed in April 1963 as to whether the Sultan's precedence should count from Malaysia Day or from his own accession, although he did not himself pursue the point at this stage. The Sultan's intention still however seemed to be to join Malaysia and the High Commissioner and Mr. Narasimhan, who visited the State in April, urged him to press forward with policies of constitutional advance and economic development and to present these and the arguments for joining Malaysia more clearly to the people of Brunei. Some steps in this direction were taken—the Emergency (Suspension of the Constitution) Order was revoked and the Executive and Legislative Councils were reconstituted, although with nominated instead of elected unofficial members, while in May the Deputy Mentri Besar was visiting kampongs to explain the advantages of merger and was arguing that the trend of opinion in the world at large would not allow the State to remain a British protectorate. But these efforts to explain the advantages of Malaysia were short-lived and insufficient to reverse a growing antagonism to merger and the Sultan at no time permitted detailed explanation of the terms proposed or agreed.

Malayan negotiations with Singapore, November 1962–March 1963

173.   On 17 November, 1962, Tun Razak proposed to Mr. Lee the setting up of an Inter-Governmental Committee between Singapore and Malaya. Mr. Lee agreed to this proposal on 20 November and on 26 November Enche Ghazali suggested the establishment of five sub-committees—constitutional, fiscal, internal security, information and broadcasting, and establishment and organisation. Despite some foreboding on the part of Mr. Lee, the Malayan Government appeared to accept the November 1961 White Paper arrangements as in general settled. There was some discussion as to whether the United Kingdom should ask to have an observer on this Committee, but Lord Selkirk took the view that it was better not to be 'involved unnecessarily in the inevitable disputes between the two Governments'.

174.   Meanwhile there had been two related developments. In the early hours of 2 February, 1963, 97 people, including leading Left-wing members of the Barisan Sosialis, were detained in Singapore at the instance of the Internal Security Council, which had authorised this step on 1 February; a further 20 arrests were made later. On 3 February Mr. Lee managed to create the public impression that this was an action which his Government would not itself have contemplated, but that he had felt compelled to fall in with the wishes of the other members in line with his intention, when within Malaysia, of always co-operating with the Federation on national issues, while remaining ready to protect the interests of the people of Singapore on local or economic issues.

175.   The Federation Government had itself arrested 50 people in Malaya on 16 December, 1962, on charges of subversive activity in support of the Communist Party. It had strongly advocated arresting the Barisan leaders and in general taking a firm hand with Communists and their sympathisers in Singapore. Mr. Lee made

much to Lord Selkirk's deputy, Mr. P. B. C. Moore, of his fear that, having achieved this, the Tunku would now be less interested in merger or at least determined to drive a harder bargain in the economic field.

176.   The arrests accelerated the decline in the influence of the China-oriented Left wing in Singapore; symptomatic of this at the time was the decline in enrolments in Chinese-language schools as against English-language schools. They also seem greatly to have increased Mr. Lee's confidence in his ability to handle his opponents—there was remarkably little public reaction to their detention. By March 1963 he was, during constituency tours, vigorously defending the retention of British bases on the argument that a third of the people of Singapore were directly or indirectly dependent on the bases for their livelihood, though he advocated a phased withdrawal over 10 or 20 years.

177.   On 10 April, 1963, the Singapore Assembly passed a motion supporting the decision of the Internal Security Council; the motion was passed without a division despite a six and a half hour speech by Dr. Lee Siew Choh, Chairman of the Barisan Sosialis. On 22 April a number of leading Barisan members took part in a violent demonstration at Mr. Lee's office and subsequently 12, including 10 members of the Assembly, were arrested. They were released on bail in May and brought to trial in August for trying to overawe the Prime Minister.

178.   The second development was perhaps more fundamental. This was the arrival of an International Bank mission to report on the economic implications of Malaysia, and especially the possibilities for a common market. Its leader, M. Jacques Rueff, made a preliminary visit to Kuala Lumpur and Singapore in October 1962. The whole mission arrived in February 1963, but jockeying for position in relation to its work began well before this. The Singapore Government strengthened its Tariff Advisory Commission and set it to examining items on which protective tariffs might be imposed, while the Federation pressed on with a policy of protecting new local industries.

179.   In December 1962 the Federation introduced restrictive new regulations affecting the import of day-old chicks and eggs for hatching from Singapore. On 9 January, 1963, the Singapore Government retaliated by requiring specific import licences on imports from Malaya of various foodstuffs and much stricter regulations on the import of meat for re-export to Malaya. After some discussion it was agreed as from 15 February that each would exempt the other from the operation of these rules and regulations and would co-operate on related veterinary issues. However the zest with which each inflicted pin-pricks of this kind on the other suggested that economic co-ordination might prove difficult.

180.   As with the Borneo Territories the main difficulty in the merger discussions between Malaya and Singapore related to finance. On 1 March, 1963, in the middle of discussions in Kuala Lumpur, Mr. Lee claimed publicly that it had been agreed that Singapore should itself carry out the collection of taxes in its territory, paying a lump sum over to the Federation. This was a position which seemed consonant with the White Paper and earlier exchanges between Mr. Lee and the Tunku. Mr. Tan however disputed this interpretation and Mr. Lee in turn reaffirmed his position. On 18 March Mr. Lee suggested to Lord Selkirk that Sir Geofroy Tory should try to persuade the Tunku that any modification of the White Paper provisions would have to be balanced by increased parliamentary representation for Singapore if they were not to be regarded in the State as unacceptable. In view of the way in which the Federal

Government had used control of revenues in Kelantan and Trengganu there was some reason for Mr. Lee's determination not to be placed in a similar position, unless Singapore was given sufficient parliamentary representation effectively to influence Federal policy. In Mr. P. B. C. Moore's view this was an issue on which Mr. Lee was prepared to refuse merger.

XIV. *The Malaysia agreement*

Domestic political pressures on the Tunku

181.   In October 1962 the Alliance won a by-election with an improved majority, but in December came under attack from the opposition in Parliament for opposing an 'anti-colonialist' revolt in Brunei. In January 1963 the former Minister of Agriculture, Enche Abdul Aziz bin Ishak, who was relieved of his portfolio on 1 October, 1962, and who was thought to enjoy considerable popularity amongst the rural Malays, launched into vigorous political opposition. In April 1963 the Opposition parties formed a 'Joint Opposition Conference' with Enche Aziz as Chairman. On 26 April they presented Mr. Narasimhan with a memorandum which complained, not so much of the proposed formation of Malaysia, as of the manner in which it was being brought into being. The town and district council election results during the summer of 1963 suggested that UMNO retained Malay support, but that the position of the MCA had weakened amongst the Chinese. This decline in support for MCA was due to differences as to the degree to which Chinese rights and interests should be asserted against the Malays. This in turn contributed to the hostility displayed by MCA leaders towards Mr. Lee and the PAP, who clearly hoped to supplant them by taking up a somewhat less compromising position in regard to Chinese claims.

182.   In these elections the Alliance lost seats in some largely Chinese towns, especially in Perak, but did well elsewhere. Nevertheless, overall its percentage of the poll dropped slightly and was still a little below the combined votes of all its opponents. These, despite the Joint Opposition Conference, were too diverse in interest and policy to unite effectively against the Alliance, but their number and the fact that many of his own supporters had sentimental ties with Indonesia induced the Tunku to be more conciliatory to Indonesia in June and July 1963. Where he had earlier, in the British view, been unduly robust, he was now thought insufficiently so.

183.   The effective restraint on the Tunku's ability to make concessions to the other prospective partners in Malaysia was however exercised not by the opposition groups but by his own party and cabinet colleagues. Many Malays in UMNO remained profoundly suspicious of the Singapore Chinese and doubtful of the wisdom of allowing them into the Federation. The Borneo Territories they had accepted purely as a counter-weight to Singapore and were therefore anxious that Malay and not just indigenous groups should be in controlling positions in North Borneo and Sarawak. The MCA leaders, who were drawn from the business class in the peninsula, had no wish to be supplanted politically by the PAP or economically by the Singapore-based entrepreneur and were equally dubious about some of the concessions extracted from the Tunku and Tun Razak.

Malayan negotiations with Singapore, April–July 1963

184.   By the middle of April 1963 the discussions on finance between Singapore and Malaya were at a standstill and there were mutual accusations of bad faith. The

public debate between Mr. Lee and Mr. Tan had shifted from the control of revenue in Singapore to the proportion of it that should be paid to the new federation. On 27 April Mr. Tan talked at a Press conference of the possibility of going ahead with Malaysia without Singapore, while Mr. Lee said that no final financial settlement could be made until the Rueff mission's recommendations on a common market had been received—it was already clear that on economic grounds the mission would favour making progress towards a customs union. Mr. Tan had laid claim to part of Singapore's financial surpluses; Mr. Lee was only willing to pay 'part of Singapore's prosperity over to the Federation' if good common market terms had been arranged.

185.   The Malayan Government was unwilling to agree to common market proposals except perhaps gradually over a period of many years. On 15 May, 1963, Tun Razak, talking to Lord Home in London, seemed to envisage promoting another Government in Singapore if Mr. Lee proved obdurate—the British Government had consistently made it clear to the Malayans that formation of Malaysia without Singapore was unacceptable. Mr. Lee made public complaint of intrigues against him by leading Malayan Chinese Association members. The MCA in Singapore was at this time trying to revitalise itself as part of the development of a Singapore Alliance, the formation of which was announced on 24 April and Mr. Lee claimed that it was trying to force a collision between him and the Tunku.

186.   On 27 May, 1963, Lord Lansdowne left London for Kuala Lumpur to try, together with a representative of the International Bank, to bring the two sides together. This mediation produced some progress. Financial negotiations were resumed on 28 May, and on 29 May Malaya agreed publicly to the principle of a common market, though remaining very vague about its form and timing, and put forward a 'package' proposal on this and the apportionment issue. This marked a considerable advance on previous proposals, but was described by the Tunku as final and by Mr. Lee, privately, as inadequate. In the middle of June the Malayans were demanding that Singapore should contribute 40 per cent of its revenues and in addition should make a grant for use in the Borneo Territories of S$50 million in the first five years of Malaysia. Singapore was willing to contribute 39 per cent of its revenues and to loan the Borneo Territories S$150 million at special rates. The control of broadcasting and television in Singapore was also a subject of dispute. By the third week in June the Malayan Cabinet was insisting that its final terms should be accepted within 48 hours [see 183]; Mr. Lee still wanted detailed provision for a common market to be written into the Constitution [see 185].

187.   By the middle of June 1963 therefore it was believed in London that Malaya and Singapore might well fail to reach agreement on the financial arrangements for Malaysia and urgent thought was in consequence being given by the Ministries concerned to future British policy. To judge by a remark by Enche Ghazali to Mr. M. J. Moynihan of the British High Commission in Kuala Lumpur, however, many other Malayans were by now 'tired of Tan Siew Sin's obstinacy'. In an effort to avert a breakdown the Tunku and Mr. Lee were invited to meet with British Ministers. The Tunku was preceded by a delegation, including Tun Razak, Mr. Tan and Dr. Lim Swee Aun, the Minister for Commerce and Industry, which left for London on 25 June, as did Mr. Lee. The function of Mr. Tan and Dr. Lim was, in Sir Geofroy Tory's view, to restrain Tun Razak from making undue concessions. Agreement was reached on the main points at issue on 5 July [see 191] and only then did the Tunku himself leave for London.

Defence and British financial aid

188. While Malaya was haggling with Singapore over financial arrangements, parallel negotiations were in progress with Britain on assistance for economic development and for the additional defence programme which would be necessary. A British team, including representatives of the Treasury and the Ministry of Defence and led by Sir Henry Lintott of the Commonwealth Relations Office, visited Kuala Lumpur from 6 to 14 April, 1963 [see 173, appendix]. Malayan financial resources were under pressure owing to falling prices of rubber, but the Malayan Government proposed to accept a running down of the country's reserves by some M$1,500 million or £175 million. The programme of capital expenditure on defence was estimated to cost some £55 million, of which £24.5 million would be spent in 1963–65. It was estimated that, with a minimum defence and development programme, the proposed running down of reserves and the use of external resources, a foreign exchange gap of about £92 million over five years would still be left.

189. The British team concluded that Malayan reserves could not be reduced further without endangering confidence in the Malayan dollar and that the defence capital programme was modest in the circumstances. They proposed however that British aid for the defence programme should be limited to the secondment of officers, to the capital programme and initially to 1963–65. It was clear that the United Kingdom could not hope to reduce its own defence expenditure in the area in the immediate future and it was already committed over the following five years to about £13 million for development aid for the Borneo Territories and Singapore and to pay the whole cost, which was expected to be £2.5 million to £3 million, of the compensation scheme for expatriate officers in Borneo.

190. These official talks prepared the way for Ministerial talks in London from 13 to 15 May, 1963, at which Tun Razak and Mr. Tan Siew Sin represented the Malayan Government [see 174 and 175]. The Malayan delegation expressed disappointment at the initial British offer of £12,350,000 for the defence capital programme for 1963–65 and on his return Tun Razak stated publicly that the British proposals fell far short of Malayan needs. The Tunku then wrote to Mr. Macmillan to ask for more generous aid and suggested that without this Britain would have to bear financial responsibility for the internal security and defence of the Borneo Territories for some time [see 177]. It was already recognised in London that the United Kingdom would have 'to provide the military and economic backing essential to keep Malaysia in being'. The British Government therefore increased its offer during the final discussions in June and a figure of M$255 million, or almost £30 million, for aid in 1963–65 was accepted by Tun Razak. He noted however that it would still fall short of Malaysia's needs and there was subsequently renewed haggling over the cost of operations in Borneo.

The Malaysia agreement, 9 July, 1963

191. The agreement for the establishment of Malaysia was signed by the United Kingdom, Malaya, North Borneo, Sarawak and Singapore on 9 July, 1963. Attached to it as annexes were the forms of Bills to be passed by the Malayan Parliament amending the existing Federal Constitution to provide for the arrangements under which Singapore and the Borneo Territories were to join the Federation and to extend and adapt the existing immigration ordinance, particularly in relation to the special needs of the Borneo Territories. Also annexed were constitutions for Sabah, Sarawak and Singapore to be introduced by British Orders in Council before Malaysia

Day and forms for Orders in Council providing for compensation and retiring benefits for officers of the existing North Borneo and Sarawak Governments and for agreements between Britain and Malaysia on conditions of service for public servants continuing to hold office in Singapore and the Borneo Territories. There were about 350 pensionable members of the Overseas Civil Service in North Borneo and Sarawak and the compensation scheme was designed to encourage them to continue to serve.

192. The timetable envisaged at this stage was that the British legislation—which which was introduced on 11 July, 1963—should be passed in July and the Malayan in August, that the formal agreement should be signed at the end of July or the beginning of August and that the British Orders in Council and the appointment of the Heads of State of Sabah and Sarawak should be made in August. Malaysia Day could then be on 31 August, 1963. The British legislation included provision for the transfer of sovereignty, for the new Constitutions of Sabah, Sarawak and Singapore and for the withdrawal of citizenship of the United Kingdom and Colonies from those in Singapore, Sarawak and North Borneo who would automatically acquire Malaysian citizenship on Malaysia Day.

The extension of the defence agreement

193. Article VI of the main agreement gave effect to the undertakings of the British and Malayan Prime Ministers in November 1961 to extend the existing defence agreement (see paragraphs 106–109). The article provided that 'The Agreement on External Defence and Mutual Assistance ... of 12th October, 1957, and its annexes shall apply to all territories of Malaysia, ... subject to the proviso that the Government of Malaysia will afford to the Government of the United Kingdom the right to continue to maintain the bases and other facilities at present occupied by their Service authorities within the State of Singapore and will permit the Government of the United Kingdom to make such use of these bases and facilities as that Government may consider necessary for the purpose of assisting in the defence of Malaysia, and for Commonwealth defence and for the preservation of peace in South-East Asia.' The application of this article was to be subject to Annex F to the agreement which related mainly to Service lands in Singapore (see paragraph 199).

194. In response to a Malayan request the United Kingdom also agreed secretly, subject to certain conditions, such as freedom from prosecution and indemnity against damage, to provide limited assistance to measures to secure internal order in Singapore after Malaysia Day. This was to include helicopters, administrative units, skilled civilian volunteers to maintain essential services and, for a few months after Malaysia Day, a company of troops for use from the outset of trouble and possibly also a stand-by battalion. It was also anticipated that counter-insurgency and other assistance would be required in Borneo for some time, since the existing Malayan forces would have to be expanded before they could take over these tasks.

195. Subsequent examination of the terms of the November 1961 statement had suggested that they would not prevent the Malaysian Government from arguing that the Singapore base could not be used under the agreement for purposes of which it disapproved, such as support for internal security operations in British dependencies. No attempt was however made to tighten up the agreement, since the existing wording would avoid political embarrassment at home for the Malayan Government. Moreover British pressure to make the terms more precise might have led to the Malayans stating objections to certain uses of the base in advance or to press for

safeguards themselves such as guarantees that the United Kingdom would maintain agreed force levels in Malaysia.

196.   On 6 August, 1963, the Tunku took the public position that 'our defence arrangements with Britain are not perpetual or permanent. They can be revoked by either party'. The formal British view at this time was that the termination or amendment of the defence agreement could only be done with the consent of both parties and posts were instructed to say so if asked. It was recognised however that effective use of the bases would depend in practice on local consent and it was believed that the wording of Article VI would permit satisfactory use so long as the existing Alliance Government, or one of similar complexion, was in office. The Malayan Government was in general anxious to play down the defence aspects of the agreement and to avoid the impression that any new commitments had been entered into. Australia and New Zealand took a similar view and on 18 September exchanged letters with Malaysia recording joint agreement that their former association with the Anglo–Malayan Defence Agreement should in future be regarded as applying to Malaysia.

197.   Nevertheless, because of the development of confrontation, defence co-operation became more active. While engaged in discussions with Malaysia on the role of British forces in Borneo, Mr. Macmillan, in a message to the Australian and New Zealand Prime Ministers towards the end of September 1963, expressed the hope that their forces would be available to participate in this effort. It was however regarded as important that the United Kingdom should seem to be helping Malaysia's own defence effort rather than to be running the war itself. Invocation of the Defence Agreement was expected to be at Malaysian request. At meetings of the Malaysian National Defence Council, the first of which was held on 10 October with the Tunku in the chair, the British Commander-in-Chief, Far East, his Political Adviser and the Defence Adviser to the United Kingdom High Commission were 'in attendance' only, while it was proposed to set up a separate *ad hoc* quadripartite body to discuss external assistance to the Malaysian defence effort, including the Australian, New Zealand and United Kingdom High Commissioners and the Commander-in-Chief, under the chairmanship of Tun Razak.

The agreement with Singapore

198.   Attached to the main Malaysia Agreement as Annex J was an agreement between Malaya and Singapore providing for the progressive establishment of a common market. It had been agreed in May 1963 that a common market must entail an erosion of Singapore's free port status as Malaysia industrialised, but the Annex provided for the harmonisation of revenue tariffs in such a way as not significantly to harm Singapore's entrepôt trade. The agreement in Annex J also provided for the setting up of a Tariff Advisory Board, whose chairman for the first five years was to be acceptable to the Singapore Government, for the apportionment of 40 per cent of Singapore revenues to the Federation, for periodical reviews of these financial arrangements with the help of an independent assessor if necessary, and for two 15-year loans totalling S$150 million to the Federation by Singapore to assist development in the Borneo Territories—the largest of these, of S$100 million, was to be interest-free for five or possibly 10 years. Annex K to the agreement provided for delegation to Singapore of day-to-day control of broadcasting and television programmes in the State.

199.   Annex F to the Malaysia Agreement provided for British Service authorities in Singapore to have security of tenure of lands held in Singapore, while a letter of 8 July, 1963, expressed the intention of the British Government to release some lands in excess of Service requirements to the Singapore Government. This was a matter of which Mr. Lee had made a considerable public issue. He had in March 1963 threatened in effect to seize one such piece of land which he claimed was wanted for a new road to Jurong. The British view at this time was that this was essentially a matter on which Her Majesty's Government could only deal with the Malaysian Government. In London Mr. Lee put forward a list of 1,947 acres of 'land made available', that is Crown land to which the Services had no normal title, and which he considered not to be in use by the Services. On such land for which use or contingent use had not been established he demanded rent at market rates. In the course of the discussions his demands were lowered to 1,365 acres and a M$15 million contribution to the cost of raising the Second Battalion of the Singapore Infantry Regiment. He finally secured promise of the release of some 1,300 acres and M$10 million; he subsequently disputed with the British Government as to whether this sum was rent or a ceiling for a British contribution towards the battalion, the raising of which in practice seemed likely to cost only M$7 million. Mr. Lee claimed publicly to have reduced his claims for the sake of the Tunku and endeavoured to convey the impression that he had been tougher and more effective in bargaining than the Malayans. This was in turn no doubt responsible for Mr. Tan Siew Sin's public statement that Singapore had made a bad bargain.

200.   During the course of the discussions in London there were a number of more informal meetings as a result of which Mr. Lee secured further concessions by exchange of letter. In particular on 7 July, 1963, the Tunku signed a very brief and loosely-worded note, written on the back of an envelope at the Ritz Hotel, of points agreed. Mr. Lee sent his expanded version of these notes to the Tunku on 10 July [see 192 and 193]. The four points he listed provided: (i) that labourers for the development projects in Borneo to be undertaken with the Singapore loans should not be engaged from outside Malaysia and that half should come from Singapore; (ii) that Singapore should be entitled to amend its Constitution so as to require a member of the Assembly to resign his seat if he left the party for which he stood when elected; (iii) that any Federal law restricting movement should be reciprocal between Singapore and Malaya; and (iv) that powers of detention under the ordinance dealing with gangsters be delegated to Singapore. These undertakings later gave rise to some dispute when Mr. Lee refused to accept postponement of Malaysia Day unless they were formalised in a supplementary agreement. This was done in an agreement signed on 12 September, 1963, though the Federal Government declined to write delegation of the gangster ordinance into the Constitution.

The end of negotiations with Brunei, June–July 1963

201.   The Sultan of Brunei visited Kuala Lumpur again in June 1963, but found the Malayans still insufficiently flexible. On 19 June a statement was issued that the Malayan Government proposed to deliver final terms for the entry of Brunei—and Singapore—into the new federation and would request an answer within 48 hours. The Sultan, and the Press, read this as an ultimatum and he left for Brunei on 21 June. The British Government then invited him to London to take part in discussions with the Tunku, but this he at first declined to do unless he received an assurance of

prior agreement to his terms. The Federation terms, contained in a letter of 21 June from Tun Razak, included, amongst other points unacceptable to the Sultan, a new proposal for a binding legal obligation to pay the equivalent of full Federal tax on new sources of revenue, including new oilfields, which might become available after the first five years of the agreement.

202.   On 2 July, 1963, nevertheless the Sultan left to take part in the talks in London, while indicating that if these should fail to produce agreement on entry into Malaysia he would wish to discuss with British Ministers the 'strengthening of Brunei's Defence Treaty with the United Kingdom'. Agreement was not reached between Brunei and Malaya. The Malayans claimed that discussions broke down, after agreement had been reached on all other matters, only when the Sultan raised the question of his precedence within Malaysia too late for the Tunku to consult the Conference of Rulers, but this was strongly denied in Brunei. There was in fact at least one financial point unresolved—the wording of the terms of reference for the eventual review of the financial arrangements—but the Malayans had made substantial concessions. It seemed evident however that the Sultan had finally concluded that he did not sufficiently trust the Malayans to enter Malaysia and that the State would be better off under the existing arrangements—a Brunei spokesman was quoted as saying that 'it was the principle of it all that Brunei found unacceptable'. In October 1963 the Tunku requested the return of the Malayan officers seconded to Brunei; there is no doubt that these officials had been one cause of revulsion against merger amongst the Bruneis.

203.   The Sultan's refusal to enter Malaysia seems to have been received in the State with satisfaction—one official report from Brunei spoke indeed of 'a certain amount of jubilation'. There were several reasons for this reaction. Amongst the general population there was a fear that merger would in effect mean becoming a vassal state of Malaya and losing the existing welfare advantages, while, owing to higher tariffs, prices would rise. There was also a naive popular belief that refusal to enter Malaysia might preserve Brunei from the Indonesian threat to Malaysia. In more sophisticated circles there was a realisation that the relatively low standard of education in the State would probably greatly reduce the opportunities open to Bruneis and this was compounded by the widespread misconception that common citizenship would result in an uncontrolled influx of more highly qualified people from Malaya and Singapore. It was suggested that this appreciation of the threat to personal prospects extended even to the Mentri Besar, Dato Marsal bin Maun.

E. *The international repercussions of the negotiations*

XV. *The Brunei revolt*

The course of the revolt

204.   At the beginning of November 1962 Sheikh A. M. Azahari and Enche Zaini bin Hadji Ahmad of the Brunei Parti Ra'ayat were in Manila, apparently under the auspices of Mr. Nicasio Osmena, who was promoting the Kiram family claim to parts of North Borneo. While there they saw Vice-President Pelaez. During the following month increasing evidence accumulated of activity in the Brunei Bay area by the 'Tentera Nasional Kalimantan Utara', or National Army of North Borneo, and other bodies connected with the Brunei Parti Ra'ayat, and also possibly with Enche Ahmad Boestamam, the leader of the Malayan Parti Ra'ayat. It was known that their aims

included unification of the British Borneo territories under Brunei sovereignty and opposition to Malaysia, by force if necessary, and it was thought, correctly as it turned out, that, though the TNKU had Indonesian affiliations and though some of its members had trained in Indonesia, it had not as yet acquired modern arms.

205.   Information was also received which suggested that Philippine Army personnel were being recruited for infiltration into North Borneo. Camps or parade grounds were discovered in Brunei and neighbouring areas of North Borneo and Sarawak and, towards the end of November, a number of arrests were made in the Fifth Division of Sarawak and uniforms, badges, charms against bullets and documents, including a plan of attack on the police station at Lawas, were seized. There were no British troops in Brunei, but small police mobile or field force units were moved into the neighbouring districts of North Borneo and Sarawak and the heads of the police Special Branch in each of the three territories met together on 28 November, 1962, to co-ordinate counter-measures, while the Governor of Sarawak offered to send a field force detachment to Brunei if requested. The strength of the TNKU was, before the revolt, thought to be somewhere between 500 and 2,000 men, but was later estimated at 2,000 to 3,000.

206.   On 1 December, 1962, the Tunku sent urgently for Sir Geofroy Tory to tell him that he had received clear evidence from the Legal Adviser in Brunei and a Malay working for Radio Brunei that an insurrection was imminent. The High Commissioner in Brunei had been on leave for some weeks—he returned as soon as the revolt broke out—and the Tunku suggested that Lord Selkirk should himself at once visit Brunei and that emergency action should be taken. He urged the same course on the Commissioner-General in person in Singapore on the following day.

207.   Lord Selkirk's first assessment of the situation was reassuring. It seems to have been based largely on the belief in the Borneo territories that the reports received by the Tunku partly reflected the hostility with which Malayan seconded civil servants were faced in Brunei, and so were greatly exaggerated, and on a lack of anxiety on the part of the Sultan and his Government. This initial optimism led the Colonial Secretary to inform Mr. Macmillan that 'there is no reason at present to expect an emergency', though the situation would have to be carefully watched and there were arrangements to bring in police forces from Sarawak and North Borneo and troops from Singapore at short notice. Lord Home's comment on all this after the event, in a minute of 11 December, 1962, was 'I think they were all very blind and complacent'. Lord Selkirk also noted, in a letter of 20 December, a certain failure to assess the situation, but added 'Nevertheless, if we had acted strongly on such evidence as we had, it might well have led to the movement being pushed underground with more serious long-term results . . . .' [See 151.]

208.   Having visited Brunei Lord Selkirk was less confident. He reported on 7 December, 1962, that he had found there a general air of complacency which he had sought to dispel; he thought the loyalty of the police 'very open to question' and their discipline uncertain, while in his view the Parti Ra'ayat represented the vast majority of the people. In general he judged the State to be 'potentially in a dangerously revolutionary condition' and noted that as he left reports had come in that an armed attack was planned on the oil installations at Miri in Sarawak for 2 a.m. on the following morning, Saturday, 8 December. He agreed on a number of counter-measures with the Brunei Government, which however were overtaken by events.

209.   It is possible that this sudden visit by the Commissioner-General to Brunei,

coupled with the arrests at Lawas, action by the police in Sarawak and North Borneo aimed at disrupting TNKU, and the postponement of the meeting of the new Brunei Legislative Council, due to be held on 19 December, 1962, 'owing to the Government's preoccupation with the situation which culminated in the revolt', may have persuaded the Parti Ra'ayat leaders to advance the date of the rising—in that event the outbreak had perhaps originally been planned to take place over Christmas. There was however no certain evidence of this and 2 a.m. on 8 December had its own significance as the time and date of the Japanese attack on Malaya in 1941.

210.   On learning of the intended attack at Miri on 7 December, 1962, the Government of Sarawak informed the Services in Singapore who were therefore placed at 48 hours' notice on the morning of 7 December and were in the event able to move within about 12 hours of a call for assistance being received from the Sultan. A police platoon from North Borneo was despatched even more rapidly and played an important part in holding the airfield. The High Commission in Brunei had also been warned and the Brunei police were on the alert on the night of 7 December.

211.   Nevertheless, although the crucial Brunei Town Police Station, under the command of the British Commissioner of Police, repulsed the rebels and prevented them capturing the Sultan himself, the police at the main police station at Seria, under a Malayan seconded officer, were, in the High Commission's view, inert and elsewhere police stations fell, with little if any resistance, to the rebels, who thereby acquired modern arms. The authorities were clearly unprepared for the weight and co-ordination of the revolt and the degree of training acquired by the TNKU forces in Indonesia. The oilfields at Seria, much of Brunei Town itself and of the rest of the State and parts of the Fourth and Fifth Divisions of Sarawak, including Limbang, were temporarily overrun; there was also minor rebel activity in several hamlets across the border in North Borneo, but Labaun, where the Government of North Borneo had expected trouble, remained quiet and was used as a staging post for Gurkha and other British troops from Singapore.

212.   The arrival of a battalion of Gurkhas and of other Army and Marine units rapidly reversed the situation. The most important centres in Brunei had been recovered by midday on 11 December, 1962, by which time some 1,600 British troops had been brought in, and the back of the revolt was broken in the next two days. By 18 December only a few rural centres had not been cleared and all hostages had been released. At this stage it was thought that casualties were, amongst civilians, at least 2 killed and 7 wounded, amongst the armed services, 7 killed and 28 wounded, and, amongst the rebels, between 50 and 60 killed and 600 to 700 taken prisoner. By 21 December no centre of population remained in rebel hands and the remnants of the TNKU were being pursued or were surrendering in jungle areas. By the end of December 1962 2,700 had been captured or had surrendered, probably comprising all but a handful of the total number engaged, but the last few dissidents were not all rounded up until 18 May, 1963, by which time many of those originally detained had been released. The British force employed consisted of the equivalent of six battalions with armour and artillery and supporting air and naval forces.

The motives of the Brunei rebels

213.   There seems no doubt that the revolt initially had the sympathy of a high proportion of Brunei Malays and of the submerged Kedayan community in the three territories and that the rebels believed that they had the support of both the Sultan

and the Indonesian authorities. Their motives seem to have been mixed. The less privileged groups were probably interested in destroying the influence of the Brunei nobility—the people of Brunei are all entitled to enjoy certain benefits such as free education, old-age pensions, medical facilities and allowances, and freedom from taxes, but the pengirans have great advantages. Others may have wished to restore some of the former influence of the State and to prevent merger with Malaya—the Tunku, who had privately offered to send both police and a battalion of infantry to Brunei, later withdrew the offer of troops, it was thought because he recognised that hostility to Malaysia was an important reason for the revolt.

214.   The rebels do not appear to have been hostile to Britain or to individual Britons, at least until British forces began to arrive. In Manila, at a Press conference held on the afternoon of 8 December, 1962, Sheikh Azahari announced that the Sultan had declared the independence within the Commonwealth of a state composed of the three Borneo territories and had designated him Prime Minister and Minister for Foreign Affairs and Defence and Enche Zaini Minister of Economics, Commerce and Industry. This was promptly denied by the Sultan in a broadcast, but British officials concerned did not at once exclude the possibility that he had had some forewarning of the Parti Ra'ayat's plans, even if he had not given them his blessing.

The aftermath of the revolt in Brunei

215.   The Parti Ra'ayat was declared illegal as soon as the revolt broke out, the Constitution was suspended and the Legislative and District Councils were dissolved. British officials, who placed much of the blame for the revolt on the failings of the 'Palace Party', subsequently spent considerable effort and thought on pressing for reforms in the State, but to little effect. The Parti Ra'ayat's recourse to violence, when it had not even tested the substantial opportunities open to it under the existing constitution, had confirmed the Sultan in his doubts about the wisdom of rapid advance to a more democratic system.

216.   In this the Sultan seems to have been of one mind with Sheikh Azahari, who was reported in the *Straits Times* of 19 January, 1963, as having stated that his 'Government' would not have elections, but would appoint a 'People's Council' and introduce 'guided democracy'. Around the turn of the year there was some discussion of the possibility of using Sheikh Azahari to reduce the Indonesian ability to create difficulties for the Malaysian proposals. This course was however not pursued and his departure for the safety of Manila before the revolt was started, the failure of the revolt itself and an interview with Nicasio Osmena in the *Straits Times* of 18 January, 1963, did much to discredit him, as did the defection of Enche Zaini, who was granted protective custody in Hong Kong towards the end of January 1963.

Precautionary measures in Borneo and the CCO

217.   After the Brunei revolt a War Executive Council was set up to coordinate operations in all three Borneo Territories with a subordinate State War Executive Committee in each. A small body of British troops had already before the revolt been spread along the east coast of North Borneo, where there had been increasing armed raids and piracies originating mostly in the Philippines. There were somewhat under 7,500 Filipino and around 31,000 Indonesian immigrant workers in this area and entry of unsponsored workers from these countries was stopped in December 1962

and January 1963—the restriction on Filipino unsponsored labourers was relaxed in April 1963. Troops were also now moved to the Kuching area of Sarawak and some 60 CCO leaders were arrested. This largely Chinese organisation was not thought to have been forewarned of the revolt. Nevertheless some of its more important leaders managed to escape arrest, while some SUPP branches in the Miri area were said to have been used as cover for TNKU activities.

218.   Whether privy to the intentions of the TNKU leaders or not, there seems little doubt that throughout the winter and spring of 1962–63 the CCO in Sarawak was engaged in preparations for armed insurrection, and it was clear by the end of January that the arrests of CCO suspects had not reduced the determination of the Communist leaders within the Chinese community, while continuing a constitutional struggle through front organisations, to prepare for armed revolution. By April 1963 *Chung Tui*, or companies, were known to have been formed in several areas and it was believed that, despite the detentions in December, an active strength of 3,500 had been organised, which might be able to count on the support of some 20,500 sympathisers. These CCO groups were thought to be centred in the Chinese rural areas of the First and Second Divisions and in the Sibu and Lower Rejang areas of the Third Division. They were also assumed to have Indonesian links, probably with the PKI, and to be receiving training in Indonesian Borneo. In April 1963 the Special Branch listed the threats to Sarawak as, in order of importance, the CCO, Indonesian action, native chauvinism, and racialism.

XVI. *Indonesian resistance and allied anxiety*

Indonesian intentions

219.   On 14 December, 1962, the Colonial Office was told that the Prime Minister wanted a most careful examination made of the part being played by Indonesia and whether a build-up of guerilla action from Indonesian Borneo could be expected. The real anxiety now related to Indonesian intentions and the lengths to which the Indonesian Government would go to prevent the formation of Malaysia, whether because they genuinely believed the Grand Design to be as they claimed an imperialist device to perpetuate British influence and military power in the area or because it might effectively prevent eventual Indonesian dominance. It was already clear that there were a variety of motives inducing influential groups in Indonesia to promote a long drawn out guerilla war along the Borneo border—expansionist ambition, a desire to divert attention from failures in the economic field, the need to have an excuse for maintaining the over-inflated armed forces, the fear that Malaya would eventually be Chinese dominated and that the formation of Malaysia would extend this threat to Borneo, anxiety over a potential source of attraction for the Outer Islands, especially Sumatra, and, not least, a desire on the part of the Indonesian Communist Party (PKI) to create confusion from which they might profit.

220.   President Sukarno, who passed through Manila on 21 November, 1962, was reported by the Ambassador, Mr. Pilcher, to have told President Macapagal that he would not tolerate the creation of Malaysia. Sheikh Azahari and Enche Zaini, while in Manila, maintained close contact with the Indonesian Embassy and it was plain that the TNKU rebels had received both training in and encouragement from Indonesia—indeed when Bekenu, near Miri in Sarawak, was recaptured the Indonesian flag was

flying over the Government offices. On 15 December the Governor of West Kalimantan, a Dyak, was reported as saying that he fully supported the struggle of his brothers in North Kalimantan and that the Dyak people had never recognised the division of their land into two parts; he again attacked the division of Borneo by 'the Dutch and British white-skinned imperialists and colonialists' in a speech on 10 January, 1963. Some caution was displayed by Her Majesty's Government about publicising these indications of hostile activity by the Indonesians, but Malayan papers at least seem to have had no doubt that Sheikh Azahari had had Indonesian aid.

221.   On 12 December, 1962, in Parliament, the Tunku referred to 'jealousy and hatred in foreign lands' from parties trying to stop Malaysia. Dr. Subandrio replied by accusing Malaya of a persistently hostile attitude towards Indonesia and on 18 December the Malayan Government issued an announcement taking 'very strong exception' to his statements. On 19 December President Sukarno, in a broadcast, called upon the Indonesian people to support the Brunei rebellion; the Indonesian representative to the United Nations was at this time pressing for an early meeting of the Committee of Seventeen, now Twenty-four, to take up the issue. On 23 December the Tunku, in a speech to the UMNO Youth Convention, claimed that the Indonesian Government and political leaders wanted to destroy the Malaysia plan; in his New Year message however he concentrated his criticisms on the PKI, rather than the Indonesian Government.

222.   Lord Selkirk, in a letter to Mr. Macmillan of 20 December, 1962, [see 151] expressed the view that military reinforcements would almost certainly be needed. He indicated that he thought the Tunku's 'provocative remarks' unwise, but said that he had himself been 'pressing the Foreign Office to make the strongest protests before Sukarno starts down the slippery path—it may well be that it is too late now'. In Djakarta Sir Leslie Fry was also urging the need for a personal message to Dr. Subandrio from the Secretary of State, while the American Ambassador had already made strong representations. These warnings, however, failed to deter the Indonesians and, in a speech on 20 January, 1963, Dr. Subandrio announced that his country was adopting a policy of 'confrontation' towards Malaya.

223.   On 24 January, 1963 the Tunku told Sir Geofroy Tory that 'intelligence from his own sources', reinforced by British and American information, had convinced him that the Indonesians intended to start guerilla activity in the next few days unless deterred by British troop movements. This view was not at the time, or subsequently, supported by British intelligence assessments, but it elicited from the Commonwealth Secretary in London a personal message to Lord Selkirk which said in part that 'Since Tunku was right on last occasion about trouble in Brunei, I am sure you will agree that we should pay some heed to his latest warning even though it may not correspond entirely with our own intelligence assessment'. Precautionary measures were thereupon taken by the Commander in Chief Far East and a brigade of the Strategic Reserve in Britain was put on 72 hours alert.

224.   The Minister of Defence, Mr. Thorneycroft, in a statement on 28 January, 1963, said that none of these troops would leave Britain for the present and made no mention of Indonesia. On the same day, however, the Tunku told a Press conference that 2,000 additional British troops were being sent to the Far East and linked these precautions directly to strained Indonesian–Malayan relations. The effect was to raise the temperature in the area to the extent that at a Press conference on 29 January U

Thant expressed concern. On 30 January the Indonesian news agency, Antara, announced that 'the legation of the Unitary State of Kalimantan Utara today disclosed the members of the complete cabinet of the Revolutionary Government' and Antara bulletins on 5 and 8 February spoke of some 10,000 Dyaks being 'ready to conduct guerilla warfare' in northern Borneo.

225. Both the Sabah and Sarawak Alliances sent messages to President Sukarno in January 1963 asking him to refrain from intervening in Borneo. Some of the substance of the Sarawak Alliance letter was published by Antara on 8 February. When the United Nations Chef de Cabinet, Mr. C. V. Narasimhan, visited Djakarta the Indonesians complained to him about the liberty allowed by Malaya to Indonesian political refugees, about supposed Malayan designs on Sumatra and complicity in smuggling from Indonesia, and about tactless comments by the Tunku. In Kuala Lumpur Mr. Narasimhan counselled a 'ceasefire on speeches', a suggestion which was well in tune with opinion in the United States, Australia and New Zealand, as well as in Britain. By the middle of February therefore relations had deteriorated further. Sheikh Azahari had arrived in Djakarta, the Malayan Embassy had been left in charge of relatively junior staff and Dr. Subandrio had categorised Malaya under the Tunku as a hostile power, while Indonesian gunboats had begun to be provocatively active in the Straits of Malacca.

Malayan politics and the Tunku's attitude to Indonesia

226. The reasons for the Tunku's 'provocative' outbursts in December 1962, and his actions in first inducing and then exaggerating British military precautions in January 1963, were not only temperamental. He was anxious to rally the country in a way that would create patriotic fervour. The opposition had attacked the Government in December for its attitude to the Brunei revolt, while Enche Ahmad Boestamam, the leader of the Parti Ra'ayat in Malaya, was arrested in February for having engaged, with encouragement from Indonesia, in preparations for violent action. In view of the widespread sympathy amongst Malays for Indonesia the Tunku may have felt that he had over-riding internal reasons to identify President Sukarno and Dr. Subandrio as hostile, under Communist influence and envious of Malaya's prosperity.

American and Australian anxieties and quadripartite talks

227. The Tunku's remarks to this end, though successful in their immediate purpose, caused concern in the United States, Australia and New Zealand and, in quadripartite talks to discuss Indonesian intentions in Washington in February 1963, [see 160–162] these countries joined in asking the United Kingdom to urge restraint on him. This was done as soon as the talks had ended. All three countries were also anxious that merger should be clearly in accordance with the principle of self-determination and should be convincingly presented as such to the world and, especially, to the United Nations Committee of Twenty-Four, the members of which the Malayans were already vigorously and effectively lobbying. All three countries tended to favour a plebiscite in Borneo and the holding of tripartite talks between Indonesian, Filipino and Malayan representatives in order to dissipate misunderstanding.

228. The United Kingdom had no confidence in either proposal, but, in order to be sure of American, Australian and New Zealand diplomatic, and possibly even

military, support, had to appear flexible and accommodating. Objections to a plebiscite included problems of administration and timing and, above all, the belief that constantly renewed consultations might suggest to the people of Borneo that the British Government itself doubted the wisdom of proceeding with merger. It was nevertheless recognised in London that it might not be possible to resist pressure for a further consultation. On the related procedural question of Malaysian membership of the United Nations there was general agreement at the talks that the Malayan delegation should merely announce a change of name to Malaysia.

229.   The basic purpose of this first round of quadripartite talks was, on the British part, to persuade the United States and Australian Governments not to veer away from support of Malaysia in face of Indonesian objections. The Americans, for their part, wished to avoid a situation in which they might be asked to participate in the task of resisting guerilla operations in Borneo and to ensure that if the Indonesians resorted to heavy infiltration adequate British forces would engage them. Both British and American minimum objectives were achieved, though little more than that in the British case. The British emphasised their intention and capacity to reinforce the area sufficiently to cope with infiltration. The Americans declined to take part in any joint warning to the Indonesians or in police action against infiltration, but reaffirmed their support for Malaysia and insisted that if infiltration turned to overt aggression their attitude of reserve would no longer apply. Meanwhile the Committee of Twenty-Four showed little interest in taking up the issue with any urgency.

XVII. *Discussions with the Philippines*

Filipino policy

230.   Malayan–Filipino relations were little better, if less menacing, and this led to the Association of South-East Asia (ASA) conference due to be held in Manila in December 1962 being postponed, first to January 1963 and then to April, despite the good offices of the Thais. The concern expressed by the Filipinos in public was at the prospect of Malaysia being created without the consent of the people affected and they raised the issue in this form in the United Nations General Assembly. Whether this concern was real or not, Mr. Pilcher put forward the view on 20 November, 1962, that President Macapagal and Vice-President Pelaez were genuinely worried by the strategic implications of merger.

231.   But President Macapagal seems primarily at this time to have been interested in projecting a new 'Asian identity' for the Philippines in the eyes of other Asian countries and a dispute with Britain as a colonial power must in this context have appeared to offer advantages and little danger. He was also in effect reinsuring with the Indonesians in case the United States should withdraw from the defence of the area and was naturally encouraged in this by the Indonesians themselves. Mr. Pilcher had no doubt that if the Brunei revolt had been successful the President would at once have recognised the State as independent. Amongst politicians recorded by Mr. Pilcher at this time as being strongly in favour of Sheikh Azahari was Mr. Marcos, then leader of the Liberal Party in the Senate.

Anglo–Filipino talks in London, January 1963

232.   Nevertheless, in the hope of persuading the Philippine Government of the strategic dangers inherent in any delay to the Grand Design and of providing them

with a face-saving way of disengaging from the active promotion of their claim, Her Majesty's Government invited a Filipino delegation headed by the Vice-President to visit London in January 1963 'for talks on problems of mutual interest affecting the security and stability of South-East Asia'. President Macapagal, however, in his State of the Nation speech on 28 January, just as the talks opened, reiterated the claim in stronger terms than before and went on to assert that Malaysia 'is not in accordance with the principle of self-determination, . . . but appears to be a continuation of colonialism'. This both destroyed the point of the London talks so far as the British Government was concerned and in Malayan eyes frustrated plans they had in train to invite President Macapagal to pay a State Visit to Malaya and for the Tunku to visit Manila.

233.   In London no real progress was made; it was however agreed to exchange documents in the case, and in particular the agreements under which Esmail Kiram and other heirs of the Sultanate of Sulu were claimed to have transferred sovereignty to the Philippine Government during 1962. A report in the *Manila Times* of 15 December, 1962, that Esmail Kiram had conferred powers of government on Sheikh Azahari suggested some confusion about the transfer. The Philippine Government in any case subsequently proved unwilling to produce these documents. This in turn enabled the British to avoid any action which might promote the wish of the Philippines, put forward at the talks and formally proposed in a note dated 21 August, 1963, to submit their claim to the International Court.

British and Malayan positions and the International Court

234.   Since the United Kingdom had, unlike Malaya, accepted the compulsory jurisdiction of the International Court, subject to certain reservations, it would have been possible for the Philippine Government to refer the issue unilaterally to the Court. It was in consequence the British purpose during the summer of 1963 to avoid an application by the Philippines for interim measures by the Court so long as the administration of North Borneo still remained in British hands. The reply of 9 September, 1963, to the Philippine note therefore, while appearing to take this seriously, did no more than to ask for clarification of Filipino intentions and to express a continued willingness to exchange documents.

235.   The Malayan Government agreed in August 1963 that the British Government should play for time until 16 September, 1963, when sovereignty would be transferred and any claim would lie against Malaysia. The Malayans had been given the documents on which the arguments in the case were based, but not the full British assessment of the strengths and weaknesses of the case. There was some discussion after 16 September between the Foreign Office, the Commonwealth Relations Office and the High Commission in Kuala Lumpur as to what the Malayans should be told. The Commonwealth Relations Office and the High Commission wished to give them a complete picture, but the view of the Foreign Office Legal Advisers that this was inadvisable, because inadequate Malayan security and the consequent probability of a leak to the Filipinos might prejudice the case, prevailed. As a result a bowdlerised version of the Research Department paper by Professor Pearn on the Sulu claims was prepared for the Malaysians.

236.   Meanwhile, on the basis of what they had been told, and no doubt their own study of the documents, the Malayans had modified their position on the claim and the basis of British sovereignty. They had at first said that they would only take the

territories on a 'clean slate' and had accepted the simple view that the 1878 Sulu document was a lease in perpetuity which clearly involved transfer of sovereignty to the British. In an *aide-memoire* of 3 October, 1962, to the Philippine Government however they justified their belief that the United Kingdom was entitled to transfer sovereignty by reference to effective British possession over a long period and to the wishes of the inhabitants, rather than to the cession of sovereignty in the 19th century. This was a position which accorded with the British official line on the issue and also with the published views of a number of Nacionalista opposition leaders in the Philippines, notably the former Foreign Secretary, Felixberto Serrano, and the Chairman of the Senate Foreign Affairs Committee, Senator Sumulong. It did, however, make it easier for President Macapagal to press for a plebiscite in North Borneo.

XVIII. *Tripartite relations, February 1963–June 1963*

Preliminary discussions, February–March 1963

237.   Indonesian pressure slackened slightly towards the end of February 1963. On 22 February Dr. Subandrio's reply to the Foreign Secretary's personal message sent in December was delivered in London. It was designed to suggest that Indonesia had no dispute with the United Kingdom, but only with the Tunku. The Commonwealth Relations Office assessment of the Indonesian Government's purpose at this stage was that they hoped to frighten the Tunku out of the Malaysia project.

238.   Early in March 1963 Tun Razak, Dr. Subandrio, Sir Garfield Barwick, the Australian External Affairs Minister, and Mr. Peter Thomas, the British Parliamentary Under-Secretary of State at the Foreign Office, were all in Manila for an ECAFE conference. The Malayans intended that Tun Razak's visit should pave the way for a rapprochement between the Tunku and President Macapagal at the ASA Foreign Ministers' Conference, which was now to be held on 2 April and which the Tunku had agreed to attend. Mr. Thomas had informal talks on the Philippine claim to North Borneo, while Sir Garfield Barwick renewed Australian efforts with Dr. Subandrio to promote a *détente* between Indonesia and Malaya in the context of a proposal by President Macapagal on 10 March for a tripartite summit meeting between the heads of government of these two countries and the Philippines. Dr. Subandrio did not attempt to conceal that his purpose was to concert action with the Philippines to prevent the formation of Malaysia; he did not meet Tun Razak.

239.   On 13 March, 1963, at a Press conference in Manila, Dr. Subandrio said that Indonesia would relax its opposition to Malaysia if relations between Malaya and Indonesia could be clarified and it could be shown that Malaysia would not be used to subvert Indonesia. The Tunku at once welcomed this statement and on 14 March the Malayan Government made known its agreement to the appointment of a new Indonesian Ambassador in Kuala Lumpur, Lieutenant-General G. P. H. Djatikusumo, and that the Malayan Ambassador would return to Djakarta. On 26 March, following discussions in Manila between Mr. Salvador P. Lopez, the Philippines Under-Secretary of State for Foreign Affairs, and Dr. Suwito Kusumowidagdo, the Indonesian First Deputy Foreign Minister, the Malayan Ambassador was called in for informal talks. The Malayan Government showed some caution about this approach—they were anxious that if formal tripartite talks should take place at Ministerial level they should be well prepared and should not delay the formation of Malaysia.

240. There was an exchange of incivilities between the Tunku and Dr. Subandrio at the end of March 1963 and statements which each country affected to regard as hostile. During March nevertheless the Indonesians welcomed reports of Malaya's willingness to take part in a tripartite meeting in Manila and there was some reduction in tension. The Indonesian interest in a tripartite meeting was partly no doubt that it provided a means of deciding the future of the area without the participation of outside Powers. This and the elimination of British and American bases seemed to be a major long-term objective of Indonesian policy at this time. Such a meeting and the negotiations leading up to it might also be used to delay or even prevent the formation of Malaysia.

Increased Indonesian pressure and the first armed action, April 1963

241. General Djatikusumo presented his credentials as Indonesian Ambassador to Malaya on 15 April, 1963. When formally appointing him, on 11 April, President Sukarno had used the occasion to reaffirm his Government's continued opposition to the establishment of Malaysia. By the end of May there were reports that the new Ambassador was engaged in trying to stir up Malay feeling against the Chinese community in Malaya.

242. On 12 April, 1963, a force of uniformed men, some of whom were clearly Indonesian Army personnel, made an attack on the police station at Tebedu, in Sarawak, 3 miles from the border—a policeman was killed, two others were wounded and some arms were removed from the post. On 23 April a Royal Marine position at Gumbang was attacked and Tebedu was fired on again on 27 April. Over 1,000 men of the Royal Marine Commandos and the Green Jackets had returned from Brunei on 1 April, but after the first Tebedu raid the flow of units from Borneo was reversed. Two other minor incursions into Sarawak were also reported in April. These incursions were mostly by groups of Indonesian 'volunteer' and TNKU guerillas stiffened or led by Indonesian Army officers and men and with a few CCO elements. A curfew was therefore imposed on areas in the First and Second Divisions of Sarawak within three hours walking distance of the frontier and in these Divisions and in the Lower Rejang area all firearms and ammunition in the hands of 'non-Natives', that is mainly Chinese, were called in. Steps were also taken to recruit a body of Volunteer Border Scouts to support the regular police and military and to supply border villages with shotgun ammunition for self-defence.

243. Meanwhile in North Borneo the Indonesian Consulate appeared to be engaged in trying to centralise the local Indonesian Associations and to develop them into an intelligence network. Its staff were also thought to be encouraging local people to go to Indonesia for training, drawing up plans for sabotage and organising petitions against Malaysia. The Indonesian Government was therefore asked in May to withdraw Major Moenardjo, the Additional Consul, and Bambang Sumali, the Publicity Officer, who had been conducting these activities. They nevertheless remained. On 19 July, 1963, they were therefore declared *personae non gratae* and left on 26 July. On 23 July 22 Indonesians were arrested in North Borneo and on 6 August the Indonesian Associations in Sandakan and Jesselton were declared illegal.

The wooing of international opinion

244. Efforts were also made in the spring and summer to bring the case against the formation of Malaysia into a wider arena and to appeal to anti-colonialist

sentiment. In general however Indonesia and the Philippines were surprisingly inactive and ineffectual in this endeavour. A number of petitions for and against the Malaysia concept were outstanding before the United Nations Committee of Twenty-four in March 1963—its predecessor, the Committee of Seventeen, had heard Mr. Lee Kuan Yew in support of the concept in September 1962. A petition, dated 28 March, 1963, calling on the General Assembly to condemn the idea of Malaysia and requesting an oral hearing as a representative of Sheikh Azahari, was sent to the United Nations Secretariat from Djakarta by Mr. Achmad Fadillah. The United Kingdom Mission to the United Nations proposed to play this down and it was decided to suggest to the Indians and Australians, who were members of the Petitions Sub-Committee, that they should indicate that they could not recognise the claim which Mr. Fadillah made to be representing a government in exile, but would raise no objection to the request being granted in a personal capacity.

245.   On 17 April, 1963, the Sub-Committee agreed to allow a hearing in place of that they had in September 1962 granted for Sheikh Azahari. The Committee of Twenty-four approved this on 18 April, but deleted from the report of the Sub-Committee a description of Mr. Fadillah's status as 'Minister of State of the Government of Kalimantan Utara'. Meanwhile a request from SUPP to be granted a hearing had already been accepted. The Committee had however a number of items on its agenda which aroused much more interest than the merger of the Borneo Territories into Malaysia. The Malayans, and especially Mr. Radhakrishna Ramani, who had been newly added to the delegation for this purpose, were effective in putting the case for Malaysia in the United Nations and Malayan and Singapore Ministers actively explained the project in the United States, Egypt and elsewhere.

246.   The 'standing and reputation' of the Malayans in the United Nations at this time was described by the United Kingdom Mission as 'far superior to that of the Indonesians'. Pakistan, after at first welcoming the proposals for merger, had, with an eye to relations with Indonesia, taken up a non-committal attitude, but countries such as India and Cambodia had come out in favour of Malaysia and the Indonesians were able to attract almost no positive support. A broadcast by Mr. Narasimhan, U Thant's Chef de Cabinet, over Radio Sabah on 22 April, 1963, was regarded as giving valuable support to the British and Malayan case. The issue was due to be discussed in June in the Committee, but was then postponed in view of the tripartite Foreign Ministers' conference and was not reviewed. Mr. Narasimhan told the United Kingdom Mission on 14 September that the bureau of the Committee had firmly rebuffed an attempt by Indonesia and the Philippines to have the matter taken up again.

Preparatory discussions, Manila, April 1963
247.   The Tunku arrived in Manila on 1 April, 1963, for the ASA meeting and subsequently had talks with President Macapagal which were reported to be cordial. The Indonesians however delayed their arrival for the tripartite talks at official level to discuss an agenda and procedure for a Foreign Ministers' meeting and these did not start until 9 April. The delegations were headed by Enche Ghazali, Mr. Lopez and Dr. Suwito. It was agreed on 16 April that a Foreign Ministers' meeting should be held in Manila in May and that there should be a prior exchange of explanatory memoranda on questions to be discussed at the meeting. It was also decided, in principle, that a meeting of Heads of Government should be held at a later date.

248.   Enche Ghazali visited Manila again on 29 April, 1963, in order to persuade the Filipinos that his Government was anxious that the Ministerial tripartite talks should be held in Manila and that the Indonesians hoped to provoke the Malayans into refusing to attend. By this time, for internal as well as external reasons, the Malayan Government was anxious to seem conciliatory and still hoped to detach the Filipinos from the Indonesians. In the second half of April 1963 therefore the Tunku's responses to hostile Indonesian statements were distinctly muted.

249.   During the spring and summer of 1963 Indonesian pressure was reduced before and during tripartite talks and the United Nations 'ascertainment' process, and in each case resumed immediately afterwards. In May there was only one armed attack, but a spate of hostile statements by Indonesians, notably President Sukarno himself, to which on the whole the Malayans did not react publicly, and by 'Lieutenant-General' Abang Zulkifli, the commander of the TNKU, some of whose statements however gave the impression of being designed to stir up Indonesian support even though ostensibly directed to urging his own men on. There was also a substantial increase in the number of young Chinese crossing into Indonesian Borneo. This flow was checked in June and, especially during the tripartite Foreign Ministers' Meeting in Manila from 7–11 June, the general pressure was reduced, though incursions did not cease.

Proposals for popular consultation in Borneo

250.   During the spring of 1963 U Thant's Chef de Cabinet, Mr. Narasimhan, had been active in trying to ease tension. In April he visited Malaya, Singapore, the Borneo Territories, Indonesia and the Philippines. In public he emphasised the degree of support for Malaysia in the Borneo Territories. In private he seems to have tried to deflate Malayan optimism and to promote the idea of some form of popular consultation in the Borneo Territories as a means of enabling the Indonesians and Filipinos, if they wished, to retire gracefully from the positions they had taken up; these positions were based publicly on the right of the people of the Territories to self-determination. In the course of this round of visits Mr. Narasimhan was unfavourably impressed by the conduct and intentions of President Sukarno and Dr. Subandrio and by July the Indonesians were aware of this.

251.   Mr. Narasimhan's favourite version of these consultation proposals seems to have been that of a plebiscite to be held some time after the establishment of Malaysia on the lines of that agreed for West Irian, although this idea does not seem to have commended itself to U Thant. Mr. Narasimhan did not however encourage a suggestion by Mr. Macapagal in April 1963 that the United Nations should take over the administration of the Borneo Territorities as they had, briefly, in New Guinea. Another suggestion, put forward by Mr. Lopez to Mr. Hilsman of the United States State Department, was that the Philippines should administer North Borneo until a plebiscite could be held. The Tunku had already, in October 1962, appeared to endorse a Philippine proposal that a referendum should be held in North Borneo to decide its future. This proposal was taken up again by President Macapagal in a statement, on 22 May, 1963, that 'we will accept the will of the people concerned' if expressed in a 'plebiscite, preferably supervised by the United Nations.'

The Maphilindo proposal

252.   On 27 July, 1962, President Macapagal had also suggested a confederation of the Philippines with Malaya, Singapore and the individual Borneo Territories. This proposal was politely received in Malaya and Indonesia. In the Anglo–Philippine talks in London in January 1963 Mr. Lopez urged it as an alternative to Malaysia and on 28 February at a Press conference Mr. Macapagal raised the suggestion again in the form of a loose grouping, which should include the Borneo Territories as individual States, thereby preventing their federation in Malaysia; he also proposed the addition of Indonesia to the original group of Territories.

The Tokyo meeting

253.   The Foreign Ministers' Meeting, which had originally been arranged for 24 May, 1963, in Manila, was postponed at the request of the Indonesians. On 25 May Dr. Subandrio told the Malayan Ambassador to Japan that it was desirable for Indonesia and Malaya to smooth out their differences and handed him a note for the Tunku signed by Dr. Sukarno. This suggested a personal meeting in Tokyo where Dr. Sukarno and Dr. Subandrio were to be until 2 June. The Tunku informed the Malayan Lower House of this approach on 28 May and left on 30 May for the meeting. The Tunku's natural optimism was greatly strengthened by this meeting, from which he concluded that the Indonesians had called off confrontation without any concession by Malaya.

The foreign ministers' meeting, 7–11 June, 1963

254.   This optimism was further strengthened by a tactical softening of the attitude of the Indonesians at the Foreign Ministers' Meeting which was held in Manila from 7–11 June, 1963, with Tun Razak representing the Tunku. The recommendations of this meeting were designed to be presented to a meeting of Heads of Government to be held by the end of July 1963. They included agreement to the formation of Malaysia on 31 August in return for what the Malayans regarded as merely face-saving concessions. Indonesia and the Philippines, in the context of the principle of self-determination, 'stated that they would welcome the formation of Malaysia provided the support of the people of the Borneo Territories is ascertained by an independent and impartial authority, the Secretary-General of the United Nations or his representative'. The Malayans undertook to approach the Governments of the United Kingdom and the Borneo Territories to enable this to be done. The Tunku, in a letter drawing U Thant's attention to this recommendation, made it clear that any move to send an assessor to the Territories would have to carry the consent of the Government of the United Kingdom and of the local Administrations and had yet to be confirmed by the Heads of Government.

255.   The three Ministers also 'supported President Macapagal's plan envisaging the grouping of the three nations of Malay origin working together in closest harmony but without surrendering any portion of their sovereignty', and agreed to establish 'machinery for frequent and regular consultations'. In particular each country was to set up a 'National Secretariat'. At this meeting the proposed grouping acquired the name of 'Mapilindo', which was soon changed to 'Maphilindo'. Its chief function subsequently was to enable the Indonesians to claim that Malayan actions contravened 'the spirit of Maphilindo' which was promoted as a valuable non-colonialist concept despite its lack of content.

256.   The Filipinos maintained their right to pursue their claim to North Borneo and it was agreed 'that the inclusion of North Borneo in the Federation of Malaysia would not prejudice either the claim or any right thereunder'. Moreover 'the three countries agreed to exert their best endeavours to bring the claim to a just and expeditious solution by peaceful means, such as negotiation, conciliation, arbitration, or judicial settlement'. From the British point of view this had at the time the advantage that it reduced any sense of urgency the Filipinos might have had about taking their claim to the International Court while the United Kingdom was still responsible for the territory. A principal, though unofficial, promoter both of the Kiram claim and of Sheikh Azahari's revolt, Mr. Nicasio Osmena, son of a former President of the Philippines, died on 21 June, 1963, and this too may have helped to reduce the Filipino sense of urgency.

XIX. *The Tripartite heads of government meeting and ascertainment*

The continuation of confrontation, June–July 1963

257.   It became clear soon after the tripartite Foreign Ministers' Meeting in Manila in June 1963 that the Indonesians did not feel themselves committed to accept anything less than a referendum in Borneo. Dr. Subandrio was soothing, but the Defence Minister, General Nasution, made plain his disapproval. He was quoted in *Merdeka* of 13 June as saying that 'There have been various interpretations given to the Foreign Ministers' Meeting . . ., but to us this is a matter of principle. We oppose Malaysia because it is neo-colonialism'; that confrontation would continue; and that 'We will assist our brothers in North Borneo to attain their right to self-determination.' The Communist Party (PKI) and its Chairman, Mr. Aidit, went further and rejected both Maphilindo and ascertainment; even a referendum was rejected unless held as well in Malaya and Singapore and after the withdrawal of British troops and the release of detainees.

258.   On 15 June, 1963, the TNKU leader, 'General' Zulkifli, spoke of launching guerilla operations in preparation for a general offensive and late in June and early in July there were incursions into Sarawak in which civilians were killed. On 10 July, as a reaction to the signing of the Malaysia Agreement, President Sukarno reaffirmed the policy of confrontation and on 16 July the Indonesian Government announced the formation of a new naval command to 'confront' Malaysia. The prospects for a summit meeting did not therefore appear encouraging. The Tunku announced on 6 July that he had told Presidents Sukarno and Macapagal that he would agree to a meeting at Manila around 30 July and on 10 July Mr. Macapagal announced that it would be held from 30 July to 2 August, but it remained uncertain until the last moment whether Dr. Sukarno would even attend.

The tripartite summit meeting, Manila, 30 July–5 August, 1963

259.   The Tunku and the two Presidents met in Manila from 30 July to 5 August, 1963. The discussions were mainly conducted by the deputies, Enche Ghazali and Senator Khaw Kai Boh, Dr. Subandrio and Dr. Suwito, and Mr. Lopez and Dr. Pelaez. Most of the heat was generated by Mr. Lopez, who, as at the Foreign Ministers' meeting, seems to have appeared much more extreme than the Indonesians. The talks were also accompanied by some anxious back seat driving—by the United Kingdom to stiffen the Tunku and by the United States and, to a much lesser degree,

Australia to urge flexibility and a willingness to accept a brief postponement of Malaysia Day in order 'to give Sukarno a fig leaf' or 'face saver'. The British position was tempered by the view, expressed by Lord Home to the Prime Minister on 4 August, [see 205] that a small postponement might be acceptable if thereby full American support could be obtained afterwards and the Tunku could be prevented from laying the blame on the United Kingdom if there was failure to agree at Manila and subsequent trouble with Indonesia. The Tunku himself was willing to accept either a form of ascertainment which took account of the results of previous elections and missions, in which case he would not object to a brief postponement of merger until the Secretary-General had completed his enquiries, or a plebiscite some years after Malaysia had come into being on the lines of that proposed for West. Irian.

260.   U Thant was also represented in Manila and was consulted on the length of time it would take, if the conference thought this desirable, to ascertain the wishes of the people of North Borneo and Sarawak 'through informed and democratic processes, impartially conducted and based on universal adult suffrage', in accordance with Principle IX of the Annex to United Nations General Assembly Resolution 1541 (XV) and without taking account of the results of previous elections or fact-finding missions. His reply seems to have been that this would require four months, US$400,000 and United Kingdom approval, which was known to be unlikely to be forthcoming, or two months, if an immediate start could be made with British consent and the General Assembly could give approval after preparatory work had been begun. U Thant subsequently pointed out, in response to a request for advice on a short method of ascertainment more in line with the recommendations of the Foreign Ministers' meeting, that the newly-elected representatives in North Borneo and Sarawak appeared to fulfil the requirements of Resolution 1541 (XV).

261.   In the event the Tunku succeeded in excluding mention of a plebiscite or of delay as such. It was agreed that ascertainment should take into consideration the recent elections in Borneo, but should verify whether Malaysia had been a major issue, whether the elections had been free and what the numbers and wishes were of those unable to vote for any reason: ascertainment was moreover to take place before the establishment of Malaysia. The Tunku also undertook to try to persuade the United Kingdom to admit observers of the process of ascertainment from Indonesia, the Philippines and Malaya—this was a new point on which the Indonesians had begun to insist.

262.   The Tunku accepted a clause in the joint statement by which the participants bound themselves to 'abstain from the use of arrangements of collective defence to serve the particular interests of any of the big powers'. He subsequently pointed out publicly that the Anglo–Malayan Defence Agreement was a 'mutual' and not a 'collective' agreement and would not therefore be affected, though SEATO would be to some extent. This clause was clearly directed at foreign bases and the State Department believed that it was inserted at the suggestion of the Philippines and directed more at bringing pressure on the United States than on the United Kingdom. Dr. Subandrio however was reported as having insisted on 3 August, 1963, that Malaya should agree that the base in Malaysia 'cannot be used in the preservation of peace in South-East Asia without the express permission of the Indonesian and Philippine Governments.' Moreover the statement insisted 'that the responsibility for the preservation of the national independence of the three countries and of the peace and security in their region lies primarily in the hands of

the Governments and the peoples of the countries concerned' and that 'foreign bases—temporary in nature—should not be allowed to be used directly or indirectly to subvert the national independence of any of the three countries'. This was read in London as enshrining the Indonesian determination to be a major South-East Asian Power in her own right, entitled to be consulted and accommodated on any defence arrangements in the area.

263. The Tunku himself regarded the meeting as a success, since he had managed to hold the Indonesians to the main lines of the Foreign Ministers' agreement, which was formally approved. He does not seem to have been under the illusion that there was any sign that confrontation would be called off. In London also there was some relief that President Sukarno had abandoned insistence on a plebiscite and had for the moment agreed, on paper at least, to accept ascertainment in some form not clearly stated, but taking previous elections into account. But Mr. Lee, who had of course an interest in presenting the Tunku as weak and irresolute, Mr. Gilchrist in Djakarta, the BBC, and Mr. Hilsman of the State Department all took the view that the meeting had been an Indonesian triumph. In the case of Mr. Hilsman this had, from the British point of view, the advantage that it made him subsequently concerned to propose firmness in dealing with such issues arising as the manner of confirmation of ascentainment by observers.

264. In addition to these central subjects the meeting agreed to establish national secretariats for the Maphilindo project, but no attempt was made to breathe real life into this concept. Once again it was agreed that the inclusion of North Borneo into Malaysia did not prejudice the Filipino claim or any right under it. A 'Manila Declaration' was issued from the meeting over the signatures of the three Heads of Government as well as the joint statement. This declaration was clearly Indonesian in inspiration and spoke of its signatories' determination 'to put an end to the exploitation of man by man or of one nation by another', and to 'combine their efforts in the common struggle against colonialism and imperialism' in their capacity 'as new emerging forces in the region'.

The British attitude to ascertainment

265. The initial British reaction to proposals for ascertainment was negative. A plebiscite in Borneo before merger or a transitional United Nations Administration had been firmly rejected in the spring of 1963, and Lord Home told Mr. Narasimhan in May that, although no formal objection could be raised to a plebiscite after Malaysia had come into being and Britain had ceased to be responsible for the territories, this was not a course which his Government could recommend to the Tunku. Mr. Sandys, in a conversation with the Malayan High Commissioner on 24 June, had taken an unfavourable view of the Manila proposal for ascertainment, though he did not reject the idea out of hand. The results of the Sarawak elections however made a form of ascertainment which took account of the elections in Sarawak and North Borneo much less unattractive to the Colonial Office. By August ascertainment was seen in London as a means of making it difficult for Indonesia and the Philippines to withhold formal acquiescence in the creation of Malaysia except by clearly accepting responsibility for a break. It was not supposed that ascertainment would persuade the Indonesians to abandon confrontation, but it was expected to consolidate American and Australian support for Malaysia and to diminish Indonesian international support by making it clear that they were the aggressors.

266.   The United Kingdom was not willing to invite ascertainment itself, but the Embassies in Manila and Djakarta were instructed on 12 July, 1963, to say that 'we foresee no objection to Mr. Narasimhan paying a return visit to North Borneo and Sarawak to complete his fact-finding mission'. After the Summit meeting, on 8 August, U Thant was informed that the United Kingdom would co-operate in such measures as he thought necessary to carry out ascertainment, on the assumptions that he could complete this task in time to allow Malaysia to be established on 31 August and that the report would not be subject to confirmation by the United Nations or by the Government of Malaya, Indonesia and the Philippines. The British Government however remained hostile to any proposal for observers. Nor did it wish the report of the Secretary-General's mission to be addressed to it—this was because it did not want to be committed to recognising the validity of the report's findings, although this was not said to the Secretary-General.

267.   U Thant's response on 8 August, 1963, to this message was that he had already made it clear that he could not complete the task before 9 September, though he hoped to finish by 14 September. In order to achieve this he proposed to enlarge his teams and to divide them between Sarawak and North Borneo. His report would not be subject to confirmation by the Manila Powers and he intended merely to inform the General Assembly of the action he had taken. He was not willing to refuse to accept observers. He would however not attach the observers to the assessment teams or permit them any advisory functions—he made this clear to the Malayan, Indonesian and Filipino Foreign Ministers on the same day—and the terms on which they would be allowed to operate in North Borneo and Sarawak would be entirely a matter for the local Governments. The United Kingdom was later persuaded by Mr. Harriman that it would be more satisfactory if U Thant were to lay down the regulations for conduct by the observers. When the observers eventually arrived in Borneo the mission itself informed them in clear terms of the limitations on their functions.

268.   On 9 August, 1963, Sir Geofroy Tory saw the Tunku and told him that before considering any question of postponement of Malaysia Day the British Government must have 'an absolutely firm undertaking' that Malaya would go ahead with merger on whatever later date should be agreed between the signatories and in any event by the end of September 1963 [see 213]. The Tunku gave this undertaking on the understanding that the United Kingdom would 'stand by the Federation Government whatever the consequences'. On the same day U Thant was told that in view of the explanations he had given he could carry out his investigation on the basis he proposed—the formal reply to the request for facilities for ascertainment was made to the Malayan Government from which the formal request had come. U Thant was also told that Her Majesty's Government wished, in consultation with the other signatories of the Malaysia Agreement, to fix a new date for merger, in order to avoid the risks involved in leaving the peoples of the territories in a state of suspense.

The issue of observers

269.   In their message of 9 August, 1963, to U Thant the British Government also agreed to the despatch of one Malayan, one Indonesian and one Filipino observer for each of the two United Nations teams; they subsequently pointed out that this was the highest number permissible if observers were not to outnumber the United Nations teams and parity was to be maintained amongst the Manila countries. The

British objection to observers was based on the conviction that the purpose of the Indonesians would be to create trouble and apprehension in Borneo, to weaken British standing in the area, and to conduct subversive and espionage activities. On 13 August, 1963, the Indonesians were informed of this British decision by the Malayans. On the same day the Indonesian Government applied to the British Embassy in Djakarta for four visas for Borneo and indicated that an application for visas for a further 15 officials was on its way. They informed the Malayan Government that they wished to send a team of not less than 30. The Filipinos were somewhat more modest in their requests. Both Governments were told that they could only be permitted one observer for each territory.

270.   During the discussions which ensued the British Government agreed to allow two observers from each country in each territory, having been told by U Thant that the two United Nations teams might both often operate in two parts; British observers would also now be attached to the United Nations teams. This concession did not satisfy the Indonesians. On 20 August, 1963, they told U Thant that they would not co-operate unless allowed five observers for Sarawak and four for North Borneo, or, in effect, parity with the United Nations teams. The Philippines supported this demand—throughout this wrangling the Filipinos, with it was suggested some embarrassment, tried to keep in step with the Indonesians. U Thant then suggested that the United Kingdom might permit each country to send, in addition to four observers, four assistants of 'junior executive or clerical/stenographic grade'. He subsequently deferred formal commencement of the ascertainment process, although the teams were already in Borneo, having told a British representative that if the United Kingdom could accept his proposal for assistants he would tell the Indonesians and Filipinos that he would proceed with the investigation whether they accepted this compromise or not—this he subsequently did.

271.   On this understanding the United Kingdom agreed, on 21 August, 1963, to permit four assistants 'of a clerical grade' for each country. There was some discussion with U Thant as to how these assistants should be described, but agreement that he would leave the Indonesians in no doubt that they must be of genuinely clerical status. This was also made plain in a British statement issued on 23 August which was designed to mollify political opinion in the Borneo Territories, where Mr. Donald Stephens was threatening to resign over concessions made on the observer issue. The Philippines accepted the compromise on 23 August and on 24 August the Secretary-General issued instructions for ascertainment to proceed.

272.   The Indonesians accepted the compromise, but then put forward as assistants men some of whom were known to be intelligence officers and tried to insist on flying their teams into Sarawak and North Borneo themselves; the Philippines also asked for, and were refused, clearance for air force planes to fly their observers to North Borneo and Sarawak. Both U Thant and the United States pressed the United Kingdom to be flexible on membership of these observer teams, but neither supported demands for the right to fly in in the observer countries' own military aircraft. It was not until 29 August, 1963, that Dr. Subandrio proposed what were thought to be acceptable names for the Indonesian assistants—though two of them were subsequently reported to be military officers from Indonesian Borneo. On 31 August agreement was reached, the Philippine Government having also proposed assistants who appeared to be of genuinely clerical grade—the assistants originally

proposed by the Filipinos included two full members of the Philippines Commission on Elections. The Indonesian teams, which included at least two intelligence officers as observers, finally arrived in Singapore to be flown on in British aircraft on 1 September, by which time ascertainment was nearing completion. The Indonesian purpose in these manoeuvres was evidently to put Britain into the position of appearing to haggle childishly over trivialities, to delay ascertainment and to cast doubt on its validity—in this they had some success.

Ascertainment, August–September 1963

273.　It had originally been supposed that ascertainment would be carried out by Mr. Narasimhan. All the parties had indeed supported this in June 1963, but by the middle of July the Indonesians and Filipinos had come to doubt whether Mr. Narasimhan would produce a report hostile to Malaysia and had informed U Thant that he would be unacceptable. The task was therefore given to Mr. Lawrence Michelmore, the American Deputy Director of the United Nations Office of Personnel, assisted by Czech, Argentinian, Ceylonese, Ghanaian, Pakistani, Japanese, Jordanian and Brazilian members of the Secretariat. The mission arrived in Kuching on 16 August, while the team for North Borneo reached Jesselton on 19 August. In announcing the appointment of the Mission on 12 August U Thant stated that he hoped 'that the Mission will be able to complete its work in approximately four weeks'. Both teams began formal hearings on 26 August and completed them on 4 September.

274.　The Sarawak United People's Party had announced on 22 August, 1963, that it would boycott the hearings, but, in Sibu, Miri and, to a lesser extent, Kuching, SUPP members organised violent, although relatively small, demonstrations to greet the United Nations Sarawak team. These demonstrations were reported to have affected the Mission's assessment of SUPP adversely. Apart from this reaction by the Left wing of SUPP, the evidence given in Sarawak was generally in favour of Malaysia. In North Borneo the teams were everywhere met with peaceful demonstrations in favour of Malaysia and the great preponderance of the evidence given favoured merger.

275.　In general the report and U Thant's assessment of it, which were published on 14 September, 1963, were highly favourable to Malaysia. Regret was expressed that a new date for merger had been fixed before the Secretary-General had reached and made known his conclusions and that facilities for observers had not been granted more promptly. Nevertheless the Secretary-General concluded that Malaysia was a major issue at the elections in Sarawak and North Borneo; that the electoral registers had been properly compiled; that the elections had been freely and impartially conducted; that votes were properly polled and counted; that the votes of those detained or absent, even if all had been hostile to Malaysia, would have had no significant effect on the result; that a majority in both territories understood and were in favour of Malaysia; that the procedures fully met the requirements of United Nations General Assembly Resolution 1541 (XV); and finally that the Mission itself had heard a cross-section of opinion, had had adequate time for its task and had been fully able to carry out its terms of reference. There was, in U Thant's view, 'no doubt about the wishes of a sizeable majority of the peoples of these territories to join in the Federation of Malaysia' [see 225].

276.　The Philippines and Indonesia had before the event indicated that they would be bound not by the Mission's findings, but by those of their own observers.

The leader of the Indonesian observers, Brigadier-General Abdul Rachman, passing through Singapore on his way home on 4 September, 1963, and later in Djakarta, said that he thought the enquiry fairly conducted, but the time allowed too short. The report of the Philippine observer team accepted that the hearings in Sarawak had been conducted 'fairly and impartially' but insisted that the Mission allowed insufficient time to complete its enquiry. Of North Borneo the Filipinos complained that the British colonial administration was so efficient and helpful that the United Nations team 'became captive' in their hands on a 'virtual guided tour'. The Indonesian observers also complained of the 'highly efficient colonial machinery' in North Borneo.

277.   Indonesia and the Philippines both subsequently concentrated their criticism on the length of the ascertainment process and the failure to adopt a 'fresh approach' and in particular to get away from the results of 'the existing colonial electoral system'. The Indonesians also claimed that the United Nations team had been too small to do a thorough job and cast doubts on Mr. Michelmore's impartiality. Dr. Subandrio said on 6 September that he did not believe that the United Nations Mission could have accomplished their task in accordance with the basis established at Manila and by the beginning of October Dr. Sukarno was talking of the need for a new and 'genuine' United Nations investigation. At the same time the Indonesians began to develop their attack on the United Nations itself.

F. *The establishment of Malaysia and its aftermath*

XX. *International reactions to the establishment of Malaysia*

The new date for merger, 16 September, 1963

278.   The proposed date for the establishment of Malaysia had, since 1 August, 1962, been 31 August, 1963. 31 August had also been written into Article II of the Malaysia Agreement, although in preparing the British and Malayan Acts care had been taken to make it possible to postpone Malaysia Day without the need for amending legislation. In the Borneo Territories and in Singapore there was reluctance to accept any postponement of this date and an increasing hostility to ascertainment and to the proposals for Indonesian and Filipino observers. On 22 August, 1963, Mr. Donald Stephens and Mr. Ningkan flew to Kuala Lumpur with the declared intention of insisting that 31 August should remain Malaysia Day. Mr. Lee Kuan Yew encouraged them and himself refused to accept the postponement, which he claimed released Singapore from its obligations under the Malaysia Agreement, until he had secured further concessions from Malaya.

279.   The Tunku's difficulty was that it was essential, if the Manila Agreement should break down, to be able to show conclusively that the blame lay with the Indonesians and that Malaya had been the reasonable party in the dispute. The time available for effective ascertainment was too short for this to be completed in August and he had therefore to accept some delay. On 15 August, 1963, U Thant informed the three Manila Powers that he hoped to complete ascertainment by 14 September. The British were anxious not to delay the formal establishment of Malaysia beyond 17 September for fear that once the representatives of the Afro–Asian States had come together for the United Nations General Assembly Indonesian opportunities for mischief would be multiplied.

280. The State Department was urging at the end of the Manila Heads of Government Conference that, although Malaysia must go ahead on a set date whatever the results of ascertainment, the United Kingdom should not say so publicly when consenting to the Secretary-General's role. This was accepted in London, but the Foreign Office told the United States Embassy that once a new date had been agreed upon this could not possibly be suppressed, though it would not be necessary to indicate what would happen if the report should prove unfavourable. It was argued that postponement from 31 August, 1963, could not be announced without a new date, since the growing resentment of people in North Borneo and Sarawak would certainly not permit indefinite postponement; a firm date was also desirable to enable invitations for the inaugural celebrations to be issued.

281. The Malayan Government were at first anxious to fix a date not later than 14 September, 1963, since some of the guests they wished to invite would be unable to attend if the celebrations clashed with the beginning of the United Nations General Assembly session. Mr. Sandys also favoured 14 September unless the Malayans themselves proposed a later date. U Thant appreciated the arguments for fixing a date, but in a discussion on 12 August insisted that 14 September was too early and suggested 20 September or a day or so later. In the course of this discussion, however, Mr. Narasimhan implied that a date in the third week in September, beginning on 16 September, would be acceptable. U Thant did not dissent from this and appears himself to have indicated to the Malayan Representative on 16 August that 16 September would be a suitable new date; he remained, however, unwilling to give any public hint of this and subsequently, in his conclusions on the Michelmore Mission's report, expressed regret that a new date had been fixed beforehand.

282. In the light of these discussions the Governments of the United Kingdom, Malaya, North Borneo, Sarawak and Singapore agreed to 16 September, 1963, and on 29 August the Yang di-Pertuan Agong signed a proclamation providing for Malaysia Day to be on 16 September. On 28 August Enche Ghazali flew to Djakarta to give advance notice of the promulgation of this proclamation. Djakarta, however, was not to be appeased. The Malayans published their notes to the Indonesians and the Filipinos explaining the announcement on 29 August and on 3 September the Indonesians responded with a strongly-worded note of protest. The Malayans, who were becoming increasingly robust in their attitude, replied firmly on 6 September, arguing that they had been scrupulous in keeping to the Manila Agreement. The Filipinos reacted more mildly. Mr. Lopez did not protest formally but on 4 September at a Press conference described the announcement as 'premature' and said that 'it does not appear to be in conformity with the letter and the spirit of the Manila Agreements to have set a new date for the establishment of Malaysia in advance of the completion of the United Nations survey'.

Indonesian reactions

283. On 14 September, 1963, the day that U Thant's report was published, Dr. Subandrio told the Malayan Ambassador in Djakarta that 'there would be no recognition of Malaysia'. On the following day he told Press correspondents that 'Indonesia could not recognise Malaysia as it is now' and the Indonesian Ambassador in Kuala Lumpur was withdrawn to Djakarta 'for consultations'. On 16 September Dr. Subandrio informed the Malaysian Ambassador that 'You have no status here.' In consequence, on 17 September, the Tunku told the Press that the Malaysian

Embassy would be withdrawn from Djakarta and the Indonesians were given seven days to remove all their diplomatic and consular staff from Malaysia. Despite this sequence of events the Indonesians had some success in suggesting that it was the Malaysians who had broken off relations.

284. The Indonesians did not confine themselves to diplomatic action. On 12 September, 1963, demonstrators invaded the grounds of the British Consulate at Surabaya and destroyed the Union Flag; a protest was made, but no apology was received. On 16 September a mob attacked British and Malaysian Embassy buildings in Djakarta causing considerable damage; despite a formal request on 13 September no attempt was made by the Security Police to give protection to the British Embassy. On 16 September also the British and Malaysian Consulates at Medan were almost completely wrecked and trade unions took over a number of British firms in the Djakarta area; these were subsequently put under 'supervision' by the authorities. Dr. Subandrio deplored the damage done at the Embassies, but declared that the Indonesian Government appreciated the militant attitude of various groups of Indonesian society and the fact that the people had shown their indignation at the formation of Malaysia.

285. There was some reaction to these events on 17 September, 1963, in Malaya when there were demonstrations at the Indonesian Embassy in Kuala Lumpur and the Consulate in Penang and the Indonesian Ambassador's residence was invaded. On the following day, 18 September, in Djakarta the Malaysian Embassy was taken over by the Indonesian Youth Front, the British Embassy was ransacked and destroyed by fire, and British property throughout the city was systematically looted and burnt. On 19 September only action by the Diplomatic Corps prevented the British Ambassador's residence being taken over. On 21 September President Sukarno announced an economic and commercial boycott of Malaysia, which *inter alia* involved stopping the entrepôt trade through Singapore.

Filipino reactions

286. In Manila the President's Office issued a Press release on 15 September, 1963, which stated that the President had decided 'to defer action on the question of the recognition of the proposed Federation of Malaysia' which, 'in effect, means that the Philippines will have no relations with the new state of Malaysia.' On the same day Mr. Lopez summoned the Malayan Ambassador and informed him of this decision and the Philippines Ambassador in Kuala Lumpur was withdrawn 'for consultation'. The Philippine Foreign Ministry subsequently told the Malaysian Embassy that they could only be recognised as a Consulate. On 17 September therefore the Tunku announced that the Embassy in Manila would also be withdrawn and the Filipino diplomatic and consular staff would have seven days to leave Malaysia.

287. On 18 September, 1963, in New York, Mr. Lopez told the Malaysian Permanent Representative to the United Nations, Dato Ong, that he had tried to persuade the Indonesians to welcome Malaysia, but without success, and that the Philippines had had therefore to withhold their own welcome for the time being. He asked that the Embassy staff in Manila should not be withdrawn. Mr. Lopez admitted that his Government had been heavily criticised for its attitude to Malaysia, but this seemed to be more a matter of disagreement over tactics and of internal political differences than of real hostility to the policy being followed by

the Administration. The Malaysians hoped at first to be able to reach agreement with the Filipinos and maintained a moderate tone in references to the Philippines attitude. By the end of 1963 however the Tunku made it plain that he had concluded that President Macapagal and Mr. Lopez were too tied to the claims in Sabah and to the desire to present a new 'Asian' image in collaboration with Indonesia to present any real basis for hope of a satisfactory resumption of relations in the immediate future.

The development of confrontation

288.   The Malaysians had by October 1963 no illusions about the Indonesian attitude towards the Federation, even though in the General Assembly on 27 September Mr. Palar had painted the British as the villains of the piece with the Malayans acting under British pressure. Soon thereafter Dr. Sukarno told the Japanese Ambassador that, unless the Tunku agreed to a new tripartite Summit meeting and a new investigation in Borneo and the British gave up their bases, he would have to consider allowing Russian bases in Indonesia. The Tunku's immediate response to this was that he could not consider attending such a meeting unless Malaysia was recognised and aggressive actions ceased. His attitude hardened further in the following months.

289.   The Tunku's greater firmness was related to the increasingly open nature of Indonesian military 'confrontation'. On 5 August, 1963, General Nasution stated that Indonesia was providing arms and training for rebels in the Borneo Territories and that the policy of confrontation would be maintained until Malaysia was 'smashed'. Raiding continued actively until 24 August, but two days earlier Dr. Subandrio told the American Ambassador that instructions had been issued to General Nasution to stop all activities on the border. After the United Nations ascertainment, however, confrontation resumed in earnest. In the middle of September the Indonesians imposed a ban on goods, ships and aircraft moving between Indonesia and the Malaysian Territories and on 25 September President Sukarno, in a speech at Jogjakarta, said that the 'Indonesians will crush Malaysia to [the] end because it is a form of neo-colonialism'. By early October Indonesian bands of up to 200 men were being recorded on the border.

290.   On 18 September, 1963, the Tunku announced that a Malaysian Defence Council was to be set up and that the Malaysian armed forces were to be increased. By late September there were six British battalions with supporting troops in Borneo, while two battalions of the Royal Malay Regiment were under orders for Borneo. The Indonesians also took over Malaysian assets in Indonesia. This probably chiefly affected a few Chinese businessmen in Singapore, while the trade boycott damaged the interests of Singapore and to a lesser extent Penang, another Chinese city, and may not therefore have been seen as excessively damaging in Malay circles. There seems also to have been a body of opinion which regarded confrontation as playing a useful role in helping to forge national unity—already, during his visit to the Borneo States in April, Mr. Narasimhan had formed the view that 'the Indonesian attitude had frightened most of the local people out of any desire for independence on their own.' Moreover the view was held by some Malayans that even without Malaysia they were bound to have trouble with the Indonesians sooner or later and that it was better to face it when they still enjoyed determined Commonwealth support.

The provenance of Malaysia

291. An issue which had caused some concern in London in the spring and summer of 1963 was the question of whether Malaysia would be an entirely new 'international personality' or merely the existing Federation of Malaya with its name changed to take account of additional territories. For Commonwealth and United Nations reasons continuity would be simpler and would provide less opportunity for obstruction, but North Borneo, Sarawak and Singapore would be better placed in, and therefore naturally preferred, an arrangement which seemed to be a compact between equal partners. The former considerations prevailed and efforts were made to avoid speaking of the 'establishment' of Malaysia. The form used in Article I of the Malaysia Agreement was that 'The Colonies of North Borneo and Sarawak and the State of Singapore shall be federated with the existing States of the Federation of Malaya . . . and the Federation shall thereafter be called "Malaysia".'

292. On 16 September, 1963, the Malaysian Permanent Representative notified the United Nations that 'the name of the State . . . has been changed from "Federation of Malaya" to "Malaysia".' The Malayan High Commission had earlier told the Commonwealth Relations Office that the Malayan Government proposed to try to avoid issuing Malaysian Representatives abroad with new letters of accreditation. As with their earlier attempts to raise the issue of Malaysia in the Committee of Twenty-four, here too Indonesia and the Philippines were neither very active nor very effective. The Indonesian Representative had intended to challenge the seating of Malaysia in the General Assembly. He was however apparently told by Sir Mohammed Zafrulla Khan that the Chairmen had agreed between themselves that, if a point of order were raised, whichever was in the Chair would rule that Malaysia was properly seated. He therefore protested at what he described as a procedural *fait accompli* without endeavouring to reverse it on a point of order. By early October it was thought that the Malaysian United Nations seat was well established.

293. Singapore, North Borneo and Sarawak all to some extent nevertheless satisfied their own need for status. On 31 August, 1963, the original Malaysia Day, the Governors of both North Borneo and Sarawak announced that they would in future follow the advice of the territory's Chief Minister or Chief Minister Designate in matters which would be State subjects under the Malaysia Constitution. In Singapore Mr. Lee, having been restrained from declaring full independence, announced that his Government had taken powers over defence and foreign affairs and was 'holding them in trust' until 16 September for the Malaysian Government. These moves were reported to have thrown the Malayan Government and the Tunku into a fury. Mr. Sandys however managed to persuade them that none of these announcements involved any legal change, or in Singapore even a *de facto* change. A joint statement by Mr. Sandys and Tun Razak confined itself to a factual recital of the constitutional position. Again on 16 September Mr. Lee issued a high-sounding proclamation repeating that Singapore on 31 August 'asserted her right to freedom and took over powers over defence and foreign affairs'. Although of no legal effect, this may well have given the popular impression that the State had entered Malaysia freely from an independent status.

The United States attitude, February to October 1963

294. After the quadripartite talks in Washington in February 1963 the maintenance of American official support for the Malaysia proposals, both in public

and in private, remained a constant preoccupation of Her Majesty's Government. In a Press conference on 14 February President Kennedy said that 'We have supported the Malaysia Federation . . . I am hopeful that it will sustain itself because it is the best hope of security for that area.' Nevertheless the United States Administration throughout doubted, on the basis of the American experience in Viet-Nam, whether the British would be able easily to contain Indonesian-promoted guerilla warfare and feared that they might be unwilling to stick to the task, so that the United States would be drawn in. There was British concern over the Mansfield Report to Congress on South-East Asia, which seemed hostile to Malaysia and suggested that the United States should pursue a policy of 'non-involvement' in the problems arising from its creation. This was however offset to some extent by robust remarks about South-East Asia made by the President with reference to the Mansfield Committee's views at a Press conference on 6 March. At a meeting with Lord Home on 7 April in Paris moreover Mr. Rusk was more reassuring than in February.

295.   By May 1963 however there was some anxiety that the luke-warm character of American support for Malaysia, especially in public, and willingness to consider further aid for the Indonesians, even if only as a lever to restrain them, might be encouraging Indonesian and Filipino intransigence. Early in May there were indications that the State Department was attracted by proposals for a plebiscite after Malaysia and they urged the British Government to keep an open mind on this proposal as a possible 'germ of a solution'. The American position was that their policy had been clearly laid down in President Kennedy's statement of 14 February. Mr. Harriman told the British Ambassador, in a letter of 23 May, that he had recently informed the Indonesians that this remained United States policy and 'that, while we were playing no part in the formation of Malaysia, we consider it the best solution available'. The ANZUS communique of 6 June, 1963, signed by Sir Garfield Barwick, Mr. Harriman and Mr. Holyoake, said that the Ministers 'noted with satisfaction that the final steps were now being taken for the early formation of the new State. They welcomed the establishment of Malaysia . . .'.

296.   On 16 July, 1963, Mr. Gilchrist was told by the French and Canadian Ambassadors in Djakarta that the American Ambassador, Mr. Howard Jones, had been advocating a postponement of Malaysia to give time for a full-scale referendum. These views seem however to have been unrepresentative of the American Administration's position. During the Manila Summit Meeting President Kennedy suggested a brief postponement to enable Dr. Sukarno to save face if he was so minded [see 204]. Thereafter the American position became firmer. Mr. Jones was instructed to make strong representations to Dr. Sukarno to persuade him to stick to the Manila Agreement and similar representations were made to the Filipinos. Mr. Harriman and Mr. Hilsman were anxious that nothing should be done to give the Indonesians an excuse for avoiding their Manila commitments, by, in particular, any statement that Malaysia would come into being on a fixed date whatever U Thant's ascertainment report might say. Mr. Hilsman agreed on 9 August that this was what must in fact happen, but on 30 August the Americans expressed the view to the Foreign Office that 'having accepted the role of the Secretary-General . . . it is inconceivable that his findings could simply be brushed away if they proved to be adverse'.

297.   Mr. Hilsman expressed the view to Mr. Greenhill of the Embassy in Washington on 3 August, 1963, that the Indonesian proposal for observers during

ascertainment was totally unacceptable and on 6 August that President Sukarno had been allowed to get away with far too much at Manila, including observers, that the United Kingdom should work on the assumption that ascertainment could be completed by 31 August and that there could be no question of the resulting report being subject to confirmation either by the General Assembly or the three Manila Powers. On 12 August U Thant was apparently strongly discouraged by the Americans when he suggested that it might be wiser to fix Malaysia Day after the Michelmore teams had reported.

298.   On the issue of observers Mr. Harriman agreed on 21 August, 1963, that U Thant should if necessary be told that the United States understanding of their function was that they were to stay with the United Nations teams and observe the manner of their enquiries and not to engage in independent investigations or other activities; he agreed that British consent to the addition of four clerical assistants to each observer team should be dependent on the laying down of bench rules by U Thant, and that if the rules were broken the attempt to reach a solution in co-operation with Indonesia might have to be abandoned. The State Department subsequently took steps to press the Indonesian Government to accept the British concession of two observers and two assistants to each territory subject to these rules and gave no countenance to the Indonesian request to be allowed to fly their observers into the Borneo Territories in their own aircraft.

299.   On 30 August, 1963, Mr. Harriman sent Mr. Sandys in Singapore a 'roughly worded' message, based apparently on what Mr. Gilchrist described as 'misrepresentations' by Mr. Howard Jones in Djakarta. This message spoke of 'arbitrary and inflexible tactics' and urged Mr. Sandys to allow the Indonesian observers and assistants to proceed 'without further dispute over their identities.' On the previous day however the American Minister in Manila had, on instructions, spoken to Mr. Lopez of his Government's 'sharp disappointment' at the Philippine Government's behaviour over the British Government's 'perfectly reasonable requirements' on observers and assistants. On 10 September Mr. Harriman agreed in principle that the United States would support publicly a favourable report by the Secretary-General as soon as it was published and this was done. It also appeared that President Kennedy had rejected a proposal for interim American aid to keep the Indonesian economy going.

300.   The violent Indonesian reaction to the formation of Malaysia led the United States again to urge conciliation. The Tunku had, in a broadcast on 20 September, 1963, while welcoming a Filipino proposal for a new summit meeting, insisted that the Indonesians and Filipinos must first resume normal diplomatic relations with Malaysia and that the Indonesians must 'stop any aggressive actions, direct or indirect, and all troops now concentrated on the border of Sarawak must be withdrawn.' The United States however pressed in Manila, Djakarta and Kuala Lumpur for a summit meeting without preconditions, though warned by Mr. Baldwin, the American Ambassador in Kuala Lumpur, that this would be pointless and dangerous, unless the Indonesians accepted the Tunku's conditions beforehand.

301.   On 27 September, 1963, President Kennedy sent a message to President Sukarno proposing 'a temporary standstill on any further provocative words and actions' and on 28 September invited Mr. Macmillan to join with him in urging restraint on the Tunku; this Mr. Macmillan agreed to do. Both in Mr. Macmillan's reply and in a subsequent talk between Sir David Ormsby-Gore and Mr. Rusk and Mr.

Hilsman in Washington it was argued that the Tunku was not, as President Kennedy believed, in a pugnacious mood and could hardly be expected to make any further concession, such as attending a new tripartite summit meeting, without at the least Indonesian recognition of Malaysia, in view of the domestic political atmosphere in Malaysia and Indonesia's continual verbal and military attacks and failure to honour previous undertakings. The chief British interest in these exchanges however was to urge an early resumption of quadripartite talks.

302.   The Tunku's reply to President Kennedy agreed to his suggestion that President Macapagal be privately informed that Malaysia would abide by its promise to consider the question of the Philippines' claims in North Borneo, but said that 'we have no further reliance on Indonesian promises' and that the Communists were strong enough to prevent any hope of successful talks with Indonesia. His earlier remarks seem already to have suggested to the Americans that the Tunku was unwilling under any circumstances to negotiate with President Sukarno and on 4 October, 1963, in New York, Mr. Rusk brusquely insisted to Dato Ong and Mr. Ramani that there must be no preconditions, that an early meeting was essential and that this would in itself amount to a recognition of Malaysia by the other two participants. In the following week the United States increased its pressure on the Tunku. He was asked again to cease making provocative statements, to demonstrate his willingness to accept further negotiation, and in particular to agree to a tripartite meeting at ministerial level. He was told that it looked as though the situation was drifting towards war, that Britain and Australia might be unable to cope and that American help might then have to be sought; before such help could be given Malaysia would have to demonstrate that it had pursued negotiation to the end.

The Australian attitude, February to October 1963

303.   The Australian position became increasingly robust after the quadripartite talks in February 1963. Sir Garfield Barwick engaged in a round of discussions early in March in Manila during which he urged moderation on Dr. Subandrio, whom he found 'evasive', and on President Macapagal, and tried to promote tripartite talks at ministerial level. He seems to have concluded that firmness in support of Malaysia was more likely to get results than any other policy. Nevertheless, so far as their claims in North Borneo were concerned, he did at this stage suggest to the Philippines that they should aim at submission of the claim to the International Court after Malaysia had been formed to be followed, if the claim succeeded there, by a referendum to resolve the issue. By early in May however the Australians were opposed to any idea of a plebiscite before or after Malaysia Day and were lobbying vigorously against the idea in Washington, using the argument that any sign of an American weakening on this point would encourage the Indonesians to increase their opposition.

304.   This firm position was maintained during the summer of 1963. In the United Nations General Assembly general debate on 3 October Sir Garfield defended the formation of Malaysia and reiterated Australia's intention of going to its defence if necessary, while Sir Robert Menzies also publicly stated that Australia had offered, if requested by the Malaysian Government, in the event of attack or externally incited subversion, to add Australian military efforts to those of the United Kingdom in aid of Malaysia. The Australians were also convinced that the Tunku had, for internal political reasons, no further room for manoeuvre and so could not be expected to

make further concessions. In discussions before the quadripartite talks in Washington they seem to have brought Mr. Harriman round to this view.

The quadripartite talks, October 1963

305. The Americans accepted the British proposal for new quadripartite talks, though without notable enthusiasm. There was some informal discussion between British and Australian officials beforehand as to the best way of leading the United States to take a serious view of long-term Indonesian policy, and some inclination to think that emphasis on the broad threat posed by the Maphilindo concept to United States as well as British bases in the area might well prove more effective than concentration on the immediate Indonesian action in Borneo. It was also thought that it would be as well to paint a black picture of Indonesian intentions in order to offset an American tendency, following Mr. Howard Jones, to believe that President Sukarno was open to persuasion and looking for a way of escape from an untenable position and that further concessions by the Tunku were needed to permit this.

306. The talks took place from 16 to 18 October, 1963, in Washington. The agenda covered an assessment of the current situation, including Indonesian and Filipino intentions and the Malaysian internal political situation, the political and military implications of this situation and Commonwealth action to deal with them, and Western policy in the area in general. It was hoped in London that, in trying to reach an agreed assessment of Western interests in the area and of Indonesian intentions towards them, it might be possible to persuade the Americans that efforts to reach a quick solution were unlikely to bring about a satisfactory settlement, either for Malaysia or for Western long-term interests. In the British view the basic Western interest was to have as wide an area as possible in South-East Asia in which to deploy military power against a Communist threat undistracted by other threats, and especially to retain full use of British and American bases. British officials were however by no means certain that the United States Administration regarded the maintenance of Singapore and other British bases as being an American interest.

307. The British inclination was to believe that the Indonesian threat could only be abated by standing up to it firmly and so demonstrating that countries with Western guarantees would be supported effectively by the United States as well as by the United Kingdom. The Americans on the other hand were expected to press the view that an effective Western presence was dependent on the goodwill of Indonesia, as the largest, most vigorous and most powerful country in South-East Asia, and that concession was therefore essential. There was also a fundamental difference of view on the internal effects within Indonesia of Western action. The Americans tended to fear that, if frustrated, Indonesia would go Communist; the British that the continued success of the existing Indonesian policy of imperial expansion would submerge moderate opinion and so play into the hands of the PKI. It was the British purpose at the talks to persuade the Americans, not so much to put pressure on the Indonesians, as to demonstrate support for Malaysia. In particular it was hoped to correct a situation in which the United States gave economic aid to Indonesia, although it gave none to Malaysia.

308. The talks proved more satisfactory from the British viewpoint than had been expected, the Americans having evidently been impressed by Australian and British insistence on the Tunku's lack of freedom for manoeuvre. The Australian and New Zealand representatives suggested that the policy of concessions to Sukarno was

leading to a Munich situation and the Americans agreed not to pursue the project of a new tripartite meeting. They still however pressed for support for Thai efforts to see if conditions for such a meeting could be created and declined to interrupt outstanding aid deliveries to Indonesia. They did agree on the other hand to consider various ways of indicating a positive United States support for Malaysia, including the sale of military equipment on credit terms, mutual visits by Malaysian and American leaders, a naval visit to Malaysia, continued full support for Malaysia's candidacy for the Security Council of the United Nations, reiterated public support for Malaysia and open encouragement of United States investment.

309.   The Americans also in effect agreed that renewed quadripartite talks should be held before they took any fresh initiatives. The United Kingdom, Australia and New Zealand for their part agreed to continue to urge on the Tunku a policy of restraint and moderation in his public statements and actions. They also accepted Commonwealth responsibility for economic and military support of Malaysia and the British confirmed their intention of maintaining their military effort in the Borneo Territories 'at such a level as the situation might require'. On balance there seemed some justice in the view expressed by both Mr. Harriman and Mr. Rusk that the decisions reached entailed 'a lot of action by the United States and very little by anyone else'. Nevertheless, although some members of the State Department and of the United States Embassy in Djakarta may have remained unconvinced, the general American attitude, and especially that of the President as expressed to Mr. Warner by Mr. McGeorge Bundy, proved to be more robust than had appeared before the talks.

XXI. *The local political scene, autumn 1963*

Malaya

310.   The London Agreement was endorsed in the Malayan Lower House by 67 votes to 18 on 12 August, 1963, and the Malaysia Bill was passed on 20 August by 73 votes to 16. Nevertheless the Alliance leadership felt compelled to make a vigorous effort to rally support for Malaysia and against the Indonesian regime. During the autumn 'Malaysian Solidarity' rallies were held throughout Malaya; these included the burning of effigies of President Sukarno, of Dr. Subandrio and of the PKI leader, Mr. Aidit. This campaign, and Indonesian actions, had the desired effect of rallying Malay, and Chinese, support behind the Government and was largely responsible for a considerable improvement in the proportion of votes secured by the Alliance in the 1964 elections as compared with those held in 1959.

Sabah

311.   Despite the unanimous adoption of the Lansdowne recommendations, there were still in April 1963 elements in North Borneo, especially in the Pasok Momogun, who were not reconciled to the Malaysia proposals. On 22 April O.K.K. Sundang sent Mr. Narasimhan, who was visiting Borneo, a letter in which he claimed that most people in North Borneo would prefer self-determination first and were worried about religious freedom in Malaysia and at opposition from neighbouring countries. Although he was subsequently persuaded to broadcast, on 12 June, a talk emphasising the safeguards in the Malaysia arrangements, there were rumours that there might be 'trouble' in the Interior Residency and it was thought wise to despatch two platoons of Gurkhas to Keningau, an area in which Pasok Momogun

was influential, to take part in the Malaysia Day celebrations—their presence was reported to have had a marked effect.

312.   The decision to grant North Borneo and Sarawak self-government, as from 31 August, 1963, in respect of rights which would later fall to them as states under Malaysia did something to assuage the desire for self-determination before merger, though it annoyed the Malayans. There were extensive and apparently virtually unanimous demonstrations in favour of Malaysia and against delay in establishing it when the Michelmore Mission team arrived in North Borneo in August 1963. At least one British Foreign Service observer in North Borneo at this time took the view, however, that for many in the State Malaysia was still only regarded as a second best alternative to continuation of British rule.

313.   On 16 May, 1963, the Sabah Alliance decided to nominate Datu Mustapha as Head of State and Mr. Donald Stephens as Chief Minister. It was by this time evident that Datu Mustapha and his Muslim supporters expected to secure a predominant position in the State in Malaysia. This was partly because of support from Federation Malay leaders and partly because Mr. Stephens had to some extent alienated the local Chinese, who were now uneasily united in the Borneo Utara National Party, or BUNAP. There were also reports that members of political parties, in disputes with the Administration, expected to benefit from party support and that USNO had attracted supporters because it seemed likely to be able to be more effective in this respect than the other parties. By October 1963 there were even rumours that USNO might affiliate directly to UMNO. In July the Alliance as a whole secured all 18 elected seats on the Legislative Council, USNO getting 8, UNKO 5, BUNAP 4 and the Pasok Momogun 1; the Council also had 4 *ex officio* and 3 nominated members. These shares were repeated on 26 September for the 16 Sabah seats in the Federal House of Representatives, except that the USNO share was cut to 6 seats.

Sarawak

314.   The unity of the parties in the Sarawak Alliance evaporated rapidly and on 15 April, 1963, the Party Negara Sarawak of PANAS, whose leader was the Datu Bandar, withdrew to fight the election on its own. Its attitude bore some resemblance to that of the Pasok Momogun, in its inclination to favour self-determination for the territories rather than direct merger. On 1 July it joined with SUPP in calling for a referendum before the creation of Malaysia, though the Datu Bandar himself subsequently said that he wanted ascertainment of the wishes of the people by the Secretary-General of the United Nations and not a referendum. On 9 July he signed the Malaysia Agreement in London. Some PANAS candidates had nevertheless talked of looking to Indonesia for support and the party was on bad terms with the other primarily Malay party, Barisan Ra'ayat Jati Sarawak, or BARJASA. By September however the Secretary-General of UMNO, Senator Ghazali bin Jawi, was trying to bring these two parties together and, it was said, to link them directly to UMNO; as a result PANAS began to lose its Chinese members.

315.   The Sarawak National Party, or SNAP, which was primarily Iban in membership, suffered from internal dissensions and from lack of funds. There were also Ibans in Party Pesaka Anak Sarawak, or PAPAS, and in SUPP, which was however primarily a Chinese party. Within SUPP the moderates were thought to have strengthened their position at the centre, largely because the CCO was preoccupied with preparations for armed action. In Sarawak, as in North Borneo, the initial

effects of Indonesian incursions, when they started in April 1963, was unsettling, but counter-action was already in May reported as having produced a recovery in public morale.

316.   The first stage of elections in Sarawak, on the three tier electoral college system, took place from 26 April, 1963, to 15 July. In the primary District and Municipal Councils, elected by full adult suffrage, the Sarawak Alliance won 138 seats, SUPP 116 seats, PANAS 59 seats and Independents, none of whom were believed to have adopted a platform hostile to Malaysia, 116 seats. These figures somewhat underrepresented the voting support for Independents and the Alliance. During July the primary level Councils elected the members of the Divisional Advisory Councils and these in turn the members of the new Council Negri. In this body, Sarawak's Legislative Assembly, the Alliance secured 19 seats, PANAS 5, SUPP 5, and Independents 7; there were also to be up to 7 nominated, *ex officio* and life members. Alliance support amongst elected members of the Council Negri subsequently rose to 23. Of the 36 elected members 9 were Chinese, 7 Malays and Melanaus, and 20 other races, especially Ibans. SUPP and PANAS had an electoral arrangement for these higher level elections.

317.   The Federal leadership had shown itself somewhat dissatisfied with some of the earlier results in Sarawak and the Tunku would not allow the election of members of the Federal House of Representatives to go ahead until he had himself approved the Alliance list. This round of the elections was therefore postponed until 22 October, 1963. Of those then elected 18 represented the Alliance, 3 SUPP and the remaining 3 PANAS.

Relations between the federal government and the Borneo Territories

318.   The Federal Government seems in general to have been contemptuous of the emerging political leaders in Borneo. Tun Razak was said to give the impression that he had a poor opinion of Datu Mustapha in Sabah. In Sarawak the Alliance unanimously elected Mr. Stephen Kalong Ningkan, an Iban, to be Chief Minister Designate and the Federation Government accepted this nomination, though its members seem to have had little confidence in Mr. Ningkan. The Sarawak Alliance however also proposed the Temenggong Jugah, the leader of another group of Ibans, as Governor—the post of Governor was on the first occasion to be filled by joint nomination by the Federation and United Kingdom Governments. The Tunku rejected the Alliance proposal on the ground that, with an Iban as Chief Minister, a Malay must be appointed Governor. He also claimed that the Temenggong was illiterate and personally unsuitable.

319.   The Temenggong nevertheless carried considerable weight with the Iban community, which was the largest racial stock [?block] in Sarawak and was becoming increasingly politically aware and active. Their importance was moreover enhanced by the presence of 2 million or so Dyaks across the border in Indonesian territory. The Governor, Sir Alexander Waddell, feared that, if Temenggong Jugah was not appointed, PAPAS and SNAP might combine to oppose Malaysia. He took the view that the Tunku should either accept the choice of the Sarawak Alliance or should convince them to the contrary.

320.   The Tunku however was under pressure from Malay feeling in the Federation. The more cautious UMNO members, who had throughout had doubts of the advantages of the Grand Design, were becoming increasingly uneasy as the

disadvantages of the scheme became more apparent and were in no mood to permit the Tunku to agree to a non-Malay Governor. They were no doubt encouraged in this attitude by the representatives in Kuala Lumpur of the Malay Barjasa Party.

321.   The Tunku therefore remained immovable throughout a series of meetings between leaders of the Sarawak Alliance, Malayan Ministers and the Secretary of State for Commonwealth Relations, Mr. Sandys, and on 7 September, 1963, he stated publicly that the nomination of the Temenggong was unacceptable. The issue was eventually resolved, on 13 September, [see 224] by appointing a Malay prominent in Islamic affairs in Sarawak, Datu Abang Haji Openg, to be Governor and by creating for Temenggong Jugah a new post of Federation Minister for Borneo Affairs[4] resident in Sarawak. At the same time an agreed statement provided that, when two years later the next Governor was to be chosen, the Yang di-Pertuan Agong would give 'favourable consideration' to the nominee of the then Sarawak Chief Minister. The episode was nevertheless not a good augury for the future.

Reactions in Singapore to the Malaysia agreement

322.   The London Agreement was criticised in Singapore by the Barisan Sosialis, by Mr. Ong Eng Guan of the United People's Party, and by Mr. David Marshall, the former Chief Minister. Their attacks were directed at the terms secured, rather than at the fact of merger, though it was this that the Barisan at least really opposed. The terms were described as 'a sell out of Singapore' a view given gratuitous support by Mr. Tan Siew Sin who claimed that the State had made a bad bargain. On 24 July, 1963, the Government, with Mr. Lee and Dr. Goh absent paired, was frustrated three times in the Assembly on Bills connected with the formation of Malaysia, including one to provide for election to the Singapore seats in the Federal Parliament. On each occasion the Singapore Alliance members voted against the Government.

323.   There was however little doubt that merger commanded wide popular support in Singapore and Mr. Lee's motion calling for adoption of the London Agreement, as amended by the Singapore Government in the light of the various exchanges between Mr. Lee, Mr. Sandys, the Tunku and Tun Razak, was passed by the Assembly by 25 votes to 17. On this occasion the 7 Alliance members and an independent abstained. Mr. Lee subsequently announced that the Assembly would be dissolved and the writ for new elections was issued on 31 August, 1963. The PAP fought the election on an anti-Communist platform, while the Barisan Sosialis argued that Malaysia should be limited to the Malaya–Singapore merger to the exclusion of the Borneo Territories, an arrangement they well knew to be unattainable. Polling took place on 21 September and the Government was triumphantly successful, winning 37 of the 51 seats as against 25 held earlier. The percentages of the poll secured by the parties were PAP 47 per cent, Barisan Sosialis 33 per cent, UPP 8 per cent and Singapore Alliance 8 per cent.

324.   On 26 September, 1963, the police, acting on the orders of the Federation Government, but with the backing of the Singapore Government, arrested a number of Nanyang University students. Seven trade unions affiliated to SATU were also asked to show cause why their registration should not be cancelled. In reaction to this pressure on the Left wing, Mr. S. T. Bani, President of SATU and a Barisan

---

[4] In fact for Sarawak Affairs.

Sosialis Assembly member, announced that the unions threatened with deregistration and 30 others would strike. He and 15 other leaders were arrested on 8 October and the Federation Government moved troops into the island. Attempts at illegal assembly were firmly dealt with and the strike collapsed, leaving Mr. Lee in a very strong position within Singapore.

Relations between the federal government and Singapore

325.   The Alliance did not secure a seat in the Singapore elections. It failed in constituencies with both Malay and Chinese majorities, despite public support by the Tunku, and Mr. Lim Yew Hock subsequently offered his resignation as its leader. The formation of the Alliance with the Tunku's active encouragement did nothing to improve Mr. Lee's relationship with the Malayan Government. Its abject failure, even in the Malay areas, and the PAP's success, had a disastrous effect on Mr. Lee's future conduct. Earlier he had accepted that it must be some years before he could begin to extend his party's influence into Malaya. Even so he had already alarmed not only the conservative Chinese partners in the Alliance, whom he aimed to displace, but, more important, the Malays, and his manner of conducting the negotiations with Malaya had led the Tunku greatly to mistrust him—at a meeting with Mr. Sandys just before the signing of the London Agreement the Tunku referred to Mr. Lee as a paranoiac.

326.   On his return to Singapore from London Mr. Lee told a welcoming crowd that the PAP would do what was right for the people, not only in Singapore, but also in the rest of Malaysia. His subsequent manoeuvres to secure changes in the London Agreement caused irritation in Kuala Lumpur, which had by now come to regard him as an untrustworthy partner and an unscrupulous opponent, as did his success in making common cause with North Bornean and Sarawak leaders and his claim on 31 August, 1963, to have taken over powers of defence and foreign affairs in trust for Malaysia. Mr. Sandys, in a message to Mr. Macmillan, spoke of Mr. Lee as 'unashamedly exploiting the delay in the establishment of Malaysia to further his political [personal] ambitions . . . his objective is to show up the Tunku as feeble and woolly-minded . . . He speaks freely about his wish to get rid of the Tunku within the next two or three years when his usefulness has been exhausted.' [See 221.]

327.   A new Cabinet was announced in Singapore on 17 October, 1963, and Mr. Lee pledged that it would work closely with the Federal Government in the higher interests of Malaysia. On 30 October he told reporters that the PAP Federal Members of Parliament would form a loyal and constructive opposition. Mr. Lee's gesture of independence on 31 August had already led influential Malays to question whether it was worth going into Malaysia with 'new friends who might be worse than their enemies.' In October the chauvinist leader, Syed Ja'affar Albar, who had been concerned with the promotion of the Singapore Alliance, was appointed Secretary-General of UMNO, a post in which he was well placed to renew his efforts to organise opposition to Mr. Lee in Singapore.

328.   On 11 November, 1963, Mr. Lee reiterated the importance of good relations with the Federal Government and insisted that the PAP would not take part in the coming elections in Malaya. The whole Malaysia arrangement rested on the agreement to limit Singapore's representation in the Federal Parliament to 15 seats. In the eyes of the Malays at least the election of PAP members for Malayan

constituencies would break this agreement. Success in the Singapore elections seemed however to have suggested to Mr. Lee that he could win both Chinese and Malay seats in Malaya in the near future. On 9 December in the Assembly he speculated on the prospect that the MCA would do so badly in the 1964 elections that UMNO would have to come to terms with the PAP on a Malaysian basis if they wished to hold the urban Chinese in the Alliance. As Mr. P. B. C. Moore, the Deputy High Commissioner in Singapore, reported in a letter of 2 December, 1963, 'He is already behaving like a caged animal, pacing up his room and restless to play a full part in the government of Malaysia. ... But he will not be prepared to wait long for a star part in the Kuala Lumpur cast and yet I can see no sign at all that Kuala Lumpur have any serious intention of letting him play an effective role. In many ways I see the Singapore/Kuala Lumpur relationship as potentially a greater threat to Malaysian stability than Indonesian confrontation.'

Appendix A

Biographical Notes

Dato Abdul Aziz bin Haji Abdul Majid
Malaya; born 1919; Principal Assistant Secretary, Defence Branch, Federal Government; State Secretary and Mentri Besar, Selangor; 1957 Permanent Secretary, Prime Minister's Department; Chairman, Public Services Commission.

Abdul Aziz bin Ishak
Malaya; born 1914; Minister of Agriculture and Co-operatives 1955–62; chaired 'Joint Opposition Conference' and formed National Convention Party 1963; arrested on political grounds 1965; released on probation 1966.

Brigadier-General Abdul Rachman
Indonesia; leader of Indonesian observer team for 'Ascertainment' in Borneo 1963.

Tunku Abdul Rahman Putra Al-Haj (Tunku Abdul Rahman Putra ibni Almarhum Sultan Abdul Hamid Halim Shah)
Malaya; born 1903; brother of former Sultan of Kedah; 1933 District Officer; barrister; 1951 President of UMNO; 1955 first Chief Minister of Malaya and 1957 Prime Minister; 1963 first Prime Minister of Malaysia; retired 1970; also Minister for External Affairs for most of the period 1957–70.

Sir Anthony Abell
United Kingdom; born 1906; Governor, Sarawak 1950–59 and High Commissioner, Brunei; Member, Cobbold Commission 1962.

Dipa Nusantara Aidit
Indonesia; born 1923; 1947 member, Central Committee and Politbureau, PKI; 1951 Secretary-General, PKI, the title being later changed to Chairman; reported killed shortly after the abortive *coup* in 1965.

Sir Denis Allen
United Kingdom; born 1910; Deputy Commissioner-General for South-East Asia 1959–63.

Sheikh A. M. Azahari bin Sheikh Mahmoud

Brunei, but not a citizen; born 1928; started unregistered film company which was declared illegal and sentenced to six months' imprisonment for leading a demonstration against this in 1953; further unsuccessful business enterprises, some supported by Government loans; 1955 organised Parti Ra'ayat in Brunei and elected Brunei representative of Parti Ra'ayat Malaya; convicted for failing to keep proper accounts for Parti Ra'ayat Brunei; 1960 organised labour union; December 1962 in Manila proclaimed 'Unitary State of North Kalimantan' to cover North Borneo and Sarawak as well as Brunei; subsequently mostly in Indonesia.

Charles F. Baldwin

United States; born 1902; 1927 Foreign Service; Deputy Assistant Secretary of State for Far Eastern Economic Affairs 1954–55; Ambassador, Kuala Lumpur 1961–64.

The Datu Bandar (Abang Haji Mustapha)

Sarawak; the traditional leader of the Malay community in Sarawak; founder of Parti Negara Sarawak (PANAS); signed Malaysia Agreement 1963; died 1964.

S. T. Bani

Singapore; born 1934 in Negri Sembilan; 1954 Government teacher; 1958 full-time union and PAP work; 1959 MP (PAP); 1961 joined Barisan Sosialis and became president of SATU; 1963 detained; released and resigned from Parliament and Barisan Sosialis 1966.

Sir Garfield Barwick

Australia; born 1903; MP 1958–64; Attorney-General 1958–63; Minister for External Affairs 1961–63; 1964 Chief Justice of the High Court.

Ahmad Boestamam bin Raja Kechil

Malaya; born 1920; 1945 Malay Nationalist Party; detained 1948–55; 1955 first president, Parti Ra'ayat Malaya; federal MP 1959–64; detained 1963–67; formed Parti Marhaen Malaya 1968.

Sultan of Brunei (Sir Muda Omar Ali Saifuddin Sa'adul Khairi Waddin)

Brunei; born 1916; succeeded as 28th Sultan 1950; introduced Constitution providing for Privy Council, Executive Council and Legislative Council 1959; introduced proposals for election of Legislative Council members and a Ministerial system 1964; abdicated in favour of son, Sultan Hassanal Bolkiah Mu'izzaddin Waddaulah, 1967, becoming Seri Bagawan.

McGeorge Bundy

United States; born 1919; Lecturer, Professor and Dean, Harvard, 1949–61; 1961 Special Assistant to the President for National Security Affairs; 1966 President, Ford Foundation.

Lord Cobbold (1st Baron Cobbold of Knebworth)

United Kingdom; born 1904; Governor, Bank of England 1949–61; Chairman of Cobbold Commission 1962.

Lt.-Gen. G. P. H. Djatikusumo

Indonesia; born 1917; from 1946 divisional commander and other senior military posts, including Defence Minister in the Djogjakarta Revolutionary Government in 1948; Consul-General, Singapore 1958–59; Minister of Land Communications 1960; appointed Ambassador, Kuala Lumpur, and withdrawn 1963; 1963 supervising subversive activities in Malaya; 1965 Ambassador, Rabat.

Achmad Fadillah
Brunei, but resident in Djakarta; petitioned United Nations Committee of Twenty-four on behalf of Sheikh Azahari 1963 under title of 'Minister of State of the Government of Kalimantan Utara', earlier described as 'Minister Without Portfolio'.

Sir Leslie Fry
United Kingdom; born 1908; Ambassador, Djakarta 1959–63.

Mohamed Ghazali bin Jawi (Tuan Haji Mohamed Ghazali bin Haji Jawi)
Malaya; born 1924; 1957 Mentri Besar, Perak; 1960 Ambassador, Cairo; 1963 Senator and Secretary-General, UMNO; 1964 Assistant Minister of Lands and Mines; 1965 Minister of Agriculture and Co-operatives; 1970 Minister of Agriculture with responsibility for Land and Forests.

Mohammad Ghazali bin Shafie (now Tan Sri Mohammad Ghazali bin Shafie)
Malaya; born 1922; family connections in Indonesia; 1956 Commissioner, New Delhi; 1957 Deputy Permanent Secretary, Ministry of External Affairs; 1959 Permanent Secretary; 1969 Member, National Operations Council; 1970 Minister With Special Functions and Senator.

A. G. Gilchrist (now Sir Andrew Gilchrist)
United Kingdom; born 1910; Ambassador, Djakarta 1963–66.

Dr. Goh Keng Swee
Singapore; born 1918, Malacca; 1940 Singapore Government Service; 1955 Director of Social Welfare; 1958 Economic Adviser to the Chief Minister; 1959 elected MP; 1959 Finance Minister; 1965 Defence Minister; 1967 Finance Minister; 1970 Defence Minister; permanent member of the Presidential Council.

Sir William Goode
United Kingdom; born 1907; 1957 Governor and later United Kingdom Commissioner and Yang di-Pertuan Negara, Singapore; Governor, North Borneo 1960–63.

D. A. Greenhill (now Sir Denis Greenhill)
United Kingdom; born 1913; 1956 Counsellor, Singapore; Counsellor and then Minister. Washington 1959–64.

W. Averell Harriman
United States; born 1891; 1943 Ambassador, Moscow; 1946 Ambassador, London; 1946 Secretary of Commerce; 1948 Special Representative in Europe; 1950 Special Assistant to President; Director of Foreign Aid 1951–53; Governor, New York State 1955–58; 1961 Assistant Secretary of State for Far Eastern Affairs; 1963 Under-Secretary for Political Affairs; Ambassador-at-Large 1965–69; Representative, Vietnam Peace Talks, Paris 1968–69.

Dr. Mohammad Hatta
Indonesia; born 1902; former Vice-President and Prime Minister; resigned Vice-Presidency 1956; Special Adviser to the President on corruption 1970.

Roger Hilsman
United States; born 1919; 1956 Library of Congress; 1961 Director, Bureau of Intelligence and Research, Department of State; 1963 Assistant Secretary of State for Far Eastern Affairs; 1964 Professor of Government, Columbia University.

Keith J. Holyoake
New Zealand; born 1904; MP National Party 1932–38 and since 1943; 1949 Deputy Prime Minister; 1957 Prime Minister; 1957 Leader of the Opposition; 1960 Prime Minister and Minister for External Affairs.

Lord Home (14th Earl of Home; now Sir Alec Douglas-Home)
United Kingdom; born 1903; 1955 Secretary of State for Commonwealth Relations; 1960 Secretary of State for Foreign Affairs; Prime Minister 1963–64.

General Sir Richard Hull (now Field Marshal)
United Kingdom; born 1907; 1958 C.-in-C. Far East Land Forces; CIGS 1961–64.

Tun Dr. Ismail bin Dato Haji Abdul Rahman
Malaya; born 1915; 1955 Minister of Commerce; 1957 Ambassador, Washington and Permanent Delegate, United Nations; 1959 Minister for External Affairs; 1960 of Internal Security; 1961 of Internal Security and Interior; of Home Affairs and Justice 1964–67; 1969 of Home Affairs and 1970 Deputy Prime Minister.

Syed Ja'affar Albar (Tan Sri Syed Ja'affar bin Hassan Albar)
Malaya, born 1913 in Indonesia; 1952 Chief Information Officer, UMNO; 1959 Assistant Minister in Prime Minister's Department for Information and Broadcasting; Secretary-General, UMNO 1963–65; retired from UMNO Central Executive Committee 1967–68.

Arthur Creech Jones
United Kingdom; born 1891; 1945 Parliamentary Under-Secretary for the Colonies; Secretary of State 1946–50.

Howard P. Jones
United States; born 1899; 1921 journalism; 1933 lecturing in School of Journalism, Columbia University; New York State Civil Service Commissioner 1939–43; 1947 Foreign Service; 1954 Head of Foreign Operations Mission to Indonesia; 1955 Deputy Assistant Secretary of State for Far Eastern Economic Affairs; 1958 Ambassador, Jakarta; 1965 East-West Center, Honolulu; 1968 Stanford University.

Temenggong Jugah anak Barieng (now Tan Sri Temenggong Jugah anak Barieng)
Sarawak; born 1900; Iban leader, Third Division of Sarawak; 1955 appointed Temenggong (Paramount Chief); Chairman, PAPAS (Pesaka) and Sarawak Alliance; 1963 federal Minister for Sarawak Affairs.

John F. Kennedy
United States; born 1917; 1947 Congressman; 1953 Senator; 1961 President; assassinated 1963.

Khaw Kai Boh
Malaya; born 1918; Special Branch Officer. Malaya and Singapore; retired 1959; 1963 Senator and Minister Without Portfolio; 1964 elected to House of Representatives; 1964 Minister for Local Government and Housing; 1969 Minister with Special Duties; 1970 asked not to be considered for Ministerial post; Secretary-General 1966–67 and later Vice-President, MCA.

Lord Lansdowne (8th Marquess of Lansdowne)
United Kingdom; born 1912; 1958 Parliamentary Under-Secretary, Foreign Office; Minister of State for Colonial Affairs 1962–64 and for Commonwealth Relations 1963–64.

Lee Kuan Yew (Harry Lee)

Singapore; born 1923; 1954 a founder and Secretary-General, PAP; 1955 Member, Legislative Assembly; 1959 first Prime Minister and 1965 of the Republic of Singapore; appointed one of the six permanent members of the Presidential Council 1970.

Dr. Lee Siew Choh

Singapore; born 1917 in Selangor; 1959 MP; 1961 Parliamentary Secretary to Minister of Home Affairs; 1961 Chairman, Barisan Sosialis; resigned 1964; 1965 Chairman, Barisan Sosialis.

Lim Chin Siong

Singapore; born 1933; accountant; 1954 secretary of various unions; 1955 Member, Legislative Assembly; detained 1956–59; 1959 Political Secretary, Ministry of Finance; Secretary-General, Barisan Sosialis 1961–69; 1963 detained; released 1969 and left Singapore.

Dr. Lim Chong Eu

Malaya; born 1919; 1953 Penang Radical Party; Alliance Chief Whip; 1958. President, MCA; resigned 1959; formed UDP 1962; merged UDP in Gerakan 1968; 1969 Chief Minister of Penang.

Dr. Lim Swee Aun

Malaya; born 1915; 1953 Perak State Executive Council; 1959 MP; 1962 Minister of Commerce and Industry; lost seat and Ministry 1969; 1966 Deputy President, MCA.

Lim Yew Hock

Singapore; born 1914; 1948 nominated Member, Legislative Assembly; elected Member 1951–63; Minister of Labour and Welfare 1955–59 and Chief Minister 1956–59; 1963 Malaysian High Commissioner, Canberra; Singapore Ministry of Foreign Affairs 1966–68.

Sir Henry Lintott

United Kingdom; born 1908; Deputy Under-Secretary, Commonwealth Relations Office 1956–63.

Selwyn Lloyd (J. S. B. Lloyd)

United Kingdom; born 1904; 1955 Secretary of State for Foreign Affairs; Chancellor of the Exchequer 1960–62.

Salvador P. Lopez

Philippines; born 1911; 1946 Foreign Service; 1956 Ambassador, Paris, United Nations and elsewhere concurrently; 1962 Under-Secretary for Foreign Affairs; 1963 Foreign Secretary; 1964 Representative, United Nations; 1969 President, University of the Philippines.

Diosdado P. Macapagal

Philippines; born 1910; 1946 Foreign Service; 1949 Member (Liberal), House of Representatives and Chairman, House Committee on Foreign Affairs 1949–53; 1958 Vice-President; President 1962–66.

Malcolm MacDonald

United Kingdom; born 1901; a former Secretary of State for Dominions Affairs and for the Colonies; 1946 Governor-General, Malayan Union, Singapore and British Borneo: Commissioner-General for the United Kingdom in South-East Asia 1948–55.

Iain Macleod
United Kingdom; born 1913; Secretary of State for the Colonies 1959–61.

Harold Macmillan
United Kingdom; born 1894; Prime Minister 1957–63.

Michael J. Mansfield
United States; born 1903; 1933 Professor of Latin American and Far Eastern History, Montana State University; 1943 Congressman; 1953 Senator; 1957 Senate Majority Whip; 1961 Leader of Senate.

Ferdinand E. Marcos
Philippines; born 1917; elected to House of Representatives 1949 and 1953; President of Liberal Party 1956; elected to Senate 1959; President of Senate; joined Nacionalista Party 1964; elected President 1965 and re-elected 1969.

Dato Marshal bin Maun (Awang Marshal bin Maun)
Brunei; Mentri Besar 1962–68.

Reginald Maudling
United Kingdom; born 1917; Secretary of State for the Colonies 1961–62.

David Marshall
Singapore; born 1908; businessman and lawyer; a founder of Labour Front Party 1954; Member, Legislative Assembly 1955–57; Chief Minister 1955–56; formed Workers' Party and won by-election 1961; lost seat 1963; 1970 a permanent member of the Presidential Council.

Sir John Martin
United Kingdom; born 1904; Deputy Under-Secretary, Colonial Office 1956–65.

Sir Robert Menzies
Australia; born 1894; 1934 Commonwealth Attorney-General; Prime Minister 1939–41, 1949–66 (and other portfolios concurrently, including Treasurer, Trade, Defence and External Affairs).

Lawrence Michelmore
United States; born 1909; Relief and Works Progress Administrations 1934–36; Wayne University and Government Research 1936–42; 1942 United States Budget Bureau; 1946 United Nations Secretariat; 1952 Deputy Controller; 1955 Senior Director, Technical Assistance Board; 1959 Deputy Director of Personnel; United Nations Mission on Malaysia 1963; 1964 Commissioner-General of UNRWA.

Major Moenardo
Indonesia; 1963 appointed Additional Consul in North Borneo; declared *persona non grata* 1963.

Philip B. C. Moore
United Kingdom; born 1921; 1960 Counsellor, United Kingdom Commission, Singapore; 1961 Deputy Commissioner, Singapore; Deputy High Commissioner 1963–65.

M. J. Moynihan
United Kingdom; born 1916; Deputy High Commissioner, Kuala Lumpur 1961–63.

Datu Mustapha bin Datu Harun (now Tun Mustapha bin Datu Harun)
North Borneo (Sabah); born 1918; 1958 Member, North Borneo Legislative Council; formed USNO 1961; 1963 first Head of State, Sabah; 1966 Malaysian Federal Minister for Sabah Affairs; elected State Legislative Assembly 1967; 1967 Chief Minister of Sabah.

Chakravarthi V. Narasimhan
India; born 1915; 1936 Indian Civil Service; 1937 District Officer, Madras; 1942 Secretariat, Madras; 1950 Central Secretariat; 1956 Executive Secretary, United Nations ECAFE; 1959 Under-Secretary, United Nations; 1961 Chef de Cabinet to Secretary-General; 1968 Under-Secretary-General.

General Abdul Haris Nasution
Indonesia; born 1918; 1949 Chief of Staff, Army; 1959 Defence Minister; 1962 Minister Co-ordinator for Defence and Security and Deputy Commander-in-Chief of the Armed Forces; 1966 Chairman, Provisional People's Congress.

Dato Stephen Kalong Ningkan
Sarawak; born 1920; Secretary-General of SNAP 1961–64; 1962 Secretary-General of the Sarawak Alliance; Chief Minister 1963–66.

Ong Eng Guan
Singapore; born 1925, Malacca; accountant; Treasurer, PAP; 1957 Mayor of Singapore; 1959 elected to Legislative Assembly; Minister of National Development 1959–60; expelled from PAP and resigned seat 1960; won by-election 1961; formed United People's Party; elected on UPP ticket 1963.

Dato Ong Yoke Lin
Malaya; born 1917; nominated to Legislative Council 1954; elected Member, House of Representatives 1955; 1955 Minister of Posts and Telecommunications; 1956 of Transport; 1957 of Labour; 1959 of Health; 1962 Minister Without Portfolio and concurrently Permanent Representative at the United Nations 1962–64 and Ambassador, Washington, from 1962; still Minister Without Portfolio in Tun Razak's Cabinet 1970; Vice-President, MCA 1965.

Dato Onn bin Ja'affar (Dato Sir Onn bin Ja'affar)
Malaya; born 1895; 1936 Member, Johore State Council; founder and first President, UMNO, 1946; Mentri Besar, Johore, 1947–50; negotiated Federation Agreement 1949; launched Independence of Malaya Party and resigned from UMNO 1951; Member Legislative Council, 1948–55; Chairman, Rural and Industrial Development Authority 1950–55; Member for Home Affairs, Federal Executive Council 1951–55; reformed IMP as Party Negara 1953; elected Member, House of Representatives 1959; died 1962.

Dato Abang Haji Openg bin Abang Sapi'ee (later Tun Abang Haji Openg bin Abang Sapi'ee)
Sarawak; born 1905; 1940 Member, State Assembly; 1955 Supreme Council; 1963 Governor; died 1969.

Sir David Ormsby Gore (now 5th Baron Harlech)
United Kingdom; born 1918; 1957 Minister of State, Foreign Office; Ambassador, Washington 1961–65.

Nicasio Osmena
Philippines; son of late President Osmena; lawyer; encouraged members of the Kiram family (the descendants of Sultans of Sulu) to make claims in North Borneo; died 1963.

L. N. Palar

Indonesia; born 1915; Member, Dutch Second Chamber 1945–47; Indonesian Permanent Representative at the United Nations 1950–53 and 1962–65; Ambassador, New Delhi 1953–56, Bonn and later Moscow 1956, Ottawa 1957–62, Washington 1965–66.

B. R. Pearn

United Kingdom; born 1900; Lecturer and Professor of History, Rangoon University 1938–47; Head, South-East Asia Section, Foreign Office Research Department 1947–64.

E. H. Peck (now Sir Edward Peck)

United Kingdom; born 1915; 1958 Counsellor, Singapore; Assistant Under-Secretary, Foreign Office 1961–65.

Dr. Emmanuel Pelaez

Philippines; born 1915; 1949 Member (Liberal) House of Representatives; joined Nacionalista Party 1953; Senator 1954–60; joined Liberal Party 1961; 1962 Vice-President; also Foreign Secretary 1962–63; joined Nacionalista Party 1963; 1966 Member, House of Representatives; 1968 Senator.

Lord Perth (17th Earl of Perth)

United Kingdom; born 1907; Minister of State for Colonial Affairs 1957–62.

John Pilcher (now Sir John Pilcher)

United Kingdom; born 1912; Ambassador, Manila 1959–63.

Radhakrishna Ramani

Malaya; born 1901 in India; constitutional lawyer; Member, Legislative Council 1948–54; Deputy 1963–64 and Permanent Representative to the United Nations 1964–68; 1969 adviser on citizenship to National Operations Council.

Tun Haji Abdul Razak bin Dato Hussein

Malaya; born 1922; 1939 Malay Administrative Service; 1950 Malayan Civil Service; 1951 Deputy President, UMNO; 1952 State Secretary and 1955 Mentri Besar, Pahang; 1955 Minister of Education; 1957 of Defence and Deputy Prime Minister; 1959 Prime Minister; 1959 Deputy Prime Minister and Minister of Defence and of Rural Development; 1969 Director of Operations and Chairman of the National Operations Council; 1970 Prime Minister and Minister of Foreign Affairs and Defence.

Jacques Rueff

France; born 1896; 1923 Inspector of Finance; 1927 Secretariat, League of Nations; 1930 Financial Attaché, London; 1934 Assistant Director and Director, Treasury, Ministry of Finance; Vice-Governor, Bank of France 1939–41; 1946 President, Inter-Allied Reparations Agency; 1952 Judge, Court of the European Steel and Coal Community; and of the European Communities 1958–62.

Dean Rusk

United States; born 1909; Associate Professor of Government and Dean, Mills College 1936–40; Army and Department of Defence 1940–46; Assistant Secretary of State for United Nations Affairs, Deputy Under-Secretary and Assistant Secretary for Far Eastern Affairs 1947–51; President, Rockefeller Foundation 1952–61; Secretary of State 1961–69.

Duncan Sandys

United Kingdom; born 1908; Secretary of State for Commonwealth Relations 1960–64 and for the Colonies 1962–64.

Dr. Ali Sastroamidjojo

Indonesia; born 1903; Prime Minister 1953–55, 1956–57; Permanent Representative to United Nations 1957–60; Permanent Deputy Chairman, Provisional People's Consultative Assembly 1960–66; General Chairman, PNI to 1966; Chairman of the Bandung Conference 1955.

Lord Selkirk (10th Earl of Selkirk)

United Kingdom; born 1906; Commissioner for Singapore and Commissioner-General for South-East Asia 1959–63.

Felixberto Serrano

Philippines; born 1906; Congressman 1946–49; Secretary for Foreign Affairs 1957–61; Chairman United Nations Commission on Human Rights 1957; 1962 Senator.

Donald Stephens

North Borneo (Sabah); born 1920; 1955 proprietor, editor and publisher of *Sabah Times*; Member, Legislative Council; 1958 Chairman, Kadazan Society; 1961 founder President, UNKO (later UPKO); 1963 Chief Minister, Sabah; 1965 Federal Minister for Sabah Affairs; dissolved UPKO 1967; 1968 High Commissioner for Malaysia, Canberra.

Dr. Subandrio

Indonesia; born 1914; 1945 Secretary-General, Ministry of Information; 1947 unofficial representative, London; 1950 Ambassador, London; 1954 Ambassador, Moscow; 1956 Acting Secretary-General, Ministry of Foreign Affairs; 1957 Minister; Second Deputy First Minister in charge of Foreign Affairs 1960–66; since 1966 under sentence of death.[5]

Dr. Sukarno

Indonesia; born 1901: first President, Commander-in-Chief and from 1959 also Prime Minister; lost most of his powers in 1966; died 1970.

Sultan of Sulu (Sultan Jamalul Kiram)

Philippines; the last Sultan of Sulu; claims to parts of North Borneo (Sabah) made on behalf of some of his heirs.

Bambang Sumali

Indonesia; 1963 Publicity Officer, Indonesian Consulate, North Borneo; declared *persona non grata* July 1963.

Lorenzo Sumulong

Philippines; born 1905; 1946 Congressman (Liberal); Chairman, House Committee on Foreign Affairs; elected Senator (Liberal) 1949: re-elected (as Nacionalista) 1955, 1961 and 1969; former Chairman, Senate Committee on Foreign Affairs.

Dato G. S. Sundang (also Orang Kaya Kaya or O. K. K. Sundang)

North Borneo (Sabah); born 1909; 1960 Assistant District Officer; 1961 formed Pasok Momogun (UNPMO); 1964 Joint President, UPKO; 1964 Minister of Local Government; Deputy Chief Minister 1964–67.

---

[5] Sentence commuted to life imprisonment in 1980; pardoned and released in Aug 1995 on the fiftieth anniversary of Indonesia's independence.

Dr. Suwito Kusumowidagdo
Indonesia; born 1917; 1957 Secretary-General, Ministry of Foreign Affairs; 1962 First Deputy Foreign Minister: 1966 Ambassador, Washington; 1968 Ambassador, Stockholm, Oslo, Copenhagen and Helsinki.

Tan Siew Sin (now Tun Tan Siew Sin)
Malaya; born 1916; 1946 Municipal Commissioner, Malacca; 1948 Member, Legislative Council; member, Rubber Producers' Council 1951–57; Honorary Treasurer, Alliance Party 1958–65; 1957 Vice-President and 1961 President, MCA; 1957 Minister of Commerce and Industry; 1959 of Finance; 1969 with Special Duties; 1970 of Finance.

(U) Thant
Burma; born 1909; 1949 Secretary, Ministry of Information; 1954 a Secretary to the Prime Minister; 1957 Permanent Representative at the United Nations; 1961 Acting Secretary-General, United Nations; 1962 Secretary-General.

Peter Thomas
United Kingdom: born 1920; 1961 Parliamentary Under-Secretary, Foreign Office; Minister of State 1963–64.

Peter Thorneycroft (now Baron Thorneycroft of Dunston)
United Kingdom; born 1909; Minister of Defence 1962–64.

Too Joon Hing
Malaya; born 1911; 1936 tin mining and rubber planting; Commandant, Perak Police Volunteer Reserve 1949–54; Member, Legislative Council 1955–59; Assistant Minister for Education 1955–57; 1959 Member, Perak State Legislative Assembly; Secretary-General, MCA; resigned from MCA 1959; won by-election 1961; helped to found UDP.

Sir Geofroy Tory
United Kingdom; born 1912; High Commissioner, Kuala Lumpur 1957–64.

Sir Alexander Waddell
United Kingdom; born 1913; Governor, Sarawak 1960–63.

F. A. Warner
United Kingdom; born 1918; Head, South-East Asia Department, Foreign Office 1960–64.

Sir David Watherston
United Kingdom; born 1907; 1952 Chief Secretary, Federation of Malaya; Special Counsellor. Malayan High Commission in the United Kingdom 1957–59; member, Cobbold Commission 1962.

Harold A. W. Watkinson (now 1st Viscount Watkinson of Woking)
United Kingdom; born 1910; Minister of Defence 1959–62.

Sir Dennis White
United Kingdom; born 1910; High Commissioner, Brunei 1959–63.

Dato Wong Pow Nee (now Tan Sri Wong Pow Nee)
Malaya; born 1911; teacher 1937–57; 1955 Member, Penang State Assembly; Chief Minister, Penang 1957–69; 1970 Ambassador, Rome.

Professor Mohamed Yamin
Indonesia; born 1903; Member, Volksraad 1938–42; adviser, Propaganda Department, Japanese administration; member, Independence Preparatory Committee 1945; involved in Communist Madiun Rising 1948; 1950 Member, Republican Parliament and 1956 MP; 1951 Minister of Justice; 1953 of Education; 1958 of State; 1959 of Social and Cultural Affairs (later Special Affairs) and Chairman of National Planning Board; died 1962.

Sir Mohammed Zafrulla Khan
Pakistan; born 1893; member, Punjab Legislative Council 1926–35; delegate, Indian Round Table Conferences 1930, 1931, 1932; President All-India Muslim League 1931; Member, Viceroy's Executive Council; 1941 Judge, Indian Federal Court; 1947 Minister of Foreign Affairs and Commonwealth Relations, Pakistan; 1954 Member, International Court of Justice; 1961 Permanent Representative at United Nations; President, United Nations General Assembly 1962–63; 1964 Member, International Court; 1970 President, International Court.

Zaini bin Haji Ahmad
Brunei; son of Brunei Privy Councillor; Member, Parti Ra'ayat; with Sheikh Azahari in Manila 1962 and named by him 'Minister of Economics, Commerce and Industry'; sought and granted political asylum, United Kingdom Embassy, Manila 1963; in protective custody, Hong Kong 1963; sent to Brunei at own request 1963; in detention from 1963.

Abang Zulkifli
Sarawak; 'Lieutenant-General', commander of TNKU and 'Defence Minister' in the 'United State of North Kalimantan' proclaimed by Sheikh Azahari 1962; 1964 relieved of his duties; thereafter mostly in Indonesia.

Appendix B

Notes on Political Parties

The Alliance
Malaya; formed early 1952 by UMNO and MCP [sic; MCA] to oppose Dato Onn's Independence of Malaya Party in the Kuala Lumpur municipal elections; won 51 out of 52 elected seats in 1955 and a majority in all subsequent federal elections; in Malaya its constituents include also MIC; related bodies also formed in other Malaysian territories.

Barisan Ra'ayat Jati Sarawak (Barjasa)
Sarawak; registered December 1961; original members mostly Malays in Government service led by Abdul Rahman bin Yacob, a Crown Counsel; originally at odds with the other Malay party, Panas, but in 1967 the two merged to form Party Bumiputra.

Barisan Sosialis
Singapore, formed summer 1961 by Communist-influenced members of PAP led by Lim Chin Siong and Dr. Lee Siew Choh, with Dr. Lee as Chairman; registered August 1961; leading Left-wing members detained during 1963; in 1963 elections won 13 seats out of 51 in Singapore Assembly, but subsequently abandoned electoral activity.

Borneo Utara National Party (Bunap)—later Sabah National Party
North Borneo (Sabah); formed October 1962 by amalgamation of United and Democratic Parties; joined Sabah Alliance November 1962; an uneasy coalition of North Borneo Chinese. (See also Democratic Party and United Party.)

Clandestine Communist Organisation (CCO)—later Sarawak Communist Organisation (SC)

Sarawak; name given by Government to the almost wholly Chinese terrorist organisation in Sarawak: connections with the Left wing of SUPP; unsuccessful efforts to infiltrate North Borneo; from 1963 engaged in small-scale guerilla warfare with Indonesian assistance.

Democratic Party

North Borneo (Sabah); formed 1961; primarily Chinese in the Jesselton and Tawau areas in membership, but also tried to attract a lower stratum of Chinese from Sandakan than the United Party and Indonesian and Filipino workers on the east coast; October 1962 agreed to merge with United Party as Bunap, which subsequently joined the Sabah Alliance.

Gerakan Ra'ayat Malaysia (Gerakan)

Malaya; formed 1968 as a multi-racial party, though primarily Chinese in composition, with the UDP as one of its components; formed the State Government of Penang following the 1969 elections.

Joint Opposition Conference

Malaya; formed April 1963 with Abdul Aziz bin Ishak as Chairman; led to formation of National Convention Party which later formed a part of the Malayan People's Socialist Front.

Malayan Chinese Association (MCA)—later Malaysian Chinese Association

Malaya; founded 1949; main interest the maintenance of Chinese economic interests and the achievement of a working relationship with the Malays to that end; formed the Alliance with the leading Malay party UMNO in 1952; 1959 a division of view in the MCA over the allocation of parliamentary seats within the Alliance and the use of the Chinese language in examinations led to the resignation of members who went on to form the UDP and the Gerakan; hostility to Singapore PAP which was a potential rival for the support of the Chinese and as a partner with UMNO: its position was weakened by Alliance losses in the 1969 elections.

Malayan Indian Congress (MIC)—later Malaysian Indian Congress

Malaya; formed 1949; a minor partner in the Alliance in Malaya and Singapore.

Malayan Communist Party (MCP)

Malaya and Singapore; formed 1930; in 1948 began guerilla-style revolt, the 'Emergency', which dwindled away after 1951 and was officially ended in 1960; the party however remained illegal and small groups continued occasional guerilla activity around the Malayan–Thai border.

North Borneo Chinese Association

North Borneo (Sabah); formed 1961; claimed to be non-political.

Pan-Malayan Islamic Party (PMIP)

Malaya; founded 1951; won the only elected seat not taken by the Alliance in the 1955 federal elections; secured control of Kelantan and Trengganu states in the 1959 elections; lost control of Trengganu in 1961; improved position in 1969 federal elections; a strongly Malay nationalist and Islamic party with its main centres of strength in the less-developed east coast states; the main rival to UMNO for Malay support and the principal Opposition party; Indonesian connections.

Partai Komunis Indonesia (PKI)

Indonesia; formed 1920, re-established 1945 and reformed in an expanded and reorganised form in 1948; the Indonesian Communist party; involved in 1948 Madiun rising and 1965 Gestapu abortive *coup*; banned 1966, but efforts have been made to revive it.

Partai Nasional Indonesia (PNI)

Indonesia; formed 1927 under chairmanship of Sukarno and reformed 1945; the Indonesian Nationalist party; Nationalist, primarily Javanese, radical and with especial appeal to the bureaucracy.

Party Negara Sarawak (Panas)

Sarawak; registered April 1960; Right-wing, Malay; failed to hold initial Iban support; at first on ill-terms with the other Malay party, Barjasa; in the 1963 elections had an arrangement with SUPP for the higher level elections; subsequently merged with Barjasa into the Party Bumiputra.

Party Pesaka Anak Sarawak (Papas or Pesaka)

Sarawak; formed June 1962; primarily based on the Third Division (or Rejang) Ibans; joined the Sarawak Alliance in October 1962 but continued to show a tendency to put up separate candidates in elections.

Parti Ra'ayat Brunei

Brunei; first congress April 1957; 1962 won 54 out of 55 District Council seats and all 16 elected seats in the Legislative Council; December 1962 organised revolt in Brunei and thereafter ceased to operate.

Parti Ra'ayat Malaya

Malaya; formed 1955; allied with the, largely Chinese, Labour Party in the Malayan People's Socialist Front until 1966; Left-wing, primarily Malay party with little following.

People's Action Party (PAP)

Singapore; formed 1954; trade union background; largest party in the City Council after 1958 elections; won 3 seats in Legislative Assembly 1955; 43 out of 51 seats 1959; Ong Eng Guan and some supporters left party 1960; the Left-wing left the party 1961; won 37 out of 51 seats in Legislative Assembly 1963; thereafter increasingly monopolised political power in Singapore.

Sabah Alliance Party (Sabapa)

North Borneo (Sabah); set up October 1962 with USNO, UNKO and Bunap as members; joined November 1962 by UNPMO and SIC; successful in December 1962 elections; thereafter increasingly dominated by USNO.

Sabah Indian Congress (SIC)

North Borneo (Sabah); joined Sabah Alliance November 1962; insignificant.

Sarawak Alliance

Sarawak; formed October 1962 as Sarawak United Front and took name of Alliance November 1962; its purpose was to support the concept of Malaysia in opposition to SUPP; constituents Barjasa, Panas, Pesaka and Snap, together with the Sarawak Chinese Association which was formed in July 1962 by a group of moderate Chinese; throughout a very loose alliance from which Panas withdrew almost immediately.

Sarawak National Party (Snap)

Sarawak; formed early 1961; primarily Second Division Ibans (or Sea Dyaks) especially from the Saribas district, but later moved its headquarters from Betong to Kuching and set out to broaden its support amongst Land Dyaks and others; member of the Sarawak Alliance until June 1966 and provided the first Chief Minister; subsequently a leading and in 1970 the only Opposition party.

Sarawak United People's Party (SUPP)

Sarawak; formed 1959; a primarily Chinese party which lost many of its Iban supporters after 1962; contained both moderates and an extremist wing linked with the CCO; entered the Government of Sarawak in 1970.

Singapore Alliance

Singapore; formed June 1961 by Singapore UMNO, the Singapore branches of MCA and MIC and the Singapore People's Alliance, which had been formed by Lim Yew Hock from the Labour Front, the rump of which dissolved in February 1960; formation of the Singapore Alliance led to defections from the SPA; a new announcement of the formation of the Alliance was made in April 1963 and it contested the September 1963 elections but failed to win a seat.

Singapore Association of Trade Unions (SATU)

Singapore; formed 1961 as a Left-wing breakaway from the PAP-linked Singapore Trade Union Council (STUC) which was shortly afterwards replaced by the National Trade Union Congress (NTUC).

Tentera Nasional Kalimantan Utara (TNKU)

Brunei, the 'National Army of North Borneo' formed as the military wing of the Parti Ra'ayat Brunei and its instrument in conducting the 1962 Brunei revolt.

United Democratic Party (UDP)

Malaya; formed April 1962 by dissidents from the MCA dissatisfied with the Chinese position within the Alliance; became a constituent of the Gerakan in 1968; its leader, Dr. Lim Chong Eu, became Chief Minister of Penang in 1969.

United Malays National Organisation (UMNO)

Malaya; formed 1946; formed the Alliance in 1952 with the MCA and has since been in effect the ruling party in Malaya and Malaysia.

United National Kadazan Organisation (UNKO)

North Borneo (Sabah); the first party in North Borneo formed following a meeting in March 1961 and inaugurated in August 1961; formed the Sabah Alliance in 1962 with USNO and other groups; merged with the other non-Muslim native party, UNPMO, to form the United Pasok-momogun Kadazan Organisation (UPKO); under increasing pressure from USNO which had Malay federal support; dissolved December 1967. ('Kadazan' is a name for the largest indigenous group in North Borneo, the Dusuns.)

United National Pasok Momogun Organisation (UNPMO or Pasok Momogun)

North Borneo (Sabah); formed late 1961; main support amongst Muruts in the Interior Residency; after healing of a split changed name to United National Pasok Momogun Party in April 1962; subsequently joined Sabah Alliance and merged with UNKO into UPKO. ('Pasok Momogun' means 'Sons of the Soil'.)

United Party
   North Borneo (Sabah); originally United Democratic Front, then Social Democratic Party; held first conference as United Party February 1962; its main supporters were the 'Towkays'[6] of Sandakan, but it also had supporters amongst the Chinese of Jesselton; united with the other main Chinese party in Bunap in October 1962.

United People's Party (UPP)
   Singapore; formed June 1961 by dissidents from PAP led by Ong Eng Guan; one of three members of Legislative Assembly rejoined PAP August 1962; only secured one seat in September 1963 elections.

United Sabah National Organisation (USNO)
   North Borneo (Sabah); formed December 1961; membership primarily Muslim though open to all natives of North Borneo; joins UNKO in Sabah Alliance October 1962; subsequently becomes the dominant group under the leadership of Datu Mustapha.

Workers Party
   Singapore; formed 1957 by dissidents from Labour Front led by David Marshall, who won a by-election for the party in July 1961; Marshall resigned from the party in January 1963 and it failed to win a seat in the September 1963 elections.

---

[6] ie, Chinese traders.

Biographical Notes

Abang Haji Openg see Openg

Abdul Kadir bin Shamsudin, b 1920
Kajang High School (Selangor), Raffles College (Singapore), one of the Inns of Court (London, 1948–1951) and Yale (1954); assistant superintendent of posts, 1939; promoted to Malayan Civil Service; secretary to the representatives of their highnesses, the Malay rulers, at the London constitutional conference, 1956; acting principal assistant secretary, Malayan Ministry of Internal Defence and Security, May 1956; seconded to the War Office, London, Oct 1956; assistant secretary, Malayan cabinet, 1957; the first Malayan to attend a course at the Imperial Defence College, 1959; deputy secretary for defence, 1960; succeeded Robert Thompson as secretary for defence, Apr 1961

Abdul Rahman Putra Al-Haj, Tunku (Tunku Abdul Rahman), 1903–1990
CH 1961; son of Sultan Abdul Hamid Halim Shah of Kedah; schools in Bangkok and Alor Star, Penang Free School, St Catharine's College, Cambridge, and Inner Temple, London; entered Kedah government service, 1931; served as director of education (Kedah) and director of passive defence during Japanese occupation; resumed law study at Inner Temple, 1946, and called to the Bar; returned to Malaya, 1949, joined Kedah legal department and became chairman of UMNO, Kedah division; seconded to Federal legal department as deputy public prosecutor, 1949; president of UMNO, Aug 1951, and left government service; unofficial member of Federal Executive Council, 1952; leader of Alliance, 1952; elected to Federal Legislative Council,

July 1955; became chief minister and minister for home affairs, Aug 1955; acquired portfolio of minister for internal defence and security, 1956; led Alliance delegation in independence talks in London, Jan–Feb 1956, Dec 1956–Jan 1957 and May 1957; prime minister of Malaya, 1957–Apr 1959 and Aug 1959–1963; led Malayan missions in London talks leading to formation of Malaysia, Nov 1961, July 1962 and July 1963; prime minister of Malaysia, 1963–70; after retirement from politics he served as secretary-general of the Islamic Secretariat in Jeddah, 1970–1973, and contributed a weekly column to *The Star* newspaper, Penang

Abdul Razak bin Hussein, Tun (Tun Razak), 1922–1976
Son of a Pahang chief; Malay school, Pekan, and Malay College, Kuala Kangsar, Raffles College, Singapore (1940) and Lincoln's Inn (1947–1949); joined Malay Administrative Service, 1939; captain in Wataniah (Malay anti-Japanese force); ADO, Raub, 1945; secretary of Malay Society of Great Britain, 1947–1948; president, 1948–1949; appointed to MCS and attached to state secretariat, Pahang, 1950; leader of UMNO Youth and a vice-president of UMNO, 1951; Federal Legislative Council from 1951; state secretary, Pahang, 1952; mentri besar, Pahang, 1955; resigned government service to contest federal elections, 1955; minister for education, 1955–1957; minister of defence and deputy prime minister, 1957–Apr 1959; prime minister, Apr–Aug 1959; deputy prime minister, minister of defence and minister of rural development, 1959–1969; director of operations and chairman of National

Operations Council, 1969; prime minister, minister of defence and minister of foreign affairs, 1970–1976

Abell, Anthony Foster, 1906–1994
Knighted 1952; Repton and Magdalen, Oxford; Colonial Administrative Service, Nigeria, 1929–1949; governor, Sarawak, and high commissioner, Brunei, 1950–1959; member, Commission of Enquiry North Borneo and Sarawak (Cobbold Commission), 1962

Azahari, Sheikh A M Azahari bin Sheikh Mahmoud, b 1928
Son of a father of Arab descent and a Brunei Malay mother; educated in Brunei; during the Japanese occupation he was sent to study veterinary science in Indonesia; participated in the nationalist struggle against the restoration of Dutch rule, 1945–1949; returned to Brunei in 1952; founded the Party Rakyat Brunei, 1956; appointed to Brunei's Legislative Council 1962; advocate of the United State of North Kalimantan; lived in Indonesia after the abortive Brunei rising, Dec 1962

Brook, Norman Craven (Lord Normanbrook), 1902–1967
Knighted 1946; cr 1st Baron Normanbrook, 1963; Wolverhampton School and Wadham, Oxford; Home Office, 1925–1940; personal assistant to lord president of the Council, 1940–1942; deputy secretary (civil) to War Cabinet, 1942; permanent secretary, Ministry of Reconstruction, 1943–1945; additional secretary to the Cabinet, 1945–1946; secretary to Cabinet, 1947–1962; joint secretary to Treasury and head of Home Civil Service, 1956–1962

Clutterbuck, (Peter) Alexander, 1897–1975
Knighted 1946; Malvern College and Pembroke, Cambridge; military service, 1916–1919; Home Civil Service, 1919–1961; entered Colonial Office in 1922; secretary, Donoughmore Commission on Ceylon constitution, 1927–1928; private secretary to permanent undersecretary, Dominions Office, 1928–1929;

member of UK Delegation to League of Nations assembly, 1929, 1930 and 1931; deputy high commissioner, South Africa, 1939–1940; assistant secretary, Dominions Office, 1940, and assistant undersecretary, 1942–1946; high commissioner, Canada, 1946–1952, and India, 1952–1955; ambassador, Ireland, 1955–1959; permanent under-secretary, Commonwealth Relations Office, 1959–1961

Cobbold, Cameron Fromanteel (Lord Cobbold), 1904–1987
cr 1st Baron Cobbold of Knebworth, 1960; Eton and King's College, Cambridge; entered the Bank of England 1933; adviser to the governor; governor of the Bank of England, 1949–1961; chairman of the Commission of Enquiry into North Borneo and Sarawak, 1962; lord chamberlain of Her Majesty's Household, 1963–1971

Dean, Patrick Henry, 1909–1994
Knighted 1957; Rugby and Gonville & Caius, Cambridge; Fellow of Clare College, 1932–1935; entered FO as assistant legal adviser, 1939; deputy under-secretary of state, FO, 1956–1960; permanent UK representative to UN, 1960–1964; ambassador in Washington, 1965–1969

Eastwood, Christopher Gilbert, 1905–1983
Eton and Trinity, Oxford; entered CO 1927 as assistant principal; private secretary to the high commissioner for Palestine, 1932–1934; secretary, International Rubber Regulation Committee, 1934; private secretary to Lord Lloyd and Lord Moyne when secretaries of state for Colonies, 1940–1941; principal assistant secretary, Cabinet Office, 1945–1947; assistant under-secretary of state, CO, 1947–1952; commissioner of crown lands, 1952–1954; assistant undersecretary of state, CO, 1954–1966

Garner, (Joseph John) Saville (Lord Garner), 1908–1983
Knighted 1954; life peer cr 1969 (Baron); Highgate School and Jesus,

Cambridge; entered Dominions Office, 1930; private secretary to successive Ss of S; served in High Commission, Canada, 1943–1948; assistant under-secretary of state, CRO, 1948–1951; deputy high commissioner in India, 1951–1953; deputy under-secretary of state, CRO, 1952–1956; high commissioner in Canada, 1956–1961; permanent under-secretary of state, CRO/Commonwealth Office, 1962–1968; head of Diplomatic Service, 1965–1968

Ghazali Shafie, Muhammad (later Tan Sri), b 1922

Clifford School (Kuala Lipis), Raffles College (Singapore), University College of Wales, Aberystwyth, and London School of Economics; member of Malay resistance organisation during the Japanese occupation; government service after 1945; assistant state secretary in Negri Sembilan and later Selangor; seconded for external affairs training to the office of UK high commissioner, New Delhi (Malcolm MacDonald), 1955–1956; Malayan commissioner, New Delhi, 1957; deputy permanent secretary, Ministry of External Affairs, Aug 1957; permanent secretary, 1959; member of Commission of Enquiry North Borneo and Sarawak (Cobbold Commission), 1962; member, National Operations Council, 1969; held senior ministerial office in the governments of Abdul Razak, Hussein Onn and Mahathir, 1970–1984

Goh Keng Swee, Dr, b 1918

Born in Malacca; educated at Singapore's Anglo-Chinese School, Raffles College, Singapore, and London School of Economics; founder and first chairman of the nationalist Malayan Forum (whose members included Lee Kuan Yew, Toh Chin Chye and Abdul Razak); civil service in Singapore until May 1959 when he resigned to stand as a candidate for the People's Action Party; minister of Finance, Singapore, 1959–1965 and 1967–1970; minister of Defence, Republic of Singapore, 1965–1967 and 1970–1979;

deputy prime minister, 1972–1984; minister of Education, 1979–1984

Goode, William Allmond Codrington, 1907–1986

Knighted 1957; Oakham School and Worcester College, Oxford; barrister-at-law, Gray's Inn, 1936; entered Malayan Civil Service 1931; prisoner of war, 1942–1945; deputy economic secretary, Federation of Malaya, 1948; chief secretary, Aden, 1949–1953; acting governor, Aden, 1950–1951; chief secretary, Singapore, 1953–1957; governor, Singapore, Dec 1957–2 June 1959; yang di-pertuan negara (head of state) of the State of Singapore and UK commissioner, Singapore, 1959; governor, North Borneo, 1960–1963; chairman, Water Resources Board, 1964–1974

Hall, Harold Percival, b 1913

Portsmouth Grammar School and Royal Military College, Sandhurst; commissioned Indian Army 1933; Indian Political Service, 1937–1947; principal, CO, 1947; assistant secretary and head of Pacific and Indian Ocean Dept, CO, 1955–1962; seconded to Reid Commission to Malaya, 1956; seconded to Office of UK commissioner-general, SE Asia, 1962–1963; secretary, Inter-Government Committee for Malaysia, 1962–1963; British deputy high commissioner for Eastern Malaysia, Kuching, Sarawak, 1963–1964; assistant secretary, CO, 1965–1966; assistant under-secretary of state, Commonwealth Office, 1966–1968; assistant under-secretary of state, MoD, 1968–1973; director of studies, Royal Institute of Public Administration, 1974–1985

Home, Alexander Frederick Douglas- (Lord Home), 1903–1995

14th Earl of Home, 1951–1963 (renounced peerage), Sir Alec Douglas-Home, 1963–1974, cr life peer 1974 (Baron Home of the Hirsel); Eton and Christ Church, Oxford; MP (Conservative), 1931–1945, 1950–1951, 1963–1974; parliamentary private secretary to prime minister, 1937–1940; joint parliamentary under-secretary of state, FO, 1945; minister of state, Scottish Office, 1951–1955; S of S for Commonwealth relations, 1955–1960; leader of House of Lords, 1957–1960; lord president of the Council, 1957, 1959–1960; S of S for foreign affairs, 1960–1963; prime minister, 1963–1964; S of S for foreign and Commonwealth affairs, 1970–1974

Ismail bin Dato Abdul Rahman, Dr Dato (later Tun), 1915–1973
English College, Johore Bahru, and Melbourne University; private medical practice in Johore Bahru, 1947–1953; member of Johore State Council, 1948–1954, and Johore Executive Council from 1954; member of Federal Legislative Council; member for lands, mines and communications, Federal Executive Council, 1953; member for natural resources, 1954–1955; minister for natural resources, 1955; minister for commerce and industry, 1956–1957; minister plenipotentiary (without portfolio), delegate to UN and ambassador to Washington, 1957; minister for external affairs, 1959; Malayan representative on Singapore's Internal Security Council, 1959–1963; minister for internal security, 1960; minister for internal security and interior, 1961; minister for home affairs and justice, 1964–1967; resigned from the Malaysian Cabinet to work in the private sector; member of Tun Razak's National Operations Council, 1969; deputy prime minister, minister for home affairs, and minister of trade and industry in Tun Razak's government, 1970–1973

Lansdowne, George John Charles Mercer Nairne Petty-Fitzmaurice (Lord Lansdowne), 1912–1999
8th Marquess of Lansdowne, 1944; Eton and Christ Church, Oxford; military service, 1939–1945; joint parliamentary under-secretary of state, FO, 1958–1962; minister of state for Colonial affairs, 1962–1964, and for Commonwealth

relations, 1963–1964; chairman, Inter-Governmental Committee on Malaysia, 1962–1963

Lee Kuan Yew, b 1923
Raffles College, Singapore, Fitzwilliam, Cambridge and Middle Temple, London; member of nationalist Malayan Forum (with Goh Keng Swee, Toh Chin Chye and Abdul Razak); legal practice in Singapore, 1950–1959; played leading role in foundation of the People's Action Party, Nov 1954; elected to Legislative Assembly, 1955; member of constitutional missions to London, 1956, 1957 and 1958; led PAP to victory in 1959 elections; prime minister of self-governing state of Singapore, 1959–1963, of Singapore within Malaysia, 1963–1965, and of the independent Republic of Singapore, 1965–1990; senior minister since Nov 1990

Lennox-Boyd, Alan Tindal (Lord Boyd), 1904–1983
cr 1st Viscount Boyd of Merton 1960; Sherborne and Christ Church, Oxford (president of Oxford Union, 1926); MP (Conservative), 1931–1960; parliamentary secretary, Ministry of Labour, 1938–1939, of home security, 1939, of Ministry of Food, 1939–1940, of Ministry of Aircraft Production, 1943–1945; minister of state, CO, 1951–1952; minister of transport and civil aviation, 1952–1954; S of S for colonies, 1954–1959

Lim Chin Siong, 1933–1996
Catholic High School , Singapore, and Chinese High School, Bukit Timah, Singapore; secretary, Changi Bus Workers Union, and Spinning Workers Union, 1953; secretary, Singapore Factory and Shop Workers Union, 1954; elected as PAP candidate to Singapore Legislative Assembly, 1955; with Lee Kuan Yew represented PAP at London constitutional talks, 1956; detained 1956–1959; political secretary in PAP government, 1959; expelled from the PAP and became secretary-general of the Barisan Sosialis, 1961; arrested

under operation 'Coldstore', Feb 1963; released from detention and went into exile in London, 1969; returned to Singapore, 1979

Lim Yew Hock (Tun Haji Omar Lim Yew Hock), 1914–1984
Third-generation Straits Chinese; Raffles College, Singapore; general secretary, Singapore Clerical and Administrative Workers Union; founder-member, Singapore Trade Union Congress; nominated by the governor to represent the interests of labour in the Legislative Council, 1948; president, Singapore Labour Party; entered the Labour Front for the 1955 elections; deputy chief minister and minister for labour and welfare, 1955–1956; succeeded David Marshall as chief minister, Singapore, 1956–1959; took strong action against Chinese high school student rebels and communist supporters in TUs, Sept–Nov 1956; led the second and third all-party-delegations to London for constitutional talks, 1957 and 1958, resulting in internal self-government; leader of the Singapore People's Alliance in the Legislative Assembly, 1959–1963; Malaysian high commissioner to Australia, 1963–1965; converted to Islam and moved to Jeddah

MacDonald, Malcolm John, 1901–1981
OM 1969; son of James Ramsay MacDonald (prime minister, 1924, 1929–1931 and 1931–1935); Bedales School and Queen's College, Oxford; member of the London County Council, 1927–1930; MP (Labour) 1929–1931, (National Labour) 1931–1935, National Government) 1936–1945; parliamentary under-secretary of state for dominions, 1931–1935; S of S for dominions, 1935–1938 and 1938–1939; S of S for Colonies, 1935 and 1938–1940; minister of health, 1940; high commissioner, Canada, 1941–1946; gov-gen, Malaya, 1946–1948; commissioner-general, SE Asia, 1948–1955; chancellor, University of Malaya, 1949–1961; high commissioner, India, 1955–1960; co-chairman, International Conference on Laos,

1961–1963; gov, Kenya, 1963; gov-gen, Kenya, 1963–1964; British high commissioner, Kenya, 1964–1965; British special representative in East and Central Africa, 1963–1966; special envoy to Sudan and Somalia, 1967

MacKintosh, Angus MacKay, 1915–1986
Knighted 1972; Fettes, Edinburgh University and New College Oxford; military service, 1942–1946; principal, CO, 1946; private secretary to the secretary of state (Lyttelton), 1950; assistant secretary, 1952; seconded to FO as deputy commissioner-general, SE Asia, 1956–1960; seconded to Cabinet Office, 1961–1963; high commissioner, Brunei, 1963–1964; assistant secretary, MoD, 1964–1965; assistant under-secretary, MoD, 1965–1966; senior civilian instructor, Imperial Defence College, 1966–1968; assistant under-secretary, FCO, 1968–1969; high commissioner, Ceylon/Sri Lanka, and ambassador, Maldives, 1969–1973

Macleod, Iain Norman, 1913–1970
Fettes and Gonville & Caius, Cambridge; military service, 1939–1945; joined Conservative Party Parliamentary Secretariat, 1946; head of Home Affairs Research Dept of Conservative Party, 1948–1950; MP (Conservative), 1950–1970; minister of health, 1952–1955; minister of labour and national service, Dec 1955–Oct 1959; S of S for colonies, 1959–1961; chancellor of Duchy of Lancaster and leader of House of Commons, 1961–1963; chairman, Conservative Party Organisation, 1961–1963; editor, *The Spectator*, 1963–1965; chancellor of the Exchequer, June 1970 (died 20 July 1970)

Macmillan, (Maurice) Harold (Lord Stockton), 1894–1986
cr 1st Earl of Stockton 1984; Eton and Balliol, Oxford; military service, 1914–1918; MP (Conservative) 1924–1929, 1931–1964; parliamentary secretary, Ministry of Supply, 1940–1942; parliamentary under-secretary of state, CO,

1942; minister resident at Allied HQ in NW Africa, 1942–1945; secretary for air, 1945; minister of housing and local government, 1951–1954; minister of defence, Oct 1954–Apr 1955; S of S for foreign affairs, Apr–Dec 1955; chancellor of the Exchequer, Dec 1955–Jan 1957; prime minister, Jan 1957–Oct 1963

Marsal bin Maun, Dato Seri Paduka Awang Haji, b 1913/1914
Sultan Idris Training College; superintendent of education, Brunei, 1935; observer on State Council, Brunei, 1954–1956; member, legislative council, 1959; deputy state secretary, May 1960; mentri besar, Brunei, Aug 1961–May 1967

Marshall, David Saul, 1908–1995
A Sephardi Jew and Singapore businessman, lawyer and politician; a founder of the Labour Front Party, 1954; member, legislative assembly, 1955–1957; chief minister of Singapore, 1955–1956; formed Workers' Party, 1957; won the Anson by-election, July 1961; lost seat in elections, Sept 1963; permanent member of the Presidential Council, 1970; ambassador, Paris, 1978

Martin, John Miller, 1904–1991
Knighted 1952; Edinburgh Academy and Corpus Christi, Oxford; entered Dominions Office, 1927; seconded to Malayan Civil Service, 1931–1934; secretary, Palestine Royal Commission, 1936; seconded as private secretary to prime minister (Churchill), 1940–1945 (principal private secretary, 1941–1945); assistant under-secretary of state, CO, 1945–1956; deputy permanent under-secretary of state, CO, 1956–1965; member, Inter-Governmental Committee (Lansdowne Committee), 1962–1963; high commissioner, Malta, 1965–1967

Maudling, Reginald, 1917–1979
Merchant Taylors' School and Merton, Oxford; joined the Conservative Parliamentary Secretariat 1945; MP (Conservative), 1950–1979; parliamentary

secretary, Ministry of Civil Aviation, 1952; economic secretary to the Treasury, 1952–1955; minister of supply, 1955–1957; paymaster-general, 1957–1959; president of the Board of Trade, 1959–1961; S of S for the colonies, Oct 1961–July 1962; chancellor of the Exchequer, 1962–1964; home secretary, 1970–1972

Melville, Eugene, 1911–1986
Knighted 1965; Queen's Park School, Glasgow and St Andrews University; entered CO, 1936; Colonies Supply Mission, Washington, 1941–1945; private secretary to S of S for colonies (G H Hall), 1945–1946; financial adviser, Control Commission for Germany, 1949–1952; assistant under-secretary of state, CO, 1952, and FO, 1961; diplomatic postings to Bonn, EFTA and GATT, 1962–1965; ambassador and permanent UK representative to UN and other international organisations, Geneva, 1966–1971

Moore, Philip Brian Cecil (Lord Moore), b 1921
Knighted 1976; life peer cr 1986 (Baron); Cheltenham College and Brasenose, Oxford; RAF Bomber Command, 1940–1942; prisoner of war, 1942–1945; assistant private secretary to first lord of the Admiralty, 1950–1951; England rugby union international, 1951; principal private secretary to first lord of the Admiralty, 1957–1958; deputy UK commissioner, Singapore, 1961–1963; British deputy high commissioner in Singapore, 1963–1965; chief of public relations, MoD, 1965–1966; assistant private secretary to the Queen, 1966–1972; deputy private secretary, 1972–1977; private secretary and keeper of the Queen's archives, 1976–1986; permanent lord-in-waiting to the Queen, 1990

Mustapha bin Datu Harun, Datu (later Tun), 1918–1995
A Suluk and a Muslim born in Kudat district of North Borneo (Sabah); primary education only; succeeded father as

headman (orang kaya kaya); member of pre-war North Borneo Legislative Council; guerrilla leader during Japanese occupation; founding president of USNO, 1961; early supporter of Malaysia; governor/head of state (Yang di-Pertua Negri) on Sabah's entry into Malaysia, 1963–1965; federal minister for Sabah affairs, 1965–1967; chief minister, Sabah, 1967–1975; made Islam official religion and conducted mass conversions, 1973; his attempt to secede from Malaysia led to fall from power and years in the political wilderness; reconciliation with the government in Kuala Lumpur resulted in his reappointment as federal minister for Sabah affairs, 1991–1994

Ningkan, Stephen Kalong, 1920–1997
Worked with police at Kapit, Sarawak, during Japanese occupation; hospital assistant in Shell Hospital, Kuala Belait (Brunei), 1950–1961; honorary secreatary, Shell Dayak Club, Brunei, 1955–1956 and 1958–1959; founder-president, Dayak Association, Brunei, 1958–1960; founding-member of Sarawak National Party (SNAP), 1961; secretary-general, SNAP, 1961–1964; president, SNAP, 1964–1975; chief minister, Sarawak, 1963–1966; ejected from office, 1966; opposition leader, Sarawak State Assembly, 1966–1974

Omar Ali Saifuddin Wasa'dul Khairi Waddin (HH Sultan Haji Sir Omar Ali Saifuddin III), 1914–1986
Malay College, Kuala Kangsar; 1937 entered service of government of Brunei, working in the forestry department and judiciary; succeeded his brother as Sultan of Brunei, 1950; introduced written constitution and new agreement with Britain, 1959; abdicated in favour of his son, 4 Oct 1967

Ong Eng Guan, b 1925
Singapore politician, born in Malaya; trained as an accountant in Australia; founder-member and treasurer of the PAP; mayor of Singapore, 1957; elected to legislative assembly, 1959; minister of National Development, 1959–1960;

expelled from PAP, July 1960; resigned seat; won the Hong Lim by-election, Apr 1961; formed United People's Party, June 1961; elected to legislative assembly as sole representative of the UPP, Sept 1963; resigned seat, 1965

Ong Kee Hui (later Tan Sri Datuk), b 1914
Member of a prominent and wealthy Hokkien family of Sarawak; St Thomas's School, Kuching, St Andrew's School, Singapore and Serdang Agricultural College; entered Department of Agriculture, Sarawak, 1935; left government service for family business, 1946; member of Kuching Municipal Council from 1953 (president, 1960–1965), Council Negri (legislature) from 1955, and Supreme Council from 1957; founding chairman of the Sarawak United People's Party (SUPP), 1959; opposed Sarawak's membership of Malaysia but in 1970 SUPP joined the ruling coalition

Ong Yoke Lin, Dato (later Tun Tan Sri Omar Yoke Lin), b 1917
Victoria Institution, Kuala Lumpur; businessman; secretary-general, MCA; member of the Alliance Roundtable and special committee of the Alliance National Convention, 1953; nominated member, Federal Legislative Council, 1954; elected member, Federal Legislative Council, 1955; minister for posts and telecommunications (later transport), 1955–1957; minister of labour and social welfare, 1957; minister of health, 1959; minister without portfolio and concurrently permanent representative at UN, 1962–1964 and ambassador to Washington, 1962–1972; vice-president, MCA; retired as minister without portfolio after the formation of Tun Razak's government in 1970 and was appointed president of the Senate, 1973–1980

Openg bin Abang Sap'iee, Abang Haji (Dato, later Tun, Abang Haji Openg), 1905–1969
Member of Sarawak State Assembly, 1940; member of Sarawak Supreme Council, 1955; governor/head of state (yang di-

pertua) of Sarawak on entry into Malaysia, 1963

Ormsby-Gore, (William) David (Lord Harlech), 1918–1985
Knighted 1961; 5th Baron Harlech, 1964; Eton and New College, Oxford; military service, 1939–1945; Conservative MP, 1950–1961; parliamentary private secretary to minister of state, FO, 1951; parliamentary under-secretary, FO, Nov 1956–Jan 1957; minister of state, FO, 1957–1961; ambassador, Washington, 1961–1965; deputy leader of the Opposition, House of Lords, 1966–1967; deputy chairman, Commission on Rhodesian Opinion, 1972; president, British Board of Film Censors, 1965–85

Perth, John David Drummond (Lord Perth), 1907–2002
17th Earl of Perth, 1951; Downside and Trinity, Cambridge University; lieutenant, Intelligence Corps from 1940 (seconded to War Cabinet Offices, 1942–1943, and Ministry of Production, 1944–1945); partner, Schroder's, 1945–1956; representative peer for Scotland, 1952–1963; minister of state, CO, 1957–1962; 1st crown estate commissioner, 1962–1977; chairman, Reviewing Committee on Export of Works of Art, 1972–1976

Poynton, (Arthur) Hilton, 1905–1998
Knighted 1949; Marlborough and Brasenose, Oxford; entered CO, 1929; seconded as private secretary to minister of supply and minister of production, 1941–1943; assistant secretary, CO, 1943–1946; assistant under-secretary of state, 1946–1948; joint deputy under-secretary of state, 1948–1959; permanent under-secretary of sate, CO, 1959–1966

Sandys, Duncan (Lord Duncan-Sandys), 1908–1987
Life peer cr 1974 (Baron); Eton and Magdalen, Oxford; Diplomatic Service, 1930; married Diana Churchill, 1935

(until 1960); MP (Conservative), 1935–1945 and 1950–1974; parliamentary secretary, Ministry of Supply, 1943–1944; minister of works, 1944–1945; founded European Movement, 1947; minister of supply, 1951–1954; minister of housing and local government, 1954–1957; minister of defence, Jan 1957–Oct 1959; minister of aviation, 1959–1960; S of S for Commonwealth relations, July 1960–Oct 1964 and S of S for colonies, July 1962–Oct 1964

Scott, Robert Heatlie, 1905–1982
Knighted 1954; Queen's Royal College, Trinidad, and New College, Oxford; entered Consular Service in China, 1927; served in Peking, Shanghai, Canton, Hong Kong, Singapore; Ministry of Information and member of governor's War Council, Singapore, 1941–1942; interned by the Japanese, 1942–1945; on staff of the UK special commissioner, SE Asia (Lord Killearn), 1946; entered FO, 1948 (attached to the Imperial Defence College); head of SE Asian Department, 1948; assistant under-secretary with responsibility for Far Eastern affairs, 1950; minister, Washington embassy, 1953; commissioner-general, SE Asia, 1955–1959; commandant, Imperial Defence College, 1960; permanent secretary, MoD, 1961–1963

Selkirk, George Nigel Douglas-Hamilton (Lord Selkirk), 1906–1994
10th Earl of Selkirk, 1940; Eton and Balliol, Oxford, and universities of Bonn, Vienna, Paris (Sorbonne); member, Edinburgh Town Council, 1935–1940; commissioner, General Board of Control (Scotland), 1936–1939; commissioner for Special Areas in Scotland, 1937–1939; military service, 1939–1945; Scottish representative peer, 1945–1963; lord-in-waiting to the King, 1951–1952, and to the Queen, 1952–1953; paymaster-general, Nov 1953—Dec 1955; chancellor of the Duchy of Lancaster, Dec 1955 – Jan 1957; first lord of the Admiralty, 1957–Oct 1959; UK commissioner for Singapore and commissioner-general, SE Asia,

1959–1963; UK council representative to SEATO, 1960–1963; chairman, Conservative Commonwealth Council, 1965–1972

Snelling, Arthur Wendell, 1914–1996

Knighted 1960; Ackworth School, Yorkshire and University College, London; study group secretary, Royal Institute of International Affairs, 1934–1936; entered Dominions Office, 1936; joint secretary to UK delegation to International Monetary Conference, Bretton Woods, 1944; accompanied Lord Keynes on missions to USA and Canada, 1943 and 1944; deputy high commissioner in New Zealand, 1947–1950 and South Africa, 1953–1955; assistant under-secretary of state, CRO, 1956–1959; high commissioner in Ghana, 1959–1961; deputy under-secretary of state, CRO/FCO, 1961–1969; ambassador to South Africa, 1970–1972

Stephens, Donald, Datuk (later Tun Mohammad Fuad), 1920–1976

Born in Kudat (Sabah), son of Australian father and Kadazan mother; on leaving school became a pupil-teacher; father was shot and he was imprisoned and tortured by Japanese during the occupation of 1942–1945; proprietor, editor and publisher of *Sabah Times* from 1955; member, North Borneo Legislative Council, 1958; member, Executive Council, 1959; chairman, Kadazan Society, 1958; founder-president, UNKO, 1961; initially opposed to Malaysia but later converted to it; chairman, Malaysia Solidarity Consultative Committee, 1961–1962; joint leader of North Borneo delegation, Inter-Governmental Committee, 1962–1963; elected to North Borneo Legislative Council, 1963; first chief minister of Sabah on entry into Malaysia, 1963; federal minister for Sabah affairs, 1965; retired from politics and was appointed Malaysian high commissioner to Australia, 1968; converted to Islam, 1971; head of state, Sabah, 1973–1975; returned to politics to lead federal supported, inter-communal party, Berjaya (Sabah People's Union), 1975; chief

minister after elections of 1976; killed with four of his ministers and son in plane crash, 6 June 1976

Tan Siew Sin (later Tun Tan Siew Sin), 1916–1988

Son of Tan Cheng Lock, a leading Straits Chinese and founder-president of MCA; Malacca High School, Raffles College, Singapore and Inner Temple; businessman particularly in rubber; spent Japanese occupation in India; adviser to British Military Administration, 1945; municipal commissioner, Malacca, 1946; member of Federal Legislative Council from 1948, elected member from 1955; founder-member of MCA, 1949, and played a leading part in the formation of the Alliance with UMNO from 1952; vice-president of MCA, 1957 and president, 1961–1974; minister of commerce, 1957–1959; minister of finance, 1959–1969, special functions, 1969, and finance, 1970–1974

Thorneycroft, (George Edward) Peter (Lord Thorneycroft), 1909–1994

Life peer cr 1967; Eton and Royal Military Academy, Woolwich; Royal Artillery, 1930–1933; called to bar and practised law, 1935; MP (Conservative), 1938–1966; parliamentary secretary, Ministry of War Transport, 1945; president of the Board of Trade, 1951–1957; chancellor of the Exchequer, 1957–1958, resigned; minister of aviation, 1960–1962; minister of defence, 1962–1964; S of S for defence, Apr–Oct 1964; president of the Conservative Party, 1975–1981; president, Pirelli General Plc, 1987–1994

Toh Chin Chye, Dr, b 1921

Born in Taiping, Malaya; Raffles College, Singapore and University of London (physiology); succeeded Goh Keng Swee as chairman of Malayan Forum (London); lecturer and reader, University of Malaya; first chairman of People's Action Party, 1954; elected member, Singapore Legislative Assembly, 1959–1988; deputy prime minister, Singapore, 1959–1968; realigned PAP on a pan-Malaysian basis, 1964–1965, for participation in the

Malaysia Solidarity Convention and federal elections; opposed Singapore's withdrawal from Malaysia, 1965; vice-chancellor, University of Singapore, 1968–1975

Tory, Geofroy William, b 1912
Knighted 1958; King Edward VII School, Sheffield and Queens', Cambridge; entered Dominions Office, 1935; private secretary to the permanent under-secretary, 1938–1939; military service, 1939–1943; principal private secretary to S of S for the Dominions (Addison), 1945–1946; served in Ottawa, 1946–1949 and Ireland 1949–1952; deputy high commissioner in Pakistan, 1953–1954 and Australia, 1954–1957; assistant under-secretary, CRO, 1957; high commissioner in Malaya, 1957–1963; ambassador to Ireland, 1964–1966; high commissioner in Malta, 1967–1970

Trend, Burke Frederick St John, 1914–1987 (Lord Trend)
Knighted 1962; life peer cr 1974 (Baron); Whitgift School and Merton, Oxford; entered the Ministry of Education 1936; transferred to the Treasury, 1937; principal private secretary to the chancellor of the Exchequer (Hugh Dalton and Stafford Cripps), 1945–1949; under-secretary, 1949–1955; seconded to the office of the lord privy seal (R A Butler); deputy secretary of the Cabinet, 1956–1959; second secretary, Treasury, 1960–1963; secretary of the Cabinet, 1963–1973; rector of Lincoln College, Oxford, 1973–1983

Turnbull, Roland Evelyn, 1905–1960
Knighted 1956; King's College, London and St John's, Oxford; entered Malayan Civil Service, 1929; served in Federated Malay States, Trengganu and as secretary to high commissioner for Unfederated Malay States; resident, Brunei, 1934; seconded to CO, 1937; controller of foreign exchange, Malaya, 1939; colonial secretary, British Honduras, 1940–1943; colonel (civil affairs), WO, 1943–1945; colonial secretary, Cyprus, 1945–1950;

chief secretary, High Commission Territories, 1950–1953; governor, North Borneo, 1954–1960

Waddell, Alexander Noel Anton, 1913–1999
Knighted 1959; Fettes, Edinburgh University and Gonville & Caius, Cambridge; entered Colonial Administrative Service and posted to British Solomon Islands, 1937; district officer, 1938; naval service, 1942–1944; district commissioner, 1945; transferred to Malayan Civil Service, 1946; principal assistant secretary, North Borneo, 1947–1952; colonial secretary, Gambia, 1952–1956; colonial secretary, Sierra Leone, 1956–1958; deputy governor, Sierra Leone, 1958–1960; governor, Sarawak, 1960–1963; UK commissioner, British Phosphate Commissioners, 1965–1977

Wallace, (Walter) Ian (James), 1905–1993
Bedford Modern School and St Catharine's, Cambridge; entered Indian Civil Service and posted to Burma, 1928; deputy commissioner, 1933; settlement officer, 1934–1938; deputy commissioner, 1939–1942; defence secretary, 1942–1944; colonel and deputy director, Civil Affairs, Military Administration of Burma, 1944–1945; commissioner, 1946; chief secretary, Burma, 1946–1947; joined CO, 1947; assistant secretary, 1949–1962; assistant under-secretary of state, 1962–1966

Watherston, David Charles, 1907–1977
Knighted 1956; Westminster School and Christ Church, Oxford; entered Malayan Civil Service, 1930; seconded to CO, 1939–1944; member, Malayan Planning Unit, 1944–1945; British Military Administration, Malaya, 1945–1946; secretary of constitutional working committee which negotiated the Federation of Malaya Agreement, 1946–1948; secretary for defence and internal security, Malaya, 1948; chief secretary, 1952–1957, and administered the government of Malaya on occasions; special counsellor, Malayan high commission in the UK, 1957–1959;

member, Commission of Enquiry North Borneo and Sarawak (Cobbold Commission), 1962

Watkinson, Harold Arthur (Lord Watkinson), 1910–1995
1st Viscount of Woking cr 1964; Queen's College, Taunton and King's College, London; family business, 1929–1935; technical and engineering journalism, 1935–1939; active service in the Second World War; chairman, Production Efficiency Panel for South England, Machine Tool Trades Association, 1948; MP (Conservative), 1950–1964; parliamentary private secretary to minister of transport and aviation, 1951–1952; parliamentary secretary, Ministry of Labour and National Service, 1952–1955; minister of transport and civil aviation, Dec 1955–1959; minister of defence, 1959–1962; president of the Confederation of British Industries, 1976–1977

White, Dennis Charles, 1910–1983
Knighted 1962; Bradfield; joined Sarawak Civil Service, 1932; senior resident, 1955; resident, Brunei, 1958, high commissioner, Brunei, 1959–1963; Brunei government agent in the UK, 1967–1983

Wong Pow Nee, Dato (later Tan Sri Wong Pow Nee), 1911– 2002
Born in Penang and Roman Catholic; St Xavier's Institution, Penang; teacher of English in a Chinese school; town councillor in 1930s; elected member (MCA), Penang State Assembly, 1955; chief minister, Penang, 1957–1969; member of Razak's Educational Review Committee, 1960; member, Commission of Enquiry North Borneo and Sarawak (Cobbold Commission), 1962; ambassador to Italy, 1970

Yaacob ibni Almarhum Sultan Abdul Hamid Halim Shah, Tunku (Tunku Yaacob), 1899–1990
Son of the Sultan of Kedah and half-brother of Tunku Abdul Rahman; Malay College, Kuala Kangsar, Queens', Cambridge and Imperial College of Tropical Agriculture, Trinidad; entered Kedah agricultural service, 1930; state agricultural officer, 1946; keeper of rulers' seals, 1950–1951 and 1954–1955; regent of Kedah, 1951; member for agriculture, Federal Executive Council, 1951–1953; chairman, Public Service Commission, 1955–1958; Malayan high commissioner in London, 1958, and later Paris

Zulueta, Philip Francis de, 1925–1989
Knighted 1963; Beaumont and New College, Oxford; military service, 1943–1947; entered foreign service, 1949; posted to Moscow, 1950–1952; private secretary to successive prime ministers (Eden, Macmillan, Home), 1955–1964; assistant secretary, Treasury, 1962; resigned from foreign service in 1962; various directorships etc, including chief executive, 1973–1976, and chairman, 1976–1981, Antony Gibbs Holdings Ltd; chairman, Tanks Consolidated Investments Plc, 1983–1989

Bibliography 1: Sources searched at the National Archives

The following classes of files were searched for the period 1957–1963 using the relevant indexes. Not all documents within these series were available for consultation.

1. *Cabinet*

    (i)   *Cabinet Committees*
          Colonial Policy Committee: CAB 134/1555–1561 (1957–1962)
          Defence Committee: CAB 131/19, 23–28
          Future Policy Committee: CAB 134/1929
          Greater Malaysia Committee: CAB 130/179, 191
          Oversea Policy Committee: CAB 134/2370, 2371 (from June1962)
          (Official) Committee on Future Developments in SE Asia:
              CAB 134/1644, 1645
          (Official) Greater Malaysia Committee: (1961–1963): CAB 134/1949–1951
          (Official) Oversea Co-ordinating Committee (July–Dec 1962):
              CAB 134/2276–2278, 2281

    (ii) *Cabinet Office*
          Cabinet conclusions (minutes): CAB 128/31–37 (1957–1963)
          Cabinet memoranda: CAB 129 /85–114 (1957–1963)
          Cabinet Office registered files: CAB 21/4626, 4770, 4847–4851, 4867,
              5350, 5520

    (iii) *Other papers*
          Greater Malaysia Discussions (Anglo–Malayan talks in London),
          Nov 1961: CAB 134/1952, 1953
          Joint Intelligence Committee:
              papers: CAB 158/39–50
              minutes: CAB 159/28–39
              weekly reviews: CAB 179/3–11

2. *Colonial Office*

    (i)   *CO original correspondence: geographical classes*
          Far Eastern: CO 1030/412–1712 (1957–1963)

    (ii) *CO original correspondence: subject classes*
          Information: CO 1027/405, 588–592
          International Relations: CO 936/839–841

Cobbold Commission: CO 947/1–61
Defence: CO 968/758–761, 807, 811
Private Office: CO 967/391, 407, 410, 413–421

3. *Commonwealth Relations Office*

(i) *CRO original correspondence*
General: DO 35/6297, 8831–8833, 8864–8866, 9817, 9818, 9864,
10019, 10034, 10035

(ii) *CRO registered departmental files*
Economic Relations (from 1959): CO 189/109–111, 122, 149, 151–153,
158–163, 195, 219–223, 256–259, 260–262, 267, 275, 351, 352, 360, 361
Far East and Pacific: DO 169/10, 11, 18, 19, 20, 24–36, 38–43, 82, 95–101,
212–237, 247–249, 255, 266, 269, 271–273, 280, 284, 287–291, 307,
320, 329, 335, 336, 338
Information Policy Department: DO 191/34, 37, 49–51, 64
United Nations: DO 181/11, 118

(iii) *CRO registered files*
Agreements, Treaties and Miscellaneous Documents: DO 118/227, 258,
265, 266, 293
Untitled series: DO 187/2, 3, 4, 14–17, 20, 21, 22, 23, 25–29, 30, 31, 32, 33

4. *Foreign Office*

Original correspondence, political: FO 371
particular attention was given to files from 1962–1963, viz: 166599–
166602, 169680, 169691, 169694, 169695, 169698, 169700,
169702, 169703, 169706, 169712–169717, 169719, 169722–
169724, 169734, 169888, 169898–169901, 169906, 169908,
169911, 169978, 173492, 173493, 173496, 175267
Commissioner-general in SE Asia: FO 1091/69, 71, 79–83, 88–91, 97,
99–101, 104–114
Information Department: FO 953/2128–2132
Private papers, Lord Selkirk (1961–1963): FO 800/897
Research, South and SE Asia: FCO 51/154

5. *Ministry of Defence, Chiefs of Staff and Service Departments*

Chiefs of Staff Committee, minutes: DEFE 4/124, 126, 127, 129, 136, 137,
139, 141, 146, 150–160, 165, 167–175
Chiefs of Staff Committee, memoranda: DEFE 5/89, 92, 104, 105, 114, 115,
128, 130–133, 143, 150–152, 154, 161
Chiefs of Staff Committee, reports of Joint Planning Staff: DEFE 6/61, 71

Chiefs of Staff Committee, registered files: DEFE 11/419, 509
Ministry of Defence, general series: DEFE 7/1187, 1698, 1724, 1726, 2190, 2193, 2232, 2235
Ministry of Defence, private office: DEFE 13/311, 399, 542

6. *Prime Minister's Office*

Correspondence and papers: PREM 11/2659, 2661, 3240, 3274, 3276, 3418–3422, 3717, 3735, 3737, 3739, 3865–3869, 4146, 4182–4184, 4187–4189, 4310, 4341–4350, 4440, 4763, 4870, 4904–4910
Correspondence and papers: PREM 13/2194

7. *Treasury*

Defence policy and material division: T 225/2353, 2354, 2407, 2431–2433, 2551, 2552, 2554, 2555
Overseas financial division: T 236/6368, 6369, 6694

Bibliography 2: Official publications, unpublished private papers, published documents and secondary sources

1. *Official publications*

    (a) *United Kingdom*
    Exchange of Letters on Internal Security Council of Singapore, Cmnd 620 (1958) *
    Federation of Malaysia. Joint Statement by the Governments of the United Kingdom and of the Federation of Malaya, Cmnd 1563 (1961) *
    Report of the Commission of Enquiry: North Borneo and Sarawak, 1962, Cmnd 1794 (1962) *
    Malaysia. Report of the Inter-Governmental Committee, 1962, Cmnd 1954, (1963) *
    Malaysia. Agreement concluded between the United Kingdom of Great Britain and Northern Ireland, the Federation of Malaya, North Borneo, Sarawak and Singapore, Cmnd 2094 (1963) *
    Release of Crown Lands made available to the Armed Services in Singapore, Cmnd 2117 (1963) *
    Supplementary Agreement to the Agreement concluded between the Federation of Malaya, the United Kingdom Government of Great Britain and Northern Ireland, the Federation of Malaya, North Borneo, Sarawak and Singapore, Cmnd 2150 (1963) *
    Public Officers' Agreement between Her Majesty's Government in the United Kingdom and the Government of Malaysia in respect of Singapore, Cmnd 2468 (1963–1964) *
    Public Officers' Agreement between Her Majesty's Government in the United Kingdom and the Government of Malaysia in respect of Sabah, Cmnd 2469 (1963–1964) *
    Public Officers' Agreement between Her Majesty's Government in the United Kingdom and the Government of Malaysia in respect of Sarawak, Cmnd 2670 (1963–1964) *
    Parliamentary Debates, House of Commons
    Parliamentary Debates, House of Lords
    The Colonial Office List (1957–1963)
    The Commonwealth Relations Office List

---

* Also published by the government presses of Malaya, Singapore, North Borneo, Sarawak, or Malaysia as appropriate.

(b) *Governments of the Federation of Malaya, Singapore, North Borneo, Sarawak, Malaysia*

Brunei constitutional documents (Kuala Lumpur, nd [1960])

Lee Kuan Yew, *The Battle for Merger* (Singapore, 1961)

Memorandum setting out the Heads of Agreement for a Merger between the Federation of Malaya and Singapore, Cmd 33 (Singapore, 1961)

Malaysia and North Borneo (Jesselton, 1962)

Malaysia and Sarawak (Kuching, 1962)

The Danger Within. A History of the Clandestine Communist Organisation, (Kuching, 1963)

Tripartite Summit Meeting – Manila, July 30 – August 5, 1963 (Kuala Lumpur, nd [1963])

Malaya/Indonesia Relations, 31st August, 1957 to 15th September, 1963 (Kuala Lumpur, 1963)

Malaya/Philippine Relations, 31st August, 1957 to 15th September, 1963 (Kuala Lumpur, nd [1963])

Malaysia's Case in the United Nations Security Council. Documents reproduced from the Official Record of the Security Council Proceedings (Kuala Lumpur, 1964)

(c) *Other official publications*

International Bank for Reconstruction and Development, *Report on the Economic Aspects of Malaysia* (Rueff Report), (Government Printing Office, Kuala Lumpur, 1963)

United Nations, *United Nations Malaysia Mission* (Department of Information, Kuala Lumpur, 1963)

2. *Unpublished collections of private papers in the UK*

Goode Papers (Rhodes House Library, Oxford, MSS Ind Ocn s 323)

Sandys Papers (Churchill College Archive Centre, Cambridge, DSND)

Waddell Papers (Rhodes House Library, Oxford, MSS Pac s 105)

3. *Published selections of documents and documentary guides*

J de V Allen, A J Stockwell & L R Wright, eds, *A collection of treaties and other documents affecting the states of Malaysia 1761–1963*, vol II (London, Rome, New York, 1981)

Peter Boyce, ed, *Malaysia and Singapore in international diplomacy: documents and commentaries* (Sydney, 1968)

British Documents on the End of Empire Project (BDEEP) (London):
  S R Ashton & David Killingray, eds, *The West Indies* (1999)
  S R Ashton & Wm Roger Louis, eds, *East of Suez and the Commonwealth 1964–1971* (2004)
  Ronald Hyam & Wm Roger Louis, eds, *The Conservative government and the end of empire 1957–1964* (2000)

John Kent, ed, *Egypt and the defence of the Middle East* (1998)
A J Stockwell, ed, *Malaya* (1995)
A Thurston, *Sources for colonial studies in the Public Record Office,*
    2 vols (1995 & 1998)
Foreign Relations of the United States, 1961–1963 (Washington):
    E C Keefer & G W LaFantasie, eds, Vol XXIII, *Southeast Asia* (1994)
J M Gullick, ed, *Malaysia and its neighbours* (London, 1967)
Nicholas Mansergh, ed, *Documents and speeches on Commonwealth*
    Affairs, 1952–1962 (London, 1963)
A N Porter & A J Stockwell, eds, *British imperial policy and*
    decolonisation, vol II *1951–1964* (London, 1989)
J Turner, ed, *Macmillan: Cabinet papers, 1957–1963, on CD-ROM* (set of
    three, Adam Matthew Publications, Marlborough, Wilts/Public Record
    Office, 1999), 'Decolonisation' intro by P Murphy
Haji Zaini Haji Ahmad, ed, *The People's Party of Brunei. Selected*
    documents (Kuala Lumpur, 1987)

4. *Select list of published books and unpublished theses*

Tunku Abdul Rahman Putra Al-Haj, *Looking back: Monday musings and*
    memories (Kuala Lumpur, 1977)
Richard Allen, *Malaysia: prospect and retrospect. The impact and aftermath of*
    colonial rule (London, 1968)
Thomas J Bellows, *The People's Action Party of Singapore: emergence of a*
    dominant party system (New Haven, Conn, 1971)
Chan Heng Chee, *A sensation of independence. David Marshall—a political*
    biography (Singapore, ed 2001)
Cheah Boon Kheng, *Malaysia. The making of a nation* (Singapore, 2002)
Chin Kin Wah, *The defence of Malaysia and Singapore: the transformation of a*
    security system, 1957–1971 (Cambridge, 1983)
Richard Clutterbuck. *Riot and revolution in Singapore and Malaya, 1945–63*
    (London, 1973)
Philip Darby, *British defence policy east of Suez*, 1947–1968 (Oxford, 1973)
John Darwin, *Britain and decolonisation: the retreat from empire in the*
    post-war world (London, 1988)
Saki Dockrill, *Britain's retreat from east of Suez: the choice between Europe*
    and the world? (Basingstoke, 2002)
David Easter, 'British defence policy in South East Asia and Confrontation
    1960–66', unpublished PhD thesis (London, LSE, 1998)
Joe Garner, *The Commonwealth Office 1925–68* (London, 1978)
Ghazali Shafie, *Ghazali Shafie's memoir on the formation of Malaysia* (Bangi,
    1998)
Willard A Hanna, *The formation of Malaysia: new factor in world politics* (New
    York, 1964)
T N Harper, *The end of empire and the making of Malaya* (Cambridge, 1999)
Heng Pek Koon, *Chinese politics in Malaysia: a history of the Malaysian*
    Chinese Association (Kuala Lumpur, 1988)

Alistair Horne, *Macmillan 1957–1986* (London, 1989)

A V M Horton, *Negara Brunei Darussalam: a biographical dictionary (1860–1996)* (ed 1996)

B A Hussainmiya, *Sultan Omar Saifuddin III and Britain: the making of Brunei Darussalam* (Kuala Lumpur, 1995)

Michael Jackson (ed by Janet Jackson), *A Scottish life: Sir John Martin, Churchill and empire* (London, 1999)

Matthew Jones, *Conflict and confrontation in South East Asia, 1961–1965: Britain, the United States and the creation of Malaysia* (Cambridge, 2002)

A H M Kirk-Greene, *On crown service: a history of HM colonial and overseas civil services 1837–1997* (London, 1999)

A H M Kirk-Greene, *Britain's imperial administrators, 1858–1966* (Basingstoke, 2000)

Albert Lau, *A moment of anguish: Singapore in Malaysia and the politics of disengagement* (Singapore, 1998)

Lee Kuan Yew, *The Singapore story: memoirs of Lee Kuan Yew* (Singapore, 1998)

Michael Leifer, *The Philippine claim to Sabah* (London, 1967)

Michael Leifer, *Dictionary of the modern politics of South-East Asia* (London, 1995)

Michael B Leigh, *The rising moon: political change in Sarawak* (Sydney University Press, 1974)

J A C Mackie, *Konfrontasi: the Indonesia–Malaysia dispute 1963–1966* (Kuala Lumpur, 1974)

Harold Macmillan, *Memoirs: volume VI. At the end of the day 1961–63* (London, 1973)

Gordon P Means, *Malaysian politics* (London, 1970)

R S Milne & K J Ratnam, *Malaysia—new states in a new nation. Political development of Sarawak and Sabah in Malaysia* (London, 1974)

Mohamed Noordin Sopiee, *From Malayan Union to Singapore separation: political unification in the Malaysia region, 1945–65* (Kuala Lumpur, 1974)

Alastair Morrison, *Fair land Sarawak: some recollections of an expatriate official* (Ithaca, 1993)

Philip Murphy, *Alan Lennox–Boyd: a biography* (London, 1999)

Ong Kee Hui, *Footprints in Sarawak: memoirs of Tan Sri Datuk (Dr) Ong Kee Hui, 1914 to 1963* (Kuching, 1998)

J P Ongkili, *The Borneo response to Malaysia 1961–1963* (Singapore, 1967)

Naimah S Talib, *Administrators and their service: the Sarawak Administrative Service under the Brooke Rajahs and British colonial rule* (New York, 1999)

Phuong Pham, 'The end to "east of Suez": the British withdrawal from Malaysia and Singapore, 1964 to 1968', unpublished DPhil thesis (Oxford, 2001)

Vernon L Porritt, *British colonial rule in Sarawak, 1946–1963* (Kuala Lumpur, 1997)

Greg Poulgrain, *The genesis of Konfrontasi: Malaysia, Brunei and Indonesia, 1945–1965* (Bathurst, NSW and London, 1998)

Robert Pringle, *Rajahs and rebels: the Ibans of Sarawak under Brooke rule, 1841–1941* (New York, 1970)

Bob Reece, *Datu Bandar. Abang Hj Mustapha of Sarawak: some reflections of his life and times* (Kuala Lumpur, nd)

R H C Reece, *The name of Brooke: the end of white rajah rule in Sarawak* (Kuala Lumpur, 1982)

Margaret Clark Roff, *The politics of belonging: political change in Sabah and Sarawak* (Kuala Lumpur, 1974)

Said Zahari, *Dark clouds at dawn: a political memoir* (Kuala Lumpur, 2001)

Graham Saunders, *A history of Brunei* (London, ed 2002)

William Shaw, *Tun Razak: his life and times* (Kuala Lumpur, 1976)

B Simandjuntak, *Malayan federalism, 1945–1963* (Kuala Lumpur, 1969)

D S Ranjit Singh, *Brunei 1839–1983: the problems of political survival* (Singapore, 1991)

D S Ranjit Singh, *The making of Sabah 1865–1941* (Kuala Lumpur, 2000)

John Subritzky, *Confronting Sukarno: British, American, Australian and New Zealand diplomacy in the Malaysian–Indonesian Confrontation, 1961–5* (Basingstoke, 2000)

Mohamed Suffian bin Hashim, *An introduction to the constitution of Malaysia* (Kuala Lumpur, 1972)

Tan Jing Quee & Jomo K S, eds, *Comet in our sky: Lim Chin Siong in history* (Kuala Lumpur, 2001)

C M Turnbull, *A history of Singapore 1819–1975* (Singapore, 1977)

R K Vasil, *Politics in a plural society* (Kuala Lumpur, 1971)

Karl von Vorys, *Democracy without consensus: communalism and political stability in Malaysia* (Princeton, 1975)

Nicholas J White, *Business, government and the end of empire: Malaya, 1942–1957* (Kuala Lumpur, 1997)

Nicholas J White, *British business in post-colonial Malaysia, 1957–70: 'neo-colonialism' or 'disengagement'?* (London, 2004)

5. *Select list of published articles and chapters in books*

S J Ball, 'Selkirk in Singapore', *Twentieth Century British History*, 10, 2 (1999) pp 162–191

Malcolm Caldwell, 'From "emergency" to "independence", 1948–57' in Mohamed Amin and Malcolm Caldwell, eds, *Malaya: the making of a neo-colony* (Nottingham, 1977)

T N Harper, 'Lim Chin Siong and the "Singapore Story"' in Tan Jing Quee and Jomo K.S. eds, *Comet in our sky: Lim Chin Siong in History* (Kuala Lumpur, 2001) pp 3–55

A V M Horton, 'British administration in Brunei 1906–1959', *Modern Asian Studies*, 20, 2 (1988) pp 353–374

Ronald Hyam, 'The primacy of geopolitics: the dynamics of British imperial policy, 1763–1963', *Journal of Imperial and Commonwealth History*, 27, 2 (1999), pp 27–52

Matthew Jones, 'Creating Malaysia: Singapore security, the Borneo territories and the contours of British policy, 1961–63', *Journal of Imperial and Commonwealth History*, 28, 2 (2000) pp 61–86

Wm Roger Louis & Ronald Robinson, 'The imperialism of decolonization',
    Journal of Imperial and Commonwealth History, 22, 3 (1994), pp 462–511
Mohamed Noordin Sopiee, 'The advocacy of Malaysia before 1961', *Modern Asian
    Studies*, 7, 4 (1973) pp 717–732
A J Stockwell, 'Malaysia: the making of a neo-colony?', *Journal of Imperial and
    Commonwealth History*, 26, 2 (1998) pp 138–156
A J Stockwell, 'Malaysia: the making of a Grand Design', *Asian Affairs*, 24, 3
    (2003) pp 227–242
A J Stockwell, 'Britain and Brunei, 1945–1963: imperial retreat and royal
    ascendancy', *Modern Asian Studies*, 38, 4 (2004) pp 785–820
Nicholas J White, 'Gentlemanly capitalism and empire in the twentieth century:
    the "forgotten" case of Malaya, 1914–1965', in R E Dumett, ed,
    *Gentlemanly capitalism and British imperialism: the new debate on
    empire* (Harlow, 1999) pp 175–195
Nicholas J White, 'The business and the politics of decolonization: the British
    experience in the twentieth century', *Economic History Review*, 53,
    2 (2000) pp 544–564
Nicholas J White, 'The survival, revival and decline of British economic
    influence in Malaysia, 1957–70', *Twentieth Century British History*,
    14, 3 (2003) pp 222–242
Yeo Kim Wah & Albert Lau, 'From colonialism to independence 1945–1965', in
    Ernest C T Chew & Edwin Lee, eds, *A history of Singapore* (Singapore,
    1991)

Index of Main Subjects and Persons:

This is not a comprehensive index, but a simplified and straightforward index to document numbers, together with page references to the Introduction, the latter being given at the beginning of the entry in lower-case roman numerals. The index is designed to be used in conjunction with the summary list of documents which begins on page xcvii. It does not cover the Appendix, 'The Origins and Formation of Malaysia'; guidance on this is provided by the table of contents at pages 581–584. As far as persons are concerned, a preceding asterisk indicates inclusion in the Biographical Notes while the countries of non-British personnel are indicated in brackets. Where necessary (eg particularly in long documents), and if possible, paragraph or section numbers are given inside round brackets. Sub-divisions of main entries are organised in document numerical order.

The following abbreviations are used:

> A – annex, appendix (thus 129 A (B) = appendix B to document 129)
> E – enclosure
> N – editor's link note (before main text of document)
> n – footnote